LET'S GO

■ THE RESOURCE FOR THE INDEPENDENT TRAVELER

"The guides are aimed not only at young budget travelers but at the indepedent traveler; a sort of streetwise cookbook for traveling alone."

—The New York Times

"Unbeatable; good sight-seeing advice; up-to-date info on restaurants, hotels, and inns; a commitment to money-saving travel; and a wry style that brightens nearly every page."

—The Washington Post

"Lighthearted and sophisticated, informative and fun to read. [Let's Go] helps the novice traveler navigate like a knowledgeable old hand."

—Atlanta Journal-Constitution

"A world-wise traveling companion—always ready with friendly advice and helpful hints, all sprinkled with a bit of wit."

—The Philadelphia Inquirer

■ THE BEST TRAVEL BARGAINS IN YOUR PRICE RANGE

"All the dirt, dirt cheap."

—People

"Anything you need to know about budget traveling is detailed in this book."

—The Chicago Sun-Times

"Let's Go follows the creed that you don't have to toss your life's savings to the wind to travel—unless you want to."

—The Salt Lake Tribune

■ REAL ADVICE FOR REAL EXPERIENCES

"The writers seem to have experienced every rooster-packed bus and lunar-surfaced mattress about which they write."

—The New York Times

"A guide should tell you what to expect from a destination. Here Let's ⌐ shines."

—The Chic

LET'S GO PUBLICATIONS

TRAVEL GUIDES

Alaska & the Pacific Northwest 2003
Australia 2003
Austria & Switzerland 2003
Britain & Ireland 2003
California 2003
Central America 8th edition
Chile 1st edition **NEW TITLE**
China 4th edition
Costa Rica 1st edition **NEW TITLE**
Eastern Europe 2003
Egypt 2nd edition
Europe 2003
France 2003
Germany 2003
Greece 2003
Hawaii 2003 **NEW TITLE**
India & Nepal 7th edition
Ireland 2003
Israel 4th edition
Italy 2003
Mexico 19th edition
Middle East 4th edition
New Zealand 6th edition
Peru, Ecuador & Bolivia 3rd edition
South Africa 5th edition
Southeast Asia 8th edition
Southwest USA 2003
Spain & Portugal 2003
Thailand 1st edition **NEW TITLE**
Turkey 5th edition
USA 2003
Western Europe 2003

CITY GUIDES

Amsterdam 2003
Barcelona 2003
Boston 2003
London 2003
New York City 2003
Paris 2003
Rome 2003
San Francisco 2003
Washington, D.C. 2003

MAP GUIDES

Amsterdam
Berlin
Boston
Chicago
Dublin
Florence
Hong Kong
London
Los Angeles
Madrid
New Orleans
New York City
Paris
Prague
Rome
San Francisco
Seattle
Sydney
Venice
Washington, D.C.

CENTRAL AMERICA

BENJAMIN KRUTZINNA EDITOR
ASHLEY KIRCHER ASSOCIATE EDITOR
CHARLENE MUSIC ASSOCIATE EDITOR
ERIN SPRAGUE ASSOCIATE EDITOR

RESEARCHER-WRITERS

MEGHA DOSHI
DANIEL ELIZONDO
SARAH GOGEL
JEREMIAH JOHNSON
PHOEBE LITHGOW
T. JOSIAH PERTZ

DAN RAMSEY
ADAM RZEPKA
TED TIEKEN
NATALIA JOSÉ TRUSZKOWSKA
ANDREA ZAYAS

NATHANIEL BROOKS MAP EDITOR
HARRIETT GREEN MANAGING EDITOR
DAVID MUEHLKE TYPESETTER

MACMILLAN

HELPING LET'S GO If you want to share your discoveries, suggestions, or corrections, please drop us a line. We read every piece of correspondence, whether a postcard, a 10-page email, or a coconut. Please note that mail received after May 2003 may be too late for the 2004 book, but will be kept for future editions. **Address mail to:**

**Let's Go: Central America
67 Mount Auburn Street
Cambridge, MA 02138
USA**

Visit Let's Go at **http://www.letsgo.com,** or send email to:

**feedback@letsgo.com
Subject: "Let's Go: Central America"**

In addition to the invaluable travel advice our readers share with us, many are kind enough to offer their services as researchers or editors. Unfortunately, our charter enables us to employ only currently enrolled Harvard students.

Published in Great Britain 2003 by Macmillan, an imprint of Pan Macmillan Ltd.
20 New Wharf Road, London N1 9RR
Basingstoke and Oxford
Associated companies throughout the world
www.panmacmillan.com

Maps by David Lindroth copyright © 2003 by St. Martin's Press.

Published in the United States of America by St. Martin's Press.

ISBN: 1-4050-0061 9
First edition
10 9 8 7 6 5 4 3 2 1

Let's Go: Central America is written by Let's Go Publications, 67 Mount Auburn Street, Cambridge, MA 02138, USA.

Let's Go® and the LG logo are trademarks of Let's Go, Inc.
Printed in the USA on recycled paper with soy ink.

WHO WE ARE

A NEW LET'S GO

With a sleeker look and innovative new content, we have revamped the entire series to reflect more than ever the needs and interests of the independent traveler. Here are just some of the improvements you will notice when traveling with the new *Let's Go*.

MORE PRICE OPTIONS

Still the best resource for budget travelers, *Let's Go* recognizes that everyone needs the occassional indulgence. Our "Big Splurges" indicate establishments that are actually worth those extra pennies (pulas, pesos, or pounds), and price-level symbols (❶ ❷ ❸ ❹ ❺) allow you to quickly determine whether an accommodation or restaurant will break the bank. We may have diversified, but we'll never lose our budget focus—"Hidden Deals" reveal the best-kept travel secrets.

BEYOND THE TOURIST EXPERIENCE

Our Alternatives to Tourism chapter offers ideas on immersing yourself in a new community through study, work, or volunteering.

AN INSIDER'S PERSPECTIVE

As always, every item is written and researched by our on-site writers. This year we have highlighted more viewpoints to help you gain an even more thorough understanding of the places you are visiting.

IN RECENT NEWS. *Let's Go* correspondents around the globe report back on current regional issues that may affect you as a traveler.

CONTRIBUTING WRITERS. Respected scholars and former *Let's Go* writers discuss topics on society and culture, going into greater depth than the usual guidebook summary.

THE LOCAL STORY. From the Parisian monk toting a cell phone to the Russian *babushka* confronting capitalism, *Let's Go* shares its revealing conversations with local personalities—a unique glimpse of what matters to real people.

FROM THE ROAD. Always helpful and sometimes downright hilarious, our researchers share useful insights on the typical (and atypical) travel experience.

SLIMMER SIZE

Don't be fooled by our new, smaller size. *Let's Go* is still packed with invaluable travel advice, but now it's easier to carry with a more compact design.

FORTY-THREE YEARS OF WISDOM

For over four decades *Let's Go* has provided the most up-to-date information on the hippest cafes, the most pristine beaches, and the best routes from border to border. It all started in 1960 when a few well-traveled students at Harvard University handed out a 20-page mimeographed pamphlet of their tips on budget travel to passengers on student charter flights to Europe. From humble beginnings, *Let's Go* has grown to cover six continents and *Let's Go: Europe* still reigns as the world's best-selling travel guide. This year we've beefed up our coverage of Latin America with *Let's Go: Costa Rica* and *Let's Go: Chile;* on the other side of the globe, we've added *Let's Go: Thailand* and *Let's Go: Hawaii*. Our new guides bring the total number of titles to 61, each infused with the spirit of adventure that travelers around the world have come to count on.

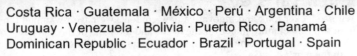

CONTENTS

How to Use This Book ix

HOW TO USE THIS BOOK

ORGANIZATION. The book starts with **Essentials,** what you need to get to, from, and around the counry, and general cultural information in **Life and Times.** Coverage is broken down into alphabetically sorted country chapters—the black tabs on the side of the book should help you navigate. Also consult the map legend at the end of the book.

PRICE RANGES AND RANKINGS. Our researchers list establishments in order of value from best to worst. Our absolute favorites are denoted by the Let's Go thumbs-up (🔲). Since the best value does not always mean the cheapest price, we have incorporated a system of price ranges in the guide. There is a table at the beginning of each country chapter that lists how prices fall within each bracket.

PHONE CODES AND TELEPHONE NUMBERS. Phone numbers in Central America have seven digits and no area codes. Phone numbers are preceded by the ☎ icon.

GRAYBOXES AND WHITEBOXES. Grayboxes at times provide wonderful cultural insight, at times simply crude humor. In any case, they're usually amusing, so enjoy. **Whiteboxes,** on the other hand, provide important practical information, such as warnings (🔲), further resources (🔲), and border crossings (🔲).

WHEN TO USE IT

TWO MONTHS BEFORE. The first chapter, **Discover Central America,** contains highlights of the region, including Suggested Itineraries (see p. 6) that can help you plan your trip. The **Essentials** (see p. 21) section contains practical information on planning a budget, making reservations, renewing a passport, and has other useful tips about traveling in Central America. For more detailed information on a specific country, see the beginning of each country chapter.

ONE MONTH BEFORE. Take care of insurance, and write down a list of emergency numbers and hotlines. Make a list of packing essentials (see **Packing,** p. 35) and shop for anything you are missing. Read through the coverage and make sure you understand the logistics of your itinerary (catching trains, ferries, etc.). Make any reservations if necessary.

2 WEEKS BEFORE. Leave an itinerary and a photocopy of important documents with someone at home. Take some time to peruse the **Life and Times** (see p. 9) of Central America, as well as the individual country histories, which have information on history, culture, flora and fauna, recent political events, and more.

ON THE ROAD. The **Appendix** contains Spanish language basics, a glossary of phrases, and a temperature chart of the capital cities of Central America. Now, arm yourself with a travel journal and hit the road.

A NOTE TO OUR READERS The information for this book was gathered by *Let's Go* researchers from May through August of 2002. Each listing is based on one researcher's opinion, formed during his or her visit at a particular time. Those traveling at other times may have different experiences since prices, dates, hours, and conditions are always subject to change. You are urged to check the facts presented in this book beforehand to avoid inconvenience and surprises.

RESEARCHER-WRITERS

Megha Doshi — *Central Costa Rica*

A developing world veteran at *Let's Go*, we knew from day one that Megha would be our *chica* to hunt down the best in Costa Rica. Always up for a challenge, this marathon runner, bioethics major, rugby player, and community service superstar has added "human typewriter" to her list of credits, as her copy was as smooth as her trip through Costa Rica. She was also our last minute godsend for maps and ice cream. *¡Bien hecho*, Megha!

Daniel Elizondo — *Western Honduras, El Salvador*

This 11th hour RW proved a champ, shifting from the study of Ancient Greek to Maya ruins, chicken buses, and *pupusas* galore. He danced his way through modern cities and highland towns, sending back marginalia that was as amusing as it was, er, personal. No barrio or volcano peak was left unexplored in the wide swath that Daniel cut across the country. His copy was precise: to a T and to the minute. Well done, Daniel!

Jeremiah Johnson — *Honduras*

Even before his first trip to Central America, Jeremiah, a member of the crew team, assured us he could "survive indefinitely." Life sure must've been rough on the paradisiacal Bay Islands and Isla el Tigre. Jeremiah really took roughing it to a whole new level as he plowed through the Mosquita, even forgetting the date and time! The Honduran ladies were surely sad to see him go, but we're happy he survived, and survived well.

Sarah Gogel — *Southern Nicaragua, Northwestern Costa Rica*

Sickness, snail mail, and rest days didn't get this *viajera* down. Quite the globe trotter, this France native spent a year traveling and volunteering in Costa Rica and Nicaragua before her stint with *Let's Go*. Sarah was proud to represent Nicaragua's developing tourism economy, and will always have a special place for *Nicas* in her heart—especially the ones who carried her heavy backpack. She's so devoted, she's probably still writing features for the book.

Phoebe Lithgow — *Northern Costa Rica*

Joining the LG team definitely brought out the inner tiger in this laidback California gal. On her third trip to Latin America, Phoebe once again shed her usual study of American history and literature for some Latina flair. Although her surfing style might not match her badminton skills, her copy definitely did. Thanks to Phoebe, every mirrored headboard in Costa Rica has now been documented. The only thing we still need to know is: 'tacos as big as your you know what?!'

T. Josiah Pertz — *Guatemala*

This traveling minstrel and salsa-dancer extraordinaire certainly earned his Central American stripes. He criss-crossed Guatemala in search of the best deals and the elusive *Robabuerguesas*. His copy was accurate, informative, and entertaining. (Check out *La Academia de Música Josiah Pertz* next time you're in Retalhuleu.) Thanks to him, some bacteria, and a few amoeba, the hospitals of Guatemala have never been so well researched. ¡Bien hecho, Josiah!

Dan Ramsey
Belize, Northern Guatemala

Thanks to Dan, coverage of Belize has been updated, clarified, and expanded, all with an eye for detail and the cheapest Internet. A world-travel veteran, he tirelessly sought out the most worthwhile eco-resort splurges, traditional Garífuna villages, and the worst— flooded roads. Even the Guatemalan Petén and PAC border strikes didn't faze this RW; he also handled more computer meltdowns than a popsicle on a hot day. Did he do his job? You better Belize it.

Natalia A. José Truszkowska
Southern Costa Rica

Hailing from Poland, Mexico, and Wisconsin, and having researched for *Let's Go: Eastern Europe 2002*, Natalia decided it was time to give her Latin American roots some attention. Natalia's study of post-modern Hispanic literature was evident in her inquisitive prose. This RW had no qualms about ditching her gear and wading up to her neck through the raging rivers of her jungle route to get the most stellar copy. Natalia loved her *viajera* lifestyle, and we loved her.

Andrea Zayas
Panama

After finishing her master's degree at the Harvard Graduate School of Education, Andrea's enthusiasm and interest were piqued from the start by Panama and its multicultural society. She ventured out into Panama's wild west, with a keen eye for cultural nuances, and always sending back well-writeen and discerning prose. Braving everything from jungle swamps to meningitis outbreaks, Andrea's time there was well spent.

Adam Rzepka
Panama

For the CEAM team this year, Adam traded one part of the Spanish speaking world for another, leaving his studies of alternative street theatre in Spain to RW through Panama. With *Let's Go: Peru, Ecuador & Bolivia 2002* and several other *LG* stints already under his belt, Adam was ready for more than the canal in the most remote regions of Panama. A recent Harvard graduate, Adam is now pursuing a masters degree in English at the University of Chicago.

Ted Tieken
Nicaragua

Growing up in Idaho, Ted spent much time outdoors, and put it to good use by taking the road less traveled through Central Nicaragua. This country was a perfect fit for this gov jock, as Ted was on the ball and down to business from day one. The only thing better than his copy were the funny anecdotes about bus rides, hostels, and SCUBA training. Now, if only Mr. Outdoorsman knew how to carry his backpack. . . rock on, Ted*ísimo*.

CONTRIBUTING WRITERS

Shannon Music. A native Costa Rican, Shannon interned at the Interamerican Court of Justice in San José, and worked the summer of 2002 at the Ethos Institute of Business and Social Responsibilities in São Paulo, Brazil. She is a psychology concentrator at Harvard College.

Zach Towne-Smith. A former Researcher-Writer for *Let's Go: USA 2000*, Zach now lives in Guatemala, where he teaches classes and conducts research in the Communications department at the Universidad Rafael Landívar.

PDAs & Travel

ACKNOWLEDGMENTS

LET'S GO

CEAM thanks: Central America for inspiring, frustrating, and enriching our lives. Thanks to our mapper Nathaniel, Kate and Harriet for their guidance, and the Asstro-naught. *Muchísimas gracias* to our fabulous RWs who toiled in the name of a better guide, leaving no tortilla unturned. Thanks to Jay, the typists, proofers, contributing writers, Leo's breakfasts, and chicken-and-cheese wraps.

Ben thanks: Ashley, Charlene, and Erin—the only women in my life—for motivating me to come into the office (literally) every day, and for their dedication, patience, and humor. Marlene por haberme dejado con tanta afición por Centroamérica. Hermann, Ursula, Jan, and Jenny for always caring about me. Everybody else who has been supportive.
Erin thanks: Ben for his knowledge, discussions, and "riiiiiiggght"; Ash for her sense of humor and mutual love of food, clothes, and coffee; and Charlita for enthusiasm and diligence all night long! Here's to A/C wars, ghetto popsicles, border, astro-naughty, and a beautiful, accurate book! Thanks to my freshman seminar and trip to Nicaragua. A quick shout-out to my summer road trip "family" and the actual one: Mom, Dad, Colleen, Cara, Kevin, and Nanny.
Ashley thanks: Guatemala, Honduras, and the Mennonites for instilling in me a deep and lasting passion for all things *rica, pura,* and unexplored; my gorgeous book team—Ben, Charlene, and Erin—how did we do it?! I am so proud. Now give me my smoothie. Love to the Fam, new bambina Stella, and Jay, my best friend and partner in adventures (and covert pool swimming). A sweet, sweet goodbye to the Big H.
Charlene thanks: Costa Rica, my homeland and inspiration. Meat and cheese. You kept me alive. Ben for the finest execution of "cheap, foreign labor" I've ever seen—wait, after *me,* that is! Erin and Ash for the fun and hard work. AEs rock. Kate, our salvation. Mom, Dad, and Shannoncita for ALL your help and for keeping me laughing late at night. Abe, for the love, motivation, and best times I had this summer.

Editor
Ben Krutzinna
Associate Editors
Ashley Kircher, Charlene Music, Erin Sprague
Managing Editor
Harriett Green, Katharine Douglas
Map Editor
Nathaniel Brooks

Publishing Director
Matthew Gibson
Editor-in-Chief
Brian R. Walsh
Production Manager
C. Winslow Clayton
Cartography Manager
Julie Stephens
Design Manager
Amy Cain
Editorial Managers
Christopher Blazejewski,
Abigail Burger, D. Cody Dydek,
Harriett Green, Angela Mi Young Hur,
Marla Kaplan, Celeste Ng
Financial Manager
Noah Askin
Marketing & Publicity Managers
Michelle Bowman, Adam M. Grant
New Media Managers
Jesse Tov, Kevin Yip
Online Manager
Amélie Cherlin
Personnel Managers
Alex Leichtman, Owen Robinson
Production Associates
Caleb Epps, David Muehlke
Network Administrators
Steven Aponte, Eduardo Montoya
Design Associate
Juice Fong
Financial Assistant
Suzanne Siu
Office Coordinators
Alex Ewing, Adam Kline,
Efrat Kussell

Director of Advertising Sales
Erik Patton
Senior Advertising Associates
Patrick Donovan, Barbara Eghan,
Fernanda Winthrop
Advertising Artwork Editor
Leif Holtzman
Cover Photo Research
Laura Wyss

President
Bradley J. Olson
General Manager
Robert B. Rombauer
Assistant General Manager
Anne E. Chisholm

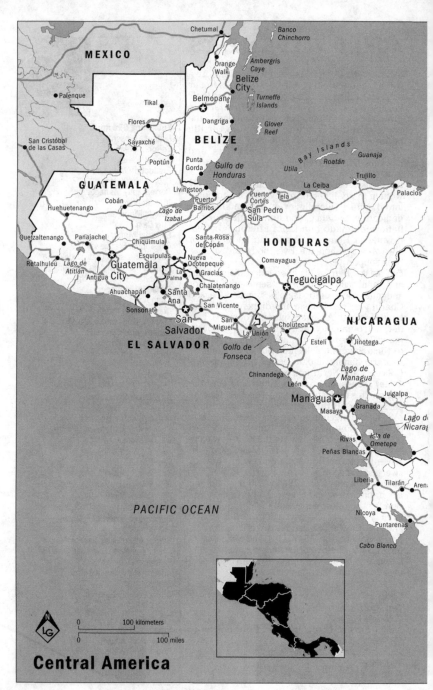

Central America

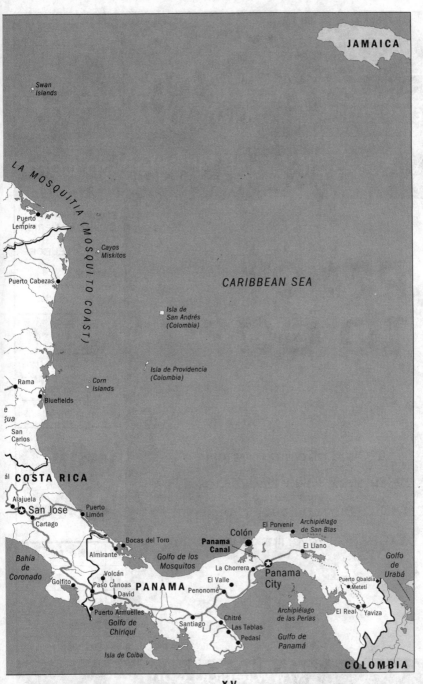

JAMAICA

Swan
Islands

LA MOSQUITIA (MOSQUITO COAST)

Puerto
Lempira

Cayos
Miskitos

CARIBBEAN SEA

Puerto Cabezas

Isla de
San Andrés
(Colombia)

Rama

Isla de Providencia
(Colombia)

Bluefields

Corn
Islands

e
ŭua

San
Carlos

ál COSTA RICA

Alajuela

San José

Puerto
Limón

Cartago

Bocas del Toro

Colón

El Porvenir

Archipiélago
de San Blas

Panama
Canal

Almirante

Golfo de los
Mosquitos

El Llano

Golfo
de
Urabá

Bahía
de
Coronado

Volcán

La Chorrera

Panama
City

Golfito

Paso Canoas

PANAMA

El Valle

Puerto Obaldía

Metetí

David

Penonomé

Puerto Armuelles

Golfo de
Chiriquí

Chitré

Santiago

Las Tablas

Archipiélago
de las Perlas

El Real

Yaviza

Pedasí

Gulfo de
Panamá

Isla de Coiba

Golfo de
Panamá

COLOMBIA

XV

DISCOVER CENTRAL AMERICA

From dripping rainforests echoing with the calls of howler monkeys to vibrant Maya markets alive with brilliant woven tapestries and fresh produce, Central America offers endless opportunities to experience and explore. The region teems with the most unique and varied of sites, people, and forms of beauty. Together, Central America's seven countries are only about a quarter the size of Mexico—but nowhere else in the world do such a wide range of geography, cultural groups, eco-systems, and recreational activities coexist within such a small space.

The nations of this narrow isthmus have emerged from decades of violent political instability into a relatively peaceful period. All have established democratic governments, and the scars left by the once-prevalent civil wars are healing. Once the domain only of bold (or foolhardy) adventurers, today's Central America—inexpensive and compact—eagerly welcomes the budget traveler.

WHEN TO GO

The most important climatic factor to consider when planning a trip to Central America is the **rainy season,** or *invierno* (winter), which generally falls between May and November. The rest of the year is the **dry season,** or *verano* (summer). On the Pacific Coast and in the highlands, the seasons are very distinct, while on the Caribbean Coast, some rain should be expected regardless of season. Temperature is determined by altitude rather than season; the highlands experience moderate highs and pleasantly cool nights while the coastal and jungle lowlands swelter. For a temperature chart, see the **Appendix** in the back of the book.

Dry season is "high season" for tourists—larger crowds and larger prices. The budget traveler may wish to consider a rainy season visit. Even then, the sun generally shines for much of the day, and most afternoon rainstorms are furious but fleeting. Dry season travel is key only for visitors in search of a dark tan or isolated areas where roads and trails can be washed out for weeks on end.

Many of the year's best parties happen during **Semana Santa,** the week-long Easter holiday. For more on when to go, see the country-specific introductions.

THINGS TO SEE AND DO

THE WILD LIFE

Thundering waterfalls. Cloudforests laced with climbing orchids and blanketed in mist. Fuming volcanoes. Miles of white-sand beach. Blessed with one of the most breathtaking and extensive park systems in the world, Central America is a nature-lover's paradise. The diversity of the region's national parks caters to every whim—whether you seek to stroll along well-maintained trails or machete your way through thousands of kilometers of jungle, Central America is sure to please.

In Belize, spelunk through **limestone caves** hollowed by underground rivers and take a dip in the subterranean waters (see p. 86). Scramble to the top of **Cerro Las Minas** (p. 458), the highest peak in Honduras, passing layers of cloudforest and gushing waterfalls on the way. Or attempt the impossible—explore the peaks and valleys of El Salvador's largest national park, **El Imposible** (p. 293), and try to spot a resplendent quetzal along the way. In Nicaragua, ascend the charred slopes of **Volcán Masaya** (p. 552) and gaze into the still-smoking Santiago crater. In Costa Rica's **Parque Nacional Manuel Antonio** (p. 212), hike along the powdery beach, stroll the forest paths, and lounge in the shade of a palm tree—all the while keeping an eye out for a resident anteaters or sloth. Or grab your binoculars and head for **Parque Nacional Soberanía** (p. 620), just an hour's reach from Panama City and yet teeming with a mind-boggling 525 species of birds.

SEX ON THE BEACH

OK, maybe not for everyone. But ocean-hungry travelers will find that Central America has everything else they might desire: snorkeling, diving, surfing, sunbathing. After all, where else are *two* oceans within such easy reach? **Bocas del Toro,** Panama (p. 662), is home to some of Central America's finest beaches, most bountiful reefs, and impressive turtle-watching. In Costa Rica, **Playa Tamarindo** (p. 196) offers the perfect combination of gorgeous beach days and wild tropical nights, while **Jacó** (p. 206) is a party-going surfer's paradise.

The world's second-largest barrier reef sits off the gorgeous Caribbean coast of Belize and Honduras. Denizens of the deep flock to Belize's **Caye Caulker** (p. 81) and **Ambergris Caye** (p. 86), to swim with sting rays and sharks. As if that weren't enough, Belize's Caribbean gems include the Blue Hole, an underwater cave 143m deep and twice as wide. The dreamy **Bay Islands** in Honduras (p. 497) offer silky white sand, elaborate coral formations, and the cheapest diving prices in the world.

El Salvador has some of the finest Pacific beaches in Central America, from the never-ending **La Costa del Sol** (p. 280) to the famed surfing at **La Libertad.** Offshore of Nicaragua's welcoming **San Juan del Sur** (p. 560), the deep-sea fishing is beyond comparison—you may hook into a wahoo or even a mighty sailfish.

DOWN THE ROAD TO RUINS

Over 2000 years ago, the inhabitants of Northern Guatemala began hauling huge slabs of limestone out of the ground and thrusting them skyward, constructing temples and palaces more than 70m high. The structures embody the mystery and grandeur of the great Maya cities, whose earliest remnants may date back more than 4000 years. The awesome temples, hieroglyphics, carvings, and statues that immortalize the ancients can today be visited at more than 30 sites in Guatemala, Belize, Honduras, and El Salvador. The most well-known is Guatemala's spectacular **Tikal** (p. 420), with more than 2000 structures and temples towering over the tropical rainforest. Equally impressive is **Copán,** Honduras (p. 463), home to intricate monuments and hieroglyphics. Less famous but still fascinating sites include **Uaxactún** (p. 424) and **Quiriguá** (p. 390) in Guatemala and **Lamanai** in Belize (p. 98).

Eventually, of course, the Spanish showed up in Central America, leaving behind an architectural legacy of their own. Ever-popular **Antigua,** Guatemala (p. 343) is a beautiful and well-preserved colonial city, with grand ruins and wonderfully atmospheric cobblestone streets. Other fine examples of colonial architecture are scattered throughout the region, from the quiet towns of Honduras's **western highlands** (p. 450) to the cities of **León** (p. 557) and **Granada** (p. 554) in Nicaragua.

PEOPLE AND CULTURE

Interactions with Central America's people are the highlight of many trips to the region. The **Western Highlands** of Guatemala (p. 343) are home to thousands of Maya who maintain many of their ancestral traditions. Visitors can glimpse modern Maya society first-hand, from the famous handicrafts at the market of **Chichicastenango** (p. 363) to the traditional villages ringing the gorgeous **Lago de Atitlán**

(p. 359). In Panama, the **San Blas Archipelago** (p. 670) is a semi-autonomous Caribbean island chain run entirely by the indigenous Kuna.

The region's recent history is crucial to its present character. Central America's people have faced immense hardship during years of civil war and governmental unrest; many are eager to share their experiences, while others would rather leave the past behind. Small but poignant museums chronicle the horrors of the wars in **Perquín**, El Salvador (p. 317) and **Estelí**, Nicaragua (p. 573), among other places.

In general, Central Americans are very warm and hospitable. Travelers who stop to chat will find locals truly excited to show what their hometowns have to offer.

COME FOR A WEEK, STAY FOR A YEAR

It's not unheard of: unsuspecting travelers get tangled up in the web of Central America's allure, and, well, just can't leave. And who would want to? For many, Central America has *it*: that one spot where the scene is just right—the people are friendly, scores of fascinating sites await exploration, and the food and culture make life a dream. These idyllic spots abound in Central America. Famous among such sites is the **Finca Ixobel** (p. 413), in the Petén region of Guatemala, where all-you-can eat dinners, tree-house accommodations, and exploration of the spectacular surroundings cast spells on wayward sojourners. **Casa Iguana** (p. 590), superbly situated on Nicaragua's Little Corn Island, combines an ecological ethic, an extensive library, a bedazzling white-sand lagoon, and light Caribbean breezes. Lounge in a hammock and laze the days away in Costa Rica at **Rancho Grande** (p. 193) and learn why black-sand **Playa Hermosa** (p. 193) deserves its name. If you don't want to spend your days twiddling your thumbs, there are numerous volunteer, work, and study options in Alternatives to Tourism .

▩ LET'S GO PICKS

BODACIOUS BEACHES: Where to begin? **Placencia**, Belize has miles of white-sand beach, as do **Tela**, Honduras, **Manzanillo**, Costa Rica, **San Juan del Sur**, Nicaragua, and **San Blas Archipelago**, Panama.

BEST DIVING AND SNORKELING: The **Bay Islands** of Honduras and **The Cayes** of Belize embrace the largest and most colorful reef in the western hemisphere.

BEST BIG ROCKS: Ruins at **Tikal**, Guatemala, are huge and impressive, but you'll avoid crowds at **Uaxactún**, Guatemala and **Caracol**, Belize. Don't miss the stunning intricacy of **Copán**, Honduras.

BEST PLACES TO GET YO' FREAK ON: Groove with the Garífuna in **Livingston**, Guatemala or merengue in **San José**, Costa Rica. Boogie all night in **Bluefields**, Nicaragua, or 24hr. in **Las Tablas**, Panama, during their Semana Santa Fiesta.

BEST HOT SPRINGS: Jump right into the healing waters of **Fuentes Georginas**, Guatemala. Soak in the Volcano's shadow at **Tabacón**, Costa Rica.

BEST NATIONAL PARKS: Explore endless trails of unique flora, fauna and bird life in **Parque Internacional La Amistad**, which extends from Costa Rica into Panama. Mimic monkeys in **Parque Nacional Corcovado**, Costa Rica. Hike through virgin rainforest in **Parque Nacional Santa Barbara**, Honduras.

BEST PLACES TO GET STEAMROLLED BY PIPING HOT MAGMA: Climb **Cerro Chirripó**, Costa Rica's highest peak. If mere height isn't enough, **Volcán Arenál**, also in Costa Rica, froths lava nightly above the town of Fortuna.

MOST FASHIONABLE BIRD: Guatemala's resplendent, ever-elusive **quetzal**.

BEST PLACE TO BUILD YOUR BATCAVE: At **Cavernas de Venado** in Costa Rica, spiders, bats, and rushing water are all that's keeping you from an underground waterworld. At Belize's **Tunich Hill Cave**, intact human skeletons are eager to greet visitors.

MOST CLICHÉD PHRASE IN THIS BOOK: "The %#*@ elusive quetzal."

DISCOVER

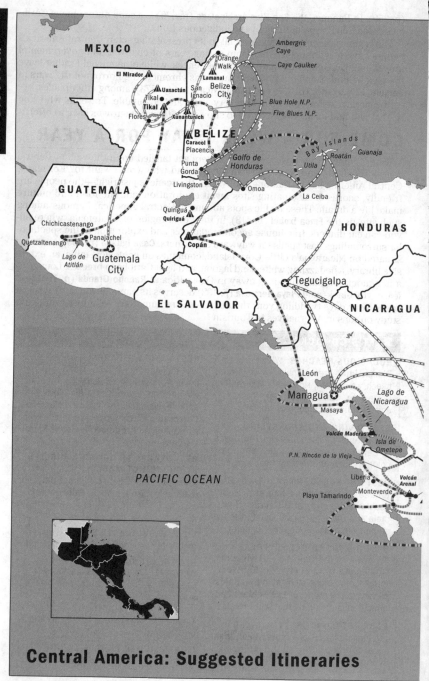

MEXICO

Ambergris Caye

Orange Walk

Caye Caulker

El Mirador

Lamanal

Uaxactún

San Ignacio

Belize City

Tikal

Tikal

Blue Hole N.P.

Flores

Xunantunich

Five Blues N.P.

BELIZE

Caracol

Placencia

Bay Islands

Roatán

Guanaja

Punta Gorda

Golfo de Honduras

Utila

GUATEMALA

Livingston

Omoa

La Ceiba

Quiriguá

Quiriguá

HONDURAS

Chichicastenango

Quetzaltenango

Panajachel

Copán

Lago de Atitlán

Guatemala City

Tegucigalpa

EL SALVADOR

NICARAGUA

León

PACIFIC OCEAN

Managua

Masaya

Lago de Nicaragua

Volcán Maderas

Isla de Ometepe

P.N. Rincón de la Vieja

Liberia

Volcán Arenal

Playa Tamarindo

Monteverde

Central America: Suggested Itineraries

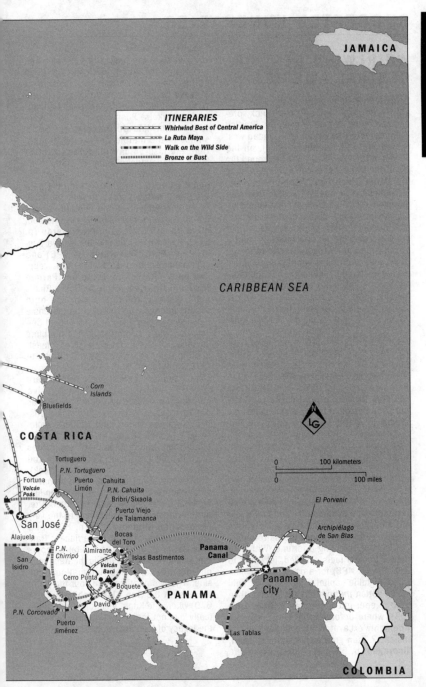

JAMAICA

ITINERARIES
- Whirlwind Best of Central America
- La Ruta Maya
- Walk on the Wild Side
- Bronze or Bust

CARIBBEAN SEA

Corn
Islands

Bluefields

COSTA RICA

Tortuguero
P.N. Tortuguero
Fortuna
Volcán   Puerto   Cahuita
Poás   Limón   P.N. Cahuita
                          Bribri/Sixaola
                          Puerto Viejo
                          de Talamanca

San José
Alajuela   Bocas
                          del Toro
San   P.N.   Almirante   Panama
Isidro   Chirripó   Islas Bastimentos   Canal
                          Volcán
              Cerro Punta Barú
                          Boquete   Panama
P.N. Corcovado   David   PANAMA   City

Puerto
Jiménez   Las Tablas

El Porvenir

Archipiélago
de San Blas

Panama
Canal

0   100 kilometers
0   100 miles

N

COLOMBIA

SUGGESTED ITINERARIES

DISCOVER

WHIRLWIND BEST OF CENTRAL AMERICA

2 MONTHS No one should try to package all of Central America into a quick, preplanned route. But we're going to. Starting in **Guatemala City** (see p. 333), head west to peaceful **Panajachel** (p. 354), on the shores of Lago de Atitlán. Cruise around the giant lake by ferry and stop in villages along the shore. Climb one of the encroaching volcanoes before heading west to **Quetzaltenango** (p. 379), a starting point for exploring western Guatemala's endless outdoor opportunities. After hiking with the howler monkeys and the elusive quetzals, find a bus headed for **Chichicastenango** (p. 363), and peruse the world-famous Maya market. Inspired by the marvels of the modern Maya, jump north to the incomparable ruins of **Tikal** (p. 420) to see the work of their ancestors. From there, hop across into Belize, spending a couple days in **San Ignacio** (p. 107), the region's up-and-coming hub for adventure tourism; canoeing, caving, Maya ruins, and waterfalls are all within easy reach. Skip out of San Ignacio on a bus down the Hummingbird Highway, stopping along the way to explore **Blue Hole and Five Blues national parks** (p. 115) and get a peek into Belize's eerie limestone underbelly—caves hollowed out by millennia of erosion. Farther south, on the coast, **Placencia** (p. 123) provides a pleasant break from a rushed itinerary. Sit on the beach and sip a fruit shake, or hire a boat out to one of the nearby Cayes to snorkel along the world's second longest coral reef. When you're ready to move on, grab a boat to **Honduras's Bay Islands** (p. 497), where you can learn to scuba dive or, if you're already certified, explore the surrounding reef without spending a fortune. With your lust for tropical reefs satisfied, jet south to **La Ceiba** (p. 486) for a party stop in Honduras' nightlife capital. Break it down until you've gotten *that* out of your system, then head deeper into Honduras to **Copán** (p. 463), where unforgettable Maya ruins lie thoroughly excavated. Had enough of the ancients? Then grab a bus south to **León, Nicaragua** (p. 557), a colonial city where you can sit in the park, enjoy the weather, and watch the young folk courting. Keep going south, and shop 'til you drop at **Masaya** (p. 549), home to one of Nicaragua's most famous (not to mention cheap) crafts markets. Push on, intrepid adventurer, to the **Isla de Ometepe** (p. 562), smack in the middle of Lake Nicaragua. Here the lush **Volcán Maderas** (p. 566) hides a tranquil lake within its crater. If all the volcano-climbing makes you hungry for some lava, roll south to Fortuna, Costa Rica, and watch **Volcán Arenal** (p. 188) belch fiery magma. Don't miss the area's hot springs and waterfalls. Move on to cool off in the cloudforests of **Monteverde** (p. 171), then wander around the Nicoya Peninsula to **Playa Tamarindo** (p. 196) and enjoy some serious beach time—surf, sleep, and party. Still farther south lies **Parque Nacional Chirripó**, home to Costa Rica's highest point, where you can see both oceans at once. The last stop on the Costa Rica leg is uncrowded Parque Nacional Corcovado, where rainforest comes tumbling into the sea. Last, but certainly not least, head to Panama, stopping first in **Boquete** (p. 652). Hike one of the area's many trails, climb Panama's highest peak, **Volcán Barú** (p. 655), and try to spot those elusive quetzals you missed in Guatemala. **Bocas del Toro** (p. 661) is next, promising pristine, turquoise waters and spotless white-sand beaches. Relax in the Caribbean atmosphere before heading to **Las Tablas** (p. 639), on the Azuero Peninsula. If you arrive during *Semana Santa* (Easter Week), you can get swept up in the wild *carnaval;* otherwise, revel in visits to the surrounding national parks and secluded islands. After all the roughing it, catch a bus to the very metropolitan **Panama City** (p. 603) and take a quick gander at the adjacent **Panama Canal** (p. 619). The capital pampers trail-weary visitors with movie theaters, hoppin' nightlife, and great international cuisine. If you've got time, end your trip far to the east in the **San Blas Archipelago** (p. 670) where the Kuna, a culturally and politically distinct indigenous group, preserve the legacy of their ancestors.

LA RUTA MAYA

3 WEEKS Beginning in **Guatemala City** (p. 333), head straight for the big one— **Tikal** (p. 420). Without a doubt the most outstanding Maya site, it can be easily explored from the nearby town of **Flores** (p. 415). From there, head deeper into the jungle to visit the stately ruins of **Uaxactún** (p. 424) that are barely resisting the encroaching jungle. Secluded **El Mirador** (p. 424), for the truly intrepid Maya enthusiast, lies farther north of Flores. Almost swallowed by the forest, it is tough to reach but remains largely unexcavated and undisturbed. Back on the road, jump east into Belize, to **San Ignacio** (p. 107), a base for two nearby ruins: **Xunantunich** and **Caracol** (p. 113). The former is easily accessible, while the latter requires a 2½hr. trek in 4x4 vehicles. The last stop in Belize is the northern ruins of **Lamanai** (p. 98), reached by a half-day river trip from the town of **Orange Walk** (p. 95). From northern Belize take a leap south to the ruins of **Quiriguá** (p. 390) in eastern Guatemala. The stelae (pillar-like carved stones) are among the finest in the Maya world. Finally, end the trip with a bang in **Copán** (p. 463), Honduras. World-famous for the research conducted there and for the complexity of the preserved artwork, the ruins offer one of Central America's (and the world's) most impressive sights.

WALK ON THE WILD SIDE

4 WEEKS Beginning in Nicaraguan capital of **Managua** (p. 531), an ecotourism jaunt through southern Central America should begin with a stop at the **Isla de Ometepe** (p. 562) for the gorgeous twin volcanoes and the world's only freshwater sharks. Jump the border to **Costa Rica** and the check out the piping hot magma of the active volcano at **Parque Nacional Rincón de la Vieja** (p. 180) just north of **Liberia** (p. 178). Continue south along the Interamerican Highway to **Monteverde** (p. 171), stopping off at **Volcán Arenal**. Eavesdrop on the local fauna in biological reserves and a superb cloudforest. Farther south, hit **Ala-** juela (p. 156) and get lost in the swirls of colorful butterflies at **Finca de las Mariposas**. Head north to **Volcán Poás**, one of the world's largest craters. Bypass San José's urban confusion and head straight to **Parque Nacional Chirripó** (p. 220), accessible from **San Isidro** (p. 216), to capture a rare view of both the Atlantic and the Pacific from Costa Rica's highest point. Soak up some luxury at the nearby *aguas termales* or the local masseuse. Tearing yourself away from that high, visit the coastal town of **Puerto Jiménez** (p. 232) and explore **Parque Nacional Corcovado** (p. 234) to witness untold varieties of birds, beasts, and botanical beauty. Journey south again to **Panama** and the town of **Cerro Punta** (p. 659) to hike Panama's highest peak through the haze of its cloudforest. From the nearby town of **David** (p. 646), hop a short flight to **Bocas del Toro** (p. 662) before cruising over to **Isla Bastimentos** (p. 666) for a glimpse of nesting turtles and other Atlantic wildlife. Lastly, fly to **Panama City** and Central America's only urban national park, **Parque Natural Metropolitano** (p. 615).

BRONZE OR BUST: A CARIBBEAN COAST TOUR

1 MONTH Arriving in Belize City, take a boat to **Caye Caulker** (p. 81) and **Ambergris Caye** (p. 86) to scuba and snorkel the 2nd largest barrier reef in the Western Hemisphere. Fly or take the Hummingbird and Southern coastal highways to **Punta Gorda** (p. 127), Belize's sleepy southern gateway to the mountains and the country's largest Maya population. Take a *lancha* to **Livingston** (p. 399), home of Guatemala's vibrant Garífuna culture, rich *tapado* stew, and *aguas calientes* (hot springs). Next, travel by *lancha* to **Omoa**, an idyllic Honduran fishing village with easy access to waterfalls, beaches, and transportation to Guatemala and inner Honduras. Use **La Ceiba** as your party port on the way to the **Bay Islands**, the best white-sand beaches in Central America. Bus it to **Tegucigalpa** and catch a flight to **San José** (p. 144), Costa Rica. (If you want to extend the itinerary, fly into **Managua** (p. 531), Nicaragua, and continue flying to either **Bluefields** (p. 585)or the **Corn Islands**(p. 588); the former a hip party town, the latter a laid-back beach scene.) From San José, fly to **Tortuguero** (p. 238), a small but increasingly popular sea-side village accessible only by boat or plane. Be sure to explore the nearby **Parque Nacional Tortuguero** (p. 241)for hiking, boating, and turtle spying. Leaving, catch a boat to **Puerto Limón** (p. 235), then head on down the coast to **Cahuita** (p. 243), home to sun worshippers, howler monkeys, and Costa Rica's largest coral reef in the **Parque Nacional Cahuita** (p. 244). The beaches are surfer-friendly. If your tan still isn't perfect, head to the ethnically eclectic **Puerto Viejo de Talamanca** (p. 246) with its numerous surfing beaches. If you can tear yourself away, journey on into **Panama** through the **Bribrí/Sixaola** (p. 670) border crossing. From **Almirante** (p. 667), take a water taxi to **Archipiélago de Bocas del Toro** (p. 662), a grouping of islands ripe for hiking, diving, and fishing. If your pocket book still allows it, head by bus from Almirante to **David** (p. 646), then fly or express bus it to **Panama City** (p. 603). From there, take a flight to **El Porvenir** (p. 673), the westernmost island of the **San Blas Archipelago** (p. 670), home of the **Kuna,** Central America's most independent, traditional indigenous population. Take your time and explore the rich and diverse culture of the Kuna; the empty white sand beaches are an added bonus.

CENTRAL AMERICA: AN INTRODUCTION

THE LAND

Central America is a land of geological and meteorological instability. Situated at the convergence of four tectonic plates and close at all points to both the Pacific and Atlantic Oceans, it has been battered by earthquakes, volcanic eruptions, tropical storms, and hurricanes. The fortunate outcome of this temperamental geology is an unparalleled array of climates and a striking variety of plant and animal life.

GEOGRAPHY AND GEOLOGY

At 523,865 sq. km, Central America is only one-fourth the size of Mexico, its neighbor to the north, and half the size of Colombia, its neighbor to the South. However, its geographic importance belies its tiny size. Serving as the land bridge between North and South America, Central America forms an important oceanic barrier, separating the Pacific from the Caribbean and the Atlantic.

In geological terms, Central America is a newborn babe. While the North and South American continents have existed as separate landmasses for nearly 140 million years, it was only five million years ago that Central America emerged heroically to connect the two. A fractured piece of the North American continental crust formed the northern isthmus, and later volcanic activity and sedimentary deposits created Southern Central America. Parts of Nicaragua and Panama were the last to fill in, perhaps as recently as three million years ago.

Central America sits atop the junction of four tectonic plates—the Cocos, Caribbean, North American, and Nazca. Geologically speaking, it's not a pretty picture. The Cocos plate pushes into the Caribbean plate at a rate of 10m per century—a veritable geological sprint. As the Cocos slides beneath it, the Caribbean plate rises and breaks up, producing earthquakes and volcanoes. **Volcanic Highlands** run from Guatemala to Panama, comprising 250 volcanoes. Although a quarter of these are extinct and half are dormant, this is still the most active volcanic belt in the Americas. Visitors can see the hot and steamy action live at volcanoes like Guatemala's **Pacaya** (p. 353) and Costa Rica's **Arenal** (p. 189) and **Irazú** (p. 166).

Besides the Volcanic Highlands, Central America has two other major mountainous regions. The non-volcanic **Crystalline Highlands,** or **Northern Sierra,** begin in Guatemala with the Sierra los Cuchumantes, stretch east through Honduras, and end with Cordillera Isabella in Northern Nicaragua. The inactive volcanoes of the **Cordillera de Talamanca, or Southern Sierra,** tower over Costa Rica and Panama.

The northernmost of the region's three major lowland regions is **El Petén,** a huge beast of a limestone shelf that encompasses northern Guatemala, Belize, and Mexico's Yucatán Peninsula. Formed by calcium remains of marine life, the shelf is over 3000m thick and pockmarked with deep caves and depressions where the limestone has eroded. Farther east along the isthmus, the Caribbean Coast of Nicaragua and Honduras form **La Mosquitia** (Mosquito Coast), a sparsely populated lowland region of swamps and rivers that comprises the largest forested region in Central America. The third major lowland is the **Nicaraguan Depression,** which cuts across the isthmus from the Gulf of Fonseca in western Nicaragua to the province of Limón in Costa Rica, including the Lago de Nicaragua and the Lago de Managua. With 2370km of Caribbean coast and 3280km of Pacific frontage, the sea is never far away in Central America—200km at the most. And at its narrowest point, in Panama's Darién, the isthmus is only 50km wide.

CLIMATE

Central America is essentially tropical, but due to variations in latitude, topography and proximity to the sea, the climate can fluctuate substantially over short distances. The Caribbean coast is much wetter than the Pacific coast. This is because of the typical easterly flow of air through the region: as it heads west, mountains trap humid air and force it to rise. Moist air is cooled past its dew point and falls as rain while drier, warmer air flows down the Pacific side. This causes higher pressure on the Caribbean side and lower pressure on the Pacific side.

Altitude divides the isthmus into four distinct and creatively titled temperature zones. Lowlands areas below 900m are termed *tierra caliente* (hot land); here the annual temperature averages over 22°C (72°F). The well-populated *tierra templada* (temperate land), at 1000 to 2000m, is a climate of eternal spring with an average temperature of 60 to 72°F (16-22°C). In the mountainous regions between 2000 and 3000m, the *tierra fría* (you guessed it—the cold land), chills below 46°F (8°C). The *tierra helada* (ice-land) exists only at the highest altitudes.

The seasons have little impact on temperature but great impact on rainfall. Beginning in May, a low-pressure system called the Intertropical Convergence Zone migrates north from its resting place in the central Pacific and sets itself squarely over Central America. This interrupts the otherwise constant trade winds and marks the beginning of the rainy season *(invierno)*, which generally lasts until December. The rainy season is marked by extremely powerful, but often quite brief, daily downpours, usually in the late afternoon. In December, the rains abate as the Convergence Zone moves back over the ocean; the trade winds resume their steady flow across the isthmus and bring the dry season *(verano)* with them.

FLORA AND FAUNA

Central America's biological diversity is due in part to its position between two continents. Both North and South American species dwell here, as do plants and animals unique to the isthmus. From the howler monkeys in the tropical rainforest to the multicolored Caribbean coral, Central America's wildlife is its biggest asset.

On land, the flora of Central America is an eclectic mix of both South American and North American species. **Tropical rainforest** covers most of the eastern lowlands of Central America, while Belize and parts of Honduras are instead **pine savanna.** Along the Pacific Coast and the inland valleys, lowland **dry forest** is most common. This forest is lower than rainforest and, as it grows on more fertile land, has been almost entirely cut down for farming. At higher altitudes, lowland rainforests blend into **montane forest**—cool evergreen woods just below timberline. Pines predominate until the highest elevations, where firs and yews are all that remain. The steep coastal slopes around 1950m harbor **cloudforest,** thickets of low, moss-covered trees, permanently dripping with moisture and enshrouded in mist.

An equally diverse crew of colorful and unusual animals, which, like their flowered friends, hail from both North and South America, making the isthmus their home. The stunning **jaguar,** typically golden with black marks, once flourished in lowland forests; sadly it is now endangered. Other exotic big cats include **jaguarundis, ocelots,** and **pumas.** The **tapir,** a fantastical, pig-like creature can also be found in the rainforest, joined by the **peccary, anteater,** and aptly named **tree sloth.** The unmistakable call of the **howler monkey** resonates through the lowlands. Squirrel, spider and white-faced **capuchin monkeys** also cavort in the trees.

Caymans, crocodiles (*not* alligators), and **boas** all inhabit Central America's lowlands, originally arriving from South America. The bright red, blue or green **poison dart frog** is omnipresent. Don't touch, though: the name isn't just for show. Another animal you may want to leave alone is the **bushmaster snake,** the massive, venomous viper with an impressive record of chasing people down. In higher altitudes, North American reptiles like **rattlesnakes** and **kingsnakes** are common.

Birds, ranging from the **violet saberwing hummingbird** to the **monkey-eating harpy eagle,** are the sole reason many come to Central America. Most famous is the resplendent **quetzal** (see **For the Birds,** p. 405), endemic to Central America and found only in isolated cloudforests. The quetzal's long, brightly colored tail feathers were treasured by Maya kings. Other prized birds of the region include rainbow-colored scarlet macaws, parrots, and toucans.

Pacific waters are colder, more turbulent, and more nutrient-rich than their Caribbean counterparts. **Plankton** thrive and support large communities of open-water fish like **tuna, mackerel,** and **jacks,** and stationary filter-feeders like **oysters** and **sponges.** This environment is not conducive to coral reef growth, however, and only in a few protected spots do reefs spring up (principally in Panama and Costa Rica).

By contrast, the Caribbean is stabler, warmer, and shallower. **Coral reefs, seagrasses,** and **mangroves** form the foundation of the Caribbean ecosystem, supporting large communities of animals, including sea urchins and stars, lobsters, sea turtles, manatees, and porpoises. The colorful fish of the Caribbean make it more attractive to snorkelers and scuba divers than the colder Pacific waters.

Five types of **sea turtles** visit Central America's beaches, coming ashore to nest in vast packs known as *arribadas.* The **green turtle** (famously on display at Costa Rica's Parque Nacional Tortuguero, p. 238), the **hawksbill,** and the rare **loggerhead** visit both coasts, while the **Olive Ridley** sticks to the Pacific.

Since Central America has been a historically impoverished region, with governments and citizens struggling to get by, the lure of a quick buck from environmental exploitation overrides the long-term benefits of preservation. A well-publicized solution to this problem is **ecotourism,** organized tourism of outdoor attractions and wildlife, theoretically done in a way that protects the environment.

HISTORY TO INDEPENDENCE

Central America's geographic fragmentation has in many ways determined the course of history on the isthmus, dividing the region into distinct cultural and linguistic groups. Between the arrival of the first people in the region at least 10,000 years ago and the Spanish "discovery" of the area in the late 15th century, the indigenous people of Central America constructed complex political and economic systems and developed agricultural and scientific technology.

PRECOLONIAL HISTORY: THE MAYA

The Maya domain stretched from Chiapas and the Yucatán in Mexico to Honduras—though never all at once or in a single unified civilization. Geographical variation divided the area into three main regions: the Pacific plain and the nearby highlands in the south; the central lowlands in Guatemala's Petén; and the northern lowlands in the Yucatán. Scholars use large-scale social changes to divide Maya history into three periods: the Pre-Classic, the Classic, and the Post-Classic.

THE PRE-CLASSIC: BUILD-IT-YOURSELF CITY-STATES

The appearance of highland cities near the Pacific Coast of the isthmus around 500 BC marked the beginning of the **Pre-Classic period**. Social stratification emerged soon after the establishment of these cities. Membership in the highest sociopolitical class did not depend on political power, which belonged primarily to the hereditary chief of a polity. The "elite," instead included priests, military rulers, or craftsmen and merchants. A pyramidal division of labor allowed the elite to delegate responsibilities to their subordinates, who passed the buck to the bottom rung, which labored to harvest the maize, beans, and manioc.

As an independent network of polities emerged in the Pre-Classic era, the elite encouraged intellectual development. Hieroglyphic writing was the fruit of this effort, but it is unknown whether the Maya created it themselves or were exposed to it through commerce with other cultures. To increase efficiency, the Maya developed new agricultural techniques, and chiefdoms vied for the best land.

SCIENCE AND TECHNOLOGY. By many accounts, the Maya were the most artistically and intellectually advanced of all the New World cultures, although their political and economic organization were rivaled by those of the Aztecs and Incas. Foremost among the Maya's developments were their complex artistic and scientific practices, many of which matched those of Europe and Asia. Arched and columned buildings in highland cities reflect precise geometrical calculations.

The Maya were also remarkable carvers, using tools of flint, obsidian, and fire-hardened wood to carve dates and pictures into blocks of stone. They were able to transport these enormous rocks across hundreds of kilometers of hilly jungle. Given this technological sophistication, archaeologists were surprised to find no evidence that the Maya ever employed the wheel except in children's games. Moreover, although the Maya never domesticated load-carrying animals, they developed advanced crop cultivation techniques such as terracing and irrigation.

THE CALENDRICAL SYSTEM. The Maya developed a working sidereal calendar— one that measures years by gauging the earth's revolution relative not only to the sun, but also to the other stars. This extremely accurate method had practical uses, such as timing the planting of maize, and more abstract ones, such as astrological calculations. The stelae (tall carved and marked altars, singular "stele") are inscribed with the date of their construction as calculated by this system.

To write these dates, the Maya established a fixed event as a chronological reference point—and created the calendar known as the **Long Count**. The Maya believed that at the end of every "great cycle" (about 5128 years) the world was created anew; the starting point of the Long Count may have been the beginning of the most recent great cycle, around 3114 BC. The dating unit was the day (rather than the year, as in modern dates), making the numbers involved fairly large. A bar equaled five and a dot equaled one in this complex, base 20, mathematical system. Since this was often cumbersome, the **Short Count** was used, in which abbreviations reduced the number of glyphs necessary, thus leaving more room for other symbolic inscriptions. Although they left a unified cultural legacy, the Maya were never politically cohesive; they lived in warring groups whose relative positions fluctuated. This did not impede the Maya's commercial interaction; trade flowed along long-distance routes, and the exchange of ideas followed the goods.

THE CLASSIC: DYNASTIC ACCOMPLISHMENTS

In the **Classic period** (AD 250-900), scientific and cultural centers emerged in the hotter, more humid lands of Belize, northern Guatemala, the Atlantic coast of Honduras, and the Yucatán Peninsula—collectively known as the "lowlands." The highland mountain regions remained populated, lorded over by the polity of Kaminaljuyú in southern Guatemala.

TIKAL. The descent into the lowlands coincided with a solidification of existing social hierarchies, as chiefdoms became kingdoms. With strong *ahau* (kings), polities swelled in population, built grander architecture, and engaged in aggressive campaigns of conquest and expansion. The archetypal Classical period polity was **Tikal** (see p. 420), located in the tropical central lowlands, in the Petén region of present-day Guatemala. Tikal rose to prominence in the wake of nearby El Mirador's demise during the Early Classic period. Like other polities of the time, Tikal exhibited a state-level organization of dynastic rule. Nearby, less spectacular remains suggest that urban sprawl is hardly a new trend; extensive "suburban" networks and reams of paved highway connected thousands of inhabitants to the larger cities. Governed by its strong rulers, the city soon reached a population as large as 100,000. One target of Tikal's expansion was its northern neighbor **Uaxactún** (see p. 424), a Maya center famed for the architecture of its ceremonial buildings, which were aligned to function as an astronomical observatory. Under Smoking Frog, Tikal usurped Uaxactún in AD 378. In the Late Classic period, however, other polities—such as **Caracol** (see p. 113), led by Lord Water—used their political alliances to help them compete with Tikal. In AD 682, when Ah Cacau ascended to the throne, Tikal experienced a brief revival. However, the city declined in the 9th century, and this time for good. (For more on **Tikal,** see p. 420.)

COPÁN. At about the time of Tikal's downfall, **Copán** (see p. 463), in modern-day Honduras, had grown from its puny Pre-Classic size into the preeminent polis of the southeast lowlands. The records reveal that heavy construction occurred during the reign of Copán's 13th king, **18 Rabbit.** The city's prosperity is thought to have been the result of sucking the life-blood out of its smaller neighbor **Quiriguá** (p. 395), in Guatemala. Apparently, 18 Rabbit stole Quiriguá's lunch money one too many times, for under the leadership of its greatest leader, **Cauac Sky,** Quiriguá kidnapped 18 Rabbit and sacrificed him in AD 738. With Quiriguá's independence, construction waned and Copán's power declined rapidly. Echoing Tikal, Copán briefly revived and then sank into permanent obscurity.

Copán is well-known for its **ballcourts.** Drawings found by archaeologists reveal that the Maya used these courts for a game in which players had to keep a hefty rubber ball aloft without using their hands or feet. Bouncing the ball from body to body, players attempted to pop it into one of the two circular stone goals mounted at either end of the enclosed court. According to hieroglyphic records, the captain of the winning team won a robe right off the back of each spectator in the audience, while the losing captain was ceremonially beheaded.

THINGS FALL APART. Of the numerous theories on why Maya civilization fragmented during the Classic period, natural disaster is among the most popular. Although there is evidence of an earthquake in Quiriguá, there is insufficient evidence to blame it; theories of volcanism suffer a similar fate, though they are considered more plausible. Epidemic disease is perhaps the most likely natural crisis; skeletons found in Tikal and Copán show that malnutrition and possibly disease increased over time. Pottery records at Altar de Sacrificios and **Ceibal** (see p. 414) show that outside forces overthrew the social order; the favored suspects are the Putun Maya, Chontal-speakers who lived on the Gulf Coast and may have monopolized trade routes. It is likely that a combination of these factors contributed to the ultimate demise of the Maya polities.

THE POST-CLASSIC: MOVE OVER, MAYA
The general decline of Classic Maya civilization followed the fall of Tikal and Copán. For reasons unknown, residents of the great focal points of the Classical

culture migrated into the outlying jungle and into Mexico, where they establishe
cities of the **Post-Classic period** (AD 900-1519). The most important of these-
Chichén Itzá, Mayapán, and Uxmal, (all in Mexico)—are popular among ruin-see
ing travelers, but less so among archaeologists; many of the fruits of Classic
Maya culture had been replaced by influences from central Mexico.

NON-MAYA INDIGENOUS PEOPLES

Non-Maya indigenous groups inhabited more than half of Central America at th
time of the Conquest. East and south of the Maya, the **Chibcha** inhabited Panam
and Costa Rica after migrating from South America; the **Kuna** populated Panam
the **Pipil** and **Nicarao** groups lived in modern-day El Salvador and Nicaragua; an
the **Miskito, Sumo,** and **Rama** tribes filled the Mosquito Coast of Honduras, whe
they still live today. These cultures were sedentary and agricultural like the May
but for a variety of reasons were slower to organize. Chieftains—instead of buil
ing the massive pyramids, stelae, or temples that existed farther north—booste
their prestige with **ornamentation.** They used their amazing wealth to import ra
jadeite (a variety of a jade) from the Motagua Valley in Guatemala and fashione
the jadeite and seashells into figurines and pendants. Around AD 600 they disco
ered metallurgy, and gold displaced jadeite and shells; the burial site **Sitio Cont**
near Penonomé in Panama, contained dozens of elaborate gold pieces. The gol
trade gained popularity in Costa Rican and Panamanian chiefdoms.

The jaguar, the cult animal of several groups in Costa Rica and Panama, co
noted fierceness, suggesting the frequency of war. Stone sculptures depict wa
riors in fighting gear, sometimes toting axes and even heads as trophies. Thes
southern groups stood up to the Spaniards, but the better-armed *conquistadore*
subdued them without much difficulty.

CONQUEST AND COLONIES

The Spanish **Conquista** (Conquest) of the Americas, from Mexico to the Cape c
Good Hope, was a tremendous, earth-shattering event, probably the most impo
tant in the history of these areas. The self-appointed task of conquering the Ne
World's land and "evangelizing" its peoples took several centuries—Some say
has not ended even today, as cultural, political, and economic elements of Eur
pean and indigenous origin continue to interface.

When Columbus first stumbled upon the area in 1502, he was intrigued by th
first few Maya inhabitants he saw—so he decided to take them back to Spain t
"civilize" them. These were among the first few losses to a native populatio
which would later be robbed of millions. Within 200 years, the total population c
Central America, including European settlers, was well below one million.

CONQUEST FROM THE NORTH

After **Hernán Cortés's** coup in Central Mexico, his forces proceeded southwar
toward Guatemala under the command of Cortés's loyal henchman **Pedro de Alva
rado,** a haughty blond notorious for his cruelty. Alvarado made his way through th
jungle, finding a Maya civilization that was concentrated in pocket-like individua
polities, vastly different from the large, imperial power structures that had bee
the fatal weakness of the Aztecs and Incas. These Maya "city-states" were able t
resist European subjugation much longer than their counterparts. The May
fought a jungle war, luring enemies into ambushes, eluding the Spanish by vanish
ing into the mountains, and setting up elaborate booby traps. Consequently, afte
subduing the Pacific Coast, the Spaniards struggled for more than 175 years t
control the jungles of the north. Several Maya communities outlasted much of th
conquest: the Guatemalan city of **Tayasal,** near modern day Flores, fell to siege onl

in 1697, and the Lacandon people of Northern Guatemala and Southern Mexico resisted subjugation or "assimilation" even until the middle of the 20th century, remaining wedded to subsistence lifestyles as late as the 1970s.

Nonetheless, many Maya polities, often weakened by smallpox, did fall under Alvarado's onslaught. In Guatemala, he allied with one Maya group, the **Cakchiquel**, to vanquish another, the **Quiché**. Alvarado continued southward, pushing into the western territories of modern-day El Salvador in 1524. The Pre-Classic Maya settlements of Tazumal and San Andrés had dissipated, but the indigenous **Pipil** remained to resist invasion. Alvarado later consolidated Cortés's control over Guatemala, Honduras, and El Salvador, founding the first Spanish capital of the region (on the old Cakchiquel site of Iximché) in July, 1524. After protracted squabbling with other *conquistadores* further south, he became the uncontested governor of Guatemala. He died in 1541, and his widow, Beatriz de la Cueva, succeeded him as governor of Guatemala. Her rule was short, however; the capital city's founders had built it squarely in the path of a volcano, and two days after Beatriz's takeover a massive flood and mudslide destroyed the city, taking the new governor with it. A new capital was constructed in present-day Antigua.

CONQUEST IN THE SOUTH

While Alvarado and Cortés's other minions marauded in Guatemala, the Conquest moved forward in the rest of Central America as well. Spain, however, did not appoint qualified leaders—the selected governors of the region were themselves *conquistadores*, petty opportunists whose rivalries furthered violence among the Spaniards and hindered unification. After **Vasco de Balboa** crossed the Panamanian isthmus and "discovered" the Pacific Ocean, his title of governor and captain general of Darién (Panama) was handed over to **Pedrarías Dávila**. Balboa and Dávila feared and hated each other, ending in the latter's decapitation of the former. After disposing of Balboa, Dávila expanded his domain, breaching royal orders further by allowing brutal treatment of indigenous groups. The **Nicarao** of the Caribbean Coast, led by the famed **King Nicarao**, rebuffed Dávila's expansionist efforts. Yet Dávila, having encroached on the region's people and gold supply, set the stage for the pillage that would accompany later European immigration to Nicaragua.

In 1524, **Francisco Hernández de Córdoba** brought the first wave of successful colonists to settle in the eastern lowlands. They named the new country Nicaragua, after King Nicarao, and much later their descendents would call the local coin "córdoba," in honor of the king's European nemesis. Confrontation between the invaders and the invaded, while fierce in places, was brief and bloodless compared to the conquests of the Aztec and Maya empires. Nevertheless, the eradication of Nicaragua's indigenous people proceeded rapidly; Those whom Old World diseases did not kill right away were sold into slavery, and an indigenous population hundreds of thousands strong disappeared within twenty years. After establishing Granada and Managua, Córdoba tried to set up a kingdom independent of Panama. Dávila rewarded Córdoba's independent thinking with a thoughtful beheading.

Costa Rica, meanwhile, was partially ignored by power- and wealth-hungry *conquistadores* because it had no large, rich indigenous empire and was thought poor in natural resources (read: gold). Nonetheless, Costa Rica's few natives did suffer from the diseases brought by the Spanish, and were unable to resist the ever larger groups of settlers who arrived to colonize the area. Juan Vásquez de Coronado established the first permanent settlement at Cartago in 1563. Colonists here enjoyed a high degree of unofficial autonomy, since European monarchs were uneager to colonize a "poor" land so far from the region's colonial centers. As a result, Costa Rica developed much differently than other colonies—serfdom and debt-peonage were not implemented because the few natives did not provide the slave-labor force available elsewhere.

COLONIAL GOVERNMENT, OR HOW NOT TO RUN A CONTINENT

Much to the *conquistadores'* dismay, colonizing efforts in Central America received little support from Spain. During the early 16th century, Spain ruled Central America with scattered *ayuntamientos* (municipal councils). In 1530, Guatemala, Nicaragua, Honduras, Chiapas, and Panama all functioned under separate royal orders. In 1535, the **Viceroyalty of New Spain** was established in Mexico City, comprised of Mexico, Guatemala, Honduras, El Salvador, Nicaragua, and Costa Rica—but its jurisdiction was unclear, thanks to a conflict with Panama over Nicaragua. In 1543, Spain managed to unify the isthmus from the Yucatán to Panama, but over the following years the capital moved from Honduras to Guatemala to Panama and back to Guatemala. Even after Central America was united as the Kingdom of Guatemala in 1548, the disorganization of its myriad administrative units, governing bodies, and magistrates belied this monolithic title.

Though the Viceroyalty of New Spain failed to unify the isthmus, it did establish an almost-united region of states recognizable from a modern standpoint: Mexico, Guatemala, Honduras, Nicaragua, El Salvador, and Costa Rica. Panama and Belize were, however, not included in the Viceroyalty. The uniformly prosperous Panama disdained its poorer brethren, remaining a loyal vassal of Spain until 1821, when it became a state within Colombia.

Belize, on the other hand, did not exist in 1535. The Spanish had penetrated the area in the 1500s and 1600s and tried to convert the Maya to Christianity but with little success. British buccaneers and logwood cutters finally settled on the unfriendly coast in the mid-17th century. Spain, and later Guatemala, regarded the British as interlopers in their territory. Britain took an unaggressive yet determined stance, referring to Belize as a "settlement," not a colony. Spain allowed the British to ply the logwood and mahogany trades, but only much later (1798) did Britain get Spain off its back, and even later (1862) was Belize declared to be the colony of British Honduras.

THE NEW LAWS

The King's **New Laws** (*Nuevas Leyes*, 1542) were the work of **Bartolome de Las Casas,** the Bishop of Chiapas who insisted on abolishing the cruel *encomienda* system. *Encomenderos* were conquistadors and Spanish settlers who received parcels of land (*encomiendas*) and the (forced) labor of the indigenous inhabitants in return for "civilizing" and "christianizing" these inhabitants. The colonists, however, vigorously protested the New Laws as an unfair infringement on their "rights," and the King was forced to create the institution of the *repartimiento*, which basically allowed forced labor to continue under a different heading.

The *repartimiento* did, however, change indigenous life by allowing some measure of freedom for the Indians. They could live in their own villages, somewhat protected from their former masters and slightly isolated from European influence. "Indian towns" developed in places like Quetzaltenango, Managua, and Masaya, and in some areas "closed, corporate communities" made communal living a tool of protection and survival in the face of oppression. In some cases, tight-knit indigenous communities could continue their pre-conquest spiritual practices while paying lip service to the Spanish missionaries. Despite this relative degree of freedom, however, tribute was still the cornerstone of colonial life, and the natives, while not enslaved, worked in conditions verging on slavery. Eventually, the *repartimiento* became the basis for the system of debt-peonage which spread throughout the area. It was a means for the Spanish to perpetuate the subjugation and manipulation of the indigenous population.

The number of Maya dwindled due to famine, disease, and overwork, and as a result, the Spanish lost their labor force. Although substantial Indian groups remained in Guatemala, Honduras, and sections of El Salvador parts farther south and west of the region suffered from native depopulation. *Indígena* villages disbanded, and the Spanish had to eke out new trades for themselves. Nevertheless, the economy weakened, and the Kingdom of Guatemala found itself ill-equipped to deal with a series of earthquakes that struck in 1717. The Kingdom withdrew into a self-sufficient, feudal existence.

INDIGO, INDIGONE

During the 18th century, Central America's economy stabilized. Immigrants arrived, the resident Spanish population grew, and the Indian population rebounded. Production and trade kicked off. Spain encouraged mining in the area, but because mineral deposits were thin, agriculture was paramount. Cacao had been the principal export of the 16th century, but indigo, needed by Peru's textile mills, replaced it. From 1760 to 1790 the indigo trade blossomed. Used as a dye, this tough legume played an essential part in the colonial economy, though it was of no use to the mostly indigenous farmers.

The indigo boom cemented the exploitative relationship between the landholding class and the indigenous *campesinos*, which has marked nearly every political and economic conflict in Central America ever since. Displaced from their traditional subsistence farming locales, the indigenous populations became a landless labor force working on export-crop plantations; they were exploited mercilessly. Because indigo farms were large plantations in the hands of very few employers living in Guatemala City, the capital city became the center of a large monopoly.

At the turn of the century, however, the indigo industry experienced the same shock as the cacao trade had decades earlier: outside competition usurped much of the international trade. Although Central American indigo production decreased in importance, it remained the organizing element of life until the boom of the coffee trade late in the 19th century.

The death of Charles II brought **Philip V** of the Bourbon family to the throne. The new king plunged the empire into a costly war, but Bourbon policy centralized authority and reasserted royal control. It also bolstered the military and promoted agricultural export of Costa Rican cacao and tobacco, and especially Salvadoran indigo. As a result of these changes, the Guatemalan mercantile and bureaucratic establishment expanded. The provincial elites cultivated strong regionalist sentiments, and the Creoles resented the favoritism in the royal policy.

The **Cádiz Constitution** of 1812, an attempt to appease Creole frustrations, granted elections for colonial offices and representation in Spanish parliament. These innovations whetted the Creole appetite for independence. Local revolutions were quelled, and later, the authoritarian Ferdinand VII annulled the 1812 constitution. Upon protest, Spain restored Creole political participation in Central American towns in 1820.

THE PUSH FOR INDEPENDENCE

With the return of sanctioned Creole politics, the Liberal and Conservative parties, destined to dominate the Central American scene for a century, emerged in embryonic form. This new political vitality, combined with a resentment of Spanish authority, yielded revolution. The members of the Viceroyalty—Guatemala, Honduras, Nicaragua, El Salvador, and Costa Rica—declared independence from Spain in 1821. Internal instability allowed **Agustín de Iturbide** to seduce the Central American republics into a brief affair with Mexico, but this ended when Iturbide left office and the Mexican "empire" crumbled. In 1823 the Central Americans formed their own federal republic, the **United Provinces of Central America,** with the capital in Guatemala City.

The factionalism that had inspired independence, however, also undermined the integrity of the federation. Each of the five completely autonomous states had its own president, who ignored the federation's constitutional laws. Tension quickly arose between Conservatives and Liberals. The federation began during a Conservative regime under which only the upper classes could vote; slavery was abolished and the Roman Catholic church was preserved. In 1830, however, the elections favored Liberal **Francisco Morazán,** who undermined the Church and took measures to enhance trade. When tension mounted, he moved the capital from conservative Guatemala City to San Salvador. Unfazed, the Conservatives incited the indigenous populations and started a revolution without him. **Rafael Carrera,** a *mestizo* rebel leader, seized Guatemala City in 1838, and the federation began to crumble. Two years later Carrera humiliated Morazán's forces on the battlefield. Morazán resigned, marking the end of the federation. Carrera and others tried unsuccessfully to reunite the states in the following years. The states went their separate ways and so did their histories; for the rest of the story, look to the **History Since Independence** section in each country's chapter.

CULTURE AND CUSTOMS

The intermingling of European colonization and Native American civilizations remains integral to the character of Central America and is clearly visible in the dozens of distinct ethnic groups, languages, and religious variations.

PEOPLE

Two-thirds of Central America's current population is of mixed race, or **mestizo.** The *mestizo* are also called **ladinos** and comprise 60% of the isthmus's people. About 5% are *mulattoes,* of mixed European and African descent, and a small number are *zambos,* of indigenous and African descent. About 10% claim to be of pure European blood. The majority of these live in Costa Rica, which had a small native population to begin with. Recent estimates place the **indigenous** population of Central America at the time of the Conquest at around 5.5 million, almost half of which was concentrated in Guatemala. The ensuing battles with European conquerors and diseases decimated these populations. Even with the population explosion of the last 50 years, the indigenous population today only accounts for about four to five million of Central America's 29 million people. The vast majority of these are the Maya of Guatemala, a country where 55% of the population is indigenous. Other native groups include the **Lenca** and **Chortí** in western Honduras, the **Pipil** in western El Salvador, the **Miskito, Pech, Sumu,** and **Rama** along the Mosquito Coast of Honduras and Nicaragua, and the relatively isolated **Kuna, Guaymí,** and **Emberá** in Panama.

In addition to the European and indigenous heritages, Central America also contains small **Chinese** and **East Indian** populations, descendants of indentured laborers brought to the area, and, more notably, large **black** populations concentrated on the Caribbean Coast. These blacks are the descendants of African slaves who were either brought to Central America as laborers or escaped from the West Indies in several waves over the last few centuries. One of these groups is the **Garífuna,** or Black Caribs, the descendants of a group of mixed African and Carib Indian peoples who were deported to Honduras's Bay Islands in 1797. The Garífuna populates the Caribbean Coast from Belize to Nicaragua.

LANGUAGE

Spanish is the official language of six of the seven Central American countries and is the most common language throughout the isthmus. For those accustomed to Castillian Spanish, Central American Spanish may take some getting used to,

QUEMAR: **TO FIND A SHORTY** Although most basic Spanish phrases are universal, plenty of regional variations exist—often making matters confusing or downright embarrassing for the traveler. One case in point: each country has its own terms for the citizens of other countries. To a Honduran, for example, a Guatemalan is a *chapine*, a Nicaraguan is a *muco*, a Salvadoran is a *guanaco*, and a Honduran is a *catracho*. Use these in some other countries, though, and you might get punched in the nose. Other vocabulary quirks pop up throughout the region. In Panama, the verb *quemar*, usually meaning "to burn," can instead mean cheating on a spouse. In Costa Rica, Guatemala, and Honduras, jail is *el bote*, not *el cárcel*. If you need a doctor in Guatemala or Honduras, better not call for a *médico*; try *matasano* instead. Above all, avoid using the verbs *coger* or *recoger*; while in some countries these mean plain old "get" or "collect," say *"Quiero coger el bus"* in Central America you may find yourself makin' whoopee with a schoolbus.

though it tends to be crisp and clear. This is one reason Central America, and Guatemala in particular, is noted for its language schools. However, each country, or even each region of a country, has its own cadence, speed, and vocabulary. The more isolated indigenous groups still speak traditional languages, sometimes exclusively. In parts of the Guatemalan highlands and along the Mosquito Coast, even a fluent Spanish speaker may find herself reduced to gestures when dealing with villagers. However, there is usually someone around who speaks Spanish, even if as a second language.

However, English is the official language of Belize and is spoken in many Caribbean towns throughout Central America. The Afro-Caribbean English is a creole that, at its most extreme, is barely intelligible to foreigners. The slang's catchy, though: you'll be greeting people with *"Allright, Goodnight"* long after you leave.

RELIGION

Roman Catholicism, the professed faith of over four-fifths of the population, is by far the dominant religion in Central America. In more urban areas where indigenous heritage has largely been effaced, a very European Catholicism is practiced, while in more rural areas, the faith is highly syncretistic, blending Roman Catholicism with indigenous beliefs. The polytheism of native religions enabled the indigenous people to integrate Catholic traditions into their own religious system.

There are a number of pilgrimage sights in Central America, the most famous being the Black Christ in Esquipulas, Guatemala (see **El Cristo Negro,** p. 391). Despite the successful integration of these religious systems, other religious forces have recently begun to undermine the dynamic relationship that has traditionally existed between Roman Catholicism and native religious beliefs. Nativistic movements are increasingly popular, advocating a rejection of the religious practices that arrived with the Conquest and a return to indigenous religions.

THE ARTS

Central America's most famous artist is probably **Rubén Darío** (1867-1916), a Nicaraguan poet whose highly experimental style was a powerful engine of Modernism in both Europe and the Americas. The Guatemalan **Miguel Angel Asturias** (1899-1974), winner of the 1967 Nobel Prize for Literature, is perhaps Central America's most famous recent writer, author of *Men Of Maize* and *El Señor Presidente.*

The folk art of Central America is ubiquitous both in use and for sale. From the blankets and *huipiles* that the highland Maya hand-weave on looms to the embroidered *molas* of the Kuna in Panama, the textiles of Central America create a constant barrage of color and design. Strong traditions of leatherwork, hammocks, ceramics, and woodcarving survive in many parts of Central America.

Vibrant traditional music flourishes on either end of Central America, in Guatemala and Panama, but can be more elusive in other places. The marimba, a type of xylophone, is heard in plazas from Guatemala to Costa Rica and ancient indigenous instruments are still played in churches in the Maya highlands. Afro-Carib music rocks all along the Caribbean coast. *Punta*, it percussion-based music and dance, is performed by the Garífuna along the Honduran coast, and Nicaragua's Bluefields Area has produced world renowned reggae bands. Panama's classic national folk dance, the *tamborito*, is performed in local.

FURTHER SOURCES

GENERAL HISTORY

Central America: A Natural and Cultural History, edited by Anthony G. Coates (1997). A recent, academically rigorous treatment of the natural history of Central America, the history of its indigenous peoples, and, most interestingly, the history of their interaction.

The Maya, by Michael Coe (1993). Of the many introductions to the Maya, this is perhaps the most readable and engaging—and one of the shortest.

Scribes, Warriors, and Kings: The City of Copán and the Ancient Maya, by William Fash (1993). An American archaeologist's account of the history of Copán, one of the most important cities of the Classic Maya.

I, Rigoberta Menchú: An Indian Woman in Guatemala, by Rigoberta Menchú (Trans. Wright, 1984). A gripping autobiographical account of *La Violencia* in Guatemala by the Nobel Peace Prize winner, Rigoberta Menchú.

Rigoberta Menchú and the Story of All Poor Guatemalans, by David Stoll (1998). An anthropologist's recent exposé refuting the authenticity of the story Rigoberta Menchú presents in her autobiography.

FICTION, NON-FICTION, AND POETRY

Men of Maize, by Miguel Asturias (Trans. Martin, 1993). Written in the 1940s, the most widely read work by Guatemala's most famous writer and 1967 Nobel Laureate.

And We Sold the Rain: Contemporary Fiction from Central America, edited by Rosario Santos (1996). A collection of short stories.

The Inhabited Woman, by Gioconda Belli (Trans. March, 1995). A tale of romance and rebellion against an oppressive government by a well-known Nicaraguan writer.

Incidents of Travel in Central America, Chiapas, and Yucatán, by John Lloyd Stephens (1992 reprint). This classic account from the 1840s by the world-traveler Stephens was one of the pioneering works of Maya archaeology.

Songs of Life and Hope, by Rubén Darío. Generally considered to be the Nicaraguan poet's masterpiece, this collection engages social, historical, and existential themes.

Volcán: Poems from Central America: A Bilingual Anthology, edited by Alejandro Murguia (1983). Published by City Lights, an excellent collection in Spanish and English.

Poesia Contemporánea en America Central, edited by Francisco Albizurez Palma (1995). A massive collection of Central American poetry in Spanish.

ESSENTIALS

FACTS FOR THE TRAVELER

ENTRANCE REQUIREMENTS.
Passport: Required for all foreign visitors to Central American countries (p. 21).
Visa: Requirements differ from country to country, but prearranged visas are generally not required for citizens of Canada, Ireland, the UK, and the US. Tourist visas are required in some countries, and can usually be purchased upon entrance. Guatemala, Honduras, Panama, and El Salvador require visas for citizens of South Africa. Visitors from New Zealand and Australia also must have visas to enter El Salvador and Guatemala(p. 22).
Onward/Return Ticket: Proof of departure is required for all travelers to Belize, Honduras, Nicaragua, Costa Rica, and Panama.
Letter of Invitation: Not required.
Inoculations: None required, but see **Health** (p. 29) for recommendations.
Work Permit: Required (p. 22).
Driving Permit: Requirements differ between countries, and enforcement of the rules may vary even in countries where permits are required (p. 49).
Exit Fee: Varies between countries, but can be as much as US$30.

EMBASSIES AND CONSULATES

CONSULAR SERVICES

For information regarding Central American **embassies and consulates** abroad, see the **Essentials** sections of the country chapters; for information regarding foreign embassies in Central America, see the **Practical Information** section in the capital cities. US citizens should consult the state department web site at www.pueblo.gsa.gov/cic_text/travel/foreign/foreignentryreqs.html.

TOURIST OFFICES

For information regarding Central American tourist offices, please refer to the **Essentials** section in each country chapter.

DOCUMENTS AND FORMALITIES

PASSPORTS

REQUIREMENTS. Most citizens need passports to enter all Central American countries. All Central American countries do not allow entrance if the holder's passport expires in under six months; returning home with an expired passport is illegal, and may result in a fine.

NEW PASSPORTS. Citizens of Australia, Canada, Ireland, New Zealand, the UK, and the US can apply for a passport at any post office, passport office, or court of law. Citizens of South Africa can apply for a passport at any office of Foreign Affairs. Any new passport or renewal applications must be filed well in advance of the departure date, although most passport offices offer rush services for a very steep fee. For US citizens, the filing and processing fee for first-time applicants older than 16 is US$60 and US$40 for those 15 and under. In addition to a completed application form, first-time applicants must also submit proof of citizenship (a birth certificate or certificate of naturalization), and a valid photo ID.

PASSPORT MAINTENANCE. Travelers who wish to renew an expired passport must pay US$40 and submit a passport renewal form, their previous passport, and two recent identical photos. Both new and renewed passports take five to six weeks to be processed. Rush services take two to three weeks and cost an extra US$35. Citizens living abroad who need a passport or renewal services should contact the nearest consular service of their home country. For more information, visit www.travel.state.gov.

Be sure to photocopy the page of your passport with your photo, your visas, your traveler's check serial numbers and any other important documents. Carry one set of copies in a safe place, apart from the originals, and leave another set at home. Consulates also recommend that you carry an expired passport or an official copy of your birth certificate in a part of your baggage separate from other documents.

If you lose your passport, immediately notify the local police and the nearest embassy or consulate of your home government. To expedite its replacement, you will need to know all information previously recorded and show ID and proof of citizenship. In some cases, a replacement may take weeks to process, and it may be valid only for a limited time. Any visas stamped in your old passport will be irretrievably lost. In an emergency, ask for immediate temporary traveling papers that will permit you to re-enter your home country.

VISAS & WORK PERMITS

VISAS. Refer to the **Essentials** sections of the country chapters for which countries require visas. Visas can be purchased from the nearest mission of the country you intend to visit. US citizens can take advantage of the Center for International Business and Travel (CIBT; ☎800-925-2428), which secures visas for travel to almost all countries for a variable service charge.

Double-check on entrance requirements at the nearest embassy or consulate of all countries you wish to visit (listed under **Embassies & Consulates Abroad,** on p. 21) for up-to-date info before departure. US citizens can also consult the website at www.pueblo.gsa.gov/cic_text/travel/foreign/foreignentryreqs.html.

Citizens of Canada, Ireland, the UK, and the US generally do not need a prearranged visa to enter Central America. Visas are required of all South African citizens traveling to Guatemala, Honduras, Panama, and El Salvador. El Salvador and Guatemala also require visas for visitors from New Zealand and Australia. See each country's **Essentials** sections for details.

WORK PERMITS. Admission as a visitor does not include the right to work, which is authorized only by a work permit. Entering Central America to study usually requires a special visa. For more information, see **Alternatives to Tourism,** p. 55.

IDENTIFICATION

When you travel, always carry two or more forms of identification on your person, including at least one photo ID. A passport combined with a driver's license or birth certificate is usually adequate. Never carry all your forms of ID together; split them up in case of theft or loss, and keep copies of them in your luggage and at home.

TEACHER, STUDENT & YOUTH IDENTIFICATION. The **International Student Identity Card (ISIC),** the most widely accepted form of student ID, provides discounts on sights, accommodations, food, and transport; access to 24hr. emergency helpline (in

North America call ☎ 877-370-ISIC; elsewhere call US collect ☎ +1 715-345-0505); and insurance benefits for US cardholders (see **Insurance,** p. 34). The ISIC is preferable to an institution-specific card (such as a university ID) because it is more likely to be recognized and honored abroad. Applicants must be degree-seeking students of a secondary or post-secondary school and must be of at least 12 years of age. Because of the proliferation of fake ISICs, some services (particularly airlines) require additional proof of student identity, such as a school ID or a letter attesting to your student status, signed by your registrar and stamped with your school seal.

The **International Teacher Identity Card (ITIC)** offers teachers the same insurance coverage as well as similar but limited discounts. For travelers who are 25 years old or under but are not students, the **International Youth Travel Card (IYTC;** formerly the **GO 25** Card) also offers many of the same benefits as the ISIC.

Each of these identity cards costs US$22 or equivalent. ISIC and ITIC cards are valid for roughly one and a half academic years; IYTC cards are valid for one year from the date of issue. Many student travel agencies (see p. 43) issue the cards, including STA Travel in Australia and New Zealand; Travel CUTS in Canada; usit in the Republic of Ireland and Northern Ireland; SASTS in South Africa; Campus Travel and STA Travel in the UK; and Council Travel and STA Travel in the US. For a listing of issuing agencies, or for more information, contact the **International Student Travel Confederation (ISTC)**, Herengracht 479, 1017 BS Amsterdam, Netherlands (☎ +31 20 421 28 00; fax 421 28 10; istcinfo@istc.org; www.istc.org).

CUSTOMS

Upon entering any Central American country, you must declare certain items from abroad and pay a duty on the value of those articles if they exceed the allowance established by your destination country's customs service. Check with the embassy of your country of destination for details. Note that goods and gifts purchased at **duty-free** shops abroad are not exempt from duty or sales tax; "duty-free" merely means that you need not pay a tax in the country of purchase. Upon returning home, you must similarly declare all articles acquired abroad and pay a duty on the value of articles in excess of your home country's allowance. In order to expedite your return, make a list of any valuables brought from home and register them with customs before traveling abroad, and be sure to keep receipts for all goods acquired abroad.

MONEY

CURRENCY AND EXCHANGE

Refer to the **Essentials** sections of the country chapters for exchange rates as of August 2002 between local currency and Australian dollars (AUS$), Canadian dollars (CDN$), Irish pounds (IR£), New Zealand dollars (NZ$), South African Rand (SAR), British pounds (UK£), US dollars (US$), and European Union euros (EUR€). Check the currency converter on financial websites such as www.bloomberg.com and www.xe.com, or a large newspaper for the latest exchange rates.

As a general rule, it's cheaper to convert money in the countries you visit than at home. While currency exchange will probably be available in your arrival airport, it's wise to bring enough foreign currency to last for the first 24 to 72 hours of a trip.

When changing money abroad, try to go only to banks or casas de cambio that have at most a 5% margin between their buy and sell prices. Since you lose money with every transaction, **convert large sums** (unless the currency is depreciating rapidly), **but no more than you'll need.**

If you use traveler's checks or bills, carry some in small denominations (the equivalent of US$50 or less) for times when you are forced to exchange money at disadvantageous rates, but bring a range of denominations since charges may be levied per check cashed. Store your money in a variety of forms; ideally, at any given time you will be carrying some cash, some traveler's checks, and an ATM and/or credit card. All travelers should also consider carrying some US dollars (about US$50 worth).

At land crossings, many Central American border guards will charge official or unofficial fees for both entry and exit. If the fee is of the off-the-books sort, it may be possible to get out of it; some travelers suggest insisting upon a receipt. Often, however, it is not worth the struggle. Meanwhile, if you fly out of Central America, you'll likely have to pay a very official departure tax of US$10-30. For more details on border and departure fees, see the **Essentials** sections of the country chapters.

TRAVELER'S CHECKS

Traveler's checks are one of the safest and least troublesome means of carrying funds, though many Central American banks, especially outside of the capital cities, may be wary to cash them. Only in the most touristed areas will local businesses and shops accept traveler's checks. American Express and Visa are the most widely recognized brands. Many banks and agencies sell them for a small commission. Record check numbers when you cash them, leave a list of check numbers with someone at home, and ask for a list of refund centers when you buy your checks. Never countersign your checks until you actually cash them, and always bring your passport and proof of purchase with you when you do so.

Check issuers provide refunds if the checks are lost or stolen, and many provide additional services, such as toll-free refund hotlines abroad, emergency message services, and stolen credit card assistance. Ask about toll-free refund hotlines and the refund centers when purchasing checks, and always carry emergency cash.

It's generally cheaper to convert money in Central America than at home. However, bring enough foreign currency to last for the first 72 hours of a trip to avoid being penniless should you arrive after bank hours or on a holiday (especially if you arrive on or just before a weekend). US travelers can get foreign currency from the comfort of home: International Currency Express (☎888-278-6628) delivers foreign currency or traveler's checks second-day at competitive exchange rates.

When changing money abroad, search around for the best exchange rate: even within towns, banks and *casas de cambio* (exchange houses) can vary quite a bit. Try to go only to exchange establishments that have at most a 5% margin between their buy and sell prices. Since you lose money with every transaction, **convert large sums** (unless the currency is depreciating rapidly), but no more than you'll need. Also ask hostels, restaurants, and shops if they can change money; they sometimes even have better rates. Keeping small bills and change will make your life easier because Central America has a noticeable shortage of currency, especially in small towns.

In most areas, the **black market is illegal;** the below information is not intended to recommend its use. Black market changers only sometimes offers better rates than banks do, and it's easy to get swindled. Don't go alone, have the money you want to change ready, and double-check what you receive. It's wise to find out competitive rates beforehand and be prepared to bargain.

American Express: Checks available with commission at select banks and all AmEx offices. US residents can also purchase checks by phone (☎888-887-8986) or online (www.aexp.com). AAA offers commission-free checks to its members. Checks available in US, Australian, British, Canadian, Japanese, and Euro currencies. *Cheques for Two* can be signed by either of 2 people traveling together. For purchase locations or more information contact AmEx's service centers: In the US and Canada ☎800-221-7282; in the UK ☎0800 521 313; in Australia ☎800 25 19 02; in New Zealand 0800 441 068; elsewhere US collect ☎+1 801-964-6665.

Visa: Checks available (generally with commission) at banks worldwide. For the location of the nearest office, call Visa's service centers: In the US ☎800-227-6811; in the UK ☎0800 89 50 78; elsewhere UK collect ☎+44 020 7937 8091. Checks available in US, British, Canadian, Japanese, and Euro currencies.

CREDIT, DEBIT, AND ATM CARDS

Credit cards and **cash (ATM) cards** are increasingly easy to use throughout Central America, especially in Costa Rica, Panama, and parts of Belize. Where they are accepted, credit cards often offer superior exchange rates. They may also offer services such as insurance or emergency help, and are sometimes required to reserve rental cars or similar big-ticket items. A credit card is a good thing to bring along— it allows for the occasional splurge and can be invaluable in an emergency. That said, many budget hotels and restaurants in Central America won't accept cards, and it's best not to count on them except in some of the larger cities. Visa and Mastercard are both good choices.

ATM cards are increasingly common in nearly all Central American countries. Depending on the system that your home bank uses, you can most likely access your personal bank account from abroad. ATMs get the same wholesale exchange rate as credit cards, but there is often a limit on the amount of money you can withdraw per day (around US$500), and computer networks sometimes fail.

Debit cards are as convenient as credit cards but have a more immediate impact on your funds. A debit card can be used wherever its associated credit card company (usually Mastercard or Visa) is accepted, yet the money is withdrawn directly from the holder's checking account. Debit cards often also function as ATM cards and can be used to withdraw cash from associated banks and ATMs. Ask your local bank about obtaining one.

The two major international money networks are **Cirrus** (to locate ATMs call in the US ☎800-424-7787 or www.mastercard.com) and **Visa/PLUS** (to locate ATMs call in the US ☎800-843-7587 or www.visa.com). Most ATMs charge a transaction fee that is paid to the bank that owns the ATM.

GETTING MONEY FROM HOME

If you run out of money while traveling, the easiest and cheapest solution is to have someone back home make a deposit to your credit card or cash (ATM) card. Failing that, consider one of the following options.

WIRING MONEY. It is possible to arrange a **bank money transfer**, which means asking a bank back home to wire money to a bank in the country you are visiting. This is the cheapest way to transfer cash, but it's also the slowest, usually taking several days or more. Note that some banks may only release your funds in local currency, potentially sticking you with a poor exchange rate; inquire about this in advance. Money transfer services like **Western Union** are faster and more convenient than bank transfers—but also much pricier. Western Union has many locations worldwide. To find one, visit www.westernunion.com, or call in the US ☎800-325-6000, in Canada ☎800-235-0000, in the UK ☎0800 83 38 33, in Australia ☎800 501 500, in New Zealand ☎800 27 0000, in South Africa ☎0860 100031.

US STATE DEPARTMENT (US CITIZENS ONLY). In dire emergencies only, the US State Department will forward money within hours to the nearest consular office, which will then disburse it according to instructions for a US$20 fee. If you wish to use this service, you must contact the Overseas Citizens Service division of the US State Department (☎202-647-5225; nights, Su, and holidays ☎202-647-4000).

ESSENTIALS

COSTS

In most respects, Central America is a great place for travel on the cheap. In the most inexpensive areas, the very savvy budget traveler can survive on US$10 a day. Most penny-pinching voyagers, however, should expect to spend between US$20 and $45 a day, with Panama and especially Belize and Costa Rica being considerably pricier than the rest of the region. If you spend a lot of time in heavily touristed areas—or travel during peak tourist seasons like Christmas and Easter—you'll wind up spending more. The rainy season (May-Nov.) typically brings the best deals. Your biggest single expense will probably be your plane ticket (see **Transportation,** p. 41). Don't forget to factor in emergency reserve funds (at least US$200) when planning how much money to take.

TIPS FOR SAVING MONEY. Considering that saving just a few dollars a day over the course of your trip might pay for days or weeks of additional travel, the art of penny-pinching is well worth learning. Learn to take advantage of freebies: for example, museums may be free once a week or once a month, and cities often host free open-air concerts and/or cultural events (especially in the summer). Bring a sleepsack (see p. 35) to save on sheet charges in hostels, and do your laundry in the sink (unless you're explicitly prohibited from doing so). You can split accommodation costs (in hotels and some hostels) with trustworthy travelers; multi-bed rooms almost always work out cheaper per person than singles. The same principle also works for cutting the cost of restaurant meals. You can also buy food in markets (or, in large cities, supermarkets) instead of eating out. With that said, don't go overboard with your budget obsession. Though staying within your budget is important, don't do so at the expense of your sanity, health, or an unexpected splurge.

TIPPING AND BARGAINING

Tipping and bargaining in the developing world is quite a different practice from what most travelers are accustomed to; there are many unspoken rules to which tourists must adhere. In tourist and upscale restaurants, a 10% tip is common. In smaller restaurants frequented by locals, tipping is rare. Tour guides generally appreciate something extra; small change is appropriate for porters in hotels and restaurants. Taxi drivers are generally not tipped. At outdoor markets, handicraft markets, and some handicraft shops, bargaining is expected and essential. On the other hand, prices at supermarkets and most indoor stores are not negotiable. Bargaining for hotel rooms is often a good idea, particularly in the low season (or if the hotel simply isn't full.) For more on bargaining, see **The Art of the Deal,** below.

SAFETY AND SECURITY

As civil wars end and armies are downsized, Central America is becoming safer. However, with a surplus of guns left over from the wars and new governments struggling to enforce laws, crime continues to plague the region. Violent crime does occur; however, the vast majority of incidents are petty theft, pickpocketing, luggage theft, and the like. As the general level of safety varies from region to region, it is wise to research the safety of a particular area before departure. For more details, consult the **Safety** section of each country. The following information provides some general suggestions and further resources to learn more about protecting oneself from crime and other mishaps.

PERSONAL SAFETY

EXPLORING. To avoid unwanted attention, try to blend in as much as possible. Respecting local customs (in many cases, dressing more conservatively) may placate would-be hecklers. Familiarize yourself with your surroundings before setting

THE ART OF THE DEAL Bargaining in Central America is a given: no price is set in stone, and vendors and drivers will automatically quote you a price that is several times too high; it's up to you to get them down to a reasonable rate. Successful merchants enjoy the haggling (just remember that the shopkeepers do this for a living and have the benefit of experience). With the following tips and some finesse, you might be able to impress even the most hardened hawkers:

1. Bargaining needn't be a fierce struggle laced with barbs. Quite the opposite: good-natured wrangling with a cheerful smiling face may prove your biggest weapon.

2. Use your poker face. The less your face betrays your interest in the item the better. If you touch an item to inspect it, the vendor will be sure to "encourage" you to name a price or make a purchase. Coming back again and again to admire a trinket is a good way of ensuring that you pay a ridiculously high price. Don't get too enthusiastic about the object in question; point out flaws in workmanship and design. Be cool.

3. Know when to bargain. In most cases, it's quite clear when it's appropriate to bargain. Most private transportation fares and things for sale in outdoor markets are all fair game. Don't bargain on prepared or pre-packaged foods on the street or in restaurants. In some stores, signs will indicate whether "fixed prices" prevail. When in doubt, ask tactfully, "Is that your lowest price?" or whether discounts are given.

4. Never underestimate the power of peer pressure. Try having a friend discourage you from your purchase—if you seem to be reluctant, the merchant will want to drop the price to interest you again.

5. Know when to turn away. Feel free to refuse any vendor or driver who bargains rudely, and don't hesitate to move on to another vendor if one will not be reasonable about the final price he offers. However, to start bargaining without an intention to buy is a major faux pas. Agreeing on a price and declining it is also poor form. Turn away with a smile and "thank you" upon hearing a ridiculous price—the price may plummet.

6. Start low. Never feel guilty offering what seems to be a ridiculously low price. Your starting price should be no more than one-third to one-half the asking price.

7. Give in. In the final blows of the deal when you are fighting over the last five *lempiras* or *colones*, give in. The vendors are trying to make a living and the small difference is probably just tiny loss for you that can go a long way for them.

ESSENTIALS

out, and carry yourself with confidence; if you must check a map on the street, duck into a shop. If you are traveling alone, be sure someone at home knows your itinerary, and never admit that you're unaccompanied.

When walking at night, stick to busy, well-lit streets and avoid dark alleyways. If you feel uncomfortable, leave as quickly and directly as you can, but don't allow fear of the unknown to deter you.

SELF DEFENSE. There is no sure-fire way to avoid all the threatening situations you might encounter when you travel, but a good self-defense course will give you concrete ways to react to unwanted advances. **Impact, Prepare, and Model Mugging** can refer you to local self-defense courses in the US (☎800-345-5425). Visit the website at www.impactsafety.org for a list of nearby chapters. Workshops (2-3hr.) start at US$50; full courses run US$350-500.

DRIVING. If you are using a **car,** learn local driving signals and wear a seatbelt. Children under 40 lb. should ride only in a specially-designed carseat, available for a small fee from most car rental agencies. Study route maps before you hit the road, and if you plan on spending a lot of time on the road, you may want to bring spare parts. If your car breaks down, wait for the police to assist you. For long drives in desolate areas, invest in a cellular phone and a roadside assistance program. Be sure to park your vehicle in a garage or well traveled area, and use a steering wheel locking device in larger cities. **Sleeping in your car** is one of the most dangerous (and often illegal) ways to get your rest.

TERRORISM. Terrorism in Central America does not pose a huge concern to most travelers. However, some countries such as Guatemala and Panama still have areas of political unrest. See **Essentials** sections of the country chapters for information on terrorism and violence. The box below on **travel advisories** lists resources to get the most updated information of your home country's government's advisories about travel.

TRAVEL ADVISORIES. The following government offices provide travel information and advisories by telephone, by fax, or via the web:

Australian Department of Foreign Affairs and Trade: ☎ 1300 555135; faxback service 02 6261 1299; www.dfat.gov.au.
Canadian Department of Foreign Affairs and International Trade (DFAIT): In Canada and the US call ☎ 800-267-6788, elsewhere call ☎ +1 613-944-6788; www.dfait-maeci.gc.ca. Call for their free booklet, *Bon Voyage...But.*
New Zealand Ministry of Foreign Affairs: ☎ 04 494 8500; fax 494 8506; www.mft.govt.nz/trav.html.
United Kingdom Foreign and Commonwealth Office: ☎ 020 7008 0232; fax 7008 0155; www.fco.gov.uk.
US Department of State: ☎ 202-647-5225, faxback service 647-3000; http:// travel.state.gov. For *A Safe Trip Abroad,* call 202-512-1800.

FINANCIAL SECURITY

PROTECTING YOUR VALUABLES. There are a few steps you can take to minimize the financial risk associated with traveling. First, **bring as little with you as possible**, and leave expensive jewelry, cameras, and electronic equipment at home. Second, buy a few combination **padlocks** to secure your belongings either in your pack or in a hostel or train station locker. Third, **carry as little cash as possible.** Keep your traveler's checks and ATM/credit cards in a **money belt**—not a "fanny pack"—along with your passport and ID cards. Fourth, **keep a small cash reserve separate from your primary stash.** This should be about US$50 sewn into or stored in the depths of your pack, along with your traveler's check numbers and important photocopies.

CON ARTISTS AND PICKPOCKETS. Beware of people who try to distract you in the street. Petty thieves may spill something on you (or claim to have done so) in order to catch you off guard. Avoid picking up anything from the street. Don't ever hand over your passport or money to a so-called official whose authority you question—ask to accompany him to a police station if he insists, but stay out of unmarked cars—and *never* let your passport out of your sight. Be especially wary in markets, buses and bus stations. Also, be alert in public telephone booths: If you must say your calling card number, do so very quietly; if you punch it in, make sure no one can look over your shoulder.

ACCOMMODATIONS & TRANSPORTATION. Never leave your belongings unattended; crime occurs in even the most demure-looking hostel or hotel. Bring your own **padlock** for hostel lockers, and don't ever store valuables in any locker. Travelers using public transportation are usually requested to store their larger pieces of luggage on top of or below the bus. Though this a considered to be a relatively safe practice, luggage locks might help protect the contents of your outer pockets.

Some travelers suggest throwing a flour sack and net over your pack; this is how locals transport goods. Any luggage brought on to the bus itself is best kept in your lap. In hotels, double-check all locks. It may be a good idea to bring along a padlock to use in lieu of the one some budget places give you. Be particularly careful on **buses** and **trains;** horror stories abound about determined thieves who wait for travelers to fall asleep. Carry your backpack in front of you where you can see it. When traveling with others, sleep in alternate shifts.

DRUGS AND ALCOHOL

Because of Central America's turbulent relationship with narcotics, penalties are severe for possession of drugs and your home embassy will be of minimal assistance should you get into trouble. Remember that you are subject to the laws of the country in which you travel, not those of your home country; it is your responsibility to familiarize yourself with these laws before leaving. If you carry **prescription drugs** while you travel, have a copy of the prescriptions themselves and a note from your doctor. Avoid public drunkenness; in certain areas it is against the law, and can also jeopardize your safety and earn the disdain of locals.

POLICE

Central American police are not uniformly helpful, but if you have anything stolen, be sure to file a report for insurance purposes. While law enforcement is still a problem, it is improving. Tourist police forces are available in some areas and corruption is being reduced. With a few exceptions, if you're in trouble, the police will try to help. However, bribing law enforcers is still common in some areas.

HEALTH

Common sense is the simplest prescription for good health while visiting Central America. Travelers complain most often about feet and stomach ailments, so take precautionary measures: drink lots of water (purified or bottled) to prevent dehydration and constipation, and wear sturdy, broken-in shoes and clean socks.

BEFORE YOU GO

In your **passport,** write the names of any people you wish to be contacted in case of a medical emergency, and list any allergies or medical conditions. Matching a prescription to a foreign equivalent is not always easy, safe, or possible, so carry up-to-date, legible prescriptions or a statement from your doctor stating the medication's trade name, manufacturer, chemical name, and dosage. While traveling, be sure to keep all medication with you in your carry-on luggage. For tips on packing a basic **first-aid kit** and other health essentials, see p. 26. The names in Central America for common drugs are: *aspirina* (aspirin), *paracetamol* (acetaminophen), *penicilina* (penicillin), and *antihistimínico* (antihistamine / allergy medicine). Brand names such as tylenol, advil, and pepto bismol are also well known.

IMMUNIZATIONS AND PRECAUTIONS

Travelers over two years old should make sure that the following vaccines are up to date: MMR (for measles, mumps, and rubella); DTaP or Td (for diptheria, tetanus, and pertussis); OPV (for polio); HbCV (for haemophilus influenza B); and HBV (for hepatitis B). Adults traveling to Central America on trips longer than four weeks should consider the following additional immunizations: Hepatitis A Vaccine and/or immune globulin (IG), an additional dose of polio vaccine, and typhoid and cholera vaccines, particularly if traveling off the tourist path. While yellow fever is only endemic to parts of South America and sub-Saharan Africa, Belize, El Salvador, Honduras, and Nicaragua require a certificate of vaccination

INOCULATION RECOMMENDATIONS

There are a number of inoculations recommended for travel in Central America:

Hepatitis A or immune globulin (IG). Hepatitis A is a series of shots so consult your doctor a few weeks in advance.

Hepatitis B, particularly if you expect to be exposed to blood (e.g. health-care workers), have sexual contact, stay longer than 6 months, or undergo medical treatment. Hepatitis B vaccine is now recommended for all infants and for children ages 11–12 years who did not receive the series as infants.

Rabies, particularly for travel in rural areas or for people expecting to come into contact with animals.

Typhoid, particularly for travel in more rural areas.

Yellow fever, for travelers to Panama who will be going outside urban areas.

As needed, booster doses for **tetanus-diphtheria** and **measles.**

Malaria pills, particularly for travel in more rural areas. These pills must be taken at least two weeks before and after your trip.

for travelors arriving from these destinations. Inoculations are recommended for travelors to Panama. For recommendations on immunizations and prophylaxis, consult the CDC (see below) in the US or the equivalent in your home country, and check with a doctor for guidance..

USEFUL ORGANIZATIONS AND PUBLICATIONS

The US **Centers for Disease Control and Prevention** (**CDC;** ☎877-FYI-TRIP; toll-free fax 888-232-3299; www.cdc.gov/travel) maintains an international travelers' hotline and an informative website. The CDC's comprehensive booklet *Health Information for International Travel,* an annual rundown of disease, immunization, and general health advice, is free online or US$25 via the Public Health Foundation (☎877-252-1200). Consult the appropriate government agency of your home country for consular information sheets on health, entry requirements, and other issues for various countries (see the listings in the box on **Travel Advisories,** p. 28). For quick information on health and other travel warnings, call the **Overseas Citizens Services** (☎202-647-5225; after-hours 202-647-4000), or contact a passport agency, embassy, or consulate abroad. US citizens can send a self-addressed, stamped envelope to the Overseas Citizens Services, Bureau of Consular Affairs, #4811, US Department of State, Washington, D.C. 20520. For information on medical evacuation services and travel insurance firms, see the US government's website at http://travel.state.gov/medical.html or the **British Foreign and Commonwealth Office** (www.fco.gov.uk). The **Pan American Health Organization,** a subgroup of the World Health Organization, 525 23rd St., NW, Washington, D.C. 20037, USA provides health information specific to Central America, in both English and Spanish (☎202-974-3000; fax 974-3663; www.paho.org).

For detailed information on travel health, including a country-by-country overview of diseases, try the **International Travel Health Guide,** by Stuart Rose, MD (US$19.95; www.travmed.com). For general health info, contact the **American Red Cross** (☎800-564-1234; www.redcross.org).

MEDICAL ASSISTANCE ON THE ROAD

In general, medical services in Central America are basic; only in the capital city of each country are you likely to find well-equipped facilities. Medical care is often available in emergency situations, but the quality of assistance varies widely by region. As much as possible, be prepared to treat small problems yourself.

If you are concerned about obtaining medical assistance while traveling, you may wish to employ special support services. The *MedPass* from **GlobalCare, Inc.,**

6875 Shiloh Rd. East, Alpharetta, GA, 30005-8372, USA, (☎800-860-1111; fax 678-341-1800; www.globalems.com), provides 24hr. international medical assistance, support, and medical evacuation resources. The **International Association for Medical Assistance to Travelers** (**IAMAT**; in the US ☎716-754-4883, in Canada ☎416-652-0137, www.iamat.org) has free membership, lists English-speaking doctors worldwide, and offers detailed info on immunization requirements and sanitation. If your regular **insurance** policy does not cover travel abroad, you may wish to purchase additional coverage (see p. 34).

Those with medical conditions (such as diabetes, allergies to antibiotics, epilepsy, heart conditions) may want to obtain a **Medic Alert** membership (first year US$35, annually thereafter US$20), which includes a stainless steel ID tag, among other benefits, like a 24hr. collect-call number. Contact the Medic Alert Foundation, 2323 Colorado Ave, Turlock, CA 95382, USA (☎888-633-4298; outside US ☎209-668-3333; www.medicalert.org).

ONCE IN CENTRAL AMERICA

ENVIRONMENTAL HAZARDS

Heat exhaustion and dehydration: Heat exhaustion, characterized by dehydration and salt deficiency, can lead to fatigue, headaches, and nausea, and dizziness. You can avoid it by drinking plenty of fluids, eating salty foods (e.g. peanut butter), and avoiding dehydrating beverages (e.g. alcohol, coffee, tea, and caffeinated soda). Continuous heat stress can eventually lead to heatstroke, characterized by a rising temperature, severe headache, and cessation of sweating. Victims should be cooled off with cool, wet towels and taken to a doctor. This is a particular concern because of Central America's hotter climate.

Sunburn: Bring a high SPF sunscreen (at least SPF 30) with you, and apply it liberally and often to avoid burns and risk of skin cancer. Protect your eyes with good sunglasses, since ultraviolet rays can damage the retina of the eye after too much exposure. If you get sunburned, drink lots of fluids and apply vinegar, or an aloe-based lotion.

Hypothermia: A rapid drop in body temperature is the clearest sign of overexposure to cold. Victims may also shiver, feel exhausted, exhibit slurred speech or poor coordination, hallucinate, and/or suffer amnesia. **Do not let hypothermia victims fall asleep,** or their body temperature will continue to drop and they may die. To avoid hypothermia, keep dry, wear layers, and stay out of the wind. In wet weather, wool and synthetics such as fleece retain heat; cotton will make you colder.

INSECT-BORNE DISEASES

Many diseases are transmitted by insects—mainly mosquitoes, fleas, ticks, and lice. Be aware of insects in wet or forested areas, especially while hiking and camping; wear long pants and long sleeves, tuck your pants into your socks, and buy a mosquito net. Use insect repellents such as DEET and soak or spray your gear with permethrin (licensed in the US for use on clothing). Ticks—responsible for Lyme and other diseases—can be particularly dangerous in rural and forested regions, but are not endemic to Central America.

Malaria: Transmitted by *Anopheles* mosquitoes that bite at night. The incubation period varies from 6-8 days to as long as months. Early symptoms include fever, chills, aches, and fatigue, followed by high fever and sweating, sometimes with vomiting and diarrhea. See a doctor for any flu-like sickness that occurs after travel in a risk area. To reduce the risk of contracting malaria, use mosquito repellent, particularly in the evenings and when visiting forested areas, and take oral prophylactics, like **mefloquine** (sold under the name Lariam) or **doxycycline** (ask your doctor for a prescription). Be

ESSENTIALS

aware that these drugs can have very serious side effects, including slowed heart rate and nightmares.

Dengue fever: An "urban viral infection" transmitted by *Aedes* mosquitoes, which bite during the day rather than at night. Dengue has flu-like symptoms and is often indicated by a rash 3-4 days after the onset of fever. Symptoms for the first 2-4 days include chills, high fever, headaches, swollen lymph nodes, muscle aches, and, in some instances, a pink rash on the face. If you experience these symptoms, see a doctor, drink plenty of liquids, and take fever-reducing medication such as acetaminophen (Tylenol). **Never take aspirin to treat dengue fever.**

Yellow fever: A viral disease transmitted by mosquitoes; yellow fever derives its name from one of its most common symptoms, jaundice caused by liver damage. While most cases are mild, severe ones begin with fever, headache, muscle pain, nausea, and abdominal pain before progressing to jaundice, bloody vomit, and bloody stools. While there is no specific treatment, an effective vaccine offers 10 years of protection. Yellow fever inoculations are currently recommended for travelers to Panama.

Other insect-borne diseases: Filariasis is a roundworm infestation transmitted by mosquitoes. Infection causes enlargement of extremities and has no vaccine. **Leishmaniasis** is a parasite transmitted by sand flies. Common symptoms are sores, fever, weakness, and swelling of the spleen. There is a treatment, but no vaccine. **Chagas' disease (American trypanomiasis)** is another relatively common parasite transmitted by the cone nose and kissing bug, which infest mud, adobe, and thatch. Its symptoms are fever, heart disease, and later on an enlarged intestine. There is no vaccine and limited treatment.

FOOD- AND WATER-BORNE DISEASES

Prevention is the best cure: be sure that your food is properly cooked and the water you drink is clean. Peel fruits and veggies and avoid tap water (including ice cubes and anything washed in tap water, like salad). Watch out for food from markets or street vendors that may have been cooked in unhygienic conditions. Other culprits are raw shellfish, unpasteurized milk, and sauces containing raw eggs. Buy bottled water, or purify your own water by bringing it to a rolling boil or treating it with iodine tablets; note however that some parasites such as *giardia* have exteriors that resist iodine treatment, so boiling is more reliable. Always wash your hands before eating or bring a quick-drying purifying liquid hand cleaner.

■ **Traveler's diarrhea:** Results from drinking untreated water or eating uncooked foods. Symptoms include nausea, bloating, and urgency. Try quick-energy, non-sugary foods with protein and carbohydrates to keep your strength up. Over-the-counter anti-diarrheals (e.g. Imodium) may counteract the problems but may also complicate serious infections. Pepto-Bismol eases the discomfort, but does not stop your body from pushing the bacteria through your system. An anti-diarrheal product should only be taken to in cases of severe pain or times when you may not have easy access to a bathroom, (e.g. a long bus ride). The most dangerous side effect is dehydration; drink 8 oz. of water with ½ tsp. of sugar or honey and a pinch of salt, try uncaffeinated soft drinks, or eat salted crackers. If you develop a fever or your symptoms don't go away after 4-5 days, consult a doctor. Consult a doctor immediately for treatment of diarrhea in children.

Dysentery: Results from a serious intestinal infection caused by bacteria. The most common type is bacillary dysentery, also called *shigellosis*. Symptoms include bloody diarrhea (sometimes mixed with mucus), fever, and abdominal pain and tenderness. Bacillary dysentery generally only lasts a week, but it is highly contagious. Amoebic dysentery, which develops more slowly, is a more serious disease and may cause long-term damage if left untreated. A stool test can determine which kind you have; seek medical help immediately. Dysentery can be treated with the drugs norfloxacin or ciprofloxacin (commonly known as Cipro). If you are traveling in high-risk (especially rural) regions of Central America, consider obtaining a prescription before you leave home.

Cholera: An intestinal disease caused by a bacteria found in contaminated food. Cholera has recently reached epidemic stages in Central America. Symptoms include diarrhea, dehydration, vomiting, and muscle cramps. See a doctor immediately; if left untreated, it may be deadly. Antibiotics are available, but the most important treatment is rehydration. Consider getting a (50% effective) vaccine if you have stomach problems (e.g. ulcers) or will be living where water purification is not reliable.

Hepatitis A: A viral infection of the liver acquired primarily through contaminated water. Symptoms include fatigue, fever, loss of appetite, nausea, dark urine, jaundice, vomiting, aches and pains, and light stools. The risk is highest in rural areas and the countryside, but it is also present in urban areas. Ask your doctor about the vaccine (Havrix or Vaqta) or an injection of immune globulin (IG; formerly called gamma globulin).

Parasites: Microbes, tapeworms, etc. that hide in unsafe water and food. **Giardiasis,** for example, is acquired by drinking untreated water from streams or lakes. Symptoms include swollen glands or lymph nodes, fever, rashes or itchiness, digestive problems, eye problems, and anemia. Boil water, wear shoes, avoid bugs, and eat only cooked food.

Schistosomiasis: Also known as *bilharzia;* a parasitic disease caused when flatworm larvae penetrate unbroken skin. Symptoms include an itchy localized rash, followed in 4-6 weeks by fever, fatigue, painful urination, diarrhea, loss of appetite, night sweats, and a hive-like rash. If exposed to untreated water, rub the area vigorously with a towel and apply rubbing alcohol. Schistosomiasis can be treated with prescription drugs.

Typhoid fever: Caused by the salmonella bacteria; common in rural villages in Central America. Often transmitted through contaminated food and water, it may also be acquired by direct person-to-person contact. Early symptoms include fever, headaches, fatigue, loss of appetite, constipation, and sometimes a rash on the abdomen or chest. Antibiotics can treat typhoid, but a vaccination (70-90% effective) is recommended.

OTHER INFECTIOUS DISEASES

Rabies: Transmitted through the saliva of infected animals; fatal if untreated. By the time symptoms (severe thirst and muscle spasms) appear, the disease is in its terminal stage. If you are bitten by an animal, wash the wound thoroughly, seek immediate medical care, and try to have the animal located. A rabies vaccine, which consists of 3 shots given over a 21-day period, is available but only semi-effective.

Hepatitis B: A viral infection of the liver transmitted via bodily fluids or needle sharing. Symptoms may not surface until years after infection. Vaccinations are recommended for health-care workers, sexually active travelers, and anyone planning to seek medical treatment abroad. The 3-shot vaccination series must begin 6 months before traveling.

Hepatitis C: Like Hep B, but the mode of transmission differs. IV drug users, those with occupational exposure to blood, hemodialysis patients, and recipients of blood transfusions are at the highest risk, but the disease can also be spread through sexual contact or sharing items (e.g. razors and toothbrushes) that may have traces of blood on them.

AIDS, HIV & STDS

For detailed information on **Acquired Immune Deficiency Syndrome (AIDS)** in Central America call the **US Centers for Disease Control's** 24hr. hotline at ☎ 800-342-2437, or contact the **Joint United Nations Programme on HIV/AIDS (UNAIDS),** 20, Ave. Appia, CH-1211 Geneva 27, Switzerland (☎ +41 22 791 3666; fax 22 791 4187). Note that some Central American countries screen incoming travelers for AIDS, primarily those planning extended visits for work or study, and deny entrance to those who test HIV-positive. Belize and El Salvador require that foreigners applying for long-term residence complete an HIV test prior to entry. Panama requires testing of those who alter their visa status while in Panama and of women seeking employment in "entertainment sectors." Contact the nearest consulate for up-to-date information.

Sexually transmitted diseases (STDs) such as gonorrhea, chlamydia, genital warts, syphilis, and herpes are easier to catch than HIV and can be just as deadly. **Hepatitis B** and **C** are also serious STDs (see **Other Infectious Diseases,** above). Though condoms may protect you from some STDs, oral or even tactile contact can lead to transmission. Warning signs include swelling, sores, bumps, or blisters on sex organs, the rectum, or the mouth; burning and pain during urination and bowel movements; itching around sex organs; swelling or redness of the throat; and flu-like symptoms. If these symptoms develop, see a doctor immediately.

WOMEN'S HEALTH

Women traveling in unsanitary conditions are vulnerable to **urinary tract** and **bladder infections,** common and very uncomfortable bacterial conditions that cause a burning sensation and painful (sometimes frequent) urination. Over-the-counter medicines can sometimes alleviate symptoms, but if they persist, see a doctor. **Vaginal yeast infections** may flare up in hot and humid climates. Wearing loosely fitting trousers or a skirt and cotton underwear will help, as will over-the-counter remedies like Monostat or Gynelotrimin. Bring supplies from home if you are prone to infection, as they may be difficult to find on the road.

Since **tampons, pads,** and reliable **contraceptive devices** are sometimes hard to find when traveling, bring supplies with you.

INSURANCE

Travel insurance generally covers four basic areas: medical/health problems, property loss, trip cancellation/interruption, and emergency evacuation. Although your regular insurance policies may well extend to travel-related accidents, you may consider purchasing travel insurance if the cost of potential trip cancellation/interruption or emergency medical evacuation is greater than you can absorb. Prices for travel insurance purchased separately generally run about US$50 per week for full coverage, while trip cancellation/interruption may be purchased separately at a rate of about US$5.50 per US$100 of coverage.

Medical insurance (especially university policies) often covers costs incurred abroad; check with your provider. **US Medicare** does not cover foreign travel to Central America. **Canadians** are protected by their home province's health insurance plan for up to 90 days after leaving the country; check with the provincial Ministry of Health or Health Plan Headquarters for details. **Homeowners' insurance** (or your family's coverage) often covers theft during travel and loss of travel documents (passport, plane ticket, railpass, etc.) up to US$500.

ISIC and **ITIC** (see p. 22) provide basic insurance benefits, including US$100 per day of in-hospital sickness for up to 60 days, US$3000 of accident-related medical reimbursement, and US$25,000 for emergency medical transport. Cardholders have access to a toll-free 24hr. helpline (run by the insurance provider **TravelGuard**) for medical, legal, and financial emergencies overseas (US and Canada ☎ 877-370-4742, elsewhere call US collect ☎ +1 715-345-0505). **American Express** (US ☎ 800-528-4800) grants most cardholders automatic car rental insurance (collision and theft, but not liability) and ground travel accident coverage of US$100,000 on flight purchases made with the card.

INSURANCE PROVIDERS

Council and STA (see p. 43) offer a range of plans that can supplement your basic coverage. Other private insurance providers in the US and Canada include: Access America (☎ 800-284-8300); Berkely Group/Carefree Travel Insurance (☎ 800-323-

3149; www.berkely.com); Globalcare Travel Insurance (☎800-821-2488; www.globalcare-cocco.com); and Travel Assistance International (☎800-821-2828; www.europ-assistance.com). Providers in the UK include Columbus Direct (☎020 7375 0011). In Australia, try AFTA (☎02 9375 4955).

PACKING

Pack lightly: lay out only what you absolutely need, then take half the clothes and twice the money. If you plan to do a lot of hiking, also see the section on **Camping & the Outdoors,** p. 37.

LUGGAGE. If you plan to cover most of your itinerary by foot, a sturdy **frame backpack** is unbeatable. Remember that packs will be left on top of buses and otherwise exposed to the elements, so bring along a waterproof pack cover or sturdy trash bags. Toting a **suitcase** or **trunk** is fine if you plan to live in one or two cities and explore from there, but a very bad idea if you're going to be moving around a lot. In addition to your main piece of luggage, a **daypack** (a small backpack or courier bag) is a must.

CLOTHING. No matter when you're traveling, it's always a good idea to bring a warm jacket or wool sweater, a rain jacket (Gore-Tex® is both waterproof and breathable), sturdy shoes or hiking boots, and thick socks. Rain gear is particularly essential during the summer months—Central America's "rainy season." Flip-flops or waterproof sandals are must-haves for grubby hostel showers. You may also want to add one outfit beyond the jeans and t-shirt uniform, and maybe a nicer pair of shoes if you have the room. If you plan to visit any religious or cultural sites, remember that you'll need something besides tank tops and shorts to be respectful. A wide-brimmed **hat** keeps the sun at bay. The Central American highlands get quite cold at night—be sure to take a sweater or medium weight fleece. Central Americans generally value a neat and clean appearance, and appreciate visitors who do likewise. This is particularly useful when dealing with officials, as at border crossings. In most areas, Central American men don't wear shorts; exceptions are beach towns and most touristed locales. Not all local women dress conservatively but the female visitor is well advised to do so.

CONVERTERS & ADAPTERS. Throughout most of the region, the standard is 110V AC current - the same as the US, Canada, and Mexico. A few areas, especially scattered parts of Panama and Honduras, have the 220V current found in Europe and Australia. The currents are not interchangeable. To be safe you should purchase an **adapter** (which changes the shape of the plug) and a **converter** (which changes the voltage; US$20). Don't make the mistake of using only an adapter (unless appliance instructions explicitly state otherwise).

TOILETRIES. Toothbrushes, towels, cold-water soap, talcum powder (to keep feet dry), deodorant, and razors are often availavle, but may be difficult to find so bring extras along. Tampons and reliable condoms are not as widely available. In addition, contact lenses are expensive and difficult to find, so bring extra pairs and plenty of solution for your entire trip. Also bring your glasses and a copy of your prescription in case you need emergency replacements. If you use heat disinfection, either switch temporarily to a chemical disinfection system (check first to make sure it's safe with your brand of lenses), or buy a converter and adapter if needed. Sunscreen and insect repellent are essential. Many travelers also suggest taking pre-moistened wipes.

FIRST-AID KIT. For a basic first-aid kit, pack: bandages, pain reliever, antibiotic cream, a thermometer, a Swiss Army knife, tweezers, moleskin, disposable gloves, decongestant, motion-sickness remedy, diarrhea or upset-stomach medication

ESSENTIALS

(Pepto Bismol or Immodium), an antihistamine, sunscreen, insect repellent, burn ointment, and a syringe for emergencies (get an explanatory letter from your doctor).

FILM. Film and developing in Central America are easy to find, but expensive. Less serious photographers may want to bring a **disposable camera** or two rather than an expensive permanent one. Despite disclaimers, airport security X-rays *can* fog film, so buy a lead-lined pouch at a camera store or ask security to hand-inspect it. Always pack film in your carry-on luggage, since higher-intensity X-rays are used on checked luggage. Be aware that in some regions of Central America, particularly among the indigenous villages of Guatemala, photography is an unwelcome activity. Ask before taking any pictures, and offer tips in some cases.

OTHER USEFUL ITEMS. For safety purposes, you should bring a **money belt** and a small **padlock.** Basic **outdoors equipment** (plastic water bottle, compass, waterproof matches, pocketknife, sunglasses, sunscreen, hat) may also prove useful. A **sleep-sack**—basically a full-size sheet folded over and sewn together—and a pillow case can be useful when lower-end accommodations lack clean bedding. **Quick repairs** of torn garments can be done on the road with a needle and thread, also consider bringing electrical tape for patching tears. If you want to do laundry by hand, bring detergent, a small rubber ball to stop up the sink, and string for a makeshift clothes line. **Other things** you're liable to forget: a **mosquito net,** an umbrella, sealable **plastic bags** (for damp clothes, soap, food, shampoo, and other spillables); an **alarm clock;** safety pins; rubber bands; a flashlight; earplugs, garbage bags; and a **calculator.**

IMPORTANT DOCUMENTS. Don't forget your passport, traveler's checks, ATM and/or credit cards, and adequate ID. Also check that you have any of the following that might apply to you: a hosteling membership card, driver's license, and/or travel insurance forms.

ACCOMMODATIONS

HOTELS AND HOSPEDAJES

WHAT TO EXPECT
Rooms in Central America can cost as little as US$3 or so per night, but usually range from US$5-10. Accommodations go by many different names; the differences between them are by no means consistent. *Hospedajes* or *casas de huéspedes* are usually the cheapest. However, there are also *hoteles, pensiones,* and *posadas.* Standards vary greatly, but generally speaking, for a basic room expect nothing more than a bed and a light bulb, perhaps a fan; other amenities are a bonus. The very cheapest places may not provide towel, soap, or toilet paper. For a slight price jump you can get a room with private bath, and for a modest amount above that you might find a place with some character and charm.

AMENITIES TO LOOK FOR
In sea level areas, try to get a room with a fan (*ventilador*) or a window with a nice coastal breeze. In more upscale hotels, air conditioning may be available. Also look for screens and mosquito netting. At higher elevations, a hot-water shower and extra blankets will be most welcome. Make safety an extra priority in urban areas; you can often get more comfort and security for only a couple extra dollars. In isolated, non-touristed areas, accommodations will often be quite basic but friendly. If you plan on staying well off the beaten path, your own mosquito net, toilet paper, towel and flashlight are a must.

BATHROOMS
Let's Go quotes room prices with and without private bath. Note that "with bath" means a sink, toilet, and basic shower in the room, not an actual bathtub. Commu-

nal baths are typically the same sort of thing, just off the hall. Hot shower is a relative term in Central America: "hot" can often be tepid at best. Quite frequently, the heating device will be electric coils in the shower head. Such devices work best at low water pressure. The electrical cord should be an easy reminder that water, electricity, and people do not mix well, so be sure to avoid the shower head or other metal objects during a shower. Toilets in Central America often do not have toilet seats. Moreover, the sewer systems generally cannot handle everything thrown in them. As a rule, do not flush used toilet paper, tampons, or other waste products. Instead, use the receptacle (usually) provided. Toilet paper always seems to be missing when you most need it; it is wise to carry some on you wherever you go.

GETTING A GOOD PRICE

Many countries have a hotel tax; double-check if this has been included in the rate. Rooms shared with other travelers usually cost less per person. Often a hotel will first show you the most expensive room. Ask if there's anything cheaper (¿Hay algo más barato, por favor?) You can sometimes bargain for a lower rate at hotels, particularly during the low season or on days when they are not full. A few places may also offer student discounts.

CAMPING

WHERE TO CAMP

With its vast tracts of wilderness, Central America might be a camper's paradise—except that the practice is not very common and there are few facilities. Some of Costa Rica's national parks have official campsites, and there are private camping sites here and there. However, beyond that you're on your own. Occasional hostel owners with a bit of land may allow travelers to camp outside and use their indoor facilities. If anyone offers this arrangement, always agree upon a price before setting up camp. Travelers do camp in remote wilderness areas, but it requires extensive equipment, knowledge of the area, and possibly a permit. In thinly populated rural areas, it's usually best to get a property owner's permission and camp on his/her land (usually for a small fee). In small towns, some travelers try talking to the town mayor, parish priest, or police chief as well as asking to sleep on public athletic fields or the like. Camping should be avoided in populated areas; hotels are almost as cheap and much safer. An excellent resource for travelers planning on camping or spending time in the outdoors is the **Great Outdoor Recreation Pages** (www.gorp.com).

EQUIPMENT. For lowland camping, a hammock and mosquito net are usually shelter enough—and both can be easily purchased in Central America. If using a hammock, bring along a generous length of rope to reach and get around any tree and a plastic tarp to keep you out of the rain. On the other hand, if you plan on camping at higher elevations, for example en route to a peak or volcano, a sleeping bag and other cold-weather gear will be essential. Because your fuel supplies are inconsistent, camping stoves should be multi-fuel models. Camping supplies are usually available only in big cities in Central America, and even then you're much better off purchasing equipment before you arrive. The web site for **Recreational Equipment Inc.** is a good place to start research (www.rei.com).

HOSTELS

Although rare in Central America, **Hosteling International** hostels give discounts to members. Log onto www.hiayh.org or www.hostelslatinamerica.org for info. There are 13 HI hostels scattered throughout Costa Rica. Check out http://www.hicr.org for more info.

INTO THE WILD. Central America has hiking trails galore—from nature walks in national parks to rural paths used by locals—and provides ample opportunity for escaping all trappings of civilization. Even more than elsewhere, any serious expedition requires much planning and research. However, even casual day-hikers will benefit from a few equipment basics. **Water bottles** are essential, as are **water-purification tablets** or a **filter**. **Raingear** in two pieces, a top and pants, is far superior to a poncho. **Synthetics,** like polypropylene tops, socks, and long underwear, retain warmth even wet (unlike cotton). For anything beyond casual walks, good **boots** with strong ankle support are a necessity; to avoid blisters, be sure to break them in before your trip and wear several layers of socks. Even if just setting out for a short hike, bring a first-aid kit, food, extra water, warm clothes, and a flashlight.

KEEPING IN TOUCH
BY MAIL

SENDING MAIL FROM CENTRAL AMERICA

Airmail is the best way to send mail home from Central America. **Aerogrammes,** printed sheets that fold into envelopes and travel via airmail, are available at post offices. Write **"Por Avión"** on the front. Most post offices will charge exorbitant fees or simply refuse to send aerogrammes with enclosures. Anything important should be sent registered mail, and duplicates should be made. **Surface mail** is by far the cheapest and slowest way to send mail. It takes about two to four weeks for regular mail to reach Central American countries. See the Essential sections of the country chapters for the standard postage rates.

SENDING MAIL TO CENTRAL AMERICA

Mark envelopes "air mail," "par avion," or "por avión" or your letter will never arrive. In addition to the standard postage system whose rates are listed below, **Federal Express** (Australia ☎ 13 26 10; US and Canada ☎ 800-247-4747; New Zealand ☎ 0800 73 33 39; UK ☎ 0800 12 38 00; www.fedex.com) handles express mail services from most home countries to Central America. See the Essentials section in the country chapter for specific rates and for examples of how to address letters.

RECEIVING MAIL IN CENTRAL AMERICA

There are several ways to arrange pick-up of letters sent to you by friends and relatives while you are abroad. Mail can be sent via **Poste Restante** (General Delivery; *"Lista de Correos"* in most of Central America, *"Entrega General"* in Panama and "General Delivery" in Belize) to almost any city or town in Central America with a post office.

The mail will go to a special desk in the central post office, unless you specify a post office by street address or postal code. It's best to use the largest post office, since mail may be sent there regardless. It is usually safer and quicker, though more expensive, to send mail express or registered. Bring your passport (or other photo ID) for pick-up; there may be a small fee. If the clerks insist that there is nothing for you, have them check under your first name as well. *Let's Go* lists post offices in the **Practical Information** section for each city and most towns.

American Express's travel offices throughout the world offer a free **Client Letter Service** (mail held up to 30 days and forwarded upon request) for cardholders who contact them in advance. Address the letter in the same way shown above. Some offices will offer these services to non-cardholders (especially AmEx Travelers Cheque holders), but call ahead to make sure. *Let's Go* lists AmEx office locations for most large cities in **Practical Information** sections; for a complete, free list, call ☎ 800-528-4800.

BY TELEPHONE

CALLING HOME FROM CENTRAL AMERICA

Central America's phone system is improving but still chock full of frustrations. National telephone offices are located in nearly every town, although in some cases better prices may be found at hotels, shops, or Internet cafes. A **calling card** is probably your cheapest bet. Calls are billed collect or to your account. **To obtain a calling card** from your national telecommunications service before leaving home, contact the appropriate company listed below.

COMPANY	TO OBTAIN A CARD, DIAL:
AT&T (US)	888-288-4685
British Telecom Direct	800 34 51 44
Canada Direct	800-668-6878
Ireland Direct	800 40 00 00
MCI (US)	800-444-3333
New Zealand Direct	0800 00 00 00
Sprint (US)	800 877-4646
Telkom South Africa	10 219
Telestra Australia	13 22 00

To **call home with a calling card,** contact the operator for your service provider in Central America by dialing the appropriate toll-free access number (listed on the inside back cover of this book). You can frequently call collect without even possessing a company's calling card just by calling their access number and following the instructions.

You can usually also make **direct international calls** from pay phones, but if you aren't using a calling card, you may need to drop your coins as quickly as your words. Where available, prepaid phone cards (see below) and occasionally major credit cards can be used for direct international calls, but they are still less cost-efficient. **MCI Worldcom** even offers collect rates that are the same as calling from the US to Central America (US$0.29-.65) with a US$6 monthly plan fee) for US customers. Some US carriers have surcharges if you are calling from a phone both as well.(See the box on **Placing International Calls** below for directions on how to place a direct international call.)

TIME DIFFERENCES

Central America is six hours behind **Greenwich Mean Time (GMT);** one hour behind New York; two hours ahead of Vancouver and San Francisco; eight hours behind Johannesburg; fifteen hours behind Sydney; and thirteen hours behind Auckland.

BY EMAIL AND INTERNET

Email and Internet access is becoming more available throughout Central America. Every capital city has Internet cafes, as do many other major cities and tourist towns. *Let's Go* lists Internet cafes in the **Practical Information** section of cities and

PLACING INTERNATIONAL CALLS. To call Central American countries from home or to call home from Central America, dial:

1. The **international dialing prefix.** To dial out of **Australia,** dial 0011; **Canada** or the **US,** 011; the **Republic of Ireland, New Zealand,** or the **UK,** 00; **South Africa,** 09; **Belize, Costa Rica, Honduras,** and **Nicaragua,** 00; **El Salvador,** 00 or 144 + 00; **Guatemala,** 00 or 130 + 00; **Panama,** 0.

2. The **country code** of the country you want to call. To call **Australia,** dial 61; **Canada** or the **US,** 1; the **Republic of Ireland,** 353; **New Zealand,** 64; **South Africa,** 27; the **UK,** 44; **Belize,** 501; **Costa Rica,** 506; **El Salvador,** 503; **Guatemala,** 502; **Honduras,** 504; **Nicaragua,** 505; **Panama,** 507.

3. The **city/area code.** *Let's Go* lists the city/area codes for cities and towns in Central America opposite the city or town name, next to a ☎. If the first digit is a zero (e.g., 020 for London), omit the zero when calling from abroad (e.g., dial 20 from Canada to reach London).

4. The **local number.**

towns where they exist. Though in some places it's possible to forge a remote link with your home server, in most cases this is a much slower (and thus more expensive) option than taking advantage of free **web-based email accounts** (e.g., www.hotmail.com and www.yahoo.com). Travelers with laptops can call an Internet service provider via a **modem.** Long-distance phone cards specifically intended for such calls can defray normally high phone charges; check with your long-distance phone provider to see if it offers this option. **Internet cafes** and the occasional free Internet terminal at a public library or university are listed in the **Practical Information** sections of major cities. For lists of additional cybercafes in Central America, check out www.planeta.com.

GETTING TO CENTRAL AMERICA

BY PLANE

When it comes to airfare, a little effort can save you a bundle. If your plans are flexible enough to deal with the restrictions, courier fares are the cheapest. Tickets bought from consolidators and standby seating are also good deals, but last-minute specials, airfare wars, and charter flights often beat these fares. The key is to hunt around, to be flexible, and to ask persistently about discounts. Students, seniors, and those under 26 should never pay full price for a ticket.

Central America's eight major international airports include: Guatemala City, Guatemala; Belize City, Belize; Tegucigalpa and San Pedro Sula, Honduras; San Salvador, El Salvador; San José, Costa Rica; and Panama City, Panama. There is also limited international service to Roatán, in Honduras's Bay Islands.

AIRFARES

Airfares to Central America peak between November and April; holidays are also expensive. Midweek (M-Th morning) round-trip flights run US$40-50 cheaper than weekend flights, but they are generally more crowded and less likely to permit frequent-flier upgrades. Not fixing a return date ("open return") or arriving in and departing from different cities ("open-jaw") can be pricier than round-trip flights. Patching one-way flights together is the most expensive way to travel. Flights between Central America's major airports will tend to be cheaper.

If Central America is only 1 stop on a more extensive globe-hop, consider a round-the-world (RTW) ticket. Tickets usually include at least 5 stops and are

valid for about a year; prices range US$1200-5000. Try **Northwest Airlines/KLM** (US ☎800-447-4747; www.nwa.com) or **Star Alliance,** a consortium of 22 airlines including United Airlines (US ☎800-241-6522; www.star-alliance.com).

Fares for roundtrip flights to Guatemala City, Guatemala; Belize City, Belize; Tegucigalpa and San Pedro Sula, Honduras; San Salvador, El Salvador; San José, Costa Rica; and Panama City, Panama from the US or Canada cost about US$600, US$350 in the off season (May through Oct.); from Australia AUS$2500.

BUDGET & STUDENT TRAVEL AGENCIES

While knowledgeable agents specializing in flights to Central America can make your life easy and help you save, they may not spend the time to find you the lowest possible fare—they get paid on commission. Travelers holding **ISIC and IYTC cards** (see p. 22) qualify for big discounts from student travel agencies. Most flights from budget agencies are on major airlines, but in peak season some may sell seats on less reliable chartered aircraft.

Council Travel (www.counciltravel.com). Countless US offices, including branches in Atlanta, Boston, Chicago, L.A., New York, San Francisco, Seattle, and Washington, D.C. Check the website or call 800-2-COUNCIL (226-8624) for the office nearest you. Also an office at 28A Poland St., Oxford Circus, **London**, W1V 3DB (☎0207 437 77 67). As of May, Council had declared bankruptcy and was subsumed under STA. However, their offices are still in existence and transacting business.

CTS Travel, 44 Goodge St., **London** W1T 2AD, UK(☎0207 636 0031; fax 0207 637 5328; ctsinfo@ctstravel.co.uk).

STA Travel, 7890 S. Hardy Dr., suite 110, Tempe, AZ 85284, USA (24hr. reservations and info ☎800-781-4040; www.sta-travel.com). A student and youth travel organization with over 150 offices worldwide (check their website for a listing of all their offices), including US offices in Boston, Chicago, L.A., New York, San Francisco, Seattle, and Washington, D.C. Ticket booking, travel insurance, railpasses, and more. In the UK, walk-in office 11 Goodge St., **London** W1T 2PF ☎0207 436 7779. In New Zealand, Shop 2B, 182 Queen St., **Auckland** (☎09 309 0458). In Australia, 366 Lygon St., **Carlton** Vic 3053 (☎03 9349 4344).

Travel CUTS (Canadian Universities Travel Services Limited), 187 College St., **Toronto,** ON M5T 1P7 (☎416-979-2406; fax 979-8167; www.travelcuts.com). 60 offices across Canada. Also in the UK, 295-A Regent St., **London** W1R 7YA (☎0207 255 1944).

COMMERCIAL AIRLINES

From the **US,** the largest gateways for flights to Central America are Miami and Houston, with other flights originating from Atlanta, Los Angeles, New York, and Washington, D.C. Charter flights sometimes run from **Canada,** but scheduled flights are routed through the US. From **Europe,** KLM flies via Mexico to Guatemala City, while Iberia has indirect service from Spain. British Airways flies from London to San José, Costa Rica. Otherwise, it's straightforward to connect through the US on American, Continental, or Delta. From **Australia** or **New Zealand,** the least expensive route is via Los Angeles or Miami. The **OneWorld network** connectsUse **Microsoft Expedia** (msn.expedia.com) or **Travelocity** (www.travelocity.com) to get an idea of the lowest published fares, then use the resources outlined here to try and beat those fares

Grupo Taca: US ☎800-535-8780, Canada ☎416-968-2222; www.grupotaca.com. Flights to Central and South America. Los Angeles to San José US$265. For last-minute offers, subscribe to their email E-Speciales.

FLIGHT PLANNING ON THE INTERNET. Many airline sites offer special last-minute deals on the Web. For travel to and within Central America, try **Grupo Taca** at www.taca.com. Other major airlines with flights to Central America include **American** (www.aa.com), **Continental** (www.continental.com), and **Delta** (www.delta.com). Other sites do the legwork and compile the deals for you—try www.bestfares.com, www.flights.com, www.hotdeals.com, www.onetravel.com, and www.travelzoo.com.

StudentUniverse (www.studentuniverse.com), **STA** (www.sta-travel.com), **Council** (www.counciltravel.com), and Orbitz.com provide quotes on student tickets, while **Expedia** (www.expedia.com) and **Travelocity** (www.travelocity.com) offer full travel services. **Priceline** (www.priceline.com) allows you to specify a price, and obligates you to buy any ticket that meets or beats it; be prepared for antisocial hours and odd routes. **Skyauction** (www.skyauction.com) allows you to bid on both last-minute and advance-purchase tickets.

An indispensable resource on the Internet is the *Air Traveler's Handbook* (www.cs.cmu.edu/afs/cs/user/mkant/Public/Travel/airfare.html), a comprehensive listing of links to everything you need to know before you board a plane.

ESSENTIALS

AIR COURIER FLIGHTS

Those who travel light should consider courier flights. Couriers help transport cargo on international flights by using their checked luggage space for freight. Generally, couriers must travel with carry-ons only and deal with complex flight restrictions. Most flights are round-trip only, with short fixed-length stays (usually one week) and a limit of a one ticket per issue. Courier flights generally depart and arrive in large cities and are not as viable in Central America as elsewhere in the world. However, good deals to places like Panama City occasionally surface.

TICKET CONSOLIDATORS

Ticket consolidators, or **"bucket shops,"** buy unsold tickets in bulk from commercial airlines and sell them at discounted rates. The best place to look is in the Sunday travel section of any major newspaper (such as the *New York Times*), where many bucket shops place tiny ads. Call quickly, as availability is typically extremely limited. Not all bucket shops are reliable, so insist on a receipt that gives full details of restrictions, refunds, and tickets, and pay by credit card (in spite of the 2-5% fee) so you can stop payment if you never receive your tickets. For more info, see www.travel-library.com/air-travel/consolidators.html.

TRAVELING FROM THE US & CANADA

Travel Avenue (☎ 800-333-3335; www.travelavenue.com) searches for best available published fares and then uses several consolidators to attempt to beat that fare. **NOW Voyager,** 74 Varick St., Ste. 307, New York, NY 10013 (☎ 212-431-1616; fax 219-1793; www.nowvoyagertravel.com) arranges discounted flights, mostly from New York, to . Other consolidators worth trying are **Interworld** (☎ 305-443-4929; fax 443-0351); **Pennsylvania Travel** (☎ 800-331-0947); **Cheap Tickets** (☎ 800-377-1000; www.cheaptickets.com); and **Travac** (☎ 800-872-8800; fax 212-714-9063; www.travac.com). Yet more consolidators on the web include the **Internet Travel Network** (www.itn.com); **Travel Information Services** (www.tiss.com); **TravelHUB** (www.travelhub.com); and **The Travel Site** (www.thetravelsite.com). Keep in mind that these are just suggestions to get you started in your research; *Let's Go* does not endorse any of these agencies. As always, be cautious, and research companies before you hand over your credit card number.

ESSENTIALS

TRAVELING FROM THE UK, AUSTRALIA, & NEW ZEALAND

In London, the **Air Travel Advisory Bureau** (☎0207-636-5000; www.atab.co.uk) can provide names of reliable consolidators and discount flight specialists. From Australia and New Zealand, look for consolidator ads in the travel section of the *Sydney Morning Herald* and other papers.

CHARTER FLIGHTS

Charters are flights a tour operator contracts with an airline to fly extra loads of passengers during peak season. Charter flights fly less frequently than major airlines, make refunds particularly difficult, and are almost always fully booked. Schedules and itineraries may also change or be cancelled at the last moment (as late as 48 hours before the trip, and without a full refund), and check-in, boarding, and baggage claim are often much slower. However, they can also be cheaper.

Discount clubs and **fare brokers** offer members savings on last-minute charter and tour deals. Study contracts closely; you don't want to end up with an unwanted overnight layover.

BY BOAT AND BUS

Except for cruise ships, there are no regularly scheduled **boats** from North America to Central America, but arrangements may be made informally on cargo ships or private yachts. When traveling from **Colombia** to Panama it's possible to trek via the Darién Gap or travel by boat (see p. 675). Note that both of these routes are currently unsafe and not recommended.

BORDER CROSSINGS

Coming overland from North America means traveling via Mexico. Mexico has an extensive **bus** system that one can take from the US border to Guatemala or Belize. It's also possible to take your own **car,** but remember that Mexican insurance should be obtained at the border and preparation and planning is essential.

GETTING AROUND CENTRAL AMERICA

BY PLANE

📖**Grupo Taca** (comprised of four of Central America's international airlines; www.grupotaca.com) offers a **Latin Pass** that may save you money if you plan on traveling between several countries on the isthmus and South America. It requires that your itinerary include seven to sixteen countries. Flying between capital cities avoids the long, arduous bus routes that would be your alternative. **Domestic flights** are common throughout the region and are reasonably priced. See country chapters for destination info:rmation.

BY BUS OR TRAIN

Everyone in Central America gets around by bus. The service varies from country to country, but the bus system is comprehensive overall. Direct, first-class trips are often available between cities; otherwise expect some harrowing adventures on "chicken buses," in backpacker lingo. Worn shocks let you feel every bump in the rough roads, and drivers have few qualms about putting it into high gear on winding down hills. Snag a window seat (unless you're tall) to enjoy the view.

AIRCRAFT SAFETY. The airlines of developing world nations do not always meet safety standards. The *Official Airline Guide* (www.oag.com) and many travel agencies can tell you the type and age of aircraft on a particular route. This can be especially useful in Central America, where less reliable equipment is often used for internal flights. The **International Airline Passengers Association** (US ☎ 800-821-4272, UK ☎ 020 8681 6555) provides region-specific safety information. The **Federal Aviation Administration** reviews the airline authorities for countries whose airlines enter the US. As of December 2001, Costa Rica was the only Central American nation in full compliance with international aviation safety standards for oversight of its air carriers. For updated info, check www.faa.gov. **US State Department** travel advisories (☎ 202-647-5225; travel.state.gov/travel_warnings.html) sometimes involve foreign carriers, especially when terrorist bombings may be a threat.

BY CAR

RENTING

Rental cars are readily available in Central America, but can be somewhat pricey, depending on the region.

RENTAL AGENCIES. In major Central American cities, national and international chains are usually easy to find. Well-known agencies and their local numbers are listed in **Practical Information** sections. You can generally make reservations before you leave by calling major international offices in your home country. However, occasionally the price and availability information they give doesn't jive with what the local offices in your country will tell you. Check with both numbers to make sure you get the best price and accurate information. Local desk numbers are included in town listings; for home-country numbers, call your toll-free directory.

To rent a car from most establishments in Central America, you need to be at least 21 years old, and most charge those aged 21-24 an additional insurance fee (about US$25 per day). Policies and prices vary from agency to agency.

Thrifty Car Rental (☎ 800-847-4389, www.thrifty.com). Rents cars in Belize (US$330 per week), Costa Rica (US$102), El Salvador (US$144), Honduras (US$168), Nicaragua (US$120), and Panama (US$143.70). In El Salvador, Honduras, and Panama there is an additional daily surcharge of US$5 for drivers aged 21-24.

Dollar Rent-a-Car (☎ 800-800-3665, www.dollar.com). Rents cars in Costa Rica (US$94 per week), Guatemala (US$800), Nicaragua (US$118.20), and Panama (US$161.70). Additional daily fee of US$5-25 for drivers aged 21-24.

National Car Rental (☎ 800-227-7368, www.nationalcar.com). Rents cars in Costa Rica (US$132 per week), Honduras (US$200), and Panama (US$161.70). Additional daily fee of US$25 for drivers aged 21-24.

COSTS & INSURANCE. Rates range from a low of around US$40 per day in Costa Rica to a high of US$140 in Guatemala, and also vary widely based on vehicle type. Expect to pay more for larger cars and for 4WD. Cars with **automatic transmission** can cost up to US$15 a day more than standard manuals (stick shift), and in some places, automatic transmission is hard to find in the first place. It is virtually impossible, no matter where you are, to find an automatic 4WD.

Most rental packages in Central America offer unlimited kilometers. Return the car with a full tank of petrol to avoid high fuel charges at the end. Be sure to ask whether the price includes **insurance** against theft and collision. Remember that if you are driving a conventional vehicle on an **unpaved road** in a rental car, you are almost never covered by insurance; ask about this before leaving the rental agency. Beware that cars rented on an **American Express** or **Visa/Mastercard Gold or Platinum** credit cards in Central America might *not* carry the automatic insurance that they would in some other countries; check with your credit card company. Insurance plans almost always come with an **excess** (or deductible) of around US$105 for conventional vehicles; excess ranges increase for younger drivers and for 4WD. This means you pay for all damages up to that sum, unless they are the fault of another vehicle. The excess you will be quoted applies to collisions with other vehicles; collisions with non-vehicles, such as trees, ("single-vehicle collisions") will cost you even more. The excess can often be reduced or waived entirely if you pay an additional charge, around per day.

National chains often allow one-way rentals, picking up in one city and dropping off in another. There is usually a minimum hire period and sometimes an extra drop-off charge of several hundred dollars.

ON THE ROAD. Petrol (gasoline) prices vary, but average about US$1.70 per gallon in Central AmericaUnleaded gasoline is available in Guatemala, El Salvador, Honduras, and Costa Rica. If you must use leaded gasoline, always use the high grade/premium kind. Park your vehicle in garages or well-traveled areas, and keep valuables out of sight. When approaching a one-lane bridge, labeled *"puente angosto"* or *"solo carril,"* the first driver to flash headlights has the right of way. .

DRIVING PRECAUTIONS. When traveling in the summer or in the desert, bring substantial amounts of water (a suggested 5 liters of **water** per person per day) for drinking and for the radiator. For long drives to unpopulated areas, register with police before beginning the trek, and again upon arrival at the destination. Check with the local automobile club for details. When traveling for long distances, make sure tires are in good repair and have enough air, and get good maps. A **compass** and a **car manual** can also be very useful. You should always carry a **spare tire** and **jack, jumper cables, extra oil, flares, a torch (flashlight),** and **heavy blankets** (in case your car breaks down at night or in the winter). If you don't know how to **change a tire,** learn before heading out, especially if you are planning on traveling in deserted areas. Blowouts on dirt roads are exceedingly common. If you do have a breakdown, **stay with your car;** if you wander off, there's less likelihood trackers will find you.

DANGERS. The durability and security of your **car** are of incredible importance for successful travel in Central America. Be careful driving during the rainy season (May-Oct.), when roads are often in poor condition and landslides are common. In some areas the luxury of a 4WD vehicle may be well worth the extra rental cost.

CAR ASSISTANCE. Make sure your vehicle is ready for theParts, gas, and service stations are hard to come by, so be prepared for every possible occurrence. Mechanically inclined drivers might want to order a "test" pipe from a specialty parts house to replace the converter so that the car can process regular fuel. *Let's Go: Central America 2003* lists the countries' automobile organization in each chapter's Essentials section.

DRIVING PERMITS & CAR INSURANCE

INTERNATIONAL DRIVING PERMIT (IDP). If you plan to drive a car while in Central America, you must be over 18 and have an International Driving Permit (IDP), though certain countries (e.g. Guatemala) allow travelers to drive with a valid American or Canadian license for a limited number of months. It may be a good idea to get one anyway, in case you're in a situation (e.g. an accident or stranded in

ESSENTIALS

a small town) where the police do not know English; information on the IDP is printed in ten languages, including Spanish.

Your IDP, valid for one year, must be issued in your own country before you depart. An application for an IDP usually requires one or two photos, a current local license, an additional form of identification, and a fee. To apply, contact the national or local branch of your home country's Automobile Association.

CAR INSURANCE. Most credit cards cover standard insurance. If you rent, lease, or borrow a car, you will need a **green card,** or **International Insurance Certificate,** to certify that you have liability insurance and that it applies abroad. Green cards can be obtained at car rental agencies, car dealers (for those leasing cars), some travel agents, and some border crossings. Rental agencies may require you to purchase theft insurance in countries that they consider to have a high risk of auto theft.

BY THUMB

 HITCHHIKING AND SAFETY. *Let's Go* urges you to use common sense if you decide to hitch and to consider all the serious risks before you make that decision. The information listed below and throughout the book is not intended to recommend hitchhiking.

Hitchhiking is common in most of Central America and may be the only way to get around in some places. Drivers expect compensation, but travelers usually pay after a ride—and rarely pay much more than bus fare. Rides are generally considered safest when offered to groups; women in particular should never hitchhike alone. Those who hitch should find out where the driver is going before getting in and think twice if he opens the door quickly and offers to drive anywhere. If you insist on hitching, don't get in without ensuring that you can get out. Letting a driver store luggage out of one's reach complicates matters should an escape be necessary—keep your luggage on your lap. *Let's Go* strongly urges you to consider the risks before you choose to hitchhike.

SPECIFIC CONCERNS

WOMEN TRAVELERS

Women exploring on their own inevitably face some additional safety concerns, but it's easy to be adventurous without taking undue risks. If you are concerned, consider staying in hostels which offer single rooms that lock from the inside or in religious organizations with rooms for women only. Stick to centrally located accommodations and avoid solitary late-night treks. Always carry extra money for a phone call, bus, or taxi. **Hitchhiking** is never safe for lone women, or even for two women traveling together. Look as if you know where you're going and approach older women or couples for directions if you're lost or uncomfortable.

You will likely be harassed no matter how you're dressed, especially in cities. While Latin American *machismo* often means that women are treated with deference and politeness, the opposite is also true, and women often find themselves the target of catcalls, whistles, and unsolicited come-ons. Your best answer to verbal harassment is no answer at all; feigned deafness and staring straight ahead at nothing in particular will do a world of good. The extremely persistent nuisance can sometimes be dissuaded by a firm, loud *"¡Déjame en paz!"* (leave me alone!), *"¡No me molestes!"* (stop bothering me), or *"¡Voy a llamar a la policía!"* (I'm going to call the police!). If need be, enlist the help of an older woman; her stern rebukes will often be enough to embarrass the most obnoxious of suitors. *Let's Go* lists emergency numbers in the **Practical Information** listings of most cities.

TRAVELING ALONE

There are many benefits to traveling alone, including independence and greater interaction with locals. On the other hand, any solo traveler is a more vulnerable target of harassment and street theft. As a lone traveler, try not to stand out as a tourist, look confident, and be especially careful in deserted or very crowded areas. If questioned, never admit that you are traveling alone. Maintain regular contact with someone at home who knows your itinerary. For more tips, pick up *Traveling Solo* by Eleanor Berman (Globe Pequot Press, US$17) or subscribe to **Connecting: Solo Travel Network,** 689 Park Road, Unit 6, Gibsons, BC V0N 1V7, Canada (☎604-886-9099; www.cstn.org; membership US$35). **Travel Companion Exchange,** P.O. Box 833, Amityville, NY 11701, USA (☎631-454-0880, or in the US ☎800-392-1256; www.whytravelalone.com; US$48), will link solo travelers with companions with similar travel habits and interests.

OLDER TRAVELERS

Central America is easy to explore, and some destinations (Costa Rica, in particular) are developing substantial tourist infrastructures for older travelers. If you don't see a senior citizen price listed, ask, and you may be delightfully surprised. The books *No Problem! Worldwise Tips for Mature Adventurers*, by Janice Kenyon (Orca Book Publishers; US$16) and *Unbelievably Good Deals and Great Adventures That You Absolutely Can't Get Unless You're Over 50*, by Joan Rattner Heilman (NTC/Contemporary Publishing; US$13) are both excellent resources. For more information, contact one of the following organizations:

ElderTreks, 597 Markham St., Toronto, ON M6G 2L7 (☎800-741-7956; www.eldertreks.com). Adventure travel programs for the 50+ traveler in Costa Rica.

Elderhostel, 11 Ave. de Lafayette, Boston, MA 02111 (☎877-426-8056; www.elderhostel.org). Organizes 1- to 4-week "educational adventures" in Belize, Costa Rica, Guatemala, Honduras, Nicaragua, and Panama on varied subjects for those 55+.

The Mature Traveler, P.O. Box 15791, Sacramento, CA 95852 (☎800-460-6676). Deals, discounts, and travel packages for the 50+ traveler. Subscription $30.

Walking the World, P.O. Box 1186, Fort Collins, CO 80522 (☎800-340-9255; www.walkingtheworld.com), organizes trips for 50+ travelers to Costa Rica.

BISEXUAL, GAY, & LESBIAN TRAVELERS

Homosexuality and bisexuality are shunned throughout much of Central America, but contact organizations give advice and help gay travelers find existing organizations. A good source is Richard Stern, reached at **Asociación Triangulo Rosa** in Costa Rica. (☎258-0214 for Spanish, ☎234-2411 for English; atritosa@sol.racsa.co.cr. Open M-F 8am-noon and 1-5pm.) **Out and About** (www.outandabout.com) offers a bi-weekly newsletter addressing travel concerns and keeps a continually updated newsbank of events in Central America. Listed below are contact organizations which offer materials addressing some specific concerns.

Gay's the Word, 66 Marchmont St., London WC1N 1AB, UK (☎+44 20 7278 7654; www.gaystheword.co.uk). The largest gay and lesbian bookshop in the UK, with both fiction and non-fiction titles. Mail-order service available.

Now, Voyager, 4406 18th St., San Francisco, CA 94114 (☎415-626-1169; fax 626-8626; www.nowvoyager.com). Travel agency for gay and lesbian travelers. Register on the website for their electronic newsletter on travel information and reservations.

Giovanni's Room, 1145 Pine St., Philadelphia, PA 19107, USA (☎215-923-2960; www.queerbooks.com). An international lesbian/feminist and gay bookstore with mail-order service (carries many of the publications listed below).

International Lesbian and Gay Association (ILGA), 81 rue Marché-au-Charbon, B-1000 Brussels, Belgium (☎+32 2 502 2471; www.ilga.org). Provides political information, such as homosexuality laws of individual countries.

> **FURTHER READING: BISEXUAL, GAY, & LESBIAN.**
> *Spartacus International Gay Guide 2001-2002.* Bruno Gmunder Verlag (US$33).
> *Ferrari Guides' Gay Travel A to Z, Ferrari Guides' Men's Travel in Your Pocket,* and *Ferrari Guides' Inn Places.* Ferrari Publications (US$16-20). Purchase the guides online at www.ferrariguides.com.
> *The Gay Vacation Guide: The Best Trips and How to Plan Them,* Mark Chesnut. Citadel Press (US$15).

TRAVELERS WITH DISABILITIES

Central America still poses a formidable challenge for the disabled traveler. Intense planning is necessary. Though few facilities are accessible to disabled persons, many attractions are trying to make exploring the outdoors more feasible. Call ahead to restaurants, museums, and other facilities to find out if they are handicapped-accessible. **Guide dog owners** should inquire as to the quarantine policies of each destination country.

USEFUL ORGANIZATIONS

Mobility International USA (MIUSA), P.O. Box 10767, Eugene, OR 97440, USA (☎541--343-1284; www.miusa.org). Sells *A World of Options: A Guide to International Educational Exchange, Community Service, and Travel for Persons with Disabilities* (US$35).

Society for the Advancement of Travel for the Handicapped (SATH), 347 Fifth Ave., #610, New York, NY 10016, USA (☎212-447-7284; www.sath.org). An advocacy group that publishes free online travel information and the travel magazine *OPEN WORLD* (US$18, free for members). Annual membership US$45, students and seniors US$30.

TOUR AGENCIES

Directions Unlimited, 123 Green Ln., Bedford Hills, NY 10507, USA (☎800-533-5343). Books individual and group vacations for the physically disabled; not an info service.

TRAVELERS WITH CHILDREN

Family vacations often require that you slow your pace, and always require that you plan ahead. If you rent a car, make sure the rental company provides a car seat for younger children. **Be sure that your child carries some sort of ID** in case of an emergency or in case he or she gets lost. Children under two generally fly for 10% of the adult airfare on international flights (this does not necessarily include a seat). International fares are usually discounted 25% for children from two to 11. Always try to negotiate for a family rate--often children can go free. For more information, consult one of the following books:

Backpacking with Babies and Small Children, Goldie Silverman. Wilderness Press (US$10).

How to take Great Trips with Your Kids, Sanford and Jane Portnoy. Harvard Common Press (US $10).

Have Kid, Will Travel: 101 Survival Strategies for Vacationing With Babies and Young Children, Claire and Lucille Tristram. Andrews McMeel Publishing (US$9).

Adventuring with Children: An Inspirational Guide to World Travel and the Outdoors, Nan Jeffrey. Avalon House Publishing (US$15).

Trouble Free Travel with Children, Vicki Lansky. Book Peddlers (US$9).

DIETARY CONCERNS

Vegetarian cuisine is not hard to find in Central America's more touristed, cosmopolitan cities, but in more remote areas, beans and rice may become the only vegetarian options. Many eateries in Central America do not consider pork or chicken to be "meat"; if you are concerned about the specific ingredients of dishes listed on the menu, be sure to ask very specific questions. For a brief lexicon of common foods, see the inside of the back cover of this guide. Living a vegetarian lifestyle while on the road might be a helpful, albeit compromised, alternative. Caution is advised in restaurants where many "vegetarian" dishes are cooked in a pork base. The **North American Vegetarian Society,** P.O. Box 72, Dolgeville, NY 13329 (☎518-568-7970; www.navs-online.org), publishes information about vegetarian travel, including *Transformative Adventures, a Guide to Vacations and Retreats* (US$15), and the *Vegetarian Journal's Guide to Natural Food Restaurants in the US and Canada* (US$12).Travelers who keep **kosher** may have trouble finding restaurants in Central America that accommodate their needs. Those who are strictly observant will probably need to prepare their own food on the road. A good resource is the *Jewish Travel Guide,* by Michael Zaidner (Vallentine Mitchell; US$17). More info on dietary concerns in Latin America can also be found through these resources:

The Vegetarian Traveler: Where to Stay if You're Vegetarian, Jed and Susan Civic. (Larson Publications; US$16). Covers only Costa Rica.

The Jewish Travel Guide, Jewish Chronicle staff (International Special Book Services; US$15.95). Lists synagogues, kosher restaurants, and Jewish institutions in Guatemala, Honduras, Costa Rica, and Panama.

Latin American Vegetarian Resources (www.vrg.org/travel/largupdate.htm) is a comprehensive resource of regional healthfully stores and vegetarian restaurants as well as books pertaining to vegetarian issues.

OTHER RESOURCES

Let's Go tries to cover all aspects of budget travel, but we can't put *everything* in our guides. Listed below are books and websites that can serve as jumping off points for your own research.

TRAVEL PUBLISHERS & BOOKSTORES

Hippocrene Books, Inc., 171 Madison Ave., New York, NY 10016, USA (☎718-454-2366; www.hippocrenebooks.com). Publishes foreign language dictionaries and language learning guides.

Hunter Publishing, 470 W. Broadway, fl. 2, South Boston, MA 02127, USA (☎617-269-0700; www.hunterpublishing.com). Has an extensive catalog of travel guides and diving and adventure travel books.

Rand McNally, P.O. Box 7600, Chicago, IL 60680, USA (☎847-329-8100; www.randmcnally.com), publishes road atlases.

Adventurous Traveler Bookstore, P.O. Box 2221, Williston, VT 05495, USA (☎800-282-3963; www.adventuroustraveler.com).

Travel Books & Language Center, Inc., 4437 Wisconsin Ave. NW, Washington, D.C. 20016, USA (☎800-220-2665; www.bookweb.org/bookstore/travelbks/). Over 60,000 titles from around the world.

WORLD WIDE WEB

Central America's information technology infrastructure is continually growing so that many aspects of budget travel are accessible via the web. Listed here are some budget travel sites to start off your surfing; other relevant web sites are listed throughout the book. Because website turnover is high, use search engines (such as www.google.com) to strike out on your own.

OUR PERSONAL FAVORITE...

Let's Go: www.letsgo.com. Our constantly expanding website features photos and streaming video, online ordering of all our titles, info about our books, a travel forum buzzing with stories and tips, and links that will help you find everything you ever wanted to know about Central America.

THE ART OF BUDGET TRAVEL

How to See the World: www.artoftravel.com. A compendium of great travel tips, from cheap flights to self defense to interacting with local culture.

Rec. Travel Library: www.travel-library.com. A fantastic set of links for general information and personal travelogues.

Lycos: cityguide.lycos.com. General introductions to cities and regions throughout Central America, accompanied by links to applicable histories, news, and local tourism sites.

INFORMATION ON CENTRAL AMERICA

Consular Information on Belize: www.un.int/belize/consular. The website of Belize's UN diplomatic mission.

Travel Documents and Visas: www.traveldocs.com. Download visa applications for any country. Will process the documents for you for a fee.

Drive to Mexico, Pan American Highway, and Central America: www.drivemeloco.com. Lots of great information and advice on driving in Mexico and Latin America.

Dirla.com: www.dirla.com. Lots of information on long-term living in Central America, including real estate listings, discussion forums, information on work visas, and statistical and cultural information.

CIA World Factbook: www.odci.gov/cia/publications/factbook/index.html. Tons of vital statistics on (your country's) geography, government, economy, and people.

Foreign Language for Travelers: www.travlang.com. Provides free online translating dictionaries and lists of phrases in (your language).

Geographia: www.geographia.com. Highlights, culture, and people of Costa Rica.

Atevo Travel: www.atevo.com/guides/destinations. Detailed introductions, travel tips, and suggested itineraries.

Alfatravelguide.com: www.alfatravelguide.com. Helpful entry and exit requirements.

World Travel Guide: www.travel-guides.com/navigate/world.asp. Helpful practical info.

ALTERNATIVES TO TOURISM

Traveling through a country or region for several weeks is an exciting and memorable experience. But if you are looking for a more rewarding way to see the world, you may want to consider more long-term opportunities. Working, volunteering, or studying for an extended period of time can be an much more enriching way to explore and understand life in Central America. This chapter outlines some of the different opportunities available to learn more about Central America: from jobs that allow you to pay your way through, to academic and volunteer programs that provide personal growth and development.

Central America is especially rich with opportunities for working and volunteering. Numerous programs operate out of all seven nations and provide a wide variety of experiences, from helping disabled children in the Honduras to studying ecology in Costa Rica and Belize. The complex issues facing Central American countries, including ecological preservation, growing economies, and their rich and colorful cultures will further enrich your extended stay abroad as you learn about a people uniquely different from Western cultures.

VISA INFORMATION

BELIZE

All visitors are automatically issued a 30-day visa upon arrival, which can be renewed at any Immigration office for US$12.50 per month for up to six months. You must have resided legally in Belize for six months to obtain a **work permit.** Your prospective employer must then submit an **Application for Permission to Employ a Foreigner** to the Labor Department (☎822 204), along with three passport photos, US$10 in stamps, a valid passport, and proof that you are qualified for the job. They must also prove that all efforts to employ a native were exhausted, including a local advertisement of the job for at least three weeks with no qualified applicants. The work permit costs US$25-500, depending on the type of work. Another type of work permit is an **Application for Temporary Self-Employment**. You must legally reside in Belize with the proper visas and permits, but the six-month residence requirement is waived. Along with application, you must provide proof of sufficient funds for the venture and a reference from the appropriate Ministry. For more information on work permits, contact the **Immigration and Nationality Department** (Belmopan ☎822 611 or 822 423). **Student visas** are not required.

COSTA RICA

A **student visa** allows a foreign individual to study at a Costa Rican school or university for a year, and can be renewed for an additional year if required by their studies. An individual must be enrolled as a full-time student in an academic educational program, language program, or vocational program accredited by the Immigration Department of Costa Rica; proficient in Spanish or be enrolled in courses leading to Spanish proficiency; have proof of sufficient financial funds; and have a permanent residency abroad that they have no intention of giving up.

To apply for a student visa, it's recommended that you first apply for a tourist visa at the Costa Rican consulate in your home country. When you arrive in Costa Rica, go to the Immigration Department **(Direccion General de Migracion y Extranje-**

ria) within 30 days of your arrival and submit the following: a Visa Student Application authenticated by an attorney; results of medical exams and tests required by the Costa Rican Health Department (the Health Department will provide a list of clinics to go to); fingerprints; four recent passport-sized photos; a guarantee deposit; proof of enrollment in an accredited school or university; a notarized guarantee letter issued by the school or university; a passport valid for at least six months; and an original birth certificate and police record, both authenticated by the local consulate of Costa Rica prior to arrival.

Foreign nationals wishing to **work** in Costa Rica must hold an **Employment Authorization Document (EAD).** To obtain an EAD, you must submit the following to the Immigration and Naturalization Services of Costa Rica: an EAD Application form authenticated by an attorney; a notarized personal letter requesting an EAD; a six-month labor contract stating the terms of the contract, the salary, job duties, working hours, and location of the job; a *Caja Costarricense del Seguro Social Employer* (CCCSS) certification that your employer is a registered CCSS tax paying company; a certified photocopy of the employer's tax ID; authenticated copies of your passport; four recent passport-sized photos; and a guarantee deposit.

EL SALVADOR

To apply for a **work permit** in El Salvador, you must legally be in El Salvador with the proper visas and permits, and then submit the following to the Ministry of the Interior: a residency request form; an original birth certificate; a good conduct certificate issued by the Salvadoran consulate of your home country and from the Ministry of Foreign Relations; two recent passport-sized photos; results of an HIV test; a health certificate; a work contract stating the terms of the contract, the salary, job duties, working hours, and location of the job; a notarized letter requesting residency; a personal data form; and authenticated photocopies of everything previously stated. Student visas are not required; however, check with the Salvadoran consulate of your home country.

GUATEMALA

A **work permit** in Guatemala is valid for one year and can be extended if necessary. Your employer must apply to the Ministry of Labor and Security with the following materials from you: an authorization of your temporary or permanent residency in Guatemala; a police record citing a lack of criminal activity in your home country during the previous six months; a notarized letter in which the employer takes full responsibility for your conduct; a certification of the number of Guatemalan and foreign employees working for the company and the wage statistics; a notarized photocopy of the letter of hire; a sworn statement of your Spanish proficiency; and documents that prove your qualifications for the job (such as high school or college diploma). All documents that come from your home country must be authenticated by the nearest Guatemalan consulate.

HONDURAS

All foreigners wishing to study or work in Honduras must first apply for a **resident visa**. The only exceptions are Canadians, who may study for 6 months before needing to apply for residency. To apply for a resident visa, submit a valid passport, 4 passport size pictures, notarized medical certificate, bank letter, income tax references, work contract (if needed), and copies of a birth or naturalization certificate, letter of good conduct, and a marriage certificate (if applicable) to the **Honduran Consulate** in your home country. Once all documents are processed at the consulate, your passport will be stamped with the appropriate visa.

NICARAGUA

For those wishing to work or study in Nicaragua, a **resident visa** is required. To apply for residency, travelers may enter with a passport, and obtain a letter from the school or place of employment. This, plus a medical certificate, birth certificate, and police record should be submitted to the Immigration Office in Managua.

PANAMA

If you are working for a foreign company in Panama, you do not need a **work permit**. However, if you are hired by a Panamanian company, you will need a permit from the Ministry of Labor; they are good for 1 year, and renewable. You must also have a passport, a police record notarized by the nearest Panamanian Consulate, an original birth certificate, 6 passport-sized photos, and a negative HIV test. If you are married, you must show a marriage certificate. You may have to hire a lawyer. Alternately, if you have lived in Panama legally for 5 years, you can become a resident alien with the right to work.

STUDYING ABROAD

Study abroad programs range from basic language and culture courses to college-level classes, often for credit. In order to choose a program that best fits your needs, you will want to find out what kind of students participate in the program and what sort of accommodations are provided. In programs that serve large groups of English-speaking students, you may feel more comfortable in the community, but you will not have the same opportunity to practice a foreign language or to befriend other international students. For accommodations, dorm life provides a better opportunity to mingle with fellow students, but there is less of a chance to experience the local scene and day-to-day life in that country.

UNIVERSITIES

Those relatively fluent in Spanish may find it cheaper to enroll directly in a university abroad, although getting college credit may be more difficult. Some American schools still require students to pay them for credits they obtain elsewhere. Most university-level study-abroad programs are meant as language and culture enrichment opportunities, and therefore are conducted in Spanish. Still, many programs do offer classes in English and beginner- and lower-level language courses. Try www.studyabroad.com, which has links to various semester abroad programs based on a variety of criteria, including desired location and focus of study. The following is a list of organizations that can help place students in university programs abroad, or have their own branch in Central America.

AMERICAN PROGRAMS

American Institute for Foreign Study, College Division, River Plaza, 9 W. Broad St., Stamford, CT 06902, USA (☎800-727-2437, ext. 5163; www.aifsabroad.com). Organizes programs for high school and college study in universities in Costa Rica.

School for International Training, College Semester Abroad, Admissions, Kipling Rd., P.O. Box 676, Brattleboro, VT 05302, USA (☎800-336-1616 or 802-257-7751; www.sit.edu). Semester- and year-long programs in Belize, Nicaragua, and Panama run US$12,250-13,550. Also runs the **Experiment in International Living** (☎800-345-2929; fax 802-258-3428; www.usexperiment.org), 3- to 5-week summer programs that offer high school students cross-cultural homestays, community service, ecological adventure, and language training in Belize and Costa Rica. US$3500-4100.

International Association for the Exchange of Students for Technical Experience (IAESTE), 10400 Little Patuxent Pkwy. Suite 250, Columbia, MD 21044-3519, USA

(☎410-997-2200; www.aipt.org). 8- to 12-week programs for college students who have completed 2 years of technical study. US$25 application fee.

PROGRAMS IN CENTRAL AMERICA

Study abroad programs in Central America are varied and numerous, ranging from week-long intensive language courses to several month-long homestays and cultural immersion. Thanks to the growing ubiquity of the internet, many programs are now on the web; what may be more difficult is gauging which programs will live up to their promises. Popular cities for study abroad programs are Antigua in Guatemala, León, Granada, and Managua in Nicaragua, Tegucigalpa in Honduras, and San José, Heredia, and Cartago in Costa Rica.

Academia Americana (☎/fax 223 7217). IPAT-recommended. Also try **Idiomas y Especialidades** (☎229 3892), **Genesis Language Center** (☎223 1137; fax 223 0947), and **Centro de Idiomas Orientación y Capacitación** (☎260 5366; fax 236 8319).

LANGUAGE SCHOOLS

Unlike American universities, language schools are often independently international or local organizations or divisions of foreign universities that rarely offer college credit. Language schools are a good alternative to university study if you desire a deeper focus on the language or a less-rigorous course load. Language programs are popular in Guatemala, Costa Rica, and Nicaragua. In general, **language study programs** are few and far between in Belize. The **Guatemalan Embassy** (☎02 331 50), located on 8A St., offers Spanish classes (call or scan newspaper ads). Guatemala is full of **language schools**, particularly in Antigua. Indigenous languages are also taught at a few institutions. Most schools offer packages of five hours of instruction per day for five days, a week of homestay with a family, and full board for US$100-140 per week. Quetzaltenango affords students immersion in a more urban environment. In Panama

City, contact **Instituto Internacional,** Apdo. 2169, Zona 9A, Panama (☎ 264 7226; fax 269 3216) for more info on programs and classes. Some good programs include:

Academia de Español Guatemala, 3a. Av. Sur #15, Apdo. Postal No. 403, Antigua, **Guatemala** (☎/fax 832 5057). Language program highly acclaimed by participants. US$200 per week covers tuition, homestay, and organized recreation.

Academia Europea, ALKE Carretera Masaya, 1c. abajo, ½c. al sur (☎ 278 0829), Managua and León, **Nicaragua.** An international language school that offers classes at every level in private (US$15 per hr.), semi-private (US$19 per hr.), and full immersion (US$222) settings.

Amerispan, 6 Av. Norte #40A, Antigua, **Guatemala** (☎ 832 0164; fax 832-1896; in the US (☎ 215-751-1100; info@amerispan.com). Language courses with homestays and meals. 1 week minimum. Offers services to pre-registered students and new arrivals.

Costa Rican Language Academy, P.O. Box. 1966-2050, San José, **Costa Rica** (US ☎ 866-230-6361, worldwide ☎ 506 280-1685 or 280-1739; fax 280-2548; crlang@crlang.co.cr; www.spanishandmore.com). Language and cultural study custom tailored for individual students. homestays and weekend excursions plus lessons in Latin dance, Costa Rican cooking, Spanish music, and conversation.

Academia Latinoamericana de Español S.A., Apdo. 1280-2050 San Pedro Montes de Oca, San José, **Costa Rica** (☎ 224 9917; fax 225 8125; recajhi@sol.rasca.co.cr; www.alespanish.com). Spanish taught in small groups. Classes start every Monday.

Casa Xalteva, (☎/fax 552 2436; casaxal@ibw.com.ni; www.ibw.com.ni/~casaxal), 5 blocks west of the *parque* on Calle Real, next to la Iglesia Xalteva, Granada, **Nicaragua.**. Approximately US$125 per week, US$425 per month plus a $25 registration fee. homestays US$60 per week. Internships available. This non-profit Spanish language school offers classes of 1-4 students, as well as activities and volunteer opportunities. US$90 per week for instruction.

Centro Nicaraguans de Aprendizaje Cultural, P.O. Box #10, Estelí, **Nicaragua** (CENAC; ☎/ fax 713 2025; cenac@tmx.com.ni; www.tmx.com.ni/~cenac), on Calle 9 S., 300m east of the Carretera Interamericana. CENAC participants choose between language classes, homestays, service projects, or any combination of the 3 (weekly costs about US$120).

Comunicare, 12086 SJO, 1601 NW, 97th Ave., P.O. Box 025331, Miami FL 33102-5331 or Apdo. 1383-2050, San Pedro, **Costa Rica** (☎/fax 506-224-4473; comunica@rasca.co.cr; www.comunicare.co.cr). A non-profit organization offering Spanish classes, cultural and Central American studies, and volunteer opportunities working with the community around San José.

Escuela de Español Ixbalanque, Copán Ruinas, **Honduras** (☎ 898 3432). Located 1km from the ruins at Copán. US$145 for one-on-one instruction 4hr. per day, 5 days per week, with homestay and full board.

Escuela Idiomas d'Amore, P.O. Box 67, Quepos, **Costa Rica** (☎/fax 777 1143; in the US ☎/fax 262-367-8598 or 310-435-9897; damore@sol.rasca.co.cr; www.escueladamore.com). "Immerse yourself in Spanish on the beaches," halfway between Quepos and Parque Nacional Manuel Antonio. Participants are primarily adults in high season, college students in low season. A percentage of tuition goes to the World Wildlife Fund.

Escuela de Español Leonesa (☎ 311 2116; nssmga@ibw.com.ni), in the *casa de cultura,* León, **Nicaragua.** Customized Spanish classes start any day of the week. Part of Nicaragua Spanish Schools in Managua (☎ 244 1699).

Escuela Horizonte, Esteli, **Nicaragua** (☎ 713-4117; http://www.ibw.com.ni/~horizont/ escuela.htm; horizout@ibw.com.ni). Focused on raising awareness of community development and is a great resource for volunteering in the area. 20hr. of morning or afternoon instruction and 7 day homestay with meals US$150; without homestay US$100.

Forester Instituto Internacional, P.O. Box 6945, 1000 San José, **Costa Rica** (☎225 3155; fax 225 9236; forester@rasca.co.cr; www.fores.com). Spanish language programs in the nation's capital.

Los Pipitos (☎713 5511; sacuanjoche@ibw.com.ni), a large language school just south of town in Estelí, **Nicaragua.** Started by parents of disabled children to raise money for the attached school for the handicapped. Two outside activities per week. 20hr. of instruction with 7 day homestay and meals included, US$170. US$150 for 3 weeks or more. US120 without homestay.

Instituto Central America (ICA), 19 Avenida 1-47, Zona 1, Quetzaltenango, **Guatemala** (☎/fax 502 763 1871; US contact 402-439-2943; ica@larutamaya.online.com; www.spanishschoolica.com). This fully accredited language school takes a "total immersion approach." US $140 per week Sept. through May, US $150 per week June through August includes homestay, meals, and 5 hours a day of one-on-one language instruction. Those willing to volunteer for a minimum of 3 weeks and 4 to 5 hours a day at ICA can pay Q225 per week to live with a family, or Q24 per week to live at the school. Intermediate Spanish required.

Proyecto Linguístico de Español/Mam "Todos Santos", main street, Todos Santos Cuchumatán, **Guatemala.** At the entrance to town. Instruction in Spanish and indigenous Mam. US$115 for a seven-day home-stay in a traditional Mam household with meals and 25hr. of language instruction. Traveler's checks accepted. Also see **Spanish and Mam Academy Hispanomaya** and **Nuevo Amenecer,** with similar services in Todos Santos.

Proyecto Linguístico Francisco Marroquín, 7a Calle Pte. #31, Apdo. 237, Antigua, **Guatemala** (☎800 552 2051; fax 502 832 3777; 502 832 2866 within Guatemala; info@plfm-antigua.org; www.plfm-antigua.org). The oldest, largest school in Antigua. A nonprofit foundation whose revenues help preserve Maya languages. Organizes regular *fiestas* and excursions to many parts of Guatemala. One-on-one instruction 7hrs. per day. 2-week minimum stay during summer. Make reservations 8-10 weeks in advance.

▧ **Spanish Learning Center,** Panama City, **Panama,** 6 blocks past Trapiche's restaurant, off Via Argentina (☎213 3121; spanishlearning@hotmail.com). One-on-one Spanish instruction tailored to your needs, learning style, and schedule (block of 10 hours distributed as you choose, US$99). Also offers intensive homestay and instruction packages (classes 4hr. per day 4 days per week) for US$950 a month. Options include daytrips and Latin dance classes.

Spanish School (☎449 0331), in La Libertad, **El Salvador,** has daily lessons and homestays.

BIOLOGY/ECOLOGY PROGRAMS

Centro Ecológico de Los Guatuzos (☎283 0139; http://www.geocities.com/guatuzos/guatuzos.html), in front of the Nazareno church in San Carlos, **Nicaragua.** El Rufugio de Vida Silvestre Los Guatuzos is one of the most diverse concentration of ecosystems, flora, and fauna in Central America. Possible volunteer options include scientific experiments and social development programs in the center and surrounding communities.

Forest Restoration Program, (kellykeefel@yahoo.com), Bocas del Toro near Bocas del Drago, **Panama.** Run by the Institute for Tropical Ecology and Conservation (ITEC), volunteers are welcome. US$15 per day includes food and facilities.

Instituto Monteverde, Apdo. 69-5655, Monteverde, Puntarenas, **Costa Rica** (☎/fax: 506 645 5053; mvi@mvinstitute.org; www.mvinstitute.org). "Education for a sustainable future." This nonprofit association provides educational and cultural resources for the local community. 10-week programs in tropical ecology, biology, architecture, landscaping, and planning. 6-week and 16-week programs also available. Accredited by CIEE and the University of California Education Abroad Program.

La Escuela del Mundo (☎643 1064; www.schooloftheworld.org). 50m east of Panadería Tosso in Jacó, **Costa Rica**. Look for a blue sign. Offers programs in Spanish, ecology, surfing, drawing and painting. All programs take weekly field trips to hike, kayak, and horseback ride. One week US$390; two weeks US$735; four weeks US$1275.

Proyecto Ecológico Escuela de Español, (☎882 3992 or 265 7225; www.guegue.com.ni/eco-nic; eco-nic@guegue.com.ni), Laguna de Apoyo, **Nicaragua**. Language classes in this beautiful dry forest and protected region. One-on-one classes start weekly on Sundays. Also offers concurrent dive instruction with prior arrangement. Bike, scuba, swim, and kayak after class. One week US$190 with lodging and meals; two weeks US$365; 3 weeks US$535; 4 weeks US$690.

Sea Turtle Conservation Program, (contact Aideen ☎757 9244; acomerford18@hotmail.com), Bocas del Toro and Isla Colón, **Panama**. Volunteers live on the archipelago and help out scientists and biologists. 1 week minimum stay.

WORKING

Some travelers want long-term jobs that allow them to get to know another part of the world in depth (e.g. teaching English, working in the tourist industry). Other travelers seek out short-term jobs to finance their travel. They seek usually employment in the service sector or in agriculture, working for a few weeks at a time to finance the next leg of their journey. This section discusses both short-term and long-term opportunities for working in Central America. Make sure you understand **visa requirements** in Central American countries for working abroad. See the box on p.1 for more information. Finding a job in Central America will take a great amount of personal initiative. In general, employers seek college graduates with some proficiency in Spanish.

For US college students, recent graduates, and young adults, the simplest way to get legal permission to work abroad is through **Council Exchanges Work Abroad Programs.** Fees are from US$300-425. Council Exchanges provides assistance obtaining three- to six-month work permits/visas and finding jobs and housing.

LONG-TERM WORK

If you're planning on spending a substantial amount of time (more than three months) working in Central America search for a job well in advance. International placement agencies are often the easiest way to find employment abroad, especially for teaching English. **Internships,** usually for college students, are a good way to segue into working abroad, although they are often unpaid or poorly paid (many say the experience, however, is well worth it). Be wary of advertisements or companies that claim the ability to get you a job abroad for a fee—often times the same listings are available online or in newspapers, or even out of date. It's best, if going through an organization, to use one that's somewhat reputable.

Casa Guatemala, 14 Calle 10-63 Zona 1, Guatemala City, **Guatemala** (☎502 25 517; fax 502 31 9408). Provides malnourished, orphaned, and abandoned children with school, a medical clinic, and farm. Seeks doctors, teachers, farm workers, nannies, and agronomist. Minimum stay 3 month-1 year. Spanish required for teaching positions.

TEACHING ENGLISH

Teaching jobs abroad are rarely well-paid, although some elite private American schools can pay somewhat competitive salaries. Volunteering as a teacher in lieu of getting paid is also a popular option, and even in those cases, teachers often get some sort of a daily stipend to help with living expenses. Even though salaries at private schools may be low compared to the US, a low cost of living makes it much more profitable. In almost all cases, you must have at least a bachelor's degree to be a full-fledged teacher, although often times college undergraduates can get summer positions teaching or tutoring. It is relatively easy for a college grad to find a position as a teacher in Central America. However, pay is very low.

Many schools require teachers to have a **Teaching English as a Foreign Language (TEFL)** certificate. This does not necessarily exclude you from finding a teaching job, but certified teachers often find higher paying jobs. Native English speakers working in private schools are most often hired for English-immersion classrooms where no Spanish is spoken. Those volunteering or teaching in public, poorer schools, are more likely to be working in both English and Spanish. Placement agencies or university fellowship programs are the best resources for finding teaching jobs in Central America. The alternative is to make contacts directly with schools or just to try your luck once you get there. If you are going to try the latter, the best time of the year is several weeks before the start of the school year. The following organization is helpful in placing teachers in Central America:

WorldTeach, Inc., Center for International Development, Harvard University, 79 John F. Kennedy St., Cambridge, MA 02138, USA (☎800-4-TEACH-0 or 617-495-5527; fax 617-495-1599; www.worldteach.org). Fees range from $4000-6000.

SHORT-TERM WORK

Traveling for long periods of time can get expensive; many travelers try their hand at odd jobs for a few weeks at a time to make some extra cash to carry them through another month or two of touring around. Another popular option is to work several hours a day at a hostel in exchange for free or discounted room and/or board. Most often, these short-term jobs are found by word of mouth, or simply by talking to the owner of a hostel or restaurant. However, it is difficult in Central America to find short term work due to the lagging economies. Even menial jobs are coveted by locals. *Let's Go* tries to list temporary jobs like these whenever possible; check the practical information sections in larger cities, or check out the list below for some of the available short-term jobs in popular destinations.

Finca Ixobel, 3km south of Poptún, Petén, **Guatemala** (☎410 4307, fax 927 7363; www.fincaixobel.com). There are a few opportunities for short-term employment, usually in 3-month stints. Volunteers usually tend bar, serve food, and help maintain the hotel 6 days a week in exchange for room and board. 6 week minimum commitment.

VOLUNTEERING

Volunteering in Central America can be one of the most fulfilling and challenging experiences you can have in life. Volunteer efforts in throughout the region range from humanitarian aid to teaching to archaeological to environmental work. Many volunteer services charge you a fee to participate in the program and to do work. These fees can be surprisingly hefty, and while they likely cover most living expenses, they may well not cover airfare. Try to research on a program before committing—talk to people who have previously participated and find out exactly what you're getting into, as living and working conditions can vary greatly. Different programs are geared toward different ages and levels of experience, so make sure the program is a good fit. Be aware that most volunteer programs in Central America will have you living at the same standard as those you are working with; the more informed you are and the more realistic expectations you have, the more enjoyable the program will be.

Most people choose to go through a parent organization that takes care of logistical details, and frequently provides a group environment and support system. There are two main types of organizations—religious (often Catholic), and non-sectarian—although there are rarely restrictions on participation for either.

AFS (formerly American Field Service), 71 W. 23rd St., 17th fl., New York, NY 10010, USA (☎212-807-8686; fax 807-1001; info@afs.org; www.afs.org). Coordinates summer, community service, and educator programs in **Costa Rica, Guatemala, Honduras,** and **Panama.** Volunteers range from high school students to teaching administrators. Minimum stays and fees vary with program.

Amigos de las Americas, 5618 Star Ln., Houston, TX 77057, USA (☎800-231-7796; fax 713-782-9267; www.amigoslink.org). Sends high school and college students in groups of 2-3 to work in rural Latin American communities for up to 8 weeks. One year of Spanish instruction required. Costs average US$3500, including airfare.

Arcas (Asociación de Rescate y Conservación de Vida Silvestre), Section 717, P.O. Box 52-7270, Miami, FL 33152 (☎/fax 502 476 6001; arcas@pronet.net.gt; www.rds.org.gt/arcas). A conservation group that works on projects in **Guatemala.** 1 week minimum stay. US$50 per week includes meals and lodging. Spanish recommended but not required.

Casa Alianza, Apdo. Postal 2704, Guatemala City, **Guatemala** (☎502 253 2965; fax 253 3003; info@casa-alianza.org; www.casa-alianza.org). Or reach them in the US: SJO 1039, P.O. Box 025216, Miami, FL 33102. Volunteers work with street children who are often victims of "social cleansing." Also in **Honduras** and **Nicaragua.**

Casa Alianza, (☎222-4503; www.casa-alianza.org), 1 block east of Iglesia El Carmen in Managua, **Nicaragua.** Works with homeless children providing shelter as well as social and educational programs. Volunteers help organize activities and lead field trips.

CODA, Attn: Noemí D. Espanoza, Colonia Florencia Sur, Av. Los Pinos, número 4022, Tegucigalpa, Honduras (☎232 82 23; fax 232 3189). Volunteer work in Honduras.

Common Hope/Familias de Esperanza, Km 2, Carretera a San Juna, outside Antigua, **Guatemala** (☎832 4111; info@commonhope.org; www.commonhope.org). This family development non-profit accepts long-term volunteers (and some short-term volunteers). Once in Antigua, get on a bus headed to San June del Obispo or Santa Maria de Jesús and ask the driver to drop you off at Km 2.

Earthwatch, 3 Clocktower Pl, suite 100, Box 75, Maynard, MA 01754 (☎800-776-0188 or 978-461-0081; www.earthwatch.org). Arranges 1- to 3-week programs in **Costa Rica** and **Belize** to promote conservation of natural resources. Fees vary based on program location and duration, costs average US $1700 plus airfare.

Elderhostel, Inc., 11 Ave. de Lafayette, Boston, MA 92111-1746, USA (☎877-426-8056; fax 877-426-2166; www.elderhostel.org). Sends volunteers age 55+ around the world to work in construction, research, teaching, and many other projects. Costs average $100 per day plus airfare.

Finca Magdalena (☎880 2041; http://www.coop.CDC.com) in Magdalena, **Nicaragua,** promotes a one month exchange of working for free lodging and food. Contact the Sister Islands Association of Bainbridge in WA in the USA who have worked closely with the cooperative (☎206 842 8148; http://www.bainbridgefoundation.org)

The Fajina Craft Center, in Punta Gorda, **Belize,** next to the post office. An organization of 21 Maya cheerleaders from southern villages who run a craft store open on market days. Volunteers needed in the areas of crafts and small business development.

Global Routes, 1814 7th St., Berkeley, CA, USA (☎510-848-4800; www.globalroutes.org). Has high school programs focused on construction and college teaching internships throughout the world; both involve homestays. Programs cost around US$4000 plus airfare.

Habitat for Humanity International, 121 Habitat St., Americus, GA 31709, USA (☎229-924-6935 ext. 2551; www.habitat.org). Volunteers build houses in over 83 countries for anywhere from 2 weeks to 3 years. Short-term program costs range from US$1200-4000.

Hogar San José (☎662 0491), in Santa Rosa de Copán, **Honduras,** run by the Misioneras de la Caridad, an order of nuns founded by the late Mother Theresa. A center for developmentally disabled and malnourished children. Volunteers pay their own expenses and do everything from playing to feeding to teaching the children to walk. Physical therapists and special education teachers are especially welcome. Volunteers can be of any or no religious faith, and decide their own schedule and length of stay.

Jubilee House (☎0 883 6634; jhc@ns.sdnnic.org.ni), c/o FUNDECI, de la Estatua, Lezcano, Managua, **Nicaragua,** 2 blocks south and 1½ blocks east. A sustainable development center that works on organic farming, micro-enterprise development, education, and health care. Takes volunteers as individuals or groups. Write them in the US at: 2425 Spice Wood Dr., Winston Salem, NC 27106, USA. (☎800-274-3845).

The NGO Connection, based in the Marine Terminal in Belize City, **Belize.** Brings together several non-governmental organizations and generates income for them by selling local handmade crafts in the Terminal. Volunteers can work in the kiosk or assist in other projects. Contact Randine for more information.

Peace Corps, Office of Volunteer Recruitment and Selection, 1111 20th St., NW, Washington, D.C., 20526, USA (☎800-424-8580; www.peacecorps.gov). Opportunities in 70 developing nations, including all Central American countries.

Plenty, PO Box 394, Summertown, TN 38483 (☎831-484-5845, plenty1@usit.net). A village-based international development agency places volunteers in **Belize, Guatemala** and **Nicaragua** in a variety of hands-on volunteer positions. No expenses paid.

The Salvadorean Association for Rural Health (ASAPROSAR), Santa Ana, **El Salvador** (☎441 0646; asaprosar@netcomsa.com; www.thegreensource.com/asaprosat/index/asp; contact Lucy Luna). Volunteer opportunities help provide health services to villagers in remote areas. F

Service Civil International Voluntary Service (SCI-IVS), SCI USA, 3213 W. Wheeler St., Seattle, WA 98199, USA (☎/fax 206-350-6585; www.sci-ivs.org). Arranges placement in work camps in **El Salvador, Guatemala, Belize,** and **Nicaragua** for those 21+. Registration fee US$65-125. Fluency in Spanish is required except for Belize, which requires no Spanish background.

Volunteers for Peace, 1034 Tiffany Rd., Belmont, VT 05730, USA (☎802-259-2759; www.vfp.org). Arranges placement in work camps in **Belize, Guatemala, Honduras, Nicaragua,** and **Costa Rica.** Membership required for registration. Annual *International Workcamp Directory* US$20. Programs average US$200-500 for 2-3 weeks.

FOR FURTHER READING ON ALTERNATIVES TO TOURISM

Alternatives to the Peace Corps: A directory of third world and U.S. Volunteer Opportunities, by Joan Powell. Food First Books, 2000 (US$10).

How to Get a Job in Europe, by Sanborn and Matherly. Surrey Books, 1999 ($US22).

How to Live Your Dream of Volunteering Oversees, by Collins, DeZerega, and Heckscher. Penguin Books, 2002 (US$17).

International Directory of Voluntary Work, by Whetter and Pybus. Peterson's Guides and Vacation Work, 2000 (US$16).

International Jobs, by Kocher and Segal. Perseus Books, 1999 (US$18).

Overseas Summer Jobs 2002, by Collier and Woodworth. Peterson's Guides and Vacation Work, 2002 (US$18).

Work Abroad: The Complete Guide to Finding a Job Overseas, by Hubbs, Griffith, and Nolting. Transitions Abroad Publishing, 2000 ($16).

Work Your Way Around the World, by Susan Griffith. Worldview Publishing Services, 2001 (US$18).

Youth Enhancement Services (☎02 325 38; yes@btl.net). An alternative learning center in Belize City, **Belize,** for girls ages 12-17 who aren't in school. Volunteers usually work on special projects (7-10 days), depending on skills. Volunteers should be flexible and pay their own expenses. No age requirement. Contact Mrs. Karen Cain.

World Teach, Center for International Development, Harvard University, 79 JFK St., Cambridge, MA 02138(☎800-4-TEACH-0, 617-495-1599; fax 617-495-1599; info@worldteach.org; www.worldteach.org). Sends volunteers to **Costa Rica** and **Panama** for 8 week to year long programs teaching English and other fields in an environmental education context. Program fees range from US $3990-5990.

BELIZE

The least inhabited country in Central America, tiny Belize is graced by nearly untouched natural beauty and stable politics. With a heterogeneous population of 250,000 and a predominantly Caribbean atmosphere, Belize is also the only country in Central America where reggae is more common than *salsa*. Though a bit pricier than its neighbors, the country is extremely accessible: English is the official language, transportation is a relative breeze, and few other places in the world offer such mind-boggling biological and geographic diversity in such a small space (8867 sq. mi.). In fact, ecotourism has bloomed into the nation's leading money-maker. Fortunately, commercial development remains modest. While Belize has its share of Maya ruins, they are less outstanding than their Guatemalan counterparts; Belize's most popular destinations are its dozens of coastal cayes and national parks, nearly twenty of which have been set aside for conservation.

In one day, a enthusiastic traveler could snorkel the 2nd-largest barrier reef in the Northern and Western hemispheres, scale Maya temples, and slide down waterfalls in a pine forest, stopping along the way at a jaguar or baboon preserve. And after savoring inexpensive lobster and sipping smooth Belikin beers on one of the country's many idyllic beaches, many find they never want to move again. Thousands of tourists come each year to explore the country's wonders and affirm the tourist bureau's slogan, "You better Belize it."

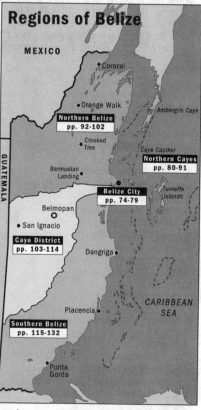

Regions of Belize

MEXICO

Corozal

Orange Walk

Northern Belize
pp. 92-102

Ambergris Caye

Crooked Tree

Caye Caulker

Northern Cayes
pp. 80-91

GUATEMALA

Bermudian Landing

Belize City
pp. 74-79

Turneffe Islands

Belmopan

San Ignacio

Cayo District
pp. 103-114

Dangriga

CARIBBEAN SEA

Placencia

Southern Belize
pp. 115-132

Punta Gorda

HIGHLIGHTS OF BELIZE

The colorful coral and fish in the **barrier reef,** minutes from **Ambergris Caye,** Belize's most popular destination, and relaxed, budget-friendly **Caye Caulker** (p. 81).

The outdoor wonderland around **San Ignacio,** where Maya ruins, spectacular caves, pine-covered mountains, and jungle rivers are all ready to be explored (p. 107).

A dozen miles of perfect beach lead to the village of **Placencia,** in which sand, coconuts, reggae, and lobster burritos combine to create a piece of paradise (p. 123).

Caracol, Lamani, and Xunantenech, three of Belize's impressive Maya sites, with an 112 ft. temple (p. 98).

SUGGESTED ITINERARIES

1-2 WEEKS: NORTHERN BELIZE AND THE CAYES. This route has the best of both worlds: Maya ruins and nature preserves, and the brilliant blue ocean of the relaxing cayes. Beginning in Belize City, head north to **Orange Walk** (p. 95), a good base camp for daytrips to the impressive Maya ruins of **Lamanai** (p. 98) and **Cuello** (p. 98). Also near Orange walk is birder's paradise **Shipstern Nature Reserve** (p. 99), home to over 22,000 species of feathered friends. From Orange Walk, catch a bus to **Corozal** (p. 100), a sleepy stepping stone for flights to **Ambergris Caye** (p. 86). This, along with **Caye Caulker** (p. 81), are the gems of Belize's Caribbean coast, offering world-famous scuba diving and snorkeling, and miles of clean beaches. Departures to **Belize City** (p. 74) via boat and plane leave from both cayes.

1 WEEK: THE CAYO DISTRICT. Leaving the beach to traverse Belize's highland region is a pleasant surprise: following the Western Highway offers an alternate read of Belizean culture along with some highlights of Belize. Leaving Belize City, Monkey Bay Wildlife Sanctuary and Guanacaste National Park are both worth a visit on your way to **San Ignacio** (p. 107), the perfect town and base camp from which to explore the **Cayo District** (p. 103). From the town, one peer into dark caves at **Actun Tunichil Muknal Cave** (p. 112), and hike the **Mountain Pine Ridge Reserve** (p. 112). One sight not to miss is **Caracol** (p. 113), Belize's largest and most impressive Maya ruin that once rivaled Tikal in importance. From San Ignacio, it is easy to slide across the border into Guatemala, or head down the **Hummingbird Highway** (p. 115) to southern Belize, itself a smooth, scenic delight.

LIFE AND TIMES

LAND, FLORA, AND FAUNA

Belize sits atop the immense limestone shelf that extends into Guatemala's Petén and Mexico's Yucatán Peninsula. The border with Guatemala is an escarpment from which the land falls east into the Caribbean. A slow, gradual slope covered by hardwood forests in the north, it becomes much steeper and somewhat tropical in the south, where the **Maya Mountains** of the Belizean Cayo District jut out of the limestone plain along the Guatemalan border. **Victoria Peak,** Belize's highest point (3681 ft.), lies in a spur of the Maya Mountains called the **Cockscomb Range.** The coast itself is characterized by inland lagoons and extensive swamp and mangrove systems with a variety of wildlife. The Cayo District is also distinguished by its many **cave** formations—water has eroded the soft limestone and shaped hundreds of tunnels which lure tourists to the region. Offshore is one of Belize's foremost attractions: the **Belize Barrier Reef,** the 2nd-largest coral reef in the world. Rising above the ocean surface are hundreds of tiny islands called the **Cayes.**

Flora has played an incredibly important role in the shaping of Belize's history, as logging once formed the basis of the Belizean economy. Today, however, only half of Belize is second-growth forest. There are over 700 tree species including logwood, chicle, and the national tree, the mahogany. Fruit trees abound: coconut, custard apple, mango, papaya, cashew, pineapple, and guava. Belize has an estimated 4000 species of native flowering plants, including 250 species of orchids; the national flower is the black orchid. As more of the forest is scientifically catalogued, some plants are being used for non-traditional medicinal purposes.

Since over 70% of Belize is covered by forest, it is not surprising that animal life flourishes. The revered jaguar has helped bring attention to the Cockscomb Basin Wildlife Sanctuary, which is now a protected area. There are also puma, jaguarundi, margay, ocelots, and the national animal "the mountain cow," or tapir. The

BELIZE

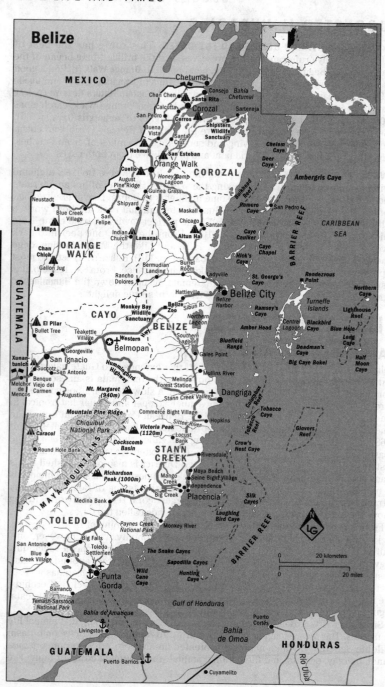

endangered three-toed sloth also lives in Belize. Over 200 species of migratory birds winter in Belize, including wood storks, herons, egrets, white ibis, orioles, and the black cat bird. The national bird is the keel-billed toucan.

Caribbean animal life off the coast of Belize is as rich as that of its on-land neighbors. The endangered West Indian manatee makes its home in the reefs off the cayes, and grows up to 12 feet long and 1000lbs. Three of the world's eight species of sea turtle, the green, loggerhead, and hawksbill, nest in Belize; nesting season is June 1 to August 31. Groupers, jacks, swordfish and snapper, stingray, and nurse sharks swim the reefs and lagoons up and down the Caribbean coast.

HISTORY

Belize's unusual status within Central America stems partly from Spain's choice not to settle the area in the 16th century due to the area's lack of minerals and the Maya's resistance to Christianity. Shipwrecked English sailors settled the still-Spanish area and took large quantities of precious mahogany and logwood to finance buccaneering ventures. After the 1655 capture of Jamaica from Spain, British soldiers and their families joined the settlement.

By the early 18th century, white settlers were importing slaves from Jamaica and other English territories to log the forests; slaves remained indebted even after emancipation in 1838. After 200 years of skirmishes with Spain, England won control over Belize at the **Battle of St. George's Caye** in 1798. Belize was declared an official colony of British Honduras in 1862, but by then, the timber supply was waning. When the economy began to decline, thousands of Creole workers were left in poverty; subsistence farming became the chief economic activity in Belize.

INDEPENDENCE AND BEYOND. Responding to the lack of democracy under British Colonial rule, unfair labor practices in the mahogany work camps, and later economic hardships from the 1930's Great Depression, Belize's workers initiated a series of strikes, calling for a Black Man's British Honduras. One consequence of this movement was the 1950s emergence of the People's Unity Party (PUP), which blazed the path to independence. The party instituted a new constitution and self-government in 1964, achieving independence from Britain on September 21, 1981 and assuming the name Belize. Although land claim disputes with Guatemala still persist, Belize is officially recognized by both the United Nations and Guatemala.

The contemporary Belizean political scene has been dominated by the centrist People's Unity Party, headed until recently by the cautious liberal **George Price.** On June 30, 1993, in an early and close election called by the PUP, the **United Democratic Party (UDP),** headed by **Manuél Esquivel,** broke PUP rule. Five years later, in 1998, the PUP regained leadership with **Said Musa.**

TODAY

Belize has made headlines in the past year mainly for its severe weather: Hurricane Iris ripped through southern Belize in October 2001, killing 15 American tourists. However, since the September 11th terrorist attacks on New York City, visitor numbers have dropped by 22% (compared to the first nine months of 2001).

In an attempt to combat the Caribbean drug trade, the Belizean government negotiated a "hot pursuit" agreement with the US, opening its territorial waters to Coast Guard vessels in pursuit of drug traffickers.

ECONOMY AND GOVERNMENT

Despite attempts at industrialization, Belize continues to rely upon timber exports and commercial export farming of sugar and citrus. The next largest and most rapidly expanding sector is tourism. The illicit cultivation of cannabis for export to the US, especially concentrated in the areas northwest of the capital, is another

BELIZE

large source of revenue. Belize continues to struggle economically, trying to man-age its resources with US and British efforts to transform it into a prosperous, democratic country. Slash-and-burn farmers are starting to accept ecotourism as an efficient income source, but new restrictions on land use continue to frustrate. Nevertheless, national pride is strong. Belizeans cite their 53 cable channels as proof that the country isn't underdeveloped, and residents sport T-shirts with the resounding phrase *"Belize da fu we"* ("Belize, there for us!").

A member of the British Commonwealth, Belize's head of state is the British Monarch, and its government is structured according to the British parliamentary system. The political leader is the prime minister, currently **Said Musa** of the cen-ter-left PUP. Locally, there are city and town councils, while some traditional Maya villages are led by mayors, or *alcaldes*.

PEOPLE

Belize's diverse population stems largely from multiethnic immigration in the 19th century. Spanish-speaking *mestizos*, mostly of mixed Maya and European heri-tage, are Belize's largest ethnic group, two-fifths of the population. Refugees from Guatemala, Nicaragua, Honduras, and El Salvador add to these numbers. The Maya flourished in Belize between AD 300 and 1000, and the **Kekchi** and **Mopan-Mayan** speaking descendants of the Maya still dwell in Belize, their numbers aug-mented by refugees from the Yucatecan **Caste War** of 1847-48. A third of Belize's population is black Creole, descendants of African slaves and British Baymen. In the country's southern districts live the **Garífuna,** Black Caribs of mixed Carib Indian and African descent. Most Garífuna speak their own Arawakan language. Descendants of South Asian and Chinese laborers who came seeking work in the 19th century, a few expatriate Americans, and several thousand German **Menno-nite** farmers round out the mix. Linguistic diversity is counterbalanced by the pro-motion of English as the official language. While the majority of Belizeans are Roman Catholic, nearly a third are Protestant, and evangelical and fundamentalist adherents are small but growing.

CULTURE

FOOD AND DRINK

There are as many types of food in Belize as there are ethnic groups. The country's residents eat a lot of rice and beans, as well as beans and rice. (Yes, there *is* a dif-ference: beans and rice consists of the two mixed and cooked together; rice and beans are separate.) Garífuna and Creole dishes combine seafood with cassava, plantain, coconut, and green bananas, and a dash of the ubiquitous Marie Sharpe's hot sauce. *Escabeche* is a potent Maya onion soup. A *garnache* is similar to a Mex-ican *tostada*, a fried tortilla covered with beans, cheese, and vegetables, whereas the more distinctive *salbute* is a fried puff-tortilla covered with chicken, fish, tomatoes, or cabbage. A *panade* is a folded tortilla fried with fish (usually shark). For breakfast, *fryjacks* are similar to Mexican *sopaipillas* (fried dough); *johnny cakes* are closer to American pancakes. Lobster is available in season (June 15-Mar. 15). "Whole fresh fish" is available, but be prepared to dissect a fully intact specimen. Fruit juice competes with Belikin Beer as the most popular beverage in Belize; Belikin is light, smooth, and goes with just about everything. Lunch is the biggest meal of the day; dinner is sometimes referred to as "tea."

THE ARTS

The artistic tradition of Belize reflects the nation's blend of cultures and the daily lives and struggles of its people. A growing body of Belizean **literature** includes **Zee Edgell's** *In Times Like These*, which explores one woman's struggle for self-defi-nition, and **Zoila Elli's** bright collection of short stories, *On Heroes, Lizards, and*

Passion. Poetry also has a strong tradition in Belize. **James Martinez's** departure from English into free-flowing Creole poetry opened the way for folk literature and expression; **Hugh F. Fuller's** pieces elegantly depict the country's natural beauty; and **Evan X. Hyde's** works, such as *North Amerikkan Blues*, are laced with biting political criticism. Internationally renowned artist **Benjamin Nicholas** is at the fore of Belizean painting; his colorful depictions of daily life among the Creoles and Garífuna hang all over the country, particularly in Dangriga, where he lives.

POPULAR CULTURE

With a population blended from such diverse backgrounds, Belize has a flourishing folk life. In fact, *mestizos* are now the largest ethnic group in Belize. Proverbs and old wives tales are known throughout the country, particularly on the coast. They come in three parts: the Creole saying, the English translation, and the universal meaning. For example: *"Weh eyes nu seh, hart no grieve"* (what your eyes don't see your heart won't grieve), also known as "what you don't know can't hurt you."

Belizeans proudly enjoy one of the best cable TV systems in the world, although it's unclear as to who is actually paying for it. International broadcasting is occasionally interrupted with congenial reminders like, "Brought to you by Social Security." Cable also broadcasts Chinese and Spanish programming. Four newspapers in Belize with online journals include *The Reporter* (www.belizereporter.com), *The Belize Times* (www.belizetimes.com), *The Guardian* (www.udp.org.bz/guardian), and *Amandala* (www.belizemall.com/amandala). The government-operated Belize Radio broadcasts in both Spanish and English.

ESSENTIALS

EMBASSIES AND CONSULATES

An updated list of Belizean embassies and consulates is available at www.belize.gov.bz/diplomats.html.

> **Embassy of Belize,** 2535 Massachusetts Ave., NW, Washington, D.C. 20008 (☎202-332-9636; fax 332-6888). Open M-F 9am-5pm. For tourist information call ☎800-624-0686.

 PASSPORTS, VISAS, AND CUSTOMS.

Passport (p.1). Required for all visitors. Must have at least 6 months left.

Visa (p.2). Not required for citizens of the US, UK, Ireland, Canada, South Africa, New Zealand, or Australia. Valid for 30 days. Extensions for up to 90 days granted by the Immigration Office in Belize City.

Onward ticket (p.1). Required of all visitors.

Proof of Funds. All visitors must demonstrate proof of sufficient funds: US$60 or more per person.

Inoculations and Medications (p.10). None required.

Work Permit (p.2). Required for all foreigners planning to work in Belize. Must be a legal resident of Belize for at least 6 months prior to application. For more information contact the Immigration and Nationality Department (☎501 82 2611, 22 423).

Driving Permit (p.23). Valid driver's license required.

Departure restrictions. Do not leave the country with fish, coral, or shells. Attempting to leave with certain marine species is punishable by jail time.

Departure Tax. BZ$27.50.

BELIZE

Consulate of Belize, 1110 Salzedo, St. 2F, Coral Gables, FL 33134 (☎305-666-1121; bzconsulmi@aof.com). Open M-F 8am-noon. Belize has missions in Los Angeles, New York (☎212-599-0233), Chicago, San Francisco, Houston, Dallas, and other cities.

Consulate of Belize in Canada, c/o McMillan Binch Suite, 3800 South Tower, Royal Bay Plaza, Toronto, Ontario, Canada M5J 2JP (☎416-865-7000; fax 416-864-7048).

High Commission of Belize in Great Britain, 22 Harcourt House, 19 Cavendish Sq., London, England W1M 9AD (☎441 71 499 97 28; fax 441 71 491 4139; bzhc-lon@talk21.com). Open M-F 9am-5pm.

MONEY

CURRENCY	
US$1 = BZ$2.00	BZ$1 = US$0.50
CDN$1 = BZ$1.29	BZ$1 = CDN$0.78
UK£1 = BZ$2.88	BZ$1 = UK£0.35
AUS$1 = BZ$1.11	BZ$1 = AUS$0.90
EURO€ = BZ$1.83	BZ$1 = EURO.55

The rates above were accurate as of June 2002. The Belizean dollar (BZ$) is locked in to the US dollar at a rate of two to one. Dollars come in denominations of 100, 50, 20, 10, five, two, and one; there are coins of one dollar and 50, 25, 10, five, and one cents. The 25-cents piece is often referred to as a shilling. American paper currency is good nearly everywhere, but US coins are not. Prices are often quoted in both US and Belizean dollars; be sure to check.

Belizean banks typically change British pounds and US and Canadian dollars at slightly less than the two-to-one rate. Border money changers and local businesses may do better. Barclay's Bank changes **traveler's checks** and does **cash advances** free of charge; it also accepts international **ATM** cards. **Credit cards** are widely accepted in Belize, but beware of extra fees. **Tips** of 10% on restaurant bills are customary. Taxi drivers are not tipped.

Belize is more expensive than most of its Central American neighbors; the same amenities you might receive in Guatemala or Nicaragua may cost you 2-3 times as much in Belize. Consider US$30 an estimated minimum daily budget.

BELIZE DOLLAR	❶	❷	❸	❹	❺
ACCOMMODATIONS	BZ$0-20	BZ$21-30	BZ$31-45	BZ$46-60	BZ$61+
	US$0-10	US$10-15	US$15-22	US$22-30	US$31+
FOOD	BZ$0-5	BZ$6-10	BZ$11-15	BZ$16-30	BZ$31+
	US$0-2.50	US$2.50-5	US$5-7.50	US$7.50-15	US$16+

SAFETY

The non-medical hazards of Belize come in three flavors—the inebriated rowdy, the on-the-make male, and the eager-to-sell-drugs heavy—and a few Belizeans who manage to wear all three hats. Particularly in English-speaking areas along the coast, expect hustlers and self-appointed "guides" to confront you. Firmly and immediately refuse their services and make it clear that you won't give them money, but don't be rude; the problem could escalate. Public drunkenness is not infrequent in Belize, and women should take more than usual precautions. Even the most careful may not be able to avoid being approached by a representative of the recently intensified drug trade. Politely refuse and continue walking. Purchasing drugs is not only dangerous, but illegal. The nearest police station can be reached anywhere in Belize by dialing ☎**911.** See **Safety and Security,** p. 26.

HEALTH

Purified drinking water is available almost everywhere except for the Cayes. In cities and big towns, municipal water is generally chlorinated and safe for brushing teeth. In rural areas, use boiled water. For fruit and veggies, follow the Peace Corps rule: "Peel it, cook it, boil it, or vomit." Though malaria is reported to be under control, precautions are advised. For general but vital info, see **Health,** p.9.

BORDER CROSSINGS

MEXICO. Buses cross at **Chetumal,** Mexico from Belize City and Corozal.

GUATEMALA. There is a land crossing at **Melchor de Mencos/Benque Viejo de Carmen.** See p. 425 for details coming from Flores, Guatemala, and p. 114 from Belize. **Boats** go from Punta Gorda and **Puerto Barrios** and **Livingston, Guatemala** (see p. 332).

HONDURAS. Weekly boats run between Placencia and **Puerto Cortés, Honduras** (see p.164) and between Dangriga-Mango Creek and Puerto Cortés (see p.206).

KEEPING IN TOUCH

The **mail** system is fairly reliable. It costs BZ$0.60 to mail a letter from Belize to the US, BZ$0.30 for a postcard. To Europe, letters are BZ$0.75 and postcards are BZ$0.40. First-class airmail takes about 10 to 15 days to travel between the US and Belize. Pharmacies sell stamps and have mailboxes. You can have mail sent to you in Belize through **general delivery.**

> Tessa ROLLO
> Poste Restante
> Orange Walk (city)
> BELIZE

Seven-digit **telephone** numbers including area codes are listed in this book. When calling from the US, dial the country code before the seven digit number. For US phone company access numbers, see the inside back cover. **Belize Telecommunications Limited (BTL)** currently owns all phone systems. One must buy a BTL phone card, sold in BZ$5 increments, to use any public payphone. To use an international calling card, first dial 115. This reaches an operator, who will help you with your call. Calls to the US cost BZ$9.60 for the first three minutes and BZ$3.20 per minute after. Calls to Europe are BZ$6 per minute. Collect calls are free.

COUNTRY CODE	501

TRANSPORTATION

The **international airport** is located 16km (10 mi.) northwest of Belize City, on the Northern Hwy. Try to share a cab to Belize City, as the fare has been set at BZ$35, but make all arrangements *before* approaching a driver; they strongly discourage the practice. Maya Island Air and Tropic Air have **domestic flights** from both Belize City international and Belize City **municipal airport** to points throughout Belize. **Buses** are cheap, efficient, and frequent, as are **boats** to and from the cayes.

ORIENTATION

Belize, forever the British oddball among its more Spanish neighbors, stands out for *not* having cities with a grid-like structure of *avenidas* and *calles*. There is, however, a preponderance of Main Streets, Front Streets, and Back Streets.

B E L I Z E

TRAVEL RESOURCES

Belize Tourist Board, 421 7th Ave., Ste. 1110, New York, NY 10001 (☎800-624-0686 or 212-563-6011; fax 212-563-6033). Exhaustive information. In **Belize City,** P.O. Box 325, New Central Bank Building, 2nd level, at the end of Queen St. (☎02 31 913; fax 02 31 943, toll free number 800-624-0686), info@travelbelize.org, www.travelbelize.org.

Belize Audubon Society, 12 Fort St., Belize City (☎02 23 5004; base@btl.net; www.belizeaudubon.org). Information about all national parks, wildlife, and birds. Sells a guide to Belize's wildlife (BZ$8). Open M-F 8:30am-5pm.

Glover's Atoll Resort and Marine Biology Station, P.O. Box 563, Belize City (☎01 483 51, fax 27 0156; www.belizemall.com/gloversatoll). 40 mi. offshore. US$149 per week includes boat trip, snorkeling, fishing, and marine science lectures. Boat leaves Su. Cabins have toilets and kitchens. Camping US$99 per week.

Triton Tours, 812 Airline Park Blvd., Metairie, LA 70003 (☎504-464-7964; fax 504-779-9015). Airfare and accommodations organized for diving and ecotourism.

HOLIDAYS

In addition to national holidays, which follow the British calendar, the Garífuna and the Maya communities have their own celebrations with traditional dancing and festivities. National holidays include: **January 1,** New Year's Day; **March 9,** Baron Bliss Day; **March/April,** Holy Week; **April 21,** the Queen's Birthday; **May 1,** Labor Day; **May 24,** Commonwealth Day; **September 10,** Belize National Day; **September 21,** Independence Day; **October 12,** Columbus Day; **November 19,** Garífuna Settlement Day; **December 25,** Christmas; **December 26,** Boxing Day.

BELIZE CITY

Despite a history of unfortunate transitions—from a graceful colonial town to an overcrowded shanty town twice reduced to rubble by hurricanes, and the official shift of the capital to Belmopan in 1971—Belize City (pop. 70,000) still remains the commercial, social, and historic center of the country. Most visitors use "Belize," as it is known to locals, simply as an arrival point before escaping the hectic and overcrowded urban center. Here streams of sewage overflow the canals that line the streets, buildings wobble on weak foundations, and masses of pedestrians, buses, cars, and bikes line the crumbling narrow roads. Gospel yells of a Seventh-Day Adventist revival meeting mingle with the roar of buses arriving at the station, while young Creole day-laborers wearing Chicago Bulls caps blast reggae music and smoke joints the size of large cigars. Furthermore, Belize City does not have the beaches, forests, wildlife, laid-back lifestyle, or Maya sites that serve as Belize's tempting tourist bait. However, others may appreciate the glimpse into the diverse contemporary Belizean culture that Belize City affords. Mestizos, black Creoles, Garinaga, East Indians, and whites speak Creole dialects, Garifuna, Spanish, and English, and sing reggae, punta, roca, and salsa. Belize City also has cultural facilities, museums, post-Maya historical sites, and colonial houses.

Belize City is by far the dirtiest and most dangerous place in Belize. Hustlers are in full force here; some will try to stop you and start a conversation, while more aggressive ones walk beside and behind you, offering information, drugs, and prostitutes, and demanding a cash payment in return. If approached, be firm but not obnoxious. In a bind, look for one of the khaki-shirted "tourist police."

✈ INTERCITY TRANSPORTATION

International Flights: Philip S.W. Goldson International Airport (☎025 2045), in Ladyville, 10 mi. northwest of Belize City; it is easier to call the airlines directly and make a reservation through their representatives. Serves: **Continental,** 80 Regent St. (☎227 8309); **American Airlines,** intersection of New Rd. with Queen St. (☎223 2522); and **Grupo Taca Airlines,** 41 Albert St. (☎227-7363).

Domestic Flights: Check with **Belize Air Travel Service,** Belize Municipal Airstrip, on the waterfront north of town (cab ride BZ$7). Serves **Tropic Air** (☎224 5671; www.tropic-air.com) and **Maya Island Air** (☎223 1403; www.mayaislandair.com). Tropic Air flies to **Dangriga** (15 min., every 1½hr. 8:30am-4:50pm, BZ$61); **Placencia** (45 min., every 1½hr. 8:30am-4:50pm, BZ$118); **Punta Gorda** (1 hr., every 1½hr. 8:30am-4:50pm, BZ$152); and **San Pedro** (15 min., every hr. 7:40am-5:30pm, BZ$52). For visitors interested in Tikal, Tropic offers a flight to **Flores, Guatemala** for BZ$176. **Maya Island Air** offers similar schedules and prices as Tropic Air. To make reservations, call the airline and speak to a representative. A **taxi** from the airport costs BZ$35.

Buses: Many companies, many stations; be careful around the terminals as streets can be confusing. Also be careful walking to the bus station at night; consider a taxi. Schedules change often, so check ahead. Buses have their destination written in the lower left corner of their front window. **Novelo's** now has a monopoly on the public market and owns both **Northern** and **Southern Transport.** Essentially, Novelo's goes to the western border (Melchor de Menchos, Guatemala) and to the northern border (Chetumal, Mexico), and Southern goes to Punta Gorda; each service stops at cities along the way. **Jex** runs only to Crooked Tree, **Russell** goes through Ladyville en route to Bermudian Landing (Baboon Sanctuary), and **James** offers the only direct route to Punta Gorda. Arrive at the station early, as buses leave ahead of schedule when they are full.

Bus companies and terminal locations:

Novelo's (Northern & Western Transport), intersection of West Collet Canal St. and King St. (☎207 2025; novelo@btl.net). Go west on King St., on the right after crossing Collet Canal.

Southern Transport (Z-line) (☎207 2025). Same building as Northern Transport.

Russell's, Cairo St. From the Swing Bridge take Orange St. W., turn left at Euphrates, and make another immediate left on Cairo St. There is no building terminal; the bus leaves from the street.

Jex, corner of Regent St. W. and W. Canal St. From the south end of the Swing Bridge, turn right on Regent St. W. and walk 2 blocks to the first canal.

James, corner of Vernon St. and Woods St.

Destinations:

Belmopan: Novelo's bound for Melchor. 1¼hr., every hr. 5am-9pm, BZ$3.50. Express (BZ$4) runs direct to Belmopan before continuing to the border (11am, 1, 3, 5pm).

Benque Viejo: Novelo's bound for Melchor. (3hr., every hr. 5am-9pm.; express 3hr.; 11am, 2:30, 3, 5:30pm; BZ$8.)

Bermudian Landing (Baboon Sanctuary): Russell's. (1½ hr.; M-F noon, 4:30pm, Sa noon, 12:15, 1, 4:30pm; BZ$3.50.)

Corozal: Novelo's bound for Chetumal. (2½hr., every hr. 4am-8pm, BZ$9; express 2hr., 7 per day 6am-6pm, BZ$11.)

Chetumal: Novelo's. (4hr., every hr. 4am-8pm, BZ$11; express 3hr., 7 per day 6am-6pm, BZ$13.)

Crooked Tree Sanctuary: Jex. (1½hr.; 10:30am, 4:30, 5:30pm; BZ$4.)

Dangriga: Southern Transport. (2-3hr., every hr. 8am-5pm, BZ$10.)

Ladyville: Russell's. (1hr., 1 per day noon, BZ$4.)

Melchor: Novelo's. (3½ hr., every hr. 5am-9pm, BZ$9.)

Orange Walk: Novelo's bound for Chetumal. (1½hr., every hr. 4am-8pm, BZ$5.)

Placencia: Southern transport to Dangriga. Catch Dangriga bus to Placencia (see **Dangriga,** p. 118).

Punta Gorda: James Bus runs only direct route 5, 10am, and 3pm. Or take Southern Transport to Dangriga. Catch Dangriga bus to Punta Gorda (see Dangriga section).

San Ignacio: Novelo's bound for Melchor. (1hr., every hr. 5am-9pm, BZ$7.)

Boats: The most frequent departures to the Cayes are from **Belize Marine Terminal,** on the northern end of the Swing Bridge. Other boats depart from the **Belize Tourism Vil-**

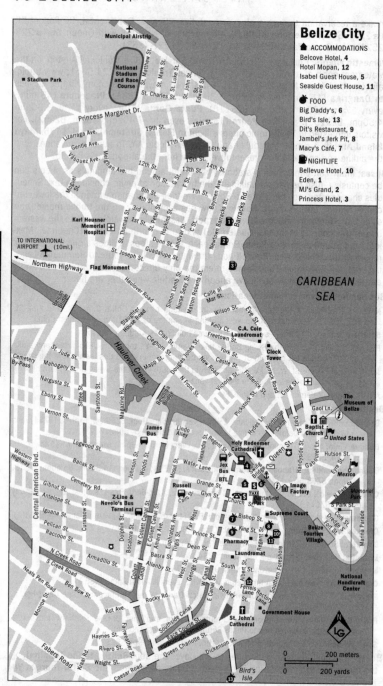

Belize City

🏠 ACCOMMODATIONS
Belcove Hotel, 4
Hotel Mopan, 12
Isabel Guest House, 5
Seaside Guest House, 11

🍴 FOOD
Big Daddy's, 6
Bird's Isle, 13
Dit's Restaurant, 9
Jambel's Jerk Pit, 8
Macy's Café, 7

🛏 NIGHTLIFE
Bellevue Hotel, 10
Eden, 1
MJ's Grand, 2
Princess Hotel, 3

lage Water Taxi Association, located in the Tourism Village, a few blocks east of the Marine Terminal. They have schedules and fares that are similar to the Marine Terminal.

Caye Caulker: from Marine Terminal. (45min.; 9, 10:30am, noon, 1:30, 3, 4, 5pm; BZ$15 one-way, BZ$25 round-trip.) All stop in Caye Chapel.

San Pedro: Marine Terminal. (1½hr.; 9,10:30am, noon, 3pm; BZ$25, BZ$45 round-trip.)

✈ ORIENTATION

UPON ARRIVAL. From the airport, it is possible to walk the 2mi. from the airport to the highway and catch a bus from there, as they run every 30min. (BZ$2). From the bus terminal, it's best to take a cab, especially at night. The bus terminals cluster around the **Collet Canal.** If you walk east, **Orange Street** leads to **Albert Street** and **Battlefield Park,** the center of town. Two blocks north lies the **Swing Bridge.** Most boats from the Cayes arrive at the **Marine Terminal** adjacent to the northern end of the Swing Bridge, others at the **Courthouse Wharf,** across the river from and slightly east of the Marine Terminal. Taxis are the only direct service to the airport; the nearest bus stop is often more than 0.6mi. away.

LAYOUT. The Caribbean Sea nearly surrounds the city. **Haulover Creek** runs southeast to the sea and splits the city into north and south parts. Most services are a short walk from **Swing Bridge,** which spans the creek mouth. South of Haulover Creek, most restaurants, hotels, and attractions are to the east of **Albert St.** To the north of Haulover Creek, they are clustered along **Queen Street** and **Barracks Road.**

SAFETY. Belize City has declared the area east of Northside and Southside Canal as the official **tourism district.** The city has successfully secured the area by stationing khaki-uniformed police officers solely in the district. It is best to look as if you are heading to a specific destination. At night, walk in groups on the main streets or take a taxi. The further one travels to the west, the more dangerous and dirty the city becomes. The basic advice is to stay within the tourism district. If travel outside is necessary, travel in a group or take a taxi, especially at night.

⊏ LOCAL TRANSPORTATION

Taxis: All have green license plates. Flag them down on any street or at the stand in Battlefield Park. Cabs in Belize City are now unionized and have the same set fares across companies. BZ$6 per stop within Belize City, plus BZ$1-2 for each extra person. Confirm fare before getting in, and never get into a car without a green plate. Take cabbies' claims that the hotel you ask for is "full" with a grain of salt. Drivers often collect a fee from hotel owners for bringing them business. Cabs from the airport to the city are expensive (BZ$35), but worth the safety and convenience. The cabs sometimes negotiate prices for longer trips, including rates as low as BZ$20 from the airport.

Car Rental: Budget Car Rental, 2½mi. Western Hwy. (☎223 2435; jmagroup@btl.net; www.budget-belize.com). **Hertz Car Rental,** 11 Cork St. (☎223 5393; safarihz@btl.net), across from the Radisson Fort George. Call 3-4 weeks in advance during high season. Remember that the companies require a large damage deposit and that gas is very expensive (BZ$7 per gallon). AmEx/MC/V.

❼ PRACTICAL INFORMATION

TOURIST AND FINANCIAL SERVICES

Tourist Information: Belize Tourist Board, Gabourel Ln., New Central Bank Bldg., 2nd level (☎223 1913; fax 223 1943; btbb@btl.net; www.travelbelize.org). Located beside the new Museum of Belize, in the huge bank building. Friendly staff offers free maps and brochures of Belize. Open M-Th 8am-noon and 1-5pm. Closes F 4:30pm.

Embassies and Consulates: The **British High Commission** (☎822 2146; brithicom@btl.net) can be reached at P.O. Box 91 in Belmopan. **Canada,** 83 N. Front St. (☎223 1060). Open M-F 9am-1pm. **US,** 29 Gabourel Ln. (☎227 7161). From the Swing Bridge, take Queen St. northeast until it meets Gabourel and turn right—the string of white colonial houses on your left is the US compound. Entrance to the consulate is around the corner, 50 ft. back. Consular services open M-F 8am-noon and 1:30-4pm.

Banks: Barclay's Bank, near Battlefield Park at 21 Albert St., offers cash advances on Visa and currency exchange. Open M-Th 8am-2:30pm, F 8am-4:30pm. The **24hr. ATM** located outside the main entrance accepts Visa. Foreign ATM cards work only inside the bank during business hours. **Belize Bank,** just south of the market building on Albert St., has cash advances and cash exchanges. Open M-Th 8am-1pm, F 8am-4:30pm. Most banks close by 1pm. A **Western Union** is located in the Marine Terminal. Changing currency is not essential, as most businesses actually prefer American dollars.

American Express: Belize Global Travel Services, 41 Albert St. (☎227 7363; bzadventure@btl.net; www.belizenet.com/gat.html), at the corner of King St. Card member services upstairs; once inside, enter to the left of the Travel Service. Open M-F 8am-5pm, Sa 8am-noon. Also arranges car rentals, tours, and air freight.

LOCAL SERVICES

Bookstores: Stock up here in Belize City; new books are hard to find in other parts of the country. **Brodie's** (see below) has cheap novels, current US magazines, and a great selection of titles on Belize. **Sunny's,** in the Marine Terminal, carries US newspapers.

Supermarkets: Brodie's, on Albert St. off Battlefield Park. Open M-Th 8:30am-7pm, F 8:30am-8pm, Sa 8:30am-5pm, Su 8:30am-1pm.

Laundry: G's, on Dean St., between E. Canal St. and Albert St., does wash (BZ$4) and dry (BZ$4). Open M-Sa 8am-noon and 1-5:30pm. **CA Coin Laundromat,** 114 Barrack Rd., across from Clock Tower, is open weekends. Open M-F 9am-9pm, Sa-Su 8am-9pm.

EMERGENCY AND COMMUNICATIONS

Emergency: Police ☎90 nationwide. **Fire** or **Medical:** ☎90 in Belize City only.

Police: (☎227 2222; emergency 90). Located one block northeast of the Swing Bridge on Queen St. A 2nd station is at 9 Racoon St. Follow West Collet Canal St. south along Collet Canal from the bus station and turn right on Racoon St. Open 24hr.

Pharmacy: Central Drug Store, 1 Market Square (☎227 2317), just south of the Swing Bridge. Open M-Sa 9am-9:30pm. The **Community Drug Store** (☎227 3842) is on the corner of Prince and Albert St. Open M-Sa 8am-1pm and 3-9pm.

Hospital: Karl Heusner Memorial Hospital, (☎223 1548 or 223 1564) on the way to the airport, along Princess Margaret Dr. Open 24hr.

Telephones: Public phones are scattered around Queen and Albert St. Public phone at the Batty Station. **BTL,** 1 Church St. (☎227 7085), off Albert St. Open M-F 8am-6pm. Only BTL phone cards are accepted, and are sold at BTL offices and general stores.

Internet: BTL, 1 Church St., charges BZ$4.40 for 30min. **Ray Communications,** 15 Regent St. West, offers faster service. BZ$3 for 30min. Open the iron gate and the entrance is the 1st door on your left.

Post Office: Queen St., north of the Swing Bridge in the old colonial Paslow building. Open M-Th 8am-5pm, F 8am-4:30pm.

⌂ ACCOMMODATIONS

Safety should be your first priority when choosing a hotel in Belize City. Beware of hotel curfews and carefully check the locks between you and those who wander the street. It is not smart to walk around Belize City after dark, especially alone.

Many hotels have an additional sales tax of between 7-12% and some hotels charge an extra 3-5% for credit card payments. Last resort budget options include **North Front St. Guest House ❶** (123 North Front St.) and **Downtown Guest ❶** (5 Eve St.).

▨ **Seaside Guest House,** 3 Prince St. (☎227 8339; seasidebelize@btl.net). Undoubtedly Belize City's most impressive combination of tranquility, safety, helpful management, and affordability. A spectacular veranda has a water view. Updated collection of books and pamphlets full of current information on Belize. Pass through a gated garden area and three locks to one of the immaculate rooms with fan and shared hot water showers. Internet access BZ$8 for 30min. Meals available. Call ahead for reservations. Dorms BZ$24; singles BZ$40; doubles BZ$60; triples BZ$72; quads BZ$96. D/MC/V. ❸

Hotel Mopán, 55 Regent St. (☎227 7351), is a friendly, family-run hotel a block from St. John's Cathedral. Rooms are sparse but spacious. Also operates a small bar/lounge with cable TV, music, and a restaurant for breakfast and lunch. Has a nice 3rd floor balcony and roof access. All rooms include private bath with hot water, linens, and fan. A/C an extra BZ$20 per room. Check-out 11am. Singles BZ$60; doubles BZ$80; triples BZ$90; quads BZ$100; 12% sales tax not included. ❸

Belcove Hotel, 9 Regent St. West (☎227 3054), is a remodeled hotel in the center of downtown, on the south side of Haulover Creek. A walk out on the 2nd floor waterfront balcony may leave some reminiscing of Venice's famed building-lined waterways. Nice, clean, spacious rooms. Can be noisy at night. Singles with fan BZ$32, with bath BZ$42; doubles BZ$43/BZ$53. Swank rooms with A/C, private bath, and cable TV are BZ$85 for singles and doubles. Check-out 11am. MC/V. ❷

Isabel Guest House, 3 Albert St. (☎227 3139; almelhado@yahoo.com), above the Central Drugstore, south of the Swing Bridge; follow signs to upstairs. Be cautious in this neighborhood after dark. This tidy guest house offers 4 spacious wood paneled rooms, each with a fan, fridge, and modern private bath. Palatial common room has cable TV. Check-out 11am. Reservations recommended. Singles BZ$45. ❷

▣ FOOD

Jambel's Jerk Pit, on King St. a few meters west of the waterfront. Free of jerks and pits, this new, hospitable eatery specializes in top quality Jamaican and Belizean food. Specializes in seafood entrees (BZ$10-20). Try the spicy Jamaican King Shrimp (BZ$15), or the conch soup, touted as an aphrodisiac. Open M-Su 11am-9pm. MC/V. ❷

Bird's Isle. It takes a bird's eye to find this Caribbean hideout located in the very southeast of Belize City out on the mini Bird's Isle. A bit out of the way, the walk is well worth it. Walk south on Regent St., past the massive colonial England Government House and the ancient St. John's Cathedral. Take the first left past the church, follow the waterfront foot bridge; it is the thatched building on the right. Burgers and sandwiches (BZ$4), seafood entrees (BZ$12-20). Karaoke on Th night. Open M-W 11am-2:30pm and 5:30-9pm, Th-Sa 11am-2:30pm and 5:30-10pm, Su 11am-5pm. ❶

Dit's Restaurant, 50 King St. One of the nicer pastry shops in town. This family-owned and operated restaurant serves up hearty dishes for breakfast, lunch, and dinner (BZ$5-8). Open M-Sa 7am-8:30pm and Su 8am-4pm. ❶

Macy's Café, 18 Bishop St. Take Albert St. south from Swing Bridge, turn left on Bishop St. At this local favorite, armadillo and turtle are regulars. . . on the menu, that is (BZ$25-30). Young River Phoenix was rumored to have shimmied up the awning while filming *The Mosquito Coast*. Fresh juices BZ$2-4. Open M-Sa 11:30am-9:30pm. ❸

Big Daddy's, in the hulking commercial center next to the mouth of Haulover Creek, on the south bank just south of the Swing Bridge, serves up the usual rice and beans fast and delicious (with chicken BZ$6.90). Big fans keep the bamboo-decorated restaurant cool. Cafeteria-style lunch is a big draw with the locals. Open daily 7am-4pm. ❶

◎ SIGHTS

While Belize City may not be the nicest place for a leisurely stroll, there are a few interesting spots, new museums, and cultural centers that warrant a visit.

SWING BRIDGE. The center of the city is the Swing Bridge, an unusual, manually operated bridge. *Two blocks north of Battlefield Park.*

ST. JOHN'S CATHEDRAL. The oldest Anglican cathedral in Central America was built in 1826 with bricks used as ballast on English ships. Today, the idyllic edifice stands out in an unhappily urban Belize City. Mrs. Elsie Evans, the caretaker, sometimes sings spirituals and gives tours. *(At the southern end of Albert St., a 10min. walk south from the Swing Bridge. Open M-Sa 9am-noon and 2-7pm, Su 6am-noon and 6-7pm.)*

THE IMAGE FACTORY. Three doors down from the tourist office on North Front St., the Image Factory is a non-profit space devoted to Belizean art. Started by Yasser Musa, son of Said Musa, current prime minister, this gallery rotates works of contemporary Belizean artists, natural history exhibits, and folkloric artifacts. *(Open M-F 8am-6pm, Sa 9am-noon. Free.)*

THE MUSEUM OF BELIZE. Opened in 2002, this worthwhile museum is housed in a fully restored edifice that formerly served as Her Majesty's Prison. There are plans to maintain rotating exhibits of Belizean interest. Currently features an exhibit on Historical Belize City and another on Maya Masterpieces. *(On Gabourel Ln., next to the massive new Central Bank Building. www.museumofbelize.org. Open Tu-F 10am-6pm, Sa 10am-3pm. BZ$5.)*

NATIONAL HANDICRAFT CENTER. One of the best places that showcases and sells goods made in Belize. *(2 S. Park St. on Memorial Park.)*

◙ NIGHTLIFE

It only takes one night on the town to be convinced of the musical and linguistic diversity of Belize City. The best nights to go out are Thursday, Friday, and Saturday. For dancing to *punta*, *soca*, and reggae, locals swear by two places. The **Bellevue Hotel** is the place to be every Friday night. Start the night upstairs with a little karaoke with the locals (5-10pm). After 11, venture downstairs to enjoy the hot live band music and to shake yo booty on the intimate dance floor. Like the rest of Belize City, the party does not get jumpin' until midnight or later. (Open 10pm-morning.) Notorious in its own right is **Eden,** on Newtown Barrack Rd., at the first intersection past the large Fiesta Inn Belize on the left. Expect DJs and dancing. (Open Th-Sa 10pm-3am, BZ$10 cover.) The **Princess Hotel** has a casino, bowling alley, swimming pool, and the only movie theater in the country (BZ$15). To reach the hotel, go north on Queen St., turn left at the end, and follow the waterfront for 10min. Investing in a cab at night is a necessity. **MJ's Grand,** also on Newton Barracks St., on the left past the Princess Hotel, recently opened and has already gained a rep as a hot dance club. It showcases live bands and DJs. There is a dress code of pants, shirt, and closed-toed shoes. Open until 4am; cover BZ$10.

NORTHERN CAYES

Few travelers overlook Belize's exquisite cayes (pronounced "KEYS"), strung along the second-largest barrier reef in the world. The Cayes are Belize's number one tourist destination, featuring some of the best diving and snorkeling in the world. Hordes of divers and snorkelers come to enjoy the colorful coral and 400 plus species of fish. Although there are several hundred cayes off Belize's aquamarine coast, visitors primarily concern themselves with Ambergris Caye, with its top-end resorts and dive shops, and more rugged Caye Caulker, a budget traveler's haven. The beaches are fine—it is the reef that truly sets the Belizean Cayes apart.

CAYE CAULKER

This haven of tranquility, which draws more European than American tourists, is just a 45min. boat ride from the grunginess of Belize City and the hustle and bustle of San Pedro. Caye Caulker is an island divided. According to legend, Hurricane Hattie split the Caye in two back in 1961. In fact, Hattie only widened a creek, which locals later deepened. A small swimming hole marks this spot, now called "the split." Locals and visitors remain on the southern half, while the northern half is home to mangroves and birds. Caye Caulker (pop. 800) cools and calms the spirit. With no cars, no cabs, and hardly any bicycles, the atmosphere consists of people strolling the sandy streets, geckos sunning in the grass, and coconut trees swaying in the afternoon breeze. For the majority of its history, Caye Caulker has made its living on lobster. Now tourism is prominent, but the annual **Lobster Fest**, held the first weekend in July, brings back the early memories. Even the most ambitious tend to sit back, nurse another rum punch, and forget what day it is. Of course, if you insist upon being active, snorkeling and scuba trips to

Caye Caulker

🏠 ACCOMMODATIONS
Albert's Guesthouse, **9**
Daisy's Hotel, **19**
Mara's Place, **2**
Sandy Lane, **8**
Tina's Backpacker Hostel, **3**
Tree Tops Hotel, **22**

🍴 FOOD
Caye Caulker Bakery, **11**
Dave's Bar & Grill, **18**
Glenda's, **16**
Marin's, **20**
The Sandbox, **14**
Syd's Rest. & Bar, **17**
Wish Willy, **10**

🍸 NIGHTLIFE
I&I Cafe & Bar, **21**
Lazy Lizard, **1**
Oceanside Bar, **6**
Sunset View Disco, **5**

→ TO BARRIER REEF (2km)

CARIBBEAN SEA

🔴 DIVE/SNORKEL
Anwar Tours, **13**
Driftwood Snorkeling, **7**
Frenchie's Diving, **4**
Juni, **12**
Paradise Down Diving, **6**
Ras Creek's Boat, **15**

0   200 meters
0   200 yards

BELIZE

the reef provide an escape from the heat, the mosquitoes, and the lethargy on the shore. Though residents are very open, crime is rising; caution is advisable.

▐ TRANSPORTATION

Flights: any flight between **San Pedro** and **Belize City** will stop on request at **Caye Caulker**; simply mention it when buying your ticket. Once on the Caye, call **Tropic Air** (☎226 0400), **Maya Island Air** (☎226 0012), or talk to one of the many agents on Front St. for the return trip. Flights leave for **Belize Municipal, Belize International Airport,** and **San Pedro** on request. It is cheapest to take a boat to either location.

Ferry: From the pier by the Sandbox on Front St., boats head to the marine terminal in **Belize City** (45min., 9 per day 6:30am-5pm, one-way BZ$15; open-ended round-trip BZ$25) and to **San Pedro** on **Ambergris Caye** (45min., 8 per day 7am-5:15pm, ,one-way BZ$15; open ended round-trip BZ$25). Buy your tickets in advance from the water taxi office off the pier on Front Street. The west pier (back) goes to the tourist village in **Belize City,** and also to **San Pedro.** It has hours and prices almost identical to those of the eastern pier. A fun, leisurely way to spend a few hours in San Pedro is to take a full-

BELIZE

Cayes

N
LG

CARIBBEAN SEA

Glovers Reef

Lighthouse Reef

BARRIER REEF

Turneffe Islands

Ambergris Caye

Caye Caulker

Belize City

Dangriga

Placencia

0   20 kilometers

0   20 miles

day snorkeling trip that stops for lunch in San Pedro (BZ$55-70) and visits **Hol Chan Marine Reserve.** Most leave at 10:30am and reach San Pedro at 12:30pm.

✴ 🗺 ORIENTATION AND PRACTICAL INFORMATION

A **creek** called **"The Split"** divides Caye Caulker into two halves. The town stands at the northern tip of the southern portion, while the northern half remains largely uninhabited. The only street signs in Caye Caulker state the obvious: "Go slow." Three parallel dirt roads, known informally as **Front Street, Middle Street,** and **Back Street,** run north-south through town. **Water taxis** drop tourists off on the east side of the island. The first street parallel to the sea and in the center of town is **Front Street,** lined with gift shops and eateries. Landmarks include the cream-colored **police station,** the **basketball court** just south of the station, and the two largest **piers** that jut out on the east and west sides of the island. The **airstrip** is at the southern end of Back St., within easy walking distance of town.

Tourist Information: Dolphin Bay Travel (☎226 2214; dolphinbay@btl.net), just up Front St. Ilna and Dianne are knowledgeable about all the island's offerings and are especially attuned to the needs of penny pinchers. Also try Diane's sister Tina, proprietor of the Backpacker Hostel (see **Accommodations,** below), for the local lowdown.

Banks: Atlantic Bank, on Middle St., parallel with the road connecting the 2 main piers. Gives cash advances on Visa (BZ$5) and exchanges traveler's checks. Open M-F 8am-2pm, Sa 8:30am-noon. **Tropical Paradise Hotel,** at the southern tip of Front St., exchanges traveler's checks at a 2 to 1 rate, as do some gift shops on Front St.

Bike Rental: Caye Caulker gift shop on Front St. rents bikes for BZ$5 per hr., BZ$24 per day. Open daily 9am-9pm.

Book exchange: Yoohoo, on Front St. next to the police office.

Supermarket: Chan's Minimarket, on the corner of Middle St. and the pier. MC/V. Traveler's checks accepted. Open daily 7am-9pm.

Police: (☎226 2120), in a green and cream house by the basketball court on Front St. Officer available 24hr.

Pharmacy: Jungle Roses (☎226 2231), on the south end of Front St., has both herbal and standard medicines.

Medical Services: Caye Caulker Health Center (☎226 2166), at the southern end of Front St. No set hours.

Laundry: Coin Laundromat on the pier road between Front St. and Middle St. Wash and dry, BZ$4 each. Open daily 7am-9pm.

Telephones: BTL (☎226 0169), directly off the eastern pier on Front St. **Fax** service. Open M-F 8am-noon and 1-5pm. Many pay phones are on Front and Middle St.

Internet: Caye Caulker Internet Cafe, on Front St. near the basketball court. Nine computers and A/C. Beverages half-price during happy hour (daily 3-6pm). Great 80s music. BZ$4.50 for 30min. MC/V. Travelers checks.

Post Office: Located at the southern end of Front St., in the same building as the health center. Open M-Th 8am-noon and 1-5pm, F 8am-noon and 1-4:30pm.

▟ ACCOMMODATIONS

Upon arrival, you will be greeted by locals asking if you need a room; it is usually best to further research their references in your trusty guide book or at **Dolphin Bay Travel** (see **Orientation and Practical Information,** above). In general, housing on Caulker is safe and secure. Look for a place on the Caribbean side where a steady ocean breeze will keep you cool and deter voracious mosquitoes and sand flies.

Campers looking for sites can wander to the more isolated parts of the island. It might also be worth inquiring at hotels to see if they allow camping.

▨ **Tina's Backpacker Hostel** (dolphinbay@btl.net), in the bright blue house at the very north of Front St., is one of the best deals on Caye Caulker. It offers 5 small rooms, each with four bunk beds. Linens provided, but no towels. Maintains the perfect backpacker environment. Communal kitchen with fridge, lounge with cable TV, radio, and a front beach yard legendary for its cricket and volleyball matches between its guests. The best place to meet other travelers. BZ$15 per person. ❶

Albert's Guesthouse (☎226 0277), a few blocks north of the front pier, on Front St. One of the best budget values on the island. Convenient, oceanfront location, if a bit noisy at night. All rooms with fan and shared bathroom. Also, shared balcony with chairs, hammock, and sea view. Singles and doubles BZ$15. ❶

Sandy Lane (☎226 2217), located just south of the soccer field, on Middle St. If you want the unbeatable price of a hostel, but the quiet and privacy of your own room, this is it. Some more expensive cabins in front. Rooms equipped with fan and shared bathroom. Singles BZ$15; doubles BZ$20. ❶

Mara's Place (☎226 0056), at the north end of Front St., just before the split. Overlooking Caulker's tiny beach, Mara's is a great value. Double-size *cabañas* come with private baths, hot water, cable TV, and a porch with a hammock. Reservations recommended. Cabanas BZ$50. ❹

Daisy's Hotel (☎206 0150), just past Big Fish, Little Fish on Front St. Spacious blue rooms with soft mattresses, high ceilings, and a pink, hot-water communal bath. Strong fans keep guests cool. Check-out 10am. 50% deposit required to reserve a room. Singles BZ$17; doubles BZ$27; triples BZ$38. ❶

Tree Tops Hotel (☎226 0240; fax 226 0115; www.treetopsbelize.com). An incredible value, this elaborately decorated hotel. Each themed room (African, Indonesian, Malaysian) has beautiful artwork, cable TV, fridge, oceanfront view, and gardens. Book exchange, purified drinking water, bike rental for guests (BZ$10 per day). Min. 2-night stay required. Reservations recommended. Room with fan and shared bath BZ$70; with fan and private bath BZ$80; with A/C and private bath BZ$85. ❺

▣ FOOD

Caye Caulker's restaurants are legendary for cheap seafood and laid-back (read: slow) service. For a quick and tasty breakfast, buy some **Creole bread** (BZ$1.50) from one of the many children and women on Front St. Also stop by the pink **Light House,** just north of the basketball court, for excellent ice cream (BZ$1.50). Caye Caulker is one of the few spots in Belize that **does not have safe drinking water;** be sure to buy purified water and ice. The **Caye Caulker Bakery,** on the corner of Middle St. and the dock street, sells excellent fresh breads and pastries. (BZ$0.50-2. Open M-Sa 7am-noon and 2-6pm).

▨ **Glenda's,** on Back St. Friendly family atmosphere with great food at great prices. Fresh orange juice (BZ$2); coffee, eggs, bacon, and warm cinnamon rolls (BZ$6); chicken burritos (BZ$2). Open M-F 7-10am and noon-1:30pm. ❶

Syd's Restaurant and Bar, on the corner of Middle St. and the back path by Glenda's. While not the most elegant dining environment, Syd's more than compensates by serving the cheapest, tastiest lunch on the caye. Chicken *tostadas* BZ$1; trio of *garnaches* BZ$1; burritos BZ$2. Dinner serves excellent fish (BZ$10) and lobster (BZ$20). Catch the island-renowned barbecue on Saturday night (BZ$8). Popular with locals. Open daily 10am-3pm and 6-9:30pm. Credit cards and traveler's checks accepted. ❶

The Sandbox, on Front St. near the dock. During happy hour (daily 3-6pm) the island congregates here for half-price drinks (BZ$2.50-4). Varied menu has some good values (*tostadas* BZ$6) and many dinner options. Open daily 7am-10pm. ❶

Marin's, at the south end of Middle St., west of I&I Cafe and Bar. Highly recommended by locals. Great veggie dinner (BZ$9.50), simple garden salad (BZ$3.50). Fried shrimp BZ$17; *tostadas* BZ$1. Open daily 8am-2pm and 5:30-10pm. ❷

Wish Willy, on North Front St., just before Albert's, has great food hidden in a unique, bizarre plywood restaurant. Heavily recommended by both locals and international gurus. However, expect unusually slow (even by Caye Caulker standards) service, up to 2hr. for food. Relax by filling up on the *free* rum punch, usually from 7-8 each night. Excellent lobster tail (BZ$18) and vegetable kebab (BZ$10). ❸

Dave's Bar & Grill, located on Middle St., one block west of Daisy's Hotel. Word on the street says this is the best place to grub on Caye Caulker's delicious fresh catch. Grilled whole lobster (BZ$25) and kebabs (BZ$12-18). ❹

⚡ WATERSPORTS

SNORKELING. Snorkeling off Caulker guarantees schools of multicolor fish and miles of coral at prices that, despite having almost doubled in the past year, still beat those of San Pedros. Tours usually leave around 10am and sometimes at 2pm. Walk-ins on the day of the trip welcome. All operators should be approved by the Tour Guide Association; ask for a license.

Caye Caulker has fixed rates on snorkeling packages throughout the island. Half-day trips to the shallow coral reef near Caulker are typically the cheapest option. This usually includes three stops: one dazzling stop to swim and play with sting rays, one at the deep coral reef, and one at the shallow coral gardens. (Half-day trips depart 10am and 2pm. BZ$40.) Full-day trips to gorgeous **Hol Chan Marine Park** and **Shark Ray Alley,** both off Ambergris Caye, run about BZ$70 and usually include a brief stop in **San Pedro.** Two reputable snorkeling companies are **Driftwood Snorkeling** (☎226 0011), located two blocks north of the basketball court on Front St., and **Anwar Tours** (☎226 0327), across from the Sandbox Restaurant.

There are two excellent independent local guides whom all travelers get to know, rave about, and generally prefer to the one-size-fits-all tour companies. For the half day tour, find **Ras Creek** (☎606 4299; rascreek@hotmail.com), or simply ask around for the big rasta guy. His trip includes the three snorkeling stops, an informational tour around the island, and a visit to see an iguana and seahorse. Ras usually leaves around 11am from the front pier in his colorful thatched-roof boat. (Tours BZ$30; snorkeling gear is not provided.) For a full-day snorkeling tour, **Juni** is praised for his knowledge and professionalism. He takes out his sail boat, "The Trinity" to the **Hol Chan Marine Park** at the cheapest rates (BZ$55). His office is located across from the police station. To explore Caye Caulker on your own, rent equipment from any of the shops. Cheap rentals are at **Big Fish, Little Fish,** at the southern end of Front St. (BZ$5 per day.)

SCUBA DIVING. Several dive companies offer similar services and prices in Caye Caulker. Four-day certification courses run BZ$500, two-tank dives are BZ$140; three dive trips to the world-famous **Ambergris Caye** (see **Ambergris Caye,** p. 91) and to Belize's other prized location, **Turneriffe Elbow** (about BZ$290). The two most reputable dive companies are **Frenchie's** (☎226 0234; frenchies@btl.net), on the dock close to the northern end of Front St., and **Paradise Down Scuba** (☎226 0437; paradisedown@btl.net), in the Oceanside Bar.

OTHER SPORTS. Caye Caulker delights with a variety of fun activities: kayaking, canoeing, fishing, windsurfing, sailing, and of course, swimming. **Kayaking** is a fun way to explore the shores of the island. Rentals are available at **Seaside Cabanas.** (1 person BZ$15 per hr., BZ$45 half-day; 2 people BZ$20/BZ$60.) **Canoes** are available at Toucan canoe rentals, located on Back St., next to the Sunset View Disco

(BZ$10 per hr., BZ$25 half day; lessons extra). **Say L King** (☎ 226 0489; www.saylk-ing.com) is a new, but already popular sailboat rental store, located in the back of Treasured Travels on North Front St. (rentals BZ$20 per hr.), includes brief, but free lessons to beginners. Fred, at the Seaview Hotel may rent **windsurfing** equipment in the high tourist season. **Fishing trips** are becoming increasingly popular. Half-day trips through **Hummingbird Tours** and other companies run about BZ$300 for 2-4 people. Local fishermen offer much cheaper trips, just ask around the village. Travelers can rent fishing rods and buy bait at the store located next to the Sandy Lane hotel office, and cast off of the split. Prized catch includes red snapper, barracuda, and the blue marlin. For **swimming,** the best spot is the split.

▶ DAYTRIPS FROM CAYE CAULKER

Day and overnight trips to surrounding cayes and gorgeous coral reefs are becoming increasingly popular, and include manatees dolphin sightings, and trips to Geoff's Caye. (Day trips BZ$75, 9:30am-5pm.) The centerpiece of the trips is the magnificent visit to the **manatee** communtiy at nearby **Swallow Caye.** Then, for a picture perfect lunch, most take you to **Geoff's Caye** (often pronounced Goff's), a perfect "Gilligan's Island." This small island, situated on top of the reef, has coconut trees, white sandy beaches, and great snorkeling. The last stop of the trip is usually at **Sargent's Caye,** where **dolphins** are the lure. Nobody does this trip like **Chocolate,** who has been protecting the endangered manatees for more than 20 years (☎ 226 2151). He can be found near Chocolate's Gift Shop close to the north end of the island. A solid alternative is **Anwar Snorkel and Tours,** in the center of town on Front St. (☎ 226 0327. Trips BZ$75 including gear.) If it's your thing, splurge on a round of golf at privately owned **Caye Chapel** (BZ$400), which includes water transportation, equipment, lunch, and use of the resort's extensive amenities including private beaches, a heated mosaic pool, and paddle boats.

▶ NIGHTLIFE

After a short time on Caye Caulker, most travelers find themselves conforming to a cheap, incredibly relaxing, and wonderful night life pattern. First, swim, fish, or delight in a beautiful Caribbean sunset at **The Split.** While there, join grizzled guides, locals, and sunburned tourists at the **Lazy Lizard's** happy hour daily from 4-6pm. Next, trek a few blocks south to the **Oceanside Bar,** which usually offers drink specials from 6-8pm, and has pool tables, cable TV, and Caye Caulker's only live music on Friday nights. A unique alternative is the **I&I Cafe and Bar** near the south end of Front St., about 50m west of Tropical Paradise. Walk up the rickety staircase to a tree house atmosphere and take a seat at one of the many swings, painted in bright, primary colors (local beer BZ$3, Cuba Libre BZ$4.) If you need to escape Bob Marley, head to the roof and chat it up with the resident dreadlocked Rasta. After too many hours sitting on their bums, or too many happy hours, tourists head to the **Sunset View Disco,** at the northern end of Back St., for some alcohol inspired bumping and grinding. (Open Th-Sa until 2am, entrance BZ$5.)

AMBERGRIS CAYE

Belize's leading tourist destination and Caye Caulker's upscale sibling, Ambergris Caye (pronounced am-BER-gris) sits offshore 36 mi. north of Belize City. Ambergris was once used as a major Maya trading port, where it is estimated that at least 10,000 Mayans lived. After the Maya disappeared, the island fell out of favor and was purchased by James Howe Blake, a wealthy Creole landowner for a paltry $625 (an amount that today will barely support a single night at the dazzling Mata Chica resort). It is the largest of Belize's 200 islands and spans some 25 mi., but the only real population center is the town of **San Pedro**, located near the southern tip. Although fishing remains an important industry for many of the town's 2500 residents, tourists have become the island's most lucrative catch. Families, honeymooners, and even backpackers (despite the price) can't get enough of the island. During the day, the most popular area is the **Barrier Reef**. At night, sunburned tourists crowd the sandy streets and putt around in golf carts.

Ambergris, usually referred to simply as San Pedro, is the most expensive area in Belize, but a few budget deals can be found. Known in Spanish as *La Isla Bonita*, Ambergris Caye has a pleasant beach, and because the Barrier Reef is right next to the island's eastern shores, snorkeling and diving are easier, though pricier, than at Caye Caulker. Ambergris Caye rose to prominence in the US when FOX turned two of the island's luxury resorts into their Temptation Island to test the limits of reality TV. If you're at a "crossroads in your relationship" and need to scour the resorts for your tempter or temptress, ask around for the secluded Mata Chica Resort (the guy's resort) or Captain Morgan's (the girls resort), but expect to pay at least US$130 a night for your acre of love (no promise of temptation).

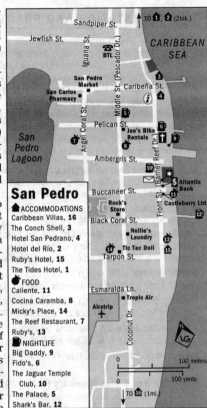

San Pedro

🏠 **ACCOMMODATIONS**
Caribbean Villas, 16
The Conch Shell, 3
Hotel San Pedrano, 4
Hotel del Río, 2
Ruby's Hotel, 15
The Tides Hotel, 1

🍴 **FOOD**
Caliente, 11
Cocina Caramba, 8
Micky's Place, 14
The Reef Restaurant, 7
Ruby's, 13

🌙 **NIGHTLIFE**
Big Daddy, 9
Fido's, 6
The Jaguar Temple Club, 10
The Palace, 5
Shark's Bar, 12

BELIZE

TRANSPORTATION

Flights: The San Pedro airstrip is located at the southwest end of town and can be reached easily by foot or taxi (BZ$5). **Tropic Air** (☎ 266 2012) flies to: **Belize City Municipal** (20min., every hr. 7am-5pm, BZ$52); **Belize International** (20min., every hr. 7am-5pm, BZ$93); **Corozal** (35min., about every 2hr. 7am-5pm, BZ$70). Flights stop on request at Caye Caulker, but it is more convenient and cheaper to get to Caye Caulker by boat. Reserve flights in advance during high season (Nov.-May).

Boats: Boats depart San Pedro for **Belize City** (1½hr.; BZ$25, round-trip BZ$45 via **Caye Caulker** (30min.; BZ$15, round-trip BZ$25). **Water taxi** boats depart from the Municipal dock on the eastern shore of the island, next to Shark's Bar (8 per day 7am-4:30pm). Boats also leave for same destinations at similar times from the Coral Beach Dive Shop pier near the center of town.

Taxis: They wait hungrily by the airport and the docks by day and near Elvi's Kitchen on Middle St., in the middle of town after 6pm. Trips in town BZ$5, outside of town BZ$7.

✦ 🔋 ORIENTATION AND PRACTICAL INFORMATION

Arriving in San Pedro, the **airstrip** is south of the center of town. **Boats** from Belize City usually pull up to the Texaco dock or the water taxi dock, both on the eastern shore of the island. A few boats do cruise around to the other side. If coming from the east, the first sandy road you will hit is **Front Street,** officially **Barrier Reef Road** The strip runs across the Caye from north to south, and is home to most accommodations, restaurants, and dive operations. Cheap restaurants and delis can be found on **Middle Street,** also referred to as **Pescador Drive,** which runs parallel to Front St. The center of town is on Front St. at the Children's Park and the Barrier Reef Hotel. Upscale resorts and homes sit south of San Pedro, while the vast stretch heading north of town is uninhabited save for a few secluded resorts.

Tourist Information: Ambergris Caye Information Center (☎206 2816) on Barrier Reef Dr. across from the San Pedrano Hotel. Has maps and info on the island's more expensive options. Unofficial but useful information is at **Ruby's Hotel** (see below).

Banks: Atlantic Bank, just south of the town center on Front St., exchanges US dollars and traveler's checks. MC/V cash advances. Fee BZ$10. Open M-F 8am-2pm, Sa 8:30am-noon. **Castleberry Ltd.,** at the **Spindrift Hotel,** next door to the bank, offers rates better than 2 to 1 for cash and traveler's checks. They exchange most currencies and have a **Western Union.** Open M-F 8am-4pm, Sa 8am-noon, Su 10:30am-noon.

Markets: Rock's Store, on Middle St., stocks everything from suntan lotion to fresh bread. Look for fluorescent purple columns. Open daily 6:30am-10pm.

Laundry: Nellie's Laundry, on Middle St., 1 block south of Rock's Market, offers wash, dry, and fold service for BZ$11. Open M-Sa 7am-8pm, Su 8am-2pm.

Bike Rental: Joe's Bike Rentals (☎226 4371), located in middle of Middle St., one block west of Fido's. BZ$5 per hr., BZ$18 per day.

Police: (☎90 or 226 2022), on Front St., just north of Atlantic Bank, next to the central park. Open 24hr.

Pharmacy: San Carlos Pharmacy (☎226 2918), on the north end of Middle St. Open M-Sa 7:30am-9pm, Su 9am-noon and 6-9pm. 24hr. emergency service.

Medical Services: Dr. Lerida Rodriguez (☎226 3197), just north of airport. Open M-F 8am-noon and 4-8pm, Sa 9am-1pm. The bright purple **San Pedro Health Center** (☎226 3668) is a 3min. walk north of the San Pedro Supermarket. Open M-F 8am-5pm; 24hr. for emergencies.

Telephones: Several **public phones** dot Front St. **BTL** (☎226 2199), at the north end of Middle St., past the loud electric generator. Free collect and AT&T credit card calls to the US; otherwise BZ$10 per min. Open M-F 8am-noon and 1-4pm, Sa 8am-noon.

Internet: Coconet, on Front St., has a full bar inside to quench your thirst. BZ$5 per 15min., BZ$15 per hr. Open daily 8am-9pm.

Post Office: on Front St. near the banks in the pink building. Open M-Th 8am-noon and 1-4:30pm, F 8am-noon and 1-4pm.

🏠 ACCOMMODATIONS

Inexpensive rooms are more scarce here than on Caye Caulker, especially during high season. During low season many proprietors are willing to negotiate prices.

🏨 **Ruby's Hotel** (☎226 2063; wamcq@cowichan.com), on Front St.'s south end, a 2min. walk from the airstrip. Ruby's is the best deal in town for budget travelers. Right on the water, this hotel provides comfortable mattresses, soap, and towels. Call to reserve.

Singles BZ$32, with bath BZ$50; doubles with shared bath BZ$50, with A/C BZ$90. Prices BZ$10 extra in high season. ❸

Hotel San Pedrano (☎226 2054; fax 226 2093), about 2 blocks north of the park on Front St. Clean, spacious rooms have polished wooden floors. All are equipped for double occupancy with large comfortable mattresses and private baths. Singles and doubles both BZ$55. Prices BZ$5-10 extra in high season. ❹

The Conch Shell (☎226 2062), is located on the waterfall, just around the corner from Hotel San Pedrano. Clean breezy rooms, with porches overlooking ocean. All rooms have private bath. Singles BZ$40; Doubles BZ$50; prices increase in high season. ❸

The Tides Hotel (☎226 2283), 10min. from central docks. Follow Middle St. north, turn right at the basketball court, and go north along the beach for several minutes until you see a three-story pink mansion on the beach. The Tides is a great medium range offering—with a shaded yard area, and nice quiet location. Singles and doubles with fan BZ$90; BZ$120 in high season; singles and doubles with A/C BZ$100/BZ$150. ❺

Hotel del Río (☎226 2286; hodelrio@btl.net), located on the beach, just north of the Tides Hotel. This hotel has a quiet, private, beach-side environment. Basic triples with private bath and fridge BZ$60; 5 person Cabana Grande with full kitchen BZ$150. ❹

Caribbean Villas (☎226 2715; c-v-hotel@btl.net), about 1 mi. south of town, set in a garden right on the waterfront. Escape the hustle of San Pedro to this peaceful shaded retreat. All rooms include fan, A/C, small fridges, beautiful views, free bikes, hot tub, and access to the bird sanctuary on the grounds. Basic singles and doubles BZ$130; more in high season. Also offers larger villas for high end travelers. ❺

▶ FOOD

Cheap restaurants are even more difficult to find than budget accommodations, especially at night. Delis usually provide the best values, though you often have to eat standing up. They are common in the center of town, especially on Middle St. The best is **Tic Tac Deli,** located just before **Micky's** on Tarpen St. During daytime, the two **La Popular Bakeries** in town serve tasty fresh pastries and donuts (BZ$1-3). (Both open 7am-8pm.) After 7pm carts offering Belizean dishes line Front St.

Micky's Place, at the intersection of Tarpen and Coconut Dr. just north of the airstrip, is an impeccably clean restaurant. Lunch doesn't get much better than this in San Pedro, with fish burger or conch fritter (BZ$7) and

THE BIG SPLURGE

DIVE IN

It's no secret that the diving sites off the coast of Belize are incredible—the waves are azure, visibility is unlimited, marine life and coral are colorful and abundant. In fact, two of the sites are ranked by experts among the world's best dive sites, the Blue Hole and Turneffe Elbow. Blue hole is a dark blue 1000 ft. circle enclosure set amidst the turquoise waters of the Caribbean. The site was made famous in the 1970s when diving pioneer Jacques Cousteau explored it in a miniature submarine. The Hole is actually a collapsed cave 470ft deep. Divers can explore mindblowing stalagmite and stalactite formations and swim in what is believed to have been a land cave about 10,000 years ago. Most companies sell 3-dive packages for the Blue Hole, with the 8 min. Blue Hole Dive, plus additional dives at Belize's Great Reef, and lunch on an island. Prices are approximately BZ$300 from Caye Caulker and BZ$350-370 from Caye Ambergris. Novice divers should be careful and seek advice before attempting this dive. Turneffe Elbow is located at the southern tip of the immense Turneffe Islands atoll. Unique in its own sense it offers the ultimate in wall diving. The dive is longer than the Blue Hole site, as it is shallower, and the Elbow features a far superior collection of incredible marine life. Turneffe Elbow is also usually included in a 3-dive package. The other 2 dives may also be in the Turneffe atoll. Lunch is included. Prices are BZ$290 from Caye Caulker and BZ$320-330 from Caye Ambergris.

fruit salad (BZ$8). Some breakfast items such as waffles (BZ$6) are also available. Dinner prices (BZ$20-30) remind you that you are in a resort town. Open daily 6:30-10am, 11:30am-2pm and 6-10pm. ❷

The Reef Restaurant, north of Rock's on Middle St. Festively decorated with sand floor and fishing decor. A local favorite. Open M-Sa 11am-2pm and 5-10pm. ❸

Papi's Restaurant, about 2min. south of the Hotel del Río, north of town. Owner Steve, known around the island as Papi, is perhaps the friendliest man in San Pedro and cooks up generous meals. Burgers (BZ$3.50); fried chicken (BZ$7). Big banana or mango *licuados* are also tempting (BZ$3). Open daily 7-10am and 11am-10pm. ❷

Ruby's, next to the hotel of the same name, on the south end of Front St., serves tasty banana bread, rum cake, cinnamon rolls, and other snacks like meat pies and burritos (BZ$2-4). For an authentic treat, try their Belizean johnny cake (BZ$1.50). Open M-Sa 5am-2pm and 4-7pm, Su 5am-11am. ❶

Caliente, located in the Spindrift Hotel on Front St. Everyone in San Pedro agrees that this is the best Mexican food and atmosphere in town. Breezy dining overlooking the water. and savory chicken and seafood burritos (BZ$12-20). Dinner prices increase, but the entrees are excellent (BZ$20-45). Open 11am-6pm and 6-9pm. ❹

Cocina Caramba, located on Middle St., just before the Palace Casino, has the only all you can eat buffet in San Pedro. Buffet served from 11am-9pm and offers excellent Belizean favorites (BZ$16). The menu entrees are overpriced. ❹

⚑ WATERSPORTS

Ambergris Caye has some of the best diving and snorkeling in the world. Even highly experienced divers are amazed by the colorful array of fish and coral found here. In low season, prices are more negotiable.

SNORKELING

Just off Ambergris, the **Hol Chan Marine Reserve** affords an opportunity to swim along the reef amid barracudas, moray eels, lobsters, yellowtail snappers, parrotfish, eagle rays, and the occasional benevolent shark. **Shark-Ray Alley** almost guarantees a swim with them: nurse sharks and sting rays come as snorkeling guides toss diced fish carcasses overboard. **Mexico Rocks** is a slightly less trafficked site. It is possible to free dive through caves and canyon walls built from the coral and swim next to Nassau groupers, lobster, horse-eye jacks, and sand sharks.

Guided trips are easily arranged. A half-day, two-stop snorkeling trip to Hol Chan and Shark-Ray Alley usually costs about BZ$50 per person (plus BZ$5-10 for equipment and BZ$5 entrance to Hol Chan.) Trips to Mexico run about BZ$55, plus equipment. Two reputable operators are **SEArious Adventures** (☎ 226 4202; SErious@btl.net), located behind Ruby's, and **SEAduced** (☎ 226 2254), located on the street running west from Ruby's. SEAduced trips are more relaxed than those of SEArious, which generally fits its namesake. Both companies also offer a three-site trip with a stop at Caye Caulker (BZ$70), where they will drop you off if requested. Meanwhile, you don't even have to get wet (though you can) on the *Southern Beauty*, a glass-bottom boat that leaves from the **Off Shore Express** dock. (☎ 322 2340. Daily 9am and 2pm for half-day excursions. BZ$40, snorkel gear BZ$8.) The **Rum Punch II**, a 38 ft. sailboat, will take you out and, yes, provide the rum punch. (☎ 322 2340. BZ$100; delightful sunset cruises BZ$40.) Look for the sign on the beach south of the town center.

For those unable to splurge, there is still hope. Most shops rent out fins and masks (BZ$5-10) for you to explore the shores of Ambergris Caye on your own. However, **never attempt to swim out to the reef on your own.** Always hire a guide.

SCUBA DIVING ON AMBERGRIS

SITES. It's possible to dive in the reefs right off the island. (US$35 for 1 tank, US$45 for 2.) The most famous site nearby, however, is **Blue Hole**. The other world-wide renowned site is the **Turneffe Elbow**.

DIVE SHOPS. The most highly recommended diving company is **Amigos del Mar** (☎226 2648; amigosdive@btl.net), just south of Hotel Pedrano on a pier. An excellent alternative is the **Coral Beach Dive Shop** (☎226 2817), located a few blocks north of Ruby's on the end of a pier. Other companies may offer lower rates, be sure to get second opinions on their quality. A great source of info on the dive companies is the **Blue Hole Dive Center.** (☎226 2982; bluehole@btl.net.)

LEARNING TO SCUBA. If you aren't scuba certified but want to dive, the cheapest option is a **Discover Scuba** or resort **course,** which lets you make one or two dives with a dive-master after a morning of basic theory. **Amigos del Mar** (see above) offers the course for BZ$250 and also offers a full menu of certification courses, including the **PADI openwater certification** for BZ$700.

DEFENSIVE DIVING The barrier reef along Belize and Honduras is the largest in the western hemisphere and second largest in the entire world. Many dive shops on the cayes offer travelers the chance to get certified and explore the fantastic reefs for considerably less than in the US. Unfortunately, competition between shops has also caused some corner-cutting. Safety awareness and quality of instruction are sometimes sacrificed for mass-output certification. Shop around before settling on a dive center. Make sure the instructor is fully certified with NAUI or PADI, the biggest divers' organizations. If some shops' deals seem too good to be true, they probably are. **Bad air or poor instruction can lead to decompression sickness and death,** so don't take chances. While preserving your own safety, make an effort to protect the well-being of the coral and sea life as well. Many dive operations in Belize have strict rules about not touching the coral or removing anything from the reef. However, some dive instructors still do not preach the importance of keeping your equipment near your body and not touching the coral or kicking your fins near it. Coral-heads that took eons to develop can be lost in a matter of seconds.

OTHER AQUATIC ACTIVITIES

If being underwater doesn't suit you, or you want to enjoy the view of the coastline, check out the other options. **Sailsports Belize** gives **windsurfing** lessons and offers **boat rentals** and **sailing instruction**. (☎226 4488. Windsurfing US$40; boards US$20 per hr., boat rentals US$30; sailing instruction US$55.) For a semi-dry caye experience, you can get a guided **kayak tour** among the Mangrove Islands from **SEAduced** (☎226 2254) for US$50 per person, including lunch. **Innovations Watersports,** on the pier next to Ramon's Resort south of town, rents kayaks. (☎226 3337. 1-person US$10 per hr.; 2-person US$15 per hr.) Many operators also have **charter fishing** trips (US$125-150 half-day, US$200 full day).

LAND ADVENTURES

ON CAYE AMBERGRIS. A great way to explore La Isla Bonita and discover its more secluded beaches and gardens is by renting a bike from Joe's (see **Practical Information,** above) or a golf cart (BZ$120 day). At the north end of Middle St., there is a ferry (BZ$1, 7am-8pm) that takes you to the beautiful beaches, and past resorts that you saw on Temptation Island. Stop for a drink or snack at Captain Morgan's (2 mi.), Mata Chica (4 mi.), or local favorite Capricora.

MAINLAND BELIZE. Those eager to dry off or escape the brunt of coastal tourism can hit a daytrip led by some of the local outfits. **Blue Hole Dive Center** organizes excursions to the zoo (approximately a 2hr. road trip) as well as to the ruins of **Lamanai** (BZ$250) and **AltunHa** (BZ$120). **SEArious** also takes people out to these ruins, though this is not the cheapest way to get there (☎226 4202).

NIGHTLIFE

For a night out, begin at the **Shark's Bar** at the end of the water taxi pier on the southern side of town. They make a mean margarita on the rocks, serve tasty pizza, and host live music every Tuesday. (Happy hour daily 4-5pm. Open Th-Tu until midnight). Meanwhile, every Friday and Saturday the party is at the **Jaguar Temple Club,** right in the middle of town, on Front St., and at the **Barefoot Iguana,** south of town. For those with a desire for something a bit different, the Barefoot is renowned for its Friday night mud wrestling (9pm-midnight). Yes, guys, its true—hot girls get naked in the mud and battle it out. (Take their free shuttle.) Back downtown, **Big Daddy** features a 2-for-1 happy hour as well as dancing and live music on weekends. During low season, opening hours are unpredictable, and the "party" can be sparse. (Cover varies, usually BZ$15.) Nightly live music at **Fido's** tends to attract an "older crowd," with its regular country music and guitar playing contests. If you are feeling lucky, head to **The Palace** on the end of Front St. for some high-stakes gambling at slot machines and tables. (Open Th-Tu 6pm. 21+.)

NORTHERN BELIZE

Northern Belize is a low-lying area of pine savannas, swamps, jungles, and coastal lagoons. The region has much more of a Mexican feel than other parts of the country, and Spanish is prevalent in many areas. Given the long stretches of cane fields, smoke stacks jutting up from refineries, and the abundance of cheap rum, it's easy to see that sugar is the basis of the northern economy. The Northern Highway turns inland after leaving Belize City and doesn't return to the coast until it reaches Corozal eight miles from the Mexican border, after reaching most of the region's landlocked Maya ruins and nature reserves. Highlights of the region include the impressive Maya site of Lamanai, accessible from mellow Orange Walk, as well as outstanding birding. Look for the rare Jaribu stork at Crooked Tree Wildlife Sanctuary, and explore the variety at the Shipstern Nature Reserve.

BERMUDIAN LANDING BABOON SANCTUARY

*Russell's **buses** leave Belize City (M-F noon and 4:30pm, Sa 12:15, 1, 4, and 5pm; BZ$3.50) from the corner of Euphrates St. and Cairo St., opposite the basketball court. Return buses leave M–Sa 5:30, 6 and 6:30am, so plan to spend the night if you come by bus. Register before entering the sanctuary at the green building with the "museum" sign in Bermudian Landing (☎220 2181; www.howlermonkey.bz). Speak to the friendly Mrs. Jessie or Mrs. Joseph. A tour is included in the BZ$10 admission fee. Local guides usually ensure at least one sighting in each 1hr. tour. At the museum, which is also the sanctuary headquarters, you can arrange more extensive guided trips into the forest (3½hr. canoe trip with guide BZ$80 for single, BZ$100 for two; night hikes BZ$20 per person).*

For the true monkey-lover! The sanctuary was started in 1985 when a concerned group founded the Community Baboon Sanctuary in Belize City to protect the endangered black howler monkey, locally known as "baboon." Farmers in the tiny village of **Bermudian Landing,** an hour northwest of Belize City, and seven other communities voluntarily pledged to abide by conservation plans to protect the

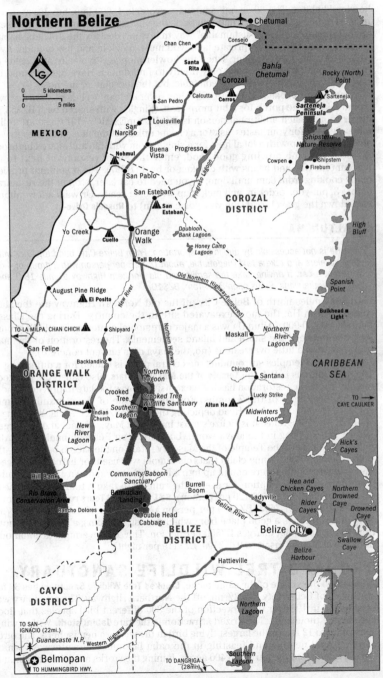

Northern Belize

MEXICO

Chetumal
Chan Chen
Consejo
Santa Rita
Bahía Chetumal
Rocky (North) Point
Corozal
Sarteneja
Calcutta
Cerros
Sarteneja Peninsula
San Pedro
Louisville
San Narciso
Shipstern Nature Reserve
Buena Vista
Progresso
Cowpen
Shipstern
Fireburn
Nohmul
San Pablo
High Bluff
San Esteban
COROZAL DISTRICT
San Esteban
Doubloon Bank Lagoon
Yo Creek
Orange Walk
Honey Camp Lagoon
Cuello
Spanish Point
Toll Bridge
Old Northern Highway (unpaved)
August Pine Ridge
El Posito
Bulkhead Light
TO LA MILPA, CHAN CHICH
Shipyard
Maskall
Northern River Lagoon
San Felipe
Backlanding
Chicago
CARIBBEAN SEA
Santana
ORANGE WALK DISTRICT
Northern Lagoon
Crooked Tree
Crooked Tree Wildlife Sanctuary
Altun Ha
Lucky Strike
Midwinters Lagoon
TO CAYE CAULKER
Lamanal
Indian Church
Southern Lagoon
New River Lagoon
Hick's Cayes
Hill Bank
Community Baboon Sanctuary
Burrell Boom
Hen and Chicken Cayes
Northern Drowned Caye
Río Bravo Conservation Area
Bermudian Landing
Ladyville
Drowned Caye
Rancho Dolores
Double Head Cabbage
Belize River
BELIZE DISTRICT
Belize City
Swallow Caye
CAYO DISTRICT
Hattieville
Belize Harbour
Northern Lagoon
TO SAN IGNACIO (22mi.)
Guanacaste N.P.
Western Highway
Belmopan
TO HUMMINGBIRD HWY.
TO DANGRIGA (28mi.)
Southern Lagoon

N
LG
0   5 kilometers
0   5 miles

New River
Northern Highway

BELIZE

howlers' habitat. The 20 sq. mi. sanctuary protects 1600 black howler monkeys. Instead of being treated as a national park, the villages share land with the reserve and attempt to live in a "sustainable" way that won't destroy the howlers' habitat. Since the sanctuary is on private land, you must check in and use a guide. Avoid trips after a heavy downpour, when the howler monkeys typically nap inside the trunks of palm trees, emerging only briefly to find dinner. Have patience and bug repellent—the monkeys are unpredictable, but the mosquitoes are not.

Nature Resort Cabañas ❹ (☎ 619 4286) has several clean, well-kept *cabañas* with hammocks on the porch for a bit more cash. (Singles with shared bath BZ$53; for larger rooms, each additional person is BZ$15. AmEx/MC/V.) If these are full or too expensive for your tastes, ask for a cheaper place at the museum. They may be able to set you up with a local host for a single room with fan and shared bathroom BZ$25. For some howling good food, enter the small restaurant next to the museum for rice and beans with chicken or beef (BZ$7). The restaurant provides ready cooking from 6am until 3pm; if you need to eat later, stop in the restaurant before 3, put your order in, and pick it up whenever ready. Or walk a few minutes back down the gravel road (the way you came in) to **Russels Drive-In.**

⚪ ALTUN HA

> *Altun Ha is not accessible by public transportation. From Belize City, band together with other travelers and take a **taxi** (negotiable, about US$25 per person with a group of 4 or 5) or rent a **car.** If driving, take the semi-paved old Northern Highway to mile 18.9 and then follow the signs. Ruins open 8am-4pm. BZ$10.*

Thirty-one miles north of Belize City off the old Northern Highway are the Maya ruins of Altun Ha, the most excavated site in the country. During the Classic Period (AD 250-900), Altun Ha was a major ceremonial center and a middle ground for trade between the shore and inland settlements. The restoration of the main ruins has been a little overzealous (no, the Maya didn't invent concrete).

Each of the 13 temples surrounding the central plaza is named for a different god. The most famous is B-4, the **Temple of the Masonry Altars,** also called the sun god's temple. While the restoration has been extensive, it was too late to prevent bandits from ransacking 5 of the 7 tombs. Fortunately, one of the remaining tombs enclosed the beautiful Jade Head depicting the sun god, Kinick Ahua. Weighing in at nearly five kilograms, it is Belize's most important Maya artifact and the largest known jade carving in the Maya world. Look for it on Belizean banknotes. Also notice the image of the Temple of the Masonry Altars on the sacred beverage—the Belize Beliken Beer. Some claim that this temple was used for human sacrifice—the fortunate victims were bound up into a ball and pushed down 150 ft. of stairs.

A more expensive option for seeing the ruins is to take a tour through one of several companies (BZ$80-120 per person). **S&L Travel and Tours** runs half-day tours of Altun Ha. (☎ 227 7593. BZ$100 per person.) The village of Crooked Tree, 7mi. west of Altun Ha, is a good place from which to visit the ruins; almost every hotel runs tours. **Sam Tillet** charges BZ$50 per person. The only overnight accommodations are at **Maruba resort** (☎ 022 2199, BZ$119 per night).

CROOKED TREE WILDLIFE SANCTUARY

Adjacent to the village of the same name, **Crooked Tree Wildlife Sanctuary** lies 33 mi. northwest of Belize City and 2½ mi. off the Northern Highway. The sanctuary was established in 1984 for the protection of the 300 different bird species that flock here by the thousands. The prized attraction is the rare **Jabiru stork.** With a wingspan of up to 12 ft., it's the largest flying bird in the western hemisphere. The birds can be found nesting and feasting in the calm lagoons and waterways which stretch inland into the park's 16,400 acres. Joining the storks are other inhabitants include boat-billed herons, kites, egrets, and ospreys. The sanctuary is best visited from late February to early June when the jabirus storks fill the park's lagoons. This is also the time when hotels are open and lagoon tours operate.

⌸ TRANSPORTATION. Crooked Tree lies 4km off the Northern Highway, which connects Belize City and Orange Walk, so you can take any **bus** between those two destinations. After the driver drops you off at the **Crooked Tree Junction** (you must ask him to do so), walk about 1hr. to get to the actual town. It is possible to get a direct bus from Belize City through **Jex** (M-Sa 10:55am from Regent St. West, 4:30 and 5:15pm from Pound Yard; return M-Sa 5, 6:30, 6:50am) and Novelo's (M-F 4pm, return M-F 6am). Arrive 15min. beforehand, as buses fill up early. Schedules change often; call the community phone for the latest update. (☎ 209 7084.)

▚ ORIENTATION. The park is accessible via tiny **Crooked Tree Village** (pop. 878). All visitors to the park must pay the BZ$8 admission fee at the **Visitors Center,** on the right as you enter the village. (Open daily 8am-4pm.) In addition to helpful guides and useful maps of trails, the Center features some interesting exhibits.

▛▐ ACCOMMODATIONS AND FOOD. For a village of its size, Crooked Tree offers an extensive selection of rooming options, each of which are signposted at the junction just past the visitors center. The buses will take you close to each of the accommodations if you ask. **Rhaburn's Rooms ❶,** a 5min. walk from the visitors center, is currently the cheapest B&B in town. It has four basic rooms with fans and a clean, communal bathroom. Turn left at the junction by the other hotel signs, cut through the field just past the blue-green Church of the Nazarene, and look for the path at the far back corner of the field. As the path turns right, enter the gate on the left of Rhaburn's yellow wooden house. (☎ 225 7035. Meals BZ$6. Singles BZ$15; doubles BZ$25.) **Sam Tillet's Hotel ❸,** in the middle of the village, is a two-story *cabaña* in a yard filled with livestock. Otherwise, follow signs from the visitors center (about 10min. on foot). Rooms are spacious, well swept, and bug-free, with modern bathrooms and A/C or fan. Suites provide the extra bonus of mosquito-netted beds and refrigerators. (☎ 220 7026. Singles BZ$40; doubles BZ$60; Jabiru Suite BZ$100.) If you want the luxury and beauty of lodging near the water without the elevated price, get a dorm room at **Bird's Eye View Lodge ❶,** a 20min. walk left from the main junction following the signs. Try their nice upstairs bar, but avoid the overpriced standard rooms. (☎ 225 7027. Dorm beds BZ$15.)

Food options in town are limited. There are two basic restaurants located to the right of the main junction. The best bet is to eat at your lodge.

⚡ ACTIVITIES AND GUIDED TOURS. The following operations offer good deals, but timing is everything. The most recommended guide is **Sam Tillet** (☎ 220 7026). He runs excellent birding/boating tours on the lagoon. Call ahead, as the water level can sometimes be too low for boats and the jabirus may be in Mexico. (BZ$120 for 1-4 hotel guests; BZ$140 for 1-4 non-guests.) He also does trips to Altun Ha. (BZ$100 for 1-4 people.) **Bird's Eye View Lodge** (☎ 225 7027) and the **Paradise Inn** (☎ 225 7044) offer the same tours for similar prices. Bird's Eye View Lodge also offers **canoe rentals** (half day BZ$15) and **horseback riding** (BZ$20 per hr.).

ORANGE WALK

When European settlers built the first church here, they planted a "walk," an orange tree orchard outside the church's front door. These days sugar, not oranges, reigns over Orange Walk, 56 mi. north of Belize City. The main road is filled with sugar cane, as are the trucks heading south to the refinery. Orange Walk is a predominately Hispanic town, as its first settlers were Mestizos fleeing the Caste Wars of the Yucatan in the 1850s. Today, the town is ethnically diverse and includes people of Chinese, Maya, and Spanish descent, as well as uniformly dressed Mennonites who periodically come into town to trade.

In the 1980s, as a result of depression in sugar prices, Orange Walk became notorious as the center of Belize's growing marijuana production. Today, with help from the US, the marijuana production has largely ceased, though an undercurrent is still noticeable. Despite being Belize's 2nd largest city, Orange Walk's main attraction is not its bustling nightlife, but rather its proximity to the Maya ruins of Lamanai and Cuello. Most visitors use Orange Walk as a way station before embarking on a river tour to visit the famed Maya ruins of Lamanai.

▐ TRANSPORTATION

Most buses leave from **Novelo**'s terminal, located at the northern end of Orange Walk. Buses go to **Belize City** (2hr., every hr. 5am-8:30pm , BZ$5) and **Chetumal, Mexico** (2hr., every hr. 6am-9pm, BZ$7) via **Corozal** (1½hr., BZ$5). Local buses also leave from Zeta's store on Main St. for **Sarteneja** (see Sarteneja for schedule) and from the lot next to the fire station for local villages.

✴ ▐ ORIENTATION AND PRACTICAL INFORMATION

Buses from Mexico and Belize City drop off along the principal north-south drag, which is called **Queen Victoria Road** north of the fire station, and **Belize-Corozal Road** south of the station. For quick orientation, remember that the **Novelo's** bus terminal is at the very north end of town, and the Town Hall is in the center of town. Both are on **Belize-Corozal Road.** Looking north from Town Hall, across the street is a lively **park.** The ill-named **Main Street** also runs parallel to Queen Victoria Rd. another block east, close to **New River** on the eastern edge of town. Don't ask locals where Main St. is; they tend to direct tourists to Queen Victoria Road. Orange Walk is not considered safe after dark. Women should be particularly cautious.

Tourist Information: The official tourist office closed after Hurricane Keith in Oct. 2000.

Banks: Bank of Nova Scotia, on Main St., next door to The People's Store (see below). Cash advances on Visa (BZ$10.80 fee); changes cash and traveler's checks. Open M-Th 8am-1pm, F 8am-4:30pm.

Car Rental: Melo's Auto Rental, 72 Belize-Corozal Rd. (☎322 2177). Head south on the Belize-Corozal Rd. to the yellow wooden house on the left, about a block past the juncture with Liberty Ave. There's no sign. BZ$50 per 12hr.

Market: The People's Store, 51 Main St. Open M-Sa 8am-noon and 1:30-5pm, F-Sa 7am-9pm, Su 8am-noon.

Police: (☎90 or 322 2022), 4 blocks north of the park on Belize-Corozal Rd.

Pharmacy: Pharmacy Lucille (☎322 0346), half a block north of the Belize Bank on Main St. Open daily 8am-9pm. **Prisma's Pharmacy** (☎322 0773) is located across from Lee's Restaurant on San Antonio Rd. Open daily 8am-noon and 1-9pm.

Hospital: (☎322 2072), 1200 ft. north of the police office. Open 24hr.

Telephones: Public phones are located at various points along Belize-Corozal Rd. **BTL** (☎322 2196) has an office above the BeliColor on Park St. at the northeast corner of the park. **Fax** and telegram service. Open M-F 8am-noon and 1-4pm, Sa 8am-noon.

Internet access: UMAX, on the left-hand side of the street with the town hall on it. BZ$9 per hr. Open M-Sa 8am-9pm, Su 10am-9pm.

Post Office: 3 blocks north of the park on Belize-Corozal Rd., in the same building as the treasury. Open M-F 8am-4:30pm.

ACCOMMODATIONS

St. Christopher's Hotel (☎302 1064), the pink building at the north end of Main St., before the bridge. Named for the patron saint of travelers, this hotel is a blessing for the weary. Large rooms are equipped with ceiling fans, cable TV, and private, hot-water baths. Doubles with fan BZ$59, with A/C BZ$91; BZ$10 per additional person. ❹

D'Victoria Hotel, 40 Belize-Corozal Rd (☎322 2518), at the south end of town, across the street from the Shell station. Offers spacious, tiled rooms with cable TV and private bathrooms. Extra perks include soap and towels, a sitting area, and a pool. There is a bar downstairs, which can be noisy on the weekends. Check-out noon. Singles with fan BZ$45, with A/C BZ$75; doubles BZ$60/BZ$86; triples BZ$85/BZ$107. MC/V. ❸

Mi Amor Hotel, 19 Belize-Corozal Rd. (☎322 2031), before the Shell station and above the **Mi Amor Lounge** (see below). Enter the office on the left. On weekends, sleep is virtually impossible because of the booming disco downstairs. Rooms have fans, cable TV, and private hot-water baths. Check-out 1pm. Singles BZ$48, with A/C BZ$74; doubles BZ$59/BZ$86. Traveler's checks accepted. ❹

FOOD

Taco carts cluster around the park and offer some of the best and cheapest meals in town, including chicken sandwiches (3 for BZ$1), hot dogs (BZ$2), and drinks. Those with a sugar craving can grab pastries, cakes, and cookies for the road at **Pontificadora La Popular,** 1 Bethias St., north of the park. On Fridays and Saturdays, locals sell excellent BBQ chicken (BZ$5 plate) on Belize-Corozal Rd.

Juanita's, 8 Santa Ana St., north of the Shell station at the south end of town. This clean, local favorite offers traditional Belizean fare in a town dominated by Chinese restaurants. Though the menu is not extensive, hungry travelers can fill up on bacon with eggs and beans, or rice and beans with chicken (BZ$5). Adventurous palates might want to try the cow foot soup. Service is friendly and the waiters even provide patrons with personal basins and soap for hand washing. Open M-Sa 6am-2pm and 6-9pm. ❶

Lee's Chinese Restaurant: 11 San Antonio Rd., 1 block west of the firehouse. The tops among local Chinese restaurants. Go for the chicken curry (BZ$12) or the conch fried rice (BZ$9). Open M-Sa 10:30am-midnight, Su noon-midnight. ❷

SIGHTS

La Inmaculada Church, a 101-year-old Catholic church at the south end of Main St., is worth a look, and the **river bank** is a great picnic spot. Although the park in the center of town is cement rather than grass, it is always conducive to resting and people-watching. A mile north of town is Trial Farm #4, the **Godoy orchid farm.** Carlos is the expert for all the dirt on the orchids. If you're lucky, he'll be around to give a tour. Call before you go. (☎322 2969.)

ENTERTAINMENT

For those yearning for nightlife, the club at **Mi Amor Hotel** has just reopened. It offers a full bar and draws a good crowd. The club offers karaoke early some evenings, and a DJ and hot dancing later, and plays a wide variety of local and international tunes. Live bands make occasional appearances. (Open Th-Su 8pm.) If you're looking for a place with smaller crowds more conducive to conversation, **Carl's** is a karaoke bar in the same building as D'Victoria. (Open Tu-Su 6pm.)

BELIZE

NEAR ORANGE WALK

LAMANAI

One of Belize's most impressive attractions, this site is believed to have been a vital agricultural and trade center of the Maya world. Archaeologists think the structures here were first erected in 1500 BC and inhabited until the 17th century, after the community had been ravaged by European diseases. Lamanai's claim to fame is that it is the only significant Maya site to be inhabited in all five archaeological classifications: pre-Classic, Classic, post-Classic, Spanish era, and English era. Originally called *Lamanain* ("submerged crocodile"), a linguistic blooper resulted in the current name, which translates as "drowned insect." Unfortunately, a short time in Lamanai confirms that the mosquitoes are alive and well.

Lamanai sits on the shore of the 20 mile long New River Lagoon. A visit usually involves a 31 mi. boat ride down the New River and a short hike on a jungle path. The reward is three magnificent temples with great panoramic views. Archaeologists are currently renovating and excavating the temples as a result of damage from Hurricane Keith; completion is expected in 2004. (BZ$5 entrance fee.)

TRANSPORTATION. Several companies offer memorable boat trips which usually start at 9am and end around 4pm. In Orange Walk Town, try **Jungle River Tours,** located in **Lover's Restaurant,** just east of the central plaza. The company is well run by the knowledgeable Novelo brothers, who lead legendary treks through the ruins, and also stop to discuss wildlife sightings on the New River. (☎ 302 2293; lamanaimayatour@btl.net. Trips BZ$80 per person with a 4-person min. Includes lunch and drinks.) A cheaper, but less recommended option is **New River Tours,** 100m or so past the bridge. They offer good tours and worthy guides. (☎ 322 3068. BZ$55 with a 5-person min. Includes lunch and drinks.) Local hotels also arrange tours, but usually use the guides of Jungle River Tours.

If a guided tour is beyond your budget, you may still be able to get to Lamanai. Buses leave from beside the fire station for the village of **Indian Church,** which is just a one mile walk from Lamanai. (Buses leave Orange Walk M, W, F 4pm, return 6am). Call the Indian Creek community phone for current schedules. (☎ 309 2015.)

THE RUINS. Boats arrive at a dock surrounded by souvenir stands. Up the hill and to the right lies a small but impressive display of pre-classic Maya artifacts, which have been collected during excavation. Bear right at the fork and follow the trail for 5min. to the first and smallest pyramid, the **Temple of the Mask.** A 13 ft. face protrudes from the front side. The mask itself was added under the reign of the powerful Lord Smoking Shell. Archaeologists who excavated the temple left it exposed in layers. The Temple of the Mask is actually four temples; each successive ruler built over the temple of his predecessor.

Five minutes farther along a windy path is the **High Temple.** At 30m, it is the third-largest building in the Maya world, dating back before Christianity. The safest (and least destructive) way to climb it is to go up the center steps, then take a left on the first platform and follow the path around the corner onto the 3 ft. wide steps that go the rest of the way. The top provides an impressive view of the jungle and the river that made Lamanai an important center of trade. Check out the finely detailed **Stela 9.** Located near the High Temple, this edifice commemorates Lord Smoking Shell's anniversary. Other attractions include the labyrinthine elite residences and the plebeians' **Temple of the Jaguar.** (Open 8:30am-5pm.)

CUELLO

Cuello can be reached by walking west from the Orange Walk Plaza (1 hr.) or by taxi (BZ$20 round trip). Call ☎ 3422 2141 for permission before visiting. Open daily 8am-noon and 1:30-6pm.

Not nearly as impressive as Lamanai, but closer to Orange Walk, Cuello was once thought to be among the oldest sites in Central America. Recent studies suggest, however, that this small, single temple, the Maya equivalent of a wine cellar, actually dates back to *only* 1000 BC. Nonetheless, excavations are reported to have uncovered more burials here than at any other Maya site. Some of the 200 skeletons had their skulls detached, suggesting that they may have been sacrifices dedicating the new temple. Today, with cattle casually grazing, Cuello retains a relatively untouristed tranquility.

SARTENEJA AND THE SHIPSTERN NATURE RESERVE

Situated across the Chetumal Bay from Mexico's Yucatán Peninsula, The **Sarteneja Peninsula** is endowed with a characteristically Yucatán climate. With some of the driest forests in Belize, much of the wildlife found in Sarteneja is unique to the area. This phenomenon led to the founding of the **Shipstern Nature Reserve.** Here, jaguars, pumas, and crocodiles are numerous. The star attraction is the spectacular bird life: over 200 species can be found in the reserve's 22,000 acres. Three miles north is the colorful fishing village of Sarteneja, where the blue bay creates an idyllic spot for an afternoon swim and a beautiful sunrise. Sarteneja itself is a sleepy little town with two hotels, one small restaurant, two bars, and a few shops.

▐ TRANSPORTATION. Located along the road from Orange Walk, the entrance to the Shipstern Nature Reserve is 5km shy of Sarteneja village. You can ask the bus driver to let you off there. **Buses** make the bumpy 2hr. trip to Sarteneja from Orange Walk in the afternoons. (3 buses between 2-5pm.) All buses depart from outside **Zeta's Ice and Purified Water Store** on Main St., one block north of the People's Store. There is also a **boat** service that leaves Corozal at 3pm, and can stop in **Sarteneja** en route to **San Pedro**. Buses return from Sarteneja to Orange Walk en route to Chetumal or Belize City (M-Sa 4, 5, 5:30am) and depart from North Front St., next to Fernando's Seaside Guesthouse. The 3 mi. walk can be hot and sticky.

▐ PRACTICAL INFORMATION. The **Visitors Center** is located at the entrance to the Shipstern Nature Reserve, 3 mi. south of Sarteneja Village. In the village, there are a few very small **grocery stores;** it is probably a better idea to stock up in Orange Walk, particularly with mosquito repellent. A pay phone is next to the basketball court in the center of town. The **police station** is on North Front Street.

▐ ACCOMMODATIONS. If you are planning on hiking the trails at Shipstern Nature Reserve, ask at the **Visitors Center ❶** for dorm rooms (BZ$20 per bed). Ranger Damien will sometimes rent out a cabin next to the Visitors Center (BZ$80). There is no phone number, and reservations can be problematic. Contact the Belize Audobon Society for more information. (☎ 223 5004; www.belizeaudobon.org.) In Sarteneja Village itself, there are several spots with *cabañas* or rooms: **Fernando's Guesthouse ❹**, on North Front St., has four spacious double rooms. Each has two queen size beds, private bath, hot water, and fan. There is also a common room with cable TV and a porch overlooking the bay. Also a native fisherman, Fernando's fresh seafood is easily the best in town. Reserve ahead. (☎423 2085. Singles BZ$50; doubles BZ$60.) If Fernando's has no vacancies, consider **Krisami's ❺**. All rooms have cable TV, A/C, private baths. (☎423 2283. BZ$82.)

▐▐ FOOD AND ENTERTAINMENT. There are limited dining options in Sarteneja. This is a bit surprising, since Sarteneja fishers deliver lobster all over Belize! The only other option is **Lily's ❷**, a two-story house a block past the bars. Lily's menu is three words long: rice, beans, chicken (BZ$8). Be sure to follow the restaurant rules written on the wall in red lipstick: eat with shirt on, do not spit on the floor, and pay for your food. **Fernando's Guest House Restaurant ❸** is set to open by October 2002 (he currently only serves guests). His seafood is incredible.

Sarteneja also offers two bars with the same menu—Belikin beer (a local favorite), a game of pool, rum, and loud music. **Noa Noa Bar** is a block north of Richies on North Front St. (Open daily 8am-11pm.) **Mira Mira Bar,** which draws a younger crowd, is around the corner on Coracol St. (Open daily 8am-midnight.)

◪ ☢! SIGHTS AND ACTIVITIES. Established in 1981 for the conservation of hardwood forests, saline wetlands, and lagoon systems, the **Shipstern Reserve** is a birdwatcher's dream and a mosquito sufferer's nightmare. Its 22,000 acres support animals indigenous to the area and over 200 species of birds, many of which are endangered or threatened. The forest is beautiful but young—all but three of the larger trees were lost to Hurricane Janet when it struck the peninsula in 1955. Today, most are less than 20m tall and many are just saplings.

Your first stop should be the **visitors center** at the reserve entrance. Knowledgeable rangers take guests through a display of animal skulls, tracks, and droppings. They also show off a peaceful butterfly house. This, and a guided 1hr. walk along the painstakingly labeled Chiclero Botanical Trail, are included in the BZ$10 admission fee. If you can tolerate the mosquitoes, the staff will guide you along a number of longer and more interesting trails through the forest for BZ$5 per hr.

Between September and June, visitors can arrange a trip out to an island in the Shipstern Lagoon to see the rare **wood storks.** In the past, the birds' eggs and babies have fallen prey to villagers who consider them a delicacy. Now, a 24hr. staff protects these endangered birds. The trip to the island is BZ$30 for fuel, plus BZ$5 per hr. to hire a guide. For a bit more money, it's also possible for groups to hire a night or even an overnight boat tour. If crocodiles are your thing, ask to visit the 1000-acre Xo-Pol Parcel crocodile pond to see saltwater crocs as well.

Aside from the stunning sunsets over the bay, Sarteneja does not have much to see. If you're looking for more, contact **Fernando.** He runs excellent fishing trips, and trips to Bacalar Chico for snorkeling.(☎423 2085. See **Accommodations,** above. Fishing trips BZ$100 for up to 4 people. Snorkeling BZ$200 1-4 people.)

COROZAL

Touching the striking turquoise waters of the Chetumal Bay, just 8 mi. south of the Mexican border, Corozal (pop. 8000) is the northernmost town in Belize. A colorful **mural** by Belizean-Mexican painter Manuel Villamor in the town hall documents the history of this laid-back, enchanting town. Corozal is a great place to spend a few relaxing days or weeks. Stroll through the town square, swim or picnic in the park-lined waterfront, visit several minor Maya sites, and delight in some of Belize's best food. Hurricane Janet ripped through in 1955 and wreaked such destruction that the people of Corozal had to rebuild from scratch. The town's well-ordered streets, paved roads, and abundance of recreational parks are the result.

▐ TRANSPORTATION

Flights: Maya Island Air (☎422 2333) flies to **San Pedro** on Ambergris Caye (20min.; 7:30, 12:30, 5pm; one-way BZ$82); **Tropic Air** (☎422 0356) does the same run. It is best to make reservations with the airlines directly, as some agencies may charge a commission. The airstrip is a 5min. taxi ride south of town (BZ$5).

Buses: All buses leave from the **Northern Transport Terminal** at the intersection of 1st St. North and 7th Avenue, 2 blocks west of Central Park. Destinations include: **Belize City** (3hr.; every hr. 4am-noon, every 30min. noon-7:30pm; BZ$8); **Orange Walk** (1½hr., BZ$4); **Chetumal, Mexico** (1½hr.; every 30min. 7:15-10:15am, every hr. 10:15am-2:15pm, express 11:20am; BZ$2.50.)

Boats: Thunderboat departs from the pier next to Corozal Visitors Center for **San Pedro** (☎ 422 2904; crivero@btl.net) and can stop in **Sarteneja.** (20min., daily 3pm, BZ$35.)

Car Rental: Hotel Maya rents cars for around BZ$100 per day. Call Hokol Kin in advance and they will have a **Budget** car waiting for you.

◼︎ ▟ ORIENTATION AND PRACTICAL INFORMATION

Despite the grid system, navigation in banana-shaped Corozal can be confusing. Major landmarks include the **Central Park** and **plaza** (home of the **town hall**) next to the **Catholic church** in the center of town. The **ocean** runs along the eastern side of the city. The avenues run parallel to the shore and are numbered consecutively starting at the bay. Streets run perpendicular to the bay and are numbered in two groups from the park. **First Street North** skirts the northern side of Central Park, and **First Street South** skirts the southern side. For quick orientation, remember that **Corozal Bay** is at the eastern edge and runs roughly north-south.

Tourist Information: The new **Corozal Cultural and Visitor Center,** 2nd South St. (☎ 422 3176; website www.corozal.com), houses a small **museum** that details Corozal's history. Head east to the sea from Central Park and turn right. It's the building with the bright orange roof. Open Tu-Sa 9am-noon and 1-4:30. Tourist info is hard to come by in Corozal, and the website is worthwhile. Museum BZ$3 for special exhibits.

Banks: Atlantic Bank, 1 block west of the south side of the central park, offers cash advances on M/VC for a fee (BZ$6) and cashes traveler's checks. However, US dollars are the preferred currency. Open M-F 8am-2pm.

Market: U-Save, 4th Ave., 2nd St. South. Two blocks south of Central Park. Open M-Th 7:30am-8pm, F 7:30am-9pm, Sa 7:30am-9:30pm, Su 7:30am-12:30pm.

Police: (☎ 422 3416 or 90) on the west side of the central park behind the post office. Open 24hr.

Pharmacy: J.R.'s Pharmacy, 1st St. (☎ 422 2982), just north of the park. Open daily 8am-10pm. Call for 24hr. service.

Hospital: (☎ 422 2076), located past the bus terminal about 200m up the Northern Hwy., on the left. Open 24hr.

Telephone: BTL, 6th Ave (☎ 422 2196), between 2nd and 3rd St. South. They also have mail service. Open M-F 8am-noon and 1-5pm, Sa 8am-noon. Public payphones scattered on the street running along the park.

Internet: ME Computer Systems, on 3rd. St. south, 3 blocks from the water. BZ$3 per 30min. Open 9am-8pm.

Post Office: On the west side of Central Park, across from the taxi stand. Open M-Th 8:30am-noon and 1-4:30pm, F 8:30am-noon and 1-4pm.

▛ ACCOMMODATIONS

Few tourists come to this area. There is currently a dearth of true budget options, as several have gone out of business or, in the case of one, burned down. However, those with a higher pricetag are worth the extra money.

Marvirton Guest House & Lounge, 16, 2nd St. North (☎ 422 3365). Budget option with basic rooms, clean bathrooms, and dry fountain area. Singles BZ$30; doubles BZ$45, with private bath and TV BZ$58. ❷

Hotel Maya (☎ 422 2082), in southern Corozal, on the shore road 1 Ave. A comfortable abode offering the friendliest service in town. Tiled, well-kept hot-water private baths have cute bars of soap. Restaurant serves breakfast; order lunch or dinner in advance.

Laundry service available. Bike rental BZ$15 per day. Singles with fan BZ$50, with TV BZ$60, with A/C BZ$85; doubles BZ$62/BZ$75/BZ$99. AmEx/MC/V. ➍

Hokol Kin, 4th Ave. South (☎ 422 3329), 4 blocks south of the park on the water. This oceanfront treasure is the perfect choice for larger groups. Spacious, bright rooms with fans and 2 ultra-comfortable queen-size beds accommodate up to 4. Modern bathrooms have hot water and the lounge has cable TV and refrigerator. Many rooms have a sliding door to a balcony complete with a hammock and a stunning view of the bay. Singles BZ$64; doubles BZ$85; each additional person BZ$10. ➎

Tony's Inn and Beach Resort (☎ 422 2055; www.tonysinn.com), Corozal's nicest hotel, set on beautiful waterfront 1 mi. south of the town center (taxi BZ$5). Offers large spacious rooms surrounding a lawn, just off the beach. Relax on Tony's sandy private beach and try the restaurant's excellent seafood in an exquisite dining area. Standard rooms have fan and private bath. Singles BZ$70, with A/C and TV BZ$100; doubles BZ$90/BZ$120. Room prices increase about 10% in high season. ➎

■ FOOD

Corozal has some of the tastiest, cheapest restaurants in all of Belize.

▨ Le Café Kéla, 3 blocks north of the Visitors Center across the street from the coast. Hidden amidst lush gardens in a thatched *cabaña*, and even harder to find open. Specializing in Caribbean cuisine with a French twist, this restaurant is recommended by locals for a reason: it's unique, daring, and delicious. Crepes BZ$4; pastas BZ$6. Fantastic ocean view. Open W-F 11:30am-2pm and 5:30-9pm, Sa 5pm-10pm. ➋

▨ Jo-Mel-Inn, on 5th St., 1 block south of the west end of the park. Named after the manager's three children, this local standby is all you'll need. The blackboard outside details the special of the day. It's a bargain: BZ$6-8 for a full meal and huge goblets of fresh fruit juice for BZ$2. Open M-F 6:30am-5pm, Sa 6:30am-2:30pm. ➋

Cactus Plaza, on 6th St. South, 2 blocks from waterfront, is the best deli in town. Mexican-style eatery allows you to eat takeout, inside, outside, or on the roof. Serves hot and cold sandwiches (BZ$2-3) and great milkshakes (BZ$2). Hidden inside is one of the nicest discos around. Open 8am-midnight. ➊

Hailey's, 2 blocks south of Hotel Maya on the waterfront. For those who like their waterfront dining cheap, fast, and rugged. Enjoy the brisk ocean breeze and occasional wave splash while munching on sandwiches (BZ$3-5) or fish and chips (BZ$6). Open daily 10am-10pm, later on weekends. ➊

Tony's Inn Y-Not Bar & Grill, the most romantic and luxurious setting in town, also serves excellent food. Located in a well-decorated breezy *cabaña* on the southern beachfront with piers leading into the ocean. Sizzling chicken fajitas (BZ$13); burgers (BZ$8); Caribbean lobster (BZ$22). For breakfast, retreat indoors to the immaculate Vista Del Sol Restaurant. Breakfast 7-11am, lunch and dinner 11am-7pm. ➌

◉ SIGHTS

SANTA RITA. The "Ancient Corozal," inhabited from 900 BC-AD 1550, is a 20min. walk from Central Park. Take Rita Rd. (Northern Hwy.) north towards Chetumal, past the bus station. As the road splits in two, stay to the right, and proceed uphill. After about 100m, make the first left. Keep going until you see the ruins on your right. Archaeologists suspect that Santa Rita may have been the once powerful Maya city of Chactemal; however, most of the ruins were demolished in building Corozal. A small pyramid is the only worthwhile remaining structure. Mr. Wiltshire, the caretaker, sometimes gives tours. Entrance fee BZ$5.

CERROS MAYA. This more spectacular ruin is more difficult to reach. Built around 50 BC as a trading center, this 8 sq. km site is featured on many a postcard. To get there, travelers need to hire a boat to cross a lagoon. All hotels offer day trips. Call ahead to secure arrangements; these trips run sporadically. Many fishers at the market are also willing to take tourists to this sight for a negotiable fee.

NIGHTLIFE

Corozal has abundant late-night options, ranging from relaxing in beach bars to grinding in two very unique discos. **Butchie's Bar and Grill,** on 1st Ave., a block north of Hotel Maya overlooking the bay, is a great place to unwind and mingle or play pool with locals under the moonlight. (Open daily 11am-9pm, later on weekends.) **The Cactus Plaza** (see **Food,** above) hides one of the best discos in Belize. Get your freak on the dance floor with beautiful neon-lit Mexican paintings on the wall. Open weekends until 3am. Has karaoke, DJs, and occasional live music. **The Purple Toucan,** on 3rd St. North, one block from the coast, is the kind of place you immediately love or hate. Yes, it is bright purple with a splash of neon yellow, and the small enclosed dance floor is not for claustrophobics. Also offers food, pool tables, and lottery games. Open daily; disco open F-Sa nights until 2am.

CAYO DISTRICT

The Western Highway bisects Belize horizontally, cutting across the Cayo District and offering an avenue to rugged jungle adventure for those who have tired of the sandy beaches of the cayes. Far from the sea and the grassy savannas of northern Belize, and nestled within the lush greenery of the Maya Mountains, this area is Belize's only highland region. Along the Western Highway, Monkey Bay Wildlife Sanctuary and Guanacaste National Park tease travelers with hints of the tropical forests to come. From Mennonite farmland to the Maya village of San José Sucotz, this may be Belize's most culturally diverse district. Cayo is a mecca for outdoor adventure tourists. San Ignacio, the main town in Cayo District, makes a good base from which to explore the ruins, caves, and rivers of the region. Highlights include the Mountain Pine Ridge Reserve, with caves, waterfalls, and refreshingly cool temperatures, and Caracol, the largest Maya site in Belize.

IN RECENT NEWS

THIS LAND IS MY LAND

The Belize-Guatemala border dispute has dominated Belizean politics for the past century and is currently threatening to erupt again. The Guatemalan claim to Belizean land is not without merit, and dates back to the 1859 Anglo-Guatemalan Treaty that defined the borders of the countries as they are known today. Article 7 of this treaty states that both parties must establish a means of transport between the Guatemalan capital to the Caribbean coast by a combination of river and road. While the issue rested peacefully for over 80 years, the connecting road was never built, and in 1940, Guatemala declared that the treaty was actually a land cession, in which they ceded Belize in return for the building of the road. Thus, as the road was never built, the treaty was nullified, and Belize land should be returned to Guatemala.

The dispute has haunted both countries and international peace-keeping organizations since. Belize refuses to cede land, stating that the treaty must compromise in other ways. In recent years, both sides have begun professional negotiations.

In the summer of 2002, Great Britain offered each country US$200 million in developmental grants on the condition that Guatemala recognizes the full sovereignty of Belize, while Belize must extend access and fishing rights to Guatemala in Southern Belize's maritime areas. As of August 2002, the treaty had been favorably received by the Belizean government. Guatemala has yet to accept.

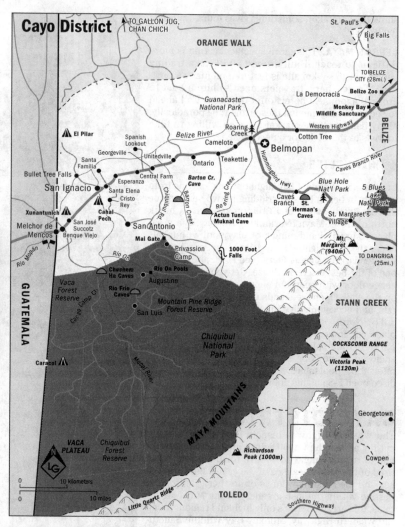

FROM BELIZE CITY TO SAN IGNACIO

🔲 THE BELIZE ZOO

*To get to the zoo, take any non-express **bus** running to the Western border. On the way back, walk to the highway and flag down a bus going in the direction you want. ☎820 2004. Open daily 8:30am-5pm. Night **tours** BZ$20 per person, 5 person min.; day tours BZ$25 per person, offered with 2 weeks notice. BZ$15, children BZ$7.50.*

American naturalist Sharon Motola opened the Belize Zoo in 1983 after the filming of the documentary *Path of the Raingods* left seven semi-tame animals in the country. Thirty miles west of Belize City on the Western Highway, the zoo has expanded to house 35 species native to Belize and more than 100 animals total, including the jaguar, the beautiful toucan, the macaw, and the tapir.

The zoo underwent massive renovation in 1991, is immaculately kept, and still refuses to capture animals from the wild. The critters arrive after injury and stay until they can be successfully released. The zoo is acclaimed for teaching the importance of wildlife conservation to Belizeans, and provides the only opportunity for many of them to see their nation's prized wildlife. The zoo is also a popular tourist spot, as many of its animals are almost impossible to spot in the wild. Check out the overpriced gift shop where the underfunded park ekes out its revenue. Traveler's checks and Visa are accepted.

🐵 MONKEY BAY WILDLIFE SANCTUARY

*Any **bus** running to the Western Border can drop you off. The research headquarters are about 100m down the gravel road. On the way back, flag down a bus on the highway. Research Station ☎820 3032. Dorms ❶ BZ$15; camping BZ$10.*

The Monkey Bay sanctuary has become a haven for those wishing to study Belize's environment. The area is rich in biodiversity, encompassing acres of tropical forest and the Sibun River, and is used mainly by students and professors conducting field research. Do not let the name deceive you; there are currently no monkeys at Monkey Bay. However, birds and mammals are abundant, and unlike many of Belize's reserves, this one is easily accessible. The **research station,** located a mile west of the Belize Zoo, was founded by a Dutch-American conservationist couple. Currently the sanctuary is under the supervision of Matthew Miller, who offers a welcoming place, meals, dorm beds (try to get one with a mosquito net), camping, and advice on visiting the sanctuary. A 30min. walk along the road to the river is a good introduction to the local flora and fauna; canoe rentals are available.

Two restaurants with outdoor terraces are near Monkey Bay along the highway. Everybody knows your name at **Cheers,** a quarter mile to the east. **JB's Watering Hole ❸** (☎820 2071) is just west, plastered with mildly amusing bumper stickers and signs. (Meals BZ$10-15.) JB's ❹ also offers *cabañas* with hot water, fans, and stunning views of the forest below. (Singles BZ$50; doubles BZ$70. MC/V.

🏞 GUANACASTE NATIONAL PARK

*For info on the park, call the Belize Audobon Society (☎223 4987). Get on a Belmopan-bound **bus** from anywhere in Belize and ask to be let off at the park. Park open M-F 8am-4:30pm. Admission BZ$5.*

At the junction of the Western and Hummingbird Highways, Guanacaste is ideally situated to break up a long bus ride or kill an afternoon around Belmopan. Founded in 1990, the 50-acre park of secondary growth forest is named after the fast-growing Guanacaste tree, one of the largest trees in Central America. The park consists of two small hiking trails. The shorter leads to the park's main attraction, a giant Guanacaste tree (about 15 min.). Used in making dugout canoes, most have long since fallen victim to loggers. Afterwards, take a dip in the two waterways that traverse the park, the cold Roaring Creek and the warm Belize River.

BELMOPAN

Situated halfway between Belize City and San Ignacio, Belmopan (pop. 8000) is politically and geographically the center of Belize. However, the city is definitely not the center of Belizean social life or any significant tourist attractions. After Hurricane Hattie destroyed much of Belize City in 1961, Belmopan was constructed as a new, more disaster-proof capital. Far too small to support any significant cultural events or nightlife, it seems to be waiting for an influx of Belizeans that has yet to come. For most travelers, Belmopan merely serves as the transfer station for those heading west to San Ignacio or south along the Hummingbird Highway toward Dangriga. Some visitors may appreciate the opportunity to quickly view Belize's Independence Plaza, which consists of the National Assembly, the Foreign Ministry, and the stately Prime Minister's Office, among others.

▐ TRANSPORTATION. Buses leave from the **Novelo's Bus Terminal** (see **Orientation,** below) to **Belize City** (1½hr., every 30min. 5am-7pm, BZ$3.50) and **Benque Viejo** (1¼hr., every 30min. 6am-10pm, BZ$2.50). Buses to **Dangriga** (1½hr., every hr. 8:30am-5:30pm, BZ$6) follow the Hummingbird Hwy.

▟ ❼ ORIENTATION AND PRACTICAL INFORMATION. The Western and Hummingbird Highway junction, just west of town, is linked to Belmopan by **Constitution Drive,** which also forms the western portion of **Ring Rd.,** making a loop around the entire town. **Independence Plaza,** the heart of the national government, is the center of the town. A pedestrian **walkway** cuts east to west through Independence Plaza and is a shortcut to nearly all places worth visiting. All buses stop at the **Novelo's** bus terminal, on **Constitution Dr.** For quick orientation, remember that the **Novelo's Bus Terminal** is west and directly east from the terminal is the **marketplace.**
The **British** and **Mexican Embassies** are next to each other at the west end of North Ring Rd. The **immigration office** can be found south of the marketplace on Ring Rd. (☎822 2423. Open M-F 8am-4pm.) North of the market, next to the walkway, in the pink building, **Barclay's Bank** exchanges cash, provides cash advances on MasterCard, Visa, and Discover, and offers one of the three **ATMs** in the country that accepts foreign cards without a fee. (Open M-Th 8am-2:30pm, F 8am-4:30pm., 24hr. ATM for Visa) The **Angelus Press** on Constitution Dr., just north of the bus terminal, offers a **Western Union,** and its bookstore offers an excellent selection of Belizean titles (M-F 7am-5pm). Look for the **hospital** at the northernmost extension of Constitution Dr., with the office around back. (Emergency ☎822 2623. Open M-F 8am-5pm.) The **police** are located northeast of the market in Independence Plaza. (☎822 2220, emergencies 90. Open 24hr.) **Internet** at **The Techno Hub** in Novelo's bus terminal. (BZ$7 per 30min., BZ$12 per hr. Open 8am-6pm.) **Telephone** and **fax** available at **BTL,** southeast of the market on Ring Rd. (☎822 2193. Open M-F 8am-noon and 1-5pm.) The **post office** lies between the bus area and the police station. (Open M-Th 8am-4:30pm, F 8am-4pm.)

▟ ACCOMMODATIONS. Due to the lack of tourist demand and inadequate competition, Belmopan's hotels are generally pricey and mediocre. **El Rey ❸,** 23 Moho, is Belmopan's only budget option, a 10min. hike (taxi BZ$5) from the market. Walk north past Caladium Restaurant and turn right onto Ring Road, then left at the sign for El Rey. Take the second right onto Moho, and you're there. Rooms have ceiling fans and private bath. (☎822 3438. Check-out 11am. Singles BZ$39; doubles BZ$49.) Belmopan sports two nicer options with significantly higher price tags. **The Bullfrog Inn ❺** is a 10 minute walk from the market; walk north to North Ring Rd. and follow it to the east. The Inn is right around the bend on East Ring Rd. Spacious rooms with A/C, private bath, cable TV and one of the nicer restaurants. (☎822 2111. Singles BZ$90, larger singles BZ$120; doubles BZ$120/BZ$150.) The oldest and most convenient option is the **Belmopan Hotel ❺,** across the street from Novelo's bus terminal. It has nice rooms with A/C, private bath, cable TV, cabana bar and pool. (☎822 2130. Singles BZ$88; doubles BZ$100-BZ$125.)

◖◗ ◪ FOOD AND ENTERTAINMENT. Burritos, tamales (BZ$3), and fresh fruit (BZ$1 per bag) are sold throughout the **market,** and several restaurants and stands cluster near the bus stop. A local favorite is speedy **Caladium ❶**, north of Novelo's. (French toast BZ$3.50, rice and beans with chicken BZ$6.75. Open M-F 7:15am-8pm, Sa 7:15am-7pm.) **Wade's Place ❸**, at the east end of North Ring Rd., next to the 99¢ supermarket, has an all-you-can-eat buffet. (Belizean flavored buffet begins at 11:30am, BZ$11. Open daily 8:30am-6pm.)

Many gather for drinks at the **Bullfrog Inn's** bar before heading out for karaoke and dancing at the **Roundabout,** close to the junction just outside of Belmopan (taxi BZ$6). Thursday night is the best time to party in Belmopan. The city comes alive when hosting popular live bands like *Griga Boyz* and *Punta Rebels.*

SAN IGNACIO

Known to many Belizeans as "Cayo," San Ignacio (pop. 8000) is the pot of gold at the end of the rainbow for the rucksack wanderer. Conveniently situated on the bank of the Macal River, 10 mi. from the Guatemalan border, the town is the starting point for many outdoor adventures and offers so much even the most overzealous traveler leaves wishing for another week. Canoe down the Macal, hike through a medicine trail, and visit the Maya ruins of Xunantunich. Guides lead expeditions to the Mountain Pine Ridge forest to view Five Sisters Falls and swim below the 1000 ft. cascade. The dense jungle to the south holds countless adventures and hidden lodges for those who like to rough it with A/C and swimming pools.

▐ TRANSPORTATION

Buses: All buses and *colectivos* depart from the **Savannah Plaza,** next to the market. Almost anything along the Western Hwy. is easily accessible by bus from San Ignacio. Destinations include: **Belize City,** with stops along the Western Hwy. (2½hr., every 30min. 4am-5pm, BZ$5), via **Belmopan** (45min., BZ$2); **Benque Viejo** (20min., every 30min. 3-11pm, BZ$1-1.50; or grab a bus to Melchor and ask to be let off at Benque); **Dangriga** (take a Belize City Bus and change at Belmopan. From Belmopan to Dangriga 2hr. 8:30am-5:30pm, BZ$6); **Melchor de Mencos** (25min., about every 30min. 7:30am-2:15pm, BZ$1.50).

Airport Shuttle: Eva's (See **Food,** below) sometimes offers shuttle service to Belize City. (10am, BZ$50 per person.) The **Watering Hole** (☎ 09 236 09) may offer cheaper rates; see if Bill or Lenny is in.

Taxis and Colectivos: Taxis travel to: **Melchor** (BZ$30); **San Antonio** (BZ$50); **Bullet Tree** (BZ$15); and **Cahal Pech** (BZ$5). *Colectivos* are cheaper.

⚹ ▐ ORIENTATION AND PRACTICAL INFORMATION

Seventy-three miles west of Belize City and a smooth 20min. east of the Guatemalan border, San Ignacio is joined to its unremarkable sister city to the east, **Santa Elena,** by the **Hawkesworth Bridge**—Belize's only suspension bridge. Built in 1949, the single-lane bridge spans the **Macal River** and boasts one of the five traffic lights in all of Belize. The Hawkesworth Bridge is one-way, heading out of town. All buses and cars entering town from the northeast arrive over a small wooden bridge. Taking a left after the bridge, you'll pass **Novelo's bus terminal** on the right and hit the heart of town. This five-way intersection is dangerous—there are no stop signs. **Burn's Avenue,** San Ignacio's main commercial strip, heads north. Be careful when driving; this place made up entirely of one-way streets. The intersection of Burn's Ave. and **Waight's Avenue** is the town's center.

Tourist Information: The legendary **Bob** of Eva's Restaurant (see **Food,** below) has served for years as San Ignacio's official unofficial source of tourist information. Ask here for anything from hiring guides to renting canoes. Open Su-Th 6:30am-11pm, F-Sa 6:30am-midnight. (See also **Guided Tours,** below.)

Banks: All establishments accept US dollars. **Atlantic Bank,** 1 block south of Eva's on Burns Ave., offers **cash advances** on MC/V. (Fee BZ$5.) Open M-F 8am-2pm, Sa 8:30am-noon. **Belize Bank,** 16 Burns Ave., stays open later, but cash advances on MC/V cost BZ$10. The closest **ATM** accepting international cards is in Belmopan.

Laundry: Martha's Laundry, 10 West St., on the other side of Martha's Kitchen (see **Food,** below). Open M-Sa 8am-6pm, Su 9am-2pm. **Mike's Laundry,** across from Venus Hotel, offers self service and drop off. Open M-Sa 8am-8pm, Su 9am-5pm.

Police: (☎824 2047, emergency 90 or 824 2047), just west of the bridge at the town park. Open 24hr.

Hospital: (☎824 2087, emergency 824 2066). **La Loma Luz Hospital,** on Waight's Ave. out of town. Open M-F 8am-noon and 1-4pm.

Pharmacy: (☎824 2510), 24 West St. Open M-Sa 8am-noon, 1-5pm, and 7-9pm, Su 9am-noon.

Internet: Cayo Community Computer Center, on Hudson St., has the best rate in town. BZ$0.10 per min., in 30min. increments. Open M-Sa 8am-9pm.

Telephones: BTL (☎824 2052). Open M-F 8am-noon and 1-5pm. **Public phones** located at the corner of Eve. St. and Church St., in front of Venus Hotel, and at the park across from Hawkesworth Br.

Post Office: Open M-Th 8am-noon and 1-4:30pm, F 8am-noon and 1-4pm.

⛏ ACCOMMODATIONS

San Ignacio boasts a high concentration of cheap, clean, backpacker-savvy hotels, and the jungle around San Ignacio hides retreats and lodges ranging from back-to-basics affairs to full-blown resorts. Make sure to reserve during the high season.

Hi-Et (☎824 2828), up Waight's Ave. across from Martha's, is not to be confused with the Hyatt. A perennial favorite with the backpacker crowd, it's the best budget hotel in San Ignacio. Four cubicle-sized rooms have private balconies and share hot-water bathrooms. Relax downstairs on the veranda or in the living room with cable TV. Singles BZ$20; doubles BZ$25. ❶

Pacz Hotel (☎824 4538; paczghouse@blt.net), on Far West St. Run by laid-back Diana, the Pacz features a nice lounge with cable TV, a book exchange, and 5 large, comfortable rooms with 2 clean bathrooms. The restaurant downstairs, Erva's, is excellent. Singles BZ$27; doubles BZ$38; triples BZ$43. ❷

Martha's (☎824 3647; www.marthasbelize.com), above Martha's restaurant and laundromat, up Waight's Ave. This guest house is truly your home away from home and most visitors feel like family with the gracious Martha as host. The guesthouse creates a special ambiance one only expects from luxury hotels— three floors of elegantly decorated hallways, high wooden ceilings, balconies, artwork, and intimate lighting. Singles BZ$48; doubles BZ$52; 4-person penthouse suite BZ$100. MC/V. ❹

Casa Blanca (☎824 2080), 10 Burns Ave., a few blocks south of the Bank of Belize. Humphrey Bogart and Ingrid Bergman would be delighted to continue their passionate romance in this newly opened guesthouse. The best value of San Ignacio's mid-range options features pristine bedrooms with private bathroom and cable TV. The elegant upstairs common room has a kitchen and beautiful mahogany tables. Join fellow visitors on the overhanging balcony or on the roof. Singles BZ$37; doubles BZ$48. ❸

Mida's Eco-Resort (☎824 3172). Walk to the graveyard at the end of Burns Ave, make a right and then a left (15min. walk from the bus stop). Concrete, thatched-roof *cabañas* with private baths set in a sparsely vegetated backyard with hammocks. Fans

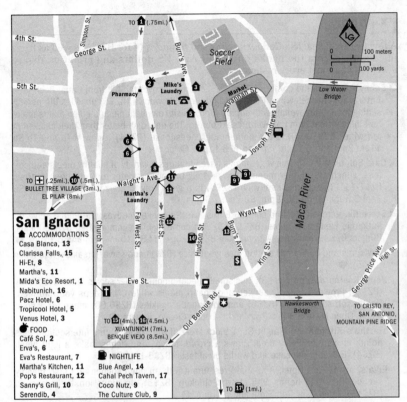

San Ignacio

⌂ ACCOMMODATIONS
Casa Blanca, **13**
Clarissa Falls, **15**
Hi-Et, **8**
Martha's, **11**
Mida's Eco Resort, **1**
Nabitunich, **16**
Pacz Hotel, **6**
Tropicool Hotel, **5**
Venus Hotel, **3**

🍴 FOOD
Café Sol, **2**
Erva's, **6**
Eva's Restaurant, **7**
Martha's Kitchen, **11**
Pop's Restaurant, **12**
Sanny's Grill, **10**
Serendib, **4**

🎵 NIGHTLIFE
Blue Angel, **14**
Cahal Pech Tavern, **17**
Coco Nutz, **9**
The Culture Club, **9**

Map labels: 4th St., George St., Simpson St., 5th St., TO ⬛1 (.75mi.), Burn's Ave., Soccer Field, Market, Savannah St., Low Water Bridge, Pharmacy, Mike's Laundry, BTL, Joseph Andrews Dr., Macal River, TO ✚ (.25mi.), ⬛10 (.5mi.), BULLET TREE VILLAGE (3mi.), EL PILAR (8mi.), Waight's Ave., Martha's Laundry, Church St., Far West St., West St., Wyatt St., Hudson St., Burn's Ave., King St., George Price Ave., High St., Eve St., TO ⬛15 (4mi.), ⬛16 (4.5mi.), XUANTUNICH (7mi.), BENQUE VIEJO (8.5mi.), Old Benque Rd., Hawkesworth Bridge, TO CRISTO REY, SAN ANTONIO, MOUNTAIN PINE RIDGE, TO ⬛17 (1mi.)

BELIZE

and mosquito netting keep you cool and bug-free. A convenient respite from the hub-bub of downtown, it also has nice **camping** facilities with toilet and shower for BZ$8.60 per person. Singles BZ$54; doubles BZ$70. Discounts in low season. ❹

Tropicool Hotel (☎824 3052), on Burns Ave., features a mini jungle-garden, low prices, and hot water in the shared bathrooms. Cheap bike rentals. Singles BZ$20; doubles BZ$25-30; cabins BZ$50. ❶

Venus Hotel (☎824 3203), on Burns Ave. just north of the Tropicool, is a place to check if everywhere else is full. The largest place around with nice open-air hallways and large balconies. Singles BZ $30, with private bath BZ$45; doubles BZ$34/BZ$53. ❷

Clarissa Falls (☎824 3916; clarifalls@btl.net), 1 mi. off the Western Hwy., 4 mi. west of San Ignacio. Easily accessible by bus. Call in advance for free pick-up from the highway. Set amidst a gorgeous cattle ranch along the banks of the scenic Mopan River. Book exchange. Horseback tours (BZ$75 for 3 hrs.). Canoes (BZ$30 per person), water tubes (BZ$20 per person). Open-air bunkhouse dorm beds BZ$15 per person. Camping and trailers BZ$15; rooms with private bath BZ$85-130, some with kitchen. ❹

Nabitunich (☎501 93 2096; www.nabitunich.com), 1 mi. off the Western Hwy., 5 mi. west of San Ignacio, just past turnoff for Clarissa Falls. Meaning "little stone cottages" in Maya, Nabitunich has basic rooms set in a beautiful 400 acre ranch complete with tours, trails, rivers, and wildlife. Camping BZ$10 per person. Rooms with private bath BZ$40 for adults, half price for students with ID. Meals half-off with ID. ❶

▶ FOOD

A few fast food shacks offer *gornachos* and *panades* (4 for BZ$1) as well as fresh juice across from the banks on Burn's Ave. US dollars and credit cards are accepted at almost every restaurant.

Sanny's Grill, on the corner of 23rd St. A short walk over the hill from Cahal Pech (see **Entertainment,** below) or a quick taxi ride from downtown (BZ$5) provides the perfect setting for a quiet evening with superb food. Music, dim lighting, and green plants make for a nice retreat from the ever-present burrito. The only dish better than their chicken in red wine (BZ$10.50) is the homemade cheesecake (BZ$4). Open M-Tu and Th-Sa 11am-2pm and 6-11pm. Su and W 6-11pm. ❶

Café Sol, on West St. This vegetarian's haven features a variety of healthy meals and coffees. Lunch and dinner menus change daily but always cater to herbivores (entrees BZ$7-11). The sunrise sandwich (BZ$5) is a great way to start the day. Open Tu-Sa 7am-2:30pm and 6:30-9pm, Su 7am-2:30pm. ❷

Serendib, across from Tropicool on Burns Ave. Sri Lankan natives, the Pieris, serve up authentic Eastern favorites (BZ$10-16) that come highly recommended by the locals. Burgers BZ$3, yellow rice with chicken BZ$10. Open M-Sa 10am-3pm and 6-11pm. ❷

Lucy's, a stand by the bus station, has great juice (BZ$1) and serves breakfast and lunch (BZ$5). ❶

Pop's Restaurant, on West St. This small, air-conditioned diner serves breakfast all day (BZ$8). Provides friendly service and cheap meals while CNN keeps you informed. Hearty sub sandwiches (BZ$6) and homemade cookies (BZ$0.50) make for a great lunch. Open M-Sa 6:30am-2pm and 6-10pm. Closed W night. ❷

Martha's Kitchen, on Waight St. 1 block west of the Waight-Burns intersection, gets points for variety. Every meal draws a crowd. Maya sandwiches make a light lunch (BZ$4). Excellent pancake and waffle breakfasts (BZ$5-12). ❷

Erva's, under Pacz Hotel. A spotless restaurant with an open kitchen and fast, friendly service. Rice and beans with stewed chicken (BZ$5); delicious lobster in season (BZ$15). Open daily 8am-3pm and 6-10pm. ❷

Eva's Restaurant, 22 Burns Ave. The food is not the cheapest nor the best, but Eva's is the pulse of tourist life in San Ignacio—come for the lowdown on the local tour scene and meet local guides and archaeologists. While investigating, try the behemoth chicken burrito (BZ$7.50) and the bigger than behemoth banana milk shake (BZ$3). Veggie options. Open Su-Th 7am-11pm, F-Sa 7am-midnight. Internet access. ❷

♫ ENTERTAINMENT

After exploring Cayo's pristine forests and natural wonders, most tourists grab a beer with their guide before hitting the showers. A group usually gathers at **Eva's** and **Martha's** after dinner to chug some Belikins before heading over to their preferred hot spot. Recently, the **Cahal Pech Tavern,** perched on the hill and hoppin' with frequent live bands, has grown in popularity. The **Blue Angel** on Hudson St. offers loud music and good times for the hard-core partier. Cover charge on weekends for live bands varies (about BZ$10-15), but it's always more for men than women. (Open Tu-Th, Su 8pm-midnight, F-Sa 8pm-3am.) Locals warn against walking back to San Ignacio from Santa Elena after dark, so take a taxi. **Coco Nutz** and **The Culture Club** are the premier hot spots downtown, located directly across from the bus station—if you get lost just follow the music. Upstairs **The Culture Club** offers a fun dance environment with live reggae. For less aerobic workout and more chilling out, **Coco Nutz** offers pool tables and a sitting area to enjoy your drink and good company (Th-Su). Another popular spot (especially on Friday) is happy hour at the **San Ignacio Hotel** (6-8pm).

GUIDED TOURS FROM SAN IGNACIO

Before beginning the quest for the perfect adventure with the best guide, a quick *caveat emptor* must be issued. In San Ignacio, anyone and everyone sells tours to any destination a naive tourist is willing to go to. There are several trips that require a guide (Actun Muknal Cave, Chechem Ha Cave, Barton Creek Cave, and Caracol). There are also several sites easily accessible by public transportation (Xunantanich, Cahal Pech, and the Macal and Mopan Rivers). Be wary of advice, as competition runs high in the San Ignacio tour industry, especially between local guides and foreign operators. The best and cheapest way to ensure a great trip is to go directly to reputable guides. Apart from the stellar *Let's Go* picks, head to **Dave "The Scotsman"** for info and guided tours. Also try **Bob** at **Eva's,** who organizes competitively priced trips to popular sites on a commission free basis. Eva's is also a great place for the solo traveler to join up with others for better deals.

OTHER ACTIVITIES AROUND SAN IGNACIO

Besides caves, waterfalls, and Maya sites, there are other exciting activities in Cayo. **Mountain biking** is quite popular; rent from the Tropicool Hotel in San Ignacio or Trek Stop (BZ$6 per hr., BZ$20 per day) on the Western Hwy. There are some excellent trips, but avoid attempting the long trip into the Mtn. Pine Ridge from San Ignacio. There are some great areas for **horseback riding.** Charlie Collins of EasyRider charges BZ$80 for a half-day (☎ 824 3743; easyrider@btl.net). Other options include saddling up at Clarissa Falls (BZ$75 per 3 hr. with guide) or Nabitunich (BZ$10 per hr.). Cayo is a mecca for **bird watching.** Excellent birding is offered on the beautiful grounds of Nabitunich (guided for BZ$10 per hr.), duPlooy's (free guide 6:30-7:30am), and Crystal Paradise.

NEAR SAN IGNACIO

From pine forests to caves, Maya ruins to medicinal trails, there's enough outdoor splendor around San Ignacio to fill an entire vacation. Many of these attractions are best visited by guided tour, easily arranged from San Ignacio.

THE HIDDEN DEAL

DUPLOOY'S

It takes planning to fit this jungle resort into one's budget, but a night in paradise at duPlooy's Pink House is certainly worth it. Take the bus from San Ignacio 3 miles west to the sign on the Western Hwy. for Belize Botanic Gardens and Chaa Creek. A BBG shuttle picks up passengers from the Western Hwy. and makes the ardous 4 mile trek to duPlooy's (9:30, 11:30am, 1:30 pm; return to Hwy. 9, 11am, 1pm; BZ$5). Arrange in advance. A taxi from San Ignacio to duPlooy's is a steep BZ$100.

duPlooy's is the best "ecotourism" facility in the area, set amidst lush and well-kept gardens, forests, and streams. Located west of San Ignacio several miles of winding roads lead into true wilderness. The hotel offers excellent daily birdwatching with a free guide (6:30-7:30am). The Macal River runs through the property, with a developed white sand beach. Also on the grounds is the **Belize Botanic Garden** (BZ$5), created by Ken duPlooy and an excellent display of local and exotic flora, with an exhibit on Plants of the Maya and an orchid house. The Pink House is a nice 7 bedroom, 2-bathroom house with a spacious veranda, full kitchen, and a nice common room with books and a piano. Excellent meals, and a wide range of overpriced rentals and guided trips are also available. ☎ 824 3101; www.duplooys.com. Singles BZ$60, BZ$20 each additional person. Offers a full range of more luxurious rooms for up to BZ$600.

BELIZE

🏔 MACAL AND MOPAN RIVERS

Starting by the Hawkesworth bridge in town, canoers can paddle, while the languid drift in tubes down the mellow **Macal River** into peaceful jungle. Any place along the bank makes a refreshing swimming spot, and there are plenty of chances to see black vultures, iguanas, and even the deadly yellow-jaw snake. The best time to see animals is at night when they head to the river to drink. In the past, a popular place to paddle to was the Ix Chel Medicine Trail, but is now closed.

The **Mopan River** flows north-south, a few miles west of San Ignacio with its source in the mountains of Guatemala. The river is quite picturesque, with some beautiful jungle stretches and minor white-water rapids. Be careful with the Mopan, especially when the water is extremely low. The Mopan is easily accessible via the hotels along it, all of which offer reasonable rental rates for canoes, kayaks, and water tubes. These include Trek Stop, Nabitunich, and Clarissa Falls.

Back in San Ignacio, you can rent a canoe on your own—**Mayawalk** or **Eva's** both charge BZ$25—or arrange a guided paddle. For tubes check with Bob at Eva's in town. Guides are not necessary unless one desires the added security or extra eyes for wildlife. **Tony** of **Tony's River Tours** is recommended, who specializes in wildlife on the Macal and works through Eva's. (☎804 2267; evas@btl.net; BZ$25.)

👁 CAVES

The hills south of San Ignacio offer some fascinating spelunking. The most impressive cave in Belize is 🗿**Actun Tunichil Muknal Cave,** meaning "Cave of the Stone Sepulchre." Excavation, featured in *National Geographic* (Apr. 2000 and 2001), has just been completed and has allowed the artifacts to remain in their original locations. Trips involve hiking (45min.) through the jungle and rivers, wading through subterranean water, tiptoeing past ancient artifacts, and coming face to face with intact human skeletons. Only two companies are allowed into Muknal (full day tours BZ$130). Try for Renan of **Pacz Adventure Tours** as your guide; he has reached prominence in a feature article in the *New York Times* (☎824 2477 or 804 2267; pacztours@btl.net). The other option is **MayaWalk** (☎824 3070).

Barton Creek Cave, only navigable by tube or canoe, is the most visited due to its accessibility and lower price tag. The entrance to the cave is enclosed by rain forest. The cave has an astonishingly high ceiling—over 100ft. in places—intricate stalactite and stalagmite formations, and fascinating Maya artifacts. Try Michael Waight through Eva's (☎804 2267; BZ$60 per person), or Richard Zul (see below).

Also fascinating is more modest **Chechem Ha,** 7 mi. south of Benque Viejo, near the Guatemalan border. Discovered by members of the Morales family, this untouched cave has Maya pots and shards. (☎823 7013. 1-3 people BZ$50, includes 3½hr. guided cave tour.) You'll need a **taxi** to get there (15min., BZ$20).

🏔 MOUNTAIN PINE RIDGE RESERVE

The reserve is not accessible by public transportation. Follow Chiquibul Rd. out of town and turn right on Cristo Rey Rd. Stay to the left and watch for signs.

Mountain Pine Ridge, south of San Ignacio parallel to the Guatemalan border, is a 590 sq. km. reserve unique for its pine forest. It is graced by tall conifers, wide mountains, ancient caves, gorgeous signature waterfalls, clear streams, and exclusive jungles lodges. Much of the forest has died due to beetle infestation, you must stomach a depressing drive to see what remains of this forest. The road into the reserve passes the Maya village of **San Antonio**—here the García sisters have a famous workshop and museum where they sell carved slate. (Donation BZ$10.) The credit card machine seems a out of place in the "traditional Maya home" and the slate is overpriced. At the entrance to the reserve, the guard at **Mai Gate** offers information and checks vehicles. The turnoff for **Hidden Valley Falls** is about a 25min. drive past the reserve entrance. Ten miles off the main road, the **1000 Foot Falls** plummet over 1500 ft. and also offer a panoramic view as far as Belmopan. Once back on the main road, it is about 1 mi. to the scenic **Big Rock Falls,** a wonderful place for a massage under the firmly pressing water. Several miles further from the reserve, the main road crosses the **Río On Pools,** at a point where giant boulders form inviting swimming holes. Five miles beyond is the town of **Augustine,** with the only official **camping** in the park at the **Douglas D'Silva Forest Station.** A mile past Augustine is a series of caves surrounded by lush rainforest. The **Río Frío Cave** is actually a huge tunnel (65 ft. high) with impressive rock formations. Nearby is a small nature trail with *chicle* (gum) producing sapodilla trees. On the return to San Ignacio, stop by the Five Sisters Lodge for a postcard-perfect view of the **Five Sisters Falls.** An over-the-top place to grab a beer (BZ$4) or an upscale meal is Francis Ford Coppola's **Blancaneaux Lodge ❹,** a few kilometers from **Mai** gate.

A highly recommended tour guide for the Mtn. Pine Ridge is **Richard Zul,** who leads cheap trips. (☎824 2545; richardzul126@hotmail.com.) An alternative option is **Angel Tours** through Eva's, which leads a trip to the Mtn. Pine Ridge that includes 1000 ft. falls, Big Rock Falls, Río Frío Cave, Río on Pools, and nature hiking for BZ$50, 5 person min. (☎824 3365 or 824 2267). An excellent way to explore Cayo and its numerous attractions is by car, with 4WD recommended in the wet season. Roads are fairly well-marked, and directions are easy to obtain. Ricard Zul (see above) and other guides charge modest rates to accompany tourists who have their own car and direct them to attractions.

MAYA RUINS AROUND SAN IGNACIO

ⓒ CARACOL

Ruins accessible only by 4x4 vehicles. Tours available; guides for hire at the entrance, or make arrangements in town. Rates run US$50 per person. **Admission** *BZ$10.*

The largest Maya site in Belize is impressive: Caracol is a secluded yet expansive metropolis, empty and isolated in the midst of the thick jungle. Led by Lord Water, it was an active hub from about 300 BC to AD 700 and rivaled Tikal in importance. In fact, many archaeologists consider Caracol to be one of the greatest of all Maya sites. An altar stone found at Caracol depicts their victory over Tikal in 562. The population of Caracol is estimated to have been almost 150,000 distributed among 30,000 structures. The Belize Government and international funding are helping to position Caracol as the centerpiece of Belize's Mundo de Maya. Currently, only about 10% of the site has been excavated. Not until 50 years after its discovery did archaeologists begin to understand Caracol's importance. Since 1985, archaeologists have discovered more than 4000 structures on the site's 88 acres, including a royal tomb, carved stone slabs depicting dwarves, and the 144 ft. **Canaa** ("Sky Palace"), which offers stunning views of the surrounding jungle-enshrouded hills.

The cheapest option to explore Caracol is **Everald's Caracol Shuttle,** available through Eva's. (☎804 2267; evas@btl.net.) His trip to Caracol leaves around 7:30am, returns at 5pm, and stops at Río Frío and Río on Pools on the way home (BZ$100). **Omar Kantun** of Maya Mystic Tours is also recommended (☎824 4524 . Visiting Caracol is more difficult during rainy season. Few tours make the trip and the road is often closed by the government; it is best not to pre-pay a guide.

ⓒ XUNANTUNICH

To get to Xunantunich, take any Western bound **bus** *and ask to be let off at the* **ferry** *in* **San José Succotz.** *From Succotz take the small, cable-drawn ferry across the Mopan River* *to Xunantunich. (M-F 7:30am-5:30pm, Sa-Su 7:30am-4:30pm. Free.) From the river it is a steep 2km to the ruins. Guides are available at the ruins, but the Visitors Center has enough info for you to guide yourself. Ruins open M-F 8am-5pm, Sa-Su 8am-4pm. BZ$5.*

Xunantunich (Maiden of the Rock) was an important city in the Maya Late Classic period (AD 700-900) and is the most accessible of any of Belize's top Maya sites. While workers lived in the more fertile Mopan River valley, within a 3km radius, the aristocracy resided here. Like many of Belize's Maya ruins, Xunantunich is only partially excavated, but the main temple, the picturesque **El Castillo** (130 ft. high), is easily accessible. From the temple's reconstructed roof, the settlements of Succotz, Benque Viejo del Carmen, and Melchor de Mencos (in Guatemala) are visible. Climb the temple's lower portion to the first platform, where you'll see a fiberglass reproduction of the elaborate **stuccofriezes** that stood on the temple's eastern and western sides. Examine the **stelae** in the **Visitors Center** next to the offices. A great place to grab lunch or dinner in an Jose Succotz is **La Plaza ❷**, right across from the ferry. Serves excellent chicken quesadillas (BZ$8).

👁 CAHAL PECH RUINS

From the Hawkesworth Bridge in San Ignacio, take an immediate left onto the first road, Buena Vista St., past the police station. You will pass the San Ignacio Resort Hotel on your left, and will soon see the road sign for Cahal Pech. Follow it and take a left onto a gravel road. Follow it all the way to the top. You will see the entry to the ruins on your left. A taxi is BZ$5. The ruins are also accessible by Melchor/Benque bus; ask to get off by the ruins (BZ$1). Ruins open daily 7am-6pm. Admission BZ$5.

A daytrip to visit Maya ruins couldn't get much easier or be much better. Located almost a mile from the Hawkesworth suspension bridge, just 800m from town, it is a 30 min. walk up a *steep* hill or a quick taxi (BZ$5) or bus ride (BZ$1) to the site Mayans named the "Place of the Ticks." Although Cahal Pech was a medium-sized Maya center, it produced some of the earliest evidence of occupation in the area (1000 BC to AD 900). Some restoration has been overly imaginative, especially the masks depicted on the temple and the main arch. The real attraction of Cahal Pech is at the rear of the plaza, where narrow paths visit the dark rooms of the royal chamber. The elite residential quarters are among the most extensive in the area. Caretakers sometimes give tours, but expect a tip.

👁 EL PILAR

Not accessible by public transportation. Taxi fare is fixed (BZ$75 round-trip), but try bargaining, and ask the driver to wait while you explore.

El Pilar, 11 mi. northwest of San Ignacio and 7 mi. past the village of Bullet Tree Falls, spans 100 acres and is Belize's newest national park. This extensive Maya archaeological site has over 25 unexcavated plazas, providing a more natural look at the virgin ruins. El Pilar is one of the least touristed Maya sites and is accessible only by taxi. **Chris** and **Theo** of the Parrot Nest lodge (see above) can help arrange transport. At El Pilar, Teo (*not* "Theo") is an extremely knowledgeable guide.

WEST TO GUATEMALA

✖ BENQUE VIEJO AND THE BORDER WITH GUATEMALA

The border with Guatemala at **Melchor de Mencos** is about 1½mi. beyond the town of **Benque Viejo del Carmen**. All buses from Belize now stop here, which is a good walk or a quick cab ride to the border (BZ$5). The **immigration office** is open from

6am to 8pm. Leaving Belize, you must pay the environmental fee of BZ$7.50. Save your receipt if you'll be returning; if you aren't, you will also have to pay the Belize departure tax (BZ$20). Be aware that the Belizean dollar decreases in value from 10-15% across the border. Guatemalan immigration may try to charge unofficial fees, usually US$10. Some travelers have demanded a receipt and been excused from such fees. Entering Guatemala, buses leave from the market in **Melchor** (a 15min. walk over the bridge, up the hill, and to the right; taxi Q5) to **Santa Elena/ Flores** (2hr., every 2hr. 7am-7pm, Q15). Entering Belize, buses depart from San Ignacio and Belize City. These leave from Benque Viejo, and not the border itself.

SOUTHERN BELIZE

Belize's southern frontier encompasses broad expanses of virgin rainforest, lush mountain jungles, miles of pristine beaches and mangroves, and small villages alive with Garífuna culture, all connected by a few rough dirt roads. Toledo, as the district is known, is a largely uncharted region where wildlife easily outnumbers people. Traveling here requires tenacity and a sense of adventure, but the few tourists who take advantage of the region's immense beauty and untouched wilds find their efforts richly rewarded. From beach villages swaying to the beat of Garífuna drums to a living Maya culture that invites you into its homes, southern Belize holds many treasures between its impressive mountains and turquoise waters.

THE HUMMINGBIRD HIGHWAY

The 89km Hummingbird Hwy., between Belmopan and Dangriga, is a lusciously green alternative to the bump-a-thon known as the Coastal Hwy. The Hummingbird cuts through citrus valleys and clear rivers, while the Maya Mountains loom in the background. Though mostly unpaved, a resurfacing project was just finished, and the ride is incredibly smooth. If you're headed to Dangriga by bus or car from Belize City or coming from the west, the Hummingbird Hwy. is not to be missed.

◪ BLUE HOLE NATIONAL PARK

*To get to Blue Hole, hop on any Dangriga-bound **bus** from Belmopan (every hr. 7:30am-5:30pm, BZ$2) and ask to be let off at Blue Hole. For Caves Branch, ask to get off at Ian Anderson's Caves Branch Lodge, then walk 10min. down the unpaved turn-off. Visitors Center, call the Belize Audobon Society (☎ 223 5004) and ask for Blue Hole. Open daily 8am-4pm. BZ$8; camping with toilets and bucket showers BZ$5 per person; flashlight BZ$5.*

Blue Hole National Park, 11mi. south of Belmopan, consists of 575 acres of pristine forest, and is home to more than 300 species of birds and, of course, the Blue Hole itself, an 8m deep limestone sinkhole that allows an underground tributary of the Sibun River to emerge briefly into a rocky pool before being swallowed up again by a cavern 50m away. There are two entrances to the park; the main entry is the farthest west and includes excellent jungle trails to St. Herman's Cave, the observation tower, and the campsite. The breathtaking view from the top of the observation tower rewards those who brave the arduous climb from the visitors center; keep an eye out for orchids on the way. Spectacular **St. Herman's Cave** is about a 20min. hike along the trail from the visitors center. Explore on your own with a strong flashlight, or hire a guard in San Ignacio for a better excursion.

The Blue Hole is right off the highway, about a 30min. walk east from the main highway, and makes a great place for a refreshing dip after hiking the 1mi. Hummingbird Loop trail that rangers have constructed near the Hole. Unfortunately, the Blue Hole can be disappointing as it is rather small and not always blue, but rather a muddy brown color most of the year due to rain.

BELIZE

THE GARÍFUNA STORY. The incredible journey of the Garífuna people in search of a home for more than two hundred years is an epic tale fit for Homer. The Garífuna culture began on the Caribbean island of St. Vincent, where the Arawak and Carib tribes of South America arrived just after the first millenium. In 1635, ships of Nigerian slaves being transported to the New World shipwrecked on the isle. The two ethnic groups eventually formed a peaceful, homogenous culture, originally referred to as "Black Caribs" in European literature. Once the British gained control of St. Vincent, the Garífuna, as they called themselves, were quickly and violently exported to Honduras. In 1823 they formed alliances with the losing side of a failed revolution in Honduras, and found themselves homeless once again. However, the Garífuna found a home in Belize, where their culture thrives today. Many carry on the traditional farming and fishing lifestyles. The Garífuna are best known for their vibrant music, *punta* dancing and knocking drums, and their colorful art and handicrafts.

Between Blue Hole and the park visitors center there is a small sign for ◙ **Caves Branch Jungle Lodge ❷** (☎/fax 822 2800; www.cavesbranch.com), mile 41.5 of the highway. Tiki torches light the pebble path to your immaculate and comfortable room. Bunks in a cozy bunkhouse and camping both have access to thatch-covered "jungle showers" and clean bathrooms with hot water. Each room comes with bottled water, mosquito netting, and a kerosene lamp. If your wallet allows, there are even nicer jungle *cabañas* and suites. There is even a rope swing hanging over the crystal clear waters of the nearby Sibun River. The lodge also offers tasty, though expensive buffet-style meals. Reserve in advance. (Meals BZ$24-34. Bunks BZ$30; camping BZ$10; *cabañas* BZ$134; suites BZ$216.) Ian Anderson and his well-trained guides lead great caving and tubing trips. (BZ150-210 per person.)

▲ FIVE BLUES LAKE NATIONAL PARK

*To get to the lake, take any Dangriga-bound **bus** from Belmopan and get off at St. Margaret's (every hr. 7:30am-5:30pm, BZ$3). Check in at the park office down the dirt road on your left. It is a 4 mi. **hike** to the heart of the park. If you're lucky, the park's only vehicle may be available to take you to the lake, a bumpy 20min. truck ride away (BZ$20 roundtrip). During the high season it is easy to hitch a ride; but Let's Go does not recommend it. Otherwise, the walk into the heart of the park is an easy 2hr.*

In the jungle-covered limestone foothills of the Maya Mountains 25 mi. southeast of Belmopan, Five Blues Lake National Park offers 4200 acres of rugged, unspoiled wilderness centered around a crystal-clear 10-acre lake. The park depends upon entrance fees (BZ$8), donations, and grants for its operation and independence from government control. Impromptu tours are provided by local village experts, usually youths who have as much—if not more—fun exploring the park as you do. Rugged hiking trails are plentiful, and bright orange markers point the way when branches and roots obscure the path. The saw-toothed caves and cliffs of Five Blues are quite unlike the smooth, slick underground caverns to the west: located mostly above ground, they form a fascinating, confusing labyrinth of rock stretching across hundreds of acres and towering into the sky.

Tread carefully if you wish to catch sight of the fleeting jungle leopard or gibnut. Spider monkeys, on the other hand, are surprisingly easy to find, and leaf-cutting ants seem to follow you no matter where you go. The real gem of the park is the pristine lake, fed by collapsed river caves hundreds of meters below. When the sun is out, the lake fragments into brilliant shades of piercing blue. **Canoes** rent for about BZ$5, and **cave diving** is allowed if you bring the proper equipment.

While you can certainly enjoy all the park's wonders in a day, you can make your visit more leisurely by spending the night in adjacent **St. Margaret's Village** (☎809

BELIZE

2005). Definitely not for the pampered traveler, the **Women Rising's Bed and Break-fast ❷** allows you to experience Belizean life by living with a rural family as a part of a community-based, ecologically minded development program that also oversees the administration of the park. A village homestay can be an eye-opening experience, as families make do with no electricity and few conveniences. Inquire at the park's visitor center or in the village itself; ask for Isabel. (BZ$25 per night. Meals BZ$7 each.) **Gladys Geldemez ❷** has *cabañas* and offers the same rates. **Camping ❶** (BZ$5 per person) in the park is cheaper but less rewarding.

DANGRIGA

Dangriga thrives today as the musical, artistic, and historical center of the Garífuna. Originally named Stann Creek, the town was renamed Dangriga ("Standing Water") to honor the Garífuna tradition. Located on the coast halfway between Belize City and Placencia, Dangriga was founded as a trading post by Puritans from New Providence who farmed Tobacco Caye and the Coastal Belt. Today, most residents are Garífuna—Black Caribs of mixed African and native Caribbean descent whose ancestors fled Honduras in 1823 in the wake of a failed rebellion. Some travelers come to learn more about the Garífuna, while most use it as a base to reach Tobacco Caye, Cockscomb Basin, or the deep South. A few even get swept away by the warm hospitality and soon call "Griga" home.

Dangriga

♦ ACCOMMODATIONS
Bluefield Lodge, 7
Chaleanor Hotel, 8
Pat's Guest House, 10
Weyhoan Hotel, 3

♦ FOOD
Kinburger Restaurant, 4
Pelican Beach, 1
Ritchie's Dinette, 2
Ruthie's, 9
Riverside Café, 5

TO TOBACCO CAYE (16km)

Boats to Tobacco Caye

Benjamin Nicholas' Studio

Val's Laundry & □

Gulf of Honduras

Austin Rodriguez's Drum Shop

TO SOUTHERN & HUMMINGBIRD HWY.,
MAYFLOWER RUINS (15km),
HOPKINS VILLAGE (16km),
COCKSCOMB WILDLIFE SANCTUARY (32km)

Southern Transport 🚌

▮ NIGHTLIFE
Griga 2000, 6

▐ TRANSPORTATION

Flights: A 20min. walk north of town or a BZ$5 taxi ride. **Tropic Air** (☎522 2124) flies to **Belize Municipal Airport** (20min., every 2hr. 7am-5pm, BZ$62), **Punta Gorda** (45min., 5 per day 8:50am-5:20pm, BZ$112) via **Placencia**. **Maya Island Air** (☎522 2659) flies similar routes at similar prices.

Buses: Southern Transport (☎522 2160) serves **Punta Gorda** (4½hr.; M-Sa 10:30am, noon, 3:30, 5:30pm; Su noon, 3:30, 5:30pm; BZ$13); **Belize City** (3hr., 10 per day 5:15am-5pm, BZ$10) usually via **Belmopan** (2hr., BZ$6); **Placencia** (2½hr.; Tu-W and Su 12:15 and 5:15pm; M and Th-Sa 12:15, 3:30, 5:15pm; BZ$10) via **Hopkins Village** (45min., BZ$4).

Boats: Captain Reyes (☎522 3227) heads to **Puerto Cortés, Honduras** (3hr., Sa 9am, US$50). Make arrangements at Catalina's or the Riverside Café a few hours early to allow for exit stamps (BZ$7.50). Boats to **Tobacco Caye** (45min., BZ$30) leave irregularly from the Riverside Café on the south bank of Stann Creek. Ask around the docks on North Stann Creek to find a ride. Capt'n Buck, a local, makes the trip regularly.

ORIENTATION AND PRACTICAL INFORMATION

The **Stann Creek River,** also called the Gumaragu River, flows east through town to the ocean. Running parallel to the coast, the main road has two names: **St. Vincent Street** south of the river and **Commerce Street** north of it. Hustlers congregate near the Stann Creek bridge and the Southern Transport Bus Station at the southern end of Dangriga. The center of town and the Stann Creek bridge are less than a half mile north of the bus station. Several blocks south of the bridge, **Mahogany Lane** connects St. Vincent St. to the sea and **Alijo Benji Park,** named after the Garífuna chief who led his people from Honduras to Dangriga. A large red-and-white sign for the Chaleanor Hotel marks the junction of St. Vincent St. and Mahogany Ln. Police warn that the "back-a-town" area by Havana bridge is unsafe at night.

Tourist Information: The **Belize Tourism Industry Association** (BTIA) has recently opened a tourist center (☎522 2277) in the Southern Transport Terminal, but is not the best source of information. Most knowledgeable are Louise at the **Bluefield Lodge** (☎522 2742) and Chadwick at **Chaleanor Hotel** (☎522 2587).

Banks: Barclay's Bank, 3 blocks north of the bridge on the east side of Commerce St., gives cash advances on credit cards and changes traveler's checks and Canadian dollars. 24hr. **ATM** accepts Visa. Open M-Th 8am-2:30pm, F 8am-4:30pm. Change US traveler's checks at **Kuylen Hardware,** 30 ft. north of the main bridge. There is a **Western Union** in the building. Open M-Th 7:30am-noon and 1:30-5pm, Sa 7:30am-1pm.

Laundry Service: Val's Laundry, 1 Sharp St. with an entrance on Mahogany across from the post office. Wash BZ$5. Wash, dry, and fold for BZ$10. Open daily 7am-7pm.

Car Rentals: Ready Rentals (☎522 2607), near the post office, has sturdy Izuzu Troopers. Reservations recommended for high season. BZ$160 per day.

Police: 107 Commerce St. (☎522 2022, emergency 90), north of the river, by Barclay's Bank. Open 24hr.

Pharmacy: St. Vincent Drugstore (☎522 3124), at 12 St. and Vincent St. just south of the bridge. Open M-Sa 8am-9:30pm, Su 9-11am and 5-7pm.

Hospital: (☎522 2078). Take the frontage road 2 blocks north and 2 blocks east of the bridge. Open 24hr. Ambulance available.

Clinic: Health Centre (☎522 2184), across from the hospital on the water. Open M-F 8am-5pm.

THE LOCAL STORY

THE ARTIST SPEAKS

Garífuna painter Benjamin Nicholas of Dangriga is one of Belize's most renowned artists. His colorful scenes of everyday life have garnered international fame, and he has been commissioned by the Queen of England and the Archbishop of Canterbury.

On his youth: In school I wouldn't be paying attention to the teacher, but rather observing the way the classroom, students, and professor looked. In the little village I grew up in, I was the only one doing these types of drawings, and the teachers soon had me helping their lessons by drawing illustrations on the board. Everyone talked about the little artist in Barranco.

On his artistic style: I mostly do colorful portrayals of everyday Garífuna life: women making casava, men fishing, and people *punta* dancing and knocking their drums.

On his art's impact: Before I started painting, the world only knew the Garífuna people as savages. But now, I am so proud that I have changed people's conception of them. People are now visiting the Garífuna because they have seen the paintings.

On Garífuna people today: Now Garifuna, Creole, Hispanics, and Indians are all mixing. It is hard to tell who is who just by looking. But the Garífuna are trying to guard against losing their culture by maintaining their lifestyle and cultural ties.

On his favorite thing about being an artist: It makes you more pronounced to the world, as paintings speak loudly about people.

Telephones: BTL (☎ 522 2065; fax 522 2038), across the street from the police. Collect and credit card calls free. **Fax** service. Open M-F 8am-noon and 1-5pm.

Internet: Val's Laundry and Internet, 1 Sharp St., at the eastern end of Mahogany Rd. Internet BZ$10 per hr. Open daily 7am-7pm.

Post Office: 16 Caney St. Open M-Th 8am-noon and 1-5pm, F 8am-noon and 1-4:30pm.

ACCOMMODATIONS

■ **Bluefield Lodge** (☎ 522 2742), 1 block south and 2 blocks west of the bridge, offers the best bang for your Belizean buck. Immaculate rooms with double mattresses come with bottled water and towels. Bathrooms have hot water and soap. Lounge with cable TV and US magazines. Singles BZ$27; doubles BZ$37, with bath and TV BZ$48. ❷

Chaleanor Hotel (☎ 522 2587), 35 Magoon St. Nice three-story hotel with balconies, roof access, and hospitable owners. Economy rooms are a good value but share rather grim bathrooms. Free drinking water, coffee, and bananas in the morning. Economy rooms have fan and shared bath. Singles BZ$17; doubles BZ$28. Nicer, large rooms have TV and private bath. Singles BZ$50; doubles BZ$60. ❶

Pat's Guest House (☎ 522 2095), south of the bridge. Far from the center of town. Some rooms are right on the water and are bright and airy, but cost more. The hot-water shower is small but clean. Singles BZ$16, with private bath BZ$32; doubles BZ$32/BZ$43; nicer rooms with verandas facing the beach BZ$5 extra per person. MC/V. ❶

Weyhoan Hotel (☎ 522 2398), on the west side of Commerce St. If the receptionist desk is closed, check the Asian convenience store downstairs. Basic singles in a modern building; shared, clean, hot-water baths. BZ$10 key deposit. No smoking. Singles with fan BZ$20; with private bath, fan, and TV BZ$36; doubles with all amenities BZ$68. ❶

FOOD

Dangriga has several tasty options and has excellent seafood. Most are fairly near the Stann Creek bridge, easily accessible from the center of town. Be aware that many restaurants are closed on Sunday and you may have to search around; grocery stores are usually open Sunday afternoons.

■ **Riverside Café,** on the south bank of Stann Creek about half a block east of the bridge. Friendly service, reasonable prices and delicious entrees make the Riverside popular with both tourists and locals. The fried shrimp (BZ$17) is a hearty meal. In season, the lobster (BZ$18) is a real treat. Breakfast and lunch BZ$6-8. Open M-Sa 7am-9pm. ❸

■ **Ruthie's** (☎ 502 3184), just north of Pat's Guesthouse and across the street from Waterfront. The locals know where to get the best Garífuna food, and Ruthie's is it. Treat yourself to fresh fish, shrimp, or lobster and plantain in delicious grated coconut milk (BZ$8-12), or the coconut roll and Belizean johnny cake for breakfast (BZ$8). Call ahead. ❷

Ritchie's Dinette Creole and Spanish Food, 84 Commerce St., 2 blocks north of the bridge on the right. Ritchie offers up the typical breakfast: fry jacks, bacon, eggs (BZ$8) and fresh-squeezed O.J. (BZ$2). For lunch, try a magnificent chicken burrito (BZ$2.50) or a fish filet (BZ$14). Open M-Sa 7:30am-10:30pm, Su 7:30am-1:30pm. ❷

Kingburger Restaurant, 1 block north of the bridge. Burger King's lesser-known brother provides an old Western standby: all-beef burgers with fries BZ$6. The ice cream (BZ$2) is a favorite with locals; so is the extensive list of fresh juices (BZ$1.50). Open M-Sa 7am-3pm and 6:30pm-midnight, but hours are lax. ❶

Pelican Beach, ½ mi. north of the village on beautiful waterfront property next to the airport, is a 20min. walk or a short taxi ride (BZ$5), but well worth it. Prices are high but the dinners are delectable. Try the Porterhouse steak for BZ$46. Tasty breakfasts served 7-9am, BZ$14-17. Dinner served 6:30-9pm. ❺

NIGHTLIFE

For a town that is the birthplace of some of Belize's most popular bands, live music and exciting nightlife are surprisingly hard to find in Griga. Ask if electric Griga Boyz and Punta Rebels are playing in town. You will find locals drinking and wandering the street at all hours of the night with no destination. Be aware that taxis don't run past 9pm. **Griga 2000**, just south of the bridge, is the most popular nightclub. Karaoke draws a big crowd (W and Su, open daily until midnight). The **Kennedy Club**, a few blocks north of the police station, popular but more run-down, and jams to *punta* and soul until 3am on Saturdays. (Open weekdays until 11pm.)

SIGHTS AND SHOPPING

The Garífuna, also known as Black Caribs, make up the majority of Southern Belize's population. **Garífuna Day,** November 19, commemorates the arrival of the Black Caribs in Belize in 1823 with the biggest party of the year. Dangriga transforms itself completely, as usually placid and unassuming streets erupt into a frenzy of wild celebrations and exhaustive merrymaking.

Dangriga is a great place to explore Garífuna culture. World-renowned artist **Benjamin Nicholas** (see **The Artist Speaks,** p. 119) often welcomes visitors to his in-home workshop, just past the post office. Take a look at his numerous works in progress, typically colorful scenes of everyday Belizean life. To get there, turn left on Mahogany St., just past Ritchie's bus station south of the bridge. Mr. Nicholas asks that you call ahead (☎522 2785) and leave behind a BZ$20-30 "courtesy" for his time. Those with a musical bent should stop by the workshop of **Austin Rodríguez** (look for the small shack at the southern end of Tubroose St. with wood shavings in the yard), who handcrafts mahogany and cedar drums in the traditional Garífuna style under the shelter of a thatched roof in his driveway. Rodríguez's daughters, Norielee and Deatha ("DAY-ta") have learned their father's craft and may share their wealth of information about Garífuna culture.

NEAR DANGRIGA

HOPKINS VILLAGE

The Southern Transport bus from Dangriga stops at the village en route to Placencia (45min., Tu, W, Su 12:15 and 5:15pm; M, Th-Sa 12:15, 3:30, 5:15pm; BZ$4). Buses heading back to Dangriga circle Hopkins and leave from its main junction at around 7am.

A traditional Garífuna village graced with beautiful beaches but slowly succumbing to paved roads and concrete buildings, Hopkins Village (pop. 1100), 10 mi. (16km) south of Dangriga and 6½km east of the Southern Hwy., is easy to get to and offers basic accommodations. **Tania's ❷,** a few minutes south of the main junction, has incredibly cheap rooms with private bath and TV. (Singles BZ$27; doubles BZ$30.) **Swinging Armadillos' ❷,** north of the junction on the beach, is a hammock-slung bar and restaurant that serves delicious meals (BZ$6-10). **Iris ❶,** south of the junction, serves food all day. (*Garnaches* 3 for BZ$1; burgers BZ$3.50-5.) North of Armadillos is **Hideaway Bar,** with weekend karaoke.

TOBACCO CAYE

*To reach the caye from Dangriga, ask boatmen near the bridge for a ride. **Captain Buck** is a reliable ride. Most boats leave between 11am-2pm at the dock by the Riverside Cafe. Boats make regular trips in high season, but low-season is more sporadic. (1hr., BZ$30*

BELIZE

*per person each way.) Boats return daily from the caye at 9am. Louise at Bluefield Lodge (☎522 2742) can help with travel plans, as can folks at **Riverside Café** (☎502 3499).*

Squarely atop the reef, Tobacco Caye (pop. 18, yes, 18) is the ultimate easy-living hideaway, with hammocks outnumbering humans. Excellent swimming, snorkeling, and fishing are the primary attractions. The island is a sandy 4½ acre palm-tree filled caye encircled by beautiful azure waters and the coral reef. It may not last forever; the ocean creeps up the shore a bit farther each year. Still, like everything else going on in Tobacco Caye, it's happening *slowly*. Despite the underwater beauty, there is a distressing amount of damaged coral, due to Hurricane Mitch, which swept by in 1998, and the possibly rising temperatures of the Caribbean.

The Caye's four hotels are solid rivals, as their room prices all include three meals a day. Make sure to have a reservation in high season. The best value is **The Gaviota ❺**, in the center of the island. Bert and his wife offer clean rooms with wood floors and three small but excellent meals per day. They also occassionally make bargains with snorkeling gear, canoes, and kayaks, especially in low season, as do many of the hotels. (☎509 5032. Snorkeling gear and fishing poles BZ$10-15 per day. Singles BZ$60; doubles BZ$100). **Lana's Hotel ❺**, offers basic rooms with shared bath and gourmet meals. (☎509 5036. Singles BZ$60; doubles BZ$100, more in high season.) Several hotels will allow **camping** on their beach; ask for permission in advance (BZ$10-20 per person). Easygoing Gerald and Mark operate the island's primary hangout, a tiny bar near the northern dock where Spice Girls karaoke jangles on the weekends. **Larna's**, by the dock, allows camping on its beach (US$10 per person). Dive-master **Andrew Muha** has an office near Reef's End.

COCKSCOMB BASIN WILDLIFE SANCTUARY

*The cheapest way to the site is by **bus**. Take any bus heading south from Dangriga in the morning (1hr., BZ$5) and ask to be let off at Maya Center. From here it is a 6 mi. (2hr.) hike to the sanctuary. Bus service back to Dangriga stops at 3pm. Or hire a taxi from Maya Center (BZ$25 each way). A more expensive option is a daytrip from Dangriga. The best company is **C&G Tours** (☎522 3641), run by Godfrey Young. His sanctuary trips return through Sittee River and Hopkins Village. (BZ$360 for 1-4 people.)*

About 20 mi. south of Dangriga, the Cockscomb Basin Wildlife Sanctuary is the jewel of Belize's extensive list of nature reserves. It is bordered on three sides by the peaks and ridges of the Maya Mountains and totals over 100,000 acres. The sanctuary's claim to fame is the title of "World's First Jaguar Sanctuary." Stop at the village of **Maya Centre,** 6 mi. before the sanctuary on the Southern Hwy. to pay the BZ$10 entrance fee. There is also an extensive collection of carved slate and handwoven baskets for sale. Head down the 7 mi. dirt path road to the Visitors Center for maps (BZ$1) and information.

Night hikes offer the best shot at a glimpse of one of the elusive cats, but even then, the most dogged visitors often see only tracks. Most of the forest residents aren't as difficult to track down as the jaguar; the trails teem with wildlife. Pumas, gibnuts, deer, pacas, and armadillos are just a few of the gang. The jungles also provide a great opportunity to view over 200 species of birds. Many visitors come for the well-developed and clearly marked trail system, including a 3km hike to a beautiful waterfall, and a 4km hike to a steep bluff overlooking the basin and the majestic **Victoria Peak.** Longer treks may require a guide; inquire at Maya Centre. **Victoria Peak,** Belize's second highest point (1120m), rises from within the sanctuary, and a four or five day journey will take prepared hikers to the summit and back. Before climbing the peak, it is best to hire a knowledgeable porter from Maya Centre (BZ$50 per day). William is a reputable guide.

There are budget accommodations in Maya Centre and in the Sanctuary. **Nu'uk Che'il Cottages ❸**, 200 yards past the Maya Centre turn-off, is run by the famous

García sisters. (☎520 3033. Bunk beds BZ$18; singles BZ$40; doubles BZ$50.) The **Visitor's Center ❶** offers beds as well. (Tent rental BZ$5-15. Camping BZ$5; dorms BZ$16; newer dorms BZ$36; cabins BZ$74-100.) For reservations contact the Belize Audobon Society (☎223 5004; base@btl.net).

MAYFLOWER RUINS AND ANTELOPE FALLS

*From Dangriga, take any bus going south and get off in **Silk Grass Village** (20min., BZ$4). From Silk Grass, it is a 5km hike to the park. There are no buses heading back to Dangriga from Silk Grass after 3pm.*

The **Mayflower** ruins and **Antelope Falls,** about 11 mi. from Dangriga are currently being excavated and promise to be one of the most important Maya sites in Belize. So far, archaeologists at the Mayflower Archeological Reserve have uncovered what they suspect were viewing platforms for ball games. There are two postclassic Maya ruins: the Mayflower and T'au Witz as well as the long wall of what was once a pyramid known as **Mainzunun,** probably built around AD 300. If you continue past Mainzunun and follow the narrow jungle trail (bear right at the fork), you'll reach the spectacular Antelope Falls. Along the way, you'll likely see hummingbirds, butterflies, and maybe an armadillo or two, but the jewel of the jungle is the 300 ft. Antelope Falls, located just under 2 mi. beyond the pyramid. The last 200m of the trail are steep and slippery, so bring sturdy shoes. Swimming here is great, but the water rushes fast and the rocks are slippery, so exercise caution.

PLACENCIA

Perched at the end of a long peninsula slipping out into the warm Caribbean, 45 mi. south of Dangriga, Placencia (pop. 800) is an inviting beach paradise. A fishing village until the lobster and conch populations began dwindling 20 years ago, Placencia retains a simple seaside charm while emerging as one of Belize's most visited areas. With good reason: miles and miles of premiere golden sandy beachfront, an impressive array of uninhabited paradisiacal islands just miles offshore, and undoubtedly some of the best seafood in the country.

Unfortunately, on October 8th, 2001, category 4 Hurricane Iris wrecked havoc on Placencia Village. The majority of hotels, restaurants, and clubs were significantly damaged or destroyed; many have yet to reopen. Locals are concerned about the destruction of the town's meandering Main St., recorded in the *Guinness Book of World Records* as the world's narrowest street. Fortunately, the town has quickly mobilized to rebuild. Despite increasing prices and painful natural disasters, the town is still remarkably hospitable and locals will openly welcome you into their home. The **Lobster Fest,** held the last week of June, is a huge attraction featuring clawed guests and the best of Belize's bands.

◩ TRANSPORTATION

Flights: Placencia's airstrip is 1¾mi. from town. **Maya Island Air** (☎523 3475) flies to **Dangriga** (20min., every 2½hr. 7am-4:30pm, BZ$69); **Belize City** (1hr., every 2½hr. 7am-4:30pm, BZ$118); **Punta Gorda** (20min.; 8:50, 10:50am, 3:35, 5:35pm; BZ$68). **Tropic Air** (☎523 3410) runs a similar schedule at identical prices. Tickets for Maya Island Air can be purchased over the phone or at the airport.

Buses: Buses leave for **Dangriga** from the gas dock (3hr.; M-Sa 5:30, 6am, 1:30pm; Su 7am and 1:30pm; BZ$8). Arriving in Placencia from Punta Gorda, you must take a bus to Independence and ferry to Placencia from there. From the Texaco dock by the tourist office, catch the ferry to **Mango Creek/Independence** (10am and 4pm, BZ$10). Then catch the bus to **Punta Gorda** (3hr., 11:30am and 5:30pm, BZ$10).

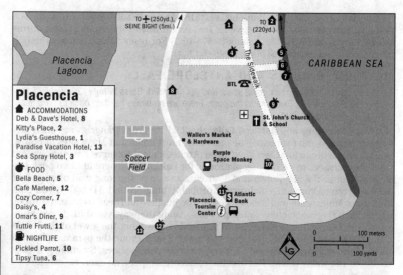

Placencia Lagoon

CARIBBEAN SEA

TO ✈ (250yd.), SEINE BIGHT (5mi.)

TO (220yd.)

The Sidewalk

BTL ☎

St. John's Church & School

Wallen's Market & Hardware

Purple Space Monkey

Soccer Field

Placencia Toursim Center ℹ

Atlantic Bank

Placencia

🏠 **ACCOMMODATIONS**
Deb & Dave's Hotel, **8**
Kitty's Place, **2**
Lydia's Guesthouse, **1**
Paradise Vacation Hotel, **13**
Sea Spray Hotel, **3**

🍴 **FOOD**
Bella Beach, **5**
Cafe Marlene, **12**
Cozy Corner, **7**
Daisy's, **4**
Omar's Diner, **9**
Tuttie Frutti, **11**

🌙 **NIGHTLIFE**
Pickled Parrot, **10**
Tipsy Tuna, **6**

0   100 meters
0   100 yards

Ferries: Ferries leave from the dock for **Mango Creek/Independence** (25min., 10am and 4pm, BZ$10). Gulf Cruza makes weekly trips to **Puerto Cortés, Honduras** (leaves Placencia F 9am arrives 2pm, BZ$100 plus BZ$20 departure tax).

⚡🔢 ORIENTATION AND PRACTICAL INFORMATION

Boats and buses disembark near the gas dock at Placencia's southernmost point. The only artery through town, a skinny sidewalk, runs north-south along the beach. Just about every place in town perches on the walkway, or announces its proximity with signs and arrows. Traversing the entire village takes only 15 leisurely minutes. The dirt road used by vehicles runs parallel to the walkway and is the only road that leaves Placencia to the north.

Tourist Information: Placencia Tourism Center (☎523 4045; www.placencia.com), is one of the best tourist offices in Belize. Produces the excellent *Placencia Breeze* with updated transportation schedules, maps, and specials. Open M-F 9am-5pm, Sa 1-3pm.

Banks: Atlantic Bank, in the white building across from the bus stop, gives cash advances on MC and V (BZ$5 charge). Open M-F 8am-2pm.

Markets: Wallen's Market, just north of the soccer field on the dirt road, is the best place for groceries. Changes US traveler's checks. Open M-Sa 8am-noon and 2-6pm.

Laundry: Cara's Laundry, in the same building as Omar's Diner (see **Food,** below). Loads BZ$8-20, depending on size. Closed Sa.

Police: (☎523 3129, emergency 90), far north of town.

Hospital: The **health center** (☎523 3129) is behind the school, west of the walkway across from Omar's. Open M-F 8am-noon and 1-5pm.

Telephones: BTL (☎523 3109), near the center of the village on the path. Free collect calls, **fax** service. Open M-F 8am-12:30pm and 1:30-5pm.

Internet: The expensive **Purple Space Monkey** charges BZ$12 per hr. Closed Su.

Post Office: Above the fishing co-op in the white building at the south end of the walkway, across from the dock. Open M-F 9-11am and 2-5pm.

ACCOMMODATIONS

The good news: budget hotels abound in Placencia. The great news: most are along the eastern shore 100 ft. from the sea, where winds keep the mosquitoes at bay. Hurricane Iris wiped out many cheap accommodations, and only the best have been rebuilt.

■ **Lydia's Guesthouse** (☎523 3117; lydias@btl.net), near the north end of the sidewalk on the west side. Lydia will cook you breakfast (BZ$7), do your laundry (BZ$8), and provide 2 fans when it's really hot. Hammocks on the porch, shared fridge, and soft mattresses are additional perks. She has also recently added an incredibly full kitchen and dining area. The common baths have hot water. High season singles BZ$31, low season BZ$25; doubles BZ$46/BZ$35. ❸

Sea Spray Hotel (☎523 3148; www.seasprayhotel.com), on the north end of the sidewalk on the east side. Though it's the oldest hotel in Placencia, the amenities in this breezy place are new: private baths with hot water for all, as well as coffee makers and fridges, and hammocks 10 ft. from the sea. Some rooms have better views and more space. Laundry service BZ$10. Low season economy singles BZ$30; doubles BZ40. High season singles or doubles BZ$50; cabañas BZ$110. D/MC/V. ❷

Paradise Vacation Hotel (☎523 3179), on the beach, a 3min. walk southwest of the dock. Comfortable rooms. The big 2nd floor deck affords a nice view. Room for 2 with shared hot-water bath BZ$27; downstairs with private bath BZ$42; upstairs BZ$49. BZ$10 extra per person. Low season discount for 3-day stay. Traveler's checks accepted. MC/V. ❷

Deb & Dave's Hotel (☎523 3207; debanddave@btl.net), has nice clean rooms with shared bath and screened verandas with hammocks. Singles and doubles BZ$36. ❸

FOOD

Superb seafood defines dining in Placencia; some of the country's most mouth-watering restaurants are located along the beach.

■ **Cafe Marlene,** a 5min. walk west of the tourist center, directly on the water in the white building. Marlene

THE BIG SPLURGE

KITTY'S PLACE

This hotel (☎523 322, fax 523 3226; www.kittysplace.com), located on the beach a mile north of town, is a great value and truly one of the nicest of all the Placencia exclusive resorts. Beautiful colonial and Belizean styled rooms are set admist well-kept gardens on the nicest stretch of waterfront on the entire peninsula. All rooms include fridge, coffee maker, veranda with hammock, ceiling fan, and complimentary bike if requested in advance. Rooms range from budget with hot-water bath, to Honeymoon suites. The restaurant on the grounds serves some of the best food in the area in a gorgeous dining room. They also offer tours of the surrounding area, including: snorkeling (full day US$45 with gear); scuba diving (2 tank dives US$80-105); sportfishing (US$225-325); jungle tours to Monkey River (half day US$35); Maya ruins tours to Nimli Punit (US$70); and trips to Cockscomb Basin Wildlife Sanctuary (US$55). Singles BZ$130-150; doubles BZ$180-200. There are economy rooms with shared bath, singles BZ$50; doubles BZ$70. All prices add 17% tax. AmEx/D/MC/V.

cooks up a delicious meal each day of the week. Portions are huge, the food is mouth-watering, and Marlene is talkative. Breakfast of eggs, sausage, fruit, and coffee BZ$15. Open M-Sa 7am-2pm and 6-10pm. ❸

Bella Beach, on the water just before Sea Spray Hotel. For a romantic splurge, Bella Beach is the place. Authentic, intimate, romantic Italian atmosphere with delicious pastas (BZ$20) and vegetarian entrees (BZ$18). Open Th-Tu 6:30-9pm. ❹

Daisy's, in the center of town west of the walkway, offers the hungry traveler a plethora of options. Sandwiches and burgers (BZ$4-5) and the seafood dinners (BZ$12-15) are delicious. Open W-M 8am-10pm. ❶

Tuttie Frutti, north of the Tourism Center, has lick-a-licious ice cream. Lauren serves up heavenly banana and fresh fruit scoops. Two scoops BZ$3. Open daily 10am-9pm. ❶

Cozy Corner, set on the beach 50 ft. east of BTL. This unassuming thatched-roof hut serves up some of the best seafood around. You can't go wrong with the fish or conch dinner (both BZ$12). In season, conch fritters are an affordable addiction (BZ$2.50 per plate). There is a nice sea breeze. Open Tu-Su 11am-10pm. ❸

Omar's Diner, in the maroon-and-white striped shack on the southern end of the walkway. Famous for its low prices and tasty seafood. The staff tends to take their time. Great burritos BZ$4.50-8, any combination of 2 types of seafood with coconut rice and juice BZ$22. Bring your own booze. Open daily during meal hours. ❷

OUTDOOR ACTIVITIES AND WATERSPORTS

NEARBY VILLAGES. Seine Bight, a small Garífuna village 5 mi. north of Placencia, and nearby **Maya Beach,** are both graced with beaches perfect for a swim, and hotels so incredible they make the visit worth it. You can rent a **bike** from **Deb & Dave's. Sunset Reef** rents kayaks. *(Deb & Dave's ☎ 523 3207. BZ$5 per hr.; BZ$25 per day. Sunset Reef BZ$5 per hr.; BZ$30 per day.)*

CAYES. Deserted tropical getaways don't get much better than this. The water is steely blue, the sand is grainy, and the cayes are uninhabited. Boaters will ferry tourists to the picture-perfect islands around Placencia for fishing, snorkeling, diving, and camping. The best cayes are generally those farthest south and closest to the reef, where the mangroves, mosquitoes, and sand-flies are less abundant. Highly recommended are the **Silk Cayes,** a series of three gorgeous palm-covered islands bordered by gleaming white sand and fantastic coral, 1hr. away by boat. **Laughing Bird Caye** is another perennial favorite. Trips to the cayes are best arranged through diving and snorkeling companies.

DIVING AND SNORKELING. Each company in Placencia offers similar services at comparable rates, most of which include lunch. Half-day snorkeling trips to the reef BZ$54. Full-day trips to heavenly **Laughing Bird Caye** and **Silk Caye** are BZ$76 and BZ$96, respectively. Two reputable operators are **Natural Mystic** (☎ 523 3278; mysticdive@btl.net) and **Nite Wind** (☎ 523 3487), both located just east of the southern dock. Prices may be discounted and negotiable in low season. You can also charter a boat. These companies also arrange camping trips to the cayes. Diving is quite popular in Placencia; rates are BZ$140 for a 1 tank dive, BZ$160 for 2 tanks, and BZ$700 for the four-day PADI certification. **Natural Mystic** (see above) is a quality operator, as is **Aquatic Adventures** (523 3182; glenmar@btl.net). For a more extreme adventure, the incredible whale sharks of the Caribbean, featured in *National Geographic*, draw divers and snorkelers to Placencia. They are most abundant from April to June, especially during the full moon. (Whale shark snorkeling US$54 per person; diving US$108.) Also popular is manatee watching in the lagoon near Placencia. **Nite Wind,** among others, runs trips for BZ$44.

KAYAKING. Kayak around the mangrove shores of the lagoon with a rental from the **Sunset Reef**, east from the dock along the beach in Dangriga. (BZ$5 per hr., minimum 2hr., BZ$30 for a full day. They also rent canoes.) For serious kayaking, **Ali and Jimmy Westby** run camping tours for up to seven days to see the Silk Cayes and the Sapodilla Range, snorkeling and fishing along the way. One stop is at a 17th-century wreck in 18 ft. of water. Meals are freshly caught seafood. (☎523 4073; pladejavu@btl.net. US$85 per day, all inclusive; 4-person min.)

FISHING. The waters off the coast of Placencia are teeming with incredible marine life. **Ocean Motion** (523 3363) runs to the inner reef for US$216, including gear and lunch. **Kingfisher Angler Adventure** (☎/fax 523 3323) is reputable and owner Charles has appeared on ESPN and the Discovery Channel for his flyfishing prowess. **Earl and Kurt Godfrey** (☎523 3433) are also recommended.

MONKEY RIVER. A popular daytrip to the nearby jungles of Monkey River, located on the coast 20km southwest of Placencia. The Monkey River Reserve is blessed with thick mangrove forests, howler monkeys haunting the canopy, and a wide variety of birds. Most trips include a guided jungle hike and a stop in nearby Monkey River Village for lunch and shopping.

ENTERTAINMENT AND NIGHTLIFE

Hurricane Iris washed away most of Belize's nightlife. Check to see if any new options have opened. In the early evening, crowds gather for happy hours at the **Pickled Parrot** (open 5-6pm), located just before Wallen's on the dirt road, and **Tipsy Tuna**, a modern sports bar with pool tables. (Happy hour 7-8pm. Open M-F until midnight, Sa-Su until 2am.) Newly opened **Sugar Reef Sunset Lounge**, on the southwest tip of town, features a diverse activities list: Saturday BBQs, kayak, and canoe races. (Happy hour daily 6-7pm. Open until midnight.)

PUNTA GORDA

In the far south of Belize, the rainforested Toledo District surrounding Punta Gorda has much to offer the adventurous traveler. Poorly maintained roads and long, bumpy bus rides have weeded out the weak, and Toledo's many natural wonders remain virtually untouched. Its mountains are home to the largest Maya population in Belize, which still uses the traditional *milpa* farming system. The commercial center, coastal Punta Gorda (pop. 4400), may be tiny, but it houses an amalgamation of Mopan and Kek'chi Maya, Garífuna, Creole, and East Indian populations, with some German Mennonites thrown in as well. Wednesday and Saturday mornings are the best time to see this eclectic melting pot, as all the surrounding villages arrive in buses to buy and sell at the market on Front St. Mass tourism is lacking and poverty abounds, but the rich cultural appeal of Punta Gorda makes a visit there time well spent.

TRANSPORTATION

Flights: Tropic Air (☎722 2008) makes at least five daily flights to each of the following: **Placencia** (20min., BZ$69); **Dangriga** (45min., BZ$112); **Belize City International** (1hr., BZ$187); **Belize City Municipal** (1hr., BZ$152). Maya Island Air (☎722 2856) offers similar rates and itineraries.

Buses: Southern Transport, on Back St., south of town, goes to **Belize City** (8hr.; 4, 5, 10am; BZ$22) via **Dangriga** (5hr., BZ$13) and **Independence** (for connections to **Placencia**). James buses (☎722 2049) make faster times along the same route from King St., in the lot opposite the police station (7hr.; 6, 8am, and noon; BZ$13). Buses leave near the clock tower in Central Park (11am-noon) to: **Maya Villages,** including **San**

Pedro Columbia (Lubaantun), **San Antonio, Blue Creek, Santa Cruz** (Río Blanco National Park), and **Laguna** (Agua Caliente National Park). The buses have their final destination on the windshield, ask driver to be certain. As return service for all village buses leaves at 3-5am on M, W, F, Sa, it is not possible to use buses for day-trips.

Ferries: Several boats go back and forth to Guatemala from Punta Gorda. North of customs on Front St. lies **Requena's Charter Service** (☎ 722 2070), which makes one trip daily to **Puerto Barrios, Guatemala** (50min., 9am, BZ$25). Go to the customs office by the wharf 30min. ahead of time to get your departure stamp and pay the BZ$7.50 conservation fee. The **Pichilingo**, a Guatemalan skiff, also heads to **Puerto Barrios** (1hr., M-Sa 4pm, BZ$26). Captain Rigoberto James goes to **Livingston** (Tu and F 10am, BZ$35). Boats to Puerto Barrios also stop in Livingston (5 person minimum, BZ$35). It's possible to get to Livingston by ferry from Puerto Barrios (BZ$10).

✈️❓ ORIENTATION AND PRACTICAL INFORMATION

Punta Gorda hugs the coastline. For quick orientation, remember that the coastline runs roughly north-south, and the major roads parallel to the coast are **Front Street, Main Street, and Middle Street.** Most activity is concentrated on these streets. Far West St. traces the western boundary of "P.G.," as the city is most frequently called. Buses arrive into the south end of town. If you do wind up at the terminal, make a right onto the road as you walk out (10min.). Look for the clock tower overhead. The tower is in the **central park,** and **Main St.** runs along it. The airstrip is northwest and the ocean is east.

Tourist Information: The **Belize Tourism Board** (☎ 722-2531) has an office on the waterfront, just south of the Customs Office. Its rarely-kept hours are from Tu-Sa 8-noon and 1-5pm. Offers maps, brochures, bus schedules, and official advice. The **Toledo Visitors Information Center** (☎ 722 2470), on Front St. behind the customs office on the wharf, in the building with the Dem Dats Doin sign. Provides details about tours, flights, activities, and up-to-date bus schedules. Open M-W and F-Sa 7am-noon. However, be warned that both of the offices keep erratic hours.

Banks: Belize Bank, on Main St., at the northeast corner of the park, changes cash and traveler's checks. Cash advances on MC/Visa (BZ$15 fee). Open M-Th 8am-1pm, F 8am-4:30pm. In emergencies **Texaco** changes traveler's checks in sums over US$100.

Supermarket: Vernon's Store, on Front St., south of customs, sells snacks and dry goods. Open M-W and F-Sa 8am-noon and 2-5pm, Th 8am-noon.

Police: (☎ 722 2022, emergency 90), next to the post office on Front St. Open 24hr.

Pharmacy: P.G. Pharmacy (☎ 722 2107), on Main St., near the bank. Open M-Sa 8am-noon, 1-5pm, and 7-9pm.

Medical Services: Punta Gorda Hospital (☎ 722 2026), at the end of Main St. near the bus station and the cemetery. Outpatient clinic and emergency room. Open daily 8am-noon and 1-5pm. The **Red Cross** is across from the hospital. Open M, W, F 9-11am.

Telephones: BTL (☎ 702 2048), on Main St., a block north of Central Park. Free collect calls. **Fax** service. Open M-F 8am-noon and 1-5pm. Most public payphones are located at the north end of Main St.

Internet Access: Carysha, on Main St., just southeast of the clock tower. BZ$3 per 15min. Open M-F 8am-noon and 1-5pm.

Post Office: Front St., across from the customs office. Open M-F 8:30am-noon and 1-5pm, F until 4:30pm.

ACCOMMODATIONS

Like much of the rest of Belize, Punta Gorda has not started catering to tourists. Rooms are adequate, but most guests stay for just a night.

■ **Charlton's Inn,** 9 Main St. (☎722 2197), at the north end of town. Big, modern accommodations a block from the sea. Rooms with TV, fan, a desk, and private bath. Singles BZ$25, with A/C BZ$50; doubles BZ$35/BZ$60. MC/V. ❷

The St. Charles, 23 King St. (☎722 2149), left on the corner of King St., 2 blocks north of the clock tower. Simple, spacious rooms with TV, multiple fans, and bed. Singles with private bath BZ$30; doubles BZ$30, with private bath BZ$40. ❷

Dem Dats Doin (☎722 2470), takes ecotourism to a new level. It's a self-sufficient "organic mini-biosphere" that runs on energy from photovoltaic cells and pig manure. To get there, take the San Pedro Columbia-bound bus (M, W, F, Sa noon, BZ$2.50) from the bank and ask to be let off at Dem Dats Doin, after the wooden bridge. There is a representative at the info box in P.G. at the dock, behind customs. 2hr. tour including butterfly ranch US$5; bed and breakfast singles US$15; doubles US$20. ❷

Punta Gorda

⌂ ACCOMMODATIONS
Charlton's Inn, **2**
Nature's Way, **6**
The St. Charles, **4**

🍴 FOOD
Earth Runnin's Café and Bakut Bar, **3**
Gomier's Foods, **1**
Punta Caliente, **7**
Titanic, **5**

Nature's Way Guest House and Restaurant (☎722 2119), at the south end of Front St. next to the large Catholic church. Excellent view of the sea, wooden floors, shiny common baths, and hammocks. You may be awakened "nature's way" at 5am by roosters next door. Bring mosquito repellent. Ultra-cool "Chet" provides info on the jungle and Maya villages. Check-out 10am. Dorm beds BZ$15; singles BZ$20; doubles BZ$30. ❶

FOOD AND ENTERTAINMENT

The large, newly built **PG Sports Bar,** across from Clock Tower, is a great place to watch major sporting events on mammoth projection TV's. Also features karaoke, dancing, and occasional live music Th-Su nights. The **Dreamlight Club,** on the top floor of the rickety building across from Mahung's, offers a pool table but not much of an atmosphere. **The Challenger's Club** is the home of the local band, *Tropical Sensation*. Both clubs are open until 3am on weekends.

■ **Punta Caliente,** 108 José María St., just north of the bus terminal, is Punta Gorda's hidden treasure. Far enough from most hotels and the rapid confusion of immigration rules, Punta Caliente remains a local secret. Fried fish with rice and beans comes in several sizes including huge (BZ$10), huger (BZ$13), and "Dear God, look at the size of that fish!" (BZ$15). Open M-Sa 7am-11pm, Su 8am-2pm. ❸

Earth Runnin's Cafe and Bukut Bar, at Middle St. and North St., is a vegetarian's dream come true, in a unique atmosphere with low lighting, soft reggae music, Belizean crafts, and carved mahogany chairs. Most vegetables cooked are grown in owner Giovanni's backyard. Excellent steamed snapper with rice, beans, vegetables, and salad (BZ$12). Locals favor the vegetarian burrito (BZ$7). Try a drink at the Bukut Bar or surf the net before eating. (BZ$12 per hr.) ❷

Titanic occupies the open-air, 2nd fl. of the southernmost market building on Front St. The simple decor and atmosphere are the big draws, second only to the price. There's no set menu, but standard Belizean rice, beans, and chicken comes in regular (BZ$3) and large portions (BZ$5). Friendly (though slow) service. Open M-Sa 6:30am-8pm. ❶

Gomier's Foods, Belize's Soybean Center. Head north about 3min. past the Texaco station until the "Y" where the 2 big roads meet. It's on the left, at the Plenty International Office. Gomier, a St. Lucian, prepares a veggie lunch special every weekday using local ingredients and soy milk. Ice cream, too. Open daily until 5pm. ❷

▶ DAYTRIPS FROM PUNTA GORDA

NIM LI PUNIT

*Take any northbound **bus** from Punta Gorda along the Southern Hwy., or any Punta Gorda-bound bus and ask to be let out at Nim Li Punit. The last bus heading north from Punta Gorda is at noon, and the last bus heading south to PG leaves Dangriga at 5:30pm. Follow the path to the visitors center. Entrance fee BZ$5. Open daily 8am-4:30pm.*

A third of a mile from the Southern Hwy., 25 mi. north of Punta Gorda, the ruins of Nim Li Punit are an easy side trip on the way between Punta Gorda and Dangriga. The site is a Late-Classic Maya center which may have had a trading relationship with Copán in Honduras. In addition to temples, Nim Li Punit is best known for its array of impressive stelae with detailed interpretations of the hieroglyphs. **Stela 14,** in the modern visitor's center, depicts the figure with a hat taller than he is, inspired archaeologists to name the site Nim Li Punit (roughly, "large headdress").

Following the path from the visitors center, the first group of structures is the **E-group.** The raised platform may have functioned as an astronomical observatory. From here, it's easy to see the northernmost structure in this group, an immaculately reconstructed **ballcourt.** The original stones were used in the reconstruction, and though the mortar is new, it was made in Maya fashion—without concrete. North of the ball court is the **Plaza of Stelae,** from which there is an excellent view of the Toledo District. Just east up the small staircase lie the tombs. The impressive **Tomb 1,** uncovered in 1986, held at least four members of the royal family, 37 ceramic vessels, and several jade items.

The **visitors center** provides a detailed look at several of the site's most impressive carved stelae. Among these is the second largest stelae in Central America. In addition, there is a small but extremely informative display describing the site and providing some background about both ancient and contemporary Maya culture.

LUBAANTUN

*You can reach the Lubaantun ruins by catching a **bus** between Dangriga and Punta Gorda on the Southern Hwy., destined for the Kekchí village of San Pedro Columbia. The bus drops you off at the dump, about 1.8 mi. from the village, but there are sometimes trucks waiting to take villagers to San Pedro from there. Direct buses run from Punta Gorda to San Pedro (M, W, F, Sa noon) but returns on the same day at 5am, making a walk back to the highway inevitable. From the village, the ruins are a well-labeled 20min. walk.*

Probably the best known of the many Maya ruins near Punta Gorda, Lubaantun is 16 mi. northwest in the village of San Pedro Columbia. Lubaantun ("Place of the Fallen Stones") indeed consists largely of what appear to be big piles of rubble.

MEET THE MAYA Although Belize's beautiful southern Toledo District isn't exactly full of budget hotels, the local Toledo Ecotourism Association (TEA), in cooperation with 13 local Maya villages, offers a more hands-on way for budget travelers to get to know the region. TEA was created over a decade ago in the hopes of bringing extra money into the poverty-stricken Toledo District and spreading cultural awareness of contemporary Maya life. TEA families and guest houses in the villages charge a flat BZ$18.50 for rustic accommodations, either in a bunkhouse or in the thatch homes of Maya families. Visitors eat meals prepared by their host families (BZ$6-8) and can participate in jungle hikes (BZ$7 per hr.), horseback riding (BZ$20 for 4hr.), canoeing (BZ$20 per 4hr.), and other activities which vary by village. The villages are generally tiny, scenic, friendly, without electricity, and relatively safe. TEA accommodations in many villages are an excellent base from which to explore nearby sights, such as Blue Creek, Lubaantun, Agua Caliente National Park, and Río Blanco Falls National Park. All villages in the Toledo district are involved in the TEA program or offer guest houses. Transportation is an additional fee. Check with the tourist office, email the Toledo Ecotourism Association (☎ 722 2096; tea@btl.net), or hop on a bus.

Thomas Gann found the ruins in 1903 and, in the manner of many "great archaeologists" of the day, blasted into them with dynamite—whether the stones had fallen before this explosive excavation isn't entirely clear. Like its somewhat more accessible neighbor Nim Li Punit, Lubaantun was recently reconstructed. The visitors center now houses artifacts and pottery, and the paths are new. Lubaantun's structures are generally a bit larger than those at Nim Li Punit, and the site is more extensive—there are two ball courts, as well as a good-sized temple. Lubaantun's edifices, as well as the buildings in some nearby communities, differ from most Maya structures in their construction; instead of using mortar, blocks were carefully sculpted and seamlessly interlocked. Besides this unique formation, Lubaantun is also famous for the finding of the Crystal Skull. If you need a place to stay, check out nearby **Dem Dats Doin** (see **Accommodations,** above).

NEAR PUNTA GORDA

MAYA VILLAGES

Buses leave from Punta Gorda for each of the Maya Villages (M, W, F, Sa, 11am-noon; returning M, W, F, Sa 4-5am, BZ$3.50). An overnight stay is inevitable. Fortunately, most of the villages have a rustic TEA guesthouse. You can check information at the TEA office, but the bus drivers usually know the location of the guesthouses.

The Toledo District is home to the Kekchi and Mopan Maya groups, who comprise most of Belize's Maya population. The area was rich in Maya sites dating back to the Preclassic Era. However, many Maya moved into the Petén as a result of Spanish persecution. In the late 19th century, the Kekchi and Mopan began moving back into the region. Most of the villages are still traditional, without electricity, and completely agricultural.

BLUE CREEK VILLAGE AND HOKEB HA CAVE

The beautiful Maya village of **Blue Creek** is 4km south of the road that branches before San Antonio. The big attraction in Blue Creek is the creek itself, which streams through lush rain forest. The creek is excellent for swimming and has a swinging tree rope for the more adventurous. Blue Creek has a **TEA guesthouse.**
Near the village is the impressive **Hokeb Ha Cave,** where the Blue Creek runs underground through the limestone. As with almost any cave in Belize, there have been

BELIZE

a variety of Maya artifacts found in Hokeb Ha. It is recommended that you find a guide in Blue Creek Village. As of September 2002, Hokeb Ha was closed due to 2001 Hurricane Iris damage, but is expected to reopen soon.

SANTA CRUZ, RÍO BLANCO NATIONAL PARK, AND UXBENKA

The Mopan Maya village of **Santa Cruz** is located 15km off the Southern Highway junction at the Dump. Santa Cruz is still traditional, with an atmosphere that seems remarkably similar to what must have been like centuries ago. The village was devastated by Hurricane Iris in October 2001, but has rebounded with help from international aid organizations. **Río Blanco National Park** is located a mile west of Santa Cruz on the only road. It has some of the area's most impressive waterfalls, including the signature **Río Blanco Falls,** with a natural 20 ft. diving board. The waterfalls and overhanging cliffs create an inviting pool. (Entrance BZ$5.)

The unexcavated ruins of **Uxbenka** lie east of Santa Cruz, and can be reached in a few minutes. Unfortunately, the caretaker left about five years ago and the village has yet to find another. In the meantime, Uxbenka remains just a muddy mound of trees and shrubs hiding a minor Maya ceremonial site that contained some excellent examples of the Maya agricultural method of raised terraces.

The place to stay in Santa Cruz is with the Marcus Sho family. While not an official member of the TEA, the family is fun-loving and hospitable, and Marcus was a founding member of both TEA and Rio Blanco National Park. (BZ$30 per night with meals, plus extra for any guided tours.) The bus driver will know the location, as everyone knows every place and everyone in these tiny Maya villages.

NEARBY CAYES

Punta Gorda is graced by several strikingly gorgeous islands with coral sand beaches that are perfect for swimming, snorkeling, and camping. The nearest island to Punta Gorda is **Moho Caye.** Though not as nice as the cayes off Placencia or Dangriga, you may want to take a day to snorkel and enjoy the water. Between March-May, **Seal Caye** in the **Sapodillo Cayes** is a great place to see whale sharks. The Sapodillo Cayes are said to be some of the most beautiful in the country. Unfortunately, as mass tourism has yet to reach the area, it can be difficult, frustrating, and expensive to get to there. Try bargaining with Paco (☎722 2246); or Tide, on Front St. If these options fail, ask at the tourist office.

LAGUNA AND AGUA CALIENTE NATIONAL PARK

Buses leave from Punta Gorda for Laguna Village (M, W, F, Sa noon; returning M, W, F, Sa 5am; BZ$3.50). It might be possible to grab a ride with Pedro Chub (see below) if you can catch him ahead of time at the SAGE office.

About 45min. from Punta Gorda by bus, the village of **Laguna** is an extremely open and welcoming community, fully prepared to help visitors relax and enjoy its amazing setting, with access to hiking, canoeing, and caving. There are two accommodation options in Laguna, a **TEA Guesthouse** or the almost-as-rustic **Friends of Lu-ha Guesthouse ❶** (☎702 2970). Both are BZ$18.50 per person, but Lu-ha has more spacious rooms and bathrooms with running water.

In the vast wilderness area surrounding Laguna, is the **Agua Caliente National Park** and its 5750 acres of wetland. An excellent 2-3hr. hiking trail starts from the information center, which is itself a 30min. hike from the village. During the dry season the trail is far more impressive. Between Feb.-May, the trail leads farther into the park to a nesting site of jabiru storks, the largest flying birds in the western hemisphere. It's possible to arrange to meet one of the park officials in Laguna, if you contact the **SAGE** office in Punta Gorda, on Far West St., beforehand. (☎722 2721.) Or ask anyone in the village for Pedro Chub, the super-helpful park coordinator. Pedro can also inform you about a hike up to a 500 ft. mountain ridge with a spectacular view. If you want to explore the nearby caves, you can rent flashlights

COSTA RICA

Endowed with dripping cloud forests, active volcanoes, lush flora and fauna, and a generous, welcoming culture, Costa Rica captivates all who dare to explore it. This tiny country unfolds new and more vibrant colors at every turn. Awe-inspiring surroundings, combined with endless recreational opportunities, easily explain why more and more curious visitors trickle in every day. Yet far too many visitors dart right for the jungle-enshrouded isolation, missing out on much of the country's true magic—its culture and people. Costa Ricans, also known as *ticos*, are proud of their country's strong democracy and outstanding social institutions. Since Costa Rica has no army, it spends an outstanding 23% of the national budget on education, while only 3% it spends on its police force. Between the exploring, take some time to enjoy the people, to kick back, and to internalize the essence of the Costa Rican mantra, *¡Pura vida!*

HIGHLIGHTS OF COSTA RICA

Playa Tamarindo has a perfect mix of nightlife, waves, and superb sunbathing (p. 196).

Monteverde Cloudforest Reserve, Central America's most famous nature reserve, where quetzals, jaguars, monkeys, and sloths strut, swing, and fly (p. 171).

Puerto Viejo de Talamanca will let you experience the eclectic mix of Afro-Caribbean, Spanish, and indigenous cultures of the west, in addition to a vibrant nightlife (p. 246).

Parque Nacional Chirripó, containing Costa Rica's highest peak, Cerro Chirripó, from whose mighty summit the view reaches to both oceans (p. 220).

Cahuita Cahuita, boasts the largest coral reef on Costa Rica's west coast, ideal for scuba and snorkeling, beautiful beaches, and turquoise waves (**p. 243**).

SUGGESTED ITINERARIES

VIVA SPRINGBREAK! Party, Party, Party! and find the fountain of youth at all of these vibrant hotspots. **SAVOR THE CITY.** By night, the tropical music in **San José** (p. 144) will keep you hopping. For a taste of tico revelry, hit Calle de la Amargura in **San Pedro** (p. 144), the heart of the *tico* college scene. Spend another wild night at the mini-disco town of Centro Comercial El Pueblo (p. 153). For more classy outings, head out to **Escazú** (p. 155). **BRONZED BOOTY AND BEACHES.** In the Nicoya Peninsula, cosmopolitan **Playa Tamarindo**'s (p. 192) endless silvery waters are prized by surfers and it has a thumping nightlife. Then head straight to **Jacó** (p. 206) for surfing in dangerous waters and wild young crowds. To experience the turquoise Caribbean and a hot nightlife, hit **Puerto Viejo de Talamanca** (p. 246).

WALK ON THE WILD SIDE. For the best of Mother Nature, first head out to **P.N. Rincón de la Vieja** (p. 180), with its active volcano, sulfuric lagoons, and boiling mud pits. Also visit **P.N. Santa Rosa** (p. 181), famous for turtle watching. **P.N. Barra Honda** (p. 198) offers breathtaking limestone caves. The **Monteverde Cloud Forest Reserve** (p. 171), is a place to explore and hike through the lush wilderness. At **Volcán Arenal** (p. 189), hike by day and, by night, loosen up in thermal waters with dazzling views of oozing magma. Guided boat tours take you to **Refugio Nacional de Vida Silvestre Caño Negro** (p. 190), an aquatic wonderland with labyrinths of mangroves and lots of wildlife. Head south and visit **Bahía Drake** (p. 227), where monkeys drip off mango trees and waves crash into jungle coasts. Finally, visit **Tortuguero** (p. 238), on the Caribbean for hiking, boating, and turtle spying.

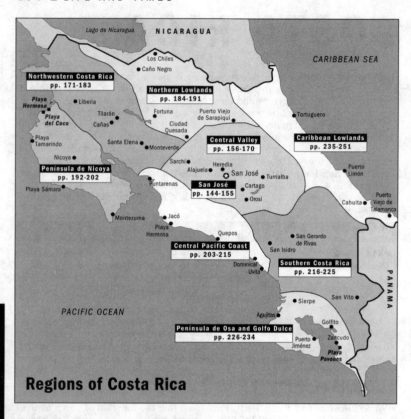

Regions of Costa Rica

LIFE AND TIMES

LAND, FLORA, FAUNA

Costa Rica contains an immense variety of landscapes within its compact area. The country is dominated by a massive arc of highlands that include more than 60 volcanoes, eight of which are active, in four distinct mountain chains—**Cordillera de Guanacaste, Cordillera de Tilarán, Cordillera Central,** and **Cordillera de Talamanca.** Between Cordilleras Central and Talamanca lies the high Central Valley, or Meseta Central, whose fertile soil is home to over half of Costa Rica's population. The mountain ranges affect the country's **climate** significantly. On the rocky peninsulas of the Pacific side there is increasing precipitation from north to south, with rain from May to October in the north and from April to December in the south. On the Caribbean side there is rainfall year-round and the climate varies with the elevation. The convergence of tectonic plates off Central America's Pacific coast makes Costa Rica prone to both **earthquakes** and **volcanic eruptions.**

Costa Rican national parks and preserves comprise more than 25% of its area, and although the country makes up only 0.03% of the world's territory, it is home to 6% of Earth's **biodiversity.** Costa Rica serves as the major intersection point on the isthmus of Central America for species from North and South America.

Roughly 25% of Costa Rica's unique geology and ecology is protected in an extensive system of national parks, biological reserves, forest reserves, and wildlife refuges; no other country in the world protects a greater portion of its territory.

HISTORY

THE COLONIAL PERIOD. 1502 was the year that **Christopher Columbus** landed on Costa Rica's eastern shores and decidedly called it "rich coast." Unlike most of its Central American neighbors, during the colonial period, the country's remoteness and lack of mineral wealth made it a forgotten land, allowing it to develop with the least colonial influence. Furthermore, there was no native population to subjugate, and subsistence farming evolved relatively peacefully.

INDEPENDENCE AND GROWTH OF THE REPUBLIC. On September 15, 1821, Guatemala declared its independence and incited the rest of Central America to do the same. This news, however, didn't reach distant Costa Rica until one month later, so without any need for uprisings, Costa Rica simply accepted its independence and had its first peaceful elections. Costa Rica already had a thriving export system, thus avoiding stratified system of land-owning elites and working peasants that characterized its Central American neighbors in the late 1800's.

Although Costa Rica has had a stable political history, it hasn't always been a perfect democracy. For most of the 19th century, literacy requirements restricted voting to about 10% of the population. In 1870 the country's most contoversial figure **General Tomás Guardia** seized the presidency. Albeit diminished civil liberties and a sizable trade deficit, his ambitious policies actually established the base for future economic progress. In 1871 he expanded the crop base to coffee, sugar, and bananas, which led to better roads and to the construction of the railroad to the Caribbean. Tomás Guardia also established free, compulsory primary education systems, securing the country's legacy of high literacy rates.

STRAYING FROM PEACE. Costa Rica has only strayed from its peaceful tradition twice. The first time happened in 1856, when **William Walker** attempted to turn Central America into a slave state of the United States. Although Costa Ricans had never fought before, they raised arms to defend their freedom. They won the first battle, **La Batalla de Santa Rosa**, in Costa Rica, and when Walker's men fled to Rivas, Nicaragua, the *ticos* followed in an effort to defend their neighbors. Costa Rica's national hero, **Juan Santamaría,** was born out of the **Batalla de Rivas,** when he sacrificed his life to set the enemy fort on fire and assure Costa Rica's victory.

The second violent event took place almost 100 years later, when incumbent **Rafael Angel Calderón Guardia** claimed an electoral fraud and refused to give up the presidency to Otilio Ulate. This resulted in a civil war led by **José Figueres Ferrer,** an intellectual who appealed to the people and headed a populist, anti-authoritarian uprising demanding respect for democracy. As head of the new **Founding Junta of the Second Republic,** Figueres banned the communist party, gave women and blacks the right to vote, established a presidential term limit of four years, created an **Electoral Tribunal,** and abolished the Costa Rican military. After 18 months in power, Figueres stepped down from the interim junta, handing over the presidency to **Otilio Ulate,** the man who had originally won the elections. Figueres was later elected president in 1953, admired for his actions.

SO LONG, SOLDIERS. Since the army was abolished in 1949, Costa Rica has enjoyed peace, political stability, and a relatively high degree of economic comfort. In addition, it has become Latin America's most democratic country. Most of Costa Rica's non-financial problems in the second half of the 20th century have been partly because of civil strife in other Central American nations, especially in

COSTA RICA

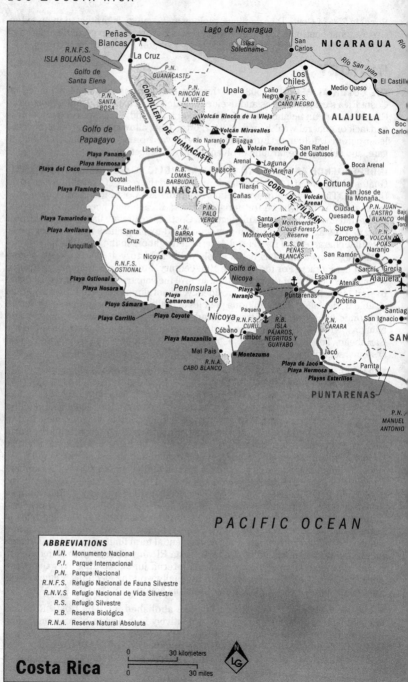

ABBREVIATIONS

M.N.	Monumento Nacional
P.I.	Parque Internacional
P.N.	Parque Nacional
R.N.F.S.	Refugio Nacional de Fauna Silvestre
R.N.V.S	Refugio Nacional de Vida Silvestre
R.S.	Refugio Silvestre
R.B.	Reserva Biológica
R.N.A.	Reserva Natural Absoluta

Costa Rica

0   30 kilometers

0   30 miles

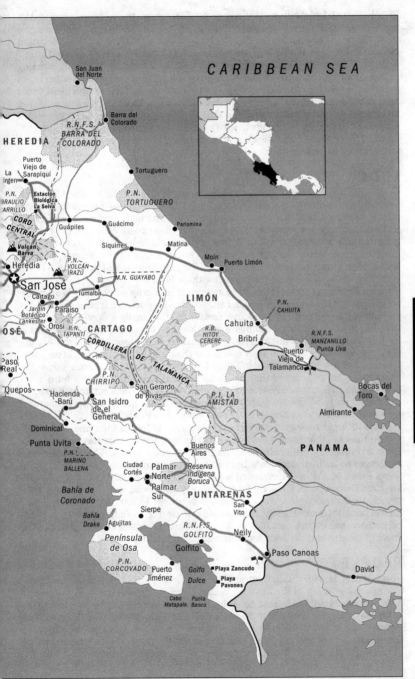

CARIBBEAN SEA

San Juan del Norte

Barra del Colorado

HEREDIA

R.N.F.S. BARRA DEL COLORADO

Puerto Viejo de Sarapiquí

La Virgen

Tortuguero

P.N. BRAULIO CARRILLO

Estación Biológica La Selva

P.N. TORTUGUERO

CORD. CENTRAL

Guápiles

Guácimo

Parismina

Volcán Barva

Siquirres

Matina

Heredia

P.N. VOLCÁN IRAZÚ

Moín

Puerto Limón

San José

M.N. GUAYABO

Cartago

Turrialba

LIMÓN

P.N. CAHUITA

Jardín Botánico Lankester

Paraíso

Orosi

P.N. TAPANTÍ

CARTAGO

R.B. HITOY CERERE

Cahuita

JOSÉ

CORDILLERA DE TALAMANCA

Bribrí

R.N.F.S. MANZANILLO Punta Uva

Paso Real

P.N. CHIRRIPÓ

Puerto Viejo de Talamanca

Quepos

Hacienda Barú

San Gerardo de Rivas

P.I. LA AMISTAD

Bocas del Toro

San Isidro de el General

Almirante

Dominical

Punta Uvita

Buenos Aires

PANAMA

P.N. MARINO BALLENA

Ciudad Cortés

Palmar Norte

Reserva Indígena Boruca

Bahía de Coronado

Palmar Sur

PUNTARENAS

Sierpe

San Vito

Bahía Drake

Agujitas

R.N.F.S. GOLFITO

Neily

Península de Osa

Golfito

Paso Canoas

David

P.N. CORCOVADO

Puerto Jiménez

Golfo Dulce

Playa Zancudo

Playa Pavones

Cabo Matapalo

Punta Banco

COSTA RICA

El Salvador and Nicaragua. As many as 500,000 **refugees** have poured across the border since the late 1970s, an overflow which has caused internal problems like unemployment swells, higher illiteracy rates, and mounting tensions between *ticos* and their new neighbors. Today this is still a complex and unresolved issue.

The 1980's brought devaluation, soaring welfare and oil costs, the plummeting prices of coffee, sugar, and bananas, and instability from the Sandinista period in neighboring Nicaragua to the region. In 1987, however, former president **Oscar Arias Sánchez** earned the **Nobel Peace Prize** when he achieved a consensus among all Central America leaders with the *Plan de Paz Arias*, a sustained cease-fire agreement that laid the groundwork for peace and a unified Central American Parliament. Since then, Costa Rica has strived to be an oasis of peace and prosperity amidst an often chaotic and conflict-torn isthmus.

TODAY

Costa Rica is now one of the most prosperous countries in Latin America. It has been and continues to be politically stable and its well-educated population maintains a strongly democratic spirit and an awareness for many environmental, political, and social issues. Economically, the country has experienced relatively stable growth and a slow reduction in inflation. Some challenges, such as unemployment, informal sector employment, and poverty still trouble the country, but to a lesser degree than in most of the region. The government and population seem generally willing and determined to tackle these issues.

Costa Rica's export-oriented economy relies primarily on **tourism.** Worldwide competition in the coffee and banana markets has increased, but Mother Nature is still the key to the country's success. **Ecotourism,** essentially a Costa Rican invention, has made the country famous worldwide, and continues to be a huge draw for foreign tourists. But not everything is sunshine in the tourism industry—while the government has plans to steer tourism in the direction of high-end, luxury ecotourism, and toward a sustainable form of "sea, sand, and sun" tourism, conservation groups are concerned that larger facilities will put too heavy a burden on Costa Rica's precious ecosystems. President Pacheco remains committed to environmental and social sustainability to preserve Costa Rica's unspoiled natural resources within its reputation for convenience and safety.

Costa Rican **technology** is modern—cell phones and Internet use are more widespread than in other Latin American countries, and the country has an unusually large and diverse media culture. Costa Rica certainly does still face **institutional challenges** to its high standards in health care, education, and welfare. Despite Costa Rica's overall well-developed welfare system, nearly 20% of the population, are classified as poor. The ugly face of poverty and social stratification becomes manifest in increasing levels of crime and sex tourism. In 2000, despite overall positive economic trends, there was increased civil unrest, including the largest political demonstrations in Costa Rica in 30 years. Citizens protested monopolies in the energy business and the need for more education funding.

PEOPLE

Costa Ricans, known within Central America as *ticos*, make up the most traditionally Spanish country in the ithsmus, both ethnically and culturally. Out of nearly 3,900,000 inhabitants, **indígenas** comprise less than 1% of the population, and those of **African** descent make up only 3% and are concentrated on the Atlantic coast. The region's largest remaining indigenous groups are the **Bribrí** and **Cabécar.** Except for **Guanacaste,** where people have darker skin due to the mix with the Cabécares, 94% of the population is of European descent. Generations of other ethnic groups, including Germans, Americans, Italians, and Chinese, have also immigrated to Costa Rica and over the past 150 years have established small communities.

Spanish, with a characteristic *tico* twist in accent and usage, is the official language. Native indigenous languages are still spoken and English is common along the Caribbean coast. The country's most popular phrases are *pura vida* (cool, awesome) and its synonym *tuanis*, from the English phrase "too nice" after Costa Ricans used it for a while. Some other unique expressions are: *mae* (dude), *quedarse bateado* (remain stupefied or baffled), and *atarantado* (wound-up).

Costa Rica is a politically secular country, with religious freedom written in the constitution. **Roman Catholicism** is the official religion and is practiced by about 90% of the population. Catholic churches exist in nearly every town in the country, and they are often at the center of cultural and religious events. Holy Week is a fervent balance of piety, pilgrimage, prayer, and partying. The majority of blacks on the Caribbean are Protestant, and there are also minority groups of Jehovah's Witnesses, Jews, Menonites, Quakers, and other denominations.

CULTURE

FOOD & DRINK

If it doesn't have rice and beans, it isn't *tico!* Rice and black beans are everyday staple foods and part of every Costa Rican's diet, whether *gallo pinto* (fried rice and beans cooked with spices) for breakfast, a *casado* (plate of rice, beans, plantains, salad, and meat) for lunch, or a black bean soup for dinner. **Comida típica** (native dishes) in Costa Rica can best be described as tasty, not spicy. The Atlantic Coast has a much stronger Caribbean influence with everything, from *gallo pinto* to chicken cooked in coconut milk. *Sodas*, the small diners you can find at almost every corner, are ideal for inexpensive, flavorful, home-style cooking.

Batidos (fruit shakes) and *frescos* (milk or water based fruit drinks) are everywhere, and don't be surprised when you see *ticos* from age 5 to 80 enjoying a big glass of Costa Rica's world-class coffee (usually mixed with milk) more than once a day. Along with coffee, *horchata*, a cornmeal drink with cinnamon, and *agua dulce*, a drink made with boiled water and brown sugar, are traditional. *Pipas*, green coconuts with chopped-off tops full of refreshing coconut water, are also popular and sold at roadside stalls. *Guaro*, the local liquor, is a clear, cheap moonshine that mixes nicely with anything, and is the *campesino's* drink of choice. Finally, when it comes to beer, anyone who's not a fan of Imperial, the Costa Rican beer, is liable to be chased out of the country.

CUSTOMS & ETIQUETTE

All Costa Ricans share a strong character regarding civil rights and liberties, and are always willing to stand up against whomever threatens these ideals. *Ticos* are very **family-oriented.** Kids live with their parents through their college years and don't leave home until they get married. In general, *ticos* are very affectionate and are often **physically expressive.** When saying hi to someone you know, young or old, it is routine to kiss the person once, on the cheek. You can also hug; it will always be well-received. It isn't unusual to see couples holding hands or walking arm in arm, and in public places like bars and discos, it isn't bad manners for couples to hug, kiss, or even for girls to sit on their boyfriend's lap. When it comes to gender relations, *machismo* has left its mark, yet women still appreciate chivalrous men.

Although times are changing, most people in the country are committed Catholics, and their religious beliefs make **sexual relations before marriage** an ongoing taboo, especially among older generations. **Homosexuality** is another hot topic, and although in general people are more open about it, public displays of affection is usually uncomfortably accepted.

COSTA RICA

THE ARTS

Long before Columbus set foot on the soil, the indigenous populations were sophisticated artisans of **gold, jade,** and **stone.** An impressive and mysterious set of artifacts from southern Costa Rica, the **Diquis stones,** are almost perfectly spherical. Although since colonization Costa Rica's arts and culture have been dominated by European ideals, Costa Ricans still take pride and an active interest in their pre-Columbian history and culture.

Prior to the 20th century, Costa Rican literature drew primarily from folk tales and colloquial expression in a movement known as *"costumbrismo."* The nation's working people were represented through *El Moto* and *Las Hijas del Campo* by **Joaquín García Monge.** Despite the strength of this movement, Costa Rican literature didn't fully bloom until 1900, when it began to give voice to political and social criticism. Playwrights **Alberto Cañas** and **Daniel Gallegos** accompanied the so-called "Circle of Costa Rican Poets" in an attempt to unite the nation's thinkers against the sociopolitical cruelties of the twentieth century. Many *ticos* revere the country's contemporary authors: **Fabián Dobles,** winner of the Premio Nacional, Costa Rica's highest distinction for artistic and intellectual achievement; and **Carlos Salazar Herrera,** poet, professor, and author of *Cuentos de Angustias y Paisajes.*

ESSENTIALS

EMBASSIES & CONSULATES

Embassies of Costa Rica: Australia, Piso 11, 30 Clarence St, N.S.W. 2000 Sydney (☎612 9261 1177; fax 9261 2953). Open M-F 10am-5pm. **Canada,** 325 Dalhousie St., Ste. 407, Ottawa, Ontario, Canada K1N 7G2 (☎613-562-2855; fax: 562-2582). Open M-F 9am-5pm. **South Africa,** P.O. Box 68140, Bryanston 2021, South Africa (☎27 11 705 3434; fax 11 705 1222). Open M-Su 8am-6pm. **UK,** Flat 1, 14 Lancaster Gate, London W2 3LH (☎171 706 8844; fax 171 706 8655). **US,** 2114 "S" St., NW, Washington, D.C. 20008 (☎202-234-2945; fax 202-265-4795; www.costarica-embassy.org). Open M-F 9am-5pm. **Consulate:** 2112 S St. NW, Washington, D.C. 20008 (☎202-328-6628; fax 202-265-4795). Open M-F 10am-1pm.

Consular Services in Costa Rica: Australia, Ireland, and New Zealand don't have embassies in Costa Rica. **US Embassy:** (mailing address: Apdo 920-1200, San José), Calle 120, Av. Central, Pavas, San José, Costa Rica (☎220 3939; after hours 220 3127; fax 220 2305; www.usembassy.or.cr). Open M-F 8am-4:30pm. Call for detailed hours of services. Canada and the UK also have consulates in Costa Rica.

ENTRANCE REQUIREMENTS

Passport (p. 21). Required of all visitors. Passports must be valid for at least 6 months after date of entry.

Visa (p. 22). Not required for citizens of Australia, Canada, Ireland, New Zealand, South Africa, UK, US, or members of the European Union.

Tourist Card. Available upon entry for US$4. Valid for 90 days; renewable at the Dirección de Migración in San José (p. 147).

Onward/Return ticket. Required of all visitors.

Inoculations and Medications (p. 29). None required.

Work Permit (p. 22). A valid **Employment Authorization Document** (EAD) is required of all foreigners planning to work in Costa Rica.

Driving Permit (p. 49). Valid foreign license and photo ID required. Vehicle permits are issued at border crossings into Costa Rica.

Airport Departure Tax. US$17. Cash only.

COSTA RICA

TOURIST OFFICES

Instituto Costarricense de Turismo (ICT), San José (☎223 1733; fax 223 5452; info@tourism-costarica.com; www.tourism-costarica.com). **Branch location:** Av. Central/2, Calle 5, Plaza de la Cultura. The national tourist bureau. Free maps and helpful hints. Publishes a comprehensive listing of tour companies and lodgings. Information in the **US:** (☎800-343-6332). Open M-F 8am-8pm EST.

Costa Rican National Chamber of Tourism (CANATUR), (www.tourism.co.cr or www.canatur.org). Extensive tourism information.

MONEY

COLONES (¢)		
	AUS$1 = ¢204	¢100 = AUS$0.52
	CDN$1 = ¢242	¢100 = CDN$0.44
	IR£1 = ¢464	¢100 = IR£0.23
	NZ$1 = ¢176	¢100 = NZ$0.61
	ZAR1 = ¢35	¢100 = ZAR3.09
	US$1 = ¢377	¢100 = US$0.28
	UK£1 = ¢574	¢100 = UK£0.19
	EUR€1 = ¢366	¢100 = EUR€0.29

The above exchange rates were accurate as of August 2002. Be advised, however, that rates are frequently changing. As a general rule, it's cheaper to convert money in Costa Rica than at home. Airports are usually good for exchanging money, but it is wise to bring enough foreign currency for the first 24-72 hours of your trip. The rates above were accurate as of June 2002. The Costa Rican currency is the **colón** (¢). Printed prices may use two periods (e.g., ¢1.234.56 means one thousand two hundred thirty-four colones and fifty-six hundredths). Taxes include a 13% **sales tax,** a 10% **service charge** on all bills, and a 3% **tourism tax** on hotel rooms; usually these charges will be included in prices cited. Particularly good service may deserve an extra **tip** of 5% or so. In smaller *sodas*, tipping is rare. Tour guides generally appreciate something extra. Small change is appropriate for porters in hotels and restaurants. Taxi drivers are not tipped. US dollars are accepted throughout the country and exchanged at most banks. Many banks **advance cash** on Visa, and/or MasterCard. **ATMs** are common, but may not accept international cards. **Traveler's checks,** on the other hand, are convenient and can be exchanged easily in most places.

While more expensive than the "norm" in Central America, the cost of traveling in Costa Rica is still relatively cheap. You can find dorm beds for US$4-6 in some cases, and more substantial lodging with private bath and perhaps A/C is available for around US$10 and up. *Sodas* offer the cheapest meals, and you can eat for as little as US$2. Staying away from the most touristed areas will keep costs down, and allow the frugal traveler to get by on a minimum of US$20 per day.

COLÓN	❶	❷	❸	❹	❺
ACCOMMODATIONS	¢380-3770	¢3770-7550	¢7550-24,500	¢24,500-37,700	¢37,700-56,500
	US$1-10	US$10-20	US$20-65	US$65-100	US$100-150
FOOD	¢380-1150	¢1150-2650	¢2650-3800	¢3800-5300	¢5300-7550
	US$1-3	US$3-7	US$7-10	US$10-14	US$14-20

SAFETY

Although the crimes aren't usually violent, travelers should be as cautious as they would be in major cities and tourist areas around the world. In March 2000, two US citizens died near the town of Cahuita, on the Caribbean Coast. Costa Rica still remains one of the safest countries in Latin America. The most prevalent problem is **theft**. Pickpockets use many clever scams to divert attention, so be wary. Keep valuable items out of site; wear discreet apparel (no flashy jewelry); and watch out for counterfeit money. It's a good idea to always have a hand on your bag or an arm through a strap when your pack is at your side. Also, always be careful to use licensed taxis, which are red and have medallions painted on the side, or which are orange at the airport, and not "pirate" taxis. As in many parts of Latin America, women are subject to more attention than might be desired—it's hard to walk outdoors without hearing catcalls, especially in the Caribbean region. Usually, the best policy is to ignore such advances. In addition, always try to travel in groups. See **Safety and Security** (p. 26).

Exploring Costa Rica's forests and wildlife can be exhilarating and fun, however, it has its risks. Ask before walking into a forest; they are dense and extremely easy to get lost in. The safest option is to always go with a guide. Always let someone— a friend, your hostel, a park ranger—know when and where you are going.

HEALTH

Life expectancy in Costa Rica is an impressive 76-plus years, a testimony to the quality of the universal medical care provided to all citizens. San José has well-equipped medical facilities and many English speaking doctors. Drinking water in major hotels and restaurants in the capital is purified. Although the tap water is usually okay, water outside San José should be purified before drinking (particularly in rural areas). Anti-malarial precautions are advised for travel in the lowlands, especially near the Nicaraguan border (see **Health**, p. 29). There have also been cases of dengue fever, which is transmitted by mosquito bites, especially in the coastal areas. Some precautions to be taken are wearing the appropriate clothes and using mosquito repellant. The names in Costa Rica for common drugs are: *aspirina* (aspirin), *paracetamol* (acetaminophen), *penicilina* (penicillin), and *antihistamínico* (antihistamine/allergy medicine). Brand names such as Tylenol, Advil, and Pepto Bismol are also well known.

BORDER CROSSINGS

NICARAGUA. There is one land crossing. **Peñas Blancas/Sapoá:** 75km north of Liberia and near Rivas, Nicaragua; for info on the Nicaraguan side, see p. 559, and for information on the Costa Rican side, see p. 183. There is also a crossing at Río San Juan near **Los Chiles,** south of San Carlos, Nicaragua. For information on the Nicaraguan side of this crossing, see p. 568, for the Costa Rican side, see p. 192.

PANAMA. There are three land crossings. **Paso Canoas:** 18km southeast of Ciudad Neily, Costa Rica, and near David, Panama. For information on crossing into Panama, see p. 225. **Sixaola/Guabito:** On the Caribbean coast 1½ hours from Puerto Viejo de Talamanca, near Changuinola, Panama; catch a bus from Puerto Viejo (see p. 246). For details on the crossing itself, see p. 251. A third crossing at **Río Sereno,** east of San Vito, is rarely used.

KEEPING IN TOUCH

Both **fax** and **Internet** service are plentiful and speedy in Costa Rica. Internet cafes are scattered throughout the country, and fax machines can be found in most post offices. **Mail** service to and from Costa Rica is quite reliable. Airmail letters to the US take about seven to 10 days, and only a bit more to Europe. Steep customs duties (up to 100% of value) can be charged for anything larger than a letter (¢90-170 for letters up to 20g), so bulky mailings can be expensive. If you do plan to receive packages, remind the sender to mark the contents and value clearly on the outside. The use of postal codes is not essential. Mail can be received general delivery through the *lista de correos*—address envelopes as follows:

> Shannon MUSIC
> a/c Lista de Correos
> 5655 (postal code) Santa Elena (city)
> Costa Rica

Costa Rica has one of the most efficient **telephone** systems and more telephones per capita than any other Latin American country. Phone numbers have seven digits and no area codes. Not many pay phones accept ¢5, ¢10, and ¢20 coins anymore, so it is a good idea to buy a pre-paid Costa Rican **phone card** to make calls within the country. These can be purchased at supermarkets, corner stores, and some banks. **ICE** cards are the most convenient and can be used on any private or pay phone. Calls from hotels cost about 30% more than calls from other phones. Dial ☎113 for **local information**, ☎911 for **emergency service** in the greater San José area, and ☎117 (or ☎127 in some areas) for the **police.** For **bilingual operator assistance** with international calls dial ☎116, and for **long distance information** dial ☎124. For more information on making international calls from Central America, see the inside back cover.

COUNTRY CODE	506

TRANSPORTATION

Two airlines, Sansa (☎231 9414; www.grupotaca.com) and the pricier but more reliable Travelair (☎220 3054; 296 2317; www.travelair-costarica.com; reservations@travelair-costarica.com), have **flights** connecting San José with destinations throughout Costa Rica. The **bus** system is labyrinthine, but thorough and cheap; from San José, you can travel almost anywhere in the country for under US$6. You can find the most accurate bus information, including detailed schedules at the **Instituto Costarricense de Turismo (ICT;** ☎506 223 1733), along Av. 2 in San José. If you're traveling by **car,** you'll have a good network of highways at your disposal. A seat belt must be used by the driver and any front-seat passenger, and a safety helmet is required when driving a motorcycle. Drive defensively. Tourists report that hitchhiking is generally safe, but *Let's Go* does not recommend it.

ORIENTATION

Landmarks are the way of the wise in most of Costa Rica, with the exception of San José. Most mid-range and larger towns have streets in an orderly grid of *calles* (streets) and *avenidas* (avenues); the *calles* run north-south and the *avenidas* east-west (exactly the opposite of the Nicaraguan paradigm). Usually odd-numbered *calles* lie to the east of the grid's center and even-numbered *calles* to the west, while odd-numbered *avenidas* increase in number to the north and even-numbered to the south. The grid is usually centered on a *parque central* (central park), and its axes are often Av. Central and Calle Central. An address given as Calle 2, Av. 3/5 means the building is on Calle 2 between Avenidas 3 and 5. Locations are often specified by a certain number of *metros* from the *parque. Metros* here refers to portions of city blocks, not meters; *100 metros al norte del parque central* indicates a building one block north of the *parque.*

TRAVEL RESOURCES

Instituto Costarricense de Turismo (ICT), Apdo. 777 1000; Av. 4/6, Calles 5/7, San José (☎506 223 1733; fax 223 5452; http://www.tourism-costarica.com; email: info@tourism-costarica.com). The national tourist bureau. Free maps and helpful hints. Publishes a comprehensive listing of tour companies and lodgings.

Green Tortoise Adventure Travel, 494 Broadway, San Francisco, CA 94133 (☎800-867-8647 or 415-956-7500; www.greentortoise.com). Their low-priced and adventurous 2-week tour visits volcanoes, waterfalls, beaches, and hot springs.

Jungle Trails por los Caminos de la Selva, Apdo. 2413, San José 1000 (☎506 255 3486; fax 255 2782). Specializes in nature tours, conservation programs, birdwatching and botany trips, and customized itineraries. Invites visitors to meet with subsistence farmers to better understand the circumstances behind deforestation. Tours: 1-15 days or longer. Portion of fee donated to reforestation groups.

The Mountaineers Books, 1001 SW Klickitat Way, Ste. 201, Seattle, WA 98134 (☎800-553-4453; fax 800-568-7604; www.mountaineers.org). Publishes *Costa Rica's National Parks and Preserves: A Visitor's Guide* (US$18.95). Also, check out *Latin America By Bike* (US$14.95).

HOLIDAYS

Most businesses and even public transportation take the day off for holidays in Costa Rica. No one wants to miss the opportunity to party. National holidays include: **January 1,** New Year's Day; **March 19,** San Jose Day; **March/April,** *Semana Santa;* **April 11,** Juan Santamaría Day; **May 1,** Labor Day; **June 20,** St. Peter's and St. Paul's Day; **July 25,** Guanacaste Day; **August 2,** Virgin of Los Angeles Day; **August 15,** Mother's Day and Assumption; **September 15,** Independence Day; **October 12,** *Día de la Raza;* **November 2,** All Soul's Day; **December 25,** Christmas.

SAN JOSÉ

Truth be told, San José (pop. 300,000) can be a disappointing starting point for travelers beginning to explore the serenity and vibrant natural beauty of Costa Rica. The streets are crowded and the air is clogged with diesel fumes. However, those who stay a few days will get to know a much livelier and charismatic version of San José and its inhabitants. Costa Rica's bustling capital is draped with a distinct *tico* flair personified by its laid-back and diverse residents. Since the 1950s, San José has grown rapidly and is now *the* transportation hub of Costa Rica and home to two major universities. Its cool weather, convenient transportation, fantastic nightlife, and sights make it a worthy stopover between the two coasts.

✈ INTERCITY TRANSPORTATION

FLIGHTS

Juan Santa María International Airport, about 15km northwest of San José in Alajuela, is most cheaply accessible by bus from San José to Alajuela (see **Buses,** below). Taxis from San José charge US$10. **Grayline Tours** (☎232 3681 or 220 2126) runs an airport shuttle that picks up from many mid-range and top-end hotels around town for US$6. Call for more info. Airlines flying to **international destinations** include **American** (☎257 1266), **Continental** (☎296 4911), **Copa** (☎222 6640), **Delta** (☎257 2433), **Iberia** (☎227 8266), **Lacsa** (☎296 0909), **Mexicana** (☎257 6334), **SAM** (☎233 3066), **Taca** (☎222 1790), **TWA** (☎221 4638), **United** (☎220 4844), **Varig** (☎257 0094). **Sansa** (☎221 9414; www.flysansa.com) offers scheduled flights **within Costa Rica.** The following are daily high season departures and one-way fares for Sansa:

Carillo near **Sámara** (75min., 8:10 and 11:50am, US$66); **Golfito** (1hr.; 6, 10:30am, 2:15pm; US$66); **Liberia** (50min., 5:15 and 11:50am, US$66); **Puerto Jiménez** (55min., 6am and 2:05pm, US$66); **Quepos** (30min., 6 per day 7:45am-4:25pm, US$44); **Tamarindo** (50min., 6 per day 5:15am-3:50pm, US$66); **Tortuguero** (35min., 1 per day 6am, US$55).

Tobías Bolaños Airport, in Pavas, serves **Travelair** (☎ 220 3054 or 888 535 8832 in US for reservations; www.travelair-costarica.com) domestic flights. Daily high season departures and one-way fares for Travelair include:

Carillo near **Sámara** (75min., 8"30am and 1pm, US$73); **Golfito** (1hr.; 6, 8:30am, 2:30pm; US$76); **Liberia** (50min.; 6, 8:30, 11:30am, 1:30pm; US$73); **Puerto Jiménez** (55min.; 6, 8:30, 11am, 2:30pm; US$76); **Quepos** (30min., 6 daily 6am-4pm, US$45); **Tamarindo** (50min., 4 per day 6am-3pm, US$73); **Tortuguero** (35min., 6:15am, US$60).

BUSES

Buses to almost every destination in the country arrive and depart from one of the city's many stops and terminals. Many cluster around **Terminal Coca-Cola**, site of an old bottling plant between Av. 1 and 3, Calles 16 and 18. The latest schedule is available at the **Instituto Costarricense de Turismo (ICT)** at the Museo de Oro (see **Tourist Information** below).

Alajuela-Airport: TUASA, Av. 2, Calles 12/14. (☎ 222 5325. 30min.; every 10min. 5am-10pm, every 30min. after 10pm; ¢210.)

Cahuita and Puerto Viejo de Talamanca: Terminal Caribe, Av. 13, Calle Central. (☎257 8129. 4hr.; M-F 6 and 8am, 4 per day 10am-4pm; return 5 per day 7:30am-4:30pm; ¢1750.)

Cartago: SACSA from Calle 5, Av. 18/20. (☎233 5350. 50 min., every 10min. 5am-midnight.) Also from Calle 1/3, Av. 2. (10:30pm-midnight; ¢210.)

Fortuna: Terminal Atlántico Norte, Calle 12, Av. 7/9. (☎256 8914. 5hr.; 6:15, 8:40, 11:30am; return noon and 2pm; ¢2300.)

Golfito: TRACUPA, Av. 3/5, Calles 14. (☎222 2666. 11hr.; 7am and 3pm, return 5am and 1pm; ¢3100.)

Heredia: Transportes Unidos 400, Calle 1, Av. 7/9; Av. 2, Calle 10/12; Calle 4, Av. 5/7; Av. 7, Calle 13. (25min., every 10min. 5am-10pm, ¢180.)

Jacó: Transportes Morales, La Coca-Cola, Av. 3, Calle 16. (☎223 1109. 2½hr.; 7:30, 10:30am, 3:20pm; return 5, 11am, 3pm; ¢650.)

Liberia: Pulmitan, Av. 5, Calle 24. (☎256 9552. 4hr., 11 per day 6am-8pm, ¢1410.)

Limón: Caribeños, Terminal Caribe, Av. 13, Calle Central. (☎221 2596. 2½hr., every hr. 5:30am-7pm, ¢1005.)

Monteverde: Autotransportes Tilarán, Atlántico Norte Terminal, Calle 12, Av. 7/9. (☎222 3854. 4½hr., 6:30am and 2:30pm, ¢1330.)

Playa Sámara and Carillo: Calle 14, Av. 5. (6hr.; M-Sa 12:30pm, return 4am, Su 1pm.)

Playa Tamarindo: Alfaro, Calle 14, Av 3/5. (☎222 2666. 5½hr.; daily 3:30pm, return 6:45am.)

Playas del Coco: Calle 14, Av. 1/3. (☎666 0138. 5hr.; 8am and 2pm; return 9am and 2pm.)

Puntarenas: Empresarios Unidos de Puntarenas, Av.12, Calle 16. (☎222 0064. 2½hr.; every 40min. 6am-5pm, return 4:15am to 7pm; ¢855.)

Quepos and Manuel Antonio: Transportes Morales, Terminal Coca Cola, Av. 1/3, Calles 16/18. (☎223 5567. Direct 3½hr.; 6am, noon, 6pm; return 6, 9:30am, noon, 5pm; ¢1375..) Only direct buses continue to Manuel Antonio.

International Buses: Guatemala: TicaBus, Calle 9, Av. 4 (☎221 8954). 60hr. with one night in Nicaragua and one night in El Salvador (6 and 7:30am, ¢10,000). **Honduras:** TicaBus. 48hr. with one night in Managua (6 and 7:30am, ¢9700). **Managua:** TicaBus (11hr.; 6, 7:30, 10am; ¢3000). TransNica, Calle 22, Av. 3/5. (☎223 4242. 11hr., 5:30 and 9am.) NicaBus, Terminal Caribe, Calle Central, Av. 13. (☎256 4248. 11hr., 1 per day 6am.) Panaline, Calle 16, Av. 3/5. (☎256 8721. 11hr., daily 4:30am.) **Panamá City:** TicaBus (16hr., 1 per day 10pm, ¢7000); Panaline (16hr., 1 per day 1pm, ¢8500).

✦ ORIENTATION

San José follows the traditional Costa Rican grid, with *avenidas* running east-west and *calles* running north-south. **Avenida Central** (called **Paseo Colón** north of Calle 22) is the main drag, with a shopping and eating area blocked off to traffic between Calles 2 and 5. Just west of the city center is the frantic **Mercado Central**, bordered by Av. Central/1 and Calle 6/8. Four blocks further west of the market is **Terminal Coca-Cola**, on Av. 1, Calle 16/18. Within the city center, **Barrio Amón**, northeast of Av. 5 and Calle 1, and **Barrio Otoya**, slightly east of Amón, are the most architecturally interesting. West of downtown past Calle 42, **La Sabana** is home to the large **Parque La Sabana.** The quiet, hilly suburb of **Escazú**, with a few gorgeous bed and breakfasts and some of San José's most ritzy restaurants, is 5km west. East of downtown past Calle 35, is upscale **Los Yoses,** followed by student-oriented **San Pedro,** home to the University of Costa Rica and some of the best entertainment.

⊟ LOCAL TRANSPORTATION

Bus: Local buses run about every 5-10min. from about 5am-10pm and go all over San José, including to the suburbs and the airport. There are no official printed schedules. Instead, ask a local, taxi or bus driver, or read the signs on the front of the bus. Most

As Central American cities go, San José is comparatively safe, yet theft, prostitution, and drugs make some areas a little shaky. Problem spots include Terminal Coca-Cola, south of Av. 8 between Calles 2 and 12, Av. 4 to 6 between Calles 4 and 12, and north of the *mercado central*. Generally, areas beyond a couple of blocks from San José center pose more of a threat after dark. The safest way to get around after dark, especially for single women, is by taxi.

bus stops are marked with the destination they serve. Carry small change. Major bus stops include: **Escazú** (Calle 16 and Av. 1/Central); **Guadalupe** and **Moravia** (Av. 3, Calle 5/7); and **San Pedro** (Av. 2, Calle 11/13 and Av. Central, Calle 9/11).

Private Bus: Grayline Tours (☎232 3681 or 220 2126) offers "fantasy buses" to and from popular destinations all over Costa Rica for US$21-25 one-way. Most leave daily between 7-8:30am. Call for reservations.

Car Rental: Prices range from US$19 (for a small sedan) to $105 (for a 4X4) per day. Minimum age to rent is 21, although many companies require drivers to be at least 23. **Avis Rent a Car,** at the Hotel Corobicí, north of the Parque La Sabana on Calle 42 (☎232 9922, at the airport 552 1321). **Budget,** Paseo Colón, Calle 28/30 (☎223 3284, at the airport 441 4444). Open 7am-6pm; airport office open daily 24hr.

Motorcycle Rental: Wild Riders, Calle 32, Paseo Colón (☎256 1636). US$40 per day, US$180 per week, includes basic insurance and helmet. Major credit card and valid driver's license required. Open 7am-10pm.

Bike Rental: EuroTours S.A. and **L&M Tours** (☎282 6817; http://mltours.cjb.net), rent mountain bikes, helmets, and bicycle carriers for US$12 per day, $56 per week.

🚪 PRACTICAL INFORMATION

EMBASSIES

Australia (☎224 1152, ext. 111), no embassy, but a representative can be found on the 2nd fl. of Building B of the Plaza del Este in front of Centro Comercial. Visa forms are available in the office or can be downloaded (www.immi.gov.au/allforms/formlist.htm). Forms must be sent to the Australian embassy in Mexico. Open M-F 8am-5pm.

Canada (☎296 4149), in Sabana Sur, Oficentro Ejecutivo building #5, behind the Contraloría. Visa and passport service before noon. Open M-Th 8am-4:30pm, F 8am-1:30pm.

UK, Av. Central, Calle 35 (☎258 2025, emergency 225 4049), Edificio Colón, 11th fl. Consular services available. Open M-Th 8am-noon.

US, Av. Central, Calle 120 (☎220 3939, emergency 220 3127), in front of the Centro Comercial. Open M 8-11:30am and 1-3pm, Tu 8-11:30am, W-F 8am-4:30pm.

TOURIST AND FINANCIAL SERVICES

Tourist Information: Instituto Costarricense de Turismo, main office Av. 4, Calle 5/7 (☎223 1733, 24hr. cell 389 7258, info service 800-012-3456). Also at Calle 5, Av. Central/2, next to El Museo del Oro, and Av. Central, Calles 5/7, 2nd fl. (☎257 3857). Free maps, intra-city bus schedules, and brochures. Open M-F 8am-5pm, Sa 8am-noon.

Guided Tours:

Costa Rica Expeditions, Av. 3, Calle Central (☎257 0766; fax 257 1665; costaric@expeditions.co.cr), 1 block east of the San José post office. Single and multi-day tours.

Ecole Travel, Calle 7, Av. Central/1 (☎223 2240), inside 7th Street Books, is a reputable and relatively inexpensive. Tours to Tortuguero (2 days US$95, 3 days US$125), Volcán Arenal and Monteverde (4 days US$260), Río Sierpe (3 days US$145), and Jacó (4 days US$169-215).

COSTA RICA

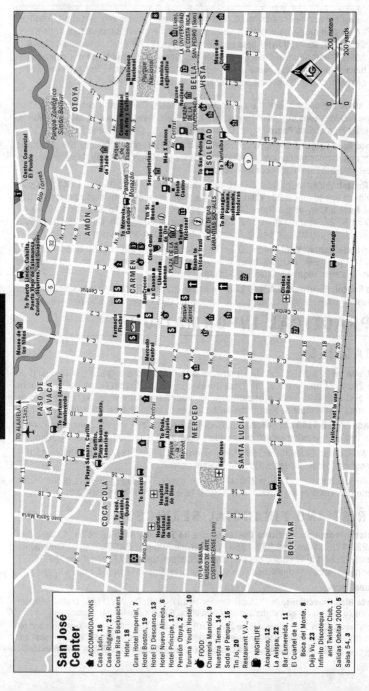

San José Center

■ ACCOMMODATIONS
Casa León, 16
Casa Ridgway, 21
Costa Rica Backpackers Hotel, 18
Gran Hotel Imperial, 7
Hotel Boston, 19
Hotel El Descanso, 13
Hotel Nuevo Almeda, 6
Hotel Príncipe, 17
Pensión Otoya, 2
Toruma Youth Hostel, 10

◆ FOOD
Churrería Manolos, 9
Nuestra Tierra, 14
Soda el Parque, 15
Tin Jo, 20
Restaurant V.V., 4

■ NIGHTLIFE
Acapulco, 12
La Avispa, 22
Bar Esmerelda, 11
El Cuartel de la Boca del Monte, 8
Déjà Vu, 23
Infinito Discoteque and Twister Club, 1
Salidas Orbital 2000, 5
Salsa 54, 3

0   200 meters
0   200 yards

Whitewater Rafting: Aventuras Naturales (☎225 3939). Open daily 7am-6pm. Class III and IV on the Río Pacuare for US$95 per person, students $75. **Ríos Tropicales** (☎233 6455). Open M-F 8am-7pm, Sa 8:30am-noon. Class III and IV on the Río Pacuare for US$95 per person and Río Reventazón for US$75 per person. **Costa Rica Expeditions** (☎257 0766). Open M-Sa 8am-5pm.

Kayaking: Ríos Tropicales (☎233 6455). Experience required. US$25 per hr.

Bungee Jumping: Latin America's oldest and safest bungee company is **Tropical Bungee** (☎232 3956; www.bungee.co.cr). Jumps daily from 9am-4pm at the 80m (265 ft.) Colorado River Bridge. No reservations necessary. US$40 per jump.

Immigration: Dirección de Migración (☎220 0355), on the Autopista General Cañas Hwy., the road to the airport. Take the red bus to Alajuela from Av. 2, Calles 12/14 or Calles 10/12, and get off at *La Oficina de Migración.*

Banks: There are dozens of banks all over San José and nearly all of them have 24hr. Cirrus/Plus/V ATMS. All require photo ID to change cash, and most require passport.

Banco Central, Calle 2, Av. Central/1 (☎243 3333). Open M-F 8:30am-3:30pm.

Banco de Costa Rica, Av. 2, Calle 2/4 (☎287 9000). Open M-F 8:30am-3pm, Sa 7am-2pm.

Banco de San José, Calle Central, Av. 3/5 (☎295 9595). Open M-F 8am-7pm.

Banco Popular, Calle 1, Av. 2/4. Open M-F 8:15am-7pm, Sa 8:15am-noon.

American Express: Calle Central, Av. 3/5 (☎257 1792), across from Banco de an José. Lost or stolen card hotline ☎0 800-011-0271 or 0 800-012-3211. Passport needed for check cashing. Open M-F 8am-4:15pm.

Western Union: Av. 2/4, Calle 9 (☎800-777-7777). Open M-F 8:30am-5pm, Sa 9am-12:30pm.

LOCAL SERVICES

English Bookstores: 7th Street Books, Calle 7, Av. Central/1 (☎256 8251). New and used books and some foreign newspapers. New books ¢5000-8000, used ¢900-2000. Open daily 9am-6pm. **Librería Lehmann,** Av. Central, Calle 1/3, has a small selection of light reading. Open M-F 8am-6:30pm, Sa-Su 9am-5pm.

Gay-Lesbian Organizations: Triángulo Rosa (☎234 2411). **Casa Yemaya** (☎661 0956) organizes all-female excursions throughout the country. Very friendly staff is knowledgeable about challenges for female travelers.

Supermarkets: Más X Menos, Av. Central, Calle 11/13. Open M-Sa 7am-midnight, Su 8am-9pm.

Laundry: Lavandería, Calle 8, Av. Central/1, next to Gran Hotel Imperial. ¢2000 per load. Open M-F 8am-6pm, Sa 8am-5pm.

EMERGENCY AND COMMUNICATIONS

Emergency: ☎911.

Police: ☎911. To report a theft, contact the **Organismo de Investigación Judicial** (OIJ), Av. 6/8, Calles 17/19. Main office at Av. 4, Calle 6. (☎295 3000). English spoken.

Pharmacies: Farmacia Fischel, Av. 1, Calle 2 (☎257 7979), near the center of town. Huge selection. Attentive service. Open M-Sa 8am-7pm, Su 9am-5pm. AmEx/D/MC/V.

Hospitals: Hospital San Juan de Dios, on Paseo Colón, Calles 14/18 (☎257 6282). Large white building where Av. Central turns into Paseo Colón, after Calle 14. 24hr. emergency service. **Clínica Bíblica,** Calle 1, Av. 14/16 (☎257 5252). 24hr. emergency care, 24hr. pharmacy. English spoken.

Telephones: Card and coin phones all over town; most phones take ¢5 and ¢10 coins. Otherwise, buy a prepaid phone card from Más X Menos (see **Supermarkets,** above) or a street vendor. **Radiográphica,** Av. 5, Calle 1 (☎287 0489). US$3 for collect calls. Also has AT&T Direct, MCI, and Sprint service. International calls only. Open daily

7:30am-9pm. Directory assistance ☎113. **Instituto Costarricense de Electricidad (ICE) office,** Av. 2, Calle 3 (☎257 7743). Open M-F 7:30am-7pm, Sa 8am-7pm.

Internet: Internet Café, Av. Central, Calle 7/9, 4th fl. ¢300 per hr. Open daily 8am-midnight. **Café Internet,** Av. Central, Calle 11/13, 2nd. fl., across from Más X Menos.

Post Office: Calle 2, Av. 1/3, in the large green building. San José has no street mailboxes, so all mail must be sent from here. Open M-F 7:30am-6pm, Sa 7:30am-noon.

Postal Code: 1000.

▐ ACCOMMODATIONS

It's best to steer clear of the cheapest lodgings; paying the relatively "pricey" US$10-12 for a dormitory bed is a trade-off for comfortable, clean lodgings and a friendly atmosphere. Accommodations listed are divided into four categories. **East** of the *parque central* is for safe, comfortable, affordable accommodations. Hotels **south** of the *parque central* are reasonably priced, but often louder. Try to avoid places **north** and **west** of the *parque central* which tend to be in dangerous areas. A pleasant alternative to downtown is **San Pedro,** a 10min. bus ride away, and the pleasant suburb of **Escazú,** a 20min. bus ride, which offers beautiful B&Bs.

EAST OF THE PARQUE CENTRAL

▨ **Costa Rica Backpackers Hostel,** Av. 6, Calle 21/23 (☎221 6191; www.costaricaback-packers.com). This inexpensive backpacker magnet has spotless rooms, common hot-water baths, night watchman, free Internet, communal kitchen, cable TV, and a pool. Baggage storage ¢50. Laundry ¢2000. Check-out 11am. Dorms ¢2500 per person. ❶

▨ **Casa Ridgway,** Av. 6/8, Calle 15 (☎222 1400, fax 233 6168; friends@racsa.co.cr), in the short, dead-end street between and running parallel to Av. 6 and 8. An active Quaker peace center, this immaculately-kept home offers a sitting area with a kitchen and dining area. Public phone (☎255 6399), laundry (US$5), and storage available. Quiet hours 10pm-7am. Dorms US$10 per person; singles US$12; doubles US$24. ❶

▨ **Casa León,** Av. 6, Calles 13/15. (☎222 9725). Turn right onto Calle 15 from Av. 2 and go up the first set of stairs to your right. Small, but homey and clean. Well-maintained rooms and appliances. Public phone, laundry (¢2000), and kitchen available. Shared hot baths. Up to 6 people in a dorm. Dorms US$10; singles US$15; doubles US$25. ❶

SOUTH OF THE PARQUE CENTRAL

Hotel Boston, Av. 8, Calles Central/2 (☎257 4499 or 221 0563). Spacious rooms with wooden beds, TVs, and clean, private, hot-water baths. Laundry service and phone available. Singles ¢3500; doubles ¢5000; triples ¢6000. AmEx/MC/V. ❶

Hotel Príncipe, Av. 6, Calles Central/2 (☎222 7983; fax 223 1589), 1 block north of Hotel Boston. The racket from the surrounding bars may be bothersome, but quiet hours after 10pm help. Big rooms are a bit worn but have bright sheets, comfy beds, and private hot-water baths. Attached bar and small lobby with cable TV. Safety deposit box available M-F 8:30am-8pm. Singles ¢4000; doubles ¢5500; triples ¢7000. ❷

NORTH OF THE PARQUE CENTRAL

Gran Hotel Imperial, Calle 8, Av. Central/1 (☎222 8463; fax 257 4922). Dirt-cheap restaurant/bar, laundry (¢1500), book exchange, TV in the lobby, Internet (¢200 per 30min.), public phone, bag storage (¢50 per bag per day), and hot water in the mornings. No smoking or visitors after 10pm. Restaurant open M-Sa noon-8:30pm; bar until 11pm. Singles ¢1500; doubles ¢3000, with bath ¢5000; triples ¢4500. ❶

Pensión Otoya, Calle 1, Av. 3/5 (☎221 3925). Spacious, bright, carpeted rooms. Hot baths are a bit worn. Laundry ¢1000. Free baggage storage. Singles ¢2700, with bath ¢3700; doubles ¢2500/¢3500; triples ¢2300/¢3300. ❶

Hotel Nuevo Almeda, Calle 12, Av. Central/1 (☎233 3551). Clean rooms, huge windows, wall-to-wall carpet, and spotless hot-water baths. Check-out noon. Singles US$15; doubles US$14 per person; triples US$10 per person. Discounts possible. ❷

WEST OF THE PARQUE CENTRAL

Hotel El Descanso, Calle 6, Av. 4 (☎221 9941), entrance on Calle 6. Safe, classy, calm lodgings with comfy beds, TVs, and clean, private hot baths. Very professional staff. The rooms and hallways are spacious. Check-out noon. Singles US$10; doubles US$20. ❶

SAN PEDRO

▨**Toruma Youth Hostel (HI),** Av. Central, Calles 29/31 (☎/fax 224 4085; reca-jhi@racsa.co.cr). Take the San Pedro bus (¢105) from Av. Central, Calles 9/11, and get off at Kentucky Fried Chicken. Toruma is the stately yellow building directly across the street. A backpacker magnet. Single-sex rooms and shared hot baths. Bright, spacious lobby with sofas, cable TV, and lockers. English spoken. Breakfast included 7:30-9am. Free Internet and luggage storage. Reception 7am-10pm. Reservations recommended. Dorms US$13, US$11 with HI card; singles US$26; doubles US$28. AmEx/MC/V. ❷

◘ FOOD

SAN JOSÉ

Black beans, rice, and fried chicken are San José's staples. Western culture has left its mark, however, and fast-food joints abound downtown, especially around Av. Central, Calle 1-3. Authentic, cheap *tico* fare can be found at the hundreds of *sodas* dotting the city. An even cheaper option is the **mercado central,** where you can snag a tasty, inexpensive, variety-filled meal or buy to cook at your hostel. Most higher-quality and pleasant *sodas* and restaurants are around Av. Central.

▨**Soda el Parque,** Calle 2, Av. 4/6. El Parque's round-the-clock hours offer delicious and inexpensive *comida típica* all day long. Medium-sized breakfasts ¢650-1000, large ¢950-1400. *Casados* ¢1000. Open 24hr. AmEx/MC/V. ❶

▨**Tin Jo,** Calle 11, Av. 6/8, is *the* place to splurge on a delicious meal. Exotic Chinese, Thai, Indian, Japanese, Indonesian, and Burmese cuisine. Veggie-friendly menu. Sushi ¢1800-3000; meats ¢3000-4000; noodles ¢2500. Open M-Th 11:30am-3pm and 5:30-10:30pm, F-Sa 11:30-3pm and 5:30-11pm, Su 11:30am-10pm. AmEx/MC/V. ❸

▨**Restaurant Vishnu Vegetariano,** main branch at Av. 1, Calles 1/3. (☎290 0119.) Other locations include Av. 4, Calle 1 (next to the Banco Popular) and Av. 8, Calles 11/13. Fresh fruits and veggies decorate your delicious *gallo pinto* (¢800) or the *plato del día* (¢1150). Main branch open M-Sa 8am-9:30pm, Su 9am-7:30pm. ❶

Nuestra Tierra, Av. 2, Calle 15. Wooden tables, *vaquero*-uniformed waiters, and meals served on palm leafs transport you 70 years back to authentic, country-style cooking in rural Costa Rica. *Plato del día* ¢750, *casados* ¢1100. Open M-Sa noon-10pm. ❶

Churrería Manolos, Av. Central, Calle 2 and Av. 1, Calles 11/13. Famous for its fresh, cinnamon-crispy *churros*. Flavored *dulce de leche* ¢150. Menu also includes standard lunch and dinner meals (rice dishes ¢900-1500). Main location open 24hr. ❶

SAN PEDRO

The heart of San José's bustling student scene, San Pedro is replete with good, inexpensive cafes and restaurants. From San José, catch a bus to San Pedro from Av. Central, Calle 9/11 (10min., every 5-10min., ¢105), ride past Mall San Pedro, and get off when you see the Outlet Mall to your right. This main drag into San Pedro is Av. Central. The street running directly perpendicular is **Calle Central.** Walk north down Calle Central with the **Parque John F. Kennedy (JFK)** to your left

COSTA RICA

and the Outlet Mall behind you. The first street on your right leads to Calle 3 (better known as **Calle de la Amargura**); a left here leads to the University campus, and a right leads back to Av. Central. This loop is usually packed with students.

Restaurante Il Pomodoro, 100m north of JFK Park on Av. Central. The aroma of garlic spills into the street. Generous crispy thin-crust pizzas (small ₡2000) and pastas (₡1900). Open M-Th 11:30am-11pm, F-Sa 11:30am-midnight. AmEx/D/MC/V. ❷

Jazz Café, 150m east of Calle 3 on Av. Central, is a more upscale place to get your toes tapping, with live jazz almost every night. Dine on salads (₡900-2000) or pasta (₡1900-2600). Cocktails attract a large late-night crowd. Open daily from 6pm. ❷

Cool Running, Av. Central, Calle 5. Dreadlocked waiters nodding to Bob Marley beats bring you plates of plantains, yucca, cassava rolls, rice and beans, and rasta salads. Most dishes ₡800-1300. M-Sa 11am-9pm. ❶

◎ SIGHTS

TEATRO NACIONAL. Built in 1897 using taxes imposed by the government in response to a national desire for cultural venues, the *Teatro Nacional* is an extravagant theater is graced with sculpted banisters overlaid in 22.5 carat gold, marble floors, and high-ceiling frescoes. Operas, dances, dramas, and music, are a real treat. *(Av. 2, Calles 3/5, off the Plaza de la Cultura. ☎ 221 1329. Open M-F 9am-5pm, Sa 9am-noon and 1-5pm. Tours ₡600. Tickets ₡2000-5000.)*

MUSEO NACIONAL. In the past 50 years, this museum, a former military headquarters, houses collections of pre-Columbian art and exhibits on colonial life, archaeology, and geology, and is a tribute to the efforts in research and education that defend the country's natural and cultural heritage. *(Calle 17, Av. Central/2. ☎ 257-1433. Open Tu-Su 8:30am-4:30pm. ₡200, students free.)*

MUSEO DE JADE. In the 11th floor of Costa Rica's Social Security building is reportedly the world's largest collection of American jade. Jade was of distinct importance to Costa Rica's indigenous groups, and artifacts dating back to pre-Columbian and Maya times are on display. Don't miss the ▨birds' eye view of San José from the museum window. *(11th fl. of INS Building, Av. 7, Calles 9/13. ₡1200.)*

MUSEO DE ORO. Established in 1950 by the Central Bank of Costa Rica to help preserve Costa Rican cultural heritage, the Museo de Oro, underneath the Plaza de Cultura, has a permanent gold exhibit with pre-Columbian items and a hall with rotating fine arts and archeological exhibits. *(Av. Central, Calle 5. ☎ 243 4202. Open Tu-Su 10am-4:30pm. Admission ₡1500, students and children ages 7-12 ₡300.)*

SERPENTARIUM. This miniature snake garden houses a collection of native reptiles, amphibians, insects, and spiders. *(Av. 1, Calles 9/11. ☎ 255-4210. Open M-F 9am-6pm, Sa-Su 10am-5pm. ₡1500, children under 13 ₡500.)*

PARQUE DE ESPAÑA AND PARQUE MORAZÁN. Complete with well-manicured laws, benches, and a majestic dome, these parks are a tranquil and cool place to rest aching feet. *(Av. 3/5, Calles 5/13. Free.)*

MUSEO DE ARTE COSTARRICENSE. Housed in a terminal of San José's old airport, this small museum is filled with over 3200 works of Costa Rican nationalist art from the 19th and 20th centuries. *(Paseo Colón, Calle 42, on the eastern edge of Parque La Sabana. ☎ 222 7155. Open Tu-Sa 10am-4pm, Su 10am-2pm. ₡400, students free.)*

CENTRO NACIONAL DE ARTE Y CULTURA. The large, tan-colored center, between Parque de España and the National Library, offers a calendar of artistic and cultural events. Check here for performances. *(Av. 3, Calles 15/17. ☎ 257 7202.)*

PARQUE ZOOLÓGICO Y JARDÍN BOTÁNICO NACIONAL SIMÓN BOLIVAR.
Although run down, it may be worth a stop to see the otherwise elusive jaguar and squirrel monkeys. Costa Rican agoutis, reptiles, a lion, jaguar, and tapirs are on display. *(Av. 11, Calle 7, 300m north and 175m northwest of Parque Morazán in Barrio Amón.* ☎ 256 0012 *or 233 67017. Open daily 8am-5pm. ₡700 per person, children under 3 free.)*

MUSEO DE CRIMEN. This peculiar crime station features a small collection of weapons, drug paraphernalia, criminal evidence, and accompanying explanations entirely in Spanish. *(Calle 17, Av. 6/8, on the 2nd fl. of the Supreme Court of Justice (OIJ).* ☎ 295 3581. *Open M-F 7:30am-noon and 1-5:30pm; the museum sometimes closes a bit earlier. Free.)*

🎭 ENTERTAINMENT

A number of 24hr. casinos have opened up in San José, many in hotels clustering on Av. 1 near Calle 5. **Fiesta Casino,** Av. Central, Calle 7/9, has a good mix of tables and slots (18+ to gamble). Several movie theaters throughout San José show recent US releases with Spanish subtitles. In the center of downtown is **Cine Omni,** Calle 3, Av. Central/1 (☎ 221 7903), in the Edificio Omni (₡1100). **Sala Garbo** (☎ 223 1960) and **Teatro Laurence Olivier** (☎ 222 1034), in the same building on Av. 2, Calle 28, 100m south of the Paseo Colón Pizza Hut, show a more artistically varied selection of older films from Latin American countries and North America (₡850). **Multicines San Pedro** (☎ 280 9585), in San Pedro Mall, has 10 modern theaters with digital sound (₡1200, ½ price on W). For fun on wheels, head to **Salón de Patines Music,** 200m west of the JFK park in San Pedro, where you can roller skate the day away and meet lots of young people. (Open M-F 7-10pm; Sa, Su and holidays 1-10pm.)

🛍 SHOPPING

You'll find the best selection of Costa Rican art, woodwork, jewelry, clothing, hammocks, and other souvenirs in a strip of vendors on Av. 2, Calle 13/15 near the Museo Nacional. (Most vendors open M-Sa 8am-6pm, some open Su.) Another option is **La Casona,** Calle 1, Av. Central/1, a collection of many souvenir stores under one roof. (Most stores open daily M-Sa 9:30am-6:30pm, some open Su.) Serious art collectors should check out San José's many wonderful art galleries, many along Av. 1 between Calle 5 and 13. For a standard Western selection of clothing and sportswear, take a San Pedro-bound bus to **Mall San Pedro** or **Outlet Mall.**

🌙 NIGHTLIFE

San Pedro pulses with life at night: the dance is salsa and merengue, the drink is either ice-cold *cervezas* or *guaro* sunrise cocktails, and the scene varies from *ticos* belting out Latin tunes in karaoke bars to American sports bars packed with tourists playing pool and chatting in English. **Calle de la Amargura** is always hopping and has the best casual atmosphere for meeting young *ticos;* **El Pueblo** is the best dancing scene; and **San José center** caters to a slightly older crowd of both locals and foreigners. Most bars and clubs charge ₡1000 for cover. Dress is usually casual; jeans and sandals are fine in San Pedro bars, but you might want to throw on some dressier threads to go to El Pueblo, San José, and Escazú. It's a good idea to bring your **passport** with you to most clubs and bars because the bouncers will require a good ID (18+) to let you in.

CLUBS

CENTRO COMERCIAL EL PUEBLO
El Pueblo, a 15min. ride north of San José center, is *the* place to be for a wild night of dancing and drinking till the wee hours of the morn. This expanded courtyard

A NIGHTLIFE FOR EVERYONE For those in search of music, drinks, and a good time in the city, there are three main night-life options you can choose from in the San José area.

San Pedro is most commonly known for *La Calle de la Amargura* (Street of Bitterness, see p. 151), which is the main hangout for students from the Universidad de Costa Rica. This street consists of an assortment of small bars and pool places. The most popular ones right now are Caccio's (especially on Tuesdays), Tavarúa, Pueblo Viejo, and Mosaikos. A lot of young people gather here to drink, dance with friends to pop and reggae music (no merengue and salsa here!), and if the time is right, enjoy a soccer match on really big screens. Prices are cheap, people are friendly, and there is no need to dress up. Very important: the action here starts early, from 3-5pm, when most classes have ended.

If you're in search of the preppy scene and classier bars, **San Rafael de Escazú** (p. 155) is the place to go. Bars like Frankie Go, Tabú, Bamboleo (especially on Thursdays), Fandango (in the Centro Comercial Trejos Montealegre), and Sambuka (in La Rambla) are all near the main drag. They offer a wide array of cocktails and dance music, and you're basically guaranteed an enjoyable night. Prices here are higher however; you usually have to pay a cover of ¢1000-2000 colones.

Want to shake your hips to some merengue and salsa? Go to **El Pueblo** (p. 153). This *centro comercial* is filled with bars of all shapes and sizes with live music and several lively restaurants. These places generally start filling up after 1am. People of all ages, places, and ideals come here, so come with an open mind and be sure to bring a lot of energy; this party lasts until the sun comes up!

filled with narrow stone paths contains gift shops, bars, and dance clubs that usually get going between 10:30 and 11pm. Although most easily accessible by taxi (¢500), you can take a bus to Calle Blancos from Av. 9, Calle 3 (until 11pm, ¢70). El Pueblo is a safe, contained area; don't wander too far outside the boundaries.

▨ **Infinito Discotheque** (☎221 9134), the most popular spot in El Pueblo. Warm and exciting interior with lamps that throw shafts of color everywhere. The larger dance room plays danceable pop and trance. Cover ¢800; W and Su ladies free; F-Sa ladies free before 9pm. Open M-W 6pm-4am, F-Su 6pm-6am. High *gringo* count in the high season. Cover Su-Th ¢450, F-Sa ¢500, including first drink. Open daily 6pm-5am.

Twister Club (☎222 7562), towards the back and on the left of El Pueblo, attracts a late-20s crowd where the music is loud and people are dressed to impress. Open daily 6:30pm until the crowd dies out..

NEAR THE CITY CENTER

San José's center is crawling with bars and clubs, many of which remain hidden between *sodas* and shops to all but the observant eye.

Acapulco, Av. Central, Calles 17/19 (☎222 1070), 1 block east of the northeast corner of the Museo Nacional. In the night, flashing lights and *salsa* and *merengue* attract a varied crowd. Cover ¢1000, ¢3000 for men on F. Open Th-Su starting at 5pm.

Salsa 54, Calle 3, Av. 1/3 2nd fl. (☎223 3814). Boogie to a mix of love songs, hits, and *salsa*. Tu and W for pool and karaoke fans. *Salsa* and *merengue* lessons Sa 10am and noon (¢5000 for 4 lessons). Tu and W no cover, Th-Su ¢1000. Open Tu-Su 7pm-2am.

Salidas Orbital 2000 (☎233 3814), right next door to Salsa 54. A younger crowd dances to pop, tango, *salsa*, and *merengue* on 3 small stages amid a sea of red plush cocktail tables. Karaoke every night 6-8pm. Male and female models wearing next to nothing dance in the Model Revue. Cover ¢1000. Open W-Su 7pm-2am.

COSTA RICA

SAN PEDRO

El Cuartel de la Boca del Monte, Av. 1, Calles 21/23, in between San José and San Pedro. One of San José's hottest spots for the burgeoning 20s scene. Live local bands with Latin rhythm on M evenings. Cover ¢1200 for live music. Open daily 6pm-2am.

Fuera de Control, Av. Central, Calle 5 (☎253-8062). Flashy lights, a raised stage, and karaoke in English and Spanish. The daily happy hour and 2-for-1 specials. Karaoke Su-Th 9-11pm, live music F, hip hop and rave Sa. Beer ¢450. Open daily 4pm-2am.

Planet Mall, Mall San Pedro, 4th fl. (☎280 4693). Mingle with a very young crowd on the huge dance floors as you gaze down on the bright lights of San José through the floor-to-ceiling windows. Cover ¢1500. Open Th-Sa 8:30pm-2:30am.

BARS

The enormous bar scene near the University of Costa Rica in **San Pedro** is student-oriented, but casual and diverse enough to accommodate just about anyone. People and loud music overflow into the streets, making the area relatively safe, but take precautions. Calle 3 north of Av. Central, known as **Calle de la Amargura** (Street of Bitterness; see **San Pedro,** p. 151), is the heart of the college scene. There are relatively few tourists, making it easier to meet the fun-loving and outgoing *tico* students. Places to try include: **Caccio's** (beer ¢450; no cover; open M-Sa 10am-2am), **Mosaiko's** for a more laid-back atmosphere (hip hop M, reggae Tu, electronic W, rock, pop, alternative Th-Sa; cover ¢1000; open 11am-2am), and **Bar Tavarúa,** a surf and skate bar which opens up a back room for dancing on crowded nights (beer ¢450; cover ¢1000; open M-Sa 11am-2am). Bars closer to San José center tend to be populated by older men. To avoid uncomfortable settings, go to:

🖾 **Raíces,** Av. 2, Calle 45, across from the Mall San Pedro and around the corner from All Stars Bar. This reggae bar draws a young, alternative student crowd who worship everything Jamaican. Jam to Fugees and Bob Marley. Beer ¢450. T and W 7-9pm 2-for-1 drinks. Cover ¢1000, includes 2 drinks. Open W-Sa 7pm till the crowds leave.

Bar Esmeralda, Av. 2, Calles 5/7 (☎221 0530). Caters to an older crowd. Mariachi music offers a soothing alternative to pop. Open daily 7pm-1am.

GAY/LESBIAN NIGHTLIFE

Déjà Vu, Calle 2, Av. 14/16 (☎256 6332). A fantastic mix of trance and reggae keeps the scantily-clad patrons moving till dawn. Don't miss the flamboyant Sa drag show. Cover Th ¢2000, F ¢1500, Sa ¢3000. Open bar 9-11pm. Open M-Sa 8pm-6am.

La Avispa, Calle 1, Av. 8/10 (☎223 5343), an attractive setting with tons of space for ultimate enjoyment: 3 dance floors, a courtyard, and pool tables (¢200 per game). Dress in your most outrageous threads. Singles night 2nd W of the month, ladies night last W of the month. Th karaoke. Cover ¢700. Open Tu and Th-Su 8pm-2:30am.

ESCAZÚ

Though just 10km west of San José, the tranquil and cozy suburb of Escazú seems worlds apart in character. Rolling hills and greenery take the place of the capital's towering buildings and grimy air. Though the town center is simple with a classic colonial feel, the lush green hills on the outskirts hide some fantastically relaxing and luxurious bed and breakfasts, while some of San José's classiest restaurants are scattered along the road to San Rafael de Escazú, 1km northeast.

From San José, buses to Escazú leave from Calle 16, Av. Central/1 (about every 15min., ¢125) and drop passengers off on Av. Central at the north side of **parque central.** The **church** is on Calle Central on the east side of the *parque.* The road to **San Rafael de Escazú** starts from Calle 5, three blocks east of the *parque,* and con-

COSTA RICA

tinues 1km northeast. Many restaurants are along this stretch of road. Local services include: **Banco de Costa Rica,** at the northeast corner of the *parque* (open M-F); **Palí** supermarket, 100m north and 50m west of the bank (open M-F 8am-7pm, Su 8am-1pm); **post office,** one block north of the bank. (Open M-F 8am-5pm.)

▨**Costa Verde Inn ❸,** just outside the town center, nestled snugly in the hills, has comfortable rooms with king size beds, private baths, hot tub, jacuzzi, a sun deck, and living room with fireplace. (☎228 4080; www.costaverdeinn.com. Internet ¢80 per min. Laundry ¢250 per piece. Singles US$45; doubles US$55.) ▨**Villa Escazú Bed and Breakfast ❸,** just down the hill, has 6 rooms with sparkling shared hot baths, and laundry service. (☎289 7971; www.hotels.co.cr/vescazu.html. Breakfast included. Singles and doubles US$26-60.) ▨**Casa de las Tías ❹,** in San Rafael de Escazú, is close enough to the town to easily walk to several wonderful restaurants, and has ceiling fans, private hot bath, laundry service, TV, tour service, and full gourmet breakfast. (☎289 5517; www.hotels.co.cr/casatias.html. Singles US$54; doubles US$65; triples US$75.)

Escazú boasts some of the country's most elegant dining options. Most come at a price, but tired travelers craving an exotic flavor won't regret the splurge. ▨**Chango ❸,** on the road to San Rafael de Escazú, serves exquisitely prepared steak, ribs, and Mediterranean entrees. (Fried calamari ¢2300; shish kebobs ¢3500-¢4800. Open daily 11:30am-2am.) ▨**Parillada Argentina El Che ❸,** at the end of the road to San Rafael de Escazú, offers an array of meats; beef, pig, tongue, and kidney grilled to perfection. (Entrees ¢4000-8000. Open noon to 10pm.) **Sabor a la Leña ❷,** on the road to San Rafael de Escazú, has delicious pizzas (personal ¢1200-1300) in creative flavors. (☎228 1941. Open daily noon-midnight.)

CENTRAL VALLEY

The Central Valley, or Meseta Central, is a high and vast region cordoned off to the north and south by the great volcanic mountain ranges that divide Costa Rica in two. Many of the volcanoes have caused the valley's residents heartache more than once, but the ash has also blessed the valley with fertile soil. It's no surprise that almost two-thirds of all *ticos* live here and that four of Costa Rica's five largest cities mark its center. Typical vacation spots on either coast are just a half-day's journey away in either direction, but that doesn't mean the country's metropolitan areas are lacking in wildlife, adventure, and authentic *tico* culture.

ALAJUELA

Alajuela, 3km from the country's international airport and 17km northwest of San José, is the home of national hero Juan Santamaría, who died burning down the fort of the US military adventurer William Walker in 1856. The town's shaded *parque central* in front of the large, colonial, red-domed cathedral is a good place to sit and relax and is in itself a fine reason to stay and visit. The town also serves as a convenient base to the Butterfly Farm, Zoo Ave, Volcán Poás, and Sarchí.

▣ TRANSPORTATION. From the TUASA station, Av. Central/1, Calle 8 (☎442 6900), 300m west of the southwest corner of the *parque central*, **buses** go to **San José** (45min., every 5min. 4am-10pm, ¢220) and **Volcán Poás** (1½hr., M-Sa 9:15am, return 2:30pm). Buses to **Sarchí** depart from 100m west of the station (1¼hr.; M-Sa every 25-30min., 5am-10pm, Su every 25min., 6:10am-10pm; ¢275).

▰▱ ORIENTATION AND PRACTICAL INFORMATION. Arriving at the TUASA bus station, Av. Central/1, Calle 8, walk to the left to the end of the block, then right for three blocks to reach the *parque central*, boxed in by Av. Central/1 and

Central Valley

COSTA RICA

TO SARCHI (10m)

TO PARQUE NACIONAL VOLCÁN POÁS

Tambor

San Antonio

ALAJUELA

Juan Santamaria International Airport

Río Segundo

Desamparados

San Pedro

Santa Bárbara

Tabarcia

Piedades

San Rafael

San Antonio de Belén

San Antonio de Belén

San Juan

Abalo

Birri

Jesús

Barva de Heredia

Ciudad Colón

Palmichal

Río Oro

Santa Ana

Salitral

Pozos

Río Virilla

San Antonio

Santo Domingo

HEREDIA

San Roque

Angeles

Concepción

TO VOLCÁN BARVA

■ Monte de la Cruz
■ El Castillo Country Club

RESERVA FORESTAL PICO BLANCO

Zona Protectora Cerros de Escazú

FILA DE CEDRAL

San Antonio

Escazú

Pavas

Tobías Bolaños Airport

La Sabana

Uruca

Tibás

Santo Tomás

San Pablo

San Miguel

San Francisco

San Isidro

San Josecito

Tarbaca

San Rafael

San Antonio

San Josecito

Alajuelita

San Juan de Dios

Aserrí

Hatillo

SAN JOSÉ

Zapote

San Pedro

Moravia

Guadalupe

San Rafael

Mirador de Cartago ■

San Miguel

San Rafael Arriba

San Rafael Abajo

Desamparados

Tirrases

Patarrá

San Sebastián

Curridabat

Sabanilla

Lourdes

Ipís

San Isidro de Coronado

San Rafael

CORDILLERA CENTRAL

San Juan

CERROS DE LA CARPINTERA

San Ramón

Rancho Redondo

Zona Protectora Carpintera

Tres Ríos

San Rafael

Dulce Nombre

Llano Grande

Tierra Blanca

Tobosí

Tejar

CARTAGO

San Rafael

Dulce Nombre

Cot

Santa Rosa

Cipreses

PARQUE NACIONAL VOLCÁN IRAZÚ

Volcán Irazú ▲

■ Jardines Lankester

Orosi

Paraíso

TO PACAYAS

TO TURRIALBA

0 ___ 5 kilometers
0 ___ 5 miles

Calle Central/2. Look for the white **catedral** on the far end and a white dome-like shelter over a stage. The streets of Alajuela form the standard Costa Rican grid, but street signs are rare and often point in the wrong direction, so it's best to count the blocks in your head or use landmarks, as locals do. To complicate things, both Av. 9 and Calle 12 are called **Calle Ancha. Banco Nacional** is on Av. Central/1, Calle 2, has a **24hr. ATM.** (Open M-F 8:30am-3:45pm.) **Banco San José,** on Av. 3, Calle Central/1, changes American Express traveler's checks. (Open M-F 8am-7pm, Sa 9am-1pm.) Supermaket **Palí** is 4 blocks west and 1 block south of the southwest corner of the *parque central.* (Open M-F 8:30am-8pm, Sa 7:30am-8pm, Su 8:30am-6pm.) The enclosed **mercado central,** 2 blocks west of the *parque,* is a crowded collection of meat, cheese, fruit, and vegetable stands. (Open M-F 7am-6pm, Sa 6am-6pm.) Other services include: **police,** 1 block north and 3 blocks east of the *parque's* northeast corner, around from the fire station (☎443 4511 from 9am-5pm, emergency 911; open daily 24hr.); **hospital,** Av. 9, Calles Central/1, 5 blocks north of the northeast corner of the *parque* on Calle Central (☎443 4042, emergency 440 1333; open 24hr.). You can find **telephones** at the *parque,* on Av. Central/1, Calles Central/2. **Internet** cafes are scattered across the city. Try **Tropicafé S.A.,** Av. 3, Calle 1. (¢300 per hr. Open M-Sa 8am-10pm, Su 1-9pm.) The **post office** is on Av. 5, Calle Central, 2 blocks north of the northeast corner of the *parque.* (**Fax** available. Open M-F 8:00am-5:30pm, Sa 7:30am-noon.) **Postal code:** 4050.

🄵🄲 ACCOMMODATIONS AND FOOD. 🄫Villa Real Hostel ❷, Av. 3, Calle 1, 1 block north and 1 block east of the northeast corner of the *parque,* has a cozy common room with cable TV. Two common bathrooms serve all rooms and there is a kitchen available. (☎441 4022; villareal@hotmail.com. Rooms US$12 per person; US$10 for a shared room with 3 other people. AmEx/MC/V.) **Hotel El Mango Verde ❶,** Av. 3, Calles 2/4, offers a garden courtyard, open-air sitting areas, cable TV, a patio, and a kitchen (bring your own food). Rooms are clean and simple. (☎441 7116; mirafloresbb@hotmail.com. Singles US$10, with bath US$15; doubles US$15/25. Cash only.) **Pensión Alajuela ❷,** is 4 blocks north of the *parque,* across the street from the judicial court and the hospital, and has TV and towels available. (☎441 6251; www.pensionalajuela.com. Internet ¢500 for 30min. Check-out noon. Reservations recommended. Singles US$18, with bath US$28; doubles US$25/32.) **Hotel Alajuela ❸,** Calle 2, Av. Central/2, south of the southwest corner of the *parque central,* is a central location with the perks and without the noise. Rooms have private bathrooms, a phone, and a fan and there is cable TV in the common area. Check-out noon. (☎441 6595. Singles US$24; doubles US$34.)

La Mansarada Bar and Restaurant ❷, 25m south of the southeast corner of the park, on the second floor, has a casual ambience ideal for its delicious fresh fish with zingy shrimp ceviche. (Ceviche ¢1700. Open daily 11am-11pm, an hr. later on F and Sa.) **La Tacareña Bar and Restaurant ❶,** Av. 7, Calle 2, has quick service and hearty portions. (☎442 1662. Burgers and sandwiches average ¢700. Entrees ¢950-2500. Open daily 10:30am-11pm. V.) **Soda El Fogón del Pollo ❶,** Calle 4, Av. 1/3, is Owned by an Argentine who knows his chicken. (☎443 1362; luvihe@yahoo.com. Delicious *casados* with *pollo asado* ¢850. Open M-F 7am-8pm.)

📓 NIGHTLIFE. Alajuela doesn't have a hopping nightlife. Not too many people go out, but those who do scatter themselves through town for beers and TV. **Cugini Bar,** 2 blocks east of the southeast corner of the *parque central,* is very lively. The restaurant upstairs serves a blend of southern Italian and American cuisine. (☎440 6893. Open M-Sa noon-midnight; happy hours Tu-F after 4:30pm.) **Spectros,** about 550m south of the park's southwest corner, is a gigantic disco with karaoke on Su, M, and W nights, live music Th nights. (Open daily 8pm-4am, except Tu.)

DAYTRIPS FROM ALAJUELA

FINCA DE LAS MARIPOSAS (BUTTERFLY FARM)

Call ahead at ☎ 438 0400; the farm provides transport from San José or Alajuela; or take the blue and white "Guácima" bus from the corner of Av. 2 and Calle 8 in Alajuela (45min.; about every 1½hr., 8:30am-4:30pm; ¢85). Open daily 9am-5pm. Tours begin at 9, 11am, 1, 3pm, and last about 2hr. US$15 includes English-speaking tour; tours with transportation from San José US$25 per person. Call ahead to find out reduced rates for groups larger than 10.

Southwest of Alajuela in La Guácima lies the renowned Finca de las Mariposas, a pleasant, rural garden that is home to countless fluttering butterflies, exotic and ordinary. The four acre farm is Latin America's oldest exporter of the delicate creatures. Genuine butterfly lovers will show you flowers and butterflies you won't see anywhere else. Come early during the rainy season; butterflies hide during afternoon showers.

ZOO-AVE

☎ 433 8989. In Alajuela, buses leave from the lot south of Calle 8, Av. Central/2. A visit takes about 45 minutes. Open daily 9am-5pm. ¢2900, children 2-10 ¢500.

The biggest bird reproduction center in Central America, Zoo-Ave breeds and rehabilitates birds, reptiles, and mammals before reintroducing them to nature. Visitors can see 100 species of birds, plus some playful monkeys and crocodiles.

VOLCÁN POÁS

To get to Poás, take one of the buses that depart daily from San José's TUASA station, Av. 2, Calles 12/14 (2hr., 8:30am, ¢600). They stop at the TUASA station in Alajuela at 9:15am and arrive at Volcán Poás at approximately 10:30am. The return bus leaves the park at 2:30pm. Bring something to do, as you may finish sightseeing before the bus is ready to leave. Park open Dec.-Apr. daily 8am-4:30pm, May-Nov. 8am-3:30pm. US$7.

Fifty-five kilometers northwest of San José, **Parque Nacional Volcán Poás** is a cloud forest easily accessible by trails full of moss, palms, orchids, and a dangling ceiling of bromeliads. A national park since 1971, Poás receives the most visitors of any park in the country, largely due to its proximity to San José and Alajuela. The area's highlight is the steam-belching crater of active Volcán Poás (2574m). Inside the crater (1320m across and 300m deep), there is a turquoise acid pool and *fumaroles* (vents in the earth's crust) that audibly release bursts of volcanic steam. The cone itself looks like a rainbow carved into the terrain, with vibrantly colored layers of gray, white, and red earth that trace the history of the volcano's eruption.

A **Visitors Center** has a small museum on preservation and appreciation of the surrounding environment. There is also a souvenir shop and a *café*. The most direct route to the crater is a 10min. walk up a gentle, paved path from the Visitors Center. **Laguna Botos**, a 15min. walk beyond the crater, is the collapsed cone of another volcano, now filled with rain water but too acidic to sustain life. Poás is most enjoyable in the morning, especially from May to Nov., when noon-time clouds and rain obscure the view. The park gets packed on Sunday.

SARCHÍ

Those who charge Costa Rica with the decay of its national culture will be stymied by this town. The nation's biggest crafts center, Sarchí, a small village 30km from San José, a 25min. drive from the International Airport, keeps an old tradition alive in the form of brilliantly decorated *carretas* (wooden oxcarts). Here you can visit the more than 200 workshops where they are made and talk with the artisans.

(Typical carts ¢51,000-91,000; minicarts ¢1050. Shipping to US US$48-82.) Sarchí also offers an opportunity to dance with the locals, visit waterfalls, and get to know local artisans. Nearby natural wonders include Bajos del Toro Amarillo, 40min. away, and Parque Nacional Juan Castro Blanco.

TRANSPORTATION. Buses to **Naranjo** (5km), **Grecia,** and **Alajuela,** pass by every 25min. (6am-11pm). Buses also go to **San José** (1½hr. direct, 5, 5:30, 6am; return 12:25, 5:15, 5:55pm). Indirect buses from San José to **Sarchí** leave from Av. 5 and Calle 18 (7 per day 5:30am-6pm, ¢350). Buses leave in front of the tourist office in Sarchí Sur for **Bajos del Toro Amarillo** (3:15, return the next day at 5:30am). **Taxis** (☎454 4028) can be found around the *parque* (6am-midnight).

ORIENTATION AND PRACTICAL INFORMATION. Sarchí is divided into **Sarchí Norte** and **Sarchí Sur.** Sarchí Norte has mainly furniture stores, while Sarchí Sur has more handicrafts and ox-cart vendors. About 1km separates the two; public buses pass by often, or you can walk between the two. **Tourist information** can be found at newly opened **Costa Tica Tours** (☎454 4146; costaticatour@hotmail.com), across from the Joaquín Chaverri factory and the *Plaza de Artensanía* in the little blue and white booth. The **Revista Sarchí Guide** has good maps, history, and up-to-date info about the town. **Banco Nacional** is in front of the soccer field on the main road, Sarchí Norte. (☎454 4126. Open M-F 8:30am-6pm.) **Supermercado El Pequeño Super** stands 50m northeast of the *parque central* in Sarchí Norte on the main road. (☎454 4136. Open daily 7am-9pm.) For emergencies, the **Fuerza Pública** (police) is at the end of La Eva part of town (☎454 4021; open 24hr.), and the **Red Cross** is 50m north of the Banco Nacional Sarchí Norte (☎454 4149, emergency 911; open 24hr.). **Farmacia Valverde Vega** is next to the west corner of the *parque central* in Sarchí Norte (☎454 4842; open daily 8am-8pm). For **Internet access,** ask Giovanni at **Costa Tica Tours** about using his Internet. The **post office** is 125m west of *parque central* in Sarchí Norte (☎454 4533; open M-F 8:30am-5:30pm).

ACCOMMODATIONS AND FOOD. Cabinas Mandy ❶, 400m north of the fire station in Sarchí Norte, has 5 rooms with TV, private hot-water baths, and parking. (☎454 2397. Rooms ¢3500-¢5000.) **Cabinas Fantasía ❷,** on Calle Trojas, 1km north of the San Pedro church, has 7 rooms with TV and private hot-water baths. Three rooms have kitchen facilities. (☎454 2007. ¢5000-¢6000 per cabin.) **Las Carretas ❸,** next to the Joaquin Chaverri factory in Sarchí Sur, is the most famous restaurant in the area, and serves up great *típica* for ¢2200-¢3000. (☎454 1636. Open daily 11am-5pm.) **Super Mariscos ❷,** 200m northeast of the *parque central* in Sarchí Norte, serves up good seafood, meat, and cheeses. (☎454 4330. ¢1500-¢5000.) **Restaurante Típico La Finca ❶,** behind the *cooperativa de artesanos* in Sarchí Norte, offers great views and *típico* food. (☎454 1602. Open daily 10am-5pm.)

SIGHTS AND SHOPPING. The **Plaza de Artesanía** is a shopping center packed with arts and crafts of different types, including leatherwork, jewelry, woodwork, textiles, ceramics, paintings, and furniture. Inside the plaza, Grettel and Henry's **Fábrica El Rancho Sarchiseño** makes and sells *carretas.* (☎454 3430, fax 454 2396. Small ox-cart US$181, largest US$1000; shipping US$60-70. *Let's Go* readers get a 20% discount with cash.) **Mueblería Quisamo** specializes in Genísaro, Cedo, and Guanacaste furniture, and is very open to answering questions from visitors. (☎454 4062. 800m south of Trojas bridge in Sarchí Norte coming from Naranjo.) The **Fábrica de Carretas Joaquín Chaverri,** dating to 1903, is one of the biggest factories and showrooms in the country. Watch selected artists paint the days away while woodcutters deftly wield the massive parts. Enjoy music, coffee, fruits, and juices. (☎454 4411; www.sarchicostarica.com. Open daily 8am-6pm.)

HEREDIA

Perched on a hilltop 11km north of San José, the town of Heredia (pop. 30,000) retains the cosmopolitan air of the capital while leaving the smog and frenzy behind in favor of a more relaxed atmosphere. A popular suburb for commuters working in the capital, Heredia attracts visitors with its friendly atmosphere, student scene, and proximity to the airport and Braulio Carrillo National Park.

TRANSPORTATION. You can flag a **taxi** down or call ☎260 3307. Taxis run throughout town, but some are reluctant to give short rides. The 15min. taxi ride from the airport to Heredia is about ₡2500. Most **buses** disembark near the *parque* or the *mercado,* although a few leave from the **Parque Los Ángeles,** two blocks west of the *mercado*'s western boundary, and others from across the **Universidad Nacional** on Calle 9. Purchase tickets upon boarding and carry small change. From the bus stop in front of the Universidad Nacional, Av. Central, Calle 9, buses go to **Alajuela** (20min., about every 15min. 6am-10pm, ₡95). Along Calle Central, between Av. 2 and 4, are the buses to **San José** (30min., every 5min. 4:50am-midnight, ₡105).

ORIENTATION AND PRACTICAL INFORMATION. Heredia is organized in a simple grid system, with *calles* running north-south and *avenidas* running east-west. However, few streets are labeled, so it's best to start exploring from the **parque central,** Heredia's hub. The *parque* is boxed in by Calle Central to the east, Avenida Central to the north, Calle 2 to the west, and Avenida 2 to the south. The town's few sights are located near the *parque central,* and the **Universidad Nacional** lies five blocks east of it, just beyond *Calle 9.* Two blocks southwest of the *parque*'s southwest corner is the bustling **Mercado Municipal.** Most of Heredia's **banks** change cash and traveler's checks for a 1-2% commission rate. **Banco Nacional,** is on Av. 2/4, Calle 2 (open M-F noon-6pm). For weekend transactions, head to **Banco Cuscatlán,** on Av. 2, Calles 4/6 (open M-F 9am-6pm, Sa 9am-noon). Both have 24hr. **ATMs.** Many covered butcher shops, fruit and vegetable stands, and small, inexpensive *sodas* are set up at the **Mercado Municipal,** Av. 6/8, Calles 2/4. (Open M-Sa 6am-6:30pm, Su 7am-noon.) Enormous **Más X Menos,** Av. 6, Calles 4/6, carries house ware, clothing, a wide variety of foods, and some medicines. (Open M-Sa 7am-midnight, Su 7am-9pm. AmEx/MC/V.) There is no self-service **laundry,** but **Martinizing Dry Cleaning,** Av. 1, Calle 2, will clean shirts for ₡950 and pants for ₡1000. (Open M-F 7:30am-6pm, Sa 8am-12:30pm. AmEx/MC/V.) Other services include: **police,** Av. 5/7, Calle Central, 4 blocks north of the *parque* (☎237 0011, emergency 911); **Farmacia Fishel,** corner of Av. 4 and Calle Central (☎261 0994; open M-Sa 8am-8pm; Su 10am-6pm. AmEx/MC/V); and **Hospital San Vincente de Paul,** Calle 14, Av. 6/10, which has an adjoining pharmacy for prescriptions (☎261 0001). Card and pay **phones** cluster the northeast and southwest corners of the *parque,* at the northwest corner of Av. 3/Calle 6, and near the Universidad Nacional on Av. Central. Purchase a phone card from **Soda El Testy,** at the *parque's* southwest corner. (Open 7am-10pm.) For **Internet access,** a few minutes from the *parque central* is **PlanetWeb,** Av. 1, Calle 6/8, next to the barber. (₡200 per hr. Open daily 9am-10pm.) The **post office** is on Av. Central, Calle 2, across the street from the northwest corner of the *parque.* (Open M-F 8am-5:30pm, Sa 7:30am-2pm.) **Postal code:** 3000.

ACCOMMODATIONS. Heredia sees relatively few tourists but maintains several good and inexpensive accommodations. ◼**Hotel Las Flores ❷,** on Av. 12, Calles 12/14, has white marble floors, private hot-water showers, comfy beds, and a large mirror. (☎261 8147. Singles US$11; doubles US$18. AmEx/MC/V.) **Hotel Colonial ❶**, on Av. 4, Calle 4/6, has a tranquil atmosphere. Tile floors, hot water in shared baths, and mid-sized rooms make it luxurious for the price. (☎237 5258. Singles ¢2000; doubles ¢3500.) **Hotel Manolo ❸**, on Av. 12, Calle 2/4, offers 8 bare but large and well-kept rooms. (☎226 3508. Singles and doubles with hot showers and fans ¢6000, with TV and music ¢8000. Student discounts available. AmEx/MC/V.)

🍴 **FOOD.** *Sodas* serving inexpensive food line every street. Nicer cafés surround the *parque central*, while a few more expensive sit-down restaurants are near the Universidad Nacional. Some American fast food joints (Taco Bell, Burger King, McDonald's, KFC, and Papa John's) are south of the Universidad near Av. 2, Calle 9. ◾**Vishnu Vegetarian/Mango Verde ❶**, on Av. Central/1, Calle 7, offers a welcome break from greasy *soda* fare. The *plato del día*, with rice, entree, salad, soup, fruit drink, and dessert, is a steal at ¢1150. (Open M-F 9am-6pm, Sa 9am-5pm.) **Fresas ❷**, Av. 1, Calle 7, does wonders for fresh fruit salads (¢260-550) and fruit desserts (strawberries with ice cream ¢1700). It also offers delicious meals. (*Casado con huevos* ¢1200-2000. Open daily 8am-midnight.) **Café-Heladería Azzura ❷**, on Calle 2, Av. Central/2, at the southwest corner of the *parque central* has delicious club sandwiches (¢1200) and breakfast is available. (Open daily 7am-10pm.)

🔲 **SIGHTS.** Overlooking the east side of the *parque* is the gray stone **Iglesia de la Inmaculada Concepción.** The church celebrated its 200th birthday in 1997—an amazing feat considering the many earthquakes it has survived. (Open M-W and F 6am-7pm, Th 3-4:30pm, Sa 4 and 7pm, Su 9, 11am, 4, 7pm.) Many *ticos*, especially school children, find refuge in shaded **Jardines de la Inmaculada,** church gardens dedicated to the Virgin Mary, tucked into the northeast corner of the *parque*.

El Fortín de Heredia, north of the *parque* near the post office, is a crumbling 13m high fort constructed in 1876 as a sentinel to guard a prison long since demolished. Surrounding the Fortín is a park with several monuments to past Costa Rican leaders and a stage where concerts are held. Check out the secretary's office at the **Palacio Municipal** and flip through a binder full of town history and folklore.

To the casual visitor, the **Universidad Nacional,** five blocks from the Fortín on Av. Central, Calle 9, resembles a large garden. Stroll under the roofed pathways to peek in on Costa Rica's college life. Young *tico* couples chat near the center of the University at the popular *Casa Estudiantil*, which offers Costa Rican style cafeteria food. (*Casado* ¢400-¢650.) Next door is a bookstore selling mostly Spanish school books and school supplies. (Open M and W-F 8am-5pm, Tu 9:30am-5pm.)

📻 **NIGHTLIFE.** Though the town itself seems to die down after 7pm, bars bustle with foreigners and *ticos* until 2am. Most students, however, go into San José or Barva for a night on the town or head to the *parque* and other venues for impromptu concerts. Check the postings all over the Universidad for current info. Students frequent **Bulevar,** an open-air bar *terraza* on Av. Central, Calle 7, and **Metamorphosis Champs,** a disco with frequent concerts at 8pm on Av. 4, Calle 9 (students with ID ¢500). Current hot spots include **Delire** (reggae) and Av. 51. Want to polish your moves before hitting the dance floor? **Merecumbé** dance instruction, on Av. 4/6, Calle 9, offers dance lessons in merengue, salsa, and swing. (☎237 0857. US$30 for 8 group classes; US$11 per hour for private classes.).

🔺 **VOLCÁN BARVA**

About 25m back from the bus stop in Paso Llano is a paved road marked with signs to Volcán Barva. This road climbs 4km to the tiny village of Sacramento, where you can refuel at a small bar/restaurant on the left side of the road (look for the Pilsen sign). From

Heredia

⌂ ACCOMMODATIONS
Hotel Colonial, **6**
Hotel Las Flores, **8**
Hotel Manolo, **7**

🍴 FOOD
Café-Heladería Azzura, **4**
Fresas, **1**
Vishnu Vegetarian/
    Mango Verde, **2**

🌃 NIGHTLIFE
Bulevar, **3**
Metamorphosis
Champs, **5**

Sacramento, it's another 4km uphill to the ranger station and entrance to the park. One kilometer out of town the road turns rough and rocky. The park entrance and ranger station (☎ 283 5906) awaits at the end of the road (open daily 8am-4pm; admission US$6, students US$1).

The 8km uphill walk to the ranger station, where the main trail to Volcán Barva begins, takes an exhausting 1½-2hrs., but idyllic cow pastures and stunning views of the valley, combined with the feel of the soothing, crisp air, make the journey up a worthy hike of its own. The main trail is a 2km, 45min. uphill hike along a shaded, well-maintained trail to three lagoons at the volcano's summit. About 300m down the trail, **Sendero Álvaro**, a 1.8km path, veers off to the right. Another 300m leads to a 900m turnoff for **Mirador La Vara Blanca.** If it's clear, you can see the Caribbean from this lookout. Back on the main route, the trail slowly transforms into a beautiful moss-covered Costa Rican cloud forest. Surrounding the trail are thick layers of *bromeliads, robles,* and the huge *gunnera insignis* plants, nicknamed *sombrillas de pobre* (the poor man's umbrella) for their wide, round leaves.

About 35min. up the trail, bear left (there's a sign) to ascend the remaining 200m to the edge of **Laguna Barva.** Creep through the mess of foliage for the best view of the lagoon. An acidic pool cupped in an extinct volcano, Laguna Barva is too harsh an environment for fish, but its waters suit a variety of aquatic insects. A second well-marked trail leads another 2km up to **Laguna Copy** (40m across). This path is especially muddy and difficult in the rainy season. The third lagoon, **Laguna Danta**

(500m across), is rather inaccessible by foot. To see the view from the rim of the volcano, fork right at the sign and turn left at the trash can when the trail ends. This is Barva's highest point (2.9km). From start to finish, the hike from Paso Llano to the summit and back takes about 5½hr. at a moderate pace. If you take the 6:30am bus from Heredia, you should have time to climb, see both lagoons, and descend the volcano to catch the 1:30pm bus. Since the volcano is at a high altitude, expect cold rain and wind. It is not advisable to stray from the trails.

⚑ CAMPING. Although camping is prohibited elsewhere in the park, it's allowed near the ranger station at Volcán Barva. Ask the ranger to show you where to camp and notify him when you leave. The facilities have space for 10 tents and provide access to potable water and toilets. Campers should bring their own drinking water in March and April and their own tents year-round. (Call 1 week ahead. Camping or 4-person cabin US$2 per person.)

CARTAGO

Cartago (pop. 30,000) had its stint of importance when it served as the nation's capital from 1563 until 1823, before the seat of power shifted to San José, 22km northwest. It has suffered since from frequent earthquakes and volcanic eruptions, reducing the once crowded, busy urban center to a quiet town with a suburban feel. Cartago's most famous sights, La Basílica de Nuestra Señora, Las Ruinas de la Parroquia, and the nearby Lankester Botanical Gardens, are easily visited on a daytrip from San José, although a smattering of rather overpriced hotels can provide a solid base for visiting nearby Volcán Irazú or Parque Nacional Tapantí.

🚍 TRANSPORTATION. Bus departure points are scattered about town. Bus and taxi drivers are a good source of information for schedules and departure points. Buses from Calle 6, Av. 1/3 depart to **Orosi** (40min.; M-Sa about every 30min. 5:30am-10:30pm, Su about every 30min. 7am-10pm; ¢215); from Av. 5, Calles 4/6 to **Paraíso** for **Lankester Botanical Gardens** (15min., every 10min. 5am-10pm, ¢85); from Av 4, Calle 2/4 to **San José** (SACSA ☎ 551 0232; in San José ☎ 233 5350. 40min.; every 10min. M-Sa 4:45am-11pm, Su 5-11pm; ¢180); from Av. 3, Calles 8/10 to **Turrialba** (1½hr., daily every hr. 6am-10pm, ¢325). For information on getting to **Volcán Irazú,** see p. 166. **Taxis** line up at the west side of the *parque central* on Calle 4, Av. 1/2.

⚑ ORIENTATION. Unlike most Costa Rican towns whose main drags are Av. and Calle Central, Cartago is anchored by Av. and Calle 1, which form the southern and western edges of the *parque central.* Just east of the *parque* stand **Las Ruinas,** the ruins of a cathedral destroyed by an earthquake, while the stately **La Basílica de Nuestra Señora de los Ángeles** is at the west end of town. Another good landmark is the *mercado central,* bounded by Calle 1/3 and Av. 4/6 slightly northwest of the *parque central.* **Volcán Irazú** soars 32km northeast of town, and the **Jardín Botánico Lankester** is about 8km southeast. Though the city is relatively safe, don't wander too far north or west of the *mercado central;* take taxis when possible at night.

🛈 PRACTICAL INFORMATION. Banco Popular, Av. 1, Calles 2/4, changes traveler's checks and cash, gives cash advances, and has **24hr. ATMs.** (Open M-F 8:15am-5pm, Sa 8:15-11:30am.) Do your laundry at **Lavandería Fabimar,** Av. 2, Calle 11. (¢475 per kg. Open M-F 8am-noon and 1-6pm, Sa 9am-3pm.) The **Palí Supermarket** is on Av. 4, Calle 6. (Open M-Th 8:30am-7:30pm, F-Sa 8:30am-8pm, Su 8:30-6pm.) Other services include: the **police,** on Av. 6, Calle 2/4, in the yellow building (☎ 551-0455); the **Red Cross,** on Av. 5, Calle 1/3 (☎ 551 0421); **Farmacia Central,** on Av. 1, Calle 2, south of Las Ruinas (☎ 551 0698; open M-Sa 8am-8pm); and you can get medical care at **Hospital Dr. Max Peralta Jiménez,** on Av. 5/9, Calles 1/3 (☎ 550 1898). You'll find **Internet** access at **Cafe Internet,** Av. 4, Calle 6/8. (¢300 per 30min., ¢500

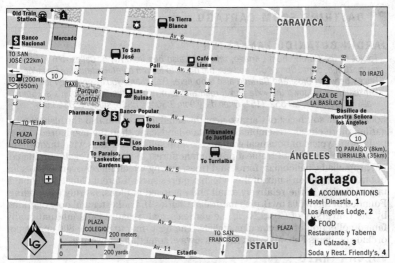

Cartago

⚓ ACCOMMODATIONS
Hotel Dinastía, **1**
Los Ángeles Lodge, **2**
🍴 FOOD
Restaurante y Taberna
La Calzada, **3**
Soda y Rest. Friendly's, **4**

per hr. Open daily 10am-10pm.) The **post office** is on Av. 2, Calle 15/17. (Open M-F 7:30am-6pm, Sa 7:30am-noon.) **Postal code:** 7050.

📵 ACCOMMODATIONS AND FOOD. Cartago's lack of safe, inexpensive accommodations makes San José or Orosi better places to stay, although there are quality lodgings in town. **Hotel Dinastía ❷,** on Calle 3, Av. 6/8, just north of the *mercado central*, has a comfy sitting area with TV and sofas. (☎551 7057. Singles and doubles with fan and shared bath ₡4500, with TV and private hot shower ₡6500.) **Los Ángeles Lodge ❷,** Av. 4, Calle 14/16, is a bit more expensive, but in a safer, more scenic location. Spotless, well-equipped rooms with private bath. (☎551 0957. Full breakfast included 7:30-9am. Singles US$20; doubles US$30; triples US$40.)

   Soda y Restaurante Friendly's ❶, on Calle 4, Av. 1/3, is one of the tastiest and most inexpensive options for a quick bite to eat. (Burgers ₡350-1000; *gallo pinto* ₡550; sub sandwiches ₡550-800. Open daily 8am-11pm.) **Restaurante y Taberna La Calzada ❷,** Av. 1, Calles 1/2, across from the ruins has good food and a laid back local bar scene. (Mexican, American, Costa Rican, and Chinese entrees ₡1200-2000. Heineken 2 for 1 ₡650. Open daily 10am-2am.)

◎ SIGHTS. La Basílica de Nuestra Señora de Los Ángeles, Costa Rica's most famous and sacred place of worship, stands at the far east end of town. Thousands of *ticos* make an annual pilgrimage to this awe-inspiring cathedral on August 2 for *El Día de la Virgen* to worship the statue of La Negrita, an indigenous image of *La Virgen,* said to have great healing powers. The interior of the church is stunning, yet the church's real treasure is hidden in a small room to the left of the main altar that is crammed full of offerings to the Virgin as appreciation for her magical blessings. The **Cripta de la Piedra** (Crypt of the Stone) contains the boulder where La Negrita is said to have been first sighted. (Open daily 5:30am-8pm. Free.)

   The crumbling walls of **Las Ruinas de la Parroquia,** Av. 1/2 and Calles 2/4, at the east side of the *parque central,* are the remains of Cartago's first parochial church. First built in 1575, the cathedral stood unharmed until 1841, when an earthquake almost completely destroyed it. It later reconstructed, only to be damaged by another tremor in 1910. Now enclosing an overgrown garden, the ruins and adjacent *parque central* are excellent for an afternoon picnic and nap.

⚡ DAYTRIPS FROM CARTAGO

JARDÍN BOTÁNICO LANKESTER

*To get to the Garden from Cartago, take a Paraíso **bus** from Av. 5, Calles 4/6 (15min., every 10min. 5am-10pm, ¢85) and ask the driver to let you off at Restaurante Casa Vieja. Buses between Orosi and Cartago also stop here. From here, you'll see a sign for Jardín Lankester. Walk down the wide gravel road and turn right at the first road; it's a 15min. walk. ☎552 3247, fax 552 3151. Open daily 9am-3:30pm. US$5, students US$3.50.*

Located 6km southeast of Cartago near the small town of Paraíso, the lush tropical garden more closely resembles a fairy tale landscape than the manicured flower beds more typical of botanical gardens. Several self-guided trails wind through the garden's 10 hectares of tropical premontane forest, nourishing vegetation including bromeliads, heliconias, ferns, and trees, among which flutter over 100 species of birds. The garden's mix of life, which requires such different climates and habitats yet exists in the relatively small and enclosed gardens, is truly astounding. Founded in the 1950s by British naturalist Charles H. Lankester and now operated by the University of Costa Rica, the garden's real treasure is its internationally famed collection of spectacular **orchids.** The best time to see the 800 species of orchids bloom is Feb.-May, but there is always something flowering.

VOLCÁN IRAZÚ

*The best time to see Volcán Irazú is on weekends; getting there during the week is difficult without private transportation. A bus leaves **San José** from 2 Av., 1/3 Calles, across the street from the Gran Hotel Costa Rica (1½hr.; Sa and Su 8am, return bus 12:30pm; round-trip ¢1500). It stops in **Cartago,** 100m south of the southeast corner of the ruins, across the street from Iglesia Los Capuchines (8:30am, ¢800 round-trip from Cartago). During the week take a taxi from Cartago or Tierra Blanca (¢7000 one-way, ¢15,000-20,000 to have the taxi wait and drive you back), or a bus to **Tierra Blanca,** then hike the remaining 20km uphill. Buses leave from the Tierra Blanca stop in Cartago for **San Juan de Chicua,** 6km from the peak. (☎219 7187; call ahead to confirm. 1hr., M and Th 11am, ¢350.) Take a taxi to return. Park open daily 8am-3:30pm. Admission US$7.*

With an elevation of 3432m, Volcán Irazú is Costa Rica's tallest active volcano. It first erupted in 1723 and has recorded 15 eruptions since, the most recent in 1994. The most famous one occurred on March 9, 1963, the day John F. Kennedy arrived in Costa Rica for an official visit, a blast which severely damaged the agriculture in the Central Valley, destroyed some 300 homes, and transformed parts of the surrounding forest into the gray, dusty wasteland they remain today. Just like out of a sci-fi movie, Irazú seams unearthly with its moon-like terrain and craters covered in black ash. If you're lucky—mornings in the dry season are best—you can see the Atlantic Ocean, Pacific Ocean, and Lago de Nicaragua from the summit.

The expansive **Cráter Playa Hermosa,** a big playpen of volcanic ash, is the first crater on the left. To the right is the **Cráter Diego de la Haya** (690m wide, 100m deep), named after the Cartago mayor who recorded the volcano's first eruption. Straight ahead is the **Cráter Principal** (1050m wide, 300m deep), the only active crater, which boasts an enormous cauldron. Bring rain gear and layers of warm clothes; temperatures range from 17°C to a bone-chilling -3°C. A small *cafetería* serves overpriced snacks and souvenirs. There is no camping or lodging.

OROSI

Regretfully overlooked by most travelers scurrying away to the more touristed coasts, small and tranquil Orosi (pop. 8000) teems with surprises that warrant at least a couple days' excursion from San José. A friendly, colonial town atmosphere makes Orosi the perfect retreat to escape the Central Valley's urban sprawl and visit nature reserves, hot springs, coffee farms, and rivers, all hidden snugly in the rolling hills and luscious waterfall-laden rainforest of the Orosi Valley.

☐ TRANSPORTATION. Buses to Orosi leave Cartago from Calle 6, Av. 1/3 (40min.; M-F every hr. 5:30am-10pm, Su about every 30min. 7am-10pm; ¢215) and return to **Cartago** from the northeast corner of the soccer field on the main road (40min.; every 45min. 4:45am-9:10pm, Su 5:45am-7:15pm; ¢200). **Taxis** also leave from the northeast corner of the soccer field. (☎ 533 3343.)

◪ PRACTICAL INFORMATION. Despite the lack of street names, Orosi is easily navigable if you keep in mind a few landmarks and directions. Buses and taxis arrive on the main drag, which runs from north to south through town; you'll be traveling south along this road past the soccer field. **La Iglesia de San José Orosi** is at the west side of the field. **Parque Nacional Tapantí** and **Purisil Park** are about 10km east of town along the main drag. The tourist office, **Oficina de Información Turística**, 200m south of the southeast corner of the soccer field on the main drag, arranges tours to Parque Nacional Tapantí, Volcán Irazú, Purisil Park, Casa Soñando, and also rents mountain bikes. (☎ 533 3825. Bikes US$7 per day.) If by chance you're in town on a Friday, **MINAE Orosi,** at the northwest corner of the soccer field, can provide information on nearby national parks. (☎ 533 3082. Open F 8am-5pm.) Groceries, fax, and photocopy service are available at **Super Anita #2,** 250m south of the southeast corner of the soccer field, where they might change US dollars if you buy something. (Open daily 7am-8pm. MC/V.) Other local services include the **police station,** directly north of the soccer field(☎ 533 3082), and the **medical clinic,** next to the police. (☎ 533 3052. Open M-F 8:30am-4pm.) You'll find **Internet** access at **PC Orosi,** 100m south of Super Anita #2 (¢500 per hr.; open M-Sa 9am-7pm).

▐▐ ACCOMMODATIONS AND FOOD. █**Montaña Linda ❶,** 200m south and 200m west of the southwest corner of the soccer field, has spotless communal bathrooms (with hot water), shared kitchen (US$1), and delicious meals (US$2-3.50). Spanish classes are offered. (☎ 533 3640. Laundry US$4. Dorms US$5.50; singles US$8; doubles US$12. **Camping** US$2.50 per person.) **Cabinas Media Libre ❷,** 300m south and 25m west of the southeast corner of the soccer field, is a luxurious bargain for a group of three. Modern triples (you can squeeze in 4) are equipped with TV, fridge, phone, private hot-water bath, and there is a restaurant attached. (☎ 533 3838. Laundry ¢1000. Singles US$20; doubles and triples US$30.)

Soda Luz ❶, 100m north of the northwest corner of the soccer field, serves some of the heartiest, most inexpensive meals in town. (Burgers ¢400; spaghetti ¢800; *casados* ¢800-1000. Open M-Th 7am-4pm, F-Su 7am-8pm.) **Bar Restaurante Orosi ❶,** at the northeast corner of the soccer field, offers good food in a relaxed setting. (Rice dishes ¢800-1200; shrimp cocktail ¢1100. Beer ¢380. Open daily 10am-10pm.)

◙ SIGHTS. Built in 1743, **La Iglesia de San José Orosi** is one of Costa Rica's oldest churches still in use, having remarkably withstood earthquakes that have wiped out nearby villages. Defying tradition, the church is also reputed to be Costa Rica's only church that faces east instead of the customary westward orientation. Adjoining the church, the **Museo Franciscano** houses a collection of Christian relics from the early 18th century. (At the west of the soccer field. Open Tu-Sa 1-5pm, Su 9am-noon and 1-5pm. US$1, children ¢100.) Orosi's hot mineral bath, **Balneario Termal Orosi,** has two simple pools at 35°C, a drastic drop from the scalding 60°C water at the source. (☎ 533 3009. 300m south and 100m west of the southwest corner of the soccer field, next to Orosi Lodge. Open 7:30am-4pm. ¢500.) **Balneario de Aguas Termales Los Patios** is more scenic and has more warm pools and a cold one. (☎ 553 3009. 2km south out of town along Orosi's main road. Open Tu-Su 8am-4pm. ¢700.)

COSTA RICA

La Casa del Soñador is an old-fashioned, intricately designed masterpiece of late Costa Rican sculptor Macedonio Quesada. The house is now filled with nativity scenes and *campesino* figures with Latin American, indigenous, and East Asian influences. (1km from Orosi on the road to the town of Cachí. From Orosi, walk east along the main road past the Balneario Los Patios until you see a sign for Hotel Río Palomo. Turn left and walk another 15min. to the hotel; make another left and continue 4.5km past the hotel to La Casa del Soñador. Most Cartago-Orosi buses will go as far as the town of Palomo. From there it's a 4.5km walk. A taxi from Orosi costs ₡2500-3000.)

The small village of Ujarrás was abandoned after it was virtually destroyed by a flood in 1833, but the ruins of the town's 17th century church, **Las Ruinas de Ujarrás,** draw a constant flow of tourists. The church is said to have been built when an Indian found a wooden box in a river. Upon opening it, he found a statue of the Virgin and was no longer able to move it from Ujarrás. The statue, known as **La Virgen de Candelaria,** has since been moved to the town of Paraíso, along with the rest of Ujarrás' residents, who continue to celebrate their sacred Virgen by holding an annual parade from Paraíso to Ujarrás in late March or early April. (From Orosi, catch a bus to Paraíso from the northeast corner of the soccer field. 20min., every 30min. 4:45am-9:15pm, ₡120. From Paraíso, buses leave every 20-30min. for La Represa de Cachí. From there it's a 1km walk to the ruins; ask the driver to point you in the right direction. To return to Orosi, confirm with the driver for a bus that can pick you up from the drop off point at Cachí. Open daily dawn to dusk. Free.)

◪ **GUIDED TOURS.** The **Montaña Linda** hotel (see **Accommodations,** above) offers guided tours of Orosi valley (US$5), Volcán Irazú (US$12), Monumento Nacional Guayabo (US$25), and white water rafting (US$70). For awesome panoramic views of the Orosi and Cachí Valley, check out the 3-4hr. "Yellow Church Walk." The **Orosi Lodge** leads combined tours of Volcán Irazú, Mirador Orosi, and La Basílica de Nuestra Señora de los Ángeles (US$40); Parque Nacional Tapantí (US$45); and Orosi Valley, a sugar cane mill, La Casa del Soñador, and the Lankester Botanical Gardens (US$40). The lodge also rents mountain bikes and canoes.

▨ DAYTRIPS FROM OROSI

PARQUE NACIONAL TAPANTÍ

The lengthy 12km hike from Orosi to Parque Nacional Tapantí passes through rolling coffee plantations. If you're short on time or energy, you can take a cab (one-way ₡3000), and arrange for pick-up. ☎ 771 5116 or 551 2797. Open daily 7am-5pm. US$7.

Twelve kilometers away from central Orosi is a 61 sq. km wildlife refuge turned national park Tapantí, famed for having the highest average rainfall (6.5m per yr.) in Costa Rica. The resulting 150+ rivers and streams intersect a pristine rainforest inhabited by an enormous diversity of wildlife and an average 80-160 species of trees per hectare. The huge amounts of rainfall that Tapantí receives are used to generate hydroelectric power for most of San José's population. From the main road, **Camino Principal** (1.6km) leads to the **ranger station,** where the park's three trails begin—the **Oropéndola** (1.2km), **La Pava** (400m), and the **Árboles Caídos** (2km), in increasing order of difficulty. The last has some steep inclines but can be finished within 1-1½ hr. Oropéndola leads up to a pool in the Río Grande de Orosi, where swimming is possible. Although camping is not permitted, the park offers very basic **rooms.** (₡1000 per person; call in advance to secure a bed.) The communal showers have warm water. Bring a sleeping bag and food to cook in the kitchen. Spanish and English maps (₡200) are available at the ranger station.

TURRIALBA

Often bypassed by travelers uninterested in adventure tours or on too limited a budget to afford them, small and suburban Turrialba generally keeps to itself. What has brought the town international recognition, however, is its proximity to the Ríos Reventazón and Pacuare, both packed with Class III-V rapids and some of the world's best river runs. Whitewater rafters and kayakers splash through while others stay a night or two on the way to Monumento Nacional Guayabo.

☎ TRANSPORTATION. Turrialba has two main bus stations. From the bus station 100m west of the southwest corner of the *parque* (☎556 0159), buses leave for **San José** (direct: 1¾hr.; every hr. 5am-4pm, 5:30pm; indirect: 2¼hr.; every 1½hr. 5am-9pm; ¢605) via **Cartago** (1½hr. ¢350) and **Siquirres** (2hr.; Tu-Th every 2hr. 6am-6:15pm, F-M every hr. 6am-7pm; ¢470) via **CATIE** (10min.; ¢80). An additional free private bus shuttles passengers to and from CATIE; pick it up at the stop opposite the Red Cross. On weekends and in the high season, you might have to buy tickets to San José in advance to ensure a seat. From the other station, 100m south and 50m west of the southwest corner of the *parque*, buses leave for **Monumento Nacional Guayabo** (1hr.; M-Sa 11am and 5:15pm, return 12:50; Su 9am, return 5pm; ¢155).

■② ORIENTATION AND PRACTICAL INFORMATION. Turrialba, 62km east of San José, is arranged in a fashion similar to most Costa Rican cities. With the *parque central* as a reference point, things aren't too tough to find. As you exit the bus station (coming from San José or Cartago), the **parque** is on the next block to your left (east), and the **church** is just south of the *parque*. There is no official office for **tourist information**, but Doña Blanca at **Hotel Interamericano** (see **Accommodations,** below), will gladly help with info about the town and nearby sights. **Banco de Costa Rica,** is 200m south and 100m east of the southeast corner of the *parque*. (Open M-F 8:30am-5pm.) **Western Union** is 100m south and 50m east of the southwest corner of the *parque*. (☎ 556 0439. Open M-Sa 8am-6:30pm.) **Supermercado Compramás** is at the northeast corner of the *parque*. (Open M-Sa 8am-8pm.) Other services include: **police station,** 200m north of the northeast corner of the *parque* (☎556 0030, emergency 117); **hospital** 300m west of the northeast corner of the *parque* (☎556 1133); **Red Cross,** 100m west and 50m south of the northwest corner of the *parque* (☎556 0191); **Farmacia,** 100m south of the southeast corner of the *parque*. (☎556 0379; open M-Sa 8am-8pm, Su 8am-6pm). You can find **Internet access** at **Turrialba.net Cafe Internet,** in the Centro Comerical Yel, 100m west and 50m south of the southwest corner of the *parque*. (¢250/30min., ¢400/hr. Open M-Sa 9am-9pm, Su 1-7pm.) The **post office** is 200m north of the northeast corner of the *parque*. (Open M-F 7:30am-5pm, Sa 7:30am-noon.) **Postal code:** 7150.

♖ ACCOMMODATIONS AND FOOD. Turrialba has a good number of budget places, although you'll be hard-pressed to find many dirt-cheap places often available in other towns. Although most of Turrialba's hotels are a touch pricier, they usually offer a few much-missed comforts like hot water and comfy beds. **✪Hotel Interamericano ❶,** the yellow building 200m south of the southwest corner of the *parque*, has small but comfortable, airy rooms. Amenities include hot showers, breakfast (entrees US$3), luggage storage, laundry (¢2000), Internet, and cable TV. (☎556 0142; www.hotelinteramericano.com. Singles US$10, with bath and TV US$20; doubles US$18/US$30.) **Hotel La Roche ❶,** 150m north of the northeast corner of the *parque*, has a few small doubles with sinking beds, and clean cold baths open up to a pleasant courtyard. (☎556 7915. Singles and doubles ¢3500.) Food in Turrialaba is much less exciting than the raging rivers that rush past it; choices are limited to basic sodas and pizza places. **Pizzería/Soda Popo's ❶,** on the east side of the *parque*, is a popular for good, inexpensive food in a simple atmosphere. (☎556 0064. Pizzas ¢1000-1500, *plato del día* ¢750. Open M-Sa 11am-11pm, Su 5-11pm.) **Cafe Gourmet ❶** is 150m west of the southwest corner of the *parque*. (Apple pie ¢500, *pinto* ¢600. Open M-Sa 7am-7pm.) **Soda Burbujas ❶**, diagonally across the street from the southwest corner of the *parque*, is a casual place popular with rafters and kayakers. (*Casados* ¢800-900. Open daily 7am-8pm.)

OUTDOOR ACTIVITIES AND GUIDED TOURS. Capitalizing on Turrialba's legendary rafting and kayaking opportunities, tour operators offer adventure trips for all abilities. If you have your own equipment or rent from a tour company, Hotel Interamericano (see **Accommodations**, p. 169) will help arrange truck transport to nearby rivers. The hotel will also set you up with information about the nearby **serpent farm** (10km away), **Volcán Turrialba,** and the **Aguiares waterfall. Costa Rica Ríos Aventuras** (☎556 9617; www.costaricarios.com), 150m north of the northeast corner of the *parque*, is the most reputable rafting and kayaking operator. (Kayaking US$41-90, mountain biking US$25-55, canyoning US$38-105, rafting US$63-150.) **Rainforest World** inside the shoe repair shop 100m west and 50m south of the northwest corner of the *parque*, has everything from tame "scenic float trips" for US$45 to hard-core Class V, "extreme" rafting and kayaking trips for US$65-90. (☎556 2678; www.rforestw.com.)

⚑ DAYTRIPS FROM TURRIALBA

MONUMENTO NACIONAL GUAYABO

*Buses to the park entrance station leave from the local bus terminal in **Turrialba** at Av. 2, Calles Central/2 (1¼hr.; M-Sa 11am, 5:15pm, Su 9am; ¢140). There is one snag: buses return from Guayabo at 5:30am and 12:30pm only, so a same-day trip requires either a very quick visit to the ruins or a 4km walk downhill to the main paved road where buses pass more frequently (7am, noon, 1:30, 4pm). Alternatively, you can hire a cab to the monument (¢4000-4500) and take the 12:30pm bus back. Monument ☎556 9507. Open daily 8am-3:30pm. US$6, children under 12 free.*

Located 19km northeast of Turrialba, **Monumento Nacional Guayabo** is Costa Rica's most important archaeological site, its only declared National Monument, and an interesting daytrip for those with extra time in Turrialba. The archaeological site is 20 hectares, yet only four of those 20 have been excavated. Much remains unknown about the civilization that built and eventually abandoned the site, believed to have been inhabited from 1500BC to 1400AD by about 10,000 people. Some scientists say that it was the Guayabo people who migrated to Columbia. The mysterious first inhabitants did leave a record of some of their technological advances. The vague remnants of these structures, at the end of an easy 1.4km trail through rainforest, are the focal point of the site, though you will pass a monolith, coffin graves, and several intricate petroglyphs on the way. There are no official guided tours, so it's worth asking the rangers for a quick briefing or shelling out ¢200 for a pamphlet. Another 1.1km trail from the park entrance leads to a rushing stream with potable water. Both trails, especially the shorter one, get extremely muddy in the rainy season; be sure to bring proper footwear and rain gear. Though the ruins are interesting, there's not much else to see, and fast hikers who take the 11am bus from Turrialba and only do the 1.4km trail to the ruins can make it back to the entrance just in time to catch the 12:30 bus back to town. If you want to stay overnight, there's a **campsite** in the monument (US$2 per person) that has a toilet, a cold shower, a clearing for tents, and barbecue pits.

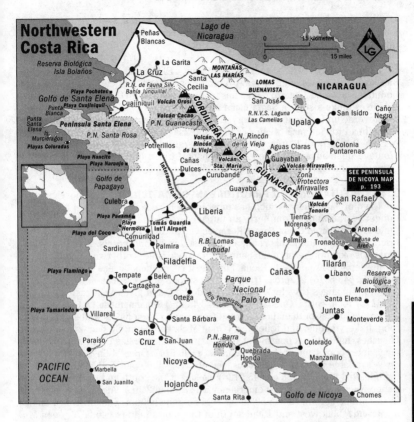

Northwestern Costa Rica

Reserva Biológica
Isla Bolaños

Peñas Blancas

Lago de Nicaragua

La Garita

La Cruz

MONTAÑAS LAS MARÍAS

LOMAS BUENAVISTA

NICARAGUA

Santa Cecilia

R.N. de Fauna Silv.
Bahía Junquillal

Playa Pochotes

Golfo de Santa Elena

Playa Cuajiniquil

Cuajiniquil

Volcán Orosí

San José

Punta Blanca

Volcán Cacao
P.N. Guanacaste

Punta Santa Elena

Península Santa Elena

P.N. Santa Rosa

Is. Murciélagos

R.N.V.S. Laguna
Las Camelias

Upala

San Isidro

Caño Negro

Playas Coloradas

Potrerillos

Volcán Rincón de la Vieja

P.N. Rincón de la Vieja

Aguas Claras

Colonia Puntarenas

Playa Nancite
Playa Naranjo

Golfo de Papagayo

Cañas Dulces

Volcán Sta. María

Guayabal

Volcán Miravalles

Curubandé

Zona Protectora Miravalles

SEE PENÍNSULA DE NICOYA MAP p. 193

Guayabo

Culebra

Volcán Tenorio

San Rafael

Playa Panamá

Liberia

Tierras Morenas

Playa Hermosa

Tomás Guardia Int'l Airport

Bagaces

Palmira

Arenal

Playa del Coco

Comunidad

R.B. Lomas Barbudal

Tronadora

Laguna de Arenal

Sardinal

Palmira

Playa Flamingo

Filadelfia

Cañas

Tilarán

Líbano

Reserva Biológica Monteverde

Tempate

Belén

Parque Nacional Palo Verde

Cartagena

Río Tempisque

Santa Elena

Playa Tamarindo

Villareal

Ortega

Juntas

Monteverde

Paraíso

Santa Cruz

San Juan

Santa Bárbara

P.N. Barra Honda

Colorado

Manzanillo

PACIFIC OCEAN

Marbella

Nicoya

Quebrada Honda

San Juanillo

Hojancha

Santa Rita

Golfo de Nicoya

Chomes

INTERAMERICAN HWY.

CORDILLERA DE GUANACASTE

COSTA RICA

NORTHWESTERN COSTA RICA

The world-famous Monteverde Cloud Forest Reserve protects the cloud forest that once covered the entire Cordillera de Tilarán. The volcanic Cordillera de Guanacaste, to the north, holds three spectacular national parks, and between these ranges is Volcán Arenal, Central America's most active volcano. Meanwhile, arid, lowland Guanacaste contrasts sharply with these lush regions, but offers a cowboy charm all its own. Here, rugged coast (preserved by Parque Nacional Santa Rosa), flowering shrubs, and folklore make the region an eclectic delight.

MONTEVERDE AND SANTA ELENA

The Monteverde area, 184km northwest of San José and due north of Puntarenas, is the sole reason for many travelers to come to Costa Rica. Several private reserves adjoining Monteverde and neighboring Santa Elena, including the famous **Monteverde Cloud Forest Reserve,** protect some of the last remaining primary cloud forest. With its mystical cloud forests now carefully protected, Monteverde is in no danger of losing its title as Costa Rica's primary tourist attraction. Luckily, conscientious locals and a set of specialists—biologists, planners, and educators—are also committed to controlling tourism's effects on the area. **Santa Elena** is a pleasant town that feeds and houses tourists who have made the pilgrimage up the unpaved roads toward tranquil Monteverdet.

⌐ TRANSPORTATION. Direct **buses** to Santa Elena and Monteverde run from **San José, Puntarenas,** and **Tilarán.** Coming from **Liberia,** you can take a San José-bound bus as far as Lagarto, and a bus to Monteverde from there (9:30am, 3, 5pm). All buses make a stop in **Santa Elena** and many continue along the road through Monteverde until the cheese factory, 2.5km from the reserve. Leaving Monteverde, buses head to: **San José** (4½hr., 6:30am and 2:30pm, ¢1475); **Puntarenas** (3½hr., 1 per day 6am, ¢795); **Tilarán** (3hr., 1 per day 7am, ¢620). Buy return tickets from Monteverde in advance at the Marza Transport ticket office half a block south of Banco Nacional in Santa Elena. (☎645 5159. Open daily 5:45-11am and 1-4pm.)

▣✚▨ ORIENTATION AND PRACTICAL INFORMATION. Arriving buses stop in the town of **Santa Elena,** which has most of the local services, budget hotels, and budget restaurants. From here, an unpaved road heads 6km southeast to the famous **Monteverde Cloud Forest Reserve.** The actual Quaker settlement of **Monteverde** is strung along this road, as are restaurants and hotels. The **Santa Elena Reserve** is 5km northeast of the Santa Elena town. Unless otherwise noted, the following services are in Santa Elena. For **tourist information, Camino Verde Information Center** (☎645 5916) is across from the bus stop. **Banco Nacional,** northwest of the bus stop, changes traveler's checks, US dollars, and gives Visa cash advances. (ATM for local cards. Open M-F 8:30am-3:45pm.) **Supermercado La Esperanza,** on the corner at the south end of the road from Banco Nacional, is well-stocked with food, bakery goods, and toiletries. (Open M-Sa 6am-8pm, Su 6am-2pm.) **Librería Chunches,** half a block southwest from Banco Nacional, has US newspapers and magazines, books, music, and local info. (☎645 5147. Open M-Sa 8am-6pm.) **Laundry** is available at **Librería Chunches,** see above. (¢1700 per load.) Other services include: **Red Cross** (☎128 or 645 6128); **police,** at the south end of the road from Banco Nacional (☎645 5127; emergency ☎117; open 24hr.); **Vitosi** pharmacy, next to the police station (☎645 5004; open M-Sa 8am-7:30pm, Su 9am-1pm); **Clínica Monteverde,** 50m west and 150m south of the sports field (☎645 5076; open M-F 7am-4pm, Sa-Su 7am-7pm). You can find **telephones** a block south of Banco Nacional in front of the church, and outside Supermercado La Esperanza. Closer to Monteverde, next to La Pizzería Johnny as well as in the Visitors Center at the reserve. **Internet Access** is available at **Desafío Tours,** across the street from the supermarket in Santa Elena, under Morphos. (☎645 5874. US$2.50 per hr.) The **post office** is up the first hill on the way to Monteverde, beyond the Serpentarium. (Open M-F 8am-noon and 1-4:30pm, Sa 7:30am-noon.) **Postal code:** 5655.

⌐ ACCOMMODATIONS. Expensive and moderate hotels line the road to the Monteverde reserve. ▨**Pensión Manakín ❶,** about 1.5km from Santa Elena toward the Monteverde Reserve, has an inviting lounge with TV and VCR, and comfortable rooms facing the forest. Veggie meals, horse tours, and Internet are available. (☎645 5080; www.monteverdeforever.com. Meals US$5. Rooms US$10 per person, US$15 with private bath. Cabin with kitchen and fridge US$50 per person. V.) **Hotel el Bosque ❷,** across from Stella's (see **Food,** below) and next to CASEM (see **Other Sights and Activities,** below), has pleasant rooms with private bath and some with fridge and TV. There are also two 2km trails and an Italian restaurant. (☎645 5158; elbosque@sol.racsa.co.cr. Doubles US$20, high season US$32.)

Most budget places in Monteverde are in or near Santa Elena. ▨**Pensión Santa Elena ❶** offers bright rooms, hot water, a communal kitchen, Internet, and infor-

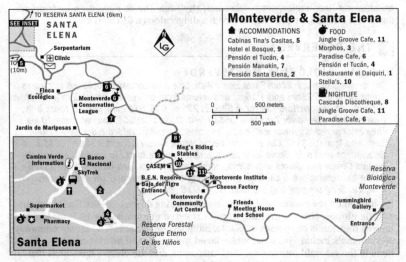

Monteverde & Santa Elena

SANTA ELENA

▲ ACCOMMODATIONS
Cabinas Tina's Casitas, **5**
Hotel el Bosque, **9**
Pensión el Tucán, **4**
Pensión Manakín, **7**
Pensión Santa Elena, **2**

🍴 FOOD
Jungle Groove Cafe, **11**
Morphos, **3**
Paradise Cafe, **6**
Pensión el Tucán, **4**
Restaurante el Daiquiri, **1**
Stella's, **10**

🎵 NIGHTLIFE
Cascada Discotheque, **8**
Jungle Groove Cafe, **11**
Paradise Cafe, **6**

Serpentarium
Clinic

TO 🅢
(10m)

Finca
Ecológica

Monteverde
Conservation
League

Jardín de Mariposas

0   500 meters
0   500 yards

Meg's Riding
Stables

Camino Verde
Information (i)   Banco
Nacional
SkyTrek

CASEM

B.E.N. Reserve   Monteverde Institute
Bajo del Tigre
Entrance   Cheese Factory

Reserva
Biológica
Monteverde

Supermarket

Monteverde
Community
Art Center

Friends
Meeting House
and School

Hummingbird
Gallery

Pharmacy

Reserva Forestal
Bosque Eterno
de los Niños

Santa Elena

Entrance

mation on the area. (☎645 5051. Dorms US$5 per person; singles with private bath US$12; doubles with private bath US$15.) 🔖**Cabinas Tina's Casitas ❶,** southwest of town, set back from the road and on the water, has bungalow-style, clean and spacious rooms with beds made of branches. (☎645 6321. Laundry available. US$7 per person, with bath US$10. High season US$10/US$20.) **Pensión el Tucán ❶** is the warmest, coziest, and most comfortable beds in budget Monteverde. Rooms and hot-water baths are small but spotless. (☎645 5017. Breakfast 5:30-9am, dinner 6-9pm. US$5 per person, with private bath US$10. No credit cards.)

🍴 **FOOD.** In Monteverde you can find 🔖**Jungle Groove Cafe ❸** down the turn-off next to Stella's. (☎645 6270. Garlic calamari stuffed with cassava ¢2800. Open for food noon-10pm. Reserve 2hr. ahead for groups of more than 5.) **Paradise Cafe ❸** is a haven for vegetarians and a rainbow of local performers on Su and W nights. (☎645 6081. Potato wedges ¢600, veggie burger ¢1800. Open daily 7am-8pm.) **Stella's ❶,** 3.25km from Santa Elena on the road to Monteverde, is a slice of heaven. (☎645 5560. Pies ¢757; organic salads ¢1146. Open daily 6am-6pm. V.)

In Santa Elena, 🔖**Pensión el Tucán ❷** has a restaurant as peaceful as the hotel itself. (Pancakes US$5, hearty *casados* US$5.) 🔖**Morphos ❷,** across the street from the supermarket in Santa Elena, offers sub-style sandwiches (¢800-1450) and fresh dinners with hearty vegetables and potatoes. (Open daily 11:30am-9:30pm. V.) **Restaurante el Daiquiri ❸,** on the main Street of Santa Elena, has prices on the high side and inattentive service, but very good food. (Sea bass in hearts-of-palm sauce ¢2500. Open 11am-9:30pm. AmEx/MC/V.)

🎵 **NIGHTLIFE. Cascada Discotheque,** a big disco with a waterfall in its parking lot, 2km from Santa Elena toward the Reserve, spouts danceable Latin and pop music. It often hosts live bands. (Cover ¢2000 on some nights. Open Tu-Sa 8pm-2am, Su 8pm-midnight.) **Jungle Groove Cafe,** down the turn-off next to Stella's in Monteverde, has an elevated catwalk-style stage, where the Cuban *dueña* sings Latin to Sadé in live-music jams with the locals. There's also fire dancing. (☎645 6270. Open for fun until midnight Tu-Su; live music F 7:30pm.) **Paradise Cafe** hosts "dinner theater" W and Su nights. Performances include breathy yogic dancing and

COSTA RICA

an amazing fire juggler, set to abstract, rhythmic music played on instruments such as jaw-harps, rain sticks, and even a didgeridoo (☎ 645 6081).

🔲 THE RESERVES

RESERVA BIOLÓGICA MONTEVERDE

*The reserve is 6km uphill from Santa Elena. Walk, take a taxi, or take a public bus that leaves Santa Elena at 6:25am and 1:15pm and returns from the reserve at 1:15pm and 4pm (45min., M-Sa). Visitors Center ☎ 645 5122, or 645 5112 for guided tours only; www.cct.or.cr. Open daily 7am-4pm. US$12, with student ID US$6, children under 10 free. The center provides general info, maps, and binoculars. 3hr. **guided tours** daily 7:30am , 8am, and 1pm (US$15). Call the night before. Night hikes 7:15 and 9:30pm (US$13; no reservations required). Some local hotels arrange private tours. To spend the night, the Visitors Center has **dorms** with bunks, communal showers, and three meals (US$26). Inside the reserve are 3 **shelters** with cooking areas, water, and showers. Reserve in advance. Bring sleeping bag and food. US$3.50-5 per night.*

Positioned on the continental divide and extending down both the Caribbean and Pacific slopes, this enthralling private reserve encompasses 10.5 sq. km and houses thousands of species of plants, animals, and insects. The most commonly seen animals include *pizotes*, white-faced monkeys, and howler monkeys. Birds include the emerald toucanette, the bananaquit, and the elusive quetzal. It can be hard to see animals in the dense cloud forest, however, guides' trained eyes and ears will help enhance the experience by interpreting your exotic surroundings. You can also explore marked **trails** on your own—highlights include **La Ventana lookout** and a long **suspension bridge.**

RESERVA SANTA ELENA

The Reserva is 5km northeast of Santa Elena village. Walk on the road north from Banco Nacional, take a taxi (¢2500 one-way) or catch the reserve's minibus in front of Banco Nacional. (6:45, 11am, 2pm; ¢700.) Make reservations for buses after 6:45am. (☎ 645 5390; rbnctpse@racsa.co.cr.) US$8; with student ID or age 10-12 US$4.50; children under 10 free. Open daily 7am-4pm. Guided tours available. The reserve information center in town is 200m north of the bank. There is a Visitors Center at the entrance.

The Monteverde cloud forest is amazing, but don't overlook the Santa Elena Reserve, established in 1992 to relieve the burden of excessive tourism from Monteverde. Home to the same flora and fauna, this impressive alternative gives its proceeds to the town's high school. The peaks within the reserve are the highest in the area (some over 1700m). There are four principal **trails,** all short enough (1-5km) to be done as day hikes. From some lookouts you can see Volcán Arenal, 19km away. **Guided tours** can be arranged a day in advance.

RESERVA FORESTAL BOSQUE ETERNO DE LOS NIÑOS

Contact Monteverde Conservation League ☎ 645 5003; fax 645 5104; acmmcl@sol.racsa.co.cr. The Bajo del Tigre entrance is open daily 8am-5pm. US$5, students US$2. Lodging US$20 per person, US$40 with meals. Student and group discounts.

Under-appreciated Bosque Eterno de los Niños is the nation's largest private reserve. The lower-elevation Bosque Eterno covers 220 sq. km, twice that of Monteverde Reserve, and less foliage makes for better bird watching and views. The **Bajo del Tigre** entrance is just 3.5km southeast of Santa Elena along the road to Monteverde and offers short 4km hikes through premontaine forest. The Visitors Center is very welcoming of children, and one of the **trails** is designed for them. Farther away, two **field stations, San Gerardo** and **Poco Sol,** have accommodations available. (Arrange with the League two weeks in advance.)

🔵 🔼 OTHER SIGHTS AND ACTIVITIES

FINCA ECOLÓGICA DE MONTEVERDE. Loop trails pass the banana and coffee plantations as well as lookouts and two cascading waterfalls, and can be hiked in 30min.-3hr. Printed guides are available at the Visitors Center. *(The well-marked turn-off from the Monteverde road is between Pizzería Johnny and Paradise Café, almost 1km from Santa Elena.* ☎645 5554; fincaecologica@racsa.co.cr. *Open daily 7am-5pm. US$7, US$5 with student ID, US$3 for children ages 6-12. Guides recommended. Call a day ahead.)*

JARDÍN DE MARIPOSAS (BUTTERFLY GARDEN). This biodiversity center focuses on the study of all sorts of insects, from the elegant to the nasty, not just the popular butterflies. Guides give a 1hr. tour of the butterfly habitats. *(Turn off the Monteverde road about 1km from Santa Elena; signs will direct you.* ☎645 5512; www.best.com/~mariposa. *Open daily 9:30am-4pm. ¢2500, student ¢2000. Tours included.)*

CANOPY TOURS. Zip-lines speed from platform to platform high above the forest canopy. The original, **Canopy Tour,** based at the Cloud Forest Lodge 7km northeast of Santa Elena, has 8 lines and 2 repelling systems. Their Santa Elena office is across from the supermarket. **Sky Trek,** across from the Banco Nacional in Santa Elena, offers a similar 2½-3hr. of zipping ecstasy along 11 longer lines. *(Canopy Tour:* ☎645 5243; www.canopytour.com. *Office open daily 6am-8pm. 2-2½hr. US$45, students US$35. Prices include transport. Sky Trek:* ☎645 5238. *Office open daily 6am-9pm. US$35, students US$28. Transportation US$1 each way. Reservations required.*)

HUMMINGBIRD GALLERY. The patio hosts hundreds of hummingbirds; the species present depend on the season. *(Just before the entrance to the Monteverde Reserve.* ☎645 5030. *Open daily 8:30am-4:30pm. Offers slide shows. Entrance US$3.)*

HORSEBACK RIDING. There are many opportunities for horseback riding in the area. **Meg's Stables,** 2.5km from Santa Elena, next to Stella's (Stella is Meg's mom), offers 2hr. rides (US$23) and a 5hr. ride to an 80 ft. waterfall (US$45). *(* ☎645 5560 or 645 5419; night 645 5052. *Call ahead for reservations.)*

CASA DE ARTESANOS. Founded in 1982 to provide economic opportunities for women in the area, Casa de Artesanos de Santa Elena de Monteverde **(CASEM)** now has 92 artisans selling their handmade crafts. *(3.25km from Santa Elena on the road to Monteverde.* ☎645 5190. *Open M-Sa 8am-5pm.)*

MONTEVERDE COMMUNITY ART CENTER. The studio offers week-long classes with artists specializing in crafts from stained glass to storytelling. Reservations must be made in advance. *(Across the road and over the bridge from the cheese factory.* ☎645 6121. *Shop open daily 9am-5pm. Classes US$235 per week, US$30-40 per day.)*

CHEESE FACTORY. The most stable business in the Monteverde community was started by Quakers. Watch the production process through an observation window as you enjoy delicious ice cream and milkshakes. *(Southeast along the road, 500m from Stella's. www.monteverde.net. Open M-Sa 7:30am-5pm, Su 7:30am-12:30pm.)*

CAÑAS

Sweltering Cañas sits on the Interamerican Hwy. amid dusty Guanacaste farm-land. It can be a transportation hub, particularly for those traveling between the Pacific coast and Volcán Arenal. The town is dull, but some use it as a base for Parque Nacional Palo Verde, 30km to the west, or for trips on the Río Corobicí.

The bus station is five blocks north of the *parque's* northwest corner behind the *mercado municipal*, a couple of blocks east of the Interamerican Hwy. **Buses** go to: **Abangares** (9:20am and 2:20pm); **Bebedero** (11am, 1, 3pm); **El Hotel** (5am, noon,

4pm); **Liberia** (1½hr., 12 per day 5:40am-5pm, ¢465); **Puntarenas** (2hr., 8 per day 6am-4:30pm, ¢450); **Tilarán** (45min., 7 per day 6am-5:30pm, ¢185); and **Upala** (6 per day 6am-5pm). Many buses between San José and Liberia (3hr., about every 30min., ¢1200) pass by on the Interamerican but do not stop at the station; to flag them down, head to a stop 200m west of the *parque's* southeast corner.

The **Banco Nacional** with **ATM** is on the northwest corner of the *parque*. (Open M-F 8:30am-3:45pm.) **Palí Supermarket** is two blocks north of the northwest corner of the *parque*. (Open M-Sa 8am-7pm, Su 8am-6pm.) The **police station** is north of the *parque* on the west side of the Interamerican. (☎ 669 0057, emergency 116.) **Farmacia Cañas** lies 1½ blocks east of Banco Nacional. (☎ 669 0748. Open M-Sa 7:30am-9pm, Su 8am-noon.) You can receive medical care at **Dr. Juan Acón Chen's clinics,** one block north and one block west of the *parque's* northwest corner. (☎ 669 0139, emergency ☎ 669 0471. Open M-F 8am-noon and 2-6pm, Sa 8am-noon.) Try **Ciberc@ñas** for **Internet** access, one block north and half a block east of the church's northeast corner. (1½hr. ¢250. Open M-Sa 8am-9pm, Su 2pm-9pm.) The **post office** is one block north and two blocks west of the *parque*, and has **fax** and **Internet**. (Open M-F 8am-noon and 1-5:30pm.)

Hotel El Parque ❶, on the south side of the *parque*, has cream-colored rooms and communal baths. (☎ 669 2213. ¢1300 per person. No credit cards.) **Cabinas Corobicí ❶**, is a good choice, three blocks east and two blocks south of the *parque's* southeast corner—the rooms are clean, spacious and have TVs and private baths. (☎ 669 0241. Singles ¢3500; doubles ¢7000.) **Nuevo Hotel Cañas ❸**, one block north and 1½ west of the *parque's* northwest corner, is more expensive, but worth it with a pool, A/C, TV, and private baths. (☎ 669 1294. Singles US$26.40; doubles US$42. AmEx/MC/V.) **Hotel Cañas Restaurant ❷**, one block north of the *parque's* northwest corner, is by far the best in town. They brag of firewood cooking, the food is simple and fresh. (Fish fajitas ¢2350; *casado* with chicken filet ¢1700. Open M-Sa 6am-10pm, Su 7am-2:30pm.) **Restaurant Paris ❷**, half a block west of the southwest corner of the *parque*, serves Chinese food. (Open daily 10am-midnight.)

Safaris Corobicí, 4.5km north of Cañas on the Interamerican, runs class I and II **float trips** on the Río Corobicí. (☎/fax 669 6091; safaris@racsa.co.cr. 2hr. trips US$37 per person, 3hr. trips US$45, half-day trips with lunch included US$60. 2 person minimum. Rafts handicapped-equipped.)

TILARÁN

About the only travelers who don't breeze in and right out of this gusty little town are windsurfers setting sail on **Laguna de Arenal,** 5km away. For everyone else, Tilarán's wide streets and reviving, fresh climate make it a convenient stopover when traveling from Fortuna to the Pacific coast. The church is east of the *parque* and windmills sit on hills north of town. **Buses** leave half a block west from the *parque's* northwest corner to: **San José** (☎ 695 5611; 4hr., 5 per day 5am-4:55pm, ¢1200); **Puntarenas** (2½hr., 6am and 1pm, ¢700); **Monteverde** (3hr., 1 per day 12:30pm, ¢800); **Ciudad Quesada/San Carlos** (4½hr., 7am and 12:30pm, ¢700); **Arenal** (1½hr., 5 per day 5am-4:30pm, ¢280); and **Cañas** (1hr., 8 per day 5am-5pm, ¢200). **Taxis** (☎ 696 5324) line the west side of the *parque* by the phones.

For **tourist information** in English, visit **La Carreta** hotel and restaurant (see **Accommodations** below). **Banco Nacional** lies across from the southwest corner of the *parque*. (Open M-F 8:30am-3:45pm.) The **police station** is half a block west of the bus station. (☎ 695 5001. Open 24hr.) The **Red Cross** is 100m east of the *parque's* northeast corner (☎ 695 5256). The **hospital** is 200m west of the *parque's* southwest corner (☎ 695 5093). For **internet access,** you can go to **Cafe Internet,** diagonally across from the bus terminal. (¢800 per hr. Open M-F 9am-11pm, Sa-Su 10am-

10pm.) The **post office** is one block north and 1½ blocks east of the *parque*'s northeast corner. (Open M-F 8am-noon and 1-5:30pm.)

Hotel Mary ❷, on the south side of the *parque*, is spacious with private baths, TV, and wall-to-wall carpeting. The restaurant downstairs is recommended and reasonably priced. (☎/fax 695 5479. Singles ¢2000; singles and doubles with bath ¢3500.) **Cabinas El Sueño ❷** sits half a block north of the *parque*'s northwest corner. Luxurious rooms surround a sky-lit courtyard. Cheaper rooms with shared bath are less comfortable. (☎ 695 5347. Singles US$8, with bath US$15; doubles US$15/US$25.) **La Carreta ❹**, behind the church, is a very convenient all-in-one souvenir shop, hotel, and restaurant. Cable TV, private baths, and ceiling fans in nice, comfortable rooms. (☎ 695 6593. Singles US$35; doubles US$45. 50% off in low season. MC/V.) **El Nilo ❷**, 100m north and 100m east of the *parque*, is a *soda* with a sofa chair, magazines, and TV. (*Platos típicos* ¢1200. Open 7am-9pm.) **La Carreta ❷**, behind the church, has an extensive Italian and American menu that includes typical *tico* options under new management. (Pizza ¢1400 small, ¢1950 large. Open daily 7am-10pm.) **Restaurante Nueva Fortuna ❷**, 50m north of the northwest corner of the *parque*, across from Cabinas El Sueño, stirs up popular Chinese food. (☎ 695 5069. Entrees ¢1500-2900. Open daily 11am-11:30pm.)

Laguna de Arenal, a man-made lake 29km long, is one of the world's premier **windsurfing** spots, especially from December to May. April is the best month. The **Hotel Tilawa,** 10km north of Tilarán, rents boards and offers classes. (☎ 695 5050. Boards US$35 half day, US$45 full day. Classes US$55 for 3-4hr.) The windsurfing center is on the lake shore and does not take reservations for non-guests; call or drop by daily from 7am-5pm (☎ 695 5710). In town, **Tour Varela,** in a garage one block north and half a block west of the *parque's* northeast corner, offers **water skiing, fishing,** and **boat tours.** (☎ 695 5292. Skiing ¢7000 per hr. Boat tour $150.)

PARQUE NACIONAL PALO VERDE

Parque Nacional Palo Verde is one of Central America's most important wetlands. The bird life is the allure: 278 species are in residence, including jabirus, egrets, ibis, and the only colony of scarlet macaws on the tropical dry Pacific. The park has an array of habitats, including lowland mangroves, riparian forest, and floodplain marsh, and is home to at least 1400 plant and animal species.

▮ TRANSPORTATION. The park entrance is 30km southwest of the town of **Bagaces,** off the Interamerican Hwy., where **buses** running between Cañas and Liberia will drop you off. There is no public transportation between Bagaces and the park, but you can get a **taxi** (¢6000 each way). When school is in session (early Feb.-Dec. save the 1st two weeks of July) there is also a **student bus** that runs from Bagaces, outside the medical clinic, to **Bagatzi,** near the park entrance. (M-F 3pm, ¢500; return at 5:15am—you will have to spend the night or call a taxi to return.) The last bus from Bagaces to STET leaves the Bagaces station at 11:30pm, from Bagaces to San José via Cañas at around 8:30pm.

▮ ▮ ORIENTATION AND PRACTICAL INFORMATION. Parque Nacional Palo Verde lies on the northwest corner of the Gulf of Nicoya, about 30km west of Cañas. From the entrance, the main road traverses the park's length. After 6km, a road branches left from the main road, leading 5km down to **La Bocana,** popular with birds, and 9km down to **Catalina,** the first ranger station. From here, a 2.5km trail ascends to lookouts on Cerro Pelón. Back on the main road, 1km past the fork, a trail leads to **Mirador La Roca.** This 570m trail offers views of much of the park. Four hundred meters farther up sits the **biological station,** an independent research facility run by the renowned **Organization of Tropical Studies (OTS).**

Although the biological station is officially for students and researchers, it's possible to negotiate for a bed when space is available. Near OTS, **Laguna Palo Verde** features hundreds of birds and ducks in December, January, and February. **Palo Verde,** the second ranger station, lies 1½km beyond the biological station. The regional Ministerio del Ambiente y Energía (MINAE) office, on the west side of the gas station on the Interamerican Hwy., has info and can contact park rangers who can guide you inside the park. The park is open daily 6am-6pm. Boat tours: US$20 per person for 2½-3hr. ride. Call **Tempisque Conservation Area** (☎/fax 671 1290) or the **MINAE** office in Bagaces in advance. (☎671 1062. Open M-F 8am-4pm.)

⛺ ACCOMMODATIONS AND CAMPING. Six kilometers from the entrance, the road branches left from the main road, leading 9km down to **Catalina,** a **ranger station** with water and camping facilities. **Puesto Palo Verde,** the second ranger station, lies 1½km beyond the biological station and has potable water and bathrooms. It is close to many of the park attractions and offers dorm rooms with fans. There is Internet access and interesting biological equipment. (US$13 per night), meals (breakfast US$3, lunch and dinner US$5 each), and horse rental (US$6 per hr.).

🥾 HIKING. A 30min. hike from the Palo Verde station leads to **Mirador Guayacán,** the best viewpoint in the park. Crocodiles laze along the banks, and nearby is **La Isla de Pájaros,** the most important breeding ground for water birds in Central America. At the end of the main road, 2km beyond the ranger station, is **Puerto Chamorro,** the park's dock along the banks of Río Tempisque. From the Catalina station, a 2.5km trail ascends to lookouts on **Cerro Pelón.** The park rangers can also arrange a **boat tour** of the park; contact them in advance.

LIBERIA

Inviting and spacious Liberia (pop. 50,000), Guanacaste's commercial center, is the heart of this dusty cowboy region. The white-washed colonial houses lining the streets, the strutting *sabaneros* (cowboys), and the rustle of the Liberia flag above the *parque central* hint at the pride, history, and tradition that make Liberia unique. Although there's little to see, it is a pleasant place and a good base for visits to national parks like Rincón de la Vieja, Santa Rosa, and Palo Verde.

🚌 TRANSPORTATION. Liberia is a convenient stop en route to Pacific beaches or the Nicaraguan border and is one of the transport hubs of the Nicoya Peninsula. **Sansa** (50min.; high season 5:15 and 11:50am, return 6:20am and 12:50pm; US$66) and **Travelair** (50min.; high season 6, 8:30, 11:30am, return 7:30, 9:55am, 3:05pm; US$73) fly from San José (see p. 144) to the airport 12km west of Liberia. The airport is accesible by taxi or any Nicoya/Playa del Coco bus, which pass by the entrance road 1.6km from the terminal.

Bus schedules change often; check beforehand. Unless otherwise noted, the following depart opposite the market, 5 blocks west and 3 blocks north of the *parque:* **Cañas** via **Bagaces** (1hr., 11 per day 5am-5pm, ¢460); **Managua, Nicaragua** (from Hotel Guanacaste; 5hr., 5 per day 8am-12:30pm, US$12.50); **Nicoya** via **Santa Cruz** and **Filadelfia** (2hr., every 30min. 4:30am-8:20pm, ¢450); Nicaraguan border at **Peñas Blancas** via **La Cruz** (1hr., 10 per day 5:30am-8pm, ¢600); **Playa del Coco** (1hr., 7 per day 5:30am-8:20pm, ¢500); **Playa Hermosa** and **Playa Panamá** (1hr., 6 per day 5am-5:30pm, ¢300); **Puntarenas** via **Cañas** (3hr., 7 per day 5am-3:20pm, ¢1000); and **San José** (4½hr., 6 per day 5:30am-5pm, ¢1600; from Pulmitán terminal a block south of the main terminal, every hr. 4-10am and every 2hr. 10am-8pm, ¢1410).

Taxis are at the north side of the *parque.* (Taxi Liberia ☎666 1778 or 666 0073.)

📑 ORIENTATION AND PRACTICAL INFORMATION. The city is built on the regular grid, with Avenida Central (or Ave. 25 de Julio) acting as the southern bor-

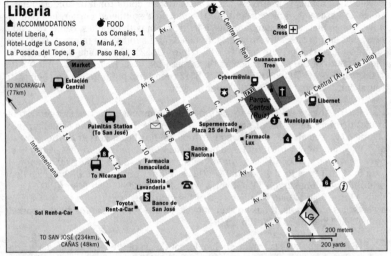

der of the **parque central** (officially known as **Parque Ruiz**). Calle Central, or **Calle Real**, is halved by the *parque*. In front of the church in the main plaza sits the **Árbol de Guanacaste,** a tree after which the whole province was named. The **Universidad de Costa Rica** is on the west side of town. The **tourist office** is 3 blocks south and 1 block east of the *parque*, and offers tours to Rincón de La Vieja, Palo Verde, and Santa Rosa National Parks. (☎665 0135. Round-trip US$40 for 3. Open M-Sa 8am-noon and 1:30-5pm.) The **municipalidad** is on the ast side of police station. (☎666 0169. Open M-F 8am-4pm.) MINAE is next to MAG after the bridge. The **Banco Nacional,** 3 blocks west of the *parque*, exchanges traveler's checks. (☎666 0259. Open M-F 8:30am-3:45pm.) There is a **Western Union** in the bamboo mall 20m north of *municipalidad*. The **market** is 5 blocks west and 3 blocks north of the *parque*, across from the central bus station. (Open M-Sa 6am-7pm, Su 6am-noon.) For groceries, go to **Plaza 25 de Julio,** half a block west of the *parque*'s southwest corner (☎666 7171; open M-Sa 8am-9pm, Su 8am-2pm). You can do your **laundry** at **Sixaola Dry Cleaning & Lavandería,** 4 blocks west and 25m south of the *parque*'s southwest corner, behind Casa Romana. (☎666 333. Open M-F 8am-noon and 1:30-5pm, Sa 8am-noon.) Other services include: **Red Cross,** on the east side of town 100m north and 200m east of *parque* (☎666 0994, emergency 118); **police,** on the *parque* (☎666 0213, emergency 911); **Farmacia Luz,** 100m west of the *parque*'s southwest corner (☎666 0061; open M-Sa 8am-10pm, Su 8am-noon); the **Health Center,** 100m west, 200m north, and 1km east of *municipalidad;* and the **hospital** (☎666 0011, emergency ext. 325). For **telephones, Telecomunicaciones Internacionales** is 3 blocks west and half a block south of the *parque*. (☎665 0403. Open M-F 7:30am-5pm, Sa 8am-11:30am.) **Ciberm@nía,** on the northeast corner of the *parque* has A/C and offers fast **Internet** connections. (¢450 per hr. Open daily 8am-10pm.) The **post office** is 3 blocks west and 1 block north of the *parque*. (Open M-F 8am-5:30pm, Sa 7:30am-noon.) **Postal Code:** 5000.

Ɍ ACCOMMODATIONS. Some rates may increase during the high season, between December and April. **Hotel Liberia ❷,** half a block south of the *parque*'s southeast corner, has simple rooms with toilets, showers, and sinks. (☎666 0161. Laundry ¢1500 per kg. Rooms ¢4500 per person; smaller rooms with private bath

¢3000; large rooms with private bath ¢5000. 10% discount for ISIC holders.) **Hotel-Lodge La Casona ❶**, 3 blocks south of the *parque's* southeast corner, has omfortable rooms, pleasant common baths, a living room with couches, cable TV, and a new restaurant especially for guests. (☎666 2971. Laundry and Internet. US$5 person; doubles with private bath US$15; triples US$21.) **La Posada del Tope ❶**, 1½ blocks south of the *parque*, across the street from Casa Real, offers cable TV for ¢500, transport to Rincón de la Vieja (US$12 round-trip per person), and help with rental cars. (☎/fax 666 3876. ¢2000 per person.)

🍴 **FOOD.** Always ask before to see if the restaurant might serve some good traditional drinks, made out of **coyol** or the flower seed called **chan** (smells really strong). **Los Comales ❶**, 2½ blocks north of the northeast corner of the *parque*, and a second, newer location three blocks west of the *parque*, offers hearty Guanacaste *típico*. (☎665 0105. *Arroz de maíz* ¢650; *casados* ¢800-1000. Open M-F 7am-5:30pm.) **Paso Real ❷**, on the southeast corner of the *parque*, has excellent seafood and a big screen TV. (Risotto with shrimp ¢2000; fish fillet ¢1800. Open daily 11am-10pm.) **Maná ❶**, 125m east of the church, serves *típica* on tree stump-style tables and stools. It has no sign in front. (☎666 8468. *Casados* ¢900; meatball soup ¢600. Open M-Sa 7am-10pm.)

🔲 **SIGHTS. Iglesia de la Ermita,** six blocks southeast of the *parque* along Av. Central, is the oldest church in town. (Open daily 2:30-3:30pm.) A small *sabanero* **museum,** now in the government building on the *parque*, displays various *sabanero* accessories and explores the historical evolution of the Guanacaste region. (Open M-F 8:30am-noon and 1:30-5pm. ¢100.) The **Camandancia Station,** north of Liberia, houses a makeshift museum for the Daniel Quiros collection, which has artifacts dating from 500BC to AD1500. (Open M-F 8am-noon and 1-4pm.)

🎭 **ENTERTAINMENT.** Apart from the wild annual celebrations organized by the town, Liberians love to go out dancing and sing karaoke. *Parranda*, the local dance, is popular in local dance halls (follow the crowd). On weekends, stop by the **Tsunami Bar and Grill,** on the road to Nicoya, 600m from center next to the Hotel Sitio, and best reached by cab. Weds. is Ladies Night. (☎666 1211). **Disco Kurú,** across the road, has kareoke and dancing. Dancers sometimes overflow into the seating area and get down between the tables to mostly Latin Music. (☎666 0769. Karaoke M, Tu, W nights. Beer on tap ¢400. Open M-Sa 8pm-4am).

NORTH OF LIBERIA

PARQUE NACIONAL RINCÓN DE LA VIEJA

While the rest of Costa Rica parties to the *tico* groove and ocean breeze, head north of Liberia for seclusion in the a park filled with waterfalls, rivers, and endless forests. A gigantic active volcano with sulfuric lagoons, boiling mud pits, thermal waters, a trail network, and birding ensure quality bonding with Mother Nature and a lasting impression of natural beauty. Rincón de la Vieja's dry climate makes this park most beautiful during the rainy season (May-Nov.), when waterfalls spill through its forests and hot springs bubble over with water.

🚌 **TRANSPORTATION AND ORIENTATION.** The park is only 25km northeast of Liberia, but public transportation covers this distance. Coming by **private car,** a dirt road leads from Liberia's Barrio La Victoria to the Santa María entrance. Another dirt road starts 5km north of Liberia on the Interamerican Hwy. and heads

10km east to the town of Curabanda; from there it is another 10km east to the Las Pailas entrance (¢700 to drive on the road). Public **buses** go only as far as Curabanda. From there, some catch a ride with occasional traffic. However, *Let's Go* does not recommend hitchhiking. More reliable **tourist shuttles** from Liberia are offered by Hotel Guanacaste (departs Liberia 6am and 4pm, returns 8am and 5pm; US$18 round trip per person for groups of 3 or more) and La Posada de Tope hotel (US$12 round trip, 3 person minimum). It's also possible to hire a 4WD **taxi** in Liberia (at least ¢10,000 each way). **Ranger station** ☎ 661 8139. (Park open daily 7am-4pm. US$6, camping US$2 per person per night.)

The park has two entrances, **Las Pailas** and **Santa María,** each with a station. Although they are fairly close, the access roads are separate. Las Pailas, with trails leading past waterfalls and up the volcano, is more visited and has a river perfect for swimming in the dry season.

▐ ACCOMMODATIONS AND CAMPING. Both ranger stations have **campgrounds** with showers and pit toilets (US$2 per person per night). You can also arrange basic room and board at the stations; call the park in advance. Near the Las Pailas entrance sit a number of **lodges** that offer meals and activities. **Rincón de la Vieja Lodge ❸** is 2.5km before the entrance, with quiet cabins, some of which come with bunk beds, and hammocks on porches. The restaurant serves a buffet and the bar occasionally has live music. (☎/fax 661 8198; www.rincondelaviejalodge.com. Canopy tour US$50; 3hr. horseback tour to hot springs US$30. Singles US$35; doubles US$51. Larger cabins US$75-110.) The **Hacienda Lodge Guachipelín ❸,** 5km before the entrance, is a 19th-century cattle ranch-turned-hotel. Activities (at a significant extra cost) include a ten-platform canopy tour and horseback tours of the park. Transportation from Liberia costs US$50 round-trip or US$10 to the park. (☎ 666 8075; www.guachipelin.com. Restaurant buffet. Breakfast included. Singles US$38; doubles US$30-45.)

▐ HIKES. East of Las Pailas ranger station is a 3km **loop trail Sendero Las Pailas,** which passes turn-offs to a picturesque waterfall (only in the rainy season), a sulfuric lagoon, and boiling mud pits. A well-marked branch about halfway around this trail, leads another 6km east to the **Santa María station.** A trail to the west of the Las Pailas leads to the park's biggest waterfalls: **Cataratas Escondidas** (4.7km) and the awesome **Catarata La Cangreja** (5km). For a swim without the 2hr. hike, there's a crystal-clear **swimming hole** just 600m down the trail toward the waterfalls. It's 8km to the **crater** of Rincón de la Vieja; allow a day for the round-trip journey (about 7-8hr.) and register at the park office. Solo hikers must be accompanied by a guide (check with the rangers or at one of the lodges). Access to the crater trail and the waterfalls is closed after 11am. From the Santa María station, a 3km trail leads west through thick, monkey-filled forests to the **hot springs,** 6km east of Las Pailas. Other points of interest accessible from the station are cold water pots, the enchanted forest waterfall, and a scenic outlook.

PARQUE NACIONAL SANTA ROSA

Established in 1971 as one of the first national parks in Costa Rica, Santa Rosa preserves the largest remaining tropical dry forest in Central America and is a UNESCO World Heritage Site. The park has isolated beaches famous for surfing and turtle-watching and unique flora such as the Guanacaste tree, Pochote, Naked Indian, and Caoba, as well as 115 species of mammals. There are many enchanting and accessible *miradores* (lookouts), or on the natural and manmade *senderos* (trails). The park also houses the famous historical sight **Hacienda Santa Rosa (La Casona).** The park is open daily (8am-4:30pm; US$6, US$2 extra for camping) and park information is available at the **Oficina de Ecoturismo** in the administration center (☎ 666 5051, ext. 219; www.acguanacaste.ac.cr; open daily 7:30am-4pm).

■▐ ORIENTATION AND TRANSPORTATION. The national park's entrance station is 35km north of Liberia and 24km south of La Cruz, on the west side of the Interamerican Hwy. From here, a dirt road leads 7km to the park's administration center, with MINAE offices and an information center. A bit farther to the left is the campground, and to the right, past the cabins, is the *comedor* (cafeteria). Beyond the administration center is a 4WD road (often closed to traffic during the rainy season) leading to the coast, 12km away. The road forks after 7km; the left branch leads 4km to **Playa Naranjo**, a popular campsite and famed surfing beach, and the right heads 8km to the turtle-hatching beach of **Playa Nancite**. On the coast, you can swim at **Bahía El Hachal, Bahía Danta, Coquito, Santa Elena**, or **Playa Blanca**, and hike on the 600m trail **(Poza del General).** You can **camp** in the area.

Buses traveling along the Interamerican Hwy. between the Nicaraguan border and Liberia (such as the Liberia-Peñas Blancas bus, leaving Liberia every 2hr. 5:30am-7pm) drop off at the entrance station (**La Casetilla**). About 12 buses per day pass in each direction. No buses run the 7km to the administration center or along the dirt road to the beach, so those without wheels walk or hitch (try asking the rangers). *Let's Go* does not recommend hitchhiking. Hotel Guanacaste in Liberia sometimes runs a shuttle to and from the park.

▐▐ ACCOMMODATIONS AND FOOD. The park offers **lodging** near the main offices (US$15 per person, students US$10) and amazing meals (¢800-1300) in the *comedor*. Reserve lodging at least 1-2 weeks before (☎ 666 5051) and give a few hours' notice for food, which is always served at noon. There's also a snack bar. A campground near the administration center has drinking water, flush toilets, and cold-water showers. The campground at Playa Naranjo has toilets and non-potable water. Ask about **camping** overnight in Nancite and in the Sector Murciélago.

◆▐ SIGHTS AND HIKING. La Casona, near the administration center (follow signs past the administration center to the left), is the main building of the historic Hacienda Santa Rosa where the battle of 1856 was fought. Invasions were also prevented in 1919 and 1955. Alas, La Casona did not withstand its most recent invasion on May 20, 2001, when two vindictive deer hunters, angered by hunting prohibitions, snuck into the park and set fire to the site. They were caught and convicted, and Costa Ricans raised ¢200,350,000 in a united effort to rebuild the fort, which now stands restored, with roof tiles from 1886 and, appropriately, a state-of-the-art fire alarm system. In front, you can view cattle being cleaned in immersion baths in preparation for their truck journey from the **embarcadero** to the **corrales de piedra.** (Open daily 8am-4pm.) The **Monument to the Heroes of 1856 and 1955** lies beside La Casona, with a windy view of nearby volcanos Orosi, Cacao, and Rincón de la Vieja. The lookouts **Mirador Tierras Emergidas,** and **Mirador Yalle Naranjo** are about halfway to the administration center from the entrance on the way to the coast, and offer some stellar views. All **trails** and points of interest are marked on a useful map available at the entrance (US$2). The short (800m) **Sendero Indio Desnudo** (a.k.a. *Gringo Pelado*, "Peeling Gringo") begins near La Casona and is a revealing introduction to the plants of the region. **Sendero Los Patos,** 5km beyond the administration center on the road to the coast, is one of the best trails for wildlife viewing. The 2km **Sendero Palo Seco** lies near Playa Naranjo, as does the 4km **Sendero Carbonal** that leads to **Laguna el Lirubo,** a crocodile hotspot.

◣ BEACHES. There is outstanding surfing at **Playa Naranjo.** Try Piedra Bruja, 3km north of the campground, with 3m waves and, according to legend, *sirenas* (mermaids). **Playa Nancite** has the country's second-largest arrival of olive ridley sea turtles. The nesting season is July-Dec. and is best in Oct-Nov., during a vague 8-day, crescent moon period when 1000-6000 turtles arrive on the 800m of beach every night at around 9pm. Access to Playa Nancite is restricted, and you need permission at the administration center. If you arrive by at the car by park, it is forbidden to drive to Nancite. Drop it off at Playa Naranjo before going on to Nancite (a guard will watch it); don't you leave your car anywhere other than with the guard.

PARQUE NACIONAL GUANACASTE

Parque Nacional Guanacaste lies on the opposite side of Parque Nacional Santa Rosa, across the Interamericana. While the west shares Santa Rosa's lowland habitats, the environment chages as the park rises toward the summits of Volcán Orosi (1487m) and Cacao (1659m). The park, created in 1991, is open mainly to students and scientists in the dry season, and is difficult to visit without private transportation. There are three well-developed research stations scattered about the park: **Marzita, Cacao,** and **Pitilla.** Tourists are sometimes permitted to stay at the stations, which have dorm beds and cold-water baths. **Camping** by the stations is permitted. For information, contact **Gisel Méndez,** in the Santa Rosa headquarters (☎ 666 5051, ext.233). About 100 groups visit the *Parque* annually, but individuals rarely visit; as such , it is best to find a group to go with.

Marzita Biological Station, is 18km off the Interamerican Hwy., along an unpaved road. The turnoff is east at the Cuanjiniquil intersection, 8km north of the entrance to Santa Rosa. Marzita has lodging for up to 32 people, electricity, and food service (request in advance). At this station, research is focused on aquatic insects and there is a 2hr. trail hike called **Pedtroglifos El Pedregal** for its approximately 800 observable petrogypls. Observations of Volcán Orosi, La Fila del Cacao, the Pacific coast, and the transition of dry to moist forest make this trail a real treat if you are allowed entrance (you have a better chance in the dry season).

A 12km trail ascends to the **Cacao Biological Station.** It begins in Potrerillos, about 9km south of the Santa Rosa park entrance. From Potrerillos, head 7km east to Quebrada Grande (take the daily 3pm bus from Libreria), then 10km north along a 4WD road to the station. During the rainy season, you will have to park 5km before the station at Río Gangora. You can lodge in Mata de Caña in Quebrada Grande or directly explore the Cacao Biological Station grounds. There is a 900m trail called **Pedregal** which leads to an observatory for forest fires. You can also climb to the top of Volcán Cacao, a 3hr. hard climb into the cloud forest that starts on the east side of the lab. You will need a permission slip.

Pitilla Biological Station, 28km off the highway near the Nicaraguan border, is the least likely to allow visitors. There is a 7pm bus from Liberia to Santa Cecilia and cheap hostels if you need to stay the night. Buses also run from La Cruz (noon, 12:30, 1:15, 7pm). At Pitilla, you can delight in incredible birdwatching and catch a glimpse of Lago de Nicaragua from the top of mini-Volcán Orosilito. Another lodging option is at the private **Volcán Cacao Base Camp,** affiliated with Hotel Guanacaste in Libreria (☎ 666 0085). It is 6km south of the park and offers bunk beds with common baths and camping. It also offers transport from Liberia (US$10 one way) and horse tours to Volcán Cacao (US$45 from Liberia).

☒ PEÑAS BLANCAS: BORDER WITH NICARAGUA

Liberia is only 1 hr. away from the border at Peñas Blancas which is not a town but a frontier. (1½hr., 10 daily 5:30am-7pm, ₡600). To reach Peñas Blancas from **San José,** catch a bus from Calle 14, between Av. 3 and 5 (6hr.; M-F 6 per day 5am-4:10pm, Sa-Su more frequent; ₡1860). To get to Peñas Blancas from **La Cruz,** catch the bus from Liberia (₡150) or take a taxi (₡500 per person if in a group).

Both Nicaraguan and Costa Rican immigration offices are "open" from 8am to 8pm, but it's wise to get there well before closing time (around noon is a good idea), as bureaucracy and transit from one to the other can take a surprisingly long time (up to 6hr.). The Costa Rica **immigration office** (☎ 677 0064) has two lines: one for entering Costa Rica (US$7) and the other for exiting Costa Rica (¢200 plus US$1.50). If you're leaving Costa Rica, buy the exit stamp from any *cambista* outside, or from the booth. For those entering Nicaragua and planning to stay more than 3 months, stamps are more expensive (US$35 for Costa Ricans and tourists and US$55 for Nicaraguan residents of Costa Rica). Entering Costa Rica for a stay of more than 3 months costs US$20.

Once you get your passport stamped, you can have a snack in **Restaurante de Frontera** inside, and change your money at the small **Banco Crédito Agrícola** (which has long lines). **Money changers** (*cambistas*) abound on both sides of the border, but the rates are better on the Nicaraguan side. Hotel Guanacaste in Liberia will also change money.**Buses** from the Nicaraguan border run to **Rivas** (1hr.; every 30min. 6am-5:30pm, 10C), and continue to **Managua.** For **San Juan del Sur,** take the Rivas bus, get off at La Virgen (30min., 4C), and change there for San Juan (30min., every 30min. 5am-6pm, 4C).

NORTHERN LOWLANDS

Costa Rica's sparsely populated northernmost region is, not surprisingly, one of its least visited. Culturally and geographically close to Nicaragua, the vegetation here was once mixed tropical forest but much of that has been replaced by pasture land. Some of this floods for much of the year, as in Refugio Nacional de Vida Silvestre Caño Negro, an aquatic wonderland teeming with birdlife.

CIUDAD QUESADA (SAN CARLOS)

Hovering amid the Cordillera Central's sloping green hills, Ciudad Quesada (San Carlos to its residents) marks the fusion of the *campo tico* with everyday small city life. The agriculture and ranching center of the north, San Carlos pumps out much of the country's beef and milk. It also serves as a major saddlery center. Northwest of San José (110km), the city is a transport hub within the Alajuela province. Travelers connect here to nearby Fortuna and Volcán Arenal (40km), as well as Los Chiles and Puerto Viejo de Sarapiquí.

■ TRANSPORTATION. The city's bus station (☎ 460 5064), referred to as *"parada nueva"* by most locals, is 500m north of town. A shuttle bus leaves from the *mercado*, 100m north of the northeast corner of the *parque*, to the terminal's side for ¢75. Here, catch **buses** to **San José** (3hr.; 11 per day M-Sa 5am-6:15pm; Su 6, 9:15, 10am, 4, 5, 5:30pm; ¢780); **Fortuna** (1½hr., 10 per day 6am-8pm, ¢375); **Los Chiles** (3hr., 14 daily 5am-7pm, ¢725); and **Puerto Viejo de Sarapiquí** (3hr., 9 per day 4:40am-5:30pm, ¢550).

■ ❼ ORIENTATION AND PRACTICAL INFORMATION. Ciudad Quesada has the classic grid layout, in which Av. 0 and Calle 0 intersect on the northeast corner of the **parque central**—but of course, none of that really matters because locals go by units of 100m *(cuadras)* up, down, right, and left. A cream-colored **cathedral** borders the park to the east. **Limited tourist information,** mostly on other destinations, can be found at **Aeronort Agencia de Viajes,** 300m north and 50m west of the northeast corner of the *parque* (☎ 460 3711 or 460 3636; fax 460 7656; ecoservi@racsa.co.cr. Open M-F 8:30am-6pm, Sa 9am-1pm). **Banco Nacional,** (☎ 460 0290) 50m east of the *parque's* northeast corner, will exchange currency and change traveler's checks. The 24hr. **ATM** at Cocique, behind the cathedral, accepts Cirrus. (Open M-F 8:30am-3:45pm.) **Western Union,** sharing a complex with Restaurant Coca Loca and another bank (tucked in the back), is on the west side of the park. (Open M-F 8am-noon and 1-5pm.) The **police station** is 1km east of the *parque* (☎460 0375). The **Hospital** is 3km north of the northeast corner of the *parque* (☎460 1176), and the **Red Cross** (☎460 0101), 150m north and 100m west of the northwest corner of the *parque*. You can find **Internet access** at **Internet Café**, 100m north and 50m east of the northeast corner of the *parque*. (¢350 per hr. Open M-Sa 9am-8:30pm, Su 3-8pm. The **post office** with fax, is 300m north and 150m west of the northwest corner of the *parque*. (Open M-F 7:30am-6pm, Sa 7:30am-noon.)

⊠ ACCOMMODATIONS AND FOOD. Hotel del Norte ❶, 100m east and 150m north of the northeast corner of the *parque central*, has small rooms, comfy beds, fans, color TV. (☎460 1959 or 460 1758. Check-out noon. Singles US$7, with bath US$11; doubles US$11/18. MC/V.) **Hotel del Valle ❶**, 200m north and 50m west of the *parque's* northeast corner, has rooms with cable TV, fans, and private baths. (☎460 0718; fax 460 7551. Singles ¢3000; doubles ¢6000.) Steak is what's for dinner in San Carlos. It is easy to miss the best steakhouse in town under its overhang, but **Restaurante Coca Loca ❸** sits directly on the west side of the *parque* and the inside sets the mood for a thick filet mignon. (☎460 32 08. Filet mignon ¢2250. Open daily 11am-11pm.) Lighter eaters can try **La Terraza ❷**, 250m north from the northeast corner of the *parque*. Besides steak, specialties include *fettuccine alfredo* (¢1000); their sea bass is recommended by locals. (Open daily 11am-midnight.) For cheaper eats, head over to the surprisingly spotless *sodas* inside the *mercado* (see **Transportation,** above).

◙ SIGHTS IN AND AROUND SAN CARLOS . El Zoológico la Marina is a fabulous zoo-park-preserve where abused, sick, or endangered wild animals are cared for. If you need/want vet experience or just love animals, Mr. Rojas welcomes volunteers. To get to the zoo, take any bus heading north from the terminal (35min.; ¢115) and ask to be let out at the Zoológico La Marina. (☎474 2100. Open daily 8am-4pm. Adults ¢1000, children ¢500). Soak in the thermal-water luxury at **El Tucano Resort and Thermal Spa**, 2 km south of the zoo. The only services to non-guests are US$13-15 thermal baths and hydrothermal therapy. (☎460 6000. Open daily 8am-6pm). To marinate in warm water with a more local (or at least *tico*) set, head 1 km south to **Termales del Bosque.** (☎460 4740. Restaurant open 7am-9pm. Singles US$32; doubles US$45.) For leather of the north, check out the **Mercados de Artesanía** on the northwest corner of the *parque*. (Open M-Sa 8:30am-6:30pm.)

PUERTO VIEJO DE SARAPIQUÍ

Eighty-two km north of San José sits Puerto Viejo, a tiny community in a majestic valley surrounded by rainforests. Though most travelers pass en route to Volcán Arenal or Tortuguero, an increasing number of nature enthusiasts are lingering in this jungle town to explore some of Costa Rica's most diverse wildlife. It is now a popular destination for those seeking adventurous white water rafting and much calmer river tours, both of which provide excellent birdwatching opportunities.

⊏ TRANSPORTATION. Buses leave from the station opposite the southwest corner of the soccer field. A schedule is posted inside at the ticket counter, from which you must purchase your tickets before boarding. Buses go to **San Carlos** (5:30, 9am, 12:15, 2, 3:30, 7:30pm), **San José** direct (2hr., 8 per day 5:30am-9:20pm, ¢920), **San José** via **Vara Blanca** (5, 7:30, 11:30am, 4:30pm), **San José** via **Heredia** (3½hr.; 7:30, 11:30am, 4:30, 9:20pm; ¢770); **San José** via **El Tunel Zurquí** (7 per day 5:30am-5:30pm, ¢920), and **Guápiles** (1hr.; 5:30, 7, 9:30am, noon, 2:30, 4, 6pm; ¢480).

Many buses stop at **Bajo de Chillamate, La Virgen,** and **Río Frío** and make additional stops along the way; ask at the ticket counter for information. **Taxis** line up along the main street just north of the soccer field. A taxi to La Virgen costs about ¢1500.

◢⚑ ORIENTATION AND PRACTICAL INFORMATION. Puerto Viejo extends along one main street for about 300m. A **soccer field** bordering this street marks the town center. The bus station is opposite a turquoise **church** that sits on the soccer field's east side. About 100m past the bus station, a small road to the right leads to the **Super Sarapiquí** supermarket. (Open daily 7am-4pm.) Another 100m down the main road, a second small road to the right leads to a few hostels and to the **port** along the Río Sarapiquí. For the most comprehensive **tourist information**, talk to Alex Martínez, owner of **Andrea Cristina Bed and Breakfast** (see **Accommodations**, below). Visit the **24 hr. ATM**, or exchange traveler's checks and dollars at the **Banco Nacional**, at the intersection of the main road and the road to the port. (☎ 766 6012. Open M-F 8:30am-3:45pm.) The **police station** is down the first small road off the main road, near the supermarket. (☎ 766 6575, emergency 911.) The **hospital** is 250m south of the soccer field on the left (☎ 766 6307). The **pharmacy** is 100m past the taxi stand. (☎ 766 3134. Open M-Sa 7am-8pm, Su 7am-1pm.) **Sarapiquí Internet** is 300m south of the soccer field, just past the hospital. (¢300 for 30min., ¢500 per hr. Open daily 8am-10pm.) The **post office** is across the street from Banco Nacional at the turn off to the port. (Open M-F 7:30am-6pm, Sa 7:30am-noon.)

◪⚏ ACCOMMODATIONS AND FOOD. Puerto Viejo offers a surprising number of decent budget options. **Mi Lindo Sarapiquí ❷**, just south of the soccer field and opposite the bus station, has spacious rooms with TVs, fans, and private warm-water baths. Laundry is available. (☎/fax 766 6074. Singles ¢3500; doubles ¢7000.) **Andrea Cristina Bed & Breakfast ❸** is 1km from the town center. Walk south (toward the soccer field) for 500m until you reach a major fork, turn right, and walk another half kilometer; the B&B is to your right. The 6 cozy, fan-cooled cabins, each with a private hot shower. (☎/fax 766 6265. Breakfast is included. US$23 per person. AmEx/MC/V.) You musn't worry about finding a place to eat at Puerto Viejo either; *sodas* line the main road. **Mr. Pizza ❷**, (☎ 766 6138), north of the soccer field next to the Clínica Santa Mónica, serves a variety of fast foods and cheesy pizzas. (Tacos ¢350. Combo plates ¢500-900. Open daily 10am-9pm.) **Restaurante Mi Lindo Sarapiquí ❸**, attached to the hotel of the same name, provides a slightly more upscale, sit-down meal. The large menu includes tasty rice dishes (¢800-1350), pastas (¢1500-2200), and seafood dishes. (Open daily 9am-10pm.)

◪ SIGHTS. Stray from Puerto Viejo de Sarapiquí or La Virgen into the maze of cages of the **Snake Garden (Serpentario)**, where a vast range of reptiles reside, from the deceptively tiny, yet venomous black and green dart frog to the Costa Rica's largest venomous snake, the rainforest-dwelling bushmaster. To get there from Puerto Viejo, take a bus to La Virgen and ask the driver to let you off at *Centro Neotrópico SarapiquiS*. From the Center gates, walk 300m south along the highway until you see the "Serpentario" sign.

▶ DAYTRIPS FROM PUERTO VIEJO DE SARAPIQUÍ

CENTRO NEOTRÓPICO SARAPIQUIS

From Puerto Viejo de Sarapiquí, take a bus to La Virgen. Ask the driver to let you off at the entrance to Centro Neotrópico SarapiquiS. Otherwise, a taxi from Puerto Viejo costs ¢1500; the entrance to the park is on the right, 300m past the snake garden. Reservations recommended. ☎ 761 1418; fax 766 6535; tirimbin@racsa.co.cr; www.tirimbina.org. 3hr. guided tours: adults US$12; students US$9; children ages 6-16 US$6. Self-guided tours: adults US$10; students US$8; children US$5. Open daily 7am-4pm.

Recently opened in 2000 by USA Wisconsin-based Tirimbina Rainforest Center, the non-profit, non-governmental ◪**Centro Neotrópico SarapiquiS** is a preserve dedicated to interactive cultural, biological, and ecological awareness and conservation. Before entering the preserve, the 1000 sq. ft. **museum** includes an informative film presentation, rainforest ecology displays, and examples of pre-Columbian architecture. Inside the park gates is the well-maintained **Alma Ata Archaeological Site**, where in Oct. 1999, 600 year old tombs and indigenous artifacts were found. The center also maintains a small **botanical garden**, where it grows an assortment of pre-Columbian, medicinal, spice, ornamental, fragrant, and edible plants.

The gem of the center is the 350-hectare **Tirimbina Rainforest Preserve**, of which 150 hectares have been developed for public use. A number of easy trails lead tour groups into the beautiful primary and secondary forest. One of Tirimbina's most unique features is its suspension bridges through the forest. The first bridge, **El Puente Colgante**, stretches 262m across the rushing Río Sarapiquí, is the largest of its kind in Costa Rica. A few trails cross the island, and crystal-clear natural pools on the island's edge are ideal for swimming.

ESTACIÓN BIOLÓGICA LA SELVA

From Puerto Viejo, take the 6:45am or 12:15pm bus headed to Río Frío to make the 8am or 1:30pm tours (15min., ¢120). Buses to Guápiles also pass this way. Ask the driver to let you off near La Selva. From this stop, follow the dirt road on your right 1km to the station's gates; signs mark the way. To get back to Puerto Viejo, have the station call you a cab (¢1000) or flag down one of the frequent buses down on the main road.

Only 6km south of Puerto Viejo, La Selva is one of the jewels of the **Organization for Tropical Studies (OTS)**, a non-profit consortium of universities and research institutions. La Selva borders Parque Nacional Braulio Carrillo to the south and boasts 1560 hectares of primary and secondary rainforest. Hundreds of scientists and students come to La Selva each year to study over 450 species of birds, 70 species of bats, and 5 species of felines. The 57km of path, 8km of which are made of concrete, make La Selva accessible to casual nature lovers; come prepared with proper hiking boots, insect repellent, and rain gear. Unless you are staying in the station's upscale lodge (singles US$75; doubles US$65 per person; meals included), the trails can only be explored with a guide. Two tours leave each day (3hrs.; 8am, 1:30pm; US$25 per person). Call the station to inquire about volunteering. (☎766 6566.) For reservations call the San José office (☎240 6696); ask for Ana Carter. (Open M-Sa 7-11:30am and 12:30-5pm, Su 7:30am-noon and 12:30-4pm.)

IN RECENT NEWS

TROUBLE ON THE SAN JUA

Nicaragua and Costa Rica are riding shaky waters on the controversial river separating the two countries The San Juan is the subject of an over 3-year-long debate that flared when the Nicaraguan government prohibited armed Costa Rican police from patrolling the river, claiming that they posed a threat to their national security. The Costa Rican government officials argue that the same 1916 ruling by the Central American Court of Justice establishing the river as Nicaraguan property, however, also upheld the Costa Ricans' right to travel the river with standard issue arms and maintain that their police presence on the river curbs illegal drug trafficking.

Though Nicaragua has threatened to impose taxes on Costa Rican goods and tensions are rising, anything more aggressive than heated debate is out of the question. Perhaps the most significant factor in the way of solidly resolving the dispute, is both country's plan to mutually develop tourism near the border. Costa Rica has planned to invest in hotel development, and Nicaragua has promised US$20 million for the project.

More interesting than the legal and business issues on the San Juan however, are the worried sentiments of citizens, who feel the severe poverty of Nicaraguans living on the river banks presents a much more serious dilemma than territorial disputes. In the face of so many social problems Nicaraguans argue that patriotism isn't a likely priority yet wish their government was nationalist in fighting the country's real problems rather than harmless Costa Ricans on the river.

RÍO SARAPIQUÍ AND RÍO SAN JUAN

*Guided tours offered by Alex Martínez (☎ 766 6265. 2-6 people US$150 per day), Yacaré Tours (☎ 238 3009; US$10 per person per hr.; 2 person min.), through Souvenirs Río Sarapiquí (see **Practical Information,** above), or Captain Mena (beeper ☎ 224 4000 or 225 2500; leave a message in Spanish; 2-4 people US$25 per hr.).*

The Río Sarapiquí, flowing calmly alongside Puerto Viejo's eastern boundary, continues north for 40km before meeting the Río San Juán, which forms the border between Costa Rica and Nicaragua. Flanked on one side by dense forest and to the other by banana plantations, the Río Sarapiquí demonstrates the constant battle between the goals of conservationists to protect the rain forest and the needs of farmers to use the land commercially. Most tours of the Sarapiquí consist of 2-3hr. rides in slow-moving, motorized boats which stop to observe the diverse river-dwelling wildlife (alligators, crocodiles, turtles, howler monkeys, and birds). Otherwise, boatmen offer day and overnight trips up to and along the Río San Juán (which is technically Nicaraguan territory), as well as to Oro Verde, Tortuguero, Barra del Colorado, and other locations along the river. Ask the boatmen at the port for more information or inquire at any of the above mentioned tour providers.

VOLCÁN ARENAL AND AROUND

On July 29, 1968, Volcán Arenal woke up from a 450-year dormancy and erupted, burying two villages and 87 people. It has been actively spewing orange lava and boulders ever since. Tourists flock to the hot springs at the base of the famous conical volcano, and hike through primary and secondary rainforest catching glimpses of lava. Rounding out the nature-lover's palette are the Volcán Arenal National Park, Catarata La Fortuna, and Las Cavernas de Venado.

FORTUNA

According to local legend, Fortuna got its name from the flotsam and jetsam that would drift down the nearby Río Fortuna during floods—*indígena* tools and relics were scooped up by villagers as signs of good fortune. The small town's luck hasn't run out yet. The lava of Arenal, 6km to the west, flows away from town yet is close enough to make the views spectacular and volcano visits easy. With good transportation connections and plenty of hotels and restaurants, Fortuna has quickly become one of the most frequented towns in the country.

⌁ TRANSPORTATION. The main street into Fortuna runs east-west; many businesses line this thoroughfare. Along its north side is Fortuna's simple central park, formerly a soccer field. The church sits on the field's west side. **Buses** pick up passengers on the south side of the field and head to: **Ciudad Quesada/San Carlos** (1½hr., 7 per day 5am-5:30pm, ¢380); **San José** (4½hr., 12:45 and 2:45pm, ¢950; or transfer in Ciudad Quesada); **Tilarán** (3hr., 8am and 5:30pm, ¢950) via **Arenal** (2hr., ¢750). **Taxis** line up on the east side of the park. **Alamo,** behind the church on the main drag, rents **cars** and **jeeps.** (☎/fax 479 9090. Open 7:30am-6pm.)

⌦ PRACTICAL INFORMATION. Banco Popular, on the main drag two blocks east of the park, has currency exchange and **ATM.** (Open M-F 8:30am-3:30pm, Sa 8:15-11:45am.) The **Super Christian** supermarket is across from the southeast corner of the *parque.* (Open M-Sa 7am-10pm, Su 8am-noon.) The **police station** is 1½ blocks east of the *parque.* (☎479 9689. Open 24hr.) For **medical service, Farmacia La Fortuna,** 25m east of the southeast corner of the field. (☎479 9778. Open M-Sa 8am-8pm, Su 8am-noon.) The **medical clinic** is 100m east and 50m north of the northeast corner of the *parque.* (☎479 9142. Open M-F 7am-4pm by appointment; Sa-Su and holidays 8am-8pm.) You can make **international phone calls** at **Sunset Tours** and **Pura Vida Tours,** both on the southeast corner of the *parque*. (Open daily 7:30am-10pm.) **Internet access** is available 100m west of the northwest corner of the *parque*, inside the Eagle Tours office. (¢400 per hr. Open daily 8am-8pm.) The **post office** with **fax** is opposite the northwest corner of the *parque*, next to Desafío. (Open M-F 8am-noon and 1-4:30pm, Sa 8am-noon.) A new office is opening just west of the northwest corner of the *parque*. **Postal code:** 4417.

ACCOMMODATIONS AND FOOD. **Cabinas Sissy ❶,** 100m south and 200m west of the southwest corner of the park, facing the Río Burío, has fresh rooms with private baths, free laundry, a kitchen, and an inviting backyard with volcano view. (☎479 9256. US$6 per person.) **La Posada Inn ❶,** 300m east of the park on the main street, is a backpacker magnet. Cheap, spotless rooms come with fans and communal hot showers. (☎479 9793. Internet ¢600 per hr. Rooms US$5 per person; camping ¢500 per person.) **Hotel Fortuna ❶,** 100m east and 100m south of the southeast corner of the *parque* offers pristine, undecorated 3-bed rooms with private baths and includes breakfast. (☎479 9197. US$8 per person, high season US$10.) **Lava Rocks ❶,** on the southwest corner of the park, is a great restaurant noted for its tasty breakfasts, milkshakes, and fish plates. (Pancakes with fruit ¢750; grilled sea bass ¢1500. Open daily 7am-10pm.) **Hotel Vagabundo ❷,** 1.5km west of the church, serves pasta and wood-fired pizza (try Pizza Olga ¢3250). It also has a disco bar with pool (¢500 per hour) and darts. (Restaurant open daily noon-11pm; bar open daily 7pm-2am. No cover. Live music on Fridays.)

OUTDOOR ACTIVITIES. In Fortuna, everyone is a "guide." Avoid individuals who approach you on the street—quality is low. Reputable operators include **Sunset Tours** (☎479 9415), **Aventuras Arenal** (☎479 9133), and **Pura Vida Tours** (☎479 9045). The most popular tour is to Volcán Arenal (see **Parque Nacional Volcán Arenal,** below), although none of the volcano tours guarantees a lava sighting. Other tours head to the caves at Venado (see below) or Caño Negro. Currently only **Eagle Tours** (☎479 9091) takes tourists into Caño Negro (US$55), and waiting for views of incredible wildlife can be tiresome. There are also **horseback tours** to La Fortuna waterfall and Monteverde (4½hr., US$45-65), but the treatment of the animals varies. Pricey **fishing tours** on Laguna de Arenal are available (half-day US$150 per person). Tircío Hidalgo (☎479 9310) comes recommended. Class III and IV **whitewater rafting** is available on rivers east of Fortuna; one of the most established operators is **Desafío Tours** (☎479 9464), opposite the field's northwest corner (full day on the Toro River US$65). Aguas Bravas rents out **mountain bikes** (☎479 9431; US$10 per half-day). Other options include **canopy tours** and **kayaking.**

PARQUE NACIONAL VOLCÁN ARENAL

*You can reach the station by bike, private car, or taxi (¢4000 one day). It's easier to take one of the **guided tours** (**Sunset Tours** offers a US$24, 2½hr. walking tour through lava trails and secondary forest, which leaves Fortuna at 8am and 3pm). Station open daily 8am-4pm. Park admission US$6.*

The volcano is the obvious centerpiece of the park. Created in 1994, Parque Nacional Volcán Arenal covers 120 sq. km including the towns of Tilarán, San Carlos, and San Ramón. The park's **ranger station** is 17km west of Fortuna (driving, head west for 15km and turn left at the sign). Just beyond the station is a lava and volcano **lookout point.** The park also has three short but pleasant trails. Since the 1968 eruption, plants have sprung up along the **Sendero Las Heliconias** (1km). **Sendero Las Coladas** (2.8km) crosses the 1993 lava flow trail. **Sendero Los Tucanes** runs through thick primary forest and delivers a stellar view of the volcano, Cerro Chato, and the Arenal dam. Hikers are forbidden to stray from the trail. The road west of Fortuna has good but more distant views of the volcano; one of the best is from Montaña del Fuego Inn, 9km from town (round-trip taxi ¢2000). Be warned that climbing the volcano is dangerous and strongly discouraged.

🐦 CATARATA FORTUNA

To reach the falls, head south on the road that runs along the west side of the church. About 1km later, a dirt road branches off to the right. After about 1½-2hr. (4km) of uphill walking, you hit the waterfall parking lot. Taxis can take you as far as the parking lot (¢1500). Pay a ¢1000 fee and follow trail to the falls.

At Catarata Fortuna, 5.5km outside of Fortuna, the Río Fortuna tumbles down through 70m of rainforest canopy. Swimming is encouraged by the fall's overseers, but beware of the thumping cold water, it can hit you pretty hard. Guided **horseback tours** are also available (US$15). From the parking lot, there is a trail to **Cerro Chato**, the dormant sidekick of Volcán Arenal. It's steep and muddy, but there's an impressive crater lake at the top. The climb takes about 2½hr. one-way.

🏔 HOT SPRINGS

Three buses per day to Tilarán pass the springs (departing Fortuna 8am, 5pm; return around 3pm). Take a taxi (¢1500 each way) or bike it. It is possible to hitchhike. Let's Go does not recommend hitchhiking.

The famous hot springs of **Tabacón**, 12km west of Fortuna, are actually a single river of hot water. The **Tabacón Resort** has 10 hot and cool swimming pools, including one with a swim-up bar, a pricey restaurant, great views of the volcano, and a man-made waterfall behind which you can sit. (☎460 2020. Open daily 10am-10pm. US$17.) **Las Fuentes Termales,** diagonally across from Tabacón, is a slightly cheaper extension of the resort's hot springs. (☎460 8050. Open M-F 10am-9pm, Sa-Su 8am-9pm. US$7.) Continue past the resort for a few hundred meters and look for trails for other options—there are no signs. Hot springs at **Baldi Termae**, 4km west of town, are closer by and, like Tabacón, feature a swim-up bar in the middle of one pool. (☎479 9652. US$10, with dinner US$15. Open daily 10am-10pm.)

🏔 CAVERNAS DE VENADO

Come by taxi (¢16,000 round-trip with wait); the ¢3500 admission includes equipment and guide. Guided tours (US$35) are the best way to visit. Bobo Adventures (☎479 9390) specializes in caves. Guides can be tricksters, so chose yours carefully.

The labyrinth of caverns extends 2km underground. Several spots are narrow like a rocky birth canal, and this born-again experience has the potential for terror if you don't appreciate the basic thrills of the dark—bats, spiders (including tarantulas), and tight spaces crowded by rushing water splashing your face. The elderly and oversized should not sign up. Comfortable shoes that you don't mind getting wet are essential and bring soap to wash off the bat guano in the on-site shower.

REFUGIO NACIONAL CAÑO NEGRO

Refugio Caño Negro is one of the wettest places in Costa Rica. The refuge is soaked by 3.5m of rain every year, and 85% of its 100 sq. km are flooded from May to December. In the heart of this aquatic wonderland is the enormous Laguna Caño Negro, a 9 sq. km lake. The swampy, canal-linked labyrinth of mangroves, rivers, and small lakes harbor one of the most important wildlife shelters in the country. Rare species of fish swim the waters, including the prehistoric gaspar. Guided boat tours are the only way to visit. (Park open daily 7am-4pm. US$6.)

TRANSPORTATION. The shortest road from **San José** by **car** is to head north on the road toward Los Chiles. The entrance to the Refugio is 1km after the Tanques Gas Zeta. Go toward "Jobo" until you reach the new bridge crossing Río Frío, turn left, and continue 12km until the Caño village. Although the road is unpaved, the public **buses** do pass by; ask and make sure you're on the right bus. Buses go from **Los Chiles** via **Caño Negro** (1½ hr.; daily 5am and 2pm, return 6:30am and 6:30pm; ¢400). Buses from **Upala** also pass by the refuge (2hr.; daily 4:30, 11am, 4:30pm; return 6:30am, 1, 3:30pm; ¢400.) Wait for the bus on the northwest side of the *parque*, or in front of the hotels on the town's main entrance road.

ORIENTATION AND PRACTICAL INFORMATION. The bus enters the village on the main road, ultimately reaching the northwest corner of the *parque*. There you'll find the only good **mini-super** in town, next to the church and across from the primary school. The **refuge** entrance, under the RAMSAR sign, is on the southeast corner of the *parque*. You can also enter from Albergue Caño Negro or Hotel Fishing Club, which are on the lagoon and have boats. The **MINAE** office, 200m west of the mini-super, provides solid **tourist information** (open M-F 8am-4pm, Sa-Su 8am-9am), as does the **information booth** in front of Albergue Caño Negro, 200m north of the northwest corner of the *parque* (open daily, no fixed hours). There is no bank and the nearest medical facility is the **Red Cross** in Los Chiles (☎471 1061). There is a **health center** on the northwest side of the *parque*. The **police station** is on the southeast side of the *parque*, 50m from school, and can be reached by radio in an emergency (with the help of a local business). The town has three **public telephones**: one at the mini super (☎461 8466; open M-Sa 7am-8pm, Su 7am-noon), the second across from the information booth (☎461 8464; open M-Sa 7am-11am, noon-5pm, and 6-8pm; Su 7-11am), and the third 100m west of the church (☎461 8442. ¢10 per min.).

ACCOMMODATIONS AND FOOD. Albergue Caño Negro ❶, 200m north of the northwest corner of the park, sits on a field that directly borders the Lago Caño Negro. Rooms have good mattresses, wall fans, and communal, cold-water bathrooms. Turn lights on downstairs to attract the harmless but annoying beetles so they'll leave you alone. (☎/fax 461 8442. US$7 per person; camping US$3 per person.) **Cabinas Martín Pescador** ❷, is 100m past the MINAE office in the field at the end of the road. Check in at the "reception" 100m north and 50m east of the park's northwest corner. The large, fanned rooms are in good shape and have tiled bathrooms and covered porches. (Beeper ☎233 3333. US$10 per person.) It is possible to **camp** ❶ on the grounds of the Caño Negro MINAE office, with access to cold-water showers and bathrooms (¢300 per person).

There are not many places to eat in Caño Negro, but **Sodita la Palmera** ❶, on the southeast corner of the *parque*, should satisfy almost any appetite. (Breakfast ¢500; lunch and dinner ¢700-900. Open daily 7am-8pm.) **Salón/Bar/Restaurante Danubio Azul** ❷, on the southeast side of the *parque*, has a nice, spacious eating area, which transforms into a discotheque from M-W. The house specialty is *guapote* fish (¢1500-2000), but meals start at ¢400. (Open daily 10am-2:30am.)

SIGHTS AND OUTDOOR ACTIVITIES BEYOND THE REFUGE. There are five *mariposarios* (butterfly farms) in Caño Negro. One farm, 100m west of the northwest corner of the *parque*, is the five-year-old project of *La Asociación de Mujeres de Caño Negro* (The Women's Association of Caño Negro, ASOMU-

CAN). Be sure to buy some of their fresh homemade bread on your way out. (Open daily, no set hours.) The other four are in homes like that of La Reinata, 10m east of the southeast side of the *parque*, and also sell crafts. (US$7 entrance fee.)

 VISITING THE REFUGE. The park is most easily accessed from Caño Negro village and is best seen by boat, though it is possible to hike. **Colibrí Tours,** runs tours of the refuge. (beeper ☎ 225 2500. 2½hr. tours for five people US$45.) **Cabinas Martín Pescador** (see above) takes people out on his canopied *lancha* (3hr., 1-3 people US$40). **Albergue Caño Negro** also leads tours (3hr., 1-4 people, US$50; 4hr. US$100). **Fishing** tours are available (1-3 people, US$80 per day). Other hotels also offer tour services such as the **Martín Pescador Hospedaje** (3hr., US$20 per hr.) and **Natural Lodge Caño Negro** (2½hr., US$25 per person; horses US$10 per hr.). **Hotel Fishing Club** specializes in sportfishing (8hr. full day US$300; See **Accommodations**)

Prices for wildlife and fishing trips do not include park entrance (US$6) or fishing license (license US$30). You can pay the fee to the ranger in the kiosk at the refuge entrance, on the southeast corner of the *parque*. Fishing is prohibited between Apr. 1-July 31. Call the Area de Conservación Huetar Norte in Upala for information on obtaining your fishing license (☎470 0100).

TOURS FROM LOS CHILES AND FORTUNA. Tour companies in Fortuna, Los Chiles, and Ciudad Quesada offer "Caño Negro Trips" along the Río Frío. The Río Frío flows south from Los Chiles and into Refugio Caño Negro, where it eventually meets Lago Caño Negro. While much of the same wildlife that's in the refuge can be seen from the river, you may have bus loads of tourists for company. The advantage of large, pre-packaged tours from Fortuna or Ciudad Quesada is that single travelers can latch on from Los Chiles for US$20-25. One such company is **Aventuras Arenal** in Fortuna. (☎479 9133; www.arenaladventures.com.) **Eco Directa** organizes trips from Los Chiles. (☎/fax 471 1414. US$60 for 1-8 people, US$70 for 8-12; US$10 per additional person.) **Servitur** offers similar trips for US$80 per person, 1-4 people with lunch and transportation included. (☎471 1055.) Adventure **fishing** companies such as **Costa Rica Jungle Tours** in Fortuna can take you for a full week of action-packed fishing. (☎469 1400; www.costaricanjungletours.com.) If you have time, it is more economical and enriching to get to the village of Caño Negro and hire a local guide.

TO NICARAGUA VIA RÍO SAN JUAN

The San Juan river-crossing into Nicaragua was a main route for Contras during the 1980s. Today, the cross-over is made by locals and the border is accessible for travelers. Those who have experienced the endless lines at the Peñas Blancas crossing might want to look into this side, as it is virtually hassle free. To leave Costa Rica, you must go through **Oficina de Migración,** 1 block west of the southwest corner of the *parque*. (☎471 1233. Open daily 8am-6pm.) The municipality charges ¢200 for dock usage. **Boats** leave frequently (9am-4pm) to **San Carlos, Nicaragua.** Contact the immigration office or police (☎471 1183) for more information.

NICOYA PENINSULA

While the roads can be difficult and the journeys hampered by backtracking, the seclusion of the Nicoya Peninsula will have you puzzling about where all those other bus passengers disappeared to. The inland is filled with rugged cowpokes and *pueblos* where the people guard a proud history. The locals share their beautiful environment with pride, and take care of it accordingly. Meander through the

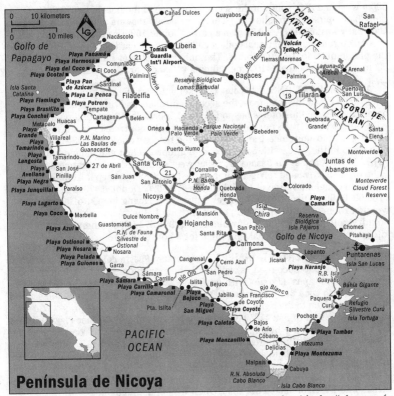

Península de Nicoya

streets, pick a favorite beach and tell everyone you meet that it's the *"playa más bonita del mundo,"* and you'll fit right in.

PLAYA HERMOSA

Wealthy and budget-minded tourists alike enjoy the clean waters, warm sands, and tame tides of Playa Hermosa. Crowds are never overwhelming, and because the beach is the attraction, the town itself is low-key. Bring a towel and swimsuit for tranquil relaxation. Hermosa is one of the best **scuba diving** beaches in Costa Rica and **snorkelers** will befriend their fair share of tropical fish around rocky points.

TRANSPORTATION. Buses to **Hermosa** depart from San José on Av. 5/7, Calle 12, one block north of the Atlántica Norte Terminal (4½hr., 3:30pm, ¢1700) and from Liberia (1hr., 6 per day 5am-5:30pm, ¢300). **Taxis** are available from El Coco to Playa Hermosa (15min., ¢2000). Out of Playa Hermosa, buses leave from Playa Panamá and pass the second entrance to Playa Hermosa. Buses depart to **San José** (4½hr., 5am, ¢1700) and **Liberia** (1hr., 7 per day 8am-7pm, ¢300) via **Sardinal**.

ORIENTATION AND PRACTICAL INFORMATION. Playa Hermosa runs north-south; the beach is to the west. There are two entrances to the beach from the main road. **Playa Panamá** is about 3km farther along the main road to the north, 5km if you're looking for the Playa Panamá **pueblo.** The **Aquatic Sports MiniSuper** is

500m west and 25m south of the second entrance to the beach. (☎672 0050. Open daily 6am-9pm. ¢200 to shower.) There are **public showers** and **toilets** at **Pescado Loco Bar y Restaurant.** A **public phone** can be found 150m east of the beach at the second entrance. International collect calls and credit card calls can be made from the phone outside Aquatic Sports. The only **Internet** is at the Villa Acacia resort, 350m east of the beach. (¢1000 per 30min., ¢1500 per hr. Open 6am-9pm daily.)

⛏ ACCOMMODATIONS. 🔲 Ecotel ❶, is set amongst the trees right on the sand. Walk 500m down the road from the second entrance, and turn left at the last road before the beach; the hotel is beyond Aquatic Sports. It offers wood-paneled room with bunks (US$10-15 per person), comfortable mattresses in an indoor loft (US$10), or mosquito net-draped beds on the balcony outdoors (US$10). You can also **camp** in the yard, with access to an outdoor kitchen and simple bathrooms. (☎672 0175.) **Cabinas La Casona** ❷, 500m west of the second entrance and to the right, offers a stove and refrigerator, and the bright rooms keep it from feeling like a random conglomeration of bunk beds. (☎672 0025. Doubles ¢7000-11,000; quads ¢10,000-17,000. Discounts on longer stays.) **The Iguana Inn** ❶, offers spacious wooden rooms that fit up to six people. Private baths, a common kitchen, pool, laundry, and taxi service are available. (☎/fax 672 0065. 6-person room with kitchen ¢10,000-15,000; ¢30,000 per night for a house for 4.)

🔲 🗗 FOOD AND ENTERTAINMENT. Restaurante Puesta del Sol ❸, on the north end of the Pescado Loco road, is well worth the extra money for its delicious Spanish *paella* and tapas. (*Paella* with seafood ¢3200 per person. Open daily noon-9pm.) **Pescado Loco Bar y Restaurant** ❶, 500m toward the beach from the second entrance and 50m to the right, has popular *tico* food at reasonable prices. (*Casado* ¢1000; orange filet of fish ¢1950. Open daily 7am-midnight.) **Cabinas Playa Hermosa** ❸ is 400m toward the beach on the first entrance (follow the road around the bend). An excellent Italian restaurant with the tempting odors of garlic and oregano. (Open daily 7-9:30am and 6-9pm. Open for lunch (in high season only) noon-2pm.) **Monkey Bar** ❶, between the two beach entrances, set back in the trees, is the only bar in Playa Hermosa that functions strictly as such. Shows sporting events on satellite TV. Beer ¢500. Pool ¢300. Open W-M 5pm-midnight.

🏄 WATERSPORTS. The calm, clear water is ideal for **snorkeling, kayaking,** or **waterskiing.** Following the signs from the second entrance to the beach, **Aqua Sport** runs waterskiing (US$60 per hr.), windsurfing (US$15 per hr.), not-to-be-missed banana-boat rides, kayak rentals, snorkeling tours, and boat trips. (☎672 0050. Open daily 6am-9:30pm.) Another option is **Diving Safaris,** 300m from the Villa Acacia complex, which offers several levels of training. (☎672 0012. 2-tank dives US$80 per person including equipment. Snorkeling US$30. Open daily 7am-4pm.) The owner of **Ecotel** (see **Accommodations,** above) offers a vast variety of guided tours to Rincón de la Vieja, Santa Rosa, Lao Verde, and the Caño Negra Wildlife Refuge, among other eco-sites. (☎672 0175. 2-person min.)

PLAYA DEL COCO

The dark and dingy Coco shore gives no indication of the treasures that lie beyond, yet divers have known for years the delightful surprises its oceans hold. The public culture of the town revolves around the snorkel, the scuba, and the boats, which can take you out to the more wondrous nature at Playas Huevo, Blanca, and Nacazcolo, and the Bat and Catalinas Islands.

🚌 TRANSPORTATION. Buses head to **San José** (5hr.; 4, 8am, 2pm; ¢1775) and **Liberia** (1hr., 8 per day 5:30am-6pm, ¢250) via **Sardinal** (5min., ¢120).

▣ ▮ ORIENTATION AND PRACTICAL INFORMATION. The main road runs from the **highway** to the **beach,** where you will find the not-very-obvious **parque central** with public phones at its center. Buses stop on the *parque's* south side. When facing the beach, the **soccer field** is about a block to the left. **Banco Nacional** is 750m inland from the beach on the main road. It exchanges US dollars and traveler's checks and provides cash advances on Visa. (Open M-F 8:30am-3:45pm.) You can also exchange currency at **Supermercado Luperón** on the west side of the soccer field. (Open M-Sa 7am-8pm, Su 7am-1pm.) For **medical services** you can go to **Medical clinic Ebais.** Walk 150m east on the road north of Lizard Lounge (see **Nightlife,** below), turn right after the bridge and left after Hotel la Puerta del Sol. (☎670 0987. Open M-Th 7am-4pm, F 7am-3pm.) Other services include: **Red Cross** (☎697 0471, emergency 911), the nearest is in Sardinal; **police station,** is across from the bus stop (☎670 0258; open 24hr. For **Internet access, Café Internet 2000** is 400m south of the *parque.* (☎670 0948. US$4.50 for 30min., US$6 per hr. Open M-F 9am-7pm, Sa 9am-5pm.) The **post office** is in the same building as the police. (Open M-F 8am-noon and 1-5:30pm.) **Postal code:** 5019.

▮ ACCOMMODATIONS. Hotel Vista del Mar ❸, 1km east on the road that runs north of the Lizard Lounge, is a ranch-style hacienda on the beach with a shaded courtyard, pool, and BBQ grill. Rooms are air-conditioned and there's a TV in the living room. ((☎670 0753; www.beach-hotels-in-costa-rica.com. Breakfast included. Doubles US$40, high season US$55; backpacker room US$10 per night. US$15 per additional person.) **Cabinas Coco Azul ❶,** 100m west and 50m south of the soccer field, has big rooms for up to 6 people with big windows and private baths. (☎670 0431. ¢2500 per person, high season ¢3000.) **Luna Tica ❶** is 10m north and 20m west of the *supermercado.* All rooms have private baths. (☎670 0127. Singles ¢4000, in high season ¢5000; doubles ¢7000/¢9000.) **Camping ❶,** 200m inland of the *parque* (look for the "camping" sign amongst the souvenir kiosks on the right), is a well-shaded site with bathrooms, showers, grills, laundry facilities, and a guard. (☎670 0151. ¢1000 per person, ¢800 for extended periods.)

▮ ▮ FOOD AND NIGHTLIFE. Marisquería La Guajira ❶, right on the beach, has a menu filled with mouth-watering descriptions. (Fried red snapper ¢1700. Open daily 10am-10pm.) **Marisquería Islas Catalina ❷,** catch a taxi for the 4km drive from Playa del Coco. Delicious fresh, cheap seafood. (*Ceviches* ¢1500-1800. Open daily noon-10pm.) **Soda Pati ❶** next to Rich Coast Diving, 300m south of the *parque,* is the best-kept secret in town. The *soda* has no sign, but it hides: *casados* at unbeatable prices (¢850-900) and other tasty *típico.* (Open M-F 7am-2pm.)

Lizard Lounge, 150m south of the *parque,* is mellow, has the snazziest decorations, and draws mostly a tourist crowd with its soundtrack of American music. (Pool ¢300. Beer ¢500. Open M-Sa 3pm-2am.) **Banana Surf Bar and Restaurant,** 300m inland, is the hot spot in town, luring locals from other beach towns. Pool (¢1000 per hr.) and darts are additional diversions. (Beer ¢500. Open daily 5pm-3am.)

▮ WATERSPORTS. Prime dive season is Apr.-Sept. The best scuba and snorkeling are reached by boat. The nearby Catalinas and Bat Islands are hot sites for turtles, sharks, and octopus. **Rich Coast Diving,** 300m south of the *parque,* offers diving, including a 3-day trip to the Bat Islands (US$495 per person), training for a variety of levels, and equipment rentals. (☎/fax 670 0176. Open daily 8am-5pm.) **Mario Vargas Expeditions,** 400m south of the *parque,* across from Café Internet 2000, is the cheapest place to rent equipment. Dive trips to the islands are a bit more expensive. (☎/fax 670 0351; www.divexpeditions.com. 2-tank dive around Catalina US$75 per person. Open daily 8am-6:30pm.) **Wahoo Tours** runs out of Cabinas Arrecife, 100m west of the southwest corner of the soccer field, and offers sportfishing trips, tours to the islands and Santa Rosa National Park, snorkeling trips, and transportation to renowned surf spots like Witch's Rock and Ollie's Point. (☎ 670 0413; wahootours@hotmail.com. Open daily 8am-5pm.)

PLAYA TAMARINDO

While the long, white shore has some rocky patches, Tamarindo is perhaps Costa Rica's most cosmopolitan beach. Few places have so much entertainment by day—scenery, sunbathing, snorkeling, surfing, and shopping—*and* such a lively nightlife. If standard activities don't suit your taste, take advantage of natural splendors, like turtle-watching at nearby Parque Nacional Las Baulas.

▐ TRANSPORTATION. Buses from Tamarindo to **San José** leave from the Alfaro office in the Tamarindo Resort driveway, 200m east down the road 200m north of the semi-circle (5½hr.; 3:30am and 5:45am, Su 12:30pm; ¢1950). Reserve tickets 3 days in advance. From the semi-circle, buses go to **Santa Cruz** (1½hr., 6 per day 6am-10pm, ¢350) and **Liberia** (9am and 4:45pm); they can also be flagged from anywhere along the main road. Coming to Tamarindo from **Nicoya,** first take the bus to **Santa Cruz** (45min., 14 buses 3:50am-6:15pm, ¢125), then walk to the *mercado* bus station, 300m south and 300m west of where the bus drops you off. Buses leave from there to **Tamarindo** (1½hr., 5 per day 4:30am-3:30pm, ¢250).

▐▐ ORIENTATION AND PRACTICAL INFORMATION. The main road in the village of Tamarindo extends 2.4km from Parque Nacional Las Baulas at the far northeast down to the main bus stop, in a semi-circle of shops and restaurants on the southwest end. The **Best Western,** on the northeast end, is a key landmark. There are two main beach entrances—one off the semi-circle, and another in the middle of the strip. Everything along the main street is geared to travelers' needs. **Centro Comercial Aster** is a small strip of white shops 200m north of the circle. A road south of it leads east to more restaurants and tour agencies. The **tourist office,** 500m north of the circle, sells a few maps and has a **book exchange** (open M-F 9am-noon). **Banco Nacional,** 375m north of the circle, changes traveler's check's and gives advances on Visa; lines are long, so get there early (open M-F 8:30am-3:45pm). The **Supermercado Tamarindo** is just south of the bank (open M-Sa 7:30am-9pm, Su 9am-8:30pm). The **police** (☎ 653 0238, emergency 911) can be found 200m east on the road and 200m north of the circle, in a bungalow in the Tamarindo Resort driveway. Tamarindo lacks a proper hospital, but **Emergencias Tamarindo** is across from Cabinas Pozo Azul, north of the Best Western. For **Internet, InterLink** is located on the circle. (¢350 per 30min., ¢800 per hr. Open daily 8am-10pm.)

▐▐ ACCOMMODATIONS AND FOOD. ▓Arco Iris ❸, hidden up the hill behind Pachanga about 500m south of the Centro Comercial Aste, has cabins with hammocks, porches, and private baths. (☎ 653 0330; www.hotelarcoiris.com. Doubles US$40 high-season; US$10-15 per additional person; 2-room apartment with kitchen US$50.) **Cabinas Marielos ❸,** across from Cabinas Doly and next to Iguana Surf, is worth a splurge. (☎/fax 653 0141. Singles US$20-30; doubles US$30-40, with A/C US$35-45; AmEx/MC/V.) **Cabinas Pozo Azul ❷,** just north of the Best Western, has clean, spacious rooms with private bath, fridge and stove. (☎/fax 653 0280. ¢3500 per person; July ¢5000.)

Whether you're seeking variety or a bargain, Tamarindo's bounty of restaurants is sure to fit the bill. **▓Pachanga ❸,** about 400m east on the road south of the Centro Comercial Aster, has an imaginative menu. (☎ 653 0404. Entrees ¢3000-5000. Open Tu-Sa 6-10pm.) **▓The Lazy Wave Food Company ❸,** on the same road as Pachanga, across from the mini-super inside a building with other establishments, incorporates Asian elements into gourmet menus. (Entrees US$10-15. Open M-Sa 11am-11pm, Su 6-11pm.) **El Pescador ❷**, on the beach 100m south of the circle serves up tasty fresh fish right on the beach. Every entree comes with a sample of *ceviche*. (☎653 0109. Filet *a la plancha* ¢1800. Open daily 6am-10pm.)

⚠🏄 OUTDOOR ACTIVITIES AND GUIDED TOURS. Surfers craving bigger waves than those in Tamarindo have a number of options: head 10km south to **Playa Avellana**, home of the reef-break "Little Hawaii," 15km south to **Playa Negra,** or just north to **Playa Grande,** another good beach break now part of the 420-hect-are **Parque Nacional Las Baulas**, on the northeast end of Tamarindo village. From mid-October to mid-February, the park is a nesting site for the *baula*, the **leather-back turtle.** Sportfishing is another great option; contact **Warren Sellers Sportfishing**, diagonally across from Frutas Tropicales. (☎653 0186; fax 653 0248.) **Agua Rica Div-ing Center,** by the bank, is the most professionally equipped when it comes to div-ing. Certification is available; half a day with 2 dives is US$85, equipment rental US$20. (☎653 0094. Open M-Sa 9:30am-6:30pm, Su 3-6:30pm.)

🎵 NIGHTLIFE. Although high-season nightlife gets thumpin', low season gener-ally consists of relaxing at beach-side bars with a beer and some music. The **Best Western** hotel often throws huge poolside parties. **Big Bazar Beach Bar,** next to El Pescador, with seats on the sand, a dance floor, and huge bonfire, heats up on Sa. (☎653 0307. Beer ¢500. Open Su-F 11am-4pm, Sa 11am-4am. Dancing starts at 11pm.) **Blue Moon Bar,** on the circle and the beach, attracts a crowd just about any night of the year. (Tu and Th nights the live blues music gets feet tapping. Try your skills at karaoke any other night. Beer ¢400. Open daily 7:30pm-12:30am.)

NICOYA

Nicoya, 78km south of Liberia, is the main settlement on the peninsula. The town was named after Chorotegan Indian Chief Nicoya, who ruled the region and wel-comed the Spaniards when they arrived in 1523. It has more tourist services and better transportation than nearby towns.

From the main bus stop, 200m east and 200m south of the *parque*, **buses** leave for **San José** (4½hr. via ferry, 6 per day 3:45am-5:20pm; 5-5½hr. via Liberia, 5 per day 5am-2:30pm; ¢1860); **Playa Sámara** (1¼hr., 5 per day 5am-6:30pm; ¢400); and **Nosara** (3½hr.; 5, 10am, 2pm; ¢560). Buy tickets at the window in advance. (Open daily 7am-5pm.) From another stop, 100m north and 150m east of the *parque*, across from Hotel las Tinajas, buses run to **Liberia** (2hr.; M-Sa 26 per day 3:50am-10pm, Su and holidays 12 per day 5am-7pm; ¢450) via **Santa Cruz** (45min., ¢140); **Fil-adelfia** (1¼hr., additional bus Su and holidays 10pm, ¢300). A 10pm departure that goes to Filadelfia on Sundays and holidays. Nicoya's **taxis** don't have meters; the standard fare is ¢100 per km.

The two landmarks in the city center are the **parque central** and the main road, **Calle 3,** which runs north-south one block east of the *parque*. The bus drops you off at various locations, so your best bet is to ask to be directed to the *parque cen-tral.* Once in the *parque*, Hotel Venecia is north, the *municipalidad* is south, Banco de Costa Rica is west, and Soda el Parque is east. **Banco de Costa Rica,** on the west side of the *parque* with Visa/Plus **ATM,** cashes traveler's checks and gives Visa cash advances. (☎685 5010. Open M-F 8:30am-3pm). There's also an ATM next door to Western Union that accepts Cirrus. **Red Cross** (☎685 5458, emergency 128) is 500m north and 50m west of the *parque.* Find the **police:** (☎685 5516, emer-gency 117), 150m south of the bus station, next to the airport. Log on to the **Internet** at **Nicoy@ Netc@fe,** next to Western Union. (Open M-Sa 7am-9pm, Su 1pm-9pm.) The **post office** is across from the southwest corner of the *parque*. (☎685 5088; fax 685 5004. Open M-F 8am-5:30pm, Sa 7:30am-noon.) **Postal code:** 5200.

Hotel Elegancia ❶, next to Hotel Venecia on the north side of the *parque*, has spacious, bright rooms with good ventilation. (☎685 5159. Meals on request. 4-bed dorms ¢1500 per person. Singles with private bath ¢3000; doubles ¢4000; triples ¢5100.) **Hotel Chorotega ❶,** 150m south of the post office, has old but clean rooms, most with very clean private baths. (☎685 5245. Singles ¢1500, with bath ¢3000; doubles ¢3500.) **Café Daniela ❶,** 100m east and 50m south of the northeast corner of the *parque*, offers the biggest selection of *comida típica*. (*Casados* ¢1000. Open M-Sa 7am-9:30pm and Su 5-9:30pm.) **Soda Yadira ❶,** 75m east of the *parque's* southeast corner, is known for its desserts and midday snacks. (Ice cream ¢250; cake ¢175 per slice. Open M-Sa 6:45am-8:30pm.)

Iglesia Colonial, on the northeast corner of the *parque*, is one of the oldest churches in Costa Rica, constructed in 1644 of stone, brick, and *cal*, a sand unique to the area and stronger than cement. Several religious artifacts are worth a look as well. If you have extra time and the heat isn't too oppressive, the folks at **Ciclo Mireya #2,** 400m north of the northwest corner of the *parque*, can rent you a bike to explore the surrounding countryside. (☎685 5391. Bikes ¢1500 per day.)

NEAR NICOYA

PARQUE NACIONAL BARRA HONDA

*Buses leave for **Santa Ana** from the main bus stop in Nicoya, 200m east and 200m south of the parque, and drop you off 2km from the park entrance. (M-Sa 1 per day 12:30pm, early Feb.-June and mid-July-Dec. 2 per day 12:30 and 5pm; ¢200). To visit the park as a daytrip, you can hire a taxi (30min., ¢3000). Buses returning to Nicoya stop at the sign 2km from the entrance 1-1:30pm. Call Nicoya's branch of the Ministerio del Ambiente y Energía (MINAE; ☎685 5667) for a guide the day before your visit (open M-F 8am-4pm). One guide speaks English. Children under 12 are not permitted in the Terciopelo cave. Park ranger station open daily 24hr. Park entrance open daily 7am-4pm; if going into the cave, you must begin by 1pm. Admission US$6. Trail guides ¢2500; cave guides ¢7000 for group of 1-4, ¢1500 for each additional person. Spelunking equipment rental US$12.*

Hidden beneath the Parque Nacional Barra Honda, 22km northeast of Nicoya, are a series of limestone caves dating back 70 million years. Only **Terciopelo,** is open to the public. With three guides, harnesses, and repelling gear, you can descend 62m underground to an amazing stalactite and stalagmite forest. The cave is about a 1½hr. hike from the park entrance—the first half is a bit of a climb, but then it levels out. Be sure to take the short **trail** to a spectacular **mirador** (lookout spot), from which you can see a large portion of the Nicoya peninsula. For many, the hike and final view are reason enough to visit. If you should visit the park in August or September when its rainy, take the 2hr. **Las Cascadas** hike to a swimmable spring with water falling down high calcified steps. If you use public transportation, you'll have to spend the night. You can **camp** in a small grassy area (¢300 per person with toilets and showers nearby), or stay in dusty cabins (one bath for 8 people; ¢1500 per person). Basic meals are available through MINAE if you call ahead.

OSTIONAL

This gritty strip of black-sand beach is Costa Rica's most important breeding ground for olive ridley turtles, and every month, at the start of a new quarter moon (usually at the end of the month), females flock by the thousands to lay their eggs. During that time, the two modest hotels fill to the brim and the fires at the two *sodas* never die down. Luckily, Ostional is an easy daytrip from Sámara, and many tourist agencies in this town can get you there and back before bedtime.

The arrival of the turtles is termed *arribada*, and on these special days, most turtles arrive between 3 and 8pm. The hordes travel in from as far away as Peru and Baja California to give give birth in the same place they themselves were born. To make sure you don't miss this event, contact biologist Rodrigo Morera (☎/fax 682 0470; adioturt@sal.racsa.co.cr) at La Asociación de Desarollo Integral de Ostional, 100m north of Soda La Plaza (see below), or check in with the tourist agencies in Nosara or Sámara. Surfing is prohibited during the *arribada*.

To get to Ostional from Nosara, contact Clemente at Cabinas Agnnel for a **taxi**. (☎ 682 0058. 20min., ¢3000.) Or, hop a **bus** from the bigger hotels in the surrounding towns. One bus makes the bumpy 3hr. ride between Santa Cruz and Ostional, stopping at small towns along the way. (Cabinas Guacamayas in Ostional 5am, Santa Cruz noon.) The bus can't make the trip during heavy rains.

Cabinas Ostional ❶, across from Soda La Plaza, has simple triples and quads with private baths and nice balconies. (☎ 682 0428. ¢1500 per person.) **Hospedaje Guacamayas ❶**, 125m left of Soda La Plaza if you're facing the beach, has darker, but clean rooms. (☎ 682 0430. ¢1500 per person.) **Camping** is allowed next to the beach behind Soda La Plaza. (Portable toilet outside. US$3 per person, 3 meals a day ¢2800. Camping fee waived for student groups who pay for meals.) For a beautiful view of Guiones, Nosara, and Ostional, and all the way to Punta India, check out **Restaurante Las Loras ❷**, up a hill about 400m south of Soda La Plaza. (Pancake-like crepes ¢700-900; vegetarian plate ¢1500. Open daily 7am-10pm.)

PLAYA SÁMARA

Not too long ago, Sámara was a tiny fishing and farming community where the hub of activity and development was limited to a few *cabinas*, *sodas*, and simple houses. But with one of Costa Rica's cleanest, prettiest, and most swimmable beaches, this little village was discovered. Luckily, Sámara isn't as busy and commercial as other hot spots, so when the waves wash away all footprints, everyone can feel like they're discovering this treasure for the very first time.

⊏ TRANSPORTATION. Since the roads along the southwestern Nicoya Peninsula are in such poor shape, getting to Sámara via public transportation from places like Montezuma in the southern Nicoya Peninsula involves going to Paquera, catching the ferry to Puntarenas, taking a bus to the town of Nicoya, and then taking one final bus to Sámara. Even if you take the first bus to Paquera in the morning, you'll likely have to spend the night in the town of Nicoya and catch a bus to Sámara the next morning. You'll be better off taking a private transfer to Sámara in a 4WD vehicle or coming via bus from San José (6hr.; M-Sa 12:30pm, return 4am, Su 1pm.), Liberia, or other points in northwestern Costa Rica. **Buses** leave from in front of Hotel Giada for: **Carillo** (25min.; 11am, 1, 4:30; 6:30pm; return 11:20am, 1:30, 5pm; ¢200); **Nicoya** (1hr.; M-Sa 6 per day 5:30am-4:30pm, Su 7am, 12:45, 4:30pm; return M-Sa 7 per day 6am-5pm, Su 8am and 3pm; ¢400); **San José** (5½hr.; M, F, Sa 4:30 and 8:45am; Tu and Th 4:30am; Su 8:30am and 1pm; ¢1780). Buses to **Nósara** leave from La Bomba, a gas station 5km from the town center (1hr., between 10:30 and 11am, ¢365).

⚠ PRACTICAL INFORMATION. Although there is no official tourist office, information is available at various accommodations, especially the Hotel Giada (see **Accommodations,** below). For essentials, the supermarket **Super Sámara** is 200m east down the side road closest to the beach. (Open M-Sa 7am-8pm, Su 7am-6pm). The **police** (☎ 656 0436) are located at the far south end of the main drag, on the beach, and for serious medical emergencies, go directly to the hospital in Nicoya; **Clínica Ebais** (☎ 656 0166), 1km west of Sámara in Congrejal, can help with minor injuries and illness. The **pharmacy Boutique L'Salud** is just west of the main drag on the side street farthest from the beach. (☎ 656 0727. Open M-Sa 8am-5pm.)

Use the **Internet** at **Super Sámara.** (¢400 per 15min. Open M-Sa 7am-8pm, Su 7am-6pm.) The **post office** is next to the police station at the far south end of the main drag. (Open M-F 8-noon and 1-5pm, but hours change often.) **Postal Code: 5235.**

🏠🍴 **ACCOMMODATIONS AND FOOD.** Casa Valeria **②**, 50m east of Super Sámara on the side street closest to the beach, has rooms with ceiling fans, shell decorations, patios, and hot-water baths are cozy. (☎656 0316. Breakfast included. Laundry ¢3000. Check-out noon. Doubles US$30; *casitas* US$40/US$60.) **Casa Paraíso ②** is down the street and around the corner from Super Sámara. The spotless rooms have bright white walls, private hot-water baths, fans, comfortable beds, and patios. (☎656 0749. Check-out noon. Singles US$25; doubles US$30.) **Hotel Giada ③**, 300m north of the beach on the main drag, is one of Sámara's nicer options and has private hot-water baths. (☎656 0132; www.hotelgiada.net. Breakfast included. Check-out noon. Singles US$26; doubles US$38.) Especially popular with nearby locals and youth are the several **campsites** along the beach.

Sámara's increasing population of foreign residents means that you'll find just as many Italian and French restaurants as simple *típico sodas.* **Soda Sheriff Rustic ①**, at the south end of the main drag on the beach, has tasty and simple *gallo pinto* (¢600-700) and rice and fish dishes (¢1000-1300). Their smoothies (¢350) are super refreshing. (Open daily 8am-7pm.) **Pizza a Go Go ②**, inside Hotel Giada, has real Italian ingredients and creativity. (Open daily noon-11pm. Closed Tu in low season. AmEx/MC/V.) Locals will direct you to **Ananas ①**, 350m north of the beach on the main drag, for a midday snack or light dinner. (Open W-M 7am-7pm.)

🎿🏄 **OUTDOOR ACTIVITIES AND GUIDED TOURS.** Several hotels and tour operators offer tours and trips for just about every interest and activity. Most center around water, as several areas nearby have excellent **fishing, snorkeling,** and **surfing.** Also popular is **dolphin watching,** as the magnificent mammals migrate along the coast and get quite close to the shore before realizing the waters are too shallow. **Hotel Giada** (see **Accommodations,** above), has a good variety of well-organized tours. Their most popular is the dolphin trip, a relaxing 4hr. boat ride with snorkeling, sportfishing, and drinks (US$35 per person). **Wingnuts Canopy Tours** (☎656 0153; canopytours@samarabeach.com), 1.5km east of Hotel Belvedere, is a family-run canopy tour operator that prefers small groups. Two 2hr. trips leave daily from Sámara. (US$39 per person, children under 18 US$30.)

MONTEZUMA

The tiny beach haven of Montezuma is stuck in somewhat of a trippy time warp. An almost exclusively foreign regimen of batik-clad flower girls and starry-eyed, dread-locked *rasta* boys are the town's most frequent inhabitants, echoing the image of a fun-loving 60s town that never grew up. Considering that Montezuma was barely discovered 25 years ago by a group of North Americans, it's no wonder that it's still in its first stages of development. Montezuma's sparse dirt roads and immaculate, endless beaches lead to some of the peninsula's most spectacular waterfalls, wildlife, and waves.

🚌 **TRANSPORTATION.** If you're coming from other towns on the north or northwest peninsula, note that backtracking to Puntarenas and taking the ferry to Paquera is the fastest way to reach Montezuma, even though other routes look shorter on a map (those roads are tediously slow, not much public transportation goes that way). **Buses** go to **Paquera** (1½hr.; 5 per day 5:30am-4pm, return 6 per day 6:15am-6:15pm; ¢700) and **Cabo Blanco** (30min.; 8, 9:50am, 2:10, 6:30pm, return 7:10, 9:10am, 1:10, 4:10pm; ¢400) via **Cabuya** (25min., ¢380). To go to **Santa Teresa** via **Mal País,** take the 10am or 2pm bus to Cóbano, where the Mal País bus to Santa Teresa will be waiting (1½hr.; 10:30am and 2:30pm, return 6:45 and 11am; ¢500).

ORIENTATION AND PRACTICAL INFORMATION. Near the southern tip of the Nicoya Peninsula, Montezuma is 41km southwest of Paquera and 8km south of the town of **Cóbano.** Most services are in Cóbano. Montezuma consists almost entirely of accommodations, restaurants, and souvenir shops. **Chico's Bar,** where the bus stops, is on the main drag and functions as the center of town. The road intersecting the main drag at Chico's points directly west and leads to a fork about 100m up. Turning right at the fork heads to Cóbano. Turning left leads to a number of restaurants, accommodations, and **Reserva Absoluta Natural Cabo Blanco,** 1km away. The road to **Cabo Blanco** can be found by walking up the hill from Chico's and turning left at the fork. There is no official **tourist information** office. A number of tour agencies offer a variety of trips (see **Montezuma: Outdoor Activities and Guided Tours,** below). Montezuma has no **banks,** but there is a **Banco Nacional** in Cóbano. (Open M-F 8:30am-3:45pm.) For groceries, go to **Mamatea Delicatessen,** next to Chico's. (Open daily 7am-9pm.) Do your **laundry** at **Express Laundry Montezuma,** by El Sano Banano on the road leading west of Chico's, which has a 3hr. turn-around. (¢700 per kilo. Open M-Sa 9am-1pm and 3-6pm.) Other services include: **police,** on the beach near Restaurante El Parque (☎ 117; Cóbano police 642 0517); **pharmacy,** in Cóbano, 100m south of Banco Nacional on the road to Montezuma. (☎ 642 0508; open M-F 8am-3:30pm; AmEx/MC/V). **Public phones** are near Chico's and next to the supermarket. **Phone cards** are sold at the supermarket. The tourist services office at **Aventuras en Montezuma,** near Soda del Monte del Sol on the road heading west of Chico's, does international calls. The cheapest **Internet** rates are at the refreshing **Pizza y Net,** next to Chico's. (¢20 per min., ¢1200 per hr. Open daily 9am-9pm.) The closest full-service **post office** is in **Cóbano,** 300m west of Banco Nacional on the road to Paquera (open M-F 8am-noon and 1-5:30pm. **Librería Topsy** (see above) sells stamps and mails letters.

ACCOMMODATIONS AND CAMPING. Camping on the beach is free, relatively safe, and popular, especially in the high season (Dec.-Apr.). ◾**Amor de Mar ❷,** a 10min. walk down the road to Cabo Blanco, offers a killer Su brunch (¢2500), laundry service, and beautiful private baths, most with hot water. (☎/fax 642 0262. High season (Nov.-Apr.) US$30-75; low-season US$20-65.) ◾**Hotel La Cascada ❶,** just before the river on the road to Cabo Blanco, has big, sparkling, private baths with hot water, and new, wood-paneled rooms to match. (☎ 642 0057. US$10 per person; prices increase during school holidays. **Pensión Lucy ❶,** about 400m from the road to Cabo Blanco, has clean rooms with shared, cold-water showers. (☎ 642 0273. Laundry ¢600 per kilo. ¢2000 per person.) **Pensión Jenny ❶,** 75m down the road to Cabo Blanco and then 50m right up the road just before the soccer field, has quiet rooms with shared, cold-water baths. (☎ 642 0306. Laundry ¢600 per kilo. Ask about the *cabina* with a full kitchen for longer stays. ¢2000 per person.)

FOOD AND NIGHTLIFE. ◾**La Playa de los Artistas ❸,** on the beach 400m down the road to Cabo Blanco, on the left, offers a romantic setting with class and style. (Entrees US$8-15. Open M, W-Sa 5-10pm, but hours subject to change in the low season.) ◾**La Creperie ❶,** 50m down the street to the right of Chico's, opposite Hotel El Capitán, has light and heavenly crepes: soft, buttery, and warm on the outside, filled with fresh fruits, vegetables, yogurt, or chocolate inside. (Original crepe ¢350, toppings ¢150 each. Open daily 7am-11pm.) **Soda Monte del Sol ❶,** just down the street leading west from Chico's, on the left, has delicious and filling *casados* come with fresh avocado. (*Casados* ¢1100. Open daily 8am-10pm.) **El Sano Banano ❷,** 50m up the road leading west from Chico's, is a good spot for families and vegetarians and shows nightly English movies. (Most entrees ¢1400-2800. Open daily 7am-10pm. AmEx/MC/V.) Everyone trickles out to either **Chico's Bar** or **Bar Moctezuma**, underneath Hotel Moctezuma, to meet up with the locals and sip on Imperiales. Music ranges from reggae to salsa to old US rap, and expect as many stray dogs on the dance floor as hip-shaking merengue experts. (Beer ¢450. Chico's Bar open daily 11am-2:30am. Bar Moctezuma open daily 8am-2:30am.) The beach is another popular hang-out, with frequent bonfires and many communal bottles of rum. For **live music concerts** usually free of charge, inquire at **Luz de Mono**.

📷 **BEACHES.** The main beach at Montezuma, to the left of Chico's, is bordered by imposing rock formations and has a strong **rip tide**, so take precautions when swimming. In the low tide, it's possible to continue farther south along the beach walking on the rocky headlands. Here you'll find safe, shallow tide pools teeming with interesting fish and aquatic plants; rent a snorkel from any tour agency (see **Outdoor Activities and Guided Tours,** below) for the best view. A hundred meters down the road to the right of Chico's is an entrance to the vast expanse of beach north of Montezuma. These beaches, the largest of them **Playa Grande,** are usually less crowded and better for swimming and long walks. Also popular is **Playa Cedros,** 2km south along the road to Cabo Blanco.

📷 ⛵ **OUTDOOR ACTIVITIES AND GUIDED TOURS.** The most rewarding and inexpensive activity is hiking to the several **waterfalls** near town. The best one is also the closest, about a 7min. walk along the road to Cabo Blanco; a sign just past Hotel La Cascada marks the entrance. From there, take the short trail through the woods to the river and hike about 20min., climbing over rocks or treading through cool water until you see the 80 ft. waterfall to your left. Past these falls is another trail that climbs through steep and dangerously loose banking and to a flatter trail that eventually leads to a smaller waterfall; you can jump off the edge and swim around in a large natural pool. Be aware that although many people complete this trail, it is extremely dangerous in some places and should only be attempted by experienced climbers. **Do not jump off the first large waterfall**—the pool is small, and many have died. Wear sturdy, waterproof footwear and be careful climbing the slippery river rocks. Many people opt to visit the falls on a **horseback tour.**

Montezuma Eco-Tours, across from Chico's Bar, offers trips to Isla Tortuga, including breakfast, snorkeling and a barbecue, kayak tours with snorkeling gear, fishing tours, scuba diving, horseback tours, and mountain bike rides to a waterfall. (☎ 642 0467; ecotoursmontezuma@hotmail.com. Isla Tortuga US$35; kayak tours US$25. Open daily 8am-8pm in high season.) **Aventuras en Montezuma** offers comparable prices in addition to a bird watching tour (US$15) and whitewater rafting. They also function as a travel agency and arrange Spanish or dance lessons. (☎ 642 0050. Open 8am-9pm in high season.)

🏔 **RESERVA NATURAL ABSOLUTA CABO BLANCO**

From Montezuma, take the Cabuya/Cabo Blanco minibus from outside Chico's Bar (30min.; 8, 9:45am, 2:10, 6:30pm; return 7:10, 9:10am, 1:10, 4:10pm; ¢400). Park ranger station ☎ 642 0093. Open W-Su 8am-4pm. Entrance fee US$8.

A bumpy dirt road runs the 8km from Montezuma to the Reserva Natural Absoluta Cabo Blanco, Costa Rica's first protected tract of land and the cornerstone of the country's reserve system. Cabo Blanco is one of the few sea-level reserves and contains plant species from both the humid Pacific region and the dry northern forests. Foliage is less dense than in other parks, so animals are easier to spot.

The bus from Montezuma will drop you off at the park's entrance, about a 1km walk from the **ranger station.** Here there is a small exhibition about the park's history, flora, and fauna, clean bathrooms, maps, a plant guide (¢200), and potable water. From the station, there are two trails. The 4.5km **Danish Loop** *(Sendero Danés)* leads into the reserve. A second trail, the **Swedish Loop** *(Sendero Sueco)*, begins about 800m from the ranger station, making a 1km loop that crosses the Danish Loop and winds over a few streams. The trip to and from the beach should take about 4hr. at a moderate pace, leaving you just enough time to catch the 1:10pm bus back to Montezuma if you arrive on the 8am bus. Be sure to bring insect repellent and closed-toe shoes. Camping is not permitted.

CENTRAL PACIFIC COAST

This region of Costa Rica sees a lot of traffic in just a few spots, and all of it is motivated by the temptation of the water. Tourists and locals alike cluster along the coast to enjoy the warm refreshment of the Pacific. Be prepared to get wet, summer or winter, and always have your sunscreen—outdoors in the only place to be!

PUNTARENAS

Once a bustling port town and major spot on tourist itineraries, Puntarenas is now a shadow of its former self. Fish are fresh, but otherwise the city feels stale. Come to catch the ferry to the beautiful beaches of the Nicoya Peninsula, but don't plan on staying long.

◪ TRANSPORTATION. Puntarenas is still a major transport hub for other beaches in the Central Pacific and Nicoya Peninsula.

Buses: From Av. 1, Calle Central/1, just east of the Palí Supermarket, buses run to the Barrio Carmen **ferry terminal** (10min., every 10min. 6am-9:30pm, ¢65) and **Orotina** (1hr., 8 per day 6am-8pm, ¢345). From the stop on Calle 2, Av. 1/3, just south of the *mercado central* and in front of the ZumZum shop, buses leave for **Caldera** (40min., 6 per day 7:30am-5:30pm, ¢220). The main **intercity terminal** is at the corner of Calle 2 and the beach front road, Paseo de los Turistas, on the northeast side of town. From inside the terminal, buses leave for **San José** (2hr., about every 40min. 4:15am-9pm, ¢620). From the stop just across the street from the terminal, buses run to: **Filadelfia/ Nicoya/Santa Cruz** (3hr., 6am and 3:45pm, ¢720); **Las Juntas** via **Monteverde** and **Santa Elena** (3hr., 8 per day 4:40am-3:30pm, ¢940); **Quepos** via **Jacó** (3hr., 4 per day 5am-4:30pm, ¢1050); **Tilarán/Cañas** (2½hr., 11:45am and 4:30pm, ¢680).

Boats: **Ferries** leave from the Contramar Terminal near Av. 3, Calle 31/33 on the far northwest side of the peninsula (☎661 1444). Ferries to **Paquera** (1½hr.; 6 per day 5am-8:15pm, return 6 per day 6am-8:30pm; ¢620, children under 5 ¢300, cars ¢4000). An additional *lancha* runs to Paquera from behind the *mercado central* (6, 11am, 3:15pm; return 7:30am, 12:30, 5pm; ¢700). From Paquera, buses connect with ferries to **Montezuma** via **Tambor, Pochote,** and **Cóbano.** Ferries (☎661 1069) also leave for **Puerto Naranjo** (1hr.; 5 per day 3:15am-7pm, return 5 per day 5:10am-9pm; ¢620, children under 12 ¢280, cars ¢4400). From Puerto Naranjo, buses connect to **Nicoya,** where you can take a bus to **Playa Sámara, Playa Nosara,** or **Santa Cruz,** for connections heading to beaches on the southern peninsula.

Taxis: (☎663 5050 or 663 2020) line the streets near the *mercado central* on the northeast side of the peninsula. (From the intercity terminal to the ferry dock ¢500.)

◪ ORIENTATION AND PRACTICAL INFORMATION. Puntarenas is a long, skinny peninsula 10km from San José. The center of town is marked by the *parque central*, bordered by Av. Central to the south, Av. 1 to the north, and Calles 7 and 3 to the west and east. The main **bus terminal** is on the southeast edge of town on Calle 2, and **ferries** arrive and depart from the dock at the northwest end near Av. 3, Calle 31/33. Along the peninsula's southern border runs the Av. 4, more commonly referred to as **Paseo de los Turistas** because it holds the more upscale restaurants and hotels once popular with wealthier tourists. Travelers should note that no part of Puntarenas is safe past dark, especially around the *mercado central*. If you must go somewhere, it's best to take a cab. The main **tourist office** (☎661 9011), just opposite the main ferry terminal, has a post office, **Internet** service, sells phone cards, and changes dollars. (Internet ¢250 per 30min., ¢500 per hr. Open daily 8am-6pm.) The peninsula's banks cluster along Av. 3 between Calles 1 and Central. **Banco Nacional** has a **24hr. ATM.** (Open M-F 8:30am-3:45pm.). The **police station** is on the northeast edge of town behind Banco Nacional, one block north of the post office (☎661 0640, emergency 911). **Farmacia Szuster** (☎661 0580), 200m east of the *parque central*, 100m south of Banco Nacional, is well-stocked. (Open M-Sa 7am-9pm, Su 8am-noon.) **Hospital Monseñor Sanabria** (☎663 0033), is 8km east of town; take any bus for Esparza, Miramar, Barranca, El Roble, or Caldera. The **Red Cross** (☎661 0184) is located 250m west of the northwest corner of the *parque.* (Open 24hr.) **Millenium Cybercafe** is on Paseo de los Turistas at Calle 17. (¢600 per hr. Open daily 10am-10pm.) The **post office** is on Av. 3, Calles Central/1, 100m north and 120m west of the *parque.* (Open M-F 7:30am-6pm, Sa 7:30am-noon.) **Postal code:** 5400.

▓▓ ACCOMMODATIONS AND FOOD. Camping on the beach is unsafe, unsanitary, and not recommended. Good, safe budget accommodations are available. Be careful of where you plan to stay, especially around the round *mercado central* area, since crime rates have risen. **Hotel Cabezas ❶**, Av. 1, Calles 2/4, is a secure option. The rooms are small, but clean, all with fans and common cold water baths, and you can watch TV in the sitting area. (☎661 1045. ¢2000 per person.) **Hotel Chorotega ❶**, Av. 3, Calle 1 , diagonally across from Banco Nacional, offers more privacy and comfort with clean rooms and fans. (☎661 0998. Singles ¢3300, with bath 5600; doubles ¢4500/¢7900.) Several decent, mid-priced restaurants serving seafood and *típico* fare line Paseo de los Turistas. Otherwise, try the *mercado central* for quick and cheap eats. A small strip of *sodas* calls to those waiting for a ferry. Most are open M-Sa 5am-6pm and some are open on Su. **◙Restaurante Kahite Blanco ❷**, Av. 1, Calle 15/17, 100m northwest of the stadium, is popular with the better-dressed locals. All seating is on a breezy patio. (Rice with shrimp ¢2200. Open daily 10am-11pm.) **Restaurante Aloha ❸**, on the Paseo de los Turistas at Calle 19, also has good seafood. (Open daily 11am-midnight.) **Pizzería ❷**, on Av. 1, Calle 3, has hot cheesy pizzas (¢1250-2350) and a large selection of pastas. (Open daily noon-10pm.) **Rincón de Surf ❶**, on the Paseo de los Turistas near Calle 15, is casual with jammin' reggae beats and a great beach-front location. Surprise your taste buds with octopus *ceviche* (¢2300) or the less daring black bean soup (¢830).

◪ SIGHTS. The **Museo Histórico Marino de la Ciudad de Puntarenas** (☎661 5036), in the *parque central*, highlights the history of Puntarenas and its inhabitants through exhibits on archaeology, customs, and trade relations and a brief display on natural resources. It is worth a glance if you have time between buses or ferries. If you prefer your water chlorinated, there's an Olympic-sized **municipal pool** at the western tip of the peninsula. Take a Barrio Carmen bus from Av. Central, Calle 1/Central (¢65). The pool is 5m from the ocean and surrounded by water on three sides. (Open Tu-Su 9am-4:30pm. ¢400, children ages 2-10 ¢200.)

PARQUE NACIONAL CARARA

Although this park only encompasses of 47 sq. km, its unique location includes three life zones, the tropical humid forest, premontane tropical rainforest, and montane rainforest. Several rare and endangered species reside in these zones, including the great anteater, fiery-billed aracari, spider monkey, American crocodile, black-and-green poison arrow frog, and phantom scarlet macaw.

⊏ TRANSPORTATION. Few **buses** pass by the reserve. From **Jacó** or **Playa Hermosa**, take any Puntarenas- or San José-bound bus (see **Transportation** sections) and ask the driver to let you off at the park entrance. If you don't see a large parking lot and the **ranger station** when you get off, chances are the driver dropped you off at the park's volunteer lodging station, 300m north (to the left with your back to the road) up the highway. To return, you'll have to rely on the few buses that pass along the highway from San José or Puntarenas to Jacó or Quepos. Ask the park ranger about what time the buses usually pass, but as the schedule is not fixed, you may have to wait anywhere between 10min. and 2hr. for a bus. If you're en route to San José or Puntarenas from Jacó, you can take an early morning bus to the park, have the ranger watch your bags while you're hiking, and then flag down a bus. Call **Freddie** (☎ 637 0523) for a guided tour of the park. (US$15 per 2hr. US$30 per 4hr. Park open daily 7am-4:30pm dry season; open daily 8am-4pm rainy season. US$8.)

▦ ORIENTATION AND PRACTICAL INFORMATION. Parque Nacional Carara, 17km northeast of Jacó and 90km west of San José, was created in a transition zone where the wet tropical jungle of the south meets the dry forest of the north. Easy-to-traverse trails are good for a quick glance at the diverse flora and fauna. Carara is best visited as a short day trip, as there is not a full day's worth to see, there is no inexpensive nearby lodging, and **camping** is not permitted in the park. The ranger station has bathrooms and a picnic area but sells only drinks.

▣ HIKING. The first two trails form a figure eight and leave from the ranger station. **Las Aráceas**, the first loop, is 1.2km and takes about 45min. if you just walk through. **Quebrada Bonita**, the second loop, is 1.5km, takes about 50min., and involves a shallow river crossing. The trail offers a greater chance of seeing wildlife. The third trail, **Laguna Meándrica**, is 4km each way and takes about 2½hr. to complete. It starts about 1km north of the ranger station and follows the Río Grande de Tárcoles. A murky lagoon about halfway along is a good place to spot wildlife. This trail is closed in Sept. when the lake floods.

◙ SIGHTS. Hidden under Carara's thick foliage are 15 uninteresting pre-Columbian archaelogical sights, some dating back to 300 A.D. One worth checking out is **Lomas de Entierro,** an ancient village with housing and funeral remains at the top of the hill facing the Río Grande de Tárcoles. About 3km north of Parque Nacional Carara, on the highway to Puntarenas and San José, is the **Río Tárcoles Bridge,** more commonly called the **Crocodile Bridge** for the dozens of crocodiles that reside in the muddy river and doze by the trail. Though it's hardly worth a visit in its own right, many private bus and transfer companies stop here for a quick peak. If you do happen to want a closer look, call **Jungle Crocodile Safari** (☎ 236 6473) for a 2hr. tour complete with a bilingual guide that will do some daring crocodile tricks. (US$25.)

SOUTH OF PUNTARENAS TO JACÓ. Further south of Caldera and before Jacó are many less-developed beaches primarily of interest to **surfers.** They are most easily accessible by car along the **Costanera Sur** highway, although any Puntarenas-Jacó bus will drop you off near the turnoffs, where you may have to walk a kilometer or two. Just south of Caldera, about 17km from Puntarenas, are **Playa Tivives** and **Playa Valor**, with reliable beach breaks off a river mouth. **Playa Escondida**, 10km north of Jacó, is an excellent point break with slow-forming lefts that crash after building to a solid peak.

JACÓ

A swimmer might be intimidated by the waves that ravage the cinnamon-colored sands of Jacó, but surfers from around the world heard the call and brought a sub-culture with them which locals now embrace. Such a young, active crowd also lures quite a number of swimmers and partiers from San José on the weekends, when the music never stops thumping. Of course, this activity comes with a price—restaurants charge a little more, budget accommodations aren't as cheap, the streets are littered, and crime and prostitution are becoming more common.

⌷ TRANSPORTATION. Buses to **San José** (3hr.; 5, 7:30, 11am, 3, 5pm; ¢935) arrive and leave from Plaza Jacó, opposite the Best Western, 1km north of the town center on the main drag. Buy tickets from the office on the southeast corner of the plaza. Other buses stop along the main drag; a good place to catch them is from the stop in front of the Más X Menos. To: **Orotina** (1½hr.; 5, 7, 9am, 12:30, 2, 4, 5pm; ¢400); **Puntarenas** (1½hr.; 6, 9am, noon, 4:30pm; ¢520); **Quepos** (1½hr. 6:30am, 12:30, 4, 6pm; ¢480). **Taxis** line up in front of Más X Menos (☎663 5050 or 663 2020). To **Playa Herradura** ¢1500-2000, **Playa Hermosa** ¢1000. Buses stopping in Jacó drop off passengers along the main road toward the center of town. Otherwise, buses passing near Jacó along the **Costanera Sur** highway will drop off pasengers at the far south end of town, from where it's about a 1km walk to Jacó center.

◪ ⑦ ORIENTATION AND PRACTICAL INFORMATION. Jacó center stretches for about 1km along its **main road,** which runs northwest to southwest parallel to the beach. For simplicity's sake, here it will be described as north-south, the far north end of town marked by the **Best Western.** Several side roads branch west off the main road and lead to the beach. **Playa Herradura** is 6.5km north of Jacó, **Playa Hermosa** about 5km south. Jacó has no official **tourist office,** but many tour opera-tors and shop owners speak English and are more than willing to help. A few par-ticularly helpful folks are Eric of **Mexican Joe's Internet Cafe** (see **Internet,** below), and George of **Chatty Cathy's Family Kitchen** (see **Food,** below). The **Banco Nacional** is in the center of town, across from Chatty Cathy's Family Kitchen, and has a **24hr. ATM.** (Open M-F 8:30am-3:45pm.) There is a **Western Union** in the north side of town near La Hacienda, inside Happy Video. (☎643 1102. Open M-F 9am-12:30pm and 1-3pm, Sa 9am-noon.) **Payless Car Rental,** formerly Elegante Rent-a-Car, is 325m north of Banco Nacional, across from Restaurante La Ostra. (☎643 3224. Min. age 23. US$1000 credit card deposit. Cheapest rentals US$42-55 per day. AmEx/DC/MC/V.) For groceries, **Más X Menos** is just south of Banco Nacional. (Open M-Th 8am-9pm, F-Sa 8am-10pm, Su 8am-8pm. AmEx/MC/V.) **Puro Blanco Laundry** is across from Más X Menos. (¢2000 per 5kg. Ironing ¢150 per item. Open daily 8am-6pm.) Other services include: **Police,** south along the main road, about 500m past Banco Nacional and right when the road forks; the police station is 200m down on a side road to the right (☎643 3011, emergency 117); **Red Cross,** 50m south of Banco Popular (☎643 3090; open 24hr.); **Farmacia Jacó,** 200m south of Banco Nacional (☎643 3205; open M-Sa 8:30am-9pm, Su 8:30am-7pm) **Clínica de Jacó,** a 5min. walk south of town along the main road, near the post office (☎643 1767; open M-Th 7am-4pm, F 7am-3pm, Sa and Su emergencies only). Public coin and card **phones** are all along the main drag; phone cards are sold at Más X Menos. **Mexican Joe's Internet Café,** about 125m south of Banco Nacional, allows international calls. US$1 per 5min. to US, Mexico, Central America, and Canada. It also has one of the cheapest **Internet** rates in town. (¢350 per hr. Open daily 8am-10pm.) The **post office** is on the south side of town, near Hotel Jacó Fiesta. Follow the main road south and turn right at the *municipalidad;* turn right on Calle Cocodrilos before the *clínica.* (Open M-F 7:30am-6pm, Sa 7:30am-noon.) **Postal code:** 4023.

⌂ ACCOMMODATIONS AND CAMPING. Jacó's main drag is lined with small *cabinas*, the majority with clean and reliable budget to mid-range rooms. A few nicer, more luxurious places cluster at the south end of town. Reserve in advance during the high season. **Camping El Hicaco ❶,** on the side street 100m south of Banco Nacional, across from Discotheque La Central (see Nightlife, below) has a shaded yard with showers, toilets, laundry basins, and rickety grills. (☎643 3070. ₡1000 per person.) **Chuck's Rooms and Boards ❶,** 700m north of the bridge; turn toward the beach at La Hacienda Restaurant; Chuck's will be on your left. (☎643 3328. Dorms ₡2700; doubles with private cold bath ₡6000; 1 triple with A/C and private hot-water bath US$30; 1 cabin with full kitchen, A/C, private hot bath, and TV US$50.) **Aparthotel los Ranchos ❹,** 100m down the first side street south of the bridge, near the beach, has spacious, apartment style rooms with kitchen, private hot-water bath, and comfy beds. (☎643 3070. Check-in 2pm. Check-out noon. Laundry ₡50 per item. Discounts available for long stays and low season. Doubles US$40; triples US$45; rooms for 6-7 US$70. MC/V.)

🍴 FOOD. A dash of surfer and a pinch of *gringo* (American) flavor most of Jacó's restaurants. That doesn't mean the food is not good, though—just expect to pay a bit more to break away from the staple rice and beans. ▊**Pasta Italiana Mónica ❶,** 50m down the second side street south of the bridge serves delicious food made by native Italians. Lasagna night draws a crowd. (Classic Italian pastas ₡1300-1700. Open M-Sa noon-2pm and 6-9pm.) ▊**Chatty Cathy's Family Kitchen ❷,** across the street from Más X Menos, upstairs, has sugary, fresh cinnamon buns (₡600) and home style breakfasts (₡1250-2200) that are mouth-watering. (Open M-Th 7am-2pm.) **Rioasis ❷,** still known by some as its former title Killer Munchies, 25m down the side street just north of Banco Nacional. Whoever dreamed up the toppings on these wood-oven baked pizzas (₡1900 for a medium) was a creative genius. (Open daily noon-11pm; bar open until midnight.) **Banana Café ❷,** about 80m south of the bridge on the right, serves unique tropical- and Caribbean-influenced rice, seafood, and meat dishes in addition to their famous *típico* breakfasts. (Breakfast ₡800-1200. Open M-W and F-Su 7am-3pm.)

🏄🏊 OUTDOOR ACTIVITIES AND GUIDED TOURS. **Intense Sunset Tours,** next to Banco Nacional, has English, Spanish, German, and French guides and special prices for students and groups. (☎643 1555. Horseback riding US$30; class IV rafting US$80; and more. Ask for Morris. Open daily 7am-11pm. V.) **Green Tours,** 50m south of Restaurante Colonial, has an extensive selection of tours and services including canopy tours, kayaking, sportfishing, among others. (☎643 1555. Open daily 7am-8pm.) **King Tours,** 150m north of Banco Nacional, arranges well-organized tours that satisfy every wildlife, relaxation or adventure craze. (☎643 2441. Scooters US$25 per day; motorbikes US$45 per day. Open daily 8am-8pm. V.) **Jacó Equestrian Center,** 325m north of Banco Nacional, has excellent horseback tours to their mountain farm. (☎643 1569. AmEx/MC/V.)

🏖 BEACHES AND SURFING. Jacó's main beach has gentle waves that break on dark sand, ideal for beginners and intermediates. Experts craving more challenging surf head to the point break in front of the Best Western and **La Roca Loca,** a rocky point with submerged rocks, about 1.5km south of Jacó. La Roca Loca is easily accessible by foot—head south along the beach on the rocks. Just 5km away, **Playa Hermosa** (p. 208) has a challenging beach break also popular with advanced surfers. Farther south of Jacó are **Esterillos Oeste, Esterillos Centro, Esterillos Este,** and **Playas Plama, Bandera,** and **Bejuco.** North of Jacó is **Boca Barranca.** Most of these have good, isolated surf spots where you won't have to wait behind dozens of others to catch a wave.

C O S T A   R I C A

■ **NIGHTLIFE.** Jacó's high season nightlife is serious business, with people packing the clubs and bars from dusk till dawn. Come low season, however, most hotspots remain relatively empty. Be aware that Jacó has had recent drug problems, and prostitutes linger in almost every bar. **La Hacienda** is located 50m north of the bridge, just past the first side street, above the restaurant of the same name. A young trendy crowd meets for pre-salsa drinks, blasting rock, and reggae. (☎643 3460. Cover ¢1500. Beer ¢500; 2-for-1 beers M-F till 9pm. Open daily 4pm-2:30am.) **Club Ole,** across the street from La Hacienda Bar plays classy *salsa* and *merengue.* (Cover ¢110. Beer ¢550. Open F-Sa 6:30pm-4am.) **Discotheque la Central,** 100m down the side street 100m south of Banco Nacional. After 11pm people head to this classic disco/bar for popular Latin and pop music. (☎643 3076. Cover Th-Su ¢800. Open daily 8:30pm-2:30am.) **Pancho Villa's,** toward the southern end of town, across the street from Mexican Joe's. After the other bars and discos close, a largely male crowd stumbles here for pricey grub and gambling. (Appetizers ¢1000-1500; hamburgers ¢738. Open daily 10am-5am.)

PLAYA HERMOSA

Surfers at Hermosa will tell you to skip Jacó and head directly to this idyllic miniature surf community. A stark contrast from the upscale beach of the same name in the Nicoya Peninsula, Hermosa is virtual paradise for those seeking long days to laze away in hammocks on the beachside or catch the perfect waves that roll onto the long, black-sand beach. Life here is as laid back as the surfers who live in it.

⌐ TRANSPORTATION. Any Quepos-bound **bus** from San José, Puntarenas, Orotina, or Jacó will drop you off in town. (See each town's **Transportation** for bus schedules.) You can also rent a **bike** in Jacó to make the trip (a hilly 30min. ride). Follow the main road to the south end of Jacó and turn right in front of the *municipalidad.* Keep straight for 1km until you reach a fork in the road, where you will turn left. At the next fork shortly after that, turn right away from the gas station. The road will lead you directly there. A slightly more expensive option is to take a **taxi** from Jacó. (☎643 2000, cell 367 9363. ¢1000.) Arrange a time to return or ask a hotel to call one when you're ready. From Hermosa, buses depart in front of Abastecedor La Perla del Mar for **Puntarenas** (2½hr.; 6:30am, noon, 4:30pm; ¢740); **Quepos** (2hr., 8 per day 6:30am-7pm, ¢560); **San José** (3hr., 5 per day 6:30am-5pm, ¢800).

⊞ 7 ORIENTATION AND PRACTICAL INFORMATION. Playa Hermosa is 5km south of Jacó and 85km north of Quepos, stretching about 1km along the **Costanera Sur** highway. The main road actually runs northeast-southwest, but all directions here are simplified to north and south. From Jacó, you will ride south into town, passing **Hotel La Terraza del Pacífico** and **Rancho Grande** (at the north end of town). The **supermarket** Abastecedor La Perla del Mar is near the center of town (open M-Sa 7am-8pm, Su 7am-7pm), and **The Backyard Bar** marks the southern end of town. The nearest **banks, pharmacies, clinics, Internet,** and **laundry** are in Jacó. (See **Jacó: Orientation and Practical Information,** p. 206.)

⋔ ACCOMMODATIONS. All accommodations are along the main road facing the beach and cater to an audience of mostly surfers. ■**Rancho Grande ❶,** made of upright wooden logs, has large, cool rooms with private hot-water bath, and a large patio and communal kitchen.(☎643 3529. US$10 per person.) **Cabinas Las Olas ❸,** near the center of town, is an amazing value for larger groups. All rooms have tile floors, private hot-water baths, fans, fridge, and kitchen. (☎643 3687. Singles US$25; doubles US$40; 6 people US$110. Discounts available.) **Costa Nera Bed and Breakfast ❷,** just north of Cabinas Las Olas, has fresh rooms with private hot-water bath and a beachfront terrace. (☎ 643 1942. Singles US$20; doubles US$30-40. Discounts for long stays.)

🏠🍴 **FOOD AND NIGHTLIFE.** As in Jacó, most food at Playa Hermosa is geared towards American visitors. ◙**Costa Nera ❷,** two doors north of Cabinas Las Olas in the Costa Nera Bed and Breakfast, has a limited menu of authentic, tasty pastas in filling portions. Creative bruscetta appetizers are included with every entree. (Pastas ₡1800-2300. Open daily 6:45-9pm.) **Soda Choy-lin ❶,** next to the supermarket, offers simple fare at the cheapest prices. (*Gallo pinto* with eggs ₡500; *casado* ₡700. Open daily 7:30am-8:30pm.) **Hard Chargers Café ❷,** behind Cabinas las Olas, has an open porch graced with beautiful ocean views and serves delicious American and *tico* breakfasts and Asian-inspired dinners. (Dinner plates ₡1500-3400. Open daily 7-9:30am and 7-9:30pm.) **The Backyard Bar ❷,** restaurant by day, bar and pool hall by night, is the place where most people congregate when the sun begins to set. (Pizzas ₡2300; beer ₡500. Open bar Sa 9:30-10:30pm. Open daily noon-2am.)

◙🐎 **SIGHTS AND GUIDED TOURS.** Hermosa's surrounding forests and tame waters nearby have enough pricey activities to keep non-surfers busy for a day or two. Budget travelers can save their money and hike the easy **Monkey Trail,** which begins across from Bar Palmeras, past the Jungle Surf Café at the north end of town. Between July and December, you have a good chance to see the 3000-4000 **Olive Ridley turtles** that emerge from the water to lay their eggs. ◙**Diana's Trail Rides** (☎ 643 3838), in the stables located on a dirt road 100m past Hotel la Terraza, offers horseback tours to a waterfall (US$45), the turtle hatchery (US$45), or the mountain top (US$25). **Hotel La Terraza del Pacífico** has a variety of activities. Ask for Randall. (☎ 643 3222. Canopy tour US$55, kayak tour with snorkeling US$50. Surf lessons with Costa Rica national champ US$45. AmEx/D/MC/V.)

🏄 **SURFING.** Intermediate and expert surfers swear by Hermosa's perfectly cascading waves, regularly reaching heights of 8-13ft. Experts flock to Hermosa for the annual **surf competition** held by Hotel La Terraza, usually in May. Those learning can sign up for surfing programs at **Loma del Mar Surf Camp** (☎ 643 1423 or 643 3908), off the road to the left past the restaurants and hotels.

QUEPOS

Three and a half hours south of San José, the city of Quepos is one of the Central Pacific's most well-trodden destinations because of its proximity to tourist-magnet Parque Nacional Manuel Antonio and to the dozens of tour operators who run adventure trips into the raging rivers and wild mountain terrain outside town. The streets are often deserted during the day when travelers are exploring, but come sunset, the chatter of an upbeat population mixes with the music: the perfect accompaniment to a nice cold beer. If adventure tours don't fit your budget, Manuel Antonio is a relaxing escape; Quepos is a convenient base with budget options.

▬ TRANSPORTATION

Flights: Sansa (30min.; high season 6 per day 7:45am-4:25pm, return 6 per day 8:30am-5:10pm; US$44) and **Travelair** (30min.; high season 6 per day 6am-4pm, return 6 per day 6:35am-4:40pm; US$45) fly out of San José (see p. 144) and arrive at the airstrip 5km northwest of town.

Buses: From **San José,** buses depart from Calle 16, Av. 1/3. (Direct 3½ hr.; daily 6am, noon, 6, 7:30pm. Indirect 5hr., M-F 5 per day 7am-5pm, ₡1230.) Only direct buses continue to **Manuel Antonio.** From the main bus station in Quepos, buses go to **Man-**

uel Antonio (25min, about every 30min. 5:30am-9:30pm, ¢80); **Puntarenas** (4hr.; 4:30, 7:30, 10:30am, 3pm; ¢800); via **Jacó** (2hr.; 4:30, 10:30am, 3pm; ¢660); **San José** (direct; 6:15, 9:30am, noon, 5pm; ¢1665; indirect; 5, 8am, 2, 4pm; ¢1300).

Taxis (☎ 777 1207) line up across the street from the bus station. A taxi to Manuel Antonio should cost ¢1000.

✈ 🛈 ORIENTATION AND PRACTICAL INFORMATION

Quepos is 144km southeast of San José, 65km south of Jacó, and 7km north of **Parque Nacional Manuel Antonio.** Most hotels, restaurants, and services cluster around the few main streets. The bus station marks the center of town; with your back to it, facing the supermarket, the beach is to your right (west), and the soccer field and road to Manuel Antonio are two and three blocks to your left (east).

Banks: Banco Popular, 100m south of the southwest corner of the bus terminal. Open M-F 8:15am-3:30pm, Sa 8:15-11:30am. Plus/V **ATMs. Lynch Travel** (☎ 777 1170), near Restaurante El Pueblo, west of the bus station, exchanges US dollars and traveler's checks. Open daily 7am-6pm.

Supermarkets: Head across the street from the bus station to **Super Más** for groceries. Open M-Sa 7:30am-8pm, Su 7am-noon. AmEx/MC/V.

Laundry: Lavandería Aquamatic (☎ 777 0972), 100m west of the southwest corner of the soccer field. Self-service wash (¢750) and dry (¢750), or have it done for you (¢900). Open M-Sa 8am-5pm. AmEx/MC/V.

Car Rental: Elegante/Payless Rent-a-Car (☎ 777 0015), 150m west of the southwest corner of the soccer field, just past the lavandería. Drivers 23+. US$1500-2000 credit card deposit required. Open M-Sa 7:30am-5:30pm. AmEx/MC/V.

Police: Organización de Investigación Judicial (OIJ; ☎ 777 0511), 100m behind the bus station. Open 24hr.

Pharmacy: Farmacia Catedral (☎ 777 0527), across from the bus station. Open daily 8am-8pm. AmEx/D/MC/V.

Medical Services: Red Cross (☎ 777 0116, emergency 128), 25m east of the bus station. Open 24hr. The **hospital** (☎ 777 0922), about 4km northeast of town on the Costanera Sur Hwy., is reachable by buses to Silencio and Londres (5-10min., M-F 5am-10pm, ¢60). Taxi ¢1000.

Public Phones: across from the bus terminal. Cards at the supermarket or pharmacy.

Internet: Quepos Diner, 75km west of the southwest corner of the soccer field, has the best deals. ¢300 per 20min., ¢600 per hr. Open daily 10am-10pm.

Post Office: Facing the soccer field on the north side. **Fax** available. Open M-F 7:30am-6pm, Sa 7:30am-noon.

Postal Code: 6350.

🏠 ACCOMMODATIONS

Budget accommodations are more plentiful and less touristy in Quepos than in Manuel Antonio, making it a nice base for visits to the park and beaches.

Mar y Luna (☎ 777 0394). With your back to the bus station, walk right to the end of the block, turn right, and then left at the next corner; Mar y Luna is a few meters down to the right. Plain fan-cooled rooms with super clean bathrooms. Common area with TV, upstairs balcony. Laundry ¢650 per kilo. Singles ¢2000; doubles with bath ¢4500. ❶

Hotel Malinche (☎ 777 0093), across from Mar y Luna. Larger, modern rooms have efficient fans, furniture, and big clean, cold-water private baths. Credit card phone available in lobby. Singles ¢3500; doubles ¢7000; triples ¢10,300. ❶

Hotel Ramu's (☎ 777 0245), a few doors from Mar y Luna, across from Barco Bar. The hallways are dark, but small bedrooms are clean and have fans. ₡2000 per person. ❶

🔲 FOOD

Restaurants in Quepos specialize in Tex-Mex, American-style breakfasts, and sea-food and are subsequently pricier than the standard *típico* fare. You can find cheaper meals at the *sodas* near the bus station.

Escalofrío, on the street just west of the bus station, next door to Los Dos Locos. Tasty and authentic Italian cuisine. Five types of bruchetta (₡600-900); pasta (₡1400-1800); huge pizzas (₡1300-1800). Open Tu-Su 2:30-10:30pm. ❶

Tropical Sushi, right by Hotel Ramu's and across from El Barco Bar, serves Costa Rica's freshest seafood in some way other than ceviche or filet. Veggie tempura ₡1200; sushi box ₡2750-3500. Open M and W-Su 5pm-1am. AmEx/D/MC/V. ❸

Gran Escape, 100m north and 100m west of the southwest corner of the bus station. The fresh fish is fantastic, and the burgers are as creative as they are filling (jurassic park burger ₡2500). Also serves a Mexican dishes and tasty cocktails. Kitchen open 7am-10pm; bar open until midnight. AmEx/MC/V. ❸

🏞 🏊 OUTDOOR ACTIVITIES AND GUIDED TOURS

The only reason tourists spend an afternoon in Quepos is to make plans for an out-ing—the surrounding environs offer numerous tempting options, including rafting, canopy tours, mangrove exploration, and some of Costa Rica's best sportfishing.

Iguana Tours (☎ 777 1262; iguana@sol.racsa.co.cr), at the southeast corner of the soc-cer field, arranges hiking and horseback tours of Parque Nacional Manuel Antonio (US$37) and boat trips to Damas Island (US$60). Experienced guides specialize in raft-ing trips (US$65-90) on Ríos Naranjo, Parrita, and Savegre. Open daily 7am-7pm.

High Tec Sportfishing and Tours (24hr. ☎ 388 6617), on the east side of the street that passes the bus station, across from the soccer field. Generally has the cheapest trips and offers other water-oriented excursions. Half-day in-shore fishing US$296.

Blue Water Sportfishing (☎ 777 1596 or 390 6759; www.sportfishingcostarica.com). Two fully equipped, custom-crafted boats to catch yellowfish tuna, snook, snapper, and more. Half-day US$550-650 for up to 4 people. US$15 per person for fishing license.

🔲 NIGHTLIFE

Quepos has quite a few bars and clubs, which get packed in the high season. In the rainy months, however, most places remain relatively mellow.

El Barco Bar, 100m west of the bus station. Sports fans flock to watch any sporting event in this chill bar and restaurant. Local bands perform on weekends in the high sea-son. They'll cook your catch for ₡2000. Tex-Mex, burgers, seafood, and steak. Beer ₡450. Open W-F 4pm-2am, Sa-Su noon-2am.

Discotheque Arco Iris, 100m west and 300m north of the northwest corner of the bus station, one block after the bridge out of Quepos. *Salsa, merengue,* and reggae beats get bodies moving. Beer ₡450; F cover ₡300, Sa ₡500. Open W-Su 10pm-2:30am.

El Tiburón, on the street just west of the bus station, is marked by a shark sign on a sec-ond story. Nutella crepe (₡350); margarita (₡1400). Open daily 6pm-1am.

Epicentro, 100m north and 100m west of the southwest corner of the soccer field, next to Gran Escape. Their foam parties attract locals and travelers that revel in suds and techno. Happy Hour 5pm-midnight.

PARQUE NACIONAL MANUEL ANTONIO

Parque Nacional Manuel Antonio offers the perfect combination of Costa Rica's best terrains: warm, jade-green waves lap at the roots of a lush tropical forest. The national park is gaining a somewhat family-vacation feel, but that doesn't make the setting any less incredible: birds fill the trees with color and iguanas and spider squirrels dodge your feet. An encounter with the park's most outgoing inhabitants, the white-faced monkeys, is virtually guaranteed. Please don't feed the animals.

■ ■ ▐ **ORIENTATION AND TRANSPORATION.** Parque Nacional Manuel Antonio is located 7km south of Quepos and is surrounded by its own little town. From Quepos, the **bus** (25min., every 30min. 5:30am-9:30pm, ¢80) will drop you off at the stop at a T intersection. From here, you'll see a street leading east, marked by the Restaurante Merlin on the left; many budget and mid-range accommodations are on this street. The direct buses from San José to **Quepos** also continue to Manuel Antonio (3½hr.; 6am, noon, 7:30pm). A **taxi** from Quepos should cost ¢1000.

▐ **PRACTICAL INFORMATION.** The **park entrance** and **ranger station** are about 1km down the road in front of the bus stop. English-speaking **guides** are available at the ranger station and can help you spot the more elusive wildlife; however, they are definitely not necessary to see the animals or enjoy short hikes. (US$15 for 2hr. Park open Tu-Su 7am-4pm. Entrance fee US$7. Park map ¢300.) In an emergency, call the **police station** (☎777 0196). Other services and conveniences can be found in **Quepos.**

▐ ▐ **ACCOMMODATIONS AND FOOD.** Staying in Quepos is cheaper than in the small and touristy town of Manuel Antonio, but isn't as convenient or scenic. **Camping** is not allowed. **Albergue y Travotel Costa Linda ❶,** on a side road a couple hundred meters up the road to the ranger station, has clean basic rooms with double beds, fans, common baths, and an area for lounging. (☎777 0304. Laundry ¢200 per item. Attached restaurant serves good breakfasts. Singles US$8; doubles US$14; triples US$18.) **Cabinas Ramírez ❶,** a short walk back in the direction of Quepos just 80m from the beach, past Restaurant Mar y Sombra, has 3 basic rooms with private cold-water baths. (☎777 5044. Singles and doubles ¢8000.)

⬛ **Restaurante Mar y Sombra ❶** sits where the road from Quepos meets the beach. Feast your eyes on the waves and your stomach on a T-bone steak (¢2500). If the crowd is big enough, the restaurant pumps out music at night. (☎777 0003. Open daily 7:30am-11pm, until 2am on dance nights.) **Pan y Net ❶,** 700m up the road to the ranger station, serves all-you-can eat pizza (every Su ¢1500). Come for breakfast and feast on pancakes. (Internet ¢1000 per hr. Closed M in May, June, and Sept.-Nov. Otherwise, open daily 7am-11pm. Live music every Th and Sa night.) **Los Almendros Steak House ❶,** just 50m down the road, is a slightly classier joint where you can dine on breaded steak (¢1400) or delicious desserts. **Internet** service also available (¢500 per 30min.). Open daily 7am-10pm.

▐ ▐ **BEACHES AND TRAILS.** Manuel Antonio is easily explored in a leisurely 2hr. jaunt through the park's several interconnecting trails. **Puerto Escondido Trail** is a 40min. up-and-down trail full of red crabs. It originates in **Playa Espadilla Sur** and circles **Punta Catedral.** It promises astonishing views of the islands off the coast. It then returns to the southern tip of Playa Espadilla Sur and leads to **Playa Manuel Antonio** and **Playa Escondida. Sloth Trail** is a 1.3km trail that originates at the same place as the Puerto Escondido trail and leads to the spectacular **mirador. Sendero Cataratas** breaks off the Sloth Trail's gravel road and leads to a **waterfall.** Walk 15min. up to a sign on your right (before the cement bridge), which marks the Sendero Cataratas. This trail winds through the forest to a small, pretty waterfall where you can take a dip. **Playa Espadilla** is a relatively large, crowded, public beach flanked by mangroves and estuaries just outside the park. The strong **rip tide** makes deep swimming risky. Get here by heading right (south) down the road when you get off the bus from Quepos. **Playa Manuel Antonio** has picnic areas, bathrooms, showers, a refreshment stand ,and is enjoyable for sunbathers and swimmers. The next big stop along the trail leads to **Plaiya Escondida** (1.6km).

DOMINICAL

With chocolate brown rocky beaches and reliable waves year-round, tiny Dominical (pop. 300), 50km south of San Isidro on the Pacific coast, is a surfer's paradise. Here, quiet evenings give way to thumping dance parties. Travelers will be pleased by a tree-canopied shore, mountainous back-drop, and expansive beach, but the overwhelming American influence might make Dominical a less than ideal vacation stop for those more interested in discovering the *tico* culture.

⬛ TRANSPORTATION. Bus: The official **bus** station is a covered bench across the street from San Clemente, in the northern part of town, but you can catch a bus anywhere along the main road. Buses head to **San Isidro** (1½hr.; 6:45, 7am, 2:45, 3:30pm; ¢440); **Uvita** (45min.; 5:45, 10:30am, 5:30, 9pm; additional buses Dec.-Feb. daily 11:30am; ¢200); **Quepos** (2½hr.; 5:45, 8:15am, 1, 3pm; additional buses May-Nov. Sa-Su 1:50pm; Dec.-Apr. daily 1:50pm; ¢400). Buses to **San José** speed down the Costanera Sur (6hr.; May-Nov. Sa-Su 5:45am, 1:30, 2pm, Dec.-Apr. daily; ¢1500). Buses don't always run on schedule, so come 30min. early. The only taxi service available with TAXI Dominical (☎ 296 2626). You can also hire **taxis** or check bus schedules at the **San Clemente Bar and Grill** (see below).

⬛⬛ ORIENTATION AND PRACTICAL INFORMATION. Dominical spreads out over a 1km stretch of the main road, which connects the **Costanera Sur** highway to the beach road. A side street that forks off the main road, forming a well-trodden shortcut to the beach. Orient yourself be remembering that the ocean is always west. There are no **banks**, but **San Clemente Bar & Grill** will exchange dollars and traveler's checks. Come to Dominical with enough cash—prices are high, and the nearest **ATM** is in San Isidro. The cheapest **laundry** service is **Lavandería Las Olas** in the town center; ask for Señora Miriam. (☎ 787 0105. ¢600 per kg. Open 7am-9pm.) Other services include: **Police,** on the main road, south of the side-street (emergency ☎ 117); **Clínica de Primeros Auxilios,** next to Diu Wok (☎ 787 0310). There are **telephones** at the southern end of the main road in front of Cabinas San Clemente. **Internet Río** is at the north end of town. (☎ 787 0156. Internet ¢1000 per hr. Also has fax. Open M-Sa 8:30am-7pm, Su 12-8pm.) There is no **post office** town, but **San Clemente Bar & Grill** can send and receive mail.

⬛ ACCOMMODATIONS. Dominical's *cabinas* range from bed-in-a-box rooms to nicer beachfront cabins. Reservations are necessary, and prices rise during the high season (Dec.-Apr.). **Camping** on the beach is possible, although belongings and equipment should not be left unattended. Campers can use showers at Cabinas El Co-Co for ¢200. **Camping Antorchas ❶,** 25m from the beach road at a turn-off beside Tortilla Flats (see below), has rooms with high ceilings or camping under low roofs outside. All guests can use cooking utensils, sink, and food storage space in the small kitchen and there is a common outdoor bath. (☎ 787 0307. Camping ¢700 per person; ¢1000 to rent a tent. Dorms ¢1500 May-Nov. per person, Dec.-Apr. ¢2000.) **Cabinas El Co-Co ❶,** at the south end of the main road, has the cheapest *cabinas* near the beach. Rooms are basic but comfortable. (☎ 787 0239.

¢2000 per person; Dec.-Apr. ¢3000. Rooms with private baths ¢7000. AmEx/MC/V.)
Cabinas San Clemente ❷, toward the northern end of the beach road, has luxurious
rooms, spacious tiled floors, and small tables. (☎787 0026. Laundry ¢800 per kg.
Doubles with fans and cold water US$20, with hot water and A/C US$40.) **Posada
del Sol ❷**, 30m south of the Dominical School, just before the fork in the road, has
quiet and clean with private baths and firm beds and hammocks. (☎787 0085. Singles US$15-20; doubles US$17-35; triples US$22-40. Apartment with kitchen
US$500 per month.) **Tortilla Flats ❹**, north of the side street on the beach road, has
spotless rooms and tiled bathrooms with hot water. (☎787 0033. Rooms with double beds and fan ¢8500 per person, with A/C ¢10,000; triples ¢10,000/13,000.)

🍴🛏 **FOOD AND NIGHTLIFE.** Locals bemoan the lack of restaurants in Dominical; everyone is awaiting the opening of new locales to enjoy good food. For **groceries** go to **Diu Wok**, where the side street splits off the main road (☎787 0087; open
daily 5am-10pm) or to the *abastecedor* across from Cabinas San Clemente. (Open
daily 8am-6pm.) **San Clemente Bar & Grille ❷** has TV, beer, and large Tex-Mex menu
in the town's center. This place dominates Dominical. Breakfast is at 7:30am
(super french toast ¢1250). The restaurant buzzes into the evening. (Bargain Taco
Tuesdays has tacos for ¢250. Restaurant open daily 7am-10pm. Shake it to *salsa*,
merengue, and funk F 10pm-2am. No cover. Bar open daily until 11pm.) **Jazzy's
River House ❸**, through the white gate to the right of the *abastecedor*, has live
music. On W nights before the show, catch a full-course veggie meal (¢1800-2000,
dessert ¢700). The house serves cinnamon rolls (¢400) to accompany the sweet
music on Sa. (☎787 0310. Shows start 7pm on W and 8pm on Sa. Reservations
required. The kitchen closes and shows begin at 7pm on W and 8pm on Sa.) **Thrust-
ers Bar & Grill ❸**, at the intersection of the main road and the beach road, is one of
the trendiest hangouts among the young and sun-bleached. (☎787 0127. Su fish
and chips special. Pizzas and burritos ¢1500 and up. Open 4pm-late.)

🏞 **OUTDOOR ACTIVITIES.** Check out **Don Lolu's Nawyaca Waterfalls** for tours that
include a horseback ride to the waterfalls and breakfast. (☎787 0198; www.ecot-
ourism.co.cr/navyacawaterfalls/index.html. Tours US$40.) **Posada del Sol** has
information about renting **horses** (¢2000 per hour). Kim at Jazzy's River House
offers lessons in everything from basket weaving to yoga (see **Food**, above). The
Surf Shack, next to San Clemente, rents boards and bikes and offers surf lessons.
(Surf boards US$7-15 per day; bikes US$15 per day. Open 7am-2pm.) **Tortilla Flats**
will take you on a **mountain bike tour** (US$40) around the surrounding area.
(Boards US$10 per day; bikes US$10 per day). Treat yourself to a massage at **OM
Massage and Meditation** or take a meditation workshop on a rainy afternoon (☎787
0101. Massage US$35 per hr.; meditation 4hrs., US$150.)

📷 **DAYTRIP FROM DOMINICAL**

HACIENDA BARÚ
*From Dominical, take a left on the Costanera Sur out of town; walk 3km past the road to
San Isidro, taking the 1st left after the gas station. From Dominical or San Isidro, any Quepos-bound bus will drop you off at the same gas station. ☎ 787 0003. Admission US$3
including guide. Breakfast included. Cabins for 2, US$40-60; additional person US$10.*

Climb into the rainforest canopy with a guide at your side or spend a night camping amidst monkeys and tree sloths at the Hacienda Barú, 3km north of Dominical.
Also, not to be missed is the beautiful butterfly garden, which includes most of
Costa Rica's colorful species. There are over 6km of carefully marked trails, which
allow for observation of nature. The 1km **Strangler Trail** features the Strangler Fig

and the 2km **Teak and Canal Trail** provides incredible sights. Six **cabins,** with hot water, fans, living rooms, and kitchenettes, are available for overnight stays. .

UVITA

The little-used highway from Dominical to Uvita, 15km to the south, has recently been paved, but the coastal village's previous isolation is still evident. The pebble and sand beach, lapped by gentle waves (no surfers here) looks like it has never seen a tourist's beach towel. A wooden sign on the beach indicates the northern boundary of **Parque National Marino Ballena,** where tortoises, whales, and coral reefs provide a few intrepid visitors with uncensored views of marine life.

E TRANSPORTATION. Buses go to **San José** (7hr.; M-F 5am, Sa-Su 1pm; Dec.-Apr. 1pm daily; ¢1500); **San Isidro** (2½hr.; 6am, 2pm); **Ciudad Cortés** (1½hr.; 5, 11am, 3pm; ¢450). An Ciudad Cortés you can connect to **Neily**—leave from the fork in Bahía, 50m north of the public phone. Also at this fork, the family with the white pickup truck gives rides. (☎743 8084; ¢1000 to Uvita.)

▄ ☷ ORIENTATION AND PRACTICAL INFORMATION. Uvita, is 1km west of Bahía along the highway (past Río Uvita), on the strip of road heading north. Uvita is split into two distinct sections: the village up on the highway, called **Uvita,** and Playa Bahía Uvita, or **Bahía,** which lies along the beach 2.5km to the northeast and borders the national park. A gravel road off the highway leads south to Bahía. Uvita boasts a couple of decent hotels that are at least a 45min. walk from the beach, but closer to the mountains and waterfalls. Some buses to Uvita continue into Bahía; the others will let you off at the start of the main gravel road.

The **public phone** is on the west side of Bahía's main road, 50m south of the fork. (Open daily 7am-noon and 1-8pm.) Local businesses and hotels have radio contact with the **police station,** 3km from Bahía. A small supermarket in the area is **Abastecedor Tatiana,** 600m up from the fork in Bahía (☎743 8080; open daily 7am-6:30pm.)

▛ ▟ ACCOMMODATIONS AND FOOD. There is a spattering of *cabinas* in Bahía, none of which are luxurious. ▨**Villa Hegalva ❶** occupies an acre of grassy land 25m before the fork on the right and is the smoothest operation in town near the beach. Screened and curtained rooms have wooden floors, huge fans, and private baths. The hotel's *soda* menu offers savory green salads (¢500), *casados* (¢900-1000), and good pastas. (☎743 8016. Restaurant open daily 7am-8pm. Rooms US$7 per person, US$10 in high season; huts ¢1500/2000 per person. **Camping** ¢750 per person.) **Cabinas Las Gemelas ❶,** 200m from the Minisuper Peri, take your 2nd left with the school on the right side of the road. Polished, private bathrooms and large fans provide cool nights. (☎743 8009. Laundry ¢1500 per load.) **Cabinas Punta Uvita ❶,** across from the public phone, has rooms with bamboo doors, fans, and outdoor hammocks. (☎743 8015. Singles ¢2000; doubles ¢3000.) **Soda y Frutería Marel ❶** next door to Cabinas Punta Uvita, sells fruit, sodas, and ice cream sundaes. (Open during high season M-Th 7am-9pm, F-Su 7am-noon.)

◪ GUIDED TOURS. There are some professional tour companies, but hotels and individuals also arrange horseback rides and snorkel excursions upon request. **Villa Hegalva** will set you up with Saúl, who will take you on a 7hr. **ride** into the mountains past lakes and a waterfall. (☎743 8016. US$20 per person, including lunch. Snorkeling 2hr. US$20 per person.) Mario of **Cabinas Punta Uvita** will also take you on horseback tours to nearby waterfalls, Punta Uvita, or the mountains. (☎743 8015. US$30, US$15, and US$55 for 2 people.) **Delfín Tour** offers a 2hr. tour of the marine park for a minimum of two people. (US$25 per person.) Jonathan

Dunam of **Ballena Adventure,** next to Soda Marel, offers snorkeling, fishing, and boat tours in English. (☎370 9482. AmEx/MC/V.)

🏞 PARQUE NACIONAL MARINO BALLENA

Ranger offices ☎786 7161. One ranger office is 200m west of the park entrance on the beach in Bahía; the other is 8km south of Uvita on Playa Ballena, which can be reached by buses heading to Ciudad Cortés. If you catch a ranger in Playa Ballena, they will request ¢600 from nationals and US$7 from foreigners plus ¢1000 for each vehicle.

Parque Nacional Marino Ballena was founded in 1989 as the first (and only) national aquatic park in Costa Rica. Of its seven beaches, only one is owned and maintained by the government. The rest are cared for by dedicated members of the community. If you enter past one of the two **ranger offices,** they will request a donation of ¢300. The park consists of 110 terrestrial hectares and 5375 marine hectares, including 5 types of coral in its extensive reef. **Snorkeling** is possible off **Punta Uvita** when the tide is right, or from a boat off the rock islands of **Piedra Ballena** and **Tres Hermanas.** If you need gear, ask at Villa Hegalva (see **Accommodations** above). From January to March, you may spot *ballenas* (whales) migrating from Southern California with their newborns. Baby tortoises hatch in a sand pit next to the ranger station from June to September. It is possible to camp in the park with permission from the rangers, but they encourage you to stay in Bahía hotels.

SOUTHERN COSTA RICA

From San Isidro and Parque Nacional Chirripó to the vast wilderness of Parque Internacional La Amistad, Southern Costa Rica retains the thrills that originally drew travelers, such as hiking through mystical cloud forests and climbing Olympian peaks. Few locations cater to tourists, but the extra effort needed to explore these isolated areas is well worth it. The warm populace makes this part of Costa Rica even more memorable for those who stop and chat.

SAN ISIDRO

About 136km southeast of San José, the small, modern city of San Isidro de El General, also known as Pérez Zeledón, is a springboard for trips into southern Costa Rica, particularly for its proximity to the unreal splendor of Parque Nacional Chirripó, whose main entrance stands in nearby San Gerardo de Rivas. Take advantage of San Isidro's urban conveniences, enjoy its small town charm, and explore the numerous plant nurseries, coffee farms, and cattle farms.

⧉ TRANSPORTATION. Finding the right **bus** out of San Isidro may seem a bit overwhelming at first—there are 6 different bus companies. The city is small, so everything within the city is within walking distance. TUASUR (☎771 0418) has service to **San José** (3½hr.; 6:30, 9:30am, 12:30, 2:30, 3:30pm; ¢870). MUSOC (☎771 0414) buses leave for **San José** from the terminal next to Vargas Rojas on the Interamerican Hwy. between Calles 2/4 (5am, every 1-2hr. 5:30am-4:30pm; ¢870). Transportes Blancos (☎771 2550) buses head to: **Dominical** (1½hr.; 7, 9am, 1:30, 4pm; ¢415); **Puerto Jiménez** (6hr.; 6:30am, noon, 3pm; ¢1330); **Quepos** (3hr.; 7am, 1:30pm; ¢655); **Uvita** (2½hr.; 9am, 4pm; ¢505) via **Playa Hermosa** (2hr.; ¢480). From the west side of the *parque* buses go to **San Gerardo de Rivas** (1½hr.; 5am; ¢400). Another bus to San Gerardo leaves at 2pm from the main terminal. TRACOPA (☎771 0486) buses go to **San Vito** (3hr.; 5:30am, 2pm; ¢925); **Golfito** (3hr.; 7am, 2pm; ¢850); the **Panamanian border** at **Paso Canoas** (2½hrs.; 7am, 1pm; ¢850). GAFESO (☎771 1523) buses leave for **Buenos Aires** (1¼hrs.; 11 per day 5:15am-5pm; ¢400). Many buses to other villages leave from the terminal on the *mercado's* south side. **Taxis** line the west side of the park. A ride to San Gerardo will cost about ¢6000.

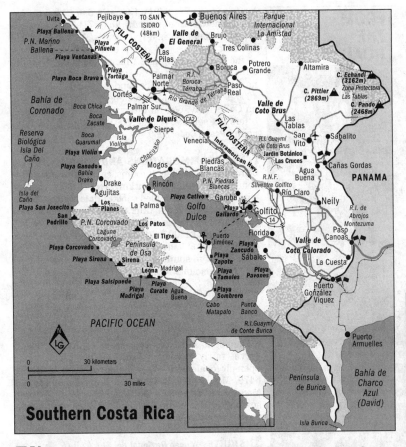

Southern Costa Rica

■ 🛈 **ORIENTATION AND PRACTICAL INFORMATION.** A fair number of streets are marked, but addresses in San Isidro do not include street names. **Avenida Central** and **Calle Central** meet at the northwest corner of the **parque central.** The modern **cathedral** borders the *parque* to the east. For **tourist information,** Ciprotur, on Av. 1/3, Calle 4, offers information about tours and activities in the surrounding area. (☎771 6096; www.ecotourism.co.cr. **Internet** services available for ¢600 per hr. Open M-F 7:30am-5pm.) **Ministerio de Ambiente y Energía (MINAE),** on Av. 2/4, Calle 2, has national park and reservation information. (☎771 4836. Open M-F 8am-4pm.) **Banco Nacional de Costa Rica,** Av. Central, Calle 1, on the northeast corner of the *parque,* changes traveler's checks, gives cash advances on Visa, and has 24hr. **ATM** service for Visa and Visa Plus holders. (☎771 3287. Open M-F 8:30am-3:45pm.) From chicks to machetes to backpacks, you can get it all at the **Mercado Municipal,** between Av. 4/ 6, Calles Central/2. (Public bathrooms available for ¢50. Open M-Sa 6am-5pm, Su 6am-noon.) **Supermercado La Corona** is on Av. 2 between Calle 3 and the Interamerican Hwy. (Open M-Sa 7:30am-8pm, Su 8am-4pm. AmEx/MC/V.) Do your **laundry** at Av. Central/2, Calle 4, across from Hotel Jerusalem. (☎771 4042. ¢400 per kg. Open M-F 8am-5:30pm, Sa 8am-3pm.) Other services include: **police,** 10km outside of San Isidro, near Río San Isidro (☎117); **Red Cross** (emergency ☎911; toll-free 128; ambu-

FROM THE ROAD

RAIN, RAIN COME BACK AGAIN

As a resident of Boston, a city grayed by clouds and rain year-round, I developed an embittered reaction to any sign of a shower, and I am always ready to shoot my umbrella open at the slightest provocation.

My experiences researching in Costa Rica, however, have completely changed my perspective on the ominous graying of skies. At the first stop in my itinerary, the fairly bustling San Isidro, I faithfully carried my umbrella during my 6hr. researching trek through the city streets. I shielded myself against the rain over the duration of the day, only to realize that I still got soaked, by my own sweat. By shying away from the rain, I not only revealed myself as the *gringa* I truly am, but also I missed the only possible respite from the grueling heat.

And after a while, however, it became more than a cure for the heat. The rain here is what every child dreams of. The huge drops really get you soaked in minutes. Yet since it's still warm, it's perfect to go out, uncovered, and just extend your arms and turn your face to the gray skies, as the rain hits your face and refreshingly crawls down, cooling your body. Not to mention the fresh smell of wet earth that inspires your journey.

Now, I have learned to look forward to the afternoon showers in this tropical paradise. My lips curl into a contented smile when I feel the familiar breeze that announces a storm. Needless to say, "dry" is no longer in my vocabulary). Forget sun worshipping—long live the rain!

—Natalia Truszkowska

lance service 771 0481); **Farmacia San Isidro,** on Av. Central across from the *parque* (☎771 1567; open M-Sa 7am-8:30pm, Su 8am-1pm; AmEx/MC/V); **Hospital El Labrador,** the blue and yellow building 5 blocks south of the cathedral on Calle 1 facing the stadium (☎771 0318). **BTC Internet,** on the south side of the *parque* next to Taquería México Lindo, has connections at ¢600 per hr. (Open M-Sa 8am-8pm.) The **post office** is on Calle 1, Av. 6/8, on the way to the hospital, and offers fax service. (Open M-F 8am-5:30pm, Sa 7am-noon.) **Postal Code:** 8000.

ACCOMMODATIONS AND FOOD. Hotel Chirripó ❶ has well-kept rooms, clean showers, a convenient café, and free parking. (☎771 0529. Singles with bath ¢2500; doubles ¢4500.) **Hotel Astoria ❶,** an airy, mint green hotel, offers small singles and good-sized doubles/triples, all with tiled bathrooms. (☎771 0914. Singles ¢1500, with bath ¢2500; doubles ¢2800/¢4000.) **Hotel El Valle ❶,** Calle 2, Av. Central/2, 100m west and 25m south of the *parque's* northwest corner, has spacious rooms, fan, TV, and a lawn chair. (☎771 0246. Singles ¢2000, with bath ¢3100; doubles ¢3700/¢5500.) **Soda Chirripó ❶,** Av. 2, Calle 1, on the southeast corner of the park, serves heaping plates of *casados* (¢500-1200) and has a fast food menu that includes tacos and hot dogs. (☎771 8287. Open M-Sa 6:30am-6pm. AmEx/V.) **La Cascada ❸,** Av. 2, Calle 2, serves fairly expensive but delicious meals in an open-air locale with TVs and cushioned seats. (☎771 6479. Meals ¢800-2950. Open daily 11am-11pm.) **Marisquería Marea Baja ❷,** Calle 1, Av. 4/6. . The best seafood in San Isidro. (☎771 4325. Fish with mushroom sauce ¢1660; seafood soup ¢1353.)

SIGHTS. Museo Regional del Sur, Calle 2, Av. Central/1, hosts three exhibits per year featuring art from southern Costa Rica. (☎771 5274. Open M-F 9am-5pm. Often closed in between exhibits. Free.) The **Fundación para el Desarrollo del Centro Biológico Las Quebradas (FUDEBIOL)** is a reserve in the mountains above the Quebradas River Basin, 7km from downtown San Isidro, which provides visitors with a chance to learn about conservation at Las Quebradas. Hike through bird-filled trails, visit the butterfly garden, and enjoy the lagoon. Students can stay for ¢5000 per night, including breakfast. To get to the reserve, take the bus to Quebradas that leaves from the main bus station (by the market) or in front of Hotel Astoria and get off at the last stop (¢75). Walk 2.5km up to the dirt road, turning right at the FUDEBIOL sign and continuing until the end of the road. (☎771 6096. Admission ¢5000. Open M-F 7am-3pm, Sa-Su 8am-3pm.)

San Isidro

🏠 ACCOMMODATIONS
Hotel Astoria, **1**
Hotel Chirripó, **4**
Hotel El Valle, **2**

🍎 FOOD
La Cascada, **3**
Marisquería Marea Baja, **6**
Soda Chirripó, **5**

COSTA RICA

CHIRRIPÓ AND SAN GERARDO DE RIVAS

A high point of many Costa Rican vacations, Parque Nacional Chirripó is home to the tallest peak in Costa Rica (3820m). From the rocky summit, you can see both the Atlantic and Pacific Oceans. Other days, you may not be able to see farther than the cloud 2ft. in front of you. But it doesn't matter; the hike up the mountain is always beautiful. The world on top of Chirripó is sure to induce chilling goose bumps and awed stares. Of course, you'll need the distraction—the trek up the peak is 20km with some 2400m-elevation gain. The route is very well marked, however, and quite accessible to the average outdoor enthusiast.

SAN GERARDO DE RIVAS

Peaceful San Gerardo de Rivas is the gateway to Parque National Chirripó. It's a place to rest up, eat up, and relax your sore muscles at the nearby hot springs.

📟 **TRANSPORTATION.** The bus from San Isidro will drop you off at the edge of town in front of the ranger station (2km from the trail), or uphill in the center of town. Catch the return bus at the ranger station (1½hr.; 7am, 4pm; ¢1000) or in front of the church 15min. earlier.

📷🛈 **ORIENTATION AND PRACTICAL INFORMATION.** The town stretches along a 1km uphill section of road. A **pulpería** (little food store) across from the soccer field at town center, has the town's only public **phone**—call it to reach anyone in San Gerardo. (☎771 1866. *Pulpería* open daily 6:30am-8pm.) Some travelers get dropped off at the station, check in, and then find a nearby hotel while most others prefer to find a hotel closer to the trail (i.e., in town), stash their gear, and then walk down to check in. Reservations are recommended during the high/dry season (Dec.-Apr.); call the town phone (☎771 1866).

ACCOMMODATIONS. Albergue Urán ❶ is 100m downhill from the trail entrance, with free pick-up available from the ranger station. An attached *soda* offers cheap, hearty food, and the small rooms line a hallway to a clean, collective bathroom. (☎388 2333; www.hoteluran.com. ¢2000 per person; triple with bath US$8 per person.) **Albergue Vista a El Cerro ❶**, the 2nd closest hotel to the trail (1km from Urán), has spotless collective rooms and shared hot-water baths. (☎373 3365. ¢2000 per person.) **Cabinas el Bosque ❶**, across from the ranger station, offers free luggage storage, breakfast, hammocks, and rides to the trail. Rooms delight with sturdy beds and warm blankets. The attached bar/restaurant is open from 10am-midnight. (☎386 2133. Rooms US$7 per person, with bath US$12.)

⚠ PARQUE NACIONAL CHIRRIPÓ

Hikers to the summit almost always stay at Base Crestones. Reservations required and can be made up to a month in advance from the MINAE office in San Isidro. ☎771 4836. Open 8am-4pm. Note that you may be required to pay by wire transfer to secure your reservation. Your first stop in the area should be the ranger station in San Gerardo, where the buses drop you off. There's an admission fee, and the rangers can update you on the latest conditions. Ranger station open daily 6am-5:30pm. Park admission US$15 per person for the first two days, then US$10 for additional days. Camping in designated areas US$5 per person per night. Hostel lodging 4-day max. stay US$10 per person per night.

The hike up Chirripó leaves from San Gerardo de Rivas, with signs pointing to the trailhead beginning at the ranger station 2km below. It is not possible to climb Chirripó in a day. It is a 16km uphill climb to the rugged yet well-equipped **hostel** at the base of the peak, which could take anywhere from 7-16hr., depending on your fitness level. The hostel, commonly known as **Base Crestones,** is a top-of-the-line facility 400m vertical below the summit with beds with mattresses, a phone, limited solar power, and (very cold) showers. It has two hours of electrical light per day (6-8pm). One thing it doesn't have is heat—the temperature at the base can drop to 7°C at night from May-Dec. and as low as 6°C from Jan.-Apr.—plan accordingly. (☎770 8040. Sleeping bags ¢500 per night. Stoves ¢300. Blankets ¢300.)

From Base Crestones it is another 6km with over 500m of altitude to climb to the summit—allow at least 2hr. even if you're fit. You'll need 2-3 days to make it all the way, climbing to the hostel on the first day, ascending the peak, and (possibly) returning to San Gerardo on the second. The last **bus** leaves San Gerardo at 4pm. Besides Crestones, the only other shelter is **Llano Bonito** (8km within the park), which has a roof, sink with potable water, flush toilet, and shower. Spending the night here is only possible with a guide hired from the ranger (US$30). Note that in the dry season, Llano Bonito may be the only **water source** until the hostel.

It's possible to do a day hike in the park and return to San Gerardo. The official park entrance is about 4km from the start of the trail in San Gerardo and the Llano Bonito shelter is the recommended turn-around point. During the dry season you can rent **horses** to carry you or your equipment up. During the rainy season, you can hire porters. (☎771 1866. Horses ¢7500 for 35kg. Porters ¢7500 for 14kg.)

◪ DAYHIKES FROM BASE CRESTONES. The second most popular trail (some say even more impressive than Chirripó itself), **Sendero Crestones** (2.5km one way), crosses the Río Talari in front of the base and ends at **Cerro Terbi** (3760m). An incredibly surreal trail runs through the **Valle de Los Lagos** (Valley of the Lakes), where crystal lagoons reflect the mountains above. Other trails include **Valle de Los Conejos** (Valley of the Rabbits), **Sabana del Los Leones** (The Lion's Savannah), and **Valle de Las Morrenas** (Valley of the Moraines). **Sendero Ventisqueros** (6km) leads to the *cerro* of the same name. All the trails are well marked and take roughly 5-6hr.

🗹 **AN ALTERNATIVE ROUTE.** Another option to the main route up Chirripó, is to take the considerably more challenging two-day hike along a newer trail and tackle the mountain from the opposite side. The trail, **Ruta Herradura,** leaves from the village of Herradura, 3km uphill from the San Gerardo ranger station. **Camping** is permitted in designated areas. Local guides are necessary for this trip and can be found through the rangers in San Gerardo (about US$25 per day, US$20 more if you would like the guide to cook or carry your pack). José Mora (☎ 771 1199), an English-speaking guide who helped build the park's facilities, will cook you hot meals of *gallo pinto* and keep you on the right trail.

BEYOND CHIRRIPÓ

A few other diversions may interest you before or after your climb. One opportunity is the soothing hot springs, **aguas termales,** tucked in the nearby forest. Take the path to the left of the white bridge 50m uphill from the ranger station. Proceed uphill about 600m, follow the trail to the right marked with a painted red tree. Cross the suspension bridge and follow the red marks uphill for 10-15min. Certified **massage therapist** Francene can be found in the conveniently located A-frame cottage right next to Albergue Urán near the trailhead (1hr. full-body massage US$25). Francisco Elizondo of Cabinas El Descanso (see **Accommodations,** above) and his family offer treks through their **Finca El Mirador,** with views of the entire valley and a lesson on coffee harvest and production (4hr., US$5 per person). Marcos Romero Valverde, of Albergue Urán, will take you on **horseback rides** to **waterfalls** or **caves** (¢3500). You can also rent horses from Cabinas El Descanso.

BUENOS AIRES

A close-knit community in the center of a major pineapple-producing region, Buenos Aires is quite a contrast to bustling San Isidro, 64km northwest. The town has few attractions, though tourists often find it a necessary layover on a southernbound bus route. The sleepy town also serves as a base for exploring nearby **Reserva Indígena Boruca** and the underappreciated **Parque Internacional La Amistad.**

The TRACOPA terminal is inside the market, while the Vargas Rojas terminal is right outside the corner of the market. From the TRACOPA terminal, **buses** leave for **San José** (5½hr.; M-Sa 5 per day 6:30am-3:30pm; Su 9:30am, 1:45, 2:45pm; ¢1450). Additional buses leave daily from the Vargas Rojas terminal. (☎ 771 0418; 6:30, 9:30am, 12:30, 3:30pm; ¢870.) Buses leave for **San Isidro** from TRACOPA and GAFESO about every hr. (1¼hr., ¢400). Call a **taxi** (☎ 730 0700 or 730 0800) or hail one from the side of the market. Both of the bus companies in Buenos Aires, TRACOPA and Vargas Rojas, drop off passengers by the market square. From here, the *parque central* Montero and the church sit next to one another, with streets stretching out from the town's center. If you need to get cash, you'll find a **24hr. ATM** for Visa inside the marketplace. The **Banco Popular** faces the marketplace. (Open M-F 9am-3pm, Sa 8:30-noon.) **Supermercado el Sol** is also near the market. (Open M-Sa 7am-8pm, Su 7:00am-noon.) Facing the church, the **police station** lies 50m down the road heading left (☎ 730 0103). The **Red Cross** sits in back of the market square, on the same block (☎ 730 0068). The **hospital** is about 2km out of town walking uphill from the church. (☎ 730 0029.) Every corner of the **market** has public

phones. (Open daily 6am-6pm, Su 6am-noon.) The **post office** is next door to the police station. (Open M-F 7:30am-6pm and Su 7:30am-12pm.)

There are few places to stay here. The best option in town is **Cabinas Violeta ❶**, next to the fire station. The motel-style *cabinas* have rooms with tables, chairs, and bathrooms. (Singles ¢2000; doubles and triples ¢3000.) Farther from the town's center and with slightly musty rooms, **Cabinas Mary ❶** has the basics: fan, bath, and cold water. There's a *soda* attached to the *cabinas*. (☎730 0187. Rooms ¢2000 per person.) **Rancho Azteca ❷** must be reached by taxi (¢300), but is the center of the town's entertainment, and has a varied menu, disco, karaoke, roller skating rink, bar, and super-relaxed wait staff. This impressive restaurant also offers delivery to any place in town for ¢250 extra. (☎730 0162 or 730 0212. *Comida típica* ¢1000-2000) With bamboo furniture, small **Soda El Dorado ❶** stands on the corner of the marketplace closest to the Vargas Rojas terminal. It has good *comida típica*. (*Casados* ¢700. *Bistec* ¢700.)

NEAR BUENOS AIRES

RESERVA INDÍGENA BORUCA

Buses leave Buenos Aires from the TRACOPA station (2hr., 2 per day 11am and 3:30pm, ¢500). Schedules are subject to change.

Twenty kilometers into the mountains south of Buenos Aires lies a welcoming and culturally rich community of indigenous people. Although the Boruca people have long since adopted modern dress and the Spanish language, some traditional customs persist. The one-room museum, **Museo de la Comunidad Indígena,** is in a thatch hut and is open for perusal at any time. If staff is given prior notice, the museum will feature many examples of crafts (both for purchase and display). Doña Marina Lásaro Morales lives next door to the museum and is in charge of the village's group of artisans. She will demonstrate the processes, sell the products, and direct you to the other families with goods for sale. The Boruca people are eager to share their artwork, but highly value the relative isolation of their village. In fact, there is an emerging trend towards preservation of their original history. If you're not traveling in a group, you may make friends with the kind villagers on the bus to Boruca and easily receive an invite to their home. (If staying with a family, it is expected that a guest leave about ¢2000.) Villagers ask that tourists in groups call at least two days ahead to the village's phone so that they may prepare the museum and the *cabinas*. (☎730 1673; 7am-5pm. Rooms ¢2000 per person; ask for Luis.)

SAN VITO

Set in the heart of the breathtaking Coto Brus Valley, refreshing San Vito stands 980m above sea level, providing a bit of a break from the oppressively hot jungles of southern Costa Rica. Marked by warm days and crisp nights, this small, sloping village fuses culture, climate, and breathtaking views. San Vito is a useful base for exploring the Wilson Botanical Gardens or Parque Internacional La Amistad.

▉ TRANSPORTATION. Buses to **San José** (8hr.; 7:30, 10am, 3pm; direct 5am) via San Isidro (4hr., ¢1000) leave from the TRACOPA terminal (☎773 3410), 400m north of the park on the main street. There are additional buses to San Isidro at 6:45am and 1:30pm. To reach **Neily,** take a bus (2hr.; 5:30, 7, 7:30, 9, 11am, 2, 5pm; ¢330) from the Santa Elena/Cepul terminal (☎773 3848), reachable by walking down the main street from the *parque*, taking your first left, and continuing up the hill 250m. Before leaving town, buses stop on the corner across from the museum to pick up passengers—look for the sign.

⊞▐ ORIENTATION AND PRACTICAL INFORMATION. The **parque central** lies in the town's center, where a charming statue of two children under an umbrella stands. The main street is **Calle Dante Alighieri.** Uphill from the park along the main street is the **Centro Cultural** and the road to the Wilson Botanical Gardens and Neily. Downhill, the main street leads to the TRACOPA bus station and post office. San Vito is surrounded by forest, and the main street continues to extend uphill out of the northern edge of town to great views. **Banco Nacional** has two ATMs and will exchange traveler's checks. (☎773 3601. Open M-F 8:30am-3:45pm.) The **Coto Brus** pharmacy has a decent selection. (☎773 3077. Open M-Sa 7:30am-7pm, Su 8am-noon.) The **hospital** (☎773 4125 or 773 4103) is 1km from the park past the Banco de Costa Rica. The **Red Cross** (☎773 3191) is just past the Cepul bus station. Slow **Internet** (by satellite) is available at **Éxitos Video.** (☎773 5029. Open M-Sa 8am-8pm; ¢600 per hour.) The **police** (☎773 3225 or 911 for emergencies) are on the main street next to the **post office** (☎773 3830), with fax. (Open M-F 8am-5:30pm, Sa 7:30am-noon.) **Postal code:** 80257.

▐▐ ACCOMMODATIONS AND FOOD. **Hotel Rino ❷,** 200m north of the park on the main street, has spacious rooms with cable TV, carved bedposts, tiled bathrooms with hot water, and towels. (☎773 4030 or 374 1214. Singles ¢3500, with A/C and king size bed ¢4775; double suite ¢6000. AmEx/MC/V.) **Hotel Colono ❶,** facing the park across from the *centro cultural,* has third floor cabinas with blankets for chilly nights. (☎773 5110. ¢2000 per person; room for 4 with private bath ¢4000.) San Vito doesn't have as many Italian restaurants as you would suspect. **Pizzería Liliana ❶,** up the taxi-lined street on the left, offers two dozen Italian favorites. (☎773 3080. Small cheese pizza ¢1300; pastas ¢1300-1700. Open daily 10am-10pm. V.) For some (relatively) swanky service and *al dente* pasta (¢1000-1300), try the restaurant in **Hotel El Ceibo ❷,** located down a driveway to the left of the main street with your back to the park. (Open daily 6:30-10pm.) In case you're missing *tico* food, there are plenty of tasty *sodas* in San Vito. Buy delicious fresh bread at the nameless Italian-owned bread shop ❶. (☎773 3174. Open M-Sa 5am-8pm, Su 5am-noon.) **Soda Familiar ❶** is a cheap, reliable *soda* on the main street. (Rice dishes ¢850-950. Open M-F 6am-8pm, Su 6am-7pm.)

◨ SIGHTS. The **Centro Cultural Dante Alighieri** is an enjoyable little museum sharing the town's Italian heritage. Black-and-white photos line the walls, and a small room off to the side houses Italian periodicals and reference books that have been sent to San Vito over the years. The center also gives classes in Italian. (Open M-F 1-7pm.) **Finca Cántaros,** 2km outside town, has a landscaped park, children's library, and crafts store. The park is 6 hectares of beautiful trails encircling a bird-filled lagoon. Picnic tables are available. The *finca* also has a splendid view of San Vito. The store sells mostly jewelry and ceramics made by the **Guaymi** (an indigenous tribe 2hr. away). The *finca* can be reached by taxi (¢500) or by any bus headed to the Wilson Botanical Gardens. (☎773 3760. Library and crafts store free. Park ¢300, children ¢150. Open Tu-Sa 9:30am-4pm, Su 9:30am-1pm. AmEx/MC/V.)

NEAR SAN VITO

◪ WILSON BOTANICAL GARDENS

*The gardens are 6km from San Vito. Only buses headed to Neily via Agua Buena head to the gardens; let the driver know you want to stop. The buses leave San Vito's Cepul terminal (10min.; 7, 9am, 2, 5pm; ¢105). Outside the park entrance, buses head back to **San Vito** (10 buses 6:30am-5:15pm). Some people walk or take a taxi (¢900). ☎773 4004; www.ots.ac.cr. Reservations ☎240 6696; reservas@ots.ac.cr. US$6. Open daily 8am-4pm.*

Founded in 1963 by tropical plant-lovers Robert and Catherine Wilson, the botanical gardens' 25 acres overflow with a mind-boggling diversity of plant and bird life. The gardens hold more than 1000 genera in some 200 plant families, along with 320 bird species and 800 species of butterflies. There are over 700 species of palms alone, the second largest collection worldwide. The park is very accessible and has a series of well-done self-guided trails. The **Natural History Trail** is a 2hr. highlight tour featuring violet-colored bananas, colossal bamboo shoots, and the delightful "marimba palm." Specialized trails include the **Palm Tour**, the **Orchid Tour**, the **Hummingbird Tour**, and the **Anthurium Trail**. The spectacular **Río Java Trail** (1.1km) runs through the adjacent secondary rainforest, which is richly populated by mammals. For a closer look, call in advance to arrange a guided tour. (☎773 4004. Half-day US$15; full day US$25; children US$10/15.) Free maps of the hikes are available with the entrance fee. You may also arrange for the more expensive overnight lodging or eat in the garden's dining room with the resident scientists.

PARQUE INTERNACIONAL LA AMISTAD

Parque Internacional La Amistad, founded in 1983, offers a breathtaking array of plants, animals, and gorgeous vistas, but due to its remote location and a lack of publicity, it remains the best-kept secret of Costa Rican ecotourism. The park's, crossing of frontiers accounts for its name, La Amistad, a natural boundary marking the friendship between Costa Rica and Panama. Recently, the park was designated a World Heritage site by UNESCO.

▓ ORIENTATION. The easiest place to begin exploring Parque Internacional La Amistad is the **Estación Altamira**. It's accessible by bus from San Isidro or San Vito. Transportation is complicated, however, and Altamira Station is not a feasible day-trip—it is best to plan on camping overnight. Park admission US$5.

▐ TRANSPORTATION. Unlike more touristed parks, Amistad has no *colectivos* running to its ranger stations. You must rely on infrequent, slow **buses** that run as far as the town of Carmen (6km from Altamira), and then get to Altamira on your own. Road conditions are extremely poor and officials are waiting for repairs before extending any public transportation to Altamira. Calling MINAE in Buenos Aires will help you obtain up-to-date transportation details. Departing from San Vito, head to the TRACOPA station and take the Autotransportes Saenz 10:00am bus to **San José**, getting off at **Las Tablas** (45min., ₡500). A bus runs from Las Tablas to **Carmen** (1hr., 2 per day 1 and 5pm, ₡350). There is also a return bus from Carmen to **Las Tablas** (1hr., 2 per day 5am and 2pm, ₡350.) Another option is to take the GAFESO bus from San Isidro to **Buenos Aires** and then switch to a bus for **Las Tablas**. There is a direct bus to **Las Tablas** from the TRACOPA station in San Isidro (1 per day, 5:30am). From Carmen, the walk is 4km up a winding road to the town of Altamira. Then turn right at the fork in the road after the church (marked by a MINAE sign) and walk 2km up a steeper incline to the ranger station and camping site. The walk is intense, but the views of the nearby valleys are breathtaking.

▐ PRACTICAL INFORMATION. Because there are fewer tourists during the rainy season, you may have **Estación Altamira**, the park station, entirely to yourself; however, it is best to call the **MINAE** office in Buenos Aires to alert them of your arrival. (☎730 0846. Open M-F 8am-4pm.) If you need more information and can't get a hold of the Buenos Aires MINAE office, try the one in San Isidro. (☎771 4836 or 771 5116. Open M-F 8am-4pm.) Estación Altamira does not have a phone of its own, but is in close radio contact with the Buenos Aires office.

⌂ ACCOMMODATIONS AND CAMPING. In Carmen, you can stay at **Soda y Cabinas Carmen de Biolley ❶** and buy limited groceries. (*Casados* ¢950, rice dishes ¢800. *Soda* open daily 6am-9pm. Rooms ¢1500 per person.) **Estación Altamira ❶** is well-equipped for camping, with bathing facilities, potable water, electric outlets, and a picnic area. There is also an exhibition room, an amphitheater, and a biodiversity lab. All facilities are in excellent condition. You'll have to bring your own food and camping equipment, though you can restock in the nearby town of Altamira, 2km down the hill. (Camping US$2 per person.) At any time, reservations are not generally necessary, but be sure to call ahead to the **MINAE** office in Buenos Aires to alert them of your arrival. (☎ 730 0846. Open M-F 8am-4pm.)

⚑ HIKING FROM ESTACIÓN ALTAMIRA. The views from the station itself are gorgeous, but several trails beckon you to explore further. Ask the rangers about the latest conditions. (Guides ¢5000 per day; can be arranged in advance through the ranger station or MINAE.) Most groups are capped at 10 people. You can also hire a local to carry your stuff along the trails. **Sendero Gigantes del Bosque** is a 3hr., 3km hike through secondary and primary forest, named after the trees that tower up to 40m. There is a bird watching observatory at the border of the primary forest along the trail. Wear long pants; the grass is hip-deep on the second half of the route. This 20hr. round-trip journey through the **Sendero Valle del Silencio** is the best known and the most highly recommended. The hike travels more than 20km each way through cloud forest and unique natural *páramo* gardens up to an altitude of 2700m. The trail has a camping area, and 15km from Altamira along the trail is a newly built *albergue*, with 4 rooms and a bath.

▚ PASO CANOAS: BORDER WITH PANAMA

Paso Canoas, the site of immigration offices at the Panamanian and Costa Rican border, is not scenic. It is easy to accidentally wander from one country to another while shopping, but the (fairly) painless passport and tourist card process is absolutely necessary for those advancing further into either country.

To get to the border from the Costa Rican side, take a **bus** to Ciudad Neily, where you can transfer to a bus for Paso Canoas. **Taxis** travel one way between the towns for US$5. Paso Canoas is 50km west of David, with buses linking the two every 10min. Leave comfortably on **LaFron**. (☎ 727 6511. US$1.50.) On either side, TRACOPA (100m west and east of the intersection) sells tickets to David and San José. (☎ 732 2119 or 727 6581. David 7-8hr.; 4, 8am, 3pm; ¢2545. San José 6½hr., 9am, ¢2625.) Even if you have no intention of visiting either city, you have to fork over the cash for this ticket. A plane ticket out of Panama is the only other accepted proof of exit. TRACOPA restaurant next door to the terminal will hold your bags while you sort things out. (¢300 per suitcase, ¢500 overnight.)

The main street, **Calle Central**, runs north-south, with perpendicular **Av. Central** neatly dividing Costa Rica on the west and Panama on the east. Stores on one side of the street use *colones* (¢), while those on the other use *balboas* (i.e. US$). The **Interamericana** from Neily and San José cuts straight through town towards David and Panama City. To leave, go to the Costa Rican **General de Migración**, 175m west of the main intersection. Fill out a worksheet at the *salida* counter and buy a ¢200 passport stamp. (☎ 732 2150. Open daily 7am-8pm.) **Customs** is next door. (Open M-Sa 6am-11pm, Su 6-11am and 1-5pm.) Entering Panama, travelers need a passport, a tourist card (available at the border checkpoint; US$5, lasts 30 days), and a return ticket. Entering Costa Rica has the same requirements. Tourist cards are sold at Instituto Panameño de Turismo on both sides. (Open 6-11am and 1-5pm, but schedule varies.) Both sides have additional checkpoints 1km down the Interamericana. **Money changers** abound. *Bolsijeros* on the Panamanian side, identifiable by the fanny packs slung across their chests, give the best exchange rate, but check the rate before you approach them to avoid getting hustled. The **police** are 50m from either border. (Costa Rica ☎ 732 3402 or 911 for emergencies; Panama ☎ 727 6521.) In Panama, the **Banco Nacional de Panamá** is 25m from the crossing and has a 24hr. ATM for US dollars. (☎ 727 6522. Open M-F 8am-3pm, Sa 9am-noon. MC/V.) Buses drop off in front of the **post office** in Costa Rica. (☎ 732 2029. Open M-F 8am-noon and 1-5:30pm.) There is another post office in Panama. (Open M-F 8-11am and 2-5pm, Sa 8am-noon.) You can find telephones at almost every corner.

Paso Canoas will not leave you hungry or homeless. **Cabinas/Restaurante/Bar Antares ❶**, across the street from TRACOPA, fulfills all basic needs. (☎ 732 21 23. Singles ¢2000; doubles ¢3000. Restaurant open daily 8am-1am.) **Cabinas El Hogar ❶**, next door, has rooms with baths and a courtyard garden. (☎ 732 2653. ¢2000 or US$5 per person.) Expect good, quick meals at the border—but nothing too authentic. In Costa Rica, next to the post office, **Tico Pollo ❶** has clean tables and fast food. (☎ 732 1075. Combo ¢995-2850. Open daily 9am-11pm.) **Supermercado San Isidro** is well-stocked and on the shopping strip.)

PENÍNSULA DE OSA AND GOLFO DULCE

If what you seek is rainforest teeming with monkeys and mysterious beasts, Península de Osa is the place to go. From the wetlands around Sierpe and Bahía Drake, to Parque Nacional Corcovado, nowhere else in Costa Rica will you find such intense and diverse tropical flora and fauna. Bounded only by long, empty beaches, the wilderness seems endless. Puerto Jiménez is the only sizeable city on the peninsula, and the most convenient base for explorations of Corcovado. If the jungle isn't challenge enough, test your surfing skills in Pavones, or sip the milk of a freshly cut coconut and enjoy the sunset on the area's secluded beaches.

SIERPE

Founded about 60 years ago, tiny Sierpe was originally a community of banana plantation farmers. However, the residents of the village now make their livelihoods through fishing, cattle-ranching, and ecotourism. Locals are welcoming and tourist-savvy in this slow-paced, small town. In addition to providing indispensable transit to Bahía Drake, Sierpe boat owners provide numerous tours.

The trip to Sierpe and ultimately, Bahía Drake, is fairly complicated. To get to Sierpe from anywhere in Costa Rica, you must first travel to Palmar Norte. **Buses** leaving Sierpe to Palmar depart across the street from Sonia's Abastecedor (every 2-3hr. 5:30am-5:30pm, ¢200). **Taxis** can be negotiated from the same spot (US$10). The **parque central** and **Bar/Restaurante Las Vegas** on the *parque*'s corner comprise the heart of the tiny village. Doña **Sonia's Abastecedor** (grocery) across from the *parque central* can also help you with bus questions and give advice for travelers to Bahía Drake. (☎/fax 786 7366; elfenix@sol.co.cr. Open M-Sa 6am-6pm, Su 6am-5pm.) The **police** station (☎ 786 7539) is located across the street from Las Vegas. **Phone** calls can be made from a pay phone outside Las Vegas or in the Pulpería Fenix (fax available). **Internet** is available at **El Fenix Dos,** the store next to Sonia's grocery. (US$5 per 30min., US$9 per hr. Open M-Sa 6am-5pm, Su 6am-4pm.)

If you do spend the night here, **Hotel Margarita ❶**, 200m inland from the left side of the *parque central* past the soccer field, is clean with tiled floors and baths, hot water showers, and a furnished patio. (☎ 786 7574. Singles with shared bath US$7; doubles with private bath US$12.) More upscale is **Hotel Oleaje Sereno ❸**, down the street from Las Vegas as you walk away from the park. All rooms have large private baths and hot water. (☎786 7580; fax 786 7111; www.oleajesereno.com. *Soda* open 6am-7pm. Laundry service. Singles US$20-25; doubles US$30-35; A/C US$5 extra.) ▧**Bar/Restaurante Las Vegas ❶** serves everything from salad (¢500-800) to American fast food (¢400-700). The *tico* food here is excellent. (Rice dishes ¢1200; fish dishes ¢1750. Karaoke Sa and every other F 7pm. Open daily 10am-11pm.)

You can also hire tours from Sierpe. **Hotel Oleaje Sereno**'s (see above) English speaking **guide**, Carlos Gonzáles, offers the most possibilities in town. You can go **hiking, bird-watching, horseback riding,** or **scuba diving.** If you do not want to stray too far, Carlos will take you on a tour of the Sierpe Lagoon (US$40) or rent you a **kayak** or **canoe** to discover the area on your own. More extensive trips include lunch; park tours include the entrance fee. **Tours Marítimo,** next door to Las Vegas, features **birdwatching** at dawn (2hr., US$70 per boat) and a **night trip** to see crocodiles, snakes, and night birds (US$70 per boat). They also rent **snorkeling** equipment for US$15 per person per day. (☎786 7591. M-Sa 7am-5pm.)

BAHÍA DRAKE

As the legend goes, Sir Frances Drake buried a treasure somewhere along this luscious coast in the 1570s. Gold, however, is not the priceless treasure you are going to find here. The magic lies in its intense natural beauty, where monkeys drip off mango trees and waves crash on jungle coasts. Bahía Drake is not conducive to budget traveling, but few who travel here regret the expense. The isolation of this town is a main draw, making it one of the only places where you can not only visit undisturbed tropical paradise, but also live amidst the breathtaking nature.

From Sierpe's *parque central*, the dock beside Bar/Restaurante Las Vegas sends a motor-boat down the Río Sierpe to Bahía Drake. (1hr.; US$15 if arranged through a hotel.) Even if you don't have a reservation, make sure to ask several captains and negotiate the price. With some effort, you can often wiggle your way onto another hotel's boat for US$15. Another option is to consult Sonia at the **Pulpería Fenix** (☎786 7311. See **Sierpe,** p. 226). She will know who is taking a boat out and at what times. Enjoy the ride as the boat winds past the legendary **Isla Violines,** where Sir Frances Drake's treasure is said to be buried.

All hotels are along the bay's coast, with farms and uninhabited jungles lying farther inland. **Agujitas,** the main *pueblecito* on Bahía Drake, lies approximately in the center of the bay. Cutting through the town is a small river of the same name. The beach serves as a thoroughfare. **Bar/Restaurant/Soda Las Brisas** lies on the ocean front in Agujitas. To its right along the beach, facing inland, is the church, the *pulpería* **La Amistad** with a radio **phone** for national calls, and the medical clinic **Hospital Clínica Bíblica.**

The following hotels are the least expensive in town, though the average resort cost is three times as much—Bahía Drake's seclusion has its price. All supplies must be brought in by boat from Sierpe and all electricity is either solar- or generator-driven. Food options are mostly limited to hotels and usually included in prices; the **restaurant** in the village is sporadically open and rarely frequented. ▧**El Mirador Lodge ❸,** a 10min. walk from Las Brisas. Facing inland, walk to the left along the beach. At the sign for the lodge, climb up onto the road and walk right where another sign will direct you left and 35m uphill. Mirador offers simple rooms with mosquito netting, private baths, and porches, and many tour options. (☎387 9138. www.mirador.co.cr. US$35 per person, includes 3 meals and laundry. Camping US$5 per person. AmEx/MC/V.) **Poor Man's Paradise ❸,** a 2hr. walk south along the shore past the beautiful beach Playa San Josecito. This resort offers one of the most nature-intensive properties in the area. (☎786 6150; poormans@cheqnet.net. Cabins with private baths and shower US$55 per person; tents with mattresses and outdoor bath US$39 per person. Camping US$7 per person.) **Albergue Jade Mar ❸,** a walk past the *pulpería* and then walk 5min. up the winding road, has 5 spacious, well-kept rooms with private baths. (☎786 7591. US$45 per person, US$35 for students; meals included. V.)

Hotels arrange **horseback riding** (US$40-60), **kayaking** (US$15-40), or trips to the stunning **Isla del Caño National Preserve** (US$70-100), an ancient burial site for the indigenous people of the region. The island also holds a local archaeological mystery—several ancient, near-perfect round stones crowd the land. However, it is best known for outstanding **snorkeling, diving**, and **kayaking.** Hotels also arrange guides into the depths of nearby **Parque Nacional Corcovado.** The cost of guides varies widely but runs at around US$70 per guide and day. It is recommended to enter Corcovado only with a guide from Bahía Drake. The park is more easily accessible from the southern part of the peninsula around Puerto Jiménez (p. 232).

GOLFITO

Golfito (pop. 18,000), home of the former headquarters of the United Fruit Company, sits on the northeast coast of the Golfo Dulce. Drastic regional cutbacks of banana production in 1984 led officials to save the town's economy by establishing a duty-free zone in the northern end of the city. Now, the famous shopping area draws *ticos* year-round and fills hotels on the weekends. For most tourists, it serves as a stopover to the beaches of Pavones, Zancudo, and Cacao, the Golfito Nature Reserve and Puerto Jiménez.

█ TRANSPORTATION

Flights: Sansa (1hr.; high season 6, 10:30am, 2:15pm, return 7:10, 11:40am, 3:25pm; low season 6, 9:30am, 12:30pm, return 7:10, 10:40am, 1:40pm; US$66) and **Travelair** (1hr.; high season 6, 8:30am, 2:30pm, return 7:20, 10am; low season 6, 8:30am, return 7:30, 10am; US$76) fly daily from San José (see **p. 144**) to the airport 4km north of Golfito. The Sansa office is 100m north of the docks.

Buses: Depart from the **TRACOPA** bus terminal (☎789 9037 or 789 9013) to **San Isidro** (4hr., 5am and 1:05pm, ¢1645) and **San José** (6-8hr., 5am and 1pm, ¢2920). Down the main street 100m north of TRACOPA, buses run to **Neily** (1½hr., about every hr. 5:30am-6pm) and the **Panamanian border** at **Paso Canoas,** 17km beyond Neily.

Boats and Ferries: For connections in the high season, plan to arrive early to secure a seat. From the *muellecito* (between Hotel Golfito and Hotel Uno in the *pueblo civil*) a **ferry** runs to **Puerto Jiménez** (1-2hr.; 11:30am; ¢1000 high season). Nearby, a **water boat** service, run by Froilán Lopez (☎775 2166), heads to **Playa Zancudo** (¢5000-7000) and **Pavones.** Similar service and prices can be found about 1km north from the gigantic *muello bananero.* For water boat services, gathering up a group reduces fares. If you are traveling alone, some small talk with the customers at Dave's (see **Accommodations and Food,** below) will probably help you accomplish this.

Taxis: (☎775 0061). Terminal next to the gas station.

█ █ ORIENTATION AND PRACTICAL INFORMATION

Golfito runs along a 5km north-south stretch of beach road, with the gulf to the west. The city is physically and economically divided into two sections. The swankier **Zona Americana** lies near the duty-free zone and airport and takes up everything north of the hospital. It's home to a mix of US retirees and better-off *ticos.* The bus terminal and the Puerto Jiménez ferry dock, called **muellecito** (little dock), along with smaller businesses and *sodas* occupy the shabbier **Pueblo Civil** to the south. Two roads run south from the *muellecito:* one forks uphill, the other stays straight. White buses (¢100) and taxis (¢300) run up and down the length of Golfito between to two areas.

Tourist Office: There is no official tourist office in Golfito, but Dave Corella at **Coconut Café** (see **Food and Entertainment,** below) is a great source of information, as is . **Club Centro** (see **Internet,** below).

Tours: There are no tour offices in Golfito. It is most convenient to hire a tour guide in Puerto Jiménez (p. 232), but if you want to stay in Golfito, adventure day trips are available. Check out the bulletin board at **Coconut Café.**

Bank: Banco Nacional (☎775 1101), 100m north of the bus terminal, changes traveler's checks and gives cash advances. Open M-F 8:30am-3:45pm. **Banco Coopealianza** (☎775 0025) has an **ATM.** Open M-F 8am-5pm, Sa 8am-noon.

Market: Super Granados (☎775 1580), 300m south of the Banco Nacional. Huge grocery store with a large liquor selection. Open M-Sa 7am-7:30pm. AmEx/DC/MC/V.

Laundromat: Lavandería Ilona, near Hotel Delfina on the flat road south of the gas station. ¢600 per kg. Open M-F 8am-5pm, Sa 8am-noon.

Emergency: ☎911.

Police: ☎775 1022, emergency 117.

Hospital: ☎775 1001.

Internet: Club Centro, north of the *pueblo civil,* on the east side of the road just past the green hospital and university, has Internet access. ¢650 per hr., ¢550 for students; ¢1200/¢1000 for 2hr. Open Tu-Su 1:30-8:30pm.

Post Office: (☎775 1911, fax 775 0373), uphill from the dock. Offers **fax.** Open M-F 8am-noon and 1-4:30pm, Sa 8am-noon.

🏠 ACCOMMODATIONS

There are cheap, simple accommodations in and around *pueblo civil.* In the quieter north end, many families take in guests. **Hotel Golfito ❶,** south of the *muellecito,* offers some of the nicest rooms in town with soft beds and A/C. (☎775 0047. ¢3000 per person with fan; doubles with A/C ¢4000.) **Cabinas Mazuren ❶,** 50m north of the soccer field on the high road, offers rooms—all with bath—ranging from singles to family-style quads. (☎775 0058. Laundry service ¢500 per kg. Rooms ¢2000 per person; doubles ¢3000.) **Cabinas El Tucán ❶,** 50m north of the *muellecito* on the right, offers rooms with private baths and fans. (☎735 0553. ¢2000 per person.) **Cabinas Isabel ❶,** farther up the road, offers slightly musty rooms with private baths and fans in a breezy house. (☎775 1774. Singles ¢1500; doubles ¢3000.)

🍽️ 🎵 FOOD AND ENTERTAINMENT

You can grab a meal anywhere along the road between the Banco Nacional and the *muellecito.* There are more *sodas* than anything else, though prices hover consistently between ¢900 and ¢1500 for a full meal. Alternatively, go to **Super Granados,** a large grocery store (see **Orientation and Practical Information,** above). ▓**Coconut Café ❶,** in the pink building across the street from the dock offers homemade pancakes (¢1220) and chocolate cake (¢350). It's a good place to gather info from the bulletin boards and use the **Internet** (¢1000 per hr.) Dave can provide information on **volunteer jobs** and **available paid positions.** (☎775 0518. Open M-Sa 6:30am-10pm, low season M-Th 6:30am-8pm, F-Sa 6:30am-10pm.) **La Eurekita ❶,** across from Cabinas Mazuren. Serves large plates of traditional fare in a breezy locale. (☎775 1524. Delivery available. Fish filet ¢1200. Open 6am-10pm.) **Pollos ❶,** across the street from Cabinas Tucán. For a good dinner and some free entertainment to boot, try Th and Sa nights—a live band will play bolero, salsa, and other Latin music for an excited local crowd in the huge open air beachside place. (☎ 775 2212. Open daily 11am-whenever.) **Restaurante Uno ❶** offers affordable chop suey (☎ 775 0061. Chop suey ¢1000-1500. Open 10am-midnight.)

⚡ OUTDOOR ACTIVITIES

PLAYA DE CACAO. Although Playa de Cacao is easily accessible from Golfito, this beach is hardly ever crowded. The nearby rainforests and calm waters provide a refreshing afternoon respite before more ambitious trips. *(6km north around the bay from Golfito or a 1½hr. walk. Taxis cost about ¢1200. A taxi boat from the muelle bananero can also take you there.)*

REFUGIO NACIONAL DE FAUNA SILVESTRE GOLFITO. Golfito also lies close to lesser-known hiking areas. Refugio Nacional de Fauna Silvestre Golfito (RNFSG) protects the steep, lush hills above Golfito. This forest area, with 125 species of trees, is visible from the entire town, and covers 13 sq. km, starting where the residential areas stop, 500m inland. The main entrance lies just north of the Golfito airport and feeds into the Sendero Naranjal trail. A more popular path begins across from the Samoa Hotel, north of the *muellecito*. A third access point starts from a gravel road 2km south of the town center, past the soccer fields but before Las Gaviotas Hotel, and heads to the radio towers 7km away. As of now, there is no fee to enter the *refugio* and services in the area are limited. Few people **camp** here, but it can be arranged. For more information and reservations, contact the MINAE office in Río Claro. (☎ 789 9092; fax 789 9292; rioclaro@ns.minae.go.cr.)

BEACHES SOUTH OF GOLFITO

◀ PAVONES

*All **buses** pick up in front of the school along the shore. Two buses per day run from Pavones to **Golfito** (2hr.; 5:30am and 12:30pm, return 10am and 3pm; ¢500). The bus heading to Golfito stops in **Conte**, where you may catch a daily 4:30pm bus to **Playa Zancudo** (¢300). On the weekends, an 11:30am bus also runs from Conte to Zancudo.*

Home to one of the longest lefts in the world, Pavones is an essential stop on any true surfer's itinerary. Surfers come here for months at a time (especially during the wet season), and the absence of anything but a spattering of *cabinas* here is a testament to their passion. For the occasional non-surfer who wanders into town, there is more sand and fewer surfers at **Punta Banco**, 5km southeast. The biggest **grocery store** in town, **SuperMares**, is 400m north of Esquinas, inland past the school. (Open M-Sa 6am-6:30pm.) **Public phones** are at Esquinas (¢100 per minute for all calls) and at Soda La Plaza. Across the street from Esquinas is the "Arte Nativo" shop with earrings, hats, posters, and, most importantly, the only **email access** (no Internet) in town from an American's cell phone. (☎ 383 6939; tamello@sol.racsa.co.cr. M-Sa 8am-8pm, ¢500 per 10 min.)

Oceanside **Cabinas Esquina del Mar ❶** in Pavones is a true surfer hangout with a popular *cantina*. Rooms here have a boxy but clean communal bathrooms. Bring a mosquito net. (☎ 383 6737. ¢2000-3000 per person.) Directly across the road is **Hotel Maureen ❶**, with fans and spacious rooms. Communal baths are in mediocre condition, but are not unpleasant. (Singles ¢2000, negotiable for longer stays.) The restaurant downstairs offers a limited selection, but the attached store offers lots of packaged food. (Open daily 3pm-7pm.) **Cabinas Cazolas ❶**, a block from Hotel Maureen on the road perpendicular to the soccer field, offers neat, homey rooms.

(Laundry ¢100 per piece. Check-out 11:30am. Access to family's kitchen. Surfboard rentals US$10 per day. Rooms US$8; with sparkling, tiled bath US$10.)

Fresh thin-crust pizza and pasta made by resident Italians make 🖼Aleri ❶, up the street from Esquina La Plaza, a local hot spot. They also offer *cabinas*. (Pasta ¢1500-2000; 2-3 person pizza ¢3000-4000. Restaurant open daily 6pm-whenever. Shared room ¢2500 per person; single with bath ¢3000.) **Soda La Plaza ❶**, up the soccer field from Maureen, has quick service of the best *tico* food in town. (Open 6am-9pm.) **Puesta del Sol ❶**, 200m past the soccer field (follow the signs) is the tourist favorite. (Homemade tortellini ¢1600. Open 10am-10pm.)

🢀 ZANCUDO

*From Golfito, boats are easiest; a **ferry** leaves from Golfito's muellecito to Zancudo (45min., noon, ¢700). It returns from the town pier, on the estuary side of the school, at 6am. A local boat captain, **Miguel Macarela,** usually departs Golfito at 5am and returns at 1pm (US$2). These schedules are variable—check at the dock ahead of time. During the dry season only, an afternoon **bus** runs between Golfito and Zancudo. Year-round, there's usually a bus from **Neily** and the Panamanian border—in **Conte** just look for it around 4:30pm along the Golfito-Pavones bus route.*

With five kilometers of spotless black-sand beach, top-notch ocean swimming, and world-record sportfishing, Zancudo feels like it should be filled with tourists and have high tourist prices—but that's not the case. This beach town yet to be discovered by foreign travelers. During Christmas and Easter weeks the town swells under an influx of hundreds of *tico* families camping on the beach. The rest of the year, it remains one of the most quiet, relaxing and beautiful beaches.

Located on a peninsula jutting out into the Golfo Dulce, Zancudo is 15km south of Golfito and 10km north of Pavones. The town runs along a 3km beach road; the gulf is to the west and the estuary to the east. On the southern end of the beach, the waves are right for some gentle surfing. Farther north, the beaches attract only bathers. The dock is located on the estuary, 500m before the northern tip of the peninsula. Most businesses have handmade signs, and may be difficult to recognize. During the dry season, a good source of **tourist information** is the gift shop and juice bar **Shangri-La** owned by an American, Sharon. (Open dry season Th-Su 10am-4pm.) For sports **fishing** information, contact **Roy's Zancudo Lodge** (☎776 008) or **Arena Altar** (☎776 0115), but expect high prices. The main *pulpería*, **Bella Vista**, lies in the center of town. (Open daily 7am-1:30pm and 2:30-7pm, but will extend hours during high season.) The **police station** (☎911 or 776 0166) is 100m from the deck, past the school on the road bearing right. One of the town's few **public phones** is located in front. **Coloso del Mar,** 2km south of the docks, offers the only **Internet** service in town. (☎776 0050, minimum ¢400 plus ¢30 per min. or ¢1700 per hr.)

Accommodations are generally divided into two categories: backpacker dives and luxurious, fully equipped cabins. The best backpacker deals are usually attached to a *soda* or bar, and are a few meters from the beach. **Cabinas, Bar y Restaurante Tío Froilan ❶**, in the center of town, offers basic budget rooms with bath and fan to a mostly *tico* clientele. (☎776 0101. ¢2000 per person.) Other backpacker rooms are found in **Bar Sussy ❶**. (☎776 0107. US$5 per person with fan and private bath.) **Soda Katherine ❶** (see below) has clean and comfortable budget rooms with private bath, TV, and fan, but you have to cross the street to get to the beach. (☎776 0124. Doubles ¢5000; triples ¢7000.)

Alberto makes large brick oven pizza at **La Puerta Negra ❷**, as well as pasta. This is a favorite spot of locals and tourists. (*La Totale* pizza with everything ¢2400. Open Tu-Su 6pm until the last customer leaves.) **Maconda ❶**, snug behind a garden decor, following the stone walkway across from Tío Froilan, also offers Italian eats. (☎776 0157. Fettuccini ¢1500. Open roughly from 3pm until last customer leaves.) Next door, **Bar/Restaurante Los Ranchitos ❶** has a thatched roof and open air seating and *tico* food. (*Casado* ¢1500-2000; beer ¢400. Open noon-midnight.)

PUERTO JIMÉNEZ

The backpacker alternative to Bahía Drake, Puerto Jiménez offers far lower prices and more options for collective transportation and tours into the **Parque Nacional Corcovado**. However, the high concentration of passing tourists has stripped the town of its character. The beach is unimpressive, and the town center is well-populated with confused foreigners and numerous stores that cater to them. It's best to stay in Puerto Jiménez as a base for exploring the nearby natural wonders.

▐ TRANSPORTATION

Flights: Sansa (☎735 5017), 300m south and 25m west of the soccer field, and **Travelair** (☎735 5062), 450m south of the southwest corner of the soccer field on Calle Comercial fly daily from San José (see p. 144). Reservations are necessary. Both airlines also arrange **rental cars** and other transportation.

Bus: Departures 100m south of arrival stop. One daily bus to **San José** (9hr., 5am, ¢1950) via **San Isidro** (6hr., ¢1400). 2 buses depart daily for **Neily** (4hr.; 5:30am, 2pm; ¢1000). Getting to Golfito is easiest by ferry, but it's possible to take a Neily bus and transfer at Río Claro.

Boat: 1 ferry daily to **Golfito** (1-2hr.; 6am; ¢1000 high season, ¢800 low season).

Taxi: Osa Natural Tours (see **Guided Tours,** below) offers their own taxi service to various sites in the peninsula. Taxis (trucks or cars) must be arranged ahead of time and hold a maximum of 5 people. Destinations are **Carate** (US$60), **Matapolo** (US$25), **Los Patos** (US$60), **La Palma** (US$40), **Puntarenita** (US$15), **Playa Preciosa** (US$7). All prices per taxi. Accessibility based on season—be sure to call and check.

✴ ▐ ORIENTATION AND PRACTICAL INFORMATION

The **Calle Comercial** (main road) runs from the **soccer field** in the north to a **gas station** in the south. Buses arrive 100m west of the soccer field. The beach road runs just north of the soccer field and heads east to the ferry pier and airstrip. The area around the airstrip is residential and is surrounded by a scattering of small farms.

Tourist Information and **Internet: CafeNet El Sol** (☎735 5718), 200m south of the soccer field on Calle Comercial. This connection to the world wide web connects visitors to good general information about area adventures. Internet ¢500 per 20min., ¢1500 per hr., Open daily 7am-10pm. For specific tour information, see **Guided Tours** below.

Bank: Banco Nacional de Costa Rica (☎735 5155), 400m south of the soccer field. Cashes traveler's checks and has an **ATM** for MC/V. The nearest source of cash for any other cardholder is Golfito. Open M-F 8:30am-3:45pm.

Supermarket: Super 96 (☎735 5168 or 735 5496), 200m south of the soccer field on Calle Comercial. Open M-Sa 6am-noon and 1-7pm, Su 6am-1pm. For mosquito nets or other essentials, try **Tienda el Record,** just south. Open M-Sa 7am-7pm, Su 7am-5pm.

Laundry: Lavandería Kandy (☎735 5347), on the northwest corner of the soccer field. Enter in the space between the buildings. ¢400 per kilo. Open M-Sa 8am-6pm.

Red Cross: (☎735 5109), across from the clinic.

Medical Clinic: (☎735 5061). 10m west of the southwest corner of the soccer field. Open 24hr.

Police: (☎735 5114, emergency 911). A few steps south of the soccer field on the main street.

Telephones: International Communications (☎ 735 5011; fax 735 5480), 200m south of the soccer field on Calle Comercial. International calls ¢1500 per min. **Fax.** Open M-Sa 8am-1pm and 2-8pm.

Post office: on the west side of the soccer field. Open M-F 7:30am-6pm; Sa 7:30am-noon.

Postal code: 8203.

ACCOMMODATIONS

Camping: Puerto Jiménez Yacht Club (☎ 735 5051), near the water at the eastern end of the beach road (and nary a yacht in sight). This place has it all: well water, bathrooms, showers, and immediate access to the beach. ¢1000 per person; a few tents available to rent. Camping on the beach is free. ❶

Cabinas Puerto Jiménez (☎ 735 5090), 50m north of the northwest corner of the soccer field. Delightfully fresh rooms wtih fans, private baths, small tables, and a spot on the gulf's edge. Singles ¢3000; doubles ¢4000. ❶

Cabinas Marcelina (☎ 735 5007; osanatur@sol.racsa.co.cr), 3 blocks south of the soccer field on Calle Comercial on the left, has clean, luxurious, and comfortably sized rooms. All rooms have private baths, and fans. Singles and doubles US$12 per person; triples US$30. Student discounts may be negotiable in the low season. ❷

FOOD

Bar, Restaurante, y Cabinas Carolina (☎ 735 5185), on the Calle Comercial, offers *tico* and American food at high prices. Open daily 7am-10pm. ❶

Soda Marrella (735 5482), 100m down from the dock, is a reliable beachfront soda. Locals enjoy this place for its generous portions and convenient location. Fried fish ¢1200, rice dishes ¢1100, casados ¢900, tacos ¢350. Open daily 11am-8pm. ❶

Juanita's (☎ 735 5056), next to CafeNet El Sol (see **Orientation and Practical Information,** above), has semi-authentic Mexican food. Taco Tuesday (¢200), half price entree Sundays (excluding fish dinners). Most entrees ¢800-1500. Open daily 10:30am-11pm, bar may stay open longer depending on crowd. ❶

GUIDED TOURS

Puerto Jiménez serves as a launching point for the Osa Peninsula, and a number of tour operators have sprung up to cater to this need. Tours are not exactly "budget," but they provide access to places difficult to reach on your own.

Escondidos Trex (☎ 735 5210; osatrex@sol.racsa.co.cr), inside Restaurante Carolina about 150m south of the soccer field on Calle Comercial. Student and group discounts, and generally has fairly flexible prices. Options include dolphin watching, mangrove kayaking, tree-climbing, waterfall rappelling, and multi-day hikes through Corcovado and the surrounding reserves. Best tourist information source in town. Open daily 8am-8pm.

Cacique Tours (☎ 735 5530; cocotero_tico@yahoo.com), next door to the MINAE office. Hikes focused on biological identification and ecosystem education. Approximately $35 per person for 8hr. Student and group discounts. Open 8am-8pm.

MINAE (☎ 736 5036 or 736 5580; fax 735 5276; corcovado@ns.minae.go.cr). Follow the beach road east until it curves inland. Take the 2nd left after the yacht club, and the busy MINAE office is 300m farther on the right. No tours, but some information available. Exhibits or Corcovado shells. Open M-F 8am-4pm.

PARQUE NACIONAL CORCOVADO

Sprawling along almost the entire western coast of the Osa Peninsula, Parque Nacional Corcovado is a virtual garden of Eden. The Peninsula, 57km in length and 25km in width, comprises only 4% of the land mass of Costa Rica, yet, it offers 50% of the biodiversity. Home to sloths, monkeys, anteaters, and almost 400 species of birds, it has earned the National Geographic title as "the most biologically intense place on Earth." Despite its popularity in the last few years, wild Corcovado still waits to be explored; some of the park's vegetation has yet to be even identified.

✥ ORIENTATION. There are four **ranger stations** inside the park boundaries, each of which has water, bathrooms, dining facilities, and campgrounds. Three of these form a triangle connected by year-round trails—**Sirena** on the southwest tip, **La Leona** on the southeast tip, and **Los Patos** to the north between them. Sirena and La Leona are the only stations with beds. **San Pedrillo,** on the northwest tip of the park, is accessible along the beach from Sirena only from December 1 to April 31. Seldom used by through-hikers, **El Tigre** is the 5th station, located outside of and detached from the park boundaries. **Los Planes,** a station in the northwest of the park, has been closed. Los Patos and La Leona are best reached from Puerto Jiménez; San Pedrillo is accessible from Bahía Drake.

▟ TRANSPORTATION. Puerto Jiménez (p. 232) is the town on the peninsula that offers the most affordable and accessible transportation into the thickets of the national park. Most independent hikers choose this town as their base for exploring the park. To get to the ranger station at **La Leona,** take the *colectivo* truck or **minibus** from Puerto Jiménez to **Carate** (2hr.; M-Sa 6am and 1:30pm, return 8am and 4pm; ¢2000), which leaves in front of Mercado El Tigre on Calle Comercial, south of the soccer field. From Carate, turn right onto the beach and walk about an hour to the park entrance at La Leona. In the dry season it may be possible to take a **taxi** from Puerto Jiménez (2hr., US$60) or a taxi tractor from the town of La Palma to **Los Patos** station (2½hr., US$50-70). From **Bahía Drake** (p. 227), the only way to get to the eastern and southern parts of the peninsula is by car or boat. Roads are very rough and often require passing through creeks. Boats, on the other hand, are very expensive. To reach the ranger station at **San Pedrillo** from Bahía Drake, either hike 18km (8-9hr.) along a trail that hugs the beach, or hire a boat from one of the Drake hotels (See **Bahía Drake: Outdoor Activities,** p. 228.) It may be necessary to take a boat when water levels are high; contact MINAE for more information. Osa Natural runs a *colectivo* on Tu during the dry season to Bahía Drake from Puerto Jiménez; call in advance to make reservations (US$20 per person).

▞ PRACTICAL INFORMATION. The park has an entrance fee. (US$8 for 1 day, US$17 for 2-3 days, US$26 for 4-6 days.) Because there are restrictions on the number of people in the park at a time, **Proyecto Osa Natural,** which handles the tourist traffic, strongly recommends making reservations one to two weeks in advance. This involves planning and faxing an itinerary to Osa Natural; call them directly for instructions and information (US$2 reservation fee). The MINAE office in Puerto Jiménez answers specific questions on the park. (For Osa Natural and MINAE contact info see **Puerto Jiménez: Guided Tours,** p. 233.)

▟ ACCOMMODATIONS & CAMPING. Most overnight trekkers hike between La Leona and Los Patos, spending the night at Sirena en route, or some other combination within that triangle. Rangers arrange lodging options and meals. (Breakfast ¢1500. Lunch and dinner ¢2500. Dorm beds US$8 high season; bring sheets and mosquito net. **Camping** US$4; only allowed inside the station.) However, at the time of writing, the ranger station at La Leona was being remodeled and fumigated and didn't offer food or lodging; check in advance whether they have reopened.

There are two other inexpensive options along the beach before the ranger station La Leona. **La Leona Lodge Camping ❷** has 12 tents with small air mattresses, sheets, and towels at no extra cost. (☎735 5705; www.laleonalodge.com. High season US$15 per person, low US$10; US$5 with own tent, US$2.50 if meals bought at lodge.) At **Corcovado Lodge ❸** you can stay in large tents with real bed frames and mattresses. (☎257 0766 office in San José US$30 per double tent.) Both camping areas are along the beach on the route to La Leona ranger station.

🖪 **HIKING.** In addition to a tide chart, guides are recommended for attempting the three major long-distance hikes inside the park. The first trail, from **La Leona** to **Sirena** (20km; 6-7hr.) is along a sandy beach. The second hike, from **Los Patos** to **Sirena** (20km; 6-8hr.), cuts right through the middle of the rainforest and is especially difficult in the rainy season, particularly the crossing of the Río Pavo. The third trail, from **Sirena** to **San Pedrillo,** is only open from Dec. 1 to May 1. It hugs the beach and ends in the forest. (25km; 8-10hr.) This is one of the most dangerous hikes because it offers little shelter from the sun. **Use proper caution and hydration.**

Shorter **day hikes** are possible from Sirena, Los Patos, La Leona, and San Pedrillo. Behind the San Pedrillo station, the short **Sendero Catarata,** on the right with your back to the sea, loops near a waterfall. **Sendero Río Pargo** begins across the Río San Pedrillo, which runs along the station. **Sendero Playa Llorona** is a 6hr. round-trip, and much of it runs along the coast.

CARIBBEAN LOWLANDS

The boggy coastal lowlands along Costa Rica's Caribbean shore contrast drastically with the Pacific seaboard. Here, coconut palms, unbroken sandy beaches, and inland tidal marshes—all kept unfathomably muggy by constant precipitation—line the relatively deserted and remote Caribbean coast. Limón, or Puerto Limón, Costa Rica's Atlantic port, serves as a hub for tourists traveling to the fantastic Tortuguero, Cahuita's coral reefs, and the placid Puerto Viejo de Talamanca. With a younger, more laidback feel, the southern Caribbean is a particularly popular for young backpackers, while the difficult-to-reach northern corners invite dozens of turtle conservation volunteers and nature enthusiasts.

PUERTO LIMÓN

Though this Caribbean city is vital for transportation and financial services, it also offers a great selection for shoppers. Surprisingly perfect rows of towering palms line the beautiful Parque Vargas. Limón is also a convenient launching point for vacations to **Tortuguero, Playa Bonita** (4km northwest), and other Caribbean towns. At night, taxis are advisable; the city has a bad reputation (many feel undeserved) for crime. The annual October 12 carnival celebrating Día de la Raza (Columbus Day), now officially named *Día de las Culturas*, especially calls for attention, as music, dancing, and drinking spill out into the streets for almost a week.

🖪 **TRANSPORTATION.** Travelair (☎232 7883) and Sansa (☎666 0306) have **flights** to San José. The airstrip, reachable by taxi, is 4km south of town. Auto Transport Caribeños and Prosersa **buses** (☎222 0610 in San José, 758 0385 or 758 2575 in Limón) leave from the new spic-and-span station **Gran Terminal del Caribe,** Calle 7, Ave 1/2, and go to **Guápiles** (100min., every hr. 6am-6pm, ₡745); **Moín,** the departure point for Tortuguero (1½hr., every hr. 6am-7pm, ₡80); **San José** (2½-3hr.; 16 per day 6am-7pm, Su 8pm; ₡1095); and **Siquirres** (1hr., every hr. 6am-7pm, ₡400). The smaller Coope Limón (☎798 0825), across the street from the Gran Terminal, south of the market, has 10 buses that leave for **San José** (2½-3hr., daily 5:30am-4pm, ₡890). Buses depart from the MEPE station (☎758 1572 or 758 3522) on the corner, one block north of the northeast side of the market, to **Manzanillo** (2½hr.;

6am, 2:30, 6pm; ¢680); the **Panamanian Border at Sixaola** (3hr., 9 per day 5am-6pm, ¢500); and **Puerto Viejo de Talamanca** (1½hr., 7 per day 5am-6pm, ¢500) via **Cahuita** (45min., ¢335). All the Sixaola buses pass through **Bribrí** (additional buses at 9, 10am, 1pm; ¢610). **Taxis** line Av. 2 and patrol the city. A taxi to **Moín** costs ¢1000.

ORIENTATION AND PRACTICAL INFORMATION. Finding street signs in Limón is nearly impossible. Orient yourself by the **mercado municipal,** Av. 2/3, Calle 3/4, where buses drop off their passengers. All hotels and restaurants are within a few blocks of here. For tourist services, go to the **Caribbean Tour Center and Store,** in the Gran Terminal. (☎ 798 0816. Open daily 7:30am-7:30pm. AmEx/MC/V.) **Banco Nacional,** at the southeast corner of the market, exchanges US dollars and traveler's checks (1% commission) and offers cash advances for Visa holders. (☎758 0094. Open M-F 8:30am-3:45pm.) For groceries, try the **Mercado Municipal,** in the center of town 300m west of the beach, or supermarket **Más X Menos,** on the northeast corner of the market (☎798 1792; open M-Sa 8am-9pm, Su 8am-8pm; AmEx/MC/V). Other services include: **Police,** 100m east of the northeast corner of the market (☎758 0365, emergency 911); **Red Cross,** one block south of the southeast corner of the market (☎758 0125 or 911; english spoken; open 24hr.); **Farmacia Buenos Aires,** 25m east of the southeast corner of the market (☎798 4732; open M-Sa 8am-7pm); and **Hospital Tony Facio,** 300m north along the boardwalk (☎758 2222). You can find **phones** on the northern side of the *mercado municipal.* For **Internet**

Puerto Limón

🏠 ACCOMMODATIONS
Hotel Continental, **1**
Hotel Miami, **7**
Hotel Tete, **4**

🍴 & 🍺 FOOD & NIGHTLIFE
Bar Acuarius, **3**
Pizzería Roma, **2**
Restaurant Doña Toda, **5**
Restaurante Mares, **6**

access, try **Cyber Cafe Interurbano,** on the 2nd floor across from the northern side of the market. (US$1 per hr. Open daily 24hr.) The **post office** is southwest of the market. (Open M-F 8am-5:30pm, Sa 8am-noon.) **Postal code:** 7300.

📕 ACCOMMODATIONS. Be cautious of ultra-cheap places; they usually don't have strong locks. Accommodations in general are well priced and comfortable. **Hotel Continental ❶** (☎ 798 0532) and **Hotel Internacional ❶** (☎ 758 0434), are on the right 2 blocks north of the northeast corner of the *mercado.* Both are 25m from the beach. Clean rooms have fans and baths. (Singles ¢2500, with A/C ¢3000; doubles ¢3600/¢4600.) **Hotel Miami ❷,** ½ block west of the southwest corner of the market, offers clean rooms with fans and hot-water baths. Other rooms come with A/C, and TV. (☎ 758 0490. Singles ¢5200-6800; doubles ¢5200-8700. AmEx/MC/V.) **Hotel Tete ❷,** 25m west of the northwest corner of the *mercado,* has a balcony, couches, daily paper, and a big TV. Comfortable beds have sparkling private baths with hot water. (☎ 758 1122. Singles ¢4000; doubles ¢7500; add ¢700 for A/C.)

📗📱 FOOD AND ENTERTAINMENT. Limón's usual grub combines standard fare with a Caribbean twist. One of the best places in town, however, is the delightful Italian restaurant **Pizzería Roma ❶,** on Av. 4 Calles 1/3, which has it all: breezy ocean views, a brick-oven kitchen, and mouthwatering pizza and pasta. (☎ 798 4305. Pizzas ¢1000-3800. Open Tu-Su 11:30am-midnight.) **Restaurante Mares ❷,** across the street from the south side of the *mercado,* has great seafood, though it's a little pricey. (☎758 4713. Vegetable and peanut shrimp ¢3200. Open daily 8am-2am. MC/V.) **Restaurante Doña Toda ❶,** on the east side of the *mercado*, offers full meal of fantastic *casado* for only ¢800. (Open M-Sa 6:30am-7pm.)

Women traveling alone at night should be cautious. **Bar Acuarius,** a dance club in the Hotel Acón, across the street from the northeast corner of the market, pounds reggae and *salsa* rhythms late into the night. (☎758 1010. Th-Sa cover ¢500; women free and 2x1 drinks Sa 8pm-midnight. Open daily 7pm-4 or 5am.)

◙ **SIGHTS.** While the **mercado municipal** seems calmer and more organized than most central *mercados*, it's still pickpocket territory. Vendors proudly display typical Caribbean fare: fresh coconuts, bananas, fish, and lobster. The market is open from dawn to dusk, though numerous *sodas* within often stay open later. **Parque Vargas,** in the southeast corner of town, is a gorgeous refuge from the town's bustling center. To get to the *parque,* head two blocks east from the southeastern corner of the *mercado* toward the dense, towering coconut palms. Make sure to check out the impressive **seaside mural** by artist Guadalupe Alvarea. On a clear day, the **Isla de Uvita,** 1km away, is visible from a *mirador* in the southwest edge of the park. The tiny **Museo Etnohistórico de Limón,** on the second floor of the post office, provides a perfect, quick introduction to the region's diverse cultural heritage. (Open M-F 9am-noon and 1-4pm. Free.) A young crowd looking for waves and rays usually heads over to **Playa Bonita,** 4km northwest of Limón. On one side, the water is calm and perfect for wading; on the other, powerful waves crash on the beach. As a result, surfers and swimmers live their afternoons in perfect harmony. To get to Playa Bonita, take the Moín bus from the Gran Terminal del Caribe (every hr. 6am-7pm, ¢50). Buy a ticket at the window and get off at one of the first stops (just ask the driver). You can also take a taxi (¢600-800).

PARQUE NACIONAL TORTUGUERO

Sheltering the most important nesting site for marine turtles in the entire Western Hemisphere, Parque Nacional Tortuguero, 84km north of Limón, encompasses 261.5 sq. km of coastal territory and 501 sq. km of marine territory and is almost exclusively accessible and navigable by boat. What has brought the park international fame and thousands of visitors year after year is its 35km beach, where thousands of turtles return every year to lay their eggs. Not content to surrender the show, howler monkeys echo in the treetops, rainbow-beaked toucans coast overhead, and leathery caimans glide stealthily through the canals intermingling with the park's swampy land areas. The village of Tortuguero, is the gateway to the park's entrance at the Cuatro Esquinas ranger station. Those who make the long and rather complicated journey will be rewarded by laid-back living and a one-of-a-kind opportunity to learn about some of the world's most fascinating animals.

TORTUGUERO VILLAGE

The village of Tortuguero has only around 700 residents, is drenched by an average yearly rainfall of 5-6m, and is accessible only by boat, yet it remains one of Costa Rica's most popular destinations. Flanked to the west by wide, glistening canals and to the east by foamy, copper-tinted Caribbean waves, the slender strip of land on which this village lies is just a few meters north of beautiful Parque Nacional Tortuguero. And if the fantastic scenery and wildlife aren't enough to hold your interest, Tortuguero's diverse population of native *ticos*, Nicaraguans, Afro-Caribs, and foreigners from all over the world mix to create a remarkably unified and unique culture anchored around the town's singular business of eco-tourism. Conservation awareness is especially encouraged here, and everyone you meet will be eager to share with you anything they can to make your stay and experience as ideal as possible. Tortuguero may be one of the few places in Costa Rica where you'll truly be an eco-tourist, learning about serious environmental problems while simultaneously actively helping to solve them.

▐ TRANSPORTATION

BY PLANE. Flying from San José to the airstrip, a few kilometers north of Tortuguero village, is faster and much more convenient than a lengthy bus-boat combo, but it's also more expensive. **Sansa** departs from Juan Santa María International Airport in Alajuela (☎221 9414; www.flysansa.com; 35min., 1 per day 6am, US$55; see **San José: Flights** p. 144); **Travelair** departs from Tobías Bolaños Airport in Pavas (☎220 3054 or 888-535-8832 in US for reservation; www.centralamerica.com/cr/tran/travlair.htm; 35min., 1 per day 6:15am, US$60; see **San José: Flights** p. 144).

VIA MOÍN. If you're traveling independently, the best-known route—from the Southern Caribbean coast via the port town of Moín—is the most scenic, but not the cheapest. Some backpackers prefer this route in spite of its cost because it practically guarantees crocodile, bird, and monkey spottings. Visitors get a good taste of the park before they even arrive, with the relaxed trip through the Tortuguero canals. From **San José**, take a **bus** from Terminal Caribe to **Limón** (2½hr., every hr. 5:30am-7pm, ¢1005) and from Limón, catch a bus to **Moín** (30min., every 30min. 6am-6pm, ¢75). *Lanchas* (small boats) depart early in the morning (8-10am, but try to arrive no later than 8:30am) for Tortuguero from Moín's small dock, behind Restaurante Papa Manuel. The *lancha* trip is 3-5hr. through canals teeming with wildlife (US$30 one-way, US$50 round-trip); it's best to arrange in advance. Large groups make for cheaper rides; if you're traveling alone, a tour guide might request up to US$180 for the trip. Arrive early to buddy up with other travelers. If you arrive in Moín too late and must spend the night, try **Cabinas Chitas ❶.** Stay on the bus coming from Limón, past the docks over a bridge, until you see the sign on the right side of the road. Every room comes with a private bath, comfy double beds, and a porch with lounging chairs. (☎798 3116. Doubles ¢2500.)

VIA CARIARI. A much cheaper route from **San José** to Tortuguero is to head to El Caribe Bus Terminal (☎221 2596) and take a direct **bus** to **Cariari** (2hr., 6:30 and 9am, ¢720). The cheapest route from Cariari is to catch the bus to **Pavona** (2pm, ¢1000) from the old bus station. From Pavona, Captain Juan Castro runs a **boat** to **Tortuguero** (4pm, ¢1000). The more traditional route from Cariari is to catch the bus to La Geest-Casa Verde (noon, ¢500), staying on until the end of the line in La Geest. A *lancha* to Tortuguero meets the bus at the river's edge at 1:30pm; most locals pay ¢1500, though tourists are charged US$8 or US$10 (2hr.). Two different captains make the trip from La Geest to Tortuguero: **Rubén Bananero** (☎382 6941 or 363 1681) and **Juan Torres** (pager ☎233 3030, #5489), who offers great tours at lower prices. Three **boats** leave daily from the main docks for **La Geest.** Bananero's boats leave at 7 and 11am, and Juan Torres' boat leaves at 7am. Juan Castro's boat leaves for **Pavona** at 6am daily. It's recommended to make reservations for all traveling arrangements the day before at Restaurante El Muellecito (opposite the dock) or with Juan Torres himself for the cheaper ticket. The connecting **bus** leaves for **Cariari** from La Geest at 9:30am (ask for hours from Pavona), and buses to **San José** leave Cariari at 11am and 1pm.

VIA GUIDED TOURS. Ecole Travel (☎223 2240; www.travelcostarica.net; see **San José: Practical Information** p. 147), offers two-day/one-night tours (US$95) and three-day/two-night tours (US$125) including transport from Moín, tours, and lodging at El Manatí Lodge. Operators in Cahuita (see **Guided Tours,** p. 244), and Puerto Viejo (see **Guided Tours,** p. 246) offer similar tours. **Fran** and **Modesto Wat-**

son's well-organized tours on their riverboat Francesca are highly recommended. Most include round-trip transportation from San José to Moín in a van and from Moín to Tortuguero in the Watsons' boat. They also include two-day/one-night lodging at the Laguna Lodge, five hearty meals, a canal boat tour, a guided turtle tour, a visit to Caribbean Conservation Center, and park entrance fees. (US$175-190 per person.) The Watsons can also arrange customized tours for cheaper budgets and travelers who chose to arrive in Tortuguero on their own. (☎226 0986.)

■ ▮ **ORIENTATION AND PRACTICAL INFORMATION.** The main village of Tortuguero is only about 500m long, with sandy gravel paths winding their way to the building scattered all about. The **airstrip** is a few kilometers north of town and is accessible only by boat. Most travelers arrive at the *lancha* dock, in the center of town. From the docks, with your back to the water, north is to your left, and south is to your right. The **main path** runs from the Caribbean Conservation Center at the far north end of the village, past the docks, all the way to the **ranger station** at the park entrance, at the far south end of town. Frequent blackouts in the rainy season make bringing a flashlight a must. For **tourist information,** check out the **kiosk,** north of the soccer field, which offers information on park activities and the turtle history. The humble guru of information in Tortuguero is **Daryl Loth** (☎392 3201; http://tortuguero_s.tripod.com), who runs ▯**Tortuguero Safaris Information Center,** 100m north of the docks, opposite the church. If the center is not open, knock on the yellow house next door. There are no **banks** in Tortuguero Village, but **Souvenirs Paraíso Tropical,** 200m north of the docks, exchanges traveler's checks *if* they have the cash. Stock up on colones before you arrive. (Open daily 8am-9pm.) For grocery shopping, head to **Super Morpho,** directly opposite the docks (open daily 7am-10pm). Other services include: **police,** in the blue building 75m north of the dock (emergency ☎117); a **doctor** can be reached at the south end of town in the central headquarters of the park service; for a serious **medical emergency,** The Jungle Shop (☎391 3483) can call a doctor in Limón. You can find **phones** at Miss Junie's (see **Accommodations,** below) and at the Super Morpho in front of the docks. (Local calls ¢20 per min. International calls with calling card only. ¢200 flat rate for connection.) The **post office** is a few meters up a side path south of Daryl's house. (Open M-F 8:30am-noon and 1-5pm.)

▮ **ACCOMMODATIONS.** All the ritzy, expensive hotels, catering mostly to organized tours, are across the canal and accessible almost exclusively by boat. In Tortuguero Village, lodging is strictly budget and minutes from the park entrance, beach, and restaurants. Camping is not allowed on the beach, but backpackers can pitch tents for US$2 at the ranger station at the southern end of town. In **Tortuguero Village, Cabinas Aracari ❶,** from the docks, south on the main path and then left 150m on the path just past the Centro Turístico La Culebra, has clean rooms with tile floors and private cold-water showers, fans, droopy beds, and porches. (Singles, doubles, and triples ¢2000 per person.) **Casa Marbella ❸,** the yellow house next door to Daryl's place, has comfortable cabins with high ceilings, soft beds, and hot water. (☎392 3201. Singles US$25; doubles US$35.) On the **canals, El Manatí ❸** is the most budget of canal lodges. Simple *cabinas* have fans and private hot-water baths.. (☎373 0330. Singles US$30); doubles US$40; triples US$50.

▯ **FOOD.** For such a small village, Tortuguero has a number of good places to eat and a variety of cuisines from which to choose. ▯**La Casona ❷,** on the soccer field, has delicious banana pancakes (¢1000) and heart of palm lasagna. (Open daily 6am-10pm.) ▯**Miss Junie's ❷,** 200m north of the docks on the main path, cooks whatever is caught that day and adds a Caribbean touch. (Breakfast ¢1000; lunch and dinner ¢2700. Open daily 7am-9pm.) **Miss Miriam's ❶,** on the soccer field, is another Caribbean wonder with uniquely flavored meals. (Breakfasts ₡1000; *casados* with rice and beans cooked in coconut milk ₡1100. Open daily 6am-9pm.)

◘ **SIGHTS.** Before going on a run to see the turtles, check out the non-profit ▨**Caribbean Conservation Corporation Natural History Visitors Center (CCC)** at the north end of town. Follow the small dirt path that jets beach-side, toward the right, for about 1km past the docks. The Center is a must-see for anyone wishing to learn about the difficult plight of the severely endangered marine turtles. A 16min. video in Spanish or English documents the history of the pressures on the sea turtle population caused by habitat destruction and poaching and tells the story of CCC founder Archie Carr's efforts to monitor the Tortuguero turtles, starting in the 1950s. Over 50 years later, the CCC has continued Carr's work and has tagged nearly 50,000 turtles, making it the world's largest green turtle tagging program of its kind. Visitors can "adopt" a turtle giving a donation of US$25 and, in turn, receive an adoption certificate, photograph, turtle fact sheet, and promise of receipt of information about the tagged turtle when it is found. (☎710 0547; www.cccturtle.org. Open M-Sa 10am-noon and 2-5:30pm, Su 2-5pm. ₡350.)

PARQUE NACIONAL TORTUGUERO

*The area that can be seen without a guide or a boat is limited. The park headquarters is at the **Cuatro Esquinas Ranger Station,** at the park's north end. To reach the station from the village, follow the main path to the south, walking through locals' yards and over a makeshift bridge, where you'll see a sign indicating that you have reached the park. The ranger station has maps (₡200), information on the park's wildlife and vegetation, and preserved turtles and turtle eggs on display. It is possible to **camp** at Cuatro Esquinas, but expect very squishy grounds. (US$2 per person, includes access to cold-water baths.) The less-frequented and less-accessible **Jalova Ranger Station** sits on the canal at the park's south end. Both park entrances open daily 6am-6pm. US$7, combination 3-day ticket for Tortuguero and Parque Nacional Barra del Colorado US$10.*

The park's claim to fame is its incredible knack for attracting multitudes of hard-shelled marine reptiles, which outdate the prehistoric dinosaurs. Tortuguero is the largest and most important turtle nesting site in the western hemisphere. Indigenous peoples thought the turtles were drawn to the black sand Caribbean beaches by nearby Tortuguero Mountain. Scientists now believe the chemical qualities of the sand and sea may contribute to some kind of imprinting. The most famous turtles are the *tortugas verdes*, which nest from the end of June through September. Three other species also nest in the park—leatherbacks (Mar.-July), hawksbills (May-Sept.), and loggerheads (June-Oct.). They now face extinction due to the oceanic jetsam that suffocates their nests, the increased beachfront development which hinders the hatchlings' return to the sea, and the poachers who steal the newly-laid eggs. In 1954, Dr. Archie Carr founded the **Caribbean Conservation Corporation** (see **Sights,** above), based 1km north of Tortuguero village, to help bring the sea turtles into the international limelight. In 1970, the Costa Rican government declared this 35km strip a national park. Today, researchers tag turtles and use satellite tracking to determine patterns of birth dates, routes, travel tendencies, in an attempt to uncover once and for all the mystery behind the tenacity of those forever-returning females. Tagging turtles has revealed absolutely amazing information about their migratory and mating habits; one turtle tagged near Tortuguero was found just one month later on the coast of Senegal, Africa, and several reports show that female turtles, after visiting hundreds of beaches around the world, return to their exact same birth site to nest 30 years later.

▨ **ACTIVITIES IN THE PARK.** Starting from the **Cuatro Esquinas ranger station,** at the park's entrance, **Sendero El Gavilán** (1hr., 2km) is not a difficult hike but can be very muddy. The trail winds through the forest and ends on the beach, where you

COSTA RICA

TOUR SMART. Some companies in the area have been known to tell unaware travelers that they can only patronize certain hotels and restaurants (from which they receive a fat commission). Some locales see incredibly good business, while others lose money due to the unfair practices of the guides. Other guides have been known to sub-contract out to dirt-cheap guides with little naturalist training that speak poor English. *Let's Go* encourages you to compare establishments before making your choices and try to visit several different businesses during your stay in Tortuguero.

can wash off and then take a left and walk back to town. **Sendero Tucán** (1.4km), runs alongside the Caño Negro Waterway. The trail starts at the **Jalova ranger station,** about 15min. from the village of Parismina by motor boat. Parismina itself is 1hr. away by canal. You will have to hire a guide to take you there (see below), but most guides and locals say that the price of the boat ride is not worth the dearth of activities at Jalova. Two other very simple mini-trails (600m) are also quite enjoyable. **La Ranita Roja** makes a semicircle around Caño Harol, while **Tragón** follows a straight, short path. Daryl also rents out **kayaks** that you can use to explore the canals yourself (US$10 for half-day; proceeds benefit Tortuguero high school).

 TURTLE WATCHING. The park's feature presentation is the nightly *deshove*, the time when turtles come to lay their eggs. The intriguing process takes about two hours. From July to October, visitors *must* be with a guide certified by the national park (ask to see a license). Even at other times, don't try to watch the *deshove* unguided; the beaches are dangerous at night due to unexpected waves and vast quantities of driftwood. There's a strategy to watching the great *deshove:* if you've already paid park admission for the day, it's best to go back to the park at night instead of the public beach. Here, there are fewer crowds and more turtles. Turtle tours leave nightly at 8 and 10pm (US$10 per person).

Talk to any of the guides mentioned below to set up a tour. Otherwise, show up (daily 5-6pm) at the Cuatro Esquinas Ranger Station, where local guides await, and obtain the necessary permission slips. Wear good walking shoes and dark clothing. Don't bring a flashlight or camera—bright lights blind the turtles and hinder their return to the sea. Official park rules state that once a tour group has seen the egg-laying process, they must get off the beach, regardless of whether or not the two hours have elapsed..

 ECO-FRIENDLY TOURS. Official park rules require boats to switch from gas to electric motors, which do not disturb the animals as much as the loud gas engines. Tour boats should glide along the canals extremely slowly to avoid disrupting animal and insect life on the shores. As an informed and eco-sensitive tourist, ask non-rule-abiding guides to slow down and keep it quiet.

 GUIDED TOURS. Entirely enveloped by water, Tortuguero is best explored by canoe or motorboat. Although it's possible to go alone, hiring a guide is much more informative and fun. Daryl from **Tortuguero Safaris Information Center** is a fantastic guide, and his boat has an electric motor that is ecologically friendly and quiet. (US$5 per hr. per person; you can design your own tour.) **Bárbara** (beeper ☎ 223 3030, dial 3761; tinamon@racsa.co.cr; www.tinamontours.de), in the purple house 100m past Cabinas Tortuguero, is a German biologist who owns **Tinamon Tours** and leads canoe, hiking, and village tours in English, Spanish, French, and German. She prefers small groups (4-5 people) and rents her canoes from older villagers who have few sources of income (all tours US$5 per hr. per person).

CERRO TORTUGUERO AND CAÑO PALMA BIOLOGICAL STATION. The flora-and fauna-filled thrills of Tortuguero can be matched at the Caño Palma Biological Station and its surrounding canals in the Barra del Colorado Wildlife Refuge.

Though the **La Palma** ranger station and the surrounding **Caño Palma** area of the refuge, managed by the non-profit **Canadian Organization for Tropical Education and Rainforest Conservation (COTERC)**, sit inside Parque Nacional Barra del Colorado (see below), they're most easily accessed from Tortuguero. Just south of the La Palma station, **Cerro Tortuguero** offers hikers a climb that is about 6km from Tortuguero village. Though rising only 390m, the summit affords a spectacular panoramic view of the lowlands and park. You will need a guide with a boat to reach the station and refuge. (US$5 per hr. per person.) There are also **volunteer** opportunities available that include research, trail maintenance, and tour guiding. (☎381 4116; canopalm@sol.racsa.co.cr. Admission to station US$2.)

CAHUITA

Warm, turquoise waves lap up on black- and white-sand beaches. Howler monkeys in the treetops of the coastal rainforest cry out broken rhapsodies. Parque Nacional Cahuita, southeast of the village, is home to the largest coral reef on Costa Rica's Caribbean coast, and the other side of the village is a comparative paradise—there, sun-worshippers bask in paradise on Playa Negra. Some warn that not all of Cahuita is idyllic, so take precautions, especially at night.

⌨ TRANSPORTATION. The MEPE **bus** company serves Cahuita (☎257 8129 in San José, 758 1572 in Limón). Buses depart from the front of the park to: **Limón** (1hr., 9 per day 6:15am-6:45pm, ¢350); **Puerto Viejo** (30min., 8 per day 6am-7pm, ¢165); **Manzanillo** (1½hr.; 7am, 3:30, 5:30pm via Puerto Viejo; ¢340); **San José** (3½hr.; 7:30, 9:30, 11:30am, 4:30pm; ¢1975). **Mr. Big J** (☎755 0328), one block southeast of the bus stop, is the most comprehensive source of info and tours in town. He has a list of **taxi** drivers, including Wayne (☎755 0078), Enrique (☎755 0017), and René (☎755 0243). Open daily 9am-noon and 3-6pm.

▚▜ ORIENTATION AND PRACTICAL INFORMATION. A road branching off the Limón-Puerto Viejo highway travels for 1km before intersecting with Cahuita's main road, in front of a small municipal park. The town's main road passes through Cahuita from northwest to southeast. Facing the bus stop (with the park in front of you), northwest is to your left and southeast is to your right. **Playa Negra** is on the northwest end of town; **Playa Blanca** lies in Cahuita National park over the bridge to the southeast. For **tourist information** the **MINAE** office (☎755 0060), two blocks northwest of the bus stop, can answer questions about parks, but isn't designed to dispense other tourist info. If you're hitting the beach for the day, store your valuables in a steel case at **Mr. Big J.** (¢1000 per day.) The closest **banks** are in Limón. The **Cabinas Safari** hotel, however, exchanges traveler's checks and over a dozen currencies. (Open daily 7am-4pm.) **Western Union** is inside Cahuita Tours, 2½ blocks northwest of the bus stop. **Mr. Big J** will do your **laundry.** (¢1500 per load. Takes 2½hr. Open M-F 8am-4pm.) Other services include: **police,** at the northwest end of the main road, 3 blocks from the bus stop right next to the post office (☎755 0217; open 24hr.); **pharmacy,** 10min. walk out of town on the main road, or hop on a bus headed for Puerto Viejo and ask to get off at the clinic on the right (☎750 0136; open M-F 7am-4pm). For medical care, contact the **Red Cross** in Limón (☎758 0125, **emergencies** 911. English spoken. Available 24hr.) There are **telephones** next to the bus stop, at **Cahuita Tours,** in Hotel Cahuita, 2 blocks northwest of the bus stop, and in front of the police station. **Palmer CyberNet,** across from Cabinas Safari offers **Internet access.** (¢1000 per hr. Open M-Sa 7:30am-10pm,

LENDING A HELPING HAND Cahuita is a town founded as an historic act of kindness. In the mid-18th century, the area was only seasonally populated by Afro-Caribbean turtle hunters, who set up camps here on their way to Tortuguero or Bocas del Toro. However, the President of the Republic Alfredo González Flores (1914-1917) had a sailing accident in the nearby waters when returning from a diplomatic meeting in Sixaola. The hunters helped the sailors with provisions and saved their lives. President González Flores bought a block of land for the settlers and allowed them to officially found the town of Cahuita.

Su 6-10pm.) The **post office** is at the northwest end of the main road, 3 blocks from the bus stop. (☎755 0096. Open M-F 8am-noon and 1-5:30pm.) **Postal Code:** 7302.

ACCOMMODATIONS. There are more *cabinas* than anything in Cahuita. Competition, unfortunately, has not created more budget options. It is only easier to get cheap rooms in groups. Most *cabinas* are very clean and comfortable. **Spencer Sea-Side Lodge ❶,** 2 blocks down the crossroads from the bus stop and right at the beach, has simple rooms have worn private baths with cold water and comfortable beds. (☎755 0027. Reef tours US$15 per person. Internet ¢1000 per hr. Basic rooms US$8 per person; doubles with fridge and hot water US$25.) **Cabinas Sol y Mar ❶,** 1½ blocks southeast of the bus stop, near the entrance to the national park, has spacious rooms with hot-water private baths. (☎755 0237. Singles US$10; doubles US$14-16; quads US$20-25. AmEx/MC/V.) **Backpackers ❶,** a half block southeast of Edith's (see **Food,** below). caters to those who need to stretch their budget, offers tidy, unexciting rooms with ceiling fans and a cold-water, concrete communal shower. (☎755 0174. Singles US$6; doubles US$10.)

FOOD. Most restaurants in town are pricey, but gourmet. A couple groceries line the main road on either side of the bus stop. ▧**Miss Edith's ❸,** 3 blocks northwest from the bus stop, then right at the end of the side road past the police, has an incredible fish with coconut, curry, and yucca. (Fish ¢2300. Open daily 7am-10pm.) **Triple Cahuita ❶,** 2 blocks up from the cross road bus stop, is one of the only places in town that will serve a cheap *casado*. (☎755 0244. Open 11am-10pm.) **Roberto's ❸,** 1½ blocks southeast of the bus stop, serves up Caribbean seafood dishes (¢2500) The restaurant will cook you a dinner made from your day's catch. (Open daily noon-10pm in the low season; high season 6am-10pm.)

GUIDED TOURS. Mr. Big J (see **Practical Information,** above) can set you up with 3hr. **snorkeling** trips (gear rental US$6, guided trips US$20 per person), **horseback riding** tours (beach 3hr., US$30 per person; waterfalls 5hr., US$40 per person with lunch), fishing trips (US$40 per person), as well as trips to **Tortuguero** (US$95 per person for 2 days). **Roberto Tours,** a block southeast of the bus stop, offers **fishing trips** (day trips for mackerel and jack 4hr., US$50). Cook up your catch in Roberto's Caribbean-style seafood restaurant next door. He also offers early-morning **dolphin tours** and **snorkeling trips.** (☎/fax 755 0117. Open M-F 7am-3pm in low season, daily 7am-8pm in high season.) **Cahuita Tours,** 2½ blocks northwest of the bus stop, offers **whitewater rafting** (US$95) and **night tours** (US$10). Rents **snorkeling** gear (¢2000 per day) and **binoculars** (¢1500 per day), and sells daily papers. (☎755 0232; cahuitat@racso.co.cr. Open daily 7:30am-noon and 1:30-7pm. AmEx/MC/V.)

PARQUE NACIONAL CAHUITA

Parque Nacional Cahuita's claim to fame is its spectacular 600 hectare coral reef. Though 22,400 hectares of the park are marine, the very accessible 1067 hectare coastal rainforest is well worth a visit. The expansive **Playa Blanca** (named for its warm white sand) stretches south of the station, where less active park visitors laze on towels and take dips in the refreshing Caribbean waves.

⌐ TRANSPORTATION. Cahuita is the gateway town for the Parque Nacional Cahuita. See **Transportation** (p. 243) for transportation to and from Cahuita. To enter the park through the Puerto Vargas ranger station, take the Puerto Viejo de Talamanca bus in Cahuita and ask to be let off at the entrance to Puerto Vargas.

■ ⁊ ORIENTATION AND PRACTICAL INFORMATION. Parque Nacional Cahuita lies on the south end of the Atlantic Coast, in the province of Limón. The park has two ranger stations, both accessible from Cahuita. The **Kelly Creek ranger station** is three blocks southeast of the bus stop just over the small bridge at the edge of town. **Puerto Vargas,** the second station, is off the main highway between Puerto Viejo and Limón. To enter, take the Puerto Viejo de Talamanca bus in Cahuita. Ask to be let off at the entrance road to Puerto Vargas. If you enter through the **Kelly Creek ranger station,** you must register in their logbook. They gratefully accept donations to enter the park (open daily 6am to 5pm). A standard US$7 national park admission fee is required if you enter from the **Puerto Vargas station** (☎755 0302; aclac@ns.minae.go.cr; open M-F 8am-4pm, Sa-Su 7am-5pm). The only trail is 5km to the tip, and 7km from there to Puerto Vargas. IMuggings have occurred; however, during station hours (M-F 8am-4pm, Sa-Su 7am-5pm) there are frequent patrols. Still, people hiking alone should be cautious.

⁊ CAMPING. Camping is permitted near the Puerto Vargas side of the park (US$2 per person). The 50 camping sites are set back from the hiking path and include an ocean vista with access to showers, sinks, and toilets at the ranger station. Places where swimming is permitted are clearly marked and strictly enforced. Surfing, as well as volleyball and soccer, are allowed in certain areas.

⁊ RAINFOREST TRAIL. An easy 9km (2½hr.) trail leads from the Kelly Creek Station in Cahuita for 4km to Punta Cahuita, and continues for an additional 3km until it reaches Puerto Vargas. The hike finishes 2km past the station. The trail seems more like a narrow road than a path, with bikers riding through and local mothers pushing babies in carriages. A little further on the path, crosses Río Suarez, which, during high tide, reaches chest-high. On one side the rolling waves of the Caribbean drum against secluded white-sand **Playa Vargas;** on the other, there's a swampy forest with brush and towering coconut palms.

⁊ FLORA AND FAUNA. The region's smaller flora and fauna are remarkable; be sure to look down and watch your step! Orange hermit crabs and white ghost crabs scurry across the path. Observe the backs of the brightly striped lizards carefully—if there are spines running down to the tail, it's an iguana; if not, then it's probably a **Jesucristo (Jesus Christ) lizard** (named for its ability to walk on water, not for any physical resemblance). The medicinal *sangrillo*'s tree trunk has thick folds that bunch up and out, making it look as though it's resting on a wrinkled pyramidal base. Look for the flaking white trees locals call *"gringo pelado"* under their breath: the trees peel from the sun like pale, blond *gringos.*

⁊ THE CORAL REEF. Fish of all shapes, sizes, and colors of the rainbow inhabit Cahuita's 600 hectare coral reef with 35 different species, and elkhorn and brain corals line the ocean floor. In the past few years, the reef has shrunk, due in part to the accumulation of eroded soil from banana plantations; the nasty chemicals sprayed on the bananas have drained into the water, contaminating the reef. Now, there's too much dead coral floating around for snorkelers to find good sites on their own. Check with the rangers or go on a guided tour (see Cahuita **Guided Tours,** above). It's a bad idea to go out the day after a heavy night storm has stirred up debris and dead coral in the water. The most popular spot to visit is **Punta Vargas.**

PUERTO VIEJO DE TALAMANCA

Puerto Viejo, 61km southeast of Puerto Limón, is all about unwinding and forgetting life's worries for a while... or forever, as the growing population of resident Europeans and gringos can attest. These recent immigrants have further added to the eclectic mix of Afro-Caribbean, Spanish, and indigenous cultures here. Though there are plenty of opportunities for surfing, snorkeling, and other outdoor activities, life here is slow, and if you're considering anything beyond catching the perfect wave or the perfect tan, you're being far too ambitious. Puerto Viejo is also the most commercially active of the Caribbean towns. Check out the open market on the main street for local crafts and the many shops for handmade souvenirs.

▛ TRANSPORTATION

Buses: Leave for: **San José** (4½hr.; 7, 9, 11am, 4pm, additional bus at 1:30pm on F and Su; ¢2300); **Limón** (1½hr., 7 per day 5:30am-5:30pm, ¢500) via **Cahuita** (45min., ¢145); **Manzanillo** (45min.; 7:20am, 4, 7:30pm; ¢4180) via **Punta Uva** (30min., ¢150); **Panamanian border** at **Bribrí/Sixaola** (Bribrí 30min., ¢200; Sixaola 1½hr., 7 per day 6:15am-7:30pm, ¢475; buses leave Bribrí at 12:30pm).

Taxis: Walk a half-block west of ATEC and you'll see a sign on the south side street for **"Charlie's Taxi Service."** Everyone knows Charlie as "Bull" (☎ 750 0112). If Bull's red minivan isn't there, ask at ATEC. Also try Sergio (☎ 750 0525) or Bruno (☎ 750 0426).

◢▟ ORIENTATION AND PRACTICAL INFORMATION

The main road comes in from the west, crosses the bridge near an abandoned barge, and cuts through town before heading east to Manzanillo 13km later. To get to the center of town from the bus stop (marked by sheltered benches), head south away from the beach one block to the main road, and turn left. The ATEC office is 1½ blocks east.

Tourist Information: Take your questions to **Talamanca Association for Ecotourism and Conservation** (**ATEC** ☎ 750 0398, fax 750 0191; atecmail@sol.racsa.co.cr) in the center of town. Open M, Tu, Th, and F 7am-9pm, W 7am-noon and 2-9pm, Sa 8am-noon and 1-9pm, Su 8am-noon and 4-8pm.

Financial Services: Pulpería Manuel León (☎ 750 0422; fax 750 0246), on the beach half-block west and 2 blocks north of ATEC, exchanges US dollars and cashes traveler's checks. Open M-Sa 7am-6pm, Su 7:30am-2pm. **Banco Nacional** (☎ 751 0068), is 30min. away in Bribrí. Visa cash advances. Open M-F 8:30am-3:45pm.

Laundry: (☎ 750 0360), 30m south of the post office. ¢2500 per load. ¢500 extra for whites washed separately. Delivery service included. Locals or extended-stay tourists often negotiate special rates. Open daily 10am-6pm.

Police: (☎ 750 0230 or 911 for emergency) a half-block east and 1½ blocks north of ATEC facing the beach. Open 24hr.

Pharmacy: Clinic Hone Creek (☎ 750 0136), 5km out of town on the main road; hop on the bus headed for Bribrí. Call ahead if possible. Open M-F 7am-4pm.

Medical Services: (☎ 750 0303), a half-block block west and 1 block north of ATEC, Dr. Rodríquez and Dr. Ríos have a small office. Open M-F 4:30-8pm, Sa 8am-noon. The

dentist is next door and shares the same phone line. For medical emergencies, contact the **Red Cross** (☎758 0125 or 911) in Limón. English spoken. Open 24hr.

Telephones: ATEC (see **Tourist Information,** above) offers international phone service. ¢274 per min. to US, ¢375 per min. to Europe and the rest of the world, ¢190 per min. in Central America.

Internet: Video Mundo (☎750 0651), next door to ATEC, has comfortable, quick connections. ¢1000 per hr. Open daily 7am-9pm.

Post Office: (☎750 0404), a half-block west and 25m south of ATEC. Open M-F 8am-noon, 1-5:30pm.

ACCOMMODATIONS

There are several extremely cheap options, but the superior conditions of the mid-range hotels are worth the extra money. US$12-16 here will get you a luxurious room with private bath and, usually, a private balcony with hammock.

Cabinas Casa Verde (☎750 0015; www.cabinascasaverde.com). From ATEC, continue half a block east on the main road and turn right, then turn left at the first street, and you'll see the green signs. Rooms have fans, mosquito nets, and porches for relaxing. Grounds have a frog farm, and the extensive tropical garden has bilingual labels. Baths, some private, have hot water. Singles US$16-28; doubles US$18-34; triples US$28-38; quads US$40-48. Prices decrease in low season. AmEx/MC/V. ❷

Jacaranda Cabinas (☎750 0069), a half-block west and 2 blocks south of ATEC. Beautiful individual cabins. Rooms are creative and varied, but make sure you get one with a fan *and* a mosquito net. A pleasant restaurant is attached. Singles US$10, with bath and porch US$15; doubles US$20/US$30; triples and quads US$25 and up. MC/V. ❶

Hotel Puerto Viejo, 1 block east and 1 block south of ATEC, is popular with surfers and tight-budget travelers. Dark rooms without fans are musty and graffiti-ridden, but those with fans are more merciful. Bright, immaculate communal baths. Try for a room away from the kitchen, which is open for your use. ¢1500 per person, ¢1900 with fan. ❶

FOOD

Soda Isma, a block west of ATEC on the main road. Famous for its *rondon,* a local dish of fish in coconut sauce that must be ordered a day in advance (¢2500). Spur-of-the-moment types can feast on tasty *gallo pinto* (¢550-700). Open daily 8am-9pm. ❶

Soda Lidia, one block east and 2 blocks south of ATEC, is an open-air restaurant with a thatched roof, offering great *casados* drizzled in Caribbean sauce (chicken ¢1000). A favorite for cheaper prices, but frequented mostly by tourists. Hours vary. ❶

Miss Sam's (☎750 0101), less cheery decor than Lidia's next door. More local customers. Breakfast ¢200-800; lunch and dinner ¢600-1400. Open M-Sa 7am-9:30pm. ❷

The Garden, attached to Jacaranda Cabinas, is a step above what you might expect to find in this tiny village. Dishes with an Asian twist. Island curry chicken ¢2400; grilled red snapper ¢3200. Open only in high season (Dec.-Apr.). ❸

SIGHTS

FINCA LA ISLA'S BOTANICAL GARDEN. Finca La Isla's Botanical Garden, a 20min. walk west of town (there are numerous signs), is an abandoned cacao plantation that has been transformed into a working tropical farm. Tours focus on education regarding the varieties of spices, herbs, and medicines produced on the

COSTA RICA

farm. Tours last 2½hr. and end with a demonstration table with juice and fruit samples. (☎ 750 0046; jardbot@racsa.co.cr; www.greencost.com\garden.html. Open F-M 10am-4pm. Admission US$3; 2½hr. guided tour including entrance US$8.)

RESERVA INDÍGENA COCLES/KEKOLDI. The most accessible indigenous reserve to outsiders, 4km west of Puerto Viejo, this reserve was established in 1977 and is home to approximately 40 Bribrí and Cabécar families. To tour the reservation, you must have an authorized guide, available through ATEC, Puerto Viejo Tours, and Terraventuras (one-day trips US$25-45). Tours include a hike on ancient trails through old cacao plantations, secondary forests, and farms. Tours concentrate more on nature than culture to create a relationship of privacy and respect between the community and the tourist. For this reason, most tours begin at Luca's house for a meeting with the family and short sensitivity introduction. Located at the entrance to the reservation is the **Iguana Farm,** two Bribrí women's project to bolster the reservation's declining iguana population. (To get there, take the bus headed for Bribrí and ask the driver to let you off at the Iguana Farm (15min., ¢100). To get back, catch the 12:45pm bus coming from Bribrí. If you miss the bus, your best bet is to walk the 4km back to Puerto Viejo, though some travelers report hitching is possible. Let's Go does not recommend hitchhiking. Farm admission ¢400.)

🏄🦎 SURFING AND GUIDED TOURS

Most surfers head straight over to **La Salsa Brava,** an extraordinary surf-hole east of the village, where waves break over a coral reef. However, if you're less experienced with a board, and getting drilled into the coral doesn't sound "far-out," a 15min. walk east along the beach is **Beach Break,** where comparable waves break on soft sand. Hotel Puerto Viejo (see **Accommodations,** above) rents surfboards and boogie boards (¢3000 per day with ¢5000 deposit). **Peter's Place,** next to Ferretería Ivon and Soda Palmer, rents snorkeling equipment, bikes, and boogie boards. (US$5. Open 7:15am-6pm.) **Terraventuras,** a half-block west of ATEC and 2 blocks north, rents snorkeling gear and offers tours, including horseback riding, snorkeling in Parque Nacional Cahuita (US$35), a hiking tour of Gandoca-Manzanillo Wildlife Refuge (US$40), and a tour of the Kekoldi and Talamanca Bribrí Indian reserves (US$40). All tours include transportation and fruit. (☎ 750 0426. Open daily 8am-1pm and 3:30-6:30pm; closed W during wet season months might be helpful. AmEx/MC/V.) **Reef Runner Divers,** a half-block west of ATEC and 2 blocks north, specializes in scuba diving and offers all types of PADI certification courses and runs diving excursions. All dives include full equipment, guide, boat, fruits, and beverages. (☎ 750 0480. Open daily 8am-6 or 7pm. AmEx/MC/V.) **Puerto Viejo Tours,** across from the bus stop, offers informal tours similar to Terraventura plus surfing lessons and gear rental. (☎ 750 0411. Surf boards US$10 per day. Scooters US$7.49 per hr., US$30 per day. All rentals include helmet.)

🄴 NIGHTLIFE

True to its reputation, Puerto Viejo is a party town, and locals and tourists pack the hot spots night after night from 10:30pm until the early morning. Every Monday and Friday, the bar/dance club **🄴Bambú,** 300m east of ATEC on the main road on the beach, explodes in a crazed orgy of dancing, drinking, and smoking until 2am. For a less intense experience, make a cameo at cocktail hour from 4-7pm or eat anytime from 8am-7pm (Caribbean *casado* ¢900-1500). From Bambú, groove at **🄴Discoteca Stanford** next door (2 beers ¢600). On Mondays and Fridays the two open-air floors of dancing pour out onto the beach. **Johnny's Place,** a half-block west of ATEC and two blocks north along the beach, is the place to be on Saturday nights, when it becomes a pulsing disco blasting rock, *salsa*, reggae, and techno.

◪ PUNTA UVA

*Buses from **Puerto Viejo** head for **Manzanillo** via Punta Uva (7:20am, 4, 7:30pm; return 5:15, 8:45am, 5:15pm). Other options for getting to Punta Uva are **walking** (about 2hr.), **taxi** (¢3000-3500), or renting a **bike** or **horse** in Puerto Viejo. Hitchhiking is also possible and fairly easy, although Let's Go does not recommend hitchhiking.*

The water is perfect for swimming, and the small waves that break close to shore are ideal for body surfing. Palm and mango trees line the beach only 50m from the water's edge. Look to the east to see the actual "grape point" for which Punta Uva is named—a small peninsula juts offshore, with a natural tunnel that acts as a window to the ocean. From the main road there are three entrances to the beach: one at the sign for Selvin's, one a 7min. walk later at Restaurant Punta Uva, and the third 3min. after that at the sign for Restaurant La Arrecife.

Most people visiting quiet Punta Uva stay in **Selvin's Cabinas ❶** (look for the sign off the road, on the western end of Punta Uva). Doubles are basic and well-maintained. Clean, large mosquito nets are draped on every bed. There is a great restaurant on the premises. (*Casados* ¢1300-2000. Restaurant open F-Su low season; W-Su high season. Singles ¢2500; doubles ¢3500.) **Cabinas Punta Uva ❸** has the advantage of being located exactly on the beach, 100m past Selvin's on the left (follow the signs). Doubles have an outdoor kitchenette and access to a communal kitchen. (☎ 750 0431. US$35 per room, with bath US$40.) There isn't a wide array of dining opportunities in Punta Uva. **La Arrecife Marisquería ❷**, an open-air bar/restaurant on the beach (you'll see a sign pointing the way 10min. past Selvin's on the main road), specializes in seafood. Mounds of rice with shrimp (¢1800) are accompanied by fries. (☎ 759 0700. Open daily 7:30am-9pm.) **Ranchito Beach Restaurant ❶** is a nice bar on the beach about 7min. past Selvin's. (Open daily 11am-5pm.)

Several hundred meters before Selvin's, you will encounter a sign for a **Butterfly Garden.** Follow the signs uphill and bearing to the left. This garden distinguishes itself from the others as a center for butterfly reproduction. The garden has up to 80 butterfly species. (Open daily 8am-3pm. US$5, children free. Tour included.)

◪ MANZANILLO

*Buses run daily from Puerto Viejo to **Manzanillo** (7:20am, 3:30, 4, 7:30pm; returns 5am, 8:30pm), passing through Punta Uva and the other beaches. You can also take a **taxi** (¢4500), rent a **bike** or **horse** (see **Orientation and Practical Information,** p. 246), or **walk** (3hr.) from Puerto Viejo. The walk along the beach, though lengthy, is gorgeous and peaceful. A bright green **MINAE office** is located on the bend of the road in Manzanillo, facing the beach. (☎ 759 0600, fax 759 0601. Open M-F 8am-4pm.) The rangers can provide details on the park and the preservation efforts inside the refuge (including dolphin and turtle projects often looking for **volunteers**). A map and history of the refuge are available with donation. The rangers are not as active with tourists because of the well-organized coalition of local guides (see below). Rangers offer beds and baths for students looking to volunteer in the Refugio.*

Bordered by a spectacular beach, the seaside village of Manzanillo is 6km southeast of Punta Uva. The original *manzanillo* tree for which the town is named fell into the sea in 1957, and the species has not been spotted since. Maybe it's for the best though, since the tree was known to be poisonous. Carelessly falling asleep beside the toxic bark meant an eternal rest for the hapless napper.

The main reason to come to Manzanillo is to visit the breathtaking **Refugio Nacional Gandoca-Manzanillo.** This dense jungle path stretches from the village through the Refuge all the way to Panama. Founded in 1985 to protect endangered flora and fauna, the refuge includes 5013 hectares of private and public land. The wetlands teem with crocodiles, alligators, sloths, pumas, and monkeys, while the coastal areas accent the refuge with five types of coral reefs, sandy beaches, and fossil-lined coral caves. A red mangrove tree swamp, unique to the Costa Rican Caribbean, sits beside the **Gandoca Lagoon** protecting the only natural population of mangrove oysters on the coast and the home of the nearly extinct manatee. The waters off rocky **Punta Mona** are frequented by tucuxi, bottlenose, and Atlantic spotted dolphins. One of the only drawbacks of the Refugio is that trails are not well-marked and heavy rains year-round make them very poorly maintained. A guide is almost always necessary.

The **police station** is behind Maxi's (see below). Make **phone calls** from the phones in front of Maxi's. **La Caribeña Lavandera** is 50m behind La Selva Restaurant in a residential house labeled "Local Guide" (☎759 0643; see below). The cheapest place to stay in town is **Cabinas Maxi ①** (☎759 0661), behind Restaurante Maxi at the end of the town road. It has basic, clean digs with private bathrooms, no mosquito netting, and mattresses, as well as large windows. (¢5000 per room with single and double bed; ¢4000 for solo traveler.) Another option is the colorful **Pangea Bed and Breakfast ②**; look 100m down from Aquamor for a sign pointing inland on a side-street between the MINAE office and Maxi's. Double rooms have ceiling fans, beautiful wood floors and walls, and hot-water baths. (☎759 0604; pangqecr@racsa.co.cr. US$25 per room includes breakfast. AmEx/MC/V.) Next to Pangea Bed and Breakfast, **Cabinas Something Different ③** offers modern, airy, luxurious cabins with cable TV, fridge, and private bath with hot water. (☎759 0614. US$25 for one person, $5 for each additional person). In the Refugio itself, it's possible to **camp** in certain areas designated by rangers. Speak to a ranger before heading in with a tent. You can also camp in **Steve Brooks' organic farm** in Punta Mona. (☎391 2116. US$5 per person; volunteer and he'll waive the fee.)

█**Restaurant Maxi ③**, in front of Cabinas Maxi in town, serves fresh seafood (catch of the day ¢2300-2700) and is the center of the town's social life. (Open daily noon-10pm.) Down the road as you enter Manzanillo is **Restaurant La Selva ②**. (☎759 0633. Seafood dishes ¢1800-3000. Open daily noon-9pm.) The cheapest food in town is 50m down the street from Aquamor at **Soda Rinconato Alegre ②**, where generous portions of pancakes and fruit (¢500) and sizable menus (¢1200-2000) attract tourists and locals. (☎759 0640. Open daily 7am-7pm.) **Más X Menos** is on the main road 50m past Restaurant La Selva. (Open daily 7am-noon and 2pm-7pm.)

◪ **GUIDED TOURS.** Guides from other Caribbean towns are often denied access, as MINAE requests that tourists only employ local guides. Local guides can be found in the office across the street from **Abastecedor Más X Menos**. Almost all guides are native to the region and founded Guis MANT (☎759 0643), a coalition uniting their profession and devotion to conserve land in Manzanillo. The guides give various tours, including trips to the refuge, turtle watching, night walks, horseback rides, snorkeling, and fishing. Most tours go for US$15-20 per person.

The 9km beach off Gandoca is the site of **marine turtle** nesting grounds. Four species colonize here: leatherback, green, hawksbill, and loggerhead. Only visitors with a guide are permitted to enter the beach and observe the turtles during nesting season (Mar. 1-Oct. 31). For more information contact **ANAI** (National Association of Indigenous Affairs; ☎750 0020; anaital@sol.racsa.co.cr).

◪ **WATERSPORTS.** If you want to explore the park from the water, check with the watersports shop **Aquamor,** the last right off the main road before Maxis in Manzanillo. They rent kayaks and snorkeling gear and offer diving trips and dolphin observation excursions. (☎359 0612; aquamorl@racsa.co.cr. Beach dives

US$30. Kayak dives US$37. Dolphin tours US$30. Open daily 7am-6pm.) Get in touch with Aquamor for information on how to volunteer for the TDF or contact them directly (☎ 586 9942; fax 586 0995; info@dolphinlink.org).

⚔ SIXAOLA: BORDER WITH PANAMA

The dusty border town of Sixaola offers a few services, but not nearly enough to make anyone stay. The Panamanian side of the border is open daily from 8am to 6pm, while the Costa Rican side is open daily from 7am to 5pm; the time zone difference assures the two coincide. You will need to buy a Red Cross exit stamp (¢200) and show an onward ticket. A tourist card is also needed (US$5). Officials reserve the right to ask for proof of economic independence. (☎ 754 2044.)

For those entering Panama, frequent **buses** run to Changuinola (15min., US$0.70) until about 7pm. Collective **taxis** cost US$1 and leave from in front of Kiosco Dalys, on the left side of the crossing entering from Costa Rica. Buses from Sixaola head back to **San José** (6hr.; 5, 7:30, 9:30am, 2:30pm; ¢2815) and **Limón** (3hr., 8 per day 5am-5pm, ¢930) via **Puerto Viejo de Talamanca** (2hr., 3pm, ¢500).

Right after the bridge on the main road is **Mercado California,** which sells the Red Cross stamps and changes US dollars to colones at a bad rate. (☎ 754 2030. Open 8am-9pm.) Next door is a **Western Union.** There's no **bank** in Sixaola; the nearest one on this side of the border is in the town of Bribrí. Costa Rican **police** sit right opposite the Migración office. (☎ 754 2160.) **Phones** are right before the bridge on the left-hand side of the tracks. If you have to stay in Sixaola overnight, walk 400m down from the bridge on the left-hand side of the tracks and bear right until the end of the road to **Hotel Doris ❶.** The musty rooms have collective baths. (*Soda* downstairs 8am-11pm; breakfast ¢600. Singles ¢2000; doubles ¢2500.)

EL SALVADOR

The smallest of the Central American countries, it is also the most densely populated. Infamous for its long and bloody civil war in the 80s and 90s, tourism has been slow to develop in El Salvador. Now that peace has been restored, the country has become much safer and visitors find that well kept mountain towns, blacksand beaches, and picturesque volcanoes await them. Salvadorans will spend endless hours helping you find a hidden hotel, discussing the state of US-Salvadoran relations, or shooting the breeze. Perhaps most rewarding about visiting El Salvador is the chance to witness a nation on the road to recovery.

HIGHLIGHTS OF EL SALVADOR

The scenic highland town of **San Vicente,** whose colonial church and dense market are watched over by the massive Volcán Chichontepec (p. 308).

The remote **Parque Nacional El Imposible,** alive with quetzals, agoutis, and anteaters, and laced with orchids and bromeliads (p. 293).

The beach town of **La Libertad,** boasting some of the best waves on the Pacific and the closest El Salvador gets to Hanging Ten (p. 275).

The city of **Santa Ana,** currently undergoing a renaissance and regaining its former stature (p. 297).

SUGGESTED ITINERARY

2-3 WEEKS: NATURE HIGHLIGHTS. If you don't mind staying in **San Salvador** (p. 261), the incredible ruins of **Joya de Cerén** (p. 273) are certainly worth it; the "Pompeii of the Americas" was covered by ash around 600 AD and is perfectly preserved. To get there, catch a bus headed for Opico. Leaving San Salvador for lush forest, take a bus through **Sonsonate** (p. 290)for **Parque Nacional El Imposible** (p.

Regions of El Salvador

GUATEMALA

HONDURAS

Metapán

La Palma

Northern El Salvador
pp. 283-288

Chalatenango

Western El Salvador
pp. 289-305

Santa Ana

Ahuachapán

Suchitoto

Perquín

Apaneca

San Salvador
and Environs
pp. 261-274

Ilobasco

Cacaopera

Sonsonate

Cojutepeque

San Salvador

San Vicente

Eastern El Salvador
pp. 306-321

Santa Rosa de Lima

Zacatecoluca

Santiago de María

San Miguel

La Libertad

Central Coast
pp. 275-282

La Unión

PACIFIC OCEAN

La Costa del Sol

Puerto el Triunfo

293). Remember to get a permit from **Salva Natura** (p. 266) in San Salvador first. Take some time to hike the park, and then head to **Santa Ana** (connecting once again in Sonsonate). This safer, rejuvenated city is an accommodating place from which to explore natural goods of the surrounding region. The sights can be daytrips or overnights. **Cerro Verde** (p. 300) and **Volcán Izalco,** the oldest and youngest volcanoes (respectively) offer different, challenging climbs, both with amazing views. If you can't get enough of Maya ruins, check out **Tazumal** (p. 302), a ceremonial center that is less impressive than Tikal, but still interesting. Last but not least, take a dip in the gorgeous **Lago de Caotepeque** (p. 302), home of fancy weekend homes, splurge hotels, and excellent swimming. For those wishing to extend the itinerary, head north of Santa Ana to **Metapán** (p. 303), a pleasant, isolated ranching village with access to the **Parque Nacional Montecristo** (p. 305), a cloud forest reserve. It is slightly difficult to get to, and requires a permit from San Salvador, but is well worth it; at one point, you can skip from El Salvador to Honduras to Guatemala in a smaller circle than you'd need for ring-a-round-a-rosy.

LIFE AND TIMES

LAND, FLORA, AND FAUNA

El Salvador's landscape is dominated by the chain of many active volcanoes that runs down its center from west to east. The mountains slope on either side toward fertile highlands and plains. A broad plain north of the highlands terminates at the edge of the Northern Sierra, otherwise known as the **Crystalline Highlands,** the mountain range that spreads north into Honduras and Guatemala.

Due to a historically high level of cultivation and current governmental disregard for the environment, El Salvador is the most ecologically damaged country in the Americas. A mere 1.5% of the original forest remains, many of the country's watersheds are polluted, and the potable water supply is running out. In spite of these ecological woes, a conscientious effort on the part of El Salvador, foreign businesses, and tourists could rectify much of the damage. Indeed, El Salvador passed its first environmental law in February 1998, and the national parks system is rapidly developing to protect resources and draw tourists.

El Salvador's varying climate provides for a high degree of plant diversity; however, since much of the country has been deforested to make way for cash crops, native species are harder to find. That said, there are remnants of oak and pine forests, mahogany, laurel, and balsa wood trees, as well as the *maquilishuat*, the national tree. There are over 200 species of orchid. The national flower is the izote.

Unfortunately, larger animals, such as jaguars and crested eagles, have either fled El Salvador's hills or have been eradicated altogether. However, there are over 400 species of birds, among them a whopping 17 hummingbird species.

HISTORY

Around 1800, the planter elite of El Salvador generated the first stirrings for independence, resentful of colonial favoritism of Guatemala in the indigo market. El Salvador rejected their Spanish status along with the rest of Central America in 1821. Following a period from 1823-1838 when El Salvador was part of the United Provinces of Central America, Salvadorans finally achieved independent status.

EL SALVADOR ON ITS OWN. Political and commercial instability marked the nation's first year of independence. El Salvador found a solution to political instability in ◪ coffee, which to this day remains the central figure in the economy and political struggles. The government forced El Salvador's indigenous population to relinquish its last remaining lands to large landowners. Coffee money in El Salva-

EL SALVADOR

El Salvador

dor tightened the already strong link between the land ownership and political power. An extremely small, and powerful elite, the "Fourteen Families," organized an effective stranglehold on the country's land, money, and might. Though their power peaked from 1913-1927, their dominance survives to the present.

During the Great Depression, El Salvador's plutocracy degenerated with plummeting coffee profits, and the oligarchy turned into a dictatorship. The pressures of the Depression were first felt among the coffee workers, who instigated a brief revolt—neither the country's first nor last, but certainly its bloodiest. Under the direction of **Augustín Farabundo Martí,** the eventually martyred founder of El Salvador's Communist Party, thousands of farm workers rebelled in 1932. In response, President **General Maximilno Hernández Martínez** orchestrated the crushing massacre known as *la matanza*—the summary execution of over 10,000 Salvadoran civilians suspected of involvement in the uprising. In total, 30,000 people are reported to have been killed. Martínez, who sought to emulate the better-known fascists of the time, stayed in power until a coup deposed him in 1948. Following the massacre, a series of dictators through the 70s took the helm as puppets of the increasingly paranoid landed elite, and the last of the indigenous peoples were forced to hide their traditions and assimilate into *mestizo* culture.

THE RISE OF THE RIGHT. By the mid-60s, El Salvador had ascended to a level of relative economic stability, and several reform programs had resulted in new levels of economic diversification and international exchange. Despite increased economic security, most laborers continued to live in poverty. An emerging middle class began to support labor rights and welfare measures, promoted by the Christian Democratic Party (PDC) and **José Napoleón Duarte,** party leader and mayor of San Salvador. Despite the shift to more liberal ideals, in 1961 the conservative landowners covertly organized a large, right-wing paramilitary force named ORDEN ("order"), which would come to play a silent yet prominent role in the ongoing repression of the Salvadoran left.

Internal strife enjoyed a brief hiatus during the **Guerra de Fútbol** ("Soccer War"), against Honduras, which lasted from 1969-1980. Meanwhile, in reaction to growing popular support for the moderate PDC, ORDEN stepped in to oversee the 1972 presidential elections. Despite obvious, nearly overwhelming support for Duarte's bid, the more conservative, actively anti-Communist candidate favored by the ORDEN troops registered victory. Following the election, the **Roman Catholic Church** joined the struggle against the conservative federal government and shifted the focus of its Salvadoran mission to "liberation theology," fueling the fires of mass movements already responsible for many public protests and strikes. The ruling regime responded as they had to the 1932 popular revolts, by increasing the scale of the brutal repression to quell dissent. Violence became extreme in 1975, when ORDEN troops gunned down students protesting the use of federal funds to promote El Salvador's bid to host the Miss Universe pageant. Another coup in 1979 marked the official beginning of the nation's infamous civil war.

THE CIVIL WAR. Duarte, in Venezuelan exile since his presidential "defeat" in 1972, returned to a hero's welcome after the 1979 coup. Unfortunately, the seizure was short-lived. In the wake of political shifts toward the left, the elite needed to align with the middle class and urban centers in order to ensure their economic, social, and political survival. With this goal in mind, the Fourteen Families organized the Alianza Republicana Nacionalista, or ARENA, to apply leverage against the extreme left wing. ARENA did not supplant the reigning junta at the time of its inception in 1981, but with military support, it managed to pressure the would-be reformist Duarte into a vicious struggle with the expanding guerrilla movement. The lines of division were drawn: the rich elite, ARENA, and the military represented the establishment that was able to unite forcefully with Duarte, a majority of the enfranchised middle class, and the remains of the PDC.

Directly opposing them were many guerrilla groups operating in the countryside and the Catholic clergy, supported by many country laborers. Although Duarte and his supporters were not interested in annihilating the rebels, the military might maintained their status as figureheads, and the struggle resulted in over a decade of conflict resulting in over 75,000 deaths, 750,000 refugees, and numerous disappearances of children. Most disappearances occurred between 1980 and 1984, when many were captured during military procedures and given up for adoption. Investigations continue into these cases, spearheaded by the Association to Support the Search for Children established in 1995.

Despite Duarte's opposition to the continued warfare, he was powerless to halt the flow of public funds to the right-wing "death squads" or into overt campaigns against the guerrillas. Furthermore, El Salvador had been singled out by the US as an example of how the military might of the West could be used to suppress "Communist insurgencies." The US government donated over US$4 billion worth of military aid to the right during the war, funding ORDEN and the death squads.

FLMN: UNITE AND CONQUER. In 1980, as ARENA was first marshaling its forces, the many-guerrilla movement unified into the FMLN (Farabundo Martípara la Liberación Nacional). FMLN was able to maintain its sabotage and attack tactics despite concentrated efforts to divide and conquer its small forces. Much of their success came from attacks on national infrastructure and actual military targets, causing an estimated $2 billion in damage and many military deaths. Fighting was always most pitched in the mountainous northeast, which was subsequently leveled by random, relentless bombings of peasant villages in the army's attempts to find the elusive rebels. Tens of thousands of innocent civilians were killed during the war, many of them by US arms wielded by soldiers trained at the School of the Americas in Georgia.One of FMLN's heroes, **Archbishop Oscar Romero,** was assassinated by the right during a Mass in March 1980; later that year, the army raped and murdered three American nuns and a volunteer who had been working on missions of mercy in FMLN-supporting territories.

The FMLN were able to maintain popular support in the country through increased political involvement, as they actively helped coffee laborers form unions and fight for higher wages. By reaching beyond their military actions, the FMLN not only maintained support during a terrible war, but also built political credibility that currently allows them to take a legitimate role in the government.

In the late 80s, more citizens were unhappy with Duarte's moderate, limping government with its repeated failures to repair a shattered economy, end an ongoing war, and implement even the most minimal of social policies. With allegations of rampant corruption in Duarte's administration, the public overlooked Duarte in the 1989 presidential elections and elected **Alfredo Cristiani,** ARENA's charismatic candidate. Cristiani punished public sedition and rebel support more openly than his allies had, but at the same time was able to maneuver with enough freedom to consider seriously the FMLN's demands for social justice. In 1992, under UN supervision, an accord was reached between the two dominant and extreme factions; though reminiscent of a failed effort in 1984, this one has thus far been effective. While the ten-year-old cease-fire is a fortunate respite, the conditions responsible for its declaration were those of a deep weariness and frustration.

In March 1994, **Armando Calderón Sol** of the right-wing ARENA party, was elected president. In 1997, ARENA lost the mayorship of San Salvador and was narrowly defeated in the legislative vote by the newly social-democratic FMLN. Interestingly, it was the religious left that emerged after the election to mediate between the two, and Sol was willing to follow the mandates of the legislative assembly.

TODAY

ARENA leader Francisco Flores won by a landslide in the March 1999 presidential elections. Since the end of the civil war in 1992 crime has spread, while support for Flores has dwindled in recent months due to unmet expectations for reducing crime and alleged party corruption. Though the country has been war-free for almost a decade, annual murder rates are as high as they were during the war.

Recently, the investigation into the murders of the American nuns was brought again to world attention when the soldiers who performed the killings admitted that they had acted on orders from high superiors. At this point it looks as though the officers who ordered those killings are living—guess where—in the US.

The new millennium brought with it another set of issues to El Salvador: natural forces as difficult as its past political ones. On January 13th and February 13th, 2001, earthquakes rocked the country. San Vicente, Santiago de María, and most of the Department of La Paz were hardest hit. The damaged reached the National Theatre, Parque National Cerro Verde, and many private businesses. Summer of 2001 followed up with a drought which slashed coffee profits and rural incomes.

ECONOMY AND GOVERNMENT

Since the end of the civil war, El Salvador's recovering economy has been plagued by high unemployment. The economy remains predominantly agricultural; however, El Salvador must import much of its food because cash crops for export occupy most of the fertile land. The industrialization that had been proceeding before the war is regaining momentum, but, in the face of extreme environmental destruction, the government must choose between industry and a non-toxic environment. Hurricane Mitch and El Niño damage have reduced the coffee yield substantially, and delivered a harsh blow to the struggling Salvadoran economy.

The current constitution was promulgated in 1983 and established the legislative, executive, and judicial branches of government. The president serves a non-renewable five-year term as head of the executive branch. The FMLN holds a narrow majority over ARENA in the Legislative Assembly, elected in March 2000. The country is organized into 14 departments, each headed by a governor.

PEOPLE

As most of its citizens have a mix of indigenous and European backgrounds, El Salvador is the most demographically homogeneous country in Central America. The **Pipil** Indians, who dominated the country before the Conquest, were aggressively driven off their lands during the last few centuries, culminating in the mid-1800s, when they were forced to become laborers on the booming coffee plantations. Surviving indigenous cultures are found in the west. In 1932, 30,000 Indians were massacred by government troops in the infamous *matanza*.

CULTURE

FOOD AND DRINK. The cuisine of El Salvador is similar to that of many other Latin American nations. Tortillas feature in every meal and beans are never far behind. Breakfast, served early, typically consists of eggs, plantains, cheese or cream, beans, and tortillas. For plain eggs, ask for *solo huevos;* otherwise, a plate of eggs with tomatoes and onions will land on the table. For lunch and dinner, replace eggs and cheese with meat and *arroz* (yellow fried rice). The meat is usually *pollo dorado* (roast "golden" chicken), *carne asada* (roast meat), or *pollo* or *carne encebollado* (stewed with veggies). *Pupusas* (tortillas filled with cheese or beans) are everywhere. As for drinks, Salvadorans prefer fruity ones. *Licuados*, fruit shakes, and *refrescos*, made of coconut and fruit juices, are rivaled only by

EL SALVADOR

Kolashanpan, an ultra-sweet local soda whose taste defies description. The most popular brands of beer are Pilsener and Suprema. For ultimate intoxication, mix Coke with Tic-Tack, a ferocious rum-like concoction distilled from sugar cane.

THE ARTS. El Salvador's early literature focused not on pressing social issues, but on sentiment. Early poets include José Batres Montúfar (1809-1844) and Arturo Ambrogi (1874-1936), who is also known for his short stories. Later writers continued in the romantic vein. Carlos Bustamante's *Mi Caso* reflected on the most intimate human feelings with the aid of overtly psychological themes, as did the works of the first acclaimed Salvadoran woman poet, Claudia Lars (1899-1974), in books such as *Tierra de Infancia* (1959). In the early days of the century, Alberto Masferrer (1868-1932) also contributed important essays and poetry to this tradition. Literature has since come to strive for progress. Rather than lambasting the recent events and current situations in this overpopulated country, popular literature strives to catalyze change by evoking impressions of what might one day be. Some of El Salvador's recent artists explore similar themes, tapping into common experience to evoke harmony and peace. Dorian Díaz's *El Pescado* and Gilberto Arriaza's *La Luna* are among the colorful, playful works which have emerged recently from the country. Some of the most well-known traditional pieces include the wicker furniture from Nahuizalco and ceramics and weavings from La Palma.

POPULAR CULTURE. US pop has made major inroads; switching on the radio often involves an encounter with Dido or Shaggy. In the country and small towns, tastes are more traditional, but there are few strictly Salvadoran groups. *La Prensa Gráfica* (www.laprensa.com.sv) and *Diário de Hoy* (www.elsalvador.com) are the best Salvadoran daily newspapers, although both tend toward the tabloid now and then with little World coverage. In San Salvador, pick up the *El Salvador News Gazette* for bilingual tips and news. There are six TV stations, most of which deliver the usual soap operas, news programs, and soccer games.

ESSENTIALS

EMBASSIES AND CONSULATES

Embassies of El Salvador: Canada, 209 Kent St., Ottawa, Ontario K2P 1Z8 (☎613-238-2939; fax 238-6940; embajada@elsalvador.ca.org). Open M-F 9am-5pm.; **UK,** 5 Gt. James Street, London WC1N 3DA (☎0171 430 2141; fax 430 0484); **US,** 2308 California St. NW, Washington, D.C. 20008 (☎202-265-9671, 265-9672, or 265-9675; fax 234-3834; corre@elsalvador.org; www.elsalvador.org). Open M-F 9:30am-5:30m.

Consulates of El Salvador: Canada, 151 Bloor Street West Suite 320, Toronto, Ontario M5S 1S4 (☎416-975-0812; fax 975-0283); **UK,** Mayfair House 3rd fl., 39 Great Portland St., Sr. London W1N 7JZ (☎44 20 7436 8282; fax 7436 8181). Open M-F 10am-5pm; **US,** 46 Park Avenue, New York, NY 10016 (☎212-889-3608; fax 679-2835); 1724 20th St., N.W., Washington, D.C. 20009 (☎202-331-4032; fax 331-4036).

MONEY

The currency of El Salvador is the **colón** (sometimes called a *peso*, denoted by a "¢"), which is divided into 100 cents. Since January 1, 2001, the US dollar is official legal tender in El Salvador and is now widely used in various transactions. US dollars can be obtained at any ATM. All shops, buses and vendors will accept either dollars or colones, but prices are not listed consistently in either currency. If you do opt for colones, change any leftovers at the border when leaving, since colones are hard to get rid of elsewhere. **Banco Cuscutlan** and **Banco Salvadoreño** will both cash traveler's checks and give cash advances on credit cards. Cuscutlan's ATM, **Cajero de Oro,** accepts the widest variety of cards.

PASSPORTS, VISAS AND CUSTOMS

Passport (p. 21). Required of all visitors.

Visas and Tourist cards (p. 22). US citizens can get a free visa from a Salvadoran Consulate on US territory, or pay US$10 for a 60-day tourist card. Canadians can get a visa for CDN$30 or can get a tourist card for US$10. Prearranged visas are required for visitors from New Zealand, Australia, and South Africa. Travelers from the UK do not need prearranged visas.

Inoculations and Medications (p. 29). None required.

Work Permit (p. 22). Required for all foreigners planning to work in El Salvador.

Driver's Permit. Drivers entering El Salvador need car registration, driver's license, and proof of insurance. Visitors can drive with their US license for up to 30 days. Permits are required for longer stays and can be purchased from the National Police; ¢100. Rental car drivers enjoy a grace period of 90 days. For more information, consult the **Auto Club of El Salvador** (☎221 0557).

Airport Exit Fee. US$27.

A 10% **tip** is appropriate for the majority of restaurants. Expect to pay more for lodgings and food in El Salvador than elsewhere in Central America, with reasonably priced rooms costing US$7-15 per night and meals costing US$5-15.

COLÓN	❶	❷	❸	❹	❺
ACCOMMODATIONS	¢1-50	¢51-80	¢81-110	¢111-150	¢151+
	US$1-5.50	US$5.50-9	US$9-12	US$12-16.50	US$16.50+
FOOD	¢1-30	¢31-50	¢51-70	¢71-100	¢101+
	US$1-3	US$3-5.50	US$5.50-7	US$7-11	US$11+

SAFETY

Violent and petty crime remains prevalent in El Salvador. Central San Salvador, San Miguel, and Sonsonate are particularly dangerous due mostly to gangs. Demonstrations and sit-ins may occur at anytime and any place in the country. A recent spate of demonstrations arose in May 2002 against the Central American Free Trade Agreement. Be vigilant and cautious while conducting financial exchanges either inside the bank or at ATMs--several armed robberies have occurred where people were followed after completing a bank transaction. A new **tourist police** is mostly found in national parks, and they will accompany travelers to volcanoes and mountain peaks for free. In some cases a formal letter may need to be written to request a police guide. In these cases the letter should be typed with the name of the destination, date, and number of people and addressed to the *Jefe Delegación de* (name of the city). The **emergency phone number** throughout the country was recently changed to ☎911. For other tips and advice, see **Personal Safety**, p. 26.

HEALTH

Stomach ailments are the main problem; it's best to watch what you eat and to drink bottled water. Malaria is present on the coast, and dengue fever has been reported throughout the country. For more information, see **Health**, p. 29.

BORDER CROSSINGS

GUATEMALA. There are four land crossings. The most northern is **La Hachadura/ Ciudad Pedro de Alvarado**, on the Pacific Coast 66km west of Sonsonate. For more on coming from Guatemala, see p.46. Farther south is **Las Chinamas/Valle Nuevo:** 25km west of Ahuachapán (see p. 296). Below that, **San Cristóbal**, 30km from Santa

Ana, with buses to Guatemala City. The most southern land crossing is **Anguiatú**, 12km north of Metapán, near Esquipulas, Guatemala.

HONDURAS. There are three land crossings. **El Poy**, in the northern highlands, is closest to Nueva Ocotepeque, Honduras (see p. 426). **El Amatillo**, in the east, is 15km east of Santa Rosa de Lima, and near Choluteca, Honduras (see p. 317). Last is **Sabanetas**, near Perquín north of San Miguel; see San Miguel for buses (p. 312). There are irregular **ferry** departures from **La Unión** to ports in Honduras and **Nicaragua** in the Gulf of Fonseca (see p. 318).

KEEPING IN TOUCH

Mail sent to the US or Europe from El Salvador is relatively reliable; air mail letters take one to two weeks. Sending a post card to North America costs US$.29, to Europe, Australia, and New Zealand US$.72; letters US$.45/US$.75; packages to North America US$1.43 per 1kg. Express mail services in San Salvador, such as DHL, tap into the US Postal Service. For example, they can get a letter from New York to El Salvador in two to three days for US$22.25. **Federal Express** (www.fedex.com; Australia ☎ 13 2610; US and Canada ☎ 800-247-4747; New Zealand ☎ 0800 73 3339; UK ☎ 0800 12 3800) can get from London to El Salvador in two to three days for UK£37. Letters sent to San Salvador's main post office should be addressed to "Centro de Gobierno, San Salvador."

> Marlene HERNÁNDEZ
> Lista de Correos
> Santa Ana (CITY)
> República de El Salvador

Salvadoran **phone** numbers have seven digits and require no area code. For major company operator access numbers see the inside back cover. The public system just went private, with **Telecom** being the most common now (with yellow booths). Calls within the country cost only about ¢0.10 for a few minutes. Calls to the US or Europe are expensive, so it's better to call collect or use a calling card. For US phone company access numbers, see the inside back cover.

COUNTRY CODE	503

TRANSPORTATION

Buses and **cars** are the easiest ways to get around El Salvador. The roads are poorly maintained and due to low enforcement of traffic laws, **driving** in El Salvador requires significant defensive skills. Drive with your doors locked and windows raised, avoid travel outside metropolitan areas after dark, and avoid unpaved roads at all times because of random banditry, carjackings, kidnappings, and the lack of police assistance. There are many local and inter-city bus systems: every bus route has a number and there is a dispatcher at every bus station who has the most recent schedules. However, drivers are not formally trained and generally do not adhere to traffic regulations. Also, assaults and robberies on buses are common. Radio-dispatched **taxis** are the safest way to travel if you don't have a car. **Pickups** have become a semi-formal mode of transport in some areas with regular schedules and fixed fares, but always be sure the vehicle is safe and that your destination and fare are agreed upon before leaving.

ORIENTATION

El Salvador's larger towns, like those of Nicaragua, Honduras, and Guatemala, have streets gridded with north-south *avenidas* and east-west *calles*—the opposite of Costa Rica. Most cities have a central *avenida* and a central *calle*. Even-numbered streets and avenues are on one side of each main drag, odd numbers on the other. In most cities (including San Salvador), odd-numbered *avenidas* and *calles* increase in number to the west and north of the center, respectively; likewise, even-numbered *avenidas* and *calles* increase toward the east and south. An address given as "3/5 Av., 2 Calle," is on Calle 2 between Av. 3 and 5.

HOLIDAYS

Each town has its own patron saint and a designated day of celebration. The country has a day of unity in celebration of El Salvador's patron saint. National holidays include: **January 1,** New Year's Day; **March/April,** *Semana Santa;* **May 1,** Labor Day; **August 3 to 6,** *Festival de El Salvador del Mundo;* **September 15,** Independence Day; **October 12,** *Día de la Raza;* **November 2,** All Souls' Day; **November 5,** the First Cry of Independence; **December 25,** Christmas. Most businesses keep limited hours during holidays; expect closures for the duration of *Semana Santa.*

SAN SALVADOR

Arriving in bustling San Salvador from more relaxed rural areas, travelers may find themselves slightly shell-shocked by the contrast. Like many Central American cities, the middle and upper classes have sequestered themselves to their own suburban neighborhoods, most notably the Zona Rosa, with nightclubs and shopping malls. San Salvador is quickly becoming one of the biggest economic players in the region, but the dilapidated downtown is a reminder of how many are being left behind. Still, with everything in the country within a 3hr. radius, the capital is a convenient base, and offers all the modern conveniences and luxuries not available elsewhere. Many parks and trees work to diminish the concrete-jungle feeling that many other big cities suffer from, and lend San Salvador a charm of its own.

✈ INTERCITY TRANSPORTATION

Flights: The international airport is 44km south of the city, reachable by bus #138 from Terminal del Sur (45min., every 5min., ¢5) and serviced by **Taca** (☎267 8222); **American** (☎298 0777; open M-F 8am-6pm); **Air France** (☎263 8101); **Continental** (☎260 3263; open M-F 8am-6pm); **Mexicana** (☎271 5936); **United** (☎298 5462; open M-F 8am-7pm). To get there, Acaya **taxis,** 19th Av., 3 Calle (☎271 4937), runs a microbus to the airport (6, 7, 10am, 2pm; ¢25). The #400 minibus departs from the south side of Plaza Barrios (1hr., every 15min. 5am-5pm, ¢8), and the #138 departs from Terminal del Sur. (1hr., every 5min., ¢5). A taxi to the airport costs ¢140 with Acaya. The Acaya office is just next door to Puerto Bus.

Domestic Buses: Terminal Occidente, on Blvd. Venezuela near 49 Av., serves destinations in the western half of the country, and can be reached by bus **#34** from *el centro,* or bus #44 from Metrocentro, exit on Blvd Venezuela. **Terminal Oriente,** the point of departure for buses headed eastward, is in the far east of the city, down Alameda Juan Pablo II and reached by bus **#29** from Metrocentro and bus #34 from *el centro* headed east. **Terminal del Sur** is the site of southward-bound travel, and can be reached by bus #26 from the National University or *el centro* including the airport. Take the bus all the way to its last stop in San Marcos. Bus listings below begin with the departure point, followed by schedule information. Most routes charge ¢1 more on weekends.

Ahuachapán: Occidente, #202 or 204. (2hr., every 18min. 4am-7:30pm, ¢7.)

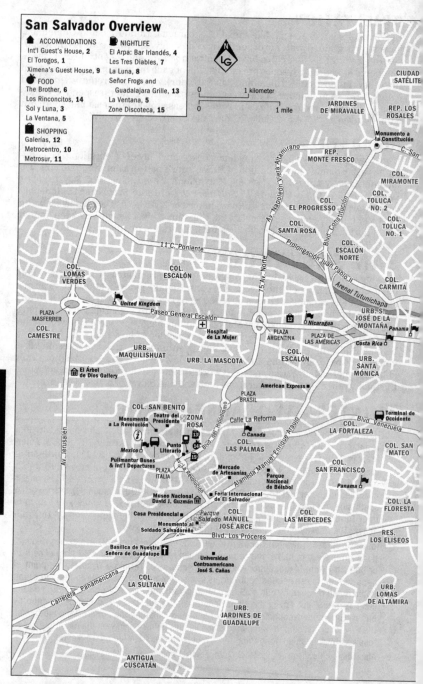

San Salvador Overview

🏠 ACCOMMODATIONS
Int'l Guest's House, **2**
El Torogos, **1**
Ximena's Guest House, **9**

🍴 FOOD
The Brother, **6**
Los Rinconcitos, **14**
Sol y Luna, **3**
La Ventana, **5**

🛍 SHOPPING
Galerías, **12**
Metrocentro, **10**
Metrosur, **11**

🎵 NIGHTLIFE
El Arpa: Bar Irlandés, **4**
Les Tres Diables, **7**
La Luna, **8**
Señor Frogs and
  Guadalajara Grille, **13**
La Ventana, **5**
Zone Discoteca, **15**

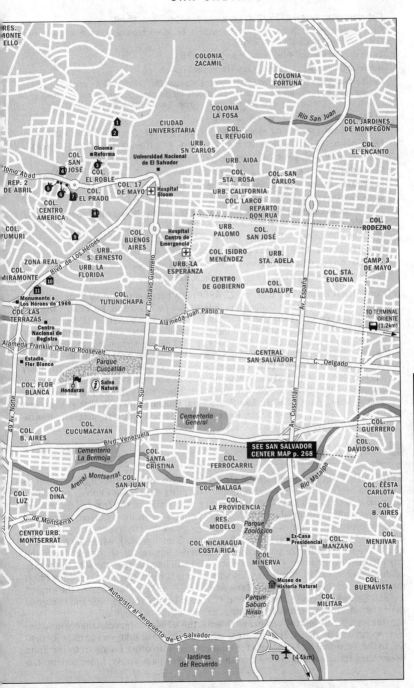

RES.
MONTE
ELLO

COLONIA
ZACAMIL

COLONIA
FORTUNA

COLONIA
LA FOSA

Río San Juan

COL. JARDINES
DE MONPEGÓN

CIUDAD
UNIVERSITARIA

COL.
EL REFUGIO

COL.
EL ENCANTO

URB.
SN CARLOS

Cinema
Reforma

Universidad Nacional
de El Salvador

URB. AIDA

COL.
SAN
JOSÉ

COL.
EL ROBLE

COL.
STA. ROSA

COL. SAN
CARLOS

tonio Abad

REP. 2
DE ABRIL

COL. 17
DE MAYO

Hospital
Bloom

URB. CALIFORNIA

COL. LARCO
REPARTO
DON RUA

COL.
EL PRADO

COL.
CENTRO
AMERICA

COL.
RODEZNO

COL.
YUMURI

URB.
PALOMO

COL.
SAN JOSÉ

Hospital
Centro de
Emergencia

COL.
BUENOS
AIRES

ZONA REAL

URB.
S. ERNESTO

Blvd. de Los Héroes

COL. ISIDRO
MENÉNDEZ

URB.
STA. ADELA

CAMP. 3
DE MAYO

COL.
MIRAMONTE

URB. LA
FLORIDA

URB. LA
ESPERANZA

COL. STA.
EUGENIA

CENTRO
DE GOBIERNO

COL.
GUADALUPE

COL.
TUTUNICHAPA

Monumento a
Los Héroes de 1969

Alameda Juan Pablo II

TO TERMINAL
ORIENTE
(1.2km)

COL. LAS
TERRAZAS

Centro
Nacional de
Registro

Alameda Franklin Delano Roosevelt

C. Arce

CENTRAL
SAN SALVADOR

C. Delgado

Estadio
Flor Blanca

Parque
Cuscatlán

COL. FLOR
BLANCA

Honduras

Salva
Natura

Av. Cuscatlán

COL.
GUERRERO

COL. FLOR
BLANCA

Cementerio
General

SEE SAN SALVADOR
CENTER MAP p. 268

COL.
DAVIDSON

COL.
B. AIRES

COL.
CUCUMACAYAN

Blvd. Venezuela

COL.
FERROCARRIL

Cementerio
La Bermoja

Arenal Montserrat

COL.
SANTA
CRISTINA

Río Matalpa

COL. ÉÉSTA
CARLOTA

COL.
LUZ

COL.
DINA

COL.
SAN JUAN

COL. MALAGA

COL.
B. AIRES

C. de Montserrat

COL.
LA PROVIDENCIA

CENTRO URB.
MONTSERRAT

RES.
MODELO

Parque
Zoológico

Ex-Casa
Presidencial

COL.
MANZANO

COL.
MENJIVAR

COL. NICARAGUA
COSTA RICA

COL.
MINERVA

Museo de
Historia Natural

COL.
MILITAR

COL.
BUENAVISTA

Autopisto al Aeropuerto de El Salvador

Parque
Saburo
Hirao

Jardines
del Recuerdo

TO ✈ (44km)

25 AV. Sur

Av. Gustavo Guerrero

Av. España

49 AV. Norte

Chalatenango: Oriente, #125. (2hr., every 10min. 4am-6:30pm, ¢6.50.)

Cojutepeque: Oriente; leaves from the roundabout, Av. Independencia, across from the terminal. #113. (1hr., every 5min. 4am-9pm, ¢3.)

Costa del Sol: Del Sur, #495. (1hr., every 30min., ¢6.)

Ilobasco: Oriente, #111. (1½hr., every 10min. 5am-7:30pm, ¢6.)

La Libertad: South of the Parque Bolívar (centro), 6a Calle Pte, between 13 Av. and 15 Av., #102. It also passes by on Blvd. Venezuela just outside the Terminal Occidente, but you have to be alert, as it doesn't always stop. (45min., every 10min. 5am-7:30pm, ¢4.)

La Palma: Oriente, #119. (4hr., every 30min. 4am-4pm, ¢12.)

La Union: Oriente, #304. (4hr., every 30min. 3:45am-7pm, ¢15; direct 7 and 8am, ¢35.)

Panchimalco: From Av. 29 de Agosto and 12 Calle Pte, #12. (Every 20min. 5:30am-7:20pm.)

Puerto El Triunfo: Del Sur, #185. (1½hr., every 30min. 9am-5:30pm, ¢9.)

San Miguel: Oriente, #301. (3hr., every 10min. 3:30am-5pm, ¢15; direct 7 and 8am, ¢35.)

San Vicente: Oriente, #116. (1¾hr., every 10min. 4:40am-9pm, ¢5.)

Santa Ana: Occidente, #201. (2hr., every 10min. 4am-5:30pm, ¢5.)

Santa Rosa de Lima: (en route to **El Amatillo**; see **El Amatillo: Border with Honduras,** p. 317) Oriente, #306. (5hr., every 40min. 3:45am-3:45pm, ¢21.)

Sonsonate: Occidente, #205. (1½hr., every 25min. 4:45am-7:45pm, ¢5.)

Suchitoto: Oriente, #129. (1½hr, every 15min. 5am-7pm, ¢4; after 6pm, ¢5.)

Usulután: del Sur, #302. (2hr., every 10min. 4am-5pm, ¢10.)

Zacatecoluca: Del Sur, #133. (1½hr., every 10min. 4am-8pm, ¢5.)

International Buses: Tica Bus (☎222 4808) has buses leaving daily from Hotel San Carlos, 10 Av. Nte., Calle Concepción. **Puerto Bus** (☎222 2158; fax 222 2138), and **King Quality** (☎271 1361) leave from their office in a strip-mall, at 19 Av., Alameda Juan Pablo II, across the street from the governmental center with the Federal Reserve Bank building. Also next to the *Zona Rosa* on Blvd del Hipodrómo #4115. **Pullmantur** (☎243 1300) departs from the San Salvador Marriott, Av. de la Revolución. Destinations include: **Guatemala City, Guatemala**(Puerto: every hr. 4am-4:30pm; ¢70, luxury bus ¢95; King Quality: US$23; Pullmantur: 7am and 3pm, US$25); **Managua, Nicaragua** (Tica: 11hr., 5am, US$25; King Quality: 5:30am, US$30); **San José, Costa Rica** (Tica: 1½days, 5am, US$35); **San Pedro Sula, Honduras** (King Quality: 6:30am and 12:30pm, US$23); **Panama City, Panama** (Tica: 5am, US$60); **Tegucigalpa, Honduras** (King Quality: 6:30, 10:30am, 1:30pm; US$25).

✠ ORIENTATION

UPON ARRIVAL. The **international airport** lies 44km south of the capital. To get to San Salvador, you have several options. The most expensive choice, and safest after dark, is to take a **taxi** (¢140). The other is to walk out the front of the airport along the main road for about 100m until it comes to an intersection; **microbuses** pass by every five minutes. **#400** microbuses go to the city center, dropping you off in front of the Cathedral (1hr., every 15min. 5am-5pm, ¢8), while the **#138** regular or microbus will take you to the Terminal del Sur, on the southern edge of the city (45min., every 5min., ¢5), from where you will have to take the **#26** to the city center (30min., ¢1.50). If it coincides with your schedule, the most reliable option may be to take the shuttle run by **Taxis Acaya** (☎271 4937), which leaves the airport for San Salvador (9am, 1, and 5:30pm; ¢25), and brings you through the center to their station, from which surrounding areas are easily accessible.

After arriving by **bus** to **Terminal de Oriente,** the **#29** local bus can take you to the Metrocentro/Blvd. de los Héroes area, while the **#34** will take you to the city center, to the Terminal de Occidente for connections with other buses, or to the Zona Rosa/Plaza Italia area in the west of the city. Buses pass on Av. Independencia, a few blocks west of the terminal, heading east into the city. The large highway signs will point you in the right direction; look for a bus stop on the side of the road. From the **Terminal de Occidente,** bus **#34** heading east will take you to the *centro* or Terminal de Oriente, while #34 heading west will take you to the Zona Rosa/Plaza Italia area. To catch the **#44** to Metrocentro/ Blvd. de los Héroes, turn left out of the terminal, walking east down Blvd. Venezuela. When that meets 49 Av. Sur after 4 blocks, turn left, cross the street, and wait for #44. **Taxis** will take you from either of the Terminals to a hotel in the Blvd. de los Héroes area (about ¢40).

LAYOUT. San Salvador employs the standard Salvadoran grid system in the older *el centro* (see map p. 261), but outside of the city center the streets to conform to the terrain, and it is easiest to navigate by major streets and landmarks. *Avenidas* run north-south, and *calles* run east-west. The northwest corner of the **cathedral,** from which the *centro histórico* radiates, is the city's origin. The main *calles* are **Calle Delgado** to the east and **Calle Arce** to the west. The principal north-south *avenida,* Av. Cuscatlán, becomes Av. España north of the cathedral. Running east-west, **2 Calle Oriente** changes into **Calle Rubén Darío** before becoming **Alameda Franklin Delano Roosevelt,** and then **Paseo General Escalón** before terminating at the **Plaza Masferrer** at the western border of the city. The downtown area, **el centro,** anchored by the cathedral and dense with markets, is on the eastern side of the city. **Zona Rosa,** sophisticated home to embassies and luxury hotels by day and full of raging clubs by night, marks the southwest. The ever-popular malls, **Metro Centro** and **Metrosur,** are conveniently located at the center of the metropolis's activity and the juncture of the major highways. **Boulevard de los Héroes** jets north of the malls, and is a haven for fast food and drive-thrus. The Boulevard heads to the **University** and towards **Calle San Antonio** with its lively international scene.

As with any big city, visitors should use caution when walking around. Crime has risen in past years, making muggings and robberies common. The city generally becomes safer the farther east from the *centro* you go. Avoid the *centro* at night. The Zona Rosa and Blvd. de los Héroes are relatively safe at night. Still, all travelers should take taxis after dark. Some gangs work the buses and bus stops, asking for small (¢2-3) donations; they usually have tattoos on their foreheads which may be covered by hats.

⊏ LOCAL TRANSPORTATION

Local Buses: Buses cruise to destinations throughout the city approximately 6am-7 or 9pm, depending on the route. Fares ¢1.50, more on weekends. Buses stop only at designated stops, which are generally clearly marked, often with route numbers. Pay when you enter and leave out the back; drivers accept *colones* or US dollars. From the center, most buses pass by either the market area or Plaza Barrios in front of the cathedral. Faster microbuses run most of these routes as well (¢2). Buses do not necessarily return via the same path; some routes loop around instead. It is generally easiest and fastest to ask locals which bus to take to your destination. Here are some key lines:

#34: Good for all east to west needs, running from the Plaza Italia in the west to the **Terminal de Occidente** through the center by the Mercado Central. Ends at the **Terminal de Oriente.**

#30b: If you're staying in the Blvd. de los Héroes area, this is your bus. It runs from the Universidad Nacional, along Blvd. de los Héroes to the stop by Metrosur, on to the Plaza Las Américas, along Paseo General Escalón, and, most importantly, the **Zona Rosa.** From **Zona Rosa,** the bus returns north via Alameda Araujo and resumes the Blvd. de los Héroes route once again.

#30: Useful north-south route from **Universidad Nacional** through Metrocentro/Metrosur, and then to the center on Calle Rubén Darío until **Parque Libertad.** Return bus on 1a Calle Poniente.

#44: Runs from the Metrocentro passing close to Terminal de Occidente before reaching the **Autopista del Sur** and **Antiguo Cuscatlán.** Microbuses reach the US embassy in Antiguo Cuscatlán.

#52: Runs from **Terminal de Oriente** via JPII, past Metrocentro, to Plaza Las Américas, and on to **Plaza Masferrer,** and back again.

#24: Connects Metrocentro to **Terminal de Oriente.**

#26: Goes to Terminal del Sur, leaving from Plaza Barrios on the cathedral's west side.

#101: Heading to the Santa Tecla southwest of the city, also connects the center to Plaza Italia. From **Plaza Barrios,** past Metrosur, down Alameda Araujo and beyond the Feria Internacional, returning along roughly the same route. **101D** goes west to Plaza Masferrer before heading south.

Car Rental: Prices range from US$50-120 per day, including insurance. **Budget,** Condominio Balam Quitze, Paseo Gral. Escalón, Local 3-A (☎263 5583); **Hertz** (☎339 8004); **Avis,** Colonia Flor Blanca, 43 Av. Sur #137 (☎260 7157). To rent from the major companies you must be at least 25 yrs. old with a valid driver's license and credit card. However, **Sandoval** will rent to anyone with a valid license and credit card.

⚡ PRACTICAL INFORMATION

TOURIST AND FINANCIAL SERVICES

Tourist Information: Corporación Salvadoreña de Turismo (CORSATUR), 508 Blvd. del Hipódromo (☎243 7835), though a little out of the way, is the best place for free maps, brochures, and info. Take bus #30b or #34 to Plaza Italia in Zona Rosa. Go past the plaza onto Hipódromo and follow it all the way up the hill. Open M-F 8am-5:30pm. They also have a branch office at the airport. Alternatively, try the **Instituto Salvadoreño de Turismo (ISTU;** ☎222 8000), located between 9a Av. Sur and 11a Av. Sur in the center of town on Calle Rubén Darío. Maps ¢10. Information on Parque Nacional Cerro Verde can be found here. Open M-F 8am-4pm. The most convenient source of information may be **Lena Johannessen** (☎260 2427), who manages Ximena's Guesthouse (see **Accommodations,** below) and is also regional manager for the Guatemala-based, English-language magazine *Revue,* which has info on goings-on in the city. Pick up a free copy of the magazine at Ximena's, or anywhere else you happen to see a stack.

Embassies: Australia and **New Zealand** have no embassies here. **Canada,** 63 Av. Sur, Alam. Roosevelt (☎279 4659). Open M-F 8am-noon and 1:30-4:30pm. **UK,** Paseo General Escalón #4830 (☎263 6520; fax 263 6516). Open M-Th 8am-1pm and 2-4pm, F 8am-1pm. **US** (☎298 1666), Residencial Santa Elena, Final Bl Santa Elena Sur, Antiguo Cuscatlán. Open M-F 8am-4:30pm. A booklet distributed by the tourist office contains a list of more embassies and consulates.

Banks: Most big banks will change travelers checks or dollars. **Banco Hipotecario,** Av. Cuscatlán, 4 Calle, changes with little fuss. Open M-F 9am-4:30pm, Sa 9am-noon. **Banco Cuscatlán,** downstairs in the Metrocentro mall, across from the Telecom office, will change checks and US dollars. Open M-F 9am-6pm, Sa 9am-2pm. **ATMs** are found at major gas stations, malls, and many banks throughout the city. All ATMs accept Visa; fewer accept Cirrus and Plus. Check out Metrocentro for a wide selection of machines.

American Express: (☎279 3844, (travelers checks help 964 6665), Calle la Mascota and Interamerican Hwy., Comercial la Mascota. Take bus #101 from the city center or bus #30b from Metrocentro. Open M-F 8am-noon and 2-5pm, Sa 9am-noon.

Immigration Office: (☎221 2111), on 15th Av. Nte. in the Centro de Gobierno just north of Alameda Juan Pablo II. Extends visas and tourist cards. Open M-F 8am-4pm.

Special Permits: Salva Natura (☎279 1515; fax 279 0220) on 33 Ave. Sur #640, in Colonia Flor Blanca. gives permits for **Parque Nacional El Imposible.** You will need to bring or fax them a letter with dates of the trip and names of those going. Permits are ¢50 per person, and include a guide who will meet you at the park. Office open M-F

8am-12:30pm and 2-5:30pm. From Av. Roosevelt (a 15min. walk from Metrocentro), head south to 16 Decima Calle to reach 33 Ave. Sur; difficult to access via bus. **Ministerio de Agricultura,** Servicio de Parques Nacionales (☎294 0566; fax 294 0575), on Canton and Calle El Matezano, in the eastern suburb of Soyapango (bus #33a from the northern edge of Parque Libertad), grants permits for **Parque Nacional Montecristo.** Again, bring or fax a letter with names and dates. Inquiries should be made at least a week ahead of departure, particularly in Aug., during *Semana Santa,* and at the end of the year. You will receive a permission slip required for overnight stays in the park and preferred for all guests. Pay the ¢50 fee at the park, not at the office.

LOCAL SERVICES

English Bookstores: Punto Literario on the North side of the Plaza Italia, near the Zona Rosa. The best place in town for English books. #30b from Metrocentro or #34 from the center to Plaza Italia. Open daily 10am-7pm. Credit cards accepted. Also check out **The Book Shop,** in Metrocentro, and **Eutopia** in the Galerías. Most luxury hotels have American magazines and newspapers at their newsstands (¢3-4).

Markets and Malls: The **Mercado Central,** Av. 5/7, 6 Calle, starts a few blocks west of Plaza Barrios and the Cathedral and branches out in a bustling web of commerce. Sells *everything.* The frenetic pace can be invigorating, but take care not to get lost; street signs, where they exist, are obscured by the vendors' booths. Open daily 7am-5pm. The **Mercado Ex-Cuartel,** 8 Av. and Calle Delgado, to the east of Plaza Barrios, features *artesanía* and handicrafts. The market is located in a somewhat dangerous area of town, so go early. Open daily 8am-5pm. Three large malls offer all modern conveniences and extensive shopping options. **Metrocentro** sits on Blvd. de los Héroes and is home to a supermarket, movie theater, and countless ATMs. By far the most ritzy, **Galerías,** is located on Paseo Escalón between Plaza las Americas and Plaza Beethoven.

EMERGENCY AND COMMUNICATIONS

Police: ☎911.

Red Cross: (☎222 5155), in the Centro de Gobierno.

Pharmacy: Farmacia Internacional, 49 Av., Blvd. de los Héroes and Alameda Juan Pablo II, in the mini-mall just south of Metrosur. Open 24hr. **Farmacia Metrosur** is a convenient option as well. Open daily 8:30am-7pm. Major credit cards accepted.

Telephones: Telecom, 5 Av., Calle Rubén Darío, just southwest of Plaza Barrios. Open M-F 8am-6pm, Sa-Su 8am-noon. A smaller branch downstairs in the Metrocentro, across from the Banco de Cuscatlan. Open M-Sa 9am-6pm.

Internet Access: Infocentros, on Blvd. del Hipodromo before Plaza Italia, is the best place for Internet access. ¢20 per hr., students ¢11 per hr. Open M-Sa 8am-8pm, Su 9am-6pm. Other internet cafes line the city streets, particularly on Calle San Antonio and in the Northwest area of El Centro. Most charge about US$1 per hr.

Post Office, on Blvd. Centro Gobierno, a couple blocks north of Alameda Juan Pablo II. Internet access is also available. Open M-F 8am-4pm, Sa 8am-noon. Another **office** in Metrocentro. Open M-F 8am-7pm, Sa 8am-noon.

▐ ACCOMMODATIONS

San Salvador's budget accommodations involve a little give and take. Consider spending a bit more, as cheap rooms are often in unsafe neighborhoods. A good compromise are dorm style accommodations, which offer cheap beds in secure neighborhoods. You might even meet some new friends. Secure, budget hotels cluster in the residential neighborhoods between Blvd. de los Héroes and the national university, the center of the city, and near the Terminal Oriente.

EL SALVADOR

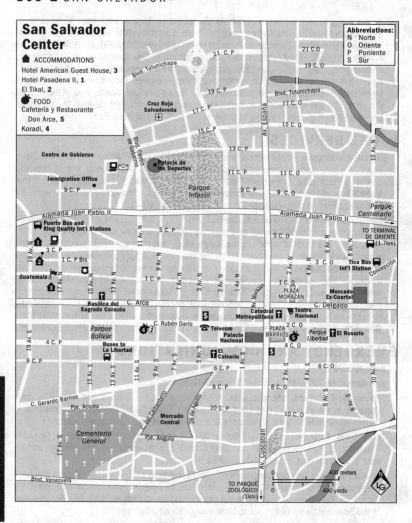

San Salvador Center

🏠 ACCOMMODATIONS

Hotel American Guest House, **3**
Hotel Pasadena II, **1**
El Tikal, **2**

🍴 FOOD

Cafetería y Restaurante
  Don Arce, **5**
Koradi, **4**

Abbreviations:
N Norte
O Oriente
P Poniente
S Sur

BETWEEN LOS HÉROES AND THE UNIVERSITY

The guest houses between Blvd. de los Héroes and the National University are safe, moderately cheap, and located in relatively tranquil and smog-free neighborhoods. The Metrocentro mall, to the south on Blvd. de los Héroes, promises to fulfill your every material need, while the university-influenced bohemian bars lining Calle San Antonio Abad to the north satisfy cravings for live music and good beer.

▨ **Ximena's Guest House,** 202 Calle San Salvador (☎260 2481), from Blvd. de los Héroes, turn west onto Calle Gabriela Mistral; take your first left and then first right. Travelers flock to the homey rooms. Manager Lena is friendly and knowledgeable. Common room has cable TV, and a kitchen is in the works. English spoken. Laundry service. The

Spanish School Cihuatán functions on the premises. Ask about the organic farm. Dorms ¢35-65; singles with hot-water bath and TV ¢190. ❺

International Guest's House, 35 Av. Nte (☎226 7343), 3 blocks north of Blvd. Universitario, is the Salvadoran version (i.e. super-friendly) of a bed and breakfast. The rooms, set in a villa with a well-tended garden, all have a private bath and fan. Also check out the small selection of books on the war (Spanish only). Breakfast included. Singles US$17; doubles US$30. Reserve a day or two in advance. Credit cards accepted. ❺

El Torogos, 35 Av. Norte north of Blvd. Universitario (☎235 4172), next door to International, is also like a bed and breakfast. Every 2 rooms share a hot-water bath, but each room (sleeping up to 4) has cable TV. Internet, laundry, and Spanish lessons. Breakfast included. US$15 per person. Credit cards accepted with 10% surcharge. ❹

CITY CENTER

Staying in San Salvador's *centro histórico* will put you in the middle of the action. Buses running to all parts of the city pass through every second and the frenetic rush of street vendors and markets wail just outside your door. It is not a safe area for visitors to walk in after nightfall when the streets empty and everything shuts down. Food and nightlife options are also limited.

Hotel American Guest House, 17 Av. Norte (☎271 0224), between Calle Arce and 1a Calle Pte. All rooms have TV, fan, and baths with hot water in this cluttered but cozy old home. Singles ¢80, with bath ¢160; doubles ¢100/¢180. MC/V. ❷

Hotel Pasadena II, 3a Calle Poniente, 17/19 Av. Norte (☎221 2782), is sparkling clean and bright. All rooms have bath, fan and TV. Singles ¢90; doubles ¢130. ❸

El Tikal (☎271 5710) right next to Casa de Huéspedes. Bare rooms have private bath. 1-2 person rooms ¢50. ❶

NEAR THE TERMINAL DE ORIENTE

The hotels around the Terminal de Oriente are convenient. However, the area is dirty and dangerous, and walking around at night is risky. For those wishing to pass through the city as quickly as possible, there are a couple relatively safe hotels about a 5min. walk from the terminal on Calle Concepción. To get there, head west from the terminal, bearing right onto Alameda Juan Pablo II where the highway splits. After a few blocks, turn right on Calle Concepción before the Esso station. You may find it worth the time to take a taxi (US$4-5) to Los Héroes.

Hotel Imperial (☎222 4920), 2 blocks north of the Esso station on Calle Concepción, has an air of faded grandeur and large, basic rooms. ¢35 per person, with bath ¢60. ❶

Hotel Yucatán, north of the Imperial. Concrete rooms are dark and dusty, but the beds are thick and comfy. Singles ¢30, with decent private bath ¢60; doubles ¢50/¢85. ❶

⊡ FOOD

Cheap, tasty food in San Salvador is always close. Small *pupusa* stands are ubiquitous, even in some of the quieter residential neighborhoods. The cheapest places to eat are the *comedores* and *pupuserías* in the *centro*. The area around **Los Héroes,** in addition to being one of San Salvador's prime nightspots, is the US fast-food row. Most restaurants are open until at least 10pm, some until midnight or later. All the malls have plenty of options, including large food courts. Pricier, higher-quality restaurants line Blvd. Hipódromo in the **Zona Rosa** and the **Paseo de Escalón** to the north. The **Zona Real,** behind the Hotel Camino Real across the street from Metrocentro, has a dozen or so restaurants, with options ranging from seafood to Chinese food to hamburgers. The selection of bars and restaurants on **Calle San Antonio Abad** has international flair and a range of price options.

▨ **The Brother**, Calle San Antonio Abad. This is the place for a great, inexpensive meal before a night on the town. Excellent, large portions of meat are grilled in front of you on the front deck, as are the baked potatoes and scrumptious garlic bread. Full dinners ¢20-35. Open daily 7pm-3am. Cash only. ❶

▨ **La Ventana,** Calle San Antonio Abad. This ultra-hip, ultra-trendy, and ultra-popular restaurant boasts fancy food and a great wine and liquor selection. Meals ¢40-70; desserts ¢15-20. Open Tu-Sa 8am-1am, Su 10am-noon. Major credit cards accepted. ❷

Restaurante Los Rinconcitos, Blvd. del Hipódromo in the Zona Rosa. Serves up gourmet meals in a cosmopolitan setting. At night, it fills with a well-dressed crowd heading to nearby *discotecas*. Meals ¢40-90. Open daily 4pm-3am. Credit cards accepted. ❸

Sol y Luna, Calle San Antonio and Blvd. Universitario. A nice vegetarian restaurant that serves typical dishes minus the meat. Soy hamburger ¢14. Open M-Sa 8am-9pm. ❶

Koradi, 11 Av. Norte in the *centro*. A small *cafeteria* and health-food store, Koradi serves veggie food at decent prices, including fresh salad (¢8) rice (¢6) and hearty rolls in a typical *comedor* setting. Vegetarians beware: the pizza may have a meat topping; don't ask, they can't explain. Open M-F 8am-5:45pm, Sa 8am-3:45pm. ❶

Cafetería y Restaurante Don Arce, 2 Av. Sur, on the southeast corner of Plaza Barrios. Grab a meal and take a reprieve from the chaos of the *centro*. Cafeteria-style setup and selection of *típico* in a spacious 2nd fl. restaurant. Lunches ¢20-25. ❶

◎ SIGHTS

Most of the historical sights in San Salvador are downtown in the *centro histórico*, while the majority of newer buildings and shopping malls are in the outlying areas of the city. All major sights are easily accessible by local buses. Some were damaged by the 2001 earthquake, so access may be limited. Check out **Planeta Alternetivo** for music, theater, and event listings for the entire country every Thursday in *La Prensa Graphica*.

CATEDRAL METROPOLITANA. Looming over the north side of Plaza Barrios, the colorful, tiled dome of the Cathedral is one of San Salvador's hallmarks. The original cathedral was begun in 1808 and destroyed by an earthquake in 1873. Subsequently rebuilt, the new church was brought down again in 1951, this time by fire. The next version was built in simple Byzantine style with drab, unadorned concrete. Oscar Romero, the Archbishop assassinated by the death squads in 1980, rests here. Yet another earthquake damaged the structure in 1986, and the building was closed until the spring of 1999, when reconstruction was finally completed. Today, the country's unique artisan style proudly adorns the exterior. The northwest corner of the cathedral serves as the origin of all street numbers in the city. *(Main entrance on 2a Calle, on the cathedral's south side. Open daily during daylight hours. Free.)*

PALACIO NACIONAL. Built in 1905, this large structure was the seat of the national government until it was ravaged by the 1986 earthquake. Since then it has been closed to visitors while undergoing a massive restoration project that has been prolonged by further damage. *(On the west side of Plaza Barrios.)*

TEATRO NACIONAL. Built in 1911 with funding from the coffee-growing elite, the elegant interior of the recently restored theater reflects the cultural aspirations of its founders. Local art adds an eclectic flair to the parlors and salons. Dance, music, and theater performances should resume early in 2002 after repairs are complete. *(☎ 222 5731. Calle Delgado.)*

IGLESIA EL ROSARIO. This striking graffiti-covered modern church holds enthralling modern sculptures (of steel rebars and other scraps) depicting religious scenes. **Father Delgado,** an important figure in Central America's independence, is entombed here. *(East of Plaza Libertad. Open daily during daylight hours.)*

MUSEO NACIONAL DAVID GÙZMÁN. The government has put a lot of money into rebuilding this museum, and the new facility is one of the best looking buildings in the city. The museum houses El Salvador's finest Maya artifacts, including the intricate **Stela of Tazumal** from El Salvador's most famous Maya site. Repairs are ongoing. *(On Av. Revolución; accessible by bus #34 and 30b.)*

MERCADO NACIONAL DE ARTESANÍAS. This market, on the site of the international fairgrounds, sells *artesanías* from all over the country. Prices tend to be quite a bit higher than in the towns where the pieces originate, but the selection is unbeatable. *(Calle Manuel Enrique Araujo. Accessible by bus #30b. Open daily until 6pm.)*

MONUMENTO A LA REVOLUCIÓN. This soaring, modernist mosaic of a figure breaking free of its shackles and reaching for the sky, surveys the whole eastern side of San Salvador. Ironically, the monument, a tribute to the peoples of Central America, is situated in the center of San Salvador's most exclusive neighborhood. *(Straight uphill from the Plaza de Italia. Accessible by bus #34 or #30b.)*

EL ÁRBOL DE DIOS GALLERY. Fernando Llort, the man famous for the simple, brightly colored designs adorning wooden *artesanía*, displays more complex and interesting work at his gallery here in the city. A large selection of Llort's painting and sculpture is on display. *(Av. Jerusalem at Calle Mascota, 4 blocks south of the Plaza de Masferrer or take #101D leaving from Metrocentro. Open M-Sa 9am-6pm.)*

PARQUE ZOOLÓGICO. Impressively large and considered one of the most modern in Central America, this zoo boasts an outstanding variety of very amusing monkeys and a bright tropical bird community. *(1.5km south of downtown. Take bus #2 from the west side of the cathedral heading south. Open W-Su 9am-4pm. ¢5.)*

BOTANICAL GARDENS. If you prefer nature without cages, the botanical gardens provide a relaxing retreat where you can walk the trails and enjoy thousands of indigenous and foreign species of plants. The gardens sit at the base of a dormant volcanic crater, which was a lagoon until an eruption in the 18th century. *(#101C bus from 3 Av. Sur and Calle Rubén Darío; get off after 45min. in Antiguo Cuzcatlán; then follow the signs. Or catch the #44 minibus from Blvd de los Héroes. Open Tu-Su 9am-5:30pm. ¢4.).*

STEPHEN HAWKING MUSEUM. This hands-on museum will give you the chance to learn about the country's geography and natural disasters while having fun with 3-D demonstrations and distorting mirrors. An awesome satellite photo of El Salvador is worth checking out, either before or after you head out to conquer the peaks and enjoy the lakes. *(Calle Reforma in Zona Rosa, 3 blocks south of Blvd. Hipódromo. ☎ 223 3027. Open M-Sa 10am-4pm. $1.14.)*

🖼 🎵 NIGHTLIFE AND ENTERTAINMENT

San Salvador can get rough at night; be on guard, particularly in the city center. Luckily, the two prime nightlife areas, the Zona Rosa and the area north of Blvd. de los Héroes, tend to be safe. City buses stop running early, so plan on taking a taxi back to your hotel. Taxi fares increase when the buses stop running.

BLVD. DE LOS HÉROES AND CALLE SAN ANTONIO

The area northwest of the Blvd. de los Héroes and in the university neighborhoods on Calle San Antonio Abad fosters a nascent bohemian scene, with a variety of fun, laid-back bars, restaurants with impressive beer, wine, and liquor selections, a live music venue, and even a couple of Irish pubs.

■ **La Luna,** 228 Calle Berlin (☎ 260 2921). The anchor of San Salvador's bohemian scene. One of the city's only concert venues. Live music W-Sa at 9pm (Jazz on W). Screenings of art-house films M 6:30pm. Beer ¢10; mixed drinks ¢22; meals ¢25-50. Cover ranges

from free to ¢50 or more. Pick up a schedule at Ximena's or at the restaurant; reservations recommended for some events. Open daily noon-2am.

Les Tres Diables, Calle San Antonio Abad. Despite the Francophilic name, this bar is
unpretentious and draws a fun, young crowd. Mid-week specials lure the local tough
guys, and on weekends the place jumps until 5 or 6am. No cover. Beers ¢11; cocktails
¢15; 2-for-1 on W; Th ¢5 tequila shots. Opens daily at 8pm. Credit cards accepted.

La Ventana, Calle San Antonio Abad (☎226 5129). A prime watering hole, with the best
selection of wines, liquors, and beers in the country. On weekends it jams until 2am.
Beers ¢12; mixed drinks ¢25 and up. Closed M. Credit cards accepted.

El Arpa: Bar Irlandés, Av. A off Calle San Antonio, behind Nash. The Guinness (¢25),
decor, and music seek to recreate the Irish pub feel. Besides the leprechaun menu, it's
a pretty cool place. Open M-Th 8am-midnight, later F-Sa. Credit cards accepted.

THE ZONA ROSA

On the western edge of the city, amid the most exclusive neighborhoods, the **"Zona
Rosa"** lines the Blvd. del Hipódromo and surrounding streets from the Plaza Italia
north to the Plaza Brasil. This is where the rich and the beautiful come to shake
their stuff until the sun rises—you haven't been to San Salvador until you've seen
this. Some clubs have dress codes, but they are generally pretty lax.

Los Rinconcitos, on Blvd. del Hipódromo. One of the more fashionable places for drinks
after sunset. The good music is barely disturbed by the cell phones of its super chic clientele. Beers ¢14; mixed drinks from ¢22. Open daily 4pm-3am.

Señor Frogs and the Guadalajara Grille. Around the block from Rinconcitos. Non-stop
partying at this branch of the famous Mexican chain. Guadalajara Grille, the bar and
restaurant in front, has a college-bar feel with rowdy groups and neon beer signs. Señor
Frogs, in the cool indoors, hosts a steamy disco at night. W ladies night with an open
bar for females 10-11:30pm. Bar open 7pm-3am. Disco open 10pm-2am.

Zone Discoteca, one block east of Rinconcitos. This disco has all the staples, from loud
bass to strobe lighting and lots of bodies heating up the dance floor. As far as discos
go, it's fairly relaxed. F, Sa US$4 cover; no cover Th. Opens Th-Sa 9pm until late.

MOVIES

The capital is a great place to catch a flick. Theaters typically show subtitled, two-
month-old Hollywood flicks, though the lag time is getting shorter. (Admission
US$3-3.50; most theaters are half-price W. Last showing 9pm.) **Cinemark,** the gigan-
tic red monster looming over Microcentro, has eight screens showing the newest
flicks in town (☎261 2001). Another branch is located in Galerías.

NEAR SAN SALVADOR

Just kilometers from the capital city are a variety of outdoor activities to suit all
moods. La Puerta del Diablo is a popular trip, and parks and lakes abound for
relaxation and enjoying the weather. Many incredible sites and activities in the
area remain unknown. For relatively untrammeled adventure, head to Volcán San
Salvador, or to get even more off the beaten path, talk to Lena at Ximena's Guesthouse. She can help you to explore an organic farm, a newly discovered site of prehistoric fossils, or the most recently uncovered Maya ruins, among other delights.

◤ LAGO DE ILOPANGO

*To the Turicentro: Take **bus** #15 from 1 Calle Pte. and 2 Av. Nte. in San Salvador centro
(45min., every 15min. until 7pm, ¢1.50). From the Terminal de Oriente or Blvd. de los
Héroes, an easier and faster option is to take the #29 bus to the town of **Ilopango** (tell*

*the driver where you're going), from where you can catch the #15 to Apulo (6am-8pm, ¢1.50). **Turicentro** open daily 8am-5pm. Boat trips ¢50 per 30min. for up to 6 people; tubing ¢10 per 30min.; water-skiing (when you can find a boat with a big enough motor to take you, is ¢100 per 30min). Admission ¢7.*

Lago de Ilopango is the largest and deepest crater lake in El Salvador and lies just 16km east of the capital. Steep lush hillsides drop rapidly to the shores of the lake, and several uninhabited islands dot the placid surface of the deep-blue water. The easily accessible **Turicentro ❶**, at Apulo on the north shore of the lake, is the destination of choice for weekenders looking for a little waterfront relaxation; on weekdays you'll have the place to yourself. Two clean pools, picnic areas, showers, changing rooms, and several restaurants line the lake shore, and small bungalows on the edge of the beach can be rented for the day. (Bungalows ¢35 per day plus ¢18 key deposit. Meals ¢15-30.) Watersports and boat trips are popular. *Lanchas* (small boast) are plentiful and their owners are willing to take you for a spin.

For the best views of the lake, the crater, and the volcanoes to the east, take the bus a few kilometers uphill back towards San Salvador to **Restaurante Mirador 70,** where you can have a drink or a relaxing meal on the terrace overlooking the lake. The restaurant is right on the highway, just ask the driver to let you off. (☎295 4768. Beers ¢12; sandwiches ¢35; appetizers ¢10-30. Open daily 8am-6pm.)

◼ VOLCÁN SAN SALVADOR

*Take San Salvador **bus #101** from Plaza Barrios to Santa Tecla (25min., ¢1.50), or **#101D,** which stops in front of Metrosur, and ask someone where the Iglesia de la Concepción is. Bus #103 heads to the town of Boquerón from 4 Av. Nte and Calle Daniel Hernández, near the church (45min., every 45min. 6am-5pm, ¢3). To arrange a pickup for the day, talk to the taxi drivers at the parque central, who can help you contact a driver and find a **guide.** José Misrael Nerios, whose house lies 5min. from the bus stop in Boquerón, on the right past the first bend in the road will guide you up to Boquerón. Machete in hand, he'll act as **bodyguard** (necessary for safety reasons;¢50) or will guide you down the trail to the bottom of the crater (¢100, includes bodyguard fee).*

Volcán San Salvador, situated northwest of the capital, 11km north of the town of Santa Tecla, offers stunning views. The most enjoyable part of a trip here is gazing down 540m into the gaping crater known as **El Boquerón** ("Big Mouth"). Thickly forested cliffs tumble down to the crater floor, from which rises a perfect 50m high cone, the result of a 1917 eruption. A path winds its way down to the bottom of the crater (about 2hr.), and another leaves from the right of the viewpoint and follows the rim of the crater all the way around (2-3hr.).

Alas, the volcano is not all pretty views and symmetrical cones. The 30min. walk from the bus stop in Boquerón to the park entrance is dangerous for foreigners and should under no circumstances be done alone. Physical assaults by thieves are not uncommon. In light of this, the safest way to see the volcano is to hire a **taxi** or **pickup truck** for the day. Don't descend into the crater without a local guide; tourists have been caught with nowhere to run as they ascend.

◉ JOYA DE CERÉN

*To get to the ruins, take **bus #108** going to the town of Opico from San Salvador's **Terminal Occidente** (40min., every 10min., ¢5). Get off immediately after crossing the bridge over the Río Sucio, at the sign for the entrance to the site. Site and museum open Tu-Su 9am-4pm. US$2.86 including guides.*

This archaeological site, situated just one hour northwest of San Salvador, is considered by many to be the "Pompeii of the Americas." While not exactly impressive in scale or grandeur, the well-preserved remains of this 1400-year-old village offer an opportunity to observe and study the daily life of common Maya people. Some 1400 years ago this tiny village was covered with ash from a volcanic explosion and entombed for centuries beneath the igneous dust. The town's extended slumber ended abruptly when bulldozers accidentally discovered it in 1976. Full-scale excavations began in 1989, yielding the discovery of 18 structures ranging from adobe houses to a steam bath to the office of the local *brujo* (shaman). Even corn, beans, and a variety of other fruits and vegetables were preserved in the volcanic ash. The inhabitants apparently had enough time to flee (no human remains have been found at the site), but not to do the dishes or put away food after their evening meal. Findings have helped to fill in the details of the daily sustenance, commerce, and familial relations of the Maya. The small but comprehensive on-site **museum** contains good examples of ceramics, utensils, and foodstuffs. The information in the museum is in Spanish, but **CORSATUR** in San Salvador gives English explanations. **Guides** sit at the picnic tables outside the museum and can take you around to the three main excavation sites, which are covered by roofs and surrounded by fences. They are quite knowledgeable, but speak only Spanish

⊙ SAN ANDRÉS

*Take **bus #201** from San Salvador's Terminal Occidente heading to Santa Ana (¢5) and ask the bus driver to let you off at the turnoff for* las ruinas *at **San Andres** (rather than the town); look for the blue signs marking the ruins on your right after 1hr. From Joya de Ceren, hop back on the #108 and ride it until the junction with the highway to **Santa Ana** (10min., ¢1) to catch a westbound #201 to San Andrés (10min., ¢1). From the highway, head down the dirt road, pay at the entrance booth, and continue to the **visitors center**. Site open Tu-Su 9am-4pm. Entrance fee US$2.86 includes guided tour.*

Veterans of Tikal or Copán might be under whelmed by the San Andrés archaeological site, though the ruins are the second largest in El Salvador behind Tazumal. The site consists of two ceremonial plazas (North and South), ringed by mounds and pyramids. Occupied by ethnic Maya and Pipil groups, San Andrés was constructed from AD 600 to 900 and originally consisted of nearly 200 structures. Little is known about the decline of San Andrés, which flourished in the heyday of Maya glory along with Tikal, Palenque and Copán. Enter the site on the South Plaza, near the **Acropolis,** a large mound of partially reconstructed concrete. The other mounds ringing this plaza have been partially restored with concrete as well, leading to a rather disappointing aesthetic appearance. The north plaza consists of mostly unexcavated and (thankfully) unreconstructed mounds. It also contains the most interesting part of the ruins: on the north end, under a thatched roof, the base of **structure 5** has been partially excavated.

The sprawling **visitors center** and **museum** complex, before the entrance to the ruins, is very well done and perhaps more interesting than the site itself. The museum gives a very informative and extensive overview of Maya culture in the area, and San Andrés in particular. You can also learn a good deal about El Salvador's colonial past and geography. There's a display on **El Obraje,** a 17th-century indigo factory recently discovered next to the visitors center. When exiting the center to the north, El Obraje is to the right and the ruins are to the left. **Guides** can be found at the entrance or exit to the museum. The visitors center has a cafeteria.

◪ LOS PLANES DE RENDEROS

*Bus **#12** leaves from Av. 29 de Agosto and 12 Calle Pte., on the southeastern edge of the mercado central in front of the government building to **La Puerta del Diablo** (30min., every 10min. 5am-6pm, ¢1.5, return ¢2). To get to **Panchimalco**, catch the **#17** at the Milcumbres junction, on the way to La Puerta and the Parques (20min., every 20min.*

6:10am-7:20pm, ¢1). Or catch the #17 in San Salvador at the departure point for the #12 to go directly to Panchimalco (45min., infrequent departures, ¢2). Parque Balboa open 24hr. Free. Parque de La Familia open Tu-Su 8am-8pm. ¢7.

A great one-day trip from the capital is to go south to Los Planes de Renderos area, where a number of great attractions are close together. Start off by climbing **La Puerta del Diablo** for one of the most impressive views in El Salvador. Continue to the **Parque Balboa** and **Parque de la Familia** to stroll through the forest, play soccer or basketball, or catch a performance at the amphitheater at La Familia on the weekends. Eat lunch at a *pupusería* along the road; the restaurants in the area are famous for their excellent *pupusas*. Further up the road from the tourist parks is **Panchimalco,** a small village suffused with hints of native traditions.

◪ PUERTA DEL DIABLO. A few kilometers from the tourist parks sits La Puerta del Diablo, a pair of gigantic rocks forming an enormous gate and providing an awe-inspiring view of the valleys below. Sadly, the ominous name is fitting—during the revolution it was the site of countless executions. The best views are from the top of the larger rock (the one on the right).

The site along the highway has a carnival feel on the weekends, attracting young and old; couples, rebellious teens and a serious rock-climber or two will likely be your company during the week. The morning hours are better to enjoy the view, which spans the countryside and even the ocean. Serious climbers can contact the Club9/a de Escalada or **Alligatours** (☎211 0967; www.alligatour.com) for information about the 35 rappelling routes set up at La Puerta del Diablo.

◪ PANCHIMALCO. Twenty minutes up the road from the tourist parks lies **Panchimalco,** a village of cobblestone streets and workshops where the locals sometimes still wear the traditional Nahuatl garb. The humble church, built in 1725, sits at the base of the valley, overlooked by the imposing Puerta del Diablo. At kilometer 12 on the road to Panchimalco, the **Mirador de los Planes de Renderos** also offers impressive views for those not inclined to climb the Devil's Door.

THE CENTRAL COAST

El Salvador's most popular beaches hug the Central Coast south of the capital. Just 34km from San Salvador, La Libertad attracts surfers from around the world. The town of Zacatecoluca is a gateway to the seemingly endless palm-fringed coastline of the Costa del Sol, the country's premier coastal resort area, and, farther east, the mangrove-lined Bahía de Jiquilisco. Largely undeveloped, the tranquil beaches remain free of gaudy tourist traps.

LA LIBERTAD

Reputed to have the best surfing in Central America, the coast of La Libertad is blessed with a rare combination of wind, current, and shore that yields constant swells of at least 1.5m. Surf culture has definitely swept over the town; even the local fishermen rush to the point after work to catch a few waves. Serious surfers rise with the sun to ride the best waves off of the famed Punta Roca. When the ocean's flat, the most interesting sight (and smell) is the bustling fish market on the pier—if it lives in the sea and can be caught and eaten, it's for sale here. But the town is not all flip-flops and bleached hair; unfortunately, drugs and crime are all too common and tourists are frequent targets. Nonetheless, the variety of beaches and seafood grants both the surfer and sunbather a pristine playground with the benefits of the sea and the beauty of the tropical coast.

▮ TRANSPORTATION. Buses depart from several points on the east side of town, although many of them cruise 2 Calle and Calle Calvario before leaving. The primary departure is around the corner of Calle Barrios and 4 Av. The bus to **San Salvador** leaves from this corner (#102; 1¼hr., every 8min. 4:20am-6:20pm, ¢6). From 4 Av. Norte and 1 Calle, on the northeast corner of town, buses head to: **Zacatecoluca** (#540; 1¾hr.; 8 per day 5:30-4:30pm; ¢6); **Sonsonate** (#287; 3hr., 6am and 1:45pm, ¢7.70); **La Perla** (#192; 1hr., every 40min. 7am-5:20pm, ¢5), via **Playas El Tunco, Zunzal, El Palmercito,** and **El Zonte** along the way; **Comalapa** (#187; 1hr., every 20min., ¢4), from where you can connect to an **airport-bound bus** in San Luis Talpa. To get to **La Costa del Sol,** take #540 and get off at **La Flecha,** where you can catch the #193 or #495 to Costa del Sol. You can also get to **Sonsonate** by taking the #261 from La Perla. Local bus #80 heads west to **Zunzal** (every 10min. 6am-6pm, ¢2), and east to **Playa San Diego** (every 20min. 6am-6pm, ¢2); ask the driver to make sure you're going the right way, since they all face the same direction.

▮▮ ORIENTATION AND PRACTICAL INFORMATION. The small, grid downtown area of this port town slopes gently toward the bay and continues to the **pier,** which is an extension of 4 Av. The slightly hidden **church** sits at the north end of the *parque central* and the main intersection is on the *parque's* northwest corner. The main *avenida* is **Av. Bolívar** to the north and **Av. Luz** to the south; the central *calle* is **Calle Barrios** to the east and **Calle Calvario** to the west. **4 Calle,** 2 blocks south of Calle Barrios/Calvario, runs along the beach and meets 5 Av. on the town's west side, and then heads toward **La Punta Roca** on the west side of the bay.

In a mini-mall next to the main bus stop, **Banco Hipotecario,** 4 Av., 1 Calle, has **Western Union** service, cashes traveler's checks, and exchanges US dollars. (Open M-F 8:30am-4:30pm, Sa 8:30am-noon.) **ATMs** in La Libertad do not take international cards. The **mercado municipal** is bordered by 2/4 Av. and Calles Barrios/1. The El Salvador **Spanish School** (☎449 0331) also operates in La Libertad, and offers daily lessons and homestays. The **police** (☎335 3121), 1/3 Av. and Calle Calvario, is open 24hr. **Dr. Stanley Moises Mendoza Jiménez** is available on Calle Barrios, east of 4 Av. on the south side of the street, 24hr. for emergencies. (☎335 3531; emergency 335 3154. Open daily 9am-6pm.) **Farmacia Jerusalem** sits on Av. 1/Bolívar, Calle Calvario. (☎335 3508. Open M-Sa 7am-6pm.) **Telecom,** at the corner of 2 Av. and 2 Calle, also offers **Internet** service. (¢13 per 30min. Open daily 8am-6pm.) **Internet** at **Infocentros,** in the mini-mall on 4 Av. north of Calle Barrios, has the best rates. (¢20 per hr. Open M-Sa 8am-5pm, Su 8am-noon.) The **post office** is on 2 Calle Oriente between 2 Av. and 4 Av. sur. (Open M-F 8am-5pm, Sa 8am-noon.)

▮ ACCOMMODATIONS. The all-important combination of safety, quality, and affordability in lodgings is hard to come by, but there are a few reasonable options. With a gate, patio and laid-back cafeteria, **La Posada Familiar ❷,** half a block up from the beach on 3 Av. provides a secure evening hang-out spot. Simple rooms have great beds and most share clean baths. (☎335 3252. Singles ¢60, with bath ¢100.) The recently renovated **Hotel Rick ❺,** on 5 Av., 4 Calle, has impeccable rooms and dainty toilet covers, all with new double beds and fans. A pool table, TV, and VCR are at your disposal. (☎335 3361. Single ¢150; doubles ¢225.) **Hotel La Hacienda de Don Rodrigo ❺,** just off Punta Roca, is a pricier alternative. (☎335 3166. Luxurious rooms US$27, available 6pm-9am.) The cheapest, safest, and certainly most appealing way to take in the coast is to stay at either **Ver Mar ❶,** in El Palmercito, or **Surf Camp Horizonte,** at Playa Zonte (see **Beaches Near La Libertad,** p. 277).

▯ FOOD. *Mariscada,* a creamy seafood chowder chock-full of every sea creature imaginable, makes for a delicious meal in itself. Cheap seafood shacks crowd

La Libertad

🛏 ACCOMMODATIONS

Hotel La Hacienda
  de Don Rodrigo, **5**
Hotel Rick, **3**
La Posada Familiar, **1**

🍴 FOOD
Mango's Lounge, **2**
Restaurante Punta Roca, **4**

PACIFIC OCEAN

the pier area; regular *comedores* and *pupuserías* huddle around the market and *parque*. Fancier restaurants have cropped up in the upscale hotels east of town on the road called *La Curva*, and above Playa las Flores (take bus #80 to San Diego).

You can't beat the views from **Restaurante Punta Roca ❷**, across from Hotel Rick at 5 Av. and 4 Calle. Though a little pricey, the food, including the best *mariscada* in town (¢40), is delicious. (Seafood dishes ¢40-125; chicken and beef ¢30-40.) To absorb a little local surf culture over good, simple food and tasty *licuados* (¢10), head to **Mango's Lounge ❶**, on 5 Av. at Calle Calvario. (Burgers ¢15; 3 tacos ¢14.) The small place is chill, though full, at night and is a prime place to meet travelers or to get surfing tips. (Restaurant and attached surf shop open Tu-F noon-10pm, Sa-Su 10am-10pm. Happy Hour 5-6pm.)

◪ **SURFING.** Standing on the pier looking back at the shore, **Playa el Malecón** is on the right side, while **Punta Roca** extends off the end of **Playa la Paz** to the left. The best and biggest waves in the area break off Punta Roca, with 1.2-4.6m swells. Surfing the point is only for experts. The smaller, inconsistent waves that come into Playa la Paz are good for beginners, but the beach is rather rocky and polluted, making **Playa Zunzal**, to the west, a more attractive option for beginners. Prime surfing months are April to October, when swells vary from 1-5m. For non-surfers, the beaches are sandiest and the waves smallest in December.

To rent *tablas* (surfboards), head to **Mango's Lounge,** which rents good boards with multi-day discounts (US$12 per day, US$5 per 2hr.) You can also rent **bikes, boogie boards, fishing gear,** and **snorkeling gear** there. Slightly more beaten-up rental boards are available at the **Hospital de Tablas,** located just north of the Posada Familiar on 3 Av. (¢75 per day or ¢20 per hr.) For lessons, **Punta Mango Tours,** run by Rodrigo at Mango's Lounge, can arrange an instructor for ¢31 per hr. or group lessons for a bit less per person. They also offer complete surf-and-stay packages and trips around La Libertad and the country's eastern beaches.

BEACHES NEAR LA LIBERTAD

*Bus #80, leaving from 4 Av. south of Calle Barrios in La Libertad, runs east to **Playa San Diego** (every 20min. 6am-6pm, ¢2) and west to **Playas Conchalio, Majahual, El Tunco,*** *and **El Zunzal** (every 10min. 6am-6pm, ¢2). Check with the driver to find out which direction the bus is headed. Bus **#192**, leaving for La Perla from 4 Av. and 1 Calle, passes the same eastern beaches but goes farther to **Playa El Palmercito** and **Playa Zonte** (35min., every 40min. 5am-5:20pm, ¢3.50). Minibuses to **Playa las Flores** cruise 2 Av. (¢3).*

If you're not a surfer, the rocky, polluted waters of the bay of La Libertad hold less appeal. Have no fear: cleaner, sandier beaches dot the coast on both sides of town. While the surfing beaches to the west are more visually stunning and better maintained by far, if you're just looking for stretches of sand and good swimming, head east. Dining options vary at each beach. Crowds vanish come Monday.

◪ **PLAYA EL TUNCO.** A fun beach with a young crowd composed of Salvadoran teens in town for the weekend, some families and tourists, Playa El Tunco is also good for swimming and surfing. A 20min. bus ride from La Libertad leads to Playa el Tunco. The beach is about 800m from the town of El Tunco (sign: "El Tunco"), so make sure to tell the bus driver to let you off at the *playa* El Tunco. It is marked by a "Pilsener" sign and signs for El Tubo surf lodge. From there, a dirt road runs down to the beach at the mouth of Río Tunco. Just left of the river mouth is the break **La Bocana,** a favorite among local surfers. To the right sit the striking rock formations of Playa el Tunco, which stretch to Punta Zunzal (see below).

A small **surf village** has sprung up along the river at Playa el Tunco. Marked just "Hotel," the folks at **Tienda Erika ❶**, along the road close to the beach, rent decent rooms with common baths (¢50). Along the road one block from the beach are two laid-back surf lodges. First is **El Tubo ❷**, where doubles with fan and shared bath cost ¢60. Here you can also collect surf information and maybe rent a board from the local surf hero **Papaya**. Just past El Tubo down a driveway is the attractive new lodge **La Tortuga Surf Lounge ❹**, with nice rooms and private beach (doubles ¢125). **Restaurante La Bocana ❸**, on the beach at the Río Tunco, has meals ranging US$3-$11, and doubles as weekend night spot (beer US$0.80).

◪ **PLAYA ZUNZAL.** West of El Tunco, this wide beach is less rocky, with consistent waves far from shore. Recommended for beginning surfers, Zunzal is also one of the best options for swimming, tanning, etc. Walk west on the beach from Río Tunco, until you reach **Punta Zunzal.** If coming by bus, get off at **Café Zunzal,** where a path by the lookout on the highway brings you to the sand.

◪ **PLAYA EL PALMERCITO.** Less crowded, this soft curve of a beach seems to be a bit of a secret. A 400m walk down a cobblestone road from the sign *Puente El Palmar,* the calm water is great for swimming after heating up on the sandy beach. **Hotel Vel Mar ❶**, a 2min. walk from the beach along the road from the highway, offers clean, cheap rooms ideal for backpackers. Ask **Mario** about special group rates, surf trips, or lessons. (☎ 867 8845. Hammocks US$3; dorms US$5; 1-6person rooms US$20, with A/C and private bath US$30. Camping US$2 per person.) **Restaurante Las Palmeras ❶** is a relaxed joint where you can also bunk up as one of the family in a cramped room upstairs. (Shrimp plates ¢35-60, soup ¢12. Rooms ¢200 for 1 or 2 people.) East on Playa Palmar, the idyllic oasis **Atami ❺** is perched on a cliff. You can enjoy the crisply manicured resort with its great beach access, three pools, deck chairs, bathrooms, showers, and requisite waterslide for only US$7; spending the night is expensive, though (US$70-80).

◪ **PLAYA ZONTE.** A slightly isolated, smaller beach, Zonte draws surfers and a small, local crowd despite the rocky shore and dark sand. Stunning trees and cliffs make up for the drab shacks along the beach. Only 15min. beyond Zunzal, buses deposit you on an unmarked road which brings you to the beach (stay to the right).

The newly opened ▓**Surf Camp Horizonte ❷,** run by friendly surfer Saburo, features the best prices in the area and provides an extremely comfortable (if not immaculate) environment in which to take in the beach. Guests may use the pool and kitchen, and the ¢80 per day board rental includes an hour of free instruction. The rooms are set around a bar with great views of the beach and cliff. (Dorms US$7; singles US$9; doubles US$10. Camping US$2.) Other accommodations can be found by asking locals about spare rooms; prices and quality vary.

◪ **BEACHES EAST OF LA LIBERTAD.** East of La Libertad lie two beaches for swimming and tanning, both large enough that you can easily find a peaceful spot to relax for the day. **Playa las Flores,** below the section of road known as La Cerra, a few kilometers east of La Libertad, has parts that are relatively clean. About 15 more minutes on Bus #80 brings you to **Playa San Diego,** a long gray beach lined with homes and public beach access paths every 100m. The beach is wide and more or less clean; at the farthest point (where the bus stops to turn around) is an estuary, a cluster of beach shacks, and *comedores.* To enjoy the beach, hop off the bus along the road to San Diego (7km after it leaves the highway) at any of the many little groups of stores or small restaurants, and take an access path to the shore. **Restaurante Carlos Mar ❷** is one of the nicer options available along the beach road (fish ¢30-45, chicken ¢30).

ZACATECOLUCA

At the foot of Volcán San Vincente, and only 1½hr. from the beach, Zacate, as the locals call it, is a launching point for trips to Costa del Sol, one of El Salvador's major vacation spots. In town, the Catedral de Santa Lucía's 45m spire, and Ichanmichen, one of the country's largest *turicentros,* are worth a look. Zacate is neither offensive nor overly endearing; travelers either pass through or use the city's hotels as a budget-friendly alternative to the upscale hotels of the Costa del Sol.

▐ **TRANSPORTATION.** From the terminal at 5/7 Calles and Av. Villacorta/Delgado, about three blocks south of the *parque central,* **buses** go to: **San Salvador** (#133, 1½hr., every 10min. 3:30am-6:10pm, ¢5); **La Costa del Sol** and **La Puntilla** (#193, 1½hr., every 30min. 4:45am-4:40pm, ¢6); **La Libertad** (#540, 1¾hr., 8 per day 5:20am-3:40pm, ¢5); **La Herradura** (#153, 2hr., every 20-30min. 4:50am-5:15pm; ¢5). Bus #177 to **San Vicente** leaves from 2 Calle, three blocks east of the cathedral (45min., every 20min. 4:45am-6pm, ¢4). Bus #171 to **Usulatán** via **Jiquilisco** from hwy. 1 block north of Av. Villacorta (50min., every 10-15min. 5:25am-5pm, ¢5).

▓ ⊠ **ORIENTATION AND PRACTICAL INFORMATION.** Most buses turn north from the carretera at the Shell station and run up Av. Villacorta to the *parque central,* passing the bus terminal at 5/7 Calles on the way. The **cathedral** is on the north side of the *parque,* whose southeast corner is the main intersection. The central *avenida* is called **Av. Villacorta** south of the *parque* and **Av. Rodríguez** north of it. The main *calle,* which runs along the south side of the *parque,* is called **Calle Peña** to the east and **Calle Osorio** to the west. Even-numbered *calles* increase to the north, and odd-numbered *calles* increase to the south.

Banco de Comercio, on the southwest corner of the *parque* changes traveler's checks and US dollars and gives advances on Visa. (Open M-F 8am-5pm, Sa 8am-noon.) The **ATM** in **supermarket Despensa de Don Juan** in the mini-mall on the highway, accepts Visa. (Open M-Sa 8am-9pm, Su 8am-8pm.) The **Santa Lucia pharmacy** is on the west side of the *parque.* (☎334 2002, line open 24hr. Pharmacy open daily 8am-1pm and 2-6pm.) Other services include: **police** (☎334 1690), 3 Calle, Av. Monterrey; **Internet access** at **Infocentros** at the mall (¢20 per hr.; open M-Sa 8am-

6pm.); **Telecom,** also at the mall (open daily 8am-6pm); and **post office** with express mail, Av. Delgado, Osorio/1 Calles, two blocks left facing the side of the church (open M-F 8am-noon and 2-5pm, Sa 8am-noon).

⌐❒ ACCOMMODATIONS AND FOOD. The **Hotel Primavera ❷,** on Av. Villacorta across from the bus terminal, has comfortable rooms with cable TV, fan, private bath, and hammock (in addition to the bed). (☎334 1346. Doubles ¢80, with A/C ¢130. Cheaper rates available for groups and stays of 2 nights or more.) Half a block away, on 7 Calle, just east of Av. Villacorta, is the **Hotel Brolyn ❶,** a yellow building with basic rooms, all including fan, clean private baths, TV, and lumpy mattresses and pillows. (☎334 1084. Singles ¢50, with cable TV ¢60, with A/C ¢80; doubles with cable TV ¢100. Additional ¢35 for the day.)

Comedores selling *comida a la vista* (buffet-style) line the streets around the *parque central,* though fast-food places like **Domino's Pizza, Pollo Campero,** and **Pollolandia** have infiltrated the area as well. **Luiggi's Pizza ❶,** a block west and 2 blocks north of the *parque,* serves up tasty tacos (3 for ¢14) and pizzas (¢15) with crispy crusts and lots of cheese. (Open M-Sa until 9pm.)

◨ SIGHTS. The imposing 45m central spire, topped by a miniature statue of Christ, of the **Catedral de Santa Lucía,** on the north side of the *parque,* is visible from most points in the city. The colonnaded facade and the statues inside have been restored, but the colonial ambience remains. (Open daily 5:30am-noon and 2-7pm.) To the south of town, **Turicentro Ichanmelchen** is one of the largest *turicentros* in the country. (*Turicentros* are tourist spots run by ISTU for Salvadorans. They generally have a clean pool, often fueled by springs. They get crowded on weekends, but during the week you can bask solo in the sun.) The crowded grotto-like main pool has a 20m-long water slide. The other two pools are off in the woods and less clean. From Zacate, board a southbound #92 bus (¢2) on Av. Delgado for the 5min. trip, but make sure the bus stopsthere first. The last bus returns at 5:30pm. (*Turicentro* open daily 7am-5pm. Admission ¢7.)

LA COSTA DEL SOL

La Costa del Sol, the most popular beach getaway of the Salvadoran elite, is an endless peninsula of grayish sand. Lacking the action of La Libertad, this beach community provides all that is necessary for a soothing escape: surf and sand with no distraction. Along with the countless summer homes and resorts, there is some reasonable lodging and beach access worth either a day trip or a week of sun.

⌐ TRANSPORTATION. Buses depart from La Puntilla and run up the peninsula road before heading to **San Salvador** (#495, 2hr., every 30min. 4:30am-6pm, ¢8); **Zacatecoluca** (#193; 1½hr.; every 30min. 6:30-9am and 3:25-5pm, departures also at 12:15 and 2:05pm; ¢7); **San Vicente** (#193-D; 2¼hr.; 8:20, 8:40am; ¢8). If you miss the Zacatecoluca or San Vicente departures, take the #495 and get off at the junction of **La Flecha,** where east bound buses pass by frequently (¢3 from La Costa).

⯀❼ ORIENTATION AND PRACTICAL INFORMATION. The beaches lie on the Pacific side of the peninsula, which is abutted by the **Jaltepeque Estuary** to the north. Bus routes bisect the peninsula and pass the town of **Las Isletas** before going on to the beaches. About 20min. after buses swing east onto the peninsula, **Playa Costa del Sol** begins where the *turicentro* straddles both sides of the road. Farther east (2km) is **Playa Los Blancos;** another 10min. on the bus carries you to the end of the peninsula **La Puntilla,** where *lanchas* depart for **La Isla Tasajera.**

Basic services can be hard to find. There are no banks in the area. There is a large **supermarket, Supermercado Costa del Sol**, just south of Las Isletas as the peninsula road curves north. (Open daily 7am-8pm.) **Clínica Fundesol** is about halfway between the *turicentro* and La Puntilla (open daily 9am-5pm). There is a **pharmacy** on the east end of Playa Los Blancos. (Open daily 8am-9pm, though hours are unreliable.) The **police** are across the street from the pharmacy. (☎338 2067. Open 24hr.) The nearest **Telecom** office is in Las Isletas, 45min. from La Puntilla. There are **pay phones** in Playa Los Blancos or outside of the *turicentro*.

▓ **TURICENTRO AND PLAYA COSTA DEL SOL.** The expansive *turicentro* conveniently offers access to the estuary as well as the beach, with pools, basketball courts, and restaurants to top it off. With a secure place to store your belongings while you swim, and plenty of showers to freshen up after, it's a cheap way to spend a day on the beach with local families. (Open daily 7am-4pm. Pools open M-F 1:30-3:30pm; Sa-Su 10-11:45am and 1:30-3:30pm. Admission ¢7. *Cabañas* ¢35.)

▓ **PLAYA LOS BLANCOS.** With good lodgings and a few stores, backpackers can enjoy the pleasures of the Pacific without the cost of nearby resorts. **Hotel Haydee-Mar ❺** has a restaurant, beach access, and nice rooms alongside a pristine pool with lounge chairs and hammocks. (☎338 2046. Doubles ¢200, with A/C ¢350.) The pool and patio of **Mini-Hotel and Restaurant Mila ❶** are somewhat less appealing, but cheaper. (☎338 2074. Doubles US$14, with bath US$20; quads US$40.)

▓ **LA PUNTILLA.** The estuary around the point of the peninsula is **La Puntilla**, where the beach is less clean than the middle strip, but lively with a cluster of *ranchos* and the bustle of fish boats. **Turicentro Rancho Los Titos,** the concrete structure with faded signs, offers bare rooms with thin mattresses. Spotty running water and no electricity will have you outside enjoying the deck and two small pools. (☎225 3670. Doubles ¢75.) **Bendición de Dios ❸,** next to Posada de Doña Emilia, rents rooms with sand floors. (☎338 0150. Rooms US$12.) On the north side, *lanchas* head to the **Isla Tasajera**. Boats go to the **Isla de los Pájaros** (US$22), a mangrove island swarming with birds, and also to the mouth (*Bocana*) of the **Río Lempa** (US$50), where the freshwater river makes for some great swimming. The captains can accommodate different trips based on your interests.

▓ **ISLA TASAJERA.** For a more intense escape, there is **Isla Tasajera** just off La Puntilla, where 250 families live and fish with plenty of beach at their fingertips. *Lanchas* to the island (¢100 roundtrip) leave from the estuary side of La Puntilla. With enough people, you can ride out on a collective *lancha de pasajeros* (¢5-10 per person) through the estuary to the island's north side at a point known as **La Palmera,** named for its rare coconut palm tree that splits three ways near its top. From the two food-and-drink stands at La Palmera, it's about a 10min. walk across the island to the isolated Pacific beach that stretches to the end of the island.

Hotel y Restaurante Oasis de Tasajera ❺ offers lodgings more pleasant than anywhere else in La Puntilla. Small cabins surround a courtyard, all with a porch, hammocks, fans, lights, and private baths. You will need to hire a *lancha* to get there, which makes your stay even pricier. (☎888 0526. Triples ¢275; quads ¢300.)

PUERTO EL TRIUNFO AND BAHÍA DE JIQUILISCO

The small fishing hamlet of Puerto El Triunfo sits on the Bahía de Jiquilisco, about 15km south of the Carretera Litoral. The pleasant port town and its buzzing marina

FROM THE ROAD

DO'S & DON'T'S OF CHICKEN BUS TRAVEL

DO:

-Be prepared for inexplicable delays. For example, your bus driver runs into a friend or a cattle crossing.

-Strategically pick your seat. Window seats provide a nice breeze. Aisle seats may tempt with extra leg room but rarely deliver.

-Make sure you're on the right bus. Sometimes destinations don't correspond with the signs on the front.

-Bring a walkman unless you enjoy hearing long sermons and sales pitches for miracle drugs (see "Vitavangelism," p. 390).

-Be willing to redefine your idea of personal space.

-Duck! If you hear the bus driver yell "Agáchense," that means the police are on the lookout for people standing illegally in the aisle. You don't know comraderie till your face is smushed in a stranger's back.

DON'T:

-Be too shy to ask for your change.

-Lose your ticket if you are given one. If you do, you may have to repay.

-Assume you can catch the last bus. Odds are, it won't come.

-Board a bus thinking you can wait to go to the bathroom. Bumpy roads can make for extreme discomfort.

-Litter. Plastics and other non-biodegradable objects are new to the older generation who are used to tossing out coconuts and banana peels that decompose. Just because locals have no compunction about littering doesn't mean you should.

-Worry. You'll get there eventually.

–Daniel Elizondo

offer a look at a local fishing industry, ranging from family-run teams who drag nets behind dugout canoes, to 45 ft. trawlers with sonar fish finders. Puerto El Triunfo is also the most convenient launching point for daytrips into the Bahía de Jiquilisco, a beautiful bay dotted with mangrove islands.

TRANSPORTATION. Coming to Puerto El Triunfo, any bus driving the *carretera* between Zacatecoluca and Usulután can drop you off near the town of Jiquilisco, where you can catch #363 to the port. From the northwest corner of the *parque*, buses leave Puerto El Triunfo bound for: **Usulután** (#363; 40min., every 10min. 4am-5:30pm, ¢3.25), passing through **Jiquilisco** near the *carretera* (20min., ¢2); **San Miguel** (#377; 2½hr., every 40min. 3:50am-2:50pm, ¢10); and **San Salvador** (#185; 2hr., every 30min. 4-7am and 3pm; ¢10), via **Zacatecoluca** (1¼hr., ¢5). It is often easier to take the #363 to the highway or to Usulután and make connections from there rather than waiting around in Puerto El Triunfo.

ORIENTATION AND PRACTICAL INFORMATION. Town is centered along two main *avenidas*. Buses enter town along the southbound and pass the church on the west side of the road before arriving a block after the *parque*, two blocks north of the marina. The northbound *avenida* is a block east.

There is no bank, so change dollars and traveler's checks at **Banco Agrícola** in Jiquilisco. The **police** are on the southbound *avenida*, just before the marina on the left, in the same building as the port's customs (*aduana*) office. (☎663 6300. Open 24hr.) There is a **pharmacy**, but no doctor (open daily 6:30am-8pm). **Telecom** is one block north and one block east of the *parque*. (☎663 6011. Open daily 7am-7pm.) The **post office** is two blocks north and a 1½ blocks east of the *parque* on the north side of the street. (Open M-F 8am-noon and 2-5pm, Sa 8am-noon.)

ACCOMMODATIONS AND FOOD. The only hotel in town is the **Hotel El Jardín ❷**, half a block north of the *parque* on the southbound Av.; knock if the door is closed. The decent rooms all have strong fans and private baths, but you'll have to use the communal sink outside. (☎663 6047. Rooms for 1-2 people US$7.) Other accommodations may be found with **Julia ❶**; call and ask if the spare room she rents is available. (☎663 6035. ¢40 per person.)

Centro Turístico El Malecón ❶, a pavilion of six little restaurants, recently opened on the marina. All six serve fantastic, affordable lunches and dinners starting at ¢25 for seafood and ¢20 for *típico*.

◎ **THE MARINA.** The marina area jumps all day with fishermen bringing in catch, women selling fish, families returning to the bay's islands, and the big fishing boats docking at the main marina. Decaying steel-hulled trawlers at the end of the main pier are remainders from the collapse of the local fishing industry in the mid-1980s, after the FMLN bombed nearby bridges, effectively cutting off the port from San Salvador. The well-kept *malecón* (sea wall) is a nice touch.

🔰 **EXCURSIONS INTO BAHÍA DE JIQUILISCO.** From a *lancha*, the water of the bay is bluer-than-blue and stunning against the lush green of the islands and peninsula. The volcanoes back on the mainland tower majestically, emphasizing the flat tranquility of the bay. Captains in Puerto Triunfo can take you to several worthwhile sights throughout the bay. **La Península de Coral de Mulas** protects the entire bay from the Pacific. **Isla Méndez,** on the peninsula's western end, has a sea turtle nursery. In town you'll have the chance to buy refreshments, and a 30min. walk brings you to the isolated Pacific beaches. There's not much to see most of the year, except mid-August through September when the 1500 eggs hatch. On the eastern end of the peninsula is the small community of **Coral de Mulas,** from where you can cross the peninsula to another deserted Pacific beach. It is a hot 30min. walk, but the scenery is wonderful.

Passenger *lanchas* run to both points on the peninsula. The schedule depends on demand; make sure to arrange for a return trip *before* you leave. You can also hire a *lancha* to Coral de Mulas (40min., ¢150 roundtrip with a 2hr. stay). Ask to be let off at Coral #2, where a sand road heads south to the Pacific. Round-trips to Isla de Mendez are a bit longer (¢200) and less frequent.

NORTHERN EL SALVADOR

North of the capital, pastures yield to remote mountain scenery. The thinly populated northern provinces of Chalatenango and Cuscatlán, war-time strongholds of the FMLN, suffered under the military's scorched-earth tactics, and as a result few visitors make the trek; locals still seem somewhat surprised at the sight of a tourist. However, the region is rich with traditional *artesanía*, which has gained international renown. Suchitoto, El Salvador's finest colonial town, sits peacefully on the shores of Lago Suchitlán, formed in 1976 by the Cerrón Grande Damn and home to more than 200 types of birds and 14 species of fish. The village of Concepción Quezaltepeque, near Chalatenango, is an example of a local handicraft into a full-blown hammock industry. More restless visitors make tracks for La Palma, heeding the call of El Pital, El Salvador's highest peak.

SUCHITOTO

With narrow cobblestone streets and fine architecture, Suchitoto has a fascinating history, and is perhaps the best-preserved colonial town in El Salvador. The town was once an important colonial center for government and commerce; in 1528, the original Villa San Salvador was located here. The 1980s brought heavy FMLN activity to the town and nearby hills, and remnants of trenches and encampments are still visible. Many residents fled to San Salvador during the war, but the town has begun a cultural rejuvenation.

🚌 **TRANSPORTATION. Buses** run from San Salvador's Terminal Oriente to Suchitoto (#129; 1½hr., every 20min. 4:30am-7:45pm, ¢4; Sa and Su and after 6pm, ¢5), and drop you off at the *parque central*. From the road along the market, you can take the #129 back to **San Salvador** (every 25min. 3:45am-5:45pm, ¢4). Leaving one block west of the *parque*'s southwest corner the #163 bus goes to **Aguilares** via a slow dirt road. (1¼hr., every 45min. 4:45am-5:30pm, ¢5.).

■ ▦ ORIENTATION AND PRACTICAL INFORMATION. The **parque central,** where buses drop off visitors, is abutted by the **Iglesia de Santa Lucía** on the eastern side. Almost everything in town is located within a few blocks of the *parque central* or along **Calle al Lago,** the street behind the church that runs north to the shore of the lake. The other park in town is **Parque San Martín;** facing the church, walk one block left, turn left and walk two blocks. The **market** building is one block in the direction opposite the right side of the church, then left one block.

Stop by the brand new **tourist office,** next to the Telecom office (see below) for **tourist information,** a free map, and bike rentals if you want to brave the bumpy streets. (☎335 1782. Bikes US$1 per hr., US$5 per day. Open daily 8am-5pm.) For the low-down, go straight to Miguel at **La Casa de Los Mestizos** (see **Accommodations,** below), who runs tours and trips in the surrounding countryside. **Casa de la Cultura,** half a block to the left of the church, has information on special events. (☎ 335 1108. Open M-F 8am-noon and 2-5pm, Sa 8am-1pm.) There is **no bank** in Suchitoto. **Farmacia Nueva,** facing Telecom, is half a block to the left. (☎335 1002. Open daily 8am-8pm, on-call 24hr.) **Hospital Nacional de Suchitoto** provides 24hr. service including ambulances (☎335 1062). The **police** are one block north of the *parque*'s northwest corner (☎335 1141). **Telecom** is across the street from the market. (☎335 1011. Open daily 8am-6pm). **Internet** at **Infocentros** on the *parque*'s southwest corner. (¢20 per hr., students ¢11 per hr. Open M-F, Su 8am-6pm, Sa 8am-noon.) The **post office,** is half a block north of the *parque* (open M-F 8am-5pm, Sa 8am-noon).

▛ ACCOMMODATIONS. Suchitoto provides a few above average options for the weary traveler. The hotel/cultural center/bar **█La Casa de Los Mestizos ❷,** 3½ blocks north of the *parque* on Calle al Lago, is *the* place to go. (☎848 3438. Singles US$7; doubles US$11.40.) Hotelito **Casa Antigua ❸** offers a peaceful garden surrounded by comfortable furniture and local *artesanía*. (☎335 1003. Singles US$11, doubles and triples US$10 per person.) The restaurant **La Fonda del Mirador ❹,** 1½ blocks north of La Casa de los Mestizos, rents out small, clean rooms, all with TV, fan, and private bath. (☎335 1126. ¢130 for 1 person, ¢140 for 2 people.)

❏ FOOD. Dining in Suchitoto stimulates mind and palate. **█Restaurante Villa Balanza ❷,** on the west side of the Parque San Martín, is a working piece of sculpture (see **The Art of War,** p. 285). Poignant works, made from the scraps of war, decorate the courtyard. Artfully presented meals are as pleasing to look at as to eat. The *picante Pollo Veracruzana* (¢40) is highly recommended. (Banana *licuado* $1.25, chicken cordon bleu ¢45. Open daily 10am-9pm.) For a meal with a view, **Pupusería Vista al Lago ❶** offers good *pupusas* and a popular Sunday lunch (¢10-20; open Th-Su 5:30-8pm) with the same views of the lake as its pricier neighbor, **La Fonda del Mirador ❸** *(plato típico* ¢55). Other *pupuserías* can be found around the *parque* and in the market.

◪ SIGHTS. Suchitoto's colonial charm is its main attraction. It also started the first school in El Salvador that teaches traditional construction methods. On the *parque*'s east side, peek into the impressive **Catedral de Santa Lucía,** which is being completely restored. The **Parque San Martín** (see **Orientation,** above) has views of Lago de Suchitlán and what has become an "open art gallery." The town's artists have transformed the small park with sculptures incorporating war "garbage" (see **The Art of War,** p. 285). Three blocks north of the *parque* on Calle al Lago, find women practicing the craft of **cigar-rolling.** A few houses down the side street to the right, women welcome visitors to watch them roll up to 400 stogies in one day.

THE ART OF WAR While the small village of Suchitoto is presently one of the most tranquil places in El Salvador, it was a stronghold of the FMLN, and the war scarred more than just the surrounding hills. Local artists have found creative ways to express their feelings about the war using discarded paraphernalia to create sculptures, many of which are on display at the Parque San Martín. Sitting atop the entrance to the Restaurante Villa Balanza, a balance scale weighing a bomb against a pile of tortillas juxtaposes Suchitoto's past and present. Across the street, a robot made of gun clips holds a trash can, symbolizing the town's growing environmental consciousness.

Lago de Suchitlán is only a 30min. walk away. Take Calle al Lago north until the three-way fork. Continuing straight ahead, you will be rewarded with views of the lake before a descent to the shore. Trucks run from the bottom of the hill for US$3, but less for a group. Bearing right makes for a longer but more gradual walk to the shore. Some travelers hitch back to town, since either route back is a 45min. uphill hike, although there are always risks involved.

A national celebrity and flamboyant character, Alejandro Coto, has recently moved his **Casa de Alejandro,** an impressive house with a garden and eclectic art collection, to town. Head towards the lake from Casa de Los Mestizos (see above), and veer to the right at the first fork. Take care not to confuse fact (pictures of Oscar Romero) with fiction (**Batistas' furniture;** open daily 9am-12pm, 2-5:30pm, ¢30). One of the area's better-known artists, **Víctor Manuel Sanabria,** also known as "Shanay," has a studio and gallery one block east of the northeast corner of the *parque central.* There are no hours; knock any time during the day, and he'll be happy to show you around. To discover more about Suchitoto's troubled past, explore **Cerro Guazapa,** a civil war battleground just outside of town. The Casa de Cultura and La Casa de los Mestizos can help you find a guide. (Tours ¢15-45.)

⚠️ OUTDOOR ACTIVITIES AND GUIDED TOURS. The **Casa de los Mestizos** organizes trips leaving every Sunday at 9am to explore the areas around the town. Caves, waterfalls, islands, and birdwatching can be arranged at La Casa. (¢20-100; prices and length vary.) Get directions to **Río Sinacanapa** and its waterfall, **Salto El Cubo,** about a 45min. hike from town for an excellent swim. For a more adventurous excursion, the folks at La Casa de los Mestizos will be happy to take you to the **Cueva Hedionda** (2½hr., ¢25 per person), a cave with three subterranean rivers running through it, that once functioned as a safe haven for FMLN soldiers

CHALATENANGO

Situated between the La Peña mountains to the north and the Lago de Suchitlán to the south is the bustling commercial center of Chalatenango, capital of the department of the same name. "Chalate," as the locals refer to it, retains some of its heritage as an FMLN stronghold during the 1980s. Town life centers around the frenetic market, where you can buy anything from socks to US pop music tapes.

The **bus** from the capital drops off two blocks down the hill from the church, which is also the spot to catch the #125 back to **San Salvador** (2hr., every 10min. 3:30am-5:40pm, ¢6.50; direct 6, 10am, 4pm; ¢12). If you're coming from the north, get off at **Amayo,** a junction on the highway from El Poy, and hop on #125 there (35min., every 15 min. 5:15am-8:15pm, ¢2.50). The highway to Chalate heads left when coming from El Poy. To get to **El Poy,** take the #125 to Amayo and there catch the #119. Buses to **Concepción Quezaltepeque** leave from the same area two blocks south of the church (#300B; 30min., every 30min. 6:30am-5pm, ¢2.50). Buses to nearby small towns leave from several other points in the town's center. A **ferry** leaves from the nearby town of **San Luis del Carmen** and crosses the Lago de Suchitlán, landing in Suchitoto on the southern side of the lake. The schedule is erratic and the ferry may or may not be operating Ask the locals on the bus for San Luis before heading out. (See **Near Chalatenango**, p. 286.) The **Banco Salvadoreño**, 1½ blocks to the right of the cathedral, has an **ATM**, changes traveler's checks and US dollars and gives cash advances on MC/V. (Open M-F 7:30am-4pm, Sa 8am-noon.) The **market** building is two blocks past the church on its right side. A **supermarket** is three blocks east of Av. Libertad on Calle Morazán. The **National Hospital** is four blocks past the Banco de Comercio; when you reach the church turn right and go two blocks. (Open 24hr.) The **police** are in a large building one block past the church on the left. (☎301 0330 emergency 24 hr. 301 0328.) To the **Telecom** office, walk across the *parque* away from the cathedral two blocks on the street that runs along the right side of the cathedral. (Open daily 8am-6pm.) **Internet** at **Infocentros**, across from the cathedral. (¢20 per hr., students ¢11 per hr. Open M-F 8am-6pm, Sa 8am-noon.) The **post office** is down the hill from Banco de Comercio. (Open M-F 7am-5pm, Sa 7am-noon.) **Postal code:** 09101.

Chalate has few accommodations. Live it up at the **Hotel California ❸**, two blocks past the church on its right side. Comfy beds in spacious rooms have fan and private bath. (☎335 3170. Check-out 9am. 1-2 person rooms ¢85. Pay an extra ¢15 to get the room for 24hr.) **Hotelito San Jose ❷** is two blocks down the hill past the garrison and one block to the right across from the basketball courts. (English spoken. Singles with fan ¢60; doubles ¢100.) ◾**Restaurante La Vieja Habana ❶**, in the pink building adjacent to the post office, is a pleasant surprise for the hungry traveler. The restaurant features live music on Thursday and Saturday nights starting at 8pm. Sample the chicken tacos (¢20) or a roast beef or *típico* dinner for ¢25. (Open M-Th 10am-10pm, F-Sa 10am-1pm).

The **Catedral de Chalatenango de San Juan Bautista** has recently received an overhaul of its massive interior. Across the street, the **army garrison** looms as a reminder of when the FMLN tried several times to take the town.

> **▼** Walks into the countryside surrounding Chalatenango, though tempting, are not advisable without local advice and accompaniment. There may still be land mines, and the area now attracts crime.

NEAR CHALATENANGO

▢ CONCEPCIÓN QUEZALTEPEQUE

> *Bus #300B runs from Chalatenango every 30min. (30min., 6:30am-5pm, ¢2.50; return buses run 6am-3:20pm). Trucks waiting at the bus stop run until 4 or 5pm, ¢2.50.*

The most easily accessible town by bus is Concepción Quezaltepeque, 12km northwest of Chalatenango and renowned for its hammock industry. Multi-colored hammocks woven in small workshops around town are sold at the **Empresa Asociativa de Artesanías Hamacas**, a cooperative of local artisans 1½ blocks south of the *parque central*, along the road the bus stops on (hammocks ¢75-¢400). Also look into **Artesanía Quezaltecas**, at the top of the hill just before the *parque central* on the right. Ask friendly owner Miguel, for a free crochet lesson (Spanish only).

▣ AGUILARES

> *Shuttling back and forth, bus #117 leaves from the parque central in Aguilares to **San Salvador** (55min., every 10min. 3:45am-7pm, ¢3). Bus #163 heads to Suchitoto (every 45min. daily 4am-5:45pm, ¢5). Regular buses service a number of other cities to the north and west. To get to the park, take any bus heading north from Aguilares, leaving*

from the Texaco station two blocks north of the parque *(¢1.50). There is no entrance fee and the attendants can provide English or Spanish information pamphlets and maps.*

Located at the intersection of the Troncal del Norte highway and the east-west *carretera* joining Santa Ana and Suchitoto, Aguilares is a busy commercial junction, with a large daily market. Take caution, as the town has had problems with crime. Nonetheless, easily accessible from Aguilares is this **Parque Arqueológico Cihuatán,** the largest site of ancient indigenous civilization in El Salvador. Dating back to the early postclassic period (AD900-1200), the remains are of unclear origin. Looking just to the right behind the pyramid, you can't miss the silhouette of a woman formed by the peaks of nearby Volcán Guazapa. The site consists primarily of a ceremonial center surrounded by a large wall. As you enter, the first structure is the **West Ballcourt.** Across the plaza is a pyramid, largely covered part by earth and grass. To the left is the **North Ballcourt.** Inexplicably, the two walls forming the channel of the playing field slant outwards, rather than toward the center. If you get stuck in Aguilares, **Hospedaje Cruzero del Amor ❷** has basic rooms with bath (1 to 3 people US$7). Grab a pizza at **Mr. Pan ❶** off the *parque central.*

LA PALMA

Just 12km south of the border with Honduras, the quiet town of La Palma sits amid dazzling flowers and mighty rivers. Below the looming El Pital, El Salvador's highest peak, villagers work at creating the brightly painted wooden and ceramic *artesanía* which have become the town's hallmark. The tradition began in the 1970s, when Salvadoran artist Fernando Llort moved to La Palma and started teaching locals how to paint simple images of Christ and mountain villages. The production of an endless array of wood and ceramic goods covered with these images—from key chains to coasters to crucifixes—has become the mainstay of the local economy. An impressive 75% of the town's 20,000 people work on these crafts. The town of **San Ignacio,** 10min. north, has accommodations with quality hikes nearby.

⛌ TRANSPORTATION. Buses pass directly in front of the *parque central* heading south to **San Salvador** (4hr., every 30min. 6am-6pm, ¢11) and north to the **Honduran border** at **El Poy** (40min., every 30min. 6am-6pm, ¢4). The bus toward the border at El Poy stops in the center of **San Ignacio** (¢1.50).

⛊ PRACTICAL INFORMATION. Banco de Cuscatlán, on the northwest corner of the *parque,* changes traveler's checks. (Open M-F 8:30am-noon and 1-4pm, Sa 8:30am-noon.) The **police station** is one block down the hill on the opposite side of the *parque* from the bank. (☎335 9184. Open 24hr.) **Farmacia Elizabeth** is a block up the hill, behind the church. (☎335 9017. Open daily 7:30am-1pm and 2-8pm.) **Laboratorio Clínica La Palma** is next door. (Open daily 8am-4pm.) **Telecom** is just up the hill from the *parque* from the front of the church off the main road. (☎335 9011. Open M-Sa 8am-7pm, Su 8am-5pm.) **Internet** at **Dinosaurias Cibernéticos** next to Cooprativo Semilla de Dios. (US$2 per hr.) The **post office** lies next to the Casa de la Cultura, west of the bank. (Open M-F 8am-noon and 2-4pm, Sa 8am-noon.)

⛭⛬ ACCOMMODATIONS AND FOOD. None of La Palma's accommodations fall in the low budget range. The best value is **Hotel La Palma ❷,** two blocks up the hill from the front after the church. The large log-cabin rooms come with hot water. (☎335 9012. ¢75 per person.) **Posada Real ❺** is half a block up the hill from the *parque,* on the road behind the church. (☎335 9009. ¢300 for 1-3 people.) For those in a jam, **Posadas Shunterun ❶** has rooms a block down the hill behind the church, before the dumpster. (Singles ¢50, with bath ¢75; doubles ¢113.)

A much cheaper choice (and better for enjoying nearby sites) is the town of San Ignacio. **La Posada de San Ignacio ❶** is located right along the north side of the *parque.* (¢35 per person.)

A varied menu, decent prices, and hearty portions await at the upscale **Restaurante La Estancia ❶**, one block up the hill in front of the church on the main road. (Breakfast ¢20; fried chicken ¢40; steak ¢45. Open daily 9am-8pm. AmEx/MC/V.) For something more *típico*, go to the retaurant at **Posada Real ❶**, where locals get their *pupusas* (¢2.50; *cena típica* ¢50). The **Pupusería El Buen Gusto ❶**, next to the *parque* in San Ignacio, keeps it simple and delicious. (*Pupusas* ¢2.25.)

◙◪ SIGHTS AND CRAFTS. The homes with workshops producing *artesanía* cluster way down the hill and to the left in *barrio San Antionio*. Of the town's artists, local painter **Alfredo Linares** is particularly renowned. His gallery, a half-block south of the *parque* along the western road, showcases canvases of rural scenes and modern pieces, all in a rich variety of colors. For a souvenir, consider a framed miniature, a lithograph copy, or splurge on an original. (Prices range from US$1 postcards to over ¢4000.) The gallery also sells paintings by other local artists like Alfredo's brother Oscar. (Open daily 9am-6pm. AmEx/MC/V.) Also catch local artisans plying their trade at the **Asociación Cooperativa La Semilla de Dios** down the hill from the front of the church one block and left two more blocks.

◪ HIKES FROM SAN IGNACIO. One hike from San Ignacio leads to the **Peña Cayaguanca**. To get there, catch an El Poy-bound bus (¢1.50) and ask the driver to let you out at **"El Desvío del Rosario,"** where a steep cobblestone road heads to the small town. Take your first left (before reaching town) on a dirt road, pass by small houses, cross an intersection and continue until you arrive at a gate that reads "Vista Hermosa." The "Beautiful View" awaits hikers from the jutting rocks above. The winding, moderately strenuous ascent breaks off to the left and continues up for about two hours. Stay to the left as you climb.

Another hike heads west from the town for 4km, leading to the **Río Nuruapa** from where you can continue to the top of a hill known as **Cerro Shuntrun**. To get to the river from San Ignacio, walk left one block north of the *parque central* and follow that road. Cross the main El Poy-La Palma road and, bearing right, follow the road down. Forty minutes of bumpy downhill lead to the river and a bridge. Cross the bridge and continue along the path up to the Cerro (1½ hr. from the bridge).

NEAR LA PALMA

◪ EL PITAL AND RÍO CHIQUITO

Bus #509 leaves from the street 2 blocks north of San Ignacio's parque central to Río Chiquito (1hr., every 2hr. 7:30am-4:30pm, ¢8). Ask the driver to let you off here. The peak is a 1½hr. hike from Río Chiquito. Entrance ¢10.

If the sight of the mountains surrounding La Palma leaves you restless, climb El Pital, the highest mountain in El Salvador (2730m). The jaw-dropping views of Honduras to the north and the cones of El Salvador's volcanoes to the south make this hike a worthwhile daytrip. It is best to leave as early as possible in the morning to beat the rain that tends to come in the afternoon. Tiny Río Chiquito, the departure point for the ascent, lies near other hikes and the neighboring town of Las Pilas. Definitely take the bus to Río Chiquito—though the town is only 10km from San Ignacio (or 10min. north of La Palma on the road to the border), you'll swear the steep, bumpy, uphill road is the longest 10km you've ever seen.

Once the bus lets you out at Río Chiquito, most of the hard work has already been done for you. The top of the peak is less than a 1½hr. hike from the town. From the main road in Río Chiquito, turn left on the dirt road (where the town's few houses are), and continue along a steep four-wheel-drive road until you reach the peak, bearing right at any forks along the way. You'll pass approximately three barbed-wire gates. During the rainy season, this road can become quite muddy and un-drivable. At the top, there is a ¢10 entrance fee (it's private property). There is a **camping area** with a toilet (¢20 per person including admission). Bring your own gear and come prepared for chilly temperatures. The summit's owner, **Arturo,** can be found here every day in the dry season, but during the rainy season, he's only around on weekends. Ask for him in Río Chiquito before heading up the peak, especially if you'd like a guide. His house is just outside of town toward Las Pilas. Arturo can arrange **guides** (¢20-30) to take you to some of the surrounding woods; ask to go to **La Piedra Rajada,** a gigantic rock formation 30min. from El Pital. The trail crosses several streams, and you must cross a log bridge over a 20m precipice to reach the rock. Going with a guide is advisable. A new option is **El Pital Highland ❺**, a restaurant and hotel set among exotic flowers and a small deer farm. The *cabañas* sleep 9 (US$125) and 4 (US$104). Reserve at least 8 days in advance. Though the hotel is only open on weekends, call in advance for a hot meal whenever you're passing by. (☎ 222 2009. Hot dog and fries US$2.85; spaghetti US$4.60.)

⚠ OTHER HIKES FROM RÍO CHIQUITO

A rewarding hike with impressive views heads up to **Miramundo.** From Río Chiquito, just past where the bus stops as the road begins to dip, bear right at the fork instead of heading down to Las Pilas. The dirt road climbs for about 45min. until the peak. The best views are from the **Hostal Miramundo** at the top. The hostal has a restaurant, bar, and rooms with a view that sleep up to 6 people (¢300). Ask and they'll gladly let you walk around their picnic area and soak up the vistas of El Salvador, Honduras, and El Pital.

From Río Chiquito, you can also take a short trip to the town of **Las Pilas,** 6km down the main road. Walk or take the same bus from San Ignacio (#509, 30min., every 2hr. 7am-5pm, ¢3). This tiny town is an international cultivation center producing potatoes, lettuce, strawberries, and apples, among other things. The town offers a great chance to see the agricultural economy and culture of northern El Salvador up close. The market in town is also the best place around to pick up some fresh fruits and veggies. You may even be able to pick the fruit yourself. There is a nice hike from Las Pilas to the **Río Sumpul,** a river that forms the border with Honduras and originates at El Pital. Turn right in the center of town, and make the 20min. walk to the river, where you can find pleasant pools to bathe in.

✖ EL POY: BORDER WITH HONDURAS

The Honduran border is 11km past El Poy and 5km past San Ignacio. **Immigration** is open from 6am to 10pm. Cars will have to make an additional stop at the *aduana* (customs house). **Money changers** on both sides of the border will change any Central American currency. Banks at the border are of little use, and those in Nueva Ocotepeque and La Palma will only change US dollars into the local currency at a standard rate about 1-2% below the actual rate. Coming into El Salvador, buses run regularly to **La Palma** (30min., every 30 min. 4am-8pm, ¢4) and continue on to **San Salvador** (3½hr., ¢10). Across the border in Honduras, buses head along a new road to Nueva Ocotepeque (every 30min. 6am-10pm, L6).

WESTERN EL SALVADOR

Coffee plantations and hilly terrain covered by national parks, lakes, and volcanoes make the west one of the most captivating regions of El Salvador. Santa Ana, the country's most pleasant city, boasts a newly renovated theater and impressive cathedral, while the small towns of Apaneca, Juayua, and Nahuizalco offer an idyllic mountain escape. Traces of the region's history are visible at the archaeological site of Tazumal. For a more extreme escape, head into the cloud forest of Parque Nacional Montecristo, near Metapán in the north, or visit El Salvador's last untouched wildlife reserve at Parque Nacional El Imposible.

SONSONATE

In contrast to its idyllic surroundings, Sonsonate buzzes with energy, chokes on diesel fumes, and swelters under the pressures of rapid modernization. The city is a transport hub; many pass through en route to the Pacific Coast, Apaneca and La Ruta de las Flores, Parque Nacional El Imposible, or the Guatemalan border at La Hachadura. Crime has become a problem in this city, especially at night.

⌨ TRANSPORTATION. Buses leave from the well-organized modern terminal on Paseo 15 de Septiembre, eight blocks east of the *parque* between 14 and 16 Av., to: **San Salvador** (#205; 1½hr., every 5min. 3:30am-6:30pm, ¢6); **Santa Ana** via **Los Naranjos** (#216; 1¼hr., every 20min. 3:30am-6:30pm, ¢5); **Santa Ana** via **Cerro Verde** (#209A; 1½hr., every 30min. 5am-5pm, ¢4.25); **La Libertad** (#287; 2½hr.; 6:15am, 3:45pm, or transfer in San Salvador; ¢6). The following buses pick up a half block south of Av. 15 de Septiembre on 10 Av.: **Los Cobanos** (#257; 40min., every 30min. 5am-6pm, ¢3) and the **Guatemalan border** at **La Hachadura** (#259; 1¾hr., every 10min. 4am-7:30pm, ¢5), which goes through **Cara Sucia** (1hr., ¢4). From there transportation heads to **Parque Nacional El Imposible** (see p. 293); **Acajutla** (#252; 30min., every 10min. 5am-7pm, ¢2). To **San Pedro Puxtlo** (#246; 1¼hr., every 30min. 6am-7pm, ¢4). To go to **Ahuachapán** directly, take #278a (1hr., every 30min. 5:30am-6pm, ¢5). To Ahuachapán and *La Ruta de los Flores*, the bus picks up along 1a Calle along the north side of the *parque* (#249; 1hr. 40min., every 35min. 4:30am-6pm, ¢6). A new bus terminal has opened recently and the bus routes are being shifted gradually; most buses will still pass the old terminal. Those heading south leave town by 10 Av., stopping for additional pickups. Local bus #53F will take you all the way to *la Nueva Terminal*, ½km down Av. 15 de Septiembre. **Local buses** travel between the *parque* and the terminal (#53F; every 5min., ¢1.50), to **Nahuizalco** (#53D; every 10min.) and to **Izalco** (#53A; every 5min.). Because of the one-way streets, buses return to the *parque* along 1 Av., one block north of the main Av. Marroquín/Av. 15 de Septiembre. A few routes of #53 also pass *Metrocentro* and are clearly marked. Bright yellow **taxis** line up on the north and west sides of the *parque* and outside the bus terminal, and charge a pricey ¢15 for travel between the two points.

⚑⚐ ORIENTATION AND PRACTICAL INFORMATION. The bus terminal is on **Paseo 15 de Septiembre,** which runs east-west, changing into **Calle Obispo Marroquín** after the river and between 14 and 16 Av. The *parque central* is eight blocks west of the terminal. The main *avenida* runs along the front of the church, **Av. Rafael Campos** to the south and **Av. Morazán** to the north. From the *parque*, odd-numbered *calles* and *avenidas* increase in number to the north and west respectively, while their even-numbered counterparts increase to the south and east. **Banco de Comercio,** on Av. Flavian Mucci one block south of the *parque*, changes traveler's checks and has an **ATM** that accepts all major cards. (Open M-F 8:30am-5pm, Sa 8:30am-noon.) Other services include: **municipal market,** Calle Marroquín between 6/8 Av., three blocks east of the *parque; police* (☎451 1099, emergency 121), a block south of Calle Marroquín on 12 Av. (also known as Av. Quiñonez); **Hospital Municipal,** 5 Av., 1/3 Calles (☎451 0200; doctor on call 24hr.); **Farmacia Fernández,** on Calle San Antonio (☎451 0465; open M-Sa 8am-6pm, Su 8am-noon). **Telecom,** Av. Campos at 2 Calle, is a block south of the *parque* (open daily 7am-7pm; Internet ¢30 per hr.); **internet** at **Infocentros,** 3 Calle between Av. Morazán and 1 Av. north of the park.

(¢20 per hr., students ¢11 per hr. Open M-F 8am-6pm, Sa 8am-noon.) The **post office** is on 1 Av., 3/5 Calles (open M-F 7am-5pm, Sa 7am-noon).

⚏⚏ ACCOMMODATIONS AND FOOD. Hotels and *hospedajes* near the bus terminal tend to be rough and dirty, while those near the *parque central* are better and only a 10min. walk from the bus station. The best place to stay is **Hotel Orbe ❷**, 2 Av. (also called Av. Flavian Mucci), 4 Calle, two blocks south of the *parque*. Private baths pass the white glove test. (☎451 1517; fax 451 1416. Singles ¢70, with A/C and TV ¢140; doubles ¢160/¢175.) For something nicer, try **Hotel Agape ❹**, a 10min. bus ride east of town on the road to Izalco. Rooms have private baths, TV, and A/C. (Singles US$16; doubles US$22. AmEx/MC/V.)

Food carts and *pupuserías* line the *parque central*, while **Pastelería Anthony ❶**, a block west, serves up good coffee, pastries, and sandwiches. (Pastries ¢2.5-7. Open daily 7:30am-6:30pm, with other branches around town.) The fast food row can be found at the intersection of 12 Av. and Calle Marroquín, near the bus terminal. From Av. 15 de Septiembre, turn left on Av. Quiñoez or catch a #53 bus headed to Izalco on Sonzocate. On your left will be **Restaurante La Terraza ❷** at Hotel Plaza, which serves good-sized meals at decent prices. (Crepes with meat or chocolate ¢15. Open daily until 9:30pm. Credit cards accepted.)

⚏⚏ SIGHTS AND ACTIVITIES. A small town north of Sonsonate, **Izalco** is home to the two oldest churche s in El Salvador. The **Iglesia de la Anunción,** the first church on your right as you proceed along the town's main road, dates back to 1580. **Iglesia de los Dolores,** at the top of the road, is 10 years older. **Turicentro Atecozol** has two pools, waterslide trails, basketball courts, and *comedores*. Bus #53A departs from the *parque central* in Sonsonate and brings you to the entrance of the Turicentro before returning. (Pool open daily 7am-4:30pm. Buses 20min., ¢1.25; last bus back leaves Turicentro at 5:30pm. Entrance fee ¢7, car fee ¢6.)

NEAR SONSONATE

⚏ PLAYA LOS CÓBANOS

Buses run from Sonsonate (#257; 45min., every 30min. from 6am, ¢3) leaving from Calle Marroquín and Av. Quiñonez (12 Av.). The last return bus leaves the beach at 6pm.

Just 25km south of Sonsonate, Playa Los Cóbanos is popular with locals for its gently curving beach. Soft, seashell-strewn sand and bits of coral yield to large black rocks at the water's edge, creating a stunning contrast. When the tide is out, you can walk hundreds of meters out to sea on the rocks. The main beach sits between rocky peninsulas. **Punta Remedios** is on the west side, and at low tide, you can walk west to the more soothing **Playa Los Remedios;** several other tranquil beaches lined with private houses await a little farther. **Beware:** high tide will block your way back to Los Cóbanos. Some of the best **scuba-diving** in the country lies offshore from Los Cóbanos, in El Salvador's largest coral reef. Conditions are good only in the summer (Nov.-May; Dec. and Jan. are best); during that time you can arrange dives with several San Salvador-based dive shops. **El Salvador Divers** organizes full-day trips that include two dives, lunch, equipment, and transportation. (☎264 0961.¢375 per person.) **Oceánico Diving School** does similar trips. (☎263 6931. US$50 per person, minimum 4 people; reserve guide 2 days in advance.)
Hotel Mar de Plata ❺, attached to the restaurant of the same name, rents dark *cabañas* with porches. Shared bathrooms are a walk away. (Rooms ¢80 per day, ¢160 per day and night.) The last hotel to the right is **Hotel Solimar ❸**, which rents *cabañas* on the beach. They also have daytime *cabañas* with a table and chairs (you can sleep there if you bring your own mattress). Solimar also has public

showers (¢3) and toilet facilities. (Beach cabañas ¢110 for a bed, with private bath, fan, and queen-size bed ¢160. Daytime cabañas ¢55 per day.)

▓ LA RUTA DE LAS FLORES

Nahuizalco, Juyua, and Apaneca, three of the towns that comprise La Ruta de Las FLores, are connected by bus #249, which runs frequently between Ahuachapán and Sonsonate (every 15min., daily 5am-7pm). Nahuizalco is also reachable by bus #53D from Sonsonate's parque central. The bus stops at the parque central of each town.

High in the mountains of the Cordillera Apaneca-Ilamatepec, between Ahua-chapán to the west and Sonsonate to the east, the towns of Ataco, Apaneca, Jua-yua, and Nahuizalco have been dubbed "La Ruta de Las Flores" by CORSATUR. These villages provide access to one of the most majestic mountain regions in the country, filled with rivers, crater lakes, coffee plantations, and, yes, a wide array of flowers. These towns have all retained a certain colonial charm as well as a rich cultural history, evident in their local traditions and especially their *artesanía*.

NAHUIZALCO. About 10km north of Sonsonate, Nahuizalco is known for its wicker baskets and carpentry, produced in homes and workshops around town by 90% of the population. Nahuizalco is one of the oldest indigenous villages in the country, although traditional dress is rarely seen nowadays. Shops selling wicker and wooden **handicrafts** (everything from full living room sets to wicker toilet-paper holders) line the street that heads out to Sonsonate. An incredible sight to behold is the unique *mercado nocturno*, where the marketplace, fed by numerous stands cooking up an array of *platos típicos*, continues to bustle by candlelight. (Open nightly 7-10pm.) Guides can be found at the Casa de la Cultura (☎ 453 0129) or at the Alcaldia; they charge only ¢5 to show you the many workshops around town.

JUAYUA. The largest of the towns, Juayua (why-YOU-ah) is about 16km from Sonsonate. The most famous sight is the sculpture of **El Cristo Negro,** sheltered in a spotless white 20th-century church on the west end of the *parque.* (Open W-M.) The most accepted history of the sculpture says it was carved by Quirio Cataño near the end of the 16th century; it continues to be a pilgrimage destination. The church itself is impressive, and the glimmering towns are a dramatic sight as you approach the valley of Juayua. Growing in popularity is the food festival and fair, **La Feria Gastronómica,** which occurs every weekend and includes music, art, and over 50 *platos típicos.* Once a month a country is chosen and its food, music, and culture are put in the spotlight. (*Platos* ¢10-35. Open Sa and Su 10am-5pm.) Close by Juayua are various lakes and a number of rivers and waterfalls. The local tour-ism committee has erected a **Caseta de Información** (☎ 452 2916; open Sa and Su only) on the *parque,* where guided tours may be arranged (guides range from ¢20-75 depending on the excursion). If you come on a weekday, ask around for **Jaime Salgado** to arrange a tour. The most popular tour is the **Ruta de las Cinco Cascadas** (Route of the Five Waterfalls), a day-hike featuring 80m high *Salto Papalunate,* and ending at *Los Chorros* with lovely swimming holes. Call the day before.

Banco de Comercio, one block west of the church on the road out of town, will change traveler's checks and give cash advances on Visa. (Open M-F 8:30am-4:30pm.) **Casa de Huéspedes Doña Mercedes ❺,** three blocks east and a block south of the *parque,* offers spotless rooms with fan, cable TV, and hot water private bath. (☎ 452 2207. Singles ¢175; doubles 225.) Two blocks behind the left-hand side of the church sits **Hotel El Mirador ❹.** Though there is no sign, the hotel furnishes clean simple rooms with private baths. (☎ 452 2432. 1-4 people ¢125.) **Pollo Rico ❶,** three blocks west and a block north of the *parque,* is the most reasonably priced restaurant in town (meals ¢20-¢30).

APANECA. The smallest and most charming of the villages on La Ruta de las Flores, Apaneca is a 40min. drive south of Ahuachapán on the road to Sonsonate. The bus drops you off along the highway and you have to walk about five blocks up the hill to get to the town center. The town, surrounded by forests and coffee plantations, gets pleasantly cool at night. Founded in 1525, the town has subsisted on its coffee industry, which still employs 80% of the population. Buses from Ahuachapán drop off facing north; those from Sonsonate drop off facing south.

The church was on the west side of the *parque*, but was leveled early in 2001 by earthquakes, and is slowly being rebuilt. On the eastern edge is an extremely well-maintained municipal park. Two hikes into the volcanic region leave from points just outside of town. don't go alone; fortunately, the local police are happy to guide and protect. The **police** are two blocks west of the *parque* (☎ 433 0037).

A 7km walk from Apaneca leads to **Laguna Verde,** a beautiful and popular crater lake surrounded by pine slopes. From the highway at the edge of town, take the dirt road to the right of the Jardín de Flores garden center; this road winds up and around the mountain and passes some viewpoints of Ahuachapán (3hr.). The smaller **Laguna Las Ninfas,** a 45min. walk from town, has good bird-watching. It can be reached by heading straight from the garden center and then, after about 20min., bearing right onto a dried-up creek bed. The lake area has nice views but dries up in times of low rainfall. It's easy to get lost—arrange a guide.

Hostal Rural Las Orquídeas ❸ is a lovely place to stay. Follow the yellow signs, go two blocks south from the church, turn left, and walk half a block. There's a sitting room, courtyard, and nice rooms with hot-water showers. (☎ 433 0061. Singles ¢100; doubles ¢150.) **Las Flores de Eloisa ❶** is probably the best known and cheapest. It sits 2km down the highway from Ahuachapán. (☎ 433 0415. Rooms about US$10.) 🖼**La Cocina de Mi Abuela ❹**, in a yellow building two blocks north of the park on 1 Av., is known as one of the best restaurants in the country. Although not open everyday, it is worth the wait; live music and beautiful gardens accompany the exquisite *típico* with a flair. (Meat dishes ¢70-85. Open Th-Sa 8am-7pm, Su 8am-5pm.) **Comedor Carmela ❶**, two blocks east of the church, has good, cheap *comida típica* and helpful maps detailing tourist sights in town. (*Pupusas* ¢2. Open daily 7am-7pm.) **El Viejo Pescador ❸**, on the main road from the highway, is famous for its seafood. (Fish plates $8. Open daily 7:30am-11pm. V/MC/AmEx.)

PARQUE NACIONAL EL IMPOSIBLE

Dubbed *El Último Refugio* ("The Last Refuge"), Parque Nacional El Imposible is El Salvador's largest and most impressive national park, home to a biodiversity that's the last of its kind. Deep green mountains and ridges covered with dense primary-growth tropical forest protect the delicate ecosystems that have been obliterated in much of the rest of the country. The park's 3600 hectares are home to nearly 400 different species of trees, 500 species of butterflies, two plant species unique to the park, and several endangered species, including the *tigrillo* and puma. The park's name derives from its pre-refuge days, when local coffee growers had to traverse a precarious mountain pass to get their coffee to market: *"El Imposible"* was a wide gap in the cliff trail, bridged by tree trunks that routinely broke, sending burros, coffee, and men falling 100m to their deaths. In 1968, however, the government built a permanent bridge over the pass and erected a sign reading: "In 1968, it ceased to be impossible."

Impressively managed by the non-governmental agency Salva Natura, the park protects three zones of vegetation and the sources of eight rivers which provide pure water uncontaminated by human and agricultural waste. Salva Natura also supports the development of local communities. Micro-enterprises with literacy programs, and water-channeling efforts are among ongoing programs.

EL SALVADOR

Visiting the park today is certainly not impossible, but it does require some planning. You will first need to secure a permit from Salva Natura in San Salvador (¢50; see **San Salvador, p. 266**). They will also arrange for a guide to meet you there. The guide service is one of the best features of the park, which is fortunate, since no one is allowed to enter without one. Service is free, but tips (about ¢50) are expected since the guides are not salaried. Upon arriving in San Miguelito, the town outside the park entrance, the guide assigned to you will either find you or will be waiting at the **visitors center.** Due to the transportation schedule, there are only two ways to tackle El Imposible. For a more thorough visit, come with the afternoon pickup, head into the park the following day, and spend a second night in San Miguelito. Alternatively, you can catch the first ride to San Miguelito, arrive by midday, have until nightfall to explore, and crash for the night in San Miguelito.

⌐ TRANSPORTATION. Getting to El Imposible can be tricky. The first step is to get to **Cara Sucia,** the nearest major town. From the terminal in **Sonsonate,** buses leave for Cara Sucia every 10min., also stopping at 10 Av. just south of Calle Marroquín on their way out of town (#25; 1¼hr., 5:30am-6pm, ¢4). About 10min. east of Cara Sucia on the *carretera*, a large park sign marks a dirt road that heads north into the hills for 13.5km to the park's **San Benito** entrance; though it's possible to wait at this junction for transportation, it's much easier to come from Cara Sucia. Two daily pickups (11am and 2pm) travel from Cara Sucia to the park entrance at **San Miguelito,** the tiny village at the San Benito entrance to the park (1¼hr., ¢7). Alternatively, you can walk to **El Refugio,** a small town 3km downhill from San Miguelito (1hr.). **Buses** run from Cara Sucia to El Refugio (1hr., daily 10am and 3:20pm, ¢4). Both the bus and the pickup leave from across the street from the bus stop in Cara Sucia, in front of Bazar Hernandez.Pickups fill up early (30min. prior).

Returns are all early in the day. A pickup from San Miguelito descends to Cara Sucia at 5:30am and a bus leaves at 7am. Buses from El Refugio return to Cara Sucia at 7am and 12:30pm. Farmers occasionally take pickups from San Miguelito to Cara Sucia, and some travelers hitch a ride to the highway, where buses for Sonsonate pass by. *Let's Go* does not recommend hitchhiking.

▲ ORIENTATION. The **San Benito** entrance, at the north end of San Miguelito, leads into the park through a gate and past several signs with park rules. Another entrance is near the town of **San Francisco Méndez** to the west, but, as of August 2002, that entrance was not open to the public.

A few minutes up the hill from the entrance gate is the **Visitors Center,** or **Casco,** with bathrooms, showers, and an ecological education center with maps of the park. Just beyond the visitors center the road splits, with the right fork heading down to the only two permissible **camping areas ❶** (free with your permit from Salva Natura). There are bathrooms with running water, firepits, and tables.

▮◪ ACCOMMODATIONS AND FOOD IN SAN MIGUELITO. Half the fun of any trip to El Imposible is spending a little time in the tranquil village of **San Miguelito,** where the people are friendly and the coffee is outstanding. The village has no electricity, and the sporadic running water is still something of a novelty.

Don Rafael and **Doña Hilda ❶,** in the last house on the right before the park entrance (marked by the painted stones forming an arrow), will cheerfully fix you up with a bed or hammock in a rustic, candlelit room (¢25). The other lodging option is **camping** at the campground within the park (see **Orientation,** above). Doña Hilda's typical Salvadoran kitchen, also known as **◪Comedor La Montaña ❶**, prepares delicious and authentic *típico* food (breakfast ¢12, lunch ¢15-25, dinner ¢12-20). **Tienda El Tucán,** down the road across the street, stocks a limited selection of water, sodas, snacks, and staples like rice, oil, and candles. Depending on the length of your stay, it may be a good idea to bring your own food, too, and water or iodine tablets, since the store may inexplicably be closed in the middle of the day.

⚑ INSIDE THE PARK. Three well-maintained main trails through the park are open; they vary in length but all are moderately strenuous, with significant uphill stretches. At the juncture beyond the visitors center, the branch heading to the right shortly becomes **El Sendero de Mulo,** a pleasant 1km forest stroll including 10 informative stations that describe the various plants and animals along the way. A few steps up the right fork lies a *mirador* offering spectacular views north and east of territory within the *parque* and the cultivated lands beyond it. In the distance, you can just make out the waterfall at a point known as **Los Enganchos.** The trail to **Los Enganchos** breaks off to the right and heads steeply downhill to a crystal-clear river and small waterfall. Swimming here is a very pleasant cooldown before the difficult ascent back (1½-2 hr. trip). The second trail brings you to the **Piedra Sellada,** one of the nine archaeological sites in the park where symbolic carvings have been found covering a large rock. It is believed that the site was of religious importance to the indigenous societies of the region (1hr. each way).

You can also try the **Cerro León** circuit. From the Sendero de Mulo, the trail branches left and winds up and down through the mountains and incredibly verdant primary and secondary forests. After 45min., a trail forks off to the right, leading to the ruins of an old church near the town of **Tacuba** on the north side of the park. Special permission from Salva Natura is required for this 3hr. hike. The panoramic views from the **summit** of Cerro León, at 1100m above sea level, stretch from the Cordillera de Apaneca to the north, to the mountains of Guatemala in the distance to the west, to the Pacific Ocean as far as Acajutla port to the south.

As you descend the Cerro, the trail that gave the park its name appears to the east as a faint cut-line in the forest skirting the top of cliffs that drop hundreds of meters to the valley floor. After retracing the trail you came up, the loop continues along another trail to the right. You will pass the small, pure **Río Ixcanal,** one of the eight rivers that originate in the park. The *río* also has a nice swimming spot. The trail heads back up and brings you home to the Visitors Center (3-4 hr. trip).

AHUACHAPÁN

Capital of its department, Ahuachapán, 35km from Santa Ana, was one of the oldest Spanish settlements in the country. There's little to see beyond the daily market and the ancient churches, but it's a convenient stop en route to the Guatemalan border and the mountain towns of La Ruta de las Flores.

▤ TRANSPORTATION. From the terminal at 10 Calle and Av. Menéndez, one block north of Parque Menéndez, **buses** head to: **Santa Ana** (#210; 1¼hr., every 10min. 4:30am-7pm, ¢6), via **Chalchuapa** (40min., ¢2); **San Salvador** (#202; 2½hr., every 10min. 3am-5:30pm, ¢7); **Tacuba** (#267, 1hr., every 30min. 3:30am-7pm, ¢4); and **Sonsonate** (#249; 2hr., every 12min. 4:30am-6pm, ¢6) via **Apaneca** (40min., ¢3), **Juayua** (1hr.; ¢8 direct, ¢6 regular), and **Nahuizalco** (1½hr., ¢5). Buses and microbuses for the **Guatemalan border** at **Las Chinamas** leave from 8 Calle and 2 Av., on the northwest corner of Parque Menéndez (#263 and #11; 30min., every 8min. 4:50am-7:30pm, ¢3-4). Be sure to get on the bus bound for the *frontera* (ask the driver); some go only as far as the town of Las Chinamas, a few kilometers short.

▧▨ ORIENTATION AND PRACTICAL INFORMATION. Arriving from El Salvador, buses will drop you in the market on **Av. Menéndez,** just above 10 Calle. **Parque Menéndez,** bounded by 6/8 Calles and Av. 2/Menéndez, the more northern of the town's two parks, is identifiable by the trees towering over the market stalls. Arriving from the border at Las Chinamas, the bus will drop you on 2 Av. on the west side of Parque Menéndez, next to **Iglesia El Calvario.** Streets are laid out in a grid:

Av. Menéndez is the main north-south artery and **Calle Barrios,** three blocks south of Parque Menéndez, is the primary east-west thoroughfare. Odd-numbered *avenidas* and *calles* increase to the east and south, respectively, while their even-numbered counterparts increase to the north and west. The other *parque,* **La Concordia,** is five blocks south of Parque Menéndez and bounded to the east by the church **Nuestra Señora de la Asunción.**

Tourist information is at **Casa de la Cultura,** Av. 2, 2 Calle and Calle Barrios. Banks and ATMs are now over-abundant; most cluster around 1a Av. Nte, Calle Barrios, and 2a Calle. **Banco Cuscutlan** has an **ATM** that takes all major cards and cashes traveler's checks. (Open M-F 8:30am-4pm, Sa 8:30am-noon.) Other services include: **De Todo Supermarket,** on the northeastern corner of Parque Menéndez (open daily 7:30am-7pm); **police,** 5 Calle between 2 Av. and Menéndez Av. (☎443 0513; open 24hr.); **Farmacia Central,** Av. 2, 2 Calle and Calle Barrios (☎443 0158; open daily 8am-7pm, call 24hr.) and next door to **medical services** at **Centro de Emergencias** (24hr. response); the **hospital,** 16 Av. Pte., Calle Zacamil (☎443 0039 or 443 0046); **Telecom,** on 3 Calle, 2 Av. (open daily 7am-7pm; internet ¢32 per hr.). Log on to the **Internet** at **Infocentros,** along the north side of La Asunción Church. (¢20 per hr., students ¢11 per hr. Open M-F 7:30am-7pm, Sa and Su 8am-5pm.) The **post office,** 1 Calle Ote. and 1 Av. Sur, also has a branch on 1 Calle Ote and Av. Menéndez. (Open M-F 8am-noon and 2-5pm, Sa 8am-noon).

❚❚ ACCOMMODATIONS AND FOOD. Hotel San José ❷, on the south side of Parque Menéndez, has comfortable rooms with clean sheets, fansc and private baths. (☎413 1908. Singles $9; doubles $15.) For affordable luxury, try **Hotel Casa Blanca ❺,** 2 Av., Calle Barrios. Spotless rooms set around a courtyard, have ceiling fans or A/C, gorgeous hot-water baths, and telephones. (☎443 1505; fax 443 1503. Singles ¢170, with A/C ¢225; doubles ¢230/¢280. AmEx/MC/V.)

Visit one of the town's ancient homes, the "Villa Carmen," for a meal at **Restaurante La Estancia ❶,** on 1 Av., 1 Calle and Calle Barrios. (Breakfast ¢7-12.) **Mixta's ❶,** half a block north of Parque Concordia on 2 Av., 1/3 Calles, has the best *licuados* in town (¢7-9). Try a *mixta* (¢12.85), pita bread stuffed with meat and a secret sauce. (Open daily 9am-8pm.) Another tasty snack is a *tostada* (or two) made on Sunday afternoons in Parque Concordia (your choice of guacamole, beans, cheese, and salsa on a crispy tortilla, ¢2).

◪ SIGHTS. The **Parroquía de Nuestra Señora de La Asunción,** on the east side of Parque La Concordia, dominates the southern part of the town with its huge dome. The facade of this 18th-century church was recently redone, with an exquisite stained-glass window that complements the marble altar and traditional tiled floor. It is presently undergoing minor repair work, but should be open well before 2003. (Open daily 6am-6pm. Free.) **Iglesia El Calvario,** on the west side of Parque Menéndez, is a rather plain church built in the 1950s, notable mostly for its altarpiece, which has a beautifully carved image of Christ. Damaged by the 2001 earthquakes, it is undergoing renovations which may limit tourist access.

Follow 8 Calle, the northern border of *Parque Menéndez,* 1.5km west to Las Chinamas, to see the still intact gate to the 16th-century Spanish town. About 4km outside of town are **ausoles,** geysers of steam and boiling mud. The nine wells are from 800-2000m deep and eject steam which is captured to generate electricity.

▨ LAS CHINAMAS: BORDER WITH GUATEMALA

A 30min. bus ride north of Ahuachapán is the busiest of El Salvador's borders with Guatemala. Las Chinamas is on the Salvadoran side, Valle Nuevo on the Guatemalan. Crossing here is the most direct route between San Salvador and Guatemala

City. The post is open daily 6am-10pm, although it's staffed 24hr. The offices on the Guatemalan side close at 9pm. Be prepared for unofficial fees. At the border, you can find **comedores,** a **Telecom** office (open daily 7am-7pm), and a last-resort *hospedaje* in the yellow house up the hill (¢30 for the night). **Money changers** abound on both sides and will change any Central American currency. Buses and minibuses head to **Ahuachapán** (#263 and #11; 30min., every 15min. 5:20am-8pm, ¢3-4). For **San Salvador** change in Ahuachapán or try to get on one of the international Pullmans. Across the border in Guatemala, buses leave for **Guatemala City** (3hr., every hr. 4am-6pm, Q30 or ¢70).

SANTA ANA

Santa Ana, El Salvador's second largest city, modestly calls itself the "Queen of the West," a claim that is not unjustified. The new luster of the cathedral, theater, and Museo Regional Occidente, as well as the town's *plazas*, exhibit the Santaneco pride. Set in a valley, friendly Santa Ana is a good base for exploring western El Salvador due to its proximity to Lago de Coatepeque, Parque Nacional Cerro Verde, Volcán Izalco, and the ruins at Tazumal. The border crossings into Guatemala at Las Chinamas and San Cristóbal are also within easy reach.

TRANSPORTATION

Intercity Buses: The main terminal is located at 10 Av., 15 Calle. **Transportes La Vencedora** runs buses from its terminal at 11 Calle Poniente and Av. Fray Felipe, a block west of Parque Colón.

Ahuachapán: Main terminal. (#210; 1hr., every 15min. 4am-7pm, ¢5.)

Cerro Verde: La Vencedora. (#248; 1¾hr.; M-Th 5 per day 8:40am-3:30pm, F, Sa, and Su 7:40pm; ¢6.50.)

Chalchuapa and Tazumal: No set departure point; passes Parque Colón before heading out of town. (#218; 20min., every 20min. 5am-6pm, ¢1.75.)

Guatemalan border at **San Cristóbal:** Main terminal. (#236; 1hr., every 15min. 5:30am-7:30pm, ¢3.60.)

Guatemala City: La Vencedora. (About every hr. 5am-5:15pm, ¢65; last bus ¢90.)

Metapán: Main terminal. (#235; 1½hr., every 15min. 4am-6:20pm, ¢5.)

San Lorenzo: Main terminal. (#277; 2hr., every 15min. 6:25am-6pm, ¢4.)

San Salvador: Main terminal. (#201; 2hr., every 10min. 4am-6pm, ¢5.)

Sonsonate: Main terminal. (#216; 1½hr., every 15min. 5am-6pm, ¢5.)

Local Buses: Slow, but useful for getting outside the center. The **#51** is the main north-south route, although it does a lot of east-west traversing, passing a block south of the cathedral and eventually heading to the **Metrocentro** on the southern edge of town. The **#55** is the main east-west route, passing a block south of the cathedral and heading to the **hospital** on the city's eastern edge. Both routes have various sub-routes, marked by letters which only increase the confusion. Most indicate their main stops on the front. Both buses pass near the bus terminal and run from 6am-8pm daily. Fare ¢1.25.

Taxis: Cluster on the north side of Parque Libertad as well as behind the Alcaldía. ¢10-20 for trips around town. At night, they are not always easy to find if you are not in the *centro* by their stands. The taxi-company's number is useful (☎ 441 1661), as walking at night is not advisable. You'll need a phone card.

ORIENTATION AND PRACTICAL INFORMATION

The central intersection of **Calle Libertad** and **Av. Independencia** is at the southwest corner of the **Parque Libertad,** which serves as the de facto *parque central.* Note that odd-numbered *calles* and *avenidas* increase to the south and east, respec-

Santa Ana

ACCOMMODATIONS
Hospedaje San Miguel, **9**
Hotel La Casita, **2**
Hotel La Libertad, **3**
Hotel Livingston, **10**
Hotel El Viajero, **1**

FOOD
Café Fiesta, **8**
Los Horcones, **5**
Pastelería Ban Ban, **7**
Pip's Carymar, **11**
Restaurante Ky'Jau, **4**
Talitunul, **6**

tively, while even numbers increase to the north and west. Most of the town lies just southwest of Parque Libertad. The bus terminal is at 10 Av., 15 Calle, 5 blocks west and 9½ blocks south of Parque Libertad, amidst a sea of market stalls.

Tourist Information: Casa de Cultura (☎ 441 0169), 2 Av. Nte. at 2 Calle, has books and info on the history and culture of the city and region. A city **map** can be bought at the theater's lobby office (¢15). Open M-F 8am-noon and 2-5pm, Sa 8am-noon.

Banks: Banco Comercio, on Calle Libertad at 2 Av., will change traveler's checks and has an **ATM** (AmEx/MC/V). Open M-F 9am-5pm, Sa 9am-noon. Second branch at Av. Delgado, 5/7 Calles. Open M-F 9am-5pm.

Market: The streets to the north and west of the bus terminal, and around Av. 6/8, 3 Calle Ote. Open during daylight hours; best avoided at night.

Mall: Super-modern Metrocentro, on Av. Independencia directly south roughly 20 blocks from *Parque Libertad*. Houses multiple ATMs (Cajero de Oro accepts all cards including AmEx, Cirrus, Diner's, and Plus), a movie theater ($3), Super Selectos grocery store, Cyber Cafe, and food court.

Supermarket: Super Selectos has a location just behind the Alcaldía, 2 Av. and 2 Calle Ote, as well as a larger store on Av. Frey Felipe and 11 Calle Ote. Open daily 7am-7pm.

Laundry: Lavandería La Solución, 8/10 Av., 7 Calle. Machine wash and dry ¢42, 2hr. Open M-F 8am-6pm, Su 8am-noon.

Police: 2 Av., 9/11 Calles (☎447 4846, emergency 911). 24hr.

Hospital: 13 Av., 1 Calle (☎447 1555), 6 blocks east and 1 block south of the *parque*.

Pharmacy: Farmacía La Asunción (☎441 2380), on the southeast corner of Parque Menéndez. Open daily 8am-6pm.

Telephones: Telecom, 5 Av., 2 blocks east of *Parque Libertad* just past the Telecom office. Open daily 7am-7pm.

Internet: Infocentros, Av. Jose Matías Delgado, 3 and 1 Calle Pte. Good rates and A/C. ¢20 per hr., students ¢11 per hr. Open M-Sa 8am-8pm, Su 9am-5pm.

Post Office: Av. 2/Independencia, 7 Calle. Open M-F 7am-5pm, Sa 7am-noon. Express mail services available. **DHL shipping** (☎441 0686), Av. Independencia, 3/5 Calles. Open M-Sa 8am-12:30pm and 1:30-6pm.

ACCOMMODATIONS

Many budget accommodations in Santa Ana are clustered along 10 Av., northeast of the bus station. Despite their attractive prices, the area is not so safe at night. Although it is still not recommended to go out alone at night, hotels around *Parque Libertad* tend to be well-maintained and relatively secure.

Hospedaje San Miguel, 12/14 Av., 7 Calle (☎441 3465). A calm refuge downtown with clean, basic rooms on a bright courtyard. Rooms without baths are small, but common bath is reasonably clean. Singles US$4, with bath US$6; doubles US$8. ❷

Hotel Livingston, 10 Av., 7/9 Calles (☎441 1801), about 4½ blocks north of the bus terminal. Popular for its spacious rooms, TVs, and water cooler. Singles with fans, TV, and private bath ¢100; doubles ¢150. Deluxe singles (same amenities but newer building, with sparkling white-tiled floors and A/C) ¢150. AmEx/MC/V. ❸

Hotel La Libertad (☎441 2358), 1 block north of the Parque Libertad; it's a bit of a hike from the bus station but convenient to anywhere else. Comfortable and classy rooms have TV, fan, and private bath. Singles US$11.50; doubles US$17.50. ❸

Hotel La Casita (☎441 1039), 1 block past La Libertad on 4 Calle Oriente, has the nicest beds and blankets in town. Rooms with private baths vary in size and are in a very cozy setting. ¢100 for 1-2 people. English spoken. ❸

Hotel El Viajero (☎441 1090), 4 blocks north of the Alcaldía on 10a Calle Pte. between Av. 4 and Av. 6. Has spacious clean rooms with cable TV. 1-2 people ¢100. ❸

FOOD

Inexpensive restaurants line Calle Libertad between Parque Libertad and Parque Menéndez, as well as Av. Independencia south of Parque Libertad. The cheapest grub is at the many food stands near the southeast corner of Parque Libertad.

Pastelería Ban Ban, Av. Independencia, located on the southeast corner of Parque Libertad. The best coffee in town (¢3.50), sumptuous pastries (¢3-8), and gourmet sandwiches (¢10-12) make this popular place hard to resist. Open daily 8am-7pm. ❶

EL SALVADOR

Los Horcones, on the east side of *Parque Libertad*, with the jungle-hut exterior. The upstairs dining area offers views of the cathedral's facade. The food's quite tasty, too. Tacos ¢23, *pollo asado* or steak ¢34. Open daily until 10pm. ❷

Restaurante Ky'Jau, Calle Libertad, 4/6 Av. Sur. Locals flock here for good Chinese food and cheap lunch combos (¢14-22). Breakfast menu has a selection of *típico* items to mix-and-match. Wonton soup ¢15; egg ¢1.75; *frijoles* ¢2. Open daily 9am-9pm. ❶

Pip's Carymar, Av. Independencia, 7 and 9 Calle (☎441 0506), is a happening place with a large menu. Known for doing typical Salvadoran food right; great service, too. *Pupusas* of all types ¢4.50. Open daily until 9pm. ❶

Café Fiesta, 1 Calle Oriente, Av. Independencia and 1 Av. Sur, is great for a vegetarian lunch (though they serve meat as well). Hearty steamed vegetables, rice, and tasty white bean soup (all under US$1). Open daily noon-2pm. ❶

Talitunal, 2 blocks east of *Parque Libertad* on the right. Run by an alternative medicine doctor and famous for its bread and vegetarian dishes. Open daily 9am-7pm. ❶

🅖 SIGHTS

CATHEDRAL. Few Central American towns can boast such a spectacular cathedral. Built in 1905, it is a testament to the once-great aspirations of local coffee magnates. The church's design sought to unite Gothic elegance and Byzantine strength; the facade is covered in ornate detail, while the imposing interior holds statues dating from the 16th century. *(Open daily 6am-6pm. Free.)*

TEATRO NACIONAL DE SANTA ANA. The impressive renaissance-style theater on the north side of the *parque* was begun in 1902, and is nearing the end of a successful restoration. See Planeta Alternativa in the Th edition of the *Prensa Gráfica* or the free English tourist magazine *Revue* for event listings. With the **Centro de Artes de Occidente,** the theater supports several cultural and artistic workshops and events. *(☎447 7270. Open M-F 8-noon and 2-6pm, Sa 8am-noon. Concerts up to ¢50.)*

PALACIO MUNICIPAL. On the west side of the Parque Libertad, the city government building is another example of the grandiose architecture popular here in the early 20th century. The courtyard in the middle centers on a nice fountain. *(Open M-F 8am-noon and 2-5pm, Sa 8am-noon. Free.)*

MUSEO REGIONAL DEL OCCIDENTE. This brand-new museum is located in the old Federal Reserve Bank. The upstairs exhibit contains artifacts from indigenous sites. Downstairs in the old bank vault, the history of Salvadoran money is on display—from the seeds of native commerce, to the Spanish *real*, through the various editions of the *colón*. Interestingly, no mention is made of the recent dollarization. *(Open Tu-Sa 9am-noon and 1:30-5pm, ¢3.)*

CASINO SANTA ANA. On the corner across from the theater and the Palacio Municipal is this beautifully maintained structure with shiny wooden floors. The casino operates today as an elite social and business club. *(Closed to the public, but check at the office for upcoming events. Peek in the window for a free glimpse.)*

🅓 DAYTRIPS FROM SANTA ANA

PARQUE NACIONAL CERRO VERDE AND AROUND

*Buses leave **Santa Ana** for Cerro Verde daily (#248; 1¾hr.; 5 per day 8:40am-3:30pm, return 6 per day 10am-5:20pm; ¢6.50). Buses drop you in the parking lot at the Cerro Verde visitors area. In Santa Ana, the #248 bus leaves from **La Vencedora** terminal. The* *park has been closed since the 2001 earthquake and will remain so until necessary repairs are made. Current information is available at the San Salvador office of ISTU (☎222 8000). Also ask about its status at the terminal La Vencedora, where you catch the bus. The park information desk is open daily 8am-5pm (☎873 3594, ¢7 entrance).*

From the El Congo junction, 15km southeast of Santa Ana, a road heads to Cerro Verde, a long-extinct 2030m volcano and now the highlight of the national park. The road that reaches all the way to the crater makes the park one of the most accessible in the country. Nearby are two other volcanoes, active Volcán Santa Ana and slightly active Volcán Izalco. The three volcanoes in such close proximity provide a fascinating lesson in volcanic development and aging. Rich vegetation and forest cover Cerro Verde, the oldest, while Izalco, the youngest, remains almost entirely composed of rough volcanic rock. Santa Ana lies in the middle, with both plant life and volcanic stone. Hiking the three volcanoes affords three very different and exhilarating experiences.

⚄🏛 CERRO VERDE VISITORS AREA. Leaving from the far side of the parking lot, the trail **Una Ventana a la Naturaleza** ascends and descends gently in a pleasant 30min. loop, passing a lookout platform toward Volcán Santa Ana and another offering very impressive views of Lago Coatepeque far below. The dense forest in the park is home to numerous species of birds and orchids. The **Hotel de Montaña** was built on Cerro Verde in 1957 to provide views of the erupting Volcán Izalco, but Izalco petered out just as the hotel was completed. It's closed now, but you can enter the grounds and enjoy the best views of the volcano. There are also two small **restaurants** off the parking lot, along with a small **orchid garden.**

> **!** Up the hill to the left is the **police station,** where you'll want to stop before heading to either Volcán Santa Ana or Izalco. Robberies have occurred in the past on both volcanoes; under no circumstances should you attempt to go up Izalco without an armed guard. Its barren slopes make it easy for bandits to spot tourists and simply wait at the bottom for them to descend. Police will accompany you for free, provided they have the personnel.

🏔 TO VOLCÁN SANTA ANA. The clearly marked trail up **Volcán Santa Ana** (2365m) departs from the Ventana a la Naturaleza trail about 100m after the *mirador* towards the volcano. It heads 200m down to a farm, behind which a narrow path leads up to Volcán Santa Ana. The trail is a creek bed; you will be finding your way among the rocks. As you reach the top, an enormous abyss unfolds: 500m deep and 1km in diameter, the crater is filled with grayish water and spews out clouds of sulfuric vapor. The highest point of the volcano lies on the opposite side, so as you circle around, views of Volcán Izalco, the coast, Apaneca, Santa Ana, Lago, and finally Cerro Verde open in front of you. This volcano, while forested at its base, is mostly bare rock and volcanic sediment by the time you reach the top. The ascent is mildly strenuous (about 3hr. roundtrip from Cerro Verde, plus another 1½hr. if you want to walk around the rim).

🏔 TO VOLCÁN IZALCO. For an idea of what the other volcanoes looked like in their infancy, and to complete a three-stage tour of volcanic evolution, head to Volcán Izalco, one of the youngest volcanoes in the world. The hike is the most dramatic and intense in the park. The barren cone rises up to the southwest of Cerro Verde. A marked path leads off the road just before the Cerro Verde parking lot, starting off on a 1km descent through the forest to the base of Izalco. The ascent begins from there, which involves strenuous rock climbing at times. For other stretches you struggle for footing among the loose, tumbling rocks. The view of the coast and the contrast between barren lava and lush forests make the trip more than worth it. Steam and sulfuric gas force their way up through holes in the rock; walk the rim or cut across the center of the crater. The descent is terrifying at first, but can be terribly fun if you learn the technique and let yourself go. Imagine you're downhill skiing, dig in your heels with toes up, lean back and slide. The entire trek to and from Cerro Verde requires 4hr. Sturdy shoes are a must.

🔘 CHALCHUAPA AND TAZUMAL

*Chalchuapa and Tazumal can be reached by the **bus** running between Santa Ana and Ahuachapán (#210; 20min. from Santa Ana, 40min. from Alhuachapán; every 15min. 4am-7pm; ¢2). There is also a bus running from Santa Ana to Chalchuapa; catch it at Parque Colón (#218; 20min., every 10min. 5am-6pm, ¢2). The bus drops you at the cemetery on the southern edge of Chalchuapa. Walk straight toward the gas station about 500m, turn left at the welcome sign and walk 2min. to the entry gate. Site open Tu-Su 9am-4:30pm. Admission ¢25. Guides ¢35.*

The Maya ruins of Tazumal are 13km west of Santa Ana, on the outskirts of the town of Chalchuapa. Though it is the most important site in El Salvador, it doesn't compare to its counterparts in neighboring countries in size or quality of restoration. Tazumal is just one of a series of sites in the larger area, which marks the southeastern border of the Maya civilization. The region's sites indicate continuous occupation from 1200BC to the present. At Tazumal, the buildings preserved at the site were the ceremonial center of a settlement that once covered more than 10 sq. km. The design of the imposing 24m **step-pyramid** has been linked to the step pyramids of Teotihuacan in Mexico. Midway up the pyramid is a reconstructed altar. On the far side of the pyramid is the **ballcourt,** and to the right of the ballcourt is **Structure 2,** a temple dedicated to the god Quetzalcoatl. The **museum,** on the left as you enter the site, displays an impressive collection of pottery from the site as well as reconstructions of the original city. The most important discovery here, the **Stela de Tazumal,** is in the Museo Nacional in San Salvador. It portrays a human figure believed to represent the goddess of waters: the wife of Tlaloc, god of rain.

The town of **Chalchuapa** supports active commerce and agriculture but has retained a certain charm. Strolling through the residential side streets, you'll see some old cobblestone streets and examples of Spanish architecture adorned by bushes and flowering trees. The **Iglesia Santiago Apostal** merits a stop, located 7 blocks west of the small park on the main road. Named a national monument in 1992, the pristine white walls and deep wooden altar and pillars are striking. The choir loft is accessible by an impressive wooden staircase in the back.

🔘 🔘 LAGO DE CAOTEPEQUE

*From Santa Ana, **bus** #220 leaves from the terminal and heads for the lake (45min., every 25min., ¢3). Coming from San Salvador, catch the #201 toward Santa Ana and get off in El Congo, where you can catch the #220 for the 5km down to the lakeshore. After descending to the level of the lakeshore, buses make a sharp left turn and follow a dirt road along the northeast shore of the lake past private estates, a few hotels and restaurants, and a few public beach access points before turning around and heading back. All the lakeside spots on this strip are within walking distance of each other. The often-full last bus to Santa Ana leaves at 5:25pm.*

Roughly 16km from Santa Ana and 5km from El Congo, Lago de Coatepeque, formed by an ancient volcanic crater and surrounded by lush slopes, is very accessible and very beautiful. The lake attracts San Salvadoran weekenders, who justifiably claim that it is among the most beautiful lakes in Central America. Although much of the prime real estate here is occupied, there are still places to soak in the scenery. There is public access to small, dirty beaches and much nicer beaches at the hotels; non-guests can usually get in for a small fee or by buying a meal or a drink. The lake is great for swimming; boats and jet-skis are available for rent.

The **Amacuilco Guesthouse ❷**, a 10min. ride from where the buses turn on to the lake road, has accommodations and a restaurant. Other offerings include canoe rental, and trips to nearby volcanoes. The beach is small but adequate, and there is a small pool; both are open to non-guests for ¢10 or the purchase of a meal at the restaurant. (☎441 0608. Hammocks ¢40; dorms ¢60; private rooms ¢140.) **Hotel Torremolinos ❺**, a well-kept hotel, has two pools, a beach, boat rental, and a restaurant. (☎447 9515. Beach and pool access free with purchase of meal or drink. Su live music 2-5pm, ¢5. 30min. boat rides, ¢10 per person up to 10. To the island, including a wait while you swim, ¢25 per person, 1½hr. Restaurant open daily 8am-8pm. Rooms ¢150; negotiate during the week.) There are two *comedores* on the lake road beyond Hotel Torremolinos. Restaurant **El Mirador** provides tables with an extraordinary view of the lake as you descend into the crater (beer $1.27).

METAPÁN

Metapán, 45km north of Santa Ana, sits in splendid isolation in the mountains of northwest El Salvador. Treacherous mountain passes didn't save the town from some of the worst action of the war, but Metapán survived largely due to its fiercely independent spirit. Ranching is the main livelihood, and older *vaqueros* still mosey into town on horseback, herding cows down the *carretera*. Serenely lording over it all is the cloud-ensconced Cerro de Montecristo. At the top of this hill, the borders of El Salvador, Honduras, and Guatemala converge in the midst of a cloud forest known as El Trifinio, part of Parque Nacional de Montecristo.

⬓ TRANSPORTATION. Buses leave from the terminal on the main highway and head to: **Santa Ana** (#235; 1½hr., every 15min. 4am-6:15pm, ¢5); **San Salvador** (#201A; 5 per day 4am-12:25pm, ¢10), the **Guatemalan border at Anguiatú** (#211A; 30min., every 30min. 5am-4:30pm, ¢3); **Citalá**, a hop, skip, and a jump from the **Honduran border at El Poy** (#463; 3½hr.; 5am bus leaves from terminal, noon and 2:30pm buses leave from 2a Calle, 2 blocks west of the terminal).

⬛ 🛈 ORIENTATION AND PRACTICAL INFORMATION. The road to Metapán comes in from the south and passes the eastern border of the town before heading north to the Guatemalan border. The bulk of the town is on **Calle 15 de Septiembre** and **2a Calle**, which run parallel to each other, perpendicular to the highway, and lead downhill five blocks to the *parque central*. If you have just crossed the border and need to change money, head to **Intercambio** (☎442 0048), on Calle 15 de Septiembre. (Open M-F 8am-noon and 2-5pm, Sa 8am-noon.) **Banco Comercio,** four blocks west from the terminal down Calle 15 de Septiembre on 2 Av., gives cash advances on Visa and has an **ATM.** (Open M-F 8am-4:30pm, Sa 8am-noon.) Other services include: **municipal police station,** seven blocks from the bus terminal down Calle 15 de Septiembre and half a block north on Av. Benjamín E. Valiente (☎442 0013; open 24hr.); **hospital** (☎442 0184), on the highway heading south to Santa Ana, (open 24hr. for emergencies); **markets,** across from the bus station; **supermarket De Todo,** next to Hotel San José on the highway (open daily 7:30am-7pm); **farmacía San Pedro,** 1½ blocks toward the highway from the park opposite the town hall (☎442 0251; open daily 7am-6pm, call 24hr.); **Telecom,** on 2a Calle, a block toward the terminal from the post office; **Internet** at **Infocentros,** behind the city hall off the *parque central* (open daily 8am-6pm). The **post office** on 2 Calle, 3½ blocks west of the terminal. (Open M-F 8am-noon and 2-5pm, Sa 8am-noon.)

⚑📷 ACCOMMODATIONS AND FOOD. Hotel California ❷ has plenty of room, a green patio, and sparkling rooms with bath and fan. To get there, walk out from the bus terminal and face the town, turn right on the highway, and walk about 500m. The hotel is on the left just before the Esso station. (☎ 442 0561. Singles ¢60; doubles ¢75.) **Hospedaje El Paso ❷**, 1½ blocks South of 2a Calle and a block west of the bus terminal, has spacious rooms near the center of town. The shared baths are immaculate, and there's a small roof-deck with impressive views of the surrounding mountains. (☎ 402 1781. Singles ¢65; doubles ¢75.) A slightly more upscale option is **Hotel Christina ❸**, located between Calles 2a and 15 de Septiembre on 6 Av., two blocks west of the terminal. All rooms in this friendly hotel have hot-water private bath, fans, and telephones. The top-floor rooms center around a roof terrace with chaise longues. (☎ 442 0044. US$11.43 per person.)

There are many *comedores* and *pupuserías* around 2 and 4 Av., all serving good, cheap breakfast and lunch for ¢15-20. **Chickenbell ❶**, located 1½ blocks west on 2 Calle, might have a fast-food feel, but the service is typical Salvadoran. (Chicken by the piece, 2 for ¢13.50; pancakes and Aunt Jemima syrup ¢4. Open daily 7am-9pm.) A standout for quality and your budget is **Tropy Jugos ❶**, on 2 Calle, 4 blocks west of the highway. Huge, super-fresh fruit drinks (¢7-10) come with a sandwich or burger and a small side dish for ¢13-20. (Open daily 7:30am-8pm.)

📷 SIGHTS. Metapán's **church,** la Iglesia de San Pedro dates back to 1743. Restored in 1963, the church has a vaulted ceiling, elaborate golden side altars, and **catacombs,** one of which is easily accessible via a wooden trap door in the tiled floor of the center aisle. To see it, stop by after 9am during the week and ask for Carlos, the caretaker, who can show you around by candlelight as he explains the church's history in Spanish. During the last week of June, the church is decorated with flowers for the nine-day **Festival de San Pedro,** celebrating the town's patron saint. The days of processions, music, carnival, and an acclaimed rodeo conclude joyously with a closing parade complete with fireworks and marching bands.

📷 NEAR METAPÁN: LAGO DE GÜIJA

*To reach the lake, take **bus** #235 south toward Santa Ana and get off at Desagüe, an unmarked but well-known village along the road about 20min. south of Metapán (ask the bus driver to drop you off; ¢3). Walk about 100m along a dirt road that forks right from the highway, bearing right until it merges with some railroad tracks. Follow the tracks across the bridge on the left and then leave the tracks and continue on the trail as it slopes gently to the right. Continue through the village until you see the lake between the houses; go towards the water. When you get to the lake, follow the shoreline to the left, where you'll see a tiny peninsula continuing out about 200m. It is possible to walk to the lake. Ask them to point you in the direction of Las Figuras. The other option is to wade through the waist-deep water. **Lanchas** are usually available for lake tours. A couple of houses advertise rentals, but gouge you ¢135 per hr. Try local fishermen who should be able to take you around for about ¢50 per hr. The last bus passes Desagüe around 6pm.*

To the south of Metapán sits the tranquil **Lago de Güija,** half of which is in El Salvador, the other half in Guatemala. While not as scenic as some of El Salvador's other lakes, Güija is much less crowded; the only people you're likely to see are local men and women fishing while their children frolic in the shallows by the shore. The lake's principal attractions are **Las Figuras,** the faded pre-Columbian rock carvings visible on boulders that line the shore of a small peninsula, and **Cerro de las Figuras,** which juts out into the lake. Though the most impressive and well-preserved carvings now sit in museums, there are still many interesting carvings of snails, men, and indecipherable designs. You get the chance to feel like an archaeologist, up close and personal, hunting for and touching the ancient art. Don't be fooled by the clever forgeries; the peace sign carved into one of the rocks is probably not pre-Columbian. If you look closely, you may notice some obsidian fragments or pieces of tools or pottery along the shore. The walk out to the point along Cerro de las Figura's west shore is a pleasant 30min. stroll encompassing all of the major carvings, as well as views across the lake to Guatemala.

PARQUE NACIONAL MONTECRISTO

The cloud forest reserve of Parque Nacional Montecristo sits in the northwestern corner of El Salvador and sprawls across with border with Honduras and Guatemala. The three countries converge at **Trifinio**, which is on **Montecristo**, the park's highest peak. The park protects an amazing variety of wildlife—quetzales, guans, agoutis, porcupines, and anteaters, to name a few. During breeding season, from May to October, the spectacular uppermost parts of the park are closed, but during the summer, from October 15th to May 1st, a 2hr. hike up to the peak will afford you the opportunity to hop childishly from El Salvador to Guatemala to Honduras without having to pay off border guards. The cloud forest is impressive, too; technically easy hiking rewards you with glimpses of sprawling forests and diverse wildlife. Get a permit in San Salvador if you plan to camp overnight.

TRANSPORTATION. Getting to the park is a more difficult task than the hiking. Vehicles are a necessity, but the park does not provide them. **Pickup trucks** leave town around 7am, but go only as far as the Casco Colonial **Visitors Center**, 3km past the *caseta* entrance gate (¢3). The **Los Planes** area of the park is 12km farther up the road, and is accessible only by vehicle, as you are not even allowed to try to walk. The road has been gradually improving with help from large amounts of international aid, but is still a rough ride. The best way to get there is to **hire a pickup.** Hang out at the corner next to the Hotel San José in the morning and ask around. A round-trip, including waiting while you hike, should cost no more than ¢450. Delivering you one day and returning to pick you up the next should cost about ¢700. Be prepared to bargain. If you are alone, make your way to the Casco Colonial, enjoy what's there, and hope that others pass by on their way up.

ORIENTATION AND PARK ENTRANCE INFORMATION. From Metapán, a painfully treacherous dirt road climbs 20km to the main tourist area of the park at Los Planes. Beginning in Metapán, the road to the park branches right from the highway at Hotel San José and continues 4km along a dirt road to the park's entrance at the **Caseta de Información,** where you will need to present your permit and pay the fee. From the Caseta, the road winds 3.5km to the **Visitors Center,** known as the **Casco Colonial.** At the foot of Trifinio, 12km past the Casco Colonial, lies the **Los Planes** visitors area, with campgrounds, picnic areas, and bathrooms. A number of well-maintained trails depart from the two visitors areas, heading to waterfalls, viewpoints, and rivers. The **Caseta de Información** is staffed 24hr., but entry hours are generally from 7am to 3pm; if you want to camp for the night, you must arrive before 3pm. Camping is allowed only in the Los Planes campgrounds, and permits are *absolutely required* if you plan to spend the night. A **permit** must be obtained at the Ministerio de Agricultura, Servicio de Parques Nacionales in San Salvador (see **San Salvador: Special Permits,** p. 266). If you plan to visit just for the day and arrive without a permit, the guards will let you pay the entrance fee and continue on (¢50 per person per day, plus ¢9 per vehicle). You will have to pay the entrance fee for your driver as well. Officials at the *caseta* will radio ahead and arrange for a guide to meet you at the Casco Colonial or Los Planes (free, but tips are appreciated). Guides are required for hiking in these areas and will jump in your car or truck and go along with you. Guides speak only Spanish.

⚑ CAMPING. Los Planes is the only location within the park where camping is allowed. Camping expenses are included in the entrance fee. The three campgrounds at Los Planes are well-equipped with bathrooms and running water, as well as plenty of trails through secondary pine and cypress forest. Try to get into camping areas #2 or 3, which are smaller and more tranquil. Warm clothes are essential to fight off nighttime cold. There are a couple of small **stores** run by locals where you can restock on camping supplies. Each day in the park is ¢50.

◉ ⚑ CASCO COLONIAL VISITORS CENTER. The well-preserved *hacienda* Casco Colonial is surrounded by beautiful flowers and lined with cobblestone streets. The interpretative center in the back explains the history of the park, gives the cultural background of its inhabitants, and provides information on animal specimens found within the park. From the Visitors Center there are also two short trails; the first, **Sendero de Curiosidades de la Naturaleza,** is a 20min. stroll that begins in front of the buildings. The other, **Sendero de los Pioneros,** is a slightly more interesting 35min. hike through secondary forest that leads to a 15m high lookout tower and the remains of a 1992 plane crash. To reach the second trail, go over the footbridge near the Visitors Center and continue a few minutes on the dirt road until you see signs for the *sendero*. Smaller paths wind behind the center around the stream trickling by. *(Open daily 8am-3pm. ¢6.)*

⚑ TRAILS FROM THE MAIN ROAD. Along the road up to Los Planes, you have the opportunity to stop and explore. Your guide should be familiar with the options that exist and can direct the driver. At km 12 a road forks off and continues 1km to a 17m high *mirador* known as **Desvío de la Torre,** which provides impressive views of the surrounding jungle. The tower is manned by a *vigilante* keeping his eyes peeled for forest fires. There is another **mirador** at km 13, with views of a beautiful waterfall, and one at km 15 with impressive views west over Metapán and the Lago de Güija. Around km 19, there is a dirt road which forks left and continues 7km up to **Trifinio.** This trail is a rewarding and intense hike, but the trail leading to Trifinio from Los Planes is a more convenient starting point.

⚑ TRAILS FROM LOS PLANES. At km 20 on the main road (after 1½hr. of driving) is Los Planes. Once there, find **El Jardín de Cien Años,** with trails winding through a well-kept garden of orchids and tall ferns. There is an educational center where each of the 74 species of orchids is labeled.

Several winding trails leave from Los Planes. **Sendero Maravillas y Procesos de la Madre Naturaleza,** a 45min. loop leaving from the soccer field at the campgrounds, passes a striking *mirador*. Another trail, **Sendero El Río Hondurano,** starting from camping area #2, continues for 1hr. before it ends outside the park at a pleasant swimming area on a river. While none of these hikes is spectacular, if you head out around dusk and stay quiet, you're bound to come across plenty of animals. The trail heading up to Trifinio leaves from the road next to the *jardín*. The trail climbs from 1850m above sea level to 2418m over the course of 7km, and should take under 2hr. Your guide will accompany you.

EASTERN EL SALVADOR

Long impoverished, eastern El Salvador was controlled by the FMLN during the war and saw some of the country's fiercest fighting. While the rebuilding continues, the wild east holds some of the country's most ruggedly beautiful scenery. The drive east along the Interamerican Hwy., from captivating San Vicente to bustling San Miguel, is a scenic delight, and several nearby peaks await conquering. South of San Miguel, El Salvador's eastern beaches reward the relatively few visitors who make the trek with miles of secluded, gray sand. In the northeast, the beautiful mountain town of Perquín is recovering from its war-torn past and offers visitors a glimpse into its turbulent history with the Museo de la Revolución Salvadoreña. The east remains slightly less safe than other parts of El Salvador; travelers should exercise more caution and find accommodations before nightfall.

 Cojutepeque, Ilobasco, San Vicente, Volcán Chichontepec, Laguna de Apastepeque, Santiago de María, and Alegría have not been updated since July, 2001.

COJUTEPEQUE

Situated 32km east of San Salvador along the Interamerican Hwy., Cojutepeque is loud, dirty, and busy, with a market that threatens to engulf the entire town, trucks constantly clamoring through, and religious pilgrims trying to make their way up the city's famed attraction, **Cerro de Las Pavas** (Hill of the Turkeys). The town itself is best left behind in favor of the more relaxing Cerro, which stands several hundred feet above the town to the south and is home to the statue of the Virgen de Fátima. The image of the Virgin appeared to shepherd children in Fátima, Portugal on May 13, 1917, and this statue was brought to El Salvador in 1949. Since then, Cerro de las Pavas has been the site where a young woman has claimed to receive messages from the Virgin Mary on the anniversary of the original apparition. The messages, including some eerie futurist warnings, have been recorded and are available for purchase at the site. The 13th of every month draws especially large crowds who pay tribute to the Virgin and appeal to her healing powers.

Buses stopping in Cojutepeque heading east along the Interamerican include those going to **Ilobasco** (#111; 30min., every 10min. 3:30am-8:30pm, ¢4), **San Vicente** (#116; 45min., every 20min. 5:30am-8pm, ¢4), and **San Miguel** (#301; 2¼hr., every 10min. 4:30am-5:30pm, ¢11). Virtually any westbound bus passing by will take you to **San Salvador** (1hr., every few min., ¢3).

To get to the hill, head south (uphill) on Av. Contreras off the southwest corner of the *parque*, through the market stalls and past the **Telecom** office. Keep going to the edge of town, where the road forks under a welcome sign; head to the right for the 20min. walk to the top. Taxis cluster around the *parque* and will take you up the *cerro* for ¢20; for ¢50 they will wait and bring you down again.

To find a prostitute-free hotel room, weave your way through the market stalls to **Motel Coscatlan ❷**, on 1 Av., 6/8 Calles, a block west and 1½ blocks south of Telecom. (Rooms ¢70.) Making up for what the town lacks, delightful **Restaurant Buena Vista ❶**, on the road up to the *cerro*, gives a sampling of traditional *cojutepecano* food. (*Butifarra* plate ¢22. ☎372 0285. Open daily except Tu, 11:30am-8pm.)

ILOBASCO

Ilobasco, with clean spacious streets and emerald-green hills, is a refreshing change after the sweltering heat and crowds of San Salvador, 54km away. The *parque central* is gorgeous, and there are numerous shops selling hand-painted ceramics, the local art specialty. Ilobasco makes a very nice daytrip from San Salvador or San Vicente and can be a pleasant place to spend the night.

▣ TRANSPORTATION. Though the official departure point for **buses** is two blocks north of the *parque*, on 7 Calle, 2/4 Av., it's easiest to wait at the bus stops (marked by signs) along Av. Bonilla. Bus #111 departs for **San Salvador** (1½hr., every 10min. 3:45am-6pm, ¢7) via **Cojutepeque** (30min., ¢3), and bus #530 heads to **San Vicente** (50min.; 5:45, 7, 9am, noon, 2, 4pm; ¢4). The #111 or the pickup service will give you a lift to the **Interamerican Hwy.** (20min., ¢2-2.50) where you can catch eastbound buses to **San Miguel.**

EL SALVADOR

🔧🛈 ORIENTATION AND PRACTICAL INFORMATION. Buses enter town from the south on **Av. Bonilla,** passing by ceramics workshops and the triangular park around **El Monumento del Alfarero,** before arriving at the main intersection, where **Calle Perdomo** heads east and **Calle Hoyos** goes west. Streets fan out in the standard grid from here. The **parque central** is a block north and a block east of this intersection, bounded by 1/3 Calles and 2/4 Av. The **cathedral** sits on the east side of the *parque.* Services include: Visa cash advances at **Banco Salvaroreño,** Calle Perdomo, Av. Bonilla/1 (open M-F 8am-1pm and 1:45-4pm, Sa 8am-noon); **DeTodo Supermarket,** 1 Calle and 1 Av.; the **police,** 4 Calle, 3/5 Av. (☎332 2418; open 24hr.); **Telecom,** Av. Bonilla at 1 Calle, 1 block west of the *parque* (☎332 1011; open daily 7am-7pm); **post office,** 1 Calle Ote, 6/8 Av., (open M-F 7am-noon, 2-5pm, Sa 7am-noon.).

🛏🍴 ACCOMMODATIONS AND FOOD. Ilobasco's best option for accommodations is the **Hotel y Restaurante Ilobasco ❶,** on 4 Calle Ote, three blocks west of Av. Bonilla. Common baths are clean, but only private baths have hot water. (Singles with fan ¢50, singles with bath and TV ¢100; doubles ¢130.) **⬛Ricky's Restaurant ❷,** Av. Bonilla, 2/4 Calles, run by a chef who learned his trade in New York and Boston, is the best in town. The food is a pleasant change from typical Salvadoran fare, with a constantly changing menu. (Open Tu-Su noon-3pm and 6-8:30pm.)

📷🛍 SIGHTS AND CRAFTS. Ilobasco's most famous attractions are the *talleres* (workshops) and shops where local ceramics are made and sold (most open daily 8am-5:30pm). Shops line Av. Bonilla from Calle Perdomo south, with many clustering in the area around the **Monumento del Alfarero.** The painting of two large hands grasping the globe bears a quotation which identifies God as the first potter (*alfarero*) and man the first earthenware jar. In the shops, look for *sorpresas,* tiny scenes of daily village life hidden within a ceramic shell made to look like an egg, fruit, or vegetable. One of the best places to see the creation process is **Kiko** at Av. Bonilla 35, 100m south of the monument. Señor Herrera has been training local artisans at this store/workshop for over 40 years, and is often around to show you the different stages of production. (Open daily 7:30am-noon, 1:30-5pm.) **Moje, Casa Artesanal,** 4 Calle, Av. Bonilla/1 Av., is another interesting stop. The shop displays the handicrafts and t-shirts made by troubled youth who benefit from the education and supportive environment provided by the organization.

Take a break in the grassy *parque central,* blanketed with flowers and shaded by trees. The **Catedral de San Miguel,** on the east side of the *parque,* dates from the 1730s and not hiding its age; renovations are progressing slowly. (Open Tu-Su 6am-6pm.) **La Iglesia de los Desamparados,** three blocks east of the cathedral at the eastern edge of a less-picturesque *parque,* has a tragic past. During the civil war, the church served as the headquarters of the local guerrilla front, the Bloque Popular Revolucionario. In 1984, government forces captured the church and executed revolutionaries and civilians here. (Open daily 6am-5pm.)

SAN VICENTE

The small city of San Vicente sits in the Jiboa Valley, in the middle of one of the most agriculturally productive areas of the country, which gives the entire region a verdant glow. Volcán Chichontepec's double cone rises sharply from the southern edge of the city and is one of the safer climbs in the country. The approach to the city from the Interamerican Hwy. through shimmering green fields is spectacular. The city itself is somewhat less so. Rocked by recent earthquakes, it suffered extensive damage. However, it remains a relatively safe city in a beautiful setting.

🚍 TRANSPORTATION. The official **bus terminal** is a little out of the way, in an abandoned railway station on the far western edge of town, on 6 Calle at 15 Av.

Luckily, outgoing buses heading north to the highway pass the *parque* on its east side. Buses go to: **San Salvador** (#116; 1½hr., every 10min. 3am-7pm, ¢6); **Zacate-coluca** (#177; 50min., every 15min. 4:30am-6:15pm, ¢4); and **Ilobasco** (#530; 50min.; 6, 7, 9, 11:30am, 2, 4:30pm; ¢4). Any bus and a regular pickup service will whisk you up the *desvio* where the buses to **San Miguel** (#301) and other points east and west pass regularly. Buses to **Tepetitán** (#191; 30min., every 30min. 5:45am-6:30pm, ¢2) leave from Calle Osorio at 9 Av., 5 blocks west of the *parque*. For the **Laguna de Apastepeque**, the #156A heads to **Santa Clara**, also from the park's east side (30min., every 30min. 6am-5pm, ¢2).

🔢 ORIENTATION AND PRACTICAL INFORMATION. Most buses arrive from the north, along **Av. Cornejo**, passing by the western side of the *parque central*, before arriving at the town's main intersection a block south of the southwest corner of the *parque*, where Cornejo changes to **Av. Miranda**. From this intersection, **Calle 1 de Julio** goes off to the east while **Calle Osorio** goes west. Streets fan out in the standard Salvadoran grid from the intersection. West is generally uphill, and south is toward the volcano. The cathedral sits on the east side of the *parque*.

    Banco Agrícola, on the northeast corner of the *parque*, changes dollars and traveler's checks. (Open M-F 8am-5pm, Sa 8am-noon.) **Banco Salvadoreño**, 1 Calle, 1/3 Av, has an **ATM**. The **mercado** occupies the block between 1/3 Av. and Calles 2/Osorio and spreads west. The **police** are at 1 Av. and 3 Calle, a block west of the *parque's* northwest corner. (☎393 4182. 24hr.) **Farmacia San Vicente,** on Calle Osorio, 1/3 Av., is open daily 8:30am-7pm. **Telecom** is on 4 Calle, Av. Miranda/ 1 Av. (Open daily 8am-6pm.) **Internet** is at **Ciber Cafe,** 3 Av., 4/6 Calle. (Open M-F 8am-6pm, Sa-Su 9am-4pm, ¢10 per hr.). The **post office** is 1½ blocks south of the *parque* on Av. Miranda, Calles Osorio/2. (Open M-F 8am-5pm, Sa 8am-noon.)

🏨🍴 ACCOMMODATIONS AND FOOD. Casa de Huéspedes El Turista ❶, 1 Av., 4 Calle (☎333 0323), is very pleasant and quite secure—the gate is locked 24hr. Downstairs, simple rooms share a cramped bath around a garden (¢50 per night plus ¢10 day), while upstairs are rooms with private baths and cable TV (¢75 night plus ¢10 day). Don't miss the views of the volcano from the roof deck. **Hotel Central Park ❶** is on the west side of the *parque* on Av. Cornejo. Clean rooms come with private baths and fans. (☎333 0383. Singles ¢45, with A/C ¢80; doubles ¢100/¢125.)

    San Vicente's homey *comedores* are a bonus. Despite the damaged exterior, **Comedor Rivoly ❶**, 1 Av., 2/4 Calle, pleases loyal customers with *comida a la vista* (buffet) in their great garden setting. (Open daily 7-9am, 11am-2pm, and 4-8pm; *platos* ¢15-20.) **Restaurante Acapulco ❶**, 4 Calle, Av. Miranda/1, is a popular lunch spot, with servings for ¢15-25. (Open 11am-2pm and 6-8pm.) The plain **Restaurante Central Park ❶** (see Hotel Central Park, above) serves typical breakfasts (¢6-18) and a wide selection of entrees (¢20-30). Although not much goes on after dark in San Vicente, **El Pueblito Viejo,** opposite the basketball court across from the El Pilar church, has cold beer, music, and a lively crowd on weekend evenings.

◪ SIGHTS. The town's hub is the sky-scraping **clocktower,** a scaled-down version of the Eiffel Tower with a clock on top which sits in the middle of the *parque central*. Unfortunately, the tower did not survive the earthquakes unscathed; though still standing, access to the spiral staircase and the panoramic views at top is limited. The **Iglesia El Pilar,** two blocks south of the *parque* on Av. Miranda, was built in 1762 and is one of the oldest churches in the country and survivor of numerous earthquakes. The main church is no longer in use, but a side chapel functions as a substitute. The lichen-encrusted facade bears a plaque dedicated to José Simeón Cañas, who abolished slavery in El Salvador.

EL SALVADOR

NEAR SAN VICENTE

⚠ VOLCÁN CHICHONTEPEC

Looming over the town, Volcán Chichontepec calls travelers to the panoramic views of its summit. The "easiest" approach is to begin from **Tepetitán,** *a small town at the base of the volcano reachable by* **bus #191** *from Calle Osorio at 9 Av. in San Vicente (30min., every 30min., 5:45am, 6:30pm, ¢2).*

Once in Tepetitán, follow the stone road that begins two blocks north of the *parque* for about 2hr. of moderate-to-steep climbing until you reach the **Finca Camón,** owned by former President Cristiani, who signed the 1992 Peace Accords. Refill water bottles from the president's water supply (with the guard's permission) before continuing along the same road for 2hr. Where the stone road begins to descend, a dirt road branches uphill. The earthquake ravaged the road along this final stretch which is not only precipitous, but rocky and uneven. One hour more will bring you at last to the antennae and helicopter landing dock where the army staff will happily let you recover as you soak in the panorama that encompasses the Pacific Coast, San Salvador, and the Honduran border. The whole trip takes 7-8hr. Start early—afternoons often bring rain. Large groups should have no safety problems; groups of less than three should contact the police in San Vicente in advance to arrange for a guide. The police guide shorter hikes to the *Inferno,* at the base of the volcano where sulfur steams and mud oozes from underground.

🗝 LAGUNA DE APASTEPEQUE

To get to the laguna, take the bus heading for **Santa Clara** *from the east side of San Vicente's parque central (#156A; 30min., every 20min. 6am-5pm, ¢2). This bus will pass through the small town of* **Apastepeque** *on the way. From there the bus heads east on the Interamerican Hwy. for 5min. before turning left (north) and arriving at the laguna a few minutes later. You'll see the laguna and a yellow sign for the turicentro on the left. Descend to the level of the lake and take the road along the lake shore for a more scenic walk. The last bus back passes at 5pm. (Turicentro open daily 8am-5pm. ¢7.)*

About 10km northeast of San Vicente, on the other side of the Interamerican Hwy., is Laguna de Apastepeque, a small, quiet lake with corn and sugarcane fields descending to its shore. Take a swim, watch the locals fish, or stroll around the lake, enjoying the view of Volcán Chichontepec. There's a **turicentro** on the other side of the lake from the bus stop. To get there, walk along the lake shore for about 10min. Though small, it is well-kept, and the pool is among the cleanest in El Salvador. The cleanest stretch of lakefront also belongs to the *turicentro,* and the on-site restaurant overlooking the water serves up ¢10 burgers, ¢20 chicken, and ¢6 beers. Two restaurants are perched along the lake across from the *turicentro* if you're looking for a nicer option. **Restaurant Casa Blanca ❶** has nice gardens and plenty of hammocks for *siestas.* (Sandwich ¢14; chicken or beef ¢35-55.)

SANTIAGO DE MARÍA

Resting in the saddle between two mountains and enveloped in thick, moist clouds, Santiago de María is a coffee-country town with easy access to spectacular hikes. Sadly, the town was hit hard by the 2001 earthquakes, and piles of stone, dangling pillars, and empty lots are all that's left of many buildings. East of town, Cerro de Tigre's summit affords Olympian views, while the Laguna de Alegría to the west in the Volcán de Tecapa crater and makes a great daytrip from Santiago. During the *fiestas patronales,* July 20-25, the small town explodes with energy.

🚍 TRANSPORTATION. From the bus terminal, buses leave for **San Salvador** (#302; 2hr.; 4, 4:30, 5am, 1:10, 2:45pm; ¢8) and **San Miguel** (#323; 3hr., every hr. 5am-

3:30pm, ¢7). It is easier to head to **Villa El Triunfo,** at the intersection of the *Inter-americana* and the road to Santiago, and catch one of the frequent **#301** buses running between San Salvador and San Miguel. To get to Villa El Triunfo, wait at the intersection of Av. M Gonzalez (extension of Av. 15 de Septiembre) and 2 Calle for bus #349 to **Usulutan** or #359 (20min., every 15min. 4:30am-5:30pm, ¢2). Bus **#348** goes to the nearby towns of **Alegría** (15min., ¢2) and **Berlín** (30min., ¢4) and leaves every 30min. from the bus terminal (6am-4pm daily).

🔛🔃 ORIENTATION AND PRACTICAL INFORMATION. Santiago lies on a hill 12km south of the Interamerican Hwy. Buses arrive from the north and pass by the main intersection of the town, where the central *avenida*, **Av. 15 de Septiembre,** is intersected by the primary *calle*, called **Calle Bolívar** to the east and **Calle Masferrer** to the west. The streets branch out in the standard Salvadoran grid, with the *parque central* a block east of the intersection, between 2/4 Av. and Calles Bolívar/2. The **church,** a concrete mass devoid of a cross, is on the east side of the *parque*, and **Cerro El Tigre** looms behind it farther to the east. The town's makeshift **bus terminal** is at the triangular *parque*, just south of 4 Calle between 3 Av. and Av. 15 de Septiembre, a block south and a block west of the main square.

   Banco Salvadoreño, on the south end of the square, cashes traveler's checks, does Visa cash advances, and has an **ATM.** (Open M-F 8:30am-5pm, Sa 8:30am-noon.) The **police** (☎ 663 0063), at their temporary office on 6 Av., 2/4 Calle, should be contacted in advance for hikes to *El Cerro*. **Telecom's** makeshift location is across from the bank. (Open daily 7am-8pm.) **Internet access** is available at **Infocentros,** Av. 15 de Septiembre, 2/4 Calle. (Open M-Sa 8am-6pm, Su 9am-5pm.) The **post office** is at 4 Calle Pte., 5 Av. Sur. (Open M-F 8am-4L30pm, Sa 8am-noon.)

🔃🔲 ACCOMMODATIONS AND FOOD. The only place to stay in town is **Motel San Antonio ❷,** on 2 Calle Oriente at 8 Av., two blocks east of the *parque's* south edge. San Antonio offers clean, simple rooms. (☎ 663 0271. Singles ¢60; doubles ¢75.) *Comedores* and *pupuserías* abound in the area near the *parque*. A surprisingly cool place with excellent food, **▨Buffalo's ❸,** Av. 15 de Septiembre one block from the *parque*, grills up a variety of tasty meats (¢25-50) in a relaxed outdoor setting around a bar, pool, and gardens. Ask if the rooms out back are open yet.

🔃 SIGHTS. Just east of town, the climb up **Cerro de Tigre** first affords views of the town, nearby volcanoes, and the Río Lempa. Head east on 4 Calle at the southeastern corner of town and follow a stone road up and down a small hill. You will pass through a gate of Finca El Tigre on the road to the top (1½-2hr.). Dense coffee plants cover the last stretch of path to the antenna marking the summit. Contact the police for safety information; often, they will send an officer with you.

🔃 NEAR SANTIAGO DE MARIA: ALEGRÍA AND THE LAGUNA

Make your way to the bus terminal at 3 Av. and 4 Calle, from where bus #348 heads to **Alegría** *(15min., every 30min. 6am-4pm, ¢2). Just shy of Alegría are a few signs marking the cobblestone turnoff to the left that leads up to the Laguna de Alegría, a 35-45min. hike away through coffee fincas and impressive views. Open daily 8am-5pm. ¢2.*

An easy and rewarding daytrip from Santiago leads to the Volcán de Tecapa, the deep green Laguna de Alegría that sits inside it, and the tiny nearby village of Alegría. The green lagoon sits in a beautiful crater, beneath the ridge of the Volcán de Tecapa, surrounded by a floor of mud and crystallized sulfur, edged by firm, rocky ground. The Alegría primary school sits on the eastern shore, detracting slightly from the tranquility of the area. If you want the place all to yourself, stick around and **camp** for ¢5 per person. Tell the caretaker when you arrive that you want to camp and he'll show you the latrine, fire pit, and best areas to pitch your tent. Swimming in the lagoon is not recommended, as it's quite shallow, and glue-like sulfurwood, which has drowned many locals, lurks on the bottom. Legend attributes their deaths to a mermaid who lies in wait for handsome young men.

For a bird's-eye view of the *laguna* and a view of surrounding volcanoes and valleys, head up the ridge of the volcano. Just return to the *laguna* entrance and follow the road up to the ridge; a 1½hr. hike will bring you to the top.

The nearby village of **Alegría**, a friendly mountain town with fresh air, expansive views, and a reputation for the mountain flowers sold at local nurseries, is a short walk away. Coming from the *laguna*, keep left on the way down the trail; once you hit the road, take a left onto it, and the town is just 5min. away. Alternatively, if you don't go to the *laguna*, the bus from Santiago will drop you off right at the *parque*. Within an overflowing wildflower garden, **Merendero Mi Pueblito ❶** is a friendly place to have a good meal while enjoying the view. (Breakfast ¢8-12, soda ¢3, *pollo* or *carne* plates ¢18. Open daily 6am-5pm.) You can climb the volcano from Alegriá, leaving from the southwest edge of town. It can be difficult to follow, however, so you may want to head to the **Centro de Desarrollo Cultural** (☎ 628 1038), next to the church, where **Narciso Marroquín** runs a guided service to the volcano, the *laguna*, and on hikes to flower nurseries in the area (¢75 per day).

SAN MIGUEL

San Miguel (pop. 200,000), is the largest city in eastern El Salvador, and the third-largest city in the country, behind San Salvador and Santa Ana. The city feels rather self-consciously second-best to its western counterpart, Santa Ana, and has dubbed itself the "Pearl of the East" in an effort to compete with the "Queen of the West." Though the pearl has lost some of its luster and the city can be dangerous after nightfall, San Miguel makes a good base for day or overnight trips around the eastern region of the country. Nearby sights include Volcán Chaparrastique, the bird-filled Laguna El Jocotal, and the largely unexcavated Maya site of Quelepa.

▐ TRANSPORTATION

Buses: Arrive at and depart from the best **bus terminal** in El Salvador on 6 Calle, 8/10 Av. Destinations include: **Border with Honduras at El Amatillo** (#330 continuing from Santa Rosa de Lima, 1½hr., 7:10am-5:30pm, ¢9); **Playa El Cuco** (#320; 1½hr., every 30min. 5:25am-7pm, ¢7); **Playa El Tamarindo** (#385; 2½hr., every 20min. 5am-5pm, ¢10); **San Francisco Gotera** (#328; 1½hr., every 30min. 4:30am-6:10pm, ¢5); **San Salvador** (#301; *normal* 3hr., every 15min. 3am-4:15pm, ¢15; *directo* 2½hr.; 7, 8am, 3pm; ¢21; *super* 2½hr; 5, 6, 7, 8am; ¢35 with TV, A/C, and bathroom); **Santa Rosa de Lima** (#330; 1hr., every 10min. 4:30am-6pm, ¢6); **La Unión** (#324; 1½hr., every 10min. 4:30am-6pm, ¢6); **Usulutan** (#373; 1½hr., every 10min. 4am-5:30pm, ¢7).

Local Buses: City buses run 6am-7pm; fare ¢1. Most buses stop at **Parque Guzmán.** **#90f,** the most useful north-south route, runs from the University, a few kilometers south of town, to the Metrocentro, up to Parque Guzmán, then over to Av. Roosevelt and up to **El Triángulo.** In the center, it runs south on 4 Av. and north on 2 Av. **#88,** the most useful east-west route, passes close to the bus terminal, heading west on 4 Calle past Parque Guzmán out to Av. Roosevelt, south on the Av. a bit, and then further west to the **hospital.** The eastbound #88 runs along 2 Calle before going to the **bus termi-nal** on 6 Calle. Both **#90b** and **#13** will get you from the center down to the **Metrocen-tro** and back. **#94** leaves from the north side of Parque Guzmán and passes the **Turicentro at Altos de la Cueva. #90-g** goes to **Quelepa. #91** travels 3 Av. from Av. Roosevelt, past the center and to the buses.

San Miguel

♠ ACCOMMODATIONS
Hotel Caleta, **6**
Hotel del Centro, **1**
Hotel Migueleños, **3**
Hotel San Rafael, **2**

BARRIO SAN FRANCISCO

San Francisco

Farmacia Brasil
Capilla de la Medalla Milagrosa
Farmacia Brasil
Mercado Central

ATM
Cathedral
Parque David J. Guzmán
Alcaldía
Telecom
Antiguo Teatro Nacional
Supermarket
Parque Gerardo Barrios
C. Sirama

BARRIO LA CRUZ
Estadio Municipal

C. Chaparrastique

Abbreviations:
N	Norte
O	Oriente
P	Poniente
S	Sur

BARRIO EL CENTRO

Av. José Simón Cañas

Supermarket
Movie Theater

BARRIO LA MERCED

El Calvario

Av. Roosevelt N

TO ✚ HOSPITAL SAN JUAN DE DIOS

♣ FOOD
Comedor El Paraíso, **4**
Restaurante Don Beto, **7**
Restaurante Mama Gallian, **5**
Restaurant La Pema, **8**

TO ⊙ (1km), METROCENTRO MALL (2km)

(not in use)

0 — 200 meters
0 — 200 yards

Taxis: Always at Metrocentro on Av. Roosevelt, the west side of Parque Guzmán, and near the bus terminal at 6 Calle and 8 Av. Cabs run well into the evening. Fares within the city range ¢10-30.

✱ 🛈 ORIENTATION AND PRACTICAL INFORMATION

The downtown area of San Miguel is bounded on the south and west by the **Interamerican Hwy.**, called **Av. Roosevelt** within the city, which enters from the south. It meets the **Ruta Militar** at the northwest corner of the city at a spot known as "**El Triángulo**" (Av. Roosevelt at 1 Calle). The city centers around **Parque Gerardo Barrios** and **Parque David J. Guzmán.** Parque Barrios gets swallowed up daily in a sea of market stalls, but the main intersection of the city is on its southeast corner. The main north-south street changes names here: **Av. Barrios** goes north while **Av. Cañas** runs south. Similarly, from this intersection the east-west street also undergoes a name change, with **Calle Sirama** heading east while **Calle Chaparrastique** goes west. It is always safer to take a cab after dark.

Banks: Banco de Comercio, 2 Av., 4 Calle, on the northwest corner of Parque Guzmán. Changes dollars and traveler's checks, gives cash advances on Visa, and has an **ATM.** Open M-F 9am-5pm, Sa 9am-noon. A variety of **ATMs** can also be found at **Metrocentro,** the mall about 2km south of *Parque Guzman.*

Markets: The *mercado central* starts at 1 Av., Calle Chaparrastique and fans west.

Laundry: Lavandería Premium, Av. Cañas, 5/7 Av.. Machine wash and dry ¢25. Open M-F 7:30am-noon and 2-5pm, Sa 7:30am-1pm.

Car Rental: Uno Rent-a-Car (☎211 2111), Av. Roosevelt, near 7 Calle Pte.. Rents cars starting at US$45 per day. Minimum age 25. Credit card and deposit required.

Police: Policía Nacional Civil (☎661 2033), 10 Av. Sur at 11 Calle, in the Centro de Gobierno complex. Second branch at 2 Calle, 3/5 Av. near the center.

Red Cross: (☎661 1771), 10 Calle Pte., #404.

Pharmacy: Farmacia Brasil (☎661 4316), has two locations on 4 Calle Poniente. Open daily 8am-6pm, emergency 24hr.

Hospital: Hospital San Juan de Dios (☎661 1425 or 661 1211), on the west of town at 11 Calle Pte. Take bus #88 from the center. 24hr. emergency service. A number of clinics and hospitals line 4 Calle Pte. between Av. Gerardo Burrios and 7Av.

Telephones: Telecom, 4 Av., 2 Calle (☎661 0814), by the southeast corner of Parque Guzmán. Open daily 7:30am-5pm.

Internet: Infocentros, 4 Calle between Av. 1/Barrios. ¢20 per hr., students ¢11 per hr. Also at **Telecom,** with lethargic Internet but frigid A/C. ¢30 per 30min.

Post Office: 4 Av., 3 Calle. Open M-F 7:30am-5pm, Sa 8am-noon.

▌ ACCOMMODATIONS

While several upscale hotels line Av. Roosevelt to the west and south of the city, most of the more affordable and convenient options lie within a few blocks of the bus terminal. You'll generally want to be in your hotel after dark, so it makes sense to choose a place with good security (usually a night watchman and a locking gate) where you won't mind spending a few hours. Cheap hotels line 10 Av. and 4 Calles as they wrap around the bus station, but gentlemen and ladies be forewarned: this neighborhood is no stranger to prostitution.

■ **Hotel Caleta,** 3 Av. Sur, 11 Calle Pte. (☎661 3233), is well worth the 15min. walk from the bus terminal, in a quiet neighborhood. Friendly management runs surf trips to secluded beaches. Singles ¢40, with bath ¢50; doubles ¢65/¢82, with A/C ¢140. ❶

■ **Hotel San Rafael** 10 Av., 6 Calle (☎661 4113), a block east of the bus terminal. One of the friendliest hotels in town with cable TV, lounge, restaurant, and decks. Front gate locks at 9:30pm. Singles US$8; doubles US$10.29, with A/C US$14.25. ❷

Hotel del Centro, 8 Calle Ote, 8 Av. Nte. (☎661 6913), 1 block north and ½ block west of the bus station. Very secure. Red-carpeted floors, TVs, phones, and sparkling private baths. Singles ¢100, with A/C ¢175; doubles ¢125/¢225. ❸

Hotel Migueleños (☎660 2737), just south of the bus terminal, has a secure pink courtyard. The beds are slightly hard, but cable TV and clean bathrooms make up for it. Gate closes 10pm. 1-2 person rooms ¢50. ❶

▐ FOOD

The paucity of decent restaurants in the center of town is offset by several great restaurants on Av. Roosevelt on the western edge of the city. **La Pema,** just south of the city, is one of the best-known eateries in the country. The *comedores* in the *centro* cluster around the Parque Guzmán and bus terminal, and fast food joints are highly visible downtown and in the Metrocentro mall, south of town.

■ **Restaurante Mama Gallian,** Av. Roosevelt at 2 Calle, across the street from the cemetery. Take bus #88 from the *centro*. A friendly place that fills with loyal customers on the weekends. The *licuados* are the best in the city (¢15), and the menu ranges from pricier entrees (¢70-120) to Mexican enchiladas (¢30). Open until 10pm. ❷

▨ **Restaurante Don Beto,** Av. Roosevelt at 11 Calle. Accessible by bus #88 from the *centro*. This Mexican-themed restaurant serves every imaginable dish in a tasteful decor. Nachos ¢20. Fajitas or *pollo en mole* ¢60. ❶

Restaurant La Pema, 1km south of the city on the road to Usulután before the University; take bus #90f from the *centro*. La Pema regularly draws visitors from San Salvador for its *mariscada* (¢85) and grilled lobster (¢125). Open daily 10am-4pm. V. ❹

Comedor El Paraíso, on the west side of Parque Guzmán, is one of the better *comedores* in the center. *Comida a la vista* (buffet) ¢15-25. Locals fill the place at lunch time. ❶

▨▨ NIGHTLIFE AND ENTERTAINMENT

While it is generally safer to amuse yourself in your hotel's TV lounge, there are several nightlife options. On Av. Roosevelt near El Triángulo are **Marquis** and **L.A. Discoteca**, with young crowds and lots of dancing. **Caribbean Discotek** jams near **Metrocentro** mall, which has two movie theaters that dish up Hollywood fare (¢30).

◉ ▨ SIGHTS AND OUTDOOR ACTIVITIES

Dominating San Miguel's center are the **Alcaldía**, on the south side of Parque Guzmán, and the **Catedral de Nuestra Señora de la Paz**, on the *parque's* east side, whose domes are visible from nearly everywhere in the downtown area. The mock-colonial-style Alcaldía dates from 1935, and gives excellent rooftop view of the cathedral, the volcano, and the entire downtown area. If in a good mood (definitely not during lunch), the guards admit anyone who wants to look around. The **Catedral de Nuestra Señora de la Paz** has an 18th-century beige and white facade topped by a statue of Jesus spreading his arms out to the plaza below. The statue of the Virgin Mary is claimed to have saved San Miguel from destruction by volcanic lava at the beginning of the century. A block east of the cathedral, on 2 Calle at 6 Av., the **Teatro Nacional Francisco Gavidia,** built in 1903, is animated by frequent performances. Stop by the office for show times. (☎661 9026. Office open M-F 8am-noon and 2-5pm, Sa 8am-noon.) The **Capilla de la Medalla Milagrosa,** 7 Av., 4 Calle, is known throughout the country because the church formerly shared the locale with a hospital where miraculous healings have been attributed to a medal of the Virgin Mary. Beautiful stained glass remains today in the ancient church.

To escape the heat of the city, head out on bus #94 (from the north side of Parque Guzmán) to the *turicentro* at **Altos de la Cueva**, where you can cool off in four clean pools and join local kids on the waterslide. (Open daily 7am-5pm. ¢7.) The most obvious challenge around town is the **Volcán Chaparrastique**, the 2100m volcano that looms over San Miguel from the southwest. You must first type a polite letter of request with your name and date of trip addressed to "Señor Jefe de la Delegación PNC San Miguel" and bring it to the Centro de Gobierno at least two days prior to departure. With this letter you can get a free guide. To get there, take bus #90D from 7 Av. and Calle Chaparrastique to **Las Placitas,** from where a road leads to the southern edge of town. It is about a 4hr. hike through coffee farms to the summit, from where you can continue into the crater.

◉ NEAR SAN MIGUEL: QUELEPA

*From San Miguel, **bus #90-g** heads to Quelepa from the west side of Parque Guzmán (20min., every 30min. 5am-6pm, ¢2) and will drop you off right in front of the **Casa de la Cultura** on the south side of Quelepa's parque central. From there, the site lies a 30min. walk (about 2km) northeast of town. If you can't get someone at the Casa de la Cultura to accompany you, head to the northeast corner of the parque (a block north of the Casa de la Cultura), turn right on 4 Calle, and follow it until you come to the Río San Esteban. Hop* *across the river on the rocks and stop to ask for directions at one of the houses on the right after you cross. The ruins are about a 15min. walk east through the fields, at the base of the Cerro Tamboral, the largest of the mountains looming to the north.*

A daytrip to the Lenca ruins at Quelepa is like seeing a film in a language you don't understand: you enjoy yourself, but most of the details go right over your head. Without a Ph.D. in Maya archaeology, only imagination will make the ruins come alive, as very little of the site has been excavated. But it is a relaxing walk through cow pastures and fields that now cover much of what was originally a 3 sq. km ceremonial center, bounded on the south by the Río San Esteban and on the north by Cerro Tamboral. Dating back to about 400 BC, Quelepa was a flourishing Lenca settlement, peaking from the 7th to the 10th centuries. The pottery, sculpture, and other artifacts found on site indicate strong trade links to Maya settlements in Mexico and Honduras. Among the nearly 40 structures identified, the main ones are a paved road, several pyramids, and a buried ballcourt.

The small village of Quelepa, about 2km southwest of the ruins, is pleasant and quiet, and the **Casa de la Cultura** in the town has a helpful, knowledgeable staff and a collection of artifacts, although most of the best artifacts from the site reside in the national collection in San Salvador. Also at the Casa de la Cultura are copies (in Spanish) of the book on Quelepa written in 1969 by Willis Andrews, a Tulane University archaeologist who remains the only expert to have done a major excavation here. Several small parts of his excavation were left uncovered when he finished (the usual procedure is to refill the earth to protect the ruins), providing a glimpse of the solid construction of one of the pyramids. Guides from the Casa de la Cultura happily show visitors these uncovered patches. (Casa de la Cultura open M-F 8am-noon and 2-5pm, Sa 8am-1pm.)

🗻 NEAR SAN MIGUEL: LAGUNA EL JOCOTAL

From San Miguel, catch bus #373 to Usulután and tell the bus driver to let you off at the lake (40min., every 10min. 4am-5:30pm, ¢3). The bus drops off at a small town on the highway. The lake is a safe 10min. walk down a road through town to the left of the hwy.

The road that runs to the laguna, which stretches out to Cerro Juguarán on the far side and affords spectacular views of Volcán Chuparrastique. Local fishermen offer *lanchas* to the tiny island of *El Espejo de Agua* (25min., ¢30 round trip). In addition to swimming and taking in the spectacular views, there are over 100 varieties of birds, including several migratory species.

SANTA ROSA DE LIMA

A half-hour bus ride from the Honduran border at El Amatillo 18km east, Santa Rosa de Lima (20,000) is a convenient spot from which to cross the border. **Bus #330** runs between **San Miguel** and **Santa Rosa de Lima** (1hr., every 8min. 5:10am-6:30pm, ¢6) before continuing to the **border** at **El Amatillo** (30min., 5:10am-6:30pm, ¢6). Arriving from San Miguel, the bus drops off on the west side of town at the intersection of the highway and **Calle Girón**, the town's main street, four blocks north of the *parque central*. Buses for the border leave from here, while buses arriving from El Amatillo meet at the same place. From Calle Girón, two blocks west of the *parque*, buses leave for **San Miguel** and **La Unión** (#342; 1½hr., every 15min. 4am-5:30pm, ¢5). The town is centered around the intersection at **Avenida Gral Arios** running north and south, and **Calle Gral Giron** running east and west of the southeast corner of the *parque central*. The *parque* also functions as the frenetic municipal market. The highway is two blocks east of the parque and most banks, hotels, and other services cluster in this area. A block south of the southwest corner of the *parque* is the **Banco de Comercio,** where you can change traveler's checks and get advances on Visa cards. (Open M-F 8am-4:30pm, Sa 8am-noon.) **Money changers** hang around the park area, but you're better off changing colones or lempiras at the border. The **Telecom** office is a block east of the *parque* on Calle Girón (open daily 7am-8pm). The **police** are a block north of there. (☎641 2072. Open 24hr.) To stock up on supplies, head to the **Despensa Familiar supermarket**, across the street from the bus stop. The national **Hospital** (☎741 3057) is about 500m up the highway toward San Miguel. **Farmacia Nueva** sits on the northeast corner of the *parque* (☎741 2335; open daily 7:30am-5pm). **Internet** is at **Infocentros**, one block west of the *parque*. (Open M-F 8am-8pm, Sa 8am-6pm, ¢20 per hr., students ¢11 per hr.) The **post office** is also one block west and south of the *parque*. (Open M-F 8am-noon and 2-5pm, Sa 8am-noon.)

Hospedaje El Salvador ❶, on Calle Girón near the buses, has spacious rooms. (☎641 2230. 1-2 person rooms ¢50.) Pricer **Hotelito El Cusco ❹**, on the highway five blocks past the *parque* has rooms with private bath, two big beds, fan, and cable TV (☎641 4433. ¢125, with A/C ¢175). *Comedores* cluster around the *parque*. Affordable meals are at **Restaurante Cancun ❶**, next to the police station. (Torta Mexicana ¢20. Open daily 10am-8pm.)

▓ EL AMATILLO: BORDER WITH HONDURAS

Along the Río Goascorán, the Honduran border at El Amatillo is crowded, dirty, and full of **money changers** who provide the only decent opportunity for exchanging currency. **Immigration** is open daily 6am-10pm. Buses leave Santa Rosa de Lima every eight minutes for the border. A whole slew of maps and **tourist info** is available at the El Salvador entrance point. The **Telefónica** office has a **Western Union** (open daily 8am-8pm). On the Salvadoran side, there is a **Telecom** office (open daily 7:30am-5pm), several **comedores**, and two hotels. The expensive **Motel Antony D'May ❺** (doubles with A/C, TV, and bath ¢200) and the basic **Motelito Dos Hermanos ❸** (doubles with fan ¢85) are both up the hill from the border to the left. There is a hotel on the Honduran side, the **Hotel Los Arcos**, a reasonable place to stay if for some reason you end up literally *at* the border for the night. (Singles L40; doubles L70.) This border crossing can be time-consuming given the crowds. From the Honduran side, **buses** depart to **Tegucigalpa** (4hr., every 30min. 4:30am-4:30pm, L26) and **Choluteca** (2¼hr., every 25min. 3:30am-5:45pm, L18).

PERQUÍN

A tiny mountain town, Perquín (pop. 500) is quite exceptional. Located in the northern region of Morazán (2½hr. from San Miguel) the peaceful village has a unique concern with its history for present and future generations. Perquín was FMLN headquarters during the war, and the mountains surrounding the town saw some of the fiercest fighting. The town began to heal with the powerful Museo de la Revolución Salvadoreña and the monument at El Mozote. Explore Río Sapo, Bailadore del Diablo, and Llano del Muerto. Perquín is one of six towns throughout the department that make up **La Ruta de la Paz**, which was created to celebrate local culture and the dawn of peace.

▟ TRANSPORTATION. **Buses** and **pickups** arrive from the south and can drop you off at either of the lodging options south of town or at the *parque central*. Throughout the morning, **Bus #332-A** departs **San Miguel** for **Torola**, passing through Perquín on the way (3hr., roughly every hr. 4:30am-12:40pm, ¢11). The easiest way to get there is to take a bus to **San Francisco Gotera** from San Miguel (bus #328; 1½hr., every 10min. 4:30am-6pm, ¢6) and from the *desvío* (detour) after the town, catch a pickup to Perquín. Run by a collective, the pickup service is reliable and safe (1hr., every 15min. 5am-6pm, ¢4).

■ ⁊ ORIENTATION AND PRACTICAL INFORMATION. Most town services cluster around the *parque central*. The church sits up the hill on the eastern side of the *parque* with the museum two blocks uphill to the left. There is a **tourist office** in the Casa de Cultura on the west side of the *parque* that has information on hikes and excursions in the area. (☎680 4086. Open Tu-Sa 7:30am-4pm.) The **police** (☎680 4040) are located near the northeast exit of town, a block north and a block east of the *parque*. (Open 24hr.) **Farmacia Fuente de Vida** is right off the park (☎680 4082; open daily 6am-7pm). The **Hospital Unidad de Salud** is below the cemetery down the hill along the highway (☎680 4082; open 24hr.). **Telecom** is on the north side of the *parque*. (Open M-F 8am-noon and 2-6pm, Sa 8:30am-noon and 2-5pm, Su 8am-4pm.) The **post office** has a desk in the *alcaldía* on the west side of the *parque*. (Open M-F 8am-noon and 1:30-4pm.)

⁊⊡ ACCOMMODATIONS AND FOOD. There are two lodging options in Perquín, both of which lie just south of town. The one closer to town, about half a kilometer downhill from the *parque* on a clearly marked dirt road, is the **Casa de Huéspedes El Gigante ❸**. (☎661 5077. 1-2 person rooms ¢100.) A few minutes walk downhill from El Gigante is the **Perquín Lenca Hotel de Montaña ❺**, with pricey, pristine cabins. (☎680 4046. Breakfast included. Singles ¢455; doubles ¢560; triples ¢630; prices higher in high season.) In addition to the few *comedores* around the *parque*, a more varied selection of meals can be found at **La Cocina de Ma Amita ❷**. The **comedor** at El Gigante serves up tasty *pupusas* (¢2 each), as well as good breakfasts (¢10) and *típico* dishes.

◨ SIGHTS. The ▨**Museo de la Revolución Salvadoreña** vividly tells El Salvador's tragic history. Events are told from the FMLN perspective on the causes for and events of the struggle Though information is only in Spanish, the language of the photos, weapons, and paraphernalia is universal. It will give every hill and village in the area new meaning as one learns of guerrillas who died fighting there. For a fuller understanding of events, ask for Carlos, a former FMLN radio operator who is willing to give his first-hand account of the war. (Spanish only. US$1-2 tip expected.) Another healing tribute to the past is the **Monumente El Mozote,** which commemorates the lives of the over 1000 people massacred at the site from December 11th-13th, 1981. To get there follow the clear signs from Perquín; a 20min. walk to the town of Arambala, followed by 1hr. along the main road.

◪ HIKES. Other attractions in the area include hikes to the **Río Sapo,** a beautiful view with prime swimming holes, and the nearby peaks of **Quebrada de Perquín** (starting from the main road just south of town) and **Cerro El Gigante** (trail begins outside the museum), each about a 30min. hike from town. Inquire at the information center in town for guides or directions on how to get to these sights.

CACAOPERA

Also on La Ruta de la Paz, Cacaopera allows travelers to immerse themselves in the pre-Maya traditions that are still maintained by locals. Local organizations support activities to educate the community about the linguistic, spiritual, and cultural traditions of their ancestors, the Kakawira people. The **Museum Winakirika** offers a detailed visual presentation of the way of life in this town before the Spanish, and the subsequent mixing of practices (religious in particular). The museum also runs a hostel where visitors can stay in an adobe room (¢50), eat traditional food (¢12-15), and learn about the indigenous people. (☎651 0251 for reservations.) A 1hr. walk from town leads to colorful hieroglyphics in **Cueva Unamá.** Find a guide and information at the tourist office in town. **Buses** leave San Francisco Gotera for Cacaopera every 30min. until 4:30pm (¢4).

EASTERN BEACHES

Along the southern edges of the departments of San Miguel and La Unión, the waves of the Pacific crash into open expanses of gray sand beaches. The long stretches of coast are perfect for walking, swimming, sunning, and in some places, surfing. Most beaches are accessible by daytrips from San Miguel or La Unión. Though they attract weekend crowds, the weekday tranquility is broken only by fishing boats rolling in and locals cooling off after a day's work.

◤ **PLAYA EL ESPINO.** Locals claim this long stretch of sand fringed with palms as their most beautiful beach. You won't find tourist facilities, but there's plenty of coast with a rolling surf. Any bus between San Miguel and Usulután drops off at the *desvío* (detour) to El Espino. Bus #321 runs to **Usulután** for the beach (2hr., 7 per day 6am-2:40pm, ¢3.50) and stops at the Hwy. juncture (1hr., ¢5). Approaching the coast, the road splits with **Arcos Del Espino** to the right and **Playa El Espino** to the left; both have similar beaches, but Arcos is more deserted. There are two *comedores* at Playa El Espino area (lunch ¢20-25).

◤ **PLAYA EL CUCO.** Located 1½hr. directly south of San Miguel, Playa El Cuco is the most developed of the eastern beaches. On weekends you'll have to walk for a bit to find a patch of gray sand to call your own. Luckily, the beach extends eastward for kilometers, so you should be able to find an empty stretch. On weekdays, the beach is deserted. **Buses** conveniently run from San Miguel (#320; 1½hr., every 15min. 5:15am-4:15pm, ¢7). The bus pulls into the center of town, from where you can walk straight ahead, taking any of the roads lined with little *tiendas* to the beach. Small restaurants, all "specializing" in shellfish, cluster near the town.

The dreary town has a **police** station, a **post office,** and a **Telecom** office, as well as a disproportionately large number of drunks. Better than the options east of town is **El Rancho Escondido ❸,** on the western side of town, along the ocean (follow the signs). The rooms are spacious and clean, and the hotel has a nice restaurant and bar, as well as a great section of the Pacific cut off from the rest by a cliff. (☎619 9017. Doubles ¢100, additional ¢100 to stay the day.) Two upscale options, **Hotel Leones Marinos ❹** and **Hotel Viña del Mar ❹,** are side by side and just up from Palmeras, closer to the town. (Double ¢150, A/C extra.) Access to hotel facilities for the day is a pleasant way to enjoy the beach (¢20).

◤ **PLAYA LAS TUNAS AND PLAYA TOROLA.** Just 4km south of the San Miguel/La Unión highway, and 20min. from El Tamarindo, the beach at **Las Tunas** attracts a weekend crowd to its gray-sand shoreline dotted with striking black rocks. A small collection of *comedores*, fishing boats, and beach shacks creates a flurry of activity on the shore by the center of the village; at high tide, the *rancho* closest to the ocean becomes a little island propped up on rocks. The most affordable hotel is the **Hotel Brisas Marinas,** 10min. from Las Tunas on the land side of the road, with clean, basic rooms with fans and private bath (¢125). There is also a small *comedor* attached, and the beach is a only a 2min. walk away.

◤ **PLAYA EL TAMARINDO.** The fishing village of Tamarindo and its tranquil and often-deserted beach sit on a gently curving point of a peninsula at the southeastern corner of the country. The sheltered, calm waters are ideal for swimming. On the horizon, the mountainous islands in the **Golfo de Fonseca** loom silhouetted against the sun. **Buses** depart from the center of the town, passing along the length of the beach, **Playas Negras,** and **Playa Las Tunas** before connecting with the *carretera* and heading to **San Miguel** (#385; 2½hr., every hr., 5am-4pm, ¢10) and **La Unión** (#383; 1½hr., every 30min., 4:30am-5pm, ¢5). The town also has a **post office**

EL SALVADOR

FROM THE ROAD

THE FACES OF WAR

I encountered a man who had lived in Mozote, a village where over a thousand civilians were massacred by the El Salvadoran army. When he was 15, he was forcefully recruited from his school into the FMLN (Frente Farabundo Martípara ae Liberación Nacional), a common practice. Not interested in dying, he deserted after a year and moved to San Salvador, where he lived until he learned that the FMLN was searching for him. Virtually penniless and disconnected from his family, the boy made his way as a *mojado* to Phoenix, Arizona. A US citizen for the past 24 years, he returned to Mozote in January 2002, unsure if his 87-year-old father and 84-year-old mother were still alive. When he arrived at his village, his mother did not recognize him, disbelieving he was still alive.

Though I don't consider myself a sentimental person, as I walked through the FMLN museum, I was nearly moved to tears. The bomb crater outside is a testament to the carpet bombing and scorched earth practices that my parents' tax dollars helped pay for.

My trip to Perquín reminded me that there aren't simply two sides to the war. It isn't just an impoverished people's struggle for social justice, but mayhem and chaos that tore people's lives apart in seemingly inexplicable ways. My mind turned to this man whose story I heard in a truck on the way to Perquín, whose flesh-and-blood story gave voice to the complexities and suffering of such a war.

—Daniel Elizondo

and a **telecom** office. The **police** are stationed just south of town on the beach side. To access the **beach,** either head to the hotel or get off the bus at the end of the peninsula and take the road to the right where the main road splits. Pass by some *comedores* and you'll arrive at a wide sandy beach.

Tamarindo is not the cheapest place to stay. Try **Hotel Tropitamarindo ❺,** along Playa El Tamarindo 2km before the town. Big, white-tiled rooms with bath, A/C, and cable TV sleep up to four. (☎ 649 5082. US$64.57 per 24hr. MC/V.) The pool, picnic area, bathrooms, and beach are ¢60 per person. The restaurant offers lunches and dinners (¢40-125) in a slightly nicer atmosphere than its downtown competitors, which are a 20min. walk away.

LA UNIÓN AND GOLFO DE FONSECA

The Golfo de Fonseca, with more than 30 islands, is bordered by the shores of Honduras, El Salvador, and Nicaragua. A 1992 decision by the International Court of Justice stated that all three countries must divide control over the gulf. Once the most important seaport in El Salvador, La Unión (pop. 36,000), has fallen on some hard times. The port has not been active since the war, and the resulting unemployment is evident in the city's swelling crime rate and the rise in panhandling. Though not a good place to walk around after dark, La Unión offers a chance to visit nearby islands or cross to Nicaragua in one of the few *lanchas.*

🚌 **TRANSPORTATION.** There are two bus terminals. **Buses** leaving from the terminal on 3 Calle, Av. 4/6, go to: **San Miguel** (#324; 1½hr., every 10min. 4:15am-6pm, ¢6); **San Salvador** (#304; 4hr., every 30min. 3am-2:30pm, ¢20); and **Santa Rosa de Lima** (#342; 1½hr., every 30min. 4am-5:45pm, ¢6). Two blocks south on Calle San Carlos, Av. 4/6 , you'll find a bus to **Playa El Tamarindo** (#383; 1½hr., every 20min. 4:30am-6:30pm, ¢6), and **Playitas** (#418; 25min., every hr. 6am-5:30pm). **Boats** to the islands of the gulf and to **Potosí** in **Nicaragua** (2-3hr.; very irregular schedule, check with immigration; ¢100 per person) leave from the waterfront at 1/3 Av. Expect to wait awhile, unless you want to shell out the cash for a private trip (as many friends as you can fit, up to ¢2000 to Nicaragua).

■ **ORIENTATION AND PRACTICAL INFORMATION.** The bay borders the northern edge of town, and most streets run downhill to the north. Incoming

buses enter from the west on 1 Calle and pass by the *parque central,* largely hidden by the market. The church is east of the *parque,* and the main intersection is on its southwest corner. The main *avenida* is **Av. Cabañas** to the north and **Av. Morazán** to the south, while main *calles* are **Calle Menéndez** to the east and **Calle San Carlos** to the west. Odd-numbered *calles* increase to the north, while even-numbered *calles* increase away from the bay to the south. Odd-numbered *avenidas* increase to the east, and even-numbered *avenidas* increase to the west.

The **immigration office**, on Av. Cabañas at 5 Calle, knows the boat schedules. Get an exit stamp here if you're heading to Nicaragua. (Open daily 6am-8pm.) **Banco Salvadoreño**, on Av. Cabañas at 3 Calle, changes traveler's checks, gives cash advances on Visa and has **Western Union** services and an **ATM.** (Open M-F 8am-5pm, Sa 8am-noon.) The **mercado** branches off the southeast corner of the *parque.* The **Despensa Familiar** supermarket sits on the east side of the *parque* (open daily 7am-7pm). Other services include: **police,** a half-block south of the marina on 1 Av. (☎ 604 3511; open 24hr.); **hospital,** on the corner of 1 Av. and 3 Calle 9 (☎ 604 4255; open 24hr. for emergencies); **Telecom phone,** 1 Calle, 5 Av. (open daily 7am-7pm); **Internet** at **Infocentros,** 1 Calle, Av. Cabañas and 2 Av. (¢20 per hr.); and **post office,** Av. Cabañas, 3/5 Calles, in a basement office (open M-F 7am-5pm, Sa 7am-noon).

⚑ ACCOMMODATIONS. Stay in a decent place, since some of the cheaper *hospedajes* rent rooms by the hour. **Hotel Portobello ❷,** on 4 Av. at 1 Calle, a block south and half a block east of the bus terminal, has a roof-top deck and cable TV. Common baths are clean, with little chance of privacy. (☎ 604 4113. Doubles ¢80, with A/C and bath ¢175.) Another good find is spotless **Hotel San Francisco ❷,** on Calle Menéndez, 9/11 Av. (☎ 604 4159. Double bed ¢80; 2 beds with A/C ¢150.) Bargain-hunters will enjoy family-run **Hospedaje Night and Day ❶,** 11 Av., 2/4 Calles. (☎ 604 3006. Rooms with fan and bath ¢40; larger doubles ¢60.)

◖ FOOD. ▧Captain John's Seafood ❶, on 3 Av. Sur, 4 Calle, is a can't-miss. The delicious food is reasonably priced (fish of the day ¢30). With a view of the bay, **Restaurante Oasis ❸,** at the end of 3 Av. on the waterfront, has seafood dinners (¢40-120) and hamburgers (¢20-30). Two blocks up from the bus terminal, **El Marinero ❷** serves excellent sea food. (Dinner plates ¢40-60. Open daily 8am-8pm.) Head to **Nevería** (ice cream) and **Lorena's** (pastries), both on Calle Menéndez, to satisfy your sweet tooth.

▨ ISLANDS OF THE GULF. The islands of the gulf—**Isla Zacatillo, Isla Martia Pérez, Isla Conchagüita,** and **Isla Meanguerita**—have deserted beaches and are serviced by *lanchas* from La Unión. Most *lanchas* travel to and from the islands before 10am (¢10), with an afternoon trip servicing Zacatillo. Comedor Montecristo on the harbor has the most *lancha* information. Ask around for **Daniel Turcios** (☎ 680 6873); he will arrange a daytrip to any of the islands and give you insider tips on the best beaches. (¢300-500 for 4 people, depending on time). Martia Perez and Meanguerra have the most highly recommended beaches, and **El Mirador** (☎ 648 8072) on Meanguerra provides the option to stay the night.

◪ PLAYITAS. Immerse yourself in the bay and soak in the riveting scenery at the little beach, **Playitas,** just 25min. south of the city. Bus #418 regularly makes the bumpy trip to the row of *comedores* along this gentle bend of sandy beach.

EL SALVADOR

GUATEMALA

In a land famed for its startling contrasts, Guatemala contains Central America's most diverse landscape and starkly visible social differences. Crisp mountain peaks, towering volcanic ridges, thick rainforest, and mellow Caribbean ports all coexist within Guatemala's borders. This manifold topography supports equally varied wildlife. With the strongest indigenous Maya presence in Central America (around 46%), Guatemala is also highly urbanized in places, with over 40% of the population living in cities. Nevertheless, a 2 hr. bus ride from the frenzy of Guatemala City transports you to the rolling western highlands, where Maya women in colorful traditional garb weave *huipiles* on the volcanic shores of Lake Atitlán. In many highland villages, travelers will find that Spanish can take them only so far. If you leave the established tourist routes, you'll soon have to learn the universal language of gestures—each of Guatemala's 23 Maya groups has its own language. Take it from the swarms of returning travelers: Guatemala is *the* place for adventurous budget travel in Latin America.

HIGHLIGHTS OF GUATEMALA

The ancient Maya pyramids of **Tikal,** one of the most awesome archaeological sites in the world (p. 420).

Cobblestoned **Antigua,** one of Central America's most beautiful Colonial towns (p. 343).

The Sunday and Thursday market in **Chichicastenango,** a lush cacophony of color, incense, and sound, with an unparalleled selection of indigenous artwork (p. 363).

The **Lago de Atitlán's** volcanoes and many indigenous villages, ranging from tourist meccas to very traditional (p. 360).

A boat ride through the spectacular gorges of the **Río Dulce** (p. 402).

The remote mountain villages of **Nebaj** and **Todos Santos Cuchumatán,** where Maya tradition is strong and the scenery superb (p. 368 and p. 381).

SUGGESTED ITINERARIES

1 WEEK: LA RUTA GRINGA. Starting in **Guatemala City** (p. 333), catch a frequent bus to **Antigua** (p. 343), the colonial city known for its cobblestone streets, elegant ruins, and ubiquity of English and language schools. Nearby are **Volcán Agua** (p. 353) and **Volcán Pacaya** (p. 353), both fun climbs. A hop, skip, and a 2½ hour jump away is the mythically important and unbelievably beautiful **Lago de Atitlán** (p. 354). Base yourself in convenient (if commercial) **Panajachel** (p. 354), and allot enough time to visit the other towns via boat—some people take years. If you yearn for the hustle of a market and the bloodrush of a successful bargain, head to **Chichicastenango** (p. 363) for its world-renowned market on Th or Su.

2-3 WEEKS: VERAPAZ HIGHLANDS, PETÉN, AND EASTERN GUATEMALA. This longer route may be done in conjunction with the 1 week itinerary if you transfer in Guatemala City. Head first to **Cobán** (p. 405), a cosmopolitan center smack dab in a wilderness paradise. Using Cobán as your base camp, visit some of the nearby *fincas*, parks, and hiking trails. Traversing north, head to **Sayaché** (p. 414) in the **Petén** region (you'll have to transfer buses in Raxrujá). Like Cobán, Sayaché is a great home base from which you can explore nearby **Ceibal** (p. 414), Maya ruins accessible by boat or pickup, and the ruins around **Lake Petexbatún** (p. 415). From

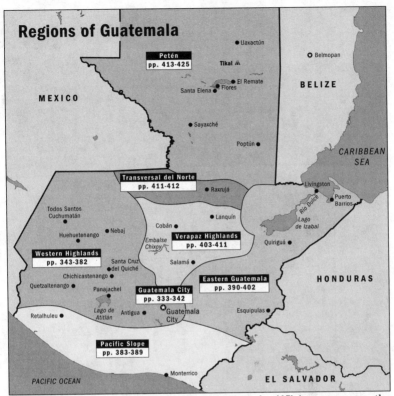

Regions of Guatemala

MEXICO

• Uaxactún

Petén
pp. 413-425

Tikal /▥

◉ Belmopan

• El Remate
Santa Elena ● ●Flores

BELIZE

• Sayaxché

Poptún ●

CARIBBEAN
SEA

Transversal del Norte
pp. 411-412

● Raxrujá

Livingston ●
● Puerto
Río Dulce ● Barrios

Todos Santos
Cuchumatán
●

● Nebaj

Cobán ●

● Lanquín

Lago
de Izabal

Huehuetenango ●

Embalse
Chixoy

Verapaz Highlands
pp. 403-411

Quiriguá ●

Western Highlands
pp. 343-382

Santa Cruz
●del Quiché

Salamá ●

Chichicastenango ●

HONDURAS

Quetzaltenango ●

Panajachel ●

Guatemala City
pp. 333-342

Eastern Guatemala
pp. 390-402

Retalhuleu ●

Lago de
Atitlán

Antigua ● ◉Guatemala
City

Esquipulas ●

Pacific Slope
pp. 383-389

PACIFIC OCEAN

● Monterrico

EL SALVADOR

Sayaché, the connection to **Flores** and **Santa Elena** (p. 415) is an easy one; the famed ruins of **Tikal** (p. 420) are 65km to the north. Though you can see Tikal in a day, give yourself enough time to soak up the tropical forest, wildlife, and the impressive ruins. Hop a bus to **Eastern Guatemala** (p. 390) via **Poptún** (p. 413) and arrive in **Fronteras** (also known as **Río Dulce**, p. 396) on the Lago de Izabal; from there, its fun to take a boat down the peaceful Río Dulce to **Livingston** (p. 399), Guatemala's plot on the Caribbean and home to the local Garífuna culture. Wash off the jungle in the local hot springs and waterfalls, shake your bon bon at beach parties, and eat your fill of coconut bread. Life is sweet. From Livingston, take a bus back to **Guatemala City** (p. 333), or a boat to **Belize** (p. 66) or **Honduras** (p. 426).

LIFE AND TIMES

LAND, FLORA, AND FAUNA

The northern third of the country—the Petén—is geographically contiguous with Mexico's Yucatán, and is part of an immense, flat, limestone shelf. Water erosion has produced an irregular limestone region with extensive cave systems and numerous depressions and *cenotes* (sinkholes) that provide the only sources of water in the dry season. The Petén is covered by a dense lowland rainforest, mixed with cleared patches of savanna. South of the Petén are the highlands, composed

GUATEMALA

Guatemala

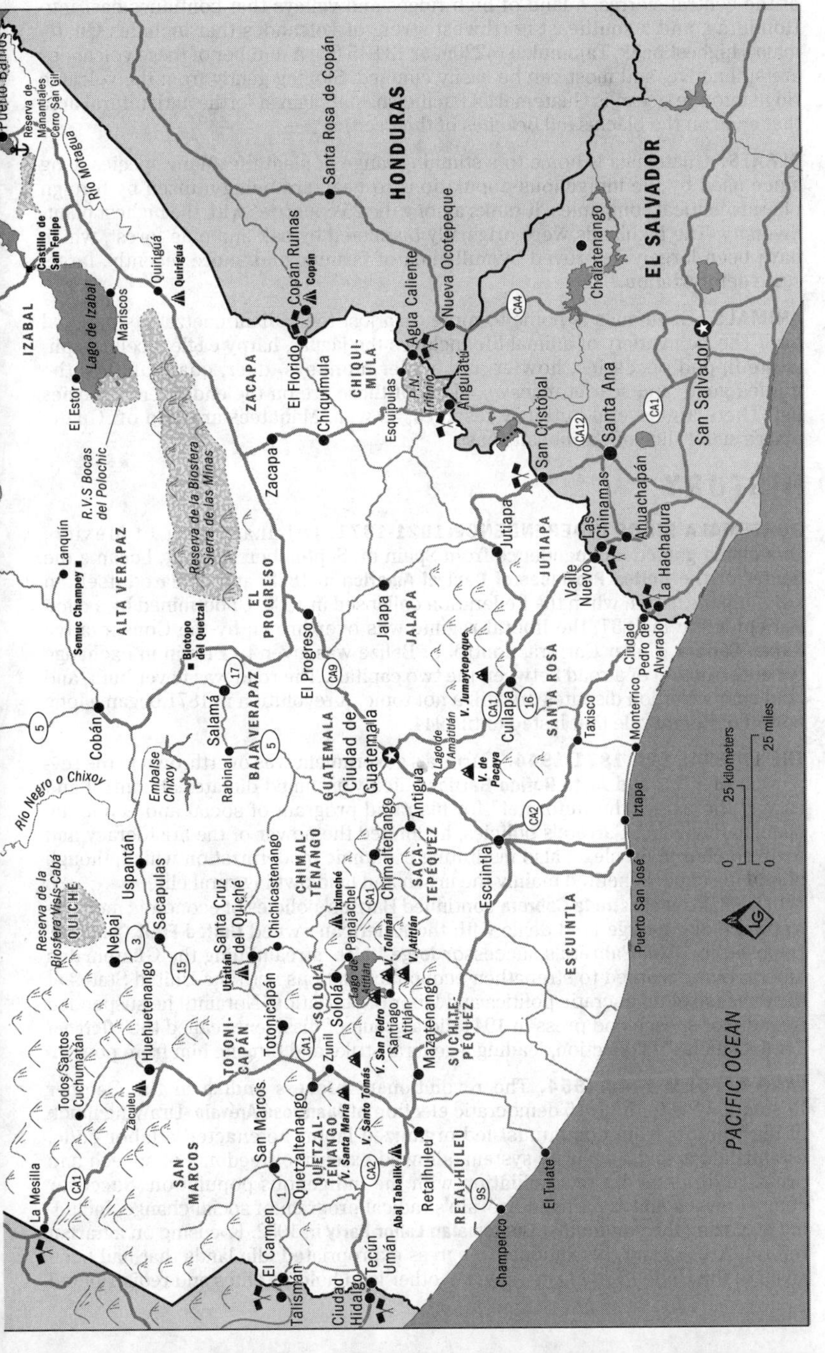
HONDURAS
EL SALVADOR
PACIFIC OCEAN
Puerto Barrios
Reserva de Manantiales Cerro San Gil
Río Motagua
Castillo de San Felipe
Quiriguá
Quiriguá
IZABAL
Lago de Izabal
Mariscos
El Estor
R.V.S Bocas del Polochic
Santa Rosa de Copán
Copán Ruinas
Copán
El Florido
ZACAPA
Chiquimula
CHIQUI-MULA
Zacapa
Reserva de la Biosfera Sierra de las Minas
Lanquín
Semuc Champey
ALTA VERAPAZ
Biotopo del Quetzal
EL PROGRESO
Salamá
Cobán
Rabinal
BAJA VERAPAZ
Embalse Chixoy
Río Negro o Chixoy
Uspantán
Sacapulas
Reserva de la Biosfera Visis-Cabá
QUICHÉ
Nebaj
Santa Cruz del Quiché
Utatlán
Chichicastenango
Huehuetenango
Todos Santos Cuchumatán
Zaculeu
La Mesilla
SAN MARCOS
San Marcos
El Carmen
Talismán
Ciudad Hidalgo
Tecún Umán
Abaj Takalik
Quetzaltenango
QUETZAL-TENANGO
V. Santa María
V. Santo Tomás
Zunil
TOTONI-CAPÁN
Totonicapán
SOLOLÁ
Sololá
Panajachel
Lago de Atitlán
V. San Pedro
V. Tolimán
V. Atitlán
Santiago Atitlán
Iximché
CHIMAL-TENANGO
Chimaltenango
SACA-TEPÉQUEZ
Antigua
Mazatenango
SUCHITE-PÉQUEZ
Retalhuleu
RETALHULEU
Champerico
El Tulate
ESCUINTLA
Escuintla
Puerto San José
Iztapa
GUATEMALA
Ciudad de Guatemala
El Progreso
Jalapa
JALAPA
Lago de Amatitlán
V. de Pacaya
V. Jumaytepeque
Cuilapa
SANTA ROSA
Taxisco
Monterrico
Ciudad Pedro de Alvarado
La Hachadura
Valle Nuevo
Las Chinamas
JUTIAPA
Jutiapa
San Cristóbal
Esquipulas
P.N. Trifinio
Anguiatú
Agua Caliente
Nueva Ocotepeque
Chalatenango
Santa Ana
Ahuachapán
San Salvador
CA1
CA2
CA4
CA9
CA12
9S
1
3
5
15
16
17
25 kilometers
25 miles
0
LG

GUATEMALA

of the central sierras, a land of high ridges and valleys that continues east into Honduras, and a southeast-northwest string of volcanoes that includes Guatemala's highest peak, Tajumulco (4220m or 13,845 ft.). A number of these volcanoes are still active, and most can be easily climbed. Sloping gently from the volcanic ridge into the ocean is Guatemala's Pacific coastal plain, a fertile agricultural area that ends on the black-sand beaches of the Pacific.

PLANTS. Guatemala is home to a stunning range of plant life. Many species, long since used by the indigenous populations to heal, are being utilized by foreign pharmaceutical companies. It ranks among the 25 countries with the highest plant-diversity. The highlands were originally blanketed by oak and pine forest, which have been largely destroyed by millennia of farming and, more recently, large-scale deforestation.

ANIMALS. Guatemala is home to more than just the radiant quetzal, its national bird. The rich variety of animal life includes the jaguar, harpy eagle, ocelot, tapir, white-lipped peccaries, howler and spider monkeys, deer, coatmundies, the horned guan, and scarlet macaws. Many of these are on the endangered species list. There are several butterfly reserves, as well. Manatees are also off Guatemala's small slice of Caribbean coast.

HISTORY

GUATEMALA SINCE INDEPENDENCE 1821-1871. Originally part of Mexico, Guatemala gained independence from Spain on September 15, 1821, became the center of the **United Provinces of Central America** in 1823, and declared itself an autonomous nation when the Federation collapsed in 1839. Undermined by a cholera epidemic in 1837, the liberal regime was overthrown by the Conservative **Rafael Carrera.** Under Carrera, control of Belize was given to Britain in exchange for construction of a road between the two capitals. The road was never built, and land compensation disputes are still a hot topic. A revolution in 1871 began a long period of liberal rule that lasted until 1944.

THE LIBERAL ERA 1871-1944. Carrera's government was overthrown in the revolution of 1871, and **Justo Rufino Barrios** quickly assumed dictatorial control and earned the name "the Reformer" for his rapid program of social and economic change. Reversing Carrera's policies, he limited the power of the aristocracy and revoked church privilege, also instituting economic modernization which, though liberal in scope, benefited mainly the urban and land owning rural elite.

In 1898, **Manuel Estrada Cabrera** continued Barrios' policies of economic modernization, making large land deals with the American-owned **United Fruit Company**. Deposed in 1920, Cabrera's successor **Jorge Ubico,** streamlining the Guatemalan Liberal State, worked to strengthen economic relations with the United States at the expense of democratic politics and labor organization. Not until he suspended freedom of speech and press in 1944 did a group of dissidents called the **"October Revolutionaries"** take action, leading a general strike and flinging him from power.

LAND REFORM 1945-1954. The revolutionary process ending in the October Revolution led to the 1945 democratic election of **Juan José Arévalo.** Drawing much of his support from communist-led organized labor, he enacted a labor code, established a social security system, allowed extensive freedoms of speech and press, and pursued a reconciliation with the indigenous population. Succesor colonel **Jacobo Arbenz** pursued Arévalo's radical program of social change, including legalizing the communist **Guatemalan Labor Party** in 1952. Focusing on agrarian reform, Arbenz and the National Congress expropriated idle lands that had been given to the United Fruit Company and other land-holding elites and redistributed them to landless peasants. United Fruit had powerful allies in the US government, and Washington quickly responded; in 1954, an army covertly trained by the US invaded and forced Arbenz to resign, ending agrarian reform before it had begun.

LA VIOLENCIA 1954-1996. The military junta that took power after the invasion reversed previously instituted social reforms , crushing any opposition through a campaign of violence, all in the interest of American big business. The military government's oppression incited increasingly violent resistance. Many workers joined oppositional guerrilla groups demanding land reform and democracy. The violence that began in the early 60s engulfed Guatemala for the next 35 years in a nearly genocidal clash over rights to land and liberty. The term **La Violencia** describes the period from the late 70s through the 80s, when the conflict extended into the most remote corners of Guatemala. A series of rigged elections and puppet presidents controlled by the military continued through the 1960s. At the same time, right-wing vigilantes formed the **Secret Anti-Communist Army (ESA)** and the **White Hand** to go after students, professionals, and peasants they suspected of leftist activity. The reign of **Carlos Arana Osorio** introduced "death squads" to the Guatemalan political landscape. These murder squads eliminated opposition, focusing on the guerrilla forces but affecting peaceful opposition as well. Meanwhile, foreign-owned business expanded, instigating social tensions. The death toll from political violence rose to the tens of thousands, as conflict polarized the nation.

As the civil war continued into the 1980s, the government--headed by 1982 coup-leader **General Efrain Rios Montt--** pursued "scorched earth" tactics against the guerrillas. Several guerrilla organizations organized in 1982 into the **Unidad Revoluciona-rio Nacional Guatemalteco (URNG).** Though Rios Montt was quickly replaced, the army razed hundreds of Maya villages, torturing and killing indiscriminately with the dual purpose of eliminating possible rebels and discouraging those left from joining the insurgency. Many were forced to relocate into camps known euphemistically as "model villages." Others sought refuge in Mexico or Honduras or wandered through the highlands in a desperate attempt to avoid the army's violence. Recently revealed Guatemalan documents state that roughly 650,000 citizens--roughly 10% of the population--were marked for death.

Under increasing financial pressure from the international community, peace negotiations finally began in the 1990s. **Alvaro Arzú Irigoyen** was elected president in 1996, and in March of that year, he signed a temporary cease-fire. Peace accords followed on December 29, 1996, ending the four decades of civil war with a death toll of 200,000, a displaced population of upwards of one million, and tens of thousands of *desaparecidos* (abducted dissidents) that were never found.

TODAY

THE STRUGGLE WITH PEACE: 1996-2002. Demobilization of the guerrillas proceeds slowly, and many of the ex-rebels and soldiers have turned their guns to the profitable enterprise of highway robbery. Recently discovered mass graves contain hundreds of bodies, and hundreds more mass burial sites are believed to exist. In one of the most horrifying acts since the cease-fire, Bishop **Juan Gerardi Conedera** was beaten to death on April 26, 1998, two days after he presented a long-awaited report on human rights violations during *la violencia*. The report, *Never Again in Guatemala*, based upon 6000 interviews with survivors, attributed 85% of the human rights abuses to the Guatemalan Army.

In February 1999, the Guatemalan Truth Commission released a report of the atrocities of the civil war, which stated that the Guatemalan military and its agents committed acts of genocide against the Maya. In spring 1999, President Clinton surprised the world by acknowledging and apologizing for the US role in the atrocities. While Guatemala is slowly building a democracy, substantial social and eco-

GUATEMALA

nomic inequalities continue to threaten peace. Current president **Alfonso Antonio Portillo Cabrera,** of the rightist Guatemalan Republican Front (FRG), has pledged to seek justice for those affected by *la violencia*, and in 2001 he asked President Bush to back legislation making it easier for Guatemalan refugees to obtain US citizenship. Justice for Bishop Conedera was served June 20, 2001, when three military officers were found guilty. Mob violence is unfortunately not uncommon. Some Guatemalans see vigilante justice as their only means of peacekeeping, often at the expense of more sanctioned means.

ECONOMY AND GOVERNMENT

Guatemala's economy is still mostly agricultural, divided between the subsistence, small-scale agriculture of the highlands, where corn and squash are the main crops, and the larger, commercial farming of the Pacific slope, where coffee, bananas, and sugar are produced for export. Industry, mostly centered around Guatemala City, is growing now that IMF stabilization plans have curtailed the slump of the 80s. Growth, however, has not resulted in equitable income distribution or the alleviation of poverty. Recently, services, especially tourism, have been the fastest growing sector of the economy.

Recently, the strength of democracy is growing. Officially, the nation is a republic, and power is divided between three branches: legislative, executive, and judicial. The entire republic is divided into 22 *departamentos*, each of which is headed by a governor. Guatemalan political parties create a constantly changing landscape. Besides the FRG, other currently visible parties include the National Advancement Party (PAN), the Revolutionary Party (PR), the centrist Guatemalan Christian Democratic party (DCG), and the right-wing National Liberation Movement (MLN). The army also continues to make its presence felt.

PEOPLE

Guatemala is home to the majority of Central America's indigenous population (7 of every 8 Amerindians live in Guatemala), and is characterized by a sharp distinction between the six million *indígenas*, who comprise over 45% of the country's population, and *ladinos* (of European ancestry) or assimilated *indígenas*. The indigenous population, concentrated in the central and western highlands, is almost uniformly Maya. Yet the Maya of Guatemala themselves consist of a number of different ethnic groups and speak 23 different languages. The largest of these groups are the **Quiché** (K'iche'), who live around Lake Atitlán; the **Mam,** who live west of the K'iche' near the Mexican border; the **Cakchiquel,** who live just west of Guatemala City; and the **Kekchi** (Q'eqchi), who live in a large area in the central and northern sierras. *Ladinos*, Spanish-speakers, live mostly in the urban centers, along the Pacific slope, and in the Petén, where they are relative newcomers.

Guatemalans consistently characterize themselves as Roman Catholic, though Protestant sects have been growing in popularity among the urban poor in the last few decades. Most Maya practice what may be the most striking syncretistic mixture of Catholicism and native religious customs found in Central America.

CULTURE

THE ARTS

The beautiful Maya weavings found in marketplaces and villages throughout the country are highly meaningful for those who make and wear the textiles (see Clothes Make the Maya, below). However, in places, their role as a tourist commodity may be eclipsing their traditional importance. Guatemala's literary tradi-

CLOTHES MAKE THE MAYA Famous all over the world, Guatemalan Maya textiles are complex tapestries of intricately woven patterns, colors, symbols, and icons. The natural dyes are fashioned from *clavel* and *heraño* flowers and then mixed with the crushed bodies of mosquitoes to keep the dye from running. The bugs themselves are often depicted in the resulting patterns, which are woven on huge, unwieldy looms specific to each village. The clothing, each piece of which can take up to six months to make, is nearly always produced and worn by women.

Travelers in search of handmade clothing in the tourist-saturated markets will be courted with machine-made replicas. Shop carefully. Some tip-offs that goods are fake: gold or silver synthetic fibers are woven into the fabric; the stitching on the back is suspiciously neat; the prices seem too good to be true. To those traditional Maya for whom the clothing signifies a particular ethnic group or status, foreigners in native dress can be downright offensive (it's especially insulting when women tourists wear traditionally male garments), so you may want to save your purchases to wear at home.

tion dates back to the Popol Vuh, an ancient Maya holy book whose existence was first recorded by the Spanish in Chichicastenango in 1701. Perhaps in recognition of these ancient precedents, Guatemalan writers have continuously tried to bridge the gap between indigenous myth and European literary forms; magic recurs in Guatemalan literature, coloring even the most modern writing with traces of indigenous beliefs. The country has produced few well-known playwrights, though Vicenta Laparra de la Cerda (1834-1905) movingly portrayed the plight of women in *Angel caído* (*Fallen Angel*, 1880) and *Hija maldita* (*Accursed Daughter*, 1895). Modern poet Rafael Arévalo Martínez (1884-1975) is said to have led the way toward magical realism through short stories such as *El hombre que parecía un caballo* (*The Man Who Resembled a Horse*, 1915). Another father of magical realism is Miguel Angel Asturias (1899-1974), the poet, novelist, and ambassador who in 1967 won the Nobel Prize in Literature, and whose novels examine the deep political realities of this century. Most notable among his writings are *El señor Presidente* (1946) and *Viento Fuerte* (*Strong Wind*, 1950), which was mentioned in his Nobel Prize citation. Guatemala's other Nobel Prize winner is the internationally known author and social activist Rigoberta Menchú, who won the Peace Prize in 1992 for her outspoken efforts to gain recognition of the plight of the country's indigenous peoples. Her world renowned testimonial *Me Llamo Rigoberta y Así Nació la Conciencia* (1983, translated *I, Rigoberta* in 1984) highlights her family's involvement in revolutionary action against the government's civil rights abuses. The book's international fame and Menchú's controversial high profile helped raise public awareness.

POPULAR CULTURE
In both circulation and sheer mass, *Prensa Libre* (www.prensalibre.com) is the biggest Guatemalan daily newspaper, followed by *Siglo XXI* (www.sigloxxi.com) and *La Hora* (www.lahora.com.gt). *Diario de Centroamerica* is the government publication. The biweekly journal *Crónica* provides in-depth analyses of national and international events. The monthly *Crítica* is a tempestuous forum for Guatemalan intellectuals.

FOOD AND DRINK
Chicken rules supreme in Central American *típico* fare; sometimes the bird is served with the feet still attached. But while the meat's the treat, meals are filled out with rice, beans, eggs, and thick tortillas. There is good reason why tortillas in Guatemala are made from corn—according to the Popol Vuh and traditional

Quiché myths, humans came from corn, and the grain is the human essence. Along the coasts, seafood is common, usually spiced with Caribbean Creole flare. Don't miss the famous *tapado* on the Caribbean coast. Despite the fruit's thorny exterior, the juicy, pulpy white core of the *guanábana* (soursop) deserves a try. Nearly every town has a tent-strewn market, stocked with fruits, vegetables, and other tasty items at a nominal cost. Coffee is the *bebida preferida* throughout Guatemala; locally grown beans are export quality and make a good gift. Fruit juice *licuados* are also favorites. Local beers include Gallo, Moza, and Dorado. If you enjoy a meal or drink, be sure to tell the cook that it was *muy rico*.

ESSENTIALS

PASSPORTS, VISAS, AND CUSTOMS

Passport (p. 21). Required for all visitors. Stamps usually valid for 30 days, but extra time may be granted upon request at entry. Extensions also can be granted at an immigration office.

Visa (p. 22). Not required for citizens of the US, Canada, UK, Ireland, or New Zealand. Visitors from Australia and South Africa need a visa.

Inoculations and Medications (p. 29). None required.

Work Permit (p. 55). Required for all foreigners planning to work in Guatemala.

Driving Permit (p. 48). No special permit is necessary; permit valid for 30-90 days issued upon arrival with valid US license. US Drivers must carry valid driver's license, title, and registration to drive across the border.

Departure Tax. US$20-25 if leaving by air, Q5-10 by land.

EMBASSIES AND CONSULATES

Embassies of Guatemala: US, 2220 R St., NW, Washington, D.C. 20008 (☎202-745-4952; fax 745-1908; http://www.mdngt.org/agremilusa/embassy.html). Open M-F 9am-5:00pm. **UK,** 13 Fawcett St., London, SW 10 9HN (☎ 441 7351 3042; fax 376 5708). Canada, 130 Albert St., suite 1010, Ottawa, Ontario KIT 5Z4 (☎613-233-7188; fax 233-0135).

Consular Services of Guatemala: 57 Park Ave., New York, NY 10016 (☎212-686-3837; fax 447-6947). Open M-F 9am-2pm for document processing. Guatemala also has consulates in Washington, Los Angeles, San Francisco, Miami, Houston, and Chicago.

MONEY

US$1 = Q7.85	Q1 = US$0.13
CDN$1 = Q5.14	Q1 = CDN$0.20
UK£1 = Q11.45	Q1 = UK£0.09
AUS$1 = Q4.19	Q1 = AUS$0.22
EURO€ = 7.33	Q1 = EURO€0.14

The above exchange rates were accurate as of June 2002. Be advised, however, that rates change frequently. The Guatemalan unit of currency is the **quetzal**, named for the elusive bird and abbreviated with a "Q." The quetzal is divided into 100 centavos, and there are coins of 25, 10, 5, and 1 centavos. Bills come as 50 centavos and 1, 5, 10, 20, 50, and 100 quetzales. Torn notes are not always accepted.

US dollars are the only foreign currency to have, though the BanQuetzal branch at the Guatemala City airport may accept others. Exchanging dollars for elusive quetzales is straightforward enough at most banks; there's also a black market, though rates are little better than the official ones. **Traveler's checks** are widely accepted in Guatemala, though American Express is slightly more difficult to change outside of the capital than Visa and Citibank. For **credit card** advances or **ATM** withdrawals, Visa (accepted at most Banco Industrials) is easy. **Tipping** is not customary in *comedores*, but if a restaurant has a menu, it's generally a good idea to leave a 10% tip; sometimes it'll be included. **Bargaining** is the norm in Guatemala's many markets and handcraft shops, but not in urban shopping centers.

Guatemala can be a very economical country to visit. The attentive traveler might come across beds for as little as US$3-4 per person and basic eateries offer up meals for US$2 or less, though you may want to treat yourself to more than this—and you'll have to in popular tourist areas like Antigua and Panajachel. Even so, the very frugal traveler could get by on about US$100 a week or less, twice that for rooms with private bath and more upscale meals. Taxis, tourist shuttles, guided tours, and tourist bars can quickly add to these figures.

QUETZAL	❶	❷	❸	❹	❺
ACCOMMODATIONS	Q1-30	Q31-45	Q46-60	Q61-80	Q80+
	US$0-4	US$4-5.50	US$5.50-7.50	US$7.50-10	US$10+
FOOD	Q1-10	Q11-20	Q21-35	Q36-45	Q46+
	US$0-1	US$1-3	US$3-4.5	US$4.50-5.50	US$5.50+

SAFETY

Although Guatemala is the safest it's been in 30 years, travel between cities after dark is still considered unsafe. **Armed bandits** have stopped city buses and tour buses along highways at night. Decrease risk by restricting travel to the daytime and, in particular, to roads the tourism industry considers safe. Local buses, moreover, are rarely subject to attacks—tour buses are more frequently targets. **Pickpockets** and purse snatchers constitute a perennial hazard in Guatemala City and elsewhere, especially in the central markets. Climbing **volcanoes** in Guatemala can be risky, as tourists have been assaulted in the recent past. It is very important to check on the safety of an area before venturing out. US citizens, particularly those staying for an extended period of time, may want to register with the Consular Section of the US Embassy in Guatemala City. An application, two photos, and proof of citizenship are required. One can register informally by mail or fax; include a local address and telephone number, itinerary, emergency contact in the US, and length of stay. Do *not* carry drugs in Guatemala. Under a 1992 anti-narcotics law, anyone caught in the possession of even small amounts of drugs can spend several months in jail—before their case is decided. Those convicted face very stiff sentences. For more info see **Personal Safety,** p. 26.

HEALTH

Although free of cost to travelers, many public hospitals outside of Guatemala City are ill-equipped to handle all emergencies. Private hospitals are generally a bit better. Avoid drinking tap water, milk, or uncooked vegetables. Also be wary of uncooked street food. There is a risk of malaria on the coast and in the Petén.

BORDER CROSSINGS

MEXICO. There are three land crossings. In the highlands, **La Mesilla**, 90km west of Huehuetenango, has buses to San Cristóbal de las Casas, Mexico. Buses from Huehue, Guatemala City, and other towns go to La Mesilla. **El Carmen/Talismán,** is west of Quetzaltenango and Retalhuleu, near Tapachula, Mexico. For info on entering Mexico, see p. 383. **Tecun Umán/Ciudad Hidalgo** on the Pacific coast, 75km

GUATEMALA

west of Retalhuleu. Buses head there from Quetzaltenango or Retalhuleu, or Tapachula, Mexico. There are several **land/river crossings** from Flores toward **Palenque, Mexico** (see p. 383 for details).

EL SALVADOR. There are three land crossings, listed from south to north. **Valle Nuevo/Las Chinamas** serves from Area 1 in Zona 4 of Guatemala City (see p. 337); **San Cristóbal** has buses from Guatemala City or Santa Ana, El Salvador. Buses run to **Anguiatú** from Esquipulas or Metapán, El Salvador.

HONDURAS. There are three land crossings. **El Florido** is along a dirt road between Chiquimula and Copán Ruinas, Honduras. Buses run on the Guatemalan side (p. 390), and pickups run on the Honduran side. **Agua Caliente** is 10km east of Esquipulas, near Nueva Ocotepeque, Honduras (see p. 394). **Corinto,** near Puerto Barrios, has connections to Omoa, Honduras (see p. 478).

BELIZE. There is one land crossing at **Melchor de Mencos/Benque Viejo de Carmen;** see p. 425 for details if coming from Flores. **Boats** run between Puerto Barrios and **Punta Gorda**, Belize (p. 127), and between Livingston and Punta Gorda (p. 399).

KEEPING IN TOUCH

Guatemala's **postal service** has improved in the last few years, after being purchased by a Canadian company. A letter costs Q0.40. If necessary, packages can be sent to the US using private mail carriers such as **DHL** (about US$30 per lb.). **First-class air mail** ought to take 10 to 14 days to reach the US, but it's not uncommon for a letter to take several months. You can receive mail general delivery at most post offices through the *lista de correos*.

> Ashley "Rockstar" KIRCHER
> Poste Restante
> Guatemala City(city)
> GUATEMALA

Guatemalan phone numbers are seven digits and require no area codes. For US phone company access codes, see the inside back cover. **Telephones** are handled by **Telgua,** the national communications network. Phoning can be difficult, so try the more expensive hotels when placing international or domestic calls. Some shops and Internet cafes have phones as well, and are often better for making calls with international phone cards. Listen for the amazing Guatemalan feedback effect; many conversations are spent listening to your own echo, and then awkwardly waiting for a response to "Hello? Can you hear me?" All calls within the country made from Telgua offices cost the same: Q3.50 for the first three minutes and Q0.35 for each additional minute. Pay phones in Guatemala City and some other places have been replaced with electronic, pre-paid calling cards which are available at many shops—look for the sign in the window.

TRANSPORTATION

Taca Inter offers **flights** between Guatemala City and a number of domestic destinations. Several airlines fly between Guatemala City and Flores (near Tikal). Common **buses,** cursed by some as "mobile chicken coops," are converted school buses that sit three to a bench. Some travelers have reported being charged a higher "gringo rate." Inquire about the price ahead of time and try to pay in exact change. **Driving** your own vehicle in Guatemala can be a hazardous experience. Some road conditions are poor. Those involved in accidents can be put in jail regardless of who is at fault, and armed car robberies are common enough that the US State Department warns against highway travel. The safest strategy if cornered by armed bandits on the road is to surrender your car without resistance.

ORIENTATION

Directions favor landmarks over addresses. Nevertheless, most Guatemalan cities, like their Honduran, Salvadoran, and Nicaraguan brethren, label streets in a grid of numbered north-south *avenidas* (avenues) and east-west *calles* (streets). Generally, *avenidas* increase in number to the west, and *calles* increase to the south. "6 Av. 25" refers to #25 on 6th Avenue. You will also see "6a Av. 25," which means the same thing ("6a" short for *sexta*). A building at 6 Av., 1/2 Calles, is on 6 Av. between 1 and 2 Calles. Guatemala's larger cities are divided into *zonas*, or zones; each has an independent grid system. In cities that are divided into zones, *Let's Go* designates the zone after the address (e.g. 6 Av. 25, Zona 1).

TRAVEL RESOURCES

Instituto Guatemalteco de Turismo (INGUAT), 7 Av. 1-17, Zona 4 (☎331 1333, or toll-free from the US 888-INGUAT1, from Guatemala ☎801 INGUAT1; inguat@guate.net; www.guatemala.travel.com.gt, www.travel-guatemala.org.gt) in the Centro Cívico just south of the Zona 1 border. Some of the staff speak English, and tourist brochures are available. There are INGUAT offices in Guatemala City, Antigua, Quetzaltenango, Pana-jachel, and Flores; see specific cities for local INGUAT listings.

The Revue, an English-language publication, has information about goings-on throughout Guatemala, although it concentrates on Antigua.

HOLIDAYS

Guatemalans are serious about festivals: patron saints' days include firecrackers, costumed dancers, and religious processions ranging from solemn to frenzied. There is, quite literally, a festival going on somewhere every day of the year. National holidays include: **January 1,** New Year's Day; **March/April,** *Semana Santa;* **May 1,** Labor Day; **June 30,** Army Day; **August 15,** Guatemala City Day; **September 15,** Independence Day; **October 20,** Revolution Day; **November 1,** All Saints Day; **December 24-25,** Christmas Eve/Christmas; **December 31,** New Year's Eve.

GUATEMALA CITY

Guatemala City, or Guate (GUAH-te), is the largest urban area in Central America. Smog-belching buses and countless sidewalk vendors, together with the sheer number of people and the volume of noise, render the city center claustrophobic. Add to this heavily armed men guarding establishments all over the city and it's easy to understand why many visitors flee the capital for the surrounding highlands. However, poking around Guate for a day or two does have its rewards. Some fine architecture and several worthwhile museums make for an engaging stay, and after camping in the countryside and hiking through jungles, the city's modern conveniences and hot showers can be quite welcoming. Poverty *is* laid bare here, standing in harsh contrast to the antiseptic shopping malls and guarded, fortress-like mansions in the wealthiest neighborhoods. This disparity is particularly evident in Guatemala's large refugee population, mainly Mayans who sought refuge from the civil violence in their home villages.

Guatemala City was named the country's capital in 1775 after an earthquake in Antigua left the government scrambling for a safer center, even though powerful tremors shook the new capital in 1917, 1918, and 1976. Yet, despite the whims of Mother Nature, the city and its three million inhabitants persevere, expanding ceaselessly into the surrounding valleys.

✖ INTERCITY TRANSPORTATION

Flights: La Aurora International Airport (☎331 8392), about 7km south of Zona 1, in Zona 13, serves all the flights listed below. Airlines with outbound flights from Aurora include: **Grupo Taca** (☎331 8222); **American** (☎334 7379); **Continental** (☎366 9985); **Delta** (☎337 0642); **United** (☎336 9900); **Mexicana** (☎333 6001); **Iberia** (☎332 0911); **KLM** (☎367 6179).

Flights to Flores: The most common domestic flight, and the only one budget travelers usually consider, is from Guate to Flores, near Tikal. Four airlines serve this route: **Grupo Taca** (☎331 8222; www.taca.com), **Tikal Jets** (☎334 5631), **Mayan World** (☎339 1519), and **Rasca** (☎361 5703 or 332 7470). Taca has the most service and the largest aircraft, followed by Tikal Jets. Specials are often available on this route—it's worth checking with a travel agent—but expect to pay US$90-120 round-trip.

Other Domestic Flights: Grupo Taca offers domestic service via its regional affiliate, **Inter.**, but only during peak seasons, which vary. It's a pricey way to go, but destinations include **Quetzaltenango, Huehuetenango, Puerto Barrios,** and **Río Dulce. Rasca** can arrange charter flights, but these also tend to be very expensive.

Domestic Buses: The **bus terminal** is located in the southwest corner of Zona 4, framed by Av. 4/Av. de Ferrocarril and Calles 7/8. Many 2nd-class services depart from here; finding an exact departure point is difficult and best accomplished by asking around. Any city bus marked "Terminal" will take you to this area. Departures are scattered throughout the city. Domestic buses that do not depart from the Zona 4 Terminal depart from various locations around Zona 1. See **Orientation,** below, for information on how to decipher addresses in Guate. Also, be advised that none of these bus "stations" has a ticket office; brace yourself for chaos. Ask a bus driver to point you toward the bus you are looking for. You pay for the trip on the road, but get money ready before you step on—you don't want to be fumbling with your wallet on a crowded bus.

Antigua: Many leave from the crowded parking lot at Av. 4, Calle 18, Zona 1. (1hr., every 5min. 5:30am-8pm, Q4.50.)

Belizean border: Fuentes del Norte, see Flores (13hr.; 2:30, 5, 9pm; Q75.)

Biotopo del Quetzal: Take any Cobán bus. (3½hr., Q20.)

Chichicastenango: Veloz Quichelense, Zona 4 Terminal; any Santa Cruz del Quiché bus runs here, too. (3½hr., every hr. 5am-6pm, Q12.)

Cobán: Escobar y Monja Blanca, 8 Av. 15/16 (☎238 1409. 4½hr., every hr. 4am-5pm, Q30.)

Esquipulas: Rutas Orientales, 19 Calle 8-18, Zona 1. (☎253-7282. 4½hr., 15 per day 2:30am-7pm, Q30.)

Flores: Fuentes del Norte, 17 Calle, 8 Av., Zona 1. (☎253 7882. 10-12hr., 1 per hr. every hr., Q60-130.) **Línea Dorada,** 16 Calle 10-55, Zona 1.(☎232 9658. departures at 10am, 2, 8, 9, and 10pm; Q240.

Huehuetenango: Velásquez, 20 Calle 1-37, Zona 1. (☎221-1084. 5hr., every hr. 8am-5pm, Q20.) Also Los Halcones, 7 Av. 15-27 (☎238 1929. 5hr.; 7am, 2, 5pm; Q30.)

Iztapa: Zona 4 Terminal. (3hr., every 20 min. 5am-6pm, Q11.)

Mexican border at Tecún Umán: Fortaleza, 19 Calle 8-70. (☎230 3390. 5hr., every 15min. 12:15am-12:30pm, Q35.) Some continue to the border at Talismán (6hr., Q40). Also try Rapidos del Sur at 20 Calle 8-55 (☎251 6678), and Chinita, 9 Av. 18-38 (☎251 9144).

Mexican border at La Mesilla: Velásquez buses to Huehuetenango (only those leaving Guatemala City from 8-11am) continue here (8hr., Q37.50).

Monterrico: Cubanita, Zona 4 Terminal. (Direct 3½hr.; 10:30am, 12:30, 2:20pm; Q15.) Alternatively, take a bus to Taxisco (from the **Pullman El Condor,** Zona 4 Terminal; 2hrs.; 6, 11am, 1:30pm; Q15) and transfer there to La Avellana (30min., every hr. 7am-2:30pm, Q3).

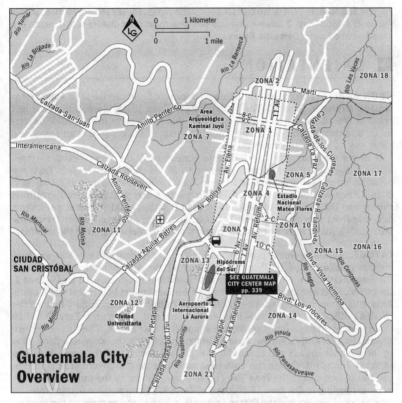

Guatemala City Overview

Panajachel: Rebulli, 21 Calle 1-34, Zona 1. (☎230 2748l. 3hr., every hr. 5:30am-3:30pm, direct at 6, 9, 10am, 3, 4pm; Q12.) Or, from the Zona 4 Terminal, take any western highlands bus and change at Los Encuentros junction.

Puerto Barrios: Litegua, 15 Calle 10-42. (☎253 8169. 5hr., 19 per day 5am-5pm, Q40.)

Quetzaltenango: Pullman service on **Marquensita,** 1 Av. 21-31, Zona 1. (☎230 0067. 4hr., every hr. 6:30am-5pm, Q25.) Other frequent first-class service on: **Líneas Americas,** 2 Av. 18-74, Zona 1 (☎232 1432); and the less desirable **Galgos,** 7 Av. 19-44 (☎253 4868). 9 2nd-class buses depart from the Zona 4 Terminal daily 7am-4:15pm.

Rabinal: Dulce María, 9 Av., 19 Calle, Zona 1. (☎250 0082. 4½hr., every hr. 5am-5pm.)

Retalhuleu: All buses running to the Mexican border at Tecún Umán stop here. (4hr., Q25.)

Río Dulce: Take any Flores-bound bus. (5hr., Q40-90.)

Salamá: Take a Rabinal bus. (3½hr.)

Santa Cruz del Quiché: Zona 4 Terminal. (4hr., every 30min. 5am-6pm, Q13.)

Tecpán: Veloz Panquileña, Calle 20 and Av. Simón Bolívar. (2hr., every 15min. 3am-7pm, Q6.)

International Buses: Buses to **San Salvador, El Salvador,** leave on King Quality (☎369 0404) from 18 Av. 1-96 in Zona 15 (5hr., 2 per day 6:30am and 3:30pm, US$23). Comfort Lines, 1 Av. 15-71, Zona 10 (☎368 0138), makes the same trip (5hr., 2 per day 8am and 2pm, US$18). Tica Bus, 11 Calle 2-72 (☎331 4279), Zona 9 leaves at 12:30pm for **Panama City,** traveling through **San Salvador, Tegucigalpa, Managua,**

GUATEMALA

and **San José.** The entire trip takes 3 days and 2 nights. For **Tapachula, Mexico,** Galgos (☎253 4868) runs 2 buses daily; Tica Bus departs at noon. Border-bound buses: see information under **Domestic Buses.**

✈ ORIENTATION

UPON ARRIVAL. Both international and domestic flights arrive at **La Aurora International Airport,** in Zona 13. The posh hotels of Zona 10 are close, but the budget spots in Zona 1 require a bit more of a trek. Bus #83 departs from outside the terminal and runs to Zona 1. Though more expensive, a taxi (Q60) is an easier and safer way of getting to your hotel.

If arriving by **bus,** prepare for some confusion. Many second-class services arrive in the Zona 4 market area, referred to as the main bus terminal. Taxis are plentiful here; if you want to take a bus to Zona 1, walk to the corner of 2 Calle and 4 Av. Other second-class and all Pullman buses arrive at scattered locations throughout the city. Most of these are in Zona 1, within walking distance or a short taxi ride from downtown hotels. Terminal addresses are listed under **Transportation**(p. 334). Avoid arriving by bus at night; if you do, take a taxi from the terminal.

LAYOUT. Although Guate is overwhelmingly large, sights and services are concentrated in Zonas 1, 4, 9, 10, and 13. The major thoroughfare is 6 Av., beginning at the Plaza Mayor in the north and continuing south through Zonas 4 and 9. **Zona 1,** the city's oldest section and the true *centro,* houses budget hotels and restaurants. **Zona 4** lies immediately south of Zona 1. An industrial area, Zona 4 houses the INGUAT office and the second-class bus terminal and market area. **Zonas 9** and **10** house the boutiques, fancy restaurants, and five-star hotels. The two zones are divided by the north-south **Av. de la Reforma:** Zona 9 is to the west, and Zona 10 is to the east. *Avenidas* run parallel to Av. de la Reforma and the street numbers increase eastward. *Calles* run east-west and increase southward. The southern portion of Zona 10 is the **Zona Viva** (Lively Zone), home to the bulk of the city's most happening clubs. **Zona 13** is south of Zona 9. Its two notable features are the international airport and the **Parque La Aurora,** which contains museums, a market, and a zoo. Some possible causes for confusion: 1a Av. of Zona 1 is different from the 1a Av. of Zona 5. Also, some streets are nameless for a block, and some *calles* in Zona 1 have secondary names. Note that many streets, especially in Zona 1, do not have street signs, so it's best to ask for directions.

 STREET-SMART. Despite the apparent disorganization, Guate's addresses are logically arranged. For example, look for "8 Av. 12-65, Zona 1" at no. 65 on Avenida 8, located above 12 Calle (between 12 and 13 Calles), in Zona 1.

SAFETY. Personal safety is of definite concern in Guatemala City. Exploring the city on your own during the day is generally not a problem, but locals warn against wandering alone at night. Zonas 9 and 10 are less problematic than others. In particular, the streets of Zona 1 are not safe after dark; even the Peace Corps forbids its volunteers to stay overnight there. If you must, travel by taxi and *never* alone. Nighttime bar and restaurant hopping in Zona 10 is reasonably safe, provided you stick with the crowds. Pickpockets are ubiquitous, especially in Zona 1 and the Zona 4 bus terminal area. Always keep your money and valuables close to your body and distribute bills among multiple pockets so that you don't lose everything if you are robbed. Thigh or waist travel pouches are recommended.

⧉ LOCAL TRANSPORTATION

Local Buses: Guate's city bus system is extensive and relatively efficient, but it takes a while to get the hang of it. The nicer and slightly more expensive buses are called *preferenciales*, which are large and red (Q1.10 officially, but everybody pays Q1), while the 2nd-class option is to ride the *corrientes* (Q0.75). Buses run from 7am until about 8pm, though you'll find the occasional bus running later. Buses have destinations clearly marked on the front, but the best places to catch them in Zona 1 are 4 Av. or 10 Av. The latter is the place to go for the more useful buses. Bus **#82** travels from the city center to Zona 4 and down Av. la Reforma between Zonas 9 and 10. Returning, it goes north on Av. de la Reforma, through Zona 4, and up 9 Av. in Zona 1. Bus **#83** runs from 10 Av. in Zona 1 to the airport and the Zona 13 sights and returns to 9 Av. in Zona 1. Any bus marked "Terminal" will take you to the Zona 4 Terminal. Bus **#101** runs from Av. de Los Proceres in Zona 10 past the INGUAT office in Zona 4.

Car Rental: Prices start at around Q300 per day for a small car, including tax and insurance. At the big chains, these prices may jump to between US$70 and US$155 per day. **Tally,** 7 Av. 14-60 (☎232 0421), Zona 1 and at the airport (☎334 5925); **Avis,** 6a Av. 11-24 (☎332 7744), Zona 9 and at the airport (☎331 0017); **Hertz,** 7 Av. 14-76, Zona 9, and at the airport (☎332 2242 for both).

⧉ PRACTICAL INFORMATION

TOURIST AND FINANCIAL SERVICES

Tourist Information: Instituto Guatemalteco de Turismo (INGUAT), 7 Av. 1-17, (☎331 1333, toll-free 801-INGUAT, or 888-INGUAT in the USA; www.guatemala.travel.com.gt), Zona 4, in the Centro Cívico south of the Zona 1 border. Some of the staff speak English and tourist brochures are available. If you're interested in volcano climbs or adventure travel, ask the front desk to direct you to the "Sillón de Guías" in the same building. Open M-F 8am-4pm, Sa 8am-1pm. There is also a branch in the **post office** in Zona 1. Another good source of information for outdoors excursions is the **Federación de Andinismo,** 21 Calle 9-31, Zona 5, in the "Ciudad de Deportes" (Sports City).

Embassies and Consulates: Belize: Av. de la Reforma 1-50 #803 (☎334 5531) Zona 9, Edificio El Reformador. Open 9am-1pm and 2-5pm. **Canada:** Embassy, 13 Calle 8-44 (☎363 4348) Zona 10, Edyma Plaza Niv. 8. Open M-F 8am-4:30pm. Consulate, 6th fl. of the same building (☎333 6140). Open M, Th, F 9am-4:30pm. **US:** Embassy, Av. de la Reforma 7-01 (☎331 1541; emergency ☎332 3347) Zona 10. Open M-F 8am-5pm. **UK:** Av. de la Reforma 16-00 (☎367 5425) Zona 10, Torre Internacional, 11th fl. Open M-Th 8am-12:30pm and 1:30-5pm, F 8am-noon. Citizens of **Australia** and **New Zealand** can report lost passports here.

Immigration Office: 41 Calle 17-36, Zona 8. Catch bus #71 from 10 Av. Open M-F 8am-3pm.

Banks: Generally, smaller bank branches, especially in Zona 1, exchange only cash; head to the larger branches for cashing traveler's checks. AmEx is by far the most commonly accepted form of traveler's check; head to any branch of **Ban Café** to exchange them. **Banco Continental,** framed by 5 Av. and 9 Calle in Zona 9, will exchange Mastercard and Visa. **ATMs** are fairly common, as long as you have Visa access. You'll usually find them beside banks. **Banco Industrial** will do cash advances with Visa. All banks are closed Su, with the exception of **BanQuetzal** at the airport, which also exchanges some European currencies. Open M-F 6am-8pm, Sa-Su 6am-6pm. Banks cluster on and around the *parque central* in Zona 1.

American Express: 2 Calle 0-93 (☎331 7422) Zona 9, Centro Comercial Montufa #22. Open M-F 8am-noon and 2-5pm.

LOCAL SERVICES

English Bookstores: VRISA Bookshop, 15 Av. 3-64 (☎761 3237) Zona 1 . Small shop with a wide range of genres in both Spanish and English. M-Sa 9am-7pm.

Supermarkets: Paiz and **Super del Ahorro,** across from each other on 7 Av., 17 and 18 Calles, Zona 1. Both open daily 8am-9pm.

Laundromats: El Siglo, 9 Av. 13-09, Zona 1, or 7 Av. 3-50, Zona 4. In Zona 10 try **USA,** Av. La Reforma 8-15, Zona 10.

Crafts Market: Central Market, 8 and 9 Av., 6 and 8 Calles, Zona 1, in a massive underground garage. Open M-Sa 6am-6pm, Su 8am-noon.

EMERGENCY AND COMMUNICATIONS

Police: 6 Av. 13-71 (☎110 or 120) Zona 1. Bilingual staff available.

Ambulance: ☎128.

Fire: ☎122 or 123.

Red Cross: 3 Calle 8-40 (☎125 or 232 2026) Zona 1. 24hr. emergency service. Also located at 4 Av. 9-38 (☎362 5237) Zona 10.

Pharmacy: Farmacia El Ejecutivo, 7 Av. 15-01 (☎230 3734) Zona 1. **Farmacia Osco,** 4 Av., 16 Calle (☎337 1566) Zona 10. Both open 24hr.

Telephones: Telgua, main office at 7 Av., Calles 12/13 (☎238 1098). **Fax** service. Cash or collect calls only. Open M-F 8am-6pm, Sa 8am-1pm. With calling cards call from public phones on the street or from hotels. Many travelers report problems using MCI and Sprint prepaid phone cards, so be prepared to call the card's office collect; Telgua offices, stores, and pharmacies sell Telgua phone cards for use in phone booths.

Internet:

Café Carambola, 14 Calle 7-39 (☎220 8080) Zona 1, has super fast connections. Q8 per 30min. Open M-Su 8:30am-8:30pm.

Planet Web Café, Blvd. Liberación 6-31 (☎339 3627) Zona 9. Q6.50 per 30 min.

Web Station, 2 Av 14-63 (☎333 4740) Zona 10, has comfy captain's chairs. Q8 per 30min. (although you could sit there longer playing Starcraft or Diablo II on the big screen). Open 24hr.

Wizard's Café, (☎332-8469), in the Centro Comercial Los Proceres, 3rd fl.,is another web cafe always packed with people hunched around tables playing *Legend of the Five Rings* (similar to *Magic: The Gathering*).

Post Office: Central Post Office, 7 Av. 11-66, Zona 1, in the huge orange building. Open M-F 9am-5:30pm, Sa 9am-1pm. **United Parcel Service,** 12 Calle 5-53, Zona 10. Open M-Sa 8am-8pm. **DHL,** 7 Av. 2-42, Zona 9. Open M-F 8am-7:30pm, Sa 8am-1pm.

⌐ ACCOMMODATIONS

Almost all of Guate's budget hotels are located in Zona 1, the city's aging downtown area. Because robberies do occur here, prioritize safety when choosing a hotel: windows should be barred, balconies secure, locks functional, and management conscientious. Given nighttime safety concerns, a reservation or an early arrival might be a good idea. Female travelers or those traveling alone may feel more comfortable paying slightly more for the safer surroundings in Zona 9 or 10. All listed hotels have hot water showers, but these can be unreliable. If none of these pan out, inquire at the **Tourist Office** for other recommendations; make safety a top priority in your choice.

Guatemala City Center

♠ ACCOMMODATIONS
Dos Lunas Guesthouse, **23**
Hotel Ajau, **7**
Hotel Carillon, **14**
Hotel Centro América, **9**
Hotel Colonial, **4**
Hotel Mayastic, **13**
Hotel Monte Carlo, **8**
Hotel Spring, **3**

🍴 FOOD
Delicadezas San
   Hamburgo, **6**
Ni-Fu Ni-Fa, **16**
Restaurante Altuna, **2**
Restaurante y Cafetería
   Cantón, **5**
San Martín and Co., **17**
El Torito Mexicano, **15**

🍸 NIGHTLIFE
La Bodeguita del Centro, **1**
Kahlua, **22**
Pandora's Box, **10**

🏛 MUSEUMS
Museo del Arte Moderno, **19**
Museo de Hist. Natural, **21**
Museo del Niño, **20**
Museo Ixchel, **11**
Museo Nacional de
   Arqueología, **18**
Popul Vuh Museum, **12**

Abbreviations:
V.   Vía
R.   Ruta

GUATEMALA

ZONA 1

▓ **Hotel Spring,** 8 Av. 12-65 (☎230 2858). Set around an elegant Spanish courtyard, the roomy, well-lit accommodations give excellent bang for the buck. Call ahead for reservations. Singles Q160; doubles Q200. US dollars accepted. MC/V. ❺

Hotel Centro América, 9 Av. 16-38 (☎220 6371 or 220 6375). Despite sterile linoleum floors and walls in need of paint, Hotel Centro América maintains its lush courtyard. Rooms are on the small side, but are reasonably priced. Internet access Q15 per 30min. Singles Q50-90; doubles Q75-100; triples Q90-Q120, depending on season. ❸

Hotel Ajau, 8 Av. 15-62 (☎232 0488). Large, tidy rooms, plus the handy conveniences of safety boxes, a *Telefónica* phone, and Internet access right in the lobby. Singles Q50, with bath Q95; doubles Q70/Q105. ❹

Hotel Colonial, 7 Av. 14-19 (☎232 6722). Gorgeous mahogany furniture. Huge rooms. Speedy Internet access in the lobby. Pricey, but if you're looking for elegance for under US$30, look no further. Singles US$18, with bath US$26. ❺

Hotel Monte Carlo, 9 Av. 16-20. Although it lacks the ambience of other establishments, Hotel Monte Carlo provides well-kept rooms at inexpensive prices. Singles Q40, with bath Q60; doubles Q70/Q120. ❸

OTHER ZONAS

▓ **Hotel y Restaurante Los Próceres,** 18 Calle 14-79 (☎368-2828) Zona 10. Safe and convenient, Los Próceres is splurge-worthy for those two reasons alone. A crystal chandelier and a large floral arrangement greet entering guests. Also on the premises are a restaurant, laundry facility, and an extensive modern art collection. Rooms are well-furnished and clean. Singles US$32; doubles US$44; triples US$53. AmEx/MC/V. ❺

Hotel Mayastic, 5 Av. 11-23, (☎331 0824) Zona 9. Pricier, but close to Zona 10 nightlife. All 14 decent-sized rooms have clean private bath, hot water, and cable TV. Try to get a room low to the ground, as noise from the nearby airport is enough to rattle the third-floor windows. Singles Q150; doubles Q175; triples Q200. ❺

Hotel Carillon, next to Hotel Mayastic (☎332 4036), offers nicer surroundings at higher prices. Singles Q215; doubles Q250; triples Q280. Includes tax and full breakfast. ❺

Dos Lunas Guesthouse, 21 Calle 10-92, (☎/fax 334-5264; lorena@pronet.net.gt) Zona 13, Aurora II. A welcoming guest house with clean rooms and a friendly, English-speaking owner. Cable TV in the living room, Internet downstairs. Free rides to and from the airport; call upon arrival. US$10 per person, with bath US$15. ❹

◖ FOOD

Sidewalk vendors offer the cheapest grub that is best avoided by the faint of stomach, but the friendly neighborhood *comedor* is usually inexpensive. Full *típico* meals run Q10-20. There's also no dearth of American fast food joints.

Restaurante y Cafetería Cantón, 6 Av. 14-29, Zona 1. Unlike many Chinese restaurants in Guate, Cantón looks and tastes authentic. Sizeable portions, friendly service, and great Chinese art on the wall. The chicken with chile sauce is without equal (Q35). Open daily 9am-10pm. AmEx/MC/V. ❸

Restaurante Altuna, 5 Av. 12-31 (☎232 0669) Zona 1. In a beautifully restored colonial home, old-fashioned, upscale Altuna has a long-standing reputation as the nicest restaurant in downtown Guate. Excellent Spanish food, and some of the dishes aren't quite as pricey as the atmosphere might suggest. Paella Q47, desserts Q15-25. Open Tu-Sa noon-10pm, Su noon-4pm. Reservations recommended. AmEx/MC/V. ❹

San Martín and Company, 2 Av. and Calle 13, Zona 10. When strolling along the posh boulevard of the Zona Viva in the late evening, stop in here for a touch of Europe. Don't miss the latte (Q8.50) and the heavenly ice-cream pastry *totito San Martín* (Q14.50). ❷

Delicadezas San Hamburgo, 5 Calle 5-34, Zona 1. Part floral cafe, part 50s diner, this downtown restaurant offers good *típico* fare (chicken with curry sauce Q38) and will grill you up a burger (Q32 with fries). Open daily 6:30am-9:30pm. ❸

Ni-Fu Ni-Fa, 12 Calle 4-05, Zona 9. Take the #83 bus from any Parque Aurora sight toward the airport. In case you didn't get your fill of animals at the nearby Aurora Zoo, this Argentine steakhouse will take care of it. Sink your teeth into a *Delmonico* (Q95) or team up with a buddy and polish off an *Asado de Tira* for 2 (Q130). Vegetarian friends can sidle up to the salad bar (Q30) and the fettuccini with tomato sauce and mushrooms (Q54). Open M-Su 5:30am-10:30pm. AmEx/MC/V. ❺

El Torito Mexicano, 5 and 6 Av., 12 Calle, Zona 9. For quick, casual Mexican eats, head to this excellent Zona 9 restaurant. The burritos are delicious (Q20) and the *tortas* with beef, ham, cheese, or chicken are a steal at Q10-15. Open M-F 9am-7pm. ❷

◉ SIGHTS

ZONA 1

PLAZA MAYOR. The Plaza Mayor consists of two large plazas—**Parque de Centenario** and **Plaza de las Armas.** Filled with barkers and barterers, this strip of concrete has been called "the center of all Guatemala," and on Sundays it is easy to understand why, as *indígenas* from all regions pour in to sell their textiles or just take an afternoon stroll. Prices are reasonable and there is room for bargaining, though the best deals are sure to be found in smaller towns near Atitlán or in Xela. Except for a fountain in the Parque de Centenario, the plaza itself is fairly bland, but is surrounded by much more impressive architecture. (*Bounded on the west and east by 6 and 7 Av. and on the north and south by 6 and 8 Calle.*)

CATEDRAL METROPOLITANA. The stately Catedral Metropolitana, constructed between 1782 and 1868, rises dramatically against the plaza. Inside the neoclassical structure, cold stone floors, lofty arches and occasional bursts of ornate gold strike a powerful balance of austerity and awesomeness. (*East of the plaza. Open M-F 7am-12:15pm and 3-7pm, Sa 7am-12:30pm and 3-6:30pm, Su 6:30am-7:30pm. Sunday services 8, 10am, noon, 1, 4, 6pm. Other services M-Sa 7:30am and 12:15pm.*)

PALACIO NACIONAL. This grand palacio was built between 1928 and 1943 under the orders of President Jorge Ubico. Currently, the public is allowed to see but a few of the imposing palace's 350 rooms, but even the corridors are magnificent. La Sala de Recepción awes visitors with its massive Bohemian crystal chandelier, replete with graceful brass and gold quetzals. The Sala de Banquetes features another chandelier, this one of 18-karat gold. In 1980, a car bomb shattered the stained glass windows (which had depicted the 10 virtues of a good nation) and some have yet to be reconstructed. The Presidential Balcony offers commanding views of the Plaza Mayor and the surrounding hillsides. You can also view the palace's Guatemalan modern art collection, which features some interesting works. (*North of the plaza. Open daily 9am-11:45pm and 2-4:45pm. Free, tip expected for guided tours.*)

MIGUEL ANGEL ASTURIAS CULTURAL CENTER. The cultural center is located at the south end of Zona 1 in the Civic Center and houses the **National Theater,** along with a chamber theater and an open-air theater. Built in 1827 on top of an old military fortress and renovated in the 1970s, the complex has a beautiful view . There's also a small military museum and art gallery. *(24 Calle 3-81. ☎ 232 4041. Tours are free, and can last anywhere from 30min. to 3hr., depending on your level of interest—an hour is probably sufficient. Open M-F 9am-5pm; museum open 7am-4pm.)*

OTHER SIGHTS. Zona 1 holds some other beautiful churches in addition to the Metropolitana. **La Merced,** at 11 Av., 5 Calle, houses sculptures, woodcarvings, and mosaics, and is worth a visit. **Cerrito del Carmen**, 12 Av., 2 Calle, is less notable for its appearance than for being the oldest church in the valley (finished 1620). The **Iglesia de San Francisco,** 6 Av., 13 Calle, is famous for its carving of the sacred heart.

ZONA 4

IGLESIA YURRITA. Decked out in vermilion, this outlandish neo-Gothic curiosity was built in 1929. The color scheme inside the church, including an unusual window painted like the daytime sky, is nearly as blinding as the exterior. *(Ruta 6 and Vía 8. Open Tu-Su 7am-noon and 4-6pm.)*

TORRE DEL REFORMADOR. Check out this smaller (and considerably less polished) take on the Eiffel Tower, named in honor of forward-looking President Justo Rufino Barrios, who held office between 1871 and 1885. *(7 Av., 2 Calle.)*

ZONA 10

MUSEO IXCHEL DEL TRAJE INDÍGENA. This modern museum is a good introduction to the textile traditions of the Guatemalan highlands. The museum is on the campus of the Universidad Francisco Marroquín in a valley with well-landscaped picnic areas. The tranquil atmosphere here makes it a nice escape from the congested city center. *(Take 6 Calle Final east off Av. de la Reforma; the museum is located at the bottom of a large hill. ☎ 331 3622. Open M-F 9am-5pm, Sa 9am-12:50pm. Q20, students Q10.)*

JARDÍN BOTÁNICO. Over 700 species of plants labeled in Spanish and Latin. Perfect for a quiet picnic. *(1 Calle off Av. de la Reforma. ☎ 333 0904. Open M-F 8am-3pm. Free.)*

POPOL VUH MUSEUM. Named after the sacred Maya text, a cosmological epic, the museum has a large collection of pre-Columbian Maya pottery, as well as exhibits on colonial art and indigenous folklore. Admission includes a booklet in either English or Spanish. *(Next to the Museo Ixchel del Traje Indígena, at the University; follow directions above. ☎ 361 2301. Open M-F 9am-5pm, Sa 9am-1pm. Q20, students Q10.)*

ZONA 13

The sights of Zona 13 are clustered within the vast **Parque La Aurora,** near the airport. Four government-run museums are here, all right next to each other, as well as the zoo. The area can be reached by bus #83.

MUSEO DE LOS NIÑOS. This museum also features colonial architecture—of a lunar colony, that is. The space-age pyramids house myriad entertaining exhibits, which teach children about peace and morality through playing (they're also a whole lot of fun for adults). Bounce around the moon simulator, play a giant game of Operation, and ride a bicycle as a skeleton mirrors your motions. The huge Guatemalan flag and R2D2 Lego models are not to be missed. Note: the static electricity generator, the centrifugal force cycle, and the earthquake room might not be approved for use in other, more safety-conscious children's museums. *(Open Tu-Th 8am-noon and 1-5pm, F 8am-noon and 2-6pm, Sa-Su 10am-1:30pm and 2:30-5pm. Q35.)*

MUSEO NACIONAL DE ARQUEOLOGÍA Y ETNOLOGÍA. This museum traces eons of Maya history through hundreds of Maya artifacts and an excellent scale model of Tikal. Descriptions in Spanish only. *(Located in the park at the corner of 7 Av., 5 and 6 Calles, Edificio #5. ☎ 472 0489. Open Tu-F 9am-4pm, Sa-Su 9am-noon and 1:30-4pm. Q30.)*

MERCADO DE ARTESANÍAS. La Aurora also holds an INGUAT-sponsored craft market. Although it's not very cheap and you can't bargain very much, the traditional textiles, ceramics, and jewelry may make good last-minute gifts for the folks back home. *(Market open M-Sa 8:30am-6pm, Su 8am-2pm.)*

OTHER SIGHTS. Museo Nacional de Historia Natural features stuffed local fauna and a mineral collection. **Museo del Arte Moderno** has national art from the last couple of centuries. The layout is confusing, but it's worth seeing if you're in the area. Also entertaining is the small **Aurora Zoo,** a great place for some last-minute photos of "wild Guatemalan" elephants. *(Both museums are next to the Archaeology Museum. Both open Tu-F 9am-4pm, Sa-Su 9am-1pm and 2-4pm. Q10 for each museum. Aurora Zoo is next to the Mercado de Artesanías.)*

🎭 🎸 ENTERTAINMENT AND NIGHTLIFE

Although the city's frenetic pace tends to die down after dark, there are several options for evening entertainment. The capital is a good place to catch an American flick. Two convenient Zona 1 theaters are the **Capitol,** 6 Av., 12 Calle, and **Palace,** across the street. Theater and opera performances (all in Spanish) are staged at **Teatro IGA,** Ruta 1 4-05 (☎ 331 0022) Zona 4, on Friday and Saturday nights. For a listing of cultural events, check *La Prensa Libre* or any local newspapers.

The best places to shake your booty are in Zona Viva, Zona 10. The pace picks up around 10pm and winds down around 2am. The hottest club is currently **Kahlua,** 1 Av. 15-06, Zona 10, which comes complete with two dance floors, a chill-out room, and a dance/Latin pop music blend. (No cover.) **Sambuka** in the Zona Viva is also popular. If you're looking for a bar with incredible live music and room to dance, visit local haunt **Bodeguita del Centro,** 12 Calle 3-55, Zona 1.

Guate also has a **gay nightlife** scene, albeit a small one. The nightspots are mostly male; no specifically lesbian clubs or bars exist. The largest gay club in town is **Pandora's Box** at Via 3 and Ruta 3, Zona 4.

WESTERN HIGHLANDS

For most travelers, the Western Highlands are the reason they come to Guatemala. The scenery alone is attraction enough: rolling hillsides and forests meet rugged peaks, while breathtaking vistas abound at every turn. But even richer than this natural splendor is the region's amazing culture; the majority of Central America's indigenous population lives here. Dialects of Mam, Ixil, and Cakchiquel echo in the vibrant markets, and men stand outside churches swinging coffee-can censers filled with smoldering resin while chanting the cycles of the Maya calendar.

Everyone visits the graceful colonial splendor of Antigua. The unsurpassed beauty of Lago de Atitlán is ringed by traditional Maya villages, while the colorful Maya market of Chichicastenango is one of the country's most famous sights. Quetzaltenango, Guatemala's 2nd-largest city, has increasingly popular language schools and easy access to hot springs and Maya markets. Two beautiful mountain towns offer a more serene highlands atmosphere: traditional Todos Santos, in the Cuchumatanes, and Nebaj, superbly situated in northern Quiché.

ANTIGUA

Antigua is one of Guatemala's most popular tourist destinations, and it's easy to see why. Picture-perfect cobblestone streets lead to grand colonial ruins, and the supremely civilized central plaza stands in striking contrast to the rugged green mountains nearby. Antigua was the third colonial capital of Guatemala and served as such from 1541 until 1773, when massive earthquakes prompted the government to flee to Guatemala City. At its height, Antigua was the capital of all of Central America. More recently, the colonial legacy and appealing locale have brought new residents—and lots and lots of travelers. Restaurants and hotels catering to them have cropped up everywhere, lending the city a cosmopolitan, if touristy, air. However, upholding Antigua's romantic facade is the true heart of Guatemalan culture: the breadth and diversity of the indigenous communities. As the main gateway to the western highlands, or *altiplano*, Antigua bears witness to the interplay between Latino and *indígena* lifestyles. Soak in the charm and enjoy the creature comforts that the city has to offer, but remember that Antigua is merely the first step in exploring a country whose beauty goes beyond the rows of tourist restaurants and gringo-filled bars.

▐▌ TRANSPORTATION

Buses: Leaving town, all services except the direct bus to Panajachel leave from the main terminal west of the *parque central*. Heading to Antigua from many western highland locales, it's often best to take a bus to **Chimaltenango** and then change there (last bus to Antigua at 6pm). Departures to: **Chimaltemango** (50min., every hr. 7am-6pm, Q2.5); **Escuintla** (1½ hr., 6 per day 6:45am-4pm, Q5); **Guatemala City** (1hr., every 15min. 5:30am-6:30pm, Q4.5); **Panajachel** from the Texaco gas station on 4 Calle Pte (2½hr., 1 first-class bus daily 7am, Q30), or go via **Chimaltenango** and change buses there (1½hr., Q10); **San Antonio Aguas Calientes** (25min.; every 30min. 7am-8pm, more frequent on Antigua market days M, Th, and Sa; Q2). For other Western Highland towns such as **Quetzaltenango** and **Chichicastenango,** take a bus to Chimaltenango and change there.

Tourist Shuttles: Available to other popular cities. Virtually any travel agent will arrange a shuttle. (For a list of recommended agencies, see **Practical Information,** below.) The shuttles are quicker and more comfortable, and more expensive than the public buses. The most frequent service is to the **airport** and **Guatemala City** (US$7-10), **Panajachel** (US$10), and on market days, (Th, Sa and Su) **Chichicastenango** (US$12). You can also arrange trips to more far-flung destinations including Río Dulce, Tikal, Monterrico, and Copán, Honduras. Most will pick you up at your hotel.

Car Rental: Ahorrent Car Rental, 5 Calle Ote. No. 113 (☎832 0968). Open daily 7am-7pm. Required deposit Q770, plus copy of passport. Cars Q250 per day. **Tabarini,** 6 Av. Sur 22 (☎832 8107). Open M-Sa 8am-1pm and 3-6pm. Variety of sedans, SUVs, and vans offered, new models only. Q460-1200 per day.

Motorcycle Rental: La Ceiba, 6 Calle Pte. 15 (☎832 0077). Q300 per day.

▐▌ ORIENTATION AND PRACTICAL INFORMATION

Antigua's streets are laid out according to the standard grid system (see p. 333). Its centerpiece is the **parque central,** bounded by 4/5 Calle on the north and south and by 4/5 Av. on the east and west. From the northeast corner of the *parque,* all *avenidas* to the north are designated **Norte** (Nte.), and all to the south are designated **Sur.** All *calles* to the east are dubbed **Oriente** (Ote.), and all to the west **Poniente** (Pte.). Segments of some of the streets have been unhelpfully reverted to their colonial names, although most businesses and residents still refer to the numbered *calle* or *avenida*. The **bus terminal** is located at the *mercado,* three

Western Highlands

MEXICO

PACIFIC OCEAN

GUATEMALA

lengthy blocks west of the *parque central*. To reach the *parque* from the bus terminal, cross the tree-lined street, Alameda Santa Lucía, and continue straight. **Volcán de Agua** looms over the city to the south. Although INGUAT-authorized "guides" roam the bus terminal, avoid the temptation to follow them to a hotel or anywhere else. While they are authorized as guides, many take tourists to travel agencies or hotels that are not authorized and often charge exorbitant rates.

TOURIST AND FINANCIAL SERVICES

Tourist Information: INGUAT (☎/fax 832 0763), on the southeast corner of the *parque*, near the cathedral, is a good first stop in town. Bilingual staff. Open M-F 8am-5pm, Sa-Su 9am-5pm. Sometimes closed noon-1pm.

Travel Agencies and Guided Tours: Local travel agents are useful for booking flights, shuttles, package deals, and (generally pricey) tours, but not all agencies in Antigua offer high-quality service. Package deals to Tikal run in the US$150 range. Always verify that the agency is approved by INGUAT and check with other travelers to see if they have had good experiences. The following are recommended: **Adventure Travel Center Viareal,** 5 Av. Nte. 25B (☎832 2928; viareal@guate.net); **Turansa,** (☎832 4703; info@turansa.com) in the Radisson Hotel at 9 Calle south of town; **Vision,** 3 Av. Nte. 3 (☎832 3293; vision@guatemalainfo.com); **Rainbow Travel Center,** 7 Av. Sur 8 (☎832 4202; myers@gua.gbm.net); and **Gran Jaguar Tours,** 4 Calle Pte. 30 (☎832 2712). Sergio García at **Eco-Tour Chejo's,** 3 Calle Pte. 24 (☎832 5464), is one of the most experienced volcano guides in town.

Banks: Banks near the *parque* have 24hr. **ATMs. BanQuetzal,** on the north side of the *parque*, exchanges traveler's checks. Open M-F 8:30am-7pm, Sa-Su 9am-1pm. **Currency exchange** closes 1 hr. before the bank closes. Note that every other Saturday is payday, so lines of check-cashing locals can be around the block.

LOCAL SERVICES

English Bookstores: The Rainbow Reading Room, 7 Av. Sur 8, has books for sale and rent. Trade in books and earn credit for new ones. Also has a pleasant cafe with several vegetarian options (Q28 each). Open daily 8am-10pm; cafe open M-F noon-2pm. **Hamlin and White,** 4 Calle Oriente, #12-A, inside Jades S.A., carries many current English magazines, as well as some NYT Bestsellers and used books. from the Texaco gas station on 4 Calle Pte. Open daily 9am-6:30pm. **Casa de Conde,** on the west side of the plaza, offers a fine selection of books about the region, as well as mystery thrillers, fiction, history, and travel literature in both paperback and hardcover.

Markets: Main market, on Alameda de Sta. Lucía next to the bus terminal, extending from 1 Calle Pte. to 4 Calle Pte. Open daily roughly 7am-6pm. **Mercado de Artesanías,** across the street, runs up and winds along 4 Calle Pte. up to the Parque Central. US$ accepted. Open daily 8am-5:30pm. M, Th, Sa are the largest market days.

Supermarket: La Bodegona, 4 Calle Pte. 27, half a block from the bus terminal. Enter through the gas station. Open M-F 7:30am-8:30pm, Sa 8am-8pm, Su 8am-7:30pm.

Laundry: Central Laundry, 5 Calle Pte. 7-B. Open M-Sa 8am-7pm. Q5 per lb., students Q4 per lb.

EMERGENCY AND COMMUNICATION

Fire and Medical: Los Bomberos Voluntarios (☎832 0234), on the north side of the bus station. 24hr. ambulance service.

Police: Policía Nacional (☎832 0251, 832 2264, or 832 2266, emergency 122 or 123), on the south side of the *parque central* in the Palacio de los Capitanes Generales. 24hr. emergency service. **Tourist Police,** 4 Av. Nte. (☎832 7290), half a block

Antigua

🏠 ACCOMMODATIONS
Backpacker's Guesthouse, **4**
Hotel Casa de Leon, **6**
Hotel Cristal, **1**
Hotel la Casa de Don
  Ismael, **10**
Posada Ruíz #2, **5**
La Sin Ventura, **21**
La Tatuana, **17**

🍴 FOOD
Café Condesa, **15**
Café Flor, **18**
Café La Escudilla, **8**
Casa de las Mixtas, **11**
Comedor Típico
  Antigüeño, **16**
Doña Luisa's, **14**

🎵 NIGHTLIFE
Casa El Escudo, **8**
La Casbah, **3**
La Chimenea, **7**
Mono Loco, **20**

🏛 MUSEUMS
Casa K'ojom, **9**
Casa del Tejido Antiguo, **2**
Museo de Arte Colonial, **19**
Museo del Libro Antiguo, **13**
Museo de Santiago, **12**

north of the *parque's* northeast corner. Open 24hr. English spoken. The tourist police will be happy to orient you. Contact the Policía Nacional in an emergency.

Pharmacy: Farmacia Roca, 4 Calle Pte. 11B (☎832 0612). There is a rotating schedule for 24hr. pharmacies; all post the *farmacia de turno* (pharmacy on call) on their door.

Hospital: Centro Médico Antigua, Calle del Manchén No. 7 (☎832 0884). Office open M-F 8am-5pm, Sa 8am-noon. Emergency service 24hr.

Telephones: The often crowded **Telgua,** on 5 Av. Sur 2 (☎832 0498), just south of the southwest corner of the *parque.* Open M-F 8am-5:45pm, Sa 9am-1pm.

Internet: Cyber cafes are all over town. **Conexion,** 4a Calle Oriente, #14, in La Fuente, delivers basic service (Q5 per 30min., Q2.50 per additional 15min.), as well as premium service with larger monitors (Q8 per 30min.). Open daily 8:30am-7pm. **Funky Monkey,** 5 Av Sur 6, inside the small complex of shops, makes going cyber cool with Q3 per 15min. Internet access, Brazilian jazz, and electronica. Open daily 8am-10pm.

Post Office: On the corner of Alameda de Santa Lucía and 4 Calle Pte. Open M-F 8am-6:30pm. **DHL** on the corner of 6 Av. Sur, 16 Calle Pte. (☎832 3718). Open M-F 8am-6pm, Sa 8am-noon.

IN RECENT NEWS

"DO YOU WANT GUARDS WITH THAT?"

I was walking down the street in Antigua one day, past yet another uniformed man with a 12-gauge shotgun, standing outside McDonalds. I did a doubletake. An armed guard outside McDonalds? Who was he guarding against, the Hamburgler? Are the Golden Arches really that valuable?

It is hardly exceptional to see an armed guard in places like Antigua and Guatemala City. They're everywhere: outside hotels, insurance agencies, and hardware stores .

My experience with guards goes beyond simply walking by them every block and hoping one doesn't sneeze and discharge his AK-47 and turn me into hamburger. After my laptop was stolen from my hotel room in Antigua, the Policía Nacional Civil gave me three armed undercover bodyguards to accompany me through the mean cobblestone streets. While it was downright hilarious looking behind me and seeing the tall guard looking completely out of place in the cowboy hat and boots they had given him as "street clothes", his short partner with the gold tooth by his side, I couldn't help feeling a little guilty. Was I actually in any danger? I had been robbed, after all, not assaulted. These situations reveal a misconception of what it means to promote safety, an easily made pitfall with possibly disastrous consequences.

ACCOMMODATIONS

From every crack in Antigua's cobblestones sprouts a budget hotel. Many families also provide homestays (usually for language school students) for about US$50 per week. For more info, contact one of the local language schools or INGUAT.

La Tatuana, 7 Av. Sur 3 (☎832 1223). Huge bedrooms, spotless bathrooms, cyprus doors and signature celeste furniture make this hotel one of the best picks of Antigua. Singles US$13; doubles US$22; quads US$35. ❺

La Sin Ventura, 5 Av 8 (☎832 0581). Three words: location, location, location. And quality. Four words. Half a block from the *parque* and next to a movie theater (see **Cinema Bistro** below) and a nighttime hot spot (see **Mono Loco** below), the high cost of the quetzal promises quality and quiet. The rooms are clean and comfortable, the bathrooms immaculate. Reservations recommended. Singles Q164; doubles Q287. 25% discount with ISIC. ❺

Hotel Cristal, Av. El Desengaño Nte. 25 (☎832 4177). A small, friendly hotel that's a long walk from the *parque central* but only 1½ blocks from the nice and under-used Plaza San Sebastián. Though it's not the cheapest option in town, you get what you pay for—gorgeous rooms, spotless surroundings, and free luggage storage. Reservations recommended. Singles Q75, with bath Q85; doubles Q90/Q110. ❹

Posada Ruíz #2, 2 Calle Pte. 25. Look for the rocky arched doorway. Bare-bones rooms are cheap and popular. Despite the communal bath and lack of colonial charm, this social *posada* is a great place to meet fellow travelers. Laundry machine available, though *lavanderías* are cheaper. Singles Q25; doubles Q35; triples Q50; quads Q60. ❶

Hotel La Casa de Don Ismael, 3 Calle Pte. 5, (☎832 1932; hdonismael@hotmail.com). Set back from the street in the 2nd small alley on your right if walking from Alameda Santa Lucía, set around a lush patio with an open terrace. Friendly staff. Free purified water, coffee, and towels. Singles Q60; doubles Q80. ❹

Backpacker's Guesthouse, 1 Calle Pte. 39 (☎832 0520). Clean rooms around a shady garden. No private baths, but a good bargain bet. Q35 per person. ❷

Hotel Casa de Leon, 7 Av. Nte 34 (☎832 4413). The friendly *dueña* here has outfitted her pleasant, plant-filled hotel with thoughtful touches. However, some rooms are less pleasant than others; check out a few. Singles Q45; doubles Q65, with bath Q85. ❷

FOOD

Dining in Antigua runs the gamut from the experimental, cosmopolitan gourmet to cheap *comedores* cuisine. No matter what your taste is, good food is easy to find: there are even more student cafes in Antigua than there are ruined churches.

Doña Luisa's, 4 Calle Ote. 12, on 2nd fl. of a 17th-century house. The basic menu is well-executed. *Huevos rancheros* Q15. Sandwiches Q20. Great homebaked desserts Q4. Open daily 7am-9:30pm. Accepts travelers checks and AmEx/MC/V. ❷

Café Condesa, on the west side of the plaza. Don't let the gringo-filled room, headset-wearing staff, or steep prices dissuade you from truly great food. Built in 1549, the building comes with a bloody legend: as rumor has it, one count returned from his travels to find his wife with the butler. He had the butler buried alive: now you too can trace the place's history through its sandwiches. Try the "Count" (beef on wheat, Q30), or the "Countess" (emmenthal and gouda on wheat with avocado dressing, Q42), and don't miss the "Butler's Revenge" (brownie with ice cream, chocolate sauce, whipped cream, and almonds, Q29). Open daily 8am-10pm. Brunch buffet Su noon-2pm. ❸

Casa de las Mixtas, 3 Calle Pte. and 7 Av. Norte. Tucked into the 1st alley off 3 Calle (coming from Calle Santa Lucía) on the right, this small, sunny *comedor* offers excellent food and generous portions. Breakfast and lunch for under Q20, try the pancake combo (includes eggs, toast, and coffee or tea, Q12). Open M-Sa 8:30am-7:30pm. ❷

Café La Escudilla, 4 Av. Nte. 4, in the Casa El Escudo (see **Nightlife,** below), a beautiful colonial house ½ block north of the northeast corner of the *parque.* Popular and cheap, the setting is leisurely with fast service. Fruit salad Q5. Rich pastas Q20. Open daily 7am-midnight. Bar open M-Sa until 1am, Su until 8pm. ❷

Café Flor, 4 Av. Sur 1, ½ block south of the southeast corner of the *parque.* Highly recommended by locals for its outstanding Asian food, suave ambience, and great service. Thai curry Q35. Vietnamese spring rolls Q23. Open M-Sa noon-3pm and 6-10pm. ❸

Comedor Típico Antigüeño, Calle Santa Lucía Sur 3, 10m to the left of the post office, if standing at the bus station facing *Correos.* Popular with locals at lunchtime, this basic *comedor* combines fast service and good food with prices that are tough to beat. Numerous lunch combos under Q15. Open daily 7am-9pm. ❷

In 1983, the government of army general **Efraín Ríos Montt** created a "security" force, the Patrulleros de Autodefensa Civil, or **PAC,** to spearhead the counterinsurgency effort. They brought "security" to the countryside by abusing, displacing, and murdering thousands of Mayans and razing their homes. On June 18, 2002, six years after the peace accords were signed, more than 20,000 ex-PACs began a three-day blockade of roads, an airport, and an oil refinery in the Petén region and demanded Q20,000 (US$2,500) each for their services during the war. Between 600 and 1000 tourists were trapped in the region. The economic effects of the demonstration crippled commerce and transportation, interrupted petroleum distribution, and dealt a blow to the region's tourism industry. The crisis ended on June 20, when the presidential commission assigned to the case agreed to meet with President Portillo to seek solutions "within the bounds of the law."

What will happen? As it stands, the government is having trouble completing the installation of a water system in Chichicastenango, much less fund an increase in veterans' benefits. If General Ríos Montt wanted security in 1983, he could have created a public works system and built a system. If McDonald's desires the good of the country, it could start serving vegetarian cuisine, and take guards off the menu.

—Josiah Pertz

🜨 SIGHTS

Although all of the following are worth visiting, perhaps Antigua's greatest "sight" is not just one location, but rather the combined effect of the colonial ruins and the multicolored buildings that line the city's rambling cobblestone streets.

THE PARQUE CENTRAL AREA

PARQUE CENTRAL. The *parque*, one of the finest in the Americas, is centered around a 250 year-old fountain, **La Llamada de las Sirenas (The Sirens' Call),** whose stony babes enthrall visitors with their leaky breasts. Locals, students, and tourists dot the *parque*'s benches as *indígenas* sell their handicrafts and wares.

CATEDRAL SAN JOSÉ. Standing to the east of the *parque*, the cathedral is a mere shadow of its colonial self. Once spectacular, the awesome edifice was leveled by an earthquake in 1773. The two restored chapels along with the ruins are collectively known as the **Church of San José.** The interior is unimpressive but holds a carving of Christ by Quirio Cataño, who also carved the famed Cristo Negro of Esquipulas. The ruins of the rest of the cathedral can be entered from 5 Calle Ote. *(Ruins open daily 9am-5pm. Q3. Church open 9am-noon and 3-6pm. Free.)*

PALACIO DEL NOBLE AYUNTAMIENTO. The *palacio*'s meter-thick walls, built in 1743 on the north side of the *parque*, were some of the few to survive the earthquakes of 1773 and 1776. Once a jail, the building now houses two museums. The small **Museo de Santiago** exhibits pottery, Mayan and Spanish weapons, and colonial paintings. The **Museo del Libro Antiguo** (Old Book Museum) displays a reproduction of the first printing press in Central America, brought in 1660, an 18th-century lexicon of Guatemala's indigenous languages, a 1615 copy of *Don Quixote*, and a gigantic manuscript of Gregorian music. *(Santiago and Libro Antiguo both open Tu-F 9am-4pm, Sa-Su 9am-noon and 2-4pm. Each Q10; Museo del Libro Antiguo free Su.)*

NORTH OF THE PARQUE

🜨 **CONVENTO DE LAS CAPUCHINAS.** The impressive and very well-preserved ruins of the convent of Las Capuchinas are definitely worth a visit. Founded in 1726 by the Capuchín nuns, the remains paint a picture of the 18th-century nuns' harsh lives. Two of the residential cells have been restored; visitors can tour the underground cellar and cloister areas. *(Northeast of the main plaza, at the corner of 2 Calle Ote. and 2 Av. Nte. Open daily 9am-5pm. Q10.)*

IGLESIA LA MERCED. One of Antigua's most memorable churches, La Merced was originally built in 1548 and survived the 1760 earthquake only to collapse in another quake 13 years later. The wonderfully restored yellow facade offers the best example of Antigua's Baroque style. Left of the entrance is the doorway to the ruined cloisters and gardens. *(Ruins open daily 8am-6pm. Q2. Church open 9am-noon and 3-8pm. Services M-Sa 5, 8am, 5, 6, 7pm; Su 5, 9, 11am, 7pm. Free.)*

CERRO DE LA CRUZ. A 15min. walk northeast of town, this hill has a fine view of the valley. Muggings have been common here, though the presence of the tourist police has improved matters; check with them before you go.

SOUTHEAST OF THE PARQUE

MUSEO DE ARTE COLONIAL. The museum building, former home of the University of San Carlos, founded in 1676 as the 3rd university in all of Latin America, is among the finest of colonial Antigua's architectural survivors. Cast your eyes heavenward to see the graceful *mudéjar* arches of the central patio or the colonial ceilings of its large gallery. (*½ block east of parque central on 5 Calle Ote. Open Tu-F 9am-4pm, Sa-Su 9am-noon and 2-4pm. Q25.*)

CASA POPENOE. This beautifully restored colonial mansion gives an excellent sense of the lives of the wealthy during Antigua's glory days. Although it's only open two hours a day the *casa's* beautiful restoration and good rooftop views are worth an hour visit. (*Corner of 5 Calle Ote. and 1 Av. Sur. Open M-Sa 2-4pm. Q10.*)

SANTA CLARA AND SAN FRANCISCO CHURCHES. At the end of a palm-lined plaza stand the church and convent of **Santa Clara.** The original building on the site was destroyed in 1717, but the 1773 surviving version is fairly well-preserved with an elaborate facade. Nearby is **San Francisco,** one of Antigua's oldest churches— built in 1579 and still in use today. The ruins of the monastery next door, which include a plaza and multiple arched doorways amongst rolling hills, are a pleasant haven. (*Santa Clara at 6 Calle Ote. and 2 Av. Sur. San Francisco at 1 Av. Sur and 7 Calle Ote. Church open daily 9am-5pm. Ruins open daily 9am-5pm. Q2.*)

WEST OF THE PARQUE

LA RECOLECCIÓN. One of Antigua's most impressive ruins, this church—once among Antigua's finest—was built between 1701 and 1708 and opened in 1717. It suffered considerable damage in an earthquake soon thereafter, and the 1773 quake was the nail in the coffin for this grand structure. In recent past this has been the site of muggings; check with the tourist office for the latest safety information. (*Calle de la Recolección. Open daily 9am-5pm. Q10.*)

MAYA MUSEUMS. Two museums west of the Plaza are tributes to the great Maya culture that thrived in Guatemala before the Spanish showed up. **Casa K'ojom** is a wonderful museum dedicated to the traditions of *indígena* music and dance. (*About a 20min. walk from the Parque Central, just past the outskirts of town. Check with the tourist office for directions and a map.*) The **Casa del Tejido Antiguo,** on the northern edge of the market/bus terminal, is small but contains some nice examples of Maya weavings from the early 20th century. (*1 Calle Pte. 51, ½ block past San Jerónimo on the left. Open M-Sa 9:15am-5:15pm. Suggested donation Q5.*)

🎭 🎵 NIGHTLIFE AND ENTERTAINMENT

You'll have no trouble running into other travelers in Antigua's bar-dominated nightlife scene. For info on special events, check bulletin boards or the English-language *Revue* (available in the tourist office). Antigua's empty nighttime streets have had some muggings; go out in a group and take precautions. Bars in Antigua close at 1am due to a law which forbids the sale of alcohol after that hour.

■ **Casa El Escudo,** 4 Av. Nte. 4, is Antigua's most popular nightspot, always packed with language school students, travelers, and locals. Besides a restaurant (see above), there are 3 bars: the lively, jazz-filled **Riki's Bar,** the low-key **Paris,** and the new Greek section **Helas.** Riki's has a happy hour 7-10pm with 2 drinks Q7.

La Casbah, 5 Av. Nte. 30. Step through the Arabic double doors into a smoky, candle-lit club with a subterranean feel. The place oozes mystery and intrigue. Beers and screwdrivers Q15. Cover F-Sa Q30, includes 1 drink. Open W-Sa 7pm-1am.

Mono Loco, 5 Av. Sur 6, #5, inside the small complex of shops. *The* place to watch gringo boys try to pick up gringa girls. The crowd gathers on the ground floor, but don't miss the upstairs terrace where you can take in some moon rays. You can also watch

FROM THE ROAD

IN DEFENSE OF THE CHICKEN BUS

As I write this, I'm traveling from Antigua to Panajachel along the old Interamerican highway—the new one is closed for some reason—in a tourist minibus. Now we're passing through Patricia, I'll give a quick play-by-play: swerve, miss the bus, swerve, miss the horse, break for the hairless dog, honk at the tractor-trailer backing into our lane. Now out of town, into the mountains. Zig-zagging, spiraling up and down a two-way one-lane road with a sheer cliff to the left at speeds I'm afraid to guess at. A road crew cuts off half the lane. We speed up.

Now, while closing my eyes might seem like the best way to keep from going bonkers, it would keep me from some of the best views in Guatemala. I'd miss the prickly pine groves of Par-ramos, the *campesinos* in the fields outside of San Andrés, the deep and winding valley of Los Chocoyos that we just came way too close to falling into. The best way to catch all of this and not have repeated heart attacks, I've concluded, is to give up riding shotgun on the tourist minibus and hop on an intercity *camioneta*, affectionately known as the chicken bus.

Often maligned by official government publications and pricey tourist agencies for their questionable safety records, chicken buses have a bum rap. Besides being cheap, they have several other advantages. First—and this gets to the root of my problem—when you're sitting by the window in the middle of the back of the

sports on TV or play darts. Burgers Q20-25. Beer Q8-12.

La Chimenea, 7a Av. Nte. 18. A lively Latin *discoteca*. Cover Q20.

Local cinemas are popular; they're mostly rooms with big-screen TVs (Q10). Check schedules at Doña Luisa or El Escudo, as shows are sporadic. Try **Cinemaya**, the Ground Zero Café, 6 Calle Pte. 7 (Dinner and movie Q32); **Cinema Bistro**, 5 Av. Sur 14 (☎832 5530); **Cinema Tecún Umán**, 6 Calle Pte. 34A (☎832 2792); and **Cinematura**, 5 Av. Nte 8 (☎832 5530). All show international flicks.

🏃 OUTDOOR ACTIVITIES

Rolando Pérez (☎832 7988) offers **horse rentals** with trail rides through the mountains. A 3hr. tour of four pueblos, accompanied by a guide, costs US$33. **La Ronda** (☎832 0857), recommended by INGUAT, also offers horse rentals. **Mayan Bike Tours**, 1 Av. Sur 15 (☎/fax 832 3383), is run by Beat, a skilled pro who gives guided **bike tours**. (2½hr.. US$15). You can also **rent a bike** for solo spins for Q12 per hour. (Open daily 8:30am-7:30pm.)

NEAR ANTIGUA

NEARBY TOWNS

Just 5.5km southwest of Antigua, **Ciudad Vieja** was Guatemala's 2nd colonial capital, but has little to show for it. However, the beautiful church is one of the oldest in Central America (1534). Five kilometers south of Antigua is **San Juan del Obispo**, with a nice view of the valley and the palace of Francisco Marroquín, the first bishop of Guatemala. **San Antonio Aguas Calientes,** a pleasant *pueblo* 8km northwest of Ciudad Vieja, is noted for weaving. A new workshop adjacent to the town plaza allows visitors to observe locals at work. Don't miss the **Valhalla Macadamia Nut Farm** on the way to San Migual (ask the bus driver to let you off at the farm). The farm is an organic, sustainable, micro-enterprise reforestation project and a small working macadamia plantation that serves up macadamia nut pancakes for breakfast. (Buses to these towns depart from the terminal between 7am and 5 or 6pm. There is more frequent service on Antigua's market days: M, Th, Sa. Q50.)

SANTA MARÍA DE JESÚS AND VOLCÁN DE AGUA

The lovely *indígena* town of Santa María de Jesús, 30min. by bus from Antigua, has a beautiful view over the valley. The trail to Volcán de Agua, by far the easiest of Guatemala's big volcanoes to climb, begins in town (4hr. uphill, 3hr. down). To reach the trailhead from the plaza in Santa María, follow the street opposite the church and walk uphill for approximately three or four blocks. Before the next church (at the end of the hill) go right and then your 1st left. No guides are available at the base of the volcano; it is best to arrange a guide in Antigua.

There are several **buses** per day between Antigua and **Santa María de Jesús,** with more frequent service on Antigua market days; to be on the safe side, catch a bus back no later than 5pm.

VOLCÁN PACAYA

Visitors to Volcán Pacaya (2552m) come face to face with one of the world's most active volcanoes. The peak, with sulfurous fumes, pockets of hot lava, and barren plains, is otherworldly, and on the way up the vistas are magnificent. The glowing lava of Pacaya is most spectacular at night and when it's more active.

Pacaya is closer to Guatemala City than Antigua—and if you want to travel there independently there are good buses from Guate. However, most people visit on a guided tour from Antigua, since it's easier. Crime against tourists on the mountain has been a problem, but due to police patrols incidents are now relatively rare; check on the latest situation. The trail can be challenging; get a guide.

⬛ TRANSPORTATION. Guided **tours** from Antigua typically leave around 1pm and return at 10pm. Security officers and guides are supplied, but bring your own water, snacks, warm clothes, and a flashlight. (US$5-15 per person. Q45 entrance fee to the national park.) Two guided companies are Eco-Tour Chejos and Gran Jaguar Tours. (For contact information see **Antigua Practical Information,** above.) Also, Eco-Tour Chejos sells two different packages: one for US$5 and the other for US$10. Although they claim to provide more security and a more flexible time schedule for the extra money, there is little noticeable difference.

From Guatemala City take a **bus** from the Zona 4 terminal to **San Vicente de Pacaya** (7am and 3:30pm), and then walk to **San Francisco** (1½hr.), the starting point for the trail. It is recommended that you walk in groups for safety reasons. You can arrange for guides in either town; your best bet is to ask for a guide upon arrival in San Francisco. The hike begins at an

chicken bus, you'll always be looking out at the green, green valley below, and never at the front of the bus, watching it head straight for the gorge. (If you do end up near the front, no matter how tempted you are to look out the windshield, don't do it.)

Second, chicken buses rarely feel the need to pass. They know they need to meander slowly down the mountain, and aren't trying to impress their few gringo passengers or their boss with how fast they can get from point A to the Afterlife.

Thirdly, you might actually get on a bus with not only chickens, but pigs, turkeys, and other domesticated animals. As I've always said, there's nothing like watching a scared *cerdo* (pig) slide squealing under the rows of seats as the bus slams on its breaks to make one appreciate life.

Lastly, everyone else around you in the bus has taken this trip a million times before, and will remain completely calm. This is unbelievably helpful.

Furthermore, they are much less likely to be stopped by fortune-seeking paramilitaries in the Petén.

So, take it from me, one who spends his summers on the road: watch the *valle* and not the *calle*, and take the chicken bus.

Oh, and bring something to write on—it helps.

—Josiah Pertz

office at the entrance to the national park. It is possible to find a place for the night by asking around; check before starting out.

🔲 **THE TRAIL TO PACAYA.** From San Francisco, the trail winds through fields and forests, and views quickly improve. About 30min. into the climb, you'll arrive at a gorgeous viewpoint with views of Guatemala City. After 1½hr., the trail emerges onto a windy ridge of volcanic rock. A few feet away, at the edge of a massive bowl of cooling lava, Pacaya's starkly beautiful cone looms above. The trail continues around the rim of the crater, and then it's a challenging 30min. scramble to the summit over loose volcanic rocks. The trek back down is equally exhilarating, as you jump and slide down the steep slope back to the base.

TECPÁN AND IXIMCHÉ

Just off the Interamerican Hwy., about 1½hr. from Guatemala City, the dusty town of Tecpán was the Spanish military headquarters during the Conquest, but today has little to offer. The nearby Maya ruins of Iximché are worth a visit: the pre-Conquest capital of the Cakchiquel people has several plazas, a palace, and two ballcourts. A few ruins have been fully excavated, while others remain covered in overgrowth. A Maya religious ceremony is sometimes conducted at the ruins. (Open to the public; no fixed schedule, just ask around in Tecpán.)

To get to Tecpán, take any **bus** running along the Interamerican Hwy. between Chimaltenango and Los Encuentros and ask to be dropped off there. From Guatemala City, Antigua, or Chimaltenango, any bus to Sololá, Panajachel, or Quetzaltenango heads past Tecpán. Coming from any of those destinations (or Los Encuentros junction), take a Guate-bound bus. Buses are frequent along this route, but dwindle toward late afternoon. Iximché is a pleasant 5km **walk** south of Tecpán along a paved road; follow the signs from town. You can also hire a taxi (Q15) or take a bus from the main road near Hotel Iximché (Q1).

LAGO DE ATITLÁN

According to Quiché legend, Lago de Atitlán was one of the four lakes that marked the corners of the world. Today, the majestic lake is indeed among the world's most beautiful. Encircled by green hills and three large volcanoes, Atitlán's waters change color constantly, from emerald to azure. Surrounding it are 3 traditional villages peopled by Maya of Cakchiquel and Tzutuhil descent. On Atitlán, the cultural and natural beauty results in a stupendous mosaic.

The tourist mecca of **Panajachel** is the first stop for almost every visitor. Several of the towns that ring Atitlán—bustling **Santiago Atitlán**, isolated **Tzununá**, and **San Antonio Palopó**, on the lake's eastern shore—are among the few in all of Guatemala in which the men wear traditional dress. **San Pedro de la Laguna** has the most established budget traveler scene on the lake, while **San Marcos**, **Santa Cruz**, and **Jaibalito** are home to beautiful lakeside hotels. **Sololá**, a traditional town, is above the lake.

PANAJACHEL

Panajachel, the rowdy ringleader of Atitlán, has long been a tourist magnet. Back in the 1960s and 70s, it was a permanent home to hippies. Today, hippies rub shoulders with busloads of tourists and retirees languishing in expensive hotels. "Pana," as it is affectionately called (or less affectionately, "Gringotenango") is one of the most touristed towns in Guatemala. It's neither the most authentic nor the most attractive town on Lake Atitlán, but that's like calling it the ugliest contestant in the Miss Universe pageant: with a little perspective, Panajachel is just more developed and heavily frequented, with the magnificent lake just steps away.

Lago de Atitlán

TRANSPORTATION

Buses: Leaving Calle Principal, buses head to: **Antigua** (Rebulli direct pullman 2½hr., M-Sa 10:45am, Q35), or take any bus heading to Guatemala City and change in Chimaltenango; **Chichicastenango** (1½hr., every hr. 7am-3pm, Q10; pullman direct 6:45am, Q15); **Guatemala City** (3hr., 10 per day 5am-3pm, Q15; pullman direct 6, 11am, 2pm; Q20) late afternoon, change in Los Encuentros. Connect to most western highlands destinations from **Los Encuentros** (1hr., frequent service, Q5); **Quetzaltenango** (2½hr.; 6 per day 5:30am-2pm, Q12), late afternoon change in Los Encuentros; **Sololá** (20min., every 30min. 5am-6pm, Q2); **Tecún Uman, El Carmen,** and the **Pacific Coastal Highway** change in **Cocales** (2½hr., 8 per day 6am-3:30pm, Q10).

Boats: See transportation sections in **Around Lago de Atitlán,** p. 359.

ORIENTATION PRACTICAL INFORMATION

Panajachel is small enough that addresses and street names are not used often, and signs point to accommodations off the main street. Buses pull into Pana along **Calle Principal** and stop at or near the town's main intersection, where it meets **Calle Santander.** Santander runs all the way to the shore has many budget establishments. **Avenida. Los Árboles** is home to a cluster of restaurants, bars, and discos.

GUATEMALA

TOURIST AND FINANCIAL SERVICES

Tourist Information: INGUAT (☎762 1392; fax 762 1106), on the walking path along the beach between Calle Santander and Calle Rancho Grande. Open daily 9am-5pm.

Travel Agencies: Agencies will arrange tours to just about any destination you desire. They also offer package deals to popular sites such as Tikal, Río Dulce, and Chichicastenango. Reliable agencies include: **Atitrans** (☎762 0146), in Centro Comercial Rincón Sai on the left side of Calle Santander facing the lake, **Servicios Turisticos Atitlán** (☎762 2075; turisticosatitlan@yahoo.com), farther down Santander toward the lake.

Banks: Banco Inmobilario, on the corner of Calle Principal and Calle Santander. Open M-F 9:30am-5pm, Sa 9am-1pm. **Banco Industrial,** near Mario's Rooms, on the right side of Calle Santander facing the lake. 24hr. Visa-friendly **ATM.** Open M-F 9am-4pm, Sa 9am-1pm. **Banca Red,** at the end of Av. de los Árboles, also has an **ATM.**

LOCAL SERVICES

Bike and Motorcycle Rental: Moto Servicio Quiché, a third of the way up Av. Los Árboles on the left. Motorcycles Q35 per hr., Q150 for 8hr. Deposit Q300 and copy of passport required. Bikes Q5 per hr., Q30 per day.

Market: The town market is at the north end of Calle Principal. From the bus stop, continue straight, passing the church on your left. Textiles, carvings, and other tourist goods are sold in stands all along Calle Santander.

Laundromat: Lavandería El Viajero, Calle Santander before the intersection with Calle Principal, above Atitrans travel agency. Drop-off service Q4 per lb. Open daily 8am-8pm.

EMERGENCY AND COMMUNICATIONS

Police: (☎762 1120), at the end of Calle Principal away from the lake, across from the church and to the left of the *municipalidad*. Limited English. The **tourist police** is located below INGUAT on the beach.

Pharmacy: Farmacia Santander (☎762 2657), across from the Banco Inmobilario, at the intersection of Calle Principal and Calle Santander. Open daily 8am-11pm.

Medical Services: There is a **hospital** located on the road between Pana and Sololá. **Dr. Edgar Barreno** is available at his office for small problems; Q50 per visit. Up Av. Los Árboles and turn right at the 1st street. Available daily 8am-noon and 2-6pm.

Telephones: Telgua, halfway down Calle Santander, on the 2nd fl. across from Banco Industrial. Open M-F 8am-5:30pm, Sa 9am-1pm.

Internet: There are a few Internet cafes on Calle Santander. **Mayanet,** across from Turisticos Atitlán, is well-priced. Q7 per 30min. Open M-Sa 9am-9pm, Su 2:30-8pm. Up the street, **Mundo Verde** is cheaper but slower. Q6 per 30min.

Post Office: Calle Santander, 200m from lake. Open M-F 8:30am-5:30pm, Sa 9am-1pm.

■ ACCOMMODATIONS

Panajachel has plenty of cheap stays, but other lakeside towns are more budget.

Mario's Rooms, Calle Santandar and Calle El Chali (☎762 2370). Recently renovated rooms are clean and nicely furnished with colorful, woven curtains and basic dressers. Good location and attached restaurant. Singles Q30, with bath Q60; doubles Q60/Q85; triples Q75/Q120. Prices slightly higher in July and Aug. ❷

Hospedaje García, Calle El Chali (☎762 2187), left off Calle Santander when walking toward the lake. Quiet, clean communal baths, hot water, and a relaxing 2nd fl. balcony. Rooms are small but very affordable. Singles Q32; doubles Q50; triples Q75. ❷

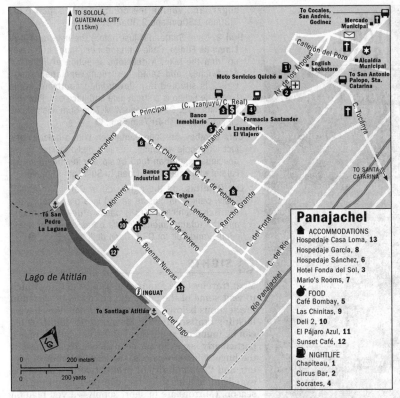

Panajachel

🏠 ACCOMMODATIONS
Hospedaje Casa Loma, **13**
Hospedaje García, **8**
Hospedaje Sánchez, **6**
Hotel Fonda del Sol, **3**
Mario's Rooms, **7**

🍴 FOOD
Café Bombay, **5**
Las Chinitas, **9**
Deli 2, **10**
El Pájaro Azul, **11**
Sunset Café, **12**

🍸 NIGHTLIFE
Chapiteau, **1**
Circus Bar, **2**
Socrates, **4**

Hotel Fonda del Sol, Calle Principal (☎ 762 1162). Near the bus station, a good deal for more upscale accommodations. Rooms on the far side of the yard are nicest and priciest. Singles Q40, with bath Q75-95; doubles Q80/Q150. ❷

Hospedaje Sánchez, Calle El Chali. Simple, cheap, and quiet, with a friendly owner and spacious rooms. Singles Q30; doubles Q40; triples Q45. ❷

Hospedaje Casa Loma, Calle Rancho Grande (☎ 762 1447), ½ block from the lake. Rooms are bare-bones, but the backyard is full of tropical flowers. Larger, more expensive units are nicely decorated. Singles Q40, with bath Q50; doubles Q70/Q80. Large units for 2 with kitchenette Q400. ❷

🍴 FOOD

The large tourist population has left its mark, and many foreign and expatriate restaurant owners gear their menus toward a healthful, cosmopolitan scene.

🔲 **Sunset Café,** at the end of Calle Santander facing the beach. A popular waterside eatery with a great view of the lake, with a local performer most nights at 7:30pm. The sizzling fajitas (chicken Q30, shrimp Q37) come highly recommended. Burritos Q35. Open M-F 11am-midnight, Sa-Su 7am-11pm. ❹

El Pájaro Azul, next to the post office on Calle Santander. This chic cafe offers delectable vegetarian options and mouthwatering crepes. Try the "Jamaican" (banana, brown

"EVERY GRAY HAIR AN EXPERIENCE"

An interview with San Perdo artist Pedro Rafael González Chauajay.

LG: Where are you from originally?

Pedro: I'm a full-blooded Mayan from San Pedro. My cradle-tongue was Tztuhil, and Spanish was my second language.

LG: How did you become interested in art?

Pedro: My grandmother painted, and she was one of the first painters in San Pedro. She started in 1938.

LG: What was going through your mind when you painted this [portrait of your grandmother]?

Pedro: I was chasing an expression. What came out was a reflection of my soul. When I painted this, with so many shadows, with so much light on her wrinkled face. . . I can't explain why, it just came out.

LG: It's very powerful.

Pedro: Yes. When someone cries, you feel it. When someone is happy, you feel it, and there is a connection between you two—that's being human. And this is what the artist draws, this is the plasma of the work.

LG: I can almost feel the wrinkles.

Pedro: Yes. Around here they say that every wrinkle is a year of life, and my grandmother also used to say that every gray hair is a year, an adventure, an experience. Everything you've done in your life—the good and the bad—is a gray hair.

Sr. González teaches painting at a local elementary school in the morning and paints in the afternoon. He lives in San Pedro with his family, where they run the Café de Arte.

sugar, and vanilla ice cream; Q19). Open daily 7:30am-1:30pm and 2:30pm-10pm. ❷

Deli 2, Calle Santander just before the lake, and **Deli Llama de Fuego,** Calle Santander two-thirds of the way up from the lake. A delicious selection of *licuados,* sandwiches, and salads—excellent vegetarian spots. Deli 2 is situated in a flower-filled courtyard, while Llama de Fuego is a street cafe and juice bar. Pita with hummus Q15. Deli 2 open W-M 7am-6pm. Deli Llama de Fuego open Th-Tu 7am-6pm. ❷

Café Bombay, on Calle Santander. With a balcony perfect for people-watching, this is a mellow place to eat delicious vegetarian food or sip a refreshing *licuado.* Falafel with salad Q18. Open Tu-Su 11am-9pm. ❷

Las Chinitas, on the right side of Calle Santander. Zesty, pan-Asian cuisine served in a pretty courtyard. The Hunan chicken (Q33) packs a delicious punch, and the rotating *menu del día* offers appetizer, main course, and fruit for Q33. Open daily 8am-9pm. ❸

🖸 SIGHTS

Most travelers use Panajachel as a base from which to visit some of the surrounding towns (covered in the sections below). However, the town does have a bustling crafts industry. Mayan crafts and textiles can be found all along the main street, but there is a particularly large cluster near the shore. Because of the huge volume of goods, the large number of sellers, and the similarity of products, there are some excellent bargains to be found, especially during low season. (Mirrors are in short supply—if you plan on buying clothes, bring your own or an honest companion.) **Museo La Custre Atitlán,** in Hotel Posada don Rodrigo, behind the Sunset Café, has a collection of Maya artifacts and a display on Atitlán's natural history. (Q35, students Q20.) **Boats** and other water sport equipment are available from **Diversiones Acuáticas Balam,** on the public beach inside the main lifeguard tower. (☎ 762 2242. Options include kayaks singles Q15 per hr., doubles Q25 per hr., canoes Q25 per hr., water bicycles Q25 per hr., and water skiing Q400 per hr.)

🖸 NIGHTLIFE

Besides the many *artesanía* vendors between your hotel and the lakefront, other entertainment options cluster on Av. Los Árboles. **Ubu's Cosmic Cantina** has ping-pong and pool tables, incredible wall art (in the back room), and a big-screen TV. (Open 10am-late.) Swing through the saloon doors of **Circus Bar** and check out live music daily at 8:30pm. (Open daily noon-midnight.) Across the street is **Chapiteau,** a bar and *discoteca*. **Socrates,** just across the way on Calle Principal, has been the hottest disco as of late (look for the yellow overhanging).

AROUND LAGO DE ATITLÁN

Boats are the best way to get around the lake; choose between ferries and smaller, faster *lanchas*. There are two docks in Panajachel. The first, by the **Hotel Barceló del Lago,** at the end of Calle del Rancho, serves Santiago Atitlán, the eastern shore, and lake tours. The second, at the end of **Calle del Embarcadero,** serves San Pedro la Laguna, Santa Cruz and all towns in between. (Some boats on this route start at Barceló del Lago pier, but they'll stop at the Embarcadero.) Schedules are lax; 45min. waits are common. Drivers wait for boats to fill up; the frequency of trips dwindles in the afternoon. You can also usually hire a (slightly expensive) private *lancha* at the dock. **Lake tours** from Panajachel are offered by the ferry companies. (To San Pedro, Santiago, and San Antonio Palopó: 7hr., 8:30am, Q50.)

SOLOLÁ

One of the largest Maya towns in Guatemala, Sololá sits beautifully in the hills and offers a gorgeous view of the lake below. Tradition is strong here, and the impressive **Friday market** (starts in the early morning) attracts *indígenas* from all over. There's a smaller market on Tuesdays as well as on the weekends. The well-priced **El Pasaje ❶,** 9 Calle, 5/6 Av., two blocks from the *parque central*, has a pleasant courtyard and clean rooms with hot water communal baths that are rough but passable. (Singles Q25; doubles Q35.) Sololá, along the road between Panajachel and Los Encuentros junction, is easily accessible by bus. On your way from Guate or any western highlands locale to Panajachel, it's an inevitable stopover.

SAN PEDRO

San Pedro has all but replaced Pana as the gringo hangout on Atitlán. At the foot of the eponymous volcano, San Pedro is an attractive base for climbing, exploring the lake, or simply relaxing. Although nothing could interfere with the mellowness of some of the town's visitors, the center erupts during its festival week of June 29.

TRANSPORTATION. *Lanchas* leave Panajachel (30min., every 30min. 7am-5pm, Q15). Ferries between Santiago and San Pedro (40min.; every hr. 8am-1pm, 3:30, 5pm; Q10). Two early buses run to **Quetzaltenango** (3½hr., 4:30 and 5:30am).

ORIENTATION AND PRACTICAL INFORMATION. There are two main docks in San Pedro; boats to and from Santiago arrive at a dock on the south side of town, while the eastern dock serves Panajachel and all other lakeside towns. (For schedule information, see **Boat Transport around Lago de Atitlán,** p. 359.) The two docks are within walking distance along a curvy **lakeside road** that runs through the lower village. The walk takes 20min., and it is best to ask for directions as you wind through the fields. From either dock, a walk straight uphill on the paved road will take you to the **town center**. In the town center, there's a **Banco Rural** that exchanges traveler's checks. (Open M-F 8:30am-5pm, Sa 9am-1pm.) **Telgua** is about halfway up the paved road from the Santiago dock. (Open daily 7am-noon and 1-6pm.) The **post office** is behind the massive gray stone church,

ACCOMMODATIONS. Close to the lakeside near the Pana dock, **Hospedaje Casa Elena ❷,** offers clean, large rooms, hot water, and a patio with views of the lake. (Q30 per person, with bath Q50.) **Hotel Ti'Kaaj ❶,** on the lakeside road close to the Santiago dock, is simple and super cheap. Offering basic cement rooms and a leafy courtyard with hammocks, this is a popular place for young backpackers. (Singles Q12; doubles Q22; triples Q32.) Another option for basic accommodations is the **Hotel San Francisco ❷**. To get there, head halfway up the paved road from the Santiago dock, go left at the fork. (Q20 per person, with bath Q30-40.)

❤❐ FOOD AND ENTERTAINMENT. When the munchies strike, head for **Nick's Place ❸**, at the Pana dock. It serves huge breakfasts for low prices (Q12) and has tasty pizzas for Q30-35. (Open daily 7:30am-10pm.) For even classier cuisine like a baguette with mozzarella and beef (Q20), as well as evening drinks and movies, head upstairs to **D'Noz ❷**. (Open 9:30am-late.) Across the street, **Restaurant El Fondeadero ❷**, has nice views and a patio. (Chicken sandwich with fries Q10. Open daily 6am-9pm.) On the uphill road from the Santiago dock is **Café de Arte ❷**, operated by well-known local artist Pedro Rafael González Chavajay (see **Every Gray Hair an Experience**, p. 358), who showcases his work on the walls. The food is good and cheap, and Pedro may even come and sit down and chat. (Open daily 7am-11pm.)

◙ ⚑ SIGHTS AND OUTDOOR ACTIVITIES. If admiring the lake isn't activity enough, you can rent **canoes** or **horses** (about Q20 per hr.; go to Pedro in Restaurante El Fondeadero or INGUAT). The 4-5hr. climb up the 3020m **Volcán San Pedro** is rewarding but not without risks. Robberies occur so it's a good idea to go with a guide; many hang out around the Pana dock. You can also ask your hotel owner to call someone trustworthy. You can vegetate in hot water at **thermal waters** or at the competing **solar pools,** both located along the lakeshore between the docks.

SANTA CATARINA AND SAN ANTONIO

An outing to Santa Catarina Palopó and San Antonio Palopó (4km and 7km respectively) from Panajachel, is an easy way to escape the bustle of Pana. The residents of **Santa Catarina Palopó** make beautiful weavings and wear an aqua and purple costume (the design of which dates back only to the disco era). The nearby ritzy, summer homes for expats and wealthy Guatemalans detract from the traditional atmosphere. Larger **San Antonio** is often included on the three-town tour of the lake offered by the launch companies. Thus residents are accustomed to peddling their wares to visitors, but there's still a sense of tradition and isolation here.

If you'd like to stay in San Antonio, options are limited. **Hotel Terraza del Lago ❺**, farther along the road past the dock, has lovely, well-kept rooms with excellent views and private hot-water baths. (☎/fax 762 0037. Singles US$24; doubles US$32.

Pickups are available every hour from the intersection of Calle Rancho Grande and Calle Tucánya (Q2). **Hiking** in from above is a far more scenic way to get there. From Pana, take any bus bound for **Cocales** (6, 7, 10am, 2 pm) or **Godinez** (6, 9, 10am, noon, 2pm). Ask to be let off at the mirador just before the turnoff to Godinez. The view is spectacular, and the steep trail on the left brings you to San Antonio (1hr.) Walk along the lakeshore road back to Santa Catarina or Pana. or grab a pickup.

 Some travelers have experienced violent crime recently in **San Pablo La Laguna**. There is limited police presence.

SANTIAGO DE ATITLÁN

The largest of the lakeside *pueblos*, Santiago de Atitlán is nestled between the San Pedro and Tolimán volcanoes. The Tzutuhil people who live here were Pedro de Alvarado's allies in subduing the Cakchiquel of Panajachel. Santiago dominated Atitlán until Panajachel eventually regained control. Although it has a busy, commercial feel, Santiago remains a traditional place. The beautiful village dress is still very much in use. You might see the striking women's *xocopes*—extraordinary,

10m long red straps worn around the head. The famed Santiago *xocop* is depicted on the 25-centavo coin. On July 25 (the festival of Santiago) and during *Semana Santa*, the entire village is awash in traditional colors.

From the boat dock, head up the hill into the village; after the initial climb, turn left and head toward the **church** in the town's main plaza. The church, with its wide, colorful nave, was founded in 1547. There isn't much else to see in Santiago, though **Maximón's Shrine** (see **A Special Sort of Saint, p. 361**) is worth a visit. **Parque Nacional Atitlán,** 5km north of Santiago, was created to protect the now-extinct Atitlán grebe, but the remaining bird life is interesting. You can get there by canoe (ask at the docks) or on foot on the road to San Lucas Tolimán (30min.).

Ferries between Panajachel and Santiago run regularly (1hr., 8 per day 5:45am-4:30pm, 7 returns per day 7am-4:30pm, Q10). **Buses** depart the plaza for Guatemala City (4hr.; 11:30am, noon, 2pm; Q15). Also near the plaza are the **Banco G&T** and **post office** (open M, Th 2-4:30pm, Sa 9am-1pm).

To find the modest **Chi Nim Ya ❶** hotel from the docks, walk up the hill and take your first left. (☎ 721 7131. Singles Q30, with bath Q50; doubles Q50/70; triples with bath Q90.) **Hotel Tzutuhil ❶** (☎ 721 7174) offers the same rates and excellent lake views. It's very close to the main town plaza; if you're facing the church, walk right and then take the first street on the right. The entrance is half a block downhill.)

A SAINT THE DEVIL WOULD LOVE Some distance from Santiago's church, lost among the houses near the edge of town, hides a sacred, alternative center of worship, one of the more striking examples of religious syncretism in a country known for its folk Catholicism. For a few quetzales, local kids will show you to the shrine dedicated to Maximón (San Simón in his Christian incarnation), a wooden figure dressed in European garb and associated with vices such as smoking and drinking. Maximón, ever a consummate enemy of the church, is quite popular in Santiago. Devotees praying, playing the guitar, and making offerings of liquor and cigarettes pack the incense-choked shrine. The saint's specialty is casting curses, so beware, but he's also been known to heal the sick. On the Wednesday of Semana Santa, a Maximón idol is paraded through the village, as the watching worshippers stand chomping on unlit stogies. For Q10, the head counter will chant at you and solemnly spit alcohol in your face. Or just let him bum a smoke or a bit of whatever you have on you.

SAN MARCOS LA LAGUNA

San Marcos's big selling point is appealing accommodations—including a respected yoga and meditation retreat—hidden in a beautiful lakeside canopy. There isn't much to do here, which is exactly why most people come. The **hiking** along the nearby shore is particularly rewarding; try the 3hr. walk to Santa Cruz. Any non-direct ferry from San Pedro to Panajachel will stop in San Marcos. If you're on a small boat, be sure to check with the captain.

There are two docks at San Marcos. The first is a five minute walk to the left (facing away from the lake). The second is right in front of the path leading to all the hotels. The best value in town is the **Hotel Quetzal ❷**. To reach it, take a left just before Paco Real, and follow the trail as it snakes to the right. Quetzal has comfortable private accommodations and dorms in a modest, 2-story house with meals and hot water. (Dorms Q25; private rooms Q30 per person.) A few steps down the path from the dock lies the **Posada Schumann ❺**. The rambling garden here holds slightly pricey but beautiful rooms and bungalows with kitchens, and hot water. Like all listed places in San Marcos, Schumann has a restaurant, but this one offers limited service in the low season. (Sept.-Mar. and May-June US$10-15 per person;

prices increase in Apr, July, and Aug.) Up the path on the left is **Las Pirámides meditation center.** The grounds are suitably inviting and peaceful, and there's a very good vegetarian restaurant. They also offer spiritual healing sessions and excellent **massages.** (☎/fax 762 080. US$9-11 per day includes lodging, courses, and use of facilities; sessions coincide with the lunar cycle.)

Captains running between San Pedro and Pana will stop in San Marcos upon request (and can be flagged down once you're here). If you're already in one of these smaller towns, flag a boat down or ask a hotel to call one. There's also a new road from San Pedro; a truck ride costs Q3.

TZUNUNA AND JAIBALITO

These two lakeside villages are notable for their lack of traffic. **Tzununa** (zoo-NOO-nah), especially, has a unique feeling of isolation and tradition. The women wear beautiful red, blue, and yellow *huipiles*. Cakchiquel is the language of choice; visitors should be willing to be creative with their means of communication.

There's little in **Jaibalito,** but the fabulous ■**La Casa del Mundo ❺** is reason enough to come. Owned and operated by an Alaskan/Guatemalan family, the house clings to a steep hillside above the water, and the views are gorgeous. Each cozy room has water views (the staff recommends rooms 1 and 3). Bill and Rosa serve delicious, family-style meals. Bill also rents out top-of-the-line river and sea **kayaks** for exploring the lake. (Q25-50 per hr.) Though most baths run cold, there's a hot tub during the high season. (☎278 5332; fax 762 1196. Doubles Q125, with bath Q230. Dinners Q65.) To get to La Casa del Mundo, ask to stop at their private dock. From the town dock, you'll have to walk to the right along the lake for 5min.

Pana-San Pedro lanchas stop here upon request (as will some ferries). If you're already in one of these smaller towns, flag a boat down or ask a hotel to call one.

SANTA CRUZ

Santa Cruz, a modest town above the lake, is home to a lovely 16th-century church. Most visitors, however, care only about the collection of hotels that line the shore below. Like other towns along the shore, Santa Cruz is a fantastic setting in which to relax, read, and meet fellow travelers. **La Iguana Perdida** (below) offers **scuba diving** in the lake; PADI certification costs only US$175 (but then again, it's not the Caribbean). They also run a catamaran to Belize. (7 days, Q380 per person. Check for schedules.) Although it's only a short hop by boat back to Panajachel, the path along the lake is almost impossible to follow. A far better **hike** is from Santa Cruz up to Sololá (about 3½hr.; take a bus back to Pana).

All of the **accommodations** listed here serve food, so you won't need to move very far from your hammock or easy chair. Note that there's no electricity or hot water. **La Iguana Perdida ❷,** right by the dock, is a backpacker's haven with an assortment of glorified bamboo huts—and even a tree-house—among the green trails of its backyard. Bring lots of repellent and a mosquito net if you want to sleep in this exposed building. The atmosphere is extremely friendly; family-style dinners are served for Q40. (Dorms Q25, in the tree Q22; singles Q40; doubles Q50.) The **Arca De Noé ❶,** run by friendly British owner Mark, next to the dock, tries to compensate for the lack of modern conveniences with daytime solar-heated water and a few hours of stored solar-powered lighting at night. Clean, comfortable rooms are set around well-landscaped grounds. Multiple-course dinners (Q65, reservations required for non-guests) are excellent. (☎306 4352; thearca@yahoo.com. Dorms Q30 per person; singles Q70; doubles Q120; single bungalows with bath Q195; double bungalows with bath Q240.)

Pana-San Pedro lanchas stop here upon request (as will some ferries). If you're already in one of these smaller towns, flag a boat down or ask a hotel to call one.

CHICHICASTENANGO

Chichicastenango's famous Sunday and Thursday markets attract travelers from around the world; tour groups flood in from nearby Antigua and nearby Panajachel. The market, ablaze with traditional costumes representing towns all across the highlands, is a sight to behold. The tourist invasion has brought with it cheap knock-offs of traditional textiles and the spirit of haggling over every last gringo quetzal. Nevertheless, "Chichi" is still very much an *indígena* town, as the soot from charcoal cookfires, the lilt of spoken Quiché, and the haze of devotional incense attest. Like the town's bustling markets, its history has been quite tumultuous. Chichi was built by the Spanish in the 16th century as a home for refugees from Utatlán, the Quiché capital they had brutally leveled. During the 19th century, the Guatemalan government used forced-labor laws written during the colonial era to pull Quiché workers from the mountains for work on coffee plantations. Tensions rose again in the late 1970s and early 80s, when guerrilla activity disturbed the area. Despite periods of persecution, the region's combination of indigenous and Catholic religious tradition continues to thrive today.

▐ TRANSPORTATION

Buses pass by the corner of 5 Av., 5 Calle, near the arch. On Th and Su market days, plenty of **tourist shuttles** run back and forth from **Panajachel** and **Antigua**. Buses head to: **Guatemala City** (3hr., every 10min. 3am-5pm, Q15); **Santa Cruz del Quiché** (30min., every 30min. 3am-5pm, Q3); **Quetzaltenango** (2½hr., 5 per day 5am-3pm, Q10); **Panajachel** (1½hr.; 9, 11am, 2pm; Q9). Any Guatemala City bus will also drop you off at **Los Encuentros** and **Chimaltenango** for transfers to other towns. Check with the tourist office for updated information and possible bus transfers.

▐▌ ORIENTATION AND PRACTICAL INFORMATION

Chichi is centered around the **parque central,** where the market is held. The *parque* is bordered by 4/5 Av. on the west and east, and 7/8 Calles on the north and south, but it is hardly discernible most of time when streets are covered by market stands. **5 Av.,** the street with most tourist services, passes in front of the church on the east side of the *parque* and runs north toward Santa Cruz del Quiché. There are many tourist services on 6 Calle. **Buses** stop at the corner of 5 Av., 5 Calle, two blocks north of the *parque*. To reach the *parque* from the bus, walk straight from the large arch for two blocks.

> **Tourist Office:** The **INGUAT** office at 7 Calle 5/6 Av. has maps, bus schedules, and recommendations on local travel agencies.
>
> **Travel Agencies:** Try **Chichi Turkaj Tours,** 5 Av. 5-24 (☎ 913 9874). Offers information and extensive tourist shuttle service to most of the country. English spoken. Another good option is **MayaChichiVans,** 6 Calle 6-45 (☎ 756 2187).
>
> **Banks: Bancafé,** 5 Av., ½ block from the *parque* toward the arch. Exchanges US dollars and traveler's checks and gives maximum cash advances of Q2000 on Visa. Open Su-F 9am-5pm, Sa 9am-1pm.
>
> **Pharmacy: Farmacia Girón,** 5 Av., 6 Calle. Open W, M-F 7am-12:30pm and 2-9pm; Tu and Th 7am-9pm.
>
> **Police:** A 10min. walk down the hill 4 blocks past the arch, next to a school.

Hospital: El Buen Samaritano, 6 Calle, 3-60 (☎756 1163). 24hr. emergency service. For more extensive services go to the hospital in Santa Cruz del Quiché (p. 366).

Telephones: Telgua, 6 Calle 5-70 (☎756 1399). Open M-F 8am-6pm; Sa 9am-1pm.

Internet Access: The **Telgua** office offers 15 min. of free access at its office. **INGUAT** also has a connected computer for use (Q0.80 per min.).

Post Office: 7 Av. 8-47. Open M-F 8:30am-5:30pm, Sa 9am-1pm.

ACCOMMODATIONS

Hotels fill up quickly on and before Thursday and Sunday market days, so if you plan on staying one of these nights call ahead for a reservation.

Hotel Chugüila, 5 Av. 5-24 (☎/fax 756 1134), a couple of blocks north of the market. A great upscale splurge with immaculate rooms with handwoven rugs and fireplaces, set around a cobblestone courtyard. All have private bath. Book at least two weeks in advance. Singles Q100; doubles Q180. ❺

Hotel Girón, 6 Calle 4-52 (☎756 1156), just off 5 Av. between the bus station and the church. Bright, oak-trimmed rooms arranged around a patio/parking lot. Super-convenient location and spotless rooms and bathrooms. Singles Q45, with bath Q65; doubles Q70/Q100; triples with bath Q130. ❸

Hotel El Machito, 8 Calle 1-72 (☎756 1343), down the hill past El Calvario. Well-kept rooms at moderate prices. Q30 per person with communal bath. ❶

Hospedaje Salvador, 5 Av., 10 Calle (☎756 1329), a couple of blocks from the church. One of the cheaper options in town, this multi-story *hospedaje* offers clean rooms with great views. Nicer rooms with private bath are spacious. Singles Q35, with bath Q70; doubles Q52/Q75; triples Q75/Q150. ❷

Hotel Posada Belén, 6 Av., 12 Calle (☎756 1244), near the edge of town. Follow 5 Av. south from the church and continue all the way until it curves left into the last main road at the town's edge (12 Calle); the hotel is 1 block farther. Though a bit farther from the market, Belén's hilltop location provides a tranquil setting and views of the countryside. Doors lock at 10pm. Basic rooms, hot showers, and laundry service (Q1 per piece). Singles Q50, with bath Q70; doubles Q60/Q80. ❸

FOOD

While the many restaurants clustered around the *parque* serve up pricey dishes, there are lots of cheap, tasty options in the market area itself. If you are facing the church, walk 10m left and then enter the market to your left. After a few stalls of *artesanía*, you will find yourself in a colorful labyrinth of food vendors. Come early in the morning (*very* early) and eat the cheapest breakfast around, and listen to the gentle muffled beat of dozens of female hands shaping the day's tortillas.

Casa San Juan, 4 Av. 6-58. Savor excellent food and service in this cozy restaurant off the park. Kick back at your candle-lit table while you enjoy grilled chicken with rice and guacamole (Q25), or sip some delicious hot chocolate (Q4). Live music by local artists on F. Open M-W, F-Sa 10am-11pm; Th, Su 7:30am-11pm. ❸

Cafe Restaurante La Villa de los Cofrades, from the north side of the *parque* on the corner of 5 Av. in the 2-story building. Entrance is 10m down 5 Av. on the left. Despite

Chichicastenango

▲ ACCOMMODATIONS   🍴 FOOD

Hospedaje Salvador, **7**
Hotel Chugüila, **1**
Hotel El Machito, **3**
Hotel Girón, **2**
Hotel Posada Belén, **8**

Cafe Restaurante La Villa
  de los Cofrades, **5**
Casa San Juan, **4**
Restaurante La Parilla, **6**

TO SANTA CRUZ
DEL QUICHÉ (18km),
✿ (300m)

Arco
Gucumatz

Cemetery

7 C.
8 C.
2 AV.
3 AV.
4 AV.
6 AV.
8 AV.
7 AV.
4 C.
5 C.

Farmacia
Girón   Telgua
       ☎ ✚ El Buen
          6 C. Samaritano

Public
Gardens
El Calvario
Chapel

Parque
Central

Museo
Regional

Santo Tomás

(i) 7 C.
8 C.

5a AV. (Av. Arco Gucumatz)

☎
✉

0   200 meters
0   200 yards

9 C.

9 C.

10 C.

11 C.

12 C.

TO SHRINE OF
PASCUAL ABAJ (300m)

the tourist-trap location, you can expect fair prices and high quality. Try the fruit salad with yogurt (Q18), and don't miss the asparagus soup (Q10). Open daily 7am-10pm. ❸

Restaurante La Parilla, 6 Calle 5-37. Surrounding a tiny, fountain-graced courtyard and tucked away from the street, La Parilla offers appetizing, filling portions with friendly service at a good price. *Pollo frito* Q25, veggie plate Q25. Open daily 7am-9pm. ❸

⚙ 🏠 SIGHTS AND CRAFTS

▨ **MARKET.** Although a few stands remain open all week, coming for the scheduled Thursday and Sunday markets (Sunday is larger) is well worth the extra planning. On these days, the otherwise calm, peaceful streets of Chichi undergo a drastic transformation, as nearly every inch of space becomes blanketed with vendors hawking their crafts and handiwork. The main vegetable market is inside the Centro Comercial on the north side of the *parque*. If you're shopping for *artesanías* (handicrafts), remember that bargaining is expected (aim for 30% off the asking price). While the prices in Chichi certainly aren't the lowest in the country, you can find some good deals. Asking prices for wooden masks (Q20-100), hammocks (Q80-300), and big, cozy blankets (Q80-150) vary greatly depending on quality. Shop around before making a purchase; bargain later in the afternoon when the market people are packing up their goods.

■ **IGLESIA DE SANTO TOMÁS.** On the southeast corner of the central market park, the church provides a fascinating glimpse into the syncretic Catholicism of the Quiché Maya. A sight of sacred ritual; an incense fire is kept burning at the base of the church's steps and on market days, brightly dressed *indígena* women blanket the stairs with hibiscus, lilies, roses, and gladiolas, selling the blooms to churchgoers as offerings. The church is built on an ancient Quiché Maya holy site and is sacred to local indigenous communities. *Indígenas* make an elaborate ritual of ascending the steps and repeatedly kneeling. Make sure you are appropriately dressed to enter. *(Use the side entrance, to the right, as the front entrance is reserved for senior church officials and cofradías or blocked by fire and other ceremonies. No photographs. Free, but small donations are appreciated.)*

SHRINE OF PASCUAL ABAJ. A lovely 20min. walk from town leads to the shrine of Pascual Abaj, a ceremonial rock surrounded on three sides by a low stone wall. There's usually a small fire burning in front, as well as a profusion of flowers and candles. The best time to go is on Sunday mornings, when gatherings are larger and more frequent. Ask before taking any photographs. *(Walk downhill 1 block from the Santo Tomás church on 5 Av. Turn right on 9 Calle and follow it as it curves downhill and to the left. When the road veers to the right, continue straight, following the large sign. Walking through a courtyard past a small museum of ceremonial masks, and enter a forested area. The trail zigzags up the hillside until flattening out in a small meadow dotted with pines. About 30m on the right is the shrine. Exercise caution as robberies have occurred.)*

OTHER SITES. The chapel of **El Calvario,** on the opposite side of the *parque* from Santo Tomás, is smaller than its counterpart, but still worth a quick look. Next to it on the west side of the *parque* are some pleasant **public gardens.** On the south side of the *parque,* the **Museo Regional** has a collection of pre- and postclassical Maya bowls and figurines. There is also a series of jade arrowheads and necklaces. *(Open W, F, Sa 8am-noon and 2-4pm; Tu, Th 8am-4pm; Su 8am-2pm. Admission Q5.)*

SANTA CRUZ DEL QUICHÉ

Located about 18km north of Chichicastenango and 40km northeast of Quetzaltenango, Santa Cruz del Quiché is the departmental capital and an important transportation hub for those heading to more remote parts of the highlands, but is neither particularly attractive nor exciting. The nearby Quiché Maya ruins of Utatlán are a perfect for a brief escape from the city.

◰ TRANSPORTATION. Buses arrive at and leave from 1 Av., 10 Calle, Zona 5. To reach the *parque central* from there, turn right on 1 Av. (with your back to the buses), and walk four blocks; turn left and walk another three blocks. Buses head to **Guatemala City** (3½hr.; every 30min. 2-10am and noon-4:30pm, 2 6am buses leave from the west side of the *parque;* Q16) via **Chichicastenango** (30min., Q3). Hop off at **Los Encuentros** for connections to **Quetzaltenango** or **Panajachel** (1hr, Q6); hop off at **Chimaltenango** to make the connection for **Antigua** (2hr., Q12). There are also a few early direct buses to Quetzaltenango (3hr.; 5, 6, 7am). Service to **Nebaj** (3hr.; 5am, noon, 6pm; Q10) goes through **Sacapulas** (1½hr., Q7). Heading to **Cobán,** take a Nebaj-bound bus to **Uspantán** and then grab a pickup truck there.

🗹 PRACTICAL INFORMATION. Banco Reformador Construbanco is on the northern edge of the parque on 3 Calle. (Open M-F 9am-7pm, Sa 9am-1pm.) **BanCafé,** next door, has a 24hr. **ATM.** One street over, **Banco Industrial** gives Visa cash advances. (Open M-F 9am-5:30pm, Sa 9am-1pm.) The **police** are on 0 Av., 4 Calle, Zona 1 (☎755 1106, open 24hr.); you can reach the **Bomberos Voluntarios** on 2 Calle 0-11, Zona 1, for **emergencies** (☎755 1122). The **pharmacy** is on 3 Calle/2 Av. (Open Su-F 8am-1pm and 2-8pm; Sa 8am-noon.) A good-sized **market** lies just south of the *parque*. **Internet, phone,** and **fax** are at **Megatel,** on la Av./3 Calle, Zona 5, in the blue Edificio Plata Azul Las Américas. (Internet Q10 per hr.; free calls to Sprint. Open M-Sa 7am-7pm, Su 7am-1pm.) The **post office,** 0/1 Av., 3 Calle, is around the corner from police headquarters. (Open M-F 8:30am-5:30pm, Sa 9am-1pm.)

🖪🖍 ACCOMMODATIONS AND FOOD. 🖾Hotel Maya Quiché ❷, on 3 Av. 4-19, a block off the *parque*, has spotless rooms in an inviting atrium. Those with private bath have cable TV, and there's a restaurant on the premises. (☎755 1667. Q40 per person, with bath Q60.) At **Hotel San Pascual ❷,** 7 Calle, 1-43, Zona 1, the clean, bright rooms are set around a courtyard. Hot water runs from 6:30-7:30am. (☎755 1107. Singles Q36, with bath Q60, with cable TV Q72; doubles Q60/Q96/Q120.) The nicest restaurant is the carnivore's heaven **El Torito ❸,** on 4 Calle, 3/2 Av., half a block from the *parque*. Though better cuts of meat are pricey, less expensive choices exist. (Filet mignon Q45. *Pollo en salsa blanca* Q28. Open daily 7:30am-9pm.) Friendly **La Toscana ❷,** on 1 Av. 1-06, serves small portions of lasagna and garlic bread for Q17, as well as pizza slices for Q7.50. (Open daily 10am-9pm.)

NEAR SANTA CRUZ DEL QUICHÉ

UTATLÁN

> To get to the ruins of Utatlán, follow 10 Calle out of town (begin at the bus terminal), eventually walking past La Colonia. At the sign for the SCEP, take a right up the hill to the park entrance. The walk is about 30min.—it's only 3km, but there are no directional signs. Traffic is light. For Q55-65 you can hire a **taxi** at the bus terminal to take you there, wait, and bring you back. **Museum** open daily 8am-4pm; gates close a little later. The only facilities are the museum's outside toilets. Admission Q10. Free camping in the parking lot.

Near Quiché lies Utatlán, the Spanish name for K'umarkaaj, capital of the Quiché Kingdom during the post-classic period of Maya civilization (AD 1250-1523). Under the rule of Q'uk'ab, the Quiché domain extended from the Pacific almost to the Atlantic, encompassing nine different nations including the Tzutuhil and Cakchiquel, two major indigenous groups around Lago de Atitlán today. The official archaeological site of K'umarkaaj—"Houses of Old Reeds"—covers an area of eight sq. km but the few discernible structures are located around a single *parque*. To reach it, follow the path right from the Visitors Center. Perhaps most interesting is a small cave 100m along an indicated trail to the right and then down from the *parque* (follow the sign saying "La dirección de la Cueva"), where religious healing ceremonies have taken place for the last 500 years. If you are lucky, you may stumble across a religious ceremony in process. You need a flashlight to see more than a few meters into the cave; bring your own, as there is only a slight chance the museum may have one to rent (Q2). Continue down the path to reach two secondary caves and a tiny museum.

GUATEMALA

NEBAJ

Situated in a fertile, stream-fed valley high in the Cuchumatanes, Nebaj is 40km north of Santa Cruz del Quiché, but winding dirt roads and imposing mountain passes lend it a far greater sense of isolation than the distance implies. The town marks the southwest point of the Ixil Triangle—the region that the Ixil (ee-SHEEL) Maya call home, defined by Chajul to the north and Cotzal to the east. Nebaj is a beautiful, traditional town of old adobe homes and one communications tower. The local clothing is striking; women dress in deep-red *cortes* (short pants) and adorn themselves with elegant, forest-green shoulder drapes with golden stripes. Nebaj celebrates the *Fiesta de Santa María Agosto* from August 12-15 with religious ceremonies, artwork displays, and sporting events. Nebaj's beauty, however, belies a difficult past. During Guatemala's civil war in the late 70s and early 80s, it became a battleground between the government and guerrillas.

▐ TRANSPORTATION

Bus service can be erratic in this remote region, so it's a good idea to check the schedules at the station. **Buses** go to **Santa Cruz del Quiché** (3hr., 9 per day 12:30am-11:30pm, Q10) via **Sacapulas**. **Cobán** can be reached via a series of windy but scenic dirt roads. The easiest first stop is Sacapulas, though the junction is actually around 30min. before that. If you feel comfortable waiting around in the middle of nowhere, ask your driver to drop you off at the road to **Uspantán**, as a reasonable number of day buses head from Sacapulas to Uspantán (1½hr.; 9:30, 10:30am, every hr. noon-4pm), as do trucks and pickups. Alternatively, you can hop into a car or pickup heading from the bus terminal in Nebaj to **El Entronque** and from there, grab a bus to Uspantán. One should always consider the risks in hitchhiking. From Uspantán, buses leave to **Cobán** very early (2 hr., 3:20 and 5am), so be prepared to spend half the night in Uspantán. If you are lucky, you might be able to find a daytime pickup heading to Cobán directly from Nebaj. Set out early; the whole trip can be done in eight hours or so, but can take much longer with missed connections. For **Cotzal** and **Chajul**, bus schedules vary, so ask at the terminal. They tend to run early, and not often. Vehicles pass by near the gas station.

◢◣❼ ORIENTATION AND PRACTICAL INFORMATION

The **church** towers over the east side of the **parque central**. Nebaj's three main streets run east-west, all more or less parallel. The road passing the *parque* on the south heads to **Sacapulas**. The road on the north side is the **road to Chajul**, and one block farther north is the **market street**. The **bus terminal** is half a block north of the market, three blocks down from the very western edge of the church. The daily **market** has mostly fruits and vegetables and is huge on Sundays.

Bank: Bancafé, on the market street, has a **24hr. ATM,** exchanges currency and traveler's checks, and gives cash advances on MC/V until noon. Open M-F 9am-4pm, Sa 9am-1pm.

Farmacia Xelaju: ½ block north of the *parque* on Cantón Batzbacá. Open daily 8am-8pm.

Police: on the west side of the *parque*. Open 24 hr., **Los Bomberos Voluntarios,** off the northeast corner of the *parque*, ½ block up on the road to Chajul, for **emergencies.** Open 24hr.

Internet: Cibercafé Turansa, off the northern edge of the *parque,* has blazingly fast computers and a satellite connection. Q10 per hr. Open daily 8am-9pm. Also **Camara de Comercio,** next to Bancafé on the market street. Q12 per hr. Open daily 8am-9pm.

Post office: 4 Av. 4-27, a block west of the *parque,* across from the communications tower. Open M-F 8:30am-12:30pm and 3-5:30pm, Sa 9am-1pm.

ACCOMMODATIONS

Many establishments are poorly marked—you may want to let one of the young guides at the bus station lead you to your destination.

Hotel Ilebal Tenam, a couple of long blocks west of the *parque* on the road to Chajul, just past the store with *Gallo* ads, is an excellent value. Family-run, friendly, and meticulously clean. Singles Q18, with bath Q43; doubles Q42/Q73; triples Q54/Q98. ❶

Anexo del Hotel Ixil (☎ 755 1091), 1 block north and 2 blocks east of the *parque* on the market street, is a more modern hotel run by the same owners of Hotel Ixil (look for the white house with black gate on the corner). Comfortable rooms with ultra-soft beds and private bath with hot water. Singles with cable TV Q48; doubles Q95. ❸

Hotel Ixil, 10 Calle, 6 Av., Zona 4, 4 blocks east of the *parque* on the road to Sacapulas. Clean rooms with common baths around a courtyard. Singles Q20; doubles Q40. ❶

Hospedaje El Viajero, next to the Quetzal gas station on the road to Chajul. Small rooms and fairly clean communal baths. Q20-30 per person. ❶

FOOD

Restaurante Asados Pasabién, on the southern edge of the bus terminal, is a classy place with low prices and hefty portions. Tasty *churrasco* with crispy potatoes, salad, and tortillas Q15. Open daily 12:30-4pm and 6:30-10pm. ❷

El Descanso, on the market street down from the bank. A touristy cafe with a varied menu, English books to read and exchange, and comfy couches. Pick up their copy of *Filosofía para principiantes* as you contemplate a veggie burrito (Q19) or pasta with mushrooms (Q17). Open daily 11:30am-9pm. ❷

Comedor Lupita, on the Chajul road a block east of the *parque.* Friendly service, and homestyle atmosphere. Pancakes and a drink Q10. Open daily 6am-9pm. ❶

Restaurante y Tacquería El Boxbolito, the lavender storefront one door down from the green building on the northeast corner of the *parque.* Serves standard *churrasco* and *pollo* dishes (Q12), as well as chicken and beef tacos. Open daily 7am-10:30pm. ❷

SIGHTS AND GUIDED TOURS

There isn't much to do in Nebaj proper beyond enjoying the scenery all around the town—which is sight enough for most. For a chuckle, check out the **Nebajenese Santa Claus**—a dinky, escaped garden gnome known as "Enanito"—on the fountain in front of the church. You can also head over to the bustling fruit and vegetable **market** (especially Su). The colorful market offers everything from coffee beans to mangos and chili peppers. For **guided tours, hikes,** and **horseback riding,** head to **Pablo's Tours,** at 3 Calle before 6 Av. Zona 1, diagonally across from Hospedaje La Esperanza. Pablo's offers hikes to San Juan Acul (6hr., Q150), visits to the lakes (2hr., Q35), and trips to Chajul and Cotzal. Avoid the lake tour, however, unless you want to fork over Q40 for a short walk to see some puny *lagunas.*

◪ HIKES FROM NEBAJ

ACUL. A challenging road hike leads to the village of **Acul** and the cheese farm **Hacienda San Antonio.** From the police station on the *parque*, head north past Comedor Irene and down the hill. Cross the bridge and follow the main road. After 15min. the main road veers left, but you'll want to continue straight over a small concrete bridge on a rougher and wider road. After about 30-45min. of hiking through corn fields and rolling cow pastures, turn right, eschewing the smaller, straight path. Soon after, the path begins to switch back and forth. Along the way, enjoy views of the town and valley below. About an hour into the hike, the path flattens out and runs past a long, thin field. At the end of the field, take the well-worn path to the right (the left path will get you there, too; it's just longer). After 10-15min., you'll go around a bend in the hillside and the village of Acul will come into sight below. Follow the road through Acul with the fields on the left and the village on the right; the road gently curves right past a small, white-washed **church** with a blue door and pink trim. About 10min. up the same road on the left is the **Hacienda San Antonio.** Set in a picturesque pasture with a forested hillside rising behind it, the *finca* looks fresh out of the Swiss Alps (well, as much as you might expect to find in Central America). The friendly folks inside will show you a room filled with circular blocks of fine Swiss cheese produced on the premises. (Q30 per lb.) The surrounding valley is scenic—perfect for a picnic. Small *tiendas* in the village sell drinks and snacks. Allow 3-5hr. for the whole trip and set out early in the morning when the air is cool and the skies are clear. While this hike is indeed beautiful, note that you can catch a bus to Acul along the same road.

LA PISTA DE ATZUMAL. A hike to the old military airfield in the tiny town of Atzumal provides a first-hand glance at the effects of the area's volatile history. Atzumal is one of the model villages, built partly by foreign volunteers in the 80s, used to house displaced Ixil families after their houses were razed during the war. The fresh new homes contrast with the traditional lifestyle of their inhabitants. At the top of town is the old military airfield, a barren and silent strip of ground surrounded by a minefield to ward off guerrillas. The minefield has been detonated, leaving the landscape awkwardly uneven. Watch out for **barbed wire.**

From the church in town, follow the road to Chajul until you reach the *Quetzal* gas station, where you should take the left fork. When this paved road ends, take a quick left, and then immediately turn right onto the dirt road heading down the hill. After following this for about 30-45min., you'll come to the only junction (at the tall *Feliz Viaje* sign); take the right fork down the slope. After another 45min. or so on this road, you'll ascend into the village. Once the road flattens at the top of the hill, pass a couple of houses and *tiendas*, and then make a left onto the path just past a blue-painted *papelería*. At the end of the path, turn right, then left. You should now see the *la pista* (airfield) in front of you.

LAS CASCADAS DE PLATA. Las Cascadas de Plata is a less rigorous hike. The largest *cascada* (waterfall), 1-1½hr. from Nebaj, is a jagged rock face carved out of a tree-lined hillside. The water here divides into many small cascades, making a beautiful display. The walk to the falls is a lovely, leisurely stroll through the pastures and valleys surrounding Nebaj. From the church in town, follow the road west to Chajul until you reach the first bridge. Follow the road that veers left just before it; you'll stay on this same road for the rest of the walk. About 10min. from the bridge, the valley narrows and the hillsides grow steeper. Less than 1hr. from the *parque*, there's a small waterfall on the left and some small waterfalls on the right. Continuing on, the road soon curves sharply to the left and drops steeply downhill to the largest fall. Allow at least 2½hr. for the round-trip.

NEAR NEBAJ

CHAJUL AND SAN JUAN COTZAL

*Chajul's market days are Tu and F, Cotzal's are W and Sa. On these days, **buses** leave the Nebaj bus station around 4am; pickups and trucks are also quite frequent until around 9am. Those who catch a **pickup** follow the road to Chajul to the Quetzal gas station and wait there. Let's Go does not recommend hitchhiking. About 20-30min. into the trip, the road branches off, veering right to Cotzal and left to Chajul. Buses return daily to Nebaj from Cotzal at 11am, and daily from Chajul at noon. A truck usually leaves Chajul for Cotzal at 11am on market days. Transportation is subject to change, so check in Nebaj first. On non-market days, buses run from Nebaj to Cotzal (30min., 9 and 10:15am).*

Chajul and San Juan Cotzal, the towns that join Nebaj to create the Ixil triangle, are stunningly set on the rolling hills of the Cuchumatanes. They are well off the standard *turista* path, and definitely worth a visit. The sense of tradition is strongly felt and their natural beauty may exceed even Nebaj.

CHAJUL. Chajul is the least bilingual of the three towns. It is made up mostly of picturesque adobe homes, in front of which women weave their fantastic *trajes*. In the plaza, the colonial **church,** Iglesia de San Gaspar, is relatively bare inside, except for the trough of fire in the aisle, between the first few rows of pews, and the gold-plated altar of *Christ of the Golgotha,* to whom pilgrimage is made on the second Friday of Lent. Two angels stand guard on either side of the altar wearing the traditional Nebaj male dress. This curious outfit is actually their third costume. Originally they were dressed as policemen, their uniforms donated by a tailor who wanted the Christ to be protected; later, during the war, they were outfitted in military garb. Many of the other religious figurines inside the church are also colorfully dressed in traditional Ixil garb, and the artfully carved wood at the main entrance displays fine Maya designs.

At **Hostal Ixil-Chajul ❶,** a family rents out two basic rooms in their fixed-up old home, has a traditional sauna for its guests, and serves local food. To get there, face the church from the plaza and take a right on the road that runs in front of the church. Follow this road to the Tienda Hernandez, make a left, and walk about 500m. The unmarked, white house will be on your right-hand side, #27. (Q20 per person for accommodations. Sauna Q15. Food Q10-15.)

SAN JUAN COTZAL. Along the road that branches away from the route to Chajul is **San Juan Cotzal,** larger, more developed, and closer to Nebaj than Chajul. It remains a tranquil town in a beautiful green valley, from which various excursions into the hills are possible. If you have to spend the night, you can check out the **Hotel Maguey ❶,** across from the police station, up from the left side of the church, which has clean, basic rooms for Q25 per person. A better option, however, is to inquire about some of the town's homestays. Ask around town or at **Cantina Las Dalias,** in the Barrio Xecuruz, for more information. While you are at the Cantina, ask for Rudy Marcelo Herincx Castillo, the friendly owner's son, who will gladly serve as a guide for local hikes or excursions. To find the Cantina, walk up the main street away from the church. Follow it all the way up the hill and at the end, near the photocopy shop, hang a left and walk down about two blocks. It will be on your left. For a quick bite to eat, head for the **Comedor Ixtil ❶,** on the main plaza. The flies are plentiful, but so are the tortillas (lunch Q7). San Juan celebrates its patron saint with a festival the week of June 24th, featuring religious ceremonies and costumed dances in the afternoon (ask around for schedules).

QUETZALTENANGO

Quetzaltenango (pop. 125,000), more commonly known as Xela (SHAY-lah), took its nickname from a shortened version of the Quiché word Xelajú, "under the 10," a reference to the 10 mountain gods believed to inhabit the peaks around the city. Gods or no, Xela is conveniently located at a junction of roads coming from the capital, the Pacific coast, and Mexico, and is the largest and most important city in Guatemala's Western Highlands. It's a pleasant place, though chilly and sometimes damp at night. A good number of gringos come, particularly for the increasingly popular Spanish language schools. There isn't a whole lot to see in town beyond the well-maintained *parque central*, but daytrips into the surrounding countryside offer hot springs, rugged volcanic peaks, and colorful markets.

▐ TRANSPORTATION

Intercity Buses: Unless otherwise noted, departures are from **Terminal Minerva**, at the northwest end of Zona 3. Some buses also depart from the **Zona 2 Terminal**, Jesús Castillo, 1/3 Av., Zona 2 (near La Rotonda). Buses depart to:

Chichicastenango: 2½hr., 8 per day 5am-3:30pm, Q8. Or take a Guate bus and change at Los Encuentros.

Guatemala City: 2nd-class from Terminal Minerva, 4½hr., every 30min. 5am-4pm, Q16. 3 companies provide Pullman service (4hr., Q28): **Galgos**, Calle Rodolfo Robles 17-43, Zona 1 (☎761 2248), 5 per day 4:15am-4:15pm; **Líneas Américas**, 7 Av. 3-33, Zona 2 (☎761 2063), 5 per day 5:15am-2pm; **Transportes Alamo**, 4 Calle 14-04, Zona 3 (☎767 7117) 5 per day 4:30am-2:30pm.

Huehuetenango: 2½hr., every 30min. 5am-5:30pm, Q10.

Mazatenango: 1½hr., about every 30min., Q8.

Mexican border at La Mesilla: Union Froteriza y Aguas Calientes. 4hr., 6 per day 5am-2pm, Q12.

Mexican border at Tecún Umán: 4hr., every hr. 5am-2pm, Q12.

Momostenango: From Terminal Minerva or the Zona 2 terminal. 2½hr., every 2hr., Q4.

Panajachel: 2½hr.,6 per day 5am-3pm, Q12. Or take a Guatemala City bus and change at Los Encuentros.

Retalhuleu: 1½hr., every 30min. 5am-6pm, Q6.

Salcaja: From Zona 2 Terminal. 15min., about every 30min., Q1.50.

San Andrés Xecul: 1hr., every 2hr., Q2.

San Francisco El Alto: From Zona 2 Terminal. 1hr., about every hr., Q3.

San Marcos: 1hr., every 30min. 6am-5pm, Q6.

Totonicapán: From the Terminal Minerva and the Zona 2 Terminal. 45 min., every 20 min., Q2.50.

Zunil: (20min., Q2) via **Almolonga** (10min., Q1.25). Departs from the corner of 9 Av. and 10 Calle in Zona 1. About every 30min. 6am-6pm.

Local Buses: They run 6:30am-7pm. Fare Q0.75. Routes are constantly changing; check with the driver. At press time, only minibuses were allowed to pass by the *parque central;* ask the driver of any full-sized bus to drop you off as close as possible.

✳ ▐ ORIENTATION AND PRACTICAL INFORMATION

Quetzaltenango follows the mighty Guatemalan Grid. The **Parque Centroamérica**, the *parque central*, is at the center of town in Zona 1 and is bordered by 11 Av. on the east, 12 Av. on the west, 4 Calle to the north, and 7 Calle to the south. Walk a few blocks east or west of the *parque* and you'll find "diagonals" thrown into the mix, but these, too, are numbered. Most hotels, restaurants and services can be found in Zona 1 within a few blocks of the *parque*.

Terminal Minerva, the 2nd-class **bus station,** is in Zona 3, northwest of the city center. If you arrive here, walk straight through the bustling market and then across an empty lot to the street on the other side. Any of the city buses heading to the left will take you to the *parque central.* (Q.50; look for one marked *"parque."*) Taxis usually wait by the buses (Q20 to Zona 1). If you arrive on a first-class Pullman bus, ask for directions at the bus office, as each company has its own terminal. Taxis also congregate at the north and south ends of the *parque central.*

TOURIST AND FINANCIAL SERVICES

Tourist Information: INGUAT, 7 Calle. 11-35, 12 Av. (☎761 4931), on the south side of the *parque.* Free city maps and list of authorized Spanish language schools. Bus schedules. Limited English. Open M-F 9am-5pm, Sa 9am-1pm.

Tours: The highly regarded **Quetzaltrekkers,** Diagonal 12 8-37, Zona 1 (☎761 5865; quetzaltrekkers@hotmail.com), located inside Casa Argentina (see **Accommodations** below), leads several multi-day trips, including a trek up Volcán Tajumulco (the highest peak in Central America at 4211m) and Lake Atitlán. Trips usually run on the weekends, and prices range Q305-460, including warm clothes, boats, tent, sleeping bags, transport, and meals. Guides are skilled, friendly, and English-speaking. Also arrange weekday trips to nearby volcanoes. Profits go to a local charity, for which donations of equipment or school supplies are warmly accepted. **Adrenaline,** located next to Salon Tecún on the west side of the *parque,* organizes trips to Volcán Santa María and throughout the region.

Mexican Consulate: 21 Av. 8-64, Zona 3 (☎767 5542 ext. 45). Open M-F 9-11am and 2:30-4pm.

Budget Travel: Xela Sin Limites, at 12 Av. C-35, Zona 1 (☎761 6043; xelasinlimit@guate.net), is a helpful source for local information.

Banks: Banco Occidente, 4 Calle 11-38, on the north side of the *parque*. Cash and traveler's check exchange, credit card cash advances. Open M-F 9am-7pm, Sa 8:30am-1:30pm. Similar services and Visa **ATM** at **Banco Industrial,** on the east side of the *parque*. Open M-F 9:30am-7:30pm, Sa 9:30am-1:30pm.

LOCAL SERVICES

Market: Next to Terminal Minerva in Zona 3. Open daily, but most gigantic on Sa. There is a flower market near Casa Argentina, 8 Calle, Diagonal 12. Open Sa.

Bookstore: URISA Bookshop, 15 Av. 3-64, Zona 1. Open M-Sa 9am-7pm. Also try **El Libro Abierto,** 15 Av. "A" 1-56, Zona 1. Open M-Sa 9:30-6:30pm.

Laundry: Laundry Tikal, Diagonal 13 8-07, Zona 1. Q12 per load.

Supermarket: Despensa Familiar, 13 Av. 6-94, Zona 1, 1 block from the southwest corner of the *parque*. Open M-Sa 8am-7pm, Su 8am-6pm. Also **Pais,** in Centro Comercial Mont Blanc.

Mall: Centro Comercial Mont Blanc, 18/19 Av. and 3/4 Calles, in Zona 3.

Car Rental: Tabarini, 9 Calle 9-21 (☎763 0418). Open M-Sa 8am-noon and 2-6pm. Q460 per day.

EMERGENCY AND COMMUNICATIONS

Police: (☎110 or 120 for emergencies, 761 4991, 761 2589, or 761 5805 for the municipal police), on 14 Av. in the *hospital antiguo* (old hospital), Zona 1. Open 24hr. Limited English.

Fire: Bomberos Voluntarios (☎761 2002 or 121). Open 24hr.

Red Cross: ☎761 2746 or 125 in emergencies. Open 24hr.

Pharmacy: Farmacia Nueva, corner of 6 Calle, 10 Av., 1 block from the *parque*. Open M-Sa 8am-8pm. The current 24hr. *farmacia de turno* (pharmacy on call) should be posted near the entrance of every pharmacy. Also **San Pablo Farmacia,** 14 Av. A-39 Zona 1, near the Teatro Municipal. Open M-Sa 8:30am-9pm.

Medical Services: Hospital Privado de Quetzaltenango, 5 Calle 12-44, Zona 3 (☎763 5421 or 763 5391), is widely regarded as the best hospital in the city. **Hospital San Rafael,** 9 Calle 10-41, Zona 1 (☎761 2956), is the closest to downtown. Clinic open daily 7am-7:30pm. 24hr. emergency service.

Internet: Upstairs at **Salón Tecún** (see **Entertainment** below) is popular and cheap. Q6 per hr. Open daily 8am-11pm. **La Cafetería,** 15 Av., 8 Calle, Zona 1, is less crowded and has a nice, breezy cafe. Q10 per hr. Open daily 7:30am-9:30pm.

Telephones: Telgua, 15 Av. "A," 4 Calle (☎763 2050). Open M-F 8am-6pm, Sa 9am-1pm. Try **Salón Tecún** (see **Entertainment,** below) for cheap international phone calls.

Post Office: 4 Calle 15-07, Zona 1. Open M-F 8am-5pm, Sa 8am-noon. **DHL** at 12 Av., 1 Calle. Open M-F 8am-5pm, Sa 8am-noon.

⌂ ACCOMMODATIONS

Budget hotels in Xela have recently started cropping up all over the city center, catering to the increasing number of students and travelers passing through. Most are quite reasonable and are located within a few blocks of the *parque*. On weekends, some hotels fill up with travelers about to enter Spanish language schools, since homestays usually start on Mondays. Xela can be quite cool at night, so check for hot water and extra blankets. All hotels are in Zona 1.

■ **Casa Argentina,** Diagonal 12 8-37 (☎761 2470). Though hard to find—look for the small sign diagonally across from Helados Danni's, near the end of Diagonal II—this is

Quetzaltenango Center

ACCOMMODATIONS
Casa Argentina, **11**
Casa Kaehler, **6**
Hotel Occidental, **10**
Hotel Villa Real Plaza, **7**
Pensión Altense, **13**

FOOD
Cardinali, **5**
Deli Crepe, **4**
La Luna Café, **9**
Rest. Royal Paris, **3**
La Salida, **14**
Sagrado Corazón, **12**

NIGHTLIFE
Cinema-Paraíso
Café, **1**
Salón Tecún, **8**
La Tasca, **2**

the most popular budget hotel in town. It's easy to feel at home: you can cook your own food, wash your own clothes, and make plenty of friends. Many guests stay months at a time. The communal baths are kept clean and have hot water. Q20 per person for dorm-style bed; Q25 per person for tiny private rooms (depending on availability). Monthly rate Q600 per person. ❶

Pensión Altense, 9 Calle 8-48 (☎761 2811). Well-appointed rooms around a flowery courtyard. Rooms with private bath. Singles Q60; doubles Q100; triples Q150-180. ❹

Hotel Occidental, 7 Calle 12-23 (☎765 4069), ½ block from the southwest corner of the *parque central*. Bland but spacious rooms have comfortable mattresses with nary a crater nor a broken spring. Excellent location. Singles Q67, with bath Q97; doubles Q74/Q100; triples with bath Q135. ❹

Hotel Villa Real Plaza, 4 Calle, half a block west of the parque. If you're looking for class, this is *the* place. A spiral staircase leads up to elegant verandas overlooking an indoor courtyard. Enormous rooms have spotless bathrooms. Singles US$35; doubles US$40; triples US$45. ❺

Casa Isabel, 3 blocks up the street from Casa Argentina, has been popular with travelers of late. Q30 gets you a bed and free meals. ❶

Casa Kaehler, 13 Av. 3-33 (☎761 2091). Newly remodeled, if generic, rooms with private bath, on the 2nd fl. balcony of a refurbished, colonial-style house. Front door locked 24hr.; guests have keys. Singles Q70; doubles Q80; triples Q90. ❹

⬛ FOOD

Xela has plenty of affordable *típico* cuisine, augmented by fast-food joints and a thriving cafe and bar scene that caters to Spanish language students, locals, and tourists alike. Unless otherwise noted, listed restaurants are in Zona 1.

⬛ Restaurant Royal Paris, 14 Av. "A" 3-06. The menu of this elegantly laid-back French restaurant quickly reveals its sophistication; try the baked camembert (Q35) or the trout a la Florentine (Q85). Service is slow; order a bottle of wine, grab a board game, and make an evening of it. Open M-Sa 11am-4pm, 6-11pm, Su noon-11pm. ❺

La Luna Café, 8 Av., 4 Calle. Each of Cafe Luna's theme rooms is decorated with unique Guatemalan antiques and newspaper clippings about Xela from the 1800s. Scrumptious desserts and a warm atmosphere make this the perfect place to relax after dinner. *Californiano* (pure hot chocolate with vanilla and chocolate ice cream) Q8. Open M-F 9:30am-10pm, Sa-Su 4-9pm. ❷

Cardinali, 14 Av. 3-25. Serves slightly better Italian food than the Guatemalan average. Pizza toppings run from mozzarella to walnuts and asparagus. Small pizzas Q20-30, large Q40-75. ❸

Deli Crepe, 14 Av., 3/4 Calles and also 8 Calle 11-29. Popular enough to have 2 locations, Deli Crepe's filling breakfasts, dinner burritos, and sweet crepes earn many a repeat customer. *Desayuno típico* Q10, banana crepe with chocolate sauce Q13, burritos Q4. Open daily 8:30am-9pm. ❶

La Salida, 9 Av., 10 Calle. Feast on a tofu burger or chickpea curry dish while relaxing to 1930s American tunes in this intimate vegetarian restaurant. The food is scrumptious and cheap. Entrees Q12-20, *lassi* Q7. Open Th-Tu 11am-9:30pm. ❷

Sagrado Corazón, 9 Calle, 9 Av. *Típico* dishes are delicious and affordable, and the family that runs the place is all smiles. *Cena del día* Q20. Plentiful portion of *pollo con papas fritas y frijoles* Q14. Open M-Sa 8am-8pm. ❷

⬛ SIGHTS

PARQUE CENTROAMÉRICA. The **Municipalidad,** on the east side of the *parque*, is an impressive structure built in 1897. There's a beautiful courtyard just inside the main entrance. On the first Sunday of each month the *parque* is the site of a big **handicrafts market,** with outdoor concerts and performances of traditional music.

MUSEO DEL FERROCARRIL. Near the south end of the *parque*, the museum presents a fascinating account of a unique electric railway that connected Xela and Retalhuleu. It opened in 1930 and closed from storm damage only three years later. *(7 Calle, 12/13 Av. Open M-F 8am-noon and 2-6pm, Sa 9am-1pm. Q6.)*

MUSEO DE HISTORIA NATURAL. Located in the **Casa de la Cultura,** the collection includes a few Maya artifacts, ceramics, an assortment of soda bottles from throughout the ages and a ragged bunch of stuffed animals. Though not the most polished museum around, the place has charm. *(On the southern side of the parque. Open M-F 8am-noon and 2-6pm, Sa 9am-1pm. Q6.)*

TEATRO MUNICIPAL. This beautiful neoclassical structure plans to someday host performances on weekends. It's under construction on a sporadic schedule; call ahead or consult the tourist office if you're interested in a show *(4 Av. "A," 1 Calle, Zona 1. ☎ 761 2181.)*

NIGHTLIFE

Salon Tecún, Pasaje Enríquez, west side of the *parque*, Zona 1. Central location and a popular hangout for gringos and locals alike. Open mic on M. Open daily 8am-1am.

La Tasca, 14 Av. 1-49 Zona 1. This cool, candlelit bar plays Spanish rock and caters to a more local clientele. Open M-Sa 6pm-1am.

Casa Verde, 12 Av. 1-40, Zona 1, lives up to its name with a greenhouse roof. The airy joint sometimes hosts poetry readings and dance classes. *Salsa/merengue* nights (Th) are packed. W is disco and F features live music. Open daily 9am-12:30am.

Cuba, on Blvd. Minerva, Zona 3, tries to emulate its Caribbean counterpart with sand, fake palm trees, and *salsa* tunes. Onlookers have no qualms about laughing at rhythmically-challenged gringos. Reachable by taxi. Cover Q15. Open Th-Sa 8:40pm-12:45am.

Cinema-Paraíso Café, 14 Av. "A," 1 Calle, Zona 1 (☎761 3546). Watch a wide selection of international movies and documentaries while sipping excellent tea. English language library, art exhibitions. Live music M. Tea Q3, nachos Q10. Admission Q10, students Q8. Open daily 4pm-midnight.

DAYTRIPS FROM QUETZALTENANGO

ZUNIL AND FUENTES GEORGINAS

Buses run to Zunil from 9 Av., 10 Calle, Zona 1 in Xela (20min., every 30min. until 6:30pm, Q1.50). Zunil's market days are M and F and the town festival is November 22-26. Cooperative open M-Sa 8:30am-5pm, Su 2-5pm. To get to Fuentes Georginas from Zunil, you can hire one of the pickups that wait in the parque across from the church (20min., Q25-40 for up to 8 people). The walk uphill is lengthy and not recommended for safety reasons. If you must, proceed uphill to the main highway and turn right. Soon on the left you'll see a sign pointing to Fuentes Georginas; from there, it's an 8km uphill climb. Fuentes open M-Sa 8am-5pm. Su 8am-4pm. Q10.

For a great daytrip from Xela, strike out to the picturesque town of Zunil, tucked in a lush river valley about 8km southeast of the city, then to the nearby **hot springs** of Fuentes Georginas. Zunil's immense white **church** is delicately crafted inside and out. The town is also notable for its idol, the infamous **Maximón.** Locals have a life-sized dummy of the figure (also known as San Simón). His outfits are changed every two days—one of the trendiest includes a cowboy hat, red bandana, and sunglasses. Maximón rotates from house to house; ask around for the present location. (A small donation is expected.) The **Cooperative Tejedoras Santa Ana,** half a block down the steep hill to your left as you face the church was founded in 1970 and employs more than 500 women of Quiché Maya descent.

A 15min. ride into the verdant hills overlooking Zunil brings you to the paradisiacal **Fuentes Georginas.** Often shrouded in mist, the hot springs sit in a steep, narrow gorge with hanging tropical vegetation. Relax in one of five steaming pools, the largest of which features a pool-side restaurant and bar. It's possible to stay overnight in one of the worn, musty *cabañas* (Singles Q90, doubles Q120).

The 30min. trek up to the steam vents in the hills above the pools makes an interesting side-trip before or after your soak. The climb takes you through lush green vegetation and at the top you can see huge vats of sulfur steaming up from the mountainside. The smell is terrible but the fluorescent green-streaked granite and the beautiful views make the trip worthwhile. The hike starts from the main road leading to the Fuentes, about 20m shy of the entrance on the left. The trail is unmarked, so it's best to ask one of the guards to show you where the hike begins.

GUATEMALA

Rain gear is highly recommended, and robberies have occurred in the area; a guide is recommended for the hike.

VOLCÁN SANTA MARÍA

To get to the start of the climb, take a bus from Xela's Minerva terminal to **Llanos del Pinal** *(about every hr. 7am-5:30pm; last bus back at 6:30pm).* **Hike** *5-7hr. round-trip.*

Visible from downtown Quetzaltenango on a clear day, the inactive Volcán Santa María (3772m) forms a perfect cone 10km southwest of the city. The climb to the top is rigorous, and robberies have occurred along the trail, but the views are spectacular. **Adrenaline** leads guided hikes if there's sufficient interest, but it's easy enough to go on your own. You can head up with camping gear and pitch a tent to catch the sunset and superior morning views, or make it a long daytrip from Xela. Be sure to bring lots of water, warm clothes, and raingear.

The trail is unmarked, so you'll have to ask for instructions or rely on the following. From the bus drop-off point, walk straight up the road toward the volcano for about 5min. When the road veers right, continue straight to a wide trail strewn with small rocks. The first section rises gently through cornfields and pasture. After approximately 30min., there's an area of exposed rock on the left and a series of long rows of stubby palm-like trees on the right. Veer left onto the gently sloping rocks after the third bunch of palm trees (away from the more worn trail) and the trail quickly becomes easier to follow. About an hour into the hike, there's a flat, grassy area and a view of the cone on clear days. To follow the correct trail to the summit, take a right at the beginning of the grassy area and follow the path through the meadow. From here, the trail becomes much narrower and steeper, leaving the farmland and proceeding up the mountain surrounded by pine trees and undergrowth. From the meadow, the climb takes 2-3hr. of tough hiking. The trail, marked by red arrows painted on rock, sometimes splits in two, but usually the two paths join within 10-15m; if in doubt, follow the more heavily worn path. The air and the forest thin, and the pines give way to a meadow on the summit.

SAN FRANCISCO EL ALTO

Buses *for San Francisco leave Xela from the Zona 2 terminal on Av. Jesús Castillo (45min., about every hr., Q4). Buses back to Xela leave from 1 Calle and 1 Av.*

On a hill overlooking Xela, 17km away, San Francisco El Alto comes alive every Friday with one of the largest weekly markets in the country selling grains and meats to locals. Catch a bird's eye view of the action from the church roof (Q1). **Hotel Vista Hermosa ❶,** on 3 Av. 2-22, Zona 1, has adequate, relatively clean rooms and views true to its name. (☎738 4010. Singles Q25, with bath Q50; doubles Q50/Q100; triples Q75/Q150.)

MOMOSTENANGO

Buses *for Momo leave from the Zona 2 Terminal in Xela (2hr., about every 2hr., Q4) and travel via Cuatro Caminos and San Francisco El Alto. The last direct bus back leaves mid-afternoon, though it is possible to change at Cuatro Caminos.*

An hour north of Xela, in the heart of Guatemala's wool-growing region, Momostenango's popular Sunday market sells—you guessed it—cheap woolen goods (blankets Q70-110, hooded pullovers Q80). Momostenango makes a pleasant daytrip on non-market days. The town is also famed for its naturally occurring **riscos,** heavily eroded clay formations that look like a sci-fi movie set. A 20min. walk on the road to the left as you face the church will take you to the **Baños de Payexú,** where boiling water literally bursts out of the river. Follow the road and take a left at the bridge. The walk to the Baños will take you past a large waterfall and a beautiful ravine. The views are far more impressive than the actual baths, which are rather dirty and reek heavily of sulfur. The nicest place to stay is **Hotel Estiver ❶**, 1 Calle 4-15, Zona 4, 3min. from the plaza. Rooms are clean and comfortable, and the upper floors boast a prime view. (Singles Q25, Q30 with bath.)

OTHER EXCURSIONS

*Zunil buses will stop at **El Recreo** (depart from 9 Av., 10 Calle, Zona 1; 10min., about every 30min. until 6pm, Q1.25), and there's also service from Minerva terminal. Beware: the baths stay open late, but the last bus back to Xela leaves at around 7pm. Buses to **Salcajá** leave Xela from the Zona 2 terminal (15min., about every 30min. Q1.50). Buses for **San Andrés** leave Xela's Minerva terminal (45min., about every 2hr. Q2).*

Another trip from Xela is a visit to **El Recreo,** the best of a number of bath houses near the town of **Almolonga** that take advantage of a natural volcanic water heater. **Salcajá,** 9km from Xela on the way to **Cuatro Caminos,** is known for its embroidered textiles and is home to one of the oldest churches in Guatemala. On a side route off the main road to Cuatro Caminos and surrounded by cornfields, is the *indígena* village of **San Andrés Xecul.** The village's canary-yellow church, complete with a technicolor collage of angels, icons, and adornments, contrasts sharply with the town's mud-brick houses. Hike uphill 15min. to a chapel with views of the whole town and surrounding farmland.

HUEHUETENANGO

More than 250km northwest of the capital and 90km north of Quetzaltenango, Huehuetenango (a Haxcalteca word roughly translated as "old folks' home") sits at the foot of the rugged Cuchumantanes mountains. With fewer than 30,000 inhabitants, Huehue (WAY-way) has an inviting small-city feel. Though there's not much to do, it's a nice stopover on the way to or from the Mexican border at La Mesilla or nearby Todos Santos Cuchumatán. Huehue began its life as a suburb of Zaculeu, the nearby Mam capital, now in ruins. Since the Spanish conquest, the area witnessed a couple of minor silver rushes and a region-wide coffee boom; the mineral has since petered out, but *café* still holds its own.

⌁ TRANSPORTATION

International Buses: From the highlands, take a bus to the **Cuatro Caminos** junction, from which it is easy to get to Huehue (2hr.). Buses to: **Antigua** (4hr., take a capital-bound bus, change at Chimaltenango); **Chichicastenango** and **Panajachel** (3hr., take a capital-bound bus, change at Los Encuentros); **Guatemala City** (5hr., every hr. 1am-9pm, Q25). Alternatively, Transportes Los Malcones (☎769 2251) offers direct Pullman service to Guate from its 7 Av., 3-62 terminal (4:30, 7am, 2pm; Q30); **La Mesilla border with Mexico** (2hr., every 15min. 3am-6pm, Q8); **Nebaj** via **Uspantán** (5hr., 11:30am, Q13); **Sacapulas,** on Rutas García (3hr.; 8:45, 11:30am; Q10); **Todos Santos Cuchumatán** (2½hr., 8 per day 3am-2pm, Q9); **Xela,** transfer at Cuatro Caminos.

Local buses: Buses run daily 5am-7pm. Bus fares within town and to the terminal Q0.65. Buses to **Zaculeu** leave from 7 Av., 2 Calle (every hr. 5am-6pm, Q1); to **Chiantla,** from 1 Calle, in front of the church (every 20min. 5am-6pm, Q1).

▨ ⮝ ORIENTATION AND PRACTICAL INFORMATION

Huehue adheres to Guatemala's typical grid system (see **map** p. 333). The **parque central** is in Zona 1, bounded by 2/3 Calles on the north and south sides and by 4/5 Av. on the east and west. Most services, hotels, and restaurants, are located within a few blocks of the *parque central.* **Buses** pull into the well-organized terminal about 2km outside of town. City buses head into Huehue from the terminal about every 15min. (Q1); to find them, walk through the building with the bus company offices (the one with an archway in the middle), cross the next dusty lot, and head through another vendor-filled building. Alternatively, take a taxi (Q15).

Mexican Consulate: the corner of 5 Av., 4 Calle (☎ 764 1366) inside Farmacia del Cid, where pharmaceuticals and diplomacy unite. Open M-F 8:30am-12:30pm and 2-7pm.

Inguat: 2 Calle past 4 Av. Open Daily 8am-noon and 1-5pm.

Banks: Banco G & T, 2 Calle 4-66, on the *parque*, changes traveler's checks and has a **Western Union** office. Open M-F 9am-8pm, Sa 9am-1pm. **Banco Industrial,** on 6 Av., 1 Calle, has a **24hr. ATM** and gives cash advances on Visa.

Supermarket: A huge **Paiz** in **Centro Comercial El Triángulo.** Open daily 8am-9pm. Also **Despensa Familiar,** corner of 1 Av., 3 Calle. Open M-Sa 7am-7pm, Su 7am-6pm.

Car Rental: Amigos Rent a Car, (☎ 764 9356) at Hotel Chachumatanes in Zona 7. Open daily 7:30am-10pm.

Market: Between 1/2 Av. and 3/4 Calles, near the *parque*. Th and Su are market days. A newer market has also been established next to the bus terminal.

Police: Policía Nacional Civil, 3 Av., 3 Calle (☎ 764 1465 or 704 0986. 24hr. emergency).

Pharmacy: Farmacia Del Cid, 5 Av., 4 Calle (☎ 764 1366). Open daily 8am-12:30pm and 2-7:30pm.

Medical Services: Hospital de Especialidades, 5 Av., 6/7 Calles (☎ 764 3980), past the old police station. Emergency 24hr.

Telephones: Telgua, on the 2nd fl. of Centro Comercial El Triángulo, out of the town center on the way to the bus terminal (look for the Campero sign). Open M-F 8am-6pm.

Internet: Ciberplanet, in Centro Comercial El Triángulo, offers fast service. From Zona 1, take a bus from 6 Av., 2 Calle. Q10 per hr. Open daily 8:15am-9pm. Closer is **Genesis Internet,** 2 Calle 6-37 Zona 1. Q12 per hr. Open M-Sa 8:30am-7pm. Across the way is **La Cabaña Del Café,** a cute cafe with two computers (Q30 per hr.) and live music.

Post Office: 3/4 Av., 2 Calle. Open M-F 8:30am-5:30pm, Sa 9am-1pm.

ACCOMMODATIONS

Unless otherwise noted, all accommodations listed are in Zona 1.

Todos Santos Inn, 2 Calle 6-64 (☎ 764 1241), 1½ blocks from the *parque*. Comfortable beds, plants, and reliable hot water make this the best budget place in town. Some rooms also have cable TV. Singles Q30, with bath Q40; doubles Q60/Q80. ❷

Hotel Zaculeu, 5a Av. 1-14 (☎ 764 1086). A more upscale option, with large, well-appointed rooms around a jungle of a courtyard. Hot water, private baths, cable TV. Eddie the house cat's eyes are ferocious, but he isn't. Singles Q100; doubles Q150. ❺

Hotel Mary, 2 Calle 3-52 (☎ 764 1618), across from the post office. Modern, pink stuccoed rooms surround a multi-story atrium. Hot water 6-9am and 6-9pm. Well-lit rooms have private bath and cable TV. Singles Q56; doubles Q87; triples Q102. ❸

Hotel Gobernador, 6 Av. 1-45 (☎ 764 1197), just north of the *parque*. Friendly management and clean, basic rooms with fair communal baths. Hot water and a *comedor*. Singles Q29, with bath Q41; doubles Q41/Q65; triples Q60/Q95. ❶

Hotel Central, 5 Av. 1-33. While the rooms are well-worn and the communal bathrooms a bit rough, these are the cheapest rooms. Singles Q18; doubles Q36; triples Q42. ❶

🔲🔲 FOOD AND NIGHTLIFE

There's not a whole lot going on in Huehuetenango by night (remember the meaning of the city's name), but there is a *discoteca*, **Cactus** (4 Ca., 6 Av.) and the laid-back and popular **Bob's Bar** (2 Ca. and 3 Av.).

Restaurante Bouganvilias, on the *parque*, across from the church. Surely one of the country's only 4-story *comedores*, Bouganvilias serves up fine views and tasty *típico* dishes. Lunches Q18 including drink. Open daily 6:30am-10pm. ❷

Café Chantilly, 4 Calle 5-28. Excellent service, tasty dishes, and a large selection of coffees, milkshakes, and liquors make this restaurant a popular draw. For breakfast, try the tortillas slathered with eggs and ham, side of pancakes, and coffee or tea (Q25), or sip the *batido de guanabana* when in season (Q12). Open M-Sa 10am-9pm. ❸

Jardín Café Restaurante, 6 Av., 3 Calle. The Jardín is popular with locals for its healthy portions and tasty grub. The well-priced menu features local and US-style food. Chicken, soup, salad, rice, tortillas, and drink Q17; hamburgers Q10. Open daily 6am-10pm. ❷

La Fonda de Don Juan, 2 Calle, between 5/6 Av. An elegant (if not as seductive as Don Juan himself) place to enjoy slightly more upscale *platos típicos*. Pancakes, fruit, and juice Q15; *pollo a la parilla* Q30. ❷

🔳 DAYTRIPS FROM HUEHUETENANGO

ZACULEU

Buses to Zaculeu leave Huehue from the small plaza at 7 Av., 2 Calle (10min., every 30min. 6am-6pm, Q1). To walk there, head west out of town on 2 Calle and look for signs pointing to the ruins. Any local will also be able to direct you. Allow 30-45min. for the walk. The last bus returns at 5pm. Open daily 8am-6pm. Q25.

About 4km west of Huehuetenango lies the ancient Mam Maya site of Zaculeu, the former capital of the Mam people. Ruled by the Quiché until the 15th century, the Mam finally managed to free themselves just as the Spanish arrived. When an army led by Gonzalo de Alvarado met the Mam on a battlefield, the Mam took a look at the fearsome Iberians and retreated to their base. Zaculeu was a study in defense; the temples, plaza, and ball court on the present site were fortified on three sides. However, the Spanish weapons proved too much, and after a few months the Mam were forced to surrender. In the 1940s, the United Fruit Company sponsored an overzealous restoration of Zaculeu. Today, Zaculeu is not what you'd expect from ancient ruins: the original stones are slathered in stucco, no jungle vines envelop the area, and the temples are free of rubble.

TODOS SANTOS CUCHUMATÁN

In a high mountain valley amid the frigid Cuchumatanes, Todos Santos is a spectacular 40km uphill ride from Huehuetenango. Ascending more than 1000m (3300 ft.), the road snakes around sharp ravines before flattening out on a harsh stretch of *altiplano* reminiscent of the Andes. Just when the land seems most desolate, the road dives into a scenic river valley, of which Todos Santos is the commercial center. The strong sense of tradition is just as striking as the setting. Among the Mam-speaking inhabitants, the men (unlike most men in Guatemala) still wear traditional clothing, sporting red and white striped pants and cowboy hats. Women dress in intricately woven *huipiles* (blouses) and dark blue *cortes* (short pants). The pueblo's determination to maintain tradition has persisted despite brutal military repression that forced many locals to flee their homes for the surrounding

(DON'T) HOLD YOUR HORSES Todos Santos residents kick off their out-of-control All Saints Day revelry with one of the wildest customs around. On the first of November, locals rent horses and ride them around in an uproariously funny, drunken race. There's no finish line per se, but whenever a rider makes it to either end of the course, he must take a shot of specially prepared moonshine; each successful lap means another two shots. Things are made even more interesting by the time-honored tradition of using chickens to whip the horses into gear. Ardent contestants actually tie themselves onto their horses to keep from toppling. The race's winner is anybody still mounted and conscious at the end. Afterwards, in the bars back in town, the marimbas belt out everyone's favorite hits while villagers hold a "no-bars-barred" competition of a similar sort. The chickens aren't invited.

mountains in the 1980s. Todos Santos is also known for its partial observance of the traditional Maya calendar, though its most famous festival, All Saints Day, has Catholic roots. The celebration lasts October 31 to November 5, and its highlight is a unique horse race on November 1 (see **Hold Your Horses**, p. 382).

TRANSPORTATION. Most **buses** pull into the town's central plaza, where the small *parque* sits. The uphill street running by the *parque* holds hotels and restaurants. Most buses back to **Huehue** leave very early (2½hr., 5 per day 4:45-6:30am, Q8), and two pass around midday (11:30am and around noon). Some pickup trucks allow tourists to hop in for a fee.

PRACTICAL INFORMATION. On the edge of the plaza, **Banrural** exchanges dollars and traveler's checks. (Open M-F 8:30am-5pm, Sa 9am-1pm.) Three **language schools** make their home in Todos Santos; as a result, there is a very small gringo scene (see **Alternatives to Tourism**, p. 60). **Nuevo Amanecer** is toward the beginning of the main street, down the hill from the church. It runs a **book exchange** and sells a small stock of textiles. The **Spanish and Mam Academy Hispanomaya** is a block up the hill from the *parque*, to the left, near the **Hotelito Todos Santos** (see below). Down the alley before the *parque* is **The Mountain Muse**, a small English bookstore with erratic hours. There are **pharmacies** up and down the main street. The **police station** (open 24hr.) is right next door to the bank, and the **post office** is at the head of the plaza (open M-F 8:30am-12:30pm and 2:30-5:30pm, Sa 9am-1pm).

ACCOMMODATIONS AND FOOD. The town's best rooms are at **Hospedaje Casa Familiar ❶**, 30m uphill from the *parque*. Small, cozy rooms have clean communal bathrooms. Perks include a terrace with great views, fresh banana bread (Q10), and a place to meet fellow travelers. (Dorms Q15; singles Q20-40; doubles Q40.) **Hotelito Todos Santos ❶** is another fine place to lay one's head. To reach the *hotelito*, head uphill from the *parque* and take your first left at a sign. (Clean rooms Q20 per person with or without bath.) Short-term homestays are available through the language schools, for around Q30 including meals.

Some of the best meals in town are the fabulous home cooked ones at the language schools (Q15 for all-you-can-eat dinner). If you're in the mood for *típico*, stop in at the **Comedor Martita ❷** across from the Hotelito Todos Santos. Walk through the tiny door, through the dark and warm kitchen, and into the back room, where social dining tables, a great view, and cheap, delicious food awaits (lunch Q12). **Comedor Katy ❷**, uphill from the *parque* and just before Casa Familiar, is also a good place for some traditional grub. (Meals Q15. Open daily 6am-9pm.) The wooden **Restaurante Tzolkia ❸**, on the main street across from the Proyecto Lingüístico School, serves a variety of tourist-oriented specialties. (Margarita pizza Q35. Screwdriver Q10. Open daily 8am-9pm.) **Café Cuchamatlán ❷**, a bar/restaurant with erratic hours next door to Proyecto Lingüístico, also serves pizza and delicious vegetable chow mein (Q15).

◙ SIGHTS AND ACTIVITIES. The normally tranquil town gets busy for the **Saturday market,** though you can shop for textiles anytime in the *tiendas* along the main street. Inquire at the language schools for information about **dance classes** (up to Q20 per hr.), **weaving classes** (Q7 per hr.), visits to a **sauna** (*chuj* in Mam; Q12 per person), daily hikes (Q10), and movies (Q5). In the upper reaches of town lies the small, unexcavated Maya site of **Tojcunanchén.** This secluded place offers great views of the valley, perfect for a picnic or a nap, and can be reached by following the road uphill from the *parque* (past Casa Familiar) for about 10min.

There are several other day hikes. Check with the folks at **Nuevo Amanecer** language school; they have excellent written directions in English and accompanying maps. One such hike is **Caminata a Tzunul,** a 4hr. roundtrip to Tzunul. Go down the steep paved road and cross the river; follow the path until it meets the main road on the other side of the valley; then take the road down the valley (3km.) to Tzunul, where families weave in their homes and welcome interested visitors. To find the houses, turn left at the soccer field. Returning, take the small path in front of the first house after the soccer field. At the fork, go left downhill and follow the zigzagging path. Follow the road downhill that the path runs into. Cross three streams in as many hills; the path eventually leads back to Todos Santos.

PACIFIC SLOPE

Guatemala's Pacific Slope is a sweltering plain that contrasts sharply with the mountain vistas of the highland region. Here, on rich fertile land divided into vast *fincas* (plantations), bountiful crops like sugarcane, bananas, and rubber make a vital contribution to the nation's economy. The Pacific slope does not, however, usually make the tourist's hit list. The dusty inland trade towns tend to be busy but unappealing, and the black-sand coast is too often marred by trash and debris. There are exceptions; along the busy coastal highway between the Mexican border and Guatemala City, **Retalhuleu** is a pleasant town with the interesting Maya ruins of Abaj Takalik and a few beaches nearby. Farther east, as the coast makes its way toward the border, laid-back **Monterrico** captivates visitors with hammock-lined stretches of fine beach and verdant nature reserve.

⚔ THE BORDER WITH MEXICO

There are two places in the Pacific slope region bordering Mexico: **Ciudad Tecún Umán** and **Talismán/El Carmen.** Tecún Umán, closer to the Pacific coast, and with slightly better service to Guatemala City, is more crowded. Both, however, stay open 24hr. and are equidistant from Tapachula on the Mexican side. The nearest Mexican consulates are in Tecún Umán and Malacatán (near El Carmen).

CIUDAD TECÚN UMÁN. From the bus terminal, take a bicycle taxi to the border (Q10) and then another across the 1km bridge from the Guatemalan to Mexican immigration posts (Q6). Foreigners entering Mexico are required to pay a Q5 entrance fee; entering Guatemala is free. In Guatemala, buses from Tecún Umán head to **Guatemala City** (5-6hr., every 30min. 1am-8pm, Q35) via **Retalhuleu** (1½hr.) and **Escuintla** (4hr.); a few are direct and faster. If you get stuck for the night, try the respectable **Maxcel ❸,** 3 Av., 4 Guillón 82, Zona 2, a few blocks from the *parque.* (Singles Q60, with A/C Q125; doubles Q90/Q175.) Or try tidy **Lourdes ❸,** 1 Av. A, Zona 1. (Singles and doubles Q50; triples Q60; all with private bath.)

Pacific Slope

GUATEMALA

TALISMÁN. It's 200m between the Guatemalan and Mexican border posts. Money changers are on both sides. The nearest town is **Malacatán;** frequent mini-buses connect this with the border (30min., Q2). In Malacatán, you can spend the night at **Pensión Santa Lucía ❷,** 5 Calle 5-25 (singles Q45; doublesQ90). There are six buses daily to **Guatemala City** (5½hr.); if you miss those, connect through Malacatán. Talismán is connected to the western highlands by way of **San Marcos** (1½hr. away).

RETALHULEU

Reu (RAY-oo), as Retalhuleu is concisely nicknamed, is the most pleasant town on the Pacific slope. Buildings surrounding the *parque central* testify to colonial pretensions, from a stately neoclassical city hall to a snow-white church flanked by royal palms. Laid-back Reu is a logical stopover on the way to or from the Mexican border. Visit the Maya ruins of Abaj Tabalik, slide down fake ruins at the Xocomil water park, or take a trip to nearby Pacific beaches.

⌨ TRANSPORTATION. Because Reu is just 5km southwest of El Zarco junction, where the coastal highway (CA2) meets the road to Quetzaltenango, there are plenty of **buses** heading toward the Mexican border and the highlands. Retalhuleu's main **bus terminal, La Galera,** is marked by food stands between 7/8 Av. on 10 Calle. A second bus terminal a few blocks west of the *parque* serves Champerico and the coast. Grab a bus along 8 Av. and ask to be dropped off at the terminal (Q1) or get a taxi (Q10 from the main bus terminal). Walking from the park, follow 5 Av. until it runs into 2aCalle, turn left onto 6a av., then right, and walk until you see parked buses. They run to the Mexican border at **Tecún Umán** (1½hr., every 30min. 4am-6pm, Q10); most continue to the Mexican border at **El Carmen** (2½hr., Q15). Buses also run to **Quetzaltenango** (1½hr., every hr. 5:30am-6pm, Q7) and **Guatemala City** (3½hr., every 30min. 2:30am-9:30pm, Q20-25) via **Escuintla** (2½hr.).

⌨ ORIENTATION AND PRACTICAL INFORMATION. To reach the **parque central,** turn left on 7 Av., walk four blocks to 6 Calle, then turn right and go straight one block. The *parque* is bordered by 6/5 Av. and 5/6 Calles. Most services are near the *parque* or on 7 Av. between the bus stop and the center of town. Exchange currency at **Banco Agrícola Mercantil,** on 5 Av. (Open M-F 8:30am-7pm, Sa 9am-1pm.) **Banca Red,** behind the G&T Continental Bank across from the church, has a Visa **ATM,** as does **Banco Industrial,** behind the church. The following services are on the *parque* unless otherwise noted: **Farmacia Las Palmas**

THE LOCAL STORY

MÚSICA EN VIVO

*Retalhuleu is home to one of the finest guitar and vocal trios in Guatemala, if not in all of Central America. The **Trio San José,** with Carlos Billagrán (1st voice, lead guitar), José Mazariegos (2nd voice, rhythm guitar), and Róblin Mijangos (3rd voice, maracas, rhythm guitar), is the house band at the restaurant in the Hotel Posada Don José, 4 Av. and 5 Calle. Combining earthy three-part harmony with soulful guitar playing, the trio plays W, F, and Sa nights 7-9pm.*

LG: What kind of music do you play?

José: Anything romantic, like boleros, rancheritas, baladas. Lots by the Mexican trios Los Panchos and Los Soberanos, who wrote "Quién Será."

LG: How long have you been playing together?

Róblin: José and I have played together for 35, 40 years. We used to record with a friend of ours, but he passed away five years ago. That's when Carlos started in with us.

Carlos: Right now, we're just trying to keep the trio alive, keep this music alive. There aren't that many trios like us these days. We're the only one in Reu.

Róblin: With every day that passes, we want to make music, romantic music, and make it with excellence.

José: Yeah, like they said, we're fighting to move forward. Music keeps us going, fuels our spirits.

FROM THE ROAD

XOCO ME THE MONEY!

My friend Chelsey and I hop off the Retalhuleu bus at Xocomil Waterpark, Xetulul, only to find it is inaugaration day, open only to the press. I smile and whip out my Let's Go press pass. After a suspicious "Who's the girl?" ("My photographer!"), we're soon strolling into the 64,000 m² park complex.

A speech given by the Recreational Institute of the Works of Guatemala (IRTRA), which owns Xetulul, informs us that the park cost Q350million and employs almost 2000 people. It consists of seven cultural mini-parks representing three periods in Guatemalan history and four European Nations that have influenced it: Spain, France, Italy, and Germany/Switzerland. Finally, the ribbon is cut in a swell of cheesy theme music, and a sea of white faces enters the park. Armed with my Rite-Aid 27-exposure disposable camera and Chelsey's slightly more high-class weapon, we set out to do as Xetulul ads suggest, and document "the experience of a lifetime."

We stroll past "folkloric dancers" in the Pueblo Guatemalteco to the Plaza Italiana. Inside the "Uffizzi" is an uncensored replica of Michaelangelo's David. How progessive! Unbridled immaturity and photos ensue.

Next is Plaza Maya with a nearly full-size plaster replica of the Temple of El Gran Jaguar in Tikal, with a live jaguar in a cage next to it. The beautiful cat is being hunted by a middle-aged woman and her camera-toting husband. The cat slinks to the side of its cage, the woman shuffling along

II (open M-Sa 8am-1:30pm and 2:30-7pm); **police** (☎771 0120; open 24hr.); **Telgua,** 5 Calle 4 Av., a block away from the *parque* (open M-F 8am-6pm, Sa-Su 8am-noon); and **Internet** at **Cafe Internet Antigua,** on the corner of 6 Av. and 5 Calle (M-Sa Q10 per hr, Su Q8 per hr; open daily 8:30am-10pm), or at **Asys Computación,** on 6 Av. 9-16 (☎771 5272; Q10 per hr.). Next to the Museo (see **Sights,** below) is the **post office** (open M-F 8:30am-5:30pm, Sa 9am-1pm).

⬛⬛ ACCOMMODATIONS AND FOOD. Hospedaje San Francisco ❶, 6 Calle 8-30 Zona 1, has mediocre rooms. (Singles Q20, with fan Q30, with bath Q50; doubles Q35/Q45/Q70.) **Hotel Modelo ❹,** 5 Calle 4-53, half a block from the *parque,* is run by an amiable older couple who provide spacious rooms with ceiling fans and cold-water private baths. (☎771 0256. Singles Q65; doubles Q85.) Across the street is upscale **Hotel Astor ❺,** a splurgeworthy indulgence. Large rooms with A/C, a pool and jacuzzi, and a cabinet of Maya relics. (☎771 6475. Singles Q130; doubles Q215.)

For cheap eats, head to the popular, clean **Cafetería La Luna ❷,** on the *parque* at the corner of 5 Av., 5 Calle. (*Almuerzo del día* Q20. Open daily 7:30am-10pm.) Or try **Restaurante El Patio ❶,** 5 Calle across from Telgua. Listen to your favorite Iglesias ballad on the jukebox while enjoying the *almuerzo del día* for Q12. (Hamburgers, filled tortillas, and sandwiches Q8. Open daily 7am-9:30pm.)

◪ SIGHTS. The **Museo de Arqueología y Etnología,** on the parque in the municipal building, has a good collection of Maya artifacts from the pre- to postclassical periods, and a rotating gallery with everything from photographs of Reu's early history, to model aircraft. (*Open Tu-Sa 8:30am-5:30pm, Su 9am-12:30pm, Q10.*)

⬛ DAYTRIPS FROM RETALHULEU

ABAJ TAKALIK

From Reu, take a bus to El Asintal (1 hr., Q1.50). Ride it to the end of the line, which leaves you at the parque central. From there, it's a 4km walk continuing up the road you were traveling, which will take you through a coffee plantation and to the ruins. Between 6am and 5pm there are pickups for hire near the parque that will take you to the site. Admission Q25, including guide.

Though only partially open and excavated, Abaj Takalik is one of the more interesting Maya sites outside of Petén. The settlement, probably occupied between 800 BC and AD 900, once covered 9 sq. km. Today you can see several temple platforms and a series of carved sculptures and stelae, including frogs and an alligator.

PARQUE XOCOMIL

The park is 15min. outside Reu; hop on a Xela-bound bus and ask the driver to drop you off. (☎771 2673 from Guatemala City. Open daily 9am-5pm. Adults Q75, kids Q50.)

Sure, Abaj Takalik sounds kind of cool, but why bother with *real* ruins when you can dive into a "Maya-inspired" wave pool or speed slide? Parque Xocomil (pronounced SHOW-koh-meal) is a well-maintained, modern water park with many theme slides and raft rides, food service, and locker rooms.

CHAMPERICO

*There are **buses** to and from Reu (1hr., about every 30min., Q3.50) with some direct morning buses to Quetzaltenango. Three early buses head directly to Guatemala City, though it's easier to change in Reu.*

Champerico, 43km southwest of Reu via paved road, once the country's third most important port, is a little more lively and developed than most other Pacific towns. It's black sand beach, while short of stunning, is welcoming and pleasant. The best place to hang out is in front of the line of beachfront *comedores*, where thieves are less likely to operate. If you need lodging, try the clean, well-priced **Miramar ❶**, 2 Calle, Av. Coatepeque. (☎773 7231, singles Q25, Q40 with bath; doubles Q50/Q70.) Across the street is nicer, slightly more expensive **Hotel Martita ❸**, with sparkling doubles with private bath. (Singles Q50, with bath Q75; doubles Q60/Q100.)

THE COASTAL HIGHWAY

East of Retalhuleu, the highway passes **Cuyotenango,** where a side road runs 45km south to the nondescript beach of **El Tulate.** Further east on the highway are the towns of **Mazatenango** and **Cocales.** Buses from here run north to Santiago Atitlán and Panajachel. After another 23km, the coastal highway reaches **Santa Lucía Cotzumalguapa,** famous for its archaeological sites. Next up on the highway is rundown **Siquinalá.** A branch road serviced by bus heads to the coast by way of **La Democracia.** The site of Monte Alto is east of La Democracia, but the town plaza is home to its highlight: massive stone heads that may be as many as 4000 years old. Before winding its way to Guatemala City, the coastal highway from Retalhuleu runs though **Escuintla,** a transportation hub. From here, one road goes to **Taxisco,** a town

with him, the husband trying to fit the two of them in the same frame. The cat gives up, and a cold camera clicks. Chelsey and I are much more interested in the fearsome plastic jaguar next to the kiddie pool (a.k.a. the "Wild River"). We take turns mounting the beast and taking pictures. Our poaching goes undetected. We ea our way through Europe until the su sets on fantasy-land.

The next day Xetulul makes the front page, hailed as a momentous cultural achievement. The *Prensa Libre* June 29th writes that "tourists o the world will find yet another reason to visit Guatemala," and that it is "another reason to be proud to be Guatemalan." Do I feel proud to be an American because of Disne World? Did I feel proud when, in 6th grade, one of my classmates was asked to name a national park and said, "Six Flags"? (After a moment o shocked silence, the teacher called on another student who answered "Jellystone.") No, there are far bette reasons to be proud to be American and far better Guatemalan parks to be proud of. I'm not saying that enter tainment needs to have redeeming social value, but that's exactly the point. Be amused by Xetulul, be proud of Tikal. Elevating a plaster temple to the level of the stone one in the words of my perceptive photogra pher "just doesn't seem *justo*." Or the other hand, Central America's largest amusement park is a place where a tourist doesn't have to feel guilty about being one. Don't check your camera at the door; just make sure you're shooting in the right frame of mind.

—Josiah Pertz

en route to **Monterrico** (p. 388) and the southernmost border with El Salvador. Another road runs to the large, scruffy beach "resort" of **Puerto San José** and the tiny beach town of **Iztapa.**

MONTERRICO

If you have time to visit just one spot along the Pacific coast, this is the place to go. Separated from the mainland by the Chiquimulilla canal, the village is removed from anything resembling commotion. Its black sand beach—hardly pristine, but certainly peaceful—is one of Guatemala's finest, and the town is encircled by a nature reserve. A sand shelf protects Monterrico from the rain but allows visitors to watch the frequent lightning storms a few kilometers offshore. Grab a hammock and let the crashing waves of the Pacific lull you to sleep.

TRANSPORTATION

Buses: To get to Monterrico, first take a bus from the Zona 4 terminal either direct to **La Avellana,** with Transport Cubanita (3½hr.; 10:30am, 12:30, 2:20pm; Q15) or first to **Taxisco** on one of many chicken buses, or try the Pullman El Condor (2hr.; 6, 11am, 1:30pm; Q15) and change there for a bus to La Avellana (30min., every hr. 7am-2:30pm, Q3), then the ferry. To leave Monterrico, take a return ferry. Buses leave for Taxisco every hr. 7:30am-3pm. To **Guatemala City,** take the Taxisco bus and transfer there or at **Chiquimulilla** (frequent buses stop across from the Esso station).

Ferry: To and from La Avenalla to Monterrico (30min.; one leaves for Monterrico right after the bus pulls in, Q3). *Lanchas* from **Iztapa** to **Puerto Viejo** (5min., Q2) from where you can take a bus to Monterrico (1hr.; 8am, noon, 2, 4, 6pm; Q15). A ferry leaves **Monterrico** for La **Avellana** 30min. before each bus to Taxisco.

Microbus: Some travel agencies in **Antigua** offer express round-trip service to La Avenalla. Try Don Quijote Travel (☎/fax 832 7513).

ORIENTATION AND PRACTICAL INFORMATION

Monterrico has one main road, which heads south toward the beach; buses or *lanchas* will drop you off at the end of it. All of the hotels and restaurants are either on this street, along the beach, or set back from the beach. There are **no banks or police** in Monterrico. Walking toward the ocean on the main street, there is a **pharmacy** 50m to the left (open daily 7am-7pm), with a **post office** nearby on the main street. (Open M-F 8am-5:30pm, Sa 9am-1:30pm.) The best source of local **tourist information** is the fabulous Frenchman Henry, owner of the bar **El Animal Desconocido** (see below). Also try either of the two language schools listed below.

ACCOMMODATIONS

Hotels tend to jack up their prices on Saturdays, during high tourist season in late June and July, and during Guatemalan holidays, especially *Semana Santa*. Make sure to get a room equipped with mosquito netting, or bring your own.

Hotel El Mangle Eco Resort (☎369 8958, cell 611 8547). Facing the ocean at the end of the main road, head to the left a few hundred meters. Though the only thing truly "Eco" about this "Resort" is its proximity to the nature reserve, its well-kept pool and antique wooden carvings make it a pleasant place to stay. Call ahead for reservations. Q50 per person, Q60 on Sat. ❸

Kaiman Inn (☎ 334 6215), on the beach about 200m to your left when facing the ocean at the end of the main road. A decent place to go for quiet surroundings. It has a good Italian restaurant. Q50 per person. ❸

The Guesthouse, off the beach. Walking toward the beach, turn left at the post office and walk a few hundred meters. The 4 double rooms come with fans and mosquito netting; shared bath, kitchen, and laundry facilities are available for guest use. Q25 per person, Q20 per night for more than two nights. ❶

Hotel Baule Beach (☎ 202 4152), next to Kaiman Inn. Shade-covered tables and relaxing hammocks front the beach; the rooms are a bit rough but passable. Ask for a room in the back. Q65 per person in low season, Q100 in high season. ❹

🔆 🍴 FOOD AND ENTERTAINMENT

The beachfront Italian restaurant of the **Hotel Pez de Oro** ❹, is probably the best bet for a nice meal, offering fresh fish (Q40-50) and banana flambé (Q15). Take a left at the end of the main road. **Kaiman** ❺ is good as well. There are several *comedores* along the main road. Near the beach, popular **Divino Maestro** ❷, has some excellent seafood (entrees Q16-25), while **Comedor Sudy** ❷ (next door), offers similarly priced meals in a clean and extremely purple setting.

There are several options for night owls. **El Animal Desconocido,** 100m to the right after the end of the main road, is a good bet. Henry, the bar's owner, speaks English, French, and Spanish, and will give you directions or other local tourist info. Try his specialty cocktail, *El Animal Desconocido* (Q15), a mix of Malibu, milk, and cacao. (Open daily 5pm-late, happy hour 8-10pm.) **El CaraCol,** 100m to the left at the end of the main road, is the main competition. (Happy hour daily noon-1pm and 5-7pm and F-Sa 9-11pm.) **Johnny's Place** has the best of all worlds: bar, Internet access, and bungalows. (Q20 for 1st hr., Q10 for each additional ½hr.)

👁 🏔 SIGHTS AND OUTDOORS

BIOTOPO MONTERRICO-HAWAII. Established to protect the turtles, Biotopo Monterrico-Hawaii also preserves one of Guatemala's last remaining mangrove swamps and is home to thousands of birds. The Biotopo encompasses 2800 hectares, including Monterrico and several smaller towns. Take a rewarding boat tour through the dense mazes of the mangrove reserve, but note that non-motorized boats are less likely to scare away the animals. *(Ask Iguanatours, down the main street, down the road across from the soccer field, to arrange a tour for you. Q10-15 per hr.)*

OTHER NEARBY SIGHTS. Reserva Natural de Monterrico is not the grandiose zoo Walt Disney would have built, but is a fun visit for those interested in iguanas and caimans. A few tanks full of little iguanas, turtles, and caimans are placed around a short path. *(Behind the Hotel Baule Beach. Open 8am-noon and 2-5pm. Q3 for nationals, Q8 all others. Some report not being charged.)*

Five kilometers east along the coast is **Hawaii,** but we're not talking Waikiki. Instead you'll find a sleepy fishing village, as well as a privately funded organization working to save turtles. *(Walk 5km; 2hr. down the beach east from Monterrico.)*

🔳 BORDER WITH EL SALVADOR

*Chiquimulilla and Taxisco are the best places to catch a ride to the border (45min., every hr. 5am-5pm, Q8). If you're entering Guatemala at this border crossing, buses head toward **Guatemala City** via Chiquimulilla and Taxisco. Pullman buses run (4hr., every 30min. 9am-4pm, Q30) as do 2nd-class buses (4½hr., every hr. 6am-3:30pm, Q15).*

IN RECENT NEWS

VITAVANGELISM

A middle-aged woman in a pantsuit steps confidently to the front of the moving bus, briefcase in hand. If first-time chicken-bus riders expect an evangelical speech, they're only half right. "God wants your family to be healthy. . . That's why I'm here to tell you about this great new vitamin."

The bottle the lady hands out looks like many others hawked by different salespeople. It's almost always ginseng, occasionally with glutamic acid to make it a "multivitamin." No matter what the composition, the large market seems to have stabilized at Q10 ("today and today only, not Q30, not Q20, but Q10!!"). So the question is, why has this particular product become so popular, and why is this sales approach so effective?

The success of "vitamins" may be the result of an underfunded and over-burdened national healthcare system. Private hospitals, almost always a cut above, are too expensive for many to afford. With health care so hard to come by, people want and have come to rely upon cheap bottled miracles.

There are more Bibles than Physicians' Desk References, so when Guillermo Graham steps up to the pulpit at the front of the bus to preach about keeping the family healthy to praise God, he gives people's judgement a one-two punch as strong as Muhammed Ali's. I'm not saying snake oil is a recent invention, or that using religion to sell unrelated products is all that original. But what role should the Vitaminister play?

---

*Taxisco is the transfer point for **Monterrico**. On the El Salvador side, frequent buses run to Sonsonate. Immigration offices open daily 6am-10pm.*

The peaceful hamlet of **Ciudad Pedro de Alvarado** sits at Guatemala's southernmost border crossing with El Salvador. **La Hachadura** on the Salvadoran side provides easy access to Sonsonate, though it's not the most convenient crossing to San Salvador. While there are no fees on the Guatemalan side, Americans and Canadians must buy a US$10 tourist visa in El Salvador. At the border, **Banrural** exchanges dollars, *quetzales*, and Salvadoran *colones*. (Open daily 6:30am-9pm.)

EASTERN GUATEMALA

Guatemala's short Caribbean coastline, squeezed into the right angle between Belize and Honduras, is a world away from the jungles and highlands of the rest of the country. Largely populated by people of African descent, the towns along the coast boast delicious seafood, numerous boating and hiking possibilities, and a distinct local culture. Laid-back Livingston is the most well known and tourist-friendly. The other major draw of the region is the Río Dulce, which begins at the northeastern end of Lago Izabal and flows into Livingston.

There are two ways to the Caribbean coast. The first is to take the Atlantic Hwy. to its end in Puerto Barrios, from where boats run to Livingston. The highway passes the ruins of Quiriguá, home to some of the best preserved Maya stelae, a branch road to Esquipulas, one of the most important pilgrimage sites in all Central America, and Chiquimula, a gateway to the Maya ruins of Copán across the border in Honduras. The second option is to head to Fronteras, at the beginning of the Río Dulce on the Lago de Izabal, and from there take the boat ride on the river.

CHIQUIMULA

Thirty-two kilometers south of the Atlantic Hwy., hot, bustling Chiquimula is primarily a transport hub and an overnight stop for those coming to and from the Copán ruins in Honduras, accessible via the border at El Florido.

⊏ TRANSPORTATION. Buses leave for: **Esquipulas** (1hr., every 10min. 5am-7pm, Q8); **Guatemala City** (3½hr., every 30min. 2am-3:30pm, Q20); **Puerto Barrios** (4hr., every hr. 4:30am-2:45pm, Q20); **Zacapa** (30min., every 30min. 4:30am-5:30pm, Q4); and the **Honduran border** at **El Florido** (2½hr.; 6:30, 7, 9:30, 10:30am, every

30min. noon-4:30pm; Q8-15). **Trucks** on the Honduran side head to **Copán** (it's best to set out early). For more information on the border crossing, see p. 469.

■■ 🛈 **ORIENTATION AND PRACTICAL INFORMATION.** Hilltop Chiquimula is laid out in a grid. *Avenidas* run across the hill, while *calles* follow the slope down. *Avenida* numbers increase as you head downhill and, facing downhill, *calle* numbers increase from left to right. The **bus station** is at 10 Av., 1/2 Calles, and the **parque central** is at 7 Av., 3 Calle. **Bancafé**, on the corner of 8Av., 4 Calle, has a **24hr.** Visa **ATM**, and changes traveler's checks. (Open M-F 8:30am-4:30pm, Sa 1-5pm.) There are **markets** at the terminal and the *parque*, and a **Paiz** supermarket on 7 Av., 3 Calle (open daily 8am-9pm). Other services include: **police** (☎942 0356), at the end of 8 Av. across from the station; **Hospital Centro Clínico de Especialidades,** 9 Av., 4 Calle (☎942 2053; open 24hr.); **Telgua**, on 7 Av, just downhill from the *parque* (open M-F 8am-6pm); **Internet** at **Contacto Digital** on 8 Av., 4/5 Calle (open M-Sa 9am-9pm, Su 9am-1pm; Q18 per hr.); and the **post office** in the alley across from the bus stop (open M-F 8:30am-5pm, Sa 9am-1pm).

🏠🍴 **ACCOMMODATIONS AND FOOD. Hotel Darío ❶**, 8 Av., 4/5 Calles, has large, clean, well-kept rooms. (☎942 0192. Q20 per person, with bath Q30, with A/C Q50; doubles Q40/Q50/Q60.) **Hotel Chiquimula ❹**, next to Paiz, across from the *parque*, has spacious rooms with private baths and fans. (☎942 0387. Singles Q60; doubles Q80.) **Hotel Hernández ❷**, 7/8 Av., 3 Calle, down the street from the *parque*, is a decent option with clean rooms and baths. The front door locks at 10:30pm, but the swimming pool keeps you entertained. (☎942 0708. Singles Q40, with bath and cable Q60; doubles Q50/Q90.)

Cheap *comedores* line 8 Av., 3/4 Calles, and the ones in the market to the left of the church off the *parque* are dirt cheap. You know a place is serious about meat when they serve it by the pound. Family-run **Parrillada de Calero ❹**, 7 Av., 4/5 Calles, specializes in grilled meats. (Q130 for 4 people. Open daily 9am-10pm.) **El Tesoro ❸**, 7Av. between 4/5 Calle, has good Chinese food. (Open daily 11am-9pm.)

ESQUIPULAS

Esquipulas holds the most important Catholic shrine in all Central America: **El Cristo Negro**, a mahogany crucifix delivered by Spanish missionaries in 1595. Ever since its arrival, the figure, now housed in the gleaming, white-domed Basílica de Esquipulas, has been revered for its miraculous healing powers. Most famously it cured the bishop of Guatemala, Pardo de Figueroa, of his ailments in 1737. More than one million visitors stream through every year, and the bustling, occasionally seedy town makes its living catering to them.

📧 **TRANSPORTATION.** The **Rutas Orientales** bus station is across from the gas station on the corner of 11 Calle, 1 Av. **Buses** leave from the stretch of Doble Vía in front of the Basílica for: **Guatemala City** (4hr., every 30min. 2:30am-4:30pm, Q24) and **Chiquimula** (1hr., minivans every 10min. 5am-6pm, Q8), where connections can be made to **Quiriguá, Puerto Barrios,** and other stops along the Atlantic Hwy. **Minibuses** also run to the borders of **El Salvador** (1hr., every 30min. 6am-3pm, Q8) and **Honduras** (20min., every 30min. 4:30am-5pm, Q5).

■■ 🛈 **ORIENTATION AND PRACTICAL INFORMATION.** Buses drop pilgrims on **Doble Vía**, also called 11 Calle, the main east-west drag crossing in front of the *basílica* and the **parque central.** The main avenue used to be the highway and has a handful of names. It is **3 Av.,** but you may hear Camino Real or Quirio Octaño. It

GUATEMALA

Eastern Guatemala

GUATEMALA

TO SAYACHÉ

Playa Grande (Ixcán)
Parque Nacional Xuctzul
Laguna de Lachuá

SIERRA DE CHAMÁ

QUICHÉ

Nebaj

Sacapulas

Uspantán

Santa Cruz del Quiché

Totonicapán

Sololá

Panajachel

Lago de Atitlán

Chichicastenango

Chimalténango

Antigua
S. Vicente Pacaya
Volcán de Pacaya

Candelaria Caves

ALTA VERAPAZ

Raxrujá

Fray Bartolomé de las Casas

Sebol

Chahal

Cahabón

Lanquín

San Pedro Carchá

Cobán

San Cristóbal Verapaz

Cubulco

BAJA VERAPAZ

San Miguel Chicaj

Rabinal

Purulhá

Biotopo del Quetzal

Salamá

San Jerónimo

El Rancho Junction

SIERRA DE CHUACÚS

TO POPTÚN (70km)

Modesto Méndez

SIERRA DE SANTA CRUZ

El Estor

Panzós

La Tinta

Montaña Rubelpec

SIERRA DE LAS MINAS

Montañas Piedras Blancas

Río Hondo

Guastatoya

Sanarate

EL PROGRESO

Los Mixcos

GUATEMALA

Mixco
Ciudad de Guatemala

Villa Nueva
Amatitlán
Lago de Amatitlán

San Pedro Sula
Omoa

Puerto Cortés

Golfo de Honduras

Pta. Manabique
Bahía de Amatique
Livingston

Biotopo Chocón Machaca

Castillo de San Felipe

Lago de Izabal

Mariscos

IZABAL

Amates

El Florido

Zacapa

BELIZE

CA13

Pta. de Manabique
Biotopo Punta de Manabique
Pta. Morena
Puerto Barrios
Finca Inca

El Cinchado

Entre Ríos

Fronteras (Río Dulce)

La Ruidosa

Bananera
Morales

Quiriguá
Quiriguá

La Unión

ZACAPA

Tecucigalpita
Cuyamelito

Azacualpa

Quimistán

San Marcos

Macuelizo

SIERRA DEL MERENDÓN

Montañas del Mico

San Francisco

SIERRA DEL ESPÍRITU SANTO

Montañas del Gallinero

La Entrada
Protección

Nueva Arcadia

Dulce Nombre de Copán

Sta. Rosa de Copán

SIERRA DEL GALLINERO

Florida

Copán Ruinas
Copán

Cuyuyagua

Corquín

Agua Caliente

Nueva Ocotepeque

OCOTEPEQUE

EL SALVADOR

Guarita

Dulce Nombre de María

La Palma

CHIQUIMULA

Chiquimula

Quetzaltepeque

Esquipulas

Concepción
Las Minas

Anguiatú

Lago de Güija

CA12

Las Montañas

JALAPA

San Luis Jilotepeque

Montaña de Pinula

Jalapa

Volcán Jumay

San José Pinula

Mataquescuintla

SANTA ROSA

Cuilapa

Barberena

Pueblo Nuevo Viñas

Los Dolores

Esquintla

Jutiapa

Yupiltepeque

Sta. María Ixhuatán

HONDURAS

TO TEGUCIGALPA (100km)

CA9

CA1

CA14

0 30 kilometers
0 30 miles

heads north and downhill from Doble Vía at the *basílica*. With your back to the church, *avenidas* increase in number left to right; *calles* increase as they near the *parque*. **Bancafé,** 4 blocks down 3 Av. from the *basílica*, changes money, accepts traveler's checks, and has a 24hr. **ATM.** (Open M-F 8:30am-7pm, Sa 9am-1pm.) Other services include: **Supermarket, Despensa Familiar,** 3 Av., 3 blocks south of the Basílica (open M-Sa 7am-7pm, Su 7am-6pm); **police,** at the end of 6a Av., across from the post office (☎943 1207); **Farmacia San Rafael,** at the beginning of 3a Av., across from the *basílica* (☎943 1216; open 24hr.); **Hospital de Especialidades Esquipulas** (☎943 1654), 9 Calle and 3Av.; **Telgua** office, 5 Av., 9 Calle, Zona 1 (open M-F 8am-6pm; after hours, use the phones outside); **Internet** at **Speedtech,** 3 Av. 8-87 (Q12 per hr.; open daily 9am-9:30pm). The **post office** is between 2/3 Calles at the northern end of 6 Av. (Open M-F 8:30am-5:30pm, Sa 9am-1pm.)

⚲ ACCOMMODATIONS. Esquipulas treats its wealthier pilgrims well with several high-class hotels. Unfortunately, many cheaper places are not as attractive or friendly. Prices double as crowds descend on the town on weekends and during festivals. Reservations are a must around the feast day of the lord of Esquipulas (Jan. 15), and during Lent. **Hotel Monte Cristo ❹,** 3 Av. and 10 Calle (☎943 1453), is one of the nicest upper mid-range hotels around. Sparkling clean rooms. (Singles Q67, with private bath Q152; doubles Q85/Q183.) **Pensión Niño de Dios ❶,** 3 Av. 9-19, has tiny, fairly clean rooms. Communal baths are slightly above average. (Q25 per person.) **Hotel La Favorita ❷,** 2 Av. and 10 Calle, has especially clean communal baths. (Singles Q40; doubles Q60. Q75 per person with private bath.)

❐ FOOD. High quality dining can be found at **Restaurante Las Fronteras ❸** on Doble Vía, across from the *basílica*. Mostly Guatemalan food with some international options. (Cheese ravioli Q30. Open M-F 7am-10pm, Sa-Su 6:30am-11pm.) **Restaurant El Angel ❸,**11 Calle and 2 Av., also below the *basílica*, has not-so-authentic but nonetheless tasty Chinese food and a very clean setting. (Duck with vegetables Q35. Open daily 11am-9pm.) Cheap restaurants line 3 Av. , and snack carts cluster on 11 Calle. Prices are reasonable farther away from the *basílica*.

◙ SIGHTS. The **Basílica de Esquipulas** and its **Cristo Negro** are the city's main attractions, easily reached through the *parque*. The entrance is outside on the left of the *basílica*. The interior, always full of praying visitors, is lit by many burning candles. El Cristo Negro is protected by glass behind the altar. The walls in the hallway are lined with small metal plaques of thanks and images of body parts that the Cristo has healed. On Sunday and religious holidays, you may wait hours for a 20-second glimpse of the statue. Remember to exit backwards down the ramp or pilgrims will think you're turning your back on the Lord. Benedictine monks bless lines of people and their souvenirs with holy water to the right of the *basílica*.
If you're lucky, you may catch a syncretic religious ceremony at the **Cueva de las Minas** (admission Q5). To get there, follow the street to the right of the *basílica* until you reach the highway, then take a left. The ticket booth is 50m up the road on the right, past the Texaco station. The 15min. walk ends at a well-maintained park, with a refreshment stand, playground, small zoo, and a cave shrouded in religious myth. Although there is significant evidence that Spanish sculptor Quirio Octaño fashioned the Cristo Negro, many still believe it was discovered in this cave. Watch your head when walking through the tunnel and don't touch the walls lest you wish to emerge black with soot. For a panoramic view of Esquipulas, climb up to the **Franciscan convent** on the opposite end of town. Follow 3 Av. north to its base where it becomes a dirt road; turn left, and after two blocks it will dead-end. Walk 1km up the rocky road on the right. Just uphill, the **Cruz del Perdón**

EL CRISTO NEGRO El Cristo Negro, a 16th-century mahogany carving of Christ on the cross, is all the rage in Esquipulas, and replicas and imitations can be found throughout the New World. It owes its inspiration to the Chortí natives living in the area, who by the mid-16th century had been converted to Catholicism by Spanish missionaries. One fateful day, a group of natives working in the cotton fields had a mass vision of Christ on the cross, which they interpreted as a call to worship. At their request, a chapel was built and the famed Spaniard Quirio Cataño was commissioned to carve a life-size emblem of their vision. El Cristo Negro has always been *Cristo*, but not always *negro*: decades of the devout burning candles and incense and rubbing their hands over the carving turned this chameleon Christ from brown to black. Local legend has it that the mahogany miracle worker was not man-made, but instead emerged from the black earth of the caves in the mountains just above Esquipulas. El Cristo is now out of reach, carefully enclosed in a glass case.

(Cross of Pardon), is surrounded by hundreds of plastic water bags filled with small rocks and hanging from tree branches. Maya pilgrims bring the rocks with them as a penance for their sins and leave them at the cross to gain forgiveness.

La Piedra de los Compadres, 2km north of town on the old highway, is another traditional holy spot. Legend has it that many years ago, two pilgrims traveling to Esquipulas became a bit too amorous and hence were turned into stone by God. A large boulder (the man) balances on the smaller one (the woman). Although some visitors are struck by the humorous nature of this site, many devout Catholic Maya still bring stones to throw at the effigy of the two sinners. To get there, take 3 Av. to where it becomes a dirt road at the church. Turn right onto the cobblestone street. After one block, turn left and follow that street up to cross a bridge built in the 16th century. Once you've passed the graveyard, continue another 5min. to the Piedra. At the summit, a 1hr. walk from the Piedra, is a vista of Central America's only triple-border; Guatemala, Honduras, and El Salvador are all visible.

NEAR ESQUIPULAS

★ AGUA CALIENTE: BORDER WITH HONDURAS

From the center of Esquipulas, *colectivo* drivers can take you to **Agua Caliente,** the site of the border crossing (10min., 5:30am-6pm, Q5). Another *colectivo* will whisk you the 2km from Guatemalan to Honduran immigration (Q2). Though money can be exchanged in Esquipulas, there are better rates at the border. Ask around for the best rate. US dollars and AmEx traveler's cheks can be changed at **Banco de Occidente** on the Honduran side. (Open M-Sa 8am-3pm, Su 8am-2pm.) The **immigration office** is open daily (3am-7pm). If you're driving across the border, go to the *tránsito* office around the corner from immigration. Which forms you have to fill out and how much you must pay depend on your plans. Standard entrance tax is L17. Guatemalan immigration officials may try to ask for an unofficial exit fee, usually of about Q10. Politely refuse, saying *"la salida no cuesta nada"* (the exit doesn't cost anything). If they insist, which they most likely will not, ask for a receipt with the officer's name on it. Once in Honduras, **buses** go to: **San Pedro Sula** (5hr., every hr. 4am-midnight, L100); **Tegucigalpa** (8hr.; 4, 6am, 4pm; L135); and **Ocotepeque** (every 30min. 4am-7:15pm, L10). The San Pedro Sula and Tegucigalpa buses crawl sluggishly over the misty hills and stop at **Santa Rosa de Copán** (2-3hr., L55) and **La Entrada** (3-3½hr., L70), where you can catch buses to **Copán Ruinas.**

QUIRIGUÁ

While Quiriguá is smaller than other sites on La Ruta Maya, it contains some of the grandest and best-preserved stelae and zoomorphs, sculptings with images of both humans and animals. Quiriguá's beginnings have been traced back to AD 300, though its exact origins are unknown. The city remained subservient to the nearby empire of Copán for several centuries and was probably valued for its strategic position on the River Motagua. Under the leadership of Cauac Sky ("Two-Legged Sky"), Quiriguá defeated Copán by AD 737 and became an independent power. During the Sky Dynasty, Quiriguá's power continued to grow, as evidenced by a the prolonged construction campaign that gave rise to a new monument every five years. Among the monuments erected were the spectacular stelae, many of which bear Cauac Sky's now-crumbling visage. Quiriguá is now a World Heritage Site.

TRANSPORTATION. To get to town from the ruins, take a bus down to the highway (Q1) and walk, or take any bus traveling the Atlantic Hwy. and ask to be let off at Quiriguá. For the Ruinas, a regular bus zips visitors 4km from the highway drop-off through a Del Monte banana plantation to the site (every 30min. 7:30am-5:30pm, Q1); the road is well-traveled, and many passing trucks will let you hop in the back for Q1 or nothing at all. Back at the highway turnoff from the main road, **buses** leave for **Chiquimula** (2hr., every 30min. 6am-6pm, Q12); **Guatemala City** (4hr., every 45min. 3am-5pm, Q35); and **Puerto Barrios** (2hr., every 30min. 5am-9pm, Q10) . Nearby Amates is a stop-off for minibuses heading all over the area, including "El Cruce," where connections can be made south and north to Petén. A minibus to **Mariscos** on Lago Izabal leaves about every 30min. (Q7.)

ORIENTATION AND PRACTICAL INFORMATION. There is one **public telephone** by the Hotel Royal and another at the bus turnoff. To the ruins, walk or catch the shuttle to the highway (.75km, Q1), turn right on Atlantic Highway or take any bus heading toward the turnoff to the ruins (1.5im, Q1, sometimes free). Then catch a bus to the ruins (4km, Q1). The combined trips take about 30min.

ACCOMMODATIONS AND FOOD. Pickings are slim for food and hotels; the ruins are best as a stop en route to somewhere else along the Atlantic Hwy. The most reasonable place to stay in the village is **Hotel Royal ❶**. The simple rooms are large and clean, providing a fine place to rest your inscription-filled head. (Singles Q30, with bath Q50; doubles Q60/Q90; 6-person suites Q120.) The **restaurant ❶** in front serves standard Guatemalan fare. (Q15-35; veg. meals available.)

THE RUINS. Thatched roofs protect the monuments from the elements. The stelae and zoomorphs (designated with letters of the alphabet) stand like sentinels in the site's plaza central. The plaza is an open field, making sunscreen and mosquito repellent a necessity. **Stela E,** a towering 12m, is the tallest in Central America, and is on the Guatemalan 10-centavo coin. **Stela D** contains some of the most fantastically designed and best-preserved artwork in the region. Also look for the **ballcourt** at the southwest end of the plaza (near the mango tree) and the **Acropolis,** the residence of the elite, to the south of the plaza. Although there are no guides to interpret the glyphs that line many of the monuments, a bilingual history of the site is available (Q10) at the entrance kiosk. (Ruins open daily 7:30am-5pm. Q25.)

LAGO DE IZABAL

Lago de Izabal, northwest of the Atlantic Hwy., is an expansive lake gradually developing into a tourist draw. The largest lake in Guatemala, it's a great place to enjoy water activities. The town of Fronteras (Río Dulce), along the Atlantic Hwy., is the launching point for excursions to the Spanish fortress El Castillo de San Felipe and the swimming holes and waterfalls of Finca El Paraíso, as well as the worthwhile boat trip down the river to Livingston. Other lake towns with accommodations are El Estor, connected by a slow bus to Cobán, and Mariscos.

FRONTERAS (RÍO DULCE)

More commonly called Río Dulce, Fronteras lies at the foot of Lago de Izabal. The town is rundown, but stands as an important transportation hub, and is pleasant enough to spend the night. It is a scenic 23km boat ride to the Garífuna village of Livingston. Buses leave regularly for Petén, Flores, and Guatemala City. Take a few minutes to admire the view from the longest bridge in Central America.

⌁ TRANSPORTATION. The main *lancha* dock, jutting off of Restaurante Río Bravo on the northeast side of the bridge, and the bus station are on the northwest side of the bridge. Most other services are along Río Dulce Rd., which leads to the bridge. **Buses** to **El Estor** depart from 2 long blocks from the north side of the bridge and to the left down the first cross street. (1hr., every hr. 11am-3pm, Q10); **Guatemala City** (5hr.; 3, 5:45, 7:45, 11:45am; Q35); **Puerto Barrios** (3hr., every 1½hr. 7am-5pm, Q12); and **Flores** (6hr.; 7 daily 7am-8pm; Q50, Q70 with a reserved seat) via **Poptún** (Q30). Inquire at **Tijax** Express near the dock for more regular departures to **Guatemala City** (every hr. 10:30am-2:30am) and **Flores** (roughly every hr. from 9am-3am). For details on the popular Río Dulce cruise to Livingston, see **Near Livingston,** p. 402. If you need *lancha* transport in the evening, the information booth 50m before the bridge on the turn-off toward the dock will call one for you until 8pm.

⌁ PRACTICAL INFORMATION. All places of interest are located on the north side of the bridge. The **INGUAT** office is 200m from the bridge. (Open M-Sa 9am-5pm.) The **Tijax Express** tourist office also offers good tourist information; English is spoken. **Bancafé** and **Banrural** 300m from the bridge, exchange traveler's checks. (Open M-F 9am-5pm, Sa 9am-1pm.) Other services include: **pharmacies; Internet** at **Captain Nemo's Communications** in Bruno's Hotel complex right before the bridge (Q20 per hr. open M-Sa 8am-8pm.), and the **post office,** a few blocks past the banks away from the bridge (open M-F 9am-5pm).

⌁⌁ ACCOMMODATIONS AND FOOD. Hotel Backpackers ❹, on the waterfront at the end of the lesser populated side of the bridge, has everything going for it except its remote location . Run by the center for troubled youth, Casa Guatemala, it offers a communal kitchen, dorm rooms, private rooms, and space for hammocks. The outdoor **restaurant ❸,** though a little pricey, has a beautiful view and excellent lasagna for Q30. (☎/fax 208 1779. Restaurant open daily 7am-9:30pm. Laundry Q20 per load. Bunks Q25; simple rooms Q60 per person, with bath Q75.) A more upscale place to stay is the **Tijax ❸.** Located on a working rubber plantation across the water, it will provide a free ferry (ask at the infobox near the dock), or you can walk in if you get off a bus at the sign 2.4km before town. Tijax offers horseback riding, sailing, hiking, and a nice swimming pool. The **restaurant ❸** is expensive, but delicious (fusilli with pesto Q34), and popular with the older crowd. Camping available. (☎930 5507; tijax@guate.com. Restaurant open daily 7:30am-9pm. Singles US$7.50; cabin with bath US$25; doubles US$12, cabin with bath US$30. 6 person bungalows with kitchen US$108.) Another option on the more populated side of the bridge is **Hospedaje Don Paco ❷,** down the cross street from the El Estor bus stop. Small, clean rooms with cement floors surround a quiet courtyard and shared bathrooms. (Singles Q40; doubles Q60; triples Q90.)

NEAR FRONTERAS

🔵 EL CASTILLO DE SAN FELIPE

Castillo de San Felipe and San Felipe are a pleasant 45min. walk from Fronteras. Heading away from the bridge, take the first left at Pollito Tienda; bear left at the fork. Frequent **pickups** *depart one block from the bridge in Fronteras (every 30min. 6am-6pm, Q2).* **Boats** *coming from Livingston will usually drop you off in San Felipe if you ask, and Río Dulce boat tours often include a stop here. Direct lancha from Río Dulce Q75 round trip.* **Castillo** *open daily 8am-5pm. Grounds open daily 7am-6pm. Q10; Q5 to use the pool.*

El Castillo de San Felipe is 3km past the bridge at Fronteras. The original Spanish fortress was built in 1651 to stave off plundering pirates intent on looting warehouses on Lake Izabal. The reconstructed version rests on the original foundations. Though moderate in size, the *castillo* has enough dungeons, cannons, and dark cramped passageways to merit a trip. The lakeside Castillo grounds have a pool, bathrooms, picnic facilities, and a restaurant. The charming village of **San Felipe** is a 5min. walk north from the castle. **Hotel and Restaurant Don Humberto ❷** is a peaceful place to plop down for the night. Humberto's small cement rooms have plush beds and private baths, and are a good budget value. (Q36 per person.)

🔺 FINCA EL PARAÍSO

The finca is occasionally included on Río Dulce boat tours. It's also reachable on any bus traveling between Fronteras and El Estor. From Fronteras, you can get to Finca El Paraíso and Boquerón by hopping on a **bus** *to* **El Estor** *and asking to be let off at either one (Q7). Or, from El Estor, grab a bus to Fronteras and tell the driver where you want to get off. From either city, it's no problem to see both the canyon and the waterfalls in one day. Buses drop passengers at 6 Av. on 3 Calle (the main drag). Last bus back to Fronteras passes the Finca at 4:30pm. Admission Q10.*

Along the north side of the lake between San Felipe and El Estor, the beautiful Finca el Paraíso is a working ranch a 10min. walk from a fascinating and beautiful hot waterfall that cascades into clear, deep pools, perfect for swimming. There are caves nearby (bring a flashlight), and horse and rowboat rentals (horses Q50 per hr., boats Q25 per 30min.). There is also **camping** (Q25; hammock rentals Q25). A bit farther down the road to El Estor is **El Boquerón** (admission Q5). Antonio, at the house by the river a bit before the bridge, will paddle you up into a spectacular canyon and drop you off on a beach near caves and river rapids (Q20).

PUERTO BARRIOS

United Fruit Company exports once made Puerto Barrios, at the end of the highway from Guatemala City to the Caribbean, the nation's most crucial port. Commerce has since shifted to Pacific ports, and the city's significance has faded. Today, the palm tree-lined streets of the city boast many pharmacies but little of interest to the healthy traveler, most of whom pass through en route to Livingston, Belize, or Honduras. Walking the streets at night is not recommended.

⌗ TRANSPORTATION. Buses wait by the railroad tracks where 9 Calle and 6 Av. intersect, 4 blocks up and 3 blocks over from the dock. Look down the line to find the bus with your destination printed on the window. Litegua buses (☎948 1172) go to **Guatemala City** (5-6hr.; every 30min. 1am-4pm; regular Q30, *especial* Q40). There's also service to **Chiquimula** (4hr., every hr. 5am-5pm, Q20) and **Río Dulce** (1hr., 6, 9, 11:30am, 1pm; Q10). Take a Guatemala City bus as far as **La Ruidosa** for connections to **Río Dulce** and the **Petén, Río Hondo** for connections south to **Esquipulas** and **El Salvador,** or **El Rancho** for connections to **Cobán** and the **Verapaces.**

The **boat** dock is at 1 Av., 12 Calle. A ferry heads to **Livingston** (1½-2hr., 10:30am and 3pm; Q10). *Lanchas* also make the trip (30min., 6:30am-5pm, Q25) and head to **Punta Gorda, Belize** (50min.; M, W-Th, Sa-Su 10am, Tu and F 8am; Q70). Paco's ferry heads to **Punta Gorda** (10am, BZ$25). Before departing for Belize, stop at the **immigration office.** From the dock, head down 12 Calle one block to the small red building on the corner of 3 Av. (Open daily 7am-7pm.)

■ ■ **ORIENTATION AND PRACTICAL INFORMATION.** The **municipal boat dock** serves as a busy stepping-stone to Livingston and neighboring Honduras and Belize. The dock lies on 2 Av. past the end of 12 Calle. *Avenidas* run north-south, increasing in number away from the water. *Calles* run east-west, increasing in number from north to south. The **immigration office** is a block from the dock on the corner of 3 Av. and 12 Calle. **Banco Industrial,** 7 Av., 7 Calle, changes currency and has a **24hr. ATM.** (Open M-F 8:30am-5pm, Sa 10am-2pm.) **Banco Internacional,** at 6 Av., 8 Calle, has **Western Union.** (Open M-F 9am-6pm, Sa 9am-1pm.) A **market** is at 9 Calle, 6 Av. **Farmacia La Fe** is on 5/6 Av., 9 Calle, next to the Litegua office at the bus terminal. (☎948 0796. Open M-F 7am-9pm, Sa 7am-8pm, Su 7am-noon). In an **emergency,** call **Los Bomberos** at 5 Av., 5/6 Calles. (☎122. Open 24hr.) **Clínica Médica** is near the bus terminal at 7 Calle, 6/7 Av. (Open M-F 7am-noon and 2-7pm; Sa 7am-noon.) The **police station** is at 6 Av., 5 Calle. (☎120 or 385. Open 24hr.) **Phones** and **fax** at **Telgua,** 10 Calle, 8 Av. (☎948 2198. Open M-F 8am-6pm.) **Internet** at **Café Internet,** across from the Texaco station on 6Av and 13 Calle. (Q10 per hr. Open daily 9am-9pm.) The **post office** is at 6 Av., 6 Calle. (Open M-F 8:30am-5:30pm.)

■ ■ **ACCOMMODATIONS AND FOOD. Hotel Miami ❷,** 3 Av. 11/12 Calles, offers simple rooms with private baths close to the dock. (☎948 0637. Singles Q40; double Q80.) Upscale **Caribbean Hotel Calypso ❹,** 7 Calle, 6/7 Av., near the terminal (look for the thatched roof across from Banco de los Trabajadores), has cable TV and A/C. (☎948 1121. Singles Q72, with A/C Q94; doubles Q107/Q136; triples Q143/Q164.) North of Hotel Miami, the **Hotel La Caribeña ❸,** 4 Av., 10/11 Calles, has parking lot views. (☎948 0860. Singles Q55; doubles Q80; triples Q100; quads Q120.) There is an attached **restaurant ❶**(Q13; open daily 6am-11pm). **Café Vistalmar ❷** on 1 Av., as it approaches 9 Calle, serves great *tapado* (Q70) and *menú del día* for Q13. (Open daily 7am-1am.) **Maxim ❷,** 6 Av., 8 Calle, is a good Chinese and Guatemalan eatery. This colorful restaurant is a clean retreat from the dirty streets. (Fried chicken Q20. Open daily 10:30am-midnight.) **Pizza Luigi ❸,** on 5 Av. and 13 Calle, is famous for its quality pies. (Small Q35. Open Tu-Su 10am-1pm and 4-9pm.)

NEAR PUERTO BARRIOS

■ **BORDER WITH HONDURAS**

Minibuses run from Puerto Barrios, across from the Despensa Familiar on 8 Calle and 6 Av., to the **Honduran** border (30min., about every 20min., Q10). The minibus from Puerto Barrios drops you off across the border in no-man's land. From there, Honduran pickup trucks (L5) shuttle you 3km to their immigration office in **Corinto,** where money changers swarm outside. From Corinto, buses leave for **Omoa** and **Puerto Cortés, Honduras** on the Caribbean coast (every hr. at about 20 past the hour). The trip from Puerto Barrios to Omoa takes about 4hr. in decent weather; rains sometimes close the road on the Honduran side. The "jungle trail" and boat crossings to Honduras are no longer used.

LIVINGSTON

Life is sweet in Livingston, where the Río Dulce tickles the waves of the Atlantic. Here live Guatemala's largest population of Garífuna, descendants of the African slaves and Carib Indians who formed a distinct language and culture. Livingston offers a sampling of the laid-back Belizean lifestyle. Once the largest port in Central America, Livingston now spends its days partying and shuttling tourists to an array of beautiful sites nearby, including the cascades of the Seven Altars and the effervescent *aguas calientes* (hot springs). The greatest tourist attraction is the beautiful Rio Dulce boat ride, which starts in Livingston and heads to Lago de Izabal. In town, steady infusions of coconut bread, fresh fish, and mellifluous reggae redefine *tranquilo*. Don't let the town's relaxed nature lull you into *too* peaceful a slumber; some crime (mainly drug-related)has found its way here. The appearance of tourist police has lowered the crime rate, but take the usual precautions.

▐ TRANSPORTATION

Livingston is accessible only by water; most arrive by ferry from Puerto Barrios or by boat along the Río Dulce (see **Up the Río Dulce,** p. 402). Leaving, **ferries** head to **Puerto Barrios** (1½hr., 5am and 2pm, Q15). Private *lanchas* leave from the same dock as soon as 12-16 people gather (30min., Q25 per person). The one departure you can count on is the first of the day—6:30am. The trip up the Río Dulce will bring you to **Fronteras,** where you can get buses to **Flores, Tíkal,** or **Guatemala City.** Other *lanchas* go to: **Punta Gorda, Belize** (1hr., 6-8 person min., Q100 each); **Omoa, Honduras** (6-person min., US$35 each); and **Puerto Cortés, Honduras** (8-person min., US$35-40 each). **Happy Fish** (see **Food,** below) has daily shuttles to **Omoa** (US$25) and **Copán** (US$30). **Exotic Travel** sends a boat to **Omoa** (2hr., Tu and F 7am, US$35). Don't forget to have your passport stamped (see **Immigration Office,** below).

▟ ▐ ORIENTATION AND PRACTICAL INFORMATION

It's almost impossible to get lost in Livingston. The town's main street—known as **Calle Principal**—leads directly up a hill from the main dock, and hooks to the left at the public school painted with big blue Pepsi signs. Most of the action occurs along Calle Principal and continues after the turn onto what is sometimes called **Calle del Cementerio** (Cemetery Rd.). **Calle Marcos Sánchez-Díaz** runs parallel to the Río Dulce. Coming from the dock, take the first left at the playground. Calle Marcos Sánchez-Díaz contains a number of good budget hotels and restaurants.

Tourist Information: Exotic Travel Agency (☎947 0151) has a small office in Bahía Azul restaurant, halfway up Calle Principal. Free maps when they've got 'em and advice on border crossings, tours, and transportation. Open daily 7am-midnight.

Immigration Office: Get your exit stamp at the **Immigration Office,** across from the Hotel Villa Caribe on Calle Principal. Open daily 7:30am-5:30pm.

Banks: Bancafé, just above Bahía Azul on Calle Principal, changes traveler's checks and gives cash advances on V and MC. Has a **24hr. ATM,** but problems have been reported using foreign cards. Open M-F 9am-5pm, Sa 9am-1pm. Beware of high transaction fees at many establishments on the main drag.

Police: (☎948 0120). 300m down Calle del Cementerio, then right 100m. Knock if the door is closed. Open 24hr.

Pharmacy: Livingston, on the right side of the main street about 50m after the split with Calle del Cemeterio. Open daily 8am-9pm, sometimes until 10pm. **Farmacia Sucey,** 350m down Calle del Cementerio, has a larger stock of goods.

GUATEMALA

Hospital: Centro de Salud. Uphill on Calle Principal, right after the Restaurant Tiburón to the end of Calle a Capitanía. Look for the large yellow building on the left. Open 24hr.

Telephones: Coming from the dock, the **Telgua** office is on the side street on the right, just past and opposite the Hotel Villa Caribe. **Fax** service available at various establishments along the main street.

Internet: Happy Fish Restaurant, up the hill about 100m from the clock, on the left. Q25 per hr. **Telgua** (above) gives 20min. of free access.

Post Office: Coming from the dock on Calle Principal, make a right after the Hotel Villa Caribe. It's on the left, next to Telgua. Open M-F 8:30am-12:30pm and 3:30-5:30pm.

ACCOMMODATIONS

During the high season, finding a room can be difficult, so book in advance.

Hotel Garífuna (☎947 0183), 100m to the right after the sign on Calle del Cemeterio. Hidden from the crowds of tourists downtown. Immaculate rooms with fan and private bath. The brick building is secured with a wrought-iron gate at night. Laundry service. Fax and international phone service available. Singles Q40; doubles Q60. MC/V. ❷

La Casa Rosada (☎947 0303), left on Calle Marcos Sánchez-Díaz from Calle Principal, a few houses after the small bridge, on the left. Exotic furniture, hammocks, a patio, and ocean views make even guests of other hotels stick around. Bungalows are artfully simple, with mosquito netting, fans, and hand-painted furnishings. Clean shared baths have hot water. Excellent food and tours available. English spoken. Beds on the open balcony are an overpriced Q50. The annex across the street is bare-bones, with cold water. Laundry Q2.50 per piece. 2-person bungalows Q150; dorms Q50; annex Q40. ❸

Hotel Villa del Mar, straight on the main road 100m after the turn off to the Calle del Cemeterio. Good, generic rooms with fan. Rooms Q40, with bath Q60. ❷

Hotel El Viajero, a couple of minutes down Calle Marcos Sánchez-Díaz, is one of the cheapest hotels. Very basic rooms with fans surround a safe, quiet courtyard. The restaurant out back overlooks the sea. Singles Q20; doubles Q32, with bath Q42. ❶

Hotel Doña Alida (☎947 0027). Turn right off Calle Principal onto the quieter part of Calle del Cementerio until it ends, then take a left and go 100m. It is on your right. With a great view, removed location, and elegant furniture, this is a high-class option. Rooms all have private bath. Q150. ❺

Rigoletto Pizzería (☎947 0772), on Calle Marcos-Sánchez Díaz, a bit farther down from Hotel El Viajero. Your friends will be impressed at your hard-core backpacker style when you tell them you slept in the back of a pizza parlor. Far from a loaf of garlic bread as a pillow, though, the one room that Brit Alex rents out feels just like home, with 2 beds and a shared bath (as in, shared with restaurant patrons). Q45 per person. ❷

Hotel Caribe, a few meters off Calle Principal down Marcos Sánchez-Díaz, is for those who can't be bothered hauling their gear up the hill. Simple rooms with tolerable shared baths are cheap, and the porch to the rear has a waterfront view, but there are no fans or mosquito nets. Singles Q20; doubles Q40, with private bath Q61. ❶

FOOD

Tapado, a local favorite of seafood and plantains drenched in a spicy coconut broth, surprises with the sheer number of critters that fit into a bowl (watch out for fish heads). Far superior than inland beans and rice, Caribbean rice and beans ("rays an bins") are stir fried in coconut milk. For dessert, the *pan de coco* and *pie de piña* will leave you wobbling back to your hammock, woozy with ecstasy. For

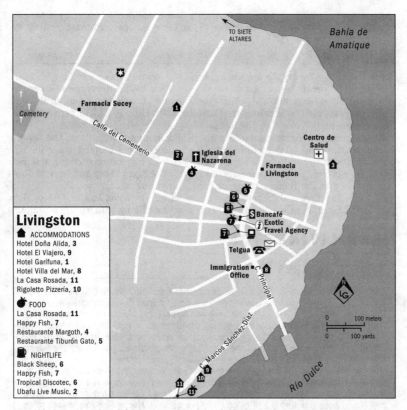

Livingston

ACCOMMODATIONS
Hotel Doña Alida, **3**
Hotel El Viajero, **9**
Hotel Garífuna, **1**
Hotel Villa del Mar, **8**
La Casa Rosada, **11**
Rigoletto Pizzería, **10**

FOOD
La Casa Rosada, **11**
Happy Fish, **7**
Restaurante Margoth, **4**
Restaurante Tiburón Gato, **5**

NIGHTLIFE
Black Sheep, **6**
Happy Fish, **7**
Tropical Discotec, **6**
Ubafu Live Music, **2**

a quick, heaping plateful of savory local food (Q10), join the *lancha* drivers at the cart by the dock between 10am and 5pm.

🔲 **La Casa Rosada** (see **Accommodations,** above), has some of the most mouth-watering dinners in town (if not Guatemala). All meals include a healthy salad and a deliciously deathly dessert. Enjoy outside dining while local chefs mix up the menu every night, though a veggie special can always be counted on. Prices range from Q35 for vegetarian pasta to Q110 for a pound of lobster. *Tapado* is offered every night (Q65). Open for breakfast and lunch 6:30am-5pm; place your dinner order before 6pm to be served at 7:30pm, though the staff sometimes accepts later orders. ❺

🔲 **Happy Fish,** just up the hill on Calle Principal on the left. Snazzy outdoor lighting makes for stylish dining under a thatched roof. Huge portions, cheap prices, and great bread. Dip in *tapado* for a real treat (Q50). Most meals Q20-30; shrimp soup Q40. Occasional live music starts at 8pm. Open daily until 7pm-9pm. ❸

Restaurant Margoth, on the cemetery leg of the Calle Principal, across from the Iglesia del Nazarena. Good, simple food served on brightly covered tables. Very coconuty rice and beans. Fish filet Q35. Open daily 8am-9pm. ❸

Restaurante Tiburón Gato, up Calle Principal on the left, is a local favorite. *Carne a la plancha* Q30; conch Q35. Open daily 7am-9:30pm. ❸

GUATEMALA

Comedor Normita, under the red Coca-Cola awning half a block down Calle Marcos Sánchez Díaz, has good stewed chicken (Q15). Eating surfaces are hard to come by. ❷

NIGHTLIFE

A mellow village by day, Livingston apparently conserves its energy for nighttime partying. The recent relaxation of the dry laws has begun to rejuvenate a party scene that had been suffering. Most establishments are now open until 3am. Things are especially wild during the Garífuna **festival** Nov 20-27. The cemetery has a happening party November 1 (All Saints Day) and 2 (All Souls Day).

The Garífuna music scene/dance party begins and ends with **Ubafu Live Music,** 50m down the Calle del Cemeterio leg of the Calle Principal. Painted to resemble a pack of Life-Savers and plastered with Bob Marley's inspirational visage, the live music here is truly alive. (Open daily until 3am.) The **Black Sheep** and **Tropical Disotec,** attached to the Bahía Azul restaurant, show movies daily at 5:30pm (Q15); happy hour is 8-9pm and the music lasts until dawn. The **Bahía Azul,** and **Happy Fish** (see **Food,** above) have excellent live music starting at 8pm, with a party ensuing.

NEAR LIVINGSTON

SIETE ALTARES

*A 90min. walk down the beach, though this stretch is not too safe. Robberies occur here almost every day; going with a guide is paramount, as guided groups are rarely assaulted. The arrival of tourist police along the walk has helped, but always use common sense. Travel in groups and leave valuables behind. Head out early, both to avoid intense heat and to ensure an early return; around 5pm a rising tide makes travel difficult. At the end of Calle Principal, make a left onto the beach. After about 40min., you'll reach the **Quehueche River.** Cross the bridge and keep walking until you reach the end of the beach. Continue up the hillside trail until you see the cascades on your left. With your back to the sea, the trail on the right side of the pools leads to more cascades. You can also go by **lancha colectiva** (9am, Q25) or hire a guide. Exotic Travel Agency's trip includes a mountain hike, canoe trip, and a bag lunch (Q50 per person). **Happy Fish Restaurant** offers similar trips, guides, and prices. (Most leave at 9am. Sign up a day in advance.)*

On the Caribbean side of Livingston cascade the **Siete Altares** waterfalls. Catching the waterfalls at their peak is a matter of delicate balance: if it hasn't rained in a while, there won't be much to see; if it's been pouring, access to the falls can be difficult and dangerous. Assuming reasonable conditions, the trip is well worth it, as the crisp, clear pools, glittering with sunlight, are light-years better than Livingston's sub-par beaches. The falls' big attraction is swimming; the water only crashes down a few feet. A cool place to stop on the way back is **Larubella,** a Garífuna bar about 10min. before town. They assault patrons with *guífiti* (bitters): *aguardiente* (strong liquor, literally translated "fire water") passed through herbs and sticks, valued both as a purgative and an aphrodisiac (Q5 for a flask).

UP THE RÍO DULCE

*Trips may be arranged in either Livingston or Fronteras/Río Dulce. Head to the docks to arrange a trip with any of the **boaters,** or book at almost any of the hotels in Livingston or Río Dulce for about the same price. (20min.; Q75 one-way, Q120 round-trip.) La Casa Rosada in Livingston offers a thorough and enjoyable tour, as does Rigoletto Pizzería.*

A boat ride along the Río Dulce offers lush green cliff faces, calm, wide stretches of water, and varied wildlife. The stretch nearest to Livingston, where the river narrows and the cliffs loom over 100 ft. high, is probably the most breathtaking. Most *lanchas* stop at the sulfur **aguas calientes** (hot springs), where scalding water surfaces along the rocky bank and mingles with the cool-flowing fresh water. They also pass by **Isla de los Pajaros,** a tiny island swarming with *garzas* (storks).

Another 15-20min. up the river is the **Biotopo Chocón Machacas,** a manatee sanctuary. The shy sea cows, however, are often elusive. Giant tree ferns and butterflies are more abundant, but the highlight of the park may be the small, eclectic museum. The *biotopo* includes several scenic lagoons and a **camping** area with bathroom and kitchen facilities. Inform the pilot of your boat *before* you leave the dock that you'd like to stop here. (Open daily 7am-4pm. US$5; includes camping.)

VERAPAZ HIGHLANDS

No great geographic divide separates the Verapaces from the western highlands. However, travelers will immediately sense the difference between Baja Verapaz's unique combination of near-desert and tropical forests, and the densely forested green hills of Alta Verapaz. **Cobán,** the capital of Alta Verapaz and the region's transportation hub, is a convenient base from which to explore the surrounding highlands. The festive towns of Salamá and Rabinal are in Baja Verapaz, near the highway from Guatemala City to Cobán. It's the magnificent outdoor opportunities, however, that put this region on the map.

It was the area's long, successful resistance to the Spanish Conquest that gave it the name Tuzuntohil, or "Land of War." Thanks to Fray Bartolomé de las Casas and the Franciscan friars, however, the region has earned its present Spanish name, Verapaz, or "True Peace." When the Fray organized a campaign in defense of the *indígenas,* the Spanish empire halted its military conquest and granted him five years for the "humane" conversion of the local people. The chiefs, assured that the friars were not interested in their gold and land, accepted them, and a peaceful conversion followed. By the end of the 19th century, however, the Guatemalan coffee boom had established large *fincas* in Verapaz, which strained available land and labor and disrupted many indigenous villages. Despite these tensions, the *indígena* presence in the region remains strong. Much of the native population speaks Kekchí and Pokomchí; a small population in the south of the region speaks Quiché. On a practical note, it takes a while to navigate this area. Transportation is like the quetzal: elusive, and most active in the early morning.

BAJA VERAPAZ

The road to the Verapaz highlands branches off from the Atlantic Highway at El Rancho junction. Up the road, at La Cumbre junction, is the turnoff to **Salamá,** the pleasant regional capital, and the smaller **Rabinal,** both of which are best visited during their annual *fiestas* (weeks of Sept 17 and Jan 25, respectively). The main road continues past the Biotopo del Quetzal before making its way to Cobán.

RABINAL AND SURROUNDINGS

Rabinal lies about 1hr. west of Salamá, in the area's next large valley. Rabinal is famous for its impressive *artesanía* and the local dances showcased during the town's annual *fiesta* from January 19-25. If you can't make it to the *fiesta,* a jaunt over to the Thursday and Sunday markets to look at the renowned carvings and pottery is worthwhile. For area **tourist information,** see the energetic Raul Fernández at the Esso gas station in Salamá, 13 Calle 9-84, Zona 1. (☎940 1780.)

Rabinal suffered a great deal during the war—hidden graves are still being uncovered—and a few sights in town memorialize the tragedy. By the altar of the

Northern Guatemala

MEXICO

El Mirador
Los Lagartos
P.N. Mirador - dos Lagunas
Río Azul
Dos Lagunas

Pozo Xan I

Biotopo Laguna del Tigre Río Escondido

Carmelita

Xultún

Uaxactún
Uaxactún

El Naranjo
Mactún
Ocultún
La Reina

Paso Caballos

El Perú

Río San Pedro

Río San Pedro

Biotopo el Zotz: San Miguel-La Pelotada

En Encanto
Tikal
Uolantún

San Diego

PETÉN

San Miguel

P.N. Cerro Cahuí

P.N. Tikal

Yaxjá
Ciudad Melchor de Mencos

Laguna Perdida

Metul de San José

Lago Petén Itzá

El Remate

Topoxte

TO BELMOPAN (50km), BELIZE CITY (94km)

San Benito

Pasajá
Sta. Rita

Flores
Paxcaman
Santa Elena
Santa Ana

CA13

Bethel

Polol

La Libertad

San Francisco

Santa Ana Vieja

Río Mopán

Planchón de las Figuras

Las Cruces

Ixponé

Sabaneta

Ixcún

Río La Pasión

Itzán
Aguas Callentes
El Caribe
La Amella
Altar de los Sacrificios

Sayaxché

El Ceibal
El Chorro
El Cedral

Dolores

CA13

Dos Pilas

MEXICO

Aguateca

Reserva Machaquila

Poptún

Reserva Aguateca-dos Pilas

Las Pozas

Finca Ixobel

N
LG

0   20 kilometers
0   20 miles

Río Salinas

Tres Islas

San Luís

BELIZE

5

Cancuén

Río Santa Isabel o Can Cuén

Playa Grande (Ixcán)

Chisaj
R.P. Franja Transversal Del Norte

Raxrujá

Sto. Domingo

Modesto Méndez

Laguna Lachuá
P.N. Laguna de Lachuá

Chisec

Candelaria Caves

Sebol

Fray Bartolomé de las Casas

Río Sarstún

IZABAL

Finca San Luís

ALTA VERAPAZ

SIERRA DE SANTA CRUZ

Río Negro o Chixoy

QUICHÉ

Grutas de Lanquín

Lanquín

El Estor

Lago de Izabal

Cobán

Semuc Champey

Río Cahabón

San Pedro Carcha

R. Polochic

7W

7E

Biotopo del Quetzal

SIERRA DE LAS MINAS

BAJA VERAPAZ

Embalse Chixoy

Rabinal

5

17

Salamá

CA14

Reserva de la Biosfera de Las Minas

CA9

TO GUATEMALA CITY (98km)

El Cumbre Junction

El Rancho Junction

Zacapa

CA9   TO GUATEMALA CITY (147km)

GUATEMALA

parque's colonial church hang two striking murals, painted in 1998. One is of the town's troubled past, with fires in the woods (the army destroyed vast areas of forest in their campaign against the insurgents) and tormented faces. The other, featuring among other things a marimba and a computer, depicts Rabinal's rich culture and anticipates a bright future. There is also a small **community museum** on 2 Calle 4 Av., Zona 3, with exhibits ranging from drawings of an indigenous anti-hyperthyroidism dance to over 300 photographs of local war victims.

Buses from Guatemala City head to **Rabinal** via **Salamá** (4½hr., about every hour). Most buses heading from Salamá to Rabinal continue west to **Cobulco**. The best place to stay in Rabinal is ◙**Posada San Pablo ❶**, 3 Av. 1-50, Zona 1. The clean rooms are equipped with top-of-the-line mattresses, and the communal baths are fair. An on-site *comedor* serves three meals per day. (Singles Q16, with bath Q25; doubles Q32/Q42.) During Cobulco's *fiesta*, around July 19, the famed *palo volador* ritual is performed. Men shuffle monkey-style up a tall tree on the mountain and spin down on a wooden triangle.

FOR THE BIRDS They are *kukul* to the Maya, *quetzaltototl* to the Aztecs, and *Pharomachus mocinnus* to international bird nerds. No matter what they call them, however, people have a universal respect for quetzals. It has always been illegal to kill the endangered bird; the offense was even punished by death in pre-colonial times. Legend has it that after the battle of Xela—another killing spree by Pedro de Alvarado—quetzals descended to the blood-stained field, thus acquiring their bright-red breasts. The quetzal's flashy beauty elevated it to godly heights in early Mesoamerica. The "quetzal-serpent" makes cameo appearances in the artwork of Tikal, Guatemala and Palenque, Mexico. Come the conquest, it wasn't long before the Spanish came to appreciate the metallic-green and bright red plume of the colorful male, and *conquistadores* quickly followed the native lead in incorporating the plumes into robes, headgear, and other adornments. Yet for all its historical gumption, Guatemala's national bird is indeed elusive; to catch a glimpse of it, you'll need plenty of time and patience.

COBÁN

Though home to plenty of cosmopolitan pleasures, Cobán gives the distinct impression that nature is never too far away. Lush hillsides appear within arm's reach as the city's edges quickly fade into country terrain. And then there's the rain—lots of rain. More and more tourists are using Cobán as a base for excursions to the natural wonders nearby, including the Biotopo del Quetzal, Rey Marcos, Semuc Champey, and the Grutas de Lanquín. When you need a break from the outdoors, Cobán is happy to oblige: here, you can sip a cup of the famous local coffee in a cafe and rest your head at one of several charming hotels.

◪ TRANSPORTATION

Buses: Unless otherwise noted, buses leave from the **main terminal** at 1/3 Av., 2/3 Calles in Zona 4. Coming into town, some buses stop conveniently to the west of the *parque*, on 1 Calle, near Café El Tirol. You may also board most buses heading south from this location, as they head out of town. Make sure to get to the terminal at least 30min. early, especially for destinations toward Transversal Del Norte and the Petén. Ask ahead for the latest info—services change frequently. Buses depart to:

Biotopo del Quetzal: Any Guatemala City bound bus. (1hr., Q8.)

Fray Bartolomé de las Casas: (6hr., 6 and 7am, Q20.)

Grutas del Rey Marcos: From 5 Calle, 5 Av. in Zona 3. Take the bus to Chamelco (20min., Q3), where you can change buses and head to Chamil, which passes by the Grutas.

Guatemala City: Transportes Escobar y Monja Blanca, on 2 Calle 3-77, Zona 4, offers 1st-class service. (4-5hr.; every 30min. 2-6am, every hr. 6am-4pm; Q26.) "Special direct" buses have TV and play movies (5 per day 4:30am-2pm). Chicken buses leave from the main terminal. (4½-5hr., 5 per day 4am-1pm, Q17.)

Lanquín: The 5 and 6am buses leave from behind the cathedral; the rest leave from between 1 and 2 Av., 2 blocks north of the *parque.* (3½hr., 7 per day 5am-3pm, Q10.)

Playa Grande: Buses, microbuses, and pickups leave from the terminal on 1 Av. (5hr.; every hr. 6am-2pm; Q25 for bus, Q40 for microbus.) They leave more frequently when there are enough passengers. Buses drop off near **Parque Nacional Laguna de Lachuá;** walk to the entrance.

Raxrujá: (5hr., 4 and 6am, Q20.) An additional bus leaves at noon from San Pedro Carchá. Some pickups also go to Raxrujá in the morning. Or take the bus to Las Casas and transfer at Sebol, where pickups leave periodically to Raxrujá.

Salamá and Rabinal: Take any Guatemala City bound bus to La Cumbre junction. (1½hr., Q15.) Minibuses leave frequently from there for Salamá. (10min., Q3.)

San Pedro Carchá: From the new terminal on 1 Av., north of the main terminal on the left fork of the road. (15min., every 10-15min. 6am-7pm, Q1.)

Sayaxché and the Petén: Either take the bus to **Raxrujá** or a pickup to **Cruce del Pato** via **Chirec** and then hop on a bus or pickup to Sayaxché. Direct buses (6 and 8am) can be caught heading south down 1 Av. in front of Ban Rural or Bancafé.

Tactic: Any Guatemala City bound bus. (30min., Q2.50.)

Uspantán: (5hr., 10am and noon, Q15.) From Uspantán, buses leave for any Western Highland locale, including **Santa Cruz del Quiché** via **Sacapulas** (where you can grab a bus to **Nebaj**).

Taxis: Around the *parque central,* at the western tip and northern side of the cathedral.

◼◼ ORIENTATION AND PRACTICAL INFORMATION

The two main streets in Cobán, **1 Av.** and **1 Calle,** adhere to the standard grid (map p.124). They divide the city into four **quadrants:** northwest Zona 1, southwest Zona 2, southeast Zona 3, and northeast Zona 4. The city's **cathedral** towers at 1 Av., 1 Calle. The neighboring triangular **parque central** is directly west in Zona 2. The cathedral and *parque* rest atop a hill that encompasses Cobán, from where the rest of the city drops off. Within the central area, numbered *avenidas* and *calles* continue through different *zonas.* Note that addresses on 1 Av. and 1 Calle may be in any of the *zonas* they run through, depending what side of the street they lie on.

Tourist Information: Hostal D'Acuña, 4 Calle 3-11, Zona 2, is a great information source and can provide maps and bus schedules.

Guided Tours: At the Hostal de Acuña, **U&I, S.A.** (☎951 0482; uisa@amigo.net.gt.) runs guided tours throughout the Verapazes, including Lanquín, Semuc Champey, and the Parque Nacional Laguna de Lachuá, as well as up to Flores (daytrips US$35). **Oficina de Transportes Tzi boney,** Diagonal 4 4-43 off the *parque* (☎617 4278), also heads to several regional locations. **Proyecto Eco-Quetzal,** 2 Calle 14-36, Zona 1 (☎952 1047), works to protect the cloud forest and organizes trips to learn about the life of Kekchí families. Guides show you the forest, its medicinal uses and agriculture, and familiarize you with the Kekchí. Proceeds benefit environmental protection. Homestays 2 days and 1 night Q210 per person; 3 days and 2 nights Q320 per person. Guide included.

Banks: Bancafé, 1 Av. 2-66, Zona 2, accepts most types of traveler's checks, advances cash on credit cards, and has a 24hr. Visa **ATM.** Open M-F 9am-7pm, Sa 9am-1pm. **Banco Continental,** across from Hotel La Posada on 1 Calle, changes all traveler's checks. Open M-F 8:30am-7pm, Sa 10am-2pm.

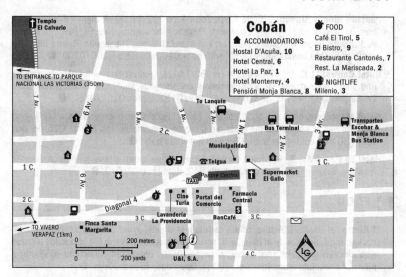

Cobán

🏠 **ACCOMMODATIONS**
Hostal D'Acuña, **10**
Hotel Central, **6**
Hotel La Paz, **1**
Hotel Monterrey, **4**
Pensión Monja Blanca, **8**

🍴 **FOOD**
Café El Tirol, **5**
El Bistro, **9**
Restaurante Cantonés, **7**
Rest. La Mariscada, **2**

🍷 **NIGHTLIFE**
Milenio, **3**

Supermarket: El Gallo, on 1 Calle. Open M-Sa 9am-8pm, Su 9am-6pm.

Laundromat: Lavandería La Providencia, Diagonal 4 2-43, Zona 2, near the movie theater. Q25.75 per load. Open M-Sa 8am-noon and 2-5pm.

Car Rental: Tabarini, 8 Av. 2-27, Zona 2 (☎951 0661). Open daily 8am-noon, 2-6pm.

Police: 1 Calle 5-12, Zona 2 (☎952 1225), past Hotel la Posada. Open 24hr.

Pharmacy: Farmacia Central, 1 Av., 2 Calle, Zona 2, on the *parque*. Open 8am-7pm.

Medical Emergency: Los Bomberos, 3 Av., 3 Calle, Zona 4 (☎952 1212). Open 24hr.

Red Cross: 3 Calle 2-13, Zona 3 (☎952 1459).

Hospital: Poliolínica Galeno, 3 Av. 1-47, Zona 3 (☎951 3175). This well-equipped private clinic has emergency service, though not always 24hr. Walk-in hours M-Sa 10am-noon and 4-8pm. Public **Hospital Nacional de Cobán** 8 Calle 1-24, Zona 4. (☎952 1315.) Open 24hr.

Telephones: Telgua near 3 Av., 1 Calle, Zona 1 (☎951 3098), in the large, unmarked white building on the *parque*. Public phones in front. Open M-F 8am-6pm.

Internet: Infocom, 2 Calle 6-03, Zona 2. Fast connections and quality machines. Open M-Sa 8am-9pm. Q15 per hr. **Infosel Cybercobán,** 3 Av. 1-11, Zona 4. Q15 per hr. Open M-Sa 8am-7pm, Su 2:30-7pm. **ORC Systems,** 1 Calle 3-13, Zona 1, in the Café El Tirol complex. Slower connection Q20 per hr. Open M-Sa 8am-7pm.

Post Office: 2 Av., 3 Calle, in Zona 3. Open M-F 8:30am-5:30pm, Sa 9am-1pm.

🏠 ACCOMMODATIONS

📝 **Hostal D'Acuña,** 4 Calle 3-11, Zona 2 (☎951 0484). With a colorful, inviting atmosphere, this is the best budget option. Bunkbeds are arranged in homey rooms for 2 or 4 people. The small courtyard garden rings with jazz, and the restaurant is sumptuous (though not cheap). Hot water and dressers with padlocks. Dorms Q40 per person. ❷

Pensión Monja Blanca, 2 Calle 6-30, Zona 2 (☎952 1712). A dignified place, with friendly service and a jungly courtyard. Elegant rooms with cable TV, free *agua pura*, and private baths with state-of-the-art hot-water showers. Those with shared bath are comfortable but basic. Singles Q50, with bath Q100; doubles Q100/Q200. ❸

Hotel Central, 1 Calle 1-79, Zona 4 (☎952 1442). Clean rooms with hot-water private baths and a courtyard. More pricey rooms are spacious, well-lit, and come with cable TV. Singles Q62, with TV Q83; doubles Q112/Q132; triples Q161/Q182. ❹

Hotel Monterrey, on 6 Av. 1-12, Zona 1, behind Hotel Cobán Imperial, is a fairly good deal. Rooms are bare, but the beds are decently comfortable and cheap. Q25 per person, Q30 with cold-water bath, Q55 with hot-water bath. ❶

Hotel La Paz, 6 Av. 2-19, Zona 1 (☎952 1358). Large, clean rooms, some with wooden furniture. Singles Q30, with private bath Q42; doubles Q60/Q72. ❶

🍴 FOOD

El Bistro, at Hostal D'Acuña, offers candlelight dining, good service, delicious home-cooked food, and plenty of *música tranquila*. Grab a table by the fire and enjoy a crepe with chicken and light parsley cream sauce (Q58), vegetarian cannelloni (Q38), or a piece of chocolate macadamia pie (Q11). Open daily 6am-8:30pm. ❹

Restaurante Cantonés, Diagonal 4 4-24, Zona 2. Authentic Chinese food served in a typical Cobán house. Some dishes are pricey, but others are a good value for their generous portions. Chicken fried rice Q26; spring rolls Q18. Open daily 11am-10pm. ❸

Café El Tirol, 1 Calle 3-13, Zona 1. Even hardened caffeine junkies will be impressed by the huge selection of coffees and teas at this relaxing cafe. Sandwiches and light meals are also served. Basic cup o' joe Q4-6; *café krupnik*—a vodka-based concoction—Q11.50; tuna sandwich on Italian bread Q17. Open M-Sa 7:30am-9pm. ❷

Restaurante La Mariscada, on 6 Av. across from Hotel La Paz, has a wide variety of seafood entrees. Stuffed crab Q60; *ceviche de concha* Q45. It is also known for its generous *bocas* (appetizers): for each beer you drink (local beer Q10), your server will bring you a shrimp cocktail, chicken tortilla, or beef taco. ❺

🏛 SIGHTS

For a bird's eye view of Cobán, stroll out to **Templo El Calvario.** The hillside church dates all the way back to 1559, but it's the expansive view from the church, reached by a climb of 135 stone steps, that makes the visit worthwhile. To reach it, continue north on 7 Av. until you reach the stairway. The nearby woods are part of **Parque Nacional Las Victorias;** the entrance is at 11 Av., 3 Calle, Zona 1. Strolling along the well-kept paths through the pine forest makes for a relaxing retreat. (Open 8am-6pm. Admission Q6.) **Vívero Verapaz** is an orchid farm where you can admire thousands of different species, including the *monja blanca* (white nun), the national flower of Guatemala. Follow the diagonal road (Diagonal 4) that begins at the end of the *parque* (left of Hotel la Posada). At the bottom of the hill turn left and continue for about 15min. (Open M-Sa 9am-noon and 2-5pm. Q5.)

Cobán's passion for **coffee** spills outside the town's cafes and into the surrounding *fincas*, many of which were once owned by wealthy Germans. For insight into the coffee culture, check out **Finca Santa Margarita,** 3 Calle 4-12, Zona 2. Guided tours of the plantation explain the *finca's* history; some provide coffee samples for visitors to savor and compare. Both Spanish and English-speaking guides are available. (☎/fax 951 3067. Tour 45min., Q15 per person. Coffee tasting US$4 per person. Open M-F 8am-12:30pm and 1:30-5pm, Sa 8am-noon.)

☜ NIGHTLIFE

If you're looking for nightlife, your best bet is probably **Milenio,** on 3 Av., half a block north of 1 Calle in Zona 4. The front bar has a more upscale feel, but the atmosphere stays pretty laid back, with *fútbol* on the widescreen TV and a pool table in back. There are two main lounges and *salsa* is the music of choice. (Open daily until 1am.) Catch a movie at **Cine Turia** at the pointed end of the *parque* (Q7).

NEAR COBÁN

▩ BIOTOPO DEL QUETZAL

Buses on the route between Cobán and Guatemala City pass the biotopo *frequently. To Guatemala City (3hr.; every 30min. 3-7am, every hr. 7am-5pm). To Cobán (1hr., about every hr. 7am-8pm, Q10). Open daily 7am-5:30pm; last entrance 4pm.*

About 30km southeast of Cobán is the Biotopo Mario Dary Rivera, commonly known as the Biotopo del Quetzal (Quetzal Reserve), an expanse of rugged cloud forest home to Guatemala's national bird, the quetzal, which cannot survive in captivity. Two trails twist their way through the park: **Sendero los Helechos** (1hr., 1.8km) is the shorter trail, while **Sendero los Musgos** (2hr., 3.5km) takes you deep into the dense forest. The longer route provides better vistas, but both give excellent tours of the forest and an equally good chance of spotting the quetzal. The road at the entrance to the reserve is actually one of the best places to catch a glimpse of the beautiful birds; they're spotted most often in April and September in the early morning. Look in the large leaves of the **aguacatillo;** its small green fruit is a favorite chow-down treat for quetzals. But even if the bird eludes you (and odds are, it will), the beautiful forest canopy and waterfalls are still worth a visit.

You can stay the night at **Hospedaje Los Ranchitos ❶,** just down the road toward Cobán from the entrance to the reserve. It offers rustic accommodations and is a good place to look for quetzals. The *hospedaje* has its own patch of forest, complete with a private trail and a basic *comedor*. (Breakfast Q15-20, lunch or dinner Q18-25. Singles Q30, with bath Q50; doubles Q60/Q80; triples Q90/Q100.)

▨ GRUTAS DEL REY MARCOS/BALNEARIO CECILINDA

*To reach the Grutas from Cobán, take a bus to Chamelco from 5 Av., 5 Calle in Zona 3 (20min., Q37), where you can find morning **buses** or **pickups** to Chamil. Ask to be dropped off at the road to Rey Marcos/Balneario Cecilinda, then walk about 500m to the entrance (follow the sign). Coming back, pickups to Chamelco are less frequent in the afternoon but still pass by. The last bus to Cobán departs in the late afternoon.*

For adventure seekers who enjoy crawling and climbing through unlit caves, the Grutas del Rey Marcos are not to be missed. Listen to the roar of a sacred, underground Maya river, and splash around under gorgeous natural waterfalls. Discovered just four years ago and open to the public since January 1999, the caves are believed to be the site of religious ceremonies that took place in pre-Columbian times; the Maya still hold the site sacred and ceremonies continue even today. The inner sanctuary of the cave is rumored to be the source of a large, mystic energy field, and Iván, the owner and occasional tour guide, warns that everyone who enters, leaves carrying a blessing or a curse. Mystics aside, a tour of Rey Marcos is an exhilarating experience and makes for a worthwhile daytrip from Cobán. After getting muddy exploring the caves, cool off in the **Balneario Cecilinda,** the natural swimming area set into the mountainside below the caves. (Open daily 8am-5pm. Admission, including guided tour, rubber boots, helmet, and flashlight Q25.)

LANQUÍN AND ENVIRONS

About 40km northeast of Cobán rests the village of Lanquín and two nearby natural wonders, the beautiful pools of Semuc Champey and the cave network known as the Grutas de Lanquín. Guided tours from Cobán, though a more expensive alternative for large groups, are convenient and often a good deal for one or two travelers; the guides are excellent and will point out the sights' hidden marvels. **Hostal D'Acuña** (see **Accommodations,** p. 407) offers a "Semuc Special," which includes a night at the hotel, transportation, breakfast, lunch, and guides. (US$35 per person, 4-person min.) Also, both **Hostal D'Acuña** and **Hostal Doña Victoria,** 3 Calle 2-38, Zona 3 (☎952 2213) organize 4x4 transport to **Semuc Champey** (US$25 per person for 4 or more; discounts for larger groups).

Many travelers make daytrips to Lanquín, catching the 6am bus from Cobán and returning on the 2:30pm bus. Buses from Cobán (2½hr., 6 per day 6am-3pm, Q10) and return buses from Lanquín (2½hr., 6 per day 3:30am-2:30pm, Q10) make several trips per day. Pickups can also be found in the mornings heading from Lanquín to Pujal, and then on to Cobán. Be ready to go a little early, and be prepared to wait. Should you want to stay the night, there are a few good options. About 100m downhill from the town entrance is **Hotel el Recreo ❶,** which offers spacious rooms with private baths. The hotel also has decent budget bungalow rooms with clean communal baths in forested grounds. (☎861 2856. Budget rooms Q25 per person. Singles Q144; doubles Q190.) Uphill and to the right of the town entrance is **Hospedaje La Divina Providencia ❶,** with plain rooms, hot water, and and an attached *comedor* and pharmacy. (Q20 per person.) Travelers rave about **El Retiro ❶,** a budget spot on the eastern side of town also recommended for its food. Free pickup at the bus stop. (Dorms Q20; private bungalow rooms Q33 per person.)

GRUTAS DE LANQUÍN

The Grutas de Lanquín are about 1.5km along the road toward Cobán and down a short drive that veers to the right off the main road. Visitors can explore the cave network, which extends more than 3km. The first segment is the only one with a walkway and lights, and even this portion is quite slippery. Before visiting, stop by the *municipalidad,* across from the *parque* near the church, and check to make sure the site is open and the power on. Some travelers enjoy waiting until dusk to see the cave's bats pour out into the night sky. However, since the park is closed then, this can only be done from outside the entrance. If you do stick around, bring a flashlight to find your way back to Lanquín, and wear clothes and shoes you don't mind getting dirty—especially if you venture out past the walkway. (Open daily 8am-noon and 1-5pm. Q20.) **Alberto and Otto Bolom Choc** (see below) provide transportation to the caves if you're taking their pickup to Semuc Champey.

SEMUC CHAMPEY

The 300m natural limestone bridge of Semuc Champey creates quite a show as the mighty Cahabón River thunders into the depths below. The top of the bridge, by contrast, is pure tranquility, and a descending series of clean pools perfect for swimming flow above the river. Framed by steep, forested hillsides, the waters turn marvelous shades of blue and green as the sun moves across the sky. Upon arriving at the Semuc parking lot, follow the trail past the small *tienda.* Alongside the pools is a covered *rancho* for camping or picnicking, changing rooms, and bathrooms. To reach the departure point for the Cahabón River, put the parking lot at your back and follow the trail that crosses over to the right side of the pools and continues past the picnic tables. Follow the slippery rocks carefully, and don't get too close to the waterfalls, as some tourists have recently come to a bad end. (Open daily 8am-noon and 1-5pm. Q20 admission fee collected in the parking lot.)

Semuc Champey is best reached by pickup truck, but you can do the 3hr. hot, uphill hike following the gravel road that heads away from the river. Bring water. **Pickups** (Q3) run from the church to a point two-thirds of the way to Semuc; you have the best chance of finding one on Mondays and Thursdays (market days). Otherwise, hire a round-trip pickup and try to team up with other travelers to split the cost. Excellent service is provided by **Otto Bolom Choc** and his father Alberto, who shuttle visitors in the family pickup(Q75). They also provide round-trip service to Champey and take you to the Grutas de Lanquín and show you around the cave (Q150). They live in the third house on the left after Comedor Shalom as you walk downhill. If you're going alone, guided tours from Cobán may be cheaper.

TRANSVERSAL DEL NORTE

Comprised of southern Petén and northern Alta Verapaz, the Transversal del Norte region consists of limestone pockmarked with sinkholes, humid tropical forest, and mammoth caves. When oil was discovered here 20 years ago, the region's first road—the Transversal del Norte—was built, and Kekchí from the war-torn highlands followed. Today, it remains a sparsely populated agricultural frontier criss-crossed by a baffling web of routes built by the oil industry. If you're looking for an off-the-beaten-path adventure, a trip through the region is worth the uncertainty and transportation hassles. Its magnificent natural sites, the Candelaria Caves and Parque Nacional Laguna de Lachuá, remain little touristed. Both can be visited round-trip from Cobán or on the way from Cobán to the Petén. Hostal D'Acuña and Doña Victoria in Cobán (see **Cobán: Accommodations,** p. 407) occasionally offer tours of the region, but it's much more economical to go on your own. A few towns scattered through the Transversal serve as small-scale transportation hubs and provide basic services. The bare town of Playa Grande (Ixcan) is near Parque Nacional Laguna de Lachuá. Raxrujá and Fray Bartolomé de las Casas are east of the Candelaria Caves and en route between Cobán and the Petén.

CANDELARIA CAVES

The beautiful and remote Candelaria Caves are part of an underground system more than 30km long. French spelunker Daniel Dreux discovered the caves in 1974, following a six-year search that began when he read about a sacred underground river in the *Popol Vuh*, the Quiché Maya holy book. The area encompassing the caves was recently declared a national park. The most accessible cave is the **Cueva Mico Uno,** at the point where the Candelaria River, sacred to the Maya, plunges into the earth. A number of cathedral-sized vaults open up to the tropical forest above, allowing light to filter in and illuminate the intricate rock formations.

The cave complex is 10km west of **Raxrujá,** which is itself a 5hr. ride from Cobán. Pickups from Raxrujá toward **Chisec, Sayaxché,** or other points west leave periodically (until about 4pm); just tell the driver you want to go to the Cuevas Candelaria. The drop-off point is the small town of **Mucibilhá** (45min., Q3); look for a yellow sign on the left side of the road marked "Proyecto Escuela Comunidad Mucibilhá." The entrance to the trail is 25m before the large "Cuevas Candelaria a 100mts" sign. Follow the trail that runs left from the road between two fenced-in pastures. Cross a small bridge and after about 5min., turn left through a gate. Follow the signs and walk for 5min. more along the stone path and up the stone steps. You'll have the best luck getting a ride back to Raxrujá in the morning, but ask around. Pickups may go by in the afternoon as well. Otherwise, walk 45min. back to Raxrujá or toward **Chisec** in the other direction until the junction with the road to **Sayaxché**, where it's possible to catch a bus or truck north to Petén or east to Raxrujá. To get to **Parque Nacional Laguna Lachuá** from the caves, take a pickup west to the junction with the road to Chisec. Try to get a Playa Grande-bound truck. It's also possible to return to **Cobán** from Chisec. Ask around, leave early, and be prepared to wait. (Cave admission including guide Q25, 2-person min.)

To see the caves, hire a guide at the **Complejo Cultural y Turístico de Candelaria ❹**, a beautifully decorated hotel. While the thatched-roof dorms and private bungalows are basic, well-maintained, and inviting, they are outrageously overpriced. If you visit on a daytrip, you may want to bring a snack, as lunch and dinner are both US$15. However, if you can afford it, the food is delicious. (Dorms US$10, with 3 meals US$40; private doubles US$40, $100 with meals.) Cheaper accommodations can be found in the tiny town of **Raxrujá**, 10km east of the caves, a 5hr. ride from Cobán. **Hotel Gutierrez ❶**, 50m down the road to the caves, is a good budget choice with simple, clean rooms and a friendly *comedor* attached. (Q25 per person.)

PARQUE NACIONAL LAGUNA DE LACHUÁ

A new road from Cobán to Playa Grande has made accessing Lachuá much easier. Microbuses or trucks from Cobán will drop you off in **San Luis,** a small settlement 5km from the park entrance—tell the driver you want to go to Lachuá. In San Luis, you might find a pickup heading east toward the park. Otherwise, it's flat walking; be aware that assaults do sometimes occur here. From the park entrance it is 4.2km to the base camp. Returning to Cobán, walk the fairly straightforward 5km back to the Playa Grande-Cobán road and wait—departures are fairly frequent in the morning.

The not-so-well-traveled road in front of the park runs east; a single bus passes by around 3:30am before taking the long road to Cobán via Chisec. To get to **Raxrujá** and the **Candalaria Caves,** the bus will drop you off at a crossing where a pickup can take you farther. For the Petén, one option is to take a microbus or pickup to **Playitas,** where an 11am bus heads all the way to **Flores** via **Sayaché.**

Laguna de Lachuá, one of the least-visited national parks in Central America, is a hidden gem. Eons ago, a giant meteor landed on this remote stretch of rainforest, creating a clear, deep, limestone-ringed lagoon. A single river feeds the lagoon, and two drain it. The park was established in 1975 to protect the area's humid tropical forest and the animals that live in it. Speedy lizards and colorful butterflies abound on the 4.2km trail leading to the lagoon and bathing/camping area. Other less visible fauna include jaguars, tapirs, wild boars, and hundreds of bird species, including parrots and toucans. The only **trail** in the 14 sq. km park is the one leading from the entrance to a tranquil lagoon. Bathe with fish and wonder how on earth this slice of the Caribbean became trapped in the wilderness. A building by the shore has rustic cooking facilities (bring your own food and water), solar-powered lighting, and bunk beds with mosquito netting (Q30). Latrines and a covered *rancho* for **camping** (Q25) are nearby. (Open daily 7am-4pm. Park admission Q20.)

Staying in nearby **Playa Grande,** which is neither a *playa* nor *grande*, is a more accommodating but less scenic option. Alternatively dusty and muddy, Playa Grande was constructed as a model village, a settlement for war refugees, and has all the grace and charm one would expect from the work of a military architect. If you stay the night, **Hotel Torrevisión ❶** is past the Municipalidad on the first road heading to the left, down the street from where the bus drops off. (Singles Q30, with private bath Q75; doubles Q60/Q100.) **Cafetería Long Beach ❷**, down the street, is clean and cheap. Across the way, **Guatemex ❸** has classier dishes (lobster Q70; steak Q22).

PETÉN

Guatemala's northernmost region once held one of the world's most advanced civilizations, but ever since the Maya mysteriously abandoned their power center at Tikal, humans have more or less avoided this forbidding area. The thick forest and thin soil kept the Spanish settlers away, and today the Petén contains a third of Guatemala's land mass but less than 3% of its population. Even so, nature's dominance is being threatened by new residents, slash-and-burn agriculture, and ranching. Conservation efforts have helped slow the destruction, most notably the establishment of the Maya Biosphere Reserve in 1940. With roads rolling over cleared grasslands now dotted with banana trees, jaguars prowling, and stone pyramids hidden behind hanging jungle vines, the Petén feels magically surreal.

The region's great attraction is Tikal, arguably the most beautiful of all Maya sites. Flores and its sister city, Santa Elena, have the most visitor services in Petén and serve as pleasant bases. El Remate, between Flores and Tikal, is a quiet lakeside village, increasingly popular with visitors to the ruins. Sayaxché provides river access to smaller Maya sites, and the famous traveler's hangout of Finca Ixobel near Poptún lies along the coastal highway to Guatemala City. North of Tikal are some isolated Maya ruins, including Uaxactún and spectacular El Mirador.

Unfortunately, in recent times political and social instability have overshadowed these magnificent sights. Petén was a constant battleground during the civil war, and shocks from the conflict still reverberate. In the 1980s and early 90s paramilitaries would frequently stop buses along the highway and rob them at gunpoint. Such incidents fell in number after the signing of the 1996 Peace Accords; however, the signing failed to address the issues of the paramilitaries (Patrulleros de la Autodefensa Civil, or PAC), scattered across the country. In June 2002 over 20,000 ex-PAC paralyzed Petén, blocking roads, the Tikal International Airport, and seizing an oil refinery. They demanded Q20,000 each for services rendered during the war, and ended their blockade of the region only after the government promised some form of compensation to be paid for by a national tax.

FINCA IXOBEL

*All buses on the Guatemala City-Flores route pass by both Poptún and the **turn-off** to the finca (from which it is a 15min. walk to the property). Microbuses from **Flores** will drop you right at the entrance. In **Poptún**, buses stop near the Shell station. Departures to **Guatemala City** (7-10hr., every hr. 9:30am-1:30pm, 3:30, 10:30, 11:30pm; Q55-190) via **Rio Dulce** (2hr., Q30). Going to **Flores**, buses leave every hr. and there is a night bus (2hr., 8:30am-6:30pm and 10pm, Q20-40). Buses heading to Flores after 10:30am are coming from Guatemala City but pass through Poptún. Finca Ixobel can also arrange minibuses, a cheaper option for large groups. Taxis from the Finca to Poptún cost Q20.*

Three kilometers south of Poptún, Finca Ixobel has become notorious for the spell it casts on travelers, who come for a day and end up staying for weeks or months. Run by American Carole DeVine, the 400-acre *finca* set in pine-covered hills is a peaceful and relaxing spot, and the homemade all-you-can-eat buffet dinners (Q45) are nothing short of delicious. The staff offers a range of excursions into the surrounding wilderness, including horse treks (2hr., Q70; 1 day Q150; 2 days with camping Q350), jungle treks (2-4 days, Q200 per day), inner tubing trips (1 day Q85), and a popular river cave trip (full day trip, Q70). However, if you tend to feel suffocated by hordes of international backpackers, the Finca is not the place for you. There are a few short-term volunteer opportunities (see **Alternatives to Tourism,** p. 62). Accommodations vary from sheltered camping and dorms to simple rooms with private bath. (☎410 4307, fax 927 7363; www.fincaixobel.com. Camping Q18 per person; blanket or hammock rental Q3. Dorms Q25; simple rooms Q55, with bath Q115; doubles Q70/Q160. Treehouse singles Q50; doubles Q65.)

SAYAXCHÉ

Sleepy Sayaxché sits on the Río de La Pasión about 50km southwest of Flores. Although there's little to do here, the town makes a great launching point for trips to Ceibal and other ruins in the southwest Petén. Sayaxché is also a good place to stop over before heading south toward Cobán and the Verapaz highlands, or Tikal.

⬛ TRANSPORTATION. Most **buses** depart across the river from town (ferries Q1) for: **Cobán** via **Raxrujá** (2½hr.; 4, 5am; Q20; departing near the *parque*, on the main side of town); **Flores** (1½hr.; 6, 8am, 1pm; Q10. Frequent **minibuses** also depart until 6pm; Q10); and **Guatemala City** (12-15hr.; 4:30 and 5pm via **Flores**).

⬛ PRACTICAL INFORMATION. Tourist Info is at the **INGUAT** office, 1½ blocks up from the waterfront and a block to the left. Open M-Sa 9am-5pm. Exchange currency or traveler's checks at **Banoro**, one block from the waterfront dock on the left. (Open M-F 9am-4pm, Sa 9am-1pm.) **Farmacia Arteaga** is two blocks from the waterfront on the right. (Open daily 6:30am-8:30pm.) With your back to the dock, the **post office** is five blocks to the left and four blocks to the right, in a small office next to the large "Fondo de Tierras" building. (Open M-F 8am-4:30pm.)

⬛ ACCOMMODATIONS AND FOOD. Hotel Guayacán ❺, by the dock, is a bit pricey, but has the most comfortable rooms in town with private bath. (☎/fax 928 6111. With fan Q110-125, with A/C Q150.) An **annex** across the street has more basic rooms with shared bath. (Singles Q40; doubles Q70; triples Q100.) **Hotel Mayapan ❶,** half a block from the waterfront and another half-block to the left, has a variety of rooms. The cheapest of them is as hot as a steam bath, and will have you engaging in the age-old budget-travel debate: "is this *really* a mattress?" The clean doubles with fan are much nicer and a better value. (Singles Q20; doubles Q40; room with private bath Q60.) A good place to eat is **Comedor Esmeralda ❷,** one block up from the waterfront and one block to the right, on the left side. Friendly owner Doña Rita and her 12 children love making friends, and the food is delicious. (Eggs, beans and tortilla Q15.)

RUINS NEAR SAYAXCHÉ

⬛ CEIBAL

*The best way to reach Ceibal from Sayaxché is a 1hr. **boat** journey along the Río de la Pasión through pastures, hamlets, and the Parque Nacional Ceibal. The short but steep trail from the landing climbs through thick forest before flattening out near the ruins; head straight until reaching the informal center. Boats are available for hire at the Sayaxché dock. **Don Mario,** a lanchero who can be found on the waterfront, offers reliable transportation (Round-trip including a few hours at the ruins Q200-250 for 1-5 people.) A faster lancha costs substantially more, but only shaves 15min. off the 1hr. ride. A slightly cheaper and faster way is to hire a **direct pickup** truck (45min., Q150 roundtrip) although this may be possible only in the dry season. The cheapest option is to take a **collective pickup** from the bus terminal across the river to **Aldea Paraíso** (10min., every 30 min., Q3) and then walk the dirt road veering left to the ruins. It's a hot, 8km walk (1½-2½hr.), so start early in the day. Ruins open daily 7am-3pm. Q25.*

The most memorable of the Maya ruins near Sayaxché is Ceibal, 15km east of town. With only 3% of the ruins restored, the site is modest. The main attractions are the wonderfully preserved **stelae.** Ceibal reached its peak around AD 900 and seems to have been strongly influenced by the Toltec dynasties of Mexico. Most of the site surrounds several plazas off to one side of the guard's quarters. A path heading in the opposite direction from the information center leads to the only other restored structure, the **pirámide circular,** a Toltec-influenced platform. Free **camping** is permitted, but bring tent, mosquito netting, water, and enough food to share with the guards (no joke). For tours of the ruins, hire a guide at the entrance.

👁 ⚠ LAKE PETEXBATÚN

*Aguateca is 1½hr. by **boat** from Sayaxché. Getting to the path to Dos Pilas takes 45min., but you must walk from there. **Servicio de Lanchas Don Pedro** and **Viajes Turísticas La Montaña** also arrange trips to Aguateca and Dos Pilas. During the dry season (Jan.-May), a 4WD **pickup** sometimes runs to Dos Pilas, leaving Sayaxché at 7am.*

From Sayaxché, a 30min. ride down the southern branch of the Río de la Pasión leads to the secluded Lake Petexbatún (Peh-tesh-bah-TOON), surrounded by forest and teeming with wildlife. The area was once an important trading center for the Maya, and the ruins of **Aguateca** overlook the southern edges of the lake. Occupied until about AD 790, the site has plazas, unexcavated temples, well-preserved stelae, and the only known Maya bridge. The ruins are undergoing restorations, scheduled for completion in 2004. The guards will show you around and let you camp if you bring food and equipment. Raingear, mosquito netting, and lots of bug repellent are advisable. Nearby is the **Petexbatún Lodge ⑤,** a well-kept hotel on the shores of the lake. (☎331 7561 or 926 0501. Dorms US$10 per person. Singles with bath US$35; doubles with bath US$36.) A second Maya site, **Dos Pilas,** is a 13km hike west of the lake. Find guides (Q300) at the Finca el Caribe. Built in a unique east-west linear pattern, these ruins include stelae and hieroglyphic stairways.

FLORES & SANTA ELENA

Surrounded by the tranquil Lake Petén Itzá, the relaxed island city of Flores (pop. 2000) serves as a welcoming base for visitors to the Petén. Flores began life as the Itzá capital of Tayasal. Cortés stopped by in 1524 just long enough to drop off a sick horse. Tayasal remained the last independent Maya city, holding off Spanish conquest until 1697. The colorful homes and cobblestone streets contrast nicely with the typical Petén town. While Flores may be the departmental capital, most of the down and dirty business gets done across the causeway in down and dirty Santa Elena (pop. 30,000), home to buses, banks, and planes.

▐ TRANSPORTATION

Flights: Tikal International Airport is 2km east of Santa Elena on the highway to Tikal. Minibuses to the airport generally leave from 4 Calle in Santa Elena (2min., Q10). Town buses leave from near the causeway in Flores (every 10-15min. 6am-7pm, Q1), and pass by 4 Calle in Santa Elena. Flights to **Guatemala City** (30min.), with the nicest equipment and highest prices on Grupo Taca/Aviateca (☎926 0451; 7:35am and 4:10pm, US$85), followed by Tikal Jets (☎926 0386; 4:30pm, US$75) and Rasca (☎926 0596; US$55). To **Belize City** (30min., US$88) on Tropic Air (☎926 0348; 9:30am and 3:30pm), Maya Island Air (☎926 3386). To **Cancún, Mexico** (1½hr., US$145) daily on Grupo Taca.

Buses: Fuentes del Norte is located along 4 Calle in Santa Elena. Its 1st and 2nd class buses depart from there. The other major companies, **Pirita** and **Rosita,** depart from deep in the market in Santa Elena behind the Fuentes del Norte terminal.

Belizean Border at Melchor de Mencos: (2hr.; every hr. 2-6am, 11am, 1, 4, 6pm; Q15.)

Bethel: (5hr., 5am and 1pm, Q40.)

Carmelita: (5hr., 1pm, Q20.)

Cobán: It's best to take a Guatemala City-bound bus as far as El Rancho Junction (6hr.) and catch a Cobán bus there (4hr.). A bumpy route is via Sayaxché and then Raxrujá. Alternatively, take the bus to Sayache (1½hr.), then catch the bus to Cobán (5hr., 3am and 4am).

El Naranjo: (5hr., 7 per day 5am-2:30pm, Q20.)

El Remate: (45min., 3 and 4pm, Q5.) The 1pm to Tikal also stops here.

Guatemala City: Best service on Linea Dorada (☎926 0070), with an office in Mundo Maya on the southern Flores shorefront road. Express luxury buses with drink service and movies depart 3 times per day. 8hr.; 8am, 8, 10pm; Q215. Also offers regular Pullman buses (Q120). Fuente del Norte (☎926 0517), on 4 Calle in Santa Elena, has frequent Pullman departures, bus quality varies. 8-12hr., about every hr. 6:30am-9pm, Q60-130.

Poptún: Any daylight Guatemala City-bound bus. (1½hr., Q15.)

Río Dulce: Any daylight Guatemala City-bound bus. (5-6hr., Q50.)

Sayaxché: (1½-2hr., 6 per day 5am-3pm, Q20.)

Tikal: (2hr., 1pm, Q10.) Continues to **Uaxactún**. (3hr., Q15.) See also **Tourist Minibuses**, below.

Tourist Minibuses: The most popular way of getting to **Tikal**. Purchase tickets in most hotels or travel agencies for hotel pickup, or catch one on the southern shore road in Flores (about every hr. 5am-noon, more sporadic in afternoon). Also run directly from the airport. **Linea Dorada** offers the best and cheapest service. (☎926 0070. Q25 round-trip.) **San Juan Travel** is slightly pricier. (☎926 0041. Q40 round-trip.) The same two companies travel into Belize and Mexico. Linea Dorada/Mundo Maya offers very low rates to **Belize City** (4hr., US$8) and **Chetumal, Mexico** (7½hr., US$15). If and when they raise their rates, they may match those of San Juan travel (US$20 and US$35).

✴ 🔁 ORIENTATION AND PRACTICAL INFORMATION

Island Flores to the north and Santa Elena to the south are connected by a paved **causeway** across the lake. In Flores, the **parque central** is on top of the hill at the center of town. Santa Elena's main street, **4 Calle**, is three blocks south of the end of the causeway. Banks, stores, and buses are all along this street. To get to Flores from the bus drop-off, head east (right as you face the lake) on the main drag until the road signs point you left across the causeway. The **airport** is 2km from Santa Elena along the highway toward Tikal; minibuses and local buses head into town.

Tourist Information: INGUAT (☎926 0669), in Flores's *parque central*. Open M-F 8am-4pm. Also in the airport (☎926 0533). More info at **CINCAP** (☎926 0718), on the north side of the *parque* in Flores. Open M-F 9am-1pm and 2-6pm. Also useful is the **Destination Petén** magazine.

Travel Agencies and Guided Tours: Recommended agents in Flores are the knowledgeable **Quetzal Travel** (☎926 3337) and **Martsam** (☎926 3225). **Evolution Adventures** (☎926 3206) and **Eco-Maya** (☎926 1363; www.ecomaya.com) have tours and community projects.

Banks: Head to a bank in Santa Elena—there's an abundant supply along 4 Calle. Try **Corpobanco**, which has a **Western Union** (open M-F 8:30am-7pm, Sa 9am-1pm). **Banco Industrial** opposite the Hotel Posada Santander, cashes Visa and Citicorp traveler's checks and has a 24hr. Visa **ATM** (open M-F 9am-7pm, Sa 10am-2pm).

Laundromat: Lavandería Peténchel, on Calle Centro América. Open M-Sa 8am-7pm.

Police: (☎110, emergency 120), just north of Flores' *parque central*.

Hospital: Hospital Privado (☎926 1140), in Santa Elena. Open 24hr.

Flores & Santa Elena

🏠 ACCOMMODATIONS
La Casa del Lacondón, **1**
Hospedaje Doña Goya, **2**
Hotel Maya, **7**
Hotel Mesa de los Maya, **6**
Hotel Posada Santander, **11**
El Mirador del Lago, **5**

🍎 FOOD
La Canoa, **9**
La Luna, **4**
El Mirador, **3**
Restaurante Las Puertas, **8**

🎷 NIGHTLIFE
Raíces, **10**

Pharmacy: Farmacia Nueva, a few doors down from Restaurante Las Puertas. Open daily 8am-9pm.

Telephones: Telgua (☎916 0397), 2 blocks south of 4 Calle in Santa Elena. Open M-F 8am-6pm, Sa 9am-1pm.

Internet: Internet Petén, on Calle Centro America in Flores has the fastest connection and best rates. Q6 per 30min. Open daily 8am-10pm.

Post Office: In Flores, one block south of the *parque central.* Open M-F 8am-noon and 2-5pm.

Car Rental: San Juan Travel (☎926 2013), in Santa Elena by the causeway, has rentals for Q450 per day. **Tabarini** (☎926 0272) and others at the airport.

ACCOMMODATIONS

Accommodations in Santa Elena are closer to the bus station, but Flores is safer and more enjoyable.

La Casa del Lacandón (☎926 4359), on the northwest side of the island. Bright, very clean tiled rooms with private bath and lukewarm water. 2nd floor balcony and pool. Singles Q50; doubles Q100, with A/C Q160. ❸

El Mirador de Lago (☎926 4363), on the east side of the island. Bright, comfortable rooms and a great dock for swimming make this hotel popular. Rooms have fans and hot-water private baths; lobby has a TV. Singles Q50; doubles Q80; triples Q125. ❸

Hospedaje Doña Goya (☎926 3538), on the north side of the island. A great budget option. Bright, spacious rooms with or without bath. There's a lake view rooftop and space to sling hammocks, plus a book exchange. Doubles Q70, with bath Q90. ❹

Hotel Maya, on the west side near Calle Centro América. Run by a friendly family, Hotel Maya has small, clean rooms with private bath and strong fans. There's a private dock for swimming and enjoying the sunset. Singles Q50; doubles Q80; triples Q105. ❸

Hotel Mesa de los Maya (☎926 1240), on Av. La Reforma, a block from Calle Centro América. Dark, elegant rooms with TV and bath. The cheapest A/C in town. Pricey attached restaurant. Singles and doubles Q135, with A/C Q195. ❺

Hotel Posada Santander (☎926 0574), near the bus terminal on 4 Calle, is the best choice in Santa Elena. Rooms are well-maintained; those in the new wing are nicer and more spacious. Singles Q40, with bath Q60; doubles Q60/Q60. ❷

FOOD AND NIGHTLIFE

■ **Restaurante Las Puertas,** on Av. Santa Ana, off Calle Centro América. A popular meeting place with just the right amount of hip (read: paint-splattered walls). Sandwiches and pastas are tasty and well-priced. Spaghetti al pesto Q24; pizzas and sandwiches Q20-25. Live evening performances from 9pm on. Open M-Sa 8am-midnight. ❸

El Mirador, on the west side of the *parque central*. Serves the tastiest budget food in Flores, with a nice balcony overlooking the town and lake. Full breakfast Q15. The real bargain is the Q14 buffet served noon-2pm. Open M-Sa 7am-9:30pm. ❷

La Luna, on the west side of the island, by Eco Maya. Excellent food, a warm ambience, and an adjacent patio with tropical plants justify slightly higher prices. Chicken *cordon bleu* Q49; burgers Q24. Open daily noon-midnight, kitchen closes at 10:30pm. ❸

La Canoa, on Calle Centro América. Inexpensive renditions of *comedor* food served in a cozy, family-run cafe. Chicken dinner Q25; tacos Q12. Open M-Sa 8am-3pm, 5-9pm. ❷

Flores has a huge supply of bars and restaurants in which to drink, eat, and enjoy the waterfront or sunset. Two of the best include **The Sports Bar,** on the south shore, and **Las Puertas.** Flores's only disco is **Raices,** on the water in southwest Flores. The popular weekday bar turns into a club with DJ on weekends, with occasional live music. Especially hopping on weekend nights is **Mega Tarro,** a disco with a prime lakefront location 100m to the right of the causeway in Santa Elena. Fridays boast *ranchero* music; Saturdays feature hip-hop, Top 40, and reggae.

SIGHTS AND OUTDOOR ACTIVITIES

Local boaters will take visitors out for **tours** of **Lago Petén Itzá,** which may include visits to the lookout point **El Mirador** or the **Peténcito** zoo. Look for boats near the causeway or at the west end of Calle Centro América, by Hotel Santana; speak directly with the captain rather than with the agents roaming the streets. (2hr., Q150-200 for small groups.) To go on your own, rent **kayaks** at La Casona de La Isla (Q12 per hr.) or Hotel Petén—both on the west side of the island.

GUATEMALA

The **Aktun Kan cave,** 2km south of Santa Elena, holds 300m of well-illuminated paths as well as several unlit kilometers (bring your own flashlight). To get to the cave, follow the causeway south; bear left at the fork and then turn right at the sign. (Open daily 8am-5pm. Q5.) Hotel Sábana, just past Doña Goya, allows non-guests to use its **swimming pool** (Q20).

EL REMATE

On the beautiful shores of Lake Petén Itzá, the village of El Remate is known for its woodcarving, but it's the location—halfway between Flores and Tikal and conveniently near the Belizean border—that makes it a popular base for visiting the region. The area has a few interesting diversions and clean lake swimming, and it's a great change of pace after the bustle of Santa Elena and tourist-centered Flores.

TRANSPORTATION. Tourist minibuses heading between Flores and Tikal stop in El Remate, and there are also direct public buses from Santa Elena (4 per day 8am, 1, 3, and 4pm). You can also take a Flores-Belize border bus and get off at **El Cruce/Puente Ixlú,** 2km south of El Remate. From there it's a 20min. walk to town along the main road. Note that en route to **Tikal,** only the 5:30am minibus stops at the hotels; later minibuses must be flagged down on the highway. Ticket sellers visit hotels in the evening; you can also buy tickets at La Casa de Don David (see below). A public bus bound for Tikal passes by around 1:45pm. Catch all buses and minibuses at the shed across the street from La Casa de Don David.

ACCOMMODATIONS AND FOOD. Budget accommodations in El Remate are more rustic than those in Flores. The standout is **La Casa de Don David ❺,** at the junction of the highway and the dirt road veering left along the lake. David Kuhn and his staff provide tourist information, good cheer, and delicious food (dinner Q30-40). Comfortable rooms have private bath. Bungalows are great for families. (Cell ☎ 306 2190; lacasadedondavid@yahoo.com. Reservations requested. Basic singles with cold bath Q120, nicer singles with hot bath Q150-175; doubles with cold bath Q150/Q200-300. Each additional person Q20.) Popular **John's Lodge ❶,** or the **Casa de Don Juan,** on the highway just before the dirt road near La Casa de Don David, offers basic dorms with mosquito nets, plus a cheap *comedor* and communal bath. (Q20 per person.) **Mirador del Duende ❷,** on a hill on the right side of the highway entering the village from Flores, has the best view in town, but the bungalows are nothing more than open-air cement shelters with mattresses. Hammock-slingers and campers are welcome. The restaurant serves veggie food. (Camping Q20; bungalows Q35 per person.) The **Biotopo Cerro Cahuí** (see below) has a few free campsites along Lake Petén where campfires are allowed.

SIGHTS AND OUTDOOR ACTIVITIES. The **Biotopo Cerro Cahuí,** 2km from the highway on the dirt road along the lakeshore, contains 651 hectares of protected lands, including ponds and tropical forest. Two interconnecting **loop trails**— 4km (2hr.) and 6km (3hr.)—traverse the reserve. Just past the first turnaround lies a *mirador* with a view of the lake. Be careful, though, as violent assaults on tourists have occurred along the road to the Biotopo and in that area as recently as 2001. Since then, tourist police have been placed to make things safer, but you should still check with locals before you go. Traveling in a group is a good idea. (Open daily 7am-5pm, though visitors may stay later. Q20.) An excellent way to explore beautiful Lake Petén is renting a **mountain bike** from La Case de Don David. (Q5 per hr.; Q30 per day.) La Case de Don Juan also offers **tours,** including the acclaimed **Night Crocodile Tour** led by Filin Oliveros. (2hr., 1-4 people Q100 each, 5 or more people Q75 each.) In the little village of Puente Ixlú (El Cruce), 2km south of El Remate, stand the largely unrestored ruins of **Ixlú.**

TIKAL

Tikal attracts visitors from every corner of the globe and elicits such a powerful reaction that the site draws nearly as many repeat visitors as first-timers. The ruins, 65km northeast of Flores, encompass more than 3000 Maya stone constructions. The site was featured in *Star Wars*—and no wonder. With five massive temples rising above the dense jungle, Tikal holds a magical, mythical quality no modern-day movie set could match. As impressive as the buildings themselves are, it's the surrounding tropical forest that distinguishes Tikal from other great Maya sites. Falling fruit gives away the spider monkeys hiding overhead, remote paths conceal parrots, iguanas, and wild boars, and lucky early risers may spot a sacred jaguar slinking through the undergrowth. And there's always the elusive quetzal…

Many package tours are scheduled so that you can visit Tikal in a single day, but while this is enough time to see the highlights, a longer visit allows for a more leisurely pace and the opportunity to savor the ruins and the jungle as they change with the light. Sunrise and sunset at Tikal are particularly magical.

▐ TRANSPORTATION

From Flores/Santa Elena, El Remate, or the airport, tourist **minibuses** are the easiest way to reach the ruins (see the Flores and El Remate sections for more details). Minibuses arrive in Tikal throughout the morning and return in the afternoon and evening as soon as they accumulate enough passengers. There's also a daily local bus from **Santa Elena** (2hr., 1pm, Q10; return 7am). If you're coming from Belize, change buses at **Puente Ixlú/El Cruce** and wait for northbound transport. Frequent minibuses pass by in the morning; the local bus from Santa Elena comes by around 1:45-2pm, but otherwise there is little afternoon traffic toward Tikal. To get to Belize from Tikal, take any Flores-bound bus or minibus to Puente Ixlú and wait for a border-bound bus (the last usually passes around 6pm).

✳ ORIENTATION

The ruins of Tikal sit in the middle of the **Tikal National Park** (550 sq. km). The road from Flores crosses the park boundary 15km south of the ruins; buses will stop so that you may pay the Q50 park entrance fee. (Tickets sold after 3pm are good for the next day as well.) The **Visitors Center** complex holds a post office, a restaurant, and one of the area's two museums. Nearby are three hotels, a camping area, three *comedores*, and a second museum. The entrance to the ruins site is near the visitors center, but from the entrance it is a 20min. walk to the Great Plaza.

▐ ACCOMMODATIONS

Accommodations at Tikal include one good campground and three expensive hotels (by Guatemalan standards). Some budget travelers commute from El Remate or Flores. An overnight stay, however, is an exhilarating treat for those who'd like to beat the crowds to Temple IV to see the sun's first rays illuminate the dense jungle foliage. All three hotels listed have restaurants and electricity during certain hours only (electricity is usually off 11pm-5am). During the night those fans make for lovely, motionless ceiling decorations, but you'll be able to enjoy the piercing sounds of the jungle. All three hotels are very popular, so book ahead.

Jungle Lodge (☎476 8775), across from the visitors center by the ruins entrance. Rooms with shared bath and fan are not too appealing but clean. Well-kept swimming pool. Singles US$26, with bath US$54; doubles US$31/US$72; triples US$86. ❺

Tikal Inn (☎/fax 926 0065), past the Jaguar Inn as you walk away from the ruins. A slight step down but still pleasant, with reasonable rooms and slightly nicer bungalows

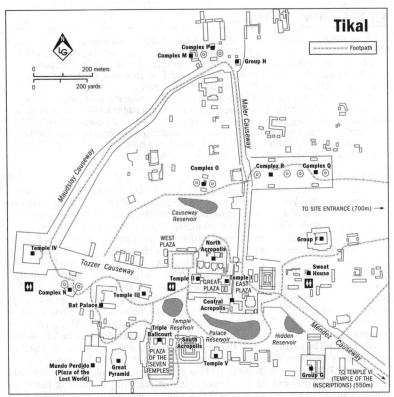

Tikal

- - - - - - Footpath

Complex P
Complex M
Group H

Complex O

Complex R
Complex Q

Causeway
Reservoir

TO SITE ENTRANCE (700m) →

WEST
PLAZA

North
Acropolis

Group F

Temple IV

Tozzer Causeway

Sweat
House

Complex N

Temple III

Temple II

GREAT
PLAZA

Temple I
EAST
PLAZA

Bat Palace

Central
Acropolis

Temple
Reservoir

Triple
Ballcourt

Palace
Reservoir

Hidden
Reservoir

Méndez Causeway

South
Acropolis

PLAZA
OF THE
SEVEN
TEMPLES

Mundo Perdido
(Plaza of the
Lost World)

Great
Pyramid

Temple V

Group G

TO TEMPLE VI
(TEMPLE OF THE
INSCRIPTIONS) (550m)

0 — 200 meters
0 — 200 yards

N
LG

set around an inviting pool. All rooms have private baths with hot water in the evenings. Singles US$25, bungalow US$50; doubles US$35/US$60. ❺

Jaguar Inn (☎926 0002; www.jaguartikal.com). The cheapest option. Simple, well-kept bungalow rooms come with cold-water private baths. Nice communal bathrooms are available for those who camp on the grounds or rent one of the hammocks with mosquito nets. Dorms US$10; hammock/net rental Q40; camping Q25; singles US$20; doubles US$32. Prices rise approximately US$20 for private rooms July-Mar. ❺

Campground. A grassy expanse across from the visitors center. Communal bathrooms with showers. Luggage storage. Check in at the restaurant inside the visitors center. Pitch a tent or sling a hammock (mosquito netting can be rented, or bring your own) under thatched-roof huts (Q25 per person) or try a tiny wooden cabin with sleeping pad. Singles Q50, with sheets and towels Q108; doubles Q100/Q170. ❸

🍴 FOOD

Three *comedores* line the road in from Flores. The best food is served at **Comedor Imperio Maya,** where portions are huge (*pollo frito* Q30; open daily 6am-9pm)—but all offer similar fare. For finer dining, head to the restaurant at the **Jaguar Inn.** Although service is a bit slow, the food gets rave reviews. (Entrees from Q26. Open daily 6am-9pm.) Also recommended is the **Jungle Lodge** restaurant, which serves tasty food in a more upscale environment (Q30-50) and features an outdoor pool.

GUATEMALA

👁 THE RUINS OF TIKAL

*Tickets (Q50) are typically purchased on the bus/minibus at the national park entrance, but may also be purchased at the entrance to the ruins themselves. The **site** is open officially from 5am to 6pm daily, although tickets can be purchased as early as 4:30am once inside the park. Both **museums** open M-F 9am-5pm, Sa-Su 9am-4pm; Museo Lítico free with park admission, Museo Cerámica Q10 extra. A few explanatory signs are scattered throughout the ruins, but hiring a **tour guide** makes for a more informed visit. Guides wait in the Visitors Center. Ask around especially if you have a particular interest, since areas of specialization vary. Tours in Spanish or English (about 4hr., 1-5 people US$40, US$5 per additional person). Israel Segura is an enthusiastic Spanish-speaking guide specializing in flora, fauna, and uses of the jungle's natural resources. Also worthwhile is William Coe's Tikal Guidebook (Q75), which includes a detailed map.*

HISTORY

The Maya settled Tikal around 700 BC; they were likely attracted by its hilltop location above the Petén lowlands and the abundance of flint useful for weapons and tools. The earliest buildings date from 500 BC, and by AD 250—the dawn of the Classic period—Tikal had been established as a major population center. At this time, the powerful city of **El Mirador** (65km to the north) fell into decline, making **Tikal** and **Uaxactún** the dominant cities of the region. In AD 378, Tikal, aided by an alliance with the mighty highland center of **Kaminaljuyú**, on the modern site of Guatemala City, and the powerful **Teotihuacán** of Central Mexico, handily defeated Uaxactún. From that moment, Tikal reigned over the Petén and grew in population and splendor. By the 6th century it spanned some 30 sq. km and supported a population of 100,000. The middle of the 6th century, however, saw Tikal's power overshadowed by that of **Caracol** (in Belize's Maya Mountains). In AD 700, the city embarked on a splendid renaissance. Led by the mighty **Ah Cacau (Lord Chocolate)**, Tikal regained its supremacy in the Petén. Ah Cacau and his successors built all five of Tikal's massive temples in the span of a single century.

Around AD 900, the entire lowland Maya civilization suddenly and mysteriously collapsed, and Tikal was largely abandoned. Contemporary theories of the Maya collapse suggest a combination of endemic regional warfare, overpopulation with declining agricultural productivity, popular uprisings, and drought. While Post-Classic descendents of the original population continued to live and worship at Tikal, they did little of lasting significance other than pillage the centuries-old tombs. By AD 1000, jungle engulfed the city. Save for a few passing references by Franciscan friars, the modern world did not rediscover Tikal until the Guatemalan government sponsored an expedition led by **Modesto Méndez** and **Ambrosio Tut** in 1848. The first photographs were taken in 1881 by English archaeologist Alfred P. Maudslay. Reprints of some of the photos are on display in the Museo Lítico.

THE MAIN SITE

THE GREAT PLAZA. One kilometer west of the entrance lies Tikal's geographic and commercial heart, the Great Plaza. Towering above the plaza is **Temple I**, the Temple of the Jaguar, built by the son of the great Ah Cacau after his father's death in AD 721. Tikal's most recognizable symbol, the 44m high temple is topped by a three-room structure and a roof comb that was originally painted in bright colors. Unfortunately, it's no longer possible to climb Temple I. You can, however, climb **Temple II** (38m), known as the Temple of the Masks and located at the west end of the Plaza. The complicated **North Acropolis** also stands on the Plaza. It was built and rebuilt and contains the remains of around 100 structures—a few dating back more than 2000 years. The two huge stone masks near the base of the North Acropolis make for another highlight. One is displayed under a thatched roof, and the other can be reached by following an adjacent dark passageway (you'll need a flashlight). To the south of the Great Plaza is the **Central Acropolis,** a complex of buildings probably used as an elite residential area. The configuration of rooms has changed over time, perhaps to accommodate different families.

THE WEST PLAZA TO TEMPLE IV. The **West Plaza,** north of Temple II, features a large Late Classic temple. Following the Tozzer Causeway north from here you'll reach **Temple III,** still covered in jungle vegetation. Continuing on, you'll come upon **Complex N,** one of seven identical temples at Tikal, all believed to have commemorated the completion of a Katun (a 20-year cycle in the Maya calendar). At the end of the Tozzer Causeway is **Temple IV,** the tallest structure in Tikal (64m). Built in AD 741 possibly in honor of the ruler Coon Chac, the temple affords a stellar view especially at sunrise and sunset. Steep stairways facilitate the ascent.

FROM MUNDO PERDIDO TO THE TEMPLE OF THE INSCRIPTIONS. The **Mundo Perdido** is signposted between Temples III and IV, includes 38 structures, and is capped by the 32m-high **Great Pyramid.** The Pyramid dates to the Pre-Classic era, and during its time was certainly one of the most impressive structures in all of Mesoamerica. If you can handle the steep climb, the top of the Great Pyramid provides one of the park's nicest views; all five towers soaring above the jungle. Just east is the **Plaza of the Seven Temples.** The visible structures are Late Classic, but the hidden complex dates back at least 2000 years. The north side of the plaza was once the site of a unique triple ball-court. To the east of the Plaza of the Seven Temples are the unexcavated **South Acropolis** and the **Temple V** (58m tall), under restoration until 2005. The contrast between the temple's condition before and after restoration is striking. Also interesting is the fact that the Temple V laborers slaved for years to build a 58m temple, then put only a few square meters of floor-space on top. A 1.2km (20min.) walk along the Méndez Causeway from the Great Plaza leads to the **Temple of the Inscriptions (Temple VI),** noted for the hieroglyphic text on its 12m roof comb. The text is unique to Tikal and dates from AD 766.

OTHER STRUCTURES

Complexes Q and **R,** between the Great Plaza and the entrance, are Late Classic twin pyramids. Complex Q has been well restored; to its left lies a replica of the beautiful **Stela 22,** which portrays Tikal's last known ruler, **Chitam.** The original is now in the Visitors Center. One kilometer north of the Great Plaza lie **Group H** and **Complex P,** additional examples of twin temples.

OTHER ATTRACTIONS

▨ **MUSEO LÍTICO.** Located in the Visitors Center, the museum has an excellent scale model of Tikal, photographs of the restoration process, and a fine collection of Tikal stelae, including intricate #16 of Ah Cacao in brilliant costume. Entrance is free with park admission, and the museum is a must-see.

MUSEO CERÁMICA. Museo Tikal, or Museo Cerámica, between the Jungle Lodge and the Jaguar Inn, features a more extensive collection of smaller artifacts, including colorful painted pottery, jade decorations, and stela #31, one of the finest Classic carvings in the Maya world. (Entrance Q10.)

RUINS NORTH OF TIKAL

Hidden in the vast tropical forests north of Tikal are several other Maya sites. The important site of Uaxactún is the most accessible. El Zotz, Río Azul, and the splendid El Mirador are all largely unrestored and uncleared, but it's precisely the isolation and mystique that make a visit memorable. Other attractions in the region

GUATEMALA

include the Maya ruins of Yaxhá, Nakum, and El Pedro—where it is actually the jungle and wildlife that are the primary attractions.

👁 UAXACTÚN

*The cheapest way to visit Uaxactún is to take the Transportes Pinita **bus** from the market in Santa Elena (3hr., 1pm, Q20) or Tikal (about 3pm, Q10), and then catch the return bus the next morning (6am). Some travel agencies in Flores organize daytrips to Uaxactún. Groups of 4 or more can ask minibuses or hotels at Tikal for transportation (US$10-15 per person). The **Jungle Lodge at Tikal** offers trips (8am, return 1pm; US$15 per person, 4-person min., US$60 total for smaller groups). Though Uaxactún is small, it may be wise to let one of the local kids show you around. Uaxactún is always open. The road passes through the Tikal entrance, where visitors heading to Uaxactún can pay the Q15 entrance fee.*

In the forest 23km north of Tikal hides Uaxactún (wah-shak-TOON), a small Petén village built around an airstrip and surrounded by Maya ruins. Uaxactún once rivaled Tikal in stature but was defeated in AD 378. Tikal retains its edge today, and Uaxactún is disappointing in comparison. However, for the Maya scholar, the site holds some of the best Pre-Classic Maya architecture in Mesoamerica.

As you come into town and hit the disused airstrip, **Group E**—the most impressive site—is about a 10min. walk to your right. There, three side-by-side temples served as an observatory: viewed from atop a fourth temple, the sun rises behind the south temple on the shortest day of the year and behind the north one on the longest day. Beneath these temples is **E-VII-Sub,** the oldest surviving building in Petén, with foundations dating to 2000 BC. On the other side of the old airstrip, a dirt road beginning at the far end of the field passes through unexcavated **Group B** and leads to the grander **Group A,** the second notable site in Uaxactún. Mainly a series of temples and residential compounds, the area is topped off by **Temple A-18,** whose broad roof peers over the jungle canopy.

The impressive Uaxactún museum is hidden within a small one-room building next to Hotel Chiclero, on the left side at the end of the retired airstrip. It features pieces of pottery, jade, and human skulls—most dating back 2000 years. Entrance is free; ask at Hotel Chiclero. The hotel offers barebones rooms (singles Q42; doubles Q82; meals Q30-40), and will arrange Spanish-speaking *niños* as guides for the ruins (Q20). Note that the village only has electricity from 7 to 9pm.

👁 EL MIRADOR

*Reaching El Mirador is no easy task; it involves a 4.5hr. **bus** journey and two tough days on foot and horseback. The cheapest option in Flores is Quetzal Travel (see the Flores section), which offers a 5-day trip for US$200 per person for a 2-5-person group and US$150 for a 6-10-person group. Another option is to take the daily bus from Flores to Carmelita, the starting point for the trek to the ruins (4.5hr., 1pm, Q25). There, you can arrange for a guide and horse (US$25 per day), but you must supply your own food and equipment.*

The most magnificent of these sites and also the most remote, El Mirador was once a tremendous city, certainly greater than Tikal in the Pre-Classic era. Archaeologists believe that the city reached its peak around 2000 years ago, making it the first great Maya city. The 16 sq. km site features a number of pyramids, including on that is 70m high, the tallest structure anywhere in the Maya world, with a base the size of three football fields.

👁 OTHER MAYA SITES AND JUNGLE EXCURSIONS

*Yaxhá is about 60km northeast of El Remate and accessible by road, with Nakum about 20km farther north. El Zotz is about a 4½hr. **walk** from Cruce Dos Aguadas (on the Carmelita bus route from Flores) and 30km west of Uaxactún along a sometimes-drivable dirt* *road. Río Azul is 95km north of Uaxactún, a journey of one day by **jeep** (if passable) or four days by **horse**. El Perú is about 100km northwest of Flores. The most competitively priced tours in Flores are offered by Quetzal Travel and Martsam.*

Located in the dense Petén jungles are several other important Maya sites and sightseeing trails. Situated in thick jungle close to the east shores of Lago Yaxhá are the ruins of **Yaxhá,** meaning "green water," or water the color of sacred jade. The third-largest Maya site in Guatemala, Yaxhá appears to have been built in an unusual grid pattern more typical of sites such as Teotihuacán, and it holds one of the Maya world's most extensive constructions, a twin pyramid complex comprising hundreds of structures. Also interesting are the ruins of **Nakum,** 20km to the north, which are also considered a bird- and animal-watching paradise.

El Zotz is a large ruin noted for its huge bat population. The bats' mass exodus from nearby caves at dusk is a famed spectacle. It is possible to hike the El Zotz-Tikal trail with guides. **Río Azul,** an unrestored mini-Tikal, is home to a 47m temple and some impressive tombs. The ruins of **El Perú** are part of the scarlet macaw trail. In addition to the ruins and the macaws, the trip also features a pleasant boat ride, during which crocodiles and turtles are regularly spotted.

BORDER WITH BELIZE

The Guatemalan border with Belize, in the town of **Melchor de Mencos,** is 101km from Flores/Santa Elena. Border-bound buses from Santa Elena pass by Puente Ixlú/El Cruce, 2km south of El Remate; coming from Tikal or El Remate you can catch a ride here. At the border, the **immigration office** is open daily 6am-8pm. Guatemalan immigration officially charges no fee, but usually does anyway—often Q10 to leave and as much as US$10 to enter. Ask for a receipt and they may let you off the hook. **Exchanging** quetzales and Belizean dollars with the countless money changers on either side. The most convenient place for food or accommodations is **Hotel Palace,** by the immigration post, along the river. The owner is a good source of information, and Internet is available for Q15 per 30min. (☎926 5196. Singles Q75; doubles Q90.) From the border, **buses** head to **Flores** (2hr., every 2hr. 7am-7pm, Q15). Three afternoon buses (3, 5, 6:30pm) travel to **Guatemala City.**

BORDER WITH MEXICO

There are two established routes from Flores to **Palenque** in Chiapas, Mexico. The quickest and easiest route is through **Bethel.** Transportes Pinta buses leave from Flores (5hr., 5am and 1pm, Q40). Once there, get your passport stamped and catch one of the fairly frequent 30min. boats (Q225 per group) to **Frontera Corozal** in Mexico. In Corozal (or even Bethel), it's possible to arrange a trip to the beautiful ruins at **Yaxchilán.** From Corozal, minibus *colectivos* leave for Palenque until about 2:30pm for the 3hr. trip. The other route begins with a bus from Flores to the Guatemalan border post in **El Naranjo** (5hr., 7 per day 5am-2:30pm, Q25). There are a few basic hotels in El Naranjo, but it's best to set out early and catch the midday boat from El Naranjo to the Mexican border post in **La Palma** (3hr., US$20-25 per person). From there, buses depart for Palenque via **Tenosique**—the last leaves around 5pm; if you miss it, there's camping and a few basic rooms in La Palma. Whichever route you choose, plan on the trip taking at least one day. It might be wise to organize the trip with the help of a Flores travel agency; **San Juan Travel** has a 5am, 6hr. trip to Palenque for US$30.

HONDURAS

Honduras, a land of jagged mountains and dense jungle, has the most rugged geography of Central America. The indomitable terrain, though it has kept the country isolated throughout history, is also the source of its huge tourist appeal. Pristine cloudforests full of wildlife, long stretches of Caribbean beach, pine-covered ridges, and tropical rainforest all beckon adventurers. Western Honduras is home to the magnificent Maya ruins at Copán. Non-Maya indigenous groups survive elsewhere in the country—amidst the splendor of less frequented locales.

Though Honduras has never suffered a civil war, the 1980s saw its people suffer the effects of military dictators funded by the US. This oppression has rendered Honduras one of Central America's poorest countries—and, for better or worse, one of the cheapest to visit. Though the flow of tourists to Honduras is slow, the *gringo* trail is very well-defined. While Copán, Tela, and the Bay Islands have well-established tourist industries, those who explore the back country are in for an experience of solitary splendor, scattered frontier towns, and engaging locals.

HIGHLIGHTS OF HONDURAS

The Maya ruins of **Copán,** an essential stop on La Ruta Maya, where the Hieroglyphic Stairway relates the divine genealogy of Copán's kings (p. 463).

The paradisiacal **Bay Islands,** boasting silky beaches, excellent snorkeling, and the cheapest diving on the planet (p. 497).

Trujillo, the last town of any size heading east along the Caribbean coast, featuring great Garífuna *giffity*, clean beaches, and all-night dancing (p. 492).

For adventure seekers, true wilderness awaits in the rugged cloudforest of **Parque Nacional La Muralla** and the expansive and diverse **Biosfera Río Plátano,** in the isolated Mosquitia (p. 515 and p. 510).

Regions of Honduras

HONDURAS

SUGGESTED ITINERARIES

ONE WEEK. Only two hours from Miami and Houston, even a short trip to Honduras can combine culture, coast, and cloudforest. Fly into the capital **Tegucigalpa** (p. 435), but spend more of your time around the city in **La Tigra National Park** (p. 445) or **Valle de Angeles** (p. 445) with its great views and galleries. Then travel northwest through the former capital **Comayagua** (p. 450) on your way to the magnificent Maya ruins of **Copán** (p. 463). Now it's time for some beach, baby. Head to **La Ceiba** (p. 486), the base for exploring paradise at the **Bay Islands** (p. 497). Of the main islands, **Roatán** (p. 502) is the largest and most popular; **Utila** (p. 497) has a distinctive young, party atmosphere. If you have time you can visit a few more coastal towns such as **Tela** (p. 481) and **Puerto Cortés** (p. 477) on your way back to **San Pedro Sula** (p. 470)for your departure flight.

TWO WEEKS. Building on the one week itinerary, spend more time at each destination and for the adventurous out there, add **La Mosquitia** (p. 508). From **La Ceiba** (p. 486) fly to **Palacios** (p. 509) or **Puerto Lempira** (p. 513) and be sure to check out the Mosquito coast and the amazing **Reserva de Biosfera del Río Plátano** (p. 510). La Mosquitia is true wilderness and truly rural. Fly back to La Ceiba or Tegucigalpa.

THREE WEEKS. From **Palacios** (p. 509), you can head to **Trujillo** (p. 492) for a last day of beach tanning, and then head into the beautiful and rugged Olancho interior. Head toward **La Unión** (p. 515), and check out **Parque Nacional La Muralla** (p. 515). Stop in **Juticalpa** (p. 516) for some city life amidst the natural beauty and then you're on your way back to **Tegus** (p. 435). If you plan to dip into Nicaragua head south from **Tegus** to the border at **El Espino** (p. 448), or **Guasaule** (p. 448). While in Southern Honduras take a boat to **Isla El Tigre** (p. 449) for some Pacific paradise.

LIFE AND TIMES

LAND, FLORA, FAUNA

Honduras, the second largest country in Central America, is predominantly mountainous, with its eastern coast jutting into the cool Caribbean. Peaks as high as 2100m are atypically non volcanic; they are part of the large Northern Sierra, or **Crystalline Highlands.** These ridges are mostly covered by pine forest and at higher altitudes by surreal cloudforest and expanses of short, gnarled trees.

The steep valleys and gorges that plunge into the mountainsides support much of Honduras's agriculture and cattle raising. The narrowest regions—the Caribbean and Pacific lowlands—are its most heavily cultivated. East of the coastal plain is the untainted **La Mosquitia,** Central America's largest intact rainforest.

Off the Caribbean coast are the **Bay Islands,** lingering above-water fragments of the continental shelf. Surrounded by an extension of Belize's reef system, the islands (particularly Roatán and Utila) are popular with snorkelers and divers.

Honduras's many ecosystems—cloudforest, reefs, mangroves, savannahs, tropical dry forest, pine forest, tropical rainforests, coral reefs, and mountainous highlands ensure an abundant wealth of **biodiversity.** With over 2000 species of fauna including monkeys, jaguars, puma, sloths, armadillos, crocodiles, snakes, fish, and birds galore, any area of Honduras is sure to be a treat for the animal lover. Even if you miss spotting that elusive quetzal, there are still over 10,000 vascular plant species to keep you entertained. With 100 protected areas, there are more tree species per square hectare in Honduras than in the Amazon jungle. Honduras is home to the most intact rainforest in Central America, including the Río Plátano Biosphere in La Mosquitia—one of the most magnificent rainforests in the world.

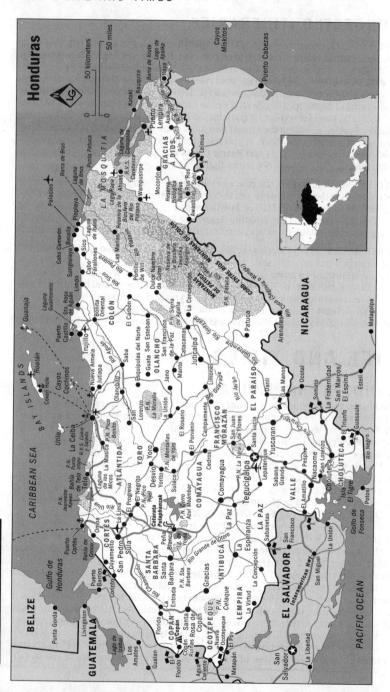

Mahogany, *indio desnudo, zapaton,* and *ceiba* are all endemic plant species important to the economy, and interesting to the traveler.

HISTORY

Honduras has always been rich in history, from the days of the Maya in Copán, through post-independence political turmoil, to its role as a pawn in the Contra War. Honduras has often been at the mercy of external interests in Central America, the US, Spain, and Great Britain. Its history has been adversely affected by its propensity for devastating natural disasters. Its namesake "Honduras," or "depths" is telling of both the coastal Caribbean waters and an intense history.

NOT SO INDEPENDENT. Columbus first sighted Honduras in 1502, and the fallen civilization of Copán over half a century later. The *conquistadores* Hernán Cortés and Pedro de Alvarado established modern day Comayagua and Tegucigalpa in their all-consuming quest for gold. When Central America finally shook off Spanish rule three centuries later in 1821, Honduras found itself in a more difficult situation than its neighbors. Steep mountains, isolated settlements, floods, and droughts frustrated farmers, and the British were attacking in the north.

After independence from Spain in 1821, Honduras briefly joined the **United Provinces of Central America**, sending liberal leader **Francisco Morazán** to head the alliance. When a group of Hondurans traveled to Europe to commission a statue of Morazán, they found themselves without enough money to pay for the monument. Instead, they bought a second-hand statue of an obscure Napoleonic military leader and erected the hand-me-down, which still stands in Tegucigalpa. Unlike the imperfect monument, the federation could not withstand its faults: under increasingly Conservative influence, Honduras declared independence on November 5, 1838, and the United Provinces collapsed two years later.

A NATION DIVIDED. The Conservative regime in Honduras struggled to establish national unity, but constant British, American, and Central American military and financial intervention ruined all chances of internal stability. After the assassination of **President José Santos Guardiola** in 1862, 20 leaders ruled Honduras in just 10 years. Six different constitutions were drafted between 1865 and 1924. As factions fought for control, the federal capital bounced between Liberal Tegucigalpa and Conservative Comayagua. Soil erosion and fire in Comayagua eventually shifted the balance toward "Tegus," where the capital has remained ever since.

In the late 1870s, the Liberal president **Marco Aurelio Soto** pacified warring factions, undertook capital improvements, and expanded the education system. But by the turn of the century, no commercial bourgeoisie had emerged in Honduras, and its absence left an economic and political vacuum. A handful of foreign companies, most notably the **United Fruit Company,** stepped in to fill the void.

BANANA REPUBLIC. United Fruit bought huge tracts of land for banana plantations, set up its own banks and railroads, and created an elaborate political machine. By 1918, United Fruit and two other companies controlled 75% of the nation's banana-growing land, much of it taken from small farmers through threats or violence. For the next 40 years, *El Pulpo* ("The Octopus," as United Fruit was known) held Honduras in its grip, with convenient military support of the USA.

Domestic unrest, combined with the Great Depression, allowed **General Tiburcio Carías Andino** to seize power in 1932 and rule as a dictator until 1948, when he was replaced by **Juan Manuel Gálvez.** He and the two following leaders, Julio Lozano Díaz and Ramón Villeda Morales, ruled until 1963 and began a series of much-needed reforms. In 1954, the famous Banana Strike took place. Beginning among dock workers, the strike spread through the foreign-owned banana industry, supported by sympathetic strikes in other industries. Though it was ultimately broken with help from the American Federation of Labor, the strike initiated Honduras's labor movement and prompted the legal recognition of unions the next year.

MILITARY MAKE-OVER. The military assumed center stage again in 1963, when **Colonel Oswaldo López Arellano** took control of the government with the support of the fruit companies. He kept control until 1975. During his rule, frustrations with neighboring El Salvador increased, and in mid-July 1969 tensions erupted after the two countries confronted each other in a match. While the **"Soccer War"** resulted in a wave of Honduran nationalism, it left 2000 Honduran civilians dead and sent 130,000 Salvadoran refugees fleeing across the border. Although Arellano did attempt to institute large-scale agrarian reform, it met with little success.

Despite a series of corruption scandals, the military ruled until 1981, when a civilian government was elected. The time was not fortuitous for peaceful civilian rule, however, as **Ronald Reagan** decided that Honduras was the perfect launching pad for attacking the new Sandinista government in Nicaragua. With the support of the commander-in-chief of the Honduran armed forces, **General Gustavo Álvarez,** the anti-Sandinista forces set up bases in Honduras using millions of dollars of American arms and the help of CIA and US military advisers. The improvement of social conditions that the Hondurans had expected from their civilian government was thus postponed even further, as the Honduran military operated from behind the scenes to extinguish any internal opposition to the presence of the Contras on Honduran soil. Victims of Alvarez's US-supported death squads included peasant leaders and priests. Growing increasingly uncomfortable with Alvarez's violence, the military ousted the president in 1984. Yet the Contra war accelerated, and was met with growing anti-US protests. Frustrated, the Honduran government ordered the Contras out of Honduras in 1988. When US-backed **Violeta Chamorro** was elected president of Nicaragua in 1990, US troops evaporated from Honduras, only to be replaced by 11,000 armed and aimless Contras seeking refuge in Honduras.

BEYOND THE CONTRAS. **Rafael Leonardo Callejas Romero's** term as president, from 1989 to 1993, was characterized by high inflation and falling wages, all in the name of economic adjustment. Callejas also favored another kind of "economic adjustment," embezzling millions of dollars from corrupt deals with foreign businesses. The Liberal **Carlos Roberto Reina** was elected in 1993 on a platform of political reform. The value of the lempira continued to shrink, however, as unemployment grew. Finally, in 1997, **Carlos Flores,** a Liberal businessman and engineer, won the presidency with a majority vote. Yet Hondurans remain skeptical: elected civilian governments have not met their promises, and the military continues to exercise power behind the scenes.

TODAY

In October 1998, Hurricane Mitch swept across Central America, and Honduras bore the brunt of the attack. More than 5000 people died and 82,000 homes and nearly 200 bridges collapsed in what is considered one of the worst natural disasters ever in the Western Hemisphere. The destruction has left this under-developed nation struggling to recover and rebuild. In May 2000, the US passed the Trade and Development Act of 2000 to increase trade with the Caribbean Basin and Sub-Saharan Africa. The act liberalizes trade between Central America and the US through the elimination of duties and quotas.

PEOPLE

Honduras is predominantly *mestizo*, Spanish-speaking, and Roman Catholic. Although western Honduras was a major Maya area centered around the city of Copán, few intact indigenous communities survive. Of the remaining communities, most are concentrated in the west and consist of the **Lenca** and **Chortí,** generally assimilated into *mestizo* culture. However, in the northeastern rainforests, the **Miskito, Pech,** and **Tawahka** live isolated from the currents of mainstream Honduras. The **Garífuna,** descendants of Carib Indians and African slaves, reside along the north coast and on the Bay Islands. They first arrived in Roatán in 1797 and from there spread out across the Caribbean coast, ever maintaining a strong cultural identity and famous traditional dances and music.

CULTURE

FOOD & DRINK

Honduran *típico* fare is a hodgepodge of rice and beans, tortillas, and fresh seafood (on the coast). Hondurans have their own word for just about every regional specialty. For starters, a *baleada* is sort of like a burrito; most often, it's a tortilla smeared with fried beans and onions. Garífuna food usually includes *casabe* (cassava) and *tapado* (soup made of fish), both drenched in coconut milk. A favorite dish on the Bay Islands, rarely seen in their restaurants, is *tapado* (or *machuka*) comprised of fish, potatoes, yucca, and vegetables cooked in diluted coconut milk, served over rice. Vegetarians will want to look for yucca, the long, slender, green vegetable sold in markets. *Guanábana frescos* must be drunk; so must Salva Vida beer, the most popular and tastiest of Honduras's brews.

CUSTOMS & ETIQUETTE

Hondurans are generally very hospitable and gracious. Social activities are often valued as part of a business deal or holiday. Conversations usually have more formalities, and are less "to the point" than in the U.S. Time is somewhat arbitrary—Hondurans are not in a rush, and lateness is both tolerated and expected. Arriving half an hour after a preset time is a good guideline. Dinner in Honduras is later, usually around 9pm. Women usually go out with a date, and men pay for meals. Women should also expect verbal cat calls whether they're alone or not. Hissing is common by both men and women toward the opposite sex. Homosexuality is generally accepted, but not overt. Rubbing index fingers together like "shame on you" in the US means "pay up" in Honduras. Handicapped access is not common. Approach conversations about politics or unrest in Central America tactfully.

THE ARTS

HISTORY. The combination of the legacy of the Mayas, international influence, and a flavorful people and culture, have created a lasting artistic impression in Honduras. Emerging from the Liberalism of the 19th century, the Romantic movement found its voice in writer-president Marco Aurelio Soto and in Ramón Rosa. This century, Modernist poet Juan Ramón Molina's pained works set the course for the more politically oriented writers of the "generation of '26," whose nationalist search for Honduran identity stressed both the Creole and the native.

ARCHITECTURE. Honduras has thus far escaped extreme earthquakes and fires that ravage the architecture of many Central American countries. The ancient architecture of the Mayas offers a rare glimpse into this calm, religious lifestyle of the past. In many urban areas such as Tegus, style is modern, but with a pervasive, Spanish colonial theme. Many buildings were destroyed by the devastating effects of Hurricane Mitch in 1998, but reconstruction efforts are underway.

FINE ARTS. Painting and the fine arts are a strong testament to Honduran culture from remnant Maya artifacts to colorful modern paintings. Fine arts first became a phenomenon in the 18th century with religious-themed paintings by **José Miguel**

Gomez. Several Honduran painters capture their culture in color, among them **Ana Isabel Acosta, Rosa María de Larios, Armando Lara,** and **Marco Rietti. José Antonio Velásquez** and his primitive paintings of Honduran life are a more modern legacy. Another common theme in paintings is the "rain of fish," - based on the tale from a north-central village where townspeople woke up one morning after a thunderstorm to find the ground mysteriously covered in fish.

Three bronze statues recently erected in San Pedro Sula by artist **Regina Aguilar** were supposed to honor the writer of the Central American Declaration of Independence—José Cecilio del Valle, but instead launched a raging controversy. Valle is depicted in the nude, and is conspicuously lacking the appropriate fig leaf.

LITERATURE. Honduran literature has bloomed more slowly, first because Guatemala was the center of 19th-century intellectual activity, and then because of the extreme poverty of the region. A rich heritage of legends folklore, and devotion to nature define Honduran literature. There is a limited market for books, and most authors are initially published in newspapers. The modern, prolific author Guillermo Yuscarán writes books in English reflecting Honduran culture.

MUSIC. Honduran musical taste is a conglomeration of Mexican, Guatemalan, and Caribbean styles; more locally grounded work can be found among the Garífuna. The classical music of the National Symphonic Orchestra is also best heard during their special spring festivals. Listen for drums, whistles, flutes of clays and wood, and the *marimba* and *caramba* stringed instruments. Cruising around on buses or in taxis, you're likely to hear Latin American and US pop from a few years back, including Shakira and Ricky Martin.

FILM. Several movies concerning Honduras have been made abroad, but there is no infrastructure for a film culture within the country. In 1999, the first major Honduran film "Anita the Insect Hunter" was a reflection of cultural and familial values. Hollywood is still a better bet for finding films on Honduras.

TV/NEWS. Particularly in the cities, Hondurans stay on top of the news through one of the country's six dailies. *La Prensa* (www.laprensahn.com), is the oldest and most respectable, but all six papers have become increasingly guilty of sensationalism over the last few decades. Fewer Hondurans have TVs than read the papers, but crowds gather around electronics shop windows when big stories break or when there's a hot soccer game on. The English-language *Honduras This Week* is comprehensive and informative (www.marrder.com/htw/).

SPORTS & RECREATION

Fútbol is the name of the game in Honduras, and with a national soccer league and international-caliber competition, soccer is more of an obsession than a hobby. Baseball is also a popular sport, and interest in basketball is growing. Although most younger girls pursue dance, national teams for women in soccer and basketball are competitive. Sport fishing and diving are obvious enjoyments in coastal areas. For more low key recreation, chill out with some locals over a game of checkers, chess, cards, or marbles. Embrace your inner child with a game of *cantarito* or "kick the can" with the kids.

ESSENTIALS

EMBASSIES AND CONSULATES

Embassies of Honduras: US, 3007 Tilden St., NW, suite 4M, Washington, D.C. 20008 (☎202-966-7702; fax 202-966-9751). **Canada,** 151 Slater St., Suite 805, Ottawa,

ENTRANCE REQUIREMENTS
Passport (p. 21). Required for all visitors.

Visa (p. 22). Not required of citizens of Australia, Canada, Ireland, New Zealand, the US, or the UK for stays up to one month (extendable). Needed for citizens of South Africa. Allow a month to issue.

Tourist Stamp. Issued upon arrival. Valid for 30 days but can be extended twice for US$25 at Immigration Offices.

Inoculations and Medications (p. 29). None required.

Work Permit (p. 22). Required for all foreigners planning to work in Honduras.

Driving Permit (p. 49). Not required. Must have foreign driver's license and proof of registration.

Airport Departure Fee. US$25. Tax flying within the country is 20L

Ontario, K1P 5H3 (☎ 613 233 8900; fax 613 232 0193). **UK,** 115 Gloucester Pl., London, WIH 3PJ (☎ 0171 486 4880; fax 0171 486 4550).

Consulates of Honduras: 1528 K St. NW, 2nd fl., Washington, D.C. 20005 (☎ 202-737-2978; fax 737-2907). Honduras has consulates in New York (☎ 212-714-9450), Los Angeles, Miami, Tampa, Atlanta, San Francisco, Chicago, New Orleans, and Houston.

MONEY

LEMPIRAS		
US$1 = L16.57		L1 = US$0.06
CDN$1 = L10.64		L1 = CDN$0.09
UK£1 = L25.66		L1 = UK£0.02
AUS$1 = L9.15		L1 = AUS$0.11

The rates above were accurate as of August 2002. The Honduran currency is the **lempira.** Bills come in denominations of one, two, five, 10, 20, 50, and 100 lempiras. The lempira is divided into 100 **centavos.** Coins are issued in values of one, two, five, 10, 20, and 50 centavos. The 10-centavo coin is sometimes called a *daime;* you'll occasionally hear a 20-centavo coin called a *búfalo* and 50-centavo pieces called *tostónes.* Large banks, exchange shops, hotels, and international airports will change **traveler's checks,** but beware of long forms and high commissions. Western Union can be found in most main towns and the banks themselves also sometimes have new money-wiring systems. Most banks give **cash advances** on credit cards. **ATMs** accept mostly Honduran bank cards. Banks do not change the currencies of neighboring Central American countries, but officials at border crossings will. Honduras can definitely be experienced on the cheap. Comfortable lodgings may be had in many places for a few bucks, and penny-pinching visitors can delight in rooms and meals for as low as US$5 and beer for $1.

PRICE DIVERSITY

PRICE RANGES AND RANKINGS. Our researchers list establishments in order of value from best to worst. Our absolute favorites are denoted by the Let's Go thumbs-up (📷). Since the best value does not always mean the cheapest price, we have incorporated a system of price ranges into the guide. The table below lists how prices fall within each bracket.

SYMBOL	❶	❷	❸	❹	❺
ACCOMM.	L0-50	L50-100	L100-150	L150-200	L200+
FOOD	L0-20	L20-70	L70-100	L100-140	L140+

SAFETY

Though Honduras is safe overall, street crime is on the rise in some areas. San Pedro Sula, rural Olancho, and parts of Tegucigalpa can be dangerous, especially after dark. The Caribbean coast has also been suffering from escalated crime. Don't walk the streets at night, and don't carry anything valuable. Villages and towns in the interior are quite safe, though women will receive unwelcome attention. For more advice on staying safe, see **Safety and Security,** p. 26.

HEALTH

As in the rest of Central America, travel in Honduras poses health risks (see **Health,** p. 29). Malaria is present in coastal regions. Cholera has become a bigger risk, so street stalls are best avoided. Throughout the country, don't drink tap water—your bowels will never forgive you. When traveling in the Mosquitia, bring all emergency supplies.

BORDER CROSSINGS

GUATEMALA. There are two land crossings. **El Florido** is along a dirt road between Copán Ruinas and Chiquimula, Guatemala; pickups run on the Honduran side (see p. 469), and buses run on the Guatemalan side. **Agua Caliente** (see p. 462) is 16km west of Nueva Ocotepeque and 10km east of Esquipulas, Guatemala (see).

BELIZE. Weekly **boats** link Puerto Cortés and coastal Belize (p. 477).

EL SALVADOR. There are three land crossings. **El Poy:** just south of Nueva Ocotepeque (p. 462). In the south near Choluteca and Santa Rosa de Lima, El Salvador you'll find **El Amatillo** (see p. 448). **Sabanetas** is 165km southeast of Gracias near Perquín, El Salvador, north of San Miguel, El Salvador. There are irregular **ferry** departures from **La Unión,** El Salvador, to ports in the Gulf of Fonseca, Honduras.

NICARAGUA. There are three land crossings. **Guasaule** is 50km southeast of Choluteca, near Chinandega, Nicaragua (see p. 448). **San Marcos/El Espino** is located 70km east of Choluteca, near Somoto, Nicaragua; buses head there from Tegucigalpa and Choluteca (see p. 448). Finally, **Las Manos** is 150km east of Tegucigalpa, south of Danlí, near Ocotal, Nicaragua (see p. 577).

KEEPING IN TOUCH

A letter sent from Honduras takes two to three weeks to reach the US. EMS offers **express mail,** but it is pricier. You can receive mail in Honduras through **general delivery** *(Lista de Correos)*; address envelopes as follows:

> Erin Erin BO-BARIN
>
> a/c Lista de Correos
>
> Tegucigalpa (town), Francisco Morazán (department)
>
> República de Honduras

Honduran **telephone** phone numbers are seven digits and require no area code. For information on making international calls from Central America, please see the inside back cover. The Honduran phone company, **Hondutel,** provides efficient service, and has an office in most towns. From the phone offices, Sprint calling cards are easiest to use, followed by AT&T. For company access codes, see the inside back cover. **Faxes** and **telegrams** are generally available in Hondutel offices.

COUNTRY CODE 504

TRANSPORTATION

Airlines including Taca, Isleña, Sosa, and Rollins Air offer flights between points within Honduras for relatively low fares. The **bus** system in Honduras is extensive. Often each destination is served by a different company and the terminals are scattered throughout the city. Be especially cautious riding the buses at night.

ORIENTATION

Landmarks, not street names, are the mainstay of directions in Honduras. The larger towns, like those in neighboring countries, have streets in a grid of north-south *avenidas* and east-west *calles* (the opposite of Costa Rica). In most cities, there is a central *avenida* and a central *calle*. A building at "3/5 Av., 2 Calle" is on Calle 2 between Avenidas 3 and 5.

TRAVEL RESOURCES

Honduran Institute of Tourism, P.O. Box 140458, Coral Gables, FL 33114 (☎1-800-410-9608; www.letsgohonduras.com; M-F 9am-5pm) Also has an office in Tegucigalpa (Av. Ramón Ernesto Cruz, Calle República de México; ☎222-2124; fax 222-6621, M-F 8:30am-4:30pm). Will mail information, brochures, and maps.

Garífuna Tours, Parque Central, Tela, Atlantida, Honduras, C.A. P.O. Box 74; ☎504-448-1069; fax 448-2904; tours@honduras.com; http://www.garifuna-tours.com/). Offer local tours and package tours (more expensive but all inclusive).

HOLIDAYS

Public holidays include: **January 1,** New Year's Day; **April 14,** Day of the Americas; **March/April,** Thursday, Friday, and Saturday before Easter, Holy Week; **May 1,** Labor Day; **September 15,** Central American Independence Day; **October 3,** Francisco Morazán's birthday; **October 12,** Discovery of America /Columbus Day **October 21,** Army Day; **December 25,** Christmas Day.

TEGUCIGALPA

Tegus, as the capital city is known, has never really lost its boom-town feel. Ever since silver was discovered here in 1578, Tegus has been creeping slowly and surely up the surrounding hills like a spider casting a web of *barrios* and *colonias*. Still, it maintains the character of a provincial seat, not a national capital. Residents continue to gather under the shade of trees in the plaza to chat and meet friends. The city's genuine interest in tourism and security makes Tegus one of the safer big cities in Central America.

Tegucigalpa became the capital of Honduras in 1880, off-the-record because the wife of then-president Marco Aurelio Soto didn't like the old capital of Comayagua, 100km to the northwest. By the end of the century, Tegus and its sister city of Comayagüela (not to be confused with Comayagua), across the Río Choluteca, had been incorporated into a "central district." Even today, though, the cities coexist uneasily, and some locals still talk of separation.

While Tegus may look picturesque from the mountain passes leading to the city, a closer look reveals the contaminated rivers, homelessness, blaring horns, and downright toxic air quality that plague the capital. However, Tegus also boasts mansions, gourmet restaurants, colorful fruit stands, and flashy malls. The city's Galería Nacional de Arte and Iglesia Los Dolores are must-sees to get a complete picture of Honduran culture and history.

La Concordia

Museo Villarey

Av. Las Delicias

C. Salvador Mendieta

C. Buenos Aires

BARRIO ABAJO

Av. Lempira

Av. Paulino Valladares

Av. Máximo Jeréz

C. el Telégrafo

Paseo Marco Aurelio Soto

Río Choluteca

C. la Concordia

C. Morelos

Parque La Leone

C. Dionisio Gutiérrez

Los Dolores

Av. Jerez

1

2

C. los Dolores

Hondutel

Av. Cristobal Colón

3

BCA

6

CáfeNet

Paseo

Cyberiada Café

C. Palace

C. la Leona

8

C. Hipólito Matute

Book.net

Av. Gutemberg

Immigration Office

4

C. Correo

C. Adolfo Zuñiga

Hotel La Ronda

C. Salvador Corleto

C. las Damas

Parque Herrera

Teatro Nacional Miguel Bonilla

Calle Peatonal

Cinema

10

Av. Miguel de Cervantes

Supermarket

13

15

Parque Central (Plaza Morazán)

14

San Miguel

17

Clinic Vier

Av. Pa

Av. La Merced

Av. La Plazuela

La Merced

C. Bolívar

Museo Histórico de la República

1 C.

Congreso Nacional

Galería Nacional de Arte

Penitencia la Central

Av. Molina

18

BARRIO SAN RAFAEL

San Isidro Market

2 C.

3 C.

COMAYAGÜELA

4 C.

5 C.

6 C.

7 C.

BARRIO MORAZÁN

7 Av.

3 Av.

2 Av.

1 Av.

Río Choluteca

Parque la Libertad

Estadio Nacional

Baseball Stadium

Hondutel ☎ ✉

20

Discovery

El Rey

8 C.

9 C.

Av. Japón

1

9 C.

6 Av.

5 Av.

4 Av.

10 C.

Parque Juan A. Laínez

Monumento a la Paz ■

11 C.

Sultana de Occidente

ETRUSCA

COTRAIBAL

Cristina

Transporte Norteño

12 C.

Parque el Obelisco

El Rey Express

Saenz

Discovery

13 C.

14 C.

Parque el Soldado

10 Av.

9 Av.

8 Av.

7 Av.

15 C.

TO MI ESPERANZA 🚌 & CRUCEROS DEL GOLFO 🚌 (500m)

16 C.

🚌 **Tica**

TO KING QUALITY 🚌 (500m), ✈ (5km)

BARRIO CASAMATA

Policía
Femenina

4 C.

BARRIO
LA CABAÑA

2 Av.

TEGUCIGALPA

COLONIA LA REFORMA

Laundry

Subida Casamata

Mercado
San Miguel

To
Jutiapa

1 C.

Av. La Paz

2 C.

Río Chiquito

arahona

Más X Menos
Supermarket

Hotel Honduras
Maya

Banco
Atlántida

1 C.

4 Av.

2 C.

TO HOSPITAL CENTRAL
(200m)

United
Kingdom

2 Av.

United
States

COLONIA
PALMIRA

Mundirama
Travel Service

3A C.

Instituto Hondureño
de Turismo (i)

Av. República de Panamá

3 C.

3 Av.

4 C.

1 C.

5 Av.

Av. República de Chile

Av. Juan Lindo

BARRIO
GUADALUPE

19

Boulevard Morazán

Blvd. Morazán

4 C.

5 C.

Río Quebrada

6 C.

COLONIA
LAS MINITAS

COLONIA
RUBEN DARÍO

7 C.

Av. Galvez

Boulevard Suyapa

8 C.

9 C.

3 Av.

2 Av.

10 C.

11 C.

COLONIA ALAMEDA

N

0   400 meters
0   400 yards

TO BLVD. JUAN PABLO II,
MULTIPLAZA MALL &
Canada

Tegucigalpa

ACCOMMODATIONS
Hotel 2002, **1**
Hotel Granada #1, **11**
Hotel Granada #2, **9**
Hotel Granada #3, **5**
Hotel Iberia, **3**
Hotel Nan King, **12**
Hotel San Pedro, **20**

FOOD
Comedor Vegetariano, **15**
El Patio, **19**
La Terraza de Don Pepe, **6**
Señor Cafe, **10**
Taco Mexi, **4**

NIGHTLIFE
Café Paradiso, **16**

PUNTOS DE TAXI
Kennedy, **17**
Loarque, **2**
San Miguel, **7**
Torocogua, **13**
Villa Olimpica, **18**

HONDURAS

◼ INTERCITY TRANSPORTATION

Domestic Buses: Most companies are clustered in the 2 blocks surrounding 8 Av., 12 Calle in Comayagüela. Arrive early, as buses fill up quickly. Buses run to:

Agua Caliente: Cristina, 8 Av., 12 Calle. (9hr., 6 and 9:30am, L143.)

Catacamas: Discovery, 7 Av., 13 Calle. (☎222 4256. 4hr.; 6:15am, 12:30, 2:15, 4:15pm; L38.)

Choluteca: Mi Esperanza, 7 Av. 24. (☎225 2863. Every hr. 4am-6pm, L29.) From Choluteca, buses run to the **Nicaraguan border.** (2hr., L25.) Executive service (A/C, TV) is also offered.

Comayagua: Mi Esperanza, (1½ hr., every hr. 6am-4pm., L19.)

Danlí: Disqua Litena, Mercado Jacaleapa. (☎230 0470. 2hr., 6 per day 6:30am-4:15pm, L38.)

Guasaule (border with Nicaragua): Mi Esperanza (4hr.; 6, 8:15am, 3pm; L40.) Discua Litena (☎230 0470. 6:30 and 11:30am.)

Juliapa: (The gateway to Parque Nacional La Tigra.) Yellow school buses leave from the corner of Calle Finlay. Buses leave when full. (6:30am-4pm, L8.)

Juticalpa: Aurora (☎237 3647. 3hr., 5am-5pm, L31.) Discovery (☎222 4256. 3hr., 6 per day 6:45am-4:15pm, L31.)

La Ceiba: Cristina, 8 Av., 12 Calle. Nonstop service. (☎220 0117. 6hr., 6 per day 6:15am-3:30pm, L110.) Etruesa, 8 Av., 12 Calle. (☎222 6881. 6hr., 9 per day 7am-4pm, L60-L110.)

La Paz: Lila, 8 Av., 12 Calle. (☎237 6870. Heading toward Marcalla 1½hr.; 7, 8, 10am, noon, 2pm; L17.

La Unión: Take an early bus to Juticalpa and from there catch the noon bus to La Unión.

Lago de Yojoa: Norteños (☎237 0706. 3hr., L32.)

Las Manos (border with Nicaragua): Discua Litena, Mercado Jacaleapa. (☎230 0470. 2hr., every hr., L38.)

Ocotepeque: Sultana Occidente, 8 Av., 12 Calle. (☎237 8101. 9hr.; 6, 7:30, 8:30, 10am; L130.)

San Marcos (border with Nicaragua): Mi Esperanza goes to San Marcos after stopping in Choluteca. (4hr.; 4, 7:30, 11am, 2, 4pm; L33.)

San Pedro Sula: El Rey, 7 Av., 12 Calle. (3½hr., every hr. 5:30am-6:30pm, L70.) Saenz, 6 Av., 9 Calle. Express first class. (☎233 4229. 3½hr.; M-Th 6 per day 6am-6pm, F-Su 6 per day 8am-6pm; L60. Norteños, 6 Av., 12 Calle. (☎237 0706. 4½hr.; 6:30, 9:30, 11:30am, 3:30pm; L45.)

Saenz: 6 Av., 9 Calle. Centro Comercial Pañsure. Express 1st class. (☎233 4229. M-Th, 6 per day 6am-6pm; F-Su 6 per day 8am-6pm; L150. Norteños, (☎237 0706. 4½hr., every 1½hr. 6:30am-6pm, L130.)

Santa Bárbara: Jungueños, 8 Av., 12 Calle. (☎237 2921. 4hr.; M-Sa 7am and 2pm, Su 8am and 2pm; L44.)

Santa Lucía: Take a bus going to Valle de Ángeles.

Santa Rosa de Copán: La Sultana, 8 Av., 12 Calle. (☎237 8101. 5½-6hr.; 6, 7:30, 8:30, 10, 11:30am; L100.)

Trujillo: COTRAIPBAL, 7 Av., 12 Calle. (☎237 1666. Direct 8hr., 1:30am and 4:15am, L132.)

Valle de Ángeles: Catch a bus from the Esso gas station near the U.S. Embassy on Avenida La Paz. (1hr., 6am-5pm, L8.)

International Buses: Ticabus (☎220 0590 or 225 0579) leaves Tegus at 9am, arrives in **Managua** at 5pm (US$20), and continues in the morning to **San José** (US$35) and the following day to **Panama City** (Panamá US$60; Ticabus hotel in Managua US$6). Other destinations include **Guatemala City** (US$23) and **San Salvador** (US$15). King Quality (☎225 5415) goes to **Guatemala City** (6am; US$48); **Managua** (6am, 9hr., US$20); **San Salvador** (7hr., 6am and 1pm, US$45).

Flights: Toncontín International Airport (☎233 9797) is 7km from downtown (L60-100 by taxi or L1 by bus). Most domestic and international airline offices are clustered around the Hotel Honduras Maya on Av. República de Chile.

Domestic: Taca (☎239 0148 or 233 9797) flies to: **San Pedro Sula** (40min., 10am and 7:45pm, L1663); **La Ceiba** (8:15am and 2:45pm, L760 plus 2.5% tax); **Trujillo** (9:40am, L1131.20);

Roatán (6 per day 7am-4pm, L280); **Palacios** (6 and 9:40am, L600); **Puerto Lempira** (6am, L1325). Atlantic Airlines (☎234 9701 or 234 9702) flies to La Ceiba, San Pedro Sula, Roatán, Utila, Guanaja, Puerto Lempira, Belize, and Guatemala.

International: American (☎232 1414), across from Hotel Honduras Maya (open M-F, 8am-4:30pm, Sa 8am-3:30pm) and **Continental** (☎220 0999), in the building next to Hotel Clarions on Juan Pablo II (open M-F 9am-7pm, Sa 9am-5pm). **Taca** (☎239 0148 or 233 9797), on Blvd. Morazán, next to Credomatic, flies to Central American capitals and Houston. Open M-F 8:30am-8pm, Sa 8:30am-4pm.

✦ ORIENTATION

The **Río Choluteca** divides Tegucigalpa into two regions, **downtown** Tegus to the north and east of the river, and **Comayagüela** to the south and west. The **airport** is a few kilometers south of town. Most buses arrive in Comayagüela, while most sights, services, and hotels are downtown. Tegus's streets, dating back to the colonial era, form a tangled web centered around the **parque central**. The *parque* contains the Cathedral and is bordered by **Av. Colón** (6 Calle) to the north and **Av. Cervantes** to the south. One block north of the *parque*, **Avenida La Paz** runs west to east and connects the center to the US embassy, and the Colonia Palmira. Across the river, Comayagüela, a more blue-collar section, contains budget hotels and the city's largest market within its independently numbered, more regular grid of roads. The central part of town surrounds 6 Av. In general, Comayagüela is afflicted with higher crime rates, especially at night.

East of downtown Tegus, **Colonia Palmira** is home to the tourist office, embassies, restaurants, and nightlife. Most clubs are on **Blvd. Morazán** and **Av. Juan Pablo Segundo**. To get there, take Av. Cervantes past Hotel Honduras Maya. If you get lost, look to Christ—his concrete statue is always visible on top of **El Picacho** to the north. Another good reference point is the **Monumento de la Paz** (Monument of Peace), which ironically looks like a prison watchtower on a forested hill just south of downtown.

▐ LOCAL TRANSPORTATION

Local buses: Local buses run from the commercial strip near the airport terminal into downtown Comayagüela. City bus #24 stops at the airport and passes through Comayagüela to downtown Tegucigalpa. Buses' signs and hollering drivers usually indicate the *barrios* or *colonias* between which they are traveling. Many stop on the north side of the *parque central* or across the bridge from Comayagüela. M-F L1.50, Sa-Su L2.

Taxis: Yellow cabs outside the airport charge L80, but walk out to the street for fares of L40-60, traveling within the city. Fares typically run L20-40. Agree on a price before departing. To the airport or the bus station from within the city L40-50. Prices are higher after buses stop running.

Collective taxis (*taxis colectivos*): This mode of transportation is ideal for the budget visitor. *Puntos de taxi* (taxi spots) are located throughout the city, and each has a specific, direct destination. Lines form while taxis make rounds. Four people collectively pay the driver, but the fares are a fraction of what the same ride would cost in a personal taxi. You can also be let out anywhere en route to the final destination. A typical fare is L6.50 per person. Taxi points include:

Punto de Taxis de la Kennedy: Behind El Prado Hotel's parking lot. Destination: Discua Litena bus station.

Punto de Taxis de la Torocagua: At a corner across from Banco Credomatic. Destination: 9 *calle* in Comayagüela, near the bus stations.

Punto de Taxis de la Villa Olimpica: Walk down the street to the national stadium, then turn left on Av. Molina. Destination: Multiplaza Mall.

Punto de Taxis de la San Miguel: On the same corner as Banco Atlántida. Destination: Valle de Ángeles bus station, Santa Lucía bus route.

Punto de Taxis del Loarque: Next to Herrera park, on Calle Morelos. Destination: Cruceros del Golfo bus station.

Car rental: Low priced agencies US$60-70 per day (with insurance); high end US$120. **Hertz** (☎234 3784), **Avis** (☎233 9548), and **Budget** are at the airport and scattered throughout the city. The minimum age for the large chains is 25.

🔢 PRACTICAL INFORMATION

TOURIST AND FINANCIAL SERVICES

Tourist Information: Instituto Hondureño de Turismo, in the Edificio Europa, on Calle República de México (☎800 222 TOUR from Honduras; 800-410-9608 from US and Canada; fax 222 6621; ihturism@hondutel.com), 2 blocks east of the US Embassy. Information, maps, and English-speaking representatives. Open M-F 8:30am-4:30pm.

Travel Agencies and Guided Tours: Mundirama Travel Service, Col. Palmira, Edificio CICSA, Av. Rep. de Chile, Paseo Rep. de Panamá (☎232 3943), a block from the Hotel Honduras Maya. Serves as the local **AmEx** office. English spoken. Open M-F 8am-noon and 1-5pm, Sa 8am-noon. **Trek Honduras** Edificio Midence Solo 218 Colonia Olmeda, Avenida Julio (☎239 0743), offers tours of Tegus, Copán, and Bay Islands.

Embassies and Consulates: Canada Edificio Comercial Los Castaños, 6th fl., Blvd. Morazán (☎232 4551). For other embassies, call the Ministerio del Exterior (☎234 1922). **UK** Colonia Payaqui, Centro Financiero Banexpo, Blvd. San Juan Bosto, 3rd fl. (☎232 0618; fax 232 5480). Open M-Th 8am-1pm and 2-4:30pm, F 8am-1pm. **US** on Av. La Paz, apartado 3463 (☎236 9320; fax 236 9037). It's a large building; folks know where it is. The US consulate is across the way. Open M-F 8am-5pm.

Immigration Office: (☎238 7367), Av. Jerez next to Hotel La Ronda. A block north and 6 blocks east of the *parque*. Get a visa extension here for L7.50. Next day service (pickup at 3pm; temporary copies available). Open M-F 8:30am-noon and 1-4:30pm.

Banks: Most banks change US dollars and AmEx Traveler's Cheques. In the Mall Multiplaza there is a *centro financiero* where all the banks have offices and keep convenient hours. Expect very long lines. **BGA** (☎232 0909), Av. Cristobal Colón, Calle Los Dolores, a block south of Iglesia Los Dolores, cashes traveler's checks and gives cash advances on Visa. Open M-F 9am-4pm, Sa 9am-noon. **Banco Atlántida** (☎232 1050) exchanges traveler's checks. At Hotel Honduras Maya, open M-F 9am-3pm; in the office at Mall Multiplaza, open M-Sa 10am-7pm. **Banco Credomatic** (☎238 7220) accepts Cirrus cards and gives Visa and MC cash advances. Two offices on Blvd. Morazán are open M-F 9am-5pm. In Mall Multiplaza, open M-Sa noon-7pm.

ATM: UNIBANC on the east side of the *parque*, at Texaco gas stations, and at Mall Multiplaza, accepts AmEx, Cirrus, and MC cards at locations throughout the city.

LOCAL SERVICES

Bookstore: Book.net, across from Hotel La Ronda, 4 blocks east and one block north of the *parque*. English used bookstore and book exchange. Open M-Sa 8am-9pm, Su 10am-5pm. **Metromedia,** 2 blocks behind the U.S. Embassy, sells new and a few used books and newspapers. **Shakespeare's Books,** on the street behind the cathedral in the Tobacco Tavern (see **Entertainment**), sells used books for half the cover price.

Markets: San Isidro, along 7 Av., 1 Calle in Comayagüela, is the main outdoor market. The **San Miguel** market is next to Hotel Granada. The area around Iglesia Los Dolores hosts a large market.

Supermarket: Mas X Menos, Av. La Paz, Colonia Palmira, 2 blocks from the US embassy. Called "Mas por Menos." Open daily 7:30am-9pm, Su 8am-8pm.

Laundry: To the right of Restaurant Eliza, below Hotel Granada #3. Offers wash, dry, and fold, usually in under 2hr. Wash or dry L60; both L130. Open M-Sa 8am-6pm.

EMERGENCY AND COMMUNICATIONS

Emergency: Red Cross ☎237 8654. **Medical** ☎195. **Police** ☎199. **Fire** ☎198.

Police: FUSEP (☎222 8736), behind Iglesia Los Dolores, a bit beyond the Hotel Imperial. Open 24hr. Female police (☎237 2184).

Pharmacy: One of the many is **Farmacia Santa Teresa** (☎237 0632), a block east of the southeast corner of the *parque central,* across from Hotel Prado. Open M-F 8:30am-6:30pm, Sa 8am-1pm. For a list of pharmacies open until 10pm and on weekends, call ☎192 or look in any pharmacy window.

Medical Services: Clínicas Viera (☎237 3160), Av. Colón. across from Hotel La Ronda. Open 24hr. Some English spoken. Visits L300. Open M-Sa 9:30am-noon and 4-6pm.

Telephones: Hondutel (☎238 3131; fax 237 9715), Av. Cristobal Colón before Calle Telégrafo, in a large castle-like building. Open daily 24hr. Also in Comayagüela (☎238 1448), next to the post office. Open M-F 8am-4pm. The phone prices are high (L97 for 3min.), so go to an Internet cafe for more reasonable rates.

Internet: Cyberiada Internet Café (☎220 0029), one block north of the *parque central,* on the corner of Av. Gutemberg and Calle Matute in a pink building on the 2nd floor. Claims to have the fastest connection in town (DSL). Also with a bookstore/exchange and snack bar. English spoken. L30 per hr.; Happy Hour: 9pm-9am L25 per hr. Open 24hr. Rates at the trendy **C@feNet** (☎237 3916), on the corner of Av. Jerez and Calle Adolfo Zuñig, are L25 per hr. Open M-Sa 8am-7pm, Su 2-7pm.

Post Office: Av. Paz Barahona, Calle Telégrafo. Open M-F 7:30am-7pm, Sa 8am-1pm. In Comayagüela, 6 Av. by Instituto Abelardo R. Fortín. Open M-F 8am-7pm, Sa 8am-1pm.

Postal code: Tegucigalpa 11101; Comayagüela 11103.

⌘ ACCOMMODATIONS

Those wanting to catch a morning bus might head to Comayagüela. In all areas, try to get a room facing away from the street to avoid bus fumes and loud traffic. Basic rooms don't have private baths, *privados* do.

DOWNTOWN TEGUS

Hotel Nan King (☎238 0291), Av. Juan Gutenberg, past Hotel Granada from the *parque central* (pagoda on the roof). In the heart of Tegus's small Asian community, Nan King has spotless rooms with private hot baths. Also in the hotel are a Chinese restaurant and Internet cafe. Singles L120; queen bed L220, with TV and A/C L350. ❸

Hotel Iberia (☎237 9267), 2 blocks down the Peatonal Dolores from the *parque central.* While lacking hot water, the rooms are clean. Clean, shared bathrooms. Upstairs lounge with TV and tables. Singles L90; doubles L170; triples L240. ❷

Hotel Granada #1, Av. Juan Gutenberg 1401 (☎222 2654), **Hotel Granada #2,** Subita Casemata 1326 (☎237 7079), and **Hotel Granada #3** (☎237 0843; hgranada@hondudata.com). Three similar hotels, around Parque Guanacaste (an area that is pleasant by day but somewhat dangerous at night), with slightly different amenities. Less expensive #1 is pleasant, although without hot water. (Singles L120, with bath L180, with TV and A/C L230; doubles L170/L230/L280.) Rooms in #2 all have private, hot-water baths. Each floor has a comfortable lobby with couches and chairs, and the upper floors have good city views. (Singles L160; doubles L270; add L50 for cable TV and A/C.) Granada #3 also has private, hot-water baths in all rooms. (Singles L160; doubles L320; add L50 for cable TV and A/C.) All 3 hotels can be accessed 24hr. ❸

Hotel 2002, Calle Morelos and Av. Máximo Jerez (☎222 3187). Ideal location. The hotel's name seems to change with the year. Singles L180; doubles L200. ❹

COMAYAGÜELA

Hotel San Pedro, 7 Av., 8/9 Calles (☎222 8987), a block from El Rey bus station. Yellow rooms, small but clean. Beware the rainy season: roofs are leaky. The 3rd fl. is high enough to pick up a breeze. Restaurant and snack bar in lobby. Singles L90, with bath L130, with TV and A/C L200; doubles L120/L190/L230. ❷

🚩 FOOD

Food in Tegus is somewhat unimpressive. The *parque central* and *calle peatonal* offer fast food chains, while Chinese restaurants are scattered throughout the city. For bargain food, head to the *comedores* set up in the *plaza* in front of Iglesia Los Dolores—one of the markets in Tegus or across the river. At either spot, you can find hearty portions at heartening prices: a *típico* meal costs about L20.

▨ **La Terraza de Don Pepe,** Av. Colón, 4 blocks from the cathedral. Sure, the bargain-priced *típico* is pretty good, but the highlight is the bathroom. On Sept. 2, 1986, the nationally sacred **Virgen de Suyapa,** which had been stolen a few weeks earlier, was found next to the toilet, wrapped in newspaper. Now, the old lavatory is a sanctuary. Along with such treats as chicken *cordon bleu* (L53), **Don Pepe** offers breakfast (L15-28), sandwiches (L18-30), and banana splits (L28). Open daily 9am-9:30pm. ❷

Comedor Vegetariano, a block from the post office at the corner of Av. Cervantes and Calle Telégrafo, is perhaps the only *comedor* in Honduras specializing in vegetarian food (L27-35). Open M-Sa 10:30am-5pm. Also offers vegetarian cooking classes. ❷

El Patio, on Blvd. Morazán. This *restaurante* is a huge (you guessed it) patio with a lively bar in the back. Excellent shish kebabs (L115-160) and fried chicken (L40-65). Open daily 11am-2am. ❹

Gyros, right next door to Pan y Mas, serves gourmet buffet-style *comida árabe* (L50-75). Open M-F 9am-6pm, Sa 9am-6pm. ❷

Señor Café, one block down from the *calle peatonal* on the right. A truly relaxing place to get coffee (L7-9), eat a snack (tasty sandwiches L8-10), or just chat. Open M-Sa 7am-8pm, Su 8am-6pm. ❶

Taco Mexi, on Av. Jerez across from Hotel La Ronda. Delicious Mexican fast food at delectable prices. Good sandwiches and *tortas*. Open M-Sa 8am-9pm. ❷

🎭🎵 NIGHTLIFE AND ENTERTAINMENT

Fear not, revelers. Tegus's nightlife heats up to a fever pitch on weekends. Most places are either on Blvd. Morazán or Blvd. Juan Pablo II. Though it's risky to walk to clubs from the town center after dark, there are enough partygoers in the nightlife district to ensure some safety, although Blvd. Juan Pablo II is notorious for gangs and criminal activity. Taxis are plentiful here, though pricey; restaurants keep late hours; and college-age Saturday night pre-partyers line Blvd. Morazán. It's best for women to go in groups. Men in the clubs are forthright even with local women; travelers should especially beware. While most discos are up and running Thursday to Sunday, Fridays and Saturdays are the biggest party nights.

The **discotecas** come and go quickly, so ask around for the latest rage. The hot disco for the chic in Tegus is **Confetti's,** at the east end of Blvd. Morazán, where a

CAGED ART You may have been warned about ending up in a Central American jail, but there's good reason to visit the **Penitenciaría Central,** Av. San Martín de Flores/Av. Molina, in southeast Tegus. The inmates sell crafts that they make on site. Previously, tourists could enter the prison bearing a small metal tag with the ominous threat, "You lose this, you're not leaving." To avoid red tape, prison officials opened a small shop outside. A guard summons the peddling prisoners, who proffer their wares with toothy smiles and modest English. More than 80 people visit the store each day. In general, the prisoners are friendly to customers and are psyched to rip into their favorite Steely Dan or Simon and Garfunkel guitar licks while chatting with guests. Most like to bargain; supposedly, all profits go to the producers. (Hammocks L250-300, guitars L180-300. Open M-Sa 8am-2pm.)

young crowd boogies to disco hits from all over the hemisphere, with a little *merengue* to remind you where you are. (Pants required for men. Cover L50-70. Open T-Su from 8:30pm.) **Rock Castle Club** (a.k.a. El Castillo) has stood the test of time as a pub, disco, and pool hall up the hill from McDonald's on Av. Juan Pablo II. Live bands play on weekends. (Cover L50, includes one free rum and coke or *cerveza;* pool L30 per 30min. Open F-S at 8pm.) **Arenas,** on Blvd. Morazán, is the hot spot for students and gringos to dance and hang out under the stars. (Open Tu-Sa, 7pm-5am. Cover L80 Sa only.) **Iguana Ranas,** Blvd. Morazán 4 blocks down from Confetti's, is a chill sports bar with a mix of locals and foreigners. (Local beers L15, imported beers L30. Open M 4pm-midnight, Tu-Su 11am-2am.) To relax, try **Café Paradiso,** a coffeehouse, bar, art gallery, and bookstore on Calle Barahona, two blocks south of Hotel Granada. This hangout attracts Tegus's artists, poets, and musicians. Café Paradiso and Cine Club Buñuel present a film every Tuesday at 7pm followed by a discussion. (Open M-Sa 9am-8pm, Tu until the movie is over.)

Pool halls are a popular entertainment choice for male locals and can be found all over the city. Playing at **Mr. Pool,** at the intersection of Calle Matute and Av. Colón, costs L35 per hr. (☎237 4444. Open daily 11am-11pm.) Other pool halls include **Billiards Navas,** across from the Hotel Nan King (☎222 3291; L25 per hr.; open daily 10am-11pm.), and the succinctly named **Pool,** two blocks from Hotel Alvi (☎222 3291; L25 per hr.; open daily 10am-11pm). If a **movie** is more your thing, check out the **Aries/Tauro complex,** just up Subita Casimata from Hotel Granada #3 (L20) or the movies at **Plaza Miraflores.** Newer releases can be found in the six-theater **Cinemark,** in the Mall Multiplaza on Av. Juan Pablo II (L40; Tu L20). **Variedades,** at the intersection of Av. Colón and Calle Mendieta, shows two recent films multiple times daily (L10). Check the newspaper for show times..

◎ SIGHTS

The city's attractions are all within a short walking distance of the **parque central.** The *parque* itself (also called the **Plaza Morazán**) is a must-see—actually, if you don't see it, you're probably in the wrong town. A statue of the hero Morazán stands in the middle, surrounded by locals relaxing under the park's shady trees. The whole city seems to converge here morning, noon, and night. The **Calle Peatonal,** to the west, is Tegus's "main street," filled with vendors and restaurants.

■ **IGLESIA LOS DOLORES.** One block north and 2½ blocks west of the *parque*, this church retains some of the flavor of its Afro-Honduran construction, with the exuberance of a sequined altar and neon John the Baptist. Two blocks east of the cathedral is the 16th-century **Iglesia San Francisco,** the oldest church in Tegus. (*Iglesia Los Dolores open daily at 3:30pm for individual prayer, Iglesia San Francisco open Su.*)

CATEDRAL SAN MIGUEL. Anchoring the eastern side of the *parque* is Catedral San Miguel. Built between 1765 and 1782, the church is full of the tombs of former Honduran presidents and other VIPs. At the heart of the cathedral's simple interior, stands a gold Baroque altar. *(Mass M-Sa 6:30, 7am, 4, 5pm; M-F additional noon mass; Su 6:30, 8, 9:30, 11am, and 4pm. Doors open from first to last mass.)*

▨**GALERÍA NACIONAL DE ARTE.** One block south of the *parque central* on Calle Bolívar is the Parque Merced, in which statues of former presidents and national heroes are guarded by uniformed soldiers, and in which the Galería Nacional de Arte, the national art gallery, a work of art in itself, can be found. Inaugurated in August 1996, this convent-turned-university-turned-museum houses Honduras' best art, new and old. Downstairs, the gallery displays works from prehistoric to colonial periods. Upstairs, fans of more modern works can sample colorful, magical realism set down on canvas. There is a pleasant, inviting courtyard with benches. *(☎ 237 9884. Open M-Sa 9am-4pm. L10, students with ID L5.)*

MUSEUMS. About three blocks north of the *parque central* is **Parque La Concordia,** a little bamboo grove resembling a miniature golf course. Just past La Concordia is **Museo Nacional de Historia y Antropología Villarey,** chronicling the history of the country from before Spanish arrival through colonization. *(Open W-Sa 8:30am-3:30pm.)* The **Museo Histórico de La República,** in the former Presidential Palace one block west of Parque La Merced, picks up where the National Museum left off, presenting Honduras's political history from independence to the present. *(☎ 237 0268. Open W-Sa 9am-noon and 1:30-4pm. L25.)*

EL PICACHO. If you have more time, climb up El Picacho, the hill in the northern part of town, to the statue of Jesus (or ascend on any bus bound for Limones). The concrete savior gazes peacefully over the sprawl of Tegus's *barrios*, inviting you to do the same. Besides the view, there's a mini zoo and replicas of Maya ruins.

NEAR TEGUCIGALPA

SANTA LUCÍA

Santa Lucía makes a pleasant stop on the way to Valle de Ángeles, with breathtaking views of the surrounding mountains—you can see as far as Tegus on clear days. The town is as tranquil as Tegus is frenetic: gardens overflowing with flowers and local pottery line a long cobblestone street. Down the hill from the bus stop is the local **church,** containing a crucifix from 1574 which was ordered to be built by the King of Spain when the silver-mine town was booming. About 1km steeply uphill on the road, to the right of the church, is a **vineyard** with marvelous views of the valley and Tegus below. Wine is sold in December, but you can ask the family who works there for a tour any time of the year.

To get to Santa Lucía, hop off the Valle de Ángeles **bus** at the "Bienvenidos a Santa Lucía" sign and walk up the hill. The only hotel in town is the pricey **Hotel Santa Lucía Resort ❺,** a beautiful getaway with views of the valley, an upscale restaurant, and a patio filled with outdoor grills, swings, and gardens. (☎236 9179; hotel_santa_lucia@yahoo.com. Rooms US$70.) **Restaurante Miluska ❷,** offers a taste of Europe with excellent Czech cuisine, outdoor dining, and swings. (*Goulash* L65; *strudel* L18. Open M-Su 10:30am-8pm.) ▨**Portal la Leyenda,** is a new cafe/bar with a patio and great antique furniture in a tastefully crumbling old house lit only by candles in the evening. You can bring your own music! (Open daily 11am-10pm.) The **Billares Cerrato** pool hall is below the municipal building (L20 per hr.; open daily 9am-10pm), while the local disco, **Club Social Santa Lucía,** is next to the school playground. (Cover L35, first 30 women free. Open 8:30pm-1am.)

VALLE DE ÁNGELES

Valle de Ángeles, a hamlet in the mountains outside Tegus, lives up to its heavenly name. The area is a getaway for Honduras's elite, and their presence keeps the roads paved, the sidewalks clean, and the villages safe. Valle de Ángeles is the capital of the country's *artesanía* trade and is the best place in Honduras to find expertly carved woodwork, intricate pottery, leather, and colorful canvases.

The town is packed with galleries and craft stores which accept major credit cards and people speak just enough English to make a deal. Valle's *parque* is flanked by the church to the north and the **Palacio Municipal** to the south. FUSEP, the **police station,** is on the north end of Calle Principal. (☎766 2151. Open 5am-midnight.) Inside the Palacio you can find **Banco de Occidente,** which exchanges cash and has **Western Union** service (open M-Sa 9am-noon and 1-4pm), and the **post office** (open M-F 7am-4pm). The **Hondutel** office is in an office connected to the *mercado.* They also have **Internet** service for L25 per hr. (☎766 2744. Open M-Sa 8am-8:30pm, Su 10am-8:30pm). **Clínica Médica del Valle** is one block away from La Casa de las Abuelas. (☎766 2820. After hours ☎766 2864.)

To get to Valle de Ángeles, take a **bus** from the Esso station on Av. La Paz past the US embassy in Tegus (1hr., every 45min. 5:30am-6:45pm, L6.) Accommodations here are sparse and generally expensive. ■**Hotel Villas del Valle Resort ❺,** offers cottages with TVs, hot water, bathtubs, and large beds. There's also a bar, restaurant, and kitchen, as well as Internet access. (Cottages US$30-60. Economy singles US$10; doubles US$12. Discounts for longer stays.) **Posada del Ángel ❺,** one block to the right and one block uphill from the church, has spotless rooms with hot bath and cable TV, and a pool. (☎766 2233. Pool L50 per person per day. Singles L300; doubles L400; triples L500.) **Los Tres Pines Bed and Breakfast ❺,** the only B&B in town, has three cozy rooms, a beautiful backyard, and welcoming hosts, who also run a souvenir/crafts store. (☎766 2879. US$25 per person.) To the right of the Palacio Municipal, **Restaurant El Anafre ❸,** has a great selection of *anafres* (a black bean and cheese fondue often with veggies) at decent prices, and seafood for L80-100. (Open Th-Tu 10am-7pm.) Next door, the antique shop/restaurant/bar **Épocas ❸,** offers *comida típica*—particularly meat dishes (L40-90)—and many kinds of liquor. (Open M-F 10am-10pm, Sa-Su 10am-midnight.) For a bit of nightlife, head to ■**Axilt Bar and Grill ❶,** behind La Casa de los Abuelos, which features a dance floor with colored lights, popular music, and specialties such as breaded *papas fritas* for L20. (Open M-F 4pm-midnight, Sa-Su noon-midnight.)

◤ PARQUE NACIONAL LA TIGRA

*To get to **Jutiapa Visitor Center** from Tegus, take one of the school buses bound for Jutiapa that leave from the corner of Calle Finlay and Av. Cristobal Colón in Tegus. Buses leave when full (1½hr., 6:30am-4pm, L8). After getting off the bus, walk uphill 1.5km to the visitors center. Buses return from Jutiapa all day until 5pm. To reach El Rosario Visitor Center from Tegus, take the bus that goes directly to San Juancito (3pm daily). Get to the bus early. Once in San Juancito, follow the signposts uphill out of town for about 4km until you reach El Rosario and the visitor center. Returns leave the cruce at San Juancito at 6am daily with an additional bus at 1pm on weekends. After that, it should be possible to hitch a ride 14km to Valle de Ángeles, but Let's Go does not recommend hitchhiking; the last bus leaves there at 5:30pm. Traffic is scarce, so don't count on hitching a ride back on weekdays. For more information, contact AMITIGRA, the organization that manages the park. Their offices are located in Tegus on the 6th fl. of Edificio Italia, on Av. República de Panamá two blocks west of Av. República de Chile. (☎235 8493. Open M-F 9am-5pm.)*

Parque Nacional La Tigra is only 21km northeast of Tegucigalpa, but the setting couldn't be more different. Covering some 238 sq. km, the park's cloud forest has orchids, more than 200 species of birds, ocelots, monkeys, pumas. The trails are gorgeous but steep—pack light, but bring rain gear, lots of water, and warm clothes (chilly nights as cold as 5°C).

There are two **visitors centers,** one by the western entrance near Jutiapa and another by the eastern entrance near El Rosario. Park ranger Olga Girón speaks English. Trails are more accessible from Jutiapa, but accommodations are available near El Rosario. Both centers, with restrooms and picnic areas, are well stocked with free maps. Guides offer tours from there (L45-75 depending on the trail). Visitors should register at the station and pay the trail fee (US$10; seniors and persons with disabilities US$5). All of the trails jut off the *sendero principal* which cuts through the park and is good for mountain bikes. (Centers and park open 8am-5pm, no entrance after 2pm.)

The most popular and hardest of the six trails is **La Cascada.** The steep up-and-down path connects both visitors centers (7km apart) and leads to the park's centerpiece, a 60m waterfall. **La Mina** (2.7km), the easiest trail, climbs to the entrance of one of the larger mines and passes some great *vistas* of the valley. **Jucuara** (2km) winds through conifer and broad leaf forests to a glorious natural spring and connects to Los Plancitos, while **Las Granadillas** makes a loop near Jutiapa visitor center and gives an introduction to the park's plant life. **La Esperanza** (2.5km) passes by a mine and ends at a peak called Rancho Quernado, offering views of the surrounding valley. **Bosque Nublado** (2km) leads to a *mirador* where you can spy on the birds below. Check to see if the sky-ride that departs from this point is ready. All trails are most easily reached by the Jutiapa visitor center.

The "town" of El Rosario is an abandoned 19th-century settlement with just a few hotels. **El Rosario Ecolodge ❸,** an old building converted into dorm-style accommodations, is in the El Rosario Visitor Center (beds US$10). Augustine Cierra at the visitor center will help with lodging and can arrange for food (L25-30). Alternatively, try **San Pablito Hotel ❶,** 1hr. away in San Juancito (mattress L20).

SOUTHERN HONDURAS

A thin extension of Honduras runs south to the Golfo de Fonseca, giving the country all-important access to the Pacific Ocean. Travelers here are usually en route to some place else: both El Salvador and Nicaragua are an easy trip down the Carretera Panamericana. Traveling south from Tegus, a road heads west to the Salvadoran border at El Amatillo from the junction at Jicaro Galán. The colonial city of Choluteca makes for a good diversion on the longer route to Nicaragua.

CHOLUTECA

Honduras's fourth-largest city, Choluteca is a well-preserved colonial center. It is also the country's hottest city, but bearable during the rainy season from May to November. Choluteca is a nice stop to break up a trip, but it doesn't have much to offer the more adventurous traveler.

⌷ TRANSPORTATION. The town has two bus stations. **Mi Esperanza** goes to **Tegucigalpa** (express service 2½hrs., 6am-6pm, L100; local service is 3½ hours, every 30min., 4am-9pm, L29) and the Nicaraguan border at **Guasaule** (35 min., every 20 min., 4am-9pm, L12). All other destinations leave from the main station. Buses head to **Tegucigalpa** (3½hr., every 30min., L26) and to the Nicaraguan border at **Guasaule** (45min., every 20min., 5am-6pm, L14) and **San Marcos** (1½hr., every 1½hr., 7am-6pm, L10). Hop a bus to the Salvadoran crossing at **Amatillo** (2hrs, every 25min., 3:30am-5:55pm, L20). **Taxis** offer flat rates of L10 to get from the bus station to the hotels.

⚅⚇ ORIENTATION AND PRACTICAL INFORMATION. Choluteca is organized along the standard Honduran grid, except the *parque central* (also called Parque Valle) is not located at the grid's epicenter; instead, it's on 6 Calle, 6 Av. N., near the suspension bridge. The main commercial strip is **4 Calle,** two blocks south of the *parque.* Parque de la madre is in the middle of the main street heading toward the *mercado viejo* area, home to the bus stations and cheaper hotels. Hotel Pacífico is three blocks away from the main **bus station,** which is located on the south edge of town at 4 Av., 5 Calle S.

Bancoahorro, 4 Av., 2 Calle N., across from the Hondutel in Barrio Guadalupe (open M-F 8:30am-3:30pm, Sa 8:30am-1:30pm), and **Banco Atlántida,** one block from the *parque,* will change traveler's checks. (☎882 0121. Open M-Sa 8:30am-3:30pm.) The **police** station is on the northwest corner of the *parque* (☎882 0951; emergency☎199. Open 24hr.) There are plenty of **pharmacies** on 4a Calle; they take turns staying open until 10pm. The public **Hospital Del Sur,** between 5 Calle and 6 Calle (☎882 0231), and the private clinic **Phillips Centro Médico,** on 4a Calle (☎882 0261) are open 24hr. for emergencies. Some doctors speak English. **Hondutel** is available to call the US at L96 per 3min. (☎882 3962. Open M-F 7am-9pm.) Next door, the **post office,** on 4 Av., 2 Calle N., has **EMS** service. (Open M-F 7:30am-4pm, Sa 7:30-10:30am). **Internet** and **fax** are available at the **Restaurante Yi Kim,** behind the police station a block away from the *parque central.* (☎882 2149. Open 11am-8:30pm. L1 per minute.) Also find service on **Av. Paulino Valladares.** (☎882 1148. L50 per hour.) Chat with the cool managers, especially Luis.

⚆⚇ ACCOMMODATIONS AND FOOD. Hotel Central ❷, though older, has spacious rooms and a patio full of flowers, trees, and hammocks. Its only drawback is its distance from the bus station. From the *parque central,* walk past the police station, then two blocks to the right. Prices include fan, bath, and TV. (☎882 0090. Singles L100, doubles L160.) **Hotel Pacifico #1** and **#2 ❸,** both located on 4a Calle, 3 blocks from the main bus station, have dozens of spotless rooms, private baths, and multiple fans. Number one has hammocks in the courtyard and is a pleasant atmosphere for the exhausted traveler (☎882 0838. One bed L120, with TV and A/C L200; two beds with fan L180, with A/C and TV L290; triples L300.) Number two is newer, but similar to number one. The lobby stocks snacks and travel supplies (☎882 3249. Singles with fan L90, with fan and TV L120, with TV and A/C L200; doubles L29; group rooms, add L30 per person to doubles rates). **Hotel Pierre ❹,** just off Vicente Williams St., has the advantage of being in downtown Choluteca. (☎882 0676. Singles L156, with A/C 273; doubles L193-L336; triples L240-L422.) The closest thing to a "resort" in Choluteca is **Hotel Centroamerica ❺,** located on Blvd. Chorotega across from Napolis, with very large rooms, amenities, a restaurant, and a pool. (☎882 3940. Singles L440; doubles L530; triples L650.)

Tío Rico ❷, on Vicente Williams, 3 blocks south and 2 blocks west of the *parque central,* is a bit more expensive but serves very good seafood and huge hamburgers (L34). Bust a move dancing on Friday and Saturday evenings. (Open Su-Th 9am-10pm, F-Sa 9am-2am.) **El Burrito ❷,** located 2 blocks from the Hotel Pacifico going away from downtown, offers some of the best Mexican food in Choluteca. The burritos are obviously the specialty (2 for 40L). The taco *gigante* is excellent, especially at L22. In addition to Internet service, **Yi Kim ❸,** has a very large eating area which fills up at night. Soups are around L60 and Chow Mein is L70-L90.

⚇⚆ SIGHTS AND ENTERTAINMENT. The pride of Choluteca is **La Iglesia de Concepción,** at the southern end of the *parque central,* and the colonial **Barrio Corbeta** that surrounds it. The church, dating from the 17th century, was destroyed by an earthquake in the late 19th century and rebuilt in 1918. It is open daily, with

FROM THE ROAD

HANGING OUT— HONDURAN STYLE

Beaches of both white and black sand create a perimeter around the tropical island *Isla el Tigre*, and invite travelers to take a romantic aside in the tropical paradise. The isolation from the "real world" offers a primitive feel for travelers not interested in Westernized and overpriced islands like those found off the Atlantic coast. When I woke up one morning to find clear skies above, I decided to climb *"La Cima"* with two other adventurers. The trail began as a cement road and then we turned onto a very rocky dirt road. The trail became very steep and narrow, and coupled with the oppressive heat it became very difficult. Along the way there were overlooks with spectacular views of the surrounding islands and the Gulf of Fonseca, and I wondered what excitement awaited at the summit. Suddenly the vegetation began to change and ecstatic with the accomplishment, I ran until I was surrounded completely by sky. I slipped through a barbed wire fence and passed a three foot snake skin through a tick infested path to an edifice with a shack and 360 degree view. Suddenly a hermit named Vicente Vasquez Garcia appeared and showed us around. He had lived on top of the mountain for 18 years. After shared stories and mangos we saw the remains of a former US military camp behind his house. Thinking about my climb and experience later that day, I realized that Vicente was truly alone up there. He lives on this tiny mountain in Honduras without companionship, conversation, and electricity. And he loves it.

—Jeremiah Johnson

mass at 5pm on weekdays and throughout the day Sunday. A stroll through the cobblestone streets, tiled roofs, and antiquated buildings might begin behind the church and then move in a counterclockwise direction back to the other side of the *parque*. To avoid the sun, wander around in the morning or late afternoon.

Both locals and travelers frequent **Disco Metro** for evening excitement. Located in town next to Banco Atlantida. (Open F-Sa 8pm-3am.)

⛏ BORDER WITH NICARAGUA

RÍO GUASAULE. From Choluteca, take a *colectivo* that goes directly to Guasaule; this route to the border passes through El Triunfo. The **crossing**, at the bridge over the Río Guasale, is open 24hr., and Nicaraguan buses continue on the other side of the border. In Guasaule, people will storm the bus offering bike rides to the border and money changing services. Hiring a bike cart isn't a bad idea, but be firm: locals pay no more than 10 córdobas, and you should do the same. There is a US$7 entrance fee to Nicaragua (payable only in US dollars).

EL ESPINO. From Choluteca, the Interamerican Hwy. heads northeast 110km to San Marcos de Colón, where there are some accommodations and restaurants. The **crossing**, 10km past San Marcos, is open 7am-6pm. From San Marcos, minibuses and *colectivos* head to the border when full. Buses leave directly for Managua from the town of Somoto on the Nicaraguan side.

LAS MANOS. This border crossing is most easily accessible from Tegus. The **bus** leaves from the station Discua Litena and travels for 2½ hr. through breathtaking mountains. There are poor rates for exchanging money here. Besides money changing and immigration services, Los Manos has little to offer. Crossing the border is easy, but requires US$7 and L20.

⛏ EL AMATILLO: THE BORDER WITH EL SALVADOR

To get to El Amatillo, take a bus from Tegus or Choluteca. Crucero del Golfo **buses** leave the station on the Blvd. de la Comunidad Europea in Tegus (3hr., L120). Direct buses to El Amatillo leave the main bus station in Choluteca (2½ hrs., L120). The border is open 7am-10pm. US citizens must get a **Visa** in Tegucigalpa at the Salvadoran Embassy or pay

US$10 to get one at the border. **Banco Atlántida,** on the Honduran side, changes traveler's checks (not lempiras) for colones, lempiras, or US dollars. (Open M-F 8am-5pm, Sa 9am-noon.) **Banco Comercio,** on the Salvadoran side, does the same. Money changers, clustered on either side, are usually above-board and offer fair rates to change lempiras directly to colones or vice versa.

ISLA EL TIGRE

Isla el Tigre offers an adventurous island paradise in Golfo De Fonseca that's only a 20min. boat ride from the port town of **Coyolito.** The main city, **Amapala,** has the cheapest hotels and restaurants, but the island as a whole has much more to offer.

■ ⁊ ORIENTATION AND PRACTICAL INFORMATION. In the Golfo de Fonseca, Isla el Tigre is the only entirely Honduran island. A neighboring, larger island is co-owned with El Salvador. From Isla el Tigre, El Salvador is to the west, Nicaragua to the southeast, and Honduras to the north and east. Because of the size and locale, there is no **tourist office** on the island. **Maps** can be obtained at the Varias store, and anywhere with an *Informacíon Turística* sign. The only bank on the island is **Banco Grupo Ahorro Hondureño (BGA).** It is located two blocks up the main street (the one you are on when you get off the boat) on the left. (Open M-F 8:30am-3:30pm, Sa 8:30am-11:30am.) The **post office** is located 2 blocks up the main street in Ampala, but try to use the one in Coyolito or San Lorenzo—Ampala's isn't always open. **Telephones** are located at the **Hondutel,** next to the bank. (A 3min. call to the US is L100. Open M-F 7am-9pm.)

⌒ LOCAL TRANSPORTATION. You must first get to **Coyolito,** the small town from where boats to Amapala on Isla el Tigre leave. Boats don't travel on a regular schedule, but instead leave when there are 10 passengers. The ride is L10 each direction and runs from sunrise to sunset. To get to Coyolito, take a **bus** to San Lorenzo first (5am-6pm, L9), and then one to Coyolito. Once on the island, the road **Calle la Marina** runs entirely around the island and is approximately 10 mi. long. In order to get around you must either walk or hire a local with a car.

⌐ ACCOMMODATIONS. With a pig, large talking parrots, roosters, a duck, a turtle, cats, dogs, and young children, the only actual **hotel** in Ampala has almost as much excitement as a zoo ❷. It is located on the right side of the main street in Ampala on the third block from the water, next door to *Pulpería Tres Hermanos.* There is no sign to tell that it is a hotel. The rooms have cement floors and walls, but are safe and clean. The bathroom is communal, and the shower is a trough of water and a ladle. L80 is a bit pricey for the conditions, but it is the only hotel option. **Apartamento Victoria ❺,** three blocks east on *Calle la Marina,* is a pseudo-apartment complex which rents rooms for the night to travelers. It is the nicest place to stay here, with private rooms, bathrooms, TV's, and fans. (L215 for one or two people, L50 for each additional person.)

⌂ FOOD. The food on the island is comparable to the rest of Honduras. There aren't vendors on the street, but the *Varias* store is sufficient. A snack for the beach of *pan* (bread) and 2 *bebidas* (drinks) will run about L20-L25. **El Faro Victoria ❷,** is located ½ block west on *Calle La Marina* near a mini lighthouse. Named after the owner's wife, it is a pleasant environment with a porch overlooking the gulf, fans, good service, and even better food. (Hamburgers and french fries L33; large breakfast L35; banana split L35. Open daily at 10am.) **Restaurante la Cueva de la Sirena ❷,** located across the street from El Faro Victoria, is complete with a large TV to watch the latest *telenovela* (popular Latin American soap operas). Try the fish for about L50. (Open daily 7am-9pm.) **Pupusa y Pollo ❷**, is 2 blocks up the main street on the left. (Chicken L33; *pupusas* (stuffed tortillas), L8; hamburgers L30. Open daily 9am-9pm.)

🏃 OUTDOORS. The island has incredible beaches surrounding its perimeter, but the two best and most popular are **Playa Grande** and **Playa Negra**. Playa Grande is always open for swimming, and Playa Negra has black sand. **Isla el Tigre** has a large mountain for an island of its size. *La cima* (the summit) at 2500ft. takes between 2-3 hours to climb. The path is quite steep but the views at the top of El Salvador, Honduras, and Nicaragua make it worthwhile. US soldiers were stationed here when Central American countries were at war, and remains of the camps can still be seen. Views of the Golfo de Fonseca are breathtaking on a clear day. Guides are cheap, but not necessary. From Amapala, travel west on Calle La Marina and turn left past the Naval Base where the sign says *Caracol*. Follow the path the entire way and bring lots of water.

WESTERN HIGHLANDS

The star attraction of the highlands is undoubtedly the magnificent Maya site of Copán, but there's *so* much more: forest-covered mountain ranges call out to the outdoor enthusiast, and time-warped colonial towns charm romantics. Along the busy highway between Tegus and San Pedro Sula, the first stop of note is colonial Comayagua, the country's first capital. Not far north lies the relaxing Lago de Yojoa, the country's largest lake, and the fabulous waterfall, Catarata de Pulhapanzak. The rest of the region's attractions are farther west, most easily accessible from San Pedro Sula or across the border in Guatemala or El Salvador. After the majesty of Parque Nacional Celaque, recoup nearby in the old colonial town of Gracias. Santa Rosa de Copán, the area's main town, also retains a sense of the past. Several hours away are the unparalleled ancient carvings of Copán, near the Guatemalan border and convenient to the inviting town of Copán Ruinas.

COMAYAGUA

The town of Comayagua, 80km northwest of the capital, makes for a colonial pit-stop on the highway between Tegucigalpa and San Pedro Sula. The first capital of Honduras, Comayagua has retained its colonial legacy and inviting atmosphere. Recent reconstruction efforts seek to preserve and highlight the city's treasures, which date back to the 16th century and incorporate Spanish and Maya influences.

🚌 TRANSPORTATION. Buses run regularly from both **Tegus** and **San Pedro Sula**, arriving five blocks south of the *parque central* in Comayagua. *Trans Rivera* bus company has a station six blocks south of the *parque* which hosts buses to **San Pedro Sula** (1½hr.; M-F every hr. 5am-4pm, Sa and Su every hr. 5am-4pm; L19).

🏛🎯 ORIENTATION AND PRACTICAL INFORMATION. The San Pedro Sula-Tegus highway is on the western edge of the town. The **parque central** is about three blocks east and seven blocks north of the Texaco station that serves as a bus stop, between Calles 5 and 4, and Av. 1 and Av. 2 de Julio. The general grid pattern is formed by the north-south *Calles* and east-west *Avenidas*.

The municipal building in the northeast corner of the *parque* provides bilingual **tourist information** and L20 maps of the city. (Open M-Sa 8am-noon and 2-5pm.) Banks are never hard to find in this town. **Banco del País,** on the park's southwest corner, cashes AmEx traveler's cheques until 4pm and accepts Visa/MC (open M-F 9am-4pm, Sa 9am-noon; window teller open M-F 4-7pm, Sa noon-4pm), while

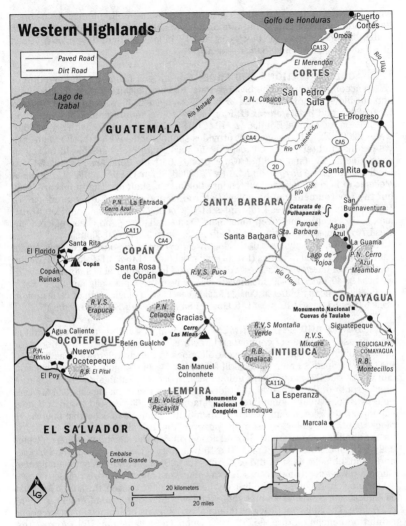

Western Highlands

Paved Road
Dirt Road

Golfo de Honduras

Puerto Cortés

Omoa

CA13

El Merendón

CORTES

P.N. Cusuco

San Pedro Sula

El Progreso

CA4

Río Chamelecón

CA5

20

Santa Rita

YORO

Lago de Izabal

GUATEMALA

Río Motagua

P.N. La Entrada Cerro Azul

SANTA BARBARA

Río Ulúa

San Buenaventura

Catarata de Pulhapanzak

Parque Sta. Barbara

Agua Azul

Santa Barbara

La Guama

CA11

CA4

Lago de Yojoa

P.N. Cerro Azul Meámbar

Santa Rita

COPÁN

El Florido

Santa Rosa de Copán

R.V.S. Puca

Río Otoro

COMAYAGUA

Copán

Copán Ruinas

R.V.S. Erapuca

P.N. Celaque

Gracias

Monumento Nacional Cuevas de Taulabe

Siguatepeque

Cerro Las Minas

R.V.S Montaña Verde

R.V.S. Mixcure

TO TEGUCIGALPA, COMAYAGUA

Agua Caliente

OCOTEPEQUE

Belén Gualcho

INTIBUCA

R.B. Montecillos

P.N. Trifinio

Nuevo Ocotepeque

R.B. Opalaca

San Manuel Colonhete

La Esperanza

El Poy

R.B. El Pital

CA11A

LEMPIRA

Monumento Nacional Congolón

Marcala

EL SALVADOR

R.B. Volcán Pacayita

Erandique

Embalse Cerrón Grande

0   20 kilometers
0   20 miles

N

Banco Ficensa, on the west side, gives cash advances on MC (open M-F 9am-4pm, Sa 8:30am-11:30am). **Banco Atlantida,** one block south of the park on Av. 1 has an ATM that accepts Visa. (Open M-F 9am-noon, 2-4pm and Sa 9-11am.) All hotels and many stores will accept US dollars. The **Red Cross** offers emergency service (☎195). For medical assistance, try **Policlínica Berlioz,** directly behind the cathedral, where a consultation is L100. (☎772 0133. Open M-Th 8am-noon and 2-5pm.) The **Farmacia San Martin** is one block south of the southeast corner of the *parque.* (Open M-F 8am-noon and 2-6pm, Sa 8am-noon.) The **police,** a.k.a. **FUSEP,** is two blocks behind the cathedral. (☎772 0080, emergencies 772 3040. Open 24hr.) **Cyber-Centro,** 2 Av., 1 Calle, offers **Internet** access for L29 per hr. (Open M-Sa 8am-7pm.) The **post office** (open M-Sa 8am-4pm), two blocks north of the *parque,* is in the same building as **Hondutel,** which provides a row of public phones from (open daily 8am-9pm, with lunch and dinner breaks; about L24 per min. to the United States). A **UPS** office is one block east and 1½ blocks south of the *parque*. (Open M-F 8am-noon and 2-5pm; Sa 8am-noon.)

▐▐ ▐ ▝ ACCOMMODATIONS AND FOOD. Comayagua has a decent selection of cheap accommodations. The best are **Hotel Norimax Colonial ❸,** four blocks south and one block east of the *parque* (☎722 1703; singles L140, with A/C L180; doubles L180/L200), and **Hotel Norimax ❸,** four blocks south and three blocks west of the *parque,* on Av. Manuel Bonilla. (☎772 1210. Single/doubles L150, with A/C and hot water L200.) Family management provides simple rooms with cable TV, fans, private baths, and telephones. Closer to the park, with nice beds in old but clean rooms, cable TV, fans, and hot water private baths is **Hotel America Inc. ❸,** two blocks south of the *parque* on Av. 1 (☎772 3060. Singles L140; doubles L195.) **Hotel Moderno ❷** is in a converted warehouse behind a restaurant. The rooms are large but the environment can be noisy. Bathrooms and showers are shared. (☎772 1077. Singles L50; doubles L70; triples L150. Open 24hr.) Across from Hotel Norimax is the recently improved **Hotel Maru ❷,** a small, cozy, and cheap place. (Singles L70; doubles L90, with private bath L112. Open 5:30am-10:30pm.)

Fruty Taco ❶, directly west of the southwest corner of the *parque,* delivers on its name with great fruit *licuados* (L10-14) and meat tacos (L16-33). **◪Palmeras ❷,** on the south edge of the *parque,* serves wonderful food in a comfortable ambience. (Sandwiches L25-45, tacos L20-30, full dinners L60-75, beer L15. Open daily 7am-9pm.) Early risers enjoy a hearty buffet at **Comida Rapida Vencia ❶,** a block south of cathedral on Calle 3 (rice L5, salad L10, meat L16. Open M-Sa 7am-7:30pm, Su 7am-1:30pm.)

◪ ▐ ▍ SIGHTS AND ENTERTAINMENT. Comayagua's 17th-century **cathedral** is an impressive example of colonial architecture. Originally made by the Moors for Spain's Alhambra palace, the 800-year-old clock in the church tower was given to the town by Spain's Philip II, and still functions. Despite ongoing renovations, you can check out the magnificent golden altar work and small side chapel. Three blocks south of the cathedral, the oldest church in Honduras, **Iglesia San Merced,** built in 1536, displays some interesting statues. The 500-year-old wooden beams supporting the roof are impressive. (Open daily 5-7pm.) **San Sebastián Church,** 11 blocks south and 3 blocks east of the *parque* (15min. walk; L10 taxi), is famed for its altar and for ex-president General José Trinidad Cabañas, buried here. (Open daily 8-10am. Service daily 6pm). The 16th-century **Iglesia de la Caridad,** 3 blocks north and 3 blocks west of the park, integrates Spanish and indigenous cultures. Current renovations limit access, but the courtyard and facade are visible.

One block north of the cathedral, on the Plaza San Francisco, the **Museo Regional de Arqueología,** resides in an incredible 400-year-old mansion and former presidential palace. The museum provides bilingual explanation of artifacts in an excellent exhibit on Lencan culture. (☎772 0386. Open Tu-Sa 8am-5pm. L20.) Across the street from the cathedral on the right is the **Museo Colonial.** This three-room colonial museum, displays 15th- and 16th-century artifacts culled from churches in and around Comayagua. (Open daily 9am-noon and 2-5pm, Su 9am-1pm. L10.)

Nightlife in Comayagua is scarce, but a **movie theater,** Cine Valladolid, a block west and two blocks north of the park, shows US hits. (Spanish subtitles. Shows daily 7pm, L20; Su 1pm, L10.)

LAGO DE YOJOA

Nestled between fertile mountains and the centerpiece of a national conservation project, serene Lago de Yojoa was originally inhabited by the Lenca. From horseback riding to bathing in waterfalls, the lake provides numerous excursions for the adventurous traveler. Three large hotels offer the best access to Lago de Yojoa, while nearby Peña Blanca is a convenient and cheaper base to explore the lake.

📧 **TRANSPORTATION.** Although the lake is huge, the northern side is the most accessible. **Buses** run regularly from **San Pedro Sula** and **Tegucigalpa** (via Comayagua) and stop at the roadside town of **La Guama.** Wait with the cluster of people at the *pulpería* for the clearly marked bus that shuttles back and forth between La Guama and **Peña Blanca** (25min., about every 30min., L5). The resort hotels lie along the route to Peña Blanca. Leaving from the north end of Peña Blanca buses marked "Mochito" head to **San Pedro Sula** or **Catarat Pulhapanzak.**

📋 **PRACTICAL INFORMATION.** In **Peña Blanca,** a tiny **Hondutel** office is inside the *Cafetería y Repostería Candy.* (Open daily 7am-noon and 1-6pm.) There is no local phone service in Peña Blanca, but long distance calls may be made from the office of hotel La Finca (see **Accommodations** below) provided you have a calling card. No banks cash traveler's checks. Hotel Maranata has a small **pharmacy,** and the **clinic** up the hill has a slightly more comprehensive pharmacy with 24hr. access. The **police** are across the street from Hotel Maranata. (Open 24hr.)

🍴🛏 **ACCOMMODATIONS AND FOOD.** *Lempira*-pinchers, beware! All three hotels off the road from La Guama to Peña Blanca are on the left overlooking the lake, and the views are pricey. **Hotel Auga Azul** ❺ may offer the cheapest rates. (☎992 7244. Doubles and triples L377. AmEx/MC/V.) However, **Las Brisas del Lago** ❺ may be your best bet if you are looking to spoil yourself with unbroken lake views, spacious balconies, air conditioned rooms, hot showers, and recreational facilities. (☎992 2937. Singles L586; doubles L732.50. AmEx/MC/V.) **Hotel La Finca** ❺, facing Hotel Maranata across from and just before the gas station, doesn't have lake views, but the rooms are in excellent condition. (☎898 8178. Singles L232; doubles L348; three or more L706.) As a last resort (and a resort it is *not*), **Hotel Maranata** ❷ is next to the bus stop from La Guama. Make sure to thoroughly inspect the bathroom before taking the room. (Singles L70, with bath L100.)

Enjoy a wonderful, quiet meal at the scenic restaurants of **Hotel Agua Azul** ❸ (above). **Las Brisas del Lago** ❸, along the road to Peña Blanca, and **Finca de las Glorias** ❸, further off the same main road, have large portions of traditional dishes (L80-150), beers (L18)

THE PERILS OF HEAVY METAL

In April 2002, *La Asociación de Municipios para la Proteccion del Lago de Yojoa,* an environmental advocacy group, released an astounding report on the state of Lago de Yojoa. Although the lake has been part of a governmental preservation project since 1971, in the last eight years 90% of the lake basin has been deforested and put to commercial agricultural use.

While for the time being the water sparkles a healthy greenish-blue, run-off from fertilizers and other agricultural chemicals threatens to damage the lake considerably. This causes eutrophication. In this process, high levels of nitrates cause an algae bloom, which not only turns the lake an unappealing green, but also uses up available supplies of oxygen, causing fish to suffocate.

The accumulation of heavy metals from both past and ongoing mining operations also threaten wildlife. Levels of copper, lead, and zinc already exceed government standards for safety, so the savvy traveler may want to think twice before stopping at one of the *comedores* for fried fish.

Finally, a hydro-electric dam threatens to drain the lake, with the result that in ten years, the advocacy group predicts, the lake will be little more than a green marsh, its aesthetic appeal and dependent ecosystems destroyed.

and desserts are available with any meal. In **Peña Blanca** many *comedores* dish up cheap fried foods. **Cafeteria la Boca ❷,** a block towards La Guama from the bus stop, is a cool place to sit indoors and enjoy a filling meal. (Hamburgers L30, standard Honduran fare L30-40. Open daily 7am-9pm.)

◙ 🄌 SIGHTS AND OUTDOOR ACTIVITIES. Guided **boat rides** carry groups of four to five people from Hotel Agua Azul and Las Brisas del Lago (L300 per hr.). Agua Azul also rents **fishing poles,** while Las Brisas has **rowboats** (L80 per person per hr.) and will arrange guided **horseback riding** (L70 per hr.) or a boat tour to the lakeside ruins of **Los Naranjos** (price negotiable). Hotel services and equipment are also available to non-guests. Beyond enjoying the lake itself, treasures hidden deep within the dense forest and steep mountains of **Cerro Azul Meambar National Park** are increasingly accessible despite the lack of visitor information. Easy access to the park begins behind the bus stop in La Guama and heads along a gravel road to the small village of **Santa Elena.** A small bus shuttles back and forth from La Guama every hr. (L5). Beyond the village, a 1hr. path rambles up through the mountains toward **Los Pinos,** a convention center ideal for group-stays.

Los Pinos is part of a larger ecological preservation project and has four well-marked hiking paths ranging in length and difficulty from 30min. to 9hr. and will help you penetrate the park to discover the flora, waterfalls, peaks, and cloud forests. The helpful staff will guide you and provide a cabin with bunks and bath. Food service for a group must be arranged in advance, since the restaurant is not in continuous operation. (Siguatepeque office ☎ 733 0539. Breakfast L40, lunch/dinner L50. Cabins for 6 people US$5.)

NEAR LAGO DE YOJOA

CATARATA DE PULHAPANZAK

*Take a Tima company bus labeled "Mochito" toward San Pedro Sula from Hotel Maranata in Peña Blanca and get off in **San Buena Ventura**. (20min., every ½hr., L6.) A yellow sign points the way to Centro Turístico Pulhapanzak. Follow the main concrete road and bear left at the fork that is about 1km up the hill. At the top of the hill, follow the sign pointing to A Pulhapanzak. The falls will be on your right after about 15min., inside the gated entrance of the Centro Turístico. There are a couple of small stores and comedores in San Buena Ventura for drinks, snacks or a cheap meal. With the exception of camping at the falls, the nearest lodging is at Peña Blanca. Return buses to San Pedro and Peña Blanca leave about every hour during daylight hours from where the bus drops you off. Park is open daily 6am-6pm. Park entrance L25. **Camping** L25; bring your own gear.*

An easy trip from San Pedro Sula or Lago de Yojoa that could last an afternoon or all day, this 43m waterfall along the Río Lindo is truly awesome. The best way to "do the waterfall" is to have a guide take you down the steep path to river-level, where the churning white water of the falls kicks up a cooling mist. The downside of this mist is that it makes the trail slippery; the descent is mildly difficult, particularly the bottom section, which involves using tree roots as a ladder. For a tip of L50 to L100, depending on how long you stay, guides can reveal the secrets of the waterfall, including a cave behind the main part of the falls, a pool to swim in below them, and some rocks for jumping. If no one appears on your way up, the men working the entrance to the park can find you a guide. It is easy to follow the trail without a guide; just follow the sound of madly rushing water to the top of the falls, where the trail begins along the right, then descends to the left. For the less intrepid, benches and viewpoints await to the right of the trail on top of a small bluff. For the even less intrepid, there is a reasonably well-maintained cement stairway that meets the river about a 100m downstream from where the steeper trail does so. This vantage point still provides an excellent view of the falls, but you miss out on the mist. The more difficult trails can last up to 1hr. and you are likely to get wet, so plan accordingly. The drier paths take 10-20min.

The area around the falls is a **public park** that allows camping and has a small **restaurant** (with public bathrooms) just upstream from the falls (meals L40-50). Next to the restaurant is the **Plaza Ceremonial,** an unexcavated archaeological site believed to have been a center of Lenca religious ceremonies.

SANTA BÁRBARA

Situated to the west of Lago de Yojoa, Santa Bárbara is a quiet town with a serene and friendly ambiance. The streets follow the landscape's contours, diving up and down the hills upon which the city sits. The ruins of a castle that dates to the time of Honduras's independence are perched on a hill overlooking the city. Moss grows on power lines above the *parque central* as a symbol of the relaxed pace of life this town has been able to preserve.

TRANSPORTATION. Most **buses** stop just down the hill from the *parque central* on the opposite side of the church. **Terminal Cotisba** (☎643 2308) runs buses to **San Pedro Sula** (2hr., every 30min. 4am-5pm, L19). There are also 3 daily buses to **Siguatepeque** (☎643 2689; 1½hr, last bus at 2pm, L20), from which you can continue on to Tegucigalpa.

ORIENTATION AND PRACTICAL INFORMATION. Santa Barbara is a small town of about 15,000, and centers around its *parque*. The street layout abides by the logic of the terrain, which means that it is entirely illogical, but the town is small enough to be easily navigable. The castle is visible from the *parque central* on a distant hill to the right of the church. **Banco Atlántida,** one block down the main street to the left of the church, cashes traveler's checks and gives advances on Visa. (Open M-F 8:30am-3:30pm, Sa 8:30-11:30am.) The **police station** is a 20min. walk from the *parque central,* down the hill to the left facing the church on the opposite side of the park. (☎643 2120, emergency ☎199. Open 24hr.) The **hospital** is just before the police station (open 24hr.). The **Hondutel** office is just behind the post office. (Open daily 7am-9pm.) Find **Internet** is at **Servicopins,** one block down the street running along the right side of the church. (☎643 3012. Open M-F 8am-5pm, Sa 8am-noon. L40 per hr.) The **post office** is on the street directly in front of the church, one block to the right. (Open M-F 8am-noon and 2-5pm, Sa 8-10am.)

ACCOMMODATIONS AND FOOD. There are a few hotels to choose from in Santa Barbara. **Hotel Ejecutino ❸** is about 1½ blocks to the left of the church on your left hand side. The rooms vary in size but have large windows. (☎643 2206. Singles L100; doubles with TV L250.) Just to the left is **Hotel Ruth ❷,** slightly cheaper with standard rooms. (☎643 2632. Singles L80, L100 with bath; doubles L150, with A/C L200.) *Comedores* line the streets of Santa Barbara, and fresh fruit can be bought in the *mercado* just behind the church. For a quiet meal in air-conditioned surroundings, try **Cafetería y Pastelería Charlies ❷,** down the street from the church on the corner of the *parque central.* (Sandwiches L24, with fries L25.)

SIGHTS. There isn't much to see in Santa Bárbara, but that may actually be part of its charm, making the town a great place for the weary traveler to relax and take in modern Honduran small-town life. The *castillo,* built at the time of Honduras's independence some 180 years ago, is a L100 cab ride away. Remember to arrange for a return trip. (Open daily 8am-5pm. Free.)

LA ESPERANZA

Atop a Western Honduran mountaintop at 1980m elevation, La Esperanza is one of Honduras's highest *pueblos*. With a population of less than 10,000 and chilly mountain nights, it is also one of the most endearing. Large stone streets lead up to a hill just a few blocks past the *parque central*, into which prisoners carved a shrine to the Virgin Mary in 1950. A large wooden cross lies inside the shrine and is brought out during *Semana Santa* just before Easter.

▐ TRANSPORTATION. The **bus** terminal is one block left of the *parque central* behind the police station. They run to **San Pedro Sula** (4hr., every 2hr. 4:30am-2:30pm, L40) and **Siguatepeque** (1½hr., L25), a transport point to **Tegucigalpa**.

▟ ▐ ORIENTATION AND PRACTICAL INFORMATION. The central street runs right past the *parque central* straight uphill where a whitewashed church-like facade frames the shrine to the Virgin Mary. Staircases hewn into the stone on both sides lead to the top of the hill, from which the entire town is visible. There is no official tourist office, but the town is so small that there is no need. **Banco de Occidente,** right off the *parque central*, cashes traveler's checks and has a **Western Union** office. (Open M-F 8:30am-4:30pm, Sa 8:30am-1:30pm.) The **police station** is in the turreted building next to the park. (☎ 783 1007, emergency ☎ 199. Open 24hr.) A **Clínica Médica** is one block from the *parque* past the right-hand side of the church. (☎ 783 0290. Open 24hr.) There is no hospital. **Internet** access can be had at **Café Recreo,** opposite the police station. (☎ 783 0598. L1 per min., 15min. minimum. Open daily 8:30am-9pm.) The **Hondutel** office is opposite the church on the *parque central*. (Open daily 7am-9pm.) Next door is the **post office.** (Open M-F 8am-noon and 2-5pm, Sa 8-10am.)

▐ ▐ ACCOMMODATIONS AND FOOD. For travelers on a tight budget, **Hotel Mejin Batres ❶** can't be beat. One block along the main road toward the shrine, the hotel provides guests with spacious rooms and hot showers, which are especially welcome on brisk mountain nights. (☎ 783 0051. Singles L50, with bath L100; doubles L80, with bath L140.) Another budget option is **Hotel Venecia ❶,** 3 blocks down the main road from the *parque* in the opposite direction of the shrine, on the left. (Singles L45, with bath L100; doubles L80, with bath L200.) The new **Gran Hotel la Esperanza ❺** is more luxurious; the rooms are large and well maintained, and a restaurant and full bar adjoin the hotel. (☎ 783 0068. Singles L250; doubles with bath and TV L350.) **Cafe Recreo ❷,** opposite the police station, provides a pleasant environment for a sip of coffee or a full meal. (Lunch and dinner L40-60; coffee L5.) It's also pleasant to stop by the *cuseta* in the middle of the *parque central* to sip a cold soda or *licuado* from the second-story balcony. (Open daily 9am-7pm.)

▣ SIGHTS. The crisp weather makes La Esperanza an ideal place to stop for a few days and soak up small-town Honduran life. In addition to the dramatic **shrine** to the Virgin Mary poised conspicuously at the end of the main street, La Esperanza boasts cool spring **baths,** *baños públicos* that are a 5min. walk just outside town to the left of the hill with the shrine. Open during daylight hours. Free.

GRACIAS

Ever since Juan de Chávez, the first settler of the region, exclaimed, "Thank God we've finally found flat land!", Gracias has served as a comfortable base camp amidst rugged terrain. Founded in 1536 as a garrison for the Spanish, the town later served as both the capital of Honduras and as a seat of government for all of

Spanish Central America. While the Honduran economy's center of gravity shifted north and east, Gracias's importance faded, but its colonial flair endures. Gracias is also known for its festival and fair (all July, peak days 19-20) celebrating the region's cultural traditions and honoring the native leader Lempira, a longtime enemy of the Spanish. Visitors typically stop en route to nearby hot springs and the breathtaking cloud forest in Parque Nacional Celaque.

⌷ TRANSPORTATION. Lempira bus company (☎656 1214) runs regular service to **Santa Rosa de Copán** (1½ hr, every 30min. 5am-4:30pm, L20). **Gracianos** buses leave irregularly from Gracias to **San Pedro Sula** with a stop in **Santa Rosa** (4hr., L50).

◼️? ORIENTATION AND PRACTICAL INFORMATION. You're never too far from where you want to be in Gracias. **Buses** chug into town from the north and drop passengers off three blocks west and one block north of the **parque central.** Another bus stop is two blocks toward Banco de Occidente from the *parque*, and then two blocks to the right. In uncommon fashion, the *parque* is not quite the center of town. Most action takes place to the west. The **Church of San Marcos** is on the south side of the *parque* and the turreted **Castillo de San Cristobal** looms on a hilltop to the west. There is no official tourist office, but **Froni** at Guancascos Restaurant (☎/fax 656 1219; see below) is a great source of information on trips around Gracias. **Banco de Occidente,** one block right of the church facing the *parque* in the northwest corner, cashes traveler's checks. (Open M-F 8:30am-4:30pm, Sa 8am-noon.) Other services include: the **police station,** on the northeast corner of the *parque* (☎656 1036, emergency 199; open 24hr.); the **hospital** with 24hr. emergency service, on the outskirts of town near the Texaco station (☎656 1425; follow the central street from the *parque* away from the church); **Hondutel,** a block south of the *parque's* southwest corner, past the church (☎656 1003. Open daily 7am-9pm); **Internet** access at **Millennium Computer School Cyber Café,** one block right of the church (☎656 1140. L1 per min. Open daily 8am-noon and 2-8pm.); **post office** (open M-F 8am-noon and 2-5pm, Sa 8-10am). **Postal code:** 1301.

⌂⌂ ACCOMMODATIONS AND FOOD. Gracias has quite a few hotels, but few budget ones. **Hotel Erick ❷,** three blocks east of the bus terminal or one block north of the *parque*, has spacious rooms with private baths and a friendly owner who can arrange rides to **Parque Nacional Celaque** and the **Aguas Termales.** (☎656 1066. Singles L65; doubles 80; with fan and hot water L150.) At luxurious **Hotel Guancascos ❹,** perched three blocks west and one block south of the *parque*, airy rooms have hot-water baths, fans, and TV. Some rooms also have dramatic views of the town, framed by distant mountains. (☎656 1219. Singles L170; doubles L240.) Froni, Guancascos's owner, also rents two nicely equipped cabins on the edge of the Parque Celaque (L250 a night for two people.) **Hotel San Antonio ❶** is not only cheap, but somehow soothing. The turquoise and baby pink building is one block west and 5½ blocks north of the *parque* on the left. It has clean, basic rooms and a common TV area, and the entrance is a terrace with unobscured views of the peaks in Parque Nacional Celaque. (☎656 1071. Singles L35, with private bath L60; doubles L65/L80.) **Hotel Colonial ❷,** one block right from the *parque* facing the church, provides a cheap central option. The large rooms have powerful fans. (☎656 1258. Singles with bath L70; doubles L174.) **Hotel Don Juan ❹,** set inside a courtyard opposite Banco de Occidente, has clean tile floors, high ceilings, and is ideal for group and family stays. (☎656 1020. Singles L156, with A/C and hot water L280; doubles L208/L405.)

Set on a balcony high above town which catches the cool morning breezes, **◼️Restaurante Guancascos ❷,** in Hotel Guancascos, is a good place to grab breakfast before heading out to tackle Celaque. (Simple breakfast L35; *cena típica* L65, beer L15; veg. options available. Open daily 7am-10pm. AmEx/MC/V.) Right behind the church, **El Mundo de la Pizza ❷** serves Italian favorites. (One-topping pizzas L35-50, vegetarian options L80. Open daily 9am-10pm.) Still in the mood for Italian food? **La Exquisita Repostería y Pizzería ❷,** half a block west of the northwest corner of the *parque,* right next to Hotel Colonial, has earned a following for its delectable pizzas (L35-65), hamburgers (L125), and baked goodies (L5-L7) that are, yes, exquisite. (Open daily 7am-9pm.)

◙ SIGHTS. Like many other Central American towns, Gracias is a great place to walk around and soak in that romantic, colonial feel. The town's two churches are both within a block of the *parque.* A short walk starting just behind the stairs to Guancascos leads up to Gracias' main attraction, the **Castillo de San Cristóbal,** with the tomb of former President Juan Lindo and magnificent views of **Parque Nacional Celanque** and the town. (Open daily 8am-noon and 1-5pm, often later. Free.)

NEAR GRACIAS

📶 PARQUE NACIONAL CELAQUE

The best way to reach the park is to arrange for a ride in Gracias, especially for groups that can split the cost. Froni at Guancascos Restaurant charges L150 for up to four people, which is the standard price. Be sure to arrange a return trip prior to departure (also L150). Otherwise, you will have to take the walk 8km back to town. From Guancascos, walk left until you pass an old church. At the intersection turn left, but stay to the right of the DIPPSA gas station. Go to the right around a pink and white church, then start on the "shortcut" indicated by a sign with the words "a pie" (on foot). The park is 2hr. straight ahead. The **Office of the Proyecto Celaque,** *located at Castillo de San Cristóbal in Gracias (see above), has the latest information on the park. (☎ 656 1362. Open daily 8am-5pm.)* **Corporación Hondureña de Desarollo Forestal** *(COHDEFOR), main office off the road to Celaque near the junction with the road to La Campa, also provides info and maps. A* **Visitor Center** *at the foot of the trails has maps, tips, and a list of regulations. (Park open 8am-4pm. Entrance L50.)*

Looming to the west of Gracias is the 66,000-acre **Parque Nacional Celaque,** whose main attraction is **Cerro Las Minas** (2849m), the tallest peak in the country. *Celaque* means "box of water" in the local Lenca dialect, and the name is apt—the top of the mountain is a cloud forest, where rains come frequently. The journey to the peak is a long, strenuous one; it's wise to spend the night at the visitor center if not along the way. Those without the time or inclination to climb will still find plenty to see on the lower reaches of the mountain, where dense forests surround the trail and birds chatter above. The park's wildlife includes pumas and white-faced monkeys and, at higher elevations, quetzals and toucans.

Guides can be arranged by both Froni at Guancascos and Ivan at the Celaque office, but the trail is easy to follow. The guides know the area exceptionally well, but they speak only Spanish. L200 to L300 per day. Plan this a day in advance.

To conquer **Celaque** there are a few strategies. If you arrive before 4pm, either stay at the visitor center for the night or hike up and camp at the first campsite, **Don Tomás** (2½-3hr.) and then rise with the sun and get moving. This option will give you a good chance to reach the peak the next day. Otherwise, arrive from Gracias early in the morning and hike as far as you can before turning around.

Any excursion into the park will require sturdy hiking boots, a light rain jacket, and warm clothes. Bug repellent and long pants might also be useful. Stock up on food, as there's none beyond the visitor center. Ample stream water is available, but bring means of purification. There are shelters along the way, but no bedding. Restaurante Guancascos rents sleeping bags (L25) and two-person tents (L50).

Note that in addition to the route described below, the peak can also be climbed from the other side starting from the villages of **Belén Gualcho** or **San Manuel Colnonhete,** accessible by infrequent buses from Santa Rosa de Copán or by hired truck. These routes are very underdeveloped and a guide from one of the villages is necessary (L200-300 per day). These routes are considerably more difficult and require several days to make the full trip. The staff at the Proyecto Celaque Office can help plan such an adventure if you contact them in advance (see above).

THE HIKE

The road stops a half-hour's walk shy of the visitor center, at the gate and a sign welcoming you to the park. Froni, at Restaurante Guancascos (see **Gracias: Food and Accommodations,** above), rents two cabins at the end of the drivable road. Note that a house on the right of the road functions as a visitors' center on the weekends, collecting the fee and pointing you in the right direction (look for the small sign). After you go through another gate along the road 25min. later, a small path to the right leads up to Alejandrina's, where you can enjoy a home cooked meal before tackling the peak. Look for the sign that reads "*Aquí se vende comida.*"

The **Visitor Center** is a few minutes farther and marks the official entrance to the park. There is a bunkhouse, running water, latrines, and a rustic kitchen. The bunks have thin mattresses and nothing else, so bring a sleeping bag, and if you want to cook, bring your own kerosene for the stove (L10 per night). In addition to the main trail up to "el cielo," the peak of **Cerro Las Minas,** there are two shorter scenic trails. Just at the start of the trail, a sign will indicate the path **"La Ventana,"** which is a fairly easy 1hr. hike. The other trail, **"El Mirador"** is reached from the main trail past the rest area. At the trail split, head right for a 2hr. hike to the scenic overlook of waterfalls.

On the main trail, the hike to the first camp, **Don Tomás,** at 2000m, is a moderately strenuous 2-3hr. hike that first follows the Río Arcagual and then a series of switchbacks. The camp is basically a snug tin shack with mattress-less bunks, a latrine, and a firepit. Be sure to get the key if you plan to use the shack. There are also flat areas in the site to accommodate about three tents.

The next campsite, **El Naranjo,** a steep 1½- to 2½-hr. hike from Don Tomás, is not much more than a firepit, a nearby creek, and some level spots. This is the beginning of the glorious cloudforest, with towering trees covered in dripping moss. The **summit** is still another two hours away. This less-trodden portion of the trail is at times camouflaged by encroaching brush and debris; keep your eyes peeled for the bright ribbons that mark the way. From the top, enjoy a breathtaking view of the valleys below, or just imagine one through the clouds.

🏔 AGUAS TERMALES

Restaurante Guancascos and Hotel Erick in Gracias (p. 456) will take groups of up to four to the hot springs (L80). If you'd like the driver to wait and bring you back, expect to pay more (around L150). The other option is an easy 1½hr. hike (not recommendable at night). From the southwest corner of the Gracias parque central, head south toward the police station. The roads merge after five blocks; make a left at the next corner, cross the street in front of you, and you'll see the path to the springs. Go through a coffee field, across a stable hammock bridge, and continue until you hit the road again. Turn right, and the springs are just ahead. Open until 10pm every day all year long. L20.

The *aguas termales* (hot springs) provide the physical therapy necessary after romping through Celaque. Nestled in a river gulch 6.5km south of Gracias, the beautifully crafted stone pools hold crystal-clear water that reaches 38°C (100°F). The springs are very popular in the evenings with locals who eat *papas fritas* (french fries) and drink beers at the small spring-side *comedor.*

HONDURAS

SANTA ROSA DE COPÁN

First-time visitors to Santa Rosa are inevitably disappointed by the sight of the town's squalid bus station. But first impressions can be deceiving: the bus station is 1km from town, and uphill awaits a charming colonial center that's a pleasant base for exploring nearby indigenous villages and the Honduran highlands. A former tobacco center, the area still produces first-rate cigars, but the nearby countryside is now devoted to another addiction: caffeine. Coffee beans from Santa Rosa are sold nationwide and are considered among the country's finest. A festival is held Aug. 30 to honor *Santa Rosa*, the city's patron saint.

E TRANSPORTATION. A transportation hub, Santa Rosa's terminal can be a frenzied place, with bus companies competing for business. **Buses** to **San Pedro Sula** leave every half-hour (3½hr., 4am-6pm, L30; express 2½hr., 4 daily, L50). To get to **Tegucigalpa**, take any bus to San Pedro and transfer there, or look for the less frequent "Sultana" (7½hr., 5 per day, L70). Two daily direct buses go to **Copán Ruinas** (3hr., 11:30am and 12:30pm, L40), but the easiest way to get there is to catch a bus to **La Entrada** (45min., every 30min. 5:30am-5pm, L20), and connect there to the ruins (2hr., every 40 min. 7am-5pm, L23). Buses also run to: **Nueva Ocotepeque** (2½hr., every hr. 9:30am-5pm, L30); **Gracias** (1½hr., roughly every hr. 7am-4:30pm, L20); **Agua Caliente** (3hr., 7 per day, L70); **San Salvador** (daily 6:30am, US$20).

■ ⁊ ORIENTATION AND PRACTICAL INFORMATION. Buses arrive at and depart from the **terminal** on the northwest outskirts of the city, about a kilometer (L10 cab ride) from the city center. A city bus marked "urbana" goes from the terminal to the center via an hour-long loop (L1), whereas a cab ride is much shorter. Walking might sound like an attractive option, but the walk up the hill is a steep one. Once you get to **El Centro**, the city is easy to navigate and most activity clusters within a short distance of the **parque central**. The main drag, **Calle Centenario**, runs east-west along the *parque's* south side, the yellow **Cathedral of Santa Rosa** marking the *parque's* southeast corner. The *parque's* north side is uphill.

While a local Commission of Tourism is getting underway, there are several reliable sources of tourist information in town. **Warren Post**, American expatriate owner of **Pizza Pizza** (see below), is very knowledgeable. Exchange AmEx traveler's checks and American dollars at **Banco de Occidente** in the southeast corner of the *parque*. (Open M-F 8am-noon and 2-5pm, Sa 8-11:30am.) There's an **ATM** at **Banco Atlántida**, on the *parque's* south side, which accepts Visa. (Open M-F 8am-3pm, Sa 8am-11am.) Take laundry to **Super Lavandería Florencia**, 4½ blocks west of the southwest corner of the *parque* on Calle Centenario. (2hr. Full service L68 per load. Open M-Sa 8am-noon and 1:30-5pm.) The **police station** is on the *parque*. (☎662 0091, emergency 199. Open 24hr.) **Hospital de Occidente** is open 24hr. for emergencies (☎662 0112). Take Calle Centenario eight blocks west of the *parque*; turn left just before the soccer field, and head up the hill one block. The **Policlínica Santa Rosa** provides 24hr. emergency service right in town, on Calle Centenario three blocks west of the *parque* (☎662 1338). **Hondutel** has phones. (Open daily 7am-9pm.) **Zeus Cyber Café**, 2 blocks from the *parque* along Calle Centenario, plays techno while you surf the **Internet**. (☎662 3535. L20 per hr. Open M-F 8am-10pm, Sa-Su 8am-9pm.) The **post office** is on the *parque*. (☎662 0030. Open M-F 8am-noon, 2pm-4pm, Sa 8am-noon). **Postal code:** 040101.

⁊ ⊡ ACCOMMODATIONS AND FOOD. Hotel Maya Central ❷ furnishes clean, spacious rooms that include private baths. The hotel can be found three blocks west of the northwest corner of the *parque*. (☎662 0073. Singles L70, with TV and hot water L120). Another cheap option is **Hotel Continental ❺**, with well-kept rooms and a restaurant. Head 4 blocks down Calle Centenario and then 2 blocks to the right; the hotel is opposite the Esso station. (☎662 0801. Doubles with bath and TV L290.) For more style, **Hotel VIP Copán ❸**, two blocks east of the northeast corner of the *parque*, has an exquisite lobby, dark wooden ceilings, great rooms, and nice baths. (☎662 0265. Singles L140, with TV L195; doubles L280/L370.) A cheaper option is **Hotel Blanca Nieves ❷**, two blocks east and two north of the *parque's* northeast corner, where you'll pay little for an uninspiring room. (☎662 3012. Singles L60-80; doubles L120, all with common bath.)

🖾Pizza Pizza ❷, four blocks east of the southeast corner of the *parque*, bakes brick oven pizza with topping choices and a cheap L30 lunch special. (Plain cheese personal pizza L21.50. Open Th-Tu, 11:30am-9pm.) **Flamingo's ❹**, half a block south of the southeast corner of the *parque*, serves up surprisingly fancy food with superb service in a tranquil, very pink setting. (*Spaghetti flamingos al horno* L60; seafood and beef L82-100. Open W-M 11am-10pm. AmEx/V.) Local secret **La Casa Vieja ❷**, one block south and five blocks west of the *parque's* southwest corner, (in a 200 year old house) serves delicious Honduran *típico* slow-cooked in a wood oven. (*Típico* L26; *baleada* L12. Open M-Sa 8am-9pm).

🖸🖾 SIGHTS AND ACTIVITIES. Not surprisingly, Santa Rosa is yet another pleasant spot for a romantic colonial stroll. Take a peek in the yellow and white **Catedral de Santa Rosa**, on the *parque's* east side, where wooden side altars display devotional items particular to the cults of the saints. The **Flor de Copán** cigar factory hand-rolls Honduran *puros*, said to rival those of Cuba. Walk around and sniff the delicious aroma at the factory, three blocks toward the city from *la terminal*. (L30 for Spanish guided tours, open M-F 10am-2pm.) The new showroom in town, one and a half blocks west of the *parque* on Calle Centenario, sells the excellent product. (Box of 25 Corona Santa Rosa L670. Open M-F 7:30am-noon, 2pm-4:30, Sa 7:30am-noon.) At the western end of Calle Centenario past the soccer fields, climb the steps to the top of **El Cerrito** to see a Maya sculpture from AD 753.

The **Balneario Ecoturístico Las Tres Jotas (JJJ)** is a swimming spot featuring mountain spring water. The pools and cafeteria lie on the site of an old fish and tobacco farm. The *balneario* is an hour up the road toward Gracias (L10 by bus). Be sure to remind the driver when you get close. (Admission and swimming L20. Lunch L45. Open daily 7am-6:30pm.) A pleasant picnic spot with swimming on weekends is **La Montañita**, a 10min. bus ride toward Gracias (L10).

🖸 DAYTRIPS FROM SANTA ROSA. For more in-depth exploration of the countryside, **Max Elvir** of **Lenca Land Trails** (at Hotel Elvir in town) can arrange a variety of custom tours starting at around US$20 per day. Possibilities include visits to small Lenca villages, horseback tours, and hikes in Celaque National Park. Contact Max (lenca@hondutel.hn) to set up a trip or ask questions. Max's great familiarity with the area, flexibility, and eagerness make him a valuable contact.

NUEVA OCOTEPEQUE AND THE BORDER

NUEVA OCOTEPEQUE

Wiped out by a flash-flood years ago, the town of Nueva Ocotepeque (what's left of Antigua Ocotepeque) has rebuilt itself into one gigantic bus depot, largely because of its location 15km from the borders of both El Salvador and Guatemala.

🖙 TRANSPORTATION. Most buses arrive and depart along 1 Calle. Within Honduras two companies travel the same route, and both have offices on 1 Calle where the buses depart. The **San José** company has the most visible bus stop (and large sign) on 1 Calle, from where it shuttles people to the **Salvadoran border** at **El Poy** (15min., every 30min. 6am-10pm, L6); the **Guatemalan Border** at **Agua Caliente** (30min., every 30min. 6am-7pm, L10); **San Pedro Sula** (5hr., 5 per day 6:15am-1pm, L70). **Torito/Copanecos,** a half block from very visible San José on the same side of 1 Calle, runs to **San Pedro Sula** (5hr., 6 per day 10am-4:40pm, L70) with stops at **Santa Rosa de Copán** and **La Entrada,** and express to **Tegus** (7½hr.; 4, 7, 8, 8:40am; L130). A third option, **Congolón,** leaves daily for **San Pedro Sula** stopping at the major cities along the way (5hr., 7 per day 5:45am-3:30pm, L73).

■✚❷ **ORIENTATION AND PRACTICAL INFORMATION. 1 Calle** is the main drag, and stretches through the town center across the **parque central** from the church. All action and transactions take place along it. **Banco de Occidente** cashes traveler's checks into colones or quetzales, but not lempiras. (Open M-F 8:30am-4:30pm, Sa 8:30am-11:30.) Get Visa cash advances at **Banco Atlántida.** (Open M-F 8am-3pm, Sa 8-11am.) The **police station** is 1 block south and 5 blocks west of the intersection. (☎ 653 3199. Open 24hr.) Facing Banco de Occidente, walk one block left and cross the street to find a **medical clinic.** (24hr. service. Open M-F 8am-5pm, Sa 8-11am.) On the same side as the bank and one block toward the church from 1 Calle, on a side street of the parque, is **Hondutel.** (Open M-F 7:30am-7:30pm, Sa and Su 8am-6pm.) **Internet** available at **Cybermax World,** next to Hondutel. (L35 per hr. Open daily 9am-8pm.) The **post office** is one more block away from 1 Calle, on a parallel side street. (Open M-F 8am-4:45pm, Sa 8am-noon.)

❏❐ **ACCOMMODATIONS AND FOOD.** Nueva Ocotepeque is best utilized as a transit town, but there are some options if you get stranded. Finding clean, affordable accommodations can be tough, particularly if you arrive at night, as hotels fill up in the early evening. The best budget choice is **Hotel Turista ❶.** Facing the church from the *parque central,* walk two blocks to your left; it is on the corner. It has an odd layout and clean rooms of varying sizes. (☎653 3659. L40 per person, with bath L60, with TV and fan L100.) **Hotel Maya Chortis ❺,** one block further away from 1 Calle on the left, has first-class lodging at somewhat affordable prices. (☎653 3377. Singles L193, with A/C L240; doubles L339/L400.) Facing the church on 1 Calle, walk two blocks and turn left to **Hospedaje San Antonio ❶.** Cheap, relatively clean rooms. (Closes at 10pm. Singles L30, with bath L60; doubles L40/L120.)

   Comedor San Antonio ❶, on 1 Calle, provides good budget food in one of the nicest *comedores* you'll see. There's no menu, but a typical plate is L30. (Open daily 8am-7:30pm.) One block toward the *parque* from Hotel Turista is clean, well-lit **Restaurante Sandoval ❷.** (Breakfasts L30-35; dinners L60-80; beers L15. Open daily 6am-9pm. MC/V.) **Restaurante Don Chepe ❸** is in the Maya Chortis hotel. (Chicken entrees L50-L80; salads L30-L80. Open daily 7am-10pm. AmEx/MC/V.)

❌ **EL POY: BORDER WITH EL SALVADOR**

*Border open daily 6am-10pm. In El Salvador, buses run regularly to **La Palma** (30min., every 30min. 4am-8pm, ¢6), and continue on to **San Salvador** (3½hr., ¢10).*

The border at El Poy is about 10km south of Nueva Ocotepeque. Banks here accept only US dollars; money changers accept Central American currencies. There are *comedores* but no hotels on either side.

❌ **AGUA CALIENTE: BORDER WITH GUATEMALA**

*Border open daily 6am-6pm. In Guatemala, minibuses run to **Esquipulas,** where you can connect to destinations throughout the country.*

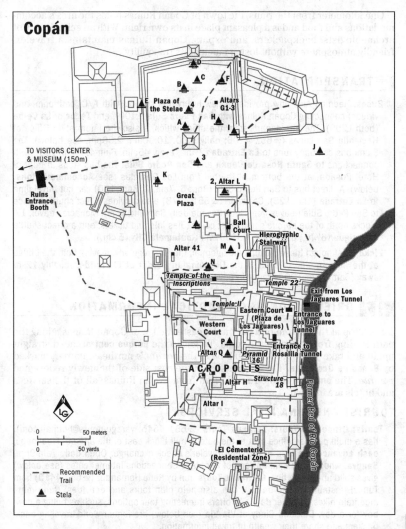

Copán

TO VISITORS CENTER
& MUSEUM (150m)

Plaza of
the Stelae

Altars
G1-3

Ruins
Entrance
Booth

Great
Plaza

2, Altar L

1

Ball
Court

Hieroglyphic
Stairway

Altar 41

Temple of the
Inscriptions

Temple 22

Temple II

Exit from Los
Jaguares Tunnel

Eastern Court
(Plaza de
Los Jaguares)

Entrance to
Los Jaguares
Tunnel

Western
Court

Altar Q

Entrance to
Rosalila Tunnel

Pyramid
16

A C R O P O L I S

Altar H

Structure
18

Altar I

Former Bed of Río Copán

0   50 meters

0   50 yards

- - - Recommended
      Trail

▲   Stela

The crossing into Guatemala is 16km from Nueva Ocotepeque, with **banks** (open
M-F 8am-4pm, Sa-Su 8am-1:3-pm), money changers, and a few lodging options if
you're stuck. **Hospedaje Hermanos Ramírez ❷** will take you in for L60.

COPÁN RUINS

Situated in a deep valley hidden by mountains, the otherworldly ruins of Copán
are a special link in the chain of ancient Maya centers that sweeps south from the
Yucatán. While some Maya ruins —notably Guatemala's Tikal— are larger, no site
can match Copán's magnificently detailed carvings of imposing deities and rulers.

One kilometer from the ruins, the town of Copán Ruinas holds the area's accommodations and food and is a pleasant place in its own right. With an eclectic mix of archaeologists, backpackers, and expats, Copán Ruinas maintains a traveler-friendly atmosphere without losing much of its tranquility.

⌐ TRANSPORTATION

Buses: Hedman Alas now provides a new luxury **bus** service (with A/C, bathroom, and videos) connecting Copán Ruinas with **San Pedro Sula** (L100), and **Tegus** or **La Ceiba** (both L200). The bus departs from the office which is also the Information Office of Hacienda San Lucas (☎651 4106; daily 5:30, 10:30am, 2:30pm, see below). The Etumi bus company runs to **La Entrada** (2½hr., every 45min. 6am-4:30pm, L23), with connections to **Santa Rosa de Copán** and **San Pedro Sula**. The bus stops in front of Hotel Posada, at the bottom of the hill from Los Gemelas (see **Accommodations,** below). A direct bus to San Pedro Sula (3hr.; 6, 7am, 2, 3pm; L60) can cut travel time to **La Entrada** (1hr., L25). Casasola (☎651 4078) also provides direct shuttle service to San Pedro Sula (leaves from Hotel Posada daily 8am and 2pm). Monacras travel, 1½ blocks north of the *parque's* northeast corner, has info and tickets, and a direct shuttle to **Antigua** (6½hr., daily 2am, US$30) via **Guatemala City** (5½hr.).

Pickups: Although these pickups are informal, they run regularly, leaving from the bridge at the western side of town to the **Guatemalan Border at El Florido,** roughly 12km away (6am04pm, L20, arrange in advance).

✳❼ ORIENTATION AND PRACTICAL INFORMATION

Buses stop at the bottom of a hill on the eastern edge of Copán Ruinas, along the path leading from town to the ruins. To get to the **parque central,** head straight uphill and take your first left; you'll be at the *parque's* northeast corner, marked by **Banco de Occidente.** The church sits on the east side of the newly redesigned *parque.* The **entrance** to the ruins is 1km from Copán Ruinas; all of the services and hotels are in town.

TOURIST AND FINANCIAL SERVICES

Tourist Office and Tours: Yaragua Tours (☎651 4645; yaraguatours@hotmail.com), has a multi-purpose office next to the hotel a half block east of the *parque.* Free maps, **cash advances** on Visa or MC and traveler's check exchange. Open daily 7am-9pm. **Sandra,** who can be found at one of her Maya Connections Internet cafes (see below) gives solid up-to-date tips. **Go Native Tours,** run by René Hernandez (☎651 4410) from Tunkel Restaurant (see below), can also help plan tours and activities. René rents mountain bikes (L25 per day) and offers interesting tour options, such as being a cowboy for a day. Dirk and Cindy at **Via Via** (see below) are former world-traveling backpackers and share their wealth of travel information.

Banks: Banco de Occidente, on the *parque's* northeast corner, cashes traveler's checks. Open M-F 8am-4:30pm, Sa 8-11:30am. Visa advances at **Banco Atlántida,** on the *parque's* south side. Open M-F 8am-3pm, Sa 8-11am. **Banco Credomatic,** along the street to the right of the church off the *parque,* has an AmEx/MC **ATM.** Open daily 8am-9pm. Establishments around town will buy and sell Guatemalan quetzals, but the border has better rates.

LOCAL SERVICES

Laundry: Maya Connections, either location (see **Internet**). L8 per lb. for a 5hr. wash, dry, and fold. Open daily 8am-6pm.

EMERGENCY AND COMMUNICATIONS

Police: FUSEP (☎651 4060), 1½ blocks west of the northwest corner of the *parque.* Open 24hr. Outpost stationed on road to the ruins.

Pharmacy: Farmacia Ángel (☎651 4603). A block south of the *parque.* Open daily 8am-9pm.

Medical Services: Dr. Luis Castro (☎651 4504), next to the Banco de Occidente at the northeast corner of the *parque.* English spoken. Open M-Sa 8am-noon and 2-4:30pm.

Telephones: Hondutel (☎651 4004), a half block south of the *parque's* southwest corner. Open daily 7am-9pm.

Internet: By far the cheapest is **Internet Copán;** facing the church, walk one block right, then turn right and walk another two blocks. L25 per hr. Open daily 8:30am-9pm. There are more computers at **Maya Connections,** with one location in **Los Gemelos Hotel** (see **Accommodations,** below) and another 1½ blocks south of the *parque's* southwest corner. L0.70 per min., 10min. minimum. Open daily 8am-9pm.

Post Office: Honducor (☎651 4447) a half block west of the southwest corner of the *parque.* Open M-F 8am-4pm, Sa 8am-noon. **Postal code:** 040401.

▐ ACCOMMODATIONS

Local kids on the street or at the border may try to steer you away from your desired hotel to a friend's guest house by claiming the hotel is more expensive than it really is; take their advice with a grain (or a shaker) of salt.

▓ **Hostel Iguana Azul** (☎651 4620; casadecafe@mayanet.hn). From the park's southwest corner go south 1 block, go right (north) 5 blocks, then turn left again toward the blue building. A welcome change of pace for the road-weary, with great hot showers (communal) and comfy beds. Bunks L65 per person; singles L100; doubles L150. ❷

▓ **Los Gemelos** (☎651 4077), take the 1st left half a block south of the bus stop. A traveler favorite for its friendly service, low prices, central location, and clean, simple rooms. The courtyard, a botanical sedative, is a great place to meet other travelers. Checkout 10am; storage is free. Singles L70; doubles L100; triples L150. ❷

▓ **Vin Vin Copán** (☎651 4652; copan.honduras@viaviacafe.com; www.viaviacafe.com). From the *parque,* walk half a block past the town hall on its left-hand side. Vin Vin's new Belgian managers are extremely helpful and keenly attuned to the needs of both backpackers and families. English spoken. Vegetarian cafe attached. (Dorms L65; singles with bath L145; doubles with bath L190.) ❷

Posada Honduras (☎651 4082). Just north of Gemelos on the same block. Standard issue, with clean rooms and baths. Large, open courtyard lacks personality. Singles L50, with bath L100; doubles L70/L120. ❶

Hotel California (☎651 4314), across from Los Gemelos. Spacious, bamboo-decorated rooms surround a leafy courtyard with an outdoor sitting area and restaurant specializing in pizza. Hot common bath. Check out anytime. Singles L80; doubles L140; triples L150. Check out anytime. ❷

Hotel San José (☎651 4472), up the hill to the left facing the church 1 block, then left 1½ blocks. Clean, cheap rooms and common baths. Singles L60; doubles L100. ❷

Hotel Clásico Copán (☎651 4040), down the hill past Banco de Occidente 1 block and then right half a block. High ceilings and hot showers make the higher price worth it. Singles and doubles L150 with bath. ❸

◐◑ FOOD AND NIGHTLIFE

▩ **Carnitas Nia Lola,** 2 blocks south of the southwest corner of the *parque,* at the end of the street. Some of the best food and music in town. Locals highly recommend *pinchos* (kabobs, L95), chicken tacos (L30), and free nachos with meal order. Happy Hour kicks off Copán nightlife (6:30-8pm with 2-for-1 margaritas). There's a book exchange. ❷

▩ **Vamos a Ver,** half a block south of the southwest corner of the *parque.* Friendly Dutch couple serves hard-to-find delicacies like fresh baked bread. Vegetarian choices. Sandwiches L30-50; muesli and fruit L35; lasagna L70. Open daily 7am-10pm. ❷

Tunkul Restaurante and Bar, 1½ blocks west of the *parque's* southwest corner, just past Via Via (see below). The place to see and be seen in Copán, whether you're gringo, expat, or local. Friendly owners play host to the town's nightlife during happy hour (7-8pm until closing, usually midnight). Delicious rum punch L30 all night. Kitchen serves good variety, including a vegetarian plate (L50), chicken fajitas (L80), and chef salad. Open daily 7am-10pm. AmEx/MC/V. ❷

Llama del Bosque, across from Tunkul, has been a Copán institution for the last 22 years. Excellent service and plates of hearty Honduran fare in a classy locale. Quick breakfasts. Meat dishes (L85), *arroz con pollo* (L60). Open daily 6:30am-10pm. ❷

Via Via Café, just in front of the hotel of the same name (see **Accommodations,** above.). Vegetarian Owners specialize in vegetarian cuisine. Veggie burgers L60; chili *sin carne* L60. Open daily 8am-10pm. ❷

◉ SIGHTS

IN TOWN. The Copán Museum, on the *parque* across from the church, contains very detailed information on countless aspects of Maya civilizations. If you can read Spanish, it's worth a visit. (Open M-Sa, L31.) The **Galería de Arte** displays and sells magnificent artwork and hand-made items by Honduran artists. The gallery can be found two blocks south of the *parque's* southwestern corner. (Open daily 8am-noon and 2pm-7pm. AmEx/MC/V.)

OUT OF TOWN. For a change of pace, slip out of town to visit the new **Enchanted Wings Butterfly House,** where a 3400 sq. ft. greenhouse is the home to exotic plants and zillions of butterflies. The owners are also adding an orchid exhibition. For a little enchantment, leave town on the road to Guatemala, pass the cemetery on your left and continue straight for about 10min. (Open daily 8am-5pm. L50.)

◉ THE RUINS OF COPÁN

*The main entrance to the ruins is a 15min. walk from town via an elevated walkway running left of the "road to La Entrada" (east out of town). Las Sepulturas archaeological site is a few kilometers farther along. The **Visitor Center** at the main entrance houses the ticket booth, a small exhibition on the site's history, a desk to arrange for guides, and is where you purchase all tickets. The fabulous **Museum of Maya Sculpture** is near the entrance, to the right of the visitors center. The main site is open daily 8am-4pm. Ruins and Las Sepulturas US$10, Museum of Maya Sculpture US$5, both tunnels US$12, two-hour guided tour with a certified, multilingual guide US$20.*

Although the ruins of Copán are not one of the peaceful sites of Central America, once stained with the blood of human sacrifice and now swarming with tourists, a visit to them will certainly be a highlight of any trip. Diego García de Palacio, who informed the Spanish crown in 1576 of the site, was the first known European to see it. Palacio remarked that the city was built "with such skill that it seems it could never have been made by people as coarse as the inhabitants of this province." In 1834, Spaniard Juan Galindo visited the ruins and drew the first map, sparking the interest of Americans John L. Stephens and Frederick Catherwood, whose 1841 book *Incidents of Travel in Central America, Chiapas, and the Yucatán* brought the ruins to the attention of the world. In 1891, the first archaeological study of the site was made, and today, Copán stands as the most studied city in the Maya world and has been designated a world heritage site by UNESCO.

HISTORY. Called Xukpi by the Maya for the ubiquitous, black-crowned mot-mot bird, Copán was first inhabited nearly 2000 years ago. This theocratic society was highly stratified, deeply symbolic, and focused on tradition. Though situated in a fertile valley well-suited for corn cultivation, Copán grew slowly. The city's Golden Age was between AD 553 and 800, when a series of strong rulers expanded their power. Under Smoke Jaguar (AD 628-695), the 12th of Copán's 16 kings, the city grew into a military powerhouse. Next came ruler 18 Rabbit (AD 695-738), who left an impressive legacy, but was captured. The Great Plaza, the Ballcourt, and Temple 22 earned 18 Rabbit the title of "King of the Arts." 18 Rabbit was succeeded by Smoke Monkey, who ruled Copán for only 11 years (AD 738-749). The reign of Smoke Monkey's son, Smoke Shell (AD 749-763), was marked by an unprecedented cultural and intellectual growth. During his reign, Maya astronomers met at Copán to pool their research on eclipses. The elaborate hieroglyphic stairway was also built under his supervision. It is thought that Smoke Shell's energy was focused on recovering Copán's pride after the assassination of 18 Rabbit.

Although Smoke Shell's successor Yax-Pac (AD 763-820) built the version of the Acropolis visible today as well as the famed Altar Q, the glory days were coming to an end. For reasons not entirely clear to archaeologists, Copán, like the rest of the Maya world, ceased to be agriculturally self-sufficient and began to decline around AD 900. With a population of 20,000 people forced to rely on foodstuffs shipped down the Copán River by satellite settlements, Copán's power waned, and by about AD 1100, the jungle began to reclaim the city.

INSIDE THE COMPLEX. More detailed information about the ruins is available in a booklet entitled *History Carved in Stone*, available in the gift shop (L60) or for less in souvenir shops in town. For the full experience, hire one of the many uniformed **guides** who wait at the visitor center (US$20). Antonio Ríos (or "Tony Rivers"), the very first guide at Copán, and Juan Marroquín are highly recommended English speaking guides. One restaurant, **Cafetería Rosalila,** to the right as you enter, serves burgers, sandwiches (L30), bottled water, and ice cream (L16).

THE MAIN SITE. The following lists the major buildings and altars in a roughly counter-clockwise order, heading to the right from the entrance booth.

THE WEST COURT AND THE RESIDENTIAL ZONE. Temple II was constructed by Yax-Pac as his channel to the supernatural world. **Altar Q,** (a replica) outlines the Copán dynasty with each of the 16 rulers occupying his own glyph. **El Cementerio (The Residential Zone).** The original theory was that these structures were ruins of burial grounds, but it is now believed that this was a residential area for the elites because of its proximity to the sacred temples and plazas.

THE EAST COURT (PLAZA OF THE JAGUARS). Structure 18 was built as the tomb for Yax-Pac, in the "Temple of the Rain." The discovery of this tomb revealed that rulers weren't buried communally with their families, but in a sacred location. **Jaguar Sculpture,** a symbol of courage and greatness, overlooks the Plaza of the Jaguars, where the dance of the jaguar was practiced to honor the governor, seated at Temple 22. **Pyramid 16** was built on top of other monuments, specifically Rosalila Temple, as a temple to the god of death, war, and sacrifice. **Temple 22,** built by 18 Rabbit, has some of Copán's most intricate carvings and elaborate symbolism. Used as the seat of the ruler in front of the plaza, the plateau reflects the mouth of a serpent; the top step has teeth carvings and the two curly structures indicate a tongue. The square arch, set at the top of the temple, depicts the life cycle. A male leg can be discerned on the right; representations of random body parts are scattered over the top of the arch; a female leg, umbilical cord and baby's head are carved on the left. The skulls on the base step clearly depict death.

TUNNELS. Admission to the **Rosalila Tunnel** and **Los Jaguares Tunnel** is extra—get your tickets at the entrance. Excavations found Rosalila Tunnel to be the best preserved underground temple. Built in AD 571, it honors the Sun God and the sacredness in which it was held is shown by the fact that it wasn't destroyed and replaced by subsequent rulers. Visible from the tunnel, carvings on the temple's facade, including a two-headed serpent. The Los Jaguares tunnel displays a tomb with side niches for offerings, macaw masks honoring the god of brilliance, and a hieroglyphic stair that serves as a dedication plaque. There is evidence of an advanced draining system and the only private bath in all Maya civilizations.

THE GREAT PLAZA. Hieroglyphic Stairway, Copán's most famous sight, is the longest known text of hieroglyphic writing in the Americas. The intricate carvings and inscriptions on the 63 steps depict the genealogy of Copán's rulers and the city's history from its mythical beginnings through the reign of its 15th ruler, Smoke Shell. **Stela M** recounts a solar eclipse in AD 756. **Temple of the Inscriptions** is an ancient astronomical lab. Don't miss the **Ball Court,** a grassy space between two sloping walls where a ballgame was played gladiator-style. Three Macaw heads are perched on each side. Both teams had the object of hitting the heads with the ball in order to defeat the forces of evil and perpetuate the life cycle. The "winner" would frequently be sacrificed. **Plaza of the Stelae** holds the altars in the plaza, which are surrounded by the ruins of a massive stadium. **Stela C** has the face of a young, unbearded man on one side, and an old man on the other, yet another symbol of the life cycle. **Stela A** seems to be the site of human sacrifices. The sculpture is of a man dressed in his ballgame attire.

OTHER ATTRACTIONS

MUSEUM OF MAYA SCULPTURE. The large, red-roofed building by the site entrance is a splendid museum that will give you an informed perspective on the ruins; you may want to come here before entering the site. Unique in the Americas, the massive complex was built to house and protect the park's most precious sculptures from the area's moisture and temperature fluctuations. Several important stelae and altars have already been relocated inside the museum and replicas left in their place in the ruins. Of these, a highlight is the famed **Altar Q,** encircled by the likenesses of 16 elaborately-costumed rulers of Copán. The centerpiece of the museum, however, is a full-sized, brightly-painted replica of **Rosalila,** a temple found buried beneath Structure 16 with all of its original paint and carvings intact. The replica suggests how flamboyant and colorful Copán truly was in its heyday.

LAS SEPULTURAS. A nearby site that is getting an invigorating reexamination, Las Sepulturas is about 2km beyond the main site on the main road from Copán Ruinas. Las Sepulturas (tombs) are not too aptly named; they were actually a residential appendage to Copán for Maya *nouveau riche*. Although it has been extensively uncovered and reconstructed, its platforms don't cause as much open-mouthed awe as the mountains to the south. Still, they've sparked a small frenzy among archaeologists intrigued with the social stratification of the Copán dynasty.

When approaching the site on foot, take the small trail rather than the dirt vehicle road. It winds through pleasant green foliage before opening up to the first series of residential dwellings. As indicated by the low-lying platforms, these were used by commoners. As you continue, buildings get taller and culminate with the residences of the elite and the impressive scribe's palace. *(Admission to Las Sepulturas is included with admission to the ruins.)*

NEAR COPÁN

▶️ LOS SAPOS

To walk to the Hacienda from Copán Ruinas, head south from the parque on the street in front of the church; stay to the right and not toward the carwash. Cross the river, turn left, and then follow the road along the river, which eventually curves right up the hill (stay right). Facing the church, turn left and walk straight about two blocks up the hill to the Hacienda's **information center** *(☎651 4106; open daily 9am-5pm). They offer round-trips on horses (US$10). Lunch at the hacienda is L50, and they also run a* **shuttle** *to San Lucas for unlimited time (US$16). Renting a horse from one of the boys who roam the parque can be a cheaper option, but the scrawny horses can be expensive. The L30 entrance fee is for using the facilities, but is included in the package trips run by the information center.*

One small piece of the Copán story, Los Sapos (The Toads) sits on the town's outlying hills, about a 30min. walk from town. A group of rock outcroppings are believed to have served as a birthing site for Maya women. The stones are carved with what seem to be images of toads, Maya symbols of fertility, as well as what many claim is the image of a pregnant woman. Some archaeologists have declared that the pregnant woman is not a woman at all, but an abnormally well-endowed man holding a perforator for self-sacrifice. You decide.

The stones sit on the grounds of the **Hacienda San Lucas ❺**, a beautifully restored *hacienda* with views overlooking the entire valley and the Copán ruins. The property also includes a network of trails and a small waterfall. Meals and lodging are available at the *hacienda*. (☎651 4106; sanlucas@honduras.com. Singles US$50; doubles US$70.) Stroll or horseback ride around the *hacienda*, and relax in the hammocks at dusk on the candle-lit front porch.

▶️ POOLS AND CAVES

The hot springs are open daily 8am-8pm, L20. Both **Vamos a Ver** *and* **Yaragua Tours** *organize trips (tours daily 2pm. US$10 per person.) Dirk at* **ViaVia** *can arrange for a truck to take a group. (L700 round-trip; most people stay about 2hr.) Caving trips are led by* **Go Native Tours** *(US$35 per person, 3 person min.) and* **Yaragua Tours** *(US$80 per group of up to 8).*

A respite from civilizations past and present can be found at the **hot springs** 23km north of town. There are several caves near town, but you must hire a guide to access them. A good option is to explore the extensive cave system and underground river of **Cueva de Boqueron**, 23km from town. Since a November 2001 machete attack at the Ruby Waterfall, no company organizes tours there. It is unsafe to visit without armed guards.

▶️ EL FLORIDO: BORDER WITH GUATEMALA

Border open daily 6am-6pm. Pickups run back and forth until 5pm (L20-30, arrange in advance). In Guatemala, buses run to **Chiquimula,** *50km away (every hr. until 6pm).*

This generally hassle-free crossing is just 12km from Copán. Monarcas in Copán Ruinas runs a direct shuttle to Guatemala City (see **Transportation,** p. 438). Another

FROM THE ROAD

THE MIDAS TOUCH

A Greek friend of mine recently pointed out what he jokingly calls the United States' "Hand Tax," i.e. anything touched by hand or handmade automatically quadruples in price. Upon arriving in Honduras, it was difficult not to notice some of the advantages of living in a country with relatively inexpensive labor: the corn tortillas are made on the same day they are eaten; freshly picked mangos beat out "Value meals" any day.

Frustrated by the notorious trappings of the developing world (an overcrowded bus that ran an hour and a half late, drivers' intimate relationships with their car horns, and the everyday adventure that is crossing a city street), I found myself longing for a quiet suburban evening draining my brain in front of cable TV. Then I walked into my first *barbería* (barber shop). Hanging on a wall, below a cross, was the most ingenious, welcoming sign I had seen all day:

Haircut L30
Shave L30
Massage L30.

For under US$6, I pampered myself with over half an hour of air-conditioned bliss. Like most things, these little treats shouldn't be overdone or they will lose their special appeal (and I can't see myself needing too many more haircuts in my next two months here anyway), but it was amazing how a little attention rubbed away the day's frustrations.

—**Daniel Elizondo**

alternative route to Guatemala is via Agua Calientes near Nueva Ocotepeque (see p. 461). Those entering Honduras just for Copán who would normally need a visa may obtain a 72hr. pass at the border but must exit Honduras from this town.

CARIBBEAN COAST

Honduras's long, hot Caribbean coastline is lined by great beaches, beautiful national parks, wildlife reserves, and old Spanish forts, interspersed with tiny Garífuna villages and La Ceiba's urban center. There's the backpacker favorite, Tela; the Caribbean hub Puerto Cortés; and the gateway to La Mosquitia, Trujillo. The region has a gregarious Caribbean atmosphere that's a world away from the rest of the country and English or Creole are as likely to be heard as Spanish.

The 17th century saw this region marred by the African slave trade. As slaves escaped or were emancipated, they intermarried with South American indigenous people. Their descendants built fishing communities along the northern shores, with a distinctive culture and language. Today the **Garífuna**, (as they came to be called) are one of the fastest-growing ethnic groups in Central America. Their thatched-roof villages, dugout canoes, and colorful *punta* music are among the most captivating highlights of the Caribbean coast.

SAN PEDRO SULA

Although it was long a sleepy provincial town, modern San Pedro Sula (pop. 415,000) is Honduras's major industrial city. The Coca-Cola sign conspicuously erected on the mountains that fringe the city's dramatic western edge serves as a constant reminder of its economic bent. *Maquiladoras*, foreign-owned factories made profitable by the low wages paid to its workers, have popped up along the city's well-maintained highway system. Still, despite its recent industrial awakening, San Pedro has a relaxed air that makes it an ideal gateway to either the ancient Maya ruins at Copán or the pristine beaches of the Caribbean. A recent crackdown has reduced crime, easily avoided by using taxis and standard caution at night.

▉ TRANSPORTATION

Flights: Villeda Morales International Airport is 15km out of town. It is best to take a taxi to and from the airport. **Continental** (☎557 4141; fax 552 9766) and **American** (☎558 0518) fly to the US. **Isleña Airlines** (☎552 8335; fax 552 8322) flies to **La Ceiba**

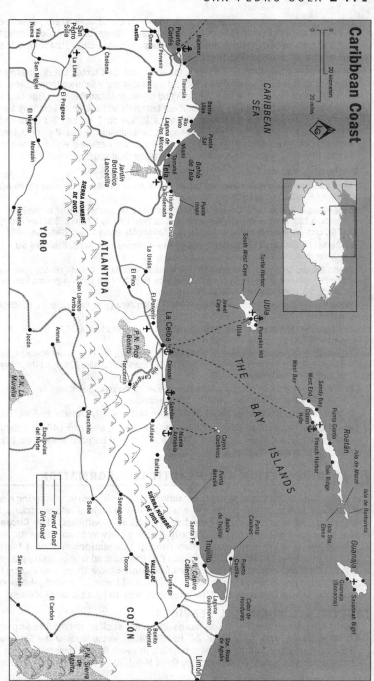

Caribbean Coast

0 —— 20 kilometers
0 —— 20 miles

CARIBBEAN SEA

THE BAY ISLANDS

Puerto Cortés · Bajamar
Castle · Omoa · El Porvenir
San Pedro Sula · Travesia
Villa Nueva · Baracoa
San Miguel · Choloma
La Lima · Berú Ulúa
El Progreso · Río Tinto · Punta Sal
El Negrito · Miami · Bahía de Tela
Morazán · Tornabé · Tela
Habana · Triunfo de la Cruz · Punta Izopo
La Ensenada

YORO

ATLANTIDA

SIERRA NOMBRE DE DIOS

Jardín Botánico Lancetilla

La Unión
El Pino
San Lorenzo Arriba
El Porvenir
P.N. La Muralla
Arenal
Jocón
P.N. Pico Bonito
Toncontín
La Ceiba · Corozal
Río Cangrejal
Esquipulas del Norte
Olanchito
Sambo Creek
Jutiapa
Nueva Armenia
Balfate
Cayos Cochinos
Sonaguera
SIERRA NOMBRE DE DIOS
Saba
Santa Fe
Tocoa
Punta Betulia
Bahía de Trujillo
Punta Caxinas
Trujillo
VALLE DE AGUAN
Calentura
P.N. Capiro
Puerto Castilla
Cabo de Honduras
Laguna Guaimoreto
Durango
Santa Rosa de Aguán
San Esteban
El Carbón
Bonito Oriental
P.N. Sierra de Agalta
Limón
COLÓN

Utila
Turtle Harbor
South West Caye
Jewel Caye
Pumpkin Hill
West Bay
West End · Sandy Bay · Punta Gorda
Coxen Hole · French Harbor
Oak Ridge · Roatán
Isla de Morat
Isla Sta. Elena
Isla de Barbareta
Guanaja (Bonacca)
Savannah Bight

Paved Road
Dirt Road

HONDURAS

(20min.; 8:30am and 2pm; one-way L380, round-trip L646), from where you will need to connect to go to **Roatán** (1¼hr.; take La Ceiba and change; one-way L667; round-trip L1220). **Taca** (☎550 2640) heads to **Tegucigalpa** (25min.; 6:55, 10:45am, 4:15pm; one-way L476, round-trip L953).

Buses: Most bus terminals are located in the southwest (SO) sector, but discovering the exact location of each terminal can be tough, as some are little more than parking lots with temporary wooden shacks in the back and no easily discernible signs. The best way to get bus information is to go to any of these terminals and ask which company travels the route you want. **Chicken buses** run from a station on 1 Av. and 2-3 Calle on the slightly sketchier side of the tracks. It is best to travel during the day. If you must make a connection between terminals at night, cabs are strongly advised even for a few short blocks; otherwise, you could arrive with less luggage than you began with.

Destinations include:

Agua Caliente (Guatemalan border): Impala school buses (☎553 3111) depart from Av. 2, Calles 4/5, SO. (7hr., every 20min. 5am-7pm, L65.)

Copán Ruinas: Bus to Santa Rosa de Copán, get off at La Entrada for transfer to Copán Ruinas. (2½ hr., L12.) Direct service with Transgama (☎552 2861), Av. 6/7, Calle 6, SO (7am and 3pm, L60); Empresa Norteña (☎552 2145), Av. 6/7 Calle 6, SO. (every 90min. 8am-3pm, L60.)

La Ceiba: Catista-Tupsa (☎552 1042 or 550 5199) departs from Av. 2, Calle 5/6 SO. (3hr., 5:50am-6pm, L51.)

Puerto Cortés: CITUL mini buses (☎553 0070) depart from Av. 6, Calles 7/8, SO. (1hr., every 15min. 5:30am-8:30pm, L15.) Expresos Del Caribe (☎553 0456) sends large vans from Av. 7, Calle 9, SO. (Every 10min. 5:10am-7pm, L15.)

Santa Rosa de Copán: Toritos school buses (☎553 4930) depart from Calles 8/9, Av. 6, SO. (4hr. every 25min. 4am-5:15pm, L25.)

San Salvador (El Salvador): King Quality (☎553 4547) departs from Av. 7/8, Calle 6, SO. 1st class with A/C. (1 per day 6:30am.)

Tegucigalpa: Empresa Norteña(☎552 2145), Av. 6/7, Calle 6, SO. (4hr., every 90min. 6:30am-4:30pm, L45.) El Rey motorcoaches (☎550 8952) depart Av. 7, Calles 5/6, SO. (4hr., every hr. on the half hr. 5:30am-6:30pm, L70.)

Tela: Catisa-Tupsa school buses and old motor coaches via **Progreso** depart from Av. 2, Calles 5/6, SO. (Tela 2hr., La Ceiba 3hr.; every hr. 5:50am-6pm.)

Trujillo: Cotraipbal school buses (☎557 8470) depart Av. 1, Calles 7/8. (8hr., 6am-4pm, L90.)

Local Transportation: Taxi rides within the city are L30-40, after dark L40-60. Establish a price beforehand. Taxis are generally safe and should be used around the city at night, even for short distances.

◼◪ ORIENTATION AND PRACTICAL INFORMATION

San Pedro Sula is organized along the standard grid, with *avenidas* running north and south and *calles* running east and west. The city is divided into quadrants: **NO** (northwest), **NE** (northeast), **SO** (southwest), and **SE** (southeast). The **Circunvalación,** a fast-food infused commercial strip, forms a beltway around the city, with highways to other cities radiating away from it. Bus stations and most budget hotels are southwest of the *parque*. Locals call the railroad tracks running alongside Av. 1 "la línea" and advise tourists not to venture across them even during the day. They also recommend that you not go south of Calle 7. The neighborhoods north of the *parque central*, near the museums, tend to be a bit more affluent.

TOURIST AND FINANCIAL SERVICES

Tourist Information: San Pedro Sula has no official tourist office, but the friendly people at **Maya Tropic Tours,** Calle 1, Av. 2-3 (☎552 2405), in the lobby of the Gran Hotel Sula by the *parque*, will help budget travelers in need, though their tours are a bit beyond budget bounds. English spoken. Open M-F 7:30-11:30am and 1:30-5:30pm,

Sa 7:30-11:30am. Extensive info on Honduras's national parks is available only in Spanish at the **Museo de la Naturaleza Biocentro** (see **Sights** below).

Travel Agency: Agencies are scattered throughout the city and especially near the *parque*. Tickets and flight info available at **Astro Tour,** Calle 2, Av. 5/6 (☎552 5649). Open M-F 8am-12:30pm and 2-5pm, Sa 8am-12:30pm. Try also **Mundirama,** Calle 2, Av. 2/3 (☎553 0142). Open M-F 8am-5pm, Sa 8am-noon.

Consulates: UK, Av. 13, Calles 10/12, SO (☎557 2046; fax 552 9764). Open M-F 8am-noon. There is no US consulate in San Pedro Sula.

Banks: Banco Atlantida, on the corner of the *parque*. Cashes traveler's checks and gives cash advances on Visa cards, but be sure to ask if you need to have your check endorsed at a separate desk before going to the teller. At a separate entrance facing the *parque* you can access an **ATM.** Open M-F 9am-3pm, Sa 9am-noon. **Creditlan,** Av. 3, Calles 1/2, NO, gives cash advances on Visa cards. Open M-F 8:30am-5pm, Sa 8:30am-noon. **Banco Credomática,** Av. 5, Calle 2, NO, has an **ATM** for Cirrus and AmEx cards.

LOCAL SERVICES

English Bookstore: Coello Bookstore, Av. 9, Calle 4, SO. Stocks only a handful of used English paperbacks and an eclectic Spanish collection that is well worth a browse. Open M-F 8am-noon and 1:30-5:30pm, Sa 8am-noon.

Laundromat: Lavandería Almich, Calle 5a, Av. 9/10, SO. Wash and dry service L5 per lb. Open M-F 7:30-11:30am and 1-5pm, Sa 8am-2pm.

EMERGENCY AND COMMUNICATIONS

Emergency Numbers: ☎199. Fire ☎198.

Police: Av. 3, Calles 9/10, SO (☎552 3171). Open 24hr.

Pharmacies: To find out which pharmacy is open late or on weekends, call the operator (☎192). **Clínica Ferraro** (☎557 6438) in Barrio Medina on Calles 12 and 13 has a 24hr. pharmacy. The massive **Superfarmacia Simón** (☎553 0321), at Calle 5 and Av. 6, SO, is extremely comprehensive. Open M-Sa 8am-5:30pm, Su 8am-noon.

Hospital: Centro Médico de Emergencias, Av. 11, Calles 5/6 (☎553 1214).

Telephones: Hondutel, Av. 4, Calle 4 (☎557 2222; fax 550 2252). Friendly representatives of AT&T Direct and Sprint compete for your business in the main lobby. Both companies have special calling card booths. **Fax** available. Open daily 8am-4pm. Phone booths around town use 20- and 50-cent coins. 3min. local phone calls cost 50 cents.

Internet: Internet Más, Av. 8, Calle 5, SO (☎550 5736), is the best deal in town at only L15 per hr. Open M-Sa 8am-9pm, Su 10am-9pm. **Informática Gerencial de Honduras,** at the south end of the *parque central* in the "Gran Villa" building (☎550 1307) provides most computer services for L25 per hr. Open daily 8am-8pm.

Post Office: Av. 3, Calles 9/10, SO, next to police station. Open daily 8am-4pm. **Express mail** next door at **E.M.S. Honduras.** Open M-F 8am-7pm, Sa 8am-noon.

◤ ACCOMMODATIONS

In the sticky, sweltering heat of San Pedro, fans are a must. The SO quadrant, where most of San Pedro's bus terminals lie, also contains a number of "bargain" *hospedajes* with lumpy beds, rank communal bathrooms, and daily outages of electricity and water at cut rates. Before committing to these understandably cheap deals, be sure to ask around and inspect them.

Hotel San José, Av. 6, Calles 5/6, SO (☎557 1208). The attentive proprietors maintain the relatively spacious rooms exceptionally well. Front door locked 11:30pm-5am; call ahead to arrange check-in during these times. Singles with double bed L112, with A/C

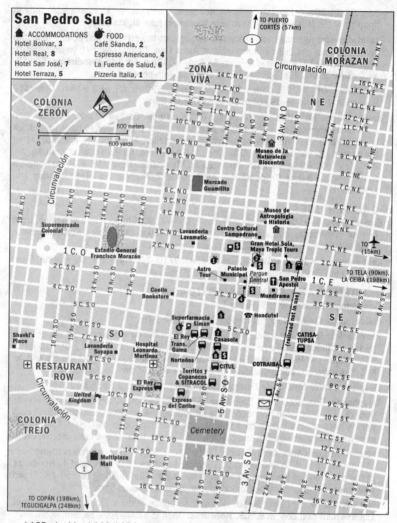

San Pedro Sula

🏠 ACCOMMODATIONS 🍴 FOOD

Hotel Bolívar, **3** Café Skandia, **2**
Hotel Real, **8** Espresso Americano, **4**
Hotel San José, **7** La Fuente de Salud, **6**
Hotel Terraza, **5** Pizzería Italia, **1**

L168; doubles L140/L196; triples L168/L252. Married couples pay single rate, so get hitched to your travel partner. ❸

Hotel Real, Av. 6, Calles 6/7, SO (☎ 550 7929). Family run and very professional. Clean rooms surround a welcoming courtyard with comfy couches and a TV. Singles with double bed and fan L150, with A/C and cable L230; doubles with A/C and cable L300. ❹

Hotel Terraza, Av. 6, Calles 4/5, SO (☎ 550 3108). Rooms vary in size so make sure to check yours out first. The hotel boasts hot water and a telephone. Additional perks include a pitcher of iced water and clean towels delivered fresh to the room every day. Singles L100, with A/C L350; doubles L265/L350. ❸

HONDURAS

Hotel Bolivar, Av. 2, Calle 2, NO (☎ 553 3224). This mid-range hotel situated just a block from the central park is ideal for families. All rooms have A/C. Wet bar off the patio overlooking the pool. English spoken. Singles and doubles L525; triples L600. ❺

🍴 FOOD

After *fútbol*, San Pedro's favorite pastime seems to be eating, and the streets are lined with restaurants and food stands. Although much of the food is expensive, careful *mochileros* (backpackers) can squeeze by on cheap local food. For a fast-food fix, head to the cluster of US chains at Av. 4 and Calle 3, SO. Fresh fruit of varying quality can be found just about anywhere in the *centro;* the best selection is at the **Mercado Guamilito,** Calle 6, Av. 8/9, NO. Aptly named **Restaurant Row,** on the southwestern stretch of the Circunvalación, has sit-down places both casual and elegant. Also, at the corner of Calle 1 and Circunvalación on the western side you can find **Supermercado Colonial** with a wide selection of items.

Pizzería Italia, Av. 7, Calle 1, NO serves a wide variety of flavors on a crispy, thin crust pizza. A much welcomed frigid A/C and fresh-squeezed juices refresh the weary after a day in the San Pedro heat. Ham and sausage pizza L62, veggie L88, lasagna L60. Open daily 10am-10pm. ❸

Café Skandia, in the lobby of Best Western. 1950s Americana with a Honduran twist. Eat at palm-shaded outdoor tables. Hamburgers L38, apple pie L18. Open 24hr. ❷

La Fuente de Salud, Av. 8, Calles 5/6, SO. Natural-remedies clinic and a vegetarian paradise all just a short walk from most hotels. Vegan *típico* L15, tofu sandwich L5. Open Su-F 11:30am-1pm. Bakery open 7am-6pm. ❶

Espresso Americano, at the south end of the *parque central.* Locals and visitors alike enjoy the entire range of hot and cold caffeinated beverages, like cappuccinos (L9) and frappuccinos (L14), in this large and air-conditioned cafe. Open M-Sa 6:30am-7pm. ❶

👁 SIGHTS

From Mayan pottery to honey-covered women, San Pedro Sula has enough to occupy inquisitive minds. For a respite from the museums, get lost in the crowd at the *parque central* or catch a local soccer game at the stadium.

▩ MUSEO DE ANTROPOLOGÍA E HISTORIA. San Pedro's pride and joy is its new museum of anthropology and history, a favorite among local kids. The modern building has both permanent and temporary exhibit spaces, a library, and a massive theater. The highlight is the museum's top floor, which displays an impressive collection of pre-Columbian pottery and artifacts, some dating back more than 2500 years. Most exhibits are translated into English. Allow 1-2hr. for a visit, and be sure to ask the receptionist about any cultural events taking place in the theater. The lush, edenic grounds merit some meandering on their own, and the outdoor cafeteria cooks up Honduran cuisine at attractive prices. (Av. 3, Calles 3/4, NO. ☎ 557 1496. Open M and W 9am-4pm, Su 9am-3pm. Closed Tu. L10, students with ID and children L5, seniors L2. Free 1st Su of every month.)

ASOCIACIÓN NACIONAL DE ARTESANOS DE HONDURAS. Besides being a good source of traditional food, the *Mercado Guamilito* houses the best Honduran artisan's market. Wander through the maze of handmade carvings and ceramics and watch traditional Honduran food be prepared before your eyes. For better quality goods at slightly higher prices, cross the road to *Casa del Sol.* Be ready to bargain at both places. (Av. 8/9, Calle 6, NO. Asociación open M-Sa 7am-5pm, Su 7am-noon. Casa del Sol open M-Sa 8:30am-6:30pm, Su 8am-noon.)

MUSEO DE LA NATURALEZA BIOCENTRO. The resourceful, English-speaking curator does the best she can with an apparent lack of funding for this museum on Calle 9, NO. Ecotourists will find the information on local flora and fauna helpful. In addition, curiosity-seekers will get a kick out of one of the biggest collections of pickled reptiles in Honduras. *(Open M-F 8am-5pm, Sa 8am-noon. L10.)*

CENTRO CULTURAL SANPEDRANO. The center has both permanent and rotating gallery space which display traditional San Pedro handicraft as well as slightly more contemporary work, two theaters, and a public library. The theaters regularly host dramatic performances, with tickets starting at L40; call for schedule information. *(☎553 3911. Calle 3, Av. 3/4. Open M-F 9am-noon and 1-6pm, Sa 9am-noon.)*

GETTING COVERED WITH HONEY. Sorry, guys, this one's for women only: a 1hr. massage is given by the all-women Seventh Day Adventists at the La Fuente de Salud (see **Food** above). The massages include a rubdown with lotion or stickier honey, which supposedly softens the skin. Health advice and other treatments are also available. *(Massages begin at 8am. Come early. Showers available. L50.)*

📷🎵 NIGHTLIFE AND ENTERTAINMENT

In the evening, San Pedro's chic set heads out to the *zona viva* **discotecas** on the western half of the Circunvalación. All have a minimal dress code (no shorts, t-shirts, or sandals), and it's standard to be frisked upon entry. Recent regulation that closes all bars and restaurants at 10:30pm and forces all minors to be inside has made evening entertainment much safer for both locals and visitors. Women should be warned that city bars are fertile breeding grounds for *machismo*, and everyone should be aware that San Pedro Sula can still be dangerous at night. Taxis are strongly recommended. Stay with a group you trust.

The place to go for the young and restless of San Pedro Sula is **Confetti's,** on Circunvalación near the Puerto Cortés exit, which shakes it to modern Latin and North American disco hits. (Beer L25. Cover L60. W ladies' night. Open Tu-Su 7pm-dawn or until the last dancer drops.) **Henry's,** just a few blocks west on the Circunvalación, offers a similar scene at identical prices but attracts a slightly older crowd. **Sr. Frogs** (no relation to the Mexican beach resort standard) has three bars and a patio, along with a small bonanza of activities including beach volleyball, foosball, pool, and sports via satellite for those who want to do more than dance. At the Tegucigalpa exit, **La Costa Bar and Grill** spins modern pop hits on a semi-open-air top level, while the bottom floor serves up snacks and drinks. Nearby at Av. 18 and Calle 8, SO, **Shauki's Place,** an upscale restaurant, has a bar under the stars in a beautiful, lush courtyard. With a more laid-back atmosphere, this is a good option for women who would like to avoid being badgered. (Open M-Sa 4pm.)

FESTIVAL: FERIA JUNIANA

San Pedro Sula is nationally famous for its **Feria Juniana** (Fair of June), which begins with a bang in the early morning on June 1 and culminates in the last week of the month. Dating back to 1846, the festival features *Garífuna* dancers, drum corps, and pre-teen beauty queens parading down the street. During the last two weekends, vendors and booths stay open late and a bevy of musical groups keeps the streets throbbing well into the wee hours. Don't forget to check out the tractor pull and rodeo events at the suburban fairgrounds (ask a taxi driver to show you; L60). The last night is traditionally *carnaval*, so grab a cardboard mask and join in, but keep your belongings somewhere safe. Some locals warn tourists against hanging out too late during the fair, especially in areas outside the main drag.

PUERTO CORTÉS

Puerto Cortés, Honduras's largest port, is situated on a deep, natural harbor 64km north of San Pedro Sula. Although visiting Puerto Cortés is most convenient for travelers planning boat trips to Belize or the Garífuna communities, the *parque central* and new waterfront park are pleasant perches for watching the constant commerce of the free trade port. Puerto Cortés is also an easy jump to the fort at Omoa or to the Guatemalan border crossing at Corinto.

TRANSPORTATION. Buses cluster in the area off the northwest corner of the *parque central* on Av. 3/4, and Calles 3/4. Impala buses run to **San Pedro Sula** (1hr., every 10min. 4:30am-10pm, L15) from their station on Av. 4, Calles 3/4, one block north and half a block west of the *parque*. Direct buses to the beach of **Omoa** leave behind the Esso station on Calle 3, Av. 3/4 (45min., every 30min. 6am-7pm, L6). CITRAL buses marked "Frontera de Guatemala" head to the **border crossing** at **Corinto** from a station 1½ blocks north of the Esso station (2½hr., every hr. 6am-4pm, L22). **Tela**-bound travelers should take a bus to San Pedro Sula and then a bus to Progreso. From there, grab a bus to Tela. An alternate way to get to Tela is the rusty old **train** that departs from the *laguna* (4hr., F and Su 7am, L50).

Departing from the *laguna* are two regularly scheduled **boats** to Belize; boats depart irregularly to ports all over the Americas from here, so ask at the docks for upcoming trips. One boat, Gulfa Cruza (☎665 5556), leaves for Belize (M 12pm), stopping at **Big Creek** (2hr.), **Placencia** (3hr.), and **Belize City** (3½hr.), with prices starting at L670. The other boat heads to **Dangriga** (Tu 11am, L600). To get to the *laguna*, either take a taxi or catch the local bus headed east from the northwest corner of the *parque*, next to Pizza Hut (L3). For both boats, you must be at the port by 8am the day of departure. It is a good idea to stop by the *laguna* the day before and talk to someone at the *comedores* on the far side of the bridge to make sure the boat is making the trip. Improved overland routes through Corinto have eliminated the regularly scheduled boats to Guatemala.

ORIENTATION. Puerto Cortés occupies a peninsula surrounded by the Caribbean to the north and west, the Bahía de Cortés to the south, and the inland *laguna* to the southeast. The docks, recognizable by the loading cranes, line the south side of downtown. *Avenidas* run east-west, parallel to the docks, starting with Av. 1 and increasing numerically as you head north away from the docks. *Calles* run perpendicular to the *avenidas*, and their numbers increase from west to east. The large *parque central* sits on Av. 2/3, Calles 4/5. Buses generally arrive on Av. 4, leaving passengers one block south of the *parque*.

PRACTICAL INFORMATION. The **immigration office** lies 3½ blocks west of the northeast corner of the *parque* (Open M-Sa 8am-12pm and 2-5pm) For provisions, head to **Supermercado Riga** on the southwest corner of the *parque* (Open M-Sa 7am-7pm, Su 8am-12:30pm). Change currency and traveler's checks at **Banco de Occidente,** Av. 3 and Calle 4 off the northwest corner of the *parque*. (Open M-F 8:30am-4:30pm, Sa 8am-noon.) **Banco Ficensa,** one block west of the southwest corner of the *parque*, has an ATM accepting American Express and MasterCard. (Open M-F 8:30am-4pm, Sa 8am-noon.) A Visa ATM is at **Banco Atlántida,** half a block back toward the *parque* from Ficensa. (Open M-F 9am-4pm, Sa 9am-noon.) The **police** (☎665 0420 or 665 1023) are at Av. 1 and Calle 9 in the southeast part of town. **Hospital Cemeco,** Av. 4/5, Calle 8 (☎665 0460 or 665 0057), three blocks east and two blocks north of the *parque*, is open 24hr. with an English-speaking doctor on call. An **ambulance** is also available (☎665 2439 or 997 9267). Different **pharmacies** take turns staying open until 10pm; check the list posted at any pharmacy. **Internet access** is available at **Rudon's Cyber Mundo,** Av. 1/2, Calle 3. Though slow,

FROM THE ROAD

FÚTBOL FANÁTICOS

By day it is an animal grazing pasture, by night a sea of strobing fireflies, and around 4pm everyday, it's a soccer field. All across the country, Honduran communities gather in the afternoon around the largest patch of flat land they can find to play soccer until the ball can no longer be seen. Goals vary from sticks connected at the top by a string to shoes and rocks dotting the ground. Nothing is regulation, and shinguards, let alone shoes, are not an option. Sometimes two friends with oppositely dominant feet will split a pair of shoes to spread the wealth" and lessen the pain. Little to no attempt is made to dodge the plate-size piles of cow pie bespeckling the field, and this even adds another element to the game as players slip and collide across el campo. Males, either too young or too old to play, linger along the sides, occasionally attempting to referee the mayhem. Talent levels vary drastically, and foreigners are welcome to play, but regarded with skepticism when passing the ball up the field. As an American sports-a-holic, I can enjoy a different professional sport's championship series practically every week of the year on TV. However, there is something about these motley afternoon pick-up games that is so much more alluring—and fun.

—Jeremiah Johnson

prices beat most other cities at L20 per hr. Open daily 8am-11pm, Su noon-11pm. The **post office** and **EMS express mail** share a building on Calle 1 between Av. 1 and 2 (open M-F 8am-4:30pm), with **Hondutel** (☎665 0010; fax 665 0017; open daily 7am-8:30pm).

⚏⚏ ACCOMMODATIONS AND FOOD. Stick to the more reputable hotels near the center of town for a full-night stay (as opposed to the hourly rate). Many visitors skip town to spend the night in either San Pedro or Omoa, just 45min. away. All rooms at **Hotel El Centro ❹**, Av. 3, Calles 2/3, have newly painted and well-maintained rooms with TV, private baths, and a fan. (Singles L170; doubles L280; matrimonial L200.) The **Formosa Hotel ❷**, Av. 3, Calles 1/2, three blocks west of the *parque*, has adequate rooms in long hallways. (☎665 0853. Singles with bath and fan L92, with TV L174, with TV and A/C L225; basic doubles L232; quads L224, A/C and TV extra.). In either hotel, try for a breezier upstairs room to get away from the noise and traffic of downtown. **Hospedaje San Juan ❶**, located next to Hotel El Centro on Av. 3, is the cheapest lodging in town. Rooms are small, poorly lit, and plain, but for the budget traveler, it's ideal. (Singles L50; doubles L80.)

Restaurants in Puerto Cortés are sprinkled around the *parque;* some of the best line Av. 2. **La Cabaña ❸**, one block east down Av. 2, serves up Honduran shish kebabs, or *pinchos* (L80-90), seafood soup (L80), and rice with shrimp for L100. (Open M-Th 10am-7pm; F-Sa 10am-2am.) **La Familia ❷**, Av. 1/2, Calle 5, serves many tasty Garífuna and Honduran dishes from simple sandwiches (L35-60) to complete seafood dinners (L70). From the Wendy's on the corner of the *parque*, pass the pharmacy on the corner and continue up the street a few steps past the *comedor* with 7-Up decoration to find Pepsi-decorated La Familia. **Restaurante Pekin ❷**, one block east of the *parque* on Av. 2, serves up dinners to please hungry travelers (L60-120). **Licuados Gladys ❶**, a good place on the south side of the *parque*, refreshes with smooth *licuados* for L10-15. Open M-Sa 6am-7pm. **Golosinas Alex's ❶**, hidden down a green tunnel-like hallway from Av. 3 between Calle 3/4, offers some of Honduras's most varied and best-tasting *típico* treats. (L5-L16. Open daily 6am-9pm.) Go to **Cinemas Vicente** for an English film with Spanish subtitles. Shows at 3, 6:30, and 9pm daily; L20.

OMOA

Situated on the tranquil Bahía de Omoa and cradled by the striking Merendón mountains, the idyllic fishing village of Omoa (pop. 2500) oozes relaxation. The massive Fortaleza de San Fernando de

Omoa, an 18th-century Spanish fort, is the best-known attraction, but the town is quickly becoming a popular tourist stopover for a variety of other reasons. The beach is a great place to kick back and go for a swim, and on the weekends, barefoot *fútbol* takes over. Two spectacular waterfalls are just a short hike from the beach. Both the locals and the expats who run the hostels are good sources of information on the land crossing to Guatemala, which is a short bus ride from Omoa. But beware: a two-day stopover in Omoa can easily extend to two weeks of hiking and catching rays.

☐ TRANSPORTATION. Get to Omoa by **bus** from Puerto Cortés. Note that only buses marked "Omoa" will go all the way to the beach; others (often marked "Frontera") drop you off 1km away along the main highway. Buses leave the beach for **Puerto Cortés** every 5-10min., but from the main road about every 20min. (45min., 6am-8pm, L6). Sunday buses only pass on the main road. If you're heading back to **San Pedro Sula**, hop a bus back to Cortés, and get off at the Texaco station just outside of town, where express vans to San Pedro stop every 10min. (1hr., 7am-7pm, L15). For details on crossing the border into Guatemala (see p. 481).

☐ ☑ ORIENTATION AND PRACTICAL INFORMATION. Omoa is a one-road town; a single road connects the highway from Puerto Cortés to the beach, snaking by the *fortaleza* along the way. At the beach, a road lined with restaurants and hotels follows the curve of the bay. The town center sits at the intersection of the highway and the road to the beach, which is 1km from the center of town.

For **tourist information,** talk to Roli at **Roli's Place** (see **Accommodations,** below). It is easier to find him in the evenings. **Banco de Occidente** has caught wind of backpacker bucks and now has a small office seated at the junction with the main road, 1km from the beach, where you can exchange traveler's checks and quetzales. (Open M-F 8:30am-4:30pm, Sa 8:30am-noon.) **Laundry** services are available at Roli's for L5 per lb. and Hotel Bahía de Omoa for L40 per load. Also, the **Clínica Médica Omoa,** next door to the pharmacy, can help with minor surgical emergencies. There's a **pharmacy** by the bank at the main junction. (☎658 9198. Open M-Sa 8am-6pm, Su 8am-2pm.) At the municipal building, across from the Texaco station near the junction, there is a **Hondutel** office. Along the beach, there's also a pay phone in front of the Hotel Bahía de Omoa. **Sunset Playa** offers **Internet** access (L2 per min.). Access is also available at Roli's from 4-7pm, but only for guests. The **post office** is near the Hondutel office. (Open M-F 8am-4pm.)

☐ ACCOMMODATIONS. Omoa, a hidden secret currently being discovered, was known as a backpacker haven with no high-dollar tourists or pesky taxis. As the plans for docks to support cruise ships developed, however, tension heightened between ideologically and economically conflicting interests. Nevertheless, the town is still largely unscathed and will be for a few more years. **☑Roli's Place ❶,** on the dirt road just before it hits the beach, is owned by a wise and warm veteran backpacker and sits on shady, lush grounds. In addition to Roli's free travel advice, free Internet access (5min. free with dorm rooms, 10 min. with rooms, L2 per min. after), and reasonable money exchange, guests get a cheap, comfortable place to stay with a common kitchen, free use of bikes and kayaks, free drinking water, a ping-pong table, a horseshoe pit, a dartboard, and a communal guitar. Bring mosquito netting. (☎658 9082. Hammocks L40; camping L30 per person; dorms L60; doubles L140.) **Pía's Place ❶,** advertised as being "on the beach," but actually about 30m away, offers free bikes, fishing rods, and kitchen access in its charming wooden cabin with ocean views from its porch-side hammocks. (Dorms

L40; doubles L110.) The Dutch-German couple who own Pía's Place also offer budget luxury next door at the **Hotel Bahía de Omoa ❺**. As you face the beach, the two are located next to each other on the left. Bahía de Omoa will make you feel at home in very nice rooms and private bathrooms complete with big bathtubs and hot water. There is a TV in the common room and A/C is available. (Singles L250, extra person L50.) **Hotel Tatiana ❸**, with a huge, well-maintained lawn and spotless rooms, is a more private backpacker joint. Rooms have powerful industrial-like fans and private bathrooms. L150 for one large or two beds for 1-3 people. **Tucán Eco Café ❷**, the hip newcomer across from Roli's, serves delicious French food at reasonable prices and offers similar room rates. Camping and kitchens are available. Enjoy crepes, wine, quiche, and singles for L80 or doubles for L140.

[] FOOD. A number of good restaurants have recently sprung up along the beach. With excellent seafood and panoramic views of the bay, these are ideal places to spend a relaxing evening. The best restaurants are on your right as you come to the beach. A little farther down, American-owned expat hangout **Stanley's Restaurante ❷** serves the best burgers and fries in town (L45), but locals flock for the *"sopa marinera"* filled with enough shrimp, lobster, crab, and fish for two people. (*sopa* L145. Open daily 9am-10pm.) For the cheapest eats on the beach, go where the locals go: **La Galera del Capo ❷**, next to Stanley's (L30-60). The **Sunset Playa Resort ❷**, a Canadian/US bar found by taking a right when you hit the beach and taking the left fork where the pavement ends, serves cheap food (*pescado* L40; tacos and pizza slices L15 each; Omoa Iced Tea L50; vegetarian nachos L35. Open F-Sa 2pm-1am.) For a splurge, **Flamingo's ❸**, a wonderful restaurant sitting high off the ground and overlooking the bay, is both well-decorated and delicious. The hammocks underneath are like a dessert of their own. Chicken (L70-80) and their famous Flamingo's rice with lobster, shrimp, and fish (L150) complement the atmosphere. (Open daily 8am-10pm.)

◙ ▶ SIGHTS AND OUTDOOR ACTIVITIES. Although the sea has long since receded and the Fortaleza de San Fernando de Omoa no longer sits directly on the water, its imposing presence is still captivating. The best-preserved Spanish fort in Honduras, this national monument was built between 1759 and 1775 to protect gold and silver shipments from buccaneers and the British navy, and it remains in good shape. It could have done a better job; the feisty Brits seized the fort for five months in 1779, and some 40 years later, famed pirate Luis Aury had a brief but glorious command of it. Once the foreign threat dissipated, the fortress's energies were turned to the "enemies" within. In the first half of the 20th century, its damp, dark cellars held the political prisoners of the Honduran government. Today, the newly remodeled museum noticeably glosses over this dubious episode in the fortress's past. Take a gander at the exhibits about pirates past as you wander among their swords and rifles. (Open M-F 8am-4pm, Sa-Su 9am-5pm; L20.)

Roli's Place (see **Accommodations,** above) offers **bike rental** (L50 per day) and **kayak rental** (L40 per day) for non-guests. Hotel Bahía de Omoa rents small **sailboats** and **surfboards.** Visit David at the Sunset Playa Resort (see above) for **birdwatching** tours to spot toucans, kingfishers, and other birds in the nearby forest.

Those wanting a little more adventure can take a short hike up to either of the two **waterfalls** nearby. Both have refreshing swimming holes and are located up the dirt road on the left-hand side of the main intersection. The closer of the two falls is about a 45min. hike from the beach; the second one is about a 15min. longer. Both hikes involve walking up the river a bit, so wear shoes that can get wet—pristine waterfalls surrounded by impossibly dense walls of lush greenery await you. The entering waterfall and exiting river seem like an island paradise disconnected with the rest of the world. Climbing up the waterfall provides an exhilarating, if dangerous experience. Successful attempts reward climbers with massages under the constantly cascading natural masseuse. To get there, take the road next to the bank and go right at the fork. When you reach the river, walk alongside until the trail ends and then trek upstream hopping between river rocks. The large waterfall is just around the corner from the first small one. From the bank, the walk takes 30-45 min.

✖ CORINTO: BORDER WITH GUATEMALA

Direct buses marked "Frontera Guatemala" head to Corinto from Omoa's main road (about every hour 6am-4pm. From there, you'll have to grab a pickup for the last 3km to the border, where buses head to Puerto Barrios, Guatemala (L10). It will take about 4hr. to get from Omoa to Puerto Barrios. In heavy rains, the crossing may be delayed or not possible; the road on the Honduras side is still being upgraded and buses must traverse a couple of small rivers. Guatemala entrance fee L20.

In Corinto, money changers stand next to the immigration center. There is a posted (yet conveniently not very visible) list of countries that need not pay the entrance fee, but the guards regularly try to charge everyone. Note that the "jungle trail" and boat crossings to Guatemala are no longer widely used. For up-to-date information on crossing, check with Roland Gussmann at Roli's Place in Omoa.

TELA

Halfway between San Pedro Sula and La Ceiba on the Caribbean coast, Tela is a former banana-growing center tucked between two nature preserves and a mountain range. The United Fruit Company has left behind some pleasant reminders of its short reign; it built the Hotel Villas Telamar, with unrivaled access to beautiful beaches, and the Lancetilla Botanical Gardens, both of which are major tourist attractions. Nearby outdoor opportunities and very traditional Garífuna villages have revealed to Tela's helpful residents the town's ever-increasing tourism potential. Due to recent unemployment, caused in part by Hurricane Mitch, street crime has been more present, but as businesses have been rebuilding and rehiring, crime has settled down. Nonetheless, common sense is important when exploring the town, especially after sunset.

⫟ TRANSPORTATION

Bus: Buses leave from Terminal Empresa de Transportes CITY, LTDA, at Av. 9, Calle 9, for **La Ceiba** (2hr. 20min., every 25min. 4:10am-6pm, L19) and **El Progreso** (1¾hr., every 25min. 4:30am-6pm, L13). For **San Pedro Sula,** head to El Progreso; buses to San Pedro depart from there until 6pm. To catch a direct bus to San Pedro Sula, try to flag one down from the main highway. Buses for **Triunfo** (1hr., every 30min. 6am-6pm, L8) and **Tornabé** (1hr., every 30min. 6am-6pm, L7) depart from Calle 10, Av. 8, 2½ blocks east of the *parque.*

Train: A loud, rusty train, one of the last in Central America, chugs to **Puerto Cortés** from the outdated and rundown station 3 blocks south of the *parque's* southeast corner (4hr., F and Su 1:45pm, L50).

◪ ⛵ ORIENTATION AND PRACTICAL INFORMATION

While navigating around Tela, remember that the sea is always north. The city is divided in two by the Río Tela. East of the river is Tela Vieja; west of the river is Tela Nueva. As in most Honduran cities, *Calles* run east and west and *Avenidas* run north and south. Calle 11 runs east to the beach, and Av. 1 begins just east of the Río Tela. The main drag is Calle 9, which forms the southern edge of the *parque central* lying between Av. 5 and 6.

Tourist Information: Alejandro D'Agostine, the enthusiastic president of the Tela Board of Tourism, is happy to share information with visitors. Though he speaks little English, his associate is often available to translate. Ask for him at **Garífuna Tours,** Calle 9, Av. 4/5 (☎/fax. 448 1069; garifuna@hondutel.hn). **PROLANSATE,** across the street and a few blocks west, is the organization that administers the national parks near Tela. It provides information about the preservation of the local environment and sells somewhat legible maps and nice pamphlets of nearby nature preserves (L1). Open M-F 7am-noon and 2-5pm, Sa 7-11am.

Banks: BGA, Av. 3, Calle 9, cashes traveler's checks. Open M-F 8:30am-3pm, Sa 8:30-11:30am. **Banco Atlántida,** across the street from BGA. Accepts Visa. Open M-F 8:30am-3:30pm, Sa 8:30-11:30am.

Bike Rental: Garífuna Tours rents **mountain bikes** (L75 per half day, L85 per day) from Mango Café. **Villas Telamar** also rents bikes for L20 per hr.

Police: DIC Av. 7, Calle 11 (☎/fax 448 2888), at the *ministerio público*. Open 24hr. **FUSEP** at the east end of Av. 7 (☎448 2079), follow the street uphill to the 1st left.

Red Cross: ☎448 2121.

Medical Services: Head to **Centro Médico Cristiano,** Av. 9, Calles 7/8 (☎448 2456. 24hr. Emergency ☎199.). Some doctors speak English. Open 24hr. Dr. Cristina Rodríguez at **Clínica Médica Suyapa** (☎448 2682, emergency ☎448 2685), half a block south of Calle 9 before the bridge. Open M-F 1-6pm, Sa 8am-noon.

Telephones: Hondutel (☎448 2063; fax 448 2942) is 2 blocks south and 1 block west of the *parque* on Av. 4, next to the post office. **Fax** available. Open daily 8am-8pm.

Internet: Available at **Garífuna Tours** (garifuna@hondutel.hn), for L30 per hr. Similar rates can be found at **Mango Café** and **Maya Vista.**

Post Office: A white building 1 block west and 2 blocks south of the *parque* on Av. 4. Open M-F 8am-3pm, Sa 8am-noon.

Postal Code: 31301.

ACCOMMODATIONS

Hotel Atlántida, Calle 8, Av. 5/6. Gigantic, spotless doubles with fans and tiled bath. Owner Juan Chávez and his grandchildren make gracious hosts. Singles L100, L50 per additional person. ❸

Boarding House Sara (☎448 1477), 1 block north and 2 blocks west of the *parque* on Calle 11, evokes memories of a childhood tree house. Popular with backpackers. Ask for a front room with a balcony view of the sea. The bathrooms are basic, and the nightclub across the street is noisy. Kitchen facilities available at a small cost. Pre-ordered meals L22. Rooms L50 per person, group and longer stay rates available. ❶

Hotel Sinai, Av. 6, Calles 6NE/5NE (☎448 1486). Six blocks from the beach in front of the train station, is cozy and tranquil. Singles L80, with private bath L150, and A/C L200; doubles L120/L200/L260. ❷

Hotel Mi Porvenir, Calle 9, Av. 8. With a little bargaining, this hotel with small rooms and communal baths can become the cheapest in town. Make sure you can sleep with bugs as it's a necessity here. Singles L50 (drop to L40); doubles L100 (drop to L80). ❶

M@ngo Hotel, Calle 8, Av 5/6. This bed and breakfast provides large clean rooms and a choice of American or *típico* breakfast at M@ngo Cafe. Hot water. Singles with private baths L170 per person, with TV L260; doubles L250/L350. ❹

FOOD AND ENTERTAINMENT

M@ngo Café, on the ground floor of the Museo Garífuna, at the west end of Calle 8. Aura, the chef, serves mouth-watering 3-course gourmet meals, ranging from traditional

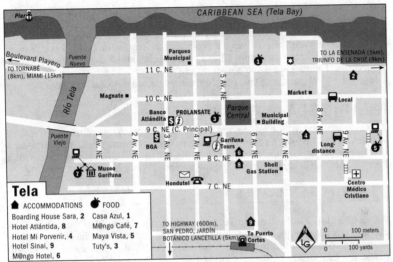

Tela

▲ ACCOMMODATIONS
Boarding House Sara, **2**
Hotel Atlántida, **8**
Hotel Mi Porvenir, **4**
Hotel Sinai, **9**
M@ngo Hotel, **6**

🍴 FOOD
Casa Azul, **1**
M@ngo Café, **7**
Maya Vista, **5**
Tuty's, **3**

Garífuna to Italian, for unbelievably low prices (L39-89). The lasagna is outstanding. Open M-Sa 8am-10pm, Su 7am-10am. ❷

Maya Vista, take Calle 8 east past the bus station to the crest of the hill, make a left, and continue to the top. Dig into a delicious entree (starting at L55) while savoring the unparalleled 30mi. panoramic views. Indeed, the view alone is well worth a visit, especially on a clear day. The building's amazing architecture and well-placed hammocks round out the perfection. Open Tu-Su 9am-9pm. ❷**Tuty's,** on Av. 9, across from Garífuna Tours. Huge breakfasts (L32) and delicious mango *licuados* (L10-14) make this a local favorite. *Taco de pollo* (L18) makes a tasty and inexpensive lunch. Open daily 7am-10pm. ❶

Casa Azul, one block north and 1 block east of the *parque central*. The bright art gallery and large collection of books welcome locals and visitors to generous portions of Italian food with especially good garlic bread. Personal pizzas with lots of toppings (L30, L5 per topping). Open W-M 4pm-midnight. ❷

Slow during the week, Tela transforms itself on the weekends from sleepy beach town to party central. Although the clubs directly alongside the beach may look like a good time, their clientele are often armed and aggressive; and it's best to steer clear, or at least ask around first. For more safety, try **Delfín** (at the Hotel Villas Telamar) where you can boogie barefoot to modern Latin pop right on the beach in a huge gazebo. Entry is free, though drinks cost an arm and a leg. Saturday nights fill **Gecko's** with a mix of locals and visitors that dance to anything from *merengue* to techno. Walk to the far end of Calle 9; it is opposite the Puente Viejo. Finally, **Magnate,** Av. 2, near Calle 11, offers modern hits, a massive dance floor, and a relatively safe environment with Christmas lights strung up for atmosphere.

👁 🏞 SIGHTS AND OUTDOOR ACTIVITIES

The beauty of Tela's public **beaches** is that there are few reasons to move a muscle. But don't bring anything you wouldn't want to lose. For more secure lounging, head to the patrolled shores in front of the Hotel Villas Telemar in Tela Nueva just past the dock. The beaches are free to customers of any store or restaurant in the facility. The pool and jacuzzi cost L50 on weekdays and L100 on weekends. The golf course is L150 per hour and the tennis courts are off limits to non-guests. The hotel also rents **horses** (L50 per hr.) and **bikes** (L20 per hr.). To get above it all, climb up to the mirador at Maya Vista (see **Food,** above) for a bird's eye view of the area. Garífuna Tours also offers package trips to **Roatán** for US$174 per person. This includes all transportation (flying) for 2 nights and 3 days at the air conditioned Hotel Pura Vida. Dive packages are available and an extra night can be added for $36. Minimum of two people required. Inquire at Garífuna Tours.

NEAR TELA

Tela is a springboard for some great adventures. A trip to one of several Garífuna villages offers a peek at a traditional culture and some quiet beach time. Nearby outdoor opportunities include the Lancetilla Botanical Gardens, the spectacular Parque Nacional Jeanette Kawas and the untamed Punta Izopo Reserve.

▶ GARÍFUNA VILLAGES

WEST OF TELA. To the west lie Tornabé and Miami. About 8km from Tela, **Tornabé** is accessible by bus or bike along the coastal dirt road and has a few restaurants and rooms rented by families for around L50. Much more beautiful and rustic, the tiny village of **Miami** is located another 7km west of Tornabé, on a spit of land no wider than 50m. Blue, Caribbean waves crash on the bright white shore to one side and a small lagoon laps gently on the other. Miami looks the way most Garífuna villages looked 50 years ago, with thatched huts and cooking fires. Delicious traditional foods (L45-50) are cooked by a family near the incongruous new PROLANSATE office, which gives out maps and tourist info on the area's national parks. Ask at the restaurant for a place to sling your hammock. *(Buses to Miami leave M-F from Av. 8/9, Calle 10.)*

EAST OF TELA. The villages of La Enseñada and Triunfo de la Cruz sit to the east of Tela. The smaller of the two and easiest villages to reach, **La Enseñada** is a perfect place to be lazy. A multitude of locals flock here on weekends, and there are eateries and a couple of small hotels. **Budani ❷,** has doubles with fans and private bath for L100. **Hotel Mirtha ❷,** located right at the entrance to the town, offers similar rooms without private baths for L100. The *champas* (huts) ❶ by the beach are mainly open on weekends and serve delicious fresh grilled fish and conch soup for around L70. Dozens are lined along the fluffy white and clean beaches inviting visitors to stay a little longer. Farther from Tela, **Triunfo de la Cruz** is the largest and most developed Garífuna village, yet the beginnings of urban influence have already begun to take their toll. The beaches aren't very safe at night, and they aren't the cleanest around either. Still, several hotels and rooms are available in town for around L70 a night, and restaurants are easy to find. Though some huts are being replaced by concrete boxes, and a ritzy luxury resort is currently under construction, thatched roofs still dominate the beach. The **Playas Miramar Restaurant ❷,** near the west end of town, serves delicious and authentic Garífuna seafood (L50 and up). Closer to the town's center but still on the beach, **Arenas "disco"** plays *punta* music for a large Garífuna crowd. Drinks L12).

To get to **villages** east of Tela, take an enjoyable 2hr. stroll along the beach from Tela to La Enseñada. If you're alone, however, it's safer to take a taxi from Tela (10min., L50) or rent a bike and travel on the main road. On the road, head toward La Ceiba for 5km until you find the dirt road that forks left to La Enseñada, and after 1km, forks right to Triunfo. Buses run to Triunfo, and any La Ceiba bus can drop you off at these junctures. Leave enough time to get back to Tela by nightfall.

BEEP BEEP! Whenever a traveler visits a new area, he or she should expect to encounter many new customs. Honduras is no exception, and in addition to the rich historical influences, there are also a few modern cultural idiosyncrasies. In Honduras, the *bocina* (car/bus horn) serves as a means of communication between drivers and pedestrians. Besides its manufactured intent of warning and alerting other drivers, pedestrians, or animals, the horn also has a language of its own. Two short blows by a bus means hello to a passing bus while a short blow followed by a long blow is a call buses make when passing through a town alerting residents of its arrival. Drivers alert all pedestrians as they pass with two short blows or a little tune on their custom made horn. Despite the direction you are walking, what deterring hand motions you make, or whether you just turned down three taxis, there will be at least five more honkings. So, the next time you're in Honduras don't just practice your Spanish; listen for the beeps.

⚑ LANCETILLA BOTANICAL GARDENS

*The gardens are 6km from Tela. Rent a bike (check the brakes) or take a taxi to get there (L40-70). Entrance on the left side of the main road toward El Progreso and San Pedro Sula. Take Av. 2 out of town to the highway, turn right, and look for the signs. Alternatively, hop on any bus headed for El Progreso and get off at the gate (inform the driver of your plans in advance). A taxi from Tela to the gate costs L10, L50 to the park. From the gate, the park is 3.5km away along a dirt road. Once you see buildings, head for the small house on the right—it's the **Visitors Center**, with maps and info in Spanish and English. Refreshment stands are inside. The **Administrative Center** (beyond the bamboo tunnel) answers questions and gives short tours and permission to camp in the park. For more info, contact COHDEFOR (☎ 448 2165) or ESNACIFOR (448-1740). Open daily 8am-3pm. Admission US$6. Tours are free M-Th but F-Su they are L50 per guide. English spoken. A self-guided tour via an informative pamphlet is another option (L5).*

Easily accessible from Tela, the Lancetilla Botanical Gardens were developed by the United Fruit Company in 1925 to determine which fruits would grow well in Honduras and to preserve the region's diverse flora and fauna. In the brainchild of **Wilson Popenoe** (whose very name has the ring of an exotic fruit), visitors can see 200 species of soaring and singing birds and a staggering variety of plant species. The reserve is divided into two sections: the Wilson Popenoe Arboretum, where experimental trees are grown, and the Biological Reserve of Virgin Forest.

⚑ PARQUE NACIONAL JEANETTE KAWAS

*The easiest way to visit the park is with a guided tour. Garífuna Tours leads guided expeditions by launch to the Punta Sal Peninsula (8am-3pm, L299 including snorkeling gear); they take a short hike through the jungle, do some snorkeling, and stop at Cocalito for some chow. The company also offers full-day bird-watching trips to Laguna de los Micos (L332, min. 5 people). Since they often go in groups, individuals should arrange ahead of time in Tela. To go it on your own, you'll need a tent, food, water, and a few free days. Arrange a drop-off and pickup by boat in Cocalito from Garífuna Tours or a local fisherman (L150 is reasonable). Garífuna Tours or **PROLASANTE** (see Tela section, above) can help with current info on getting to either place on your own.*

To the west of Tela, Parque Nacional Jeanette Kawas (formerly called Parque Nacional Punta Sal) supports rare species and diverse ecosystems, from jungle to coral reefs. There's Laguna de los Micos, with its mangrove waterways and abundant birds, and farther west, the white sand beaches of the Punta Sal Peninsula. On the west side of the peninsula, Puerto Escondido, a sheltered cove, provides great snorkeling in a pristine coral reef. On the east side by the beach, in the tiny

Garífuna village of Cocalito, you can find meals (L50). From Cocalito, you can take a steep 0.6km trail to the top of a cliff for panoramic views from the Punta Sal lighthouse. The park's namesake, naturalist Jeanette Kawas, was the most ardent and eloquent defender of the preserve until she was murdered here in 1995. Many think she was killed by profiteers interested in developing the land.

⚠ PUNTA IZOPO RESERVE

Garífuna Tours leads excellent if brief daytrips (L265) here, and local guides can be found in Triunfo de la Cruz; ask at the Pulpería Soraya and try to give one day's notice. Be sure to bring long pants and bug repellent.

One of Honduras's 77 wildlife preserves, this 1100-hectare (28,000-acre) reserve is home turf for a prodigious number of plant and animal species. The birding in particular is great—parrots, toucans, blue herons, tiger herons, and kingfishers all make their homes here. Within the park's mangrove forest lies a vast and mysterious network of canals accessible only by kayak or canoe. Paddling silently through these labyrinths increases the chances of spotting the extremely shy creatures. Though tempting, it's best not to venture here alone. Describing Punta Izopo, the local Garífunas often say *"entra si quieres, sal si puedes"* (enter if you want, leave if you can); it's easy to get very lost very quickly, and even local fishermen avoid the area for that reason. Go with a guide.

LA CEIBA

La Ceiba is the largest city on Honduras's north coast and the country's third-largest overall. Although the town lost its trademark tree, the giant, umbrella-shaped *ceiba* (silk-cotton tree) long ago, tourists still visit to catch a plane to the Bay Islands or the Mosquito Coast, or simply to enjoy the city's famous *carnaval.* La Ceiba has one of the country's best nightlife scenes—a popular Honduran saying goes, "Tegucigalpa thinks, San Pedro Sula works, and La Ceiba parties."

🚍 TRANSPORTATION

Flights: Aeropuerto Goloson, 6km from town on the road to Tela. Snag a bus (L1) and ask to be let off by the airport, or get a taxi from the *punto de taxis* at the corner of the *parque*—for L10 they'll go to Confite, 2 blocks from the airport terminal. Most airlines have offices east of the *parque.* Call a day or two ahead, but pay upon arriving at the airport. **Isleña** (☎ 441 2521 or 441 2522) goes to: **Guanaja** (40min., daily 9:30am and 4pm, L330); **Palacios** (80min., daily 6am, L600); **Puerto Lempira** (80min., daily 6am, L800); **Roatán** (20min., 7 per day 7:20am-6pm, L325); **San Pedro Sula** (30min.; daily 7:30, 10am, 1:40pm; L500); **Tegucigalpa** (45min., daily 7:15am and 2pm; L680); **Trujillo** (M and F 9:40am, L300); **Utila** (15min., daily 6am and 4pm, L275). **SOSA** (☎ 441 2519 or 440 1364) flies to: **Guanaja** (20min., M-Sa 10am and 4pm, L461); **Roatán** (20min., M-Sa 6 per day 6:10am-3:30pm, L308); **San Pedro Sula** (25min.; M-Sa 7:30, 10am, 1:30pm; L461); **Utila** (15min., M-Sa 6am and 3:30pm, L307). **Rollins Air** (☎ 441 2560) flies to: **Guanaja** (2 daily, L390); **Tegucigalpa** (2 daily, L513). **Taca** (☎ 441 2519) has flights to: **Belize City, Belize** (daily, US$157); **San José, Costa Rica** (daily, US$180); **Tegucigalpa** (6, 6:40am, 3:30pm; L539).

Buses: The **terminal,** halfway to the airport on Blvd. 15, is accessible from town by **taxi** (10min., L10). **Buses** go to **Nueva Armenia** (2hr., 11:30am, L10); **Tegucigalpa** (6½hr.; 3, 10am, 2pm; L70); **Trujillo** (3hr., every 45min. 5:30am-3:50pm, L38); **Sambo Creek** via **Corozal** (30min., every hr. 6am-6:30pm, L3); **San Pedro Sula** (3hr., every 30min. 5:30am-6pm, L51); **La Unión** (30min., every hr. 8:30am-3pm, L6); **Tela** (2½hr., every hr. 4am-6pm, L17).

La Ceiba

⌂ ACCOMMODATIONS
Hotel Amsterdam 2001, **1**
Hotel Caribe, **9**
Hotel Rotterdam, **2**
Hotel San Carlos, **8**

🍴 FOOD
Cafetería Cobel, **10**
Expatriates Bar & Grill, **14**
Masapan: Comida Rápida, **12**
Mixers, **11**
Pupusería Universitaria, **3**
Ricardo's, **13**

🍷 NIGHTLIFE
Alejandro's, **7**
El Mussal, **4**
Safari, **5**
Sépticos Europa, **6**

Ferries: Nuevo Muelle de Cabotaje (Yacht Harbor) serves as a departure point for boats to the Bay Islands. The harbor is 22km from La Ceiba; you'll need to take a cab (15min., L25). The Galaxy (☎445 1795) heads daily to **Utila** (1hr., 9:30am, L185) and **Roatán** (2hr., 3pm, L140). With a little luck and lots of patience, you can catch a cheaper, longer ride on a cargo boat or motorized *cayuco*—ask around at the dock or at the other pier at the end of Av. San Isidro. **Beware hustlers** at the harbor who carry luggage a few meters and then demand an huge tip.

Local Transportation: Taxis cluster at the southwest side of the *parque*. Fares are usually L10, including to the airport, but always ask before hopping in.

✦ 🔁 ORIENTATION AND PRACTICAL INFORMATION

Residents of La Ceiba get around by a weblike system of airtubes, which suck them at lightning speed over buildings and beneath ground. Just kidding. Actually, La Ceiba uses that same old grid system (see p. 435). *Avenidas*, however, are labeled by name, not number. From the airport or bus terminal, you'll have to take a taxi. They typically head east along **Blvd. 15 de Septiembre** and drop passengers off at the *parque central*. The parque, between Calles 8 and 9, is adorned with benches, palms, and statues of Latin American heroes. Extending from the east side of the *parque* toward the water is **Av. San Isidro**, the main drag. One block west is **Av. La República**. One block north of the *parque* and a block east is **Av.**

Atlanta; another block east is **Av. 14 de Julio.** Calle 1 lies along the shore. The cathedral is southeast of the *parque*.

Tourist Information: Consejo Municipal de Turismo, Calle 1, (☎440 3045), a block from Av. San Isidro. Provides *carnaval* information. Open M-F 8:30am-5pm, Sa 8am-noon. Alternatively, **La Moskitia Ecoaventuras** is on Av. 14 de Julio, (☎442 0104), 1½ blocks from the beach. English spoken. Open M-F 8am-noon and 1:30-5pm, Sa 8am-noon. A city-run tourist information booth is open sporadically on the west side of the *parque central.* **FUPNAPIB,** Av. La República and Calle 11, on the 2nd fl. of the Plaza del Caribe is also a good source of information.

Tours: Transmundo (☎443 2840), on the north side of the *parque*, next to the Gran Hotel Paris. English spoken. Open M-F 7:30-11:30am and 1:30-5pm, Sa 8-11:30am. **Caribbean Travel** (☎443 1360; ctravel@caribe.hn), located next to Hotel San Carlos. Open M-F 7:30-11:30am and 1:30-4:30pm, Sa 7:30-11am. **Agencia de Viajes Laffite,** Av. San Isidro, (☎443 0115), next to the Hotel Iberia. English spoken. Open M-F 7:30-11:30am and 1:30-4:30pm, Sa 7:30-11am.

Banks: BGA, in the Plaza de Sol shopping mall, 2 blocks north of the *parque* on Av. San Isidro, cashes traveler's checks. Open M-F 9am-4pm, Sa 9-11:30am. **Banco Atlántida,** across the way, offers the same along with an **ATM.** Open M-F 9am-4pm, Sa 9-11:30am. **Banco Credomatic,** Av. San Isidro, across the street from Hotel Iberia. Cash advances on MC and V. Open M-F 9am-5pm, Sa 9am-noon. **ATM** on the corner of Av. San Isidro and Calle 5 for AmEx/MC/V.

Market: Palmira, Calle 6, 2 blocks east of Av. San Isidro. Spilling onto the street is one of the biggest indoor markets in Central America. Open M-Sa 7am-7pm, Su 7am-noon. **Supermarket Super Ceibeño,** 2 locations: one next to Palmira, the other 1 block north of the northwest corner of the *parque*. Both open M-Sa 7am-7pm, Su 7am-noon.

Police: FUSEP (☎441 0995), Blvd. 15 de Septiembre, by the bus terminal. Open 24hr.

Hospital: Calle 8 (☎442 2195), 4 blocks east of the *parque*. 24hr. emergency service.

Telephones: Hondutel, Calles 5/6 (☎443 0024; fax 443 0700), 3 blocks east of Av. San Isidro, under the red and white radio tower. 24hr. Sprint and AT&T services. **Fax** available M-F 8am-noon and 1-3:30pm. **Intercon,** above Cafe@Cafe in Plaza del Sol. L3 per min. to US. Open Su-Th 7am-8pm, F 7am-5pm, Sa 6-9pm.

Internet: Internet Café, Calle 7, Av. San Isidro/14 de Julio (☎443 4152; fax 440 0904; hondusof@glom.hn), in the Panayoti shopping mall, 1 block north and 2 blocks east of the *parque*. L30 per hr.; each additional minute L1. L20 per hr. for email only. 20% discount with ISIC card. Open M-F 8am-10pm, Sa 8am-6pm. **Cafe@Cafe,** Av. San Isidro, Calles 5/6, in Plaza del Sol, central and very classy. With A/C and gourmet pastries. L0.50 per 1min. Open M-Sa 8am-8pm, Su 8am-1pm.

Post Office: Av. Morazán, Calle 13, in Barrio Independencia in the southwest part of town. Open M-F 8am-3pm, Sa 8am-noon. **EMS Express Mail** in the same building. Open M-F 8am-3pm, Sa 8am-noon.

♪ ACCOMMODATIONS

The cheapest spots in town lie on Av. San Isidro and Av. 14 de Julio; be careful at night. There are occasional power failures here. Some hotels have deceptively attractive lobbies; if in doubt, ask to see a room first.

■ **Hotel Rotterdam** (☎440 0321), 7 blocks east of Av. San Isidro on Calle 1. A newer off-shoot of the older Amsterdam 2001 (see below). Half a block from the beach, freshly painted rooms, all with private cold-water baths, open out onto a grassy courtyard. Singles L100; doubles L130. ❷

Hotel Amsterdam 2001 (☎443 2311), A large dorm room above owner Jan's wood-working shop. Jan invites you to haggle with him for group discounts. Singles L55; dark, simple doubles with bath L112. L37 per additional person. ❷

Hotel Caribe, Calle 5, Av. San Isidro/Atlántida (☎443 1857), provides spacious but poorly lit rooms. Singles and doubles with private cold-water bath L100, with cable TV L150, with TV and A/C L220. ❷

Hotel San Carlos, Av. San Isidro, Calles 4/5 (☎443 0330), is hidden away behind a restaurant. Lug your bags through their inventory room to get to the stairs. Rooms are basic but well kept and feature "chopper-size" ceiling fans. Singles L70; doubles L100. If the restaurant is closed, check next door at Hotel Iberia. ❷

🍴 FOOD

La Ceiba boasts enough mid-priced *comedores* to keep budget travelers healthy and wealthy. **Barrio La Barra,** an entertainment district on the east end of Calle 1 along the beach, is home to a good number of traditional places. Vendors sell *platos típicos* and fruit in the *mercado* on Calle 6.

▩ Expatriates Bar and Grill, Calle 12, at eastern end. As the name suggests, sit under Expats' thatched roof for some buffalo wings while listening to Bob Dylan and catching the latest baseball game. Meals from the grill L30-90. Many vegetarian options; veggie platter L35. An excellent cigar emporium is housed here. Open Th-M 4pm-midnight, Su 11am-midnight during American football (NFL) season (Sept.-Jan.). ❷

▩ Cafetería Cobel, on Calle 7a between Av. Atlántida and Av. 14 de Julio. Cheap Honduran fare in a dining room that's become a *ceibaño* institution. Breakfast and lunch L32-35. Open M-Sa 6:30am-6pm. ❷

Masapan: Comida Rápida, 1 block north of the northwest corner of the *parque*. A cafeteria line with stations for sandwiches, meats, and fruits. Great for large groups of people with many tastes. Meals L40-60. Open daily 5:30am-11pm. ❷

Ricardo's, Av. 14 de Julio, Calle 10. The perfect place to get a dash of unpretentious elegance. The steaks, seafoods, and pastas are considered some of the best in Central America, and the chef has the awards to back it up. Dressy casual attire (i.e. no jeans or sandals) required. Meals L140-330. Open M-Sa 11am-1:30pm and 5:30-10pm. ❺

Mixers, next to Cafeteria Cobal, on the 2nd floor. Inexpensive, filling breakfasts L20-50 and lunches L25-35 attract large crowds. Open daily 8am-4pm. ❶

Pupusería Universitaria, at the intersection of Ave. 14 de Julio and Calle 1. At the west end of the Zona Viva, this cool restaurant is a good place to start the evening. *Pupusas* (stuffed tortilla) L10; tacos L27. Beer L14. Open daily 10am-11:30pm. ❶

👁 SIGHTS AND FESTIVALS

La Ceiba might be the third largest city in Honduras, yet there's surprisingly little to see when it's not *carnaval* time. Not even the beaches are a big asset; for clean, swimmable shores, head to the Garífuna villages of **Corozal** or **Sambo Creek.** Buses go back and forth every hour (45min., L6). Garífuna meals (L30-50) and simple rooms (L50-80) are available in both towns.

One block northwest of the *parque central,* the influential United Fruit Company has maintained a modest but beautiful **botanical garden** curiously combined with a **railroad museum.** A free stroll around the lush grounds will reveal a dozen engines, cabooses, and handcars. You can also ride the passenger train next to the park. (Round trip 30min., L4. Open daily 6am-6pm.) In La Ceiba's southern residential area, three blocks south of La Quinta Hotel, the small **butterfly and insect**

museum is worth a visit, featuring 6200 butterflies and moths, including the moth with the world's largest mouth. Robert Lehman, primary provider of local specimens, is frequently in the office and available to chat. (☎442 2874; www.hondurasbutterfly.com. L15. Open M-Sa 8am-noon and 1-4pm.) Also consider soaking in some *fútbol* at the local **stadium;** cheap seats are only L30. (Ask about local schedules and times at the tourist office.)

During the *carnaval*, in the 2nd and 3rd weeks of May, La Ceiba fills with over 100,000 visitors, who enjoy the wild tangle of parades, costumes, and tributes to local patron San Isidro. The great *ceibaño* pride pours into the many parties in the different neighborhoods, especially for the many youth beauty pageants.

🎇 NIGHTLIFE

If you're looking for a good time, Honduras's biggest party town will not let you down. Large crowds keep the sidewalk safe and buzzing all night in the **Zona Viva,** the heart of La Ceiba's action. In addition, most clubs hire private security to keep an eye on things on weekends. Still, use common sense: stay alert, take taxis, and leave valuables behind. Thanks to a La Ceiba ordinance, minors (17 and under) aren't allowed in nightspots, so have your ID ready.

Most of La Ceiba's hip nightspots are near the beach along Calle 1, in the Zona Viva. Clubs rarely have dress codes, but few people wear sandals or shorts. The popular **Arenas** pumps out a mix of Latin and US Top 40. (Cover L20. Open Th-Su 8pm-4am.) For *punta* music, the Garífuna crowd packs into ⊠**Centro Satuye,** next to the bridge behind Queen Burger on Calle 1, with a live band. (Open 9pm-4am. Cover L30.) Pricey drinks at **El Mussal,** a popular beach dance club, pay for extra security and air conditioning. (Cover Th-Sa L40-L170. Women free except F-Sa after 11pm. Beer L20.) The mix of an express restaurant, sports bar, and disco have made **Crash** another hip disco, especially on weekends. **Safari** is probably the only club between here and Texas that plays country-western music. (Open daily 6pm-6am. Pop music on Sa.) Another popular but pricey disco is **Alejandro's.** (Cover F-Sa L40-50. 6 beers L50. Open Tu-Sa from 8pm.)

A collection of bars dots the city. **Expatriates Bar and Grill** (see **Food,** above) is a fun place to mix with other foreigners. **My Friend Bar** is a beachside locale perfect for a nightcap accompanied by the sound of crashing waves and Latin music. Next door, the well-decorated **Sépticos Europa** bar plays an eclectic selection of local, European, and American music of recent and older vintage. (Open W-Sa 8pm-5am.) Try your luck on the one-armed bandits at **El Palacio Casino,** in La Quinta Hotel at the southern end of Av. San Isidro; take a cab. (Open daily 7pm-4am.)

🏔🤝 OUTDOOR ACTIVITIES AND GUIDED TOURS

La Ceiba makes a great base for expeditions into the wilderness, and there are many tour operators in the city. Ask around about reputations and remember that what may seem a super-cheap deal may be lousy. **La Mosquitia Ecoaventuras,** one block from Calle 1 on Av. 14 de Julio, has a very good reputation. They run a variety of daytrips to nearby **Pico Bonito, Cuero y Salado** (US$50 and US$60 respectively from La Mosquitia.), and just about every other site of interest in the local area. La Mosquitia also runs some of the best-planned trips around to the **Mosquito Coast,** ranging from two-day jaunts to two-week, 500km expeditions through the entire region. Though these tours are a bit pricey, they feature jungle hiking, Garífuna dancing, and petroglyph-viewing. La Mosquitia can airlift sick or injured adventurers to civilization. (☎442 0104; moskitia@caribe.hn; www.honduras.com/moskitia. 5 day all-inclusive tours US$545.) La Mosquitia and **Ríos of Honduras,** located in Caribbean Travel Agency next to Hotel San Carlos, also run **white water rafting** excursions on the Cangrejal River, which has some of the best rapids in all of Central America, reaching Class III in the dry season and Class IV in the rainy season. (☎443 1360. Rafting US$45-50 per person, lunch included.)

NEAR LA CEIBA

If La Ceiba's vibrant nightlife tires you, how about some teeming wildlife? Parque Nacional Pico Bonito and Cuero y Salado wildlife refuge offer great opportunities. Both can be done as independent daytrips or with guided tours, but Cuero y Salado requires some advance planning.

◪ PARQUE NACIONAL PICO BONITO

*To go with a guide, call FUPNAPIB (☎443 3824) a few days in advance to arrange one for a day-hike along unmarked trails. Alternatively, more expensive La Mosquitia Ecoaventuras and Eurohonduras (see **Guided Tours,** above) provide one-day hikes and multi-day treks which include all meals and supplies. To get to the **Visitors Center**, take the "1 de Mayo" bus from either the parque central or the Parque Bonilla in La Ceiba to the last stop in **Armenia Bonito.** (1hr., every hr. from 6am, L5.) Any taxi can get to the **Zacate Waterfall** or take any westbound bus toward Tela, and ask the driver to let you off at the Zacate trailhead just past El Pino (L5, most drivers will know where it is). To get to the **wildlife rehabilitation center**, take any westbound bus toward Tela to the entrance signpost of El Pino village, 8km from La Ceiba.*

Parque Nacional Pico Bonito, southwest of La Ceiba, can be explored with or without a guide. Trails wind through the park's untouched rainforest as butterflies flit and jaguars prowl nearby. The park's sheer cliffs, deep canyons, and mist-enshrouded peaks are jaw-dropping and easily accessible.

VISITORS CENTER AREA. The Visitors Center, at Campamento del CURLA, serves as a base for hiking several of the trails that wind through the foothills of the mountain. If you get the key from the ranger and bring your own food, you can stay here overnight and use the center's bare mattresses and grill. The quality of the facility is improving. Call Ricardo Stiner, president of the Pico Bonito Foundation, for more information. (☎443 3824.) From the center, follow the signs up the dirt road toward the mountain. The ranger's home is the last house along the road before it enters the park; pay the L100 (L50 for students) entrance fee here. The road soon becomes a footpath, and if the water isn't too high, it's possible to walk upstream along the river on huge, slippery boulders. If you can't follow the river, take the trail along the bank until you reach the *Campamento del CURLA.* If you are on the river, look for the stairs to your left.

ZACATE WATERFALL. Probably the most popular sight in the park, the 40m cascade is easily accessible to view or even to swim below. From the beginning of the trailhead, walk down the road until you reach the guardhouse for the Dole Pineapple plantation. When you pay the L30 entrance fee, the guard will point out the trail. After about 250m, you'll see a small waterfall called **Cascada Ruidosa** ("noisy cascade"). Another 1km along the trail will bring you up to the Zacate falls.

AMARAS WILDLIFE REHABILITATION CENTER. To see the park's animals up-close, stop at this center on the park's outskirts. AMARAS was founded in 1993 to house animals rescued from the grips of criminals who attempt to sell them on the black market. After their stay here, the animals are released into national parks. Visitors might find the staff working with white-faced monkeys, macaws, sloths, or even baby jaguars. To get there, once in town, cross the street and proceed down the palm-lined drive; go right at the fork, and look for the buildings on your left. AMARAS is less than 1km from the road. This trip can be easily combined with a visit to the Zacate Waterfall (see above). Although there is no fee, gifts of food (carrots, bananas, meat) are greatly appreciated to help support the center.

TROPICAL BUTTERFLY FARM AND SERPENTARIUM. Located at the base of the Pico Bonito National Park and on the grounds of the lodge at Pico Bonito is a farm where these beautiful creatures thrive by the hundreds. There's also an extensive exhibit of Honduran snakes. (☎443 2716. Butterfly farm L30, children L15; serpentarium L20, children L10. Open W-Su 8am-4:30pm.)

THE PEAK. Climbing the park's primary peak is extremely difficult and requires extreme technical climbing. Only eight expeditions have summited in recent history. Experienced climbers interested in attempting the feat should contact **Germán Martínez** before going to Honduras. (☎443 3824.)

▓ CUERO Y SALADO WILDLIFE REFUGE

Only 30 people may enter the refuge per day. If you're planning a visit, call or email the ***Fundación Cuero y Salado (FUCSA),*** *which administers the refuge, a week ahead of time to reserve a spot. (☎443 0329; fucsa@laceiba.com). Take any westbound bus from La Ceiba and ask to be let off at* ***La Toronjera,*** *or take the direct bus to* ***La Unión*** *(every hr. from 6:30am, L6). From La Toronjera a 30min. walk through a grapefruit farm ends at La Unión, where you can catch a burra, a small hand-operated railcar (1 hr., first person L120, L20 each additional person). The railcar will take you into the park near the* ***Visitors Center.*** *Alternatively, call* ***Ferrocarril Nacional*** *the day before for a faster motocarro to take up to 20 people (☎443 3235. First person L150, L60 each additional person). If you're not spending the night, keep in mind that the last bus from La Unión leaves at 3pm. 2hr. guided tour for up to 7 people. Park admission fee US$10, students with ID US$5.*

The Cuero y Salado Wildlife Refuge, one of the most biologically diverse regions of Honduras, lies 30km west of La Ceiba, spilling out into the Caribbean Sea. The 133 sq. km of freshwater wetlands, saltwater marshes, and coastline protect 350 different species of animals, including jaguars, ocelots, sloths, boa constrictors, and, in the water, the park's mascot, the **manatee.** Almost 200 species of birds, more than a quarter of all those in Honduras, can be found here. The best way to tour the park is by boat. FUSCA rents thatched roofs with tents for L150 per night for four people; bring your own sheets. Camping on the beach is allowed. Bring food, water, and plenty of bug repellent. (L25 per night.)

TRUJILLO

Cradled between densely forested tropical peaks and powdery, white Caribbean beaches, Trujillo has long attracted travelers. It was near here that Columbus set foot for the first time on the American mainland. Founded in 1525, the town was the first Spanish settlement in Honduras and among the first in all of Central America. The Spaniards knew a good thing when they saw it: laid-back, uncrowded Trujillo is one of the most inviting towns on the Honduran coast. With El Olancho to the south and La Mosquitia to the east, Trujillo is a popular launching point for adventurous expeditions into the interior.

▐ TRANSPORTATION

Flights: The **airstrip** is a few kilometers west of the town's center. **Isleña Airlines** flies M and F to **Palacios** (10:15am, L462) and **La Ceiba** (11am, L365). From La Ceiba, connections can be made to the rest of the country. Buy tickets at the front desk of the **Christopher Columbus Beach Resort** (☎434 4965) on the runway (desk open M-Sa

7am-noon). You must buy the tickets at least one day in advance, as planes only stop if passengers are waiting. Schedules vary and it's best to check times in advance.

Buses: Transport Lesly buses leave from the Texaco gas station, a 10min. walk or L10 taxi ride from the *parque*. Express bus to **San Pedro Sula** (6hr., every hr. 3am-3pm, L83) via **La Ceiba** (3hr., L30) and **Tela** (3hr., L55). There is also a non-express bus to **La Ceiba** (5hr., 5 per day 6:30am-2pm, L29). An express bus goes to **Tegus** (8hr., 1 per day 1am, L143). Buses leave for **Tocoa** (1hr., every hr. 3am-3pm) via **La Ceiba** (1½hr., 5am-3pm, L16). Buses also go to **Jutiapa** (2½hr., every 1hr. 3am-3pm). To get to **La Unión,** take a bus to **Saba** (every 30min. 1am-3pm, L30). It is best to leave on the 5:30am bus in order to make the transfer from Mame to La Unión. From Saba, catch a bus to Mame (L30), and at Mame wait for the noon bus to La Unión (L50). To get to La Unión, take a bus to La Ceiba and then to La Unión (3hr., 5am-5:30pm) or to Olanchito (1hr.) and then La Unión. Catch the Empresa López direct bus to **Juticalpa** at the edge of the park (10hr., 3am). Buses to **Santa Fe** leave in front of the old cemetery (20min; 9, 10:45am, noon, and 3pm, returns 6:30 and 11am; L10). **Puerto Castilla** (30min., 7am-6pm, L5).

Boats: A collection of commercial vessels leaves from Trujillo to the Bay Islands, and from there to **Jamaica.** Ask at the docks for information. **FUCAGUA** (☎434 4294) sends boats to **Cayo Blanco** (L470) for day trips. Boats also travel to Palacios, Everta Lempira and other places in La Moquitia at irregular times. Ask at municipal docks.

Taxis: They queue at the southeast corner of the *parque* and cost L10 to any point in the city, including the bus station and airport. At night, prices jump to L20-40. Taxis are recommended for anyone going to or from the bus stop outside daylight hours, even in the early morning. Arrange for a taxi to pick you up in advance and expect to pay L70-L100 no matter the distance.

⊞🔁 ORIENTATION AND PRACTICAL INFORMATION

Trujillo's main street, **2 Av.,** parallels the beach one block inland from the **parque central.** *Calles* run north to south, beach to mountains. **Barrio Cristales,** a *Garífuna* neighborhood, sits west of town. The beaches in Barrio Cristales are excellent, but best avoided at night. The area east of town is home to new tourist developments and **Puerto Castilla,** offshore at the east end of the bay, is a major shipping center.

IN RECENT NEWS

HAPPY ANNIVERSARY

In the small village of Puerto Castilla 12km from Trujillo, a little known monument pays homage to Barthalomew Colón Columbus. This unrecognized brother of Christopher Columbus also sailed the ocean blue with his brother across the ominous and mysterious Atlantic Ocean to "the new world." After Christopher's fourth and final voyage to the Americas Barthalomew was the one who conducted the first mass in North America while his brother remained on the ship. The historic religious service which took place on August 14, 1502, has come to symbolize the inauguration of Catholicism in the Americas. The Catholic faith is still a huge force in the lives of many Central Americans today. The 500 year celebration was this past summer and boy, was it a party. The anniversary attracted various religious and political dignitaries from all over the world to celebrate this monumental event both abroad and on site in Honduras. The president of Honduras, a papal representative, and various governors from the 18 departments joined locals and others in the two day celebration.

Tourist Information: Turtle Tours (☎/fax 434 4431; ttours@hondutel.hn), at the Villas Brinkley Hotel. Detailed info. on attractions in and around Trujillo. English, German, and Spanish spoken. Open M-F 8-11am and 2-5pm, Sa 8-11am.

Banks: Banco de Occidente, on 2 Av., 2 blocks south of the *parque.* Open M-F 8:30am-4:30pm, Sa 8:30-noon. Cashes traveler's checks and Western Union. **Banco Atlántida,** on the *parque* facing the ocean, gives Visa cash advances and cashes traveler's checks. Open M-F 9am-4pm, Sa 8:30-11:30am.

Supermarkets: There are 2 in town—one on the southwest corner of the square, the other 1 block south. Open daily 7am-7pm.

Laundry: Lavandería Colón, west on the main drag heading toward Barrio Cristales. L50 for full cycle. Open M-Sa 7am-6pm.

Police: FUSEP (☎434 4038), at the western edge of the *parque.* Open 24hr.

Pharmacy: Farmacia Almim (☎434 4243), on Calle Conventillo. Open M-Sa 8am-noon and 2-9pm.

Hospital: (☎434 4093) east of the *parque.* Little English spoken. Open 24hr.

Telephones: Hondutel is next door to the post office, 1 block behind the main church. Direct line to Sprint to make collect calls to the US. Open daily 7am-9pm.

Internet: Compu-Pro (☎434 4517). Closest Internet place to the *parque,* next to the bus station toward the Hondutel office. L40 per hr. Open M-Sa 8am-6pm. **Trujillo Online** (☎434 4694), 1 block east of Hondutel, is the cheapest of several places in town. L50 per hr., L40 for students. Open M-Sa 8am-noon and 1:30-5:30pm.

Post office: Next to Hondutel. Open M-F 8am-noon and 2-4pm, Sa 8-11am.

ACCOMMODATIONS

▨ **Hotel Emperador,** Av. Mercado, 3 Calle (☎434 4446). 2 blocks south of the *parque,* is well-kept and colorful hotel. The owner, a professor, has useful knowledge about the area. He also offers clean rooms with TV and private baths. Fans and a sagging bed round out the low cost. Open 24hr. Singles and doubles L120-150. ❸

Hotel Cocapanda, at the bottom of the hill on the road next to the beach. This hotel has a restaurant, disco, and the upper floors have unbeatable views. Rooms have private baths and two beds. L100. ❷

Hotel Mar de Plata, right next to the most popular disco in town, has a friendly management and nice rooms with city views. Though loud on weekends, it may appeal to the party hardy traveler. Singles L120, doubles L150. ❷

Cabana's Campamento. These peach colored "casitas" right on the beach are ideal for a group of 4 or 5 wanting a rural location and ocean access. With A/C and private baths, these can't be beat. Quads L450; quints L650. Accessible by taxi (L40) or bus from Texaco station or the old cemetery. ❺

Casa Kiwi, in Puerto Castilla is ideal for budget travellers. The location is gorgeous and transit to and from Trujillo is easy. With a bar, restaurant, pool table, and bikes, this place has everything. Take the bus in Trujillo to Puerto Castilla. Dorm bed L50. ❶

FOOD

In addition to what's below, several places in Barrio Cristales offer *Garífuna* specials, and there are a number of bar-restaurants along the beach.

Granada, on Calle Conventillo across from Banco Occidente, is owned by a Garífuna family and serves excellent seafood and meat dishes with a touch of elegance. Hamburgers L25; seafood L65-135. Open daily 7:30am-10:30pm. ❸

Trujillo

▲ ACCOMMODATIONS
Hotel Cocapanda, **2**
Hotel Emperador, **6**
Hotel Mar de Plata, **4**

🍖 FOOD
Granada, **5**
Rincón de los Amigos, **1**

🎵 NIGHTLIFE
Truxillio Paradise, **3**

Comedor Caballero: Peter's Place has the best seafood dishes on the coast, and is tucked away in the Gantuna community of Santa Fé. All dishes prepared by an excellent ex-cruise ship chef who whips up huge, savory platters that easily feed two. Fish cakes L75; garlic shrimp L150; mixed veggie plate L60. Open daily. ❸

Rincón de los Amigos, right on the beach with the sea breeze around you, this Italian place serves wonderful, brick oven pizza. Pizza L50-70. Open M-Sa 10am-10pm. ❷

Ports of Call is a beachside bar next to the airport, charming and well-maintained. The beach is right there and the eating area is ideal. Beer L15. Open daily 9am. ❶

SPICY VIAGRA As long as you're in Barrio Cristales, follow the locals and try a shot. Reminiscent of earthy Christmas seasonings with a burning kick, *gifty* is made from young white rum. This powerful concoction plays a part in many Garífuna rituals from *novenarios* (wakes held nine days after a death) to weddings. The rum is seasoned with 17 herbs and spices, including garlic for an added kick. Supposedly, the herbal additives increase the potency of the rum in just 24hr.; leave it brewing longer, and it becomes strong enough to knock over an elephant. It's also said to be a powerful aphrodisiac: locals say its "better than Viagra, and cheaper too." The Garífuna often jokingly blame their notably high birth rate on the mix. Almost all the beachfront bars sell healthy *octavo* (one-eighth liter) shots for about L5; locals do the shots in rounds, and will often buy a visitor a glass "just to see the look on his face."

🔆 **SIGHTS**

Beyond its mesmerizing beach, Trujillo has an eclectic private museum, simply called ◪**El Museo.** More like Trujillo's collective attic, it comes complete with antique household appliances, undetonated bombs, parts of a crashed US Air Force plane, and 19th-century farm machinery. From the town's center, walk along the main street with the sea to your right until the Hotel Mar de Plata; take the next left, then the first right, and follow that road past two cemeteries. Ten minutes later you'll see creatively painted signs. If the guide is there, take the

HONDURAS

walking tour. L30 includes access to the swimming holes out back. (Museum open daily 8am-5:30pm. Swimming holes open Sa-Su.) On the way, stop by **Cementerio Viejo** to check out the grave of ambitious North Americans William Walker, executed in 1860 after unsuccessfully trying to impose plantation slavery in Central America.

La Fortaleza de Santa Bárbara, next to the *parque*, was built nearly 400 years ago to repel pirate attacks, but failed on the numerous occasions when the city was sacked. The fort's faded ramparts are one of the most poetic spots in the region. (L15, students L3 with ID. Open daily 8am-noon and 1-4pm.)

■ NIGHTLIFE

If there's one thing Trujillo's Garífuna crowd knows how to do well, it's party. Barrio Cristales throbs until dawn, with beachfront bars whose patrons spill out onto the sand (sometimes face-first). Beers are an unbelievable L5 to L10, and the nightspots are often the sites of authentic and spontaneous *punta*, the trademark Garífuna dance. **Truxillio Paradise,** up the main road past Hotel Mar de Plata, is currently the hottest disco. Cover L50 open daily. Locals also flock to **Bahía Bar** on the beach on Fridays and Saturdays. To dance *punta*, head to **El Black,** the disco in front of the Hotel Cocapanda.

▲ ■ OUTDOOR ACTIVITIES AND GUIDED TOURS

For information on the nearby parks and lagoons, stop by the **FUCAGUA** office on the road to Villas Brinkley. Visitors to the two nearby national parks are expected to stop by the office to pay a fee. (☎/fax 434 4294. L50 per person. Open M-F 7:30am-noon and 1:30-5pm.) Although not necessary, FUCAGUA can arrange for a guide (L100) with a day's notice. **Turtle Tours** (see **Practical Information,** above) sells trips to the top of Cerro Calentura in a 4X4 vehicle (1¼hr., US$20 per person.) It also offers guided hikes ($15 per person) and **canoe** trips in the Guaimoreto Lagoon (US$20 per person). Though pricey by backpacker standards, guided tours are a worthwhile way to visit the **Crocodile Reserve** at the **Hacienda El Tumbador** because the roads are unmarked (US$20 per person plus $5 entrance fee).

Parque Nacional Capiro Calentura, which includes the mountain Cerro Calentura, covers the forested slopes behind Trujillo. The best time to go is early in the morning, around 4am, when jaguars, howler monkeys, and boa constrictors may appear. If you go in the afternoon, the animals won't show, but the view from the top is still worth the effort; on clear days you can see Roatán. To reach the summit, walk (or take a 4x4 taxi) up the hill past Villas Brinkley Hotel. It's a 3hr. hike to the top (9km). **Parque Nacional Laguna Guaimoreto,** a lagoon northeast of Trujillo, is an excellent place to birdwatch and spot the occasional crocodile. It is best seen very early in the morning or late afternoon via a guided boat tour (L400 for a boat and L100 for guide for up to 5 people). Make arrangements a day in advance through the FUCAGUA office or a tour company.

A 9km trek west along the beach from town or a 20min. bus ride through the campo, is the beautiful, clean, and friendly Garífuna community of **Santa Fé,** with picture perfect beaches, excellent food (see **Comedor Caballero**), and great hotels. **Hotel Orquídeas ❷,** a 2-story white hotel at the end of town, is a great beach-hotel find, with well maintained, spacious, clean rooms with private bath and fan. (L100 for one bed, L150 for 2.) Santa Fé celebrates the *Virgen del Carmen* with three weeks of festivities including sports tournaments and a range of dramatic and celebratory dance beginning the first weekend of July.

From Sante Fé, talk to Raul or FUCAGUA, and visit the reserve of **Cayo Blanco,** a five kilometer Caye which is said to be sinking. Bring food and water. (L400 boat and L100 guide.) **Cabo de Honduras,** accessible by the Puerto Castilla bus (see **Transportation,** above) has excellent beaches. To explore the area, rent a motorcycle from Turtle Tours (US$35 per day).

Starting June 21-29, Trujillo has its annual festival where each *barrio* holds a block party at night. Huge speakers, contests, beer, and dancing means free fun for everyone. The last night culminates in a huge party with the biggest bands in Honduras coming to play.

BAY ISLANDS

Though the silky white-sand beaches and world-class diving off the Bay Islands are Honduras's biggest tourist attractions, the islands feel less commercialized and developed than many other Caribbean destinations. Dive prices are low and the marine life colorful and plentiful. For those leery of the certification process, snorkeling is almost as fantastic, but then again, diving certification here is among the cheapest in the world. If all this activity makes you long for a hammocks and some swaying palms, have no fear: the Bay Islands have plenty of both. Utila, just 32km by boat from La Ceiba, is the most budget-friendly island, low-key and inviting. Roatán is the most developed of the islands, with some gorgeous beaches and diving spots as well as phenomenal snorkeling. Though home to some wonderful dive sites, Guanaja was devastated by Hurricane Mitch and is now much less of a tourist draw. The Cayos Cochinos are an isolated version of the main Bay Islands, with beautiful tropical vegetation.

HISTORY AND CULTURE

Stunning natural beauty aside, the Bay Islands are worth a visit just for the colorful ethnic, cultural, and linguistic patterns that distinguish them from the mainland. In 1502, Spain claimed the area and proceeded to ship the indigenous islanders into slavery, all the while struggling against pirates, who hid in the reefs and harbors. Britain and Spain fought over the islands throughout the late 18th century, and in 1852, the islands joined Belize as a British possession. Eventually, under US pressure, the islands were returned to Honduras. Although the islands were once solely populated by English-speaking descendants of African and British settlers, masses of mainland *hondureños* (Bay Islanders do not consider themselves Hondurans) have recently moved in, resulting in some racial tension. For the most part, Garífuna culture survives, and Creole English peppers the expressive island dialect. Spanish, however, is becoming just as common on the streets.

TRANSPORTATION TO THE BAY ISLANDS

La Ceiba is the launching pad for most visits to the Bay Islands; air and boat service runs to Utila and Roatán. Travelers can also reach Cayos Cochinos relatively easily through La Ceiba, although there are pricier options from Roatán and Utila. It is possible to fly to either of the bigger islands from San Pedro Sula and Tegucigalpa, and Roatán is reachable by air from more far-flung locales like Belize City, San Salvador, and the USA. Guanaja is accessible only by air from La Ceiba. There are no direct flights between the islands. (See **Transportation,** below.)

UTILA

Legend has it that if you drink the water in Utila, you're destined to stay (and not in a hospital). Inexpensive yet excellent seafood, partying, and diving combine to make this quite the backpacker pilgrimage site. While Roatán has seen some price inflation due to the influx of *gringos*, and Guanaja is still rebuilding since Mitch's destruction, Utila is still simple, intimate and extremely budget-friendly.

That said, swimming and sunbathing here are not especially good, but Utila revolves around the appeal of island relaxation and especially diving—most can't leave until they have had a taste of scuba. Then again, some can't leave at all: it's said that the most frequent lie on Utila is "I'm leaving tomorrow."

▛ TRANSPORTATION

To catch a **flight**, buy tickets at the trailer on the main pier, Morgan Travel. **Atlantic** (☎425 3241) flies daily to **La Ceiba**, as does **Isleña** (☎425 3364) and **SOSA**. (☎425 3166. 15min, M-Sa 6am and 3:30pm, L300.) The Galaxy **yacht** leaves daily for La Ceiba (11am, L185) and the Easy Going yacht makes a weekly trip to **Livingston, Guatemala** (overnight, US$90). Get more information at **Gunter's Dive Shop.** (☎/fax 425 3350; ecomar@hondutel.hn.) Call a **taxi** at ☎425 3187.

▟ ▛ ORIENTATION AND PRACTICAL INFORMATION

All of Utila clings to the **East Harbour,** on the southeast side of the island. **Main Street** starts at the **airstrip** on the eastern lip of the harbor and hugs the bay until it reaches the Blue Bayou Restaurant. Ferries land at the **Municipal Dock,** on the middle of main street. The road leading inland from the dock, called **Cola de Mico Road,** leads to the only hill around, **Pumpkin Hill.** Nearly everything is located on the main road. Many major services on the island will be quoted in US dollars; they can be paid for in American greenbacks or in lempiras at the going exchange rate.

Tourist Information: For info, go to www.utilainfo.com. Also, stop by the **Bundu Café** (see **Food,** below), always packed with hungry divers eager to share a tip or two. Bundu has the best **book exchange** on the island, with selections in a number of languages.

Banks: BGA (☎425 3117), on the main street's only intersection. Exchanges traveler's checks and gives cash advances on Visa. Long lines form in the afternoon. Open M-F 8:30am-3:30pm, Sa 8:30-11:30am. **Banco Atlántida,** diagonally across the street from BGA, also accepts Visa. Open M-F 9am-4pm, Sa 8:30-11:30am. Cash traveler's checks and exchange money at **Bundu Café** (see **Food,** below), or **Henderson's Grocery Store,** in mid-town. Open daily 7am-noon and 2-6pm. For MC advances, try the **Reef Cinema,** east from the dock on the main road (6% commission).

Police: (☎425 3255), upstairs from the post office by the Municipal Dock in the *municipalidad*. Open M-F 9am-noon and 2-5pm. For off-hour **emergencies,** call **FUSEP** (☎425 3145), next to the football field. Open 24hr.

Medical Services: The **health clinic,** in the yellow house across from the Lodge Resort, is always staffed by a doctor, usually an English-speaker. Open M-F 8am-noon. For emergencies, go to the *pulpería* next to the Health Clinic for a doctor. The **medical store** (cell 997 6527), a pharmacy in the center of town, close to the dock. Open daily 8am-7pm. The **Community Methodist Medical Clinic** (☎425 3137), with a small pharmacy inside, is on the main road 5min. west of the dock. Open M-F 8am-noon.

Telephones: Hondutel (☎425 3101), west from the dock on Main (look for the tower). Open M-F 7am-noon and 2-5pm, Sa 7-11am. To call the US or make collect calls, go to **Reef Cinema** for cheaper rates, or to the Internet cafe across from Hondutel.

Internet: Bay Island Computer Services (☎425 3124; bicomput@hondutel.hn), east of the dock on Main St. L100 per 30min., L180 per hr. Open M-Sa 9am-5pm. Same prices at **Howell's Internet,** east on Main. Open M-Th 8am-noon and 1:30-6pm, F 8am-noon and 1:30-5pm, Su 9am-noon and 1:30-4:30pm. Same prices also at the nameless cafe above the ice cream store west on the main road.

Post Office: Next to the Municipal dock. Open M-F 9am-noon and 2-5pm, Sa 9-11:30am.

Postal code: 34201.

▌ ACCOMMODATIONS

Accommodations are being built at warp speed to satiate growing legions of travelers. Reservations are strongly advised during the high season (mid-July to Sept. and mid-Dec. to Easter). Hotels offer 24hr. electricity unless otherwise mentioned. Some dive centers will put you up for free as part of their course package, usually during the low season; check around for the latest deals. In addition to those listed, some good, cheap hotels to look for are **Margaritaville** to the west of the dock (rooms US$10), **Trudy's Hotel,** and the **Cross Creek Dive Center,** to the east. **Blue Berry Hill,** up Cola de Mico Road, has basic accommodations at rock-bottom prices. **Mango Hotel,** just past Blue Berry Hill, has resort-like rooms with fan for US$25.

Freddy's Place (☎ 425 3142), the 1st hotel up from the airport, but farthest east from the boat dock, is run by a British islander family. Suites with 2 doubles, full kitchen, bath, and a great big porch, including hammocks that catch the evening breeze. Reservations recommended. US$15 per room, with A/C US$20. ❹

Rubi's (☎ 425 3240), east of the main dock, next to the water. Brand new wooden rooms, fans, and large tiled hot-water bathrooms. Singles US$12; doubles US$18. ❸

Tany's (☎ 425 3376), on the left before reaching the Mango Inn. *The* cheap place on the island, with very basic rooms and shared bath. Rooms L60. ❷

Cooper's Inn (☎ 425 3184), east of the dock past Rubi's, is a friendly spot with a communal kitchen and hangout area. Singles US$5; doubles US$7. ❷

Hotel Celena (☎ 425 3228), a few houses east of Cooper's. Great rooms at good prices. Get a fan that works—you'll need it. Singles and doubles US$6, with bath US$10. ❷

Seaside Inn (☎ 425 3150), a 10min. walk west of the dock in a less-developed area. Clean rooms include private bath and fans. Doubles US$6-8. ❷

▐ FOOD

Heaping fruit salads and vegetarian entrees are refreshingly common among an assortment of local, European, and North American menu choices. Street eats like *baleadas* (a whole lot of tortilla, beans, and cheese) are a godsend. Catch fresh-fruit breakfasts all day long at Munchi's or giant shakes at the Zanzibar Cafe.

RJ's BBQ and Grill, east on the main road, before Alton's. This is the island's most popular BBQ. Get here early. With famous grilled wahoo (L70), barracuda (L70), hamburgers (L40), and heaping portions of vegetables and rice, it's no wonder that RJ's fills up quickly. Open W, F, Su 5:30pm. ❷

Bundu Café, east of the dock. One of the most popular hangouts for lunch, thanks to great veggie sandwiches, tailored to your taste on French baguettes, croissants, or bagels. Beat the heat with fruit salads (L30-42) and freshly squeezed juices. Friendly Canadians Jen and Jackie stock tea directly from Canada. Open M-Sa 7am-2:15pm. ❷

Thompson's Bakery, up Cola de Mico Rd. Thompson's reigns supreme in the morning, with fresh cinnamon rolls, *pan de coco* (coconut bread), and delicious banana pancakes (L20). It is best to arrive early—the bread goes quickly. Open daily 6am-noon. ❶

Mermaid's Corner, a bit past Bundu, is famous for its milkshakes and offers a buffet-style selection of "soul food:" fried chicken, mashed potatoes, greens, and cole slaw. Friendly staff also serves pizza and tasty rice and beans. A la carte meals are available for under L50. Open daily 10am-10pm. ❷

Delicious Food Café, right before Munchies walking west. Great prices. Fruit pancakes L15; sandwiches L10; tacos and Coke L30. Open daily 7am-2pm and 4-9pm. ❶

Neptuno's (☎ 425 3190), across the bridge toward the airport, The island's classiest restaurant. Grilled conch L130, fish and chips L55. Free refills on natural juice. Free delivery. Open Th-Tu 7am-3pm and 5-10pm. ❸

🎵 📷 ENTERTAINMENT AND NIGHTLIFE

For nightlife, head to **Coco Loco's,** a thatched-roof bar on its own pier, where party-goers start out their evening. Dip your feet in the ocean through the jacuzzi-like hole in the pier, laze in a hammock overlooking all the action, or dance to an eclectic mix of music. **Bar in the Bush** is popular for cheap drinks and late-night sand volleyball. (Open W, F, Su.) At the opposite end of the pier from Neptuno's Chinese Restaurant lies **Tropical Sunset Bar,** whose claim to fame is its excellent location and beer; this was the first bar to bring draft beer to the island. (Happy Hour daily 4-7pm.) Party hard, but whatever you do, don't forget your **bug repellent.**

On the weekend, locals go to the **casino,** across from the bank. (Open F and Sa 8-11:30pm.) The **Bundu Café** and **Reef Cinema** both draw crowds to their daily **movies.** At Bundu Café, movies start at 7pm with British comedy, videos on Hurricane Mitch, or other short films. The evening's main film starts at 8pm (L30). On Sa and Su, there are two shows per night (6 and 8pm). Bundu rents videos (L30) and the owners will even rent out their cinema for a minimum of 4 people (L30 per person). At **Reef's Cinema,** movies play Tu-Th and Su at 7:30pm and Sa at 6:30 and 8:30pm (L35). Non-members can rent videos for L35 with a L200 deposit. (Video rental open M-F 8:30am-noon and 1:30-5pm, Sa 4:30-5:30pm.)

🏔 🎣 OUTDOOR ACTIVITIES

A trail from the airport leads to the beaches and tidal pools of **Big Bight,** on the eastern shore. It's also possible to canoe through the mangrove-lined canal that runs from the lagoon near Blue Bayou and Cross Creek. Rent **bikes** from **Delco Bikes** west of the dock (L100 for 24hr., L200 for 4 days; open Su-F 8am-6pm), or **Utila Bike Rental,** east on the main road, behind Howell's Internet (bikes L100 per day, L500 per week). **Kayaks** can be rented from every dive center with a deposit. Guided **horseback rides** to nearby caves and Pumpkin Hill are offered by **Jo Jo.** Ask at Bundu Café for directions. To check out Utila's iguanas, head for the preservation project at **Iguana Station,** at Jenco's, near Stuart's Hill. (Free. Open M, W, F 2-5pm.) **Gunter,** left at the Mango Inn and up the second road on the right to the iron gate, can take you on a personal tour of the island and an adventurous romp through mangrove swamps and secret caves. Call ahead (☎452 3113).

🤿 SCUBA AND SNORKELING

Many backpackers come to Utila to get their open-water certification; others are here training to be dive masters; and then there is everything in between. If you want to try out scuba diving, do a one hour "Discover Scuba" session (US$99). The session counts toward the open water certification, and it's easy—all you have to do is breathe, and a dive master will do the rest.

GETTING CERTIFIED. Utila has recently standardized prices for certification courses, and though this eliminates the real cheapies, the set price is still low—open water certification, which takes three to five days, is US$171, including insurance. Certification courses typically include classroom instructions, five or six instructional dives, and sometimes two free fun dives after the course. During low season, some dive shops provide free or discounted hotel rooms. Most dive shops offer free use of snorkeling and kayaking equipment during courses, and many conduct training in several languages, from Hebrew to Maori.

Try the 5-star, PADI-certified **Utila Dive Centre,** halfway to the airport on the main drag. Known for their professionalism, the experienced divemasters here are conversant in six languages. The divers who own the place take the condition of their

CHOOSING A DIVE SHOP. The best way to start is by asking local divers. Some dive centers have become well-respected institutions over the years; others have reputations as yahoo outfits. Always check out the equipment room and take note of the wear on the gear and how well it's organized. Make sure there are no patches or tape on the BCD vests and that the two parts of the octopus-like ventilators are different lengths. Also, ask about the boats; faster ones can take students out to less-disturbed training sites. If you are learning however, it can be easier to go out on a bigger boat where you have enough space to put on your gear. If you're training, find out how many dives an instructor has done; novices will have had only a couple hundred, while a veteran will have had 500 or more. Small class size (2-4 students) is also a plus. Anything over six is unacceptable. Most dive shops are reputable, but don't forget the individual instructor—many people choose the dive shop because of a rapport with a particular individual.

equipment seriously. (☎ 425 3325; info@utiladivecentre.com; www.utiladivecentre.com.) **Captain Morgan's Dive Shop,** in the center of town, has a good reputation, small classes, and a staff that eats, sleeps, and breathes diving. (☎/fax 445 3349. Open M-F 6:30am-6pm, Sa 8:30am-6pm.) **Alton's Dive Shop** also has a reputation for quality on the island. (☎ 425 3108. altons@hondutel.hn.)

SITES. For those already certified, the standard prices are US$30 for a "fun dive" or US$125 for a package of 10 dives. Morning trips to the **north side** afford some of the best diving in Utila. Unbelievable wall drops are accompanied by not-so-rare sightings of gigantic bespeckled **whale sharks,** which are plentiful in the region. The **south side** has fewer big fish but compensates with greater coral diversity; the **east side** is known for **eagle ray** visits and for **Black Hill,** an underwater mountain that several sea turtles call home.

SNORKELING. Snorkeling is free for those taking a scuba course, and rentals cost US$15 at dive centers. The **Snorkeling Center,** up the main road near the airport, provides a half day of snorkeling and transportation to any of dozens of marvelous sites around the island (L185). Those who want to strike out on their own can rent gear, get snorkeling sight orientation and fish identification, and safely leave stuff at the Snorkeling Center. (Rentals L45 per day.) The rocks just off the airstrip offer some sweet sites accessible on foot. Pay L15 admission fee to snorkel at the **Blue Bayou Hotel,** a 30min. walk past Gunter's. (Rental L35 per hr.) Also explore the inlet just after Margaritaville Hotel, west on the main road.

▶ DAYTRIPS FROM UTILA

For relaxation and snorkeling on an even more deserted island, you can arrange to spend the night on one of several nearby cayes. **Water Caye** is popular for beach BBQs and star-gazing at night. Before heading out, ask your guide to stop at Pigeon Caye to buy the requisite fresh fish, and then sway the night away in bug-free bliss on rented hammocks. (Use of Water Caye is L25 per day.) Always wanted a private island? Try one for the night: **Sandy Caye** is up for grabs from about US$85 per night. **Tropical Travels,** east of the dock, and Bundu Café have boat connections, and can help arrange the rentals. (☎ 425 3241. L100 per person; does not include entrance fee.) A boat leaves every morning at 9:30am and will stay as long as the wind permits (approx. 25min to Water Caye, 45min. return). Trips to Water Caye with **Munchies** include a full BBQ meal, snorkeling, and volleyball (L250). Munchies also offers half-day trips to explore the island's freshwater caves

(L150). Talk to **sailing** instructor Captain Erick about paying to sail to the Cayos Cochinos. (Lessons US$150.) Be advised, however, that it's cheaper to get there from La Ceiba (see p. 486).

ROATÁN ISLAND

For many travelers, Roatán is paradise. The largest and most populous of the Bay Islands, Roatán is blessed with glorious powder-soft beaches, world-renowned diving and snorkeling, and a well-manicured beachfront town. While this gem was once a well-kept secret, word has gotten out, and the influx of international tourists has spawned the arrival of the all-inclusive resort, the US$1.50 Coke, and superb but pricey international menus. However, budget travelers can still find a home, particularly in West End, near stunning beaches like West Bay. Coxen Hole, home to the airport and most of the local services, is a crowded, unpleasant little settlement. Sandy Bay is Roatán's third major town.

▐ TRANSPORTATION

Three **airlines** fly to **La Ceiba:** Isleña (☎445 1833), SOSA (☎443 1154), and Atlantic Airlines (☎440 2343) have similar flight schedules and the same price. (15min., 7 per day 6:50am-5pm, L364.) Isleña also flies to **Belize City**; **San Pedro Sula** (70min., daily 6:50am and 1pm, L912); and **Tegucigalpa** (M-Sa, 7am and 1:30pm, Su 1:30pm; L927.75). Taca (☎445 1918) has service to and from **El Salvador, San Salvador,** and the US cities of **Houston** and **Miami** once a week. **Paradise Tours,** next door to H.B. Warren's in Coxen Hole, on the 2nd floor, sells tickets, or you can buy tickets directly at the airport. (☎445 0392; fax 445 1267. Open M-F 9am-5pm, Sa 9am-noon.) The *Galaxy* **yacht** leaves daily for **La Ceiba.** (☎445 1795. 2hr., 7am, L195.)

Microbuses traverse the island, ferrying passengers between West End, Coxen Hole, and Sandy Bay. You have to take a **taxi** from the airport to Coxen Hole in order to catch the bus out to West End or Sandy Bay. Beware of taxi drivers taking advantage of you; the trip to Coxen Hole should be L15-20 per person. To get from Coxen Hole to West End or Sandy Bay, catch a minibus in front of the little park by H.B. Warren's supermarket (30-45min., daily every 10min. 6am-6pm, L10). Taxis go from Coxen Hole to West End (L30 per person); negotiate a fare in advance.

◀ ▐ ORIENTATION AND PRACTICAL INFORMATION

Coxen Hole is the regional capital and site of the international airport. To the west, the road passes **Sandy Bay** en route to **West End** village, the best place to stay on the island. The sandy beach of **West Bay** is just beyond. The main road east of Coxen hole, going the other direction, leads to **French Harbour,** the Garífuna village of **Punta Gorda,** and the fishing community of **Oak Ridge.**

Arriving by air, catch a public microbus from the main road to your destination. If you take a taxi from the airport, walk out to the main road to avoid surcharges. Arriving by boat from the mainland, you'll be in the center of Coxen Hole.

COXEN HOLE

Coxen Hole (also just known as Roatán) is the capital of the Bay Islands, but it's hard to tell by looking at it: the charmless, bustling town is perhaps the single blemish along Roatán's picture-perfect coastline. Almost all travelers will need to pass through here; however most will want to conduct their business as quickly as possible and move on to greener pastures.

Coxen Hole has a simple layout: **Front Street** runs along the beach, while **Back Street** runs parallel to and behind it. **Thicket Road,** a few blocks to the west of H.B.

Roatán

Reef
Paved Road
Dirt Road

CARIBBEAN
SEA

Marble Hill Farms
Camp Bay
Paya Bay
Morat Island
Big Bight
Mangrove Swamp
Barbareta Island
Crawfish Rock
Punta Gorda
Ross Key
Palmetto Point
New Port Royal
Santa Helena Island
Man O' War Key Bight
Oak Ridge
Old Port Royal
Anthony's Key Resort
Jonesville
Mangrove Bight
French Harbour
Sandy Bay
Roatán Airport
Bahía de Honduras
Half Moon Bay
Brick Bay
West End
Coxen Hole
Dixon's Cove
West Bay
Flowers Bay
FERRY TO LA CEIBA

0 5 kilometers
0 5 miles

Warren's, cuts through both streets and connects to the highway for West End. For environmental education and tourist information, go to the **Bay Islands Conservation Association (BICA),** on the second floor of the Cooper Building, next to the *municipalidad.* (☎445 1424. Open M-F 8am-noon and 1:30-5pm.) **Exchange currency** and traveler's checks at the **BGA bank,** halfway down Front St. next to the *municipalidad* and across the street from the post office. (Open M-F 8:30am-3:30pm, Sa 8:30-11:30am.) For cash advances, try **Banco Credomatic,** on the first floor of the Cooper building. (Open M-F 9am-5pm, Sa 9am-noon.) **H.B. Warren's,** the grocery store, also cashes traveler's checks. (☎445 1208. Open M-Sa 7am-6pm.) Other services include: **police/FUSEP** (☎445 1138); **Dima Pharmacy** (☎445 5000), near the center of town, opposite the Cooper Building; **Hospital Roatán,** on Thicket Rd. a few blocks from Back St. (☎445 1499; open 24hr., English spoken); **Wood Medical Center,** downtown (☎445 1080; doctor on call daily 6am-7pm; English spoken; L300); and **Hondutel,** down the alley to the right of BGA (☎445 1001; open daily 7am-noon and 1-9pm). **Hondusoft Internet Cafe,** in the building next to H.B. Warren's, has free coffee. (☎445 1415. L45 per 15min. Open M-Sa 8am-6pm.) The Roatán **post office,** across from the bank, will hold packages but cannot send any. (Open M-F 8am-noon and 2-5pm, Sa 8am-noon.) **Postal code:** 34101.

For travelers staying in Coxen Hole, **Hotel Sarita ❶,** sitting partly over water on Front St. near BGA downtown, offers clean and comfortable rooms with TV, private bath, and fans. (Rooms with one large or two small beds L230.) **Hotel Coral ❶,** on the second floor of the green building across from the school, has small and simple rooms, with common bath. The empty lots around the building are dirty, but the hotel is clean. (Singles L150, with TV L180; doubles L180/L240.) The supermarket **H.B. Warren ❷** also has an attached diner with rotisserie. (Daily special L47.) **Tirza's Snacks and More ❶,** on Front St., has reasonable prices. (Breakfast L20-35; hot wings L40; dinner L30. Open daily 7am-10pm.)

SANDY BAY

A small community 7km west of Coxen Hole and halfway to West End, Sandy Bay holds a few interesting diversions, including outstanding snorkeling in the well-protected **Sandy Bay Marine Reserve.** You can also visit the **Carambola Botanical Gardens,** where just about every kind of plant and lizard in the tropics thrives. One of

HONDURAS

the best trails ascends about 20min. to the summit of Carambola mountain, from which you can see Roatán's reefs and Utila in the distance. Bring a camera. Bilingual guided tours are available. (☎445 1117. Ask for Bill or Irma Brady. US$4, with **tour** US$6. Open daily 7am-5pm.) Make sure to check out the **Tropical Bird Park,** between Anthony's Key Resort and Coxen Hole. (Tell the bus driver that you want to go there and he'll drop you off.) The large collection of tropical birds includes some which have been rehabilitated and saved from hunters. (☎445 1314. Open Tu-Sa 10am-5pm.) **Roatán Butterfly Garden** is the newest attraction, offering sights of butterflies native to Honduras and the Bay Islands. Hop on a bus to Coxen Hole and get off after about 2min. (Open M-Sa 9am-5pm, US$5.) Across the road at Anthony's Key Resort are the **Roatán Museum** and the **Roatán Institute of Marine Sciences,** two options for a rainy day. The museum has a small display on the archaeology and history of the island, with exhibits in English. (US$5. Open Th-Tu 8am-5pm.) The Institute features a dolphin enclosure with dolphin shows. (US$3. Open M-F 10:30am and 4:30pm; Sa and Su 11:30am and 1:30pm.) Sandy Bay is a 2hr. walk from Coxen Hole; buses depart regularly in front of the park (every 5min. 6am-7pm, L5).

WEST END

Near the island's west tip, Roatán's "gringo central" is home to international-style restaurants, a variety of lodgings, and gringofied prices. You can't blame people for coming—nearby beaches are phenomenal, especially West Bay (see below), and there is no shortage of opportunities for diving, snorkeling, and lazing around.

⚡ PRACTICAL INFORMATION

Tourist information: Speak to island veterans Susan and Henrik Jensen at **Rainbow Cafe** (☎445 1548; jensens@hondutel.hn), across from Foster's and Papagayo's Restaurant. Open M-Sa 8am-8pm, Su 9am-noon.

Bike and Motorcycle Rental: Captain Van's, on main road toward West Bay. Bikes US$9 per day, US$36 per week; mopeds US$29/US$116; motorcycles US$39/US$175. Open daily 9am-4pm.

Car Rental: Roatán Rentals (☎445 1171; d-Jackson@hondutel.hn). Jeeps $45 per day. Open M-Sa 7:30am-6pm.

Banks: Cash traveler's checks up to US$100 at **Woody's Grocery Store,** close to Chillie's Hotel. Open Su-F 7am-7pm.

Market: Woody's Grocery Store, next to the restaurant at Posada Arco Iris. Open Su-F 7am-7pm. **Supertienda Chris,** near the south side of town. Open M-Sa 8am-6pm.

Laundry: Bamboo Hut Laundry, behind Tony's Pizza. Open daily 6:30am-7pm.

Police: (☎445 1199 or 445 1138). Open 24hr.

Medical Assistance: Cornerstone Emergency Medical Service (☎/fax 445 1049 or 445 1003; radio CH26), at Anthony's Key Resort, has a hyperbaric chamber, 2 doctors who speak English, and one who speaks French.

Telephone and Internet Access: Rainbow Cafe offers email, phone, and fax. Email L4 per min., 5min. minimum. Phone also at Supertienda Chris (see above).

⚡ ACCOMMODATIONS

"Rooms for rent" signs dot the village's single street; prices are seasonal but generally US$5-15 per room.

▨ **Chillie's** (☎445 1214), north of the main junction. Rooms accommodate up to 3 people each. The "dorms" are in fact bedrooms. Ritzy communal bathrooms, a nice porch, picnic tables, and a backyard sweeten the deal. Storage, phone and fax service, and free kitchen use. Office open 9am-12:30pm and 4-7pm. Beds US$7.50 per person; doubles US$15; one-bedroom cabin with kitchen US$20; camping US$5 per person. ❹

Valerie's Youth Hostel. To get there, head uphill at Tyll's Dive Shop and follow the path for about 20m. Sweet-natured Valerie has a wide variety of cheap beds, from dorms to apartments. Safe and laundry service available. Free snorkel equipment for guests. Communal bathrooms and kitchen. Mosquito nets available. Dorms US$5; private rooms with 1 large or 2 small beds US$10-15; apartments with A/C and cable TV US$35. Huge tents for 2 US$8. ❸

Mango Hotel. Offers a backpacker alternative to Valerie's. Bar out front. Dorms L100; doubles and triples with private bath US$20, with A/C US$30; quads US$30. ❸

Pinnochio, 20m off the middle of the sandy street. High ceilings are hidden amidst jungle foliage, and contain 1 double and 2 single beds, fans, and private hot-water baths. The restaurant downstairs serves outstanding international cuisine, with several vegetarian specialties. Rooms US$25-35 for 2 people; add US$10 per extra person. ❹

Posada Arco Iris, on the main street toward the north side of town, away from West Bay. Gorgeous, new, large rooms with full kitchens, tile bathrooms, hot water, and A/C. Rooms US$20-50 (depending on season). 10% discount for week-long stays. ❺

🍴 FOOD

It seems every restaurant in town has a gourmet cook in the back kitchen, generating a gourmet menu accompanied by —you guessed it—gourmet prices.

Lighthouse Restaurant, by Half Moon Bay, is popular among locals for its inexpensive *típico* foods and fun atmosphere. Fish *a la coco* (L120); conch soup (L70); calamari rings (L75); shrimp pasta (L135); veggie stir fry (L50). Sample the fresh-squeezed lemonade and heavenly desserts. Open daily 7:30am-10pm. ❸

The Boulangerie is a French bakery with an ocean view. Cinnamon rolls (L16), peach tarts, fruit plates, and chocolate croissants (L14), make for great breakfast on the go. Vegetarian sandwiches on freshly baked bread (L30). Open 7am-4pm. ❶

Rudy's Coffee Stop, near the middle of the road, has great breakfast. Banana pancakes L40; French toast L25; omelettes L35-50; Fruit smoothies L50. Open Su-F 6am-5pm. ❷

The Big Blue, above the West End Divers shop, serves Thai dinners for those craving a bit of spice. Fish cakes (L75); vegetarian spring rolls (L75); red Thai curry (L140); lemon snapper (L160). Lunch menu changes entirely: giant chicken burrito-wrap (L50). Open M-Sa breakfast until 9:30pm in high season, 6-9:30pm in off-season. ❸

Brick Oven Pizza, down the dirt road and through the fields behind Pinnochio's, is worth the 5min. walk. Locals rave about the white pizza (L110), gourmet vegetarian lasagna (L95), and eggplant parmesan. Free movies nightly 5 and 7pm. Open daily 5-10pm. ❹

Argentinian, connected to the hotel Posada Arco Iris. Packed on weekend nights. Conch soup L45; entrees L115-160. Open W-M 7am-9:30pm. ❹

Cindy's Place, in a beach-view shack toward the south end of the road, offers some of the cheapest meals in town. Chicken or fish sandwiches L50. ❷

🤿 SNORKELING AND OTHER ACTIVITIES

You don't have to blow a lot of cash to enjoy the offshore remarkable reefs, since two of the best dive spots are even easier to reach by snorkeling. All dive shops rent snorkeling equipment. The **Sea Breeze Inn,** in the center of town, rents snorkeling gear and kayaks. They also offer kayak and snorkeling trips, as well as equipment and trips for kneeboarding and waterskiing. (☎445 0020. Snorkeling US$10 for 24 hr.; double kayaks half day US$16, full day US$22; single kayaks US$12/$18.) The **Lighthouse Restaurant** rents out equipment for the best prices. They also rent an underwater camera for US$25 per day. They provide the battery and flash and you bring the film. (☎445 1209. 1 snorkel set L100 for the 1st 24hr. and L75 for each extra day. Single kayaks US$10 for a half day and US$22 for the full day. Free snorkel gear with kayak rental. Open daily 7:30am-10pm.) **Half Moon Bay,** at the north end of town, is sinfully easy to jump into and delightfully impossible to avoid—roll out of bed anytime you want and wade into its refreshing waters for a swim around the coral megalopolis at its mouth. Some of the best snorkeling on the island is in nearby West Bay (see below). **Horseback** trips can be arranged at **Keifito's,** at the end of the road, past Lunas beach and over the bridge (US$25).

SCUBA DIVING

During the high season, the price for a dive is US$150-170. **West End Divers** is the oldest shop in town. (☎445 1531; open daily 8am-5pm.) **Para Vida Dive Center** has the newest equipment, fastest boats, and very experienced instructors, including the well-known PJ. (Open daily 8am-7pm.) **Native Sons Diving,** at the end of the road on the beach, specializes in individual attention and is flexible working around the diver's schedule. (☎445 1335.) **Ocean Divers** tailors the classes to students, has a classroom with A/C, and claims to go to sites farther along the reef. It is the only outfitter (apart from resorts) that includes emergency hyperbaric chamber treatment in its price. (☎445 1925; oceandivers@globalnet.hn. Open daily 8am-5pm.) **Reef Glider** is known for being the cheapest high-quality place around, and even has a few rooms available for divers as part its packages. (reefgliders@yahoo.com. Open 8am-6pm.) **Sueño del Mar,** in a large wooden building on the water, has some of the island's best prices. (Open 8am-5pm.) All of these operations offer night dives and wreck dives on request at slightly higher prices.

As for dive sites, an oft-frequented spot is **Peter's Place,** at the end of Marine Park, where tons of big fish, deep canyons, and vertical walls wow divers. Also popular is **West End Wall,** which features drift-diving along a wall densely packed with marine life. The famous **Hole in the Wall,** a sand-chute that qualified swimmers can wriggle through, is suited for advanced and very cautious divers. **Bear's Den,** which offers cave-like, enclosed canyons ready for exploration, is also appropriate only for highly skilled divers. A popular, recently installed mooring is **Blue Channel,** a shallow dive (35ft.) through a natural channel packed with bright fish and an occasional octopus. It is considered a perfect "tune-up" dive spot for rusty divers. For an interesting wreck dive, check out **El Águila,** near Sandy Bay.

NIGHTLIFE

Officially, live music and dancing are only allowed on Fridays. However, the **Twisted Toucan** rocks every night except Sunday (they're closed), and if the crowd here feels like dancing, few object. Near the center of town, this locale is hard to miss; the patrons inevitably spill out into the streets when the stools run out. The Toucan is famous for its well-stocked bar. Grab a "Jamaicanmecrazy" or a chocolate-banana daiquiri and pop in your music of choice. Tuesday is Curry Night (L70; come early, around 6pm). Happy Hour (daily 4-7pm) features two-for-one cocktails. Thursday is ladies' night (L30 cocktails). The newly opened **Cardiac Kitchen,** part of the Toucan, serves tasty basics: fish, chips, and cheeseburgers. It is the only restaurant open until 11pm and nothing costs more than L100. **Reggae Bar,** on the beach one minute past Jimmy's Lodge, has solid beers (L10) and *cuba libres.* (Open M-Th noon-midnight, F and Sa noon-2am.) Head to **Loafer's,** on the beach, a bit beyond Reggae Bar, for a beer on the beach or to play pool. Look for the Papagayo's sign to find **Foster's,** a good place to kick back and ponder the stars above.

(It's technically called "Foster's" only on Fridays.) Beer and philosophy are standard weeknight pastimes, while Fridays feature a more lively atmosphere. (Beer L25; mixed drinks L60-80. Cover F-Sa after 9pm L40, includes one free drink.) **Luna Beach,** the latest Roatán hotspot, features several bars, great music, and a pier stretching out into the water. (Mixed drinks L60, beer L15. Open Sa. Cover L30.)

WEST BAY

Can one beach possibly deserve to be this good? Powder-white sand, swaying palms, and crystal-clear water with phenomenal snorkeling—West Bay has it all. The **snorkeling** is particularly good on the west part of the beach, where the reef is just 10 or 20m off the shore. West Bay is becoming more and more developed. Those traveling on the cheap might want to bring their own food and drink.

From West End, West Bay is a 30min. walk along the beach. One can also take a **water taxi** from the dock (5min., L15). Bring repellent to ward off the sandflies.

EAST OF COXEN HOLE

French Harbour, the island's biggest fishing port, lies 10km east along a curvy paved road that traverses green rolling hills and has great views of the ocean. Yachts stop here, but there is no beach. For those who find the place alluring, there are some inexpensive hotels; try **Britos** or **Dixon's Plaza.** From French Harbour, the main road runs across the mountain ridge at the center of the island. Along the way, a side road branches out to **Oak Ridge,** a charming fishing village. From here, boat tours hit the beautiful **Jonesville mangroves** and go through a mangrove tunnel. Stop and get a snack at the **Hole in the Wall** restaurant. An 1½hr. boat ride will cost around US$20-25. A good place to spend the night in Oak Ridge is the comfortable **San José Hotel ❺.** (☎435 2328. L250 with fan and private bath, L220 with shared bath.) Buses run to Oak Ridge from Coxen Hole (about 1hr., L15). Once in Oak Ridge all transport is by water taxi (L20). The rustic, small **Reef House Resort ❺** may be too expensive for budget travelers, but its attached restaurant is a great place to grab a drink and watch the dolphins pass by. (All-inclusive package US$100.) Around 5km from Oak Ridge, the paved road ends at **Punta Gorda,** the oldest town on the island and the oldest Garífuna community in Honduras. The village celebrates its founding every year from April 8 to 12, and Garífuna from all over come to join the celebration. **Ben's Restaurant,** along the coast south of the village, rents moderately priced **cabins.** Beyond Punta Gorda a dirt road continues past new resorts to **Camp Bay,** a beach now partially closed. It ends at **Port Royal,** site of the remains of a British fort surrounded by the rather inaccessible **Port Royal Park and Wildlife Refuge.**

GUANAJA

In November 1998, Mitch the Bitch (known more formally as Hurricane Mitch) unleashed its fury on Guanaja, by far the hardest hit of the Bay Islands. 30 straight hours of 180-mph sustained winds turned the island into a picture of mass destruction. Though determined to reconstruct the town, the hard-working community is still reeling in the aftermath of the hurricane "made especially for Guanaja." The island is still not especially visitor-oriented; the few available lower-priced accommodations can be found with most of the local services in Bonacca, or Guanaja town, a small caye a kilometer off the southern coast of the big island.

CAYOS COCHINOS

Those looking for an isolated alternative to the Bay Islands need look no further than Cayos Cochinos (the Hog Cayes), 19km offshore from La Ceiba. A cluster of 13 mostly uninhabited islands, the cayes are technically a part of the Bay Islands group, and include Cayo Grande and Chachahuate. The spectacular coral directly offshore is considered to be some of the best in Honduras, and the Smithsonian Institute, which has been conducting marine research here since 1994, owns nearly half of the real estate on the islands. (For more information about research projects email fundacayos@caribe.hn or the director at acubas@caribe.hn.) The shore itself beckons, too, with beautiful hardwood forests.

A posh dive resort occupies most of **Cayo Grande,** the largest caye, but the island's trails and lighthouse are accessible to all. Most backpackers, however, will want to aim for the tiny caye of **Chachahuate,** a small community no larger than 300m across. The islanders keep a basic hut and cook for visitors; prices for each are negotiable, but L50-70 for the hut and L60-70 for the meal is reasonable. Families can also put you up in their lofts. It is best to bring a hammock and sling it under a rented thatched hut. There's no electricity or running water, and the only phone is at the **Plantation Beach Resort** (☎442 0974), several kilometers away.

Getting to the islands requires a bit of patience and an extra day for travel. You must arrive in one of the villages opposite the cayes a day early and head over to the Cochinos the next morning. **Sambo Creek** is easier to reach from La Ceiba (45min., every hr., L6), but is not the best base for reaching the cayes, since the direction of the waves can make transport difficult. **Nueva Armenia** (reachable by 11:30am and 3:15pm buses from La Ceiba: 2hr., L16), a village across from the cayes, is more likely to have transportation to them. Once you get in town, begin asking around for someone to take you out and back. René Arzu is recommended in Nueva Armenia; a reasonable price for the trip is L150-300.

Having found someone with a motorized canoe and made the necessary arrangements, secure a room for the night. In Sambo Creek, it's possible to stay at **Hotel Avila** (L100-120). In Nueva Armenia René Arzu's sister keeps a few basic rooms for visitors (L50). The next morning, meet your guide down at the dock at sunrise; early-morning departures are necessary to avoid the wind that kicks up later. The trip to **Chachahuate** takes about two hours, if the weather cooperates.

The new **Caribbean Sands Resort** (☎443 0035), 22km east of La Ceiba, offers tours. For about US$40 per person, they offer day-long, guided snorkeling trips to the main island. Call ahead to check schedules and reserve a spot. In Roatán, Henrik and Susan Jensen at the Rainbow Cafe (see p. 504) in West End have trips to Chachahuate every Saturday (7:30am-5pm; US$85, including lunch).

Even after all the details of arranging transport to Cayos Cochinos from the mainland, two pitfalls remain. First, if the wind picks up around the islands, it's no longer safe for small craft to make the trip. You could wind up stuck on an island for up to a week, so plan accordingly. Second, some canoe operators have a nasty tendency to charge visitors inflated prices for the ride back to the mainland, when alternatives are no longer possible. Get recommendations on reputable operators before leaving, and hold your ground for as long as possible, but be prepared to pay a "fee" (US$10-15) in order to get off the islands.

THE MOSQUITIA

The vast Mosquitia (Mosquito Coast), encompassing the entire northeast coast of Honduras, is like nothing else in the country—endless stretches of roadless, uninhabited terrain hold magnificent tropical forest, coastal marshlands, and flat savannah. Travel here can be half of the adventure; the few towns are frontier settlements, and getting to the villages requires patience, good Spanish, and tolerance for sandflies and mosquitoes. The region is not as impenetrable as it may seem, and getting here and around is not hard enough that it should deter interested visitors. Villages offer food and shelter and local guides are eager to show the way. For many who visit, this is a favorite part of Honduras.

Most travelers to the Mosquito Coast set their sights on the **Biosfera Río Plátano,** which holds some of Central America's most pristine rainforest and a number of Pech, Garífuna, and Miskito villages. The park begins at the coast, where most of its inhabitants live, and reaches deep into the interior, where the lowland rainforest gives way to mountainous cloud forest. Those who make it that far will find themselves in virtually unexplored territory. **Palacios,** the most accessible town in the region, is the gateway to the Biosfera. From there, it's possible to journey to **Las Marías,** at the heart of the reserve. Also, **Brus Laguna** is then an exciting boat ride away across a large lagoon. **Puerto Lempira,** the largest town in the Mosquitia, offers accommodations and access to remote, rarely visited villages.

Some travelers visit the Mosquitia on **guided tours;** these are expensive but often allow you to visit otherwise inaccessible regions. Two good companies are **Mesoamerica Travel** in San Pedro Sula (☎557 0332; fax 557 6886; www.mesoamerica-travel.com) and **La Mosquitia Eco Aventuras** in La Ceiba (☎/fax 442 0104).

There are a number of details to bear in mind while in the Mosquitia. The Miskito people have a rather unique schedule: most villages are awake and dressed by sunrise, and tucked soundly into bed by 7:30pm. In addition, most of the Biosfera, including Las Marías, is dry: no alcohol may be bought here, and bringing your own is a no-no as well. Some indigenous residents are sensitive about being photographed; it's courteous to ask permission before taking snapshots of them. Also, malaria is a problem here, so consult with your doctor before arriving in Honduras. As for money, bring all necessary cash, in the smallest bills possible—don't forget to take into consideration the boat ride to Las Marías (L2000) and plane tickets out of Palacios (L672) or Puerto Lempira (L892).

PALACIOS

Palacios serves as the first and last stop on the way into the jungle of the Río Plátano. Originally a Miskito village, this frontier town on the banks of a small, quiet lagoon is a blend of Miskito, *mestizo*, and Garífuna cultures. The constant rumble of the nearby ocean, almost like a waterfall, is soothing while you prepare for your hardcore excursions. The main things to do here are stock up on provisions and arrange transit into the reserve.

TRANSPORTATION. The **Isleña** office in Palacios is in Río Tinto Lodge (☎441 0794); **SOSA airlines** has an office in the Moskitia Ecolodge (see below). Most travelers fly to Palacios from **Trujillo** (L462) or **La Ceiba** (L672). Isleña flies this route from La Ceiba (1hr., M-Sa 6am; arrival in Palacios 7 and 11am.) Sami Air, Isleña, and Grupo Taca connect Palacios with **Ahuas, Puerto Lempira,** and **Brus Laguna.** The schedule is irregular, so check with the Isleña office.

For travelers who want to check out the Garífuna villages along the way, a **truck** begins in **Tocoa** and makes a hair-raising 8hr. trip along the coast. From La Ceiba, take the bus to Tocoa (L35) and wait for the **car** from Palacios to arrive (usually around 8am). Listen for drivers yelling destinations at the bus station in Tocoa. Find Don Pedro Blanco's car, which goes directly to Palacios (L300). To get back to Tocoa, talk to the very same Don Pedro Blanco in Palacios and reserve a space in the car. Keep in mind that after a hard rain—usually in June and July—the coastal route from Tocoa to Palacios may not be passable.

PRACTICAL INFORMATION. Right next to the grass runway is **Hospital Bayan.** (Open M-F 8am-noon, Sa-Su 2-5pm; walk-in 10-11am and 3-4pm; 24hr. For emergencies, L20.) A **clinic/pharmacy** is 5min. from the runway. (Open M-F 8am-noon and 2-4pm, Sa 8am-noon.) Two **pulperías** coexist with a few small grocery stores. Ana Argelia Marmol, owner of the Río Tinto Lodge and the *pulpería* closest to the runway, can help you set up transportation. Make **phone calls** at the Pulpería Yadira, across from the Río Negro Hotel. (L45 per min. to US or Europe.)

☗ ACCOMMODATIONS. By far the nicest of the hotels, **Hotel Mosquitia ❸** has moderately decorated rooms with tile and painted walls, large satellite TVs, and an extremely classy lounge, considering its location (☎ 443 3161). Before La Mosquitia there is a blue and pink hotel called **Hotel Dais ❸**. Probably the best deal around with clean double beds and private bath (L100). They have a place to wash clothes, a yard to set up tents and a well-kept and friendly *comedor*. **Hotel Río Negro ❹**, located down the main path past the Isleña Airlines office on the right, has a nice balcony overlooking the river (1-3 beds L150). **Hotel Soby ❸** (☎ 979 2015), down the main path on the right, has it all: nice rooms relaxing views, a restaurant, pet monkey, and TV's. (Singles L100; doubles and triples L150; all rooms with private baths.) **Hotel Samira ❸**, about 200m from the Isleña Airlines office at the end of the runway, is cheaper than all of the rest, but you can see why. Though rooms are clean and simple, bathrooms are shared and not as clean. However, the owner is extremely nice, knowledgeable, and may offer to show you around Palacios on his boat. (1-2 people L180).

☖ FOOD. A few restaurants exist in town with comparable, or slightly higher, prices than the cities because of its remote location. In the same building as the Isleña Airlines office and the movie store, the **restaurant ❶** has hamburgers and chicken for L20-30. (Open daily 5am-9pm.) Connected to the hotel, the classy **Comedor Soby's ❷** comes with white tablecloths and centerpieces. Excellent seafood includes *sopa de pescado* (fish soup) for L40 and *pescado frito* (fried fish) for L50. (Open daily 5am-2am.) Right next door to the Hotel Mosquitia and at the end of the runway, the **Restaurante Mosquitia ❷** has an electric generator for evening entertainment. (Fish L45-50. Toast L10).

BIOSFERA RÍO PLÁTANO

Most visitors to La Mosquitia spend their time in Biosfera Río Plátano, a massive swath of jungle designated a World Heritage Site by the United Nations in 1980. It has since been the focus of major environmental preservation efforts by the World Wildlife Federation, Nature Conservancy, USAID, and other organizations.

Palacios is the gateway to the entire region. A good trip into the Biosfera, described below, begins with an easy journey to the towns of **Raistá** and **Belén** or beyond, followed by a pricey boat ride or difficult trek to Las Marías, from where many excursions can be arranged. The towns that follow are on the way into the reserve; note that in addition to the route outlined here, express boats can be arranged to Las Marías or elsewhere in Palacios; try the Río Tinto Lodge.

⚑ FROM PALACIOS TO BELÉN

To explore deeper into the Mosquitia, you'll first need to get to the Miskito villages on the spit of land separating Laguna de Ibans from the sea. A *colectivo* (public tuk-tuk) leaves Palacios M-Sa sometime after the SOSA, Isleña, and Atlantic flights come in (7:30am), usually 8-10am. It reaches the first village, **Plaplaya,** (45min., L40), then continues to **Ibans** (1hr., L70), **Cocobila** (1.5hr., L80), and **Raistá** (2hr., L50). Ride the *colectivo* all the way to Raistá or hop off in Plaplaya and walk there on foot. The easy, flat walk makes for a leisurely afternoon exploring nice beaches and coastal Garífuna and Miskito life. Belén is right near Raistá and is a good place to arrange guides and transport farther into the reserve to Las Marías.

PLAPLAYA

Garífuna Plaplaya abounds with *punta* dancing and beautiful beaches. **Doña Cedi** offers five single rooms in a two-story wooden house near the water (L60 per person). Doña Cedi's kids are always ready to play and take travelers around town.

She cooks excellent Garífuna meals in a giant, open-air *comedor* overlooking the river and sells cold *refrescos* (1.5 liters, L25) and beer. Bottled water is not sold in Plaplaya, so bring purification equipment or your own. Plaplaya is most famous for the **Giant Leatherback Turtle Project.** Since 1996, the community has been involved in preserving the endangered turtle population that nests in the sands near Plaplaya. The group collects the eggs, lets them hatch in a fenced-off area of the beach, protected against both human and animal predators, and then releases the young turtles. The turtles nest from March to June, and visitors can partake in a 3.5hr. egg collection trip (free). To sign up, ask Doña Cedi for directions.

IBANS AND COCOBILA

From Plaplaya, follow any of the footpaths to the beach, turn right, and walk for a 60-90min. until you see a scattering of dugout canoes, which leads to **Ibans.** Any of the paths over the dunes will lead into this picturesque Miskito village, nestled along the lagoon of the same name. You may come to a smaller neighboring village first, but just turn left (the same direction you were going) on the path until Ibans. From Ibans to Río Plátano, there are constantly houses and the divisions between towns is unclear. Just ask around for locations and distances. From Ibans, continue east along the truck path to **Cocobila,** a slightly more developed Miskito village. Here, you'll find a cheerful blue dormitory (beds L40), the police and administrative headquarters for the villages, a few *comedores*, and, improbably enough, an Isleña airlines office.

RAISTÁ, THE BUTTERFLY GARDEN, AND BELÉN

From Cocobila, a short walk along the same path will lead to **Raistá.** Cecilia Boden and her family run an excellent, clean *hospedaje;* there's no electricity or running water, but the porch is inviting and Ceci, her 8-year-old daughter, will help you catch fireflies (L70). Eat meals of fried fish, rice, beans, and *pan de coco* (L30-45) at the cozy, clean *comedor* on the water. Hang around long enough and you'll meet legendary patriarch Willy Boden, who is sometimes called the "Abraham of la Mosquitia." He founded the village of Raistá 46 years ago and since nurtured the area. **Belén,** a small community near the mouth of the lagoon, has a small *hospedaje* (L40 per bed) and *comedor*. **Hondutel** has just installed a phone in Belén. The walk from Plaplaya to Raistá or Belén can be made in a leisurely afternoon.

RÍO PLÁTANO

This town, located on a point of land stretching out into the ocean, is the last community in this string of villages. Trips can be arranged from here to Las Marías (3 days roundtrip, with motor L2000; 5-6 day roundtrip renting a 4 or 5 man wooden canoe to paddle, L100 per day). Boats also run to **Brus Laguna** (L150). They leave on a completely random schedule so you may have to wait by the river for one to stop. Morgan Debbins can be found here and is an excellent resource for getting more information on travel in the area. Two nameless **hotels** exist in Río Plátano. The first is on the bank when you enter (L70 per bed) and the second is next to the soccer field (L50 per bed). They also serve large meals, including amazing tortillas for L23. To cross the river to Río Plátano, take the small wooden canoe (L10). Don't attempt to ford across; it is extremely dangerous.

LAS MARÍAS

Las Marías, 25km up the Río Plátano from Belén, is a jungle outpost at the heart of the Biosphere. A trip to Las Marías and the interior of the Biosphere is unforgettable, but be prepared to part with a significant chunk of cash: gas is expensive and local residents have a monopoly on transportation and guide services. For the journey from Raistá or Belén, you can travel by land or up the Río Plátano. Boats leave from all of the towns on the river but stop at the mouth of the river in Río Plátano. There you switch boats to finish the 4hr. trek. There is a small *pulpería* in town, but it is necessary to bring all camping supplies, food for the excursion, and bottled water or means of purification with you. The town does have a medical facility: the white **Centro de Salud** (open M-F 7am-5pm).

TRANSPORTATION. Motorized **pipantes** (canoes) make the trip to Las Marías upon request and arrive in 4hr.; unmotorized *pipantes* take up to 12hr. Both methods of transportation cost a painful L2000-2500 round-trip, can hold four to six people depending on the boat, and leave from either Raistá, Belén, Palacios, Plaplaya, Cocobila, or Kury. Going upstream, the trip takes 2-3 days, while the return trip can be completed in a day. (L100 per day, talk with Morgan Debbins.) Try to make these arrangements the night before, as river guides may want to leave early; trips can be arranged by Mandarino, Marvin, or Tinglas in Palacios, Eddy Boden in Raistá, Mynerto Castillo in Cocobila, Rollins in Kury, Humberto Marmol in Cocobila, Morgan Debbins in Río Plátano, among others. **Mandarino** is well connected all along the river and will arrange friendly, professional service. **Mynerto** is said to provide the cheapest rates. **Omar Holness** in the Isleña office in Palacios can provide general guidance, as can hotel owners in Palacios. The journey is long and you need to come prepared; bring both a raincoat and sun protection.

A scenic way to reach Las Marías is to **hike** in. The breathtaking 7-8hr. walk winds through dense jungle on the far side of the lagoon, skirts the foothills, passes through several indigenous farming communities, and finally breaks through the forest into Las Marías. You may have to walk through waist-deep water or mud at several points during the rainy season. Eddy Boden in Belén can arrange the trip (L250 per day for the guide, two days minimum; L200 for the canoe across the laguna). To get back out of the region, float or hike back to the Belén/Raistá area for the night. The *colectivo* back to Palacios leaves the towns between 4:30 and 5am, in time to catch a flight out of Palacios; Eddy Boden in Raistá or the Isleña office in Cocobila can radio ahead and reserve a spot on the plane.

ACCOMMODATIONS. Everything in Las Marías is organized with military efficiency by a tourism committee. Upon entering town, you will be directed to one of the three hospedajes: **Ovidio Martínez, Tinglas,** or **Las Cabañitas.** All are clean dormitories of equally excellent quality, with meals of beans, rice, a stack of super-thick tortillas (L40), and drinking water. A bed with mosquito net will cost L70 at Ovidio's and L80 at the other two per night. Mariano and his family at Las Cabañitas are very hospitable and their *cabañas* are charming.

EXCURSIONS. Though Las Marías is fascinating in itself, the wilderness areas that surround it are beyond description. Guided adventures are precisely planned and coordinated by the committee, yet they cater each trip to the group size and experience level of the travelers. Arrangements and payment are made through the village's *saca-guía* (guide coordinator), who is currently a gentleman named Ofracio. First, speak to the owner of your *hospedaje* and she or he will put you in contact with the *saca-guía.* **Canoe trips** (L70) to **petroglyph sites** further up the Río Plátano are very popular. (1 or 2 days, depending on the traveler's time constraints; requires 3 guides at L100 each for 2 people.) The glyphs have yet to be deciphered, and the trip offers excellent chances to see river wildlife and swim.

A more difficult two-day trek crosses the lowlands to the northwest of Las Marías and ascends to the shoulder of **Cerro Baltimore,** the highest peak in the region (1083m). From this viewpoint, the hiker can enjoy sweeping views of the Laguna de Ibans and the sea beyond. The true peak can be ascended by special arrangement, but requires much more physical stamina. The two-day Baltimore trek requires two guides. The most grueling of the regularly arranged trips is a three-day trek to **Pico Duma** (863m), requiring up to three guides, depending on the size of the group. After a 1-2hr. canoe ride upriver, the trail leads through farmland and forests, before turning steep and muddy as it heads into the mountains. The top, reached on the second day, affords spectacular views of the entire region.

Customized trips to more remote destinations can be arranged by sitting down with the *saca-guía* and a map. With the exception of the one-day petroglyph trip, none of the treks includes food; hikers are expected to bring their own supply unless special arrangements are made. There is basic protection from the rain but a tent is a good idea, though the guides can throw a lean-to together if necessary.

You can count on paying L100 per guide per day, as well as some nominal fees for forest preservation and overnight trips. The number of guides required for each trip is not flexible, nor are their rates. Tips are generally not expected.

PUERTO LEMPIRA

Located 250km southeast of Palacios, Puerto Lempira is the administrative capital of the Mosquito Coast, and is surrounded by Miskito and Pech indigenous villages. The settlement is fascinating for its rustic frontier-trading-town character, but the real attraction is just over the horizon: thousands of square kilometers of untouched wilderness and a culture that exists almost completely out of contact with the rest of the world. Travel here is no piece of cake: visitors should plan ahead and arrive in Puerto Lempira well-informed and well-prepared.

█ **TRANSPORTATION.** Almost all visitors travel to and from Puerto Lempira by **plane.** Atlantic Airlines flies directly from **Tegucigalpa** to Puerto Lempira (Tu and F 7:30am). Isleña makes daily direct flights from **La Ceiba** (6am, L896); SOSA (☎898 7467) leaves La Ceiba at the same time and for the same price, but makes a 7am stop in **Trujillo.** SOSA and Isleña tickets can be bought at the airstrip (cash only on all airlines). There are no roads that connect Puerto Lempira with the rest of the country, but roads do lead to the surrounding areas.

█ █ **ORIENTATION AND PRACTICAL INFORMATION.** Puerto Lempira follows a grid system, but the streets lack names. Commercial activity is concentrated near the street leading to the dock, and a *parque central* sits four blocks away from the water. From the airstrip, walk past the pavilion that serves as a "waiting room"; make a right, and walk until the water. Turn left here (or at any of the two previous blocks) and walk two more blocks to reach "downtown."

Banco Atlántida, underneath the Gran Hotel Flores, cashes traveler's checks and accepts Visa. (☎898 7580. Open M-F 7:30am-noon and 1-3pm, Sa 7:30-11:30am.) The **police station** is located alongside the airstrip. (☎898 7500. Open 24hr.) Basic **Kias Clinic** (☎898 7587), a block west of the *parque*, is open for emergencies and has an attached **pharmacy.** (☎898 7634. Open 24hr.) There are two **Hondutel** offices: one is in the south of the city and the other is one block north of Billares El Recreo. (Open M-Sa 8am-noon and 1-8pm, Su 10am-noon.) The **post office** is located inside the *municipalidad* on the southwest corner of the *parque;* remember that mail will take longer due to the remote location. (Open M-F 8am-noon and 2-5pm.)

█ █ **ACCOMMODATIONS AND FOOD.** Neither of Puerto Lempira's hotels is especially palatable, but they'll do for a night. The **Gran Hotel Flores** ❸ (☎898 7421), three blocks south of the dock, offers snug rooms with private bath, TV, and A/C. (Singles L150; doubles L250; triples L350.) **Hotelito Central** ❷, one block north of Flores at the main intersection in town, offers austere rooms and one basic common bath with no running water (L100 per night). **Hospedaje Modelo** ❸, one block east of Flores, is a good choice, with the recent addition of six rooms. (Older rooms with queen bed L120, 2 double beds L140; newer rooms L160.) The only restaurants in town are on either side of the main pier. **Lagún View ❷**, next to the dock, serves up filling *típico* breakfasts (L30-35). Lunch and dinner options depend on what the supply boat has brought lately, but usually includes fried chicken and steaks for L50 to L70. (Open daily 8:30am-11pm.) The town is packed with modest *comedores*, offering local staples like chicken or beans for under L30.

NEAR PUERTO LEMPIRA

Most travelers to Puerto Lempira use it as a "launching pad" to some exotic destination. It is best to plan what village to visit far in advance. Map out a route and a backup itinerary. Miskito communities like **Krata** and **Katski** are relatively easy to reach from Puerto Lempira and offer beach camping and an opportunity to see an indigenous ocean-fishing community at work. **Raya,** near the Nicaraguan border, is an even more remote coastal experience. **Rus Rus,** over 160km inland in a savannah-like landscape, is a village few visitors ever see. To get there, talk to the owner of Hotel Flores and hire a car (3-4hr., L1000 1-way). Bring a tent and all supplies. Ingri runs a *comedor* in the south part of the village (L30). Ask for Tomás Manzanares, who leads hikes into the surrounding area (L100 per day). Another day hike is to the **Savannah del Pino,** a unique feature inhabited by spot parrots and hawks. The trip into the broad leaf forest requires two to five days, but you'll see lots of animals, including jaguars and tapirs. The best time to visit is the dry season (Feb.-Apr.) There is an **Amigos de las Americas** (Friends of the Americas) **clinic** in Rus Rus that treats snake bites and has radio communication.

After hitting one of the town's general stores for supplies (it's better to get your equipment well before that), head down to the dock. As the largest port in the Mosquitia, Puerto Lempira sees hundreds of *tuk-tuks* and motorboats every day. One will undoubtedly be headed to your destination; the earlier you get there, the better your chances. Trips can take anywhere from several hours to several days, depending on your destination. The price is between you and the boater, who is always ready for a good haggle (made more difficult by the fact that many of these boaters speak neither English nor Spanish).

In the vast expanses that make up this part of the Mosquito Coast, there are few trail systems and fewer guides; enjoy it by simply venturing to an isolated Miskito village, setting up camp, and soaking it in. Visitors can set up a tent or hammock just about anywhere without having a special permit, provided they do so responsibly and follow the universal "leave no trace" ethic. Miskito and Pech villagers are, on the whole, warm and outgoing and, in some cases, you may be one of the first foreigners they've seen in living memory. Sometimes informal arrangements can be made for food and accommodation, but don't count on it.

OLANCHO

Known as the "wild east" of the country, the Olancho's far-flung cattle ranches and coffee plantations are bisected by imposing mountain ranges. Comprising hundreds of square kilometers of dense pine forests, parts of Olancho have a strangely un-Central American appearance. Olancheños are known for their independence; the department, which makes up more than 20% of Honduras's land area, is nicknamed "The Independent Republic of the Olancho." Although the region was a staging ground for the Nicaraguan Contra War of the 1980s, the communities in Olancho are small, friendly mountain towns. Travelers ought to stick to day buses, as private transportation has been a target of assault in the past, especially during holiday seasons. The vast expanses of raw wilderness in the area draw visitors for some of the best untamed adventures in Central America and the towns in this region have great accommodations and services.

LA UNIÓN

La Unión, a village halfway between Tegus and Trujillo in the heart of the Olancho province, is the main entry point for the **Parque Nacional la Muralla**, 14km away. The town survives on—and only exists because of—tourism so stop in to enjoy the good facilities and friendly locals.

TRANSPORTATION. Buses stop at the corner of the church in the *parque* and pass through town before leaving. From Tegus, take any Juticalpa-bound bus, get off at **Limones,** and from there make the hour-long ride to La Unión. If you have to spend the night along the way, get off at the stop in **Campamento,** about 15min. before Limones, where **Hotel Granada** has beds (L30). You can also catch the La Unión-bound Tegus bus in **Trujillo** (5hr., 1 per day 1am, L60). From **Juticalpa** there is a noon bus to La Unión. Leaving La Unión there are daily buses to **Tegus** (5 and 7am) and to **Juticalpa** (9am and 4pm). It's also possible to take either Juticalpa bus to **Limones** and then hop on one of the frequent buses to Tegus. The bus to **Trujillo** passes through town at 9am. Or take the **Aurora** bus (☎237 3647; 3hr., every hr. 5am-5pm, L35) and get into Juticalpa in time to take the bus to La Unión. A final option is **Discovery bus.** (☎222 4256. 2½hr; 12:15, 2:15, 4:15pm; L45.) From Trujillo take a Tegus-bound bus to **Tocoa** (5am).

PRACTICAL INFORMATION. Ban Café will change a few US dollars to lempiras. (Open M-F 8:30am-3:30pm, Sa 8am-1:30pm.) The **police station** is five blocks down from the *parque* on **Calle Principal.** To find **Hondutel,** walk down Calle Principal away from the central part of town. Before the school, turn right and walk to the end. Make a left, go two blocks, and turn right. Go to the end and turn left. Then take the right fork and follow the road until you reach the cement building. (☎885 0032. Open M-Sa 6:30am-6pm, Su 7am-noon.) Near the *parque central*, the house of trustworthy Nuemi Tejeda houses the **post office.**

ACCOMMODATIONS AND FOOD. The best deal in town is at the small **Hotelito La Posada,** across the street from the CODHEFOR office, which has good-sized rooms with private bath and fan. (L400 a month.) **Hotel La Muralla ❶,** two blocks below the *parque central* on the left, has clean rooms behind a flowery garden. (Singles L40, with private bath L70; doubles L80/L120; with TV and private bath L100 for 1 person, L160 for 2 people.) Just behind Hotel La Muralla is the cheaper **Hotel Los Arcos ❷,** with decent, dark rooms and bathrooms outside. (Singles L50-L70, with TV and hot water L100-L120.) Across the street from Hotel La Muralla is the **Restaurant y Repostería Ruth ❶,** where you will find arguably the best *pastelitos de piña* and other sweet breads in the country. (Fried chicken L22. Open daily 6am-9pm.) **Restaurant Oasis ❶,** has great cheap food with late weekend hours. (Chicken L30; taco L7; beer L10. Open M-F 3pm-10pm, Sa-Su 3pm-2am.)

NEAR LA UNIÓN

PARQUE NACIONAL LA MURALLA

*To get to the **Visitors Center** from La Unión, there are several options. First, ask at the COHDEFOR office to see if there is a **truck** going up any time soon. A car usually goes up daily. Some try to catch a ride at the parque central. Most trucks, packed with coffee plantation workers, pass throughout the day. Some drivers might ask for L15-25 to help with gas; even if they don't, it's polite to offer. You can also hire a **private vehicle;** expect to pay L350 to L400 for the day. Alternatively, it's a rigorous, but very pleasant, 14km (3-4* *hr.) hike through pine forests and coffee plantations to the park entrance. To return, either wait by the road for a car to pass (best before 3pm), or have scheduled a pickup. The park is managed by the Departmento de Areas Protegidas y Vidas Silvestres de* **COHDEFOR,** *whose La Unión office is 4 blocks down the road to Tegucigalpa from the parque central and 1 block to the left.*☎*885 2252. Open M-F 7:30am-noon, 1-4:30pm. Information is also available at the COHDEFOR office in Tegus (*☎*223 4346). Go to the COHDEFOR office for a guide; ask for Eduardo Ferrera (L100 per day). Admission and camping free, but donations are appreciated. COHDEFOR in Campamento* ☎*889 0196.*

High in the hills behind La Unión, the pristine cloud forest of Parque Nacional La Muralla conceals some of Honduras's most stunning wildlife. The park is best known for its birds, including toucans, peacocks, parrots, eagles, and the elusive quetzal. There are monkeys, white-tailed deer, jaguars, and pumas. Over 800 species of plants, almost 200 species of birds, and almost 300 species of mammals call this tropical rainforest home. La Muralla boasts well-marked trails, fairly easy access from La Unión, a helpful COHDEFOR office, expert guides, and mountain accommodations. A few beds are available in the Visitors Center for L40 a person.

◪ **TRAILS.** There are four marked trails, two campsites for overnight trips, and a dormitory at the Visitors Center. The shortest trail is **Sendero el Liquidambar,** a 25min. nature path. **Las Bromelias,** a very accessible hike, was wrecked for a while after a hurricane, but has now been restored. **Sendero El Pizote** makes a 3.78km (2hr.) loop around the top of the hill. The challenging 14km hike along **Sendero Monte Escondido,** is 5-6hr. and climbs up the mountain through several different levels of primary forest. The Visitors Center has a small exhibit hall, maps, bathrooms, drinking water, and a trail register. Ask the caretaker, who also works as a guide (L100) to unlock the building. Quetzales are plentiful during March and April when they flock right by the Visitors Center. Beautiful *cantos de pájaros* can be heard year-round near the visitors center and throughout the forest. Two excellent **campgrounds** with latrines, benches, and fire pits are located along the trails. Those without a tent can stay in the cabin-like dorm (L40) at the Visitors Center. There is a place to cook but no electricity. Bring your own food and water.

EMBEZZLING QUETZALES Beneath the tranquility of its natural setting, La Muralla National Park harbors a turbulent past. Though COHDEFOR, a government agency, is officially responsible for administering the park, a number of concerned locals complained in the early 1990s that the agency did not keep the park's best interests at heart. Tensions peaked in 1994, when locals stormed the COHDEFOR office and held it for 10 days. When the demonstrators were arrested, they submitted piles of evidence that revealed a scheme of bribes and profit-sharing that allowed illegal timber harvesting within the boundaries of the park. In the national scandal and government investigation that followed, several top regional COHDEFOR officials were forced to resign. Though today COHDEFOR works in cooperation with private local ecological groups, the relations between the two continues to be tense.

JUTICALPA

Deep in Honduras's central mountains, Juticalpa is the capital of the Olancho department and the largest city in eastern Honduras. Juticalpa offers the luxuries as well as the hustle and bustle of a city in the midst of untouched forest and coffee plantations. It is a great launching point for adventures into the mountains where glowing caves, crystal clear swimming holes, and exotic wildlife await. Known for its "wild-west" persona, travelers can easily roam the rainforest range in search of high adventure in the awesome beauty surrounding Juticalpa.

TRANSPORTATION. There are two bus stations, **The Regional Transport Center** (known commonly as the main bus station) and **Aurora**, both located on the **Boulevard** across the street from each other. Discover buses (☎ 885 2237) run three levels of service to **Tegus** from Aurora (3½hr., 9am-11am, L50). Buses to **Catacamus** leave from both stations (1hr., every 30min. 6am-5pm, L12). There is only one bus at noon from the main station to **La Unión,** and it completely fills up (3hr., noon and 1pm, L35). Buses run from Catacamus to **Juticalpa** (1hr, every 30min. 4am-5pm, L12). Buses leave from the main bus station to **Gualaco** (2½hr., 1 per day 5am, L20) and **San Esteban** (3½hr., 1 per day 5am, L35).

ORIENTATION AND PRACTICAL INFORMATION. Juticalpa is set up on the standard Honduran grid system around the leafy *parque central*, which has a cathedral to the east. The main north-south artery is **1A Av.**, usually referred to as the **Boulevard,** which runs along the *parque's* east side, and goes directly to the bus station (about 8 blocks south of the *parque*). Buses roll into the surprisingly organized and centralized Regional Transport Center. The main east-west drag is **Calle Perulapan** (running along the *parque's* south side) which passes in front of the *Casa de Cultura* and the Shell station and leads to the hospital. The other main street runs along the west side of the *parque* in front of the *municipalidad*.

Tourist and Park Informations can be found at **COHDEFOR,** specifically the *Departmento de Coordinación de Áreas Protegidos y Vidas Silvestras*. From the bus station, walk one block away from town on the Boulevard, and two blocks north, close to the stadium. (☎ 885 2252. Open M-F 8am-4pm.) Go to **Greko Tours,** adjacent to the post office, for travel information or pre planned tours to Roatan, Montelimar, or La Ceiba. (☎ 885 2775. Open M-F 8am-noon and 1:30-5pm.) **Banco Atlántida,** on the northeast corner of the *parque*, changes traveler's checks and gives Visa cash advances. (Open M-F 8am-3:30pm, Sa 8:30-11:30am.) Most stores will exchange dollars for lempiras as well. Medical services are available at **Clínica PMQ** (☎ 885 2086) and **Hospital San Francisco** (☎ 885 2655); take the street that runs in front of the Shell station until it ends, make a left, walk until the "Venta de Golosinas" is on your left, then turn right. Take the left fork and you will see the oddly-shaped tall and cylindrical hospital ahead. **Farmacia Teresita** is on the *parque central* next to the *centro de cultura*. (☎ 885 2181. Open M-Sa 8am-12:30pm and 2-6pm.) The **police station** is located in the offices along the western side of the *parque* (☎ 199). **Sico's,** across the street from Shell, above the post office, has **Internet** service. (L40 per hr., L5 per min. for calls to U.S. Open M-F 8am-8pm, Sa 8am-5pm.) **Hondutel,** a half block west of the *parque* before the Hotel Antunez, in an unmarked orange building, offers Sprint services and collect calling. (☎ 885 2297. Open daily 8:30am-8:30pm.) The **phones** located in the *parque central* work well to make international calls (L97 for 3min. to US). The **post office** is 2½ blocks west of the *parque* on Calle Perulapan in front of the Shell station. (Open M-F 8am-noon and 1:30-5pm, Sa 8am-noon.)

ACCOMMODATIONS. Most of Juticalpa's hotels are west of the *parque* behind the *municipalidad*. The best is **Hotel Honduras ❹,** on 1A Av. NO, one block west of the *parque*. It is clean with lots of amenities. All rooms have TV, telephone, and private bath. (☎ 885 1331. Singles L160, with A/C L170; doubles L180-185.) A cheaper option, **Hotel Reyes ❷,** two blocks west and half a block south of the *parque*, is well-kept and friendly, and only accepts guests arriving before 10pm. (☎ 885 2232. L60 per person, with private bath L80.)

FOOD. ▨**Antonioni's Pizza ❶,** next to Hotel Reyes, has fast, cheap, great pizza, complemented by friendly service. (Personal pizzas L20; warm focaccia bread L20;

salad-pizza-soda combo L55. Open daily 7am-9pm.) **Ole-Ole ❷,** one block from the *parque*, walk past Dirro's Restaurant, make a right and walk 1½ blocks to enjoy the authentic Mexican food of this hip restaurant. (Fajitas L50-85; nacho platter L40; burritos L40; vegetarian quesadillas L27. Open M-Sa 11am-11pm, Su 2-11pm.) **Casablanca ❶,** one block down the boulevard away from the church, toward the bus station, and a half block to the left, serves cheap buffet-style breakfast, lunch, and dinner in an outdoor setting (rice L4; soup L25). Also try **El Nuevo Rancho ❷,** one block east of the *parque*. This western BBQ restaurant is over 100 years old and specializes in meat entrees. (☎885 1202. entrees around L65; fried fish L70; *picho al rancho* L80; beer L13. Open M-Sa 10:30am-midnight.) **Fat Burger's ❷,** 1 block north and 1 block east of the church, has a chill environment, good American burgers, and cheap beer. (☎885 1316. Hamburger L25; club sandwich L40; beer L10. Open daily 11:30am-midnight.) **Comedor Los Arcos ❷,** four blocks from the park, serves large *platos típicos* and a drink for L22-35. Patrons get the bonus of great views through the arches of the surrounding town and hills. Several cheap food stands also line the *parque central*.

NEAR JUTICALPA

🔼 GUALACO

Gualaco is a good base for your jaunt through these natural hot spots. **Hotelito** by the *parque central* is clean and has communal bathrooms (L25 per person). There are *comedores* throughout town but **Comedor Sharon** (dressed in clown-like attire) is known for being friendly and helpful to travelers. There are *pulperías* in town, but it is best to stock up on food in Juticalpa for more variety and better prices. There are no phones in town but the COHDEFOR office has a radio. The most rewarding hike, which abounds with quetzals, is to the peak of **Cerro La Picucha** (2354m), which passes through five different ecosystems including a cloud and dwarf forest. It is a steep, hard hike (4 days). There are two camp sites along the way. Arrange the necessary guide through Francisco Urbina (L80-100 per day).

🔼 PARQUE NACIONAL SIERRA DE AGALTA

*Access the park through Gualaco by catching a **bus** from Juticalpa going to either Gualaco or San Esteban (2hr; 4:30, 5:30, 8:30am, 1pm).*

The park is one of the largest remaining stretches of untamed cloudforest in all of Central America. The COHDEFOR office in Gualaco can help you plan a hike.

🔘 CUEVAS DE TALGUA

*Take a **bus** from Juticalpa to Catacamus (1hr., every 30min, L12). In Catacamus, contact Jorge Yanez by phone (☎cell 988 1827) or find him at the NED office between the municipalidad and the church. Here you can arrange for transport to the Visitors Center (3km). It is also possible to walk (15min.) or take a taxi (L100). The entrance fee (L20) includes a mandatory guide.*

The famous **Cuevas de Talgua** at the Archaeological Park in the Parque National Sierra de Agalta are easily reached from **Catacamus.** These caves are known for the glowing skulls which date back to 3000BC. Be prepared with footwear that can get wet and shorts because currently there are parts of the cave where the water is knee-high. Ask a park worker to show you the trailhead for the 30min. hike to the second cave with its enormous, dramatic mouth.

🏛 MONUMENTO NATURAL EL BOQUERÓN

El Boquerón is easily accessible from Juticalpa—hop on one of the frequent Catacamus **buses** *and ask to be let off at El Boquerón, a small community at the base of the mountain. The ranger and guide, José People, needs a couple days notice to arrange a hike; contact him through the COHDEFOR office in Juticalpa.*

Halfway between Juticalpa and Catacamas, El Boquerón captures a broad cross-section of Olancho's ecological diversity in a relatively small area. Dry tropical forests, wet tropical forests, and cloud forests are nestled around **Agua Buena** mountain (1433m) and bisected by the Río Olancho. An abandoned little cement house, located at the entrance by great swimming holes, can be used as shelter from the rain, however it is best to bring a tent. There are three marked trails as well as innumerable hikes once in the mountains. The most popular, rewarding, and accessible hike is **Sendero Río Arriba** (6km, 3½hr.), which is great to spot birds and blue morph butterflies. This hike follows the river up the mountain to some caves. There are crystal-clear swimming holes and 2-3 ft. waterfalls all along the trail, even at the entrance. Bring a flashlight if you want to crawl into the caves for a fun but dirty adventure. **Sendero Tempiscapa** (4km, 2hr.), the shortest and most accessible of the hikes, is a nature trail with frequent toucans amidst the medicinal plants.

NICARAGUA

Nicaragua, for many travelers, is a dream come true: a tropical paradise largely undiscovered by tourists, complete with picturesque colonial towns, spectacular natural phenomena, and a vibrant, welcoming population. At peace for more than a decade now, Nicaragua is shedding its reputation for the Contra war of the 1980s. Outside the messy urban jungle of Managua, the country clearly deserves recognition as one of the most beautiful and fascinating places on the continent.

Nicaragua is the largest country in Central America, but one of the least densely populated; more than 90% of its citizens live in the Pacific lowlands, less than 15% of its territory. Unfortunately, it also remains the poorest country in the region, in part because of the political unrest from the past few decades and the devastation unleashed by Hurricane Mitch in November 1998. As the tourist industry is practically nonexistent in many parts of the country, exploration requires initiative. Much of the volcanoes on the Pacific coast, beaches on the Caribbean, and tracts of rainforest that dwarf even Costa Rica's park system remain untouched. Those willing to leave the tourist trail and tolerate fewer amenities will find these destinations extremely rewarding.

HIGHLIGHTS OF NICARAGUA

Lago de Nicaragua, Central America's largest freshwater paradise. On **Isla de Ometepe,** ancient petroglyphs adorn the rocky landscape amidst perfectly conical twin volcanoes beckoning hikers. For untouched nature and a unique artisan colony head to the **Archipiélago de Solentiname** (see p. 562).

León and Granada, two beautiful, well-situated colonial cites with strikingly different politics. Liberal León has a vibrant student culture and conservative Granada lights up the shores of Lake Nicaragua (see p. 540 and p. 554).

Masaya, the site of the country's most famous handicrafts market (see p. 549).

The Corn Islands, off the Caribbean coast, where the tourist facilities are minimal, the beaches empty, and the reefs undisturbed (see p. 588).

Selva Negra, a natural park and coffee plantation amidst the natural beauty of the northern highlands. Hike through the cloudforest and learn about environmentally sound farming techniques (p. 581).

SUGGESTED ITINERARIES

ONE WEEK. After flying into **Managua** (p. 531), you'll only want to spend about a day here before moving on. Ask around to see if there's a baseball game, eat some quality Nicaraguan fare, and check out the hip night scene. Keep partying right on through the next day or two with the young, educated crowd in **León** (p. 540). Continue on to the picturesque **Granada** (p. 554) whose colonial charm will tempt you to stay forever. An easy day trip from Managua or Granada is **Masaya** (p. 549), where the famed markets and handicrafts are a shopper's paradise. If nature is more your thing, you can also climb the Masayan Volcano and check out the national park. By now you should have a day or two left, and should plan to spend it along the shores of **Lago de Nicaragua** (p. 562). Take a boat to **Isla de Ometepe** (p.

Regions of Nicaragua

HONDURAS

★ Tegucigalpa

Northeast Nicaragua
pp. 591-594

Puerto Cabezas

● Siuna

● Ocotal

Central Highlands
pp. 572-583

● Somoto

● Estelí

Pacific Lowlands
pp. 540-561

● Matagalpa

Caribbean Coast
pp. 584-587

Corn Islands (Islas de Maíz)

● Chinandega

● Boaco

● León

Lago de Managua

Managua
pp. 531-539

Managua ✪

Juigalpa

Rama ●

Bluefields ●

The Corn Islands
pp. 588-590

Pochomil ●

Masaya ●

Granada

Isla de Ometepe

Lago de Nicaragua
pp. 562-571

Rivas

CARIBBEAN SEA

PACIFIC OCEAN

San Juan del Sur

Archipiélago de Solentiname

San Carlos

San Juan del Norte

COSTA RICA

NICARAGUA

562) for some volcanoes, beach, and the ultimate relaxation before you head back to Managua for your flight home.

TWO WEEKS. If you have more time, you should definitely check out both the volcano and the market in **Masaya** (p. 549). Extend your trip from **Isla de Ometepe** (p. 562) on Lake Nicaragua farther down the lake to the **Archipielago de Solentiname** (p. 567). You will be amazed by the unique artist colony in the natural setting. Head back to Managua for a flight to the cool, Caribbean atmosphere of **Bluefields** (p. 585) and the **Corn Islands** (p. 588) for more tropical beach time.

THREE WEEKS. Building on the one week and two week itineraries, a flight back into **Managua** (p. 531) from a respite in the **Corn Islands** (p. 588) is recommended. You can then journey into the central highlands, where the fresh air and natural beauty make this one of the most impressive areas in the country. If you want to hop into Honduras for a bit, head to the border at **El Espino** (p. 578). Next you can city hop through Central Nicaragua, starting with its largest city **Estelí** (p. 573), and then through **Matagalpa** (p. 578), and **Boaco** (p. 581) before heading back to Managua. Check out the **Selva Negra** (p. 581) near Matagalpa and play cowboy in the ranching town of Boaco. Once back in Managua for your return flight, if you have any time left you can dart over to some Pacific coast beaches.

LIFE AND TIMES

LAND, FLORA, AND FAUNA

Nicaragua is divided into three distinct regions: the **rugged highlands** of the northern and central part of the country from Matagalpa to the Honduran border, the volcanic **Pacific Lowlands** complete with the Lago de Nicaragua and most of the country's arable land, and the immense, forested **Caribbean lowlands** of the east known as the *Mosquitia.* With volcanic mountains and island chains, pristine freshwater lakes, wildlife reserves, coasts bordering two different oceans, central highlands, forest river jungles, and tropical rainforest, Nicaragua is a paradise of biodiversity. There are 12,000 classified species of plant life, and 5000 more that have been identified but not classified. Nicaragua's natural treasures stem from three distinct ecosystems within the country: the volcanoes, low altitude forests, and lakes of the Pacific region; the mountains and agriculture of the Central region, and the rainforests and coral reefs of the Atlantic region. Northeastern Nicaragua is home to the **Bosawas Biosphere Reserve** the biggest rainforest in Central America. The greatest diversification is found in the Atlantic region. Hang out with the monkeys, jaguars, toucans, parrots, macaw, poison-dart frogs, eyelash vipers, and green iguanas. Always stick to the trail, and look but don't touch.

HISTORY

Ask anyone about Nicaraguan history and you're sure to launch a complex political debate. Nicaragua has been a political battleground for power from the days of Spanish conquest and William Walker, through the last century of Somoza dictators, Sandinista socialists, and U.S. influences. Governments seem erupt but the coups and earthquakes are no match for the enduring kindness and vitality of the people, and breathtaking natural beauty.

THE FIRST FOREIGNERS. When the Spanish arrived in Central America in the 16th century, they found three major cultural groups in Nicaragua: the **Niquirano,** the **Chorotegano,** and the **Chontal.** These groups vied for dominance in their shared territory and were frequently involved in violent skirmishes. The influx of the Spanish and European diseases into the country's western highland areas effectively wiped out indigenous populations. In the areas where Europeans did not settle, the indigenous population remained relatively unharmed.

In 1524, the first permanent Spanish settlement was established in Nicaragua and the country was named after a powerful indigenous chief, **King Nicarao**. The cities of León and Granada were founded shortly thereafter and quickly became the main centers of the territory, sharing a rivalry that continued for three centuries. Spain retained control of the colony until the early 1800s, instituting colonial rule and establishing permanent settlements. By 1820, Spanish rule over Central America was threatened by nationalist independence movements and within the year Nicaragua was brokering its separation from European control.

INDEPENDENCE DAY (1821-1857). Nicaragua gained independence from Spain in 1821 as part of the Mexican empire, and joined the short-lived **United Provinces of Central America** before becoming fully independent in 1838. Without the Spanish presence, British and North American influence grew as Britain re-established control over the Mosquito Coast. American Cornelius Vanderbilt started the Accessory Transit Company, which carried thousands of forty-niners from New York City and New Orleans by boat and stage coach to California via Nicaragua during the 1849 California Gold Rush. With the support of the city of León, **William**

Walker, a renegade North American, attacked Granada in 1855 with 56 men, captured the city, and declared himself president. After drawing Vanderbilt's ire by seizing the transit company, Walker was expelled from Nicaragua by the US Navy, the transit company, and five other Central American republics in 1857, only to make two subsequent unsuccessful attempts to recapture the country.

AUTOCRATS AND ASSASSINATIONS. In 1857, **Managua** was chosen as the fledgling nation's capital city, a compromise between rival cities León and Granada. Following Walker's overthrow, conservatives gained power and held it until 1893, when the left-leaning **José Santos Zelaya** overthrew the government and proclaimed himself dictator. An autocrat with leftist ideas, Zelaya became Nicaragua's first nationalist leader, and his overthrow would mark the beginning of a succession of US military interventions in the country. The US State Department was especially alarmed to hear rumors of Zelaya's plans to grant land to Japan.

In 1909, resorting to a rather sneaky brand of imperialism, the US government encouraged Zelaya's conservative opponents to overthrow him and sent in the Marine Corps, eventually forcing his resignation. Although the White House refused to recognize Zelaya's successor, José Madriz, the US supported the subsequent three conservative regimes. The Americans retained a military presence with a 100-person Marine guard at the US embassy and in 1916 they signed a treaty granting the US exclusive canal building rights in Nicaragua.

During most of this period of de facto occupation, three liberal leaders maintained a steady resistance. In 1927, **Juan Bautista Sacasa, José María Moncada,** and **Augusto César Sandino** led their troops into fiery rebellion in response to the new conservative president and an additional infusion of US Marines. Six months of fighting was enough for Sacasa and Moncada, who both settled peacefully with the US-backed government in exchange for a pre-packaged presidency for each (1928-1933 and 1933-1936, respectively). Sandino, on the other hand, continued to fight against the US and the later US-sponsored dictatorship until his assassination.

THE SOMOZAS (1934-1979). The Marines left their replacements, the brutal **Guardia Nacional,** under the command of **Anastasio Somoza García** (a.k.a. "Tacho"), who used it to support the Somoza family dictatorship for 50 years. In 1934, Somoza had Sandino assassinated. The Somozas and their associates began amassing huge fortunes and land holdings while the rest of Nicaragua wallowed in poverty. To remain in power, Somoza implemented vicious repression in the form of torture, murder, and "disappearances." The Somoza monopoly became so extensive than even Somoza's counterparts among the elite grew resentful. Nonetheless, US support for the regime was unfaltering. (US President Franklin D. Roosevelt once said of Somoza, "He may be a son of a bitch, but he's our son of a bitch.") Opposition grew as the Somoza dynasty continued. In 1961, **Carlos Fonseca Amador,** a radical student leader and prominent Somoza opponent born in Matagalpa, formed the socialist **Frente Sandinista de Liberación Nacional (FSLN)** in honor of Sandino. Faced with growing opposition and ineligible to succeed himself, Somoza agreed in 1972 to cede his power to a ruling triumvirate, of which he was a key member. However, this reduced power structure would not last long.

FROM RUBBLE TO REVOLUTION. In 1972, a massive earthquake virtually leveled Managua, killing 6000 Nicaraguans and leaving over 300,000 others without food and shelter. Somoza exploited the opportunity to marshal the Guardia Nacional into a "National Emergency Committee" and declare martial law. Before the rubble from the quake had settled, he had altered the constitution, and re-installed himself as president in 1974. As the Somozas embezzled most of the international relief money, opposition to his regime solidified. Both the **Unión Democrática de Liberación (UDEL)** and the FSLN were gaining ground. In response, the government waged a counter-insurgency campaign which cost the lives of thousands of uninvolved peasants. In January 1978, the Guardia Nacional assassinated **Pedro Joaquín Chamorro,** leader of the UDEL and publisher of the popular and respected newspaper *La Prensa.* The cold-blooded murder of such a popular figure galvanized the population, and the revolution began in earnest.

The Sandinistas seized the national palace in August, successfully winning many of their demands in return for the release of 1000 hostages. For over a year, strikes and armed standoffs plagued the nation. Several thousand innocent Nicaraguans were killed, mostly by government troops. In some cases, Somoza's troops conducted summary executions of hundreds of teenage boys. Such abuses became untenable even for an ally as durable as the US. On July 17, 1979, Somoza fled the country as the Sandinistas again advanced upon the capital with the support of the Nicaraguan people. Two days later, on July 19, the Sandinistas marched victorious into Managua. Towns all over Nicaragua are still named "17 Julio," and "19 Julio." Somoza was assassinated a year later in Paraguay.

THE CONTRAS AND THE SANDINISTA REGIME. After the euphoria of victory subsided, the victors set about resuscitating a country in sorry shape; over 40,000 people had been killed, 100,000 were wounded, and 500,000 were homeless. During their first few years of control, the Sandinistas expropriated land held by members of the Samoza government, nationalized banks and natural resources, and brought food trade under government control. Throughout the 1980's, the FSLN improved agriculture, health care, and literacy rates.

Repairing the nation was the first formidable challenge facing the Sandinistas. The second was the US. In 1981, the US government, embroiled in a "Cold War hysteria," was angered to discover that Nicaragua had formed ties with Cuba and other communist countries. Newly elected president **Ronald Reagan** decided to bring an end to the leftist Sandinista government. To accomplish this, he resorted to well-worn US interventionist tactics, setting in motion covert CIA operations and pouring US tax dollars and supplies into the counter-revolutionary group who came to be called the **Contras.** The Contras were ex-Guardia Nacional members, mercenaries, scared teenagers pressed into service, and civilians ideologically opposed to the Sandinistas. Trained by the Argentine army and supported by US funds, the Contras set up camps in border towns of Honduras and Costa Rica, which they used as bases for their sporadic attacks on the country.

Throughout the 80s, the Contra-Sandinista war ravaged Nicaragua, making it virtually impossible for the Sandinistas to focus on repairing the battered country. In 1984, **Daniel Ortega** of the FSLN won a popular presidential election that was neutrally monitored and generally accepted as honest. The US, in response, mined Nicaraguan harbors and spearheaded an economic embargo. Food and supplies ran short and inflation spiraled to a staggering 30,000%. Revolutionary idealism began to wane, and the war became one of attrition. With the acquisition of expanded military equipment, forces, and tactical information, however, the Sandinista government was able to contain the insurrection. In 1987, Costa Rican president **Oscar Arias Sánchez** negotiated an end to the civil war.

A NEW ERA. As the 1990 elections approached, US President George Bush made it clear to Nicaraguan voters that if a new party were to take office, the US would consider lifting the embargo and provide badly needed aid. Sure enough, the nation replaced the Sandinistas with **Violeta Chamorro** of the Unión Nacional Opposición (UNO), a coalition of 14 smaller parties. Chamorro, the widow of Pedro Joaquín Chamorro, carried 55% of the vote. When she assumed office, the majority of the Contras disarmed, but the Nicaraguan government has continued its struggle to disarm the last remaining groups, termed *recontras*, ever since.

When Chamorro took the reins, Nicaragua was still a very poor, if peaceful, country where a few families controlled the nation's little wealth and employment was as high as 70%. No longer burdened with an economic embargo, however, the UNO government attempted to promote market-driven capitalism, a trend opposed by the socialist Sandinistas.

TODAY. In March 1998 the International Monetary Fund and the Nicaraguan government agreed on a loan package totaling almost US$150 million to finance the restructuring of the Nicaraguan economy. This loan package took place during the presidential administration of Arnoldo Alemán, of the rightist **PLC (Partido Liberal Constitutionalista) party,** and was a hopeful precursor to further foreign investment. Former president Daniel Ortega remains at the healm of the still powerful Sandinista movement, despite accusations of sexual abuse by his stepdaughter in 1998. In the most recent elections in 2001 **Enrique Bolaños** of the **PLC** narrowly defeated Ortega in free, democratic elections. The election was a bitter struggle, and largely influenced by promises of economic reform, especially in the tourism sector. Alemán, as former president and according to Nicaraguan law, is now the leading figure in the Nicaraguan legislature. Bolaños was vice president during the administration of Alemán, but their current relationship is not entirely harmonious. Despite recent peace, occasional Sandinista-motivated violence does erupt in the Atlantic coastal, rural region. The balance of power between the different

NICARAGUA

political parties and headstrong leaders in the next few years will determine Nicaragua's potential or plight for many years to come.

PEOPLE

The **Nicarao** people who resisted Spanish forays into Nicaragua in the 16th century have essentially disappeared in the intervening 400 years, as have most of western Nicaragua's indigenous peoples. As a result, the western half of the country is almost exclusively populated by **mestizos,** who live in and around the urban cores. The next largest population groups are the descendants of Europeans, and then blacks, the descendants of slaves imported to the Caribbean coast by the British. Nicaragua's indigenous population makes up the smallest part of the population and is concentrated in the eastern half of the country. The most prevalent group is the **Miskito,** who enjoy a degree of self-rule in the **North Atlantic Autonomous Region,** created by the Autonomy Statute of 1987. Other indigenous groups in the east include the **Rama** and the **Sumu,** though neither is as large as the Miskito. Although Nicaragua has no official religion, the country is predominantly **Catholic,** with a minority of Protestants. The official language is a clear, well spoken **Spanish,** and English is also common due to lingering British influences along the Caribbean coast, and greater American commercialization in the country.

CULTURE

FOOD & DRINK

Chicken, fruit, and tortillas—standard fare throughout Central America—are Nicaraguan staples. However, regional specialties abound: *gallo pinto* is rice and beans, usually fried, which most Nicaraguans eat two to three times a day, every day; *plátanos* (plantains) are served up fried as **maduros** (greasy and sweet) or **tostones** (crispy, like potato chips); *carne asada* is code for barbecued, marinated meat; and *mondongo* is tripe (stomach) cooked with beef knuckles. Most restaurants offer a lot of meats. For vegetarians, *ensaladas* usually consist of cabbage with tomatoes, beets, and vinegary dressing. The average mealtimes are 7-10am for breakfast, noon-3pm for lunch, and 6-9pm for dinner.

Scrumptious rums are produced and drunk locally in huge quantities. *Flor de Caña*, produced in Chinandega, is the most popular brand. Luckily, it's also very cheap and makes a great gift for friends at home. Victoria and Toña are the national beers. *Refrescos naturales* are fruit juices mixed with water and sugar.

CUSTOMS & ETIQUETTE

Etiquette in Nicaragua is very similar to the rest of Latin America. Rules are more relaxed in cosmopolitan cities than rural areas. Sorry girls, you're still going to see some lingering effects of **machismo,** a cultural attitude subordinating women. Women are advised to dress conservatively. Gifts should be accepted with great thanks. Table manners are standard, and public displays of affection are acceptable. When greeting someone, it is customary to kiss them on one cheek or both. Handshakes are also acceptable, but less personal. Always use the *usted* form of Spanish when addressing someone you don't know or an authority figure. Address friends or more informal acquaintances with the *tú* form.

THE ARTS

Nicaraguan art mirrors the country's natural beauty and political strife. Sculpture, pottery, and paintings all have a distinctive tropical/island flair. Political murals and advertising adorn the side of almost every building. The bright colors and detailed charm of Nicaraguan art tell its complicated but optimistic history.

LITERATURE. Probably the greatest known Central American literary figure is Nicaragua's own **Rubén Darío** (1867-1916), an inventor of the modernist style (see **National Hero, Wandering Soul,** p. 546). His definitive works include *Blue* (1888) and *Songs of Life and Hope* (1905). Darío had a turbulent and emotional relationship with Nicaragua. He spent much of his life outside the country, and feared at times that he had become estranged from his native land. His poetry, therefore, is a curious and unique blend of Nicaraguan and foreign influences. Subsequent Nicaraguan writers have been primarily concerned with the urgency of their country's sociopolitical condition. Vanguardist **Pablo Antonio Cuadra,** born 1912, and poet **Ernesto Cardenal,** born 1925, are both eminent examples.

ARCHITECTURE. Much architecture was destroyed by the huge earthquake in 1972, subsequent mudslides and floods, and Hurricane Mitch in 1998. The effects are particularly notable in Managua, where there really is no "downtown" type area. The largest buildings are usually international businesses or hotel chains. For a glimpse of the beauty of Nicaraguan architecture, visit **Granada (**p. 554) or **León** (p. 540) where the quaint streets, colonial charm, and religious atmosphere will leave a lasting impression. Individual residences range from impressive, gated compounds to heart-breaking, poverty-stricken shanty towns.

MUSIC. Native musicians jam on a variety of instruments, including the *chirimía,* a primitive clarinet, and the fearsome, thunderous *juco,* played by pulling a string through a drum head. Nicaragua is the southern terminus of "marimba country." Lucky travelers may see **El Güegünse,** a farcical, musical street drama about an old man who repeatedly outwits authorities. Young Nicaraguans groove to the sounds of a variety of Latin pop artists, including the ever present Shakira and Elvis Crespo. Clubs and bars often feature a mix of *salsa, merengue,* and Latin house. US pop music and techno are also common.

TV AND NEWS. Nicaraguans stay abreast of news through TV programming from the US. *Telenovelas,* the tumultuous, heartwrenching soap operas broadcast throughout Latin America, are popular. For local news (and the latest baseball standings and statistics), the most popular newspapers are *La Prensa,* which leans to the right (www.laprensa.com.ni), *La Barricada,* which leans to the left, and *El Nuevo Díario,* which rides the fence (www.elnuevodiario.com.ni).

SPORTS & RECREATION

While soccer is an obsession in most of Latin America, **baseball** reigns supreme in Nicaragua. Managua is home to a huge stadium and "world series" in May. In 2002, after rainy season induced washouts, Chinandega triumphed over Managua in an exciting, fan-filled game. Tickets are cheap by comparison - great seats for under US$20. **Water sports** (diving, surfing, snorkeling, fishing, etc.) are also very popular on Lake Nicaragua and along both coasts of beaches.

HOLIDAYS

Holidays in Nicaragua are often accompanied by spirited folk dancing, particularly during celebrations for each town's patron saint. Easter is traditionally spent at the beach; shops and businesses close for most of Holy Week, or *Semana Santa.* This is one of the most popular weeks for tourism in Nicaragua. The anniversary of the revolution is celebrated by Sandinistas with fireworks, revelry, marches, and a huge rally in downtown Managua. Holidays include: **January 1,** New Year's Day; **March/April,** *Semana Santa* (Holy Week). **May 1,** Labor Day; **July 19,** Anniversary of the Revolution; **September 14,** Battle of San Jacinto; **September 15,** Independence Day; **November 2,** All Souls Day *(Día de los Muertos);* **December 7 and 8,** Immaculate Conception; **December 25,** Christmas.

ESSENTIALS

NICARAGUA

PASSPORTS, VISAS AND CUSTOMS
Passport Required for all visitors, must be valid for at least 6 months. Visitors can stay for 90 days; extensions granted at an immigration offices.
Visa Not required for citizens of Australia, Canada, Ireland, New Zealand, South Africa, the UK, and the US.
Inoculations and Medications None required.
Work Permit Required for all foreigners planning to work in Nicaragua.
Driving Permit No special permit is needed—just a valid drivers license, registration, and title to the car. **Entrance Fee:** US$5 airport tax/tourist card; US$20 immigration fee.
Airport departure fee: US$30 by air; US$5 by land.

EMBASSIES AND CONSULATES

Embassies of Nicaragua: US, 1627 New Hampshire Ave., NW, Washington, D.C. 20009 (☎202-939-6570; fax 939-6545). **UK,** Vicarage House, 58-60 Kensington Church St., London W8 4DB (☎00 44 207 938 2373; fax 937 0952).

Consulates of Nicaragua: Honorary Consul in Canada: 87 Beausoleil Dr., Ottawa, Ontario K1N 8W3 (☎613-241-0682). **US,** 1627 New Hampshire Ave. NW, Washington, D.C. 20009 (☎202-939-6531; fax 939-6574). Nicaragua also maintains consulates in Miami, New York, and Los Angeles.

MONEY

CÓRDOBAS	US$1= 14.35C	1C =US$0.07
	CDN$1= 9.21C	1C =CDN$0.12
	UK£1= 22.24C	1C =UK£0.05
	AUS$1= 7.92C	1C =AUS$0.13

The above rates were accurate as of August 2002. The Nicaraguan unit of currency is the **córdoba** (C). There are 100 **centavos** to one córdoba. Colloquially, córdobas are sometimes referred to as *pesos* and 10 *centavos* are referred to as one *real*. Coins come in 1 and 5 córdoba pieces. Large bills are hard to break. US dollars are usually accepted and welcome at larger banks, hotels, stores, and even street vendors/markets. Changing dollars to *córdobas* is never a problem and most banks will exchange at the official rate. Nicaragua's **coyotes,** the guys on streetcorners with a calculator in one hand and a wad of bills in the other, will also change dollars at comparable rates. While technically illegal, this black market is usually not dangerous; avoid changing currency at night, and make sure the bills are genuine.

Many Nicaraguan cities have at least one bank that changes traveler's checks. Watch out for long lines, forms, and service charges. Most hotels and restaurants do not accept traveler's checks, though some take credit cards. *Coyotes* are less willing to change traveler's checks than cash. Most cities have **Western Union** offices, but some still route their orders by phone to Managua, sometimes with a one-day delay. **ATMs** are found in Managua and most other larger cities. ATMs are generally linked to Visa, Master Card, American Express, and Cirrus. There's no withdrawal charge, but there is a 2000C maximum per day. Tipping policies vary—

use discretion. Prices often include gratuity of 10-15%. A 15% sales tax is frequently ignored, unless you pay with a credit card. Taxi drivers are not usually tipped.

PRICE DIVERSITY

PRICE RANGES AND RANKINGS. Our researchers list establishments in order of value from best to worst. Our absolute favorites are denoted by the Let's Go thumbs-up (■). Since the best value does not always mean the cheapest price, we have incorporated a system of price ranges into the guide. The table below lists how prices fall within each bracket.

SYMBOL	❶	❷	❸	❹	❺
ACCOMM.	0-50C	50-100C	100-150C	150-200C	200C+
FOOD	0-20C	20-70C	70-100C	100-140C	140C+

SAFETY

As always, the smart traveler will stay alert and check the latest US State Department warnings before departing. Managua, like any large city, demands a certain degree of caution and common sense, especially if you want to avoid pickpockets. Touristed areas are often hot spots for crime; poorer neighborhoods and political demonstrations are best avoided entirely. Buses are notorious for their deft-fingered thieves. Avoid traveling alone in rural areas. Sporadic armed violence is reported throughout the country, and bandits have been known to operate on the roads, especially in the rural northeast, where the US State Department warns against travel. Call the US State Department's Travel Advisories Hotline for safety information (☎202-647-5225), or check out their web page at http://travel.state.gov. See **Safety and Security,** p. 26, for more tips.

HEALTH

Nicaragua carries the same health risks as other Central American countries. For descriptions of disease prevention, see **Health,** p. 29. Nearly every Nicaraguan town has a host of pharmacies; hours usually span from 8am to 6pm. Throughout Nicaragua, it is best to avoid tap water, uncooked vegetables, and fruit that has already been peeled. Malaria and dengue fever are present.

BORDER CROSSINGS

HONDURAS. There are three land crossings. **Guasaule** is 77km north of Chinandega, near Choluteca, Honduras. For details on entering Nicaragua, see p. 448. **San Marcos/El Espino** is 25km west of Somoto, near Choluteca, Honduras. **Las Manos** is 25km north of Ocotal, and 150km east of Tegus, Honduras. For details on the San Marcos/El Espino and Las Manos crossings, see p. 577. It's also possible to cross by boat via the Caribbean port town of **Puerto Cabezas** (p. 593).

COSTA RICA. There is one land crossing, **Peñas Blancas/Sapoá,** 36km southeast of Rivas, near Liberia, Costa Rica; for info on the Costa Rica side see p. 183, and for the Nicaragua side see p. 559. There is also a river crossing at **Los Chiles,** south of San Carlos. For info on Nicaragua see p. 568; for Costa Rica see p. 133.

KEEPING IN TOUCH

Nicaraguan **mail** is comparable to other Central American postal systems. Allow a good 15 days for addresses within the US and 20 days for Europe. **Correos de Nicaragua,** the national mail system, uses the private company EMS. You can receive general delivery *(Lista de Correos)* mail at any Correos de Nicaragua office. In most cases, mail will be held for one month, though sometimes for only two weeks. Mail should be addressed as follows:

Lauren WILSON

Lista de Correos

San Carlos (town name), Río San Juan (department name)

Nicaragua

Nicaraguan **phone numbers** use seven digits and require no area codes. For US phone company access codes, see the inside back cover. Many hotels and shops let patrons use their **telephones** for local calls (about 5C per call). Generally, your link with the rest of the world will be through **ENITEL**, the national communications service often still known by its old name, **TELCOR**. Most every city and town in Nicaragua has an ENITEL/TELCOR telephone office, usually identifiable by a tall radio tower; offices are generally open daily from 7am to 9pm. Important phone numbers are: ☎ 112 for information, ☎ 114 for international information, ☎ 110 for a national long-distance operator. To make long distance-national calls (for example, to call Bluefields from Managua), dial 0, then the seven-digit phone number. The general country code is 505, but several cities also have individual codes. Chinandega is 341; Diriamba is 42; León is 311, and Managua is 2.

COUNTRY CODE	505

TRANSPORTATION

Buses are the primary mode of transport in Nicaragua. Most of Nicaragua's bus fleet is composed of yellow school buses retired from North America. All the buses usually leave from one main terminal in town (except Managua, where there are five terminals), and each terminal has a small office with info on schedules. The roads, if paved, are usually in decent condition. Don't drive at night unless absolutely necessary. La Costeña offers **flights** to several destinations in Nicaragua, including Bluefields, the Corn Islands, Puerto Cabezas, and San Carlos. The main office is in Managua, but most travel agencies will sell tickets. Within cities, taxis are the easiest mode of transport.

ORIENTATION

Street directions inevitably revolve around landmarks rather than names. A town's *parque central* is the most common marker; it's also usually the focal point of the grid system by which the *avenidas* (avenues) and *calles* (streets) are laid out. Generally, *avenidas* run north-south, while *calles* run east-west. Often *calles* above and below a focal point have the same number, but are distinguished by *norte* (north) and *sur* (south), as in 3 Calle Nte. and 3 Calle Sur. Often, as in the case of Managua, words like *arriba* (up) and *abajo* (down) are understood to refer to certain compass directions; in other towns, they refer to elevation. In Managua, north becomes *al lago*, and some of the cardinal landmarks haven't existed for years. Another directional device is *al salida* or *al entrada*, as in *"al salida a Juigalpa."* Look for this address where the road for Juigalpa leaves town.

TRAVEL RESOURCES

Guía Interamericana de Turismo, a comprehensive website covering all of Central America. In Spanish. http://www.guiainteramericana.com.

Ministerio de Turismo (☎ 222 6652; fax 222 6618), a block south and a block west of the Inter in Managua. Friendly, helpful staff speaks English.

Nicaragua's Best Guide, http://www.guideofnicaragua.com.

MANAGUA

With a series of massive, disorganized *barrios* in place of tall buildings, the city feels more like an overgrown suburb than the capital of Central America's largest country. Downtown Managua was leveled by an earthquake in 1972 and the revolution swept through to destroy much of what remained. Today, empty dirt lots surround shopping centers and bustling markets border gutted buildings. Nonetheless, Managua remains the entertainment, commercial, and transportation hub of Nicaragua. Vitality also remains in the public art that saturates the city—revolutionary murals and radical graffiti. Although the city may be less safe than other parts of Nicaragua and many museums and galleries have been closed due to inadequate funds, Managua does have bright spots: the famous Teatro Rubén Darío, the impressive Palacio Nacional, and, in season, baseball games.

◾ ORIENTATION

UPON ARRIVAL. Arriving by air, you'll land at **César Augusto Sandino International Airport,** 12km east of the city on the Carretera Norte. **Taxis** from the airport to hotel-rich *barrio* Martha Quezada cost US$15-20; walk 100m right or left after exiting the terminal to the highway and the price suddenly drops to US$5-7. **Arriving by international bus** from another Central American capital, you'll most likely be at the well-located Ticabus terminal in Martha Quezada, two blocks east of the Casino Royale and near numerous hotels. Sirca buses from San José arrive in the south of the city, on Av. Eduardo Delgado. **Arriving by domestic bus,** you'll find yourself at one of four markets scattered about the city. Oft-crowded local buses lumber between the markets and the hotel areas; taxis are usually easier to find (15-20C).

LAYOUT AND ADDRESSES. Managua has dispensed with the annoyance of naming its streets. "Addresses" are given in terms of their proximity to landmarks—a Texaco station, a statue, where a cinema used to be—and their proximity to the rotunda. Even the cardinal points have Managuan pseudonyms: the direction "south" remains *al sur,* but "north" becomes *al lago* (toward the lake), "east" is *arriba* (i.e. where the sun rises), and "west" is *abajo* (where it descends). For example, *"De Tica Bus una cuadra abajo y media cuadra al lago,"* means find the Tica Bus Station, then walk one block west and half a block north.

Managua lies on the south shore of **Lago de Managua** (locally and more properly called **Lago Xolotlán**). Managua expands in all directions away from the lake. The effective center of the city is the pyramid-like **Hotel Intercontinental,** locally called the "Inter." Just north of the hotel is **Plaza Inter,** a US-style shopping mall complete with speciality stores, a cinema, and a food court. To the east, on the same hillside, looms the somber silhouette of sombrero-clad Sandino.

Just west of the Inter, **Av. Bolívar** runs north to south 1km north from the hotel to the lake shore and the old city center, where it meets the **Teatro Rubén Darío.** Along the way, it passes the **Asemblea Nacional** and the Bank of America skyscraper (the only skyscraper in the city), the **Palacio Nacional,** and the **Santo Domingo Cathedral.**

Across Av. Bolívar from the Inter is **Barrio Martha Quezada,** the neighborhood that houses most of Managua's budget hotels and *hospedajes.* Situated in the center of the *barrio* is the **Tica** bus station, an important directional landmark. The western border of the *barrio* Martha Quezada is **Av. Williams Romero,** with the now defunct **Casino Royale,** another popular reference point. The northern border of the *barrio* is **Calle 27 de Mayo.** Both of these streets are larger and busier than the bumpy byways of Martha Quezada. Eight blocks south of Calle 27 de Mayo, on Av. Williams Roberto, is the **Plaza de España,** home to a number of banks, several travel

NICARAGUA

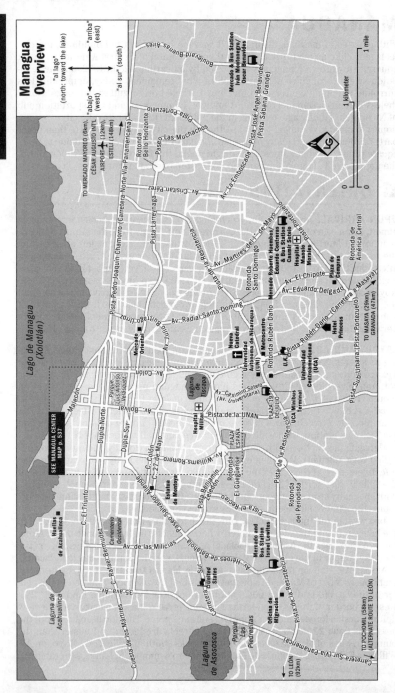

Managua Overview

"al lago"
(north: toward the lake)

"arriba"
(east)

"abajo"
(west)

"al sur" (south)

Lago de Managua
(Xolotlán)

SEE MANAGUA CENTER
MAP p. 537

Laguna de
Acahualinca

Laguna de
Asososca

Laguna de
Tiscapa

Parque
Las
Piedrecitas

TO MERCADO MAYOREO (6km),
CÉSAR AUGUSTO INTL
AIRPORT (12km),
ESTELÍ (148km)

Rotonda
Bello Horizonte

Las Muchachos

Paso

Pista-Portezuelo

Boulevard Buenas Aires

Mercado & Bus Station
Iván Montenegro/
Oscar Benavides

Pista-José-Ángel-Benavides
(Pista Sábana Grande)

Av.-La-Emboscada

Av.-Martires-del-1º-de-Mayo

Rotonda
Santo Domingo

Mercado Roberto Huembes/
Eduardo Contreras
& Bus Station

Hospital
Casmir Sotelo

Hospital
Manolo
Morales

Plaza de
Compras

Rotonda de
América Central

Av.-El-Chipote

Av.-Eduardo-Delgado

Hotel
Princess

TO MASAYA (29km),
GRANADA (47km)

Pista-Rubén-Darío-(Carretera-a-Masaya)

Orlanzaogá-Peae

Universidad
Autónoma de Nicaragua
(UNI)

Nueva
Catedral

Metrocentro

Rotonda Rubén Darío

U.A.M.

Universidad
Centroamericana
(UCA)

Pista-Sub-Urbana-(Pista-Portezuelo)

Av.-Casimiro-Sotelo
(Av. Universitaria)

PLAZA 19
DE JULIO

UCA Minibus
Terminal

Pista-de-la-UNAN

Pista-de-la-Resistencia

Rotonda
del Periodista

Pista-Pedro-Joaquín-Chamorro-(Carretera-Norte-Vía-Panamericana)

Av.-Cristian-Pérez

Av.-Radial-Santo-Doming

Pista-de-la-Resistencia

Pista-Larreynaga

Av.-Martires-del-1º-de-Mayo

Mercado
Oriental

Av.-Julio-Buitrago-Uriez

Av.-Colón

Malecón

Dupla-Norte

Dupla-Sur

Av.-Bolívar

Parque
Luis Alfonso
Velásquez

C.-Colón

C.-27-de-Mayo

Hospital
Militar

PLAZA
ESPAÑA

Rotonda
El Güegüense

Av.-William-Romero

Pista-Benjamín
Zeledón

Pista-el-Recreo

Estatua
de Montoya

Paseo-Salvador-Allende

C.-El-Triunfo

Cementerio
Occidental

C.-Rafael-Bermúdez

C.-El-Chico

Av. de las Milicias

Av.-Heroes-de-Batahola

Mercado and
Bus Station
Israel Lewites

Huellas
de Acahualinca

35-ava.-Sur

Carretera-Sur

Oficina
de Migración

United
States

Carretera-Sur-(Vía-Panamericana)

Pista-de-la-Resistencia

Cuesta-de-los-Mártires

TO LEÓN
(92km)

TO POCHOMIL (58km)
(ALTERNATE ROUTE TO LEÓN)

TO LEÓN
(92km)

1 mile

1 kilometer

0

In general, travelers are safe in Managua, although there have been more robberies recently. Pickpocketing is particularly a problem on city buses. Take a taxi at night even for short distances or when you are unsure of the directions. The **Mercado Oriental** and the surrounding *barrio* **Ciudad Jardín** are dangerous and best avoided day or night. Although the **Barrio Martha Quezada** prides itself on safety, there have been a significant number of assaults in front of *hospedajes* at night

NICARAGUA

agencies, and a supermarket. Most of the discos, chain restaurants, and the Metrocentro Mall are located on the **Carretera a Masaya.**

■ INTERCITY TRANSPORTATION

FLIGHTS

Domestic Flights: César Augusto Sandino International Airport is 12km east of the city. La Costeña (☎263 1228 or 263 2142) flies to **Bluefields** (1hr.; 6, 6:30, 10am, 2pm; 6 and 10am not serviced Sunday; one-way 680C, round-trip 1210C); the **Corn Islands** (1½hr.; 6:30am and 2pm; one-way 850C, round-trip 1570C); **Puerto Cabezas** (1¼hr.; 6:30, 10:30am, 3pm; 3pm not serviced Sunday; one-way 800C, round-trip 1420C); **Siuna** (1¼hr.; 1 per day 9am; one-way 675C, round-trip 1210C) and **San Carlos** (50min.; M-Th and Sa 9am, F and Su 12:30pm; one-way 650C, round-trip 1110C). **Atlantic Airlines** (☎233 2791 or 233 3103) has flights for the same prices to **Bluefields** (1hr.; 6:45, 10:30am, 2pm); and **Corn Islands** (1½hr., 6:45am and 2pm).

International Flights: International carriers include: American (☎266 3900; open M-F 8am-6pm and Sa 8am-1pm); Continental (☎278 2834), on Carretera Masaya (open M-F 8am-6pm and Sa 8am-noon); Grupo Taca (☎266 3136); Copa (☎267 0045), on Carretera Masaya, (open M-F 8am-12:30pm and 2-5:30pm); and Iberia (☎266 3136).

BUSES

Domestic Buses: Buses depart from 4 widely scattered markets (see map): **Mercado Roberto Huembes** and **Mercado Israel Lewites,** both in the southwest of the city; and **Mercado de Ivan Montenegro** and **Mercado Mayoreo,** both in the eastern part of the city. Next to the **UCA,** a small lot on the highway also has a few minibuses leaving for points south. Your station depends on where you're going. It's best to take a taxi or a local bus from one station to another.

Bluefields: Ivan Montenegro; Costa Atlántica runs a bus/boat combo. (☎817-0073 in Rama. 12hr., 9pm, 200C).

Boaco: Mayoreo; (2hr., every 30min. 6am-6pm, 30C).

Chinandega: Israel Lewites; (2½hr., every 30min. 4am-6:30pm, 25C). Minibuses: Lewites, (2¼hr., every 15-30min. or when full, 5am-6pm, 30C).

Estelí: Mayoreo; (3hr., every 30min. 4am-5:45pm, 22C; express 2½hr., 30C).

Granada: Roberto Huembes; (1¼hr., every 15min. 5:30am-9pm, 9C). Minibuses: (UCA, 50min., every 15min. 5:30am-8pm, 10C).

Jinotepe: Israel Lewites; (1¾hr., every 15min. 5:25am-7:30pm, 7C). Minibuses: (UCA, 50min., every 15-20min. 5:30am-9:30pm, 10C).

Juigalpa: Mayoreo; (3hr., every 30min. 4am-5:45pm, 25C; express 2hr., 30C).

León: Israel Lewites; (2¼hr., every 20min. 5am-7:30pm, 13C). Minibuses: (2hr., every 15min. 4am-8pm).

Masaya: Roberto Huembes; (Direct: 40min., every 15min. 4:30am-5:30pm, 6C. Indirect: 1hr., every 10min. 5C.) Minibuses: UCA, (30min., every 20min. 5:50am-7:30pm, 10C).

Matagalpa: Mayoreo; (2¾hr., every 30min. 4:15am-6:15pm, 22C).

Ocotal: Mayoreo; (4hr., about every hr. 5:10am-5:15pm, 42C).

Pochomil: Israel Lewites; (1½hr., every 30min. 6:30am-4pm, 10C).

Rama: Mayoreo; (8hr., every hr. 4am-10pm, 80C).

Puerto Cabezas: Mayoreo; (24hr., 2pm and 5pm, 200C).

Rivas: Roberto Huembes; (2½hr., every 30min. 8:30am-5pm, 13C, express 1½hr., 1 per day 4pm, 30C).

San Jorge (for **Isla de Ometepe**): Roberto Huembes; (2½hr., every 30min, 8:30am-5:30pm, 30C).

Siuna: Mayoreo; (10hr.; 4am, 5, 8pm; 100C). Best to stop by the night before to reserve a seat.

Somoto: Mayoreo; (3½hr.; 7:15, 9:45am, 1:45, 3:45pm; 37C).

International Buses: Catch Tica buses (☎222 6094), 2 blocks east of the Casino in Barrio Martha Quezada, to: **Panama City** (16hr., 7am, US$35); **San José, Costa Rica** (9hr.; 6, 7am, 12pm; US$10); **Tegucigalpa** (8hr., 5am, US$20); **San Pedro Sula** (12hr., 5am, US$28); **San Salvador** (12hr., 5am, US$25); **Guatemala City** (18hr., 5am, US$33); **Tapachula, Mexico** (24hr., 4:45am, US$48).

⊑ LOCAL TRANSPORTATION

Local Buses: Cost just 2C, and once you get the hang of it, they are invaluable. Routes are tricky and there's no published schedule; ask locals. While the city recently got $2.5 million to modernize the bus system, the current equipment is aging; crowding, pickpocketing, and violence are frequent problems. The **#119** stops at the Mercado Roberto Huembes, Carreterra Masaya, Universidad Centroamericana, Plaza España, and Iglesia Lezcano. The **#118** can be caught on Av. Williams Roberto and serves Mercado Ivan Montenegro, Mercado Israel Lewites, and the Red Cross. The **#109** runs from Barrio Martha Quezada and the Hotel Intercontinental to the attractions of the Plaza de la Democrácia. The **MR4**, passing along Calle 27 de Mayo, is the quickest way to Mercado Huembes from Martha Quezada. The **#110** lumbers between 3 markets: Israel Lewites, Roberto Huembes, and Ivan Montenegro.

Taxis: There's no problem flagging one down; they honk at all pedestrians to show their availability. Arrange price in advance and beware of "gringo fares." A crosstown ride should *never* be more than 25C. A trip to the airport is about 40C. Bargaining is often easier if you offer the initial price rather than ask for it. A typical fare is 10-20C during the day and 15-40C at night, depending on distance.

Car Rental: Budget (☎222 2336), **Dollar** (☎222 2275), and **Hertz** (☎222 2320), all in the lobby of Hotel Intercontinental, rent to people over 25 years old. All rent supercompacts for US$20 per day plus tax and insurance, 4x4's start at US$45-60. Open daily 7am-7pm. All have airport branches.

⚠ PRACTICAL INFORMATION

TOURIST, FINANCIAL, AND LOCAL SERVICES

Tourist Information: Ministerio de Turismo (INTUR; ☎222 6652, fax 222 6618), 1 block south and 1 block west of the Inter. Staff speaks English, but offers little substantive advice. Sells a variety of maps and guides and gives out free INTUR literature if they have them. Open M-F 8am-2pm. **Airport office** (☎263 3176), open daily 7am-7pm.

Travel Agencies and Guided Tours: The big complex southeast of the traffic rotary in the Plaza de España houses several travel agencies, including **Viajes America** (☎266 1130 or 266 0968. Open M-F 8am-6:30pm, Sa 8am-1pm). **Tours Nicaragua** (☎/fax

266 6663), 2 blocks south and a half block west of the Inter, in Edificio Bolívar, is not budget, but well-informed about tours throughout the country.

Embassies and Consulates: US (☎266 6010, 268 0123 for consular services), 4.5km down Carreterra Sur in Barrio Botahola Norte, southwest of Barrio Martha Quezada. Open M-F 8am-noon. **Honorary Consul of Canada** (☎268 0433). Open M-F 8am-noon. **UK** (☎278 0014 or 278 0887), on Reparto Los Robles, south of Av. Rubén Darío. Open M-F 9am-noon.

Banks: Banco de Finanzas (BDF; ☎222 2444), Av. Bolívar across from Plaza Inter. 3% commission on traveler's checks. Open M-F 8am-4pm, Sa 9am-12:30pm. Inside the Metrocentro mall's financial center, **Bancentro** and **Banco de America Central** have branches with extended hours, including Sunday service until noon. Both banks change traveler's checks and offer credit card cash advances. Most other national banks also have branches here. **ATMs** accept MC, Visa and AmEx at all **Texaco Star Marts** and **Esso on the Run** stores. The nearest to Martha Quezada are in the parking complex on the ground floor of Plaza Inter, and at the Esso station just west of Plaza Inter.

Western Union: (☎266 8126), south from the Inter on Av. Bolívar; turn right at the fork. The office is 400m down the hill and around the bend on the right. Open M-Sa 8am-8pm, Su 8am-3pm.

Bookstores: Hispamer (☎278 1210), 3 blocks west and 1 block south of Metro Centro, boasts an excellent Spanish-language collection. Open daily 8am-6pm.

Supermarket: La Colonia, in the Plaza España, above the roundabout. Huge, US-style supermarket with 15 aisles. Open M-Sa 8am-8pm, Su 9am-7pm.

EMERGENCY AND COMMUNICATIONS

Police: (☎249 8342, emergency 118 or 126), at the Mercado Oriental.

Red Cross: (☎265 2081, emergency 128), in Belmonte at km 7 of Carretera Sur. 24hr. ambulance service.

Hospitals: Hospital Bautista (☎249 7070 or 249 7277). **Hospital Militar** (☎222 2763). For nearby help in an emergency, **Farmacia del Buen Pastor** (see below) has a small clinic alongside. Clinic is open daily for consultations (10am-noon, 100C). Emergency visits available 24 hr. (emergency cell ☎884-3481, emergency visit 150C). Doctors can make home visits (300C).

Pharmacies: Farmacia del Buen Pastor (☎222 6462), 1 block north and 1½ blocks east of the Casino, has the best hours. Open M-Sa 8am-8pm, Su 7am-noon.

Telephones: At the Palacio de Comunicaciones, the **Correos de Nicaragua** offers all phone services. Open M-Sa 7am-9pm and Su 7am-6pm. There are phones with a direct connection to Sprint all around the city, including on the 2nd fl. of the Plaza Inter. Pick up public phones and dial access codes (**Sprint** ☎161, **ATT** ☎174, **MCI** ☎166) to connect to a bilingual operator. **Information:** ☎112. Public phones work with coins or **phone cards** that can be bought at gas stations. **FonoCenter** (☎222 2611), on the bottom fl. of Plaza Inter, has local, national, and international phone service (calls to the US 60C per min., to Europe 130C per min.). You can also use the **Internet** (40C per hr.), or send **faxes,** and there is a **Western Union** representative. Open M-Sa 10am-10pm, Su 10am-8pm.

Internet: Banisa Cyber@Center (☎222-5383) 1 block north of the Casino, 40C per hr., 32C with ISIC card. M-Su 8:30am-10pm, Su 8:30am-5pm. **Kafe@Internet** (☎264 0252), 2½ blocks north of the Casino. 20C per hr., measured in ½hr. increments. Open M-Sa 8am-8pm, Su 9am-6pm. Internet calls 3-10C a minute to most countries.

Post Office: In Palacio de Comunicaciones just west of the Old Cathedral and the Palacio Nacional. **Fax, Internet, phone service**, and express mail. Open M-F 8am-5pm, Sa 8am-12pm for mail services.

ACCOMMODATIONS

All the hotels and *hospedajes* listed below are in the **Barrio Martha Quezada,** a neighborhood of comfortable homes, bohemian lodgings, and the occasional wandering pig. The *barrio* lies eight blocks north of the Plaza España, between the Hotel Intercontinental to the east and the stadium to the northwest.

As soon as you hop out of your taxi or bus, you'll be swamped by young children. Nothing but the most forceful telling-off is likely to disperse them; it's probably easier to just go with it. A 1C tip is standard. Recently, there have been numerous assaults by young neighborhood gangs in the area right in front of *hospedajes*. Walk in groups, don't carry large amounts of cash, and ride in a taxi after dark. As a general rule, the farther west of the Inter, the cheaper the lodgings.

Casa Vanegas, formerly known as Hotel Bambú (☎222 4443), on the southwest corner of the intersection a block east of the Tica bus station (no sign) in a peach-colored house. Feel right at home in this clean hostel. Availability determines if you get a room with a private or shared bath. US$6 per person. ❶

Hospedaje Quintana (☎228 6090), a backpacker favorite, very clean and well-kept rooms with a patio in front. Private bath 70C per person. Prices subject to change. ❷

Guest House Santos (☎222 3713), a block west of Hospedaje Quintana, near Av. Williams Romero and Calle 27 de Mayo. A favorite with travelers, who lounge in hammocks in the spacious covered courtyard. The small *comedor* inside serves basic meals at rock-bottom prices. Some rooms have private baths. 50C per person. ❶

Hospedaje El Dorado (☎222 6012), half a block east of the Casino Royale. The homey, fanned rooms clustered around an indoor patio are tight and stuffy but comfortable. Communal bathrooms are kept clean, and the friendly owners are security-conscious. 70C per person, 140C with private bath; doubles with private bath 180C. ❶

Hotel El Conquistador (☎222 4789, www.hotelelconquistador.com), a block and a half north of the office of tourism. Carved wooden doors, bright yellow walls, tile floors, A/C, hot water, refrigerators, free breakfast, and free airport shuttle. US$40 one double bed, US$55 for two double beds, US$5-10 discount with ISIC card. ❺

Hotel Los Felipe (☎222 6501), 1½ blocks west of Tica Bus, is a bit on the high end. Garden, pool, restaurant, and rooms are well-maintained. Single rooms with private bath US$15; with A/C US$25; US$5 extra for each additional person. f❺

FOOD

Managua has an abundance of *fritangas*—sidewalk *comedores* that offer traditional, deep-fried buffets. You point at something, they throw it into a pan of boiling oil. The stews and *platos típicos* dished up at the city's markets are another cheap, authentic option, while the food courts at Plaza Inter and Metrocentro will satisfy those homesick for Happy Meals and Subway subs. The streets around Hotel Intercontinental are also home to more upscale spots.

Café Mirna, a block east and a block south of the Casino Royale. Every morning, the city's expatriate crowd packs in for the best pancakes in Managua (22C). *Gallo pinto* with eggs and toast 22C; omelettes 20C; *batidos* (milkshakes) 12C. Open M-F 6:30am-3pm, Sa-Su 6:30am-1pm. ❶

Ananda, across from the Montoya statue. A popular vegetarian restaurant with garden seating, especially known for its tropical fruit drink blends. Delicious *ensaladas* (20-40C) and *jugos* (10C); *Plato del día* (25C); Open M-Sa 7am-8:30pm. ❷

Comedor Sara, right across the street from Guest House Santos, serves up hot and tasty spaghetti or curry to a packed crowd of travelers (20-30C). Open daily for dinner. ❷

NICARAGUA

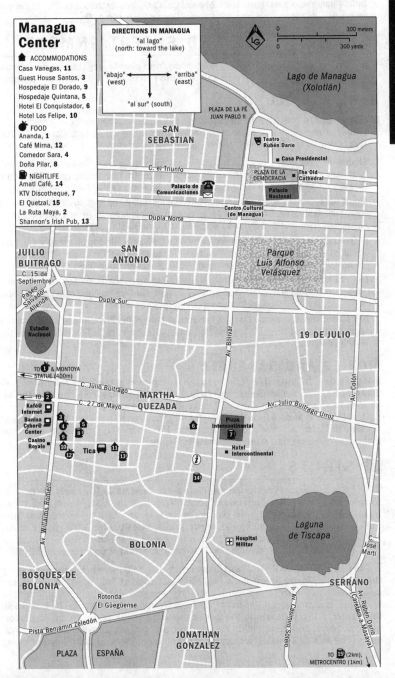

Managua Center

🛏 ACCOMMODATIONS
Casa Vanegas, **11**
Guest House Santos, **3**
Hospedaje El Dorado, **9**
Hospedaje Quintana, **5**
Hotel El Conquistador, **6**
Hotel Los Felipe, **10**

🍴 FOOD
Ananda, **1**
Café Mirna, **12**
Comedor Sara, **4**
Doña Pilar, **8**

🎵 NIGHTLIFE
Amatl Café, **14**
KTV Discotheque, **7**
El Quetzal, **15**
La Ruta Maya, **2**
Shannon's Irish Pub, **13**

DIRECTIONS IN MANAGUA
"al lago"
(north: toward the lake)

"abajo" ←→ "arriba"
(west)   (east)

"al sur" (south)

0   300 meters
0   300 yards

Lago de Managua
(Xolotlán)

PLAZA DE LA FÉ
JUAN PABLO II

SAN SEBASTIAN

Teatro
Rubén Darío

Casa Presidencial

C. el Triunfo

PLAZA DE LA
DEMOCRACIA

The Old
Cathedral

Palacio de
Comunicaciones

Palacio
Nacional

Centro Cultural
(de Managua)

Dupla Norte

JUILIO
BUITRAGO

SAN
ANTONIO

Parque
Luis Alfonso
Velásquez

C. 15 de
Septiembre

Paseo
Salvador
Allende

Dupla Sur

Estadio
Nacional

19 DE JULIO

Av. Bolívar

TO 1 & MONTOYA
STATUE (400m)

C. Julio Buitrago

MARTHA
QUEZADA

Av. Colón

TO 2
Kafé@
Internet

C. 27 de Mayo

Av. Julio Buitrago Urroz

Banisa
Cyber@
Center

3

5

6

Plaza
Intercontinental

7

Casino
Royale

9

8

Tica

11

Hotel
Intercontinental

10

12

13

ℹ

14

Av. Williams Romero

Laguna
de Tiscapa

C.
José
Martí

BOLONIA

✚ Hospital
Militar

BOSQUES DE
BOLONIA

SERRANO

Rotonda
El Güegüense

Av. Casimiro Sotelo

Av. Rubén Darío
(Carretera a Masaya)

Pista Benjamín Zeledón

JONATHAN
GONZALEZ

PLAZA   ESPAÑA

TO 15 (2km),
METROCENTRO (1km)

Doña Pilar, ½ block west and south of Hotel Quintana, this restaurant bustles in the evenings with its cheap, fast, and good *típico*. Open daily 5-10pm. ❶

🎭🎵 NIGHTLIFE AND ENTERTAINMENT

Managua has something to satisfy all tastes; from classic large discos to international music venues. You'll need a cab to get to places for safety and convenience.

BARS AND CLUBS

■ **Hippa-Hippa,** a beach bar in the city, is the hottest disco at the moment, attracting the young, socio-economic elite of Managua; slick attire suggested. Cover 40-120C depending on DJ, drink specials, and special events. Open W-Sa 8pm-whenever.

Shannon's Irish Pub, 1 block east and ½ block south of Tica Bus. An authentic Irish pub with cold cider, Guinness, darts, tasty snacks (excellent homemade chili 37C), and a friendly mix of locals and foreigners. Open M-Th 5pm-midnight, F-Sa 5pm-3am.

Amatl Café, 1 block south of the Hotel Intercontinental. A cozier atmosphere; hip bands play this trendy spot. Students, older folks, and a fair number of *gringos* all mix here on weekends. Live music every Th-Sa 6pm-12am. Cover 30-50C.

El Quetzal, on Carretera Masaya across from La Colonia Supermarket, draws an all-ages local crowd that dances the night away to live *salsa* music. Come early if you want a table. Full service kitchen (chicken tacos 35C). No cover. Open Th-Su 6pm-3am.

La Ruta Maya, just east of the Montoya statue behind the *parque*. An open-air bar and dance club with classic rock and *salsa*. Sa night stand-up political comedy (in Spanish). Occasional cultural performances. Open Tu-Sa 5pm-2am. Cover 40-80C.

KTV Discotheque, a classy disco in the bottom floor of the Plaza Inter. Private karaoke rooms with large-screen TV. There is also a casino in the hotel. 50C cover and 50C minimum drink order. (Foreigners get in free.) Open Th-Sa 7pm-4am.

MOVIES AND BASEBALL

For the latest Hollywood flick, head to the multiplexes at the Plaza Inter or Metrocentro. (40C, 35C for students, 35C before 4pm and all day Tu.) The Centro Cultural shows movies during the day. Unlike its *fútbol*-crazed neighbors, Nicaragua's national sport is **béisbol** (see **¡Jon-Ron!,** p. 552). You can join the fun by going to the stadium in Martha Quezada to watch a game. Pro teams play from October to June and college teams duke it out from June to September.

◎ SIGHTS

The sights in Managua surround the **Plaza de la Democracia** (formerly Plaza de la Revolución), on the northern end of Av. Bolívar, near the lake. A restored monument to Rubén Darío sits on the *plaza's* north side. To reach the *plaza* from Martha Quezada, walk 12 or so blocks north or take bus #109 from the corner of Av. Bolívar and Calle Julio Buitrago. Head to the *plaza* to see the colorful light show choreographed to classical music in the central fountain at 6 and 9pm nightly.

■ **TEATRO RUBÉN DARÍO.** About 200m north of the Plaza de la Democracia along the lakeshore, **Teatro Rubén Darío** is a 1200-seat concert hall hailed as one of the best venues in Central America. It regularly welcomes groups from all over the world and is permanent home to the National Symphony Orchestra. The **Experimental Theater,** a 200-seat studio theater in the same building, hosts dance performances, plays, and great children's costume and puppet shows that anyone will enjoy. The **Sala de Cristales,** a chandeliered hall on the second floor, hosts rotating international art exhibitions, which are usually free of charge. (☎ 222 3630. Main theater: national groups and symphony US$5-10; international performances US$10-40. Experimental Theater 20-50C. Stop by the box office or check the papers for schedules and prices.)

■ **FERIA EXPLICA.** One of the biggest annual events in Managua and in all of Central America, the Feria Explica is held for 11 days at the end of July on fairgrounds west of the city center, near the Huellas de Acuahalinca, an archeological excavation about ten blocks west of the Teatro Rubén Darío. Thousands of farmers and ranchers from all seven Central American countries come to show off their prize livestock and horses and buy the latest equipment and supplies. The event also features daily rodeos, food stands, night clubs, live music, and a vast array of artisan booths from all over Central America. (Admission to fair 10C, 20C after 4pm.)

THE OLD CATHEDRAL. On the eastern side of the Plaza de la Democracia, this building was nearly destroyed by the 1972 earthquake. It has been partially restored with a new fiberglass roof. The shadowy (empty) crypt, located underneath the altar, is an eerie sight. (Closed to the public at publication. Check to see if open.)

CATEDRAL DE LA IMACULADA CONCEPCIÓN. At the Rotonda Rubén Darío across from the Metrocentro Mall, sometimes called *Nueva Catedral.* Although it looks more like a moon base camp than a cathedral, this earthquake-proof church still maintains a mystical quality. (Services M-F 6pm, Su 8am, noon, 4, 7pm.)

PALACIO NACIONAL. Due to budget cuts, Managua's museums have been consolidated into the Palacio Nacional, on the south side of the *plaza.* The **Hall of Natural History,** on the first floor, has displays national parks and Nicaragua's natural history. A small **art gallery** exhibits the work of current local artists. and collections of pre-Columbian pottery and stonework. The second floor boasts the **National Library** and **National Archives;** much of Rubén Darío's work is exhibited here. The museum tour (in Spanish and English) includes a guide. (☎ 222 2905. Open M-F 8am-5pm. $1.)

⬚ SHOPPING

In Managua's excellent *mercados*, the city comes to life. ■**Mercado Roberto Huembes,** also called Mercado Central, east of the universities, is an enormous market where you can find just about anything you're looking for and a whole lot more, from a Masayan hammock to a skinned pig's head. **Mercado Israel Lewites,** commonly called "Israel," in the southwest of town, offers a notable array of sizzling *comedores*, as well as a pharmacy and a wide selection of apparel from such fine manufacturers as "Rebok" and "Adibas." **Mercado Ivan Montenegro** and **Mercado Mayoreo,** visited mainly for bus departures, don't have anything that Mercado Roberto Huembes doesn't. **Mercado Oriental,** a sprawling labyrinth of shops closer to downtown, is one of the city's most dangerous areas and **should be avoided.**

⬚ DAYTRIPS FROM MANAGUA

BEACHES

Buses to *Pochomil* (2hr., every 30min., 8C), leave from Mercado Israel Lewites in Managua. You can also **walk** between the two beaches (30min.; walk on the road during high tide). To get to Montelimar from Masachapa walk about 3km north up the road (rocks block the beach route) or take a **bicycle taxi** (10C). The last sure ride home is at 4:30pm.

About 60km southwest of Managua, the adjacent Pacific beaches of Pochomil, Masachapa, and Montelimar make a great daytrip for travelers and residents overfrenzied by the capital. On weekdays, you'll have the beach to yourself. The view of the city is spectacular. ■**Pochomil,** managed by INTUR (the Nicaraguan tourist board), is the southernmost beach; it is wide, clean, and has a boardwalk full of seemingly identical restaurants. Restaurant owners will bombard you to eat and laze in their *rancho* (a palm covering on the beach. Fish 50C; shrimp 70C; lobster 80C.) Hammocks (30C per day) are usually free if you eat. Restaurants tend to be cheaper south of the estuary (left as you face the sea). There is an unmarked *corriente* (undercurrent) that should be avoided. If you're unsure, just ask any local "*corriente?*" and point to the sea. Waves can get huge here. Many of the restaurant owners have a few rooms behind their kitchens, varying in quality. **Hotel Altamar ❸**, on the hill just south of the estuary, has basic, well-kept rooms. (☎ 269 9204. 1-3 people 100-150C, with bath 150-200C.) **Hospedaje Johana ❷**, about 100m north of the estuary on the right, is dark and small, but the proprietor is very friendly. (☎862 7410. 1-3 people without bath 50-120C.) There is an unmarked *corriente* (undercurrent) that should be avoided. Waves can get huge here. **Masachapa** and **Montelimar** are less clean and touristy, but have a pleasant fishing atmosphere

XILOA

Ten kilometers west of Managua, Xiloa (heel-WA or eel-WA) is a **volcanic lake** with a lush mountain backdrop. Lined by picnic tables and *refresco* stands, the lake has cool and inviting waters. On weekends, intoxicated Managuans make it much less appealing. To get there, catch one of the **buses** from Israel Lewites headed for Mateare, Nagorote, or León, and ask to be let out at the *entrada principal a Xiloa* (2C). Alternatively, take city bus #113 (2.5C) from the road in front of Israel Lewites or the Metrocentro to Sandino, 5km shy of Xiloa. A **taxi** to the laguna should run 40-80C. (Use of the lake's facilities 2C.)

PACIFIC LOWLANDS

The Pacific lowlands, stretching from Chinandega in the north to Rivas in the south, is Nicaragua's population center. A long string of volcanoes along the coast has made the lowlands the most fertile farmland in the country. Shielded from the Caribbean rains by the mountains, the lowlands are hot and dry. For a breeze, migrate to any body of water—Lago de Nicaragua or the Pacific. León, where student radicals keep things lively, and Granada, a tourist favorite for its architectural wonders, are both steeped in history. Artsy Masaya is a gold mine of local crafts, while San Juan del Sur offers visitors a taste of beach bum life.

LEÓN

In the streets of León, the colonial blends with the new at every step. Cobblestones traveled by horse-drawn carriages are trod by hundreds of liberal students, bells from the 19 local churches are often outdone by the horns of the taxis and *camionetas* that crowd around the markets, and prayer to the saints is never far from parties where spirituality is easily forgotten. Despite the constant mixing of eras, the echoes of the town's Spanish founders remain loud and clear.

León Viejo was founded on the shore of Lake Xolotlán in 1524. This city was destroyed by an earthquake in 1610, and León (full name: León Santiago de los Caballeros) was rebuilt 30km to the west. Though poor, the new León soon became a cultural and intellectual stronghold and the capital of Nicaragua for more than 300 years. The heady atmosphere fueled the imagination of its favorite son, Rubén Darío, whose poetry launched the modernist movement in Latin America. As bumper stickers on many cars proclaim, León is *orgullosamente liberal* (proudly liberal). The Universidad Nacional Autónoma de Nicaragua (UNAN), the country's first university, sharpens León's politics to a radical edge.

NICARAGUA

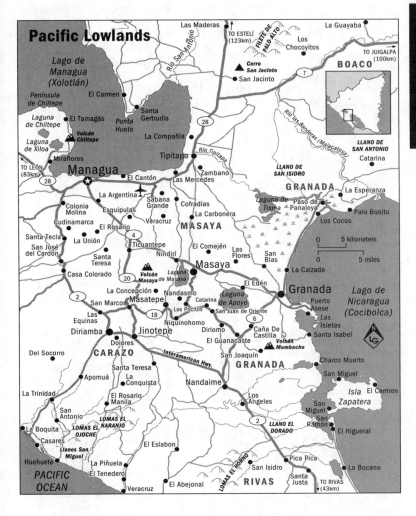

Pacific Lowlands

TRANSPORTATION

Buses leave from the main terminal, 6 blocks north and 7 blocks east of the *parque central*, to: **Managua** (bus: 2hr., every 16min. 4am-6:30pm, 13C. Express 1½hr.; every hr. 5am-noon, 2, 4pm; 15C. Minibus: 1¼hr., every 20min. 4am-8pm, 20C); **Estelí** (3hr., 3:10pm, 25C); **Matagalpa** (2½hr., 2:45pm, 24C); **San Isidro** (2½hr., every 30min. 4:30am-5pm, 16C) via **San Jacinto** (35min., every 30min. 4:30am-5pm, 7C); **Chinandega** (bus: 1½hr., every 11min. 4:30am-5:40pm, 7.50C; minibus: 30min., every 20min. 4am-9pm, 10C); **La Paz Centro** (1hr., every 35-40min. 5:50am-6:40pm, 6.50C); and **Nagarote** (1¼hr., every 35-40min. 6:10am-7pm, 7.50C). For local transportation,

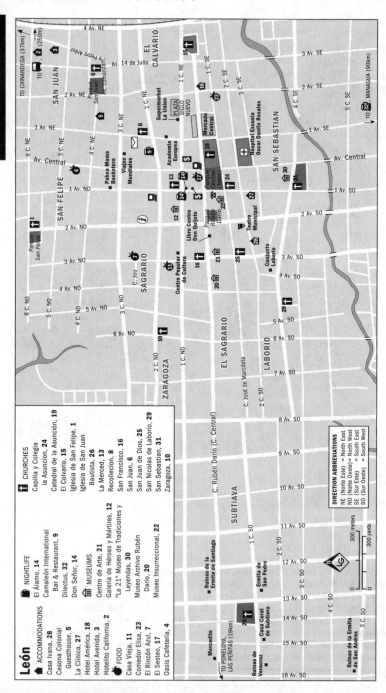

the #101 bus and *camionetas* (30min., every 10min., 2C) run between the Terminal on the east side of town and El Mercadito on the west side, where buses depart for the beach. The bus travels along Calle Central and passes through the *parque central*. **Taxis** to the center from the bus station are 6C.

■■ 🛈 ORIENTATION AND PRACTICAL INFORMATION

One of the few cities in Nicaragua where street names mean anything, León is surprisingly easy to get around, and most people choose to do so on foot. León's center is the *parque central* **(Parque Jerez)**. If you're standing in the *parque* (with the fountain of lions), the massive **cathedral** is to the east, and the imposing **ENITEL** antenna is to the west. León's *calles* run east and west and *avenidas* run north and south. **Calle Central Rubén Darío** fronts the north side of the *parque*. **Av. Central** would run right between the *parque* and the cathedral, except that the *avenida* is discontinued for a block at this point. León's 19 churches dot the landscape every few blocks and are frequently used as reference points in directions farther away from the *parque* or cathedral. **La Iglesia de La Merced,** a block north of the *parque central's* northwest corner, and **La Iglesia de La Recolección,** one block east and two north of the *parque central's* northeast corner, are useful landmarks. The **bus terminal** lies on the edge of town, six blocks north and seven blocks east of the *parque central*. To get to town from the bus station, take a right onto the main street that you came in on, walk past the market, and continue for several blocks, then take a left on 1 Av. Noreste. The walk to the center of town can be a hot and dusty 20min. trek, but it's manageable. Take advantage of the shade provided by overhangs at almost every hour of the day and you'll be thankful.

Tourist Office: Instituto de Turismo (☎311 3682), 1 block west and 2½ blocks north of the *parque*. Open M-F 8am-12:30pm and 2-5pm.

Travel Agent: Viajes Mundiales (☎311 5920 or 311 6920), 3 blocks north and ½ block west of the *parque central's* northeast corner. Good for international flights and travel within Nicaragua. Open M-F 8am-6pm, Sa 8am-12:30pm.

Banks: BanCentro, ¾ of a block north of the *parque's* northwest corner. Open M-F 8am-4:30pm, Sa 8am-noon. **Banco de America Central,** 1 block north and 20m east of the cathedral's northeast corner. Open M-F 8:30am-5pm, Sa 8:30am-12:30pm. Both cash traveler's checks and give cash advances on AmEx/MC/V. **ATMs:** Visa Plus ATMs located inside **La Unión Supermarket** and **Plaza Siglo Nuevo,** both 1 block north and ½ block east of the *parque's* northeast corner.

Western Union: (☎311 2426), 1 block north and 1 block east of the cathedral's northeast corner. Open M-F 8am-12:30pm and 2-5pm, Sa 8am-12:30pm.

Supermarket: La Unión, in Plaza Metropolitana, 1 block north and ½ block east of the cathedral's northeast corner. Open M-Sa 7:30am-8pm, Su 8am-6pm. **Supermercado Salman,** 1 block north and 3 blocks west of the *parque's* northwest corner. Open daily 7am-8:30pm.

Police: (☎311 3137, emergencies 115), 2km from Central León, on Carretera Chinandega (taxi 10C).

Hospital: Hospital Escuela Oscar Danilo Rosales (☎311 6934), 1 block south of the cathedral, in a big grayish, yellow building.

Telephones: ENITEL, on the west side of the *parque central*. Open daily 7am-8:45pm.

Internet: Puerto Café Ben Linder has the best prices. (30C per hr., students 20C.) Open daily 8:30am-11pm. **El Sesteo** is on the northeast corner of the *parque*. 30C per hr., 15C minimum. Open daily 8am-11pm.

Post Office: Correos de Nicaragua, 2½ blocks north of the cathedral's northwest corner. **Fax** and **telegram** service available. Open M-F 8am-noon and 2-5pm, Sa 8am-noon. *Lista de correos* open M-F 8-11am and 2-5pm.

ACCOMMODATIONS

Hotels in León vary from colonial lodgings near the center to cheaper places a short hike away. Prices shrink as distance from the cathedral grows. If you're willing to hike past the *parque* to the south and west, you should find a good deal.

■ **Casa Ivana** (☎311 4423), 1 block south and 1½ blocks west of the southwest corner of the *parque,* across from Teatro Municipal. Hidden behind the steel gate and a small sign, Casa Ivana offers great value. Rooms tend to go quickly. Laundry area, clean towels, and cable TV. Singles 70C; doubles 100-120C; triples 180C. ❷

■ **La Clínica** (☎311 2031), almost 2 blocks south of the southwest corner of the *parque.* A newly built annex to the friendly Dra. María Mercedes Galo's clinic. Rooms and bathrooms are basic but clean. For the proximity to the *parque*, the price can't be beat. Self-service lunch. 50C per person, with private bath 60C. ❶

Hotel Avenida (☎311 2068), 4 blocks west and a half-block south of the bus station (across from the Esso gas station), is a popular resting spot for locals and foreigners. Self-service laundry, fans, cable TV, and a *cafetín* that serves basic breakfast (12C). Singles 50C, with bath 70C; doubles 75C/80C; triples with bath 150C; quads with bath 180C. ❶

Casona Colonial Guesthouse (☎311 3178), 4 blocks north and half a block west of the cathedral's northwest corner. Rooms are luxurious, with hand-sewn quilts and sparkling private baths. Large sitting area with color TV and a pleasant garden. Guests get a key to the front door when they check in. Singles and doubles US$10; triples US$15. ❸

Hotelito California (☎311 5074), borders the south side of the market and bus station. These relatively secure, cozy rooms are certainly the most convenient place for weary travelers to crash. Baths are clean. There's a welcoming sitting room with fruit and juice in the morning, and the owners are caring. 40C per person, 70C with bath. ❶

Hotel América (☎311 5533), 2 blocks east of the *parque*'s east corner. The extra money affords guests a great location and pleasant comforts. Rooms have private baths and towels. Singles 115C; doubles 200C; triples 270C; quads 360C. ❷

FOOD

Like any college town, the city has plenty of pizza joints. But you can do better: most restaurants in León provide equally enjoyable atmosphere and food. The market is a great option for hot grilled and fried snacks (0.5-20C).

■ **Casa Vieja,** across from the west side of Casa de Cultura, 2½ blocks west and 2 blocks north of the *parque central*. Dishes piled high with colorful vegetables and other *nica* food that shows off all the country has to offer. Soft music and relaxed atmosphere draw many local couples. Entrees 20-50C. Open Th-Tu 4-10:30pm. ❷

El Rincón Azul, 2 blocks west and 2½ blocks north of the northwest corner of the *parque*. A trendy student hangout. The food is typical but served up hot and fresh. The management encourages writing on the walls, and students' musings accompany travelers' insights. *Bocas* 10-30C, entrees 40-60C. Open daily 10am-2am. ❸

El Sesteo, on the northeast corner of the *parque,* has the perfect setting for people watching and even a few delicious entrees that won't break the bank(23-98C). The *leche con cacao* (16C) is refreshing. Purified ice. Open daily 8am-10:30pm. ❷

Comedor Elisa, ½ block east of the cathedral's southeast corner, has a good lunch buffet (12-25C) that attracts crowds. Open daily for lunch 10am-2pm. ❶

Oasis Cafetería, 4½ blocks north of the *parque's* northwest corner, serves reasonably priced traditional food (10-50C) to a mostly local crowd. Check the freshness before ordering seafood. Open daily 10am-9pm. ❶

🅖 SIGHTS

León is a great walking city because churches and murals border every block. Start a walking tour of León at the *parque central,* **Parque Jerez.** A striking **mural** curves around the walls of the miniature plaza across the street from the northeast corner, tracing the path of Nicaraguan history. Set in a surrealistic desert landscape, the story is told in the form of objects strewn in the sand. Another mural, **El Gran Pedido** (the Great Request), on the east side of the basketball courts, ½ block from the northwest corner, is an expression of the frustration Nicaraguans feel because of corruption and exploitation.

▧ MUSEO INSURRECCIONAL LUIS TORUÑO CHARATA. A tiny gem, this shrine to the Sandinista Revolution is hard to forget. The museum's owner, Marvin Benito, participated in the insurrection of 1979. He'll take you through photos and faces of Sandinista leaders and martyrs, but he speaks only Spanish. *(10m west of the southwest corner of the parque central. Open daily noon-2pm. Suggested donation 10C.)*

▧ CENTRO DE ARTE. In a large colonial building, the impressive collection covers the walls of three beautiful courtyards—complete with roses and fountains—and those of almost a dozen rooms. The collection spans numerous genres, from pre-Columbian ceramics to European religious paintings to Latin American and Cuban works. The atmosphere is relaxing, especially at sunset. *(2 blocks east and 15m south of the northeast corner of parque central. Open Tu-Sa 11am-9pm. 10C; written Spanish guide 20C.)*

CATEDRAL DE LA ASUNCIÓN. The huge, restored **Catedral de la Asunción,** which lies on the *parque's* east side, is the largest cathedral in Central America, and boasts a very imposing facade that dwarfs the city. Rubén Darío rests here, on the right side of the altar, his tomb guarded by a giant lion statue. The church is also famous for *Stations of the Cross,* a series of paintings by Antonio Sarria. There are over a dozen other churches around town to check out, too.

MUSEO ARCHIVO RUBÉN DARÍO. Three blocks west of the *parque* is this museum and former home of the country's favorite poet, Rubén Darío. The museum contains some of his clothes, paintings of his family, his death mask, and a collection of manuscripts and first editions. The collection is a complete representation of this well respected literary figure. With permission, you can read the books in the archive. *(☎311 2388. Open Tu-Sa 9am-noon and 2-5pm, Su 9am-noon. Free.)*

MUSEO DE TRADICIONES Y LEYENDAS. Don't let the pleasant garden in front fool you. The building was a prison for political enemies of Somoza between 1921 and 1979. Converted in 2000 into a museum, it is a mixture of the happy, the superstitious, and the violent history of León. *(3 blocks south and ½ block east of the cathedral's southwest corner, across from San Sebastián Church. Open Tu-Sa 8:30am-noon and 2-5:30pm, Su 8:30am-3pm. 5C.)*

GALERÍA DE HÉROES Y MÁRTIRES. The gallery contains a sobering collection of black and white photos of León residents who died during the Sandinista revolutio, respectfully reminiscent of a shocking era. The caretaker, Concepción Coruño, lost her husband, a son, and a daughter in the war and gives a moving account of the stories behind the pictures. *(1 block north and 1½ blocks west of the north-*

NATIONAL HERO, WANDERING SOUL According-
ing to official reports, he died in 1916, but in Nicaragua, Rubén Darío still lives—parks,
streets, schools, and landmarks everywhere bear his name. Born in 1867 in Metapa
(now Ciudad Darío), he gained almost instant fame in Spain and Latin America for his
inventive, modern style. In fact, Darío is thought to have initiated Latin American Modernism, perhaps single-handedly, with his poem "Azul." The resulting poetic movement
was dubbed "rubendarismo." Darío reveled in the aesthetic and believed in art for art's
sake. Some of his most poignant poetry (including "Sonatina" and "A Roosevelt")
expresses the conflicting emotions Darío, who spent most of his life abroad, felt toward
his homeland. After serving as Nicaraguan ambassador to Spain and France, and living
in Panama and Chile, he died penniless in León. Despite his reputation as Latin America's greatest poet, later poets have tried to distance themselves from the man who
urged Latin America to "learn constancy, vigor, and character from the Yankee."

west corner of the parque, under a sign that says "La Galería Bazar de Artesanía." Open M-Sa
8am-5pm. Donations appreciated.)

🎭 🎵 NIGHTLIFE AND ENTERTAINMENT

Nighttime is when León really comes alive. University students often spend weekend nights dancing until dawn—or at least until authorities shut the clubs down (1-
2am), after which the party moves to bars for the rest of the night. Popular areas
are well lit and patrolled by *vigilantes* (watchmen hired by the town to keep public areas safe at night). The local tourist board sponsors **Tertulias Leonesas** in the
parque central every few Saturdays. The events—part concert, part culture, part
fiesta—are free to the public and draw huge crowds. Artisans and street vendors
set up mid-afternoon, and the music usually starts around 6:30pm.

Don Señor, 1 block north of the northwest corner of the *parque*, is a popular university
dance spot. Two dance floors provide slightly different atmospheres: *Arriba* (upstairs) is
larger, darker, air-conditioned, and plays more Latin music, while *Abajo* (downstairs) is
a cabana bar with a small but packed dance floor in the corner, playing a mix of Latin
and US pop and rap. Open W-Su 8pm-2am. Cover W-Th 15C, F 20C, Sa 25C.

Camaleón International Bar/Restaurant, 2 blocks north and ½ block east of the northeast corner of the *parque*. A popular bar that almost always has live music. Colorful bar
with palm trees, zebra-striped entryway, and owners who practice and play at all hours.
Delicious pasta dishes, including vegetarian options, also available (15-45C). 10% student discount. Open M-F 4pm-midnight, Sa-Su 4pm-2am.

Dilectus, on the highway to Managua (taxi 20C), is a little more expensive than other
clubs in town. The European-style disco draws an upper-class crowd. Music features
local DJs on the tables. 80s and *mariachi* music draws an older crowd on Th; rock and
pop groove F-Sa. Cover Th-F 20C, Sa 30C. Open Th-Sa 8pm-1am.

El Álamo, in the same building as Don Señor, above. The most popular bar in town. Perfect atmosphere for those who would rather converse than boogie, with lots of local traffic. Karaoke by demand early on W and F. Open W-Su 7pm-2am.

NEAR LEÓN

🔘 LEÓN VIEJO

From León, take a **bus** to **La Paz Centro** (1hr., every 35-40min. 5:50am-6:40pm, 7C).
From there, catch a bus for the town of **Momotombo** and ask to be let off at "Las Ruinas"

(30min., 9 buses per day 6:30am-5pm, 5C). From Managua, take a bus from Mercado Israel Lewites to La Paz Centro (1¼hr., every 20min. 4am-6pm, 9C). Buses return to La Paz Centro every 1-2hr. (8 buses 8am-5pm, 5C). Once in Momotombo, follow the blue-and-white signs to Las Ruinas de León Viejo for about 10min. The road veers to the left. Site open daily 8am-5pm. 10C, with ISIC 5C.

León Viejo (Old León) lies 30km southeast of León, on the shores of Lago de Managua. Founded in 1524 by Francisco Hernández de Córdoba, it was the colonial capital of Nicaragua until early 1610, when **Volcán Momotombo,** standing at the edge of town, caused an earthquake that destroyed the city. Hurricanes have since taken their toll on the partially excavated ruins. To prevent further damage, the brick foundations that remain have been covered with cement, so all that remains are footprints of buildings. A pleasant Spanish-speaking guide will tell you the story of their past splendor. Tours take 45min. and start at the foundations of the cathedral, a 5min. walk past the museum, where a statue marks the spot where Hernández de Córdoba was beheaded. Córdoba's remains were exhumed from the Iglesia de La Merced here in May 2000 and are now entombed below the statue.

▶ BOILING MUD PITS

*Take the **bus** bound for San Isidro from León and ask to be let off at Los Hervideros in San Jacinto (35min., every 30min. 6-7C). The bus driver will let you off on the road just above the arch that marks the mud pits' entrance.*

For an untouristed geothermal outing, head to **Los Hervideros (The Boiling Springs) de San Jacinto,** a small field full of vigorously boiling pits of muddy water and holes spewing sulfuric steam, located 25km west of León on the road to San Isidro. For a small tip, eager local kids will show you where to step to avoid breaking through the earth's crust and being boiled alive—avoid the white clay. If you ask, your guide will show you a nearby hot spring where you can bathe with the locals.

▶ BEACHES

*Take the #101 bus or a camioneta (10min., every 10min., 2C) from the main bus station in León to **El Mercadito,** on the outskirts of town, or walk about 15min. west down Calle Rubén Darío. Buses run from El Mercadito to Poneloya and Las Peñitas (40min., every 55min. 4:45am-6pm, 6C). The bus first stops in Poneloya, farther west, and then retreats east to Las Peñitas. If you get off in Poneloya, Las Peñitas is to the left (facing the beach). The main road splits right before Poneloya, and the left branch leads to Las Peñitas. You can walk between the two beaches either on the sand or on the road 35m away (30-45min.) Buses heading back to **León** leave about every hr. 6:15am-6:40pm.*

The peaceful and deserted twin beach communities of **Poneloya** and **Las Peñitas** lie 21km southwest of León, distinguished solely by their position in relation to a rocky outcropping known as La Peña del Tigre. Facing the water, Poneloya is to the right, Las Peñitas to the left. Killer waves and currents make swimming risky; the best spots are the south end of Las Peñitas and the north end of Poneloya.

There are two hotels in Poneloya. **Hotel Lacayo ❶,** on the beach one block north to the right of La Peña, has creaky floors and old cots but great ocean views. (☎887 7747. 50C per person.) **La Posada ❺,** a block inland, has clean rooms and thick mattresses, as well as private baths. (☎031 7377. 3 or 4 beds with A/C US$20; sometimes US$15 if you swear not to use the A/C. AmEx/MC/V.) The **hotel restaurants ❶** both serve a basic breakfast (20-25C). **Restaurante Pariente Salidas ❷,** one block to the right of Hotel Lacayo as you face the ocean, is the best-known restaurant in Poneloya. (Entrees 50C. Plate of the day 25C. Open daily 7am-9pm.)

Las Peñitas offers a few more options, all within a short walk of the bus stop. **Hotel Barca de Oro ❸** has basic rooms with sturdy locks and mosquito netting. One of the owners is a turtle activist and can organize trips to the nearby **Isla Tuan Uenado Reserve.** The restaurant and bar share *la torre* (the tower), which overlooks the sea, serving French and local food for 30-60C. (☎317 275; tortuga@bw.com.ni. 2 beds US$5-7; all-inclusive packages available.) **La Montaña ❶** offers rooms and hammocks for every price range, and the attached restaurant serves breakfast (25C) and the usual array of local foods. (☎317 264; mirthamer@hotmail.com. Hammocks 40C. Basic rooms 50C per person; doubles and triples with A/C, hot water, and TV US$10, with private bath US$20.) **Mi Casita Bar Cafetín ❸** has a few newly redone and brightly colored rooms. The sitting area is attractive and the small yard well maintained. (☎776 0873. Breakfast 25C, other food 35-70C. Doubles and triples US$12.) The **Suyapa Beach Hotel ❹** has a pool, a delicious restaurant (70-115C), and a number of clean, brightly colored rooms. (☎885 8345. Restaurant open Su-F 7am-8pm and Sa 7am-9pm. Doubles US$15; with A/C US$25-30.) You can rent **body boards** at La Montaña (30C per hr., less for guests), and Hotel Barca de Oro (20C per hr., less for guests).

CHINANDEGA

Chinandega, 36km northwest of León, is one of Nicaragua's hottest, driest, and flattest towns. However, its proximity to Honduras, the port of Corinto, León, and Chichigalpa (where thousands of gallons of Nicaragua's famous *Flor de Caña* rum are produced), make Chinandega a bustling commercial center. Other than a stop on the trail to and from Honduras or the difficult ascent to the top of Volcán Cristóbal, Nicaragua's tallest volcano, the town itself has little interest for visitors.

◨ **TRANSPORTATION. Buses** leave from Mercado Bisne to **León** (1¼hr., every 11min. 5am-6pm, 7.50C), by **minibus** (30min., every 10min. 5am-9pm, 10C); the border at **Guasaule** via **Somotillo** (2½hr., every 30min. 4am-7:30pm, 13C); **Corinto** (45min., every 15min. 6:40am-6:40pm, 4.50C); **Chichigalpa** by minibus (15min., every 10-15min. 6am-6pm, 5C); **Managua** (2hr., every 30-45min. 4:15am-6pm, 25C).

▚▞ **ORIENTATION AND PRACTICAL INFORMATION.** Most **buses** pull into El Mercado Bisne. To get to the *parque* walk north from the bus station for 5 blocks, then turn left for eight blocks. The *mercado central* is between the fourth and fifth blocks. **Supermarket Palí** is on the southwest corner of the *parque*. (Open M-Sa 7:30am-8pm, Su 8am-6pm.) Exchange currency, traveler's checks, and advance money on AmEx/MC/V at **Bancentro,** two blocks east of the southeast corner of the *parque*. (Open M-F 8am-4:30pm, Sa 8am-noon.) **Western Union** is 2½ blocks east of the southeast corner of the *mercado central*. (☎341 2455. Open M-F 8am-5pm, Sa 8am-12:30pm.) The **Red Cross** (☎341 3867, emergencies 341 3132), 5 blocks east and 5 blocks south of the *parque*, offers 24hr. ambulance service. Other services include: **police** (☎341 3456, emergency ☎118), on the west side of the *parque;* **Hospital Mauricio Abdalab** (☎341 4902), on the southwest corner of the *parque;* **ENITEL,** one block east and half a block north of the *parque* (☎341 0156. Open daily 7am-9pm.); **Internet** at **Cybernogs,** 2½ blocks east of the southeast corner of the *mercado central*. (Open M-Sa 9am-9pm, Su 9am-5pm; 20C per hr.); and **post office,** one block west and half a block north of the northwest corner of the *mercado central*, with **telephone** and **fax** service. (Open M-F 8am-noon and 2-5pm, Sa 8am-noon.)

▐▐ **ACCOMMODATIONS AND FOOD.** Hotels are scarce. 1½ blocks south of the southwest corner of the *mercado central*, **Hotel Chinandega ❶** offers simple rooms with communal bathrooms (45C per person). **Hotel California ❷,** 2 blocks east and 1½ blocks south of the *mercado central*, has clean baths and comfortable rooms, as well as a nice common area and a kitchen that serves breakfast. (☎341 0936. Rooms 110C per person, with bath 140C. Reservations recommended.) The pricier **Hotel Glomar ❸**, 1 block south of the southwest corner of the *mercado central*, offers rooms with decent beds and large, clean bathrooms. (☎341 2562. Singles 120C, with A/C 180C, with A/C and private bath 250C; doubles 180C/240C/300C; triples 240C/280C/350C.) **Comedor Reyes ❷**, 2 blocks south and 1½ blocks east of the southeast corner of the *mercado central*, is the most popular place in town. Portions are generous. (*Comida corriente* 20C; chicken 28C. Open daily 6:30am-9pm.) Another option is **Doña Leo ❷**, on the corner two blocks east of the southeast corner of the *mercado central*, where they grill the food right out front. Food is fast, filling, and cheap. (20-30C. Open daily 6-10pm.)

NEAR CHINANDEGA

▟ VOLCÁN SAN CRISTÓBAL

*From Mercado Bisne in Chinandega, take the **bus** headed toward Guasale on the Honduran border. Ask to be let off at the Campusano stop in El Ranchería (40min.; every 30min. 4am-7:30pm, return every 30min.; 6C). Buses leave for El Bolsa from El Mercadito in Chinandega (30min., every hr. 5am-6pm; return every hr. on the hour; 4C).*

There are no trails up Volcán San Cristóbal, and some routes are impassable after the midway point, so it is best to get a guide. The 8-10hr. round-trip is steep and mostly above the treeline. The first route to the top is via **El Ranchería**. From the bus stop, walk northeast along the highway (toward Guasale) for one block. Turn right onto the first road and walk two blocks toward the mountain. The house across the second road on the left corner belongs to Denis Chávez, the *guardabosque* or *hombre verde*, i.e. the forest ranger. If you call a few days in advance, he can get horses to take you to the summit. He likes to begin early in the mornings, as the heat becomes intense very quickly. Denis and his wife open up their home for climbers. (To reach him, call his neighbor at ☎883 9284 and he will return your call. 100C for both horses and a guide).

The other route to the volcano is via **Las Bolsas.** From Las Bolsas, it's 11km up the road to **Hacienda Rosas,** at the foot of the volcano. No buses pass this way, so if you don't have a car, you'll either have to walk or borrow a horse from Socorro Pérez Alvarado (☎883 9354) who lives at the Las Bolsas stop. It's best to go with a guide to the summit. Vincente Pérez Alvarado (Socorro's brother) is a knowledgeable person in the area and can arrange to meet you. (5hr. round trip climb from the base of the volcano; 9hr. walk from Las Bolsas.) There is no water on either route, so bring plenty. The intense climb is rewarded by the spectacular views on top of Nicaragua's tallest volcano.

MASAYA

Any souvenir you could possibly be seeking can be found in hundreds of crowded stalls of the two overflowing markets in Masaya. With more than 65% of Nicaragua's handicrafts, making decisions is a challenge and your bargaining prowess will be put to the test. T-shirts, festive blouses, polished woodwork and ceramics, leather, and the infamous Nicaraguan, hand-woven hammocks are just some of the goodies waiting for you in Masaya's markets.

Outside the bustle of the market, Masaya is a simple town, with long *siestas* when the streets are empty but the parks are full of loungers. With its proximity to **Granada** and **Managua,** Masaya is the perfect opportunity for a day-trip. Even if you don't plan to scale the nearby **Volcán Masaya,** the **Malecón** on the west edge of town will provide ample opportunity for serenity and beautiful views.

NICARAGUA

▐ TRANSPORTATION

Times will definitely vary, despite what the schedule says. Prices listed here are for school buses. Faster minibuses called *luaus* are double the price.

Buses: Leave from east of the Mercado Nuevo to: **Managua** (indirect 1hr., 5C; direct 40min., every 15min. 3:30am-8pm, 6C.); **Granada** (40min., every 20min. 4:40am-6pm, 4C.); **Carazo** (1¼hr., every 20min., 10C) via **Catarina** (20min., 4C.); **Laguna de Apoyo** (40min.; 3 per day 5:30, 10:30am, 3:30pm; 6C); **Niquinohomo** (25min., every 20 min., 6am-6:45pm, 10C.); **San Marcos** (45min. every 20min, 5am-6:30pm, 5C.)

▟█ ORIENTATION AND PRACTICAL INFORMATION

All of Masaya's main thoroughfares run into the geographic and directional center of town the **Parque 17 de Octubre**. The *parque's* eastern border is **Av. Sergio Delgadillo,** which runs north and south. **Buses** arrive and depart from the lot just east of the Mercado Nuevo. To get to the *parque,* exit the bus lot at the northwest corner and hang a left on Calle Ernesto Fernández. Walk 6 blocks west, past the **Mercado Viejo** on your right, until you reach the *parque.* You can also catch a town bus (2C), a horse drawn carriage (4C), or a cab (4C).

Tourist Information: The **Tourist Office** (☎ 552 7615), in the Mercado Viejo on the northern edge, is very helpful and has information about festivals and regional attractions. Open M-F 8am-12:30pm and 2-5pm. The friendly proprietor of the **Hotel Regis** (see below) has a wealth of knowledge of the city, and he speaks slow, clear Spanish.

Banks: BanCentro (☎ 522 4337), on the west side of the *parque.* Changes traveler's checks and gives cash advances on AmEx/MC/V. Open M-F 8am-4:30pm, Sa 8am-noon. **Banco de América Central,** one block east of the *parque's* northeast corner. Changes traveler's checks and gives cash advances on MC/V. Open M-F 8:30am-2:30pm, Sa 8:30am-2:30pm. **ATM** available in the *mercado viejo.* **Western Union** (☎ 522-6410) inside the Palí supermarket. Open M-Sa 8am-6pm, Su 8am-noon.

Supermarket: Palí, west side of the *parque.* Open M-Sa 7:30am-8pm, Su 8:30am-5pm.

Police: ☎ 522 4222, emergency ☎ 118. ½ block east of the *parque's* northeast corner, in a blue complex on the south side of the street.

Red Cross: ☎ 522 2131 or 522 2556. 1 block south on the street that bisects the *parque's* southern edge. Look for the flag, on the left corner.

Pharmacy: Farmacia Masaya ☎ 522 2780. ½ block east of the *parque's* southeast corner. Open M-Sa 8am-6:30pm.

Hospital: Hospital Hilario Sánchez (☎ 522 2778), 9 blocks east of the *parque.*

Telephones: ENITEL (☎ 522 2599 or 522 2499), on the west side of the *parque.* Open daily 7am-9pm. Phone cards and public phone at **Farmacia Emilia Arrieda** (☎ 522 2501), on the northeast corner of the *parque.* Open M-F 8am-8pm, Sa 8am-7pm.

Internet: Servicios Computarizados, 3½ blocks north of the *parque,* next to Hotel Regis. Open M-F 8am-8pm, Sa 8am-noon. **Cyber-1** (☎ 522 3022), 1½ blocks east of the northeast corner of the *parque.* Open M-Sa 8am-10pm, Su 9am-10pm.

Post Office: 1½ blocks east of the northwest corner of the *parque.* **Fax** service. Open M-F 8am-noon and 1-4:30pm.

▐ ACCOMMODATIONS

Since many visit Masaya as a daytrip, the city has relatively few accommodations.

Hotel Regis (☎522 2300), 3½ blocks north of the *parque* on Av. Sergio Delgadillo. Manager Francisco Castillo is a source of regional information. Shared baths, fan, and storage included. Huge breakfast 20C. 10pm curfew. Singles 60C; doubles 120C. ❷

Hotel Maderas Inn (☎522 5825), 4½ blocks north of the *parque* on Av. Sergio Delgadillo. The enterprising management speaks English and is happy to provide information (and a ride for a fee) to tourist sites in the surrounding area. Breakfast 25C. Laundry US$2 for up to 12 pieces. Check-out 11am. Communal baths. Single US$6; triples $5; quad with bath US$20. AmEx/MC/V. ❷

Hotel Monte Carlo (☎522 2166), 5 blocks north of the *parque* on Av. Sergio Delgadillo, has well-proportioned rooms and a small sitting area with cable TV. Large restaurant (open W-Su 6pm-2am) and discotheque (open Th-Su 9pm-2am; no cover) attached. Singles/doubles 100C; doubles with bath and TV 250C; triples 150C; quads without bath 200C. AmEx/MC/V. ❸

🍴 FOOD

Besides the abundant street vendors, restaurants are oddly scarce in Masaya.

La Criolla, two locations: across from the southwest corner of the park and on Av Sergio Delgadillo 5 blocks north of the park. Breakfast until 11am (20C) and cheap and tasty meals all day (25-30C.) Open daily 7am-5pm. ❷

Restaurante Che-Gris, 3 blocks north of the *parque* on Av. Sergio Delgadillo then a ½ block east. An outside patio and well-done cuisine. The waitstaff is attentive and polite. Che-Gris chicken 70C. Open daily 10am-10pm. AmEx/MC/V. ❸

Pizza Hot, 3 blocks north of the *parque* on Av. Sergio Degadillo. If you're longing for more American food during your stay, Pizza Hot has spaghetti, fried chicken, and of course pizza from 30C-95C for a large pie. Open W-M 11am-11pm. AmEx/MC/V. ❷

👁 SIGHTS

MERCADO NUEVO. The main place to browse for Masaya's famed arts and crafts—especially Nicaragua's famed hammocks. The hammocks are complemented by shoes, bicycles, fruit, and even haircuts. The market can be intimidating at first as most of the *artesanías* are clustered on the western end, but signs outside the market will direct you. Wander around a bit first, as much of the merchandise is similar but can vary in quality. Don't accept the first price offered—bargaining is expected. *(At the east end of town, 6 blocks east of the parque on Calle Ernesto Fernández. Open M-Sa 5am-4pm, Su 5am-noon.)*

MERCADO VIEJO. The tourism department has poured untold funds into restoring this castle-like edifice, that resembles more of an open-air mall than a *mercado.* The artisans who display their wares here are carefully chosen and the quality is unbeatable. Local children are glad to translate and help for a small tip. The atmosphere here is easier on the nerves than the chaos of Mercado Nuevo, but you pay for sophistication, and bargaining is not always taken so well. There is a Visa/Plus **ATM** in the market. *(1 block east of the parque. Open daily 9am-6pm. AmEx/MC/V accepted by most merchants.)*

OTHER ARTESANÍAS. Artisans sell goods right out of their workshops in the mostly indigenous **Barrio Monimbó.** To the west of the city, between the *parque* and the Malecón, a number of artisans weave and sell hammocks out of their homes. Prices can be higher than those you'll find in the market, but these are some serious hammocks. Try **Ramiro Suazo y Familia.** The family has been in the international hammock business for 48 years. *(Walk past the Red Cross and continue two*

¡JÓN-RÓN! Nicaragua is one of the few Latin American countries where soccer doesn't reign supreme. Here, baseball (in Nicaragua, *base*) is the overwhelming favorite. As in the Dominican Republic, the sport is a legacy from US Marine occupation in the 1920s, when soldiers passed on this pastime. Pitcher Dennis (Denny) Martínez is one *nica* who has had some success in the US major leagues and at home; he's recently been offered a government position heading the athletics department. The country has glorified another Latin American baseball player, Roberto Clemente, whose name lives on in Masaya's stadium. The famed outfielder died in a plane crash on his way to deliver aid to Nicaraguan earthquake victims in 1972.

blocks past the Colegio Salesiano. The neighborhood extends west one block to the Magdelena church and south three blocks to the cemetery. 7 blocks south on the street bisecting the southern edge of the parque. Hammocks with wooden bars about 300-1500C, cocoon style about 250C. With embroidered message 50C extra, AmEx/MC/V.)

MALECÓN. The breathtaking Malecón, next to the baseball fields, is a 10min. walk directly west from the *parque*. The city ends here and the land drops off a ledge into the Laguna de Masaya, with Volcán Masaya in the background. The view is truly spectacular and attracts admirers of all ages. You can take in a baseball game along the way, too, as there is almost always at least one game in progress.

FORTALEZA COYOTEPE. Reaching this ancient fort just outside Masaya requires a 1.5km climb up a a steep asphalt road, but it's worth it: the view is great, and you can explore the spooky, labyrinthine depths of this former military fort (a flashlight is helpful) and prison, now managed by the Nicaraguan Boy Scouts. *(Any Managua-bound bus passes by here, 2C. Disembark just outside Masaya at the stone archway "Campo Escuela/Scout/El Coyotepe." The fort will up to your right. Open daily 8am-5:30pm, 5C.)*

FESTIVALS. Masaya has a number of cultural events well worth seeing if your timing is right. You can always pick up a schedule at the tourist office or ask around. Nicaraguans flood in from Managua (p. 531) and Granada (p. 554) for these events, and the city really comes alive. Every Thursday night, Masayans young and old turn out for the fiesta **Verbena**, held in the Mercado Viejo. Local musicians play lively Latin music while masked dancers court one another on stage. Food stands sell exotic delicacies and local favorites. Every Sunday from late September through November, Masaya commemorates **San Jerónimo,** its patron saint, with festivals, parades, and street dances. The third Sunday of September and the last Sunday of October are marked by **bull runs** and on the last Friday of October locals disguised in handmade papier mâché masks parade around town in the **Procesión de Ajüezote.** For **Bailes de Negras** on the fourth Sunday of November, only men can perform the dances, meaning that half the performers are dressed in drag and wear wigs. *(Food begins at 5pm, traditional dancers and musicians 7-9:30pm, disco 9-11pm, entrance 3C.)*

NEAR MASAYA

◤◢ PARQUE NACIONAL VOLCÁN MASAYA

The entrance to the park is 7km northwest of Masaya on the highway to Managua; any of the frequent buses between the two will drop you off. Two kilometers past the entrance are an impressive **museum** and **visitors center.** There's no public transportation, but catching a ride with one of the passing tourists is easy, especially on weekends. Also, park rangers sometimes give rides to visitors who arrive just before the park opens at

9am. **Taxis** *from Masaya will take you to the top of the volcano and back for 80-100C, plus the entrance fee for you and your driver. Walking up and back to the highway is 3-5hr.* **Ranger station** ☎ *522 5415. Open daily 9am-4:45pm. Foreigners 50C, children under 4 free.*

Parque Nacional Volcán Masaya boasts a pair of spectacular twin volcanoes, Volcán Masaya and Volcán Nindirí, along with five craters. The *parque* offers bedazzling views of the Lago de Managua. The 16th-century Spaniards thought the volcano was the mouth of Hell and put a cross there to keep the devil in its place.

From the museum (1.5km past the entrance) it's 5km along a shadeless paved road to the rim of the Santiago crater. Once at the top, the best view of the crater is from the replica of the **Cruz de Bobadilla** (the cross placed by those devil-fearing Spanish). A 40min. hike around the Volcán Masaya to the left leads to a *mirador* with a marvelous vista including Volcán Mombacho, La Laguna de Masaya, and El Lago de Nicaragua. Check with the rangers before entering, as some of the paths are closed for maintenance. The **Coyote Trail** and **Bat cave/Tzinaconostoc Cave,** and the path to **El Comalito** (a small volcanic cone emitting vapors) are open to visitors with a guide arranged at the visitor's center (5C per person).

🌋 LAGUNA DE APOYO

The turnoff for Laguna de Apoyo is just south of Masaya at km 37.5 on the highway to Granada (it is the first triangle as you exit Masaya to the south). There are a few small stores on the edge of the crater and it is a hair raising 2km descent through thick jungle to a small triangle symbol in the road on the north edge of the Laguna. Turning left at the triangle symbol, the main restaurant and public beach area is 1km away. **Buses** *go to the bottom of the Laguna from the Mercado Nuevo in Masaya and return 3 times a day. (40 min.; leave 5:30, 10:30am, 3:30pm; return 6:30, 11:30am, 5pm; 6C.)* **Taxis** *will cost 40-50C one way and a hike from the Catarina lookout is about 3hr. round trip.*

A protected lagoon with a view of Volcán Mombacho and teeming in tropical birds and howler monkeys, Laguna de Apoyo is the largest crater lagoon in Nicaragua. To spend the night check out the 🏠 **Proyecto Ecológico Escuela de Español ②.** Clean rooms, hot water, a large open house and garden are supplemented by bike rentals (US$5-10) and scuba gear (tanks US$20, masks US$5). Breakfast is included. (☎ 882 3992; econic@guegue.com.ni. US$12 per night, AmEx/MC/V.) **Hospedaje Los Clarineros ❸** has an attached restaurant open weekends for the general public and daily for guests. There are clean rooms and large baths. (☎ 522 6215. Singles US$10; doubles US $15.) The resort-like **Hotel Norome ❺** has landscaped grounds, private baths, hot water and a price tag to match. The restaurant, bar, and boat rentals are expensive. (☎ 833 9093; noromeresort@yahoo.com. Breakfast 48C, lunch and dinner 100-130C, national beer 20C, kayaks 128C per hour.) If you are looking for instant relaxation, massages are US$10 per hour. A number of restaurants offer food and drink right on the beach (30-60C).

📷 PUEBLOS BLANCOS

Buses *to Jinotepe and Carazo can be found in the main bus area of Masaya, both of which will get you to Pueblos Blancos. They leave approximately every 20min. and charge 3C for a school bus and 5C for a mini bus for each town along the way.*

Although bus fees can add up quickly, *Pueblos Blancos* (White Towns) is a string of distinctive villages that pop up 5km south of Masaya on the road to Carazo. Each one has a "specialty" that makes for an entertaining but not amazing daytrip. The road splits after Catarina (which is the closest to Masaya); the left branch leads to San Juan del Oriente and Diriamba, while the right branch leads to Niquinohomo, Masatepe, and Jinotepe. The towns are each about 20min. apart.

CATARINA. This village closest to Masaya boasts an incomparable lookout over Laguna de Apoyo, Lago de Nicaragua, Granada, and Volcán Mombacho: follow the signs to the *mirador* (10min.). The *mirador* has a number of fairly expensive (70-110C) restaurants where you can eat and enjoy the view. Also check out the ice cream stand (6-12C) for yummy fruit flavors. Nurseries abound and potted plants hang from lampposts. There is a very steep trail leading down to the Laguna de Apoyo, which is perfect for swimming (Round-trip hike 3hrs.).

SAN JUAN DEL ORIENTE. The town of San Juan del Oriente, an easy 0.5km walk southeast of Catarina, is noted for its pottery and indigenous population. The well-known **Cooperativa Quetzalcóatl** has a small selection of high-quality pots and English explanations. (☎ 558 0337. Open M-Sa 8am-6pm.)

GRANADA

Granada's prime location has long been recognized. Francisco Hernández de Córdoba founded the city in 1524, and though the Spanish soon exhausted the region's supply of gold, Granada continued to prosper as a trading center. A bitter rivalry soon emerged between Granada, the country's conservative stronghold, and León, the liberal capital of Nicaragua, which continues to this day.

The colonial city of Granada is proclaimed by many travelers to be their favorite town in all of Nicaragua. Worlds away from the chaos and grime of neighboring Managua, colonial architecture lines the palm-shaded boulevards of this peaceful city. Granada nestles at the foot of the cloud-covered Volcán Mombacho and on the western edge of the gigantic Lago de Nicaragua, which supplies a refreshingly cool breeze all day. A favorite tourist pastime is strolling the city or lake shore, kicking down the same cobblestones revolutionaries, pirates, mercenaries, and colonists did in the city's past. Granada is also a good base for a trip to Isla de Ometepe or elsewhere on the lake.

▐▀ TRANSPORTATION

Buses: Buses (☎ 552 4069) to and from Managua use a terminal 700m west of the *parque*, near the old hospital, while most others leave from 1 block south of the market south of the *parque*. Buses to: **Managua** (1½hr., every 20min. 4am-7pm, 9C); **Masaya** (30min., every 20min. 5am-6:15pm, 5C); **Rivas** via **Nandaime** (1½hr., every hr. 5:05am-3:10pm, 13C). Fast **minibuses** to Managua use a lot just south of the southwest corner of the *parque*, near Banco Central (1hr.; M-Sa 5:45am-8pm, Su 5:45am-7pm; 18C).

Ferries: Boats (☎ 552 8764) leave from the dock at the foot of **La Calzada**, 1km from the center. To **San Carlos** (15½hr., M and Th 2pm, 40C) via **Ometepe** (4hr., 20C); **San Miguel** (12hr., 35C); **Morillo** (14hr., 40C). A new rapid ferry to San Carlos (4hr.) should be running some time in 2003.

Taxis: Trips around Granada cost 5C during the day and 10C after 10pm.

Car Rental: Budget (☎ 552 2323), at the Shell station at the entrance to the city.

▐▌▐ ORIENTATION AND PRACTICAL INFORMATION

The centerpiece of Granada is the spacious and verdant **parque central**, or **Parque Colón**. To find the *parque*, look for the looming white dome of the cathedral on its eastern edge. Granada's main north-south street, **Calle Atravesada**, runs one block west of the *parque central*. **Calle La Calzada**, the main east-west street of mostly *hospedajes*, leads toward the lake off the eastern side of the *parque*. Volcán Mombacho is to the south of town and to the west of Lago de Nicaragua.

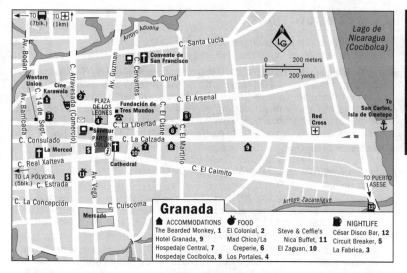

Granada

🛏 ACCOMMODATIONS
The Bearded Monkey, 1
Hotel Granada, 9
Hospedaje Central, 7
Hospedaje Cocibolca, 8

🍴 FOOD
El Colonial, 2
Mad Chico/La
Creperie, 6
Los Portales, 4

Steve & Ceffie's
Nica Buffet, 11
El Zaguan, 10

☕ NIGHTLIFE
César Disco Bar, 12
Circuit Breaker, 5
La Fabrica, 3

Tourist Information: When the staff decides to come in, **Oficina de Delegación del Turismo (INTUR;** ☎/fax 552 6858), on the southeast corner of the *parque,* has info about cultural events in town. Open M-F 8am-noon and 2-5pm, Sa 8am-noon.

Guided Tours: Servitur (☎/fax 552 2955), on the northwest corner of the *parque* next to Hotel Alhambra, offers tours in English to the Isletas (US$10-15 per person), Volcán Mombacho (US$55 per 2 people), or the main sights of Granada (US$25 per hr.). Open M-F 8am-noon and 2-5pm, Sa 8am-noon. For a view of the city from horseback, take a tour with **Coches de Caballo** (30min., 70C).

Banks: Banco del Café, 1 block west of the *parque* on Calle Atravesada, changes US dollars. Open M-F 8am-5pm, Sa 8am-noon. **Banco de América Central,** at the *parque's* southwest corner, changes traveler's checks. Open M-Sa 8am-5pm.

Western Union: (☎552 2654), 2 blocks west and a half block north of the *parque.* Open M-F 8am-1pm and 2-5pm, Sa 8am-1pm.

Market: Supermercado Lacayo, 2 blocks west on Calle Real. Open M-Sa 8am-8pm, Su 8am-noon.

Laundry: 1 block west of the *parque,* next to the Teatro González.

Police: (☎552 2929), 1km north of the *parque,* near the old train station.

Red Cross: (☎552 2711 or 552 2131), 6 blocks east down La Calzada toward the lake.

Hospital: Armistad Sapon (☎552 7050 or 552 7049), 1km on the road to Managua.

Telephones: ENITEL (☎552 2090; fax 552 2190), in an unmarked, pale-turquoise building across from the northeast corner of the *parque.* Open daily 7am-10pm.

Internet: Binary Base, across from the Museum of the Convent of San Francisco, has the fastest connections in town, the cheapest international calls (30C per hr.) and satellite phone service (2C per min. to North America, 6C to Europe, Australia, and New Zealand.) Delicious freshly squeezed juice (12-22C). Useful tourist info website www.thebinarybase.com. Also try **InterC@fe,** just west of the northwest corner of the *parque.* 30C per hr. Open daily 8am-9pm.

Post Office: On Calle Atravesada, 1 block west of the *parque,* across from the old theater. Phone cards for local calls sold here. Open M-F 7am-5pm, Sa 7am-noon.

ACCOMMODATIONS

Calle La Calzada, the long road that runs east from the *parque* to the lake shore, is lined with a number of budget and not-so-budget accommodations.

■ **The Bearded Monkey** (☎552 4028; thebeardedmonkey@yahoo.com; www.thebearded-monkey.com), on Bamba del Mono, 2 blocks west and 2 blocks north of the *parque*. The many amenities make up for the dorm's foam mattresses: bar, restaurant, communal cable TV, nightly movies, book exchange, laundry, Internet access, pool table, bike rentals, free transportation to and from ferries, and loads of tourist info. Ask about part-time jobs. Dorms 35C; singles 70C; doubles 110C; triples 135C; suites 210C. ❶

■ **Hospedaje Central** (☎552 7044; hcentral@tmx.com.ni), on La Calzada, 1½ blocks east of the *parque*. The walls are covered with tourist info, stories, and paintings. Good vegetarian restaurant open 7am-midnight. Laundry 60C. Dorms 30C; rooms with shared bath 70C per person. ❷

Hospedaje Cocibolca (☎552 7223), 3 blocks from the cathedral toward the lake, features living room with TV, well-stocked kitchen, and Internet. Helpful owner ensures a comfy stay. Breakfast 14-35C. Singles 60C; doubles with bath 165C, with bath and cable TV 210C; triples with bath 168C. ❷

Hotel Granada (☎552 2974), just past Hospedaje Cocibolca, has simple rooms and a welcoming swimming pool. Singles US$12; doubles US$25, with bath US$35. ❹

FOOD

Comedores abound at the market (3 blocks south of the *parque*); a few are one block west of the southwest corner of the *parque* in a courtyard with a fountain.

Los Portales, on the Plaza de los Leones just northeast of the *parque*, across from the ENITEL building. View of the *parque* and the cathedral. Good for a quiet dinner. Meals are mostly *nica* (30-50C); try the chicken in salsa (70C). Open daily 7am-10pm. ❷

El Colonial, 1 block north and 1 block west of the *parque*, has an American jukebox and local food. Dishes 40-60C. Open daily 11am-midnight. ❷

Mad Chico/La Creperie, on the corner of Calle La Calzada, across from Hospedaje Cocibolca. The town's only French-owned *creperie*. *Crepe* with butter, cheese, ham, and eggs 39C; with mushrooms and ham 59C. Fruit cocktails 20-32C. Open M-F noon-midnight, Sa-Su noon-2am. Mention *Let's Go* for a 10% discount. ❷

Steve and Ceffie's Nica Buffet, 1 block south and 1 block west of the southwest corner of the *parque*. Serves American-style breakfasts (bagel and cream cheese 25C; pancakes and juice 35-40C; omelette and coffee 35-40C). Open M-Sa 6:30am-11am. ❷

Asadero.com, on Calle La Calzada, across from Farmacia Loyola. Stylish gourmet, vegetarian restaurant. Fried zucchini with yogurt salsa and ratatouille 45C; papaya dessert 20C. The grill outside serves carnivores. Open M-Sa 6-11pm. ❷

El Zaguán, behind the cathedral. Well-prepared meals with garlic bread and salad include charbroiled top sirloin (100C) and fresh pasta with fish (80C). Leave room for the honey-soaked coconut *flan* (15C). Open Tu-Su 11:30am-3pm and 6-11pm. ❸

SIGHTS

LA CASA DE LOS LEONES. This beautiful colonial house with two lions on its facade was spared when the city was burned down in 1857. It presently houses the **Fundación de Tres Mundos,** which has art exhibits, performances, and offers classes. Pick up a program of the week's events at the office. Occasionally, the walkway in front is a stage for more large-scale cultural events on weekends. *(East from the southeast corner of the* parque. *Fundación* ☎ *552 4176. Open daily 6am-6pm. Free.)*

CONVENT OF SAN FRANCISCO. Next door to the shockingly bright-blue facade of the **Iglesia de San Francisco** (the first church founded by Córdoba and one of the oldest in the Americas), the yellow Convent holds a museum with great displays on indigenous life and a collection of well-preserved statues of humans and their animal alter egos. Also exhibited are early religious images, a photo history of Granada, and excellent primitivist art. *(1 block north and 2 blocks east of the* parque. ☎ *552 4237. Open daily 9am-6pm. 12C, includes guided tour.)*

LA PÓLVORA. This white fortress, built in 1749 and later used by Somoza forces as a military base and a prison, has been partly restored and allows for impressive city views. *(8 blocks west of the* parque. *Free.)*

THE LAKE. Head down the wide La Calzada for about 1km to reach the town pier on the lake. A block west of the pier is a touristy plaza, the *complejo turístico*, lined with restaurants and discos. About 30min. south from the pier lies **Puerto Asese,** where you can hire a *lancha* (boat) to see **Las Isletas,** lake islands teeming with birds. *(Lanchas US$15 per hr., hold up to 10 people. You can hire a cab to Puerto Asese, 10C each way. A* **horse-drawn carriage** *costs 50C.)*

▓ ♫ NIGHTLIFE AND ENTERTAINMENT

La Fábrica, 1½ blocks west of the northwest corner of the *parque,* is a chill bar where a young crowd and older regulars drop in every night and mingle to North American rock. (Open Tu-Su 6:30pm-2am.) The bar at the **Bearded Monkey** (see **Accommodations,** above) bustles every evening until around 11pm with a tourist crowd. (Happy Hour 4-7pm.) **Circuit Breaker,** Granada's new rave bar, is on the corner of Calle El Martijo and Calle La Libertad, one block north of Calle La Calzada. Crowds dance to techno in surroundings featuring the eclectic combination of hammocks, TVs, and the only licensed tattoo parlor in Nicaragua. (Open M and W-F 6pm-midnight, Sa-Su 6pm-2am.) Discos flank the lake shore; the most popular with locals is **Cesar Disco Bar,** featuring live *música nacional*, merengue, and salsa. (Cover 20C F-Su.) Take a taxi home at night (10C).

Each Friday night (6pm-midnight) near La Casa de Los Leones is **Noche de Serenada de Granada.** Local restaurants set up stands and sell traditional food and beer, and wandering musical trios serenade diners. Granada also hosts an annual **Folklore and Gastronomy Fair** (the third weekend in March) and celebrates its patron saint, la Virgen de la Asunción, on August 15. They also have a **running of the bulls** the second week of August.During the first nine days of December, Granada celebrates **Concepción,** the Patron Saint of Nicaragua.

◖ BEACHES NEAR GRANADA

The beaches of **La Boquita, Casares,** and **Huehuete** offer three very different atmospheres. They are relatively easy to get to and bus schedules are compatible with day trips. Take any bus to Diriamba; from Masaya and Granada you'll go via Catarina. Once in Diriamba, buses and minibuses leave to Casares via La Boquita and occasionally continue on to Huehuete. (From Diriamba to Casares: 30min.-1hr., every 20min., 6-9C. From Diriamba to Huehuete: 50min.-1½hr., 10am and 4pm. Minibus 7:40am and 1:40pm, 9-12C.)

LA BOQUITA. The farthest north and first stop on the bus route, this beach is on the most touristy of the bunch. It is run by the national tourist board INTUR and is relatively well maintained. When it rains, the ocean near the beach takes a dark brown color from all the run-off. Public bathrooms cost 2C. Expect to pay double high season prices if you go during *semana santa*. **Hotel Puertas del Cielo ❸** has small, well maintained rooms. (☎552 8717. Mid-May to Nov. 1-3 people, 150C; Dec-mid-May 200C; AmEx/MC/V.) **Hotel and Club Las Palmas del Mar ❺** is more expensive, but compensated by amenities such as a big screen TV, pool, private baths, and A/C. (☎522 8715 or 522 8716; palmasdelmar.com.ni. Mid-May-Nov. US$35 per night; Dec.-Apr. US$25-30.) A number of similar restaurants line the edge of the beach. In the low season, most give a group rate. (*Comida corriente* 30C; beef or chicken 60-70C; seafood 100-150C; AmEx/MC/V.)

CASARES AND HUEHUETE. Casares is a small fishing village just south of La Boquita, with a fish market just off the beach. (Open 8am-noon.) North of the fishing boats, the beach gets considerably cleaner. **Huehuete** is the farthest south of the three beaches and least frequented, 7km past Casares. Mid-way between Huehuete and Casares lies ■**Costa del mar Hotel/Restaurant ❹**. Attractive grounds, clean rooms with private baths, and a laid back atmosphere on the beach are ideal. Surfboard rentals are available—ask in advance. (Breakfast 25C, lunch and dinner 50C. ☎278 3235 or 522 2003; hoteleco@interlink.com. May-Sept. doubles or 2 bunk beds 200C, Nov-May 400C). **Restaurante Don Sergio Cruz ❷** is the only place to eat in town. (*Carne asado* 30C, fish 40C, lobster 120-150C.)

RIVAS

Rivas, known as "the city of mangos" and the infamous launching point of William Walker and his troops in the early 19th century, has the same aura of history and culture as Granada, but less tourists. Rivas was once a stop along the fortune seeking route during the California gold rush. Today, with its culture and proximity to the Costa Rican border, San Juan del Sur, and Lago de Nicaragua, the town is convenient for a quick stop and further exploration if you have time.

▐ TRANSPORTATION. Buses to Rivas drop off passengers in the market at the north end of town. Buses continuing on to Managua or the border will probably drop off near the Shell station on the highway, 7 blocks east of the market. Buses head to the border at **Granada** (1¾hr., every 75 min. 6:15am-4:25pm, 13C); **Managua** (2hr., every 25min. 3:30am-6:15pm, 20C); **Sapoá** (45min., every 30min. 5am-4:30pm, 10C); and **San Juan del Sur** (45min., every 45min. 6am-5:40pm, 8C). To get to **Isla de Ometepe,** take a bus to the launching point **San Jorge** (30min., every 30min. 6:30am-6:30pm, 3C) and then either a *lancha* (1hr., 6 per day, 9:30am- 4:30pm, 15C) or **ferry,** which have *cafeterías* and a smoother ride (1hr.; 10:30am, 2:30, 5:30pm; 20C). Either buy your ticket at the office at the port or pay on the boat. Around Rivas, **horse carts** are 20C, **tricycles** are 5C, and **taxis** are 50C.

▐▐ ORIENTATION AND PRACTICAL INFORMATION. If you arrive in the market, cardinal directions can be a bit flustering. Go straight ahead to the exit (in the direction of the yellow Western Union sign), from which right is south and straight is east. **Parque Arriba,** (the *parque central*) is three blocks south and three blocks east of that point. **Iglesia San Francisco** is on the east side of the *parque*. If you get off at the Shell station on the highway, south is toward the Texaco gas station and east is toward San Jorge 5km away.

The **tourist office** is two blocks south and 4½ blocks east of the market. (☎453 4914. Open M-F 8am-noon and 2-5pm.) The **MARENA** headquarters, on the west side of Colegio Berto Méndez, is a good source of information about ecotourism. (☎453 4264; delrivas@ibw.com.ni.) Head to **BanCentro,** 300m west of ENITEL on the southwest side of the *parque*, to change traveler's checks or US dollars. (Open M-

F 8am-6pm, Sa 8am-noon.) To buy or sell Costa Rican *colones*, go to the *coyotes* who hang around the market. Follow the signs to **Western Union**, 1½ blocks south of the market in the mini Arco Iris mall. (Open M-F 8am-5pm, Sa 8am-noon.) The **police station** (emergency ☎118) is 3½ blocks south of the market. Other services include: **Red Cross**, two blocks south and five blocks east of the bus stop (☎453 3415. 24hr. emergency service); **Farmacia Auxiliadora**, in the market (open daily 7am-5:30pm) and **ENITEL**, on the west corner of the *parque*. (☎453 3499. Open M-F 8am-8pm, Sa 8am-7pm, Su 8am-6pm.) Access the **Internet** at **Librería y Papelería**, next to the ice-cream store, on the northeast side of the *parque* (☎453 3345; 40C per hr. Open M-F 8am-9pm, Sa-Su 8am-5pm); and the **post office**, ½ block west of the gym Humberto Méndez. (Open M-F 8am-noon and 1-5pm, Sa 8am-1pm.)

⌂ ACCOMMODATIONS. Hospedaje Primavera ●, on the south side of the Shell gas station on the highway, is clean and spacious. Breakfast is 15-20C. (☎453 3982. Singles 40C, with private bath 50C; matrimonial 70C/80C.) **Hospedaje Internacional ●**, on the highway 1½ blocks south of the Shell station, has family style ambiance. (☎453 3652. Típico meals 20-30C. Singles 50C; doubles 80C; triples 120C.) **Cacique Nicarao ●**, 1½ blocks west of the northwest side of the *parque*, next to the old cinema, is the fanciest in town. (Restaurant open daily 7am-10pm. TV, A/C, hot water, breakfast, and taxes included. Singles US$40; doubles US$51; triples US$63. V.)

⯐⯐ FOOD AND NIGHTLIFE. For chicken, beef, or pork cooked in any style, head to **Pollo Dorado ●**, ½ block west of the northwest corner of the *parque*. (Half-chicken roasted 30C. Open daily 10am-10pm.) **Restaurante Chop Suey ●**, on the southwest side of the *parque*, serves chop suey, beefsteak, and seafood all for 60C. (Open daily 10am-9pm.) **Pizza Hot ●**, on the north side of the San Francisco church in the main plaza, serves family size (95C), medium (55C), and single slices (30C) of pizza. (Open Tu-Su 10am-midnight.) **Soda Rayuela ●**, on the north side of the national police) and **Antojitos Rayuela ●**, next to the Pellas house, are good bets for fast food (10-25C.) **Bar y Restaurante Ivania**, 1 block west and 2½ blocks south of the *alcaldía*, serves great seafood. Party from 8pm to dawn at **Discotheque Río**, next to the Cucarao store. (Ladies night Th; F, Sa, Su 25C cover.)

◙ SIGHTS. The imposing **Iglesia San Francisco** is on the east side of the *parque*. Rivas's history is on display at the **Museo de Antropología e Historia de Rivas**, two blocks west of the market, complete with ceramics and mounted animal heads. (Open M-F 8am-noon and 2-5pm, Sa 8am-noon. US$1.) **Nicarao Canopy tour**, offers a beautiful 2hr. flight crossing creeks and nature 70 ft. above ground on 7 safe, steel cables. (☎886 7548; www.nicaraolake.com.ni; nlf@nicaraolake.com.ni)

⛰ PEÑAS BLANCAS: BORDER WITH COSTA RICA

*In Nicaragua, **buses** leave Peñas Blancas from behind the pink hostel walls for **Rivas** (45min., every 30min. 7:30am-6pm, 10C). Buses from Peñas Blancas go to **Costa Rica** via **San José** (5½hr. to San José, 9 per day 5am-5pm, ¢1500) and **Liberia** (1½hr., 5 per day 6:30am-5pm, ¢500). Costa Rican **Immigration** open for regular services M-F 8am-5pm. Also open M-F 6-8am and 5-8pm, Sa 6-8am and noon-8pm, Su 6am-8pm; US$2 extra for services during those times. If entering Nicaragua from Costa Rica, try to arrive before 3pm. Expect long lines. Only US dollars accepted (typical fee US$7).*

Sapoá was the border town before the migration offices moved to Peñas Blancas in September 1999. Note that to enter Costa Rica you may be asked to show an onward ticket; this may be purchased at the Tica Bus counter nearby. There are **money changers** on both sides of the border (double-check what they give you), a **bank** on the Nicaraguan side exchanging US dollars, three small **hospedajes** (all

100C), and a helpful **tourist office** on the Costa Rican side. Check out the **Dirección General de Servicios Aduaneros** (DGA) for the most recent frontier policy information. (☎454 0041; apblancas@dga.gob.ni; www.dga.gob.ni)

SAN JUAN DEL SUR

In the days of the gold rush before the Panama Canal, Nicaragua was the quickest route between the Atlantic and Pacific. Money-hungry prospectors would sail from the US east coast, proceed up the Río San Juan, and disembark at Granada to San Juan del Sur for the northbound ride. Most of the year, this port and fishing town is packed with local tourists, backpackers, and surfers. In May 2002, it hosted Nicaragua's first international surf competition on Playa Madera.

▐ TRANSPORTATION

Buses leave from the *mercado* two blocks east of the beach. Coming to town from the Costa Rican border at Peñas Blancas, take the Rivas bus via **La Vírgen** (30min., 5C), and catch an inbound San Juan bus from there. Buses to **Rivas** (45min., about every 45min. 5am-5pm, 8C); **Managua** (3hr., every hr. 5am-8pm, 30C; express 2hr.; 5am, 5:45, 7:15am, 3:30pm; 40C). To the **beaches:** Buses leave for the northern beaches (40min., 10, 10:30am) and the southern beaches (1½hr., 12:30 and 4pm, 10C). Ask to be dropped off. **Transporte Jorge,** in the first house on the dirt road to the left of Texaco on the northwest side of town, runs express **car** trips. (☎458 2116; baloy28@hotmail.com. Minibuses to La Flor 300C, Madera 200C, and other destinations, up to 5 person max.)

◢✷ ⁊ ORIENTATION AND PRACTICAL INFORMATION

Entering San Juan del Sur, the school, Indian stone, and Finca Holman are to your right (north). Continue on this road to the beaches of **Marsella** (5km), **Madera** (12km), and **Majagual** (14km). The road to the left (south) coming in from Rivas after the bridge leads to the southern beaches: **Remanso** (6km); **Tamarindo, Hermosa, Yankee** (12km); **Coco** (18km); **Braselito** (24km); and **Refugio de Vida Silvestre La Flor.** The town's "main intersection" is where the main street hits the beach.

> **Tourist Information:** Check out the town's website (www.sanjuandelsur.org.ni). Info at **Ricardo's Bar** (☎458 2502), 3 blocks north of the main intersection, and **Marie's Bar** (☎458 2555), 1 long block north of the main intersection.

> **Banks:** There are no **banks;** few places accept traveler's checks; change money in Rivas.

> **Police:** (☎458 2382), 4 blocks south of the main intersection.

> **Medical: Servicios Médicos** (☎458 2402), 2½ blocks east of Marie's in the Clínica Farmacia Comunal. Private **doctors** and **pharmacy** (open M-Sa 7am-7pm, Su 8am-noon).

> **Telephones: ENITEL** (☎458 2261), 2 blocks south of the main intersection. For collect and international calls, use the red Sprint phone in the corner (wait for the operator to help you, no dialing necessary). Open daily 7am-5pm.

> **Internet:** Cheapest at **Comsis Internet,** 50m west of the Texaco station. (Open M-F 8am-10pm, Sa-Su 9am-8pm. 1C per min.)

> **Post office:** Next to the ENITEL building. **Fax** service. Open M-F 8am-5pm, Sa 8am-1pm.

▐ ACCOMMODATIONS

Accommodations here are usually geared toward the beach-loving backpacking crowd.

▨ **Guest House Elizabeth** (☎458 2279), across the street from the bus stop. Basic rooms have thin beds, a bar, tables, TV downstairs, and sunset views from the hammock on the upstairs patio. Additional amenities include bike rental (US$5 per day), breakfast (25C) and a photogenic pet monkey named Tuty. Singles 50C; doubles 100C. ❶

▨ **Casa el Oro** (☎458 2415; rockettom@hotmail.com; www.casaeloro.com), 1 block south of General Store Sánchez, tailored toward the backpacking crowd. Hammocks, book exchange, transportation (US$4 to beach), bag deposit, laundry, tourist info, and breakfast. Friendly owners. Singles 50C. Tent rental 70C. ❶

Hotel Estrella (☎458 2210), on the corner of the main intersection on the beach, is in a breezy and pleasant house. Bright and airy rooms, some with balconies and great views, warrant the hotel's name. 60C per person. ❷

Hospedaje Nina (☎458 2302) rents out two rooms with sparkling tile floors in the back of a *pulpería,* straight across from the bus station. US$10 per person. ❸

Hotel Casablanca (☎450 2135; www.sanjuandelsur.org.ni/casablanca/; casa-blan@ibw.com.ni), in front of the sea on the *paseo marítimo,* one block north of the main intersection. Indulge in the hot water, A/C, cable, and pool. Singles US$53; doubles US$58; triples US$69. Special rooms for backpackers US$30. ❺

🄵 🄿 FOOD AND NIGHTLIFE

Ricardo's Bar, three blocks north of the main intersection, is the evening social center. Locals and tourists alike will often spend all evening here listening to music and sipping cool beers (Beer 8C. Open M-W noon-midnight.) On Saturday nights, many migrate to **La Casa de Cultura,** 2½ blocks south of the main intersection, to dance to rock and reggae until the sun comes up. (Cover 12C. Open 8pm-dawn.) Dance to the most modern and VIP music in style at **Otangani Beach Bar/Restaurant/Disco.** (Cover 20C, 100C on special nights with open bar. Open Th-Su at 5pm.)

▨ **Marie's Bar,** 2 blocks north of the main intersection on the corner, has outstanding food and a friendly atmosphere. The knowledgeable staff speaks some English. Try some foods you might not have enjoyed for a while: curry chicken (60C) and sweet crepes (35C). Open Tu-Sa 5:30pm-midnight. ❷

▨ **Comedor Ixtel,** the *comedor* with yellow walls, inside the market, is the cheapest and best of the town's *típico* food. The breakfast is outstanding and the accompanying *café con leche* particularly hot (18C). Lunch and dinner 20-25C. ❶

▨ **Doña Elena,** in a red Coke stand 2 blocks south of the bus station, serves great chicken and beef grilled right in front of you, accompanied by fantastically thick tortillas and savory side dishes. Meals from 15-30C. Open daily for lunch and dinner. ❶

Iguana Beach Bar, one block north of the main intersection, has a pleasant location on the beach and serves good-sized portions. The fish-burgers are grilled expertly (40C). The staff is friendly and the bar is popular in the evenings. Open daily 7:30am-11pm. ❷

🄲 BEACHERS AND WATERSPORTS

The further north you walk along the beach, the less driftwood and coconut shells you'll have to move aside before staking your claim in the sand. **Hot Sand,** 1½ blocks north of the bus stop, rents surfboards. (20C per hr., 80C per day. Open daily 7am-5:30pm.) Better surfing can be found at beaches a bit north and south of San Juan del Sur—plenty of locals will drive you for a fee. A number of locals take travelers out on the water for an afternoon of sportfishing or coast exploration. **Seeger's Fishing Trips** runs a tight ship, and captain Andy Seeger knows the waters well. Regular catch includes tuna, jacks, roosterfish, wahoo, and sailfish. (☎458

2104, or inquire at Marie's or Ricardo's Bar. US$210 for groups up to 6.) **Pelican Eyes** can bring you to explore the coasts of southern beaches for a day trip with fishing, barbecue, and relaxation until sunset. (☎458 2511; pelican@ibw.com.ni. US$55 per person, US$25 for children under 10; sunset tours US$20 per person.)

⚠ REFUGIO DE VIDA SILVESTRE LA FLOR

The reserve contains mangroves, tropical dry forest, and a beach where up to 3000 sea turtles come to lay their eggs during an *arribada* every quarter moon in high season (Admission 60C). Two **buses** run there from **San Juan del Sur** via **La Flor** (1¼hr; 1 and 4pm, return 5:30pm; 10C). You can also hire a **taxi** or walk.

LAGO DE NICARAGUA

Fed by more than 40 rivers, streams, and brooks from Nicaragua and Costa Rica, Lago de Nicaragua is the largest lake in Central America and the tenth-largest freshwater body in the world. Four hundred thirty islands dot the lake's surface, notable for everything from wildlife to the myths of the pre-Columbian petroglyphs. The lake is home to bullsharks, the only freshwater sharks in the world. It is believed that many years ago the bull sharks migrated up **Río San Juan,** from the Caribbean Sea, and slowly adapted to the freshwater environment.

Farther south, the **Archipiélago de Solentiname** is renowned for its natural beauty and minimalist paintings. On the southeastern side of the lake sits **San Carlos,** where the Río San Juan begins its lazy trek toward the Caribbean. Four hours from Granada is one of Nicaragua's most treasured spots: the two enormous volcanoes and paradise of the **Isla de Ometepe.**

ISLA DE OMETEPE

In **Náhuatl,** the ancient language of the Aztecs, *ome* means "two" and *tepetl* means "hills" or "volcanoes." On Ometepe, the tallest freshwater island in the world, the twin volcanoes are **Volcán Concepción** (1610m), still active with a perfect cone, and **Volcán Maderas** (1394m), extinct with an exquisite crater lake. Ometepe is one of Nicaragua's jewels, with pre-Columbian petroglyphs, notoriously friendly inhabitants, great fish dinners, and above all, natural beauty. With the exception of the two main towns of Moyogalpa and Altagracia, the island is glorious primary forest in the upper elevations and small villages and farms on the coast. Ometepe is great for hiking the volcanoes and basking in the peaceful, slower way of life.

▣ TRANSPORTATION. Ometepe can be reached on a **ferry** from **Granada** (p. 554) to **Altagracia.** (☎552 4313. 4hr., M and Th 3pm, 20C.) You can also take a bus to **Rivas** (see p. 558), from there travel to **San Jorge** (bus 30min., every 30min. 2C; taxi: 8min., 10C), and then take a *lancha* (small boat) to **Moyogalpa** (1hr., M-Sa 6 per day 9am-4:30pm, 15C). Strong winds and currents can mean delays or cancellations. **Boats** also leave for **San Carlos** (9hr., M and Th 7pm, 40C) and **Granada** from **Altagracia** (4hr.; W, some Tu, F, 11am; 20C). Once on the island, a bus circles **Volcán Concepción,** going between Altagracia and Moyogalpa on both the long (1½hr.) and short (1hr.) routes. (About every 90min. 6:30am-7:30pm, return 4:30am-5:10pm.) From Moyogalpa, there are two buses to **Balgüe** (daily 8am and 2:30pm). From Altagracia, there's more frequent service to Balgüe (6 per day 5am-6pm) and one bus to **San Ramón** (1½hr., M-Sa 10:30am, 10C). On Sundays, service is minimal. For reliable **taxi** service call Marvin Arcia (☎459 4114) or Romel Gómez (☎459 4112). Many hotels and individuals also rent bikes (US$7 per day) or boat (US$2 per hr).

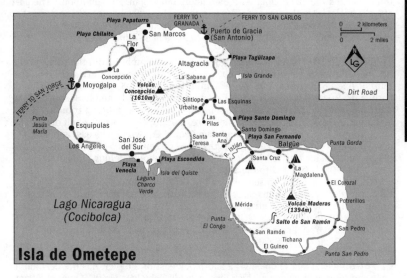

NICARAGUA

Isla de Ometepe

ORIENTATION AND PRACTICAL INFORMATION. A decent road circles the Concepción (northwest) volcano, while a much poorer road to Balgüe in the north and Mérida in the south makes it halfway around the Madera (southeast) volcano. The island's two largest towns, **Moyogalpa** and **Altagracia,** both lie on the Concepción side. Although these towns contain several *hospedajes*, many travelers skip them for the hotels on the beaches of Santo Domingo or San Ramón.

MOYOGALPA

Moyogalpa is the second largest town on Isla de Ometepe, on the western coast near the entry point from San Jorge. Apart from the eating, dancing, and revelry of its annual celebration on July 23rd called the *Fiesta Patronal de Santa Ana* (a boat race and domestication day of the bulls), Moyogalpa is a peaceful port town. Those who like to groove might be lucky enough to assist in the weekend dances, called *cochamambas.* Moyogalpa is an ideal a base to climb Concepción.

ORIENTATION AND PRACTICAL INFORMATION. As you step off the dock, east is straight ahead and to your right is a large, three dimensional fountain model of Ometepe. Back up the central street where there are hotels and *hospedajes* for two blocks, a right turn leads to the newly constructed Hospedaje Central. The elegant white Catholic church stands at the end of the main street behind the colorful park, five blocks from the bus station.

The **tourist office** *(Oficina de Información Turística or CANTUR)*, left of the dock, is the only tour operator and office on the island, and is complete with the informative Hugo Navas (☎045 4218). **Comercial Hugo Navas,** 1½ blocks up main street on the left, changes dollars and traveler's checks. (☎459 4244. Open M-Sa 7am-7pm, Su 8am-noon.) **Hotel Ometepe** (see **Accommodations,** below) is the only other option, but changes traveler's checks for poor rates. The **police** is 1½ blocks south and three blocks east of the pier. (☎459 4231. Open 24hr.) The **hospital** is five blocks east and three blocks south of the pier behind a fence. (☎459 4247. Open 24hr. for emergencies.) **Doctor Pedro Bejaranom,** on the south side of the park, is also available. (☎459 4137. Open M-Sa 4am-7pm.) **ENITEL phone service** is next to the police. (☎459 4277. Open M-F 8am-noon and 2-5pm, Sa 8am-noon.) The **post office** is in Hotelito Aly. (Open M-F 8am-noon and 1-4:30pm.) Access the **Internet** at La Curaco Isla Area Comercial, two blocks east from the center of the main street. (☎459 4137. 60C/hr.; 4C/page to print. Open M-Sa 8am-7pm.)

▐ ACCOMMODATIONS. Hotelito Aly ❶, 1½ blocks uphill from the pier, on the left, has 10 pleasant rooms set around a shady patio restaurant. (☎459 4196. Restaurant open 6am-10pm. Internet 60C/min. Rooms 40-50C per person, 60C with bath and TV.) At **Casa Familiar ❶**, three blocks uphill and one block south of the pier, the owner offers spacious rooms with bunk beds, a living room with TV, clean bathrooms, kitchen access, and a restaurant. (Restaurant open daily 6am-9pm. Rooms US$5 per person.) **Hospedaje Central ❷**, two blocks east and south of corner, is also in Granada and carries the same charm. (☎095 4262. Dorms are 30C per person, singles 70C-100C. Ask Valeria Petrone about pitching tents in the backyard.) **Hotel Bahía ❶**, next to the **Shell** gas station 1½ blocks east. The hotel offers a 5% discount for *Let's Go* readers. (☎459 4273. Restaurant service 15C-50C, day boat trips 60C; cheap rooms 30C, 40C with bathroom.) **Hotel la Isla ❶**, is a good option for families or large groups. (☎459 4258. Tiny cubicles with fans 35C, US$10 a night for 10 people. AmEx/MC/V.) **Hotel Ometepe ❺**, right ahead as you step off the dock ☎459 4276 has a restaurant with breakfast for US$2 and lunch for US$3-5. (☎459 4276. Rooms US$20-US$30 per night.)

▐ FOOD. Restaurant El Chele ❷, a half-block east of the pier, has the best ambiance and food in Moyogalpa. (Fish dishes 25-50C; chicken 35-40C. Open M-F 9am-9pm, Sa 9am-10pm.) **Restaurante Los Ranchitos ❷**, is two blocks east and a half-block south of the pier. (Breakfast 20-25C, entrees 18-40C. Open daily 7am-9:30pm.) The hotel restaurants above are mostly reasonable. Hotels and the local *pulperías* also serve cheap food.

◪ SIGHTS. Don't miss **Sala Arqueológica**, 3½ blocks east from port, which sells paintings and art by famous locals (280C-1120C). Ask Ligia de García or Siria Aguilar about the historic artifacts. (☎459 4225. Open M-Sa 8am-5pm. US$1.) On your way out of the mini museum stop by the new, popular **Sorbetería Hugo Navos** for 20 flavors of original Eskimo ice cream flavors and fast food. (☎459 4244. Open M-Th 11:30am-9:30pm, F 10am-9:30pm, Sa-Su 9am-9:30pm.) Most hotels have tourist information and can arrange guides (US$5). A recommended tour service is **Ecflorin Ometepe**, at Hotel Ometepe (see **Accommodations** above). (☎777 3835. US$6 per person for a waterfall trip; US$15 for a tour around the island by car or boat.)

ALTAGRACIA

Altagracia, on the northeast coast of the Concepción side of the island, is a more charming and convenient base from which to explore most of the island's sights. October 28 and November 18, one month apart, are the annual patrimonial festivals in honor of Saint Diego, when traditional folkloric dances in the park and loud celebration transform the usually calm atmosphere on the island's biggest town.

▐ TRANSPORTATION. Buses head to Altagracia from **Moyogalpa** via the north road stopping in **El Flor** (40min., 6C) and via the south road stopping in **Charco Verde** (30min., 4C) and **Santo Domingo** (50min., 6C).

Buses leave Altagracia to all sites on the oriental side of Ometepe: **Moyogalpa south** (1½hr., every hr. M-Sa 4:30am-5:30pm 10C), via **Santo Domingo** (45min., 4C); **El Quino** (50min., 5C); **Charco Verde** (1hr., 8C); **Moyogalpa north** (1¼hr., every 3¼hr. M-Sa, 8:30am-4:30pm, 10C), via **San Marcos** (25min., 2C); **El Flor** (40min., 4C). Señor Carlos Guillén rents **horses** (next to the Hotel Don Kencho, 35C per hr.) Hotel

Castillo rents **trucks** for the day (500C) and Luis Acosta rents **motorcycles** for the day. (1½ blocks west of Hotel Castillo. US$30) **Soda Paraíso,** two blocks north of the park, rents mountain bikes (☎552 8758. 120C per day. Open M-Sa 6am-6pm.) Many of the beaches, including **Paso Real** (1km north) and **Playa Taguizapa** (2km northeast), are also within walking distance.

■ ▄ **ORIENTATION AND PRACTICAL INFORMATION.** The **church** is on the east side of the parque and the **pier** is 2km to the north. The best source for **tours** and guides is **Hotel Castillo,** half a block west of the *carretera* and one block south of the *parque*. The Castillo brothers, Manuel, Carlos, and Julio, are authorities on the island's petroglyphs. (Julio7464@hotmail.com. Guided tours to Maderas 50C per person, to Concepción 60C per person. Next door to Hotel Castillo in **Tienda Fashion,** Gustavo Condega (gustavoc@tmx.com.ni) can give valuable tourism information (and information about the gay scene in Ometepe/Nicaragua). The **Centro de Salud** (health center) is one block north of the mayor's office. (Open 8am-noon and 1-5pm for appointments. Open 24hr. for emergencies.) **Farmacia María Auxiliadora** is half a block south of the *parque*'s southeast corner. (☎552 8758. Open M-Sa 8am-8pm, Su 8am-noon.) **Farmacia Jany,** in front of the south side of the parque, sells medicine, repellent, etc. (Open M-Sa 8am-9pm.)

Exchange traveler's checks in the **post office** building one block south of the *parque*. (Open M-F 8am-5pm, Sa 8am-noon.) The **Ometepe Museum** is located in Altagracia next to the *alcaldía* to the south side of the *parque* and west of the Centro de Salud. (☎552 8745. Open M-Sa 9am-5pm. 10C.) Two computers in Altagracia "officially" connect to the **Internet,** one in Hotel Castillo (70C per hr.) and one in Tienda Fashion (80C per hr.). **Post office** and **telephone** services are in the Enitel building, next to the Alcaldía. (Open M-F 8am-5pm, Sa 8am-noon.)

▐ ▐ **ACCOMMODATIONS AND FOOD.** Hotel Castillo ❶, 1 block south of the park and ½ block to the west, offers hammocks, spacious and clean rooms, and a spotless and tasty restaurant space. (☎/fax 552 8744; hotcatll@hotmail.com. Meals 20-70C. Rooms 40C per person, with private bathroom 70C.) **Hotel/Bar Restaurante Central ❶,** two blocks south of the *parque*'s southeast corner, has a beautiful garden and comfortable rooms and restaurant. (☎552 8770. Standard rooms 40C per person, with private bath 50C; private cabins 80C.) **Hospedaje Kencho ❶** (☎552 8772), one block south of the *parque*'s southeast corner, has a balcony and hammocks. (Rooms 35C per person, with bath 40C.) **Hospedaje Ran Luna ❶,** one block east of Hotel Castillo and run by Gustavo from the Tienda fashion (see **Orientation,** above), offers a kitchen, TV, and six cheap rooms (35C).

Buen Gusto ❷, is Hospedaje Kencho's nice, outdoor restaurant, serving *comida corriente* (12-15C); entrees (20-35C). (Open daily 6:30am-9:30pm.) There are six *comedores* set around the parque. **Soda Bar "Altagracia ❶,"** ½ block in front of the basketball court of the parque, offers good breakfasts and lunches (15C-38C. Open M-Sa 7am-10pm.) When it is not under construction the **kiosk** in the park is also good for a snack. (Open daily 8am-10pm.)

SIGHTS AROUND THE ISLAND

To access much of the island, it is best to hire a guide (see **Practical Information** under Moyogalpa and Altagracia for suggestions). Everyone on the island is a guide for something, and prices are generally reasonable.

SANTO DOMINGO. Along the isthmus between the two islands, Santo Domingo is the island's most popular and biggest beach. It's a pleasant place to relax for a few days, and a number of hotels can help you hang out in style. ▨**Hotel Villa Paraíso ❷,** near the south end of the beach, is the most luxurious place on the island, with fresh rooms, hammocks, gardens, a TV, bar room, and an excellent restaurant. (☎453 4675. Restaurant open daily 7am-9pm.) The owners offer horse rental, windsurfing, and guided tours. (Doubles US$18; doubles or triples with bath US$18; quads US$20; *cabañas* US$30-40.) **Hotel Finca Santo Domingo ❷**, just next door on the right, has a volleyball net on the beach and a young crowd of vacationers. Dark rooms have portals that let in light and sea air. (☎881 6603. Restaurant open daily 7am-8:45pm. Rooms US$6 per person, with bath for 2-5 people US$25.) The newly constructed **Hospedaje el Bosque Tropical ❶**, across the street from Villa Paraíso and once a discotheque, now offers eight well sized and well lit rooms. (50C per person with fan and private bathroom.) For cheap food and good company, walk up the main street north at the entrance of Playa Santo Domingo to **Comedor Carta al Mundo ❶**, where Mama Ana Julia will cook for you. (15C-25C. Open daily 7am-9pm.) A 30min. (1.5km) walk north of the playa Santo Domingo is the beautiful **Presa Ojo de Agua**, on your left before crossing the bridge. It is a $1 entrance fee to bathe in the crystalline water.

VOLCÁN MADERAS. Reaching Maderas's summit requires an early start; it's 5-8hr. of fairly steep hiking to the top and back, not including stops. The hike to the top passes first through tropical dry forest, then dense tropical rainforest, and finally cloud forest. On the way to the lagoon in the crater, deer, howler monkeys, white-faced monkeys, and many wild flowers cross your path. The trails can be very muddy and chilly near the summit. It is possible to continue down into the crater with a rope to assist you; this is better with a guide. Unless you're staying overnight, you'll want to be on the first bus to Balgüe (5am from Altagracia).

Ask the bus driver to drop you off at the entrance to Magdalena, from which a 15min. walk up the path leads to **La Finca Magdalena ❶**, an organic coffee farm, that sells quality cups of joe and 100% pure bee honey. Workers live off the ecologically friendly solar-energy system. It is very popular for tourists to stay overnight here, especially for work during November and December. The restaurant serves delicious, typical food (12-25C), but is only open until 8pm. (Hammock 20C; dorm bed 25C; private room 30C; matrimonial room 60C; camping 20C.) Climbing the volcano is 20C solo and 100C for a guided group.

VOLCÁN CONCEPCIÓN. The taller of the two volcanoes (1610m), Concepción is said to have the most perfectly conical shape of all the volcanoes in Central America. Concepción is still active and the terrain near the top consists primarily of loose rocks and sand, so it is less popular than Maderas. Low visibility, especially during the rainy season, often makes reaching the crater difficult (and pointless). The lower half of the volcano is covered with tropical dry forest. **Floreana** (about 2hr. to the top) is a good destination and offers the first clear, breathtaking *vista* from the volcano. Most hikes begin at **La Flor**, 6km northeast of Moyogalpa and reachable by bus (6:30, 10am, 1:30pm; return every hr. 12:10-5:10pm.) Trails also start at **La Concha**, 4km from Moyogalpa on the road to La Flor, **La Sabana**, a 1km walk from Altagracia, at **Cuatro Cuadras**, 2km from Altagracia, and at **San Ramón**. A guide is essential; paths on Concepción are unmarked and hard to find.

PETROGLYPHS. Most of the petroglyphs lie between **Balgüe** and **Magdalena**, on the Maderas side of the island. Another group is located near **El Porvenir**, a 30min. walk from Santo Domingo and 10min. from Santa Cruz and La Palma. Carved between the 11th and 13th centuries, these simple etchings contain spirals and circles of unknown significance—take advantage of this glimpse into the pre-Columbian world. Find them yourself by renting a bike or car and asking around (most children will be willing to show you the way for a few *córdobas*) or hire a guide.

SAN RAMÓN. On the south side of the Madera cascades is the **Salto de San Ramón**, a waterfall accessible from the village of San Ramón. The pleasant hike to the falls through tropical dry forest takes about 2hr., and the return about half that. There are two possible trails; the old one is to the right of the Enitel bus stop and the renewed one, which one can supposedly go up by car or bike is to the left. There is only one bus to San Ramón (M-Sa leaves Moyogalpa 8:15am, Altagracia 10:45am. The infrequent bus schedule means you might have to stay overnight. ☒**Biological Station of Ometepe ❺**, 300m north of the chapel across from the only dock with coconut trees, is a luxurious place to stay, and is often crowded with biologists. The stay includes three delicious buffet-style meals, kayaks, guides to Volcán Madera, and snoozing rights to a hammock on the dock. (☎/fax 453 0875. Meals 30C for non-guests. Stay US$20 per day.) **Francisco Jarcín ❶**, a block north of the bright turquoise church behind the Enitel bus stop, rents a few dimly lit, unfanned rooms with communal baths. (☎ 453 4023. 25C per person.)

CHARCO VERDE LAGOON. On the south side of Volcán Concepción, near the town of San José close to the beach, hides the marshy pond and hidden myths of Charco Verde lagoon. Apparently, every Friday night at midnight, *Chico Largo*, a devil-like ghost of a former Rivas shaman, comes out of the lagoon to give money to those who pray to him and take the souls of those who don't. Ask local legend José del Carmen García Aquire to tell you more. He always hangs out at the lagoon (except on Fridays, perhaps). Charro Verde offers excellent **birdwatching** and occasional freshwater **turtle spotting**. A path leads around the lagoon (1hr.), passing the very private **Playa Escondida** or **Playa Balcón** with beautiful views of Isla Quiste up at the mirador. Entrance is free but donations are appreciated.

Look for the Charco Verde sign on the main Moyogalpa-Altagracia road (ask the bus driver to let you off at Charco Verde). Another option is to get free transportation from Moyogalpa to Charco verde by *camioneta* (bus) with Conny and Ramiro, who bring you directly to their **Posada de Chico Largo ❶**. The three private rooms in a house next door are right on the lake, with the perks of gorgeous views and croaking bullfrogs. (Meals 25-50C. Rooms 50C per person.) Next to the Posada is the charming **Playa Venecia Hotel ❸**. (US$10 per person.) Five minutes left along the beach from the end of the signed road is **Hospedaje Charco Verde ❶**. (**Boat** tours 30C per hr.; **horseback** rides 20C per hr.; rooms 40C per person, private baths 70C.)

PUNTA DE JESÚS MARÍA. On the west side of Volcán Concepción sits simple Punta de Jesús María, a pebble spit extending into the lake near the town of Esquipulas, an hour's walk (3km) from Moyogalpa. On top of its breathtaking views, it sports a small cafetería, which serves no food but lots of rum. (Half bottle 50C. Open Sa-Su 8am-8pm.) You can swim on both sides of the point, but beware of strong currents at the point itself. The most popular time to come for both locals and tourists is during *Semana Santa* for both locals and tourists. The *punta* is accessible via the Moyogalpa-Altagracia bus. The turnoff on the right side of the road is unmarked, but if you see the green-and-white sign for Esquipulas, you have gone too far. From the road it's a 15min. walk to the point (1.5km).

ARCHIPIÉLAGO DE SOLENTINAME

The Solentiname Archipelago, comprised of 36 small, sparsely populated islands, and only 20km northwest of San Carlos, is one of Nicaragua's best hidden treasures. The name Solentiname, in *Nahuatl* means "site of/for many guests." But with Nicaragua's slowly increasing tourism and the few local residents, the only true guests to return annually are the 10 species of migratory birds. *Padre* **Ernesto Cardenal** arrived in 1966 and changed Solentiname forever. Poet, sculptor and evangelical priest, he taught his first 12 farmer "disciples" the unique art of primitivist painting and balsa carving (which soon became infamous both nationally and internationally). The artisans live on the main islands of **San Fernando** (also known as **Elvis Chavarría**) and **Isla Macarrón.** Mancarrón has the best tourist accommodations, and is a great base for an extended stay. Other islands include: **Macarroncito** with its impressive primary forest, **El Venado** with its well known petroglyphs and caves, **Isla del Padre,** which hosts the majority of the mammalian species of the whole archipelago, and **Isla el Zapote,** also known as "Bird Island."

▐ TRANSPORTATION. Public *lanchas* **(boats)** leave San Carlos for Solentiname on Tu and F at 12:30pm, return around 4am, and stop at Mancarrón and San Fernando. (2½-3hr., 25C one way.) If you miss the *lanchas*, hire private transportation, although it is much more expensive (usually 50C; ask around for Silvio). Plans for public service on Th and Su are underway. **Hotel APDS** on Mancarrón can provide transportation from San Carlos. (see **Accommodations,** below. US$90 round-trip.) **Solentiname Tours,** in Managua: km8 Carretera Sur (☎265 2716; zerger@ibw.com.ni), runs from Granada to Solentiname, passing through Moyogalpa, Ometepe (10½ hr. F from Granada 7am) and back again (Su from Solentiname 8am). The main islands have Italian-built *senderos* (paths) that are especially useful with the sporadic *lancha* schedule. The art colonies of **San Fernando** and **La Venada** are a 10min. boat ride from Macarrón (US$45 round-trip).

▌ PRACTICAL INFORMATION. Tours Nicaragua (☎228 7063; www.toursnicaragua.com; nicotour@nic.gbm.net) and **Careli Tours** (☎278 2572; www.carelitours.com; info@carelitours.com) are two reliable **tour operators** that offer complete packages to Solentiname. There is only one **health center** on the Isla de Mancarrón, a grey cement house 20km to the left of the hospedaje/pulpería the Lidia Castillo. (Open M-F 8am-noon and 1:30pm-5pm.) In an emergency, hotel APDS has a cell **phone.** You will have to wait until San Carlos to send any **letters.**

▌ ACCOMMODATIONS. On Mancarrón, **Hotel APDS ❺,** (☎283 0083; ramses@ibw.com.ni) is a good place to stay and offers daytrip packages to the museum in San Fernando (US$25) and tours of **Los Guatuzos Wildlife Refuge** near Río Papachure, 4km south of Isla Zapote (US$50). **Hotel Mancarrón ❺,** has rooms with private baths and good meals. (☎/fax 265 2716 in Managua; 453 0294 in Solentiname. Singles US$75; doubles US$100.)

◙ SIGHTS. Museo Archipiélago de Solentiname, a five min. walk on the along the path from Julio Cesar's cabinas, after the *taller* and up the stairs. Constructed in 2000 by the Italian Association **Asociación de Cooperación Rural en Africa y America Latina (ARCA)** and the local artisans, this sight introduces the guest to the flora, fauna, art, location, history and geology of Solentiname in three colorful rooms. (In San Carlos ☎/fax 283 0095; musasni@yahoo.com; www.una.edu.ni/soleiname. Open M mornings, T-Su 7am-noon and 2pm-5pm. Admission US$1.)

SAN CARLOS DE NICARAGUA

San Carlos sits at the head of the Río San Juan, on the southwestern shore of the Lago de Nicaragua. There's not much to do in the town itself—a former Spanish fort on the north side of the *parque* is now just a few moss-covered walls. Most travelers use the town as a launching point for adventures to the artistic culture and abundant wildlife of the Archipiélago or down the Río to the tropical rainforest of the Reserva Biológica Indio-Maíz and the Spanish outpost of Castillo Viejo. It's also possible to cross into Costa Rica through the Río Frío and Los Chiles.

▐ TRANSPORTATION. La Costeña planes take off from an airstrip 10min. from town by taxi (10C) to **Managua** (M-Th and Sa 9:30am, F and Su 1pm; round-trip US$75). The ticket office (☎283 0271) is two blocks northwest of the main ENAP port. **Buses** stop in a lot 30m northeast (right) of the main port across from the new market, about five blocks east of the *parque*. Buses from San Carlos leave for **Managua** (8hr., 5 per day 2am-9pm, 80C) via **Juigalpa** (5hr.; 10, 10:30, 11am,

12:40pm; 60C); and **Granada** via **Managua** (9½hr., Tu and F 4pm, 90C). **Boats** leave from the main ENAP dock behind the gate just west of the new market, and head to **Castillo Viejo** (via *lancha* 2¾-4hr.; M-Sa 8am, noon, 1:30, 3pm, Su 1pm; 40C) via cargo boat (4hr., 1pm, 35C); and **San Juan del Norte** (10hr.; Tu and F 6am, return Th and Su leaving San Juan 5am; 160C). Buy tickets at the pink booth. (Open daily 8am-4pm.) A speed boat to **Granada** should start running sometime in 2003. (4hr., F and Su 1pm, US$15-20.) Boats to the **Archipiélago de Solentiname** leave from the floating dock in front of the tourist kiosk on the *malecón* (boardwalk; 3hr., Tu and F 2pm, 25C) and stop at **Isla San Fernando** and **Isla Mancarrón**. Private *pangas* are also available at the floating dock. Talk to Armando Ortiz (see below). Boats for **Los Chiles, Costa Rica** leave from the immigration office 30m west of the main ENAP dock (1hr.; 10:30am, 1:30, 3:30pm; 80C).

▚▞ ORIENTATION AND PRACTICAL INFORMATION. The **church** tower is on the west side of the *parque;* the fort on the north side. The *malecón* is to the south, and the new market to the east. For tourist information, try **INTUR**, two blocks east of the *parque* across from Clínica San Lucas. (☎283 0301. Open M-F 8am-5pm.) **Viajes Turísticos Armando Ortiz** (☎283 0039), two blocks south of the *parque*'s southwest corner, runs tours throughout the area. No place changes traveler's checks, but to change US dollars try **Banco de Finanzas**, one block southeast of the east side of the *parque*. (☎283 0144. Open M-F 8:30am-4pm, Sa 8:30am-noon.) There are three **Western Union** offices in San Carlos; the main one is opposite the Kaoma restaurant. (☎283 0250. Open daily 7am-8pm.) The main **police** station (☎283 0365) is a 15min. bus ride on the *carretera* out of town; the downtown office (☎283 0092) is in the Antiguo Telcor building. Other services include: **Red Cross** (☎283 0234), 3½ blocks north of the park's northwest corner; **hospital** (☎283 0362), a block beyond; **Farmacia Fabiola**, about 200m south of ENITEL, with 24hr. emergency assistance (☎283 0025, open daily 10am-9pm); **ENITEL**, 1½ blocks north of the *parque*'s northwest corner on the *carretera* out of town (☎283 0001, open daily 7am-9:30pm); and **post office**, two blocks south of the *parque*'s southeast corner (open M-F 8am-noon and 1-5pm, Sa 8am-1pm).

▛ ACCOMMODATIONS. The nicest place is **Hotel San Carlos ❷**, on the *malecón*, 50m south of the immigration office, next to Clínica San Lucas. The clean rooms have fans, and a porch faces the lake. (☎283 0265. Singles 60C; doubles 100C.) **Hotel Costa Sur ❶**, about 300m from the main ENAP port on the road leading east and north, has comfy mattresses and quiet, stuffy rooms. (☎283 0224. Singles 50C; doubles 85C, with bath 100C.) The tiny rooms of **Hospedaje Peña ❶**, one block east of the *parque*, all have lake views. (☎283 0298. 30C per person.)

▚▞ FOOD AND NIGHTLIFE. *Comedores* and *sodas* line the so-called Calle Comercial from the new market to the end of the *malecón*. **El Ranchón ❷**, with views of the lake, serves fast food for 10C and larger meals for 30-50C. (Open daily 5am-midnight.) Play pool while waiting for your meal at **El Granadino ❷**, one block south of the southeast corner of the *parque*. (Food 25-70C. Open M-Th 10am-midnight, F-Su 10am-1am.) **Kaoma**, 1½ blocks southwest of the tourist kiosk on the *malecón*, features a loud older crowd and dancing. (Open M-F noon-midnight, Sa-Su 10am-2am.) San Carlos's only disco is **Bar-Disco La Champa**, on the first corner west of the tourist kiosk on the *malecón*. (Open Th-Su 10am-1am.)

RÍO SAN JUAN

Río San Juan runs over 200km connecting Lake Nicaragua and other tributaries to the Caribbean Sea, it marks the border between Nicaragua and Costa Rica and is one of the biggest ecotourism attractions in Nicaragua. Swirling, expanding, and churning from San Carlos to San Juan del Norte, the waters wash away history and legends since the sixteenth century and it counts many admirers, including the American author Mark Twain. The lucky visitor is sure to find a mini-Amazon full of natural wildlife fauna, such as the *sábalo real* (giant fish) and endless tropical flora like the *lechuga*, a type of lettuce that grows on floating vegetation. Apart from the sited main attractions, there are also many hidden places—farms, mountains, *pueblos*, and *comarcas* like **Boca de Sábalos** and **Raudal del Toro.**

BOCA DE SÁBALOS

The first stop from San Carlos or San Juan del Sur down the Río San Juan, this small town has both natural charm and a splash of adventure. Build your own boat out of wood (US$100) or fiber glass (US$1000), fish with the locals(100C in wood boat; 200C in motorboat), and enjoy this untouched treasure.

E TRANSPORTATION. Public boats leave San Carlos from the main dock to **Castillo Viejo,** stopping first in Sábalos. (1½hr.; M-Sa 8am, noon, 1, 3pm; Su 1pm; 35C). Private *lanchas* are more expensive but convenient; all leave before 4pm. If you stay at Yaro's place in **Raudal del Toro** (see below), free transportation to Sábalo is available (9am and 4pm, return 10:30am and 5:30pm). This is a good option if you want to get a quick taste of this small but interesting town.

█ █ ACCOMMODATIONS AND FOOD. Past the pharmacy and Nintendo game room is **Hotel Central ❶,** run by Lillia Martínez. The restaurant downstairs serves meals in the breezy shade. (Restaurant open daily 8am-midnight, 20C. Rooms 30C per person without fan, 50C with fan; 80C for fan and matrimonial bed.) **Hospedaje y Comedor Katiana ❷,** has clean, breezy rooms with shared bathrooms and ceiling fans (60C, with a mini TV 100C). Similar conditions are next door at **Hospedaje Clarissa ❶.** The mini restaurant downstairs serves great fruit salad for 25C-125C. (Rooms 50C per person with shared bathroom.) Another hotel is currently being built across the river, but until then dance the night away at disco parties every other Saturday in the hills of Sábalos (10C). At the entrance of Sábalos, past the fish fountain and town general store (with phone and basic necessities), **Parates' Miscelanea Mi Favorita,** the **Comedor Koma Rica ❶,** serves cheap, typical food.

EL CASTILLO VIEJO

Some 60km down the Río San Juan lies the small, picturesque river town of El Castillo, home to various points of interest for foreigners and locals. The town is the site of the **Fortaleza de la Inmaculada Concepción,** a Spanish fort built in 1675 to prevent pirates from coming up the river and sacking Granada. Perched on a hill next to an especially shallow and dangerous stretch of the river, its location is well-suited for defending against attackers. In 1780, English troops led by Horace Nelson captured the fort, only to abandon it a year later. In 1993 it was renovated, and now visitors are free to wander its stony walkways.

E TRANSPORTATION. The best option is to travel via public *lancha*, which leaves from the main dock across from the bus station, next to the new market in **San Carlos** (2¾hr.; M-Sa 8am, noon, 1, 3pm; Su 1pm; 40C). A private *panga* (boat) from San Carlos to El Castillo (with a stop in Bartola) is a three-day trip. (US$250, 8 person max.) You can also try to catch any cargo boat; they leave at various times from the main dock until 4pm. Buy your ticket at the pink office in the corner of the *fortuaria.* (Open M-Su 8am-4pm.) Once in El Castillo, you can rent a horse for a day and ride to nearby **Costa Rica** through mountains and small *comarcas.* (Ask Danny at Hotel Richardson. US$10 per person, five person max.) One hour by foot is enough time to do a tour of the small town.

◄ █ ORIENTATION AND PRACTICAL INFORMATION. As you get out of the boat onto the dock, a faded red and gray Sandinista flag greets you at the bottom of the steep stairwell leading straight up to the Hotel-Albergue El Castillo, which dominates the primary view of the entrance to the city. You can catch a glimpse of the impressive *fortaleza* to the left above the mountain, but the clearest open view of the fort is when coming downstream toward San Carlos looking up from the rapids, known as the *Diablo* (Devil) rapids. There is only one main street which runs parallel to the river and uphill. The **tourist office** in front of the dock offers tour packets and two bilingual guides, Gilbert Haragón and Efraín Gonzales. (Open Tu-Sa 8am-noon and 2pm-5pm, Su 8am-11:30pm and 2pm-4pm. 4hr., US$15.) There is one **health center** (one block from the *fortaleza* on the right) and one *pulpería*, Variedades Ruiz (across from El Cofalito), for pharmacy-type needs (open M-Su 6:30am-8:30pm). The ENITEL **phone** company, 50m up right from the dock, usually functions (☎283 0200). The only other public phone is at Hotel Albergue El Castillo (US$1 per minute for local calls, US$6 for international calls). There is neither **internet** access in El Castillo nor an official **post office**.

ACCOMMODATIONS AND FOOD. El Castillo ❸, up the hill from the dock, puts you closest to the lap of luxury with resort-style accommodations—sprawling decks, sparkling communal bathrooms, and a delicious restaurant (☎892 0174. US$10 per room, US$15 with breakfast). Find the clean and well lit **Hotel Richardson ❸**, by turning left at the dock and then right after the Catholic church. Decorated by the famous Nicaraguan painter Ricardo Peña, its amenities include a TV lounge, bar, and restaurant. (Rooms US$10 per person.) Cheaper options are **Hotel Aurora ❶**, right on the water 50m from the dock (30C per person), and **Hotel Manantial ❶**, near the dock. (Restaurant attached. 30C per person.) Newly constructed **Hospedaje Nena ❶**, a green house to the right 100m south of the Catholic church, offers family style ambiance and meal service. (Rooms 40C per person.)

The best and cheapest meal in town is served by **Doña Luisa Jerez ❶** in her house; turn left from the dock and follow the road straight to its end. The house will be on the left. She rents out three rooms. (Heaping *comida corriente* 15C; shrimp 75C; chicken 50C. Rooms 30C per person.) A bit more expensive but worth it is **Restaurante El Cofalito ❸**, to the right of the dock. (*Comida corriente* and beverage 45C; *camarones* 100C; *pescado* 70C. Open daily 7am-10pm, Sa-Su later.) **Restaurante Narayito ❸**, also on the river, is 400m down the dock to the left. (☎552 8829. *Comida corriente* 25C; steak 50C; *camarones* 100C.) For late-night food and drink, try reasonably

COUNT ON MONTECRISTO

On the Río San Juan, the plush thrives along the shores of the lush. The resort of Montecristo is bound to be one of the most luxurious resorts on the Río San Juan, if not in all of Nicaragua. Travel in proper style to Montecristo using the island resort's private boats (US$100), or if your visit alone might bust the bank, by public *lancha* (40C). In addition to stones spelling "Montecristo" visible by air and 64 steps leading up to the resort, it will be hard to believe you are in the middle of the Nicaraguan jungle with all the modern imports from Miami including a jacuzzi, swimming pool, and jetskis. Carlos Dronte can show you around the *manzana* (apple) farm, which displays three caged tigers, deer, and green-house cultivations. Ride the resorts beautiful horses and laze or fish along the river in guided boat tours. After working up an appetite in paradise, eat at the delicious outdoor restaurant for up to US$10 a meal. (Horses US$10-20 per ride; jacuzzis US$40; boat tours US$40-US$300 for up to 10 people. Doubles with fridge, kitchen, hot water, cable TV, and private bath US$45; matrimonial room US$80; luxury cabins for 4-6 people US$180.) However long your stay, Montecristo is sure to be the perfect escape from it all, in the lap of luxery.

priced **Bar y Restaurante La Brisa del San Juan,** 150m after the bridge (M-Su 10am-1pm, 6pm-midnight.)

⑥ SIGHTS. The **Fortaleza de la Inmaculada Concepción** gives the town both its namesake and principal sight. Tours are given by Eddy in Spanish. (Open M-Su 8am-noon and 2-5pm; US$1 entrance fee.) One of the chambers is now a first-rate **museum** which covers the fort's history and the importance of the Río San Juan in European exploration (10C). Rumor has it that the infamous ex-Nicaraguan president Arnoldo Alemán plans to build a five-star hotel across the river. Upstairs from the museum to the left is a **library.** For education about the environment and natural beauty of the Río San Juan region, check out the **Centro de Interpretación de la Naturaleza del Río San Juan.** Turn right after the health center and listen to Doña Teresa impart her wisdom (in Spanish) on the region's water cycles, deforestation, and dangerous monkeys. If butterflies are more you thing, a dozen steps up out the back door of the Centro de Interpretación is the beautiful **Mariposario,** preserving and raising five local species. (US$1. Open M-Su 8-11am and 1-4pm.)

GÜISES DE MONTAÑA AND REFUGIO BARTOLA

Six kilometers away from El Castillo is protected **Reserva Indio Maíz.** At the entrance of the **Río Bartola,** on the left side, is the center **Güises de Montaña** and **Refugio Bartola,** where there are more species of trees, insects, and birds than in all of Europe combined. This mountain **hospedaje** functions on solar energy, and is the last "civilized" spot before the 7hr. ride to **San Juan del Norte** (see below). It is an ideal spot for pure relaxation in the jungle and a huge center of interest for Nicaraguan and international researchers and biologists. University students come every year to study the infinite critters, but– fear not, layman tourist!—there are guides to bring you for a cool dip and bird watch on the Río Bartola, see the small indigenous village of **Buena Vista Comarcas,** and protect you from the occasional chance encounter with the *chancho de montes,* or wild boar. (US$10 group rate.)

SAN JUAN DEL NORTE (NEW GREYTOWN)

This town is most noteworthy for its strategic position at the mouth of the Río Indio, between the Río San Juan and the Caribbean Sea. The town has burnt down three times and Contra warfare has forced evacuation once. Today, the area is very poor and underdeveloped, but there are about 2000 inhabitants in this beautiful region of both coast and nature preserve. An airport and US$60 million road are currently being constructed in San Juan del Norte, but until they are finished the only mode of transport is by *panga* (boat). The public *lanchas* come and leave this town only twice a week from **San Carlos** (9-12hr.; Tu and F 6am, return Th and Su 5am; 160C.) From **El Castillo** (Tu and F 10am, return Th and Su 2pm). There are no passages to **Costa Rica.** If you find yourself stuck here for a night, **Tío Poon's Place ❷,** on Calle Primera across from Disco Fantasía, has rooms with shared bathrooms. (Rooms 60C.) **Bar y Restaurante los Delicias del Indio ❶,** on Calle Primera, serves cheap *corriente* (20C) under a gazebo along the Río Indio. **Soda Comedor Christian ❷,** next to Pulpería la Tequita on Calle Central, serves copious *comida corriente* with a soft drink (40C) outside at the one table available (with a mini TV). There are two disco-bars which entertain the locals: **Discoteca Tropical,** a cabin-hut across from the Casa de Compaña on Calle Central, and **Disco Fantasia,** in front of Tío Poon's on Primera Calle. (Open M-Su 6pm-11:30pm. No cover.)

CENTRAL HIGHLANDS

The central highlands are a region of rugged mountains accessible by steep, curving, scenic roads. They were the political stronghold of the *Contras* in the late

NICARAGUA

Central Highlands

Jalapa
FILA EL VENADO
VALLE SAN DIEGO
El Paraíso
Las Manos
Santa María
Volcán Viejo
Dipilto
Cerro de Tizal
Santa Clara
San Fernando
Murra
El Jícaro
Cerro Chachagua
Susucayan
Cerro California
FILA DE BUDNA
Cerro el Perro
Wiwilí
Cerro el Marimacho
Macuelizo
Mosonte
Ocotal
Cíudad Antigua
RÍO COCO
Totogalpa
Cerro Montañita de Santa María
Telpaneca
Quilalí
Cerro el Careto
San Juan de Río Coco
HONDURAS
Yalagüina
Palacagüina
FILA LAGUNA SECA
RÍO COCO
El Espino
Somoto
Cerro la Ilusión
Las Práderas
San Marcos
San Lucas
Pueblo Nuevo
Condéga
La Rica
Pueblo las Sabanas
RÍO ESTELÍ
SIERRA LOS CEDROS
San José de Cusmapa
El Bosque
San Sebastián de Yalí
San Rafael del Norte
Asturias
La Dalia
San Francisco del Norte
LLANO VALLUCÚN
El Regodío
LLANO SANTA ANA
La Concordia
Lago de Apanás
RÍO TUMA
San Juan de Limay
RÍO NEGRO
LOMA LA PEÑA DE AGUA SARCA
Estelí
Jinotega
El Tuma
San José de Achuapa
El Salto de Estanzuela
Santa Cruz
La Trinidad
Selva Negra
Matagalpa
Interamerican Hwy.
San Isidro
San Ramón
El Sauce
San Nicolás
Sébaco

0   10 kilometers
0   10 miles

1980s, and fighting continued here long after it had died out in the lowlands. Nearly every individual over age 25 has a story to tell about the war's impact. The fiercely free-thinking highlanders have always been difficult for the government to control, with passionate viewpoints from all across the political spectrum.

Estelí, the largest city in the north, has some compelling reminders of the war and is easily visited en route from Managua to the Honduran border along the Interamerican Hwy. South of Estelí is a turnoff for the beautifully situated town of Matagalpa, gateway to Selva Negra, one of Nicaragua's most accessible forest preserves. A separate highway running east from Managua toward the Caribbean coast passes near Boaco, a mountainous cowboy town, before reaching Juigalpa, a good place to stop if you're making the trip all the way to the coast.

ESTELÍ

The amicable, agricultural town of Estelí (pop. 100,000) lies about halfway between Managua and the Honduran border, and is a welcome escape from the pounding heat of lowland cities. While it is the largest town in northern Nicaragua, its cobbled streets turn to dirt roads just a few blocks from the *avenida central*, and the verdant countryside nearby remains fairly unsettled. Estelí is the principle tobacco center in Nicaragua, producing volumes of hand rolled cigars which rival the quality of those made in Cuba. The town also has a lively coffee industry. Many foreigners can be found in Estelí, volunteering or sharpening their Spanish skills at the town's many language schools (see **Alternatives to tourism** p. 55). The past has not been entirely buried—in July of 1993, violence erupted between former Sandinistas and rebellious *Contras* frustrated with the government.

▐ TRANSPORTATION

Buses going north and an express to León leave from **Terminal Norte** on the *carretera*. Destinations include: **Condega** (1hr., take any bus that goes to Somoto or Ocotal, 6C); **Ducuale Grande** (5min.; ride north from Condega, ask to be let off; 7C from Estelí, 2C from Condega); **Ocotal** (2¼hr., every hr. 4:10am-5:35pm, 13C); **Somoto** (2hr., every hr. 5:13am-6:10pm, 12C). **Express Managua** (2¼hr., ten daily stops every 30min. 4:45am-3:15pm, 30C), and **León** (2½ hr., 6:45am and 3:10pm, 30C). Buses to the **Honduran border** at **Las Manos** can be caught from Ocotal, and for the **Honduran border** at **El Espino** from Somota (see p. 578). Buses going south leave from **Terminal Sur** to: **Matagalpa** (1¾hr., every 30min. 5:20am-4:20pm, 12C); **Managua** (indirect: 3hr., every 30min. 3:30am-5pm, 22C; express: leave from *Terminal Norte*, 20C); **León,** take a Managua or Matagalpa bus to San Isidro (45min., 7C) and change there to a León bus (2hr., every hr., 18C).

Local Buses run north-south, 1 street west of Av. Central, from Barrio Rosario to the new hospital, including a stop at the bus terminal. The same buses, usually marked "Rosario-Hospital" return south to north along Av. Central (2C).

Taxis are regulated by the mayor's office and should charge the mandated price. Watch out for cabbies trying to up the price. They will pick up other passengers so don't be surprised (5am-5pm, 5C; 10pm-5am, 10C; slightly more for leaving the city.)

▐ ▐ ORIENTATION AND PRACTICAL INFORMATION

Av. Central, Estelí's main street, runs north-south along the length of the city. **Calle Transversal** runs east-west near the center of town, one block south of the *parque*. *Avenidas* (running north-south) and *calles* (running east-west) are numbered in increasing order away from Av. Central and Calle Transversal. The **Esquina de los Bancos** (financial district) sits at the intersection of Av. 1 SO and Calle Transversal. Addresses listed below often refer to the direction from this main intersection. In addition, the town is divided into quadrants (NO, NE, SO, SE). Almost all streets are labeled. The **Interamerican Hwy.** runs along the eastern edge of town, six blocks east of Av. Central. The **Terminal Norte** is at the south end of town, five blocks west from Terminal Sur. **Bus Terminal Sur** is at the south end of town, on the Interamerican Hwy. and Calle 14 SE. The **Terminal Norte** is also at the south end of town, five blocks west from Terminal Sur. The *parque central* lies one block north of Calle Transversal (15 blocks north of the bus terminals), with Av. Central running along its western edge. People will refer to the entrances to Estelí as the *cametera al norte y al sur* when giving directions.

Tourist Office: INTUR (☎ 713 6799).

Travel Agency: El Tisey (☎ 713 3099), 1 block north of the northeast corner of the *parque*, next to the Hotel Mesón. Open M-F 8:30am-5:30pm, Sa 8am-12:30pm.

Banks: Banco de América Central (☎713 7101), on the Esquina de los Bancos on Calle Transversal, serves as a Credomatic. Changes traveler's checks and advances cash on AmEx/MC/V. Open M-F 8:30-5pm, Sa 8:30am-12:30pm.

Western Union: (☎713 6756) 2 blocks north and about 25m west of the *bus terminal sur*. Open M-F 8:30am-5pm, Sa-Su 8:30am-4pm.

Supermarket: Super Económico, Av. Central, 4 blocks south of the *parque central*. Open daily 7:30am-9pm.

Library: Biblioteca Pública Dr. Samuel Meza Brones, 1 block south of the Esquina de los Bancos. Open M-F 8am-noon and 2-5pm.

Police: INTUR (☎ 713 2615, emergency 118), southeast of town, near the *carretera.*

Red Cross: INTUR (☎ 713 2330), 8 blocks south and 1 block east of the southeast corner of the *parque.*

Pharmacy: Farmacia Abdalah (☎ 713 2820), Av. Central, 7 blocks south of the *parque.* Open daily 7am-10pm.

Hospital: (☎ 713 6305 or 713 2439), about 1km south of town on the *carretera.*

Telephones: ENITEL, Calle Transversal, Av. 1/2 SE (☎ 713 3308), 1 block south and 1 block east of the *parque.* Open M-Sa 7am-9pm, Su 7am-8pm.

Internet Access: Cyber Pl@ce (☎ 713 2475), 1½ blocks north of the northwest corner of the *parque.* Has the fastest connection, free coffee, and a 20% discount for ISIC cardholders. 0.75C per min. Su 2hr. for the price of 1. Open M-Sa 8am-8pm and 10am-3pm. **Cafe@net,** on the north side of the park, is slightly cheaper and open a bit later. 0.65C per min.; 30C per hr., 25C for students. Open daily 8am-9pm.

Post Office: (☎ 713 5632; fax 713 2240) Half a block west of Av. Central on Calle Transversal. Open M-F 8am-noon and 1:30-4:30pm, Sa 8am-noon.

▐ ACCOMMODATIONS

▨ **Hotel Nicarao,** Av. Central, Calles Transversal/1 S (☎ 713 2490), The lush open-air courtyard is a relaxing place to sit and the rooms are pleasant. The door closes early at night; knock to be let in. Reservations are highly recommended. Large breakfast 25C. Singles 80C, with private bath 145C; doubles 92C/145C; triples 138C/207C. ❷

Hotel Mariela (☎ 713-2166), one block north and one block west of bus terminal *sur.* It is the farthest from the *parque,* but closest to the two terminals. The tile floors, rooms, bathrooms, laundry area, and cement courtyards are immaculate. Singles 50C; doubles 80C, with bath 150C. ❶

Hospedaje San Francisco, Av. Central, Calles 7/8 S (☎ 713 3787), 4 blocks north of the bus station. Rooms are small but clean. Room 7 is the secret hiding place of the real Mona Lisa. Front door locks at 11pm. 25C per person. ❶

Hotel Mesón (☎ 713 2655; fax 713 4029), 1 block north of the northeast corner of the *parque.* Travel posters and art fill rooms around a garden with two cabañas. Ceiling fans and hot, private baths. Singles 115C; doubles 165C; triples 230C. AmEx/MC/V. ❸

⚬ ▣ FOOD AND ENTERTAINMENT

The dozen *comedores* at the terminals are clean and cheap. Take advantage of the options in the city; there is little variety in the rest of the region.

▨ **La Casita,** located on the Finca "Las Nubes," on the southern entrance to Estelí; take a taxi (7C) or the Urbano bus. Get off at the hospital stop and walk up the highway 10min. An organic farm, La Casita sells its goods at great prices. Come early to dine on warm whole-wheat bread and incredible brie cheese in the peaceful garden. Excellent Nicaraguan coffee. Open M 1-7pm, Tu-Sa 7am-7pm, Su 9am-7pm. ❶

Taquería Beverly, 1 block east of the southeast corner of the *parque.* Mexican specialties grilled before your eyes. Tacos (24C), burritos (15C), and quesadillas (12C). Portions are modest. Open Tu-Su 6-11pm. ❷

Comedor Popular la Soya, south on Av. Central, Calles 1/2, in a small, tan building across from La Baguette. Estelí's champion of vegetarian meals. Soy steaks, grilled soy, soy with potatoes, soy milk. Swing open the doors and say, *"Soy vegetariana!"* Omnivores don't be dissuaded: under new management, *Soya* has started serving beef and chicken alongside the tofu. Meals about 15C. Open daily 7am-7pm. ❶

El Rincón Pinareño, ½ block east of Av. Central on Calle Transversal. Offers delicious Cuban food. Glass-covered tablecloths are complemented by matching plastic chairs. Try the smoked chicken with cheese and bacon (40C). Entrees 40-90C; sandwiches 25-40C. Open daily 7:30am-9:30pm. ❶

Cinema Estelí plays long-outdated Hollywood flicks and random "foreign" flicks, changing every four days (20C; 8pm). Both the young and old just can't stop raving about **Rancho de Pancho.** No cover, two big dance floors, full restaurant menu, *salsa*, *merengue*, reggae, and pop hits, and a safe, fun environment keep everyone happy and returning every weekend. For a more typical discotheque, try **Traksig.** Thursday, ladies night, means two free beers. (Beer 10C; rum and coke 10C. Cover 20C.) The new kid on the block, **Tomcats,** is on the highway across from Calle 3 SE in the Eskalibur casino complex, and has two rooms separated by a dance floor and a very large circular hole in the wall. Party from dusk to dawn to latin dance music and huge crowds. (Beer 13C. No cover. Open daily 5pm-5am.)

👁 SIGHTS

▨ GALERÍA DE HÉROES Y MÁRTIRES. This memorial, operated by the Madres de los Héroes y Mártires, has exhibits that trace the lives and writings of some key revolutionary figures. There's also a display of weapons and a stunning abstract mural. If you have the time, ask to see the poignant testimonies of the mothers translated into English and the photos of the young men and women. Contact Gloria Castillo (for more info. (☎ 713 3753; emmayorga70@yahoo.com. ½ block south of the southeast corner of the parque. Open M-Sa 8am-4pm. Donations appreciated.)

CASA DE CULTURA. This *casa* houses a modest and constantly rotating display of local art, plus a museum with some of the more important finds from Las Pintadas, an archaeological dig at a prehistoric cave outside of town. The staff will tell you about upcoming cultural events in town. (☎ 713 3021. From the Galería, above, continue south on the same street to the end of the block. Open M-F 8am-noon and 2-5pm, Sa 8am-noon. Museum open M-F 9-11am.)

ESTELÍ CIGAR. Watch the workers hand roll cigars at one of Estelí's many cigar companies. The manager on duty will usually explain the process if you ask. They also sell blocks of 25 cigars or singles if they have extras (US$20-25). (5 blocks east of the southeast corner of the park just across from the highway, Open M-F 6am-5pm.)

ARTESANÍAS LA ESQUINA. Though geared toward tourists, this shop brings together handmade pieces from all over Nicaragua into its five rooms, covering almost every aspect of the country's artistic traditions. Prices are reasonable, but the owner drives a hard bargain. (☎ 713 2229. A block off Av. Central on Calle 3NE, across from the Hotel Mesón. Open daily 8am-noon and 2-6pm.)

📷 EL SALTO DE ESTANZUELA

Seven kilometers south of Estelí, El Salto de Estanzuela, a beautiful 30m **waterfall,** spills into a deep pool excellent for swimming. Though Hurricane Mitch made a bit of a mess here, most of it has been cleaned. Definitely worth a visit, especially during the rainy season (May-Nov.). The 1½hr. walk to the falls offers great views of Estelí. Bring lots of water, not much money or baggage, and never leave your belongings unattended, as the unscrupulous have been known to lighten the loads of distracted swimmers. (Catch a city bus running south, get off at the hospital, and walk from there. The parks department has recently added large signposts at the major intersections and forks along the way. Continue south and take the first right onto a dirt road. As you come down the second large hill on the route—about a 1hr. hike from the hospital—there will be a wooden gate beside the road where another road branches to the right. This point—the camioneta drop-off point for those choosing to ride—is easy to miss, so just keep asking as you go. Head downhill to the right for 10min. sticking close to the trail, until you hear and see the waterfall on your left. Check at the bus station for info on the occasional camionetas that make the trip (5C).

NORTH TO HONDURAS

North from Estelí, the Interamerican passes the villages of **Condega** and **Ducuale Grande,** an agreeable afternoon visit, and approaches Honduras. There are two routes across the border. The first is to beautiful **Ocotal** and the nearby border at **Las Manos,** the most convenient crossing for Tegucigalpa. The second goes to **Somoto** and then across the border at **El Espino;** this will put you in southern Honduras (near Choluteca), more convenient if you want to go directly to El Salvador.

CONDEGA

*All **buses** from Estelí to Somoto or Ocotal stop here. Museum donations accepted.*

The main attraction in Condega, 30min. north of Estelí, is the government-sponsored **Museo Arqueológico Julio César Salgado,** with a fine collection of pre-Columbian ceramics. The prized possessions of the museum are the **Incensarios Indígenas**—large, spike-covered ceramic incense burners. The **Casa de la Cultura** of Condega, where local children undertake apprenticeships in leather-working and instrument making, shares the museum building. If you walk north on the highway from the city, turn right up the path beside the blue-toned cemetery, and proceed to the top of the hill, you'll find the fuselage of a military **aircraft** downed by Sandinista guerrillas on its way back from bombing Estelí in the early 1980s.

Hospedaje Framar ❶, on the south side of the *parque,* has basic, well-kept rooms. Owner speaks some English. (☎752 2393. 10pm curfew. 30C per person.) **Bar y Restaurante Linda Vista ❶,** on the highway, has good food and friendly service. (*Comida corriente* 20C.)

DUCUALE GRANDE

*The turnoff to Ducuale Grande is a 20min. walk north of Condega along the highway; look for the "Taller Communal de Cerámica" sign. **Buses** heading between Estelí and Somoto or Ocotal also pass by.*

The *pueblito* of Ducuale Grande is famous for its ceramics. From the bus drop-off on the highway, follow the gravel road for 20min., past tobacco sheds and across a small river into town. Continue straight and soon you'll see two signs by a latrine. Take the road to the left and after 200m, you'll be at a quiet but busy **cooperative factory,** where 40 Ducualians dig, throw, rub, bake, paint, and carve the rich clay into everything from earrings (15C) to owl-shaped pots (25C). Visitors are welcome to observe the whole process and look through the final products in a tarp-covered lean-to. Bring a variety of bills; they don't carry much change.

OCOTAL AND THE BORDER AT LAS MANOS

Buses from Ocotal run to: **Managua** (3hr., eight daily stops 6:30am-3:15pm, 42C); **Estelí** (2½hr., every hr. 4:45am-6pm, 12C); **Somoto** (45min., every 30 min-1hr. 5:15am-5:30pm, 6C); the border at **Las Manos** (45min., every 35min. 5am-4:20pm, 6C). **Nicaraguan immigration/customs** open daily 7am-7pm. US$7 to enter, US$2 to leave Nicaragua, US$2 extra after noon Sa-Su. 10L to enter and 25L to exit Honduras. Customs will inspect luggage. **Money-changers** convert between US dollars, colones, and lempiras at fair rates. Meals are available at the comedores on either side. Buses continue on from the Honduran side.

Ocotal has perhaps the best *parque central* in Nicaragua, which makes it an attractive and notably clean first or last stop in Nicaragua. To get to the *parque* from the bus station, walk 1km north along the highway (to the Texaco station) and five blocks east, or take a taxi (5C). **Banco Mercantil**, 1 block west of the *parque's* northwest corner, changes US dollars. (Open M-F 8:30am-4:30pm, Sa 8:30am-noon.) Emergency services include the **police** (☎732 2333) and a **hospital** (☎732 2491). **INTUR** has a satellite office here, 1 block west of the northwest corner of the park (☎782 3429). **Western Union** is 1 block north of INTUR. (☎732 2918. Open M-F 8am-12:30pm and 2-5pm, Sa 8am-noon.) **Enitel** is 1 block north and ½ block east of the northwest corner of the *parque*.

Try the cheap and slightly noisy **Hospedaje Viajero ❶**, about 500m north and ½ block east of the bus station. (☎732 2040. 50C per person; doubles with bath and TV 150C; Amex/MC/Visa.) **Hotel El Mirador ❷**, across the highway from the bus station, is a solid option. Comfortable rooms have private baths and some have TVs. (☎732 2040. Breakfast 20C. Singles 100C; doubles 120C; triples 160C.) The most popular eatery is **Restaurante La Merienda ❷**, 6½ blocks north and two blocks east of the bus station. Look for the sign north on the *carretera*. (Most meals 50-70C; *comida corriente* 20C. Open Tu-Su 10am-11pm.) For a cheap, fast meal try **Cafetín Llamarada del Bosque ❶**, on the *parque's* south side. (Open M-Sa 6:30am-8pm.)

■ SOMOTO AND THE BORDER AT EL ESPINO

Buses from Somoto run to: **Managua** (indirect 5hr.; 4, 4:45, 7:20am; 33C. Express 3½hr., 5 per day. 5am-3:10pm, 40C); **Estelí** (2hr., every 40min. 4am-5:20pm, 11C); **Ocotal** (45min., every 30min. 5:45am-4:30pm, 7C); the Honduran border at **El Espino** 20km from Somoto (45min., every hr. 5:40am-5pm, 6C). The **Nicaraguan Immigration** is 100m from the Honduran border. Open daily 8am-noon and 1-5pm. **Money changers** and **comedores** pack the Honduran side of the line; you'll need to take a taxi (L10) into the village of **San Marcos, Honduras** to catch an ongoing bus. It is US$7 to enter/exit Nicaragua, L10 to enter Honduras and 25L to exit.

Somoto is a small, quiet mountain town. The *parque central* is four blocks south and one block west of the bus station (which lies along the *carretera*). **BDF**, one block south of the *parque's* southwest corner, changes traveler's checks and converts US dollars to cordobas. (Open M-F 8:30am-4pm, Sa 9am-noon.) **Western Union**, is ½ block south of the southeast corner of the *parque*. (☎722-2038. Open M-Sa 7am-7pm, Su 8am-noon.) Emergency services include the **police** (☎722 2252) and a **hospital** (☎722 2247). **ENITEL** is five blocks south of the bus station. (Open M-Sa 7am-8:30pm, Su 10am-8pm.) If you're stuck here for the night, **▨Panamericano ❶**, on the *parque's* northern edge, has clean, bright rooms and relaxing common areas. (☎722 2355. 50C per person; singles with bath 80C; with bath, TV, hot water, and fridge 150C; doubles 200C.) The spotless **Hospedaje Solentiname ❶**, 1½ blocks east of the bus station on the *carretera*, is cheaper. Rooms are a bit tight, with very thin beds. (☎722 2100. 40C per person, with bath 120C.) For good food and relaxing atmosphere, try **El Almendro ❷**, 1½ blocks south of the southeast corner of the *parque*. (*Comida corriente* 30C. Open Tu-Su 10am-10pm.)

MATAGALPA

In the heart of coffee country, 25km east of the Interamerican–one third of the way from Managua to the Honduran border–Matagalpa is one of Nicaragua's most visually arresting towns. Fluffy clouds descend from the mountains and graze the town's rooftops while raining a thin mist. Many visitors come for nearby Selva Negra National Park, but Matagalpa itself is a pleasant place to spend time. Originally settled in the 19th century by European immigrants, Matagalpa was an FSLN (Sandinista) stronghold during the revolution against the Somoza regime, and like the rest of Nicaragua, locals still take their politics very seriously.

TRANSPORTATION

From two blocks south and five blocks west of Parque Rubén Darío **buses** run to: **Managua** (2¾hr., every 30min. 3:35am-5:55pm, 30C; express: 2hr., every hr. 5:20am-4:50pm, 35C); **Estelí** (1¾hr., every 30min. 5:15am-6:15pm, 12C); **Jinotega** (1½hr., every 30min. 5am-7pm, 12C); and **León** (2½hr., 6am and 3pm, 30C). You can also get to León by taking an Estelí bus and getting off at **San Isidro** (7C), from where buses to León leave every 30min. (2½hr., 19C). For **Boaco,** take a Managua bus to San Benito (2hr., 15C) and change there. **Taxis** within town cost about 5C.

ORIENTATION AND PRACTICAL INFORMATION

Unlike many Central American towns, Matagalpa has not one *parque central*, but two: **Parque Rubén Darío** in the south, and **Parque Catedral** in the north (across from a cathedral and sometimes called **Parque Morazán.**) The bulk of "downtown" lies between them: the main street, **Calle de los Comercios,** begins at the northwest corner of Rubén Darío and continues north for seven blocks before ending in the middle of Parque Catedral. One block east, **Av. de los Bancos** (Av. Central) also connects the two parks, and contains most banks and some *artesanías.* The **bus terminal** is five blocks west and two blocks south of Parque Darío, along the river.

Tourist office: INTUR (☎612 7060), 3 blocks west and 3½ blocks north of northwest corner of Parque Darío. Open M-F 8am-12:30pm and 2-5pm.

Travel Agent: Viajes America (☎612 2259), 1 block south and half a block west of Parque Darío's southwest corner. Open M-F 8am-noon and 2-5pm, Sa 8am-noon.

Banks: Banco de América Central, 2½ blocks south of the *Catedral* on Av. de Los Bancos is lord of the credit cards. Open M-F 8am-6pm, Sa 8am-1pm. **Credomatic,** 1 block east of the southeast corner of Parque Catedral. Open M-F 8am-5:30pm, Sa 8am-1pm.

Western Union: in **Comercio Calero Mendieta** (☎612 4984; fax 612 3245), 1 block south and half a block west of the southwest corner of Parque Darío. Open M-F 8am-12:30pm and 2-5:30pm, Sa 8am-1pm.

Supermarket: Palí, 1½ blocks north of the NE corner of Parque Catedral. Open daily 8am-8pm.

Police: (☎612 3511 or 612 3870) on the south side of the Parque Catedral. Open daily 24hrs. **Emergency:** ☎118.

Red Cross: (☎612 2059 or 612 3786), just over the river, 2 blocks west of the southwest corner of the Parque Catedral by the hospital. **Emergency** ☎119.

Pharmacy: Farmacia Alvarado (☎612 2830), opposite Parque Darío's northwest corner. Open M-Sa 8am-1pm and 2-9pm, Su 8am-1pm.

Hospital: (☎612 2081), on the north edge of town, taxi 5C.

Telephones: ENITEL (☎612 3656), near its antenna 1 block east of the Parque Catedral's northeast corner. Open M-Sa 7:30am-9pm.

Internet: CompuAcSer, 1 block north of Parque Darío. 0.63C per min., 38C per hr. Open M-F 8am-9pm, Su 10am-5pm.

Post Office: Correos de Nicaragua (☎612 2004), 1 block south on the Calle de los Comercios, and ½ block east. **Fax** service. Open M-F 8am-6pm, Sa 8am-1pm.

FROM THE ROAD

THE VILLAGE PEOPLE

Only 45min. south of Matagalpa lies the indigenous village of Chagütillo, Nicaragua. Its namesake comes from the indigenous language *Náhuatl*, and holds the connotation of dedication, love, and delicacy, appropriate for this struggling yet hopeful rural village. Deep in the surrounding mountains are hundreds of original petroglyphs, chiselled in pre-Columbian times, and revered by the villagers. I have spent time in Chagütillo volunteering with women, children, and agriculture in the community, and have found the experience very rewarding. Initially many villagers simply stared at me, calling out *rubia*, amazed by my blond hair and blue eyes. Soon though, the villagers welcomed me into their culture with warm hearts and nightly festivals on the own *cancha*. Overlooked by the average tourist, the town is quite different from Nicaragua's classic colonial towns. This rural, indigenous village in s accessible by the bus from Matagalpa toward Managua. Ask to be dropped off in Chagütillo, 5min. before the town of Sébaco. If you are interested in tours of the mountains or helping grassroot development, contact the ADCH organization at (☎ 622 2151; adch@ibw.com.ni) The time taken to explore a small community truly reveals the generous spirit of the local villagers.

—**Sarah Gogel**

ACCOMMODATIONS

Due to citywide water rationing, there is access to fresh water only every other day. Most accommodations have storage facilities. The number and variety of accommodations are overwhelming.

Hotel Fuente Azul (☎ 612 2733), 4 blocks north and 2½ blocks west of the northwest corner of Parque Catedral, just across the river. Undoubtedly the cleanest and nicest hotel in town. White tiled floors and ample gardens give a very bright feel. 24hr. hot water in all baths, laundry services, and breakfast (7-9am) included. Doubles 150C, with private bath 250C; triples 350C; quad 500C, 6-person 750C. AmEx/MC/V. ❷

Hotel Matagalpa (☎ 612 3834), 1½ blocks east of the northeast corner of Parque Rubén Darío and down one very long passageway. Friendly and immaculate, but with thin mattresses. Upstairs rooms have pleasant views, and downstairs there are common areas with cable TV. Singles 50C; doubles 80C. ❶

Hotel Plaza (☎ 612 2380), on the south side of Parque Rubén Darío. Very basic, well-kept rooms but bright and dazzlingly white sheets. Relaxing common area with cable TV. Singles 50C, with bath 60C; doubles 100C/120C. ❶

Hotel Bermúdez, 2 blocks east of the NE corner of Parque Darío. Beds are comfortable and baths are clean. Very basic. Breakfast 15C, lunch 20C. Bargaining or student status pose possible discounts. Rooms 30-40C per person. ❶

FOOD

Nicky's Cafetín, 1 block south of the southwest corner of Parque Catedral. With a small gazebo view, generous portions are served for cheap prices. Pancakes 15C; breakfast 15-20C; *comida corriente* 15-20C. Open daily 8am-8pm. ❶

La Casona, on Calle de Comercios, 2½ blocks south of the Parque Catedral, is all *pollo*, all the time (20-45C). Sit inside or outside. Open daily 8am-midnight. ❶

Delicias, 1 block west and 3½ blocks north of the NW corner of Parque Rubén Darío, with fine food and service and intimate, riverside ambiance. Try the garlic or jalapeño steak (82C). Soup on Mondays 30C. Open daily 7am-9pm. ❷

La Posada, half a block west of the northwest corner of Parque Darío. Elegant, dimly-lit dining. If you're brave enough, try the *huevos de toro* (bull's testicles; 60C). *Comida corriente* 40C. Open M-Th 10am-10pm, F-Su 10am-midnight. ❶

◎ ⚑ SIGHTS AND CRAFTS

Casa Museo Carlos Fonseca, one block east of the southeast corner of Parque Rubén Darío, has a small exhibit tracing the life of Fonseca, Matagalpa's favorite revolutionary son and the founder of the FSLN. (Open M-F 1-3:30pm. Free; donations accepted.) The **Casa de Cultura,** 2½ blocks south of the southwest corner of the Parque Catedral, houses the usual assortment of local artwork and workshops. (☎612 3158. Open M-F 7am-12:30pm and 2-5pm.)

Fine examples of Nicaragua's **cerámica negra** can be found in Matagalpa. One workshop, **Tradicional Cerámica Negra,** is located four blocks south and four steep blocks uphill east of the cathedral. (Open M-F 8am-6pm, Sa 8am-noon.)

⚟ NIGHTLIFE

Matagalpa really hops on the weekends. **La Posada** restaurant turns into the most popular local disco from Friday to Sunday night. On Fridays, head to **Noche Cultural en la Casena** for live music. **Rancho Escondido,** two blocks west of the southwest corner of Rubén Darío, has a spacious dance floor which sometimes hosts nationally famous groups. (30C cover when live bands play.) The last weekend of every month, the local restaurants set up shop at one of the *parques* for **Noches Matagalpinas,** full of traditional dance and music (Sa-Su 5-11pm). The new **Cinema Margot,** on Av. de los Bancos, two blocks south of Parque Catedral, gets Hollywood flicks a few weeks after their Managua openings. Local festivals include the **Fiesta Patronales de la Merced** on September 24, and the **Festival de Polkas, Mazurcas y Jamaquellos** on the last weekend of September.

NEAR MATAGALPA

SELVA NEGRA

*From Matagalpa, any Jinotega-bound **bus** will drop you off at the Selva Negra turnoff (marked by a rainbow-painted army tank; 25min., every 30min., 6C), from where it is a 2km hike to the restaurant, hotel, and visitors area. Entrance fee to park 25C. You can take a **taxi** (130C) from town to the restaurant. (breakfast 40-70C; entrees 90-130C; cakes 25C; coffee 10C. Open daily 7:30am-8pm.) Reservations are recommended for the hotel. (☎612 3883. Horse rentals 25C per 30min. US$30-50 per night.)*

Selva Negra (Black Forest), 12km north of Matagalpa, is a coffee plantation, hotel, and private forest reserve. Nearly 80% of the 2000-acre estate is protected, with a marvelous network of labeled hiking paths. Vibrant toucans, howler monkeys, and even the elusive quetzal inhabit the 150m canopy of dense foliage. Try the **Peter and Helen** trail (1¾ hr.) ascending to the reserve's highest point. Signs are in English and a free map is available at the hotel desk. Between November and February you might see the attached coffee plantation in action. On Sundays, horses are available for rent. The coffee and local history museum is also worth a peek. It includes Sandino's marriage certificate to Blanca Aránz, a relative of the owners.

Regular rooms, albeit expensive, called *apartamentos*, are available at the charming, comfortable ▧**Hotel and Restaurant Selva Negra ❺.** With hot-water baths, soft sheets, and fluffy towels, you are sure to enjoy this needed respite from the trails. A **youth hostel ❸** opens up for groups of 6 or more. (US$10 per person.)

BOACO

A *pueblo* amidst the clouds, Boaco is a beauty with a vibrant cowboy culture, which it shows off every 7th of July with the *Hípica*, a horse parade where almost everyone in town either rides or shows up to watch. Residents are proud of the place and they show it during the annual *fiesta patronal* for the apostle

FROM THE ROAD

HIRD WORLD MEDICINE?

About a month into my first trip to Latin America I woke up one morning with an intense pain in my right side. Hmm. Was the spicy *nica* food from the night before coming back to haunt me? Nah. It was way too good. Brushing it off, I decided to continue with my trip and hopped on the bus. Two hours of bumps and thoughts of "why didn't I take that cab" later, I arrived at my destination in rough shape. In agony, I hobbled to the nearest medical clinic. On my way in I noticed a funeral home directly across the street, and wasn't exactly filled with a spirit of optimism. However, I was immediately impressed by the hospital's facilities. Albeit small, the office and lab were well apportioned and had none of the duct tape and rugged machinery I stereotypically thought would be in a Latin American medical clinic. A few bad jokes aside, my doctor was kind and very knowledgeable. He told me I had been carrying too heavy of a pack, and had strained a muscle. He gave me some "muscle relaxants" in a small, unmarked bottle. To this day I don't know what was in that bottle, but it definitely did the trick. A few days later I was back in action, tackling every Nicaraguan volcano that dared to cross my path. Besides learning how to carry my pack, I also learned that not every stereotype about the third world is up to date. Even in the middle of the mountains, medical service in Nicaragua can be clean, kind, and competent.

—Ted Tieken

Santiago from July 21-25. Soak up the scenery and talk to the friendly locals.

TRANSPORTATION. Buses head to **Managua** (2hr., every 30min. 4am-5pm, 20C) and **Río Blanco** (3hr., every 30min. 5:15am-4:30pm, 35C). To catch buses to **Estelí, San Isidro, Matagalpa,** or the **Honduran border,** take a Managua bus as far as **San Benito.** For **Juigalpa** or **Rama,** take a Managua bus 20min. to the *enpalme de Boaco* (intersection of Boaco).

ORIENTATION AND PRACTICAL INFORMATION. Boaco is known as the *ciudad de dos pisos* (city of two floors) because of the economic and physical gap between the wealthier *ciudad alta* (high city) atop a hill to the north and the progressively poorer *ciudad baja* (low city) to the south. The highway, home to the bus station, runs along the southern edge of town. Boaco's main street, one block west of the bus station, runs directly up into *ciudad alta* and the main *parque*, **Parque Niebrowsky** (about 5 blocks from the bus station). Cash travelers checks at **BanCentro** on the main street. (Open M-F 8am-4pm, Sa 9am-noon). The **police station** (☎842 2574), is across from the northwest corner of the *parque*. The **Red Cross** (☎842 2200) is one block west of the main street. **Healthcare** facilities include the **Clínica El Socorro** (☎842 2543) on the main street, and **Hospital Niebrowsky** (☎842 2301 or 842 2302), following the signs from the bus station. **ENITEL** is one block east of the southeast corner of the *parque* (☎842 2490; open M-Sa 8am-5pm), and the **post office** can be found a block and a half north of the *parque's* church (open M-F 8am-noon and 1-5pm, Sa 8am-1pm).

ACCOMMODATIONS. Most hotels are surprisingly rustic and have running water only in the mornings. **Hospedaje Alma ❶** has some of the best rooms in the city. (☎842 2620. Breakfast 20C. Singles with fan, TV, and shared bath 50C; with private bath, new beds, and cable TV 150C. AmEx/MC/V.) **Hotel Sobalvarro ❶,** on the *parque's* south side, is the best place for gorgeous views and prime location in the center of town. Anticipate very basic rooms, communal baths, and a cable TV lounge. (☎842 2515. Breakfast 25C. Singles 50C; doubles 80C; triples 100C.) Spring-green **Hospedaje Boaco ❷,** just north of the bus station, has fairly bright rooms with thin beds and dark private baths. (60C per person.)

FOOD AND ENTERTAINMENT. The best restaurants are in the *ciudad alta*, while the best street cuisine is in the market near the bus station. **El Alpino**

❷, 1 block east and 1½ blocks north of the *parque's* northeast corner, is a popular, laid-back place. (Breakfast 30C; sandwich 12C; chicken and beef 65-90C. Open Tu-Su 8am-10pm.) The **Sorbetería Sobalvarro** ❶, an eskimo ice cream parlor in the Hotel Sobalvarro, is a local hot spot serving huge hamburgers (15C), sandwiches, yogurt, and coffee. **La Cueva** ❸, east of the south side of the *parque central*, has good *ranchero* provisions. The place becomes a full scale **disco** on weekend nights, with all the latest music and a large dance floor. Its location is ideal, as most nights crowds of people gather in the park just to be social, especially on weekends and holidays. (Beef dishes 75-120C. Beer 12C. Restaurant open Tu-Su 11am-10pm. Cover 15C. Disco open Th-Su 8pm-midnight. AmEx/MC/V.)

🅖 **SIGHTS.** The *ciudad alta* has many *paseos* (small lookout points) that provide great views of *ciudad baja* and the surrounding mountains. **Parque el Cerrito,** 1 block west and 2 north of the northwest corner of the main *parque* is a well maintained park in the highest part of the *ciudad alta*, with a tower offering 360° views. **Paseo los Poetas,** 1 block north and 1 east of northeast corner of *parque*, and **Paseo del Balaute,** 1 block east of the southeast corner of *parque*, are also worth a visit. The **Termales Aguas Claras** (☎244 2916), 4km west of the *Enpalme de Boaco*, is a sprawling complex of brightly painted cement swimming pools and thatched *ranchos*. Take any Managua bound bus and ask to be dropped off. (40 min., 8C.) The 6 adult and 4 kiddie pools of thermally heated water range in both size and temperature in the clean, well-maintained complex. The attached hotel is spotless but expensive, with a large sitting area and pool table in the main building. The restaurant is fairly expensive. (Swimming W-Su 8am-7pm, 20C; Restaurant open daily 11am-7pm, 55-95C. Rooms for 1-3 people with A/C and TV US$25.)

JUIGALPA

A tranquil place between Managua and the Caribbean, Juigalpa makes a great stopover to enjoy the surrounding mountains and fresh air. The city contains impressive views of the surrounding peaks, an archaeology museum, and a zoo.

🅕 **TRANSPORTATION.** Buses drop off passengers at the **bus station/mercado,** two blocks east of **parque central.** The *parque* is easily recognized by the two tall steeples of the cathedral on its eastern edge. Everything of interest lies within a few blocks of the *parque*. Buses head to: **Managua** (3hr., every 15min. 4am-5pm, 25C; express 2 hr., 5:45am and 2:40pm, 35C); **San Carlos** (7hr., 9 per day 3am-2:30pm, 45C); and **Rama** (5hr., every 30 min. 4:30am-2:45pm, 45C). For **Estelí** and **Matagalpa,** take the **Managua** bus as far as **San Benito** (2½hr., 20C). For **Boaco,** take the Managua bus as far as the **Enpalme de Boaco** intersection (1½hr., 13C), and hop a bus into town from there (30 min., 7C).

🅔🅕 **ORIENTATION AND PRACTICAL INFORMATION. INTUR** is inside the *alcaldía* (mayor's office), 2 blocks north of the northeast corner of the *parque*. (☎812 3066. Open M-F 8am-noon and 1-5 pm.) The **Viajes Universe** travel agency is 3½ blocks east of the *parque's* southeast corner, under the Nica Airlines sign. **BanCentro,** a block north of the *parque's* northwest corner, exchanges traveler's checks. (☎812 1504. Open M-F 8am-4:30pm, Sa 8am-noon.) **Western Union** is inside the Ferretería Reinaldo Hernández, 2 blocks east of the northeast corner of the *parque*. (☎812 2621. Open M-F 7:45am-6pm, Sa 7:45am-5pm.) Other services include: **police** (☎812 2945 or 812 2727); **Red Cross** (☎812 2233; open daily 8am-5pm); and **Hospital Real Asunción** (☎812 2332), all on the highway at the exit to Rama. **ENITEL** is three blocks north of the *parque's* northwest corner (☎812 7777. Open M-Sa 8am-noon and 2-6pm) and the **post office** is a block east of the southeast corner of the *parque* (Open M-F 8am-6:30pm, Sa 8am-1pm.)

ACCOMMODATIONS AND FOOD. ◘**Hospedaje el Nuevo Milenio ❶,** two blocks east of the *parque's* northeast corner, has bright, clean rooms, strong ceiling fans, and sparkling, modern common baths. Downstairs has cable TV. (☎812 0646. 50C per person.) **Hospedaje Angelita ❶,** just west of the *parque's* northwest corner, is a friendly, family-run place. Relaxing public areas make up for cramped, rooms with thin beds. All beds have mosquito netting. Doors close at 10:30pm. (☎812 2408. Singles 30C; doubles 80C.) **Hotel Casa Country ❸,** 4 blocks east of northeast of *parque,* is a more high class option with good mattresses, and private baths. (☎812 2546. Doubles 150C, with A/C 200C. AmEx/MC/V.)

◘**Palo-Solo ❸,** five blocks east of the northeast corner of the *parque,* inside Parque Palo-Solo, is the classiest place in town for food, drinks, and breathtaking views. (Beef and chicken 60-80C; shrimp 100C; fajitas and other *bocas* 35C; beer 10C. Open daily 10am-10pm. AmEx/MC/V.)**Rotícería El Pollito ❷,** 4 blocks south of the southwest corner of the *parque,* then 10 meters east, serves tasty food at great prices. Try the huge bowls of shrimp or if you have the balls, the bull's testicles soup. (Soup 35C; chicken 27-35C. Open 10am-11pm daily. AmEx/MC/V.) **Cafetín Arco-Iris ❶,** on the northwest corner of the *parque central,* offers good food and quick service. (Breakfast 15-18C; sandwiches 15-20C; *comida corriente* 17-35C. Open daily 8am-8pm.)

◧ **SIGHTS.** At the far east end of town, the ◘**Parque Palo-Solo** offers unparalleled views of the Cordillera de Amerrisque, the southernmost extension of the central highlands. The *parque's* bubbling fountain, shady trees, and promenade are a great place to relax. ◘**Jardín Zoológico Thomas Belt,** 8 blocks south of the southeast corner of the *parque,* is a large, well-maintained zoo. Some 95% of the 60 species represented are from Nicaragua and include primates, cats, reptiles, rodents, and birds. Founded in 1958 and run by the city, they just added a *cafetería* with reasonable prices. Avoid walking under the corners of the monkey cage, they've been known to use visitors as targets practice. (Entrance 5C, 10C for video, 5C to take pictures. Open daily 8am-5:30pm.) The **Museo Arqueológico Gregorio Aguilar Barea,** 2½ blocks east of the *parque's* northeast corner, has Nicaragua's largest collection of pre-Columbian statues, though the cluttered, faded displays inside aren't great. Don't miss the sideshow of…er…"interesting" stuffed animals, including the two-headed cow. (Open M-F 8am-noon and 2-5pm, Sa 8am-noon. 3C.)

CARIBBEAN COAST

Accessible by boat or plane, Nicaragua's Caribbean coast is unlike the rest of the country. The region is part of a geographical area known as the Mosquitia (Mosquito Coast), a sparsely populated expanse of rainforest, plains, and coastland extending the length of Nicaragua's east coast and north into Honduras. The Mosquitia is home to the country's largest remaining group of *indígenas,* the Miskitos, who maintain their own language and have a semi-autonomous system of government. Other groups, including the Sumos, Garífunas, and Ramas, also reside here. Most Caribbean-coasters identify more strongly with their West Indian heritage or indigenous community than with Nicaragua. Travel here is tricky, as there are almost no roads. Unless you're flying, getting from one place to another involves a great deal of puttering around in small boats. The extra effort is rewarded by relaxing beaches and remote, colorful villages.

RAMA

Rama's *fama* comes not from its panorama, but rather from its position as the land gateway to the Caribbean coast. The highway heading east from Managua ends here, and boats leave for Bluefields, Nicaragua's most important Caribbean port. There's nothing to do in Rama, and if you get in after 10am you'll probably have to stay the night in order to catch a boat down the river to the coast.

TRANSPORTATION. **Buses** stop at Rama's *mercado*, two blocks north of the *parque central*, called Parque Parrochial. The tall hill with communications towers is to the north. **Buses** depart for **Managua** (8-9hr., about every hr. 3-9am, 80C) via **Juigalpa** (4½hr., 45C). **Boats** leave from the dock one block west of the market to **Bluefields**: (slow boats 5hr.; Tu, Sa, Su noon; 43C, 3C dock fee. Express 2hr., 1 per day 6am, 120C, sometimes 30C fee for large luggage.) An office near the dock sells tickets for *expreso* boats (open at 8am).

PRACTICAL INFORMATION. There is no **bank,** but other services include: **police** (☎817 0026), one block north and five blocks east of the *mercado;* **Red Cross** (☎817 0181), one block north and two blocks east of the *mercado;* **hospital** (☎817 0019), 6km north of town on the highway; **ENITEL,** one block east of the bus stop (☎817 0100; open M-Sa 7am-9pm); and the **post office,** across the street from ENI-TEL (open M-F 8am-noon and 2-5pm, Sa 8-11am).

ACCOMMODATIONS. While you're waiting for your ship to come in, you might as well grab a *cama* in Rama. All the options below are 30C per person. **Hospedaje Jiménez ❶,** on the northwest corner of the town's main intersection on the same street as the dock, has a clean building. The mid-*mercado* location ensures a sunrise wake-up call. The **Hospedaje Central ❶,** just west of the post office, is near the bus and boat stations. Rooms with fans share pit toilets and bucket showers. **Hotel Johanna ❶,** one block east and half a block south of the *parque,* has clean rooms with fans, and the showers and bathrooms here are the best of Rama's lot. There's a cheap *cafetín* (cafeteria) across the street.

FOOD AND NIGHTLIFE. There are good *comedores* are near the *mercado.* **El Expreso ❷,** three blocks east of the *mercado,* serves steak (45C) and shrimp dishes for 50-60C. (Open daily 11am-10pm.) Locals come to **Los Vindes ❷,** half a block south of the market, for the jukebox. (shrimp 70C; enormous steak 50C. Open daily noon-midnight). In the evening, the bars in **Hotel Johanna** and **Hotel Manantial,** one block south and one block west of the market, are local hot spots.

BLUEFIELDS

Lively Bluefields is Nicaragua's most important Caribbean port, though the port itself is actually across the bay in Bluff. The easiest way to get to Bluefields is by boat or plane. Due in part to its isolation, the city is a fascinating urban jungle: On the streets you'll hear English with a sonorous West Indian lilt, Spanish, Miskito, and other indigenous languages. Come nightfall and you'll hear and see some of the most vibrant nightlife around as reggae rhythms and Caribbean sounds provide relief from the usual Top-40 grind. Bluefields lacks any swimming beaches or big tourist attractions, and is often used as a launching pad to the Corn Islands or other, more remote points on the Caribbean coast.

TRANSPORTATION

Flights: From the airstrip 3km south of town, **La Costeña** flies to: **Managua** (1hr.; 7:30, 8:30, 11:40am, 4pm; one-way 680C, round-trip 1210C); the **Corn Islands** (30min.; 8:40am, 3:30pm; one way 540C, round trip1020C); and **Puerto Cabezas** (1hr., 12:10pm, one-way 770C, round-trip 1420), with additional flights to Puerto Cabezas upon demand, sometimes via Managua for same price. **American Airlines** flies to:

Managua (9:10, 11:45am, 4:30pm; one-way 680C, round trip 1210C); and the **Corn Islands** (8am, 3:25pm; one-way 540C, round-trip 1020C.) Arrive at the airport early.

Boats: Boats to **Rama** leave from the main pier. Choose between slow, covered *expreso* boats (4hr.; Tu, Th, Sa, Su 5am; 43C) and speedier *pangas* (2hr., 120C). A *panga* run by the **Vargas y Peña** company leaves M, W, and F at 5:30am, all other days at 6am; boats leave throughout the morning as they fill up, but past mid-morning the chances of catching a Rama-bound *panga* are virtually non-existent. Arrive at least 30min. early to buy a ticket and be prepared to endure some jostling for a seat. Be sure to bring rain gear. Buy a *panga* ticket to Rama and then catch a bus to Managua or to other cities from Rama. Or buy a *panga*/bus combo ticket to Managua. For the same total price (200C) you get a guaranteed seat on the bus. For **El Bluff** (15min., 15C), take a *panga* from the dock 3 blocks south of the main pier. The *pangas* leave intermittently but more frequently early in the morning (starting at 6am, every 20min.). It's also possible to hitch a ride on a passing supply boat. There are 2 boats a week to **Big Corn Island.** From the main pier, Promar 45 leaves on Sa (6hr., 9am, 60C) and returns on M (departs 8am). Isleño departs from El Bluff on Su (6hr., 7am, 60C), and returns on Tu (departs 8am). These are freight boats and not conventional passenger boats; be prepared to claim your grain sack on deck for the trip.

◆ ❷ ORIENTATION AND PRACTICAL INFORMATION

The murky Caribbean borders Bluefields on the east. **Calle Central** runs north to south, curving along the coast. At the north end of this road, just north of the tall, red-roofed **Moravian church,** is the town's **main pier.** Three main streets run east to west. The northernmost is **Av. Reyes,** followed by **Av. Cabezas** and **Av. Aberdeen** to the south. The market and the pier for boats to El Bluff are on Av. Aberdeen, the only avenida that extends east past Calle Central. The **airstrip** is 3km south of the town center (taxis make the trip for 10-20C).

Tourist Office: INTUR (☎ 822 0221).

Banks: Banco Caley Dagnall, across from the Moravian church. Open M-F 8:30am-4pm, Sa 8:30am-noon. **BanCentro,** across from Mini-Hotel on Calle Cabezas cashes traveler's checks and is the only place on the Caribbean coast where you can get a credit card cash advance. Open M-F 8:30am-4pm, Sa 9am-12:30pm.

Police: (☎ 822 2448), on Calle Central, 4 blocks south of the Moravian church.

Pharmacy: Godoy Farmacia (☎ 822 2471), on Calle Cabezas, 1 block west of Calle Central. Open M-Sa 8am-9pm, Su 9am-5pm.

Red Cross: (☎ 822 2582), south of town on Calle Patterson.

Hospital: (☎ 822 2391 or 822 2621), about 2km southwest of town, past the airport.

Telephones: ENITEL (☎ 822 2222), 3 blocks west of Calle Central in the municipal building on Av. Reyes. Telephones open M-Sa 8am-8:45pm, Su 8am-6pm.

Internet: Internet Cafe, 2 blocks west of Calle Central on Av. Aberdeen, then ½ block north. Free coffee. 40C per hr. Open M-F 8am-8pm, Sa 8am-6pm, Su 10am-6pm.

Post Office: 1½ blocks west of Calle Central on Av. Aberdeen. **Fax** service. Open M-F 8am-noon and 1-5pm, Sa 8am-noon.

⌂ ACCOMMODATIONS

During high season (Jan.-May), there's a rush on the town's already crowded hotels, so reservations are recommended. The surplus of tenants forces prices up.

▨ **Caribbean Dream** (☎ 822 0107), on Calle Central, ½ block south of Av. Aberdeen. Light-green walls lend a bright, clean feeling to the place. Large, clean rooms and pleasant social area in front. There is a direct line to Sprint on the patio. All rooms have private baths. One double bed US$12, 2 double beds US$18. More for rooms with A/C. ❹

Hotel Marda Maus (☎822 2429), half a block east of Calle Central on Av. Aberdeen. This sparkling place has a breezy balcony upstairs. All rooms have fans. Rooms 100C, with private bath and cable TV 150C. ❸

Mini-Hotel Cafetín Central (☎822 2362), ½ block west of Calle Central on Calle Cabezas. Spotless rooms and tile floors. Rooms with fans, private bath, private phone, and TV. Singles 100C; doubles 150C, with A/C 250C. ❹

Hotel Hollywood (☎822 2067), on Calle Central, ½ block south of Av. Aberdeen. Maintenance leaves a little to be desired, but the price is one of the lowest in town. Singles 70C; doubles 100-110C. ❶

FOOD AND NIGHTLIFE

▨ **Mini-Hotel Cafetín Central** (see **Accommodations,** above) is one of the most popular eateries, thanks to frosty beer mugs, wide-screen cable TV, and constant table-wiping. Fish, chicken, and beef dishes 21-40C, milkshakes 15C. Open daily 8am-10pm. ❷

▨ **Cafetín "Pesca-Frita,"** in an unmarked building on the southwest corner of the intersection of Calle Central and Av. Aberdeen. Funky Caribbean decor, and an army of fans fighting to keep you cool. Fish is succulent (45C). Ask for the "super-económico" full meal (30C). Lobster (70C). Open daily 8am-1am. ❷

Restaurante Bella Vista, at the south end of Calle Central (about 6 blocks south of the Moravian church) and a few meters downhill toward the water. Tasty lunches and dinners with a great view of the Caribbean. A variety of comida económica options for 20-40C. Fuller meals 60-90C. Open daily 10:30am-10pm. ❷

La Fogata, right across the street from Mini-Hotel, with buffet-style típico (heaping plate 37C) and thick slices of pizza for meat lovers (10C per slice). Open daily 8am-11pm. ❶

At night, Bluefields turns up the juice. The best place for real Caribbean reggae is ▨**Cuatro Hermanos,** a famous open-air joint right on the water, popular with foreign volunteers. To get there, walk two blocks west of Calle Central, then south to the water. (No cover.) More upscale **Bacchus,** just south of the parque, plays salsa, merengue, and disco. (Cover 10C.) **Bella Vista,** inside Bella Vista restaurant (see **food,** above), is the fanciest of the clubs. Its intimate dance floor overlooks the water south of town, at the end of Calle Central.

NEAR BLUEFIELDS

About one hour from Bluefields by boat, **Ramaqui** is a small island community home to descendants of the Rama Indians. Corrugated metal buildings stand next to traditional bamboo huts, and dugout canoes pull up next to more modern fishing vessels. Though the island sees few visitors, local families are usually willing to host guests for a negotiable price; an ecotourism ranch is also planned. You'll have to hire your own boat; recruit a group to split the cost (600-700C).

Laguna de Perlas (Pearl Lagoon) is a small community on the southern edge of a large lagoon of the same name 80km north of Bluefields. The 1-2hr. trip here is an excellent way to get a look at Caribbean coast culture and coastal wildlife. In the village, local boats can take you to these even smaller communities around the lagoon. 18 pearl cayes—small, uninhabited off tropical islands with white sand and coral off the coast—are ideal for snorkeling. (Bring your own snorkeling equipment, food, and drinks. US$100-120 for the panga.) Basic hospedajes are available in town. **Green Lodge Guesthouse** ❶, has basic, clean rooms with fans and outside baths (85C) and excellent food (shrimp 30C). Electricity is limited. Pan-

gas leave Bluefields' main pier each morning for Laguna de Perlas (1hr., up to 3 boats per day leave when full, first one at 6am, last one at 10am, 70C). *Pangas* return to Bluefields at 6am, noon, and occasionally 10am for 70C.

THE CORN ISLANDS

The Corn Islands, 70km off the coast from Bluefields, offer white sand beaches, warm turquoise water, and a uniquely untouristed Caribbean atmosphere. Most visitors stay on Big Corn Island (pop. 6000), with a small but reasonable selection of hotels and restaurants. With no resorts and no cars or roads, splendid Little Corn Island (pop. 500), 18km away, feels even more untouched. The islands, populated by English speakers of British West Indian descent, have excellent fishing and colorful coral reefs, but most of all they simply offer the chance to curl your toes in pure Caribbean sands and do absolutely nothing.

BIG CORN ISLAND

The tourism industry is slowly becoming more popular on Nicaragua's Caribbean coast, with Big Corn Island leading the way. The Corn Islands are not as frequented as the other Caribbean hotspots in Central America due to lacking infrastructure and drug trafficking in the area. However with greater development and the island's natural beauty, Big Corn might be the next big thing in Nicaragua.

▐▀ TRANSPORTATION

La Costeña and **Atlantic Airlines** (offices on airstrip open daily 7am-4:30pm) have daily flights to **Managua** (8:30am and 3:30pm) that stop in **Bluefields** along the way. (One-way 475C, round-trip 900C.) From Managua, planes leave at 6:30am and 1:15pm, stopping in Bluefields at 7:30am and 3pm for the same prices. It is best to make reservations and get tickets in advance. Arrive one hr. early. Unlike other businesses on the islands, the airlines accept credit cards. **Boats** depart from the main pier in Briggs Bay, five blocks from the airstrip, to: **Bluefields** (4-6hr.; Su 9am, Tu 11am, other days at 8am; 100C) and **Little Corn Island** (daily 9am and 4pm, return 6:30am and 2pm; 70C). The *pangas* are synchronized with arriving aircraft, and will usually wait if a plane is late. The airlines however, are not as nice. **Buses** circle the island all day (every 40min. 6am-6pm, 4C).

✳▐▀ ORIENTATION AND PRACTICAL INFORMATION

Big Corn Island is approximately 6 sq. km. The island's main road runs all the way around its coast, and a few dead-end drives branch off either inland or out to the ocean. The **airstrip** runs southwest to northeast, marking off **Briggs Bay** and the western quarter of the island, where most of the businesses and hotels are. In the eastern part of the island are the beach communities of **North End** and **South End,** with **Sally Peachie** in between. Pick up **maps** of the island at Nautilus Ecotours about 5 blocks north of Fisher's Cave Restaurant. **Banco Caley Dagnall,** is at the south end of the airstrip just up from the pier. **Credit cards** are generally not accepted on the island. Bring traveler's checks or cash. (☎285 5107. Open M-F 8am-4:30pm, Sa 8am-noon.) Other services include: **police station** (☎285 5201), two blocks north of the road from Fisher's Cave Restaurant; a **pharmacy** on the road south from the airport to Briggs Bay (open daily 6am-9pm) and another available 24hr. for emergencies in the **hospital** (☎285 5236), 1km down the road leading east across the airstrip; and **ENITEL**, three blocks north of the Fisher's Cave restaurant (open M-Sa 8am-noon and 1-5pm). The **post office** is in the pharmacy just south of the airline offices.

ACCOMMODATIONS

Big Corn abounds with overpriced hotels that offer little to warrant their price tags. Budget digs are available however, and few hotels warrant the extra money.

Casa Blanca, on the southeast side of Briggs Bay (the unpaved road is right next to Reggae Palace), offers the best deal for budget travelers. Large porches overlook the water amidst a cool breeze. Thin beds, mosquito netting, and self-service laundry. Doubles US$10. ❸

Hospedaje Angela (☎285 5134), just south of the airline offices, has small, clean rooms and notably clean bathrooms. Beds are thin but the price is right. Singles or doubles 100C; doubles with two beds 120C; triples 150C. ❷

Hospedaje Sunrise (☎285 5187), on the northwest corner of the island in Sally Peach, known locally as Marcus Gómez, the name of the owner. Basic rooms, but near some of the best snorkeling on the island. One main house and a few private *cabañas*. Rooms have access to a kitchen. Singles 150C; doubles 200C. 70C per extra person. ❸

Hotel Paraiso (☎285 5111), on the southern edge of Briggs Bay, is the nicest hotel on the island, and the only one that accepts credit cards. It has manicured gardens and a lively monkey named Irma. Singles US$33; quads US$55. US$10 extra for A/C. ❺

FOOD AND NIGHTLIFE

Impatient personalities beware: Big Corn's "relax, take it easy" attitude definitely applies to its very leisurely restaurant service. **Hotel Paraíso Club** ❹ (see above), has one of the nicest restaurants in town, set on a thatched-hut patio with soft background music. (Pasta dishes 40C; fish 60C; meat dishes 125-175C. Open daily 7am-10pm.) **Fisher's Cave Restaurant** ❸, a 10-sided concrete building, sits at the foot of the pier, overlooking Briggs Bay. The outdoor seating area affords fabulous sunset views. Try the surf and turf shish kebob for 90C. (Fish 55-65C; meats 60-75C; shrimp or lobster 85-90C; beer 12C. Open daily 7:30am-9:30pm.) **Restaurante Seva** ❸, on the northeast side of the island, overlooking the sea, has cozy dining rooms and a balcony with a nice view. The food is no slouch either. (Fish 50-70C; lobster or shrimp 100C; beer 12C. Open daily 10am-10pm.) Two small discos come alive with local fishermen and visitors grooving to the island, reggae music. **Morgan's Reggae Palace** is a large concrete building in town. **Island Style** is on Long Beach, on the southeast side of the island. This open-air disco spills right onto the beach and is especially popular on Sundays at sunset.

BEACHES AND OUTDOOR ACTIVITIES

A walk around the road that circles the island is worthwhile and takes about 3hr.; you can always catch a bus if you get tired. The **Picnic Center,** a restaurant and hotel east of the south end of the airstrip, is a nice place for a...picnic on the most tranquil beach on the island. **Long Bay,** just south of South End, is a sweeping crescent of white sand, turquoise water, and coconut palms, perfect for sunbathing and relaxing. Water currents, however, make the swimming less than ideal. The best place to **snorkel** on the big island is **Sally Peachie Beach,** on the east side of the island. Here you can swim among schools of iridescent fish and drift over reefs teeming with marine life. On the west side are many sunken ships ripe for exploration. A number of places rent snorkel equipment. Marcus Gómez at **Hospedaje Sun-**

NICARAGUA

rise (see **Accommodations,** above) rents new gear (30C per day, US$10 deposit.) **Yellow Tail House,** in Sally Peachie, also rents gear (US$5 per day, $10 with a 2hr. tour.) **Nautilus Ecotours,** five blocks north of Fisher's Cave Restaurant, offers a menagerie of activities. It is primarily a dive shop run by a retired diving instructor/trainer (2 tank dive US$45), but they also rent snorkel gear (US$4 half day, US$7 full day), new bikes (US$6-10), and horses (US$12 per day). A guided hike around the island runs US$4 for a half day, and boat excursions are US$65-US$125 (☎/fax 285 5077).

LITTLE CORN ISLAND

Little Corn Island is an unexpected, hidden delight. On *La Islita*, as Spanish-speakers refer to it, footpaths wind through lush palm forests and reach uninhabited beaches. Splendid coral reefs sit just offshore, and a small, close-knit community welcomes visitors. The swimming and snorkeling are great on the far side of the island, and a shipwrecked fishing boat, just visible above the surface of the reef awaits exploration. The 50ft. lighthouse on the island's highest point may be climbed and yields a gorgeous *vista*. Sportfishing is excellent; snag some giant barracuda and get a free dinner. Ask around, and you may be able to tag along on a local fishing boat for free or a for a gas contribution.

▐ TRANSPORTATION. Four daily **pangas** run from Big Corn Island (9am and 4pm; return 6:30am and 2pm; 70C), 18km away. There are no cars or bikes, so you might need some pedestrian power on your trip.

▐ ACCOMMODATIONS. ▨**Casa Iguana ❹,** up a 1km trail from the *panga* drop-off, is reason enough to come to the island. It's the zenith of ecotourism lodgings: the American owners grow or catch most of their own food, generate their own electricity, and collect rainwater to drink and use. The hotel can also arrange for fishing. (US$35 one person, US$10 each additional person.) With its family-style meals and a guest lodge stocked with books and CDs this is a great place to meet fellow travelers. But the secret is out: during high season (Dec.-Mar.), Casa Iguana is booked solid up to six months in advance, but sometimes there is space for walk-ins. They serve full breakfasts (US$4.50) and dinner (US$7) for guests. (casaiguana@mindspring.com. Basic *cabaña* singles US$14; doubles US$17; furnished *casitas* US$40, US$50 with reservation. Credit cards accepted with a 4% surcharge.) On the other side of the island is "hidden" ▨**Hotel Derrek's Place ❺,** on the beach with thatched *cabañas*. Breakfast and dinner are US$3-5 and available sporadically. (Dorms US$5. Tents US$4 per person. US$10-20 for raised rooms, US$12 for ground level.) The brand new **Hotel Delfines ❺** is the deluxe option on the island with comfortable rooms, balconies, A/C, immaculate gardens, and a beach view, full-service restaurant and bar. (Singles US$25; doubles with fan US$35, with A/C US$40.) If these are booked or out of your price range, **Bridgette ❹,** in the small village at the Comedor First Stop, offers somewhat beaten-up rooms with fans and outdoor bathroom facilities (US$10).

▐ FOOD. A few **comedores** in the village will serve lunch and dinner with a few hours advance notice. **Comedor Aries ❷** has personable service, tasty, large portions, and refreshing juices. (Lobster 70C; tacos 12C; fried fish 60C; *filete jalapeño* 60C; and tasty crab soup. Open Tu-Su 10am-9pm.) **Comedor First Stop ❷,** run by Ms. Bridgette, cooks up great food, but a bit of patience is necessary. (Fish 50C; lobster 78C. Open daily 8am-7pm.) The **Little Commercial Center ❶,** stocks snacks, sandwich supplies, and cereal. Stop by around 4pm to pick up warm coconut bread. (Open daily 5:30am-8pm.) The **Happy Hut ❶** bar/disco is the island's social magnet that plays reggae, pop hits, and *salsa*. (Beer 15C; also serves finger foods.)

◪ DIVING. Little Corn Island, has its very own healthy barrier reef and a professional and fully equipped dive shop. **Dive Little Corn** (www.divelittlecorn.com) is staffed by friendly and professional PADI-certified instructors and dive masters who speak English and Spanish, with all-new equipment that is available for rent with scheduled dives. They offer morning, afternoon, and night dives as well as PADI certifications from one-day resort courses to dive master. (one tank dive US$50; two tanks US$78; five tanks package US$165; discover scuba/resort course US$60; open water certification US$315. (Snorkel gear US$5 per day, guides additional US$5. Credit cards accepted with a 4% surcharge.)

NORTHEAST NICARAGUA

Northeast Nicaragua, largely encompassed by the Northern Atlantic Autonomous Region (RAAN), is one of the least developed areas in Central America. It is a difficult region in which to travel, and few make the effort. The large Miskito village of Puerto Cabezas is the capital and second largest Caribbean port in Nicaragua, but offers little of interest to the average traveler. The town of Siuna is part of RAAN but actually lies significantly inland. This former gold-mining settlement is notable for the flawless rainforest of the nearby Bosawas Reserve. This area has a legacy of Sandinista instability, but has become more safe in recent years. The adventurous traveler looking for untouched, natural perfection and seclusion will find it in the Bosawas Reserve and northeast Nicaragua.

SIUNA

The frontier outpost of Siuna sprang up almost overnight as a gold rush town back in the day. The mine shut down in 1979, causing an economic slump. Locals continue to mine gold by hand, denting the once lush hillside. The large pit was excavated by the company and the smaller pit right next to it has been dug completely by hand. The real reason to come all the way here is for the untouched rainforest that begins near town. The environmentally conscious locals proudly call their forest—the largest swath of unbroken rainforest north of the Amazon—the "lungs of Central America." A serious visit will take "roughing it" to a whole new level, but the plants and animals that await are astounding.

> The Siuna area is still plagued by armed and active bands of Sandinistas and Contras. Recent incidents include a politically motivated massacre of 11 locals in May 2000. Recent efforts to curb the rogue groups seem to be working, but the danger of unpredictable and unprovoked attacks still exists. Travel in the region is currently not advisable. Check the latest situation before considering a visit.

▤ TRANSPORTATION. *La Costeña* has daily **flights** to Siuna from: **Managua** (1hr.; 9am, returning at 2:30pm; one-way 595C, round-trip 1070C) and **Puerto Cabezas** (1 hr.; 10:30am, returning to Siuna at 1:30pm; 510/900C). Flights to and from Puerto Cabezas stop in **Bonanza** and **Rosita** (from Siuna 355C/500C, from Puerto Cabezas 510/900C). Siuna, Rosita, and Bonanza are often referred to collectively as **Las Minas.** Flights operate subject to demand; always have a reservation or show up a few hours early. There is a small ticket office on the runway. A Siuna bound **bus** leaves Managua's Mayoreo market daily and makes a bumpy trip through the forest. Reserve a seat earlier that day. (10hr., 5pm, 80C; 8hr., 8pm, 100C.) **Buses** leave the market daily for: **Managua** (9hr., 8pm; 10½hr., 5:30pm, 70C; 12hr., 4pm, 100C.); **Puerto Cabezas** (12hr., 4am, 100C); **Rosa Grande** (2hr.; 6, 11am, 1pm, 30C); **Hormiguero** (1¼hr., 6:30am and noon, 15C). Road conditions and transit schedules in northeast Nicaragua are poor and constantly changing. **Taxis** are 5C. Transit is never guaranteed and often cancelled due to weather, road conditions, broken equipment, or lack of passengers. Always check in the market for the latest information and budget extra time and money for travel in the region.

■■ ☎ **ORIENTATION AND PRACTICAL INFORMATION.** It's hard to describe Siuna's tangled web of roads, but luckily, the town is small. The north side of the runway contains large portrait **murals.** The main cement road runs parallel to and then north from the runway. It winds around and up the hill, past the mine ruins, and turns to dirt after the market. There is then a small *parque* and the road winds around the opposite side of the hill, passing the mayor's office and eventually intersecting itself just north of the airport. Just south of La Costeña another dirt road runs east for a block then turns north. The **Bosawas Reserve Office** is one block after it turns north. (☎273 2036 in Siuna, 233 1594 in Managua. Open M-F 8am-noon and 1:30-5pm.) The **Caruna Bank,** just next to the mayor's office, doesn't offer traveler's check or credit card advances, but does offer **Western Union** services. (☎273 2016. Open M-F 8:30am-noon and 1-4:30pm, Sa 9-11am.) The **police station** is just south of the mayor's office (☎273 2000). **Hospital Carlos Centeno** is just west of the *parque* and has a 24hr. emergency pharmacy (☎273 2003). Other pharmacies are available in the market. **ENITEL** is on the west side of the *parque*. (☎273 2005; fax 273 2101. Open M-F 8am-noon and 1:30-5pm.) The **post office** is just beyond the reserve office (open M-Sa 8am-8pm.)

☎☐ **ACCOMMODATIONS AND FOOD.** The town lacks running water, but all places listed compensate with cleanliness. The only place with 24hr. running water is **Hospedaje Siu ❷,** a few blocks west of the mayor's office. (Singles 75C; doubles 120C). **Hotel Cauta Gallo ❸,** east of the park on top of the hill, was the club/bunkhouse for mine executives. Cherrywood floors and walls and the best beds in town tell of its former glory, but water and electricity are sporadic. It can be difficult to get a room. (☎273 2019. Reception open 7am-4:30pm only, best to call a day or more ahead. US$8.50 per person.) **El Desnuque ❷,** along the airstrip, has large basic rooms with bucket-flush private baths. Attached restaurant has the largest portions and best food in town for 40-80C. (☎273 2049. Singles 60C; doubles 80C.) **Hospedaje El Costeño ❶,** ½ block east of La Costeña going toward the reserve office, also has basic rooms. (☎273 2131. Singles 50C; doubles 80C.)

NEAR SIUNA

▩ **BOSAWAS RESERVE**

*To gain access to the Bosawas Reserve you must have a guide and permission from the reserve office in Siuna. The Bosawas Reserve Office (see **Practical Information,** above) has a very friendly and helpful staff who can assist you in planning a route and will organize a knowledgeable guide. They will also assist in figuring out the sporadic transportation to **Rosa Grande** or **El Hormiguero**, the entrances to the park. You should call one week in advance so that the office has time to organize a guide. A strenuous one-day hike into the park is feasible from either entrance if you take the early van; but to truly experience Bosawas you'll need three to five days. **Guides** 80C per day. Cooking about 75C per person. Horseback excursions 80C per person.*

Five-hundred-year old trees, monkeys, mountains, waterfalls, parrots, rivers, natural medicinal flowers, and even a few elusive quetzales await in the isolated Bosawas Reserve, where diehards come for the deep, dark primary rain forests. Two ecotourism camps, covered shelters with latrines and garbage cans, are used as launching points for those wishing to delve deeper into the wilderness. From Rosa Grande, the camp at **Salto Labú** is 4km, right next to a waterfall (a 10 foot cliff is perfect for jumping into the deep pool of emerald green water at Labú's base). From El Hormiguero, the camp at **El Magague** is 6km and is rich in monkeys, parrots, and wildlife. While guides will prepare meals if you've made prior arrangements, visitors should come stocked with a water filter or purification tablets, first aid kit, lots of bug spray, rain gear, and sturdy waterproof hiking boots (suffer with the thin plastic boots you can buy at the market, 80C.) Visits here are amazing at any time of year, but best in the dry season.

PUERTO CABEZAS

Far from Managua, in the country's northeastern corner, Puerto Cabezas (locally called Bilwi) is visited more often by volunteers and business people than tourists. It takes some effort to get to, and there's not too much to see once here. Even though the town is right on the ocean, its Caribbean beaches are seldom visited, and it lacks the natural beauty of the rest of northeastern Nicaragua. Still, one might stay here for practical reasons—it's the largest town in the entire Mosquitia.

La Costeña and **Atlantic Airlines** fly into the airport a few kilometers north of town. Flights to: **Managua** (1¼hr.; LC M-Sa 8am, noon, 4pm; AA M-Sa 8am, noon. One-way 850C, round-trip 1570C); **Bluefields** (1hr.; LC daily 11am; one-way 770C, round-trip 1420C); **Siuna/Las Minas** (30min.; LC daily 11am or 1pm; one-way 510C, round-trip 900C). **Buses** leave for **Managua** (24hr., daily noon, 200C). Fishing and cargo **boats** sometimes run to and from Bluefields and Trujillo, Honduras. A **taxi** to either spot shouldn't be more than 15C. It's possible to hire a boat at the dock to go to one of the dozens of tiny, uninhabited **Cayos Miskitos**. *Pangas* (small boats) can fit 12-14. (4hr. one way, 150-400C; express 3hr. one way, 3000C) Inquire a day or two in advance at the dock south of town.

The nearest **beach, La Bocana,** is a few kilometers north along the coast, near the airport. The town has a **bank** that changes traveler's checks. (☎282 2272. Open M-F 8am-4:30pm.) Other services include: **police** (☎282 2257), **hospital** (☎282 2259), **ENITEL** (☎282 2300; Open M-Sa 8am-9pm, Su 8am-5:30pm), and **post office**. The best bet for lodging is ◪**Hospedaje El Viajante ●**, on the main street, with friendly, English-speaking owners. (☎282 2237. Rooms with fan and shared bath 60C; with private bath, cable TV, fridge, and A/C 175C.) **Hotel Pérez ●**, is north on the main street. (Singles with shared bath and TV 150C, with private bath, A/C, and TV 375C.) If you're by the beach stop in at **Kabu Payaska/Aires del Mar/Seabreezes ❸** (tri-named in Miskito, Spanish, and English) for verdant grounds right on the ocean with, of course, a breeze. (*Bocas* 30-35C, beer 13C, entrees 85C.) Closer to town is **Disco Bar Miramar ❸**, a four story building above the ocean affording unmatched views of the Caribbean. The restaurant turns into a bar/disco at night. If you decide to go dancing, be careful. Puerto Cabezas is not known for the character of its nightowls. (Entrees 70-85C; beer 13C; rum and coke 10-15C. Restaurant open 10am-3am. Disco open 7pm-3am.)

PANAMA

Forget the canal for a moment and discover the real Panama—lush mountain forests, Caribbean beaches surrounded by coral reefs, a thriving, skyscraping metropolis, and vast ranches and farms below highland villages. Panama's 2.5 million people form a diverse culture, from the vibrant indigenous groups to recent international immigrants. Now remember that canal—the money it has pumped into the economy has had a clear effect: roads are well-maintained, buses run efficiently, electric power is reliable, and only the most remote locations lack indoor plumbing. Pristine Caribbean shores are within a few hours' drive of Panama City, Central America's most modern city. The capital's cosmopolitan influence extends over the country, dwindling only in the far east of San Blas and Darién. Here, dugout canoes provide access to hidden remote villages, and images of American pop culture are replaced by the Kuna's *molas*, traditional patched cloth panels. With both the traditional and the modern to tempt them, it's a wonder so few budget travelers come to Panama. Prices, though higher than in other parts of Central America, are still affordable and the political situation is stable.

HIGHLIGHTS OF PANAMA

Beautiful beaches, clear water, and a Caribbean atmosphere make **Bocas del Toro** one of the most popular sites in Panama. (p. 662).

Parque Nacional Volcán Barú, where stunning cloud forest, resplendent quetzals, and Panama's highest peak all await. (p. 655).

The sprawling cosmopolitan capital of **Panama City,** where discos and museums compete for attention, and international restaurants adjoin bohemian cafes. (p. 603.)

The **San Blas Archipelago,** home of the semi-autonomous Kuna Indians, whose tiny villages atop tropical isles provide a unique Caribbean adventure. (p. 670).

The **Azuero Peninsula,** often called the heartland of Panama, where Spanish influence is strongest and the traditional festivals are raucous. (p. 636).

SUGGESTED ITINERARIES

NORTH SOUTH. Explore **Panama City**—don't miss **Panamá Viejo** (p. 615) and **Parque Natural Metropolitano** (p. 615). Party the night away in **Bella Vista**'s clubs and bars (p. 612). See the Panama Canal at **Miraflores** (p. 619), and visit nearby **Parque Nacional Soberanía** (p. 620). Relax in **Portobelo** (p. 627) and enjoy the Caribbean flair of **Isla Grande** (p. 629) to the north. If you're back in Panama City with some time left, spend a few days and a lot of money treating yourself to the luxuries of **Isla Contadora** (p. 622) in the **Archipiélago de las Perlas** (p. 622).

EAST WEST. From Panama City head out west to hike in nearby enchanted **El Valle** (p. 631) for a day. Buy one of the world famous Panama hats in **Penonomé** (p. 633), and pay pristine **Parque Nacional Omar Torrijos** (p. 634) and its many wild animals a deserved visit. Explore Panama's traditional heartland, the **Azuero Peninsula** (p. 636), and don't miss **Las Tablas** and the peninsula's many *fiestas.* Continue west to **Volcán** (p. 657) or **Boquete** (p. 652) via David, climb Panama's highest peak, **Volcán Barú** (p. 655) and hope to catch a glimpse of one of the rare **quetzals** in the surrounding rain and cloud forest **national parks.** After the arduous hikes in thin air, hop on a bus along the scenic drive from David to Almirante, and embark on a water taxi to **Bocas del Toro** (p. 661). Explore the amazing marine life around **Isla**

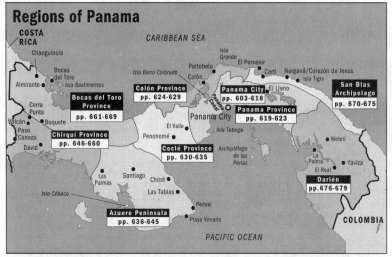

Regions of Panama

COSTA RICA

CARIBBEAN SEA

Changuinola

Bocas del Toro

Almirante ●

Isla Bastimentos

Isla Barro Colorado

Isla Grande

Portobelo

Colón

El Porvenir

Cartí

Narganá/Corazón de Jesus

Isla Tigre

Colón Province
pp. 624-629

Panama City
pp. 603-618

El Llano

San Blas Archipelago
pp. 670-675

Bocas del Toro Province
pp. 661-669

Cerro Punta

Volcán ●

● Boquete

Paso Canoas

David ●

Chiriquí Province
pp. 646-660

El Valle

Penonomé ●

Panama City

Panama Canal

Panama Province
pp. 619-623

Isla Taboga

Coclé Province
pp. 630-635

Archipiélago de las Perlas

Meteti ●

La Palma ●

El Real

● Yaviza

Darién
pp. 676-679

Las Palmas

Santiago

Chitré

Las Tablas ●

Isla Cébaco

Azuero Peninsula
pp. 636-645

Pedasí

Playa Venado

COLOMBIA

PACIFIC OCEAN

PANAMA

Bastimentos (p. 666) or simply relax on empty picture book Caribbean beaches. If by now you haven't decided to burn your return ticket, just hop on a plane or bus back to Panama City. If you are still craving sand and sun, fly to one of the islands of the **San Blás Archipelago** (p. 670) and stay with the **Kuna**, the indigenous people who govern the San Blás region, and experience a different lifestyle in a paradisiac tropical setting. Alternatively, if you feel adventurous and ready to leave the beach behind and, fly into the **Darién** (p. 676), where Panama's most untamed wilderness awaits at **Río Sambú** (p. 678) and **Parque Nacional Darién** (p. 679).

LIFE AND TIMES

LAND, FLORA, AND FAUNA

Panama is shaped like a sideways S running from west to east with the Caribbean Sea to the north and the Pacific to the south. The western half is split into northern and southern slivers by the southern end of a volcanic chain—the **Cordillera Central** (or Tabasará Mountains), while the non-volcanic **Cordillera de San Blas** divides the eastern half. Between the two mountain ranges lie lowlands, home to the **Panama Canal**, bounded by Colón in the north and Panama City in the south. The **Azuero Peninsula** juts out and elongates the Pacific coast in central Panama. Constellation of islands, including the **Pearl Islands** and the **Bocas del Toro Archipelago**, can be found on both coasts. Panama's unique geographic location has contributed to both its economic and natural wealth. Harboring literally thousands of plant and animal species, ecotourism in Panama is a fascinating possibility for the environmentally conscious traveler.

HISTORY

Panama's fate has always been tied to the interest of other nations in its strategic position as a land bridge between the Americas and the Atlantic and Pacific Oceans. Panama declared its independence from Spain in 1821, and shared closer ties with South America than Central America. While the other Central American

PANAMA

Panama

COSTA RICA

COLOMBIA

DARIÉN

SAN BLÁS

PANAMÁ

COLÓN

COCLÉ

VERAGUAS

HERRERA

LOS SANTOS

CHIRIQUÍ

BOCAS DEL TORO

CARIBBEAN SEA

PACIFIC OCEAN

CORDILLERA DE SAN BLÁS

SERRANÍA DE MAJÉ

SERRANÍA DEL SAPO

CORDILLERA CENTRAL

CORDILLERA DE TALAMANCA

Bahía de Panamá

Golfo de San Miguel

Golfo de Panamá

Golfo de Chiriquí

Golfo de Montijo

Golfo de los Mosquitos

Laguna de Chiriquí

Archipiélago de San Blás

Archipiélago de las Perlas

Archipiélago de Bocas del Toro

Península de Azuero

0   20 kilometers
0   20 miles

Highway from Chepo to Yaviza is suitable only for 4x4 vehicles, and is largely impassable during the rainy season.

Acandí
Zapzurro
Palo de las Letras
Puerto Obaldía
Capurganá
Yaviza
Río Tuira
El Real
P. N. del Darién
La Palma
Río Sambú
Punta Patiño
Sambú
Mansucum
Ustupo
Agua Fría
Santa Fé
Cañi
Nargana
Archipiélago de San Blás
El Llano
Bayano
Piñati (reti Colóno)
El Porvenir
Chepo
Tocumen
San Miguelito
Ciudad de Panamá
Balboa
Isla Taboga
Islas Taboga y Urabá
R.F.S.
Isla Contadora
San Miguel
Isla del Rey
Isla Grande
P.N. Chagres
Portobelo
P.N. Portobelo
Sabanita
Gatún
Lago Gatún
Panama Canal
Gamboa
Arraiján
La Chorrera
Chame
San Carlos
Colón
Ft. San Lorenzo
Isla Barro Colorado
P.N. Interoceánico Las Américas
La Arenosa
Altos de Campana
P.N.
El Valle
Nata Río Hato
Farallón
Penonomé
Aguadulce
Bahía de Parita
P.N.
Divisa
Chitré
Los Santos
Macaracas
Las Tablas
Pedasí
Playa Venado
Isla Iguana Wildlife Refuge
Isla Cañas Wildlife Preserve
Tonosí
Cañas
La Tronosa Forest Preserve
P.N. Cerro Hoya
El Caño
El Copé
P.N.
Calobre
Santiago
Las Palmas
Seriagua
Reserva Forestal Montoso
Isla Cébaco
Playa Sta. Catalina
P.N. Isla Coiba
Isla Cébaco
San Félix Tolé
Playa Las Lajas
La Concepción
David
Boquete
Boquerón
Volcán
Bella Vista
Cerro Punta
Cerro Volcán Barú (3475m)
La Barqueta
Puerto Armuelles
Cañas Gordas
Punta Burica
Bahía de Charco Azul
Isla Sevilla
Isla Parida
Neily
Bella Vista
Sixaola
Guabito
Changuinola
Bocas del Toro
Almirante
Parque Nacional Marino Isla Bastimentos
Parque Internacional La Amistad
R.F. Palo Seco
P.N. Volcán Barú

1
2
3

nations became completely independent by the 1840s, throughout the next century Panama was controlled by Colombia and then other nations' interests. From 1850 to 1900, Panama had 40 different governments and 13 US interventions.

EARLY HISTORY. In 1502, Columbus set foot on the shores of Central America in present day Portobelo, Panama. Vasco Nuñez de Balboa established the first colony, became governor, and "discovered" the Pacific Ocean in 1513, and thus Panama's distinctive place in the world. The isthmus soon became the route through which the riches of the Incas were transported back to Spain. With the decline of the Spanish empire, Scottish attempts toward colonization failed to obtain the same level of domination in Panama, and trade declined. In 1821, Panama became part of the **United Nations of Gran Colombia**. The construction of a US owned transcontinental railroad through Panama in 1855 brought greater intervention from the US, whispers of a future canal, and an impetus for the creation of the independent Republic of Panama by 1903.

A MAN, A PLAN, A CANAL: PANAMA. The railroad was successful enough to prompt the construction of a canal, first attempted by the French in 1848, who ultimately failed. Because Colombia opposed a deal between the US and France that would get the US the canal, the US stoked Panamanians' resentment of Colombia; the result was a revolutionary junta that declared the independence of the **Republic of Panama** in 1903. Within two weeks the rights to the Canal Zone were traded away to the US, which began work in 1904 and finished the canal 10 years later.

US-PANAMA RELATIONS. Along with control to the waterway, Panama's new constitution granted the US intervention rights. These were exercised several times throughout the century, despite Panama's increasing interest in canal control. In 1936, five years after an insurrection and coup against the oligarchy's political elite, the US agreed to abandon intervention rights and increased the fees paid for the Canal Zone. In response, Panama built a fortress near the city jail and militarized the police. As World War II approached, the US tried to arrange for the use of various Panamanian locales outside the Canal Zone. The new Panamanian executives eventually allowed the use of the sites—largely in light of the Pearl Harbor attack—but ousted the US military forces soon after the war. In 1964, US presence provoked student riots against both the Panamanian and US governments. In 1968, the Guardia Nacional nullified the presidential election. **General Omar Torrijos Herrera** of the Guardia emerged as dictator of Panama and splurged on the country's public works, despite a steadily growing debt. He developed housing for the poor, raised wages, sponsored a program to expand nationalism, and established the banking secrecy regulations that enabled Panama to become a money-laundering paradise. To encourage jingoist sentiment, he signed a treaty with US President Jimmy Carter ensuring total Panamanian control of the canal by the year 2000. A mysterious 1981 plane crash ended Torrijos's life, opening the door to a new political crisis: the leadership of **General Manuel Noriega,** Torrijos's head of intelligence.

NORIEGA AND OPERATION JUST CAUSE. Hired by the US as a spy in Perú and a CIA operative in contact with the Nicaraguan Contras, Noriega eventually became head of Panamanian intelligence. Upon seizing control of the Guardia Nacional in 1983, the Panamanian General granted himself dictatorial powers. He controlled the press, created military goon squads, and managed Panama's drug traffic. In 1984, Noriega permitted a national election; popular Arnulfo Arias seemed a clear winner, but Ardito Barlett, Noriega's candidate, emerged victorious and became a puppet president. In 1988, Noriega was indicted in the US for drug trafficking. As US President Ronald Reagan tightened sanctions on Panama, Noriega closed his grip, nullifying another election that his candidate had lost.

No sooner did Noriega declare himself president than word spread that Panama was at war with the US. After a confrontation between Panamanian soldiers and four unarmed US Marine officers **President George Bush** ordered 24,000 troops to Panama to remove Noriega. Noriega fled into the Papal Nuncio, where American soldiers assailed him with a bizarre form of psychological torture: they blared "Voodoo Child" and other rock tunes to flush him out. A few days later, Noriega (who claims not to have heard the music) surrendered and was flown to Florida to await trial. In 1992, he was found guilty on eight charges of "conspiracy to manufacture and distribute cocaine" and sentenced to 40 years in prison.

Despite its stated goals of liberating Panama from tyranny, protecting American lives, and bringing Noriega to justice, **Operation Just Cause** (known in some circles as Operation "Just Cuz") was criticized internationally as bullying, self-interested foreign policy. Panamanians are divided on what they call "the invasion"; they are thankful to the US for having gotten rid of Noriega but resentful of the bombings. The newly installed government of **Guillermo Endara** faced high post-invasion poverty, unemployment, and crime rates. Endara successfully engaged Panama in Central American affairs, establishing the country's membership in the **Central American Parliament** in 1993 and committing Panama to economic integration in the Central American Common Market. **Ernesto Pérez Balladares** replaced Endara in 1994. Balladares's administration increased privatization and improved health care, education, and the country's overall infrastructure. However, the new president encountered scandal in 1996 amid reports that he received campaign money from a reputed drug trafficker. Balladares confirmed the reports but claimed ignorance of how it had happened. As Panama privatized its economy, Balladares came under fire again for excluding US companies from the bidding process.

In May 1999, **Mireya Moscoso** was elected as the first female president. The victory was particularly sweet for Moscoso and the Arnulfista party: she defeated Martín Torrijos, whose father Omar deposed Moscoso's husband Arias from the presidency in the 1968 military coup. The election also marked the second peaceful transition of the 1990s. Despite new leadership, the country remains a center for drug trafficking due to inadequate border and airport security.

TODAY

After almost a century under US jurisdiction, the **canal** was officially handed over to Panama on December 31, 1999. Symbolically handing over the canal to Panama on December 14th, former US president Jimmy Carter provided closure to the treaties he signed in 1978, which described the gradual and systematic removal of US presence. The patriotic ceremony celebrating the inception of a new era of complete Panamanian self-sovereignty was accompanied by nationwide celebration. Huge renovation and development programs are currently underway for the canal equipment and the land left from the US. These include new locomotives, tugboats, and even a flashy hotel, golf, and casino resorts. The two most ambitious projects, however, are a conservation effort for the canal's watershed (which keeps it from drying up), and a widening of the Gaillard Cut. The project is to be completed next year and would allow large vessels to traverse the canal simultaneously in both directions.

The most pressing concern for Panama's leaders has been how to deal with the canal. With the US gone, illegal drug trafficking, money laundering, and airport security problems have increased. Contamination also remains from US presence in the area, with toxic waste buried beneath the zone's military bases and explosives in the rain forest that make the region dangerous. Moscoso's government has complained about the US's slow efforts in the clean-up process. Both countries are currently investigating the severity of the damage to determine a plan of action.

President Moscoso has worked to strengthen social programs, particularly in education. She successfully presided over the transfer and administration of the canal. She has helped pass counter-narcotics, counter-money laundering and intellectual property rights legislation. Panama supports the "Free Trade for the Americas" proposal and is the host of the official negotiations until 2003. Panama is currently negotiating free trade with its Central American neighbors and Mexico.

PEOPLE

Survivors from Pre-Colombian days—most notably, the **Ngöbe Buglé** (also called the Guaymí), **Kuna**, and **Chocó Indians**—are few but widespread and still speak their traditional languages. Generally, these indigenous descendants live by subsistence agriculture. Most Panamanians are *mestizos*, people of mixed American Indian and European heritage, and are concentrated in the lowlands on either side of the canal. The slave trade and the canal brought other groups into the country, including Africans, East Indians, Chinese, and Jews. These groups contribute to the international flavor of the region. Spanish, the official language of Panama, is spoken by over 90% of the population. The clearest exception to this rule is in the San Blas archipelago, where Kuna is the predominant language and Spanish won't get you very far. As in many other Latin American countries, Roman Catholicism is the dominant religion. However, Protestants have a foothold in the country, especially among the indigenous population and African descendants, among whom Santería, a mixture of Catholic and West Indian rites, can also be found.

CULTURE

FOOD & DRINK

The typical Panamanian meal is rice, beans, and beef or chicken. This is usually available at *típico* restaurants and is known simply as *comida*. *Sancocho*, a spicy chicken and vegetable stew cooked in a big pot, is the national dish. On the coast, seafood, like the *corvina*, is very popular and very good—while more expensive than *comida*, its high quality makes it a bargain. Panama City boasts some of the most diverse fare in Central America, offering plenty of alternatives to the standard rice and beans. At kiosks throughout the country, you can find *frituras*, bits of deep-fried dough and meat; and *empanadas*, fried dough shells stuffed with chicken, beef, or cheese. Panama produces a number of fine beers—a great dark beer is Balboa, or for a light option, try Atlas. Soberana, Panama, and Cristal are also popular. The national liquor is *seco*, potent stuff rated on a scale from two to eight. The most popular type, Seco Herrerano, is nicknamed *nueve letras*, (because of the nine letters in "Herrerano").

CUSTOMS & ETIQUETTE

Etiquette in Panama is very similar to the rest of Central America. Rules are more relaxed in cosmopolitan cities than rural areas. Usually non-threatening *machismo* still lingers. Gifts should be accepted with great thanks. Table manners are standard. Public displays of affection are acceptable. Between female or opposite sex friends, it is customary to give a hint of a kiss on one cheek or both. Handshakes are acceptable, but less personal.

THE ARTS

Panamanian art is graphic, colorful, and a reflective mix of Central American, South American, and indigenous art. Nearly every town has a *mercado artesanal*, where you can purchase and admire Panamanian art. Pottery with geometric patterns fills the markets in western and central Panama; many replicate the folk art of the Guaymí Indians. Predominant in the east are *tagua* nut carvings, and the

Kuna's intricately patterned and hand-stitched cloths, called *molas*. Check out the Museum of Contemporary Art in Panama City.

Panama's position as a continental bridge has opened it to artistic influences from all sides. The lyrical melodies of indigenous chants continue to thrive. Panama's distance from the cultural centers of Guatemala and Colombia left its literature small-scale until the 20th century. Prior to then, poetry, such as that of José María Alemán (1830-1887) and Darío Herrera (1870-1914), was mainly an outlet for Romantic and Modernist thought. Since the building of the canal, foreign nations' roles in Panamanian affairs have become the dominant themes of authors like Renato Ozores and Carlos Francisco Changmarín.

Panamanian architecture combines the best aspects of Spanish, French, Caribbean, and indigenous architecture into a new distinct form. Look for Spanish colonialism and tiled roofs, French balconies, and the rustic look of the traditional Panamanian *quincha*, elements made of mud and clay. Panama City has been dubbed the most modern city in Central America—complete with skyscrapers and attempted sophistication. The most impressive piece of Panamanian architecture certainly isn't any building or city, but 82km of water connecting two oceans.

The most popular music in Panama is certainly *merengue* and *salsa*. If that's not enough, you can also shake your groove thing to symphony, jazz, and even reggae. The most famous Panamanian dance is the *tamborito*, which is accented by claps, drums, and men using hats to fan women. Other characteristic forms are the *mejorana*, with two guitars and a square dance; and the quicker *punta*.

ESSENTIALS

FACTS FOR THE TRAVELER

ENTRANCE REQUIREMENTS
Passport (p. 21). Required for citizens of all countries.
Visa. (p. 22). Not required for citizens of Australia, Canada, Ireland, New Zealand, UK, or the US. Required for citizens of South Africa—available at nearest consulate.
Tourist Card Required for citizens of Australia, Canada, Ireland, New Zealand, UK, or US. Available upon arrival; issued for 30 days, may be extended for up to 90 days (US$5).
Onward ticket. Visitors must have an onward/return ticket.
Inoculations and Medications (p. 29). None required.
Work Permit (p. 22). Required of all foreigners planning to work in Panama.
Driving permit (p. 49). An international drivers' license is recommended.
Airport Departure Fee. US$20.

EMBASSIES AND CONSULATES

Embassies of Panama: Canada, 130 Albert St. #300, Ottawa, Ontario K1P 5G4 (☎613-236-7177; fax 236-5775). **US,** 2862 McGill Terr. NW, Washington, D.C. 20008 (☎202-483-1407; fax 483-8413). Open M-F 9am-5pm; consulate closed noon-2pm.

Consulates of Panama: UK, 40 Hertford Street, London W1J 7SH (☎+44 20 7409 2255; fax 7495 0412). **US,** 1212 Av. of the Americas, 47/48 St., 6th fl., New York, NY 10036 (☎212-840-2450; fax 840-2469). Open M-F 9am-2pm. There are other consulates in Atlanta, Chicago, Houston, Los Angeles, Miami, New Orleans, New York, Philadelphia, or Tampa..

MONEY

<table>
<tr><td rowspan="8" style="writing-mode: vertical-rl">BALBOAS</td><td>AUS$1 = US$0.55</td><td>US$1 = AUS$1.82</td></tr>
<tr><td>CDN$1 = US$0.64</td><td>US$1 = CDN$1.56</td></tr>
<tr><td>IR£1 = US$1.25</td><td>US$1 = IR£0.80</td></tr>
<tr><td>NZ$1 = US$0.47</td><td>US$1 = NZ$2.14</td></tr>
<tr><td>ZAR1 = US$0.10</td><td>US$1 = ZAR10.5</td></tr>
<tr><td>US$1 = US$1</td><td>US$1 = US$1</td></tr>
<tr><td>UK£1 = US$1.55</td><td>US$1 = UK£0.65</td></tr>
<tr><td>EUR€1 = US$0.98</td><td>US$1 = EUR€1.02</td></tr>
</table>

The rates above were accurate as of August 2002. All prices in this book are quoted in US dollars, as the Panamanian currency, the **balboa,** is directly linked to the dollar. Effectively, the balboa *is* the US dollar. Panama uses actual US bills, but mints its own coins. A huge 50¢ piece, known as a **peso,** is used regularly, and a nickel is often called a **real. ATMs** (marked by red "Sistema Clave" signs) are everywhere in Panama City and common in David, and though uncommon in rural areas, can be found in a number of towns west of Panama City. They don't always accept foreign cards. There are several **Western Union** offices in the country. Some more pricey hotels and department stores accept **traveler's checks,** but few budget establishments or businesses will honor them. Many banks are willing to exchange AmEx checks and sometimes other types. Bring proper ID and be prepared to pay a fee unless you are exchanging AmEx at the AmEx office. Outside Panama City, national banks satisfy money needs, but at border crossings, money is exchanged at very bad rates—in other words, bring US dollars. **Visa** and **Mastercard** are easier to use than other cards, but many hotels and restaurants demand cash. Visitors can often obtain **cash advances** with Visa, American Express, and Mastercard, and there are a number of US banks (Citibank, Fleet, HCSB) where charges may be less substantial. All international cards work, but PINs should be in numbers (no letters). **Tipping** is not expected, except at touristed locations, where a 5-10% tip is standard. "Free" guides usually expect a tip.

The most significant costs for travelers in Panama will be accommodations, which can be notably more expensive than those in other parts of Central America. While basic rooms can usually be found for under US$7, more elaborate lodgings will cost closer to US$15-20. Food can be found cheaply, with *típico* usually available for US$1-3. While the assiduous traveller may be able to scrape by on US$15-20 per day, a safer bet would be US$25-30.

SYMBOL	❶	❷	❸	❹	❺
ACCOMM.	US$1-7	US$7-15	US$15-25	US$25-50	US$50-100
FOOD	US$1-3	US$3-6	US$6-9	US$9-12	US$12-15

SAFETY

The regions west of Panama City are very safe for travelers and politically stable. In Panama City, standard big-city rules apply; some neighborhoods are best avoided at night, and a few are best avoided altogether (see **Panama City: Orientation,** p. 606). Colón outside the free trade zone is generally unsafe—take taxis from the bus station and don't walk (see **Colón,** p. 624). Guerrillas and paramilitaries are active in the Darién area along the Colombian border, especially after the US military left in 1999. Both the US and Panamanian governments warn travelers not to enter the region (see **Darién,** p. 679). **Women travelers** will find the same *machismo,* catcalls, and stares as in the rest of Central America, although Panama is no worse than other countries (see **Women Travelers**, p. 50). While public displays of homosexuality are not accepted anywhere in Panama, **Gay and lesbian travelers** shouldn't have any major problems. There is a large but disorganized gay population, especially in Panama City, where there is also gay nightlife.

HEALTH

For details on diseases, see **Health,** (p. 29). **Malaria** is of special concern in Panama, as there are strains of mosquitoes that are **chloroquine-resistant;** if traveling east of Panama City, travelers should take an alternative anti-malarial. Malaria risk is greatest in rural areas of the Bocas del Toro, San Blas, and Darién provinces. A **yellow fever** vaccination is recommended. Contact the Centers for Disease Control for updated info (see **Health,** p. 29). Water is generally safe to drink, except in Bocas del Toro. Almost no travelers have problems with the tap water in Panama City; it's among the best urban water supplies in the world.

BORDER CROSSINGS

COSTA RICA. There are three land crossings. **Paso Canoas** (p. 651) is 50km west of David, Panama, and near Ciudad Neily, Costa Rica. To get there, catch a bus from David. **Sixaola/Guabito** (p. 670) are on the Caribbean coast 15 minutes from Changuinola, Panama, and near Puerto Viejo de Talamanca, Costa Rica. **Río Sereno,** at the end of the Concepción-Volcán road, is rarely used.

COLOMBIA. The Darién Gap, in the far east of Panama bordering Colombia, is the only break in the Interamerican Hwy. as it makes its way from Argentina to Alaska. Transport to and from Colombia, short of flying, is difficult at best. The ferry service between Colón and Cartagena has been discontinued, but occasional passage can be found on **cargo ships** from Panama. There are currently two land/sea routes into Colombia. One involves island-hopping through the San Blas Archipelago via **Puerto Obaldía** (see p. 675). The other involves a trek through Panamá's Darién. As of August 2002, both these routes were considered prohibitively unsafe due to local guerrilla and paramilitary activity.

KEEPING IN TOUCH

Mail from Panama takes about two weeks to get to the US, although occasionally a letter slips through and makes it in a few days. Postage is cheap (US$0.10-1). To receive mail in Panama, *Lista de Correos* is *not* the phrase of choice; instead, use *Entrega General*. Also, be sure to write *República de Panamá* and not just *Panamá*, since Panama City is referred to as *Panamá*. Address letters as follows:

> Benjamin KRUTZINNA
> Entrega General
> David (City), Chiriquí (Province)
> República de Panamá

Phone numbers in Panama have seven digits with no area codes. Generally reliable public phones are everywhere and often take calling cards. Panama's only phone provider, Cable & Wireless, sells pre-paid phone cards, but doesn't have public phones in its offices. International calls are fairly priced (US$0.30-0.40 per min.). Phones as a rule don't give change. **Internet** is widespread (about US$1 per hr.).

| COUNTRY CODE | 507 |

TRANSPORTATION

The major domestic airline is **Aeroperlas** (☎ 315 7500; www.aeroperlas.com). There are a few smaller airlines connecting Panama City to San Blas and Darién. **Buses** are the major means of budget transport and the only means of reaching remote interior locations. Bus quality is generally good, and long trips tend to be served by luxury coaches. Other intercity routes are run by mini-buses, while in remote areas vans provide service. A bus's destination is almost always written on the front of the vehicle. If there's no terminal, many buses linger around the *parque central.* Pay when getting off, but confirm the fare before getting on. Consider taking some warm clothes to your seat to protect yourself from the chilling strength of the air conditioning or the constant breeze from wide-open windows. Travelers say **hitchhiking** becomes easier the farther one gets from the Interamerican Hwy., but *Let's Go* does not recommend hitchhiking. Truck drivers have been known to offer *"un lif"* from gas stations.

ORIENTATION

As in all of Central America, directions favor landmarks over addresses. Nevertheless, most Panamanian cities label streets in a grid of numbered north-south *avenidas* (avenues) and east-west *calles* (streets). Generally, *avenidas* increase in number to the west, and *calles* increase to the south.

HOLIDAYS AND FESTIVALS

Regardless of the official date, most holidays are celebrated on Monday to create a long weekend. The largest festival is Carnaval, the Panamanian equivalent of Mardi Gras, which is celebrated during the four days prior to Ash Wednesday. Holidays include: **January 1,** New Year's Day; **January 9,** Martyr's Day; **March/April,** Good Friday, Easter Sunday; **May 1,** Labor Day; **August 15,** Founding of Old Panama (Panama City only); **November 1,** National Anthem Day; **November 2,** All Souls' Day; **November 3,** Independence Day (independence from Colombia); **November 4,** Flag Day; **November 10,** First Cry of Independence; **November 28,** Emancipation Day (from Spain); **December 8,** Mother's Day; **December 25,** Christmas; **December 31,** New Year's Eve.

PANAMA CITY

Few cities in the world have a history, fortune, and character so intimately and singularly related to their geography. Indelibly marked by the canal and the commerce it brings, not to mention a century of partial US occupation—Panama City is unlike anything else you'll find in Panama or the rest of Central America. This is a metropolis that defines the word "cosmopolitan," where Spanish and indigenous traditions coexist with the cultures of immigrants from around the world. Panama City's location, a calm harbor on the narrow bridge between two continents, has made it a transit point for people and wealth for over 300 years.

Originally the gateway for the gold of all of Spain's Pacific colonies, Panama City was settled in 1673. The residents of Panamá Viejo (Old Panama) became irritated by pirates and infertile swamps and consequently moved to Panama City's modern-day site. During the California gold rush hordes of prospectors flowed in from North America, fattening the pockets of the steam-ship barons and fostering dreams of a more ambitious interoceanic connection. By the 20th century, plans for a water passage were complete, and the first ship passed through the canal's Miraflores Locks in 1914. Since then, the canal and favorable tax regulations have made Panama City an international banking and commercial center. The US

PANAMA

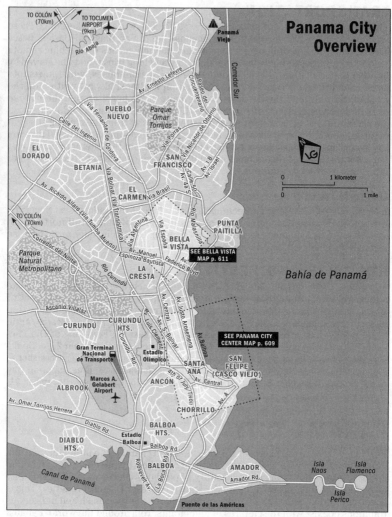

Panama City Overview

turned over complete control of the canal zone to Panama in December 1999 and so far Panama has experienced positive trends and relative stability.

✈ INTERCITY TRANSPORTATION

Domestic Buses: Most buses to the rest of the country leave from the brand-new **Gran Terminal Nacional de Transporte** near Marcos Gelabert Airport (☎ 232 5803). Services include 24hr. ATMs, Internet, and luggage storage. Despite the following schedules, buses may depend on demand and sometimes wait to fill up. Buses head to: **Almirante** (9hr., 8 and 9pm, US$23); **Chitré** (4hr., every hr. 5am-11pm, US$6); **Colón** (2hr., every 30min. 4:45am-10pm, US$1.25; express US$2); **David** (6hr., US$10.60;

express 5hr., US$15); **El Valle** (2hr., every 30min. 7am-7pm, US$3.50); **Gamboa** (40min., every hr. 5am-11pm, US$0.60); **Metetí** (7-8hr., 6 per day 4:15-1:30pm, US$9); **Paso Canoas:** (10hr., every 1½-2hr. 7am-8pm, US$12; express 8½hr., 11pm and midnight, US$17); **Penonomé** (2½hr., every 20min. 4am-10pm, US$3.70); **Sabanitas** (1-2hr., US$1); **Santiago** (3½hr.; every hr. 2am-11pm, and midnight; US$6); **Yaviza** (10-13hr., US$14). Buses to Metetí continue to Yaviza when the road is dry enough. If the road is muddy, there are 4WD *chivitas* in Metetí (2 per day, US$5).

International Buses: Tica Buses (☎262 2084) go to **San José, Costa Rica** (18hr., 1 per day 11am, US$25).

Domestic Flights: Marcos Gelabert Airport (☎315 0400) handles all domestic flights and is a US$2 taxi ride from Santa Ana. Airlines and their destinations are:

Aeroperlas (☎315 7500; www.aeroperlas.com) has flights to **Bocas del Toro** and **Changuinola** (M-F 8:30am and 1pm; Sa 7am and 3pm; Su 8am and 3pm; US$49.35 to Bocas, US$52.50 to Changuinola); **Chitré** (M-F 7:40am and 4:15pm, US$31.50); **Colón** (daily 8:45am, US$25); **Contadora** (M-F 8:45am and 5pm, Sa 8am and 5pm, Su 8:50am and 3:50pm; US$26.25); **David** (M-F 6:30, 10:30am, 4:30pm; Sa 7, 10:30am, 3:30pm; Su 8am and 3:30pm; US$56.70); **El Real** (M, W, F, Sa 9:10am; US$39); **La Palma** (1 per day, US$36). They also fly M-F mornings to **San José, Costa Rica** (US$115).

Aviatur (☎315 0311) also serves **Bocas del Toro, Changuinola, Chitré, Contadora, El Real,** and **La Palma** with 1 flight per day for the same prices as Aeroperlas. It also flies to **San Blas**—including **El Porvenir** (daily 6am, US$30) and **Puerto Obaldía** (daily 12:30pm, US$46.20).

Aerotaxi (☎315 7520), a subsidiary of Aeroperlas, flies to **El Porvenir** (daily 6am, US$58) and other **San Blas** islands.

Mapiex Aero (☎315 0888) flies west to **Bocas del Toro** and **Changuinola** (M-F 8:50am, Sa 6:30am, Su 1:30pm; US$49.50 to Bocas, US$52.50 to Changuinola); and **David** (M-F 6:25am, noon, 4pm; Sa 9:15am and 4pm; Su 8am and 4pm; US$56.70).

International Flights: Tocumen International Airport (☎238 4322) lies 30min. east of the city and can be reached by cab (US$15) or any bus marked "Tocumen" (US$0.20-0.30). Buses depart from Calle 12, Av. Perú, Via España, Av. Balboa, or Calle 50 to the airport parking lot. Airlines and local numbers include: **American** (☎269 6022); **Continental** (☎263 9177); **Copa** (☎227 2672); **Delta** (214 8118); **Lacsa** (☎238 4084); **Taca** (☎238 4116); and **United** (225 3087).

Boat: The Panama Canal is a major transit point for cargo ships and yachts, and with plenty of time and even more luck, travelers *may* be able to hitch a ride. *Let's Go* does not recommend hitchhiking. To get to the **Yacht Club**, take a red bus marked Balboa (US$0.25) from Plaza 5 de Mayo in Santa Ana. Open M-Sa 8:30am-5pm. From Balboa, commercial boats travel to **Isla Taboga** on Expreso del Pacífico (☎261 0350. 20min.; M-F 6, 8:15am, 3, 5pm, Sa-Su 7, 8:15, 10:15am, 3, 5pm; US$8) or Calypso Queen (☎264 6096; ½hr.; Tu 8:30am, Sa-Su 7:30, 10:30am, 4:30pm; US$8), and to **Isla Contadora** on Expreso del Pacifico (1¾hr., US$25 roundtrip, high season only).

✈ ORIENTATION

UPON ARRIVAL. After arriving at Tocumen International Airport, head to the parking lot to catch a bus (45min. to Santa Ana, US$0.35) or a taxi (30min.; US$25 for 1 or 2 people, US$30 for 3, US$15 for a shared van). The domestic airport is a US$2 taxi ride away from the center. Most **buses** arrive at the new Gran Terminal.

LAYOUT. The Canal provides the far southwestern border of the city, running inland to the northwest. The city's main sprawl runs west-east along the Bahía de Panamá (Panama Bay), east of the canal's mouth. The peninsula of **San Felipe** (also known as Casco Viejo), on the west side of the bay, is home to many budget hotels and sights and is centered around Plaza de la Independencia. The city's largest

PANAMA

street, **Av. Central,** runs from the tip of San Felipe northeast into the neighborhood of Santa Ana (often pronounced "Santana"). Between Parque Santa Ana, just north of San Felipe, and Plaza 5 de Mayo, in the heart of Santa Ana, it becomes a pedestrian mall. Beyond the plaza, cars return as the road runs east through Calidonia before becoming Vía España and entering the quieter residential neighborhood of Bella Vista. The bay-side skyscrapers of downtown stand south of Calidonia, and Bella Vista merges into the swanky "banking district" on its southeastern side.

SAFETY. While Panama City is welcoming to visitors, it is a big city and certainly has its share of dangers, including crime. Problems have been reported in San Felipe, Panamá Viejo, and Calidonia, especially at night. This is no reason to avoid these parts of the city, but take extra care when going out at night - don't flaunt your wallet, watch, etc. The city's poorest and most dangerous section is El Chorillo, bordering San Felipe and Santa Ana to the west. *Gringos* in particular are advised not to venture here, since US troops burned many area residences to the ground during the 1989 invasion. Curundu, San Miguel, and Santa Cruz, north of Santa Ana and Calidonia, are also best avoided.

▛ LOCAL TRANSPORTATION

Local Buses: Stops are generally unmarked, and you won't find maps of routes. Instead, find a bus that has your destination painted on the front windshield and wave it down. Most buses run through Plaza 5 de Mayo, or along Av. Perú, Calle 50, or Vía España. The cost within the city is always US$0.25 (Tocumen Airport, US$0.35); pay the driver or the bus-jockey as you get off. Luxury buses, which are so marked on the front, are more expensive (US$0.75). If the bus doesn't seem to stop where you want, yell *¡parada!* (stop!). Buses run 24hr., but from 11pm-4am they are much less frequent.

Taxis: Taxis can be found everywhere. Fares are based on a 6-zone system spanning from Balboa to just beyond Río Abajo. Rides within a zone for one person cost US$1.00; every zone boundary crossed adds US$0.25. Each additional person adds US$0.25, and there is a US$0.15 surcharge from 11pm to 5am and on Su. A US$0.40 surcharge applies for called cabs (radio cabs ☎223 7694 or 220 8510). Certain "sites" (Marcos A. Gelabert Airport, Muelle 18, Parque Natural Metropolitano) are supposed to be US$2.00 more, though this is often overlooked. A ride from San Felipe to Vía España is US$1.50 for 1 person; to Panamá Viejo US$2. Settle on a price before getting in, as tourists are prime targets for price hikes.

Car Rentals: Prices range from US$50 to US$100 per day, depending on car size and insurance options. At major chains, drivers must be 25 or older. Companies include: **Avis** (☎264 0722); **Barriga** (☎269 0221); **Budget** (☎263 8777); **Dollar** (☎270 0355); **Hertz** (☎264 1111); **National** (☎265 2222); **Thrifty** (☎264 2613). Website reservations are often easier.

▞ PRACTICAL INFORMATION

TOURIST AND FINANCIAL SERVICES

Tourist Information: Instituto Panameño de Turismo (IPAT). National office at the Atlapa Convention Center, Zona 5 (☎226 7000 ext. 112, 113, or 278), on Vía Israel just off Calle 77 and the Hotel Caesar Park. Open M-F 8:30am-4:30pm. Other branches at both airports, the green-and-yellow kiosk in the pedestrian mall, the kiosk across from Hotel Continental on Vía España, and at Panamá Viejo. Branches open daily 8:30am-4:30pm. **ANAM** (☎315 0855) has an office housing its Areas Protegidas division in Albrook airport facilities. Info on the parks is available here, although there's more at regional offices and park headquarters. Open M-F 8am-4pm.

Travel Agencies and Tour Companies: Ancon Expeditions, Calle Elvira Méndez at Calle 49 A Este (☎269 9414), in Edificio El Dorado, offers a wide range of option. Open M-F 8am-5pm, Sa 9am-1pm. **Adventure Panama** (☎263 3077), on Calle Ricardo Arias, just up the street from Voyager International Hostel, offers many excursions, including San Blas and Darién tours. Open M-Sa 8am-5pm. **Argo Tours** (☎228 4348), in Balboa, has half- and full-canal cruises. Other companies include: **Agencia de Viajes Continental,** in the Hotel Continental on Vía España (☎263 6162); **Viajes Panamá S.A.,** Calle 52, Av. Federico Boyd, Edificio Costa del Sol (☎223 0630); and **Mía Travel S.A.** (☎263 7835), farther down the same street.

Embassies and Consulates: Canada (☎264 9731), Calle 53 Este, Edificio World Trade Center, 1st fl. Open M-Th 8:30am-4:30pm, F 8:30am-1pm. **Colombia** (☎220 3535; fax 223 2811), Calle 53 near Calle 50, Edificio World Trade Center, 18th fl. Open M-F 8am-1pm. **Costa Rica** (☎264 2937; fax 264 6348), Edificio Plaza Omega, 3rd floor. Open M-F 9am-3pm. **UK** (☎269 0866; fax 223 0730), Calle 53, Edificio Swissbank, 4th fl. Open M-Th 12:30-6pm and 7-9pm, F 12:30-5:30pm. **US** (☎207 7000; fax 207 7278), Av. Balboa, Calle 39, Apdo. Postal 6959 Zona 5. Open M-F 8am-noon.

Immigration: Av. 2 Sur (Av. Cuba), Calle 29, in Calidonia, 1 block south of Machetazo on Av. Central (☎225 1373). Visa extensions and exit stamps. Show up early and wait forever. Open M-F 8am-3pm. For **passport photos,** go across the street or to a supermarket. Super 99 on Av. Central has 4 photos for US$1.25.

Banks: All over the city, particularly around Vía España in Bella Vista. **Sistema Clave** 24hr. **ATMs** tend to have the widest range of link-ups. **Banco General** and **Banco del Istmo** give cash advances on V, MC and have 24hr. ATMs. Both open M-F 8am-3pm, Sa 9am-noon. **Banco General** has offices in Santa Ana, the pedestrian mall on Av. Central and Calle 10; Calidonia on Av. Cuba and Calle 34 and Vía Argentina and Calle D. **Citibank** is on Vía España. 24hr. ATM. Open M-F 8:30am-2pm, Sa 9am-noon.

American Express: In Torre Banco, on Av. Balboa, 9th floor (☎264 2444). Ask for customer service. Open M-F 8am-5pm, Sa 8am-1pm.

Western Union: Several locations. On Vía España in Plaza Concordia across from the Supermercado El Rey (☎269 1055). Open M-F 8am-6pm, Sa 8am-5pm. In Santa Ana, the pedestrian mall has 3 Western Union locations: in Machetazo on the 2nd fl., in Rock City Appliances, and in the Dorian's department store. All open M-Sa 9am-6pm.

LOCAL SERVICES

Supermarkets: In Panama City, super-supermarkets—multi-story behemoths—sell it all. Try **Machetazo,** near the west end of the pedestrian mall in Santa Ana. Open M-Sa 8:30am-7:30pm. **El Rey** is a popular chain; there's a location on Vía España across from the Plaza Concordia near Voyager International Hostel. Open 24hr.

Bookstores: It's not easy to find foreign-language books in Panama City. **Exedra Book,** a large, brown stucco building with a red-tile roof, located on Vía España and Vía Brazil, has a modest selection of English books, a cafe with reading area, an ATM, and Internet (US$1.50 per hr.). Open M-Sa 9am-9:30pm, Su 9am-8:30pm. **Gran Morrison** (☎269 2211), at Vía España across from Plaza Concordia. Open daily 9am-6:30pm.

Markets: A large open market, **El Mercado Público,** hosts vendors selling all types of fresh food and souvenirs. Centered around Av. Alfaro and Calle 12 in Santa Ana. Beware of pickpockets, and carry purses in front, clutched close to the body. Open M-Sa 6am to mid-afternoon. **Seafood market** on the coast, at Av. Balboa and Calle 24E. Open M-Sa early morning to early afternoon.

Laundromats: Machine laundromats (many provide drop-off, pick-up service) are called *lavamáticos;* dry-cleaning services are *lavanderías.* Both are everywhere. In San Felipe, try **Lavandería Plaza Herrera,** off Plaza Herrera on Calle 9, or **Lavamático Luchín,** on

Av. Central, Calle 87, across from the Cathedral. Each charges US$0.50 per washer and US$0.50 per dryer, and both sell detergent for US$0.25-0.40.

EMERGENCY AND COMMUNICATIONS

Police: Emergencies (☎104). **Calidonia, San Felipe, Santa Ana** (☎262 4539); **San Francisco** (☎226 5692); **Bella Vista** (☎223 4411); **Balboa** (☎272 6503); **Tocumen** (☎295 1327).

Firefighters: ☎103.

Red Cross: (☎228 2187) ambulance service.

Pharmacy: Farmacia Arrocha is everywhere; the Bella Vista branch (☎223 4505), just off Via España on Calle 49 across from the Hotel Panamá, is open 24hr.

Hospital: Hospital Nacional, Av. Cuba and Calle 38/39 (☎207 8100 or 207 8337), three blocks from the US embassy. Offers extensive services and modern facilities in cooperation with Harvard Medical School.

Telephones: Public phones are everywhere, though they may not always work. **Cable and Wireless** (☎269 3933), on Vía España in Plaza Concordia offers **fax** services. Open M-F 7:30am-5pm, Sa 7:30am-2:30pm. **Phone cards,** for sale at supermarkets, pharmacies, and airports, are a good option since public phones rarely give change. Information/Directory Assistance ☎102.

Internet access: Web cafes are now almost as common as pay phones in many parts of the city, especially in Calidonia and Bella Vista. Rates hover around US$1 per hr. In Santa Ana, try the **Internet Panama Cafe**, on Plaza Santa Ana. Open M-Sa 9am-11:30pm, Su 10am-11pm.

Post Office: On Av. Balboa and B. Open M-F 7am-6pm, Sa 7am-5pm.

⌂ ACCOMMODATIONS

SAN FELIPE (CASCO VIEJO)

Casco Viejo, at the western end of Av. Central, is a lively colonial neighborhood with a few spartan budget options clustered between Plaza de la Independencia and Plaza Herrera. Renovation projects seek to revitalize the neighborhood, but for the foreseeable future, lodgings here are uniform: very cheap, locked-gate, gritty places retaining few traces of their colonial grandeur. During the day, when Tourist Police abound, the streets are relatively safe, but it's dangerous after dark.

Hotel Herrera, Av. Central and Calle 9 (☎228 8994), 2 blocks west and 1 block south of Plaza de la Independencia, in a yellow and white building on Plaza Herrera. One of the better, safer budget deals. Spacious, but unimpressive common room with TV. Ask for a room with a fan at no extra cost. Singles US$6; doubles US$8, with bath US$11, with TV, A/C, and fridge US$15.75. ❶

Hotel Foyo, Calle 6, near Av A (☎262 8023). A blue and white building on the left, 1½ blocks from Plaza de la Independencia, between the Palacio Municipal and the Museo del Canal. Good location and the cheapest liveable place in the city. Bare-bones rooms with fans. Run by the same owners as Hotel Herrera. Popular with backpackers. Rooms vary in quality. Singles US$5, with bath US$8; doubles US$8.89. ❶

Casa Grande, Av. Central Calles 8/9 (☎211 3316), in a mint green and white building. Basic rooms with high ceilings that keep it cool. Communal baths, tiny showers. Decent location. Rooms US$6, with fan US$7, with A/C US$9; dorm beds US$3.30. ❶

Pensión Panamérica (☎228 8759), a green and white hotel to the right of the horse statue on Plaza Herrera. Stuffy rooms and small bathrooms. Rooms have fans, but windows don't open. Singles US$7.70, with bath US$10, US$2 per additional person. ❷

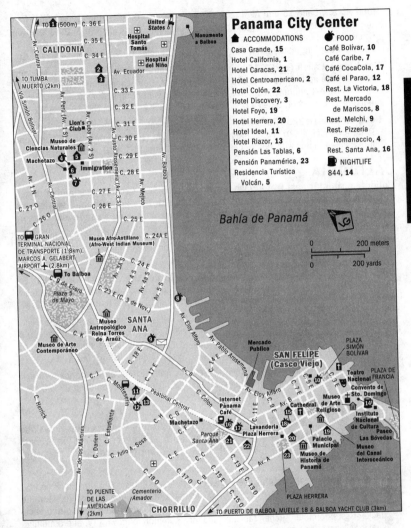

Panama City Center

🏠 ACCOMMODATIONS
Casa Grande, **15**
Hotel California, **1**
Hotel Caracas, **21**
Hotel Centroamericano, **2**
Hotel Colón, **22**
Hotel Discovery, **3**
Hotel Foyo, **19**
Hotel Herrera, **20**
Hotel Ideal, **11**
Hotel Riazor, **13**
Pensión Las Tablas, **6**
Pensión Panamérica, **23**
Residencia Turística
Volcán, **5**

🍴 FOOD
Café Bolívar, **10**
Café Caribe, **7**
Café CocaCola, **17**
Café el Parao, **12**
Rest. La Victoria, **18**
Rest. Mercado
de Mariscos, **8**
Rest. Melchi, **9**
Rest. Pizzería
Romanaccio, **4**
Rest. Santa Ana, **16**

🍸 NIGHTLIFE
844, **14**

PANAMA

SANTA ANA

Noisy, bustling Santa Ana, closer to the city center, has hotels a step above those in San Felipe. It's slightly safer, though don't stray far from Av. Central at night.

Hotel Colón (☎ 228 8506), on Calle B and Calle 12, a short block away from the gate of the pedestrian mall at Plaza Santa Ana. On the far side of the Plaza from the pedestrian mall, face San Felipe, follow the trolley track 1 block, and turn right; it is the blue building with white trim. Colón has been offering basic, cheap, dependable accommodations since 1915. Includes bar and multiple common areas with TV. Roof access offers a great harbor view. Singles with fan US$8.80, with fan and bath US$12, with A/C, bath, and TV US$15.60; doubles US$12/US$14.40/US$18. ❷

Hotel Riazor, Calle 16 and Av. I (☎228 0777; fax 228 0986), around the corner from the Banco Nacional building in the pedestrian mall. Good deal in a good location. Offers 46 comfortable, spotless rooms, all with TV, A/C, and baths with hot water, as well as a bar and restaurant on the ground floor. Singles US$16; doubles US$18. ❸

Hotel Ideal, Calle I (☎262 2400). Turn off Av. Central onto Calle I at Banco Nacional and continue up the street about 200m on the right. Quirky and friendly. Intensely floral rooms have A/C, phones, cable TV, and private hot-water baths. Common rooms, snack machines, restaurant. Singles US$14, with bath US$16; doubles US$18/US$20. ❷

Hotel Caracas (☎228 7232). With your back to the gate of the pedestrian mall at Plaza Santa Ana, facing San Felipe, the hotel is on the right, 100m up the street. Three floors of big, clean rooms with TVs, phones, and baths. Doubles US$10, with A/C US$12. ❷

CALIDONIA

Calidonia, running east from Plaza 5 de Mayo along Av. Central, has many full-service hotels in the US$15-25 range, particularly along Calles 29 and 34 near Av. Perú. It's easy and worthwhile to shop around here. Prices may rise in high season.

Residencia Turística Volcán, Calle 29 (☎225 5263), between Av. Perú and Cuba. Comfortable rooms, popular with backpackers, all with baths and sporadic cable TV. Singles with fan US$12, with A/C US$14; doubles with A/C US$16; triples US$18. ❷

Pensión Las Tablas, Av. Perú, between Calles 28 and 29, across from Machetazo, marked by a tiny sign. Small, clean rooms have fans, TVs, and baths. Some face Av. Perú—these can be noisy. Singles US$8, with bath and TV US$10; doubles US$12. ❷

Hotel Centroamericano, Calle 34 (☎227 4555), just north of Av. Justo Arosemena. More expensive than the neighbors, but definitely a step above the rest. Fountain, elevator, and large rooms with bathrooms so sparkling white you need sunglasses. TV, A/C, phone, hot water. Singles US$20; doubles US$25; triples US$30. MC/V. ❸

Hotel Discovery (☎225 1140), Calle 34 across from Hotel Centroamericano. Basic rooms with A/C, TV, phone, and hot-water baths. Singles US$15; doubles US$20. ❷

BELLA VISTA

Bella Vista is as close as you can get to the action around Vía Argentina and Calle 50 without spending a fortune. Attractive, well-priced hotels sit along Vía España as it enters Bella Vista. This area is safer than the other neighborhoods that offer budget accommodations.

🖪 **Voyager International Hostel,** Calle Manual María Icaza, Edificio Di-Lido, Apt. 8 (☎260 5913; www.geocities.com/voyagerIH), 100m from Hotel Continental and Restaurante Jimmy's. Voyager is the only place in Panama City that follows the tried-and-true backpacker-hostel formula. Kitchen facilities, laundry, common room with TV, and a multilingual book exchange complement clean, simple rooms with bunkbeds and common baths. Airport pick-up US$12. Price includes breakfast and 30min. of Internet access. 6 person rooms US$8.80 per person, US$8 with ISIC card. ❷

Hotel Montreal (☎263 4422), on Vía España, across from Hotel California. Montreal offers A/C, phone, TV, hot-water baths, a restaurant, and a rooftop pool. Upper floors have great view of the city. Singles US$22; doubles US$27.50; triples US$33. ❸

Hotel California (☎263 7736), on Vía España at Calle 43, 300m east of Av. Perú, beside Teatro Bella Vista. Quality place at a good price. Firm beds, A/C, TV, phone, and hot-water baths. Some views of the bay. Singles US$20 with a 2 night minimum stay, US$25 for one night only; doubles US$33; triples US$38.50. AmEx/MC/V. ❸

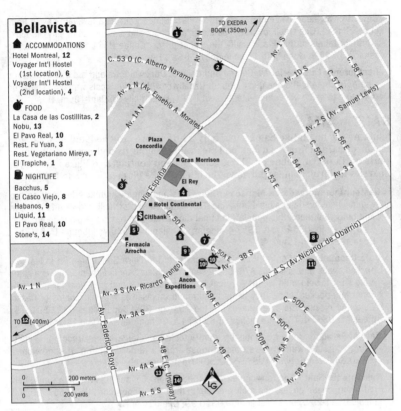

Bellavista

🏠 ACCOMMODATIONS
Hotel Montreal, **12**
Voyager Int'l Hostel
(1st location), **6**
Voyager Int'l Hostel
(2nd location), **4**

🍴 FOOD
La Casa de las Costillitas, **2**
Nobu, **13**
El Pavo Real, **10**
Rest. Fu Yuan, **3**
Rest. Vegetariano Mireya, **7**
El Trapiche, **1**

🍷 NIGHTLIFE
Bacchus, **5**
El Casco Viejo, **8**
Habanos, **9**
Liquid, **11**
El Pavo Real, **10**
Stone's, **14**

🍽 FOOD

Panama City is the heart of international cuisine in Central America, from the cheap *típico* food of San Felipe and Santa Ana to the international flavors of Bella Vista and Marbella. Throughout the city, street vendors sell hot dogs, *frituras* (Panamanian deep fried specialties), fresh fruit, and *chichas* (a sweet, fruit juice concoction). You can find vendors around Calle 13, the pedestrian mall, Plaza 5 de Mayo, in the *mercadito* at Av. Perú and Calle 34, or the giant market on Av. Alfaro.

SAN FELIPE (CASCO VIEJO)

With the exception of a few new, chic cafes on Plaza Bolívar, establishments serve cafeteria-style *típico*; grab a tray and point to what you want, with choices usually including *arroz* (rice), *frijoles* (kidney beans) or *lentejas* (lentils), *carne* (beef), *pollo* (chicken), *sopa vieja* (shredded beef stew), or *pescado* (fish). When you're finished, leave your tray and dish on the table.

Raspados de Chico, a metal cart usually located in the alley of Calle 10, off Av. Central, 2 blocks above the Plaza de la Independencia. Sr. Chico has been selling *raspado,* a fantastic Panamanian version of a snow cone, in the same spot for decades. Chico is also a fount of information about the surrounding area, so don't hesitate to ask him for local recommendations. Usually open daily mid-morning until evening. ❶

Café Bolívar, near the Teatro Nacional on Plaza Simón Bolívar (a few yards away from Café Simón). One small room with stained-glass doors and shelves full of nifty old junk. Outdoor tables on the Plaza justify the higher prices. Coffee US$1.50; beer US$2.50; snacks US$5-8. Open M-Th 11am-midnight, F-Sa 11am-1am. ❷

Restaurante La Victoria, Av. Central and Calle 9. Dark windows and a dark interior, but the *típico* here is the cheapest around. Usually crowded with locals watching soaps or listening to *salsa*. Rice, beans, and meat US$1. Open daily 9:30am-10pm. ❶

SANTA ANA

Santa Ana is much like San Felipe, only a little more crowded and upscale. Ice cream, pizza, and American fast food are available along its pedestrian mall, which starts north of San Felipe on Plaza Santa Ana and continues to Plaza 5 de Mayo. Bakeries and fruit stands spill down the hill from the Plaza toward San Felipe.

🔲 **Restaurante Mercado de Mariscos,** a big, blue and white warehouse building on the water, where Av. Balboa hits Santa Ana. For seafood that practically crawls off the boats and onto your plate, this popular, informal dining hall and bar is the place to go. Seafood cocktails US$4; fish US$3-4; shrimp or calamari US$6-7; lobsters US$10-15. Open M-Sa 10am-10pm. ❸

Café CocaCola, Av. Central, Calle 12, across from the Plaza Santa Ana. Sit in leather-backed chairs and enjoy the A/C. Supposedly the oldest cafe in Panama, this is a gathering spot for old men wearing typical Panamanian caps and *guayaberas*, the traditional four-pocket shirts. They come to surround themselves with old photos of Casco Viejo and discuss the cafe's heyday in the 20s and 30s. Sandwiches US$1.50-2.75; breakfast US$1-1.75; meat dishes US$2.50-4.50. Open daily 7:30am-11:15pm. ❶

Café el Parao, on Calle I, 2 doors up from Hotel Ideal. A large, open-air room and chattering waitstaff welcome patrons. Choose from a huge selection of sandwiches (US$0.65-2.25) or *típico* (US$1.50-2.50). Open M-Sa 24hr. ❶

Restaurante Santa Ana, on the *peatonal* (pedestrian) Central at Plaza Santa Ana. Varied menu, cheap prices, and a billiards bar in the back. Sandwiches US$0.55-2.25; full meals US$1-2.25; breakfast combo US$0.90. Open 24 hr. ❶

Restaurante Melchi, Av. B and Av. Balboa, 3 blocks towards the bay from Plaza 5 de Mayo. The cool, open-air restaurant serves full *típico* meals that include meat, rice, salad, plantains, and beans (US$1.75-2.50). The discotheque above the restaurant attracts famous names in Panamanian music on weekends (cover US$3). Open 24hr. ❶

CALIDONIA

Calidonia's establishments serve the same fare as in other areas for slightly higher prices (*comidas* US$1.50-2.75), but many close at 4pm when the workers in the area go home. Eateries cluster on Calles 29-32, between Central and Arosemena.

Café Caribe, Av. Central between Calles 28 and 29, across from Machetazo. Caribe has a local crowd and a large variety of *típico*. It's near many Calidonia accommodations. Breakfast specials US$3.50; chicken with rice US$2. Open daily 7am-10pm. ❶

Restaurante Pizzería Romanaccio, on Calle 29 and Perú. A bit overpriced, this quality Italian eatery has pasta, calzones and pizzas (US$3-6). Open M-Sa 10am-10pm. ❷

BELLA VISTA

From Vía España near Vía Argentina, down past Calle 50 to the bay, international and upscale cuisine flourishes. Be prepared to shell out extra cash for anything but fast food, but know that it will probably be worth it.

La Casa de las Costillitas, on Vía Argentina, 1½ blocks from Vía España. Good seafood and BBQ. The 15-page bilingual menu includes witticisms on literature and philosophy. Seafood US$5-9, half-chicken US$4, ribs US$5-9. Open daily noon-11pm. ❸

El Trapiche, on Vía Argentina, 1½ blocks off Vía España. Serves a variety of dishes from across Panama. Entrees US$3.25-8. Cheaper but equally filling *hojaldra* sandwich (melted cheese and meat in fried bread) US$2.25-4. *Sancocho* (traditional chicken and vegetable soup) US$3. Beer US$2. Open daily 6:30am-11pm. AmEx/MC/V. ❷

Restaurante Fu Yuan (☎223 8002), in a little storefront on Calle 55, just off Via España and across from the side entrance to Hotel Panama in Bella Vista. Classic Chinatown style, from the chintzy decor to the authentic menu—parts of it aren't even translated. #51-54 are delicious hot-pot concoctions; #77-90 are desserts; #53 is eggplant in ginger; #77 is coconut tapioca. Cheap (US$2-5) and huge. Open daily 9am-9pm. ❷

El Pavo Real, at the end of Av. 3a Sur, 2 curvy blocks from Voyager International Hostel, is a fully convincing English pub with big, hearty hamburgers and fish and chips (US$5-7). Open Tu-Su 4:30pm until the bar empties out. ❷

Nobu, at Calle Uruguay and Av. 4a Sur. Small but perfect Chinese and Japanese menu and a tranquil dining room make it a fully justifiable splurge. Appetizers US$3-7; sushi US$2-5; US$7-9 for hand rolls. Full bar. Open Tu-Su, noon-3pm and 6-11pm. MC/V. ❸

Restaurante Vegetariano Mireya (☎269 1876), at the base of Calle Ricardo Arias, just down from Voyager International Hostel. Simple, cafeteria-style selection of ultra-cheap veggie concoctions (US$1.25 per portion). Open M-F 6am-8pm, Sa 6am-6pm. ❶

◙ SIGHTS

SAN FELIPE (CASCO VIEJO)

The original settlement in Panama City, Casco Viejo is a striking blend of lively community and grand, crumbling history. Though the whole neighborhood seems to be under renovation, it is loaded with striking memorials to politicians and heroes. Begin at **Plaza de la Independencia,** on Av. Central and Calle 7.

THE CATHEDRAL. Facing the Plaza de la Independencia is the huge Cathedral, which features whitewashed, mother-of-pearl towers and domes. Be sure to check out the intricate sacrament inside. The cathedral has been around since 1798 and was one of the few buildings in the city to survive the earthquake of 1882. If the front doors are closed, try the side.

MUSEO DEL CANAL INTEROCEÁNICO. The museum offers tons of info about the canal's construction, history, and operations, as well as colonial weapons from the *Camino de Cruces.* Displays are in the standardized government collage format. Even if you can't read Spanish, the museum is worth seeing for the pictures of the canal's construction. (*With your back to the cathedral, the museum is on your right.* ☎211 1649. Open Tu-Su 9:30am-5:30pm. US$2, students US$0.75.)

PASEO LAS BÓVEDAS. This walkway, with great views of the Pacific, was once used as a buffer against pirates and prisoners. Now, the arbor-covered footpath offers breathtaking views of the skyline, as well as cool shade. At the end of the Paseo lie the *bóvedas,* vaults which once held prisoners but now house a restaurant and a small, but impressive collection of art. The gallery fronts on **Plaza Francia,** which was engineered by Leonardo de Villanueva and built in honor of the Frenchmen who died during the 19th-century attempt to build a canal. In the plaza lies a small park where chamber orchestras sometimes play. (*From Plaza de la Independencia, walk south away from the Cathedral along Av. Central until the street winds past the*

Pacific. The Paseo begins just after the big, ruined house by the water. Gallery open Tu-Sa 8am-4pm, Su 1-5pm. US$0.75, students US$0.25. Paseo always open. Free.)

THE CHURCH AND CONVENT OF SANTO DOMINGO. Dating back to 1678, the church's **Arco Chato** is famous for its mortar construction and lack of internal supports. Panamanian leaders used the arch's survival to prove the country was earthquake-free, important in the fight for the transisthmian canal. is Connected to the old church ruins is the **Museo de Arte Religioso Colonial,** a modest hall that contains a gigantic altar, sculptures, and religious paintings. (Av. A, Calle 3. 1 block south and 2 blocks east of the Plaza de la Independencia. Museum ☎ 228 2897. US$0.25.)

PALACIO MUNICIPAL. Formerly the legislature of the country, it now houses city government on the 2nd floor and the **Museo de Historia de Panamá** on the 3rd. The museum traces Columbus's landing in Panama through recent times. An attendant can give you a tour. (☎ 228 6231. The Palacio is right next door to the Museo del Canal, on the Plaza de la Independencia. Open M-F 8am-4pm. Museum US$1, children US$0.25.)

TEATRO NACIONAL. The neoclassical theater was built at the turn of the century and was reconstructed after part of the ceiling caved in. Speak with administrators to sink into the heavenly red velvet balcony chairs overlooking the grand theater. Performances in the theater range from classical to folk. (☎ 262 3525. Av. B, Calle 3. From the Plaza, stand with your back to the Cathedral and walk east 2 blocks down Av. Central and turn left. Open M-F 8am-4pm. Call for a schedule of concerts and shows. Tickets US$5-30.)

OTHER SIGHTS. **Parque Simón Bolívar** features a monument honoring the namesake liberator, with friezes depicting his feats. There are also a number of cafes here (see **Food,** above). (1 block east and 1 block north of Plaza de la Independencia.) The Moorish-style **Palacio Presidencial,** also known as the "Palace of the Herons," is home to La Presidenta, and security is extremely tight. (On Av. Alfaro, 2 blocks north of the Plaza de la Independencia.) The **Iglesia de San José** houses the **Altar de Oro.** According to legend, a priest covered the magnificent golden altar in mud to disguise its worth from pirate Henry Morgan, who sacked Panamá Viejo in 1671. (Av. A and Calle 8, 1 block south and 1 block west of the Plaza.) San Felipe's biggest collection of fresh food kiosks crowd Av. Alfaro, northwest of the Plaza de la Independencia in the **Mercado Público.** A great area to find souvenirs is **Sal Si Puedes** (literally "Get out if you can!"), which runs from the Mercado Público to the Pedestrian mall. Note the name and take precautions against pickpockets and thieves.

KIDS RULE! Turn left upon entering the Palacio Municipal in the Casco Viejo and look at the second photo from the door in front; you will see what looks like children sitting at the table of the Municipal Council housed upstairs. This, and the other photos nearby, are scenes from **El Gobierno Municipal Infantil,** which occurs every year on November 1st. On this day, the regular representatives from each of the city's neighborhoods step down, and a neighborhood kid steps up to take the reins for a day. The acts and measures passed by this "infant government" have all the legitimacy of acts passed by the normal council, and are entered into the books just like any other law. This day kicks off the "Month of the Motherland" (November), which is full of celebrations and ceremonies honoring the history and heroes of the Republic.

SANTA ANA

Santa Ana's busy pedestrian mall runs north from San Felipe to **Plaza 5 de Mayo.** The mall was erected in honor of the firemen who battled the flames of an exploded gunpowder warehouse in 1914.

MUSEO ANTROPOLÓGICO REINA TORRES DE ARAÚZ. Overlooking Plaza 5 de Mayo, the museum documents Panamanian ethnography from pre-Columbian times and is home to 15,000 pieces of artwork in gold, ceramic, and stone. English-speaking guides are available. (☎ 262 8338. Open M-F 9am-4pm. US$2, students and children US$0.50.)

MUSEO DE ARTE CONTEMPORÁNEO. A small collection of modern Panamanian and other Central American artwork. (☎ 262 8012. West of the Plaza 5 de Mayo on Av. de los Mártires. Open M-F 9am-4pm, Sa 9am-5pm, Su 11am-5pm. Free.)

CALIDONIA

MUSEO AFRO-ANTILLANO. Housed in a tiny gray church, this one-room museum recounts the history of Panama's Afro-West Indian population with photos, antiques, and parts of the old Panamanian railroad that brought immigrants looking for work. (☎ 262 5348. From Plaza 5 de Mayo, continue east 1-2 blocks along Av. Justo Arosemena. Open Tu-Sa 9am-3:30pm. US$1, students US$0.25.)

MUSEO DE CIENCIAS NATURALES. The museum's small displays hold regional birds, mammals, and insects. Most interesting to a biology or taxidermy fan. (Av. Cuba, Calle 30 Este. ☎ 225 0645. Open Tu-Sa 9am-3:30pm. US$1, children US$0.25.)

PANAMÁ VIEJO

*Getting to Panamá Viejo is easy—take any city **bus** with "Panamá Viejo" on the front window; a good place to wait for one is Plaza 5 de Mayo. (45min., 7am-11pm, US$0.25.) Get off when you see the ruins and walk 5min. along the coast to the entrance. **Market** open Tu-Su 9am-6pm. **Museum** open Tu-Sa 9am-5pm, Su 9am-1pm. US$1. **IPAT office** ☎ 221 5494. Open daily 8:30am-4:30pm.*

Panamá Viejo, the original Panama City, once flourished as the Pacific terminus of Spain's Camino Real, the trans-isthmian pipeline for the gold of all of Spain's Pacific Colonies. Its importance was brief, and after a near raze by Pirate Henry Morgan in 1673, Panamá Viejo was abandoned. Today, it offers an intriguing peek into a 16th-century city. A fort, several convents, a hospital, and other structures still stand. Most impressive are the 15m-high **cathedral tower** and the **Bridge of Kings,** one of the oldest bridges in the Americas.

Inside the gate at the bend in the road is the **Mercado Nacional de Artesanías,** several touristy mini-shops that sell souvenirs from different regions of the country. Also inside is a small **museum** with a model of the town, and an equally small but colorful IPAT office, which supplies walking tour maps. There's a pricey restaurant in the same building as the museum, yet some better, cheaper *típico* places lie near the gas station. Wear bug spray, as the ruins still border on swampland.

PARQUE NATURAL METROPOLITANO

*The easiest way to get to Metropolitano is to take a **taxi** (US$1.25-2). **Park trails** open daily 24hr.; dusk and dawn are the best times to see wildlife. **Ranger station** open M-F 8am-4pm, Sa-Su 8am-1pm. Trails US$1, map US$0.75.*

Panamanians boast it's "the most accessible rain forest in the world," and that just might be true. It's certainly the only natural park in Central America within the limits of a metropolitan city. Though occupying 265 hectares of forest—75% of which is fragile Pacific dry forest—the park is just minutes northwest of the city's "downtown" areas and is home to hundreds of plant and animal species.

There are five **trails** in the park, four of them named after a particular plant or animal often seen from the trail. Trails include, in order of increasing difficulty: **Los**

Momótides (700m), named after the motmot bird; **El Roble** (700m), named for an oak tree; **Los Caobos** (1.1km), named after the *caoba* (mahogany) tree; **Mono Tití** (1.7km), named for the *tití* monkey; and **La Cienaguita** (1.1km), named for its oft-swampy nature. This last trail also contains a lookout point 150m above sea level featuring spectacular views (best in dry season) of the city, canal, and bay. Guides can escort you during ranger hours for free, but a tip is expected. Call ahead.

🎵 ENTERTAINMENT

Theater: **Teatro Nacional** (☎ 262 3525), in San Felipe, is the city's biggest theater, showing plays and concerts. Call for a schedule. Admission US$5-30. Also try **Teatro en Círculo** (☎ 261 5375), near Vía Brazil and Transísmica. A cheaper option for live music and dancing is **Mi Pueblito** (☎ 228 7154), where you can see performances of the national dances by children in flowing *polleras* (traditional Panamanian costume) every Friday night for US$1. Call for other showings. Park open daily 10am-10pm.

Cinema: Movie theaters abound; a few major ones are located on Vía España or near the pedestrian mall. Most show American hits with subtitles soon after their US release. Try **Cine Alambra** (☎ 264 3515), on Vía España at Via Argentina, or **Cine Universitario** (☎ 264 2737), which shows artsier fare, on the campus of Universidad Nacional de Panamá, behind Iglesia del Carmen (US$3-4). For older American films, head to **Teatro Amador**, Av. Central, Calle 12 (☎ 262 5472. US$0.75).

🛍 SHOPPING

For upscale shopping, try **Vía España** near Via Argentina or Calle 53E from Calle 50 towards Punta Paitilla. The best prices in the city for typical crafts can be found in the *artesanía* markets of Balboa and at **Casa de la Pollera** in San Felipe, across from the Altar de Oro on Av. A and Calle 8. Panamá Viejo offers the chance to bargain for sweet deals. **Flory Saltzman's Artesanía**, across from Hotel El Panamá on Calle 49B Oeste, offers many multicolored *molas* (traditional Kuna reverse appliqué embroidery), both individual and sewn in quilts and wall hangings. (☎ 223 6963. Open M-Sa 8am-6pm, Su 8:30am-noon.) Those who get the chance, however, may want to go to San Blas (p. 670) and purchase *molas* directly from the Kuna.

🌃 NIGHTLIFE

Whether you're looking to strut your stuff on the dance floor or just to sit back and watch the locals network, this metropolis has it all—from quiet back rooms to full-tilt fashion raves. Panamanians dress well most of the time, but especially for their nightlife—men wear long pants and collared shirts, and women aren't afraid to show some skin. Jeans and short-sleeve shirts are OK for bars and discos, but shorts and sandals are not. San Felipe can be a blast, but it's worth taking extra care at night—if you're alone, stick to taxis and avoid walking anywhere. Bella Vista is considerably safer. The action usually picks up around 11pm.

Live Music: Good bets include: for jazz, **Restaurante Las Bóvedas** (☎ 298 8068) on Plaza de Francia (F and Sa nights 9pm); for *salsa*, **El Casco Viejo** (☎ 293 2306) at Av. 4a Sur and Calle 53; and for *típico* (traditional) music, **Las Tinajas** (☎ 263 7890) on Av. 3a Sur near Av. Federico Boyd. Covers are high, often over US$10. Many of the luxury **hotels** have shows (with a cover) in their bars and cafes. Bars and discos sometimes have live music/show, too.

844, on Calle 2a Oeste, just off Plaza Francia in Casco Viejo. Classy bar/club in a restored section of the old city. Young, hip, local crowd. Music ranges from *salsa* and *merengue* into heavier dance grooves. Cover US$8-10. Open T-Sa at 9pm.

Stone's, at Calle 5a Sur and Calle Uruguay in Bella Vista. A somewhat more laid-back spot, with plenty of tables, a long bar, and a small dance floor. Draws a good crowd on weekends. No cover except for special events (US$8). Open Tu-Su at 8pm.

Bacchus (☎ 263 9005), on Calle 49A off Vía España between Citibank and Bank of Boston. Big, busy, fully-loaded club with a karaoke bar and Greek disco. Most nights women enter free; F women US$10, men US$15; Sa live music, cover varies. Open M-Sa karaoke from 5pm, disco from 9:30pm.

Mangos Pub and Grill (☎ 321 0075), in Edison Plaza, on Tumba Muerto behind the Edison Tower, right around the corner from Voyager Hostel. Mangos fills a nightly dance floor and plays Friday *salsa* and *merengue*. Beers US$2.50; cocktails US$4-6 and up. Open daily 11am until 3-4am on weekends.

Liquid, in the big shopping center diagonally across from El Casco Viejo, takes young and chic as far as they go in Bella Vista. World-class DJ's spin stripped-down drum and bass to the golden children of the city's elite. Cool steel and blue light complete the scene. Don't bother showing up until 11pm (Tu-Sa). Cover US$10.

El Pavo Real (see **Food,** above) has free pool-tables and pitch-perfect live classic rock (F and Sa nights). No cover.

Habanos (☎ 265 5292), a tiny storefront across from the Mariott on Av. 3 Sur. Cigar shop with two womb-like smoking rooms and a full bar. Wood-panelling, plush leather chairs, strong A/C, and storied history hung on the walls soothe the over-heated mind. Dress and act like you smoke expensive cigars. Open M-Sa 8am-11pm, Su 1pm-7pm.

GAY AND LESBIAN NIGHTLIFE

El Hidalgo (☎ 269 3317), on Vía Brazil between Vía España and Calle 50, across from a Texaco station. Mostly males, plus a few heterosexual couples. Laid-back and friendly. Cover Tu-Th US$3, F-Su US$5 with transvestite comedy show and occasional strippers.

◪ DAYTRIPS FROM PANAMA CITY

LA ARENOSA

*Getting to isolated Arenosa by bus involves transfers and patience. From **Panama City** take a bus to Parque Feulliet in the city of **La Chorrera**. Buses leave for La Arenosa from the greenish-yellow building of the* Corregiduria de Barrio Colon *one block west of the parque (45min., every hr., 7am-7pm, US$1). Another option is to take one of the army-style **chivitas** that barrel down the Interamerican between Panama City and western Panamanian destinations. Get off a few km west of La Chorrera where a green sign marks the road to La Arenosa. Boats and guides can be hired at the docks in Arenosa, one block from the church (US$25-30 for approximately 4hr.).*

Heads up, fishing aficionados—the name "Panama" means "abundance of fish" in an indigenous tongue. The country is famous for expensive deep-sea fishing tours, but a more budget option is La Arenosa, a small fishing spot on Lake Gatún. Even if the fish aren't biting, the view is ample compensation. Boat tours with a local guide are also possible. Tree trunks and other obstacles stand as reminders of the land that was flooded during the canal's construction—a guide will know how to avoid them and find good fishing areas. The most common catches are a type of bass referred to as *sargentos*. Since services are limited in the tiny town, a daytrip to Arenosa works best. Bringing poles, bait, and food is also advisable, although a few food stands hover around the church plaza and near the docks.

ISLA TABOGA

With clear blue waters, sandy beaches, and lush greenery, Isla Taboga (about 20km offshore from Panama City) earns its name, "Island of the Flowers." Discovered by Balboa in 1513 before the founding of Panama City, Taboga is rich in history: it served as a base for Pizarro's journeys to South America, and the church in the town center, founded in 1550, is said to be the oldest in the Americas. Taboga's proximity to the capital results in some overcrowding, especially on weekends.

⎗ TRANSPORTATION. From Balboa (in Panama City), **Expreso del Pacífico** (☎261 0350) heads to **Taboga** (20min.; M-F 8:30am, 2pm, Sa-Su 8:30, 10:15am, 4pm; US$4), and from Taboga back to **Panama City** (M-F 10am, 3, 5pm, Sa-Su 10am, 2, 4, 5pm; US$4, children US$3). **Calypso Queen** also runs to **Taboga** (☎264 6096; 1hr.; Tu 8:30am, Sa-Su 7:30, 10:30am, 4:30pm; US$4) and back (Tu-F 4pm, Sa-Su 9am, 3, 5:45pm; US$4, children and seniors US$2.50).

⬛ ORIENTATION. The town clusters around the dock. There are no roads; the main walkway passes by the dock. Getting off at the dock, most of the town is to the left, while the **main beach** is to the right.

⬛◻ ACCOMMODATIONS AND FOOD. With only two pricey hotels, Taboga is best as a daytrip. Nonetheless, if you want to unwind, **Hotel Chu ❸** is the place to go. Ten minutes from the dock toward the left, it has rustic rooms with fans and tiny communal bathrooms. The hotel's restaurant has a large and varied menu. (☎250 2035, in Panama City 263 6933. Singles US$20; doubles US$24; triples US$30; quads US$36.) **Hotel Taboga ❺,** a block to the right off the dock, offers more amenities for more money: dimly lit rooms with A/C, private baths, access to a pool, basketball courts (US$1 per hr.), ping-pong table (US$1 per hr.), kayaks (US$10 per hr.), and trips to the main lookout point. (☎250 2122; in Panama City 264 6096. Rooms US$60-70, depending on season.) The hotel also has a rather expensive restaurant (sandwiches US$2.40-4, dinners US$8-18). Meal prices are better at **El Mirador de Taboga ❶,** to the right of the dock, just before the entrance to Hotel Taboga. (Hamburger US$1, *empanada* US$0.35. Open daily 7am-10pm.)

◪◾ BEACHES AND SNORKELING. Playa Honda is to the left of the dock, while **Playa La Restinga** is to the right. Don't be fooled by Hotel Taboga's near-monopoly on beachgoers—La Restinga is a public beach. To get there without entering hotel property, turn toward the beach at the sign just before the grounds. Go through a narrow alley between the *batido* stand and El Mirador restaurant. Bathrooms (US$0.50) and changing rooms (US$0.25) are on the right as you exit the passage. Hotel Taboga has showers, changing rooms, lockers, and bathrooms by the beach, but day visitors must pay to enter the grounds (US$5). At the gate you receive a plastic bracelet and five "Taboga Dollars" to spend anywhere on the grounds.

Right in front of La Restinga, connected to the main island at low tide, is **Isla El Morro,** the 19th-century headquarters of the Pacific Steam Navigation Company. Don't get stranded by the tide; while it's not far from shore, strong currents make swimming back dangerous. For **snorkelers, Playa Piedra Llana** and **Playa El Mobo** are more secluded, rocky beaches with good coral reefs; walk 45min. down the road that passes behind Hotel Taboga to the right of the dock. Beyond the white apartments next to Hotel Taboga, bear left at the fork and then left again. Follow the wheel tracks to the beaches. Schools of fish congregate in front of **Playa La Restinga** near a sunken ship, whose mussel-encrusted frame is visible at low tide. During high season (Dec.-Apr.), you may be able to find **Sr. Perea** cruising the beaches renting equipment, though he is often away from the island the rest of the year (mask, snorkel, and fins US$2 per hr.; US$5 per day).

⚄ **OUTDOOR ACTIVITIES.** There's a lookout point at a former US army bunker, **La Vigia**, with a view of the surrounding hills. While Hotel Taboga offers transport to the vista, the best way up is on an hour-long trail through the forest. At the church, facing the phone booth from the basketball court, take the path to the left of the booth and follow ANAM's black-and-yellow signs to the trailhead. The climb is tough. Along the way up to La Vigia, you'll pass **Cerrot Tres Cruces** (the three crosses in the ground); either head left up to La Vigia, or go straight ahead and follow the trail down to the other side of the island. This entire side is forested, and protected by the **Refugio de Vida Silvestre Islas Taboga y Uraba**. It's a major nesting area for migratory seabirds, especially from December to March, when the island is mobbed by pelicans visiting from California. It's possible to hike through the reserve alone, though ANAM recommends a guide. Before you go, visit ANAM's small blue-and-yellow office to the right of the dock to pick up **trail maps.** (☎250 2082. Usually open M-F 8am-4pm, weekends if you call ahead.) The trail from Cerro Tres Cruces goes to **San Pedro Playa** as well. A guide can accompany you on these routes; call ahead and ask for Christian Pérez. Another way to see the island is to hire a **boat** at Playa Honda or Hotel Taboga (US$25 for 4 people).

PANAMA PROVINCE

Panama Province encloses a wide range of amazing spots, both natural and engineered, all within easy range of the metropolis. The most famous of the area's attractions, the canal, is neighbor to sultry tropical islands and superb national parks. Most visitors head north first, along the road to Gamboa toward the canal locks at Miraflores and the amazing birdlife at Parque Nacional Soberanía. To the west lie the sweeping views of Parque Nacional Altos de Campana, while offshore in the Golfo de Panamá is the paradisiacal gem, Archipiélago de las Perlas.

PANAMA CANAL

The Panama Canal, comprising the 80km stretch of water connecting the Atlantic and Pacific Oceans, is one of the greatest engineering feats in the history of the world. Locomotives carry the ships through the different locks. Commercial ships pay an average of US$40,000 each to pass through the canal, and over 30 vessels do so every day. More than a technological marvel, the Panama Canal is both the defining feature and the economic basis of modern Panama.

👁 VISITING THE CANAL

Take a bus from Plaza 5 de Mayo toward **Gamboa** *and ask the driver to let you off at* **Miraflores.** *Walk across the bridge and up the road for 10min. to get to the* **Visitors Center.** *☎272 8325. Open daily 9am-5pm. Free. Presentations in English and Spanish are given every hour or so, depending on demand. Partial boat tours of the canal through* **Argo Tours** *(☎228 4348) leave every Sa at 7:30am from Muelle 18 in Balboa. US$90 per person. Full tours one Sa per month. US$135 per person.*

The best dry-land spot to see the canal in action is the Visitors Center at **Miraflores Locks,** the largest locks on the canal and the closest to Panama City. The center includes a topographical model and film about the canal (try to count the number of synonyms for "engineering marvel") and a viewing deck with commentary in

Spanish and English. The largest ships tend to pass between 7-9am and 2-4pm; call ahead for details. **Contractors Hill,** on the western side of the canal, is the most accessible place from which to see the **Gaillard Cut,** but even this is reachable only by private vehicle. On the Atlantic side, you can view the **Gatún Locks** (see p. 624). The best way to experience the canal is **by boat**—it a great way to see the locks in action and the surprisingly gorgeous scenery. Panama City travel agents book the tour, but the main operator (and the one most other agencies use) is **Argo Tours.**

THE ROAD TO GAMBOA

Taking this route north out of Panama City will eventually bring you to Gamboa, where the Río Chagres enters Lago Gatún. Combining a visit to Miraflores Locks with a stop at Summit Gardens and a short hike in Soberanía makes a great daytrip from Panama City. Overnight trips are difficult; Gamboa has no budget rooms.

To access the area, take a Gamboa-bound **bus** from the SACA terminal at Plaza 5 de Mayo in Panama City (40min., every 30min. 5am-11pm, US$0.80). If your first stop is Miraflores, you can take a bus headed to Paraíso as well—these also leave from 5 de Mayo. Eight kilometers from the city is the turnoff to the Miraflores Locks (see above). The harder-to-see **Pedro Miguel Locks** are 1.5km farther up the road, beyond which the road continues past the town of Paraíso before reaching the headquarters of the densely forested and wildlife-rich Parque Nacional Soberanía (see below). Various trailheads farther down the road provide access to the park. Farther on, the road passes the **Summit Botanical Gardens and Zoo,** on the Continental Divide. **Gamboa** itself is near the entrance to one of the park's best hikes and is a good place to arrange a boat for Lago Gatún or up the Río Chagres.

▓ SUMMIT BOTANICAL GARDENS AND ZOO

Take the Gamboa bus, and hop off at the entrance, about 9km shy of Gamboa itself. ☎ 232 4854. Open daily 8am-4pm. US$0.50, children 12 and under US$0.10.

Some 15,000 different plant species populate the spacious grounds of this park, but most visitors come for the expansive and well-maintained zoo, with its impressive harpy eagle compound and up-close views of many of the endangered animals of the Panamanian rain forest. The gardens and zoo provide a valuable supplement to walks in the rain forest proper.

▓ PARQUE NACIONAL SOBERANÍA

*The **Ranger station** (☎ 232 4192) is located where the road forks, with Chilibre to the right and Gamboa to the left. To get to the trails from here, hop on a bus or passing passenger van. Admission US$3, camping US$5 per night. **Station** open daily 8am-4pm, but rangers are there 24hr. for emergencies. **Guides** can be arranged in advance through the ranger station or with naturalist companies in Panama City—they generally run US$40 for an afternoon, and are well worth it.*

Encompassing the Río Chagres, part of Lago Gatún, and rich tropical rain forest, Soberanía is the most accessible National Park in Panama, just 40min. from Panama City and with several good trails. It protects the canal's watershed and harbors an abundance of wildlife and a notably diverse assortment of birds: more than 500 species are here, including the endangered harpy eagle, Panama's national bird and the world's most powerful bird of prey.

Stop by the **ranger station,** where rangers collect the admission fee and provide helpful maps. About 10min. toward Gamboa from the station and past the Summit Gardens, **Sendero El Charco** is a well-maintained 4km loop through the forest and

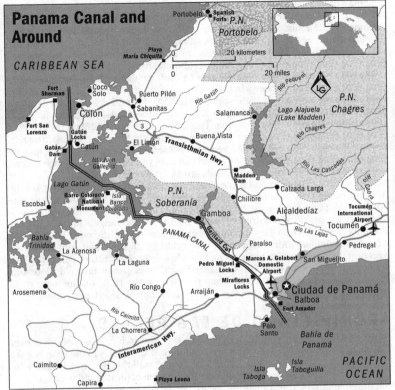

Panama Canal and Around

Not a bad place to camp. The walk takes about an hour and gets crowded on weekends. Fifteen minutes farther along the main road, turn right down a side road onto **Plantation Loop;** follow the blacktop, then the dirt road off the blacktop for a trail that, though mosquito-ridden, weaves through good secondary forest.

The park's longest trail, **Pipeline Road** (Camino de Oleoducto), has the best bird-watching around. To get to the trail, continue on the main road to Gamboa (15min. by bus). Take a look at the awe-inspiring view of the canal from the bridge into town. After walking straight 10min. through town, bear left at the fork and continue 5min. up a dirt road until you see the trail's sign. Strikingly colorful butterflies, howler monkeys, and phenomenal bird life surround this hilly hike. Spanning 17km, it's not easy to hike the entirety in one day. If you don't know a tanager from a tangerine, it might behoove you to get a guide who knows the region's birds.

PARQUE NACIONAL ALTOS DE CAMPANA

Buses heading west on the Interamerican Hwy. can drop you off at the turnoff for the park, and should cost no more than US$1. The main entrance and **ranger station** are 6km up a steep dirt road (Carretera Chicá) from the Interamerican Hwy, where 4WD taxis often pass (US$3). The entrances to the park's trails are all a 1½hr. hike past the station. **Park admission** US$3 per person. Camping US$5 per tent. Open daily 8am-4pm, but rangers are there 24hr. in case of emergency. Whether you plan to camp or hike, check in with the rangers for updates on weather and guided walks (tips appreciated).

Panama's oldest national park is in western Panama Province and extends over 48 sq. km of the Cordillera Central mountain chain. Altos de Campana, 1½hr. from Panama City, is a mix of cloud forest and deforested rolling grasslands. Deforestation has threatened many of the park's animals, but at this elevation (600-1000m) also creates brilliant views of the Pacific, as far as Isla Taboga or the Azuero Peninsula. On the Atlantic side colorful birds abound, from trogons to hummingbirds.

The park's most popular trail, **Sendero La Cruz,** winds uphill for 1hr. to **Cerro La Cruz,** which has the best views in the park. Climb another 30min. to forest-covered **Cerro Campana,** the park's highest point (1007m). From there you can continue another hour, this time downhill, to get back to the road—you'll end up about 15min. uphill from the ranger station. This is the park's most difficult trail, but the cool temperatures, views, and abundance of different birds make it worthwhile. **Sendero Panamá** (1hr., 1.4km) and **Sendero Podocarpus** (30min., 1km) are both considered easy. A ranger truck or 4WD taxi can take you part of the way if you don't want to hike. The entrances to the trails are all 1½hr. past the station.

The park has 6 **refugios** and 2 **camping** areas. To get to the closest refugio from the start of the trails, continue 10min. down the hill and to the right, where concrete wheel tracks head up to the right. There are no beds, but it will keep you dry, and there's a latrine and untreated water nearby. Let the rangers know if you are planning to stay here so they can open it up for you. For a little more comfort and a lot more company, American expat Richard "de Campana" rents out a cool old **house** on the park boundaries and can provide a few meals. Either call his paging service and leave a message for "Richard's Place," or just show up on his doorstep. It's the large white house, 15min. past the sign for the trails on the main road. (☎236 7444. 10 beds US$120 per night; individual suites US$5-10 per person.)

ARCHIPIÉLAGO DE LAS PERLAS

Between 64 and 113km southeast of Panama City, the archipelago consists of over 200 islands, only about 10 of which are inhabited. Most visitors to the islands go to Isla Contadora, the only public island with tourist facilities that aren't strictly for the super-rich. The history of the islands is chock-full of pirates and pearls, including the gigantic 31-carat "Peregrina" pearl, currently owned by Elizabeth Taylor.

ISLA CONTADORA

Contadora, the primary tourist destination in the Archipiélago de las Perlas, may just be paradise on earth. Beneath an intense sun await soft beaches, crystal-clear waters full of rainbow-colored fish, and some of the friendliest, most easy-going people ever assembled in one locale. Like many of Panama's island locales, Contadora is home to increasing tourism developments (witness the "Contadora Mall"), but most of the island is still quite peaceful.

■ TRANSPORTATION. Aeroperlas (☎315 7500) has **flights** from Panama City (Marcos A. Gelabert Airport) to **Contadora,** some via **San Miguel,** on Isla del Rey twice daily on weekdays (25min., 8:30am and 5pm, US$26.25) and four times each on Saturday and Sunday. The planes turn right around and fly back. Aviatur (☎315 0311) has daily flights to and from Contadora for the same price. Expreso del Pacifico (☎261 0350) runs a **launch** once a week from **Muelle 18** in Panama City, leaving Saturday morning and returning Saturday afternoon. (1¾hr., US$20-22.50 depending on the boat.) This boat often only runs during high season; call in advance.)

■ ⊠ ORIENTATION AND PRACTICAL INFORMATION. The airstrip cuts across the entire island on the eastern side. Most tourist facilities cluster around the north end of the airstrip (where the planes stop). Follow the road around the end of the strip and into **Hotel Contadora,** along the brown-and-white fence, to get a free map. Heading up the road on the airstrip's western side leads to a small circle with the **police station,** and, to the right of the radio tower, the new blue-and-white **health center.** (Open M-F 7am-noon and 2-5pm, weekends for emergencies only.) The main **market** is down the hill to the left of the police station. (Open daily 8am-8pm.) **Public phones** are in front of the radio tower and beside the airstrip.

■■ **ACCOMMODATIONS AND FOOD.** Lodging on the island is not cheap unless you camp. Provided you don't build fires, **camping** on the beaches is legal for short periods of time and safe. The cheapest lodging, ■**Cabañas de Contadora** ❸ offers four small suites, each with two rooms and a small kitchen. From the end of the airstrip, bear left at the police station, and continue to bear left for about 1km. Cabañas de Contadora is on your left, just as the road takes a sharp dip down toward the sea. (☎250 4214. Ask for Henri. US$30.) For larger groups (4-6 people), the beach-front **Pacific Perlas Village** ❸ is still partly under construction, although some villas are already available. The colorful villas include kitchen, A/C, and hot baths. The more expensive villas have beautiful views of the sea. The complex also offers a bed and breakfast (US$45, with breakfast US$50). Pacific Perlas is the white-and-brown villas to the north end of the airstrip on the eastern side. (☎250 4240; ammaene@excite.com. English, French, Spanish spoken. Villas for 4 people US$25-40 per person, for 6 people US$22-40 per person.)

The two cheapest restaurants are near the airline offices and the police station, in the "town" on the western side of the airstrip. At the top of the hill is **Restaurante Sagitario** ❶, with a menu of *comida típica.* (US$2-3; open daily 6am-7pm.) A few yards farther down toward the airstrip **Mi Kioskito** ❶ serves ice cream (US$1), beer (US$1), and good US$2-5 fish and pork dishes. (Open daily 9am-9pm, sometimes later.) For a quieter, more romantic atmosphere, try **Gerald's** ❺, on the hill above the entrance to Hotel Contadora. A guitar player serenades diners by candlelight (entrees US$8-24, beers US$1.50). Especially during low season, there is basically **no nightlife,** and many places won't even open unless you warn them in advance.

■ **SUN AND SAND.** With 13 different beaches, it's hard to choose. All beaches are consistently clean, with relatively clear water (except after heavy rain) and gentle currents. At the northern tip of the airstrip is **Playa Galeón,** with coral formations perfect for snorkeling, but often less than secluded due to the looming presence of the nearby Hotel Punta Galeón. In front of the Hotel Contadora, **Playa Larga** is the longest and usually the most crowded. Many of the rental shops and bars along the beach are closed during low season. If you follow Playa Larga south to the end past Hotel Contadora, a small path leads to **Playa de las Suecas,** which has more rocks... and less clothes. It's the only official nude beach in the country. A road branching off the path between Larga and Suecas, leads around the southern end of the airstrip, past the dilapidated former pier to **Playa Cacique.** This gorgeous expanse of sugar-white sand is framed by rocky cliffs and dark blue waters.

The most perfect beach on the island, if not the Pacific, is about a 10min. walk from town. Heading uphill from the airstrip, fork right at the police station, and continue to bear right. Continuing along the road, take a right at the soccer field and the first right past the lake. At the bottom of the hill lies ■**Playa Ejecutiva,** nestled among the cliffs of a turquoise cove; it is now the perfect place to laze through an afternoon, a day, a week, or a year.

■ **WATERSPORTS AND GUIDED TOURS.** Cabañas de Contadora, near Hotel Contadora, rents jetskis (US$15 per 15min.), lends snorkel equipment (free), and runs various tours, including a 1hr. jetski/snorkel tour (US$70) to surrounding islands and a deep-sea fishing tour (US$200 per half day). The owners of Pacific

Perlas also offer sailing trips to surrounding islands on a 44 ft. sailboat (☎250 4240. US$50 per person for 4hr., beer and soda included). Rent diving and snorkeling equipment at **Las Perlas Diving and Aquatic Sports Center** on Playa Larga, and fishing tours and info available from **Salvatore Morello** (☎250 4109); ask for him in town.

COLÓN PROVINCE

Historically, Colón Province has lured people for one reason: money. In the 16th and 17th centuries, the Spanish used the region to transport gold and silver across the Atlantic. In 1948, Panamanian entrepreneurs established what has become the world's second-largest free-trade zone in the city of Colón. What is more noteworthy to the traveler is the legacy of Spanish bullion—some of the highlights of the region include the well-preserved ruins of the forts used by colonists to protect their stashes. At Sabanitas, 10km shy of Colón, the road from Panama City forks—one side continues to Colón, and the other heads to the Caribbean *costa arriba* and seaside Portobelo, home to several fort ruins. Off the coast near Portobelo, the diving and snorkeling of Isla Grande is popular with weekenders. West of the city of Colón, the Gatún Locks are the largest on the Panama Canal.

COLÓN

> Much of daily life in Colón is lived on the street–from balcony musicians to domino games to dumpster-pickers. The city is vibrant and active, but can also be quite dangerous for visitors. Though Colón, like any city, has good and bad areas, most of the good areas are behind the walls of the **Zona Libre.** Most city residents can't even enter unless they have specific business there, and it has its own post office and police force. If you are forced to walk through the city, avoid Calle 8 and Calle 3, as these are some of the worst areas. Extreme caution should be used at all times. In general, it is not advisable to walk on the street, even for just a few blocks. Take taxis whenever possible.

When most Panamanians are asked about Colón, they simply reply, "Don't go there." Poverty, desperation, and danger mark the city, which suffers the highest rate of violent crime in the country. Colón's former elegance has faded throughout the century, as has the hope of its citizens. Muggings occur in broad daylight and most visitors might as well steer clear. The **Zona Libre** (Free Zone), the second-largest duty-free zone in the world (behind Hong Kong), is generally of interest to mass wholesalers. At the city's **yacht club,** where smaller boats wait to pass through the canal, it is often possible to get a crew job on boats heading south.

▐ TRANSPORTATION

Buses: All buses in Colón come and go from the terminal on Calle 13 and Av. Bolívar. Buses leave to: **Coco Solo** (20min., every 15min. 5am-8pm, US$1); **La Guayra** (2½hr., every 2hr. M-Sa 9:30am-5:30pm, Su 10:30am and 3:30pm); **Panama City** (2hr., every 15min. 5am-midnight, US$1.50; express service 1½hr., every 30min. 5am-midnight, US$2); **Portobelo** (1½hr., every 30min. 5am-6pm, US$2) via **Sabanitas** (30min., every 15min. 5am-6pm, US$1).

Flights: France Field airport, also called Enrique A. Jiménez (☎430 6736), lies just southeast of the city. Aeroperlas (☎430 1038) has 6 flights daily to **Panama City** (US$35.70). Taxis are best; take one directly to your accommodation (US$2).

Boats: Linehandler jobs can sometimes be found at **Cristóbal Colón Yacht Club,** a few blocks behind the bus terminal. Boats heading east to **San Blas** or **Colombia** are found at **Puerto Coco Solo,** reachable by bus from the terminal. These trips are negotiated with the vessel captains, but be careful; a number of dangers make it inadvisable to journey from here to Colombia by boat. Drug busts have occurred on such boats, and *Let's Go* does not recommend this method of travel. Smaller, private boats north into San Blas can occasionally be negotiated in Colón or on the Costa Arriba. Marco, who runs Adventure Youth and Traveler's Hostal (see **Accommodations,** below), is a great resource in planning boat trips out of Colón Province.

Train: Train service between Panama City and Colón is scheduled to resume as of August 2002. Once a major passage way for young men seeking gold in California in the mid-1800s, this historical route across the isthmus now provides a more scenic option to get to Colón. Daily trips between the cities are US$25.

✦ 🛈 ORIENTATION AND PRACTICAL INFORMATION

Colón is laid out in a north-south grid pattern on a roughly square piece of land that was once an island, with a bulge in the southeast corner occupied by the **Zona Libre** and a bulge in the southwest that is the former US-occupied area of Cristóbal. The city is connected to the mainland by a bridge from the Zona Libre to the airport, and by a strip of land in the southwest corner. The southwest strip has two main roads running parallel to each other: **Av. Bolívar,** and five blocks east, **Paseo del Centenario,** or **Av. Central.** In general, *avenidas* and *paséos* run north-south, and numbered *calles* run east-west, from Calle 1 in the north to Calle 16 in the south. **Av. Amador Guerrero,** between Bolívar and Central, has some budget eating and lodging in a *relatively* better neighborhood, from Calle 9 to Calle 12. The massive **Colón 2000** shopping center is on the east side of town at the end of Calles 13-18. The **yacht club** is in the southwest, near the bus station.

Tourist Information: IPAT (☎441 9644), on Calle 13 in Edificio del Correo, next to the **Registro Civil** and near Port Cristóbal. Through the black gate at the corner of the building, 1st glass door on the left. Open M-F 8:30am-4:30pm.

Banks: Several cluster just north of **IPAT** and all over the Zona Libre. **Banco General** (☎441 7301), at Av. del Frente (all the way west) and Calle 10, has an **ATM,** but it's dangerous to walk out of it unless you have a taxi waiting right there.

Western Union: Various locations. Across from Banco General on Av. del Frente and in the Colón 2000 complex. Open M-F 8:30am-12:30pm and 1:30-5:30pm, Sa 9am-12:30pm. Also in Zona Libre.

Supermarket: Several, including **Super 99** in Colón 2000.

Laundry: Many, including **Lavamático/Lavandería Luis N-2,** on Av. Guerrero near Calle 11, next to several hotels and restaurants. Open M-Sa 7am-8pm, Su 7am-6pm. It's safest to use hotel laundry services (around US$5 for a load) or not do laundry here.

Police: Main station (☎441 5833, emergencies 104), Av. Meléndez, 4 blocks east of Av. Central, on Calle 11. Also in Zona Libre (☎441 4036).

Hospital: Hospital Manuel A. Guerrero (hospital and ambulances ☎441 5077), Paseo Gorgas (all the way east) and Calle 10. Pretty run-down, but works for emergencies.

Pharmacy: Farmacia Galencia (☎441 4683), on Av. Guerrero and Calle 11. Open M-Sa 8am-11pm, Su 8am-7pm.

Post Office: On Calle 9, around the corner from IPAT. Open M-Sa 7am-6pm.

PANAMA

▛ ACCOMMODATIONS

Lodgings ranging from budget to classy cluster around Av. Guerrero and Calles 10 and 11, near restaurants, the pharmacy, and the laundromat. The town's only budget hostel is more removed, but the following options have advantages in security.

Adventure Youth and Traveler's Hostel (☎685 6347; marcossailing@yahoo.ca), #37 on Calle 5 in the upscale enclave of Nuevo Cristóbal. A family home with two bare but comfortable shared rooms. The owner **Marco Polito** is well-connected in the local shipping and sailing world and eager to help plan boat trips. US$6 per bed. ❶

Pensión Acrópolis (☎441 1456), on the corner of Guerrero and Calle 11. The best cheap place in town. Rooms come with a sink, fan, desk, and solid bed. Gate is locked at night. Across the street from 2 budget restaurants and next to a bakery. Communal bath is small and lacking in water pressure but gets the job done. Rooms US$6.50. ❶

Hotel Sotelo (☎441 7703), on Guerrero and 11, across the street from Acrópolis. Great value for quality accommodations. Cable TV, A/C, phones, bright private baths, wood paneling, and an icebox in every hall. Everyone must pass the front desk to get inside. Restaurant on the ground floor (see below). Singles US$22; doubles US$30. V/MC. ❸

Hotel Carlton (☎447 0349; fax 447 0114), on Av. Meléndez and Calle 10. One of the 2 best hotels in the city. With the extra cash comes a great location near the Zona Libre, peace of mind, and many amenities. In-house restaurant, pharmacy (open 8am-2am), and laundry. Singles US$35; doubles US$40; triples US$45; suite US$55. ❹

▛ FOOD

Eat at or near your hotel if possible. Though restaurants abound all over the city, the following are near or inside the accommodations listed above.

Restaurant Sotelo, on the bottom floor of the Hotel Sotelo. A loud, active atmosphere with the best sandwiches in the city, if not the country. Ham and egg sandwich US$1.50; chicken and rice US$3.75. Open Su-F 8am-9:30pm. ❶

Cafetería Nacional (☎445 2403), on the corner of Guerrero and 11, catty-corner from Acrópolis. Cool interior and English menu with a large selection. Chicken soup US$1.50; sandwiches US$1.75-3.25; full meals US$3-6. Open M-Sa 7am-10pm. ❶

Restaurante Carlton, on the bottom floor of the hotel. More expensive, but a huge choice of international foods including Italian, Middle Eastern, and veg. options. Veg. fried rice US$4.50, seafood US$7-14. Open M-Sa 6:30am-10pm, Su 1-10pm. ❸

▛ DAYTRIPS FROM COLÓN

GATÚN LOCKS AND GATÚN DAM

*From the main **bus** terminal in Colón, catch a bus to **Cuipo** or **Costa Abajo** (both 20min., every hr. 5am-10pm, US$1) and get off either right before crossing the locks or 5min. down the road at the dam. From the locks' bus stop, head up the hill alongside the locks to the **Visitors Center**, the white building with the Panamanian flag. (Open daily 8am-4pm.) To reach the dam, wait for the next bus (US$0.25) or walk (20min.). For the impressive walk, cross the locks and go left after the gate. When the road forks to the right, follow it all the way to the dam. Fairly frequent buses head back toward Colón 5am-11pm.*

Just 10km south of Colón, Gatún Locks and Dam make a good half-day trip. The **Gatún Locks,** on the northern end of the Panama Canal, raise and lower ships a total of 26m between the Caribbean and Lago Gatún. There are three pairs of locks and the two locks in each pair allow simultaneous passage of two ships in opposing directions. The unique characteristic of the Gatún Locks is the small bridge that allows cars and buses to pass across the canal, which brings visitors within meters of the enormous locks as vehicles travel along the bottom of the great metal gates. The Visitors Center, a tower above the middle lock, has a great view of the boats passing through the entire length of the locks (almost 2km) as well as Lago Gatún. Only by seeing the chambers empty of water can you truly appreciate their monstrous size. By the entrance is one of the retired *mulas*, the electric locomotives that pull each ship through the locks. Ships pass through 24hr. a day.

Gatún Dam, 2km away, was the largest earthen dam in the world when it was built in 1906. Over 800m wide and 2km in length, the dam formed the largest artificial body of water in the world, Lago Gatún. The dam's construction caused Río Chagres to flood, covering villages, the Panama Railroad, and 262 sq. km of forest.

FORT SAN LORENZO

*The fort is not accessible by public transportation. It is possible to take a **taxi** from Colón, but drivers dislike making the 1hr. trip because there are no emergency facilities. Expect to pay US$40 or more (including round-trip fare and exploring time); be sure to agree on the price beforehand.*

The faster of the two original trans-isthmian routes for Spanish colonial gold was overland from Panama City to Las Cruces and then by water down the Río Chagre to the Caribbean. North of the river, on a high point overlooking the river and the sea, the Spanish built Fort San Lorenzo to protect their gold and silver against pirates. Apparently their plans didn't work out so well; the fort was sacked three times, most notably in 1671 by the Welsh pirate Henry Morgan, who then sailed up the Chagres and routed Panamá Viejo. The beautiful, haunting ruins encompass moats, walls, and a row of cannons. Fort Sherman, a former US base now in Panamanian hands, stands in between Gatún Locks and San Lorenzo, and is closed while its future is debated (it may become the base for a National Park). Since San Lorenzo is so difficult to access, the ruins in Portobelo may be a better option.

PORTOBELO

Verdant hills gently bend down through Spanish ruins to meet azure Caribbean waters in a combination that creates the quiet allure of this "beautiful port." For 200 years, it was the commercial center of the Spanish colonies, where the Spanish built forts as bulwarks against pirates and the English navy to protect outgoing gold supplies. Today the ruins of the forts are one of the main tourist attractions of the area. Diving, snorkeling, ruins, the patron saint, and a mix of Panamanian and Caribbean cultures are also golden, drawing crowds to Portobelo. Attendance swells during the winter months, but in mid-summer Portobelo enters a deep, dreamless sleep, and many establishments may be partly or completely shuttered.

▄ TRANSPORTATION. To get to Portobelo, take a *ruta* bus from Panama City toward Colón (1-2hr., US$1); A faster but slightly costlier option is to take any Colón bus from the main bus terminal (these often have A/C and movies (1½ hr., US$2). In either case, ask your driver to drop you off at **Sabanitas** (look for shops with "Sabanitas" signboards, or for the new McDonald's on the left side of the road and the pedestrian bridge overhead). From the turn-off in front of the El Rey supermarket, catch a bus marked **"Portobelo"** or **"Costa Arriba"** (1hr., every 15-30min. 6:30am-9pm, US$1). Returning from Portobelo, buses travel down the main road toward **Colón** (1-2hr., every 30min. 4:30am-6pm, US$1) via **Sabanitas,** where you can catch buses heading to **Panama City.**

⛏🏄 ORIENTATION AND PRACTICAL INFORMATION. Portobelo itself is 22km east of Sabanitas, but the dive shops and higher-class establishments lie a few kilometers before the town on the main road. To go directly to one of these places, get off the bus when you see the "Scuba Portobelo" or "Diver's Haven" sign on your left. From the first dive shop along the road, Diver's Haven, the tiny town is a 30min. walk east along the main road past the ruins of Santiago de la Gloria.

There are few services, but there is a pleasant, friendly IPAT office (☎448 2200) 20m to the left of the **aduana** (the large old tan building on the *parque central* in the center of town). Open M-F 8am-4pm. There are several **mercaditos**—two near the *parque central* and two between the two dive shops. The **medical clinic** (☎448 2033) is near the town center toward the church, and the **police** (☎448 2038) are next to the Diver's Haven entrance, 2km west on the main road.

🏠🍴 ACCOMMODATIONS AND FOOD. There are four options for accommodations in Portobelo, only one of which is actually in town. Above **La Aduana ❷** bar on the *parque* are four tidy singles and doubles, each with a sink, fan, cement walls, and access to a small shared bathroom (US$10 per person). Inquire about rooms in the bar. Along the road west of town are a hotel and two dive shops that offer co-ed dorm rooms. A 25min. walk from town are **Cabañas El Mar ❸** (☎448 2102). Big, pretty doubles with fan are US$30, while quads with A/C are US$35. Five minutes past El Mar on the way into town, **Diver's Haven ❷**, right behind the police station, offers concrete dormitory rooms, most with four beds per room, and a large shared bathroom. (☎448 2914. US$10 per person. English spoken.)

The cheap eats are in town, while larger menus, more ambience, and higher prices are on the road west. Seafood is the specialty of the area, but most restaurants also offer non-seafood options. When business is slow, restaurants tend to close earlier than posted. For conch and other Caribbean delights, try **Restaurante Los Cañones ❸**, two minutes west of Scuba Portobelo. Named after the rusting cannons that dot the Portobelo region, the restaurant has a great atmosphere and a view of the bay. (Seafood with salad and rice US$6-8. Open M-F 11am-10pm, Sa-Su 8am-10pm. MC/V.) In town, there are several cheap restaurants within one block of the *parque*. **Restaurante La Torre ❷**, two minutes west of the police station on the road out of town, serves seafood and beer in the well-lit dining room or on a cool terrace. (US$4.50-6. Open M-F 10am-7pm, Sa-Su 7:30am-8pm.)

📷 SIGHTS. Portobelo boasts at least nine major ruins of old **Spanish forts**, along with others interspersed among the town's houses. **Santiago de la Gloria,** on both sides of the road just before entering town, comprises a number of evocative ruins and makes for an excellent spot to wander or just lounge about. Its tremendous walls, cannons, moats, and dark hallways beckon intrigued travelers. **San Geronimo,** with cannons, vultures, and a harbor view, rests behind the *aduana* (see below) near the ocean. **San Fernando,** with a great view and an intact colonial bathroom, is across the bay (catch a boat at the dock behind Fort Santiago for a 5 min. ride, US$2 each way). Be sure to arrange a pickup time for the return, allowing yourself half an hour to an hour to explore. The **Iron Castle** (a.k.a. **San Felipe** or **Todo Fierro**) once guarded the entrance to the harbor, but it was dismantled earlier this century to provide stones for the Gatún locks of the Panama Canal and the breakwater at Colón. Other, less complete fortresses in the area, including **Punta Farnese, La Matrinchera,** and **La Batería de Buenaventura,** crowd along the ocean.

El Nazareno, the sacred statue of Christ carrying the crucifix, rests in the large, white church of San Felipe, one block east of the *parque* (see **Festivals,** below). The **aduana** (royal customs house), built in 1630 out of the same coral reef blocks used for the forts, recently underwent a joint Panamanian-Spanish restoration effort. It now houses a modest **museum** on the second floor. One room has a collection of replicated colonial weapons, and the other displays scores of purple cloaks worn by El Nazareno (The statue is dressed in a new, luxuriously decorated cloak each year). (Free. Open M-F 8am-4pm, Sa-Su 8am-5pm.)

FESTIVALS. The El Nazareno statue first arrived in Portobelo in 1646 en route to Cartagena, Colombia. During a furious storm, the ship captain tossed everything overboard, including a statue of christ. Miraculously, the cholera epidemic that had been ravaging Portobelo disappeared when fishermen recovered the statue and brought it to town. On October 21, as the last 40 men were healed, they carried the statue around town on a heavy platform. This same procession, with the steps now ritualized, occurs throughout the year, notably for **Cristo Negro** on October 21, when thousands of purple-robed, black-faced believers descend on Portobelo to celebrate. Another lively celebration is the performance of the **congo,** an upbeat Afro-Caribbean dance performed during *Carnaval* (November 25). Women wear long dresses and men decorate themselves with bottles, old radios, and just about anything else. Then they take turns dancing with the *rey* and *reina* (king and queen). As part of the ritual, participants walk and talk backwards.

WATERSPORTS. Portobelo's diving isn't stellar, but it is cheap and offers some great wreck-dives. Beautiful **beaches** and prime **diving** and **snorkeling** are a short boat ride away—the dive shops are happy to take you. **Scuba Portobelo,** the only shop still in full operation, offers rides to nearby beaches (US$5-10), 2-dive days (with divemaster and equipment US$50), and a PADI-certification class including full equipment and lodging (4-5 days US$150). They also rent snorkel equipment. A popular spot is **Salmedina Reef,** a 3m deep reef featuring a shipwreck, complete with cannons and anchors. The region's coral reefs are full of the remnants of the many naval battles fought above. Sir Francis Drake was buried at sea here, and his lead coffin is somewhere on the bottom, still undiscovered.

ISLA GRANDE

Isla Grande, 20km east of Portobelo and just 100m off the coast, is busy compared to most other Panamanian islands in the Caribbean—active villagers and vacationing mainland families splash around and relax until late at night. The island offers good surfing and even some peaceful moments, but most of all a chance to kick back and have a cocktail on the beach with locals and north-coast Panameños.

TRANSPORTATION. During daylight hours, **boats** travel frequently between Isla Grande and **La Guayra,** the closest mainland town (5min., US$1). Buses to La Guayra leave **Colón** (M-Sa every 2hr. 9:30am-5:30pm, Su 10:30am and 3:30pm; US$3), passing through **Sabanitas** (connect here to and from Panama City) and **Portobelo** (1hr., US$1 to La Guayra). Buses return from La Guayra (daily 8, 9am, 1pm).

PRACTICAL INFORMATION. Directly in front of the main dock sits a green building called **Bodega Jackson.** The store has a large selection of liquor and a few groceries. Facing inland, walk 100m to the right to find a **medical clinic, Sub-Centro de Salud** (open M-F 8am-4pm, emergencies only after 4pm), next to a **public phone.**

ACCOMMODATIONS AND FOOD. Most places to stay here are either modest, bland buildings in the village or busy vacation complexes on the outskirts. The sprawl of concrete hotels at the western end of the island is crowded and overpriced, but the sheer number of rooms may allow you to negotiate a steal.

Prices at all accommodations can shoot up during high season (Nov.-Apr.), and during Panamanian work or school vacations. **Cabañas Cholita ❸** caters mostly to mainland vacationers and their kids, with a common patio, mini-boardwalk, bar, and restaurant. A few rooms have a balcony and harbor view. (☎448 2962. Singles US$20; doubles with A/C and private bath US$30.) **Villa Ensueño ❸**, next door, has similar rooms at slightly higher rates. **Sister Moon ❹**, a complex of beautiful *cabañas* spread along the hill a short kilometer east of town (follow the path around the rocky point), overlooks the main set of surfing breaks on the island. The beach here is rocky, but the surf is decent and the bar is well-stocked. (☎448 2182; www.hotel-sistermoon.com. *Cabañas* US$50, with ocean view US$60.) **Cabañas Jackson ❷**, behind Bodega Jackson, has clean, comfy *cabañas* (cabins) with private baths, but not always hot water. (Doubles with fan US$20; triples with A/C US$35; 6-person cabins with A/C US$50.) Next to Cabañas Jackson, **Candy Rose ❸** offers clean cabins with private baths at similar prices. Residents of the island sometimes rent out rooms (around US$15-25). Ask around or look for the occasional sign. Facilities and privacy are often limited, and security can be less than ideal. For the cheapest option, **camp** on the beach. (Free; bring mosquito net.)

Pleasant, open-air restaurants line the center of the island and serve average coastal *típico*. The best value is **Restaurante Teletón ❶**, two buildings east of Sub-Centro de Salud. Seafood with *patacones* or coconut rice is US$2-3.50. There's usually a good crowd at **Villa Ensueño ❷**, 5min. east of the dock (*comida* US$2.50-6). Five minutes west of the dock is a local favorite, **Rotisería Esperanza ❶**, a restaurant and pool hall on a patio over the water (half chicken US$2.50).

Nightlife on Isla Grande consists primarily of sitting around talking or splashing around laughing, with a constant flow of cocktails facilitating both. **Ensueño** and **Cholita** (see above) both run bars popular with vacationers and play loud Panamanian Top-40 (or nothing at all). For a few more locals, an enormous range of drinks, and an unbroken stream of dub and reggae, stop by **Punta Prou** (aka Pupy's), an inviting thatch structure just east of the clinic.

🏄🛶 **ISLAND ACTIVITIES.** For a view of the ocean and the northern islands, climb to the lighthouse on top of the island. Walk about 15min. east from the main dock until the path splits at the surfers' beach. Turn left and continue up the rough path for about 15min. You can't enter the lighthouse itself, but just past it is a small **lookout** point. Wear adequate shoes; it can get slippery during the rainy season.

Other than **surfing, snorkeling** is the activity of choice, especially on the reef in front of Villa Ensueño, where schools of fish gather around a striking black Christ (on the cross) in the water. The crucifix stands near a breach in the reef where the current is strong. For better, though less accessible reefs, follow the path west until you reach the point of the beach. Then swim 200m across the inlet toward the pink house on the hill. Beware: this can be a hard swim. In front of the house are the best reefs on the island. **Villa Ensueño** (☎448 2964) rents snorkeling equipment (US$2.50 per hr.), while **Centro de Buceo** (☎448 2298; beeper 263 5044), 100m west of the dock, has snorkeling and scuba gear and offers scuba courses.

COCLÉ PROVINCE

With intense rain forest in the highlands and a friendly rural atmosphere along the coast, this region is an important part of Panama's breadbasket. Grains and sugar dominate the fertile lowland plain and coffee and fruit reign on the mountain slopes. Weekend visitors escape the city to flood El Valle's Sunday market, birdwatch in Parque Nacional Omar Torrijos, or peek into the Iglesia de Natá.

EL VALLE

Seated in the crater of a volcano which last erupted 35 million years ago, El Valle is a pleasant village set in a well-groomed nature paradise. It offers easy access to day hikes to powerful waterfalls or the distant mountains that form the giant silhouette of the sleeping India Dormida. Situated 27km north of San Carlos and the Interamerican Hwy., El Valle is also a weekend and summer home for well-off *panameños*. With its beautiful sites, the village is a popular destination and perfect weekend trip. Go during the week for better prices and availability.

TRANSPORTATION

Buses: Often fill up in El Valle; it's best to catch them at the market. Buses run by TUVASA (☎983 6446) and head down the main road to **Panama City** (2½hr., every hr. 4am-3pm, US$3.50). To get anywhere later in the day, take the buses heading to **San Carlos** (45min., every 30min. 6am-7pm, US$1) on the Interamerican Hwy. From there, you can catch buses going just about everywhere. The **La Mesa** bus runs west past the waterfalls (5min., every 30min. 6am-7pm, US$0.25).

Local buses: Buses marked "La Campaña-El Hato" loop through the town's few streets (US$0.25).

Taxis: Easy to find and should never cost more than US$2.

ORIENTATION AND PRACTICAL INFORMATION

The main road enters town from the east and runs west. The open *mercado* is in the middle of town. Generally, sights are to the west and lodgings to the east.

Tourist Office: IPAT (☎983 6474), with helpful maps. Unreliably open Tu-Su 8am-4pm.

Banks: There are **no banks**; there is an **ATM** on the corner of Av. Principal and the street to El Níspero. Cirrus/Plus/MC/V.

Supermarket: Supercentro Yin, across the street from the *mercado*. Open daily 8am-noon and 1-7pm.

Laundry: Lavamático Mary, ½km east of *mercado*. Open M-Sa 8am-5pm, Su 8am-1pm.

Public Bathrooms: Hotel Don Pepe (see **Accommodations,** below). US$0.25.

Police: (☎983 6222 or 104), down the road to El Níspero.

Health Clinic: Centro de Salud (☎983 6112), down the street behind the church. 24hr. assistance available.

Internet: Email at **FSR Technology Systems** (☎983 6688), next to Lavamático Mary. US$2 per hr. M-Sa 8am-5pm, Su 9am-1pm.

Post office: Behind the *mercado*. Open M-F 8am-4pm.

ACCOMMODATIONS AND FOOD

In response to weekend crowds from Panama City, *cabañas* and hotels are opening up all over town, though most are not budget. You can **camp** unofficially in the woods to the west of town, but there are no facilities. **Restaurants** cluster all along the main road. The **bakery** across from the church offers cheap baked goods.

Hotel y Restaurante La Niña Delia (☎983 6110), just down the block and across the street from the Lavamático. These newly renovated rooms are squeaky clean. *Comedor* in the back serves *típico* for US$1.75. Rooms sleep 2 for US$8; 4 for US$12. ❶

Santa Librada (☎983 6376), a few hundred meters east of the *mercado,* down a short pathway behind the restaurant. One bare-bones cell and a couple of rooms with TV and private baths. The restaurant in front serves great desserts, seafood, and meat dishes (US$2-7.50). Basic rooms US$6, with TV and bath US$20, Apr.-Nov. US$15. ❶

Hotel Don Pepe (☎983 6425), across from Supercentro Yin, caters to families. Huge, gorgeous rooms sleep up to 5, and include fan, TV, and clean, new, private hot-water baths. Restaurant serves *típico* for US$2.50-4. Rooms M-Th US$25, F-Su US$50. ❸

Apartamentos El Valle (☎264 2272). Hang a left just past the *mercado,* up the road on the left before Calle los Millonarios. Apartment-style rooms with living room, cable TV, hot water, A/C, pools, and jacuzzis. Some have kitchens. Largest apartments sleep up to 12. Doubles US$39; quads with kitchen US$69; US$5 for each additional person. ❹

Panama Campsite (☎983 6750), far to the west of town. Take a taxi from the *mercado* to the campsite (US$2). More of a complex than a simple campsite, El Valle's first official camping facilities include bathrooms, hot water, Internet, kitchen, and bicycle and ATV rentals. Count on s'mores by the nightly campfires. Call owner Arturo Carreño to reserve a day ahead. Tents US$5; air mattresses US$5; use of kitchen US$2. ❶

👁 🏔 SIGHTS AND OUTDOOR ACTIVITIES

To get to the sights, follow the blue signs that lead from the main road toward the west. The best hiking is in the woods west of town.

PIEDRA PINTADA

Hop on the La Mesa bus at the mercado or walk 20min. to the western end of the main road. When the paved road ends near some kiosks, take the path to the left, but don't cross the 1st bridge. Instead, follow the river 200m and cross there; the 10m-high rock is 5min. farther up the path. For the waterfall, continue along the path past the petroglyphs, sticking to the river. After about 10min., you'll see it on the right. Guide US$0.50-1.

Petroglyphs adorn this giant rock. Nearby is a splendid **waterfall,** less famous but more accessible than El Macho. Near the top of the falls is a small grotto with a mini-cascade of its own. On weekends, local school boys act as guides (in Spanish only) to the *piedra* and give a history and explanation of the petroglyphs. Created by the original inhabitants of the town, the petroglyphs are a map of El Valle, and tell the story of the struggle against the Spaniards during the 16th century.

EL MACHO

The La Mesa bus will take you there, but it's walkable in 30min.; follow the signs from the western end of the main road. Refugio ☎983 6547. Admission US$2. Open daily 8am-4pm. Admission and guided hike US$10. 3hr. guided hike US$15 per person. Canopy Adventures ☎983 6547. US$40 per person. Short canopy tour US$10. Natural bathing pool US$2.

To view this waterfall, guides lead a great 5min. hike via suspended log walkways overlooking the Río Guayago (the water source for El Valle) and lush primary forest. From a platform 20m away, the 36m high cascade is very impressive. A 3hr. hike through the surrounding **Refugio Ecológico Chorro El Macho** brings you to the top of the falls. The refuge also runs **Canopy Adventures,** which allows fearless tourists to see the falls and surrounding forests while speeding along a zipline.

LA INDIA DORMIDA. Legend has it that when an *indígena* maiden, Flor del Aire, fell in love with a conquering Spaniard, her previous lover killed himself. The girl, tormented and disgraced, wandered into the hills to die, lying down to stare forever at the skies. With a little imagination, her silhouette can be deciphered in the hills to the west. The more difficult of two trails takes you to her head, where you can explore some small caves full of bats. Follow the signs to Piedra Pintada at the western end of town. From the rock, continue on the trail for 1hr., staying on the south side of the river until you get to the top. The hike is steep, but cuts through incredible forest and has amazing views. The other way up is less steep and less exciting; head to the western end of the main road and bear left after the small bridge. At the first street, turn right, then left when you see a brightly painted school on your left. The walk continues for about 1hr. up La India's arm to the top.

EL NÍSPERO. El Níspero, the local botanical gardens and zoo, houses capybaras, *titi* monkeys, iguanas, scarlet macaws, giant sleeping tapirs, and leopards. *(1km north down the road by the ATM; the first right after the fire station. ☎ 983 6142. Open daily 7am-5pm. US$2, children US$1.)*

POZOS TERMALES. After a long day hiking, relax in the hot springs, natural pools, and mudbaths. Picnic at the tables nearby. *(Turn south at the sign at the west end of town and walk 10min. past houses to the entrance. Open daily 8am-5pm. US$1, children US$0.50.)*

SUNDAY ARTS FAIR. The Sunday Arts Fair takes place in the **Mercado El Valle.** Artisans swarm in from surrounding farms to sell sculpted pots, soapstone trays, intricately woven chairs, and more. The rest of the week the market sells fresh produce. *(Open M-Sa 7am-4pm, Su 7am-2pm.)*

PENONOMÉ

This provincial capital was once important enough to be the capital of the country, after the sacking of Panamá Viejo. Now it is only known as *the* place to buy the famous Panama hats—though fashion historians agree that the hat actually hails from Montecristi, Ecuador. Other than a good selection of hats, Penonomé is a rather unappealing transportation and service hub for the rest of the province.

⌐ TRANSPORTATION. **Buses** leave from the **terminal** on the Interamerican Hwy. across from the Esso station to **Panama City** (2½hr., every hr. 4:30am-7pm, US$3.75). Buses coming from Panama City and heading to **Chitré, Santiago,** and **David** stop if you wave them down (every hr. to Chitre and Santiago; more frequently to David). Sometimes these buses stop at **Restaurante Universal,** 300m east of the Esso gas station on the Interamerican Hwy.; check there first as fares can be slightly less. **Local minibuses** head to local destinations including **Aguadulce** (US$1.50); **Caño** (US$1); **Chiguiri Arriba** (US$1.50); **El Copé** (US$1.50); **El Valle** (US$2.50); **La Pintada** (US$0.70). They leave regularly from behind the Mercado Público, two blocks southeast of the *parque* on Av. Guerrero. Buses to **Playa Farallón** (US$1.50) leave from Supercentro El Combate on Av. Principal.

⌘🖪 ORIENTATION AND PRACTICAL INFORMATION. Central Penonomé lies about 1km north of the Interamerican Hwy. The town is connected to the highway by the main street, **Av. Juan Demostenes Arosemena,** known as **Av. Principal,** which runs northwest from an Esso station on the highway. Principal ends at the church. On the opposite side of the *parque,* **Av. Amador Guerrero** runs parallel to Principal, merging with it about halfway to the highway at the Delta gas station.

Four **banks** with **ATMs** crowd the Interamerican, but **Banco Nacional de Panamá,** at the merger of Av. Guerrero and Av. Principal, is the only one that changes traveler's checks other than American Express. **Western Union** is located on Av. Principal in the Casa Peter building. (Open M-F 9am-noon and 1-5pm, Sa 9am-1pm.) The top of Av. Guerrero is packed with **grocery stores. SuperCentro Coclé,** at the highway next to the Hotel Dos Continentes, has a **pharmacy.** (Open M-Sa 8am-9:30pm, Su 8am-6:30pm.) The only laundromat is **Lavamático Central,** just past CITA on the same side on Av. Central. (☎ 997 8333. US$0.50 to wash or dry. Open M-Sa 7am-7pm.) Primarily a jail, the **police** station (☎ 997 8430 or 104) is on the northwest end of the *parque*. The new **Hospital Aquilano Tejeira** (☎ 997 8455) is on the Interamerican Hwy., east of the bus station. **Internet access** is available at **CITA**, about a block up Av. Principal on the right. (☎ 996 1846. US$3 per hr. Open M-F 8:30am-6:30pm.) The **post office** is around the corner from the police, at the top of Av. Principal behind the church. (Open M-F 8am-4pm.)

▐▌ ACCOMMODATIONS AND FOOD. New hotels are popping up around the town center, and along the Interamerican Hwy. **Residencial El Paisa ❷** lies on Av. Guerrero, one block off the *parque*. Rooms have two beds, a fan, and a private bath with full-size towels. (☎ 997 9242. Singles US$8; doubles US$16.) **Hotel Dos Continentes ❸** is across from the bus terminal. Rooms come with fan or A/C, TV, hot water, phone, and private balcony. (☎ 997 9326; fax 997 9390. Singles with fan US$16; 1-bed doubles with A/C US$25; 2-bed doubles US$33; triples US$34.)

Many locals recommend **Gallo Pinto ❶** as the best and cheapest *típico* around, with locations at the bus station and on Av. Principal behind the Esso station. (Meals US$1.65. Open daily 6am-9pm.) For *típico* in an a-*típico* atmosphere, try **Restaurante Las Tinajas ❶**, across the Interamerican Hwy., just west of the bus terminal in a thatched tiki lounge. (Meals US$2-3. Open daily 7am-10pm.) For *emparedados* (grilled sandwiches), try the **panadería ❶** to the left of the Super-Centro. (US$0.75-1.50. Open daily 6am-7pm.)

▣▐ SIGHTS AND SHOPPING. Commune with nature by taking the Chiguiri Arriba bus from the **Mercado Público** to get to the **Albergue Ecológico La Iguana**, a haven for regional wildlife. Alternatively, grab a bus to Panama City or El Valle and get off in **Playa Farallón** or **Playa Santa Clara** to soak in the sun. Farallón is the former site of one of Noriega's Panama Defense Force bases. At the beginning of Operation Just Cause, it became the first combat target ever of the new US F-117A stealth fighters. You can still see the runway from the Interamerican.

The finer and tighter the braid, the better and more expensive the **hat**. Start outside the Shell station, west of the Esso. Across the highway, the **Mercado de Arte-sanías Coclé** has hats along with other woven whatnots. (Open daily 8:30am-4:30pm.) The nearby town **La Pintada** is home to the **Artesanía de Sombreros**, where they sell—yes—hats. Take the La Pintada bus (US$0.70) from behind the **Mercado Público** and get off at (then cross) the soccer field in the town.

NEAR PENONOMÉ

▲ PARQUE NACIONAL OMAR TORRIJOS HERRERA

*To get to El Copé, take a bus from the Mercado Público in Penonomé (1hr., every hr. 6am-5pm, US$1.50). Or, take any bus along the Interamerican Hwy., get off at the turnoff for El Copé, and wait for the next northbound bus into town (45min., every 30min. 6am-6pm, US$1). In El Copé, go to **park headquarters** at the uphill end of the main road, for information and possibly a ride to the park. (☎ 983 9089; open M-F 8am-4pm, but call ahead because rangers are often in the park.) Barring a ride from friendly rangers, look for a chivita (minibus) bound for **Barrigón**, the last community before the park entrance (20min., every hr. 6am-7pm, US$0.30). Call ahead for a 4WD taxi from Barrigón to the park entrance. (☎ 983 9077. US$5.) From the van's last stop, it's a steep 30min. hike to the park's main entrance, ranger station, refugio, and cabañas. To get to **La Rica** and the Navas family residence, rendezvous with a member of the family at their home in Barrigón. (☎ 983 9130. US$20 per day includes lodging, 3 meals, and guided hikes of your choice.) Ask the driver of the van from El Copé to let you off at la casa de Navas. Park* *admission US$3; camping US$5; refugio US$5 per person; cabañas US$15 per person (negotiable for groups). For all lodging, notify the rangers at least 5 days ahead.*

Straddling the continental divide in northern Coclé, Parque Nacional Omar Torrijos Herrera, known to locals for its nearby village **El Copé**, protects 253 sq. km of four different forest zones. The park also houses large tracts of primary forest and watersheds, home to many species of birds and frogs found nowhere else in Panama. Scientists can often be found staying in one of the *refugios* while collecting samples. Despite its beauty and proximity to Panama City, the park remains mostly unknown to tourists, allowing visitors to experience both pristine nature and rural Panamanian lifestyles in the remote communities.

Accessible from **El Copé** (just west of Penonomé), the park entrance is near **Cerro El Calvario** (a.k.a. El Aserradero), on the continental divide. Near the **ranger station** is a camping platform and a refugio with bathrooms and running water (bring a warm sleeping bag, as temperatures can drop to 12°C at night). The camping platform affords gorgeous views of the valleys below, as do two short trails. The newly constructed *cabaña* has two bunk beds, solar-powered energy, a hot-water bathroom, a full kitchen with gas stove, a living room, and attic space for sleeping. Much of the furniture is made by local artisans, creating an elegantly rustic setting. Wide, easy **Sendero Los Helechos** is a 30min. loop. It has been made accessible for hikers of any level, through the installation of wooden hand rails, stairs, and path demarcations. For more of a challenge, take **Sendero La Rana**, which winds down to an idyllic mountain creek (30min.). Ask the rangers about more ambitious undertakings, such as a day-long hike to **Cerro Marta**, the park's highest point.

A 1½hr. hike beyond the entrance leads to **La Rica**, a village of 40 or so families who farm and raise cattle in the middle of the park under ANAM's watchful eye. The community offers the opportunity to stay with a local family and experience rural Panamanian life, while exploring the park's dense inner reaches. The **Navas** families are great hosts, providing lodging, meals, and guided hikes.

PARQUE ARQUEOLÓGICO DEL CAÑO

*Any **bus** on the Interamerican will drop you off at the entrance to El Caño village; sometimes the chivitas will drive 1km into town to the park's driveway. From here, follow the signs—it's a 25min. walk to the entrance. Otherwise, you can get a US$3 **taxi** from Natá (see below) or a US$1 taxi from the Interamerican. Open Tu-Sa 9am-4pm, Su 9am-1pm. Adults US$1, students and children US$0.25. Bring protection against mosquitoes.*

The most notable pre-Columbian site in Panama pales in comparison to those elsewhere in Central America, but makes an interesting break from a long Interamerican trip. A sacred burial ground is part of the remnants of the Nató nation, named after their *cacique* (chief) Nató. There are burials on display, which have been excavated from the large funerary mounds, and it is estimated that there are hundreds more in the surrounding area. Near the burials stand the ruins of what is thought to have been a solar calendar. A small **museum** has stone and ceramic artwork dated between AD800-1500. See the mural and captions inside for a glimpse of Nató life and their first contact with Europeans.

NATÁ

Natá holds the **Basílica Menor Santiago Apóstol de Natá,** thought to be the oldest church still in use in the Americas. The church was completed in 1522, though the regal white facade was renovated in 1998. Pre-conquest Natá was a huge *indígena* town, first discovered by **Gaspar de Espinosa** in 1517. Natá comes alive on July 25, when locals celebrate the **Fiesta de Santiago el Apóstol** with parties and processions. **Hotel Rey David** ❸ (☎993 5149), on the main road just behind the cheap

Supermercado Vega on the Interamerican, has very new rooms with all the amenities (US$18). Buses along the Interamerican will stop here (from Penonomé 45min., US$1.50; from Chitré 1¼hr., US$2.50).

AZUERO PENINSULA

The Azuero Peninsula is Panama's heartland, the center and origin of *típico* music and the *pollera* (traditional Panamanian dress). It's also the location of Panama's grandest *fiestas*, involving drinking, bullfighting, drinking, traditional music, drinking, religious processions, and drinking. *Campesinos* (peasants) continue to wear *guayaberas* (the traditional men's shirt) and classic straw-hats, and the horse is a preferred mode of transportation. The peninsula's flatlands and rolling hills have been inhabited for thousands of years; as a result, very little of the area remains forested. Despite this, natural attractions lure many visitors to the area. There is snorkeling and diving on Isla Iguana, world-class surfing at Playa Venado and Playa Santa Catalina, and sea turtles by the thousands on Isla de Cañas. The towns of most interest—Chitré, Las Tablas, and Pedasí—all lie on the eastern side of the peninsula. They are linked by the Carretera Nacional, which branches off the Interamerican Hwy. at Divisa. Santiago lies farther west along the Interamerican Hwy., inland from the peninsula, heading to David and Costa Rica.

SHAKE WHAT YO' MAMA GAVE YOU The Azuero Peninsula is, in no uncertain terms, Panama's party central. Grab your dancing partner and be prepared to get down at the many fiestas. Parades, beauty pageants, religious ceremonies, revelry, drinking, and dancing are all par for the course. If you're planning to spend any extended period of time on the peninsula, or are just passing through, and your feet are itching for action, get out your calendars and red pens—here's every planned hootenanny from Parita to Pedasí. It's still a good idea to call IPAT (☎966-8072) in Los Santos beforehand to make sure dates have not changed.

Jan. 6	**La Fiesta de los Reyes:** Macaracas	
Jan. 19-22	**Feria de San Sebastián:** (patron saint) Ocú	
Feb. 24-27	**Carnaval:** all over, but best in Las Tablas or Los Santos	
Apr. 13	**Semana Santa:** all over, but best in Las Tablas, Pedasí, Los Santos, Pesé	
May 24	**Corpus Cristi:** Los Santos	
June 24	**Fiesta de San Juan:** (patron saint) Chitré	
July 19-22	**Festival de la Pollera and Fiesta de Santa Librada:** Las Tablas	
Aug. 9	**Festival de Manito:** Ocú	
Aug. 25-29	**Semana del Campesino:** Los Santos	
Sept. 24	**Festival de la Mejorana:** Guararé	
Oct. 19	**Anniversary of the Founding of Chitré District:** Chitré	
Nov. 10	**Cry of Independence:** Los Santos	
Nov. 25	**Fiesta de Santa Catalina:** (patron saint) Pedasí	

CHITRÉ

The largest town on the Azuero Peninsula, Chitré itself does not offer much, but is a gateway to the *fiestas* in the rest of the Peninsula. Set up camp here and head out to nearby Los Santos, Guararé, or farther south to get a taste of Panama's best parties. Chitré itself gets going on June 24th for the *Fiesta Patronal*.

E TRANSPORTATION. The **bus terminal** is south of town (15min. walk; taxi US$1; local bus from behind the terminal US$0.15). **Buses** leave the terminal for: **Divisa** (30min., every 30min. 6am-7pm, US$1); **Las Tablas** (40min., every 10min. 6am-9pm, US$1) via **Guararé** (30min., US$0.80); **Monaure** and **Monagre** (30min., every 30min. 8:30am-6pm, US$1); **Ocú** (1hr., every 30min. 7am-6pm, US$2); **Panama City** (4hr., every hr. 1:30am-6pm, US$6) via **Penonomé** (2hr., US$3.30); **Parita** (10min., every 20min. 6am-6pm, US$0.50) via **La Arena** (5min., US$0.25); **Santiago** (1¼hr., every 30min. 4am-6:30pm, US$2); **Tonosí** (4hr., every 10min. 6am-7pm, US$4). South-bound buses stop in **Los Santos** (5min., US$0.25). Local buses (not *chivitas*) stop at Panadería Chiquito, two blocks north of the cathedral. The **airport** is north of town, up Av. Central. Aeroperlas has two daily **flights** (1 on Sunday) to **Panama City** (US$32) and one to **Santiago** (M-Sa 4:30pm, US$9.20). **Taxis** are common. (☎ 996 7996. 24hr.)

■ ◪ ORIENTATION AND PRACTICAL INFORMATION. Just about everything in Chitré can be found on the two main roads. Hwy. 2, the **Carretera Nacional,** enters from the west, where it becomes **Calle Manuel Correa.** Near the center of town, Calle Correa intersects **Av. Herrera** (or Av. Central) which runs north-south. Two blocks south is the **cathedral,** next to the **parque central.** Three blocks farther south, Av. Central bends east and becomes the Carretera Nacional again, heading south to **Los Santos** and **Las Tablas.** To get to the *parque* from the bus terminal, turn left out of the front parking lot and continue on the road about 500m. Turn left on the Carretera Nacional at the hospital and follow this road until it forks, then bear right onto Av. Central. The cathedral is three blocks up.

The most convenient **IPAT** office in the area is in Los Santos, 5km down Av. Nacional from Chitré. To get there, take a bus heading to Los Santos and get off at the *parque central;* the office is next to the church. (☎ 966 8013; fax 966 8040. Open M-F 8:30am-4:30pm.) **ANAM** also has an office in Los Santos, but it is 2km past the turn-off for the center on Av. Nacional. To get there, take a bus going toward Las Tablas; get off when you see the sign on the right. (☎ 966 8296. Open M-F 8am-4pm.) The **immigration office** is one block south and three blocks east of the cathedral; look for the Panamanian flag. (☎ 996 3092. Open M-F 8am-3:30pm.) **Banco del Istmo,** three blocks west of Av. Central on Calle Correa, changes traveler's checks, gives Visa and MC cash advances, and has a 24hr. **ATM.** (Open M-F 8am-3:30pm, Sa 9am-noon.) Three blocks north and one block west of the cathedral, on a little *parque*, is **Lavamático La Estrella.** (Open M-F 8am-4pm, Sa 8am-5pm.) Other services include: **police** (☎ 996 4333 or 104), west of town; **Hospital Cecilio Castillero** (☎ 996 4444), four blocks southeast of town on the Carretera Nacional; **Internet** at **PC Brains,** on Av. Central across from Panadería Chiquita (US$1 per hr.; open daily 8am-11pm); and the **post office,** 4 blocks west and one block north of Av. Central on Calle Correa, tucked under a Cable and Wireless building and across from a gas station (open M-F 7am-6pm, Sa 7am-4pm).

▉ ◪ ACCOMMODATIONS AND FOOD. The best of the many budget hotels is **◪Pensión Central ❷,** a half-block north of the cathedral on Av. Central. Large, clean rooms have cable TV, private baths, and those puffy toilet seats everyone loves. (☎ 996 0059. Breakfast included. Singles US$10, with A/C US$15; doubles US$13; triples US$19, with A/C US$22; add US$2 on weekends.) Rooms in **Hotel Santa Rita ❷,** on Calle Correa just off Av. Central, are decently clean, with TV, *lavandería*, and a restaurant downstairs. (☎ 996 4610. Singles with fan US$11, with A/C US$15.40; doubles US$15.40/US$19.80.) **Hotel Hawaii ❸,** around the corner from Machetazo, is a full-service hotel at self-service prices. (☎ 996 3524. Singles US$20.25; doubles US$28.80.) **Pensión Lily ❶,** one block east of the post office, offers basic rooms with baths and fans. (Singles US$6; doubles US$10.)

For good *típico*, head to **La Estrella #2 ❶**, right in front of the cathedral, where *comida* is US$1.50 and a giant mound of *arroz con pollo* is US$2. (Open daily 6am-11pm.) **Manolo ❶**, across Calle Correa from the Machetazo department store, specializes in hot sandwiches (US$0.75-2.75), but also offers *típicos* (US$1-5) and a range of Italian dishes (vegetarian calzone US$2.50). (☎996 5668; call for delivery. Open daily 6:00am-11pm.) Get American food at **Tastee-freez ❶**, just down from Manolo. (Chili dog US$1.10. Open daily 24hr.) **Restaurante y Panadería Chiquita ❷**, two blocks north of the cathedral on Av. Central, offers pizzas (US$2-5), delicious *chichas* (US$0.25), and baked goods. (Open daily 5am-10:30pm.)

◻ SIGHTS. Check out the town's **cathedral**, which features a beautiful mahogany and gilded altar. The pleasant *parques* that dot the city are also worth a stroll. **Museo de Herrera,** on Av. Manuel Correa two blocks west of Av. Central, has exhibits on the archaeology, history, and traditions of the Herrera province. (☎996 0077. Open Tu-Sa 9am-12:30pm and 1:30-4pm, Su 9am-noon. US$1.)

▶ DAYTRIPS TO GUARARÉ AND OTHER VILLAGES

To get to **Guararé** from Los Santos, take a bus to Las Tablas (30min., US$0.80). 1hr. by bus east of Los Santos is **Ocú**. **La Arena** is north, reachable by car or bus to Parita (US$0.25).

In addition to the shenanigans during *Carnaval*, the week before Ash Wednesday, and *Semana Santa*, the week before Easter, the small town of **La Villa de Los Santos,** 5km south of Chitré, really goes crazy for *Corpus Cristi* (see p. 603) and their Independence Day (Nov. 10, 18 days before the rest of the country). All four occasions call for gargantuan no-holds-barred parties, with assorted revelry and debauchery galore. Of interest to those in Los Santos during the rest of the year is the small **Museo de la Nacionalidad** (☎/fax 966 8192), on the *parque central*, across from the church. The museum features Panamanian artifacts and items from their struggle for independence. (US$1. Open Tu-Sa 9am-4pm, Su 9am-1pm.) The center of attention during the *fiestas*, the ◼**Iglesia de San Ignacio**, is worth a peek at any time. Beautiful, white-washed woodwork frames a life-size, wooden statue of San Pedro (Saint Peter) which stands to the left of the altar.

If Los Santos's *fiestas* aren't enough, check out **Guararé**, 18km south of Chitré. The *Festival de la Mejorana*, every September 24th, celebrates the region's traditional music, played on accordions, tambourines, and the *mejorana*, a small guitar-like instrument made from mango wood. Guararé's *Semana Santa* festivities are more intricate than most. Dancing and singing form the backdrop for a reenactment of the Easter story, culminating in a bonfire in which an effigy of Judas is burned amid great celebration. The village of **Ocú** is where most of the hats sold in Penonomé (p. 633) are actually made. Ocú's *Festival de Manito* (Aug. 9) honors the folklore and traditions of the region's farmers, complete with the celebration of traditional weddings. To the north, artisans in the small village of **La Arena** produce some of the finest ceramics in Panama. Stores line the highway from Chitré, only five minutes away by car or bus. Prices are very affordable; most vendors won't bargain unless you're buying more than a couple of pieces. For a look at the hundreds of years old process and tradition of ceramics, follow the street to the right of the church about two blocks. You will find *talleres de cerámica* (ceramics workshops) where the pieces are made. Custom work is welcome, so bring your ideas and designs. The closest **beach** to Chitré is **Monagre**, near Los Santos, or **El Rompío** right next to it. The Monagre bus leaves from the Chitré terminal to either beach (every 30min. 8am-5pm, US$1). The black sands are home to many crabs, so look out for the little holes when you put your towel down. Enjoy freshly

DANCING DEVILS At 4am on the Thursday six weeks after Easter, most of the Republic of Panama is fast asleep. In Los Santos, however, people are busy running and dancing through the streets, chasing a giant papier-maché bull's head. The celebration of **Corpus Christi** is one of the most raucous festivals in the country, though the day's Catholic significance is barely visible through the chaos of nine different traditional dances. **La Danza del Torito Santeño** (Dance of the Little Los Santos Bull) kicks it off, but the 10am mass is where things get interesting. Dances begin in the church, then spill out into the square and streets. Among these performances is **La Danza de Los Diablicos Sucios** (the Dance of the Dirty Little Devils). Historically, the Dirty Devils wore clothing striped red (with mud) and black (with charred corn), as well as intricate masks. In those days, the violent, leaping devil dance caused the dancers to sweat profusely, which mixed with mud and corn soot to make the name choice pretty clear. Nowadays, the Dirty Devils' papier-maché masks and striped silk outfits are easier to clean up. Every dance comes with an accompanying story; to get the lowdown on the hoedown, buy a wise local a beer and enjoy the narration.

caught fried fish and plantains (US$2.50) at *Complejo Turístico Monagre*, which has bathrooms, showers (US$5.25) a full bar, pool, and billiard tables.

LAS TABLAS

Las Tablas is often considered the symbolic center of Panama. The country's national dress, the *pollera*, originated here, and is celebrated annually in the joint Fiesta de la Pollera/Fiesta de Santa Librada (July 19-22), the most famous festival in the country. It begins with a procession from the church through the town on the 19th, continues on the 20th and 21st with 10am mass, and ends with an all-day street party on the 22nd where the *reinas* (queens) are chosen for the parade. In addition to the *reina* is the best *pollera* contest, and there are violin and *sombrero* contests for men. *Carnaval* time comes once a year, and starts the Friday before Ash Wednesday and Mardi Gras; much like Río and New Orleans, Las Tablas is a nonstop festival with beautiful, ornate costumes and competitions. When the town isn't partying, it is crowded with vendors and sidewalk markets until sundown, as older folks chat in the park and younger people cruise around town bumping the newest *salsa* or *cumbia* from their stereo systems. *Tableños* know how to mix religious tradition with lots of fun—religious processions followed by fireworks occur frequently at night.

TRANSPORTATION. Buses leave from various spots in town. Four blocks north of the *parque* the big green gas station serves as the terminal for buses to **Panama City** (5hr., every hr. 4am-5:30pm, US$6.50). Two blocks south, **Chitré**-bound buses pick up by the Supermercado Las Tablas (45min., every 15min. 5am-7:30pm, US$1). Those going to **Pedasí** and other points south on the peninsula, leave from in front of Restaurante Praga, on the main road three blocks east of the *parque* (45min., every hr. 6am-6pm, US$2). Note that not every bus from Las Tablas to Cañas passes through Pedasí. To **Santiago** or farther west, either take a bus to **Chitré** and transfer, or take a **Panama City**-bound bus as far as the Interamerican Hwy., then look for a westward bus. With lots of luggage, the former is easier.

ORIENTATION AND PRACTICAL INFORMATION. The main road comes in from the north and turns left at the southeast corner of the *parque central* (across from the church). It travels east through town before heading out to Pedasí. An **ANAM** office is about 2km out of town on the road to Pedasí in a large government compound. (☎994 0363; fax 994 6676. Open M-F 8am-4pm.) To get there, take a taxi (US$0.75) or a bus heading to Pedasí and get off when you see the sign on your right, or walk 25min. past Restaurante Praga. Banks are plentiful; **Banco Nacional de Panamá** is three blocks north of the *parque* on the right and has a 24hr. **ATM.** (Open M-F 8am-3pm, Sa 9am-noon.) Other services include: **Western Union,** next to the new Hotel Manolo (☎994 6279; open M-F 8:30am-4pm, Sa 9am-2pm); **Lavandería y Lavamático El Éxito,** two blocks east of the northern end of the *parque* (☎994 6765; wash and/or dry US$0.75; open M-Sa 8am-5:30pm); **police station** (☎994 7000 or 104), across from the big green gas station; **hospital** (☎994 8181; open 24hr.), right across from the hospital; **Café Internet,** facing the church, down 1½ blocks to the left (US$1 per hr., open M-Sa 9am-10pm); and the **post office,** half a block west of Supermercado Las Tablas (open M-F 7am-6pm, Sa 7am-5pm).

⌂☐ ACCOMMODATIONS AND FOOD. It's a good idea to make reservations during *fiestas* (or stay in Chitré). **Hospedaje Zafiro ❷,** on the southeastern corner of the *parque central*, offers a balcony overlooking the *parque*, and spacious, clean rooms with private baths and A/C. (☎994 8200. Singles US$14.30; doubles US$19; triples US$21.) **Hotel Manolo ❹,** about a block farther east than Zafirol, has nine brand new rooms with cable, A/C, hot water, and a restaurant with US$0.90 tacos downstairs. (☎994 6372. Singles US$27.50; doubles US$33; triples US$30.)

Among Las Tablas's indistinguishable eateries, **Restaurante Praga ❶** and **Salón Popular ❶** next door, three blocks east of the *parque*, serve large meals. (*Típico* US$2. Open daily 7am-12am.) A block farther east and half a block north, **Restaurante El Caserón ❷** is a nicer environment, with an extensive menu, including pasta, burgers, pizza, and sundaes. (US$2-8. Open daily 7am-11pm.) **Restaurante Aida ❷,** half a block farther on the main drag, is open 24hr. **Portofino ❶,** provides a break from the *típico* and is an excellent location for watching the town's activities on the *parque*. (☎994 7605; call for delivery. Small cheese pizza US$1.50; family size vegetarian US$7.25; hamburgers US$1.50. Open daily noon-10pm.)

◙ SIGHTS. Built in 1679, the recently renovated **Iglesia de Santa Librada,** with its gold-leaf altar, massive wooden doors, and a statue of the crucified saint, is the focal point of the town's cultural and religious energy. A short biography of *"La Moñona,"* (the saint's nickname, derived from her long locks), is posted by her altar. The one-room **Museo de Belisario Porras,** facing the *parque* to the south, stands as a monument to the visionary three-time president of Panama, born and raised in Las Tablas. (☎994 6326. Open Tu-Sa 8am-4pm, Su 9am-noon; US$0.50.)

PEDASÍ

Populated by people earning their living from the sea and a sprinkling of tourists looking for excellent angling, Pedasí is a quiet fishing town 41km southeast of Las Tablas. The birthplace of President Moscoso has yet to spawn an honorary museum, though a monument at the town entrance greets all visitors. Most visitors come here to fish, visit nearby Isla Iguana, or venture to Punta Mala to try to get a glimpse of "La Presidenta," the (female) president of the Republic of Panama.

⊏ TRANSPORTATION. Buses to **Las Tablas** head up the main street (45min., every hr. 6am-6pm, US$2) from the municipal building. Note that not every bus from Las Tablas to Cañas passes through Pedasí. As of June 2002, there were no buses running to **Playa Venado** or **Isla de Cañas.** The most feasible way of getting there from Pedasí is to take a taxi (around US$12). **Taxis** leave three blocks south of the municipal building on the main road.

⊞ ⊠ ORIENTATION AND PRACTICAL INFORMATION. Av. Central is a continuation of the Carretera Nacional that hugs the east coast of the peninsula, and Av. Central enters town running north-south. The municipal building marks the rough midpoint of the main road. The **parque central** is two blocks south and one block east of the municipal building.

The **ANAM** office in charge of Isla Iguana is about a block north of the municipal building on a street just before the gas station. (☎995 2134. Open M-F 8am-4pm.) **Buzos de Azuero,** a snorkel/dive shop, is next to the gas station and has maps of Isla Iguana, and Jeff, a Californian expat, dishes out the inside scoop on Pedasí. (☎995 2405; bdazuero@hotmail.com. Snorkeling gear rental US$10 per day, scuba US$30 per day.) **Banco Nacional de Panamá,** is directly across the street from the Hotel Residencial Pedasí, near the town's entrance. (Open M-F 8:30am-3:30pm, Sa 8:30am-12pm.) Do laundry at the **lavamático,** a block east of the southeast corner of the park. (Open daily 8am-noon and 2-4pm.) Other services include: **police station** (☎995 2122 or 104), two blocks south of the western side of the *parque* in the unmarked yellow building with a flag; **Farmacia Sael,** across from the southeast corner of the *parque* (open M-Sa 7am-noon and 1-8pm, Su 9-11am and 3-8pm); the **health clinic** (☎995 2127), past the laundromat, east of the park; the **post office** behind the municipal building (open M-Sa 7am-noon and 2-5pm).

⊞ ⊡ ACCOMMODATIONS AND FOOD. All three budget hotels in Pedasí are clean and well-kept, with friendly staff. **⊠Dim's Hostel ❷,** across from the police station on Av. Central, is a cozy bed and breakfast. All rooms have private hot-water bathrooms and A/C. Great buffet-style breakfast is included and served in a communal outdoor living space beneath the branches of a mango-tree. (☎995 2303. Singles US$15; doubles US$20, additional US$5 for third person.) **Residencial Moscoso ❷,** on the main road about three blocks south of the municipal building, rents impeccable rooms with fans. The owners know Pedasí well. (☎995 2203. Call ahead to reserve a room. Singles US$12; triples with bath US$12, with TV and A/C US$16.50; quads with TV and A/C US$22.) Three blocks farther north along Av. Central is **Hotel Residencial Pedasí ❸,** offering a common TV and clean rooms with private bath and A/C. (☎995 2322. Singles US$17; doubles US$22; triples US$28.)

Most restaurants open only around mealtimes. Get good food at **Restaurante Angela ❶,** across the street from the municipal building (*comida* US$1.50) or **Panadería y Refresquería Bethel ❶,** across the park from the church. Besides fresh baked goods, they fire up a mean chicken sandwich (US$1) and a host of pizzas (US$4) in front of DirecTV. (Open M-F 7am-7pm, Sa-Su 8:30am-12pm.)

⊡ BEACHES. Though most beachgoers make tracks for Isla Iguana or Playa Venado, **Playa El Toro** and **La Garita** both lie 3km east of town, providing isolation and good swimming, and are reachable by taxi (US$2.50) or foot. Follow the road east from the signs at Pensión Moscoso. Every July or August, **Playa El Arenal** hosts an huge fishing tournament. Call **IPAT** (☎966 8072) in Los Santos for more info.

NEAR PEDASÍ

🐠 ISLA IGUANA

*The owners of all three hotels in Pedasí are happy to find you transportation to the island and can do it at a moment's notice. Expect to pay a local fisherman US$30 plus US$10 for gasoline. Find a group to share the cost (boats hold up to 7 people). **Boats** leave from Playa El Arenal, a 5min. ride from the gas station at the northern edge of Pedasí. You can take a **taxi** (US$2; arrange a ride back). From the beach, it's a 25min. boat ride to Isla*

Iguana, where you will probably be dropped off in front of one of the best coral fields. Entrance fee US$3.

Pedasí's big draw is nearby **Refugio de Vida Silvestre Isla Iguana,** a diving and snorkeling hotspot 8km from Pedasí's closest beach. This island has the largest coral mass in Panama, covering some 16 hectares to a depth of 8m. Snorkelers and divers should bring their own equipment or rent equipment at the dive shop in Pedasí. Isla Iguana also has two fantastic white-sand **beaches** with clear water, bordered by dark rocks that look like baked mud castles.

The island boasts a small **refugio** for spending the night, with an outhouse and some hammock posts under a roof. **Camping** is possible if you bring everything you need, including drinking water. There are some very rough **trails** leading from the *refugio;* one leads to the lighthouse; another to a secluded beach. Be sure not to stray off the trails, as there are several unexploded **landmines** left over from when the US Navy used the island for target practice. ANAM (☎ 995 2734) asks that visitors register at the office in Pedasí before visiting.

◢ PLAYA VENADO

*Getting to **Playa Venado** requires a **taxi** (US$12) or hitchhiking. Let's Go does not recommend hitchhiking. As of July 2002 there was no reliable bus service to Playa Venado. Check with Pedasí's ANAM office for up-to-date transportation information (☎ 995 2134; open M-F 8am-4pm).*

Thirty minutes southeast of Pedasí by bus, "Playa Venao," as it is often pronounced, is one of the greatest surfing breaks in Panama. Even on a bad day, constant sets of three or four waves are good for bodysurfing. Venado's waves are big enough (2-3m, breaking both ways) to host the annual Billabong Pro Panama International Surfing Contest during *Semana Santa.* The 1.5km crescent of soft black sand is flanked by two points of land and backed by verdant hills that roll right up to the beach. The best break (and the worst trash) is at the end of the road. The constant waves make casual swimming here impossible.

In the center of the beach, where the road ends, there is a **restaurant/bar** and some **cabins** ❸ for rent. These have two beds and a private bath, and stand barely 20m from the water. The relaxed owner doesn't mind if you camp on the beach or hang a hammock. It's free, but you must wait for the locals to clear out at night (usually by 9pm) and you must clean up by 10am the next morning. (US$16 per person, US$14 in low season.) The **restaurant** ❶ serves *típico,* often with fresh seafood, and has some limited snack food (beef, rice, beans, and salad US$2).

◤ ISLA DE CAÑAS

*Combining a trip to Isla de Cañas and Playa Venado is wise, as you'll cut your transportation costs considerably. **Taxis** from Pedasí will run US$15 each way, but will leave you at the boat pickup. At the end of the dirt road, bang the wrench against the wheel rim hanging from the tree to let someone know you're there and then wait for a boat to show up. If the creek at the end of the road doesn't look big enough to allow a boat to travel up it, it's low tide. Remove your shoes, think happy thoughts free of snakes and crocodiles (which aren't a threat—during low tide), and trudge left down the creek and then left again about 50m to a small bank on the right side; wait here for the boat. The ride itself (5min., US$0.50) is spectacular and goes past thousands of crabs congregating among the mangrove roots. Island admission US$3, when ANAM is open.*

West of Pedasí and Playa Venado lies Isla de Cañas, a large island off the southern coast of the Azuero Peninsula. The southern coast of the island boasts 14km of beautiful beaches, the chosen nesting ground of four of the world's eight species of sea turtle. The reproductive antics climax in the *arribadas* (arrivals), when more than 10,000 turtles hit the beach in just two or three nights to lay their eggs. Apart from the *arribadas*, there are many nights in the egg-laying season when 100 or more turtles lay eggs on the beach. The island is managed cooperatively by ANAM and the local community, which subsists mainly on turtle egg sales. The community cooperative has established a nursery program: every morning all the eggs are collected, and a portion are reburied in a hatchery next to the beach, while the rest are sold. The egg-laying season is generally May-Dec. (leatherbacks are primarily Dec.-Mar.) though *arribadas* are usually October or November. Tours of the island's mangrove forests are also available (half day US$10). The public phone (☎995 8002) on the island, just outside the ANAM office, is always answered by someone knowledgeable. Staying overnight is necessary if you want see the *tortugas*. The island cooperative rents out three **cabañas ❶**, thatched huts with fans and an outhouse (US$8-10 per cabin, each sleeps 3). There is a **restaurant** nearby at the *cabañas*. ANAM asks that visitors call ahead.

SANTIAGO

Halfway between Panama City and David along the Interamerican Hwy., Santiago is a convenient base for forays to the waterfalls, wilderness areas, beaches, and smaller villages of the Veraguas Province. Aside from the **Fiesta Patronal de Santiago Apóstol** (July 22-25), Santiago itself doesn't offer much to visitors.

⎗ TRANSPORTATION. Transportes David-Panamá (☎998 4006) goes to **David** (3½hr., every 1½hr. 9:30am-2:30am, US$6; after midnight US$7.50) and **Panama City** (5hr., every 1½hr. 9am-2am, US$6; express 10:45pm US$7.50). The terminal is near Hotel Piramidal on the Interamerican Hwy. east of the fork. **Buses** also leave from the main terminal, on Calle 10 halfway between Av. Central and the Interamerican Hwy. to: **Arenas-Las Flores** (3hr., 8 and 9:30am, US$7); **Atalaya** (30min., every 15min. 5:30am-8:30pm, US$0.45); **Chitré** (1¼hr., every 30min. 5:30am-6pm, US$2); **Las Palmas** (1¼hr.; 5, 6, 8:20am, 6:30pm; US$2.50); **San Francisco** (30min., every 30min. 6:30am-6pm, US$0.65); **Santa Catalina** (1½hr.; 5am, noon, 4pm; US$3); **Santa Fe** (1½hr., every 30min. 5am-6pm, US$2); and **Soná** (1hr., every 20min. 6:30am-6pm, US$1.50). In Santiago, air-conditioned **taxis** provide a cheap and convenient means of transportation (fare around US$0.75). Slightly cheaper **buses** are also available.

▆▐ ORIENTATION AND PRACTICAL INFORMATION. The main road, **Avenida Central**, branches off from the Interamerican Hwy. and runs west about 2km to the **cathedral** and the town's **parque central**. *Calles* run north-south between Avenida Central and the Interamerican, with Calle 2 next to the *parque* and Calle 10 about halfway between the *parque* and the fork. To get to the *parque central* from the main **bus terminal**, turn right on Calle 10 out of the front of the terminal and continue for 5 blocks. Turn right at Av. Central and continue straight to the cathedral.

Santiago has an **IPAT office** in the white Plaza Palermo shopping complex, on Av. Central just east of Calle 10. (☎998 3929; fax 998 0929. Open M-F 8:30am-4:30pm.) On the Interamerican Hwy. fork, in the Galería shopping center, is **Mary's Tours,** a **travel agency.** It is mostly useful for booking or confirming domestic flights (US$5 fee) or for extending your visa (US$10 fee). It also offers a few one-night trips. (☎998 0072. Open M-Sa 8am-6pm.) The most comprehensive and convenient **supermarket** in town is **Los Compadres,** under the huge pink sign, four blocks east of the *parque*. (Open daily 8am-9:30pm). The Santiago **immigration office** is across from the Escuela Normal, on Calle 7, four blocks north of Av. Central. (☎998 7447. Open M-F 8am-4pm.) **Banco General,** three blocks east of the *parque* on Av. Central, cashes traveler's checks and gives Visa cash advances. (Open M-F 8am-3pm, Sa

9am-noon.) Sistema Clave **ATMs** are on Av. Central between Calles 2 and 10 and at the bus station. **Western Union** is just south of the Interamerican on Calle 10. (Open M-F 8am-5pm, Sa 8:30am-2pm.) There's a **Budget car rental** at the fork. Next to Super 99, on Calle 8 just north of Av. Central, is **Lavamático El Carmen #3.** The **police station** is east of town past the fork, as well as at a stand on Av. Central and Calle 4. (☎998 2119 or 104. Open 24hr.) The local **Farmacia Elysin** chain has branches all over town, with the largest at Av. Central and Calle 7 (☎998 3411. Open daily 8am-9pm). For emergencies, the **Hospital Regional de Veraguas** (☎999 3146) is past the fork to the east. For less dire medical (or dental) problems, **Clínica Médica Coopeve**, near the fork on Av. Central, across from the Plaza Palermo shopping complex, does consultations for US$4. (☎998 6421. Open M-F 7am-5pm, Sa 7am-1pm.) **Hal's Internet** runs a small but fully up-to-date web cafe on Calle 10, 10min. from Avenida Central (☎998 0996; fax 998 2663. US$1.50 per hr. Open M-Sa 8:30am-11pm, Su 1-10pm). There is a **DHL** inside Mary's Tours (see above). The **post office** is on Calle 8, five blocks north of Av. Central. (Open M-F 5am-7:30pm, Sa 7am-4:30pm.)

⬛⬜ ACCOMMODATIONS AND FOOD. Accommodations range from luxurious (along the highway) to basic (in the middle of town). **Hotel Santiago ❷,** one block south of the southwestern end of the cathedral, in a classic house with an interior garden, offers quiet, bare-bones rooms with private baths. Ask to look at a few rooms before settling on one, as some lack a fan. (☎998 4824. Singles US$8; doubles US$11, with A/C US$13; triples US$13.) The newly remodeled **Hotel Plaza Concord ❷,** three blocks east of the *parque* on Av. Central, has large rooms with TVs and private baths. (☎998 0644. Singles with A/C US$14; doubles US$18.80.) The **Pensión Central ❶,** 5½ blocks east of the *parque*, is noisier but a good value, with big, drab rooms and clean private bathrooms. (Singles US$7; doubles US$8.)

Típico places huddle around the center of town, between Av. Central and Calle 10. All stick rigidly to the standard cafeteria formula: chicken (roast or fried) and various forms of potato. For a nicer spot, try the wicker and tiki patio at the **Restaurante Mar Caribe ❸,** across from Hotel Gran David, west of the fork on the Interamerican, which has good seafood and meat. (Entrees US$4-9; beer US$0.60; view of the Interamerican free. Open daily 8am-midnight.) International cuisine in Santiago doesn't exactly span the globe, but there are a few places that bring some culinary diversity. Half a kilometer toward town on Av. Central, across from the Plaza Palermo shopping center, **Restaurante Tropicalísimo ❷** offers Cuban versions of the Panamanian standards (think pork and plantains instead of *pollo* and *papas*). Choose between sit-down service (entrees US$3-5) or cafeteria-style (slightly cheaper) and the A/C dining room or the expansive patio. (☎998 3661. Open daily, 9am-11pm.) One block south of the bus terminal on Calle 10, **Restaurante, Bar y Discoteca Nuevo Quo Vadis ❶** feels like Old Spain. Try the US$1.25 chicken taco. (Open daily 7am-10:30pm.) There are daily **fruit markets ❶** all over town. A central one where breakfasts are especially budget is four blocks east of the cathedral on Av. Central (*fritura* and coffee, US$0.50).

◪ SIGHTS. There isn't much to explore in Santiago, but the ⬛**Escuela Normal Juan Demóstenes Arosemana** is an excellent diversion. Built between 1936 and 1938, it is a fully functioning school for teachers that displays dazzling architecture, sculpture, and painting. The facade is a gorgeous hodgepodge of stone carvings hiding miniature figures of *pollera*-clad girls amid columns and faces. Head through the archway of the entry hall, framed by the Allegory of Time and Philosophy (that's Plato and Aristotle leaning on the clock) and through the doors to the **Aula Máxima.** This huge room was illustrated by Roberto Lewis, the famous painter responsible for the Palacio Presidencial in Panama City. The school is in the middle of Calle 7, four blocks north of Av. Central. (Free. Open M-F 8am-3:30pm.)

NEAR SANTIAGO

SANTA FÉ AND OTHER VILLAGES

Buses run between Santiago's main bus terminal and Santa Fé's center (1½hr., every 30min. 5am-6pm, US$2).

To the north of Santiago, the mountain village of **Santa Fé** is an ecotourist's dream. With waterfalls, mountains, plantations, and wildlife, not to mention the enchanting Orchid Fair in August, Santa Fé has a little of everything, though not many tourist facilities exist. The town is laid out in a rough V-shape along the top of a ridge, with Cerro Tute looming on the western side and a deep, lush valley on the east. The Santiago-Santa Fé road enters along the ridge from the southeast and splits into three roads at the "Bienvenidos a Santa Fé" sign. The left branch heads off toward the forested area of Alto de Piedra and the Hotel Jardín Santafereño (see below). The central branch leads uphill 500m to the town's modest church and the cluster of **Santa Fé-Santiago buses.** The right branch takes you toward the Orquideario (see below). No amount of directions is likely to save you having to ask—luckily, the local residents are extraordinarily friendly. **Hotel Santa Fé ❷** occupies a lovely piece of land 1km south of town on the Santiago-Santa Fé road. (*Comidas* US$2-3.) **Guides** into the verdant forests of **Cerro Tute** and **Alto de Piedra,** and to the many nearby waterfalls, can be hired here (US$20 per day). The hotel also runs tours of **El Salto,** a nearby organic farm rich in waterfalls, and to a local **coffee processing** business for US$3 per group. (☎954 0941. Singles and doubles US$13, with DirecTV US$25.) More removed and rustic **Hotel Jardín Santafereño ❷,** at the northwest corner of town (ask for directions to the *cabañas*), rents well-worn *cabañas* for US$10 each.

Santa Fé's chief assets are its tranquility and its virgin forests, but there are a few eclectic human enterprises worth checking out. Just downhill from the bus cluster, in an open concrete structure, is a modest **Artisan's Market** where a lonely scattering of handicrafts from Veraguas and Chiriquí are for sale. (Open M-Sa 9am-6pm.) Further up, 100m past the bus station, veer right to find the **Santa Fé Cooperativa** (don't be fooled by the big, concrete store of the same name—you want the little thatched building 20m away). This tiny collective project sells staples like beans and plantains, but most visitors are more interested in taking home a souvenir bag of locally grown coffee (strong and bitter, US$0.95 per ½ lb.) or a classic Panama hat (US$9-20). It's a good opportunity to support the community that's sup-

THE HIDDEN DEAL

PLAYA TORIO AND ISLA CÉBACO

Take the bus from Santiago to Mariato (3hr., 7am-5pm, US$4) and tell the driver you want to go to Cabañas Torio. Buses also run to and from Mariato (every 2hr. 9:30am-6:30pm) via Torio. There are six spotless cabañas with concrete floors, double beds, private bath, and thatched roof. ☎620 3677; yolandaf16@hotmail.com. Meals US$3. Cabaña US$15 per night. Spanish owners Yolanda and Fernando offer river float/swim days and trips to Isla Cébaco (US$40 for full-day trips).

If you want an untouristed island paradise all to yourself, head to **Isla Cébaco.** Cébaco and and its surrounding islands are covered by pristine tropical vegetation and lined by soft, white-sand beaches. Find your own small bay to make you feel like the first human being on it.

Isla Cébaco is privately owned, but its beaches are public, which means that you can **camp** there without problems. Stay at **Cabañas Torio** and go on a full day excursion to the islands. Its crystal-clear waters invite travelers to surf and snorkel (no board rentals). If you don't have the money for a boat to islands, **Playa Torio** is right by the cabañas, though a better beach is a 20-30min. walk down the coast.

Take only photos and leave only footprints. That way others will have the chance to marvel at the striking beauty of Isla Cébaco.

porting your peace of mind. Santa Fé's original attraction, however, is the mesmerizing and obsessive **Orquideario** (☎954 0916; zaguiji15@cwpanama.net), an intricate private garden containing hundreds of orchids of all shapes, sizes, and species.

San Francisco and **Atalaya,** both nearby villages, have gorgeous churches; the ceiling of the latter is covered in Biblical paintings. Southwest of Santiago, **Soná** comes alive during *La Feria de Veraguas* in February or March, and *La Fiesta de San Isidro Labrador* on May 15, but is otherwise not very exciting.

PARADISE, NEXT EXIT. If your rear is falling asleep for the 11th time since Muehuekenango, Guatemala, take a break from the Interamerican Hwy. 2hr. east of David and stop by **Las Palmas,** a small town that hides a dazzling waterfall. Well-marked but scarcely visited, this 30m waterfall is the stuff of fairy tales. (Buses run to Las Palmas from Santiago hourly (1¼hr., 5am-6:30pm, US$2.50), or get any bus on the Interamerican to drop you at la entrada de Las Palmas, and wait there for the next bus going to the town (US$1). Get off at the church and, facing the front door, head left 100m. Take a right at the brown El Salto sign and then a left at the T and a right 100m past that. From there, follow the main road down and to the right 10min. until you reach a major fork. Bear left and paradise awaits 5min. farther.)

CHIRIQUÍ PROVINCE

Chiriquí represents all what travelers come to Central America for: enticing rain forests, endless beaches, and sky-scraping volcanoes. Playa Las Lajas draws the beach crowd to its stretches of Pacific pleasure, but it is the northern highlands that put Chiriquí Province on the map. The indigenous Ngöbe named it "Valley of the Moon," and the cloud-enshrined hills above the valley cloak hot springs, lakes, and the elusive quetzal. A few hours' drive north from the provincial capital David leads to refreshingly cool villages rife with gorgeous mountain trails.

DAVID

The capital of Chiriquí Province, David functions for most travelers as a semi-urban pit stop on the Panamerican Highway. Fitness gyms, low-rider trucks, and a Top-40 radio station (Mega-Mix) hint at the town's cosmopolitan aspirations, but the nascent party scene here is mostly limited to dimly lit beer-holes and a few brothels. David steps out of its routine of lethargic days and down-and-dirty nights once a year for 10 days around March 19, when it hosts its rowdy patron saint festival, La Feria de San José.

✵ ORIENTATION

David is laid out in a grid, cut off northeast of the **parque central** by the busy diagonal **Av. Obaldía** and to the north and west by the **Interamerican Hwy.** North-south *avenidas* are numbered with *Oeste* and *Este* designations, starting on either side of **Av. Central.** East-west *calles* have similar *Norte* and *Sur* designations with letters, increasing to the north and south from **Calle Central.** Many of the streets are now labeled by names instead of numbers—for example, Av 3E is now Av. Bolívar, Av 1 E is 9 de Enero, and Calle A Sur is called Ruben D. Samudio. (Locals usually stick to the old number/letter combinations.) The *parque central*, **Parque Cervantes,** lies between Av. 3/4 Este and Calles A/B Norte. The major shopping zone is north of the *parque*, between Calles 3/5 Este.

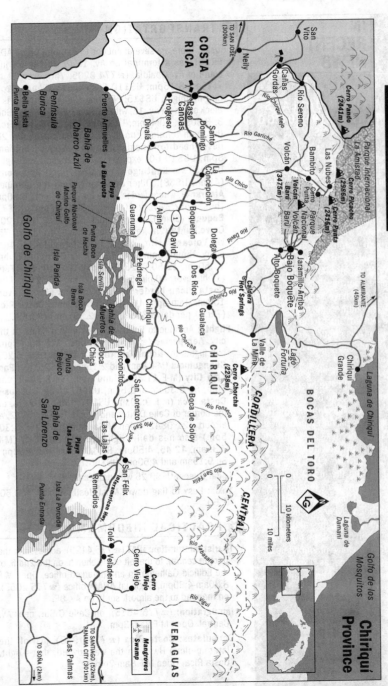

IN RECENT NEWS

600 MILLION DOLLARS WILL MAKE CHIRIQUÍ GO BANANAS!

A new law passed in Panama will pump millions of dollars into the province of Chiriquí. Blessed with substantial ecotourism around the city of Boquete and the National Park Volcán Barú, Chiriquí nonetheless is much less economically stable than the Panama and Colón provinces, with their lucrative connection to the canal. Most vegetables, fruits, and coffee come from the Chiriquí region, but recent years have seen a drop in profit for agriculture and many farmers have pulled out of the area in search of more secure economic futures. Abandoned and ill-used land is abundant.

However, with the new plan set forth by Diana de Kieswetter, the national director of the banana industry, 600 million US dollars will be pumped into Divalá (in Chiriquí) over the course of the next five years to reactivate 2 million hectares of banana plantations. The law has already approved the first 28 million dollar investment plan for this year and 8 of the 13 banana plantations have each been given 8 million dollars. The benefits of this ambitious project will soon be seen—in five years each hectare will have produced up to 2700 crates of bananas. Experts are predicting lots of yellow, and, of course, green.

⌷ TRANSPORTATION

Buses: There are several options to **Panama City**. PADA-FRONT has a terminal on Av. 1E (9 de Enero), just south of Av. Obaldía. (☎774 9205. 7hr., every 1½hr. 7:15am-8:15pm, US$10.60. Express 5½hr., 11pm and midnight, US$15.) Expreso Cinco Estrellas is 1 block south on Av. 1E, with movies. (☎774 7702. 6hr.; 3, 8:30am, 10:45pm; US$7.50, luxury US$13.) From the main terminal, north of Av. Obaldía on Av. 2E, buses head to Panama City (7hr., every hr. 6:45am-8pm, US$10.60; express 10:45pm and midnight, US$15) via **Santiago** (3hr., US$6) and **Penonomé** (4½hr., US$8). Other departures from the terminal: **Almirante**, where ferries leave for Bocas, until 6:30pm (bus 3½hr., every 30min. 4:30am-7pm, US$7); **Boquete** (50min., every 25min. 5am-7pm, US$1.20); **Cerro Punta** (2hr., every 15min. 5am-7pm, US$2.75) via **Volcán** (1½hr., US$2.30); **Changuinola** (4hr., every 45min. 5am-6pm, US$8) via **Chiriquí** (1½hr.; 11:50am, 12:50, 4:25, 5:25pm; US$20); **San Félix** (1½hr., every 40min. 5:30am-7:20pm, US$2); and the **Costa Rican border at Paso Canoas** (1½hr., every 10min. 4am-8pm, US$1.50); **San José, Costa Rica** (7hr., 1 per day 8:30am, US$12.50) on TRACOPA.

Flights: Aeropuerto Enrique Malek is 4km south of the city. **Aeroperlas** (☎775 7779; open M-F 8am-5pm) has flights to: **Bocas Isla** (daily 2:15pm, US$25.20); **Changuinola** (M-F 8am and 2:15pm, US$25.20); **Panama City** (M-F 11:30am and 5pm, Sa 8:30am and 5pm, Su 9:30am and 5pm, US$57); and **San José, Costa Rica** (M-F 9:20am, US$91). **Mapiex Aero,** on the corner of Calle D Nte. and Av. 2E (☎775 0812, at airport 721 0842. Open M-Sa 8am-10:30am, 1:30-5pm) also has daily flights to **Panama City** (M-F 7:35am, 12:45, 4:50pm; Sa 10:30am and 4:50pm; Su 9:15am and 4:50pm; US$56.70).

Local Buses: US$0.25 within the city.

Taxis: Easy to flag down. Most destinations US$0.50-1.50.

ⓘ PRACTICAL INFORMATION

Tourist Information: IPAT (☎775 4120), across from the *parque central,* to the left of the church, on the 2nd fl. of the Edificio Galherna, in an unmarked office. Open M-F 8:30am-4:30pm. Regional **ANAM** office (☎775 2055), on the road to the airport, south on Av. 8E.

Immigration: (☎775 4515), on Calle C Sur, near Av. Central. Open M-F 8am-3pm.

Consulates: Costa Rica (☎779 1923), just off the Interamerican Hwy., on the way toward, that's right, Costa Rica. Open M-F 8am-2pm.

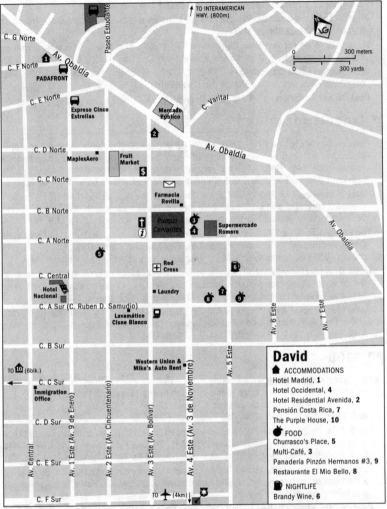

Banks: Of many, **Banco General,** at the corner of Calle C Norte and Av. 3E, cashes traveler's checks. Visa and MC advances. 24hr. **ATM.** Open M-F 8am-3pm, Sa 9am-noon.

Western Union: 3½ blocks south of the *parque* on Av. 4E. Open M-Sa 8am-6pm.

Supermarket: Supermercado Romero, behind Romero's clothing store east of the *parque.* Open M-Sa 9am-11pm, Su 8am-1pm. A 24hr. branch is on Calle F Sur.

Market: Mercado Público, 3 blocks north of the *parque* on Av. 4E.

Laundry: Lavamático Cisne Blanco, on Calle A Sur, between Av. 2/3E. Open M-Sa 7am-7pm, Su 7:30am-1:30pm. Around the corner on Av. 3E between Calles Central/A Sur, dry-clean only.

Car Rental: Mike's Auto Rent (☎775 4963), in the Western Union building. **Budget** (☎721 0845), at the airport.

Police: (☎775 2121, emergency 104), on Calle F Sur and Av. 4 Este.

Pharmacy: Farmacia Revilla (☎775 3711) has a 24hr. branch across from the *parque*'s northeast corner. MV/V.

Hospitals: Hospital Regional Chiriquí (☎775 2161), about 3km from the *parque* on the Interamerican Hwy. Take the bus toward Paso Canoas (10min., US$1).

Internet: Speedlán Ciber Café (☎774 2572), 2 blocks south of the park on Av. 3E. Fast new computers and A/C. US$1 per hr. Open 24hr.

Post Office: A block north of the park. Open M-F 7am-6pm, Sa 7am-4pm.

▐ ACCOMMODATIONS

Pensión Costa Rica (☎775 1241), on Av. 5E between Calles Central and A Sur. Popular, convenient joint with a wide range of clean, basic rooms, each oddly named for a Panamanian town. Beds and fans vary in quality. Common room with TVs. US$3.85, with bath US$6.60, with A/C US$10; doubles US$9-17; triples US$15-23. ●

Hotel Madrid (☎775 2051), on Calle F Norte, near the bus station. Each room centers around a courtyard and smells like perfume. Private hot-water bath, A/C, phone, cable TV. Laundry service. Restaurant/bar. Singles US$17.60; doubles US$23.65. ❸

The Purple House (☎774 4059; www.purplehousehostel.com), on Calle C Sur and Av. 6 Oeste. Popular hostel with many amenities. Free Internet. Dorms US$8.80; singles and doubles US$19-21; triples US$27.90. Discounts for students and volunteers. ❷

Hotel Occidental (☎775 4695), right on the *parque*, next to Multi-Café (see below) in the small shopping arcade. Great location and comfort. 60 rooms with hot-water bath, A/C, cable TV, and phone. Singles US$17; doubles US$21; triples US$25. ❸

Hotel Residencial Avenida (☎774 0451), on Av. 3E, south of Av. Obaldía. Private baths, TVs, and phones. Good location between the *parque* and buses. All rooms have A/C. Singles US$12.50; doubles US$15; 3 beds US$27. ❷

▐ FOOD

▨ Churrasco's Place, an open-air dining room on Av. 2E just south of Calle A Norte, that caters to carnivores. The huge menu includes hearty breakfasts (US$1.25-2.50), but people come for the *churrasco* (like a T-bone; US$6). Su features Panama's national dish, *sancocho* (chicken stew; US$1.25). Open 24hr. ❷

Multi-Café, on the *parque*, right underneath Hotel Occidental. Very popular, cheap *típico* in town. A blend of Mexican (tacos US$0.75), Chinese (chicken lo mein US$1), and Panamanian dishes. Everything under US$2. Open M-Sa 7am-10pm, Su 7am-1pm. ●

Panadería Pinzón Hermanos #3, on Av. 5E across from Pensión Costa Rica. By day, it's a mild-mannered bakery, but when darkness falls, it emerges as a happening sandwich and burger joint (US$0.75-1.50). Open M-Sa 7am-9:30pm, Su 4-9pm. ●

Restaurante El Mio Bello, around the corner from Pensión Costa Rica on Calle A Sur. Italian place with decent food. Try the *gaucho* (rice and seafood stew; US$2.25), tasty pasta, or their signature pizzas (US$2). Open daily from 9am. ●

♫ ▐ ENTERTAINMENT AND NIGHTLIFE

Ritzy **Hotel Nacional's** multi-screen **cinema**, on Av. 1E, Calle A Sur, two blocks west and two blocks south of the *parque*, shows recent US films with subtitles. (☎775 7887. US$3-3.50, Tu and W half-price). Blow some cash at the hotel's **casino.** (Open daily noon-4am). For more action, check out popular **Brandy Wine**, one block east and one block south of the *parque* on Av. 5E. It's divided into two buildings, one with a 12-table **billiards** hall (billiards US$1.50 per hr.; open daily 2:30pm-4am), the other with a mixed-music **dance club** called **Gótica** (open Tu-Sa nights). The party picks up after 10:30pm and rages until 2:30am. (W-Sa US$5 cover, changes often.) Thursdays are **open bar** nights (cover US$9 for men, US$8 for women).

NEAR DAVID

PLAYA LAS LAJAS

Any bus trawling the Interamerican will drop you off or pick you up at the road to Las Lajas, a 13km taxi ride south to a small cluster of buildings on the beach. From the highway drop-off, taxis run to the beach (US$5); be sure to agree on prices beforehand.

Almost halfway along the Interamerican, between David and Santiago, lies Las Lajas, an unremarkable town north of a remarkable beach. Though only about 15m wide, the smooth, palm-lined strip of sand stretches straight along the Pacific as far as the eye can see, disappearing into the mist on either end. Waves are good for bodysurfing but not big enough to prevent swimming, and during the week the beach is nearly empty. For day-trippers from David, the **El Carrizal** complex rents palm-covered *ranchitos* (US$5, low season US$3), bathrooms (US$0.25) and showers (US$0.50) to the public, though there may be no one around to take your money. To reach the only accommodation at the beach, turn right at the end of the paved road and follow a dirt road 1km along the beach (you can also walk *on* the beach). **Las Lajas Beach Cabins ❶** rents out a row of bamboo cabañas, with lights, picnic tables, and paper-thin mats in the loft above (US$7 per night). One kilometer down the beach, at the end of the road from the highway, a lonely **restaurant ❶** produces *típico* with the catch of the day and *patacones* (fried green plantains) for US$2. For less proximity but a little more formality, **Restaurante Hotel El Cruce ❷** stands at the entrance to Las Lajas on the Interamerican, where most buses drop off for the beach. Upstairs, well-worn rooms have fans and private baths (US$10), and downstairs cheap *típico* is served. The town of Las Lajas, stretched out south of the highway, also hides a few *típico* kiosks and restaurants, the most notable of which is **Mayra's ❶** at the southern end of town.

Though Las Lajas has few facilities for the visitor, basic services await 1km north of the highway entrance in **San Félix.** This long town follows the one main road north, becoming a Ngöbe village. There is a **police station** (☎727 0531), a **Banco Nacional** with **ATM** (open M-F 8am-2pm, Sa 9am-noon), and a **Centro de Salúd** (☎727 0522), as well as some assorted **supermarkets.** Of note is **Restaurante Ferjomar,** across from the Centro de Salud, which serves tasty *típico* (US$2.50).

PASO CANOAS: BORDER WITH COSTA RICA

Unappealing Paso Canoas, on the Interamerican Hwy., is the principal crossing between Panama and Costa Rica. To get to the border, take a bus from **David,** 50km east of Paso Canoas. You may have to buy a rather expensive bus ticket as proof of exit; a plane ticket out of Costa Rica is the only other accepted proof.

Entering Costa Rica, travelers need a passport, a tourist card (available at the border checkpoint; US$5, lasts 30 days), and a return ticket. Entering Panama has the same requirements. Tourist cards are sold at the Costa Rican **General de Migración,** 175m west of the main intersection (☎732 2150; open daily 7am-8pm), and at the **Instituto Panameño de Turismo** on both sides (open 6-11am and 1-5pm, but schedule varies). **Money changers** abound. *Bolsijeros* on the Panamanian side, identifiable by the fanny packs slung across their chests, give the best exchange rate, but check the rate before you approach them to avoid getting hustled. The **police** are 50m from either border. (Costa Rica ☎732 3402 or 911 for emergencies; Panama ☎727 6521.) In Panama, the **Banco Nacional de Panamá** is 25m from the crossing and has a 24hr. ATM for US dollars. (☎727 6522. Open M-F 8am-3pm, Sa 9am-noon. MC/V.) Buses drop off in front of the **post office** in Costa Rica. (☎732 2029. Open M-F 8am-noon and 1-5:30pm.) There is another post office in Panama. (Open M-F 8-11am and 2-5pm, Sa 8am-noon.) For accommodations and food, see **Paso Canoas: Border with Panama,** p. 225.

BOQUETE

Thirty-eight kilometers north of David, mountain scenery and fresh air envelop Boquete, an increasingly popular destination for international travelers and day-trippers from David, all eager to hike, horseback ride, bird watch, or escape the heat. As tourists become more frequent, prices are rapidly rising in the city itself. Despite this recent change, Boquete remains a backpacker's heaven and usually keeps them longer than they planned! The rainy season presents some difficulties in ascending the volcano, and impressive, roaring rivers tend to flood, causing landslides to block nearby trails. In these situations, it is often still possible to explore the nearby countryside through the many pebbled roads that loop out of and back into the town center. Indigenous areas, coffee farms, and many creative gardens make this alternative equally attractive.

TRANSPORTATION

Buses leave from the western side of the *parque central* for **David** (1hr., every 25min. 5am-11:15pm, US$1.20). Local Buses: Zona Urbana and Zona Rural buses serving the local area leave one block up the main street. (US$0.35-$2.) The mini-buses are yellow, with "Boquete Palmiro" painted on the front. Many **taxis** are 4WD and can be hailed in front of the park. Fares vary.

ORIENTATION AND PRACTICAL INFORMATION

Boquete is laid out in a near-grid, with the main north-south *avenida* running along the western side of the **parque central.** The main *avenida* comes in from David and continues north, where it splits and splits again through the surrounding countryside. Numbered *calles* run east-west. The **Quebrada Grande** cuts through town. The **Avenida Central** runs parallel to **Avenida Cincuentenario,** and the road west is labeled **Hacia Valle Escondido** (across the bridge).

Tourist Information: For the best info, talk with multilingual Frank at **Pensión Marilós** (see **Accommodations,** below). However, all hostel owners are full of suggestions, phone numbers, and self-drawn maps. The official tourist center, **Cefati** (☎720 4060), about 1.5km south of town on the main road, offers maps, brochures, and kind assistance, as well as an awesome view. The classy building and staff don't have much information for backpackers. Open Tu-Su 8am-4pm. Another option for free tourist information is **Gringos,** though tours suggested here may be comparatively pricey.

Banks: Banco Nacional (☎720 1328 or 720 2776), 1½ blocks south of the *parque* on the main *avenida,* across from the Delta gas station on the main road, cashes AmEx traveler's checks and has free coffee. They have a 24hr. MC/V **ATM.** Open M-F 8am-3pm, Sa 7am-noon. **Global Bank,** across the street, has an ATM and will change Visa and Master Card checks as well. Open M-F 8am-3pm, Sa 9am-noon.

Supermarkets: Supercentro El Mandarín (☎720 1815), across the main street just north of the *parque.* Open Su-F 8:30am-9pm, Sa 8:30am-10pm.

Laundry: Lavamático Las Burbujas, across from the church at the town's northern end. Wash and dry US$2.25. Clorox US$0.20. Ironing US$0.60-$2 per item. Open M-Sa 8am-6pm.

Pharmacy: Farmacia Amy (☎ 720 1296), 3 blocks north of the *parque*. Open daily 8am-9pm.

Police: (☎ 104 or 720 1222), 1 block east and 1 block south of the *parque*.

Emergency: Ambulance ☎ 720 1356.

Medical Services: Centro Médico San Juan Bautista (☎ 720 1881), near the bridge, 1 block east of the *parque*. Open M-F 7:30am-6pm, Sa 9am-1pm. Doctor on call 24hr. For a bilingual doctor call ☎ 720 1881 and ask for Dr. Pretel.

Internet: Professional Center (☎ 720 2047), next to the laundromat, across from the church. US$2 per hr. Open M-Sa 8am-9pm, Su 9am-6pm. **Kelnix** (☎ 720 2803; kevilgo@hotmail.com), across the street from the southwest corner of the *parque*. Fewer computers and slower connections. US$0.60 per 15min.; US$1 per 30min.; US$1.90 per hr. Open M-Sa 8am-8pm, Su 1pm-7pm. **Gringos** (☎ 720 2720), 2 blocks south of the *parque*, has the most expensive connections but good coffee. Coffee US$0.40-$2. Internet US$3 per hr. Open daily 9am-8pm, Oct.-Jan. 8am-9pm.

Post Office: (☎ 720 1265) Large green building across from the east side of the *parque*. Fax available within Panama, US$1 per page. Open M-Sa 7am-6pm.

ACCOMMODATIONS

Boquete has the best backpacker hostels in Panama. Rooms are often shared and cheap. Hostel owners are often eager to help and make connections between travelers and tour guides. Boquete locals are especially helpful people, but beware. Although hostel owner's suggestions may be of use, they cannot be blindly relied upon. Be prepared for overbearing treatment at all accommodations.

Pensión Marilós (☎ 720 1380), 2 blocks south and 1 block east of the *parque*. Comfort and cleanliness make it the best hostel in town. Hot water, beautiful common area, kitchen, book exchange, and a multilingual owner (Frank) with encyclopedic knowledge of the area. Free use of laundry machine with 2-day stay. Reservations recommended year round. Singles US$6.60, with bath US$9.90; doubles US$10/US$15.40. ❶

Hostal Palacio (☎ 720 1653, cell 633 8512), off the northwest corner of the *parque*. Shared rooms tightly packed with beds. Common kitchen, common baths, garden, hammocks, and an uncommonly helpful owner, Pancho, who will probably solicit your stay as you get off the bus. US$5-6 per person depending on season and other factors. ❶

Pensión Topás (☎ 720 1005; schoeb@chiriqui.com), 3½ blocks south of the southeastern corner of the *parque*. Large bright and clean rooms surround a garden with pool and original murals. Knowledgeable owners speak English and German. Massive breakfasts US$3.90. Singles US$7.70, with bath US$15; doubles with bath US$17.60-19.80; triples US$26.40; quads US$33. Tax included. Dec.-May prices 20% higher. ❶

Hostal La Estancia (☎ 720 4260), 2km out of town on the Volcancito route, after Hostal Mozart, has an enormous swimming pool open to the public during the day (US$1; open 10am-6pm) and classier rooms. US$30 for a room with two beds and bath. ❸

FOOD

If you can't say no to *típica*, **El Sabrosón** on Av. Central near the northern end of town is as cheap as they come. (*Comida corriente* US$1-2. Open M-F 6:30am-11pm, Sa-Su 6:30am-midnight.)

Punto de Encuentro (☎ 720 2123), 1 block south and 1 block west of the *parque*. Follow the blue sign for Hotel Rebequet and then turn right, down a small driveway. Superb breakfast in a relaxing setting. Open-air dining area. Omelettes US$3.25; french toast with fruit US$3; coffee US$0.50; and yogurt US$1. Open daily 7-11:30am. ❶

La Volcánica Pizzería (☎720 1063), a block south of the *parque* on the main road. Good thin crust pizza. Not authentic Italian recipes, but fun favorite locale among tourists. Small US$3.50-4.50, medium US$4.50-6.50, large US$7.50-8.50. Milkshakes US$1.25. Open M-Th 3pm-10pm, F and Su 10am-10pm, Sa 10am-11pm. ❶

La Casona Mexicana, 1½ blocks south of the *parque*. Nice locale attracts its fair share of tourists. Debatably authentic Mexican cuisine. Tacos US$2.50-3.50. *Entradas* US$1.50-4; *Arroz con leche* (rice pudding) US$1. Open daily noon-11pm. ❶

Casa Mozart (☎720 3768). A romantic dinner getaway in the mountains west of Boquete (see above). Reserve a dinner, which for US$8.50 per person includes transportation to and from the mountain cabin and a full meal. Gorgeously painted dining area and patio. Menu also includes hot chocolate (US$0.75), sandwiches (US$1.50-2.50) and *comida del día* for only US$2.50. Open daily 8am-8pm. Cash only. ❷

▲ OUTDOOR ACTIVITIES

HIKING. Plenty of trails head into Parque Nacional Volcán Barú (see below), but there is much to see without even entering the park. North of town are *fincas*, worked mostly by indigenous **Ngöbe** (NO-beh) people, recognizable by the women's long, colorful dresses, called *naguas*. One of the best circuits is known as **Bajo Mono;** follow the signs to the left at the fork north of town. This 4-5hr. hike skirts the Río Caldera past Los Ladrillos rock formation, San Ramón waterfall, a castle, and numerous bridges. If you don't have time to hike the whole route, take the bus through part of the loop to see the views. Almost all roads starting in Boquete loop back into the town center, so it's hard to get lost. The president of Panama, **Mireya Moscoso,** has a farm along this road, which locals proudly mention.

GARDENS. Mi Jardín es Su Jardín, 1km north of town, is a private garden with almost 100 varieties of flowers, ponds, and fountains. As the name implies, the family generously opens their grounds to the public for free. (Open daily 9am-6pm.) **El Explorador** is 2km south out of town. Follow the road to Palo Alto, turn right at the Jaramillo Arriba school, and then take a right at the Explorador sign. The entrance is a decorated fence on your left across from the radio tower. The garden has clearly marked paths and views of all of Boquete. The garden is essentially the fantasy land of its creator, with profound quotes, silly faces on recycled junk, and beautiful flower beds. On weekends, the *café* opens and there is music in the garden. (☎627 6908; ammsa7@cwp.net.pa. Open daily 8:30am-6pm. US$2.)

CALDERA HOT SPRINGS. Locals and tourists alike adore these seven natural springs. Most visit the swimming holes at night. However, the intricate hikes along the surrounding area, which pass the five more hidden springs, are best attempted during the day. Take a bus south toward David and ask to be let off at the turnoff for Caldera. It is easiest to hitchhike the remaining 14km to Caldera, since buses are irregular and infrequent along this road. However, *Let's Go* does not recommend hitchhiking. During the day, Caldera has plenty of 4WD taxis (follow the signs). These travel up an extremely rocky road and drop you off at a bridge that is a 15min. hike to the first set of holes. (45min.-1hr., US$15.) You can walk this stretch about as fast as a car can manage it. The best option is to find a few other interested folks at any hostel and hire a guide. Most locals provide the service (more of a taxi service than a tour) for US$15 per car. The path to the first spring passes a small farm with horses and an abandoned house; turn right here to find the holes. Almost all backpackers hire a local for this trip. *(US$0.50, rarely charged.)*

COFFEE PLANTATIONS. Cafe Ruiz is a local coffee factory about a 10min. walk along the left fork of the road north of town. They offer a tour demonstrating the coffee-making process, with samples at the end (25min., US$4). For true coffee lovers, they have a tour through the farms and the factory (3hr., US$12.50). Tours in Dutch, English, German, and Spanish. Full tours daily at 9am. (☎ 720 1000; tours@caferuiz.com.; www.caferuiz.com.) **Café Sitton** in Alto Quiel, out the left fork of the Bajo Mono loop, offers more in-depth but less organized tours that include picking beans in the field. (Go in advance to arrange a tour. Prices negotiated at the site.)

GUIDED TOURS

Boquete offers many excellent tour guides, though few have offices and it may be hard to distinguish between their merits.

Chiriquí River Rafting (☎ 720 1505 or 720 1506; rafting@panama-rafting.com; www.panama-rafting.com), has an office across the street from the southwest corner of the *parque*. Amazing (though pricey) Class II-IV rafting trips on Río Chiriquí Viejo and Chiriquí. Trips begin at 7am sharp; departure from Boquete. Return around 5:30pm. US$80-100 per person; negotiable student discounts. Open M-Sa 8:30am-5:30pm.

Feliciano's Tours (☎ 624 9940, ask for Feliciano González in the evenings). Local guide is well regarded in town and offers several hiking tours. His 4WD truck will also get you to the hot springs. Special trips across the Cordillera into Bocas del Toro (2-3 days one way; US$130) can be arranged with advanced notice. Most tours (US$20) can be split between a maximum of four people. Negotiable prices for students.

Poirier Tours (☎ 626 9354; panahikes@yahoo.com). Another one-man tour company, Denny comes highly recommended by tourists. Denny speaks English, French, and Spanish, and offers many more creative excursions than most. Several smaller hikes for those whose energy or pocketbooks are easily drained (3hr., US$25). Transportation to trailhead not included. 10 people maximum per excursion. Variable prices.

Horse Tours (☎ 720 1750, 642 6290, or 720 3013), with Señor Eduardo, can be arranged through **Gringos** for a US$5 fee or directly with the guide. US$12 per person per hr., US$18.50 for 2hr. US$5 additional for every hr. with guide.

AJ Tours (☎ 624 0350; anaj07@hotmail.com or anaj07@yahoo.com), with Ana Julia Serracín, specializes in nature hikes. US$20-40 for 2-3 people. Student discounts.

Gringo's (see **Internet** above) will connect you to several tour guides, but also rents bikes and scooters for a minimum of 2hr. Bikes US$2.95 per hr. Scooters US$7.95 per hr. Deposits (US$25-75) are strictly required.

PARQUE NACIONAL VOLCÁN BARÚ

Protecting the slopes of Volcán Barú, Panama's highest point (3475m), Parque Nacional Volcán Barú offers panoramic views and the nation's highest concentration of quetzals. During the dry season, you can see both oceans at once from the Volcano's peak. The ascent of Barú is best done from Boquete, though a guided hike is possible from Cerro Punta. Keep careful note of weather conditions, because you could face hours of cold rain. On the other hand, captivating Sendero Los Quetzales, a hike through cloud forest, is easiest from Cerro Punta. Many other hikes are possible with guides, available in both Cerro Punta and Boquete.

◪ **CLIMBING THE VOLCANO.** The easiest, most popular way to climb Volcán Barú starts in Boquete, from which a rough dirt road (barely passable even in a 4WD) climbs 2500m in about 14km. Ask about road conditions during the rainy season (Apr.-Nov.), lest a river suddenly materialize beneath you. If you've got US$100 or so to spend, you can hire a car to take you up there; contact the tour guides listed in Boquete. Locals will try to dissuade you from making the ascent during the rainy season because they have seen plenty of miserable, cold, wet travelers come back down to Boquete. However, if you leave early and dress prepared, you can have an excellent experience year-round. Camping up top is possible but very cold. Various people head up the mountain, mostly to work on the antennae up top. If you hit the road by 6am, you have a decent shot of scoring a ride all the way (some trucks leave as late as 10 or 11am), although *Let's Go* does not recommend hitchhiking. The entrance to the park, with an occasionally-staffed ranger station, is 8km from Boquete on a paved road—turn left on Calle 2 Nte., 1½ blocks past the church. A taxi will take you as far as the ranger station for US$5 (ask to go *al fin del pavimento*), but most locals will do it for free if you start walking.

Another option is to climb the other side from a village called **Paso Ancho,** a few kilometers from Volcán on the road to Cerro Punta. However, this trail can be hard to find and parts have been washed away by landslides, so you'll probably need a guide (ask in Volcán). It's a full-day hike up this side, but you can camp.

◪ SENDERO LOS QUETZALES FROM CERRO PUNTA.

This trail connects Cerro Punta and Boquete, but it's easier to start in Cerro Punta. Either take a 4WD taxi from the town's center to Respingo (US$10), or catch a Ruta Urbana bus and explain where you're going, then walk to Respingo, a steep 45min. hike on the rocky road. **Respingo,** a ranger station, has beds, a kitchen, and bathroom facilities (bring food and sheets). Rangers are friendly and will do everything possible to get you shelter for the night, including letting you crash on the couch. Grounds are beautifully kept and bunk beds are clean. (US$5 to camp per tent, US$5 per bed; US$2 park entrance). From Respingo, the trail, well-marked at the beginning, winds mostly downhill for about a half-day's hike to **Bajo Mono,** in Boquete (8km). Along the way, a 90m detour to the **Mirador,** is a well-marked elevated wooden porch with views spanning most of the park. You will also pass a possible camping area, **Respinguito,** 3km from the ranger station, which has picnic tables. Once you reach **Bajo Mono,** a bus usually passes every hour. In Cerro Punta, you can arrange guides through **Hotel Los Quetzales** (☎ 771 2182). The trail is extremely popular during all seasons, though recent rains will create deep mud along the path.

◪ SENDERO LOS QUETZALES FROM BOQUETE.

From Boquete, the trail is harder and longer. It begins at the top of the Bajo Mono road 3km north of town. Take a taxi (US$5) or bus (US50¢) to the entrance, and follow the main path to the right across the creek. Follow the red pipeline that runs alongside the rough road for about 30min., until a smaller gravel trail veers left uphill. There are four fixtures in a row on top of the pipe at that fork; take the left up the hill. That brings you to the beginning of the park at **Alto Chiquero** (12km from Cerro Punta, 3km from Boquete), where there is an unstaffed ranger station (unless you call ANAM in advance). You'll find beds, bathrooms, and kitchen facilities, but bring a sleeping bag; temperatures can drop as low as 4°C. The road continues for 45min. until a barbed wire fence, where an easy-to-miss sign points out the path to the left.

The difficult but extremely rewarding hike truly begins at this point. The path reaches a clearing and an empty house and continues to the right. Twenty minutes later, you must fork off the main path to the left at a patch of bamboo and some tree stumps. This path leads directly to the creek, which you then continue along, crossing often, uphill to La Victoria, where there's an awesome view of the valley. This is two-thirds of the way through the hike. From here, two paths diverge, one through the valley and one climbing farther uphill. Both lead 5km more to Respingo, where the trail ends. From Respingo, it's about a 45min. walk downhill to the paved road, where it's possible to get a ride from a taxi, a bus, or any car that stops. Keep in mind that during rainy season, the creek becomes harder to cross and the mud becomes harder to trudge through.

VOLCÁN

An hour north of David, the town of Volcán lies on the eastern slopes of its namesake, Volcán Barú, and can be reached only by bus from David or through the Sendero los Quetzales from Boquete. With similar access to countless natural attractions, but fewer travelers, Volcán is the perfect alternative to touristy Boquete. Not as many guides are available and night stays can be pricey, but Volcán is certainly worth the extra trouble, offering a tight-knit and kind community where the helpful locals are eager to share outdoor adventures with their visitors.

TRANSPORTATION. From the kiosk at the main intersection, buses go to **Cerro Punta** (30min., every 15min. 5am-7pm, US$0.90) and the Costa Rican border at **Río Sereno** (45min., every hr. 5am-6pm, US$2.85). The bus to **David** comes from Cerro Punta and stops at the Shell station, but will also stop wherever it is flagged on the southbound road. (1½hr., every 15min. 5:30am-7pm, US$2.30.) **4WD taxis** patrol the main road and hang out at the intersection. (☎771 4288.)

ORIENTATION AND PRACTICAL INFORMATION. The main road comes in from Concepción (a little west of David on the Interamerican Hwy.) from the south, heads northwest through town, and then heads out toward Río Sereno, on the Costa Rican border. At the main intersection, a road branches right to Cerro Punta in the north, 20km away. Most of the town's services cluster around this intersection. The town itself is divided into two districts: **El Hoto** to the southeast and **Nuevo California** past the intersection. Locals often refer to these districts to point you in the right direction, but street names are never used.

The local **ANAM** office, the main office for Volcán Barú and La Amistad, is on the left side of the road to Cerro Punta, 300m north of the main intersection. (☎771 5383. Open M-F 8am-4pm.) They offer some information, but not nearly as much as private offices in town, and do not offer guided tours. One well-respected guide in town, **Arturo Rivera,** will take you to Las Lagunas or Los Pozos for US$15, and offers tours to other attractions, such as La Amistad or Sendero los Quetzales for US$20-80. His house is 200m past the ANAM office on the road to Cerro Punta; look for the "Guía" sign. (☎771 5917; coraliagonzales@hotmail.com.) A pricier option for guided tours is **Highlands Adventure,** just across the street from the intersection on the main road, offers 43 organized tours in the area. (☎685 1682 or 771 4413; ecoaizpurúa@hotmail.com. Open daily approximately 8am-8pm. No student discounts.) Next door, **Finca Guardia** rents fairly expensive horses for adults and kids. (☎616 2521. US$10 for 30min., US$15 per hr., US$40 per day.) **Wild Adventures,** on the main road before the intersection right next to the school, sells rafts, backpacks, and other outdoor gear, and rents camping equipment at good rates. (☎771 5501; xpedition@aol.com. Tents US$4-10, sleeping bags US$2.50-4 per day. Bikes US$4 per hr., US$14.50 for 24hr. Open daily 9am-4pm.)

Other services include: **Banistmo,** a block south of the main intersection, changes traveler's checks and gives cash advances on Visa (☎771 4711; open M-F 8am-3:30pm, Sa 9am-noon); **laundry** at **Lavamatico Volcán,** 500m south of the intersection (☎695 4168; US$1.25 per wash; open M-Sa 7am-8pm; the owner lives in the house next door and will open shop for travelers desperate for Sunday cleaning); **police,** at the fork in the road (☎771 4231; emergency ☎104); **Farmacia Celina,** next to the gas station at the main intersection (☎771 5075; open M-F 7:30am-11pm, Sa 9am-11pm). Get **medical attention** at the **Centro de Salud,** left at the church on the Cerro Punta fork. (☎771 4283. Open M-F 7am-3pm.) Access the **Internet** at **Volc@net.place,** on the main road 800m west of the intersection (☎771 5482; US$1 per hr.; open daily 8am-10pm), and 200m farther west at **CyberCafé** (☎771 4461;

US$0.75 per hr.; open daily 7:30am-11pm). The **post office** is on the main road. (☎771 4222. Open M-F 7-11am and 1-4:30pm, Sa 8am-noon.)

Γ ACCOMMODATIONS. Most lodgings in Volcán are well-furnished but pricey *cabañas*. Reservations are recommended during the high season (Jan.-May). Many families rent rooms, though, so ask around town. A little south of town, ▨**Talamanca Ecolodge and Restaurante Cerro Brujo ❸**, a mother-daughter business, offers a small, luxurious *cabaña* with kitchenette, and a gourmet creole restaurant on site. Gorgeous grounds invite campers. (☎629 5604; cerrobrujo@hotmail.com. Restaurant open daily 11am-10pm. Meals US$6-10. Breakfast included with stay. US$55 for 4 people; camping US$8.) **Hospedaje Sr. Tomás Rivera ❷**, across the Centro de Salud has flimsy mattresses with private baths and small black-and-white TVs. (☎771 5917. US$8.) **Hotel Oasis ❷** is on the first left after the intersection along the westbound road. Its restaurant serves medium-priced meals and the disco is a local hangout, especially during the rainy season. (☎771 4644. Singles with hot-water bath US$12; doubles US$15; triples US$20; discount for large groups and longer stays.) **Cabañas Bonanza ❷**, 2km (US$0.75 by taxi) north of the intersection, has hot water, spacious rooms, and homey decor. (☎771 4435. Singles US$12, with kitchen US$15; doubles US$18; quads with kitchen US$25.) For **Cabañas Reina ❷** head south from the intersection on the main road; turn right at the sign for the *cabañas*, then bear right and follow the paved road. This place is quite isolated, but the *cabañas* have small living rooms with TV, kitchens with fridge, and hot water. (☎771 4338. 2-person cabin US$22, 4-person US$30, 5-person US$38.50, 10-person US$75.) Similar *cabañas* are along the road to Río Sereno.

Camp for free behind the **fire station**, on an uncovered cement platform; take the first right on the road to Cerro Punta and bear left at the *parque*. There's a toilet and sink in the station, but no shower. If you ask nicely, especially if it's cold and rainy outside, the fireman on duty may let you **crash on the couch** in the meeting room. (For camping equipment rental see **Practical Information**, above.)

◘ FOOD. Most of the action centers around the **Panadería-Dulcería-Rosticería Mole ❶**, right at the bus stop at the main intersection in town, serving ice cream pastries (US$0.15-0.45) and luscious baked loaves. (Open daily 8am-10pm.) Pleasant wooden benches draw many local families. *Comida típica* is fired up at the **kiosk ❶** right outside (US$0.50-2). **Restaurante Don Tavo ❶**, next to CyberCafé, offers good *típico* (*comida del día* US$2.50) and more exotic options such as tacos for US$1.50. (☎771 4258. Open Tu-Su 8am-9pm.) **Pizzeria Las Cananias ❶**, 500m west of the intersection, is a local family favorite with friendly and fast service. Pizzas are US$5-12. (☎771 5399. Open daily 8am-8pm.)

◙ SIGHTS. ▨**Sitio Arqueológico Barriles,** 5.5km west of Volcán, is one of the famed archaeological sites in Panama. The location of the civilization of Barriles was named after the rounded stone barrels first found on the site. The volcano destroyed the civilization, but ironically helped to preserve the stone items. Although some of the artifacts were stolen from the site during the 1950s and sold to museums in the United States and Europe, much more has been found hidden in the surrounding gardens in recent excavations. Figures include representations of sacrificial tables, maps of the area (with symbolic notations of the volcano and other peaks), whistles, urns, and outdoor statues. The owner of the farm on which the site sits offers 1½hr. tours. Accommodations geared toward **agrotourism** are planned for January, 2003. To get to the site, take a bus marked **Caizah** (30min., US$0.75) and get off when you see the black-and-white sign. (☎633 2911. Open daily 7am-8:30pm. Free. Donations accepted.) **Las Lagunas,** two placid lagoons popular with migrating birds, are only 5km southwest of town. Many families frequent the lagoons to relax, picnic, or hike the lakeside trails. To get there, continue on the main road a few blocks west of the main intersection (the road after the turnoff for Motel California), and turn left at the road where a sign points to the airport. Follow signs all the way down this road until you see the lakes. You can also take a taxi (US$2 each way). Hikers can soak their bunions in the medicinal hot springs of **Los Pozos**, 19km from Volcán. Holes suitable for swimming are hard to find, but the river that cuts through the area, Río Colorado, will lead you to a couple. To get to Los Pozos, take the Río Sereno bus and ask the driver when to get off. Right after Silla de Pando, a large hill, you'll make a sharp right off the main road; continue on this road until the end, keeping left at three forks (3.5km, about a 2hr. walk). It's easier to take a four-wheel-drive taxi (US$12-15), which will wait to bring you back. Or hire a guide, as there are no signs marking the way and generally nobody around to point you in the right direction. **Arte Cruz**, 3km south of town on the main road, accessible by taxi (US$2) or any bus heading toward David, is the studio of local artist José Cruz, who specializes in wood carving, sculpture, and crystal etching. (☎ 680 0626. Open W-Su 8am-noon and 1:30-6pm.)

The amazing gorge of **Macho de Monte,** where orchids and birds abound, has yet to be discovered by tourists, but many locals consider it their favorite natural getaway. The nearby *mirador* is private property, but you can descend into the gorge for the best views of the rapids rushing through it. Some picnic and swim in the basin, but since the gorge is extremely isolated, it is best to exercise extreme caution. Some wooden planks and fences have been put in place to keep visitors from danger. To reach Macho de Monte from Volcán, hop on a David-bound bus and ask to get off in Cuesta de Piedra. (US$0.65, 15min.) Then grab a taxi to Macho de Monte (US$1.50-2) or ask locals about the bus that passes about every 2hr. on its way to Concepcíon (US$0.50, 20min.). If you take the bus, make sure to ask to be let off. Both the bus and the taxi will drop you off at a bridge 50m above the river. From here, various hikes encircle the gorge and lead to its basin.

CERRO PUNTA

Twenty kilometers north of Volcán, tiny Cerro Punta is tucked in a valley between Volcán Barú and the Cordillera de Talamanca. The village is surrounded by beautiful mountains dotted with plantations and, just a bit farther off, pristine cloud forest. It was originally settled by Swiss immigrants, as the architecture attests. At almost 2000m, Cerro Punta's cool climate and picturesque scenery provide an ideal base for exploring the nearby national parks of Volcán Barú and La Amistad. The nearby farming villages of Guadalupe (2km north), Las Nubes (3km west), and Nueva Suiza (1km south) are equally charming.

▐ TRANSPORTATION. The main road comes in from Volcán and continues to **Guadalupe** a few kilometers north (and also to Respingo and Parque Nacional Volcán Barú). At the main intersection, just north of the police station, a road turns left into the countryside, heading west to the village of **Las Nubes** at the entrance to **Parque Internacional La Amistad** (see below). The little yellow Ruta Urbana **buses** stop at the main intersection (US$0.25) and provide the best transportation around the region, taking you almost anywhere. Schedules vary, but the buses usually pass by in either direction every 15min. Other buses head to **David** (2hr., every 15min. 5am-8pm, US$2.65) via **Volcán** (30min., US$0.95).

▐ PRACTICAL INFORMATION. All vital services are within a block of the main intersection, except the closest **bank,** which is in Volcán. Guides are hard to come by—it's better to arrange one in Volcán. Get **tourist information** at **FUNDICCEP**, 800m west of the intersection on the road to Las Nubes, on the left. (Open M-F roughly 8am-4:30pm. Spanish only.) The supermarket **Supercentro Cerro Punta** is south of the intersection on the main road. (Open Su-F 8am-10pm, Sa 8am-11:30pm.) The **police** (☎ 771 2013; emergency ☎ 104) are at the intersection and **Farmacia Zarina** is on the left a block west of the intersection on the road to Las Nubes (☎ 771 2012; open M-Sa 7:30am-8pm, Su 11am-7pm). Get **medical attention** at the **Centro de Salud**, across the street from Zarina. (☎ 771 2159. Open M-F 7am-3pm.) **Public telephones** are in front of the police station and in front of the Centro de Salud. The **post office** is two doors left of the police. (☎ 771 2052. Open M-F 8am-2pm, Sa 8am-noon.)

⚑ ACCOMMODATIONS. The best housing might be in the nearby parks, which have beds, showers, and cooking facilities; the closest ranger stations are at Respingo and at the entrance to Parque La Amistad. Locals recognize the area's lack of budget accommodations and often open their homes to lone travelers. A few kilometers to the north in Guadalupe (ask the driver when to get off the bus) is the **🏠Hotel Los Quetzales ❷**, with luxurious rooms that have phones, hot water, queen-sized beds, small sofas, and some bathtubs. Newly built dormitories run by the hotel, in a separate building across the playground, have the expensive feel of the rest of the hotel with comfortable rooms and hot water, but are much cheaper. (☎ 771 2182; fax 771 2226; stay@losquetzales.com; www.losquetzales.com. Continental breakfast included. Dorms divided by gender, US$12 per person. Hotel rooms US$50, with bathtub US$60. AmEx/MC/V.) The cheapest accommodations in Cerro Punta proper are at the comfortable **Pensión Eterna Primavera ❷**, a few minutes west of the intersection on the road to Las Nubes, on the right in the light blue-and-white house. Marked only by a "Bienvenidos a Tierras Altas" sign, the house has two rooms, both with balconies, and a well-kept garden. (Double with hot-water communal bath US$12.50; triple with private bath US$12.50.) Just south of the main intersection is **Hotel Cerro Punta ❸**. The clean, luxurious rooms have private bath, hot water, and a sweet view. (☎ 771 2020. Reception open 7am-9pm. Singles US$22; doubles US$28; triples US$33. MC/V.) The hotel also houses a pleasant **restaurant and bar ❷** (US$3 to US$9; open daily 7am-9pm). Inquire about transportation to the **Los Quetzales Cloud Forest Retreat ❺**, a phenomenal "hotel" actually located in the cloud forest 20min. away. Quetzals are no longer elusive here, as they appear almost daily late November to April, and frequently the rest of the year. Guides lead frequent tours into the Parque Nacional Barú, and hiking equipment is available to rent. (☎ 771 2182. Cabins for 6-8 people US$125-150.)

🍴 FOOD. There are a couple of *típico* restaurants around the intersection in Cerro Punta. A couple distinguish themselves from the rest, such as **Restaurante Anthony ❶**, 100m west of the intersection on the road to Las Nubes. Heaping plates of *comida corriente* are US$1.75. (☎ 627 5979. Open Su-F 7am-6pm, Sa 7am-8pm.) Another favorite is across the street from Hotel Cerro Punta, **Restaurante y Refresquería Doña Nella ❶**, which offers fast food (US$1.25-2.50) and delicious sweets. (☎ 632 0472. Open daily 7am-7:30pm.) For a glorious local specialty tasty enough to be illegal, hop a bus south (10min., US$0.50). Get off just before the second bridge in the town of Nueva Suiza by a small yellow building marked **El Sombrero ❶**. The specialty here is strawberries and cream, but Liliana, the owner and main chef, makes all sorts of tasty treats, such as fresh bread and cakes, which can be enjoyed on the wooden chairs outside. (☎ 649 2190. Sandwiches US$1-2.50, strawberries and cream parfait US$1.75.)

⛰ PARQUE INTERNACIONAL LA AMISTAD

To reach the ranger station, take a Ruta Urbana bus from **Cerro Punta** *to* **Las Nubes** *(15min., US$0.50), then walk 30min. uphill. During the rainy season, buses don't run often, in which case a taxi is US$1-3. Park admission is US$3.*

Parque Internacional La Amistad, together with its adjoining Costa Rican sister park, form **La Amistad Biosphere Reserve,** the largest protected area in Central America. The reserve is mostly undeveloped—the trails near Cerro Punta and Wetzo, in Bocas del Toro province (see p. 669). In addition to the famed quetzal, visitors may lay eyes on jaguars, pumas, tapirs, snakes, frogs, and butterflies. Most of the park is in Bocas del Toro province, but Chiriquí houses the park offices and the easiest access to the park on the Panamanian side, with clean trails supported by wooden stairs, bridges, and stepping blocks.

The **trails** at the ranger station near Cerro Punta provide a taste of the park. The best way to enjoy La Amistad is by making an expedition to the beautifully untouched forest of the park's interior. To arrange this, talk to the rangers. You can also enter the park from the Costa Rican side. The four main trails on the Panamanian side, which are extremely well maintained, leave from right next to the ranger station. **Sendero El Retoño,** an easy trail with the most primary-forest views, cuts a circular path through secondary forest near the station (2km, 1hr.). If you take a right onto a small trail 500m after the start of this *sendero*, you will hit a series of abandoned barracks built by Noriega's military. **Sendero La Cascada,** a difficult but more rewarding trail, climbs along an old cattle path through forest to the Mirador La Nevera at 2500m, offering gorgeous views of the nearby mountains, including the very imposing Volcán Barú. Fifteen minutes later, you will reach Mirador El Barranco, slightly lower at 2488m, with impressive views. From here you can see the mountain ranges 360 degrees around the park, including the Cerro Cordillera, Cerro Picacho, Cerro Derrumbe, and Cerro Respingo. Finally, you will reach a serene waterfall (2.7km; 2hr. round-trip). The third and fourth trails are short easy loops (20 and 45min.), the larger of which is ideal for birdwatching. Talk to rangers about longer hikes—you'll need a guide and machete. **Guides** are available through the Hotel Los Quetzales (☎771 2182), the Grupo Ecoturístico La Amistad in Las Nubes, Amigos del PILA in Guadalupe, or FUNDICEP (☎771 2171). Rangers are reluctant to guide tourists anymore, but have many maps in their station and will give clear directions to hikers.

The **ranger station** has sheetless beds, a kitchen, bathrooms with cold water, and a toasty fireplace. You can **camp** outside the station or anywhere in the park. (Lodging per person or camping per tent US$5.) It gets chilly at night; be sure to bring a sleeping bag. For more info, contact ANAM in David (☎775 3163) or FUNDICEP in Cerro Punta (☎771 2171). **Los Quetzales Cloud Forest Retreat,** mentioned above under Cerro Punta, is a fantastic place at the border of the park.

BOCAS DEL TORO PROVINCE

North of Chiriquí Province, Bocas del Toro (the communal name of the province, archipelago, and provincial capital) sings a different siren song than its neighbor, promising not rugged high-altitude thrills, but the allure of the Caribbean. If you're arriving from the interior or from the Pacific coast, you'll hear Spanish give way to a dense mix of English creoles and indigenous languages, and see rugged forests and ranchlands ease into the beaches, mangroves, and sea-warm docks that frame life on the islands. Once a haven for British and French pirates, the archipelago is still home to the Ngöbe (NO-beh), Bribrí, and Naso tribes. Other inhabitants include a mix of Latino, indigenous, and Afro-Caribbean peoples. Many islands, reflecting the local lingual stew and Columbus's overzealous naming practices, have more than one name. Weather here changes quickly and dramatically. It's drier mid-August through mid-November and mid-January through mid-March.

For visitors, the islands' diving, hiking, beaches, and lifestyle are the main attractions. The archipelago is made up of six large islands and many smaller ones. Sometimes called "Bocas Isla," charming Isla Colón is the main base for visiting the archipelago. Besides the town of Bocas itself, **Isla Colón** has a few other tiny towns (notably Boca del Drago on the opposite side) and plenty of natural attractions. The mainland, including half of Parque Internacional La Amistad, teems with wildlife and spooky swamps, and is perfect for hardcore exploration.

BOCAS DEL TORO AND ISLA COLÓN

Bocas is the essence of small-town Caribbean life, seamlessly melding a welcoming atmosphere of easy aimlessness with the energy and drive of a tightly-knit community. It's also the best place in Panama to launch for a tropical reef-and-beach vacation without the ritzy resorts. Throw your watch off the ferry and get ready for real relaxation—breathe deeply, slice open a mango, and stare at the sea and the palms. Ambitious visitors can work a few side trips into their visit, including Isla Bastimentos, Boca del Drago, and other nearby islands.

☞ TRANSPORTATION

Flights: Airport is on Av. F, Calle 6. From the *park,* walk a block north and a couple of blocks west. Open M-Sa 7am-5pm, Su 2:30-5pm. Aeroperlas (☎ 757 9341) has daily flights to **Panama City** (M-F 9am and 2:30pm, Sa 8:10am and 4pm, Su 9:50am and 4pm; US$49.35) and **David** (M-F 9:50am, US$25.20) via **Changuinola** only if the demand is high enough (US$10.50). Mapiex Aero (☎ 757 9841) runs daily to **Panama City** via **Changuinola** for the same prices.

Water Taxis: Galápagos Tours (☎ 757 9073), next to Bar Le Pirate in the middle of Calle 3, and **Taxi 25** (☎ 757 9062), next to the police station on Calle 1, have water taxis about every hr. to **Almirante** (30min., 6am-6pm, US$5 one-way). Because of the new road between Almirante and Chiriquí Grande, there are no boats from Chiriquí Grande.

Ferry: (☎ 758 3731), leaves from the dock at the southern end of Calle 3 for **Almirante** (W and F-Su 5pm, US$1).

Local Boats: Locals with *botes* hang out at the **public docks** south of the police station or at the **pier** next to Le Pirate Bar on Calle 3 (especially in the morning). Prices are negotiable, though the price to Old Bank on Isla Bastimentos is set (US$2).

✴ ⁊ ORIENTATION AND PRACTICAL INFORMATION

Tiny Bocas is laid out in an L-shaped grid; numbered *calles* run north-south and lettered *avenidas* run east-west. With the docks at your back, north is to the right and south to the left. Just about everything is on **Calle 3**, the main street, or on **Calle 1**, further east. The water cuts across the grid from Calle 3 at the South end of town to Calle 1 at the East end. A small park lies between Calles 2 and 3 and Av. D and F. **Av. G**, at the northern end of town, is the only route out to the rest of the island. Billboard maps are posted around town.

Immigration: (☎ 757 9263), in the government building north of the *parque.* Open M-F 9am-noon and 12:30-4pm.

Tourist Information: IPAT (☎ 757 9871), near the police station, in a large yellow house on Calle 1, has a small exhibition about the history and ecology of Bocas and provides cheap Internet access (US$1.50 per hr., students US$0.75). Open M-F 8:30am-4:30pm. **ANAM** (☎ 757 9244; www.bocas.com), on Calle 1 north of the police station, with info and permits for Parque Nacional Isla Bastimentos. Open M-F 8am-4pm.

Banks: Banco Nacional, Av. F, Calles 1/2, a block north and 1½ blocks east of the park. Cashes traveler's checks. Open M-F 8am-2pm. **ATM** one block north of the *parque,* near La Ballena.

Laundry: Don Chicho's restaurant on Calle 3, across from the *parque.*

Supermarkets: Av. H and Calle 6. Open M-Sa 9am-8pm, Su noon-7pm. Scattered fruit and vegetable markets on Calle 3, just south of the *parque.*

Police: (☎ 757 9217; emergency 104), on Calle 1 by the water.

Hospital: (☎ 757 9201), on Av. H, a few blocks west of town. 24hr. emergency.

Internet Access: El Mirador (☎ 757 9834), across from the water taxis on Calle 3, has fast connections and a pleasant balcony cafe that serves breakfast and sandwiches for US$2-3. Internet US$1.50 per hr. Open M-Sa 8am-9pm, Su 8am-8pm. **Don Chico's** (☎ 757 9838), across from the *parque* on Calle 3. US$3 per hr. Open M-F 8am-9pm, Sa 9am-8pm, Su 9am-4pm. Also available at the **IPAT** office (see above).

Post Office: in the government building just north of the *parque.*

🏠 ACCOMMODATIONS

Bocas is strewn with tons of excellent, inexpensive hotels (US$5-10), but they fill up in high season (make reservations in advance). There are also a number of relatively high-end places that offer breezy, polished luxury for very reasonable prices. Another option is to find a house or small family establishment that rents rooms, either on Calle 3 or around the northern corner along Av.'s G and H.

■ **Casa Max** (☎ 757 9120), on Av. G 50m west of Calle 3, has perfected the higher end of the classic backpacker hostel. Live the sweet life in the multi-colored hammocks and dreamy rooms of this "old Caribbean house put in a new coat." Book exchange and common stereo. Private baths. Singles US$18; doubles US$20. ❸

■ **Modo Taitú,** (☎ 757 9425), across from Casa Max on Av. G. If Casa Max perfects the fancy side of backpacker lodging, friendly and communal Modo Taitú does the same for the budget set. Dorm US$5 per person; private doubles US$7 per person. ❶

Hotel Swan's Cay (☎ 757 9090), on Calle 3, a block north of the *parque,* has a selection of carpeted, wood-paneled rooms with cable TV, phone, and A/C, built around a flower-filled courtyard. The hotel runs tours to the nearby beaches (US$5-10), and fishing excursions (US$115). Snorkel equipment free for all guests. Singles US$40.50; doubles US$60.70; triples US$80.90. AmEx/MC/V. ❹

Hostal Familiar La Concha, on Calle 3 across from the *parque.* Five rooms with communal or private bath, A/C, TV, and kitchen access. Common space upstairs doubles as a pleasant 4-bed dorm room (US$5 per person). Bring ear plugs if you plan to stay in the dorm beds. Singles US$5.50-15; doubles US$11-28.50; triples US$22. ❶

🍴 FOOD AND NIGHTLIFE

Restaurants, almost all on Calle 3 or just off of it, range from *típico* to classy Italian. *Bocatareño* food means lots of seafood with spicy coconut-lime juice flavoring. Bocas doesn't have clean tap-water, but some places have a filter on their tap. To paraphrase the advice of the Peace Corps: peel it, wash it, cook it, or vom-it.

■ **The Reef,** at the far southern end of Calle 3, is one of the few places left in Bocas Town to get tasty *bocatareño* food. Excellent meals of seafood accompanied by rice, potatoes or *patacones* can be had for US$5-7. After 8pm or so, the restaurant shifts into bar mode. Open daily 9am-midnight. ❷

La Ballena (☎ 989 9089), on Av. F, just off Calle 3. Authentic Italian food known as the best on the island. La Ballena imports the food, the cooks, and the owners directly from Italy. Dinners, from butterfly pastas to lobster *risotto* are US$10-15. Reservations necessary during high season. Open daily 8-11:30am, 12-2:30pm, and 7-10pm. ❹

Buena Vista Deli & Bar (takeout ☎ 757 9035), next to Starfleet on Calle 2. A foreigner favorite, with great sandwiches (US$4.50-5), veggie treats, clean water and ice, DirecTV athletics, mellow music, and mean margaritas (US$3.50). Open W-M noon-10pm. ❷

Don Chicho's, on Calle 3 across from the *parque*. This mini-empire (laundry, Internet, and cafeteria) is a popular local hangout with the cheapest meals around. *Comida* US$2. Big breakfasts US$1-3. Open daily 6:30am-midnight. ❶

The bar scene, like everything in Bocas town, swells hugely in the winter months (especially around Christmas). But even the rainy summer nights bring an amiable mix of locals, tourists, and ex-pats out to the dock-side *cabañas* and comfortable pool halls. Things generally pick up (if they pick up at all) around 9 or 10pm, and run until 1 or 2am. Sunday nights are often quiet. **Loop**, across from the park, has pool tables and a cool indoor/outdoor bar. Farther down Calle 3, across from Hospedaje EYL, is **Bar El Encanto**, a local favorite which cranks thunderous dance hall and *cumbia*. On Calle 1, near Taxi 25, is **Barco Hundido** (aka Wreck Bar), a great place to dry off after snorkeling. If you're in luck you might catch the **Beach Boys de Bastimentos**, the local calypso band known to have jammed for 15hr. straight.

WATERSPORTS AND GUIDED TOURS

DIVING AND SNORKELING AROUND THE ISLAND. In a local economy almost entirely dependent on tourism, nearly every hotel, restaurant, dock, shack, and patch of grass offers some form of tour or rental. The listings here provide an overview of what's available and a few unique or particularly dependable businesses.

For **diving**, the best rental/tour operator is PADI-certified **Starfleet Eco-Adventures** (☎/fax 757 9630), on Calle 1 where it curves east at the southern end of town. A 2-tank dive costs US$45, including boat and all equipment. A PADI open water certification course is also offered (3-4 days about US$195, half/full-day crash course US$65-95). Dive also vary depending on the time of year, time of day, and weather—though operators can try to arrange your choice. The **Playground** is an open-water dive just 5min. from Bocas town with tons of standard reef fish (angels, damsels, butterflyfish, hamlets, and triggerfish) as well as the occasional giant moray eel. **Big Bank** is for advanced divers, with coral formations as deep as 40m that eagle rays, jewfish, and standard reef fish call home. **Hospital Point,** on Cayo Nancy, is a shallow wall dive offering scorpionfish, toadfish, octopi and Giant Brain coral. **Dolphin Rock,** another open-water dive, has some of the largest, brightest schools of fish around, including parrotfish and barracuda. Also ask about **Bahía Bocatorito,** south of Isla Cristóbal, directly south of Bocas town, to see **bottle-nose dolphins** year-round.

For **snorkeling,** most dive shops rent gear (US$5-8 per day) and offer tours (US$15-20, equipment included). At **Bocas' Best Tour** (☎ 620 5130), Christian, a knowledgeable guide, captains one of the area's better boats. For snorkeling, local boat owners who hang out by the Le Pirate Bar docks on Calle 3, are often cheaper than tour companies—try to bargain a little.

BIKE, MOTORCYCLE, AND BOAT RENTALS. Check bikes for quality. Rent **bikes** at: Galápagos Tours (US$2.50 per hr., US$10 per day); Hotel Laguna, on Calle

3 by the park (☎757 9091; US$2 per hr.); and **Spanish by the Sea Language School,** behind the Hotel Bahía at the southern end of Calle 4 (US$4 per half-day, US$6 per day); or the stand near Modo Taitú on Av. G. Rent **kayaks** at **Galápagos Tours** and **Bocas Water Sports** (US$5 and US$10 per half-day, respectively). Spanish by the Sea also rents **canoes** (US$10 per day, US$7.50 per half-day). A few beat-up **motorcycles,** dirt bikes, and surf boards can be rented on a patch of grass next to the handicrafts stands across from the *parque* on Calle 3 (motorcycles US$8 per hr., surfboards US$2 per hr.).

OTHER TOURS. Many of the snorkeling tour shops offer half- and full-day **jungle tours** on the mainland. **Ancon Expeditions** (☎757 9850; www.anconexpeditions.com), at the northern end of Calle 3, offers more scientific tours of the snorkel and **wildlife sites;** many are guided by botanists and biologists. (Bastimentos National Park tour, 1 day, US$12-72 depending on group size.) Ancon can also connect you with **Eliseo Vargas** (☎620 0192; turismonaso_odesem@hotmail.com), who leads day trips up an inland river to a **Teribe Indian village** (US$70 per person). **Bocas Adventures** (☎757 9594), next to the park on Calle 3, offers **ecological tours** of the area and some diving tours.

🔵 SIGHTS AROUND THE ISLAND

From Bocas Town, Av. H leads west across a small isthmus to the main body of the island. From here, the road forks; the left side leads 15km through the middle of the island past La Gruta to Boca del Drago, and the right fork follows the eastern coast, passing Big Creek, Punta Puss Head, Playa Paunch, and Playa Bluff along the way. Many of these beaches are infested with *chitras* (tiny sandflies with an irritating bite), especially in the late afternoon. Walking and biking are the cheapest transportation options around the island, but roads are alternately bumpy and muddy—bring sturdy shoes or a well-maintained bike, especially after rain.

EASTERN BEACHES. The best of these beaches is relatively *chitra*-free **Playa Bluff.** The sand beach stretches almost 2km, with good surfing and casual swimming on more mellow days. Between March and September (especially June-July) the beach attracts **sea turtles** laying their eggs. To arrange a trip to see nesting turtles on the island's eastern coast, go to the CARIBARO office, 2 blocks north of the park on Calle 3, across from the church in an unmarked green-and-yellow building. *(Trips depart 8pm or midnight; stop by earlier in the day. Office is sporadically closed off-season (June-Aug.). Playa Bluff is on the eastern shore about 8km north of Bocas town; biking takes about 45min.)*

LA GRUTA CAVE. A small cave with plenty of bats and bat guano, **La Gruta** is considered a religious shrine and is the site of a annual pilgrimage celebrating *Nuestra Señora de la Gruta,* the Virgen del Carmen. A torchlight parade down Calle 3 takes place every July 16th in celebration of the Virgin; the pilgrimage to her cave happens the following Sunday. *(La Colonia Santeña, where a trail leads to the cave, is about a 45min. bike ride from town. Bring a flashlight and good boots.)*

BOCA DEL DRAGO. On the western side of the island, 8km past La Gruta on a hilly road, sits the little town of Boca del Drago. Here you'll find beautiful beaches and a coral reef walkable at low tide. The town has lodging and food, but no services in town. Look left near the end of the road for **Cabañas Estefany ❷,** where most cabins have their own kitchen, bath, and mosquito nets. From May 15 to August 15, they are generally rented out to a school program, but you may be able to scrounge an extra room or camp on the property. (☎626 7245. Ask for Chino Fátima. 5-person *cabaña* US$30.25; 6-person US$38.50; 8-person US$60.50. Reservations recommended.) Next door is the gringo-tour favorite **Restaurante Yarisnari ❷**, which also rents snorkel gear and a paddle boat. (Lentils and rice US$3.50; seafood US$7-10. Open daily 7:30-9:30am and noon-7:30pm.)

About 15min. by *bote* from Boca del Drago sits **Isla de Pájaros,** or **Swan Caye,** where hundreds of seabirds circle a huge rock and a few hardy trees. There's a coral reef with excellent deep-water snorkeling right off Isla de Pájaros, although the water isn't always that clear, particularly after rain. Tour operators in Bocas all offer trips here. Just past Swan Cay are two smaller rocky islands: **Wreck Rock,** which looks like the wreck of a ship, and **Sail Rock,** a phallic rock sticking straight out of the water. *(A taxi between Boca del Drago and Bocas del Toro runs round-trip US$25. There's also a bus that leaves Drago at 7:30am, waits in front of the mercado in Bocas, and returns to Drago at about 2pm (US$3 each way). If there are a few people who want to go, you might be able to convince the driver to make another run. Otherwise, hire a bote for the day—a trip to Boca del Drago and Isla de Pájaros costs US$25.)*

ISLA BASTIMENTOS

For a little less of the touristy, gringoesque flavor of Bocas, and more Caribbean authenticity, head to Bastimentos, only 10min. from Bocas. Here you'll find the small village of **Old Bank** (where most boats arrive), oodles of beautiful, deserted beaches, an indigenous Ngöbe village, and **Parque Nacional Marino Isla Bastimentos,** the region's largest and most important protected natural area. In fair weather, Bastimentos hosts a party on Monday nights—ask in Bocas town for the latest.

OLD BANK

The village of Old Bank (also known as **Bastimentos**) has no roads, only a semipaved 1km footpath running along the water. With your back to the water, east is to your right and west to your left. The little park is toward the western end, as are most of the docks, where you can catch a *bote* to Bocas del Toro.

▐ TRANSPORTATION. Getting to Isla Bastimentos from **Bocas del Toro** is easy. Regular boats leave Bocas del Toro from the pier next to Le Pirate Bar and head to Old Bank (more frequent in the morning, 6am-6pm; US$2). To reach **Cayos Zapatillas** or the other side of the island or your best bet is one of the tour operators. An equally dependable option is to ask around near the docks for a boat—independent operators are everywhere. Agree on a fare beforehand.

▐▐ ACCOMMODATIONS AND FOOD. All the accommodations in town are fairly budget, though facilities vary widely. **Pensión "Tío Tom" Bastimentos ❷,** near the park in a green building with a red roof, has pleasant wooden rooms on stilts over the water. (☎/fax 757 9831. www.puntacaracol.com. Singles US$10; doubles US$10, in high season US$12, with private bath US$20; each additional person US$7.) **Pelícano Cabinas ❷,** at the far eastern end of the path, has the nicest rooms in town. (☎ 757 9830. Singles US$10; doubles US$16; triple with bunk beds US$18.) Between Tío Tom and Pelícano is **Hospedaje Sylvia ❷,** with fanned rooms, shared baths, and a basic restaurant run by a local family. (☎ 757 9442. US$10 per room.)

▐ BEACHES. The island's beautiful beaches lie in a string on the northern and eastern coasts, connected by trails. To get to **Playa Primera,** take the path (marked with a sign for "1st Beach") that branches inland near the eastern end of Old Bank's main cement path and proceed for 20min.; after rain, it might be worth taking a boat to avoid the 1½hr. walk through mud (US$2). Beware: extremely strong currents make swimming dangerous. The next beach to the east is **Playa Segunda,** also known as Red Frog Beach for the little red frogs found only here (harder to spot on sunny days). This is a favorite tour destination from Bocas and a good surfing spot during the dry season. Two beaches farther is **Playa Cuarto,** one of the best beaches in the entire archipelago. Also known as Ola Chica or Don Polo, the eastern end of the beach is sheltered by **Wild Cane Key,** a small offshore island.

At the opposite end of the island from the town of Old Bank lies **Punta Vieja,** a secluded beach that offers astonishingly clear water and awesome snorkeling. Not only do many turtles nest here during the night, but there is an awesome reef right out front and the Ngöbe village of **Salt Creek** is nearby. Many of the tour operators in Bocas run tours to both the reef and Salt Creek (US$15-25).

⚡ PARQUE NACIONAL MARINO ISLA BASTIMENTOS. After a 3hr. hike along the beach and trails from Old Bank, you'll reach the spectacular 14km **Playa Larga,** an important **turtle nesting** site. The beach holds a ranger station and an entrance to **Parque Nacional Marino Isla,** which protects Playa Larga, the interior of Isla Bastimentos, the extensive mangrove swamps on the island's western side, and the two **Cayos Zapatillas** farther out in the ocean to the southeast. The inland forest on Isla Bastimentos is home to fantastic wildlife, and the southern of the two Cayos Zapatillas has a forest trail that leads to golden beaches and underwater cave formations. The crowded ranger stations on the island and on the southern Cayo Zapatillas both have simple **refugios** and allow **camping.** There are no facilities; bring everything you need, including mosquito nets (or heavy-duty repellent) and something to purify water. Before heading to the park, you have to get permission from ANAM in Bocas and pay an entrance fee. They can ensure that rangers will be there. Park rangers guide for no fee, although a tip is expected. Talk to the Ancon office at the Bocas Inn (see **Watersports and Guided Tours,** above) for info on turtle-watching. (Camping US$5 per person. Park admission US$10.)

🏝 OTHER ISLANDS

ISLA CARENERO. Isla Carenero is just a few hundred meters east of the docks on Calle 3 in Bocas. There are three good seafood **restaurants** on the island, all along the beach (meals US$5-8; all open daily 1-9pm): **Restaurante Pargo Rojo** (☎ 757 9649), **Restaurante Ocean Queen** (☎ 757 9360), and **Doña Mara** (☎ 757 9552). All restaurants will pick you up at the public dock in Bocas if you call, and *botes* make the trip as well (US$2). To get back, ask at the restaurants or stand on the dock and wave to catch passing boats. For groups, Pargo Rojo and Doña Mara also offer good deals on *cabinas.* Pargo Rojo's are larger and cheaper (cabin for up to 5 people US$25), but Doña Mara's are newer with more facilities (quads with A/C, TV, hot water US$50). On the eastern end of Carenero is a small point with decent snorkeling and a few good breaks for surfing. New construction is at full-tilt in this part of the island, however, and it can get noisy.

CAYO NANCY. Cayo Nancy is famous for **Hospital Point,** near one of the best, most accessible snorkeling spots. You'll find a variety of corals, some barely submerged, others 100 ft. deep, and enough bright fish to keep you ooohing and aaahing all day. Any *bote* can transport you, but bring your own snorkeling gear. There are a few good places to snorkel in the protected waters between Bocas, Isla Carenero, Isla Bastimentos, and Cayo Nancy. If you go by private boat, ask the driver to wait rather than return, because these are open-water sites.

ALMIRANTE

People visit small, run-down Almirante either to buy immense quantities of green bananas (grown and shipped in the area) or to hop a boat out to the Bocas del Toro archipelago. The town has few eating options and only one accommodation.

From the terminal, **buses** leave for **Changuinola** (30min., every 30min. 6am-9pm, US$1) and **David** (4hr., every 45min. 5am-6pm, US$8). A more colorful, though less luxurious, route to Changuinola is to jump on the **Banana Train.** This rattling machine leaves from the tracks between the terminal and the water taxi docks and is a great way to get to know all the locals and their farm animals. (2hr.; 7am, 2, 5pm; US$0.40.) Two **water taxi** companies, Taxi 25 (☎757 9062) and Galapago's Tours (☎757 9073), compete to take passengers to **Bocas del Toro** (30min.; every hr. or when boats are full 6am-6pm; US$5 each way). For those with more time than money, a **ferry** leaves from the opposite side of town four days a week. (1½hr; M, W, F, Sa 9am; US$1.) For the ferry, turn right at the T across the tracks and take the first left. Follow that road along the tracks and turn right just before the road crosses back over the tracks. **Taxis** charge US$1 to run from the bus station to the water taxi docks. Walking takes about 15-25min. From the **bus terminal,** head left down the main road and then bear left on a dirt track over the railroad at the sign "Taxis Marítimos." To get to the main street from the **dock,** face away from the water and go left along the gravel road until the dirt path veers right. The bus terminal is to the right. On the other side of the terminal the road forms a T.

To get to **Banco Nacional de Panamá,** bear right at the T, cross the train tracks, turn left at the first street, and continue one block. (Open M-F 9am-3pm, Sa 9am-2pm.) The **hospital** (☎758 3745) is in front of the bank. **Farmacia San Vicente** is two blocks down after you bear right at the T coming from the terminal. (Open M-Sa 8am-8pm.) To reach the **police station** (☎758 3721 or 104), start off toward the ferry but cross the tracks instead of turning off. The **immigration office** is next door. **Phones** are on the road near the bus terminal, at the post office, and in front of immigration. **Carisma** (☎758 3198), to the right of the bus station has **Internet.** The **post office** is a block past the bank. (Open M-F 9am-noon and 1:30-4:30pm.)

The only place to stay is **Hospedaje San Francisco ❷,** between the bus station and the road to the water taxi docks, with large, dark rooms with fan, private baths, and a lounge. (☎758 3779. Singles US$11, with A/C US$15; doubles US$15/US$20.) A number of *típico* restaurants line the road between the terminal and the water taxis. Snacks are also available at the taxi docks.

CHANGUINOLA

Changuinola is hot and dirty, but houses the bureaucracy for the nearby Costa Rican border crossing. The city survives on merchants and banana plantations (many open to visitors), including a Chiquita plant.

◉ **TRANSPORTATION.** The **airport** is at the north end of town, bearing right past the gas station and crossing the railroad tracks. **Aero** (☎758 9241) sells tickets from its office adjoining the nearby gas station. (Open M-F 8am-noon and 1-5pm, Sa 8am-noon.) **Aeroperlas** (☎758 7521) has its office at the airport. Both have flights to **Bocas del Toro** (US$10.50). Aero also flies to **Panama City** (1hr., 2 per day, US$52.50), and Aeroperlas flies to **David** (30min., M-F 10am, US$25.20). Changuinola has two **bus** terminals, located within 300m of each other on opposite sides of the street. **Terminal La Piquera,** next to the Shell station in the center of town, handles short-distance travel. There is no office and schedules vary significantly. **Collective taxis** are parked under specific destination signs. **Buses** leave from the terminal to the **Costa Rican border at Guabito** (35min., every 45min. 7am-7:45pm, US$0.70); **El Silencio** (40min., every 15min. 6am-7pm, US$0.50); **Finca 44** (25min., every 30min. 5am-9pm, US$0.65) via **Almirante** (45min., US$1); and many other destinations in the surrounding farmland. **Taxis** to Guabito take 20min., and cost US$1. **Terminal Urraca** (☎758 8127), north of Terminal La Piquera, is less chaotic. **Buses** head to **David** (4hr., every 40min. 5am-7pm, US$8) and **Panama City** (12hr., 7am, US$18).

⬛🔃 ORIENTATION AND PRACTICAL INFORMATION. Changuinola is strung out along the road from Guabito and the border in the northwest to Almirante in the southeast. The road to Almirante curves along a traffic circle around a large white statue. The northern end of town is full of enormous inexpensive stores, while the southern end hosts expensive hotels. Outside of town, unpaved roads cut through many *fincas*, which are referred to by numbers.

The **ANAM** office runs the San-San wetlands and the Wetzo entrance to Parque Internacional La Amistad—contact them for details. To reach the office, head three blocks north of the terminal, turn left at Hotel Hong Kong, bear left, and take the first right at the mosque. The office works closely with rangers but provides little hard information. (☎758 6603. Open M-F 8am-4pm.) If you've been in Panama more than 30 days and have a valid extension, go to the **Ingreso office** at Finca 6, at the northern end of town past the airport, to get your documents in order to **cross the border** (tax US$1, taxi ride US$1). This is also the place to go if you want to extend your stay in Panama. For those heading to Costa Rica, the next stop is **Migración,** at the southern end of town past Hotel Carol, for an exit stamp. (☎758 8651. Open M-F 8am-noon and 1-3pm.) If you have been in Panama for fewer than 30 days, you can skip both these offices and get your passport stamped in Guabito.

Banks in Changuinola don't change Costa Rican colones—do that at the **Almacén Zona Libre,** a block south of bus terminal La Piquera. (☎758 8493. Open M-Sa 8:30am-8:30pm, Su 8am-2pm.) The rates aren't great, but Sixaola doesn't offer anything better. Across the street from the Almacén is **Banco Nacional de Panamá,** for Cirrus/MC/Visa withdrawals. (☎758 8445. Open M-F 8am-3pm, Sa 9am-noon.) Cash traveler's checks or get a Visa or MC cash advance at **Banistmo,** a block north of the bus terminal La Piquera. (☎758 7477. Open M-F 8am-3:30pm, Sa 9am-2pm.) There's a 24hr. **ATM** and a **Western Union** (☎758 8644) in the **Mini Super Baseline** across from the La Piquera terminal (both open M-Sa 8:15am-12:45pm and 1:15-8:15pm, Su 8:30am-12:30pm). This supermarket and some others change colones with a purchase. The **police** (☎758 8970 or 758 7585, emergency 104) and **hospital** (☎758 8232) are down the paved side road in front of Almacén Zona Libre, south of the La Piquera terminal. **Farmacia Juan de Dios,** in the terminal, can take passport pictures. (☎758 8265. 4 pictures US$3. Open daily 8am-9pm.) **Public phones** are scattered around the La Piquera terminal and in front of the airport. **Librería, Refresquería, Internet Bezaisa** has fast **Internet access** and many computers in air-conditioned surroundings. (☎758 8640. US$1 per hr. Open M-Sa 8am-11pm, Su 8am-6pm.) The **post office** is on the north end of town in the governmental building.

🔲🔳 ACCOMMODATIONS AND FOOD. There are few hotels in Changuinola and no truly budget ones. **Hotel Carol ❷,** two blocks south of the terminal La Piquera, has a common room with TV, and simple rooms off a dark hallway with A/C and private bath. (☎758 8731. Double beds US$11; more spacious triples with TV US$24; quads US$30.) **Hotel Changuinola ❷,** just north of the airport, is more comfortable but farther out of town. (☎758 8678. Singles with fan US$12.50, with A/C US$14.30; doubles US$13.50, with TV and A/C US$19.80; king-size bed US$16.50.) The best among the higher-end accommodations is **Hotel Ejecutivo Taliali ❷,** two blocks south of the terminal behind the Caja de Ahorros. (☎758 6010. Singles US$15; doubles US$16.50; triples US$20; quads US$22.50.)

A few small kiosks on the main drag serve standard Panamanian fare for slightly inflated prices. If you like bakeries, you'll love 🔳**El Buen Sabor ❶,** just past Banco del Istmo in the storefront covered by foliage, with assorted flaky, fresh-from-the-oven treats clearly labeled with prices and English translations (US$0.30-1). (☎758 8422. Open M-Sa 8am-9pm, Su 10am-9pm.) The **Refresquería ❶** at Mini Super La Huacia (not to be confused with the larger Super La Huacia), one block north of the terminal La Piquera on the opposite side of the street, has some of the cheapest *comida corriente* in town (US$2) and delicious ice-cold *chichas* for US$0.30. (☎ 758 8461. Open M-Sa 8am-9:30pm, Su 8am-4pm.)

NEAR CHANGUINOLA

✖ GUABITO: BORDER WITH COSTA RICA

Guabito is 16km from Changuinola; Sixaola is across the border in Costa Rica, where you'll get an entry stamp after showing your passport and an onward ticket. The Panamanian side of the border is open daily from 8am to 6pm, while the Costa Rican side is open daily from 7am to 5pm; the time zone difference assures the two coincide. Both close for lunch (noon-12:30pm).

When you enter Costa Rica, **Sixaola** provides basic necessities, but most people don't waste time here before catching a bus north. Buses run to **San José** (6hr.; 5, 7:30, 9:30am, 2:30pm; ₡2815) and **Limón** (3hr., 8 per day 5am-5pm, ₡930). The 3pm bus enters **Puerto Viejo de Talamanca** (2hr., ₡500), while the others will drop you at the intersection 5km from the town. Frequent buses cover the remaining distance (15min., ₡200). Buy bus tickets with colones or US dollars. Passengers leaving Sixaola must show their papers, so don't tuck your passport away. There is no money exchange here. The nearest bank is in Bribrí (1½hr. away). For those entering Panama, frequent buses run to **Changuinola** (15min., US$0.70) until about 7pm.

Comercial Tucán, on the left side of the border crossing, changes money, but often runs out of colones. (☎ 759 7944. Open 9am-8pm.) **Zona Libre**, 200m away from the border crossing on the right side, is well stocked with everything a backpacker doesn't need, such as a huge selection of perfumes. (☎ 759 7944. Open 8am-8pm. MC/V.) A single phone sits in front of the **Aduanas** (customs), next to the migration office. The **migration offices** are across the street from national **police** posts (☎ 759 7940, emergency ☎ 104), which are connected by a decrepit bridge. Guabito has no accommodations and almost no restaurants; Sixaola, just across the border, has better options. **Kiosco Dalys ❶**, in Guabito, serves *comida corriente* (US$2), directly to the right of the border crossing. (Open 5:30am-10pm.)

SAN BLAS ARCHIPELAGO

The *Comarca Kuna Yala* ("Land of the Kuna"), on the Caribbean coast between Colón and Colombia, is a distinct province run entirely by the region's indigenous inhabitants, the Kuna. There are 50 autonomous Kuna communities in Kuna Yala, 45 of them crowded onto the tiny islands of the San Blas Archipelago. With their white sand beaches, coconut palms, and coral reefs, the archipelago's mostly uninhabited islands radiate calm, tropical splendor. The region remains isolated because transportation here can be difficult and expensive, but tourism is growing in rapid but controlled bursts. Although the beaches are lovely, the real reason to come is to experience the culture of one of Central America's most independent indigenous people.

HISTORY

By the 1500s the Kuna had migrated into Darién from Colombia, and by the 19th century, war with the Spanish and the rival Emberá tribe had forced them onto the San Blas Islands. Here, the Spanish left them in comparative peace, but in 1925 a newly independent Panama launched attempts to "civilize" the Kuna. Fed up, the Kuna revolted against the Panamanian police force, and with the help of a US bat-

CAN YOU KUNA? Kuna originally had no written alphabet, and writing was limited to hieroglyphics. Missionaries developed a westernized writing system about 50 years ago, forcing the language into the Roman alphabet. Strict spelling rules never caught on; hence, the letters d and t are interchangeable, as are the pairs b/p and k/g, while the sounds are somewhere in between. Vowels are pronounced as in Spanish.

Yes/no	Eye/suli
Hello/Goodbye	Na/Deguimalo
Hi, bye, thanks, you're welcome, good	Nuedi
I'd like a ride.	An wis urabege.
I want to go to Nalunega.	An Nalunega se nabie.
What's your name?	Iguibe nuga?
My name is Jenny.	An nuga Jenny.
Do you speak Spanish?	Be wagaga wisi?
How much does it cost?	Igey mani?
I love you.	An be abege.
I'm a gringo.	An mergi.

tleship offshore, successfully gained a degree of autonomy. In 1952 San Blas was officially recognized as self-governing. The Kuna are outside of Panamanian taxation, own all of the region's property, and send a representative to the National Assembly. Even so, today the older generation is fighting once again (this time without violence) to preserve traditions in the face of growing westernization of the people. On many Kuna town congress halls a banner proclaims, "People who lose their tradition lose their soul," but there are certainly signs of modernization. While the Kuna once survived by trading coconuts with Colombian ships, today the balboa (a.k.a. US dollar) reigns supreme on the islands, and tourists have become the new trading partners. As a result, the number of amenities and establishments is constantly on the rise and prices continue to increase.

CULTURE AND CUSTOMS

Each Kuna community elects a chief, called the *sáhila*. Twice a year, these chiefs travel to the Kuna General Congress, the main governing body. The Kuna have their own language, but most speak at least some Spanish. Men typically wear western clothes, while women wear golden nose- and earrings and beautiful traditional clothing. Their blouses feature the famous *mola*, reverse appliqué embroidered artwork (sold also to tourists). With few exceptions, the Kuna live on the beach—the same golden sand makes up town footpaths and the floors of their thatched-roof huts. Despite the presence of Christian missionaries, most of the Kuna maintain their traditional religion. Kuna theology revolves around a series of gods and creation stories featuring Mother Earth and a divine human, Ibergun, sent especially to the Kuna to teach them how to live traditional lives enlightened by the underlying principle of sharing within the community. More recent events, such as the battles fought against the Emberá, the Spanish, and the Panamanian army, have also become part of a semi-mythic Kuna cosmology. The culture of Kuna Yala includes customary puberty rituals, marriage ceremonies, funeral rites (in which the deceased is put to rest in an underground hammock), and traditional medicine. If you hang around long enough, you could run into a **chicha fuerte** feast. *Chicha fuerte* is an alcoholic drink made from maize and lots of sugar. When a Kuna girl hits puberty, her hair is cut short and she receives her name. The family invites the town over for a several-day party, with a tremendous batch of *chicha fuerte*, sugar cane, coffee, and cacao. The biggest parties of the year are in February, particularly the 25th, the anniversary of the 1925 Kuna revolution.

Travelers, particularly if visiting the more isolated islands, should learn about the Kuna before coming. Those arriving on an island that has no hotel should first go see the *sáhila* to ask permission to stay (an entrance fee of US$1-3 is typically charged). Meeting the *sáhila* also provides an opportunity to ask about meals.

✈ VISITING SAN BLAS

Rather expensive to get to and expensive to stay in, with little opportunity for independent exploration, San Blas is not for every budget traveler. It is, however, one of the most remarkable places in Central America, and well worth the more-or-less fixed price (about US$60 to fly round-trip from Panama City, and about US$35 per night). Note that tourism is developing rapidly here, so prices and facilities are subject to change. There are a number of hotels in the more populated and touristed Kuna islands (see **The Islands,** below). Since boat travel between islands is so expensive, these places—whose prices typically include meals and daily trips with some degree of flexibility—are the cheapest and best ways to see Kuna Yala. They provide a representative slice of Kuna life while incorporating some sinfully perfect beaches and snorkeling. There isn't much value in doing a highlights tour of the islands; the attractions of each are fairly similar, and picking one or two will give you a good sense of what Kuna Yala is about.

Given the above considerations, **guided tours** of the archipelago are generally not worth the expense, unless you're looking for a specific bonus, such as sailing or fishing. All visitors should keep in mind that most Kuna islands (except the one your hotel is on) require visitors to pay a US$1-5 **fee;** this may be paid at governmental offices or with the local *sáhila.* Even uninhabited islands are privately owned, and a fee may be required. In addition, photographers who want to take pictures of the Kuna will normally be charged US$1 per shot.

☰ TRANSPORTATION

FLIGHTS

The simplest and easiest way to reach San Blas is to fly. Many islands have airports, and one-way flights to or from Panama City range from US$29.40 (El Porvenir) to US$46.20 (Puerto Obaldía). Service is offered by the more comfortable and organized **Aerotaxi** (☎315 7500) and the much smaller **Aviatur** (☎315 0311), with flights typically departing at 6 or 7am in either direction. For more information, see **Panama City: Transportation,** p. 604. Since planes make multiple stops in the islands, they may be used to get around San Blas; however, these island-hops are improvised on demand—you may have to wait until close to your flight date to see what's available. Note that airports are often not on the destination island itself; you'll need boat transport, and you may want to arrange for this in advance. If you make a hotel reservation (also a good idea), the hotel may help with this.

BOATS

Boats island-hop along the coast from Colón to Cartagena, Colombia. You may have to wait on an island up to a week, as there is no schedule. Negotiate with the captain and take a good look at the boat before getting on. Deposit your pack with the captain and keep valuables on your body. Food is generally included, though a place to sleep isn't; bring a hammock or inflatable pad. Catch boats to the islands from Puerto Coco Solo in **Colón** (check in with Marco at Adventures Youth and Traveler's Hostel for the latest info, p. 626). The **Sugdub** goes to Cartí every Saturday (☎228 8917; call for exact time and return schedule. 7hr., US$10 per person includes breakfast and lunch). Otherwise ask for ships leaving to San Blas at the *sarpe* (ship documents) office and negotiate with the captains at the docks. An overnight ride to **El Porvenir** should cost US$10, while a ride to **Puerto Obaldía** runs US$30-50 and takes two to seven days, depending on the number of stops. These boats are a great way to see a lot of islands, as they stop at each one for about an hour to load goods. However, in past years a few foreigners traveling on Colombian boats have been killed or kidnapped—many are involved in smuggling. Captains may still take passengers, but the guards at Coco Solo may prohibit such hitchhiking. *Let's Go* does not recommend this mode of transportation.

Between close islands, you can use pricey local **motorboats**. Short hops between airports and nearby islands are affordable, but longer trips add up quickly. Try to haggle, but if the boat isn't going there already, don't expect to get very far.

▓ THE ISLANDS

Heading the list of popular islands, **El Porvenir** is the farthest west in the archipelago, right next to the well-touristed **Wichub Wala** and **Nalunega,** both US$1-2 boat rides from El Porvenir. All three are densely inhabited and quite traditional. Twenty minutes south of Nalunega by boat is **Cartí-Sugtupu,** a slightly more developed Kuna village, just across the bay from the only land route to San Blas (the El Llano-Cartí road, which is barely negotiable with a 4WD vehicle, even in the dry season). Two hours east by fast boat are **Narganá** and **Corazón de Jesús,** the most westernized of all the islands. Fifteen minutes beyond lies **Isla Tigre,** a traditional village becoming a tourist hotspot. Near El Porvenir, ▓**Achutupu** (Dog Island)—not to be confused with the other Achutupu halfway to Colombia—boasts an offshore shipwreck with colorful tube and staghorn corals growing on the hull that makes for stunning snorkeling. **Coco Blanco,** between Achutupu and El Porvenir, is tiny and perfect and has a new set of lodgings. **Río Sidra** and **Nusatupu** are good halfway points between Cartí and Narganá. **Tikontikí,** another traditional island, lies 45min. to the east of Isla Tigre by boat. **Mauki** is a group of 40 uninhabited islands farther away. **Islas Aligandi, Achutupu, Ustupo Ogobsucum, Ustupo,** and **Mulatupu,** in order from west to east, are more traditional Kuna villages.

EL PORVENIR

*Two morning **flights** to **Panama City** (US$29.40) leave the airport between 6:30 and 8am. Flights coming in from Panama City arrive daily around 6:30 or 7:30am. It's possible to find a flight to another island, but it's a good idea to go to the airport the day before. Whether you've already bought a ticket or not, go to the government building a day before your flight and put your name on the list of people leaving. (Hotels take care of this for guests.) **Boats** to **Wichub Wala** and **Nalunega** may be arranged at the dock. When arriving by plane, make sure to sign in with the immigration official who meets each flight.*

El Porvenir, which consists of little more than an airstrip and a few administrative huts, is not the place to see a Kuna village. It does, however, have air service and easy access to the decent hotels on Wichub Wala and Nalunega. Directly in front of the docks there's a government building with a **police station,** an **immigration office** (☎299 9056; open daily 8am-noon), and public **phones.** The airport serves as a **post office;** give letters to the pilot heading out on the morning flight, and he'll drop them off (and buy stamps, if necessary) in Panama City. The only hotel on the island is **Hotel Porvenir ❷,** practically on the airstrip. Nightly rates include three meals and daytrips for snorkeling, hiking, or sun-bathing. (☎221 1397, ask for Mrs. Bibi. US$30 per person, US$15 without food.) The only place to eat on the island is at the hotel. (Seafood US$4 and up).

WICHUB WALA

Wichub Wala has two hotel options. On a separate island on the way to Nalunega is one of the area's best hotels, the ▨**Hotel Ukuptupu ❹**. This very accommodating hotel has clean, breezy bamboo rooms, each with light inside and hammocks outside, a small library of English books and a small walled-in aquarium on the reef where you can pick the lobster that you want for dinner. Rates include three meals and a daily tour. (☎220 4781. Rooms US$38-40 per person, depending on size. Students with ISIC, US$25 per person.) Five minutes from the public docks on the path heading east into town, **Kuna Niskua Lodge ❹** (☎227 5308), a bamboo-thatched building, offers nice rooms with communal bath, hammocks, and an all-inclusive rate of US$35 per person. The island has a **health center** and a community **general store** next to the public docks. (Open daily 7am-9:30pm.)

NALUNEGA

Nalunega is home to the relaxing **Hotel San Blas ❷**, which offers 25 spacious rooms in Kuna-style cabins or in a more modern building. The owner, Luis Burgos, speaks English and Spanish and can provide information on the Kuna or the surrounding islands. There are plenty of hammocks and the clean, communal baths have running water. Prices include three meals and two tours daily. (☎262 9812 in Panama City. Rooms US$35 per person, US$10 without food or tours.) Another option is **Archimedes Iglesias ❶**, who rents a hut near his house; look for the "We sell cold beer" sign off the basketball court behind Hotel San Blas. Prices start at US$5 for lodging only and US$15-20 for lodging, seafood meals (less for Kuna meals), and tours, but negotiating for the final price is half the fun. Even if you're not staying at Hotel San Blas, you can still go on their **tours.** (Daily 8am and 2pm. US$5 per person. Ask at the hotel.) The hotel's great **food** costs as little as US$3 for lunch or dinner (lobster US$10) and US$1 for breakfast (just coffee and bread). The hotel also rents **snorkel equipment** (mask and flippers US$3 each per day).

CARTÍ-SUGTUPU

*Daily **flights** from **Panama City** to El Porvenir often stop at Cartí airport, a 3min. boat ride away (usually arriving M-Sa around 6:30am, Su around 7:30am; US$27.40). This airport is the northern terminus of the El Llano-Cartí road, which is only barely passable, even in the dry season. To reach someone on the island, call one of the public phones (☎299 9088, 299 9074, or 299 9002) or San Blas Adventures (see below).*

Near the southern shore of the gulf that forms western San Blas, Cartí-Sugtupu is the largest, most thickly settled and developed island in Cartí Bay. It's flanked by several smaller islands, including Cartí Tupile and Cartí Yantupu. Cartí-Sugtupu's accessibility and services make tourist visits relatively easy, yet the community remains mostly true to traditional Kuna life. The island is crossed by two **east-west footpaths**. The **public docks** are on the north side, near the middle of the island; walk straight 10m until you come to the first main path. Two minutes west of the dock on this path is the marked house of Eulogio Pérez, who runs **San Blas Adventures** (☎299 9074 or 641 4909; sanblasadventures@hotmail.com). He runs beach, snorkeling, and rain forest daytrips (US$20 per person), as well as multi-day adventures throughout San Blas (call for prices). He speaks English and Spanish and is a good source of information on Kuna culture. If he's not there, his brothers or father can also orient and direct you. The town's **health center** is at the eastern end of the southern path. (Open M-F 7:30am-noon and 1-4pm, Sa-Su 7:30am-noon.) There are **public phones** by the dock, next to the cafeteria.

Cartí-Sugtupu boasts a friendly community-run **dormitorio ❷** on the east end of town, past the hospital. The colorful building has four simple rooms centered around a sitting room; the communal bathroom is built over the ocean in the Kuna style: a toilet seat over a hole in the floor. (☎ 299 9088; ask for Tito Lopez or Tomás Morris. US$8 per person.) The town's **cafeteria ●** (also owned by the community), directly next to the public dock, serves flavorless *comida* for US$2.35 and sells basic groceries. (Open daily 7am-10pm.)

Also in town is the **Kuna Museum**, 5min. east of the public dock on the northern main road. The one-room museum is cluttered and dusty, but offers a truly bizarre blend of Kuna culture and eccentric personal vision. Owner, curator, and guide José Davies leads visitors on a 1½hr. progression through Kuna artifacts and his own illustrations of Kuna myths and rituals. Tours are in Spanish and, if necessary, broken English. (Open daily 8am-9pm. US$2.)

COCO BLANCO

This tiny, gorgeous island, 20min. east of El Porvenir, offers nothing but a paradisiacal remove from cultures of any description. The snorkeling is mediocre, but the swimming is superb. New, basic *cabañas* **❸** are US$20 per night with meals.

ISLA TIGRE

Flights to and from Panama City are available at the airstrip (US$27.95). *Boats* are best arranged from Narganá.

Less westernized than Narganá and Corazón de Jesús, Isla Tigre approximates traditional Kuna life. The main dock is on the southern side of the island, near a cement **general store**. The two main **east-west footpaths** are straight ahead. Some 20m to the east on the first path is a **public phone** (☎ 299 9092). About 100m east on the second path is a more complete **general store**. The **airstrip** is to the west, and **Cafeteria and Cabañas Digir ❸**, with locally famous lobster (US$6.50; open 5-11pm, earlier upon request), sits next to it. The *cabañas*, tightly wedged between the airstrip and the beach, have Western bathrooms and hammocks for sleeping (US$20). Isla Tigre is renowned for its dances, which erupt during celebrations and fiestas. The biggest is the late October celebration of a former *sáhila*, with practices occurring most Friday nights for months in advance. Even outside dancing season, most nights bring festivities of some description.

TO COLOMBIA BY SEA

San Blas offers an adventurous land/sea route from Panama to Colombia that skips the two-week trek through the Darién jungle. This is the cheapest and quickest non-air route between Central and South America. However, this route goes to the Gulf of Urabá, the epicenter of Colombia trafficking and guerrilla activity.

> ❗ Due to the degree of criminal activity on the waters of the Panamanian-Columbian border region, this route to Colombia is **not recommended.** If you must undertake the journey, check with the Panamanian, Colombian, and your home country's government for the latest security information.

Travelers **heading to Colombia** must first get to Puerto Obaldía, either by plane or by boat. Aviatur (☎ 315 0311) has daily flights from Panama City (1hr., 12:30pm, US$46.20) and Aerotaxi (☎ 315 7500) flies three days per week for the same price. Kuna boats can occasionally be found in San Blas for high rates, though more common and potentially more dangerous are Colombian boats, most of which can be found in Colón's **Puerto Coco Solo** for around US$30. You'll have to haggle with the captain of the boat there and bring a hammock to sleep. In Puerto Obaldía, clear Panamanian and Colombian border formalities before finding a boat heading to **Zapzurro,** the first town in Colombia (US$5-15). From Zapzurro you can continue on to the Colombian resort town of **Capurganá**, and from there, if possible, to **Cartagena**, a major tourist destination safely away from the unrest. Though more frequented, the port town of **Turbo** is considered by many travelers a den of iniquity, and despite its connections to Colombian roads, is best avoided.

Heading to Panama from Cartagena, visit the docks outside Cartagena to find a boat, and port-hop north through Turbo, Acandí, Capurganá, or Zapzurro, or go straight to Puerto Obaldía (24hr.). Despite assurances to the contrary by the Panamanian consulate in Colombia, travelers report that Panamanian border officials demand an onward ticket for entry. You can buy a ticket from Panama City to San José at the Aerotaxi office in town, although it takes a few days. You'll have to wait up to a week for a boat heading north, and once you find one it will take up to seven days to get to Colón. You can also get out of San Blas on the El Llano-Cartí road by foot, by 4WD in the dry season, or by plane.

DARIÉN

Paramilitary groups, drug smugglers, and bandits, most from across the Colombian border, have affected large areas of Darién, and have become even bolder since US patrols left in 1999. Travel is prohibitively dangerous in the regions east and southeast of Yaviza and El Real. Recently, travelers have been **abducted** and **murdered** in the area. Before traveling in Darién it is imperative to obtain current security information. In Panama City, ANAM, Ancon Expeditions, IPAT, and the police are all good places to check. When you get to any town in Darién, first **check in with the police,** who will take down your passport information and advise you on how to proceed. Keep all your documents with you at all times.

The Interamerican Hwy., otherwise stretching unbroken from Alaska to Tierra del Fuego, meets its undoing in Darién, Panama's largest but least populated province. Many who come here are lured by the mystique and risk associated with crossing the dangerous Darién Gap into Colombia. *Let's Go* does not recommend any attempt to cross the Darién Gap. Those of us without a death wish can still enjoy the region. **Parque Nacional Darién**, running along the entire border with Colombia, is one of the most biologically rich regions in the world. Amid the jungle live the indigenous **Emberá** and **Wounaan** peoples (often collectively called the Chocóes). Still holding to their traditional lifestyles, they wear colorful loincloths, stain their bodies bluish-black with the fruit of the *jagua* tree, and only recently put down their poisonous blowdarts in favor of more mainstream hunting weapons.

From **Metetí** a side road and river route lead to **La Palma**, a relatively safe gateway to the wilderness around the Golfo de San Miguel and the Río Sambú. In **Yaviza** the 400km roadless Darién Gap begins. Nearby **El Real** is the best gateway to Parque Nacional Darién. The safest, most effective, and most expensive way to visit Darién is on a guided tour. Ancon Expeditions and Eco-Tours de Panamá are recommended (see **Panama City: Practical Information,** p. 607). Even without a guided tour, it is worth the money to fly into Darién. If you do fly, head straight to El Real or Sambú—Darién's towns offer nothing of interest in and of themselves.

METETÍ

Fifty kilometers shy of Yaviza along the highway from Panama City, Metetí is little more than a bump on the already bumpy road. From a junction here, a side road leads 10km west to **Puerto Quimba**, where there is boat access to La Palma. During the rainy season, bus routes from Panama City end here; only 4WD *chivitas* can continue to Yaviza. Though there isn't much to do, trails and a small cabin are under development in the **Reserva Filo del Tallo,** 248 lush square kilometers surrounding the road to Puerto Quimba. For information on the reserve, talk to Nobel Castro at the **ANAM** office (☎ 299 6183), just north of the junction on the highway.

If you're staying here awhile, go to the **police station** south of the junction to show your passport. At the junction, there's a **transportation center** with bus schedules. The best of the three decent lodging options is **Hospedaje Las Nashiras ❷,** 20m down the road to Puerto Quimba, offering big, airy rooms with bathrooms and fans for US$10. North of the junction on the highway, **Hotel Restaurante Felicidad ❷** has enormous, if spartan, rooms with fans, and a general store and restaurant below. (☎ 299 6188. Singles US$10, with bath US$15; doubles US$20; triples US$24.) At the junction is **Comisariato Restaurante Pensión Tres Hermanos Ortiz ❷,** with dark rooms with fans. The water sometimes runs dry in the late morning. (Singles US$8, with A/C US$15; doubles US$10, with bath US$13; triples US$15.) Meals can be found in the numerous **restaurants** and **kiosks** in town. Pensión Tres Hermanos runs a restaurant next door with passable *comidas*. Buses heading to **Panama City** and **Yaviza** stop in town every hour. In the rainy season, bus service terminates here, and several 4WD *chivitas* (minibuses) per day run between Metetí and Yaviza (4hr., US$5). *Chivitas* also run to **Puerto Quimba** (30min., every 45min. 5:30am-7pm, US$1.25), for connections to La Palma.

LA PALMA

La Palma is not much more than a good place from which to launch a boat trip farther south into the Gulf or down the Río Sambú. Even this prospect is little reason to stop here, though, as Sambú has its own airstrip.

Aeroperlas (☎ 315 7500) and Aviatur (☎ 315 0311), in the blue-and-white building next to the airstrip, have morning **flights** M-Sa between **Panama City** and La Palma for US$35. (Open M-Sa 8-9am and 1-4pm.) La Palma is accessible by land. From **Metetí**, on the highway between Panama City and Yaviza, grab a *chivita* to **Puerto Quimba** (30min., every 45min. 5:30am-7pm, US$1.25), where **water taxis** make the jaunt across the Río Tuira to La Palma (40min., every 1½hr. 7:30am-6:30pm, US$2.50). Return trips from La Palma to Puerto Quimba run 5:30am-5pm. Cargo boats also travel between Panama City and La Palma on an irregular basis.

Nearly all visitor services are on the main street that extends from the airstrip for about 1km along the Tuira River. Boats disembark at a ramp in the middle of the main street, between the town's two *pensiones*. The **ANAM office** on the main road answers questions and recommends guides for excursions to nearby destinations, primarily the Reserva Filo del Tallo, between Puerto Quimba and Metiti. (☎ 299 6373. Open M-F 8am-4pm.) **Banco Nacional de Panamá** is near the police station next to the airstrip and exchanges AmEx Traveler's Checks. (Open M-F 8am-3pm, Sa 9am-noon.) Upon arrival, check in at the **police station** (☎ 299 6200), around the corner from the airport in a large tan building. The only service not on the main drag is the **hospital,** atop the first hill on the other side of the airstrip. (☎ 299 6219. Open daily 7-11am and 1-2pm; emergencies 24hr.) Minibuses make the 5min. run to the hospital (US$0.20). **Super Farmacia** is on the main road. (Open M-F 8am-noon and 1-5pm, Sa 9am-noon.) **Public phones** are plentiful. The **post office** is on the hill just above the airport. (Open M-F 8am-noon.)

The best place to stay is **Hotel Biaquiru Bagara ❷** (with the Casa Ramady shop in front), near the top of the main street. The country-inn atmosphere is welcoming, with two large porches, hammocks, and common TVs. It's very clean and worth the money. All rooms have fans. (☎ 299 6224. US$10, with bath US$15; doubles US$15/US$20.) **Pensión Tuira ❷,** a little farther down the street, has bright rooms. (☎ 299 6316. Singles with fans US$8, with private bath US$10, US$15 for 2.) **Pensión**

Takela ❷, nearer the airstrip, has dark rooms with small windows but large beds. (☎ 299 6490. With common bath US$8, with bath US$12; doubles US$12/US$14.) La Palma has four very basic **restaurants,** on the main road, open 7am-7pm.

NEAR LA PALMA

🐾 RÍO SAMBÚ

For a trip down the Río Sambú, arrange for a guide and a piragua (shallow canoe) in Sambú. Ask for Juan Murillo. The journey is hot and tiring, and toilets, mattresses, and potable water are almost nonexistent. The 2hr. boat ride from La Palma to Sambú runs around US$200. Aviatur flights from La Palma (check the schedule, US$15) or Panama City (departures M, W, and F; US$35.70) are a much better option. A trip from Sambú to **Pavarandó,** *the farthest village from Sambú, should run US$80-90, plus food and lodging for yourself and your guide (around US$15 per person per day, unless you've brought camping supplies). You may need to bring gasoline from Sambú to fuel your piragua.*

Farther south along the coast from Punta Patiño is the mouth of the Río Sambú. The Emberá community of Puerto Indio is the first of a string of villages along the river that forms the backbone of the Comarca Emberá Sambú. Boats from La Palma follow the river as far as the town of Sambú. The voyage is like entering another world; the jungle crowds the banks of the winding river. In the past, residents were hired by the US Army as consultants for jungle survival skills. Your guide will be able to set you up with some form of lodging in the villages. Nonetheless, camping equipment can be a huge help.

🐾 GARACHINÉ AND CASA VIEJA

ANAM owns cabins near Garachiné for US$10 per night, plus a US$3 entrance fee, payable at the office in Garachiné. Make reservations in advance at ANAM offices in Panama City, Metití, or La Palma. Hire an ANAM guide to take you on the 3hr. hike to the cabin (US$10). Boats also make the trip from La Palma to Garachiné (1½hr., US$150). Aeroperlas flies there from La Palma (US$15) and Panama City (Tu and F US$35.70).

A relatively inexpensive way to get a taste of the jungle near La Palma is to visit Garachiné, a small town 15km southeast of the mouth of the Río Sambú. Casa Vieja, complete with kitchen and bathroom, sits by the muddy beach, near a web of jungle paths. It's used primarily by scientists studying the local environment.

YAVIZA

The Interamerican Hwy. comes to an unceremonious end here, the beginning of the infamous 400km long Darién Gap. Yaviza remains the best starting point for intrepid souls looking to cross the gap, although the trek is dangerous and currently not advisable due to the unrest. It is next to impossible to find a guide willing to go. There are interesting Emberá villages near Yaviza, but they, too, are in very dangerous areas. **Buses** arrive from **Panama City** almost hourly during the dry season. During the rainy season, *chivitas* make the final leg from **Metetí** (3-4hr., usually 3 per day, US$5). Between Yaviza and **El Real,** you can catch a **boat** ride for US$5; head to the dock around 7:30am (45min.). **Pensión 3 Américas** takes *piragua* trips north up the Río Chico, a relatively safe area, to visit the village **El Común** (trips from US$40). Check the latest on security with ANAM and the police before embarking on any trip. Register with the **police** upon arrival in Yaviza. Local services include: a **pharmacy,** a **hospital** (across the river), public **telephones,** and a **post office.** The only place to stay is the **Pensión 3 Américas ❷**, across from the basketball court. Ten large rooms and two shared bathrooms with feeble water pressure perch above a decent restaurant and loud bar. (☎ 299 3245, a public phone located right beside the hotel; ask for the *pensión* when someone answers. Singles US$10, with A/C US$20; doubles US$15; 5-person room with private bath US$35.)

EL REAL

El Real is the gateway to Parque Nacional Darién. El Real is divided into two parts: one a rough grid, the other a path that snakes away from the grid. There are no street names; ask around for directions. Aeroperlas has **flights** to El Real (1hr.; M, W, F, and Sa 8:45am; US$38.85) from Panama City. Between El Real and **Yaviza** (accessible by land from Panama City), boatmen will take passengers for around US$5 (45min., best to go in the morning). Along the path are services, including: the **ANAM office; police station** (☎ 299 6136), where you should check in and show your passport; **health center;** and **post office.** Within the grid section, you'll find a **general store, Aeroperlas office,** and the only hotel in town, the scruffy **Hotel El Nazareno ❶,** with fans but sagging beds and poor plumbing (US$7 per room). There are two restaurants in town. The better of the two has no name; it's on a path near a makeshift basketball court (ask around).

NEAR EL REAL

⚑ PARQUE NACIONAL DARIÉN

*The Rancho Frío **ranger station** is a 6hr. walk from El Real in the dry season; during the rainy season, you can take a **boat** trip (1hr., around US$50) up the river to the Emberá town of Pijibasal and then **hike** 1hr. from there. Guides are a must and cost US$10 per day, plus food. There's very basic lodging at the park (US$10 per night), but bring food. Entrance fee US$3.*

With 5970 sq. km of primary tropical forests, Parque Nacional Darién boasts the second-richest neotropical biodiversity in the world after the Amazon. Thousands of plant and animal species are found here, including 64 species native to the area, and some 450 species of bird. The park stretches along most of the border between Panama and Colombia and is most accessible from El Real. **Rancho Frío,** the closest ranger station to El Real, offers good animal and bird-watching paths to nearby waterfalls and cassette-tape-guided walks. The **Pirre** station is known for some of the finest birding in the world. A 4-6hr. hike from El Real, it offers the same amenities and prices as Rancho Frío. The station is near the towns of Pirre 1 and Pirre 2; the latter has a police station. Getting to **Cruce de Mono** station, with its monkey colonies, requires an expensive 2-3hr. boat trip to Boca de Cupé and a 6hr. hike from there. The area is dangerous and the trip is currently not advisable.

PANAMA

APPENDIX

CLIMATE

Avg. Temp. (lo/hi), Precipitation	January			April			July			October		
	°C	°F	mm	°C	°F	mm	°C	°F	mm	°C	°F	mm
Guatemala City	12/23	54/73	10	14/28	57/82	30	16/26	61/79	200	16/24	61/75	170
Belize City	19/27	66/81	135	23/30	73/86	55	24/31	75/88	165	22/30	72/86	300
San Salvador	16/32	61/90	10	18/34	64/93	45	18/32	64/90	290	18/31	64/88	240
Tegucigalpa	14/25	57/77	12	17/30	63/86	26	18/27	64/82	70	17/27	63/81	87
Managua	20/31	68/88	5	23/34	73/93	5	22/31	72/88	135	22/31	72/88	245
San José	14/24	57/75	15	17/26	63/79	46	17/25	63/79	210	16/25	61/77	300
Panama City	22/31	72/88	35	23/32	73/90	60	23/31	73/88	190	23/30	73/86	265

LANGUAGE

Spanish pronunciation is very straightforward. Each vowel is pronounced only one way: **a** ("ah" in father); **e** ("e" in "convey"); **i** ("ee" in "beet"); **o** ("oh" in "tote"); **u** ("oo" in "boot"); **y**, by itself, is pronounced like the English "ee." Most consonants are pronounced the same as in English. Important exceptions are: **j** ("h" in "hello"), **ll** ("y" in "yes"); **ñ** ("ny" in "canyon"); **rr** (trilled "r"); **h** (always silent); **x** (either "h" in Spanish words or "sh" in Maya words). The letter **c** is pronounced like an English s before "soft vowels"—e and i—and like the English k before "hard vowels"—a, o, and u. In Central America, **z** is pronounced like the English s.

By rule, the stress of a Spanish word falls on the second-to-last syllable if the word ends in a vowel, n, or s. If the word ends in any other consonant, the stress is on the last syllable. Any word in which the accent does not follow the rule carries an accent mark over the stressed syllable.

BASICS

ENGLISH	SPANISH	ENGLISH	SPANISH
Hello. [morning]	Buenos días.	How are you?	¿Cómo está?
Hello. [afternoon]	Buenas tardes.	I'm fine, thanks.	(Estoy) bien, gracias.
Hello. [evening]	Buenas noches.	Please/Thank you.	Por favor/Gracias.
Good-bye.	Adios.	You're welcome!	De nada/ No hay de que
Sorry. Forgive me.	Lo siento. Perdóneme.	Yes/no.	Sí/no.
What's your name?	¿Cómo se llama?	I would like...	Quisiera.../Me gustaría
My name is Gabrielle.	Me llamo Gabrielle.	I need...	Me falta.../Necesito...
I'm from...	Soy de...	I don't speak Spanish.	No hablo español.
No problem.	No hay problema.	I don't understand.	No entiendo.
OK.	OK. Perfecto. Muy bien.	Please repeat.	Repita, por favor.
Who?	¿Quién?	Let go of me.	Suéltame.
When?	¿Cuándo?	I don't know.	No sé.

ENGLISH	SPANISH	ENGLISH	SPANISH
What (did you say)?	¿Cómo?	Go away/Leave me alone.	Vete/Déjame.
Where is...?	¿Dónde está...?	Stop/enough.	Basta.
Why?	¿Por qué?	Help!	¡Socorro!
Do you accept traveler's checks?	¿Accepta cheques de viajero?	I would like to make a call to the US	Quisiera llamar a los Estados Unidos.
How much does this cost?	¿Cuánto vale (esto)?	Where is the bathroom?	¿Dónde está el baño/los servicios?
That's too much.	Es demasiado.	Excuse me.	Con permiso/Perdón.
What time is it?	¿Qué hora es?	I like Let's Go.	Me gusta Let's Go.
many/few	muchos/pocos	several	varios, algunos
a couple	un par de	a ton of	un montón de

DIRECTIONS AND TRANSPORTATION

ENGLISH	SPANISH	ENGLISH	SPANISH
(to the) right	a la derecha	(to the) left	a la izquierda
next to	al lado de	across from	en frente de
straight ahead	todo derecho	to turn	doblar
near	cerca	far	lejos
above	arriba/encima de	below	abajo/debajo de
traffic light	semáforo	corner	esquina
street	calle/avenida	block	cuadra
How do I get to...?	¿Cómo llego a...?	Where is...street?	¿Dónde está la calle?
How far is...?	¿A cuántos kilómetros está... ?	What bus line goes to...?	¿Qué línea de buses tiene servicio a...?
When does the bus leave for...?	¿A qué hora sale el bus para...?	From where does the bus leave?	¿De dónde sale el autobús?
I'm getting off at...	Bajo en...	Is this bus going to...?	¿Es este bus para...?
How long does it take?	¿Cuánto tarda?	I'm lost.	Estoy perdido(a).

ACCOMMODATIONS AND FOOD

ENGLISH	SPANISH	ENGLISH	SPANISH
I'd like to see a room with one bed.	Quisiera ver un cuarto con una cama.	Is there a fan/private bath/hot water?	¿Hay abanico/baño privado/agua caliente?
Are there rooms?	¿Hay habitaciones?	I would like a room.	Quisiera una habitación.
Where is the bathroom?	¿Dónde está el baño?	Check, please.	La cuenta, por favor.
breakfast	desayuno	lunch	almuerzo
dinner	cena	Bon apetit	Buen provecho
drink	bebida	water (purified)	agua (purificada)
bread	pan	rice	arroz
vegetables	legumbres/vegetales	chicken	pollo
meat	carne	milk	leche
eggs	huevos	coffee	café
juice	jugo	tea	té
wine	vino	beer	cerveza
ice cream	helado	fruit	fruta
soup	sopa/caldo	vegetarian	vegetariano(a)
fork	tenedor	cup	una copa/taza
spoon	cuchara	knife	cuchillo

GLOSSARY

aduana: customs
aeropuerto: airport
agua pura/purificada: purified water
aguas calientes: hot springs
aire acondicionado: air-conditioned
alcadía: mayoral district
altiplano: plateau
arena: sand
arroz: rice
artesanía: handicrafts
asado: roast
autobús: bus
avenida: avenue
avería: (car) breakdown
avión: airplane
aviso: warning, advisory
bahía: bay
baleada: a soft, taco-like food
balneario: bathing area
baño: bathroom
barrio: neighborhood
batido: milkshake
bebida: drink
borracho: drunk
bote: boat
cabaña: cabin
cabina: cabin (CR)
caliente: hot
calle: street
cama: bed
cambio: change
camioneta: small truck
campamento: camp area
candado: padlock
candela: candle
cantina: rowdy bar
carne: meat
caro/a: expensive
carretera: highway
casado/a: married
casado: rice & beans (CR)
cascada: waterfall
catarata: waterfall
catedral: cathedral
cayuco: dugout canoe
cena: dinner
cenote: sinkhole
centro: city center
cerveza: beer
champa: a thatched-roof hut with no walls
cheques viajeros: traveler's checks
chichas: sandflies
chicle: chewing gum
chófer: driver
ciudad: city
coche: car
colectivo: bus/van
colón: name of currency in EL Salvador and Costa Rica
colonia: suburb
combi: collective taxi
comida: food, meal
comedor: a small diner
conductor: driver
consulado: consulate
correo: post office

córdobas: Nicaraguan currency
coyotes: money changers
cuadra: (street) block
cuarto: room
cuenta: restaurant bill
cuevas: caves
de ida y vuelta: round-trip
desayuno: breakfast
día: day
dinero: money
discoteca: disco
dorado: fried
edificio: building
embajada: embassy
emergencia: emergency
enfermo/a: sick
entrada: entrance, admission
estación: station
este: east
extranjera/o: foreign
farmacia: pharmacy
finca: plantation-like farm
fría: cold
frijoles: beans
frito: fried
frontera: border
FUSEP: federal police (H)
fútbol: soccer, football
gallo pinto: fried rice & beans
Garífuna: Caribbean ethnic group **gaseosa:** soft drink
general: shared (bath)
grande: big
gringo/a: white person; North American
grutas: caves
hacienda: ranch
hombre: man
hospedaje: inn
hospital: hospital
huipil: an embroidered garment
iglesia: church
INGUAT: tourist info (G)
IPAT: tourist info (P)
isla: island
indígena/o: indigenous
inundacíon: flood
invierno: winter; rainy season
ladrón: thief
lancha: launch (boat)
lago: lake
laguna: lagoon; lake
lavandería: laundromat
leary: a puto
licuado: fruity shake
linterna: flashlight
llamada por cobrar: collect call
lista de correos: *poste restante*
llave: key
malecón: boardwalk
mañana: morning; tomorrow
marisco: shellfish; seafood
matrimonial: bed for two
médico: doctor
menú del día: meal of the day
mercado: market
merendero: snack bar

MINAE: park info (P)
mirador: view, lookout
Miskito: indigenous group in Honduras and Nicaragua
molas: patched cloth panels (P)
mondongo: innards
montaña: mountain
monte: mountain
moto: motorcycle
mujer: woman, wife
niño: child
norte: north
novio/a: fiancé/fiancée
oeste: west
ola: wave
oriente: eastern
palapa: palm-thatched hut
pan: bread
panadería: bakery
panga: skiff (boat)
parada: stop, bus stop
páramo: barren plain
parque: park; plaza
pasaporte: passport
peligroso/a: dangerous
pensión: hostel
pequeño: small
picop: pickup truck
piedra: stone, rock
pincho: meat shish kebab
pipa: seed; pipe
playa: beach
pollera: a traditional woman's garment (P)

pollo: chicken
poniente: western
pueblo: town
pulpería: grocery store
pupusa: fried tortilla with beans and cheese
pupsería: vendor of *pupusas*
privado: private (bath)
rebaja: bargain
refugio: shelter
resaca: hangover
restaurante: restaurant
río: river
ropa: clothes
sábanas: sheets
salida: exit
santo: saint
semana: week
sendero: path
soda: roadside eatery (CR)
sopa: soup
stela: stele, stone monument
sur: south
taquería: taco stand
tico: Costa Rican
tienda: store
típico: traditional (food)
tortuga: turtle
vegetales: vegetables
verano: summer
verde: green
vuelo: flight
zapatos: shoes
zona rosa: red light district; prostitution zone

APPENDIX

INDEX

A

Actun Can Cave (G) 419
Actun Tunichil Muknal Cave 112
Acul (G) 370
aerogrammes 38
Agua Buena mountain (H) 519
Agua Caliente (G) 394
Agua Caliente (H) 462
Agua Caliente National Park 132
Aguas Termales (H) 459
Aguilares (ES) 286
Ahuachapán (ES) 295
AIDS 33
airplane travel
  courier 45
  courier flights 45
  fares 41
Alajuela (CR) 156
  Butterfly Farm 159
  Zoo-Ave 159
alcohol 29
Alegría (ES) 311
Almirante (P) 667
Almolonga (G) 379
Altagracia (N) 564
Altar de Sacrificios 13
Altun Ha (B) 80, 94
Alvarez, General Gustavo 430
Amapala (H) 449
El Amatillo (H) 448
Ambergris Caye (B) 86
American Express 24, 38, 49
American Red Cross 30
Antelope Falls (B) 123
Antigua (G) 344
Apaneca (ES) 293
Apastepeque lagoon (ES) 310
Archipiélago de las Perlas (P) 622
Archipiélago de Solentiname (N) 567
Arena (P) 638
arts
  Belize 70
  Honduras 431
  Nicaragua 526
  Panama 599
Asturias, Miguel Angel 19

Atalaya (P) 646
ATM cards 25
Atzumal (G) 370
Augustine (B) 113
Azuero Peninsula (P) 636–646

B

Baboon Sanctuary (B) 92
Bahía de Jiquilisco (ES) 281
Bahía Drake (CR) 227
Baja Verapaz (G) 403
ballcourts 13
Balneario Cecilinda (G) 409
Baños de Payexú (G) 378
bargaining 26
Barton Creek Cave (B) 112
Battle of St. George's Caye 69
Bay Islands (H) 497–508
beaches
  Bahía Bocarito (P) 664
  Bahía Uvita (CR) 215
  Balcón (N) 567
  Beach Break (CR) 248
  Big Bight (H) 500
  Bluff (P) 665
  Bonita (CR) 238
  Cacique (P) 623
  Cahuita (CR) 243
  Cedros (CR) 202
  Conchalio (ES) 277
  Corn Islands (N) 588
  Costa del Sol (ES) 281
  Cuarto (P) 667
  de Cacao (CR) 230
  de las Suecas (P) 623
  del Coco (CR) 194
  Dominical (CR) 213
  Ejecutiva (P) 623
  El Arenal (P) 641
  El Cuco (ES) 319
  El Espino ES) 319
  El Mobo (P) 618
  El Palmercito (ES) 278
  El Rompío (P) 638
  El Tamarindo (ES) 319
  El Toro (P) 641
  El Tunco (ES) 278

MAP INDEX

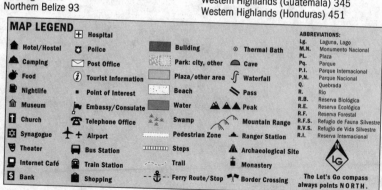

MAP LEGEND

Hotel/Hostel	Hospital	Building	Thermal Bath	
Camping	Police	Park: city, other	Cave	
Food	Post Office	Plaza/other area	Waterfall	
Nightlife	Tourist Information	Beach	Pass	
Museum	Point of Interest	Water	Peak	
Church	Embassy/Consulate	Swamp	Mountain Range	
Synagogue	Telephone Office	Pedestrian Zone	Ranger Station	
Theater	Airport	Steps	Archaeological Site	
Internet Café	Bus Station	Trail	Monastery	
Bank	Train Station	Ferry Route/Stop	Border Crossing	
	Shopping			

ABBREVIATIONS:
Lg.   Laguna, Lago
M.N.   Monumento Nacional
PL.   Plaza
Pq.   Parque
P.I.   Parque Internacional
P.N.   Parque Nacional
Q.   Quebrada
R.   Rio
R.B.   Reserva Biológica
R.E.   Reserva Ecológica
R.F.   Reserva Forestal
R.F.S. Refugio de Fauna Silvestre
R.V.S. Refugio de Vida Silvestre
R.I.   Reserva Internacional

The Let's Go compass always points NORTH.